Accounting

NINTH EDITION

Charles T. Horngren
Stanford University

Walter T. Harrison Jr.
Baylor University

M. Suzanne Oliver
University of West Florida

Prentice Hall

Boston   Columbus   Indianapolis   New York   San Francisco   Upper Saddle River
Amsterdam   Cape Town   Dubai   London   Madrid   Milan   Munich   Paris   Montréal   Toronto
Delhi   Mexico City   São Paulo   Sydney   Hong Kong   Seoul   Singapore   Taipei   Tokyo

VP/Editorial Director: Sally Yagan
Editor-in-Chief: Donna Battista
Director of Marketing: Kate Valentine
Director of Editorial Services: Ashley Santora
VP/Director of Development: Steve Deitmer
Editorial Project Manager: Rebecca Knauer
Editorial Assistant: Jane Avery
Development Editor: Shannon LeMay-Finn
Director of Product Development, Media:
  Zara Wanlass
Editorial Media Project Manager: Allison Longley
Production Media Project Manager: John Cassar
Marketing Manager: Maggie Moylan
Marketing Assistant: Kimberly Lovato
Senior Managing Editor, Production:
  Cynthia Zonneveld

Production Project Manager: Lynne Breitfeller
Permissions Project Manager: Hessa Albader
Senior Operations Specialist: Diane Peirano
Senior Art Director: Jonathan Boylan
Cover Design: Jonathan Boylan
Cover Photos: Sideways Design\Shutterstock;
  iStockphoto; Bruno Ferrari\Shutterstock;
  Francesco Ridolfi\Dreamstime LLC -Royalty Free
Composition: GEX Publishing Services
Full-Service Project Management:
  GEX Publishing Services
Printer/Binder: Courier Kendallville
Cover Printer: Lehigh Phoenix
Typeface: 10/12 Sabon

Credits and acknowledgments borrowed from other sources and reproduced, with permission, in this textbook appear on appropriate page within text.

Sonica83\Dreamstime LLC -Royalty Free pp. 773, 813, 880, 924, 962, 1010, 1050, 1105, 1151

Library of Congress Cataloging-in-Publication Data

Horngren, Charles T.
  Accounting / Charles T. Horngren, Walter T. Harrison Jr., M. Suzanne Oliver. -- 9th ed.
    p. cm.
  Includes bibliographical references and index.
  ISBN 978-0-13-256905-7 (casebound : alk. paper) -- ISBN 978-0-13-256901-9 (pbk. : alk. paper) -- ISBN 978-0-13-256904-0 (pbk. : alk. paper) 1. Accounting. I. Harrison, Walter T. II. Oliver, M. Suzanne. III. Title.
  HF5636.H667 2012
  657--dc22

                      2010053113

10 9 8 7 6 5 4 3 2 1

Prentice Hall
is an imprint of

www.pearsonhighered.com

ISBN-13: 978-0-13-256905-7
ISBN-10: 0-13-256905-1

About the Authors

Charles T. Horngren is the Edmund W. Littlefield professor of accounting, emeritus, at Stanford University. A graduate of Marquette University, he received his MBA from Harvard University and his PhD from the University of Chicago. He is also the recipient of honorary doctorates from Marquette University and DePaul University.

A CPA, Horngren served on the Accounting Principles Board for six years, the Financial Accounting Standards Board (FASB) Advisory Council for five years, and the Council of the AICPA for three years. For six years he served as a trustee of the Financial Accounting Foundation, which oversees the FASB and the Government Accounting Standards Board.

Horngren is a member of the Accounting Hall of Fame.

A member of the AAA, Horngren has been its president and its director of research. He received its first annual Outstanding Accounting Educator Award.

The California Certified Public Accountants Foundation gave Horngren its Faculty Excellence Award and its Distinguished Professor Award. He is the first person to have received both awards.

The AICPA presented its first Outstanding Educator Award to Horngren.

Horngren was named Accountant of the Year, in Education, by the national professional accounting fraternity, Beta Alpha Psi.

Professor Horngren is also a member of the IMA, from whom he has received its Distinguished Service Award. He was a member of the institute's Board of Regents, which administers the CMA examinations.

Walter T. Harrison, Jr., is professor emeritus of accounting at the Hankamer School of Business, Baylor University. He received his BBA degree from Baylor University, his MS from Oklahoma State University, and his PhD from Michigan State University.

Professor Harrison, recipient of numerous teaching awards from student groups as well as from university administrators, has also taught at Cleveland State Community College, Michigan State University, the University of Texas, and Stanford University.

A member of AAA and the AICPA, Professor Harrison has served as chairman of the Financial Accounting Standards Committee of AAA, on the Teaching/Curriculum Development Award Committee, on the Program Advisory Committee for Accounting Education and Teaching, and on the Notable Contributions to Accounting Literature Committee.

Professor Harrison has lectured in several foreign countries and published articles in numerous journals, including *Journal of Accounting Research*, *Journal of Accountancy*, *Journal of Accounting and Public Policy*, *Economic Consequences of Financial Accounting Standards*, *Accounting Horizons*, *Issues in Accounting Education*, and *Journal of Law and Commerce*.

Professor Harrison has received scholarships, fellowships, and research grants or awards from PriceWaterhouse Coopers, Deloitte & Touche, the Ernst & Young Foundation, and the KPMG Foundation.

M. Suzanne Oliver is an accounting instructor at the University of West Florida in Pensacola, Florida. She received her BA in accounting information systems and her MA in accountancy from the University of West Florida.

Oliver began her career in the tax department of a regional accounting firm, specializing in benefit plan administration. She has served as a software analyst for a national software development firm and as the Oracle fixed assets analyst for Spirit Energy, formerly part of Unocal. A CPA, Oliver is a member of the AAA, AICPA, FICPA, IAAER, IMA, TACTYC, and the Florida Association of Accounting Educators.

Oliver has taught accounting courses of all levels for the University of West Florida, state colleges, community colleges, and to practitioners since 1988. She has developed and instructed online courses using MyAccountingLab, WebCT, D2L, and other proprietary software.

Oliver lives in Niceville, FL, with her husband, Greg, and son, CJ. She especially thanks her husband, Greg, her son, CJ, and her uncle and aunt, Jimmy and Lida Lewis, for their unwavering support and encouragement. Oliver donates a portion of royalties to www.raffieskids.org, a charitable organization that assists children.

Brief Contents

ONLINE MATERIAL: located at pearsonhighered.com/horngren

APPENDIX C—Check Figures

SPECIAL JOURNALS

INVESTMENTS

Contents

Changes to This Edition

Students and Instructors will both benefit from a variety of new content and features in the ninth edition of *Accounting*:

ADDED impairment coverage to Chapter 9, Plant Assets and Intangibles.

IMPROVED Liabilities Coverage: Now Split into Two Chapters. Based on reviewer demand, we split Chapter 10 into two chapters:
- Chapter 10: Current Liabilities and Payroll
- New Chapter 11: Long-Term Liabilities, Bonds Payable, and
            Classification of Liabilities on the Balance Sheet

We also added long-term notes payable, mortgages payable, and allocation of payments between principal and interest coverage to new Chapter 11.

ADDED Ratio Coverage. Based on reviewer demand, we added more ratio coverage to the Financial Statement Analysis, Chapter 15, and additional individual chapters.

ADDED Excel Formulas in Chapter 21, Capital Budgeting, to complement the blue/green formula boxes.

REVISED Budget Coverage. Chapter 22: The Master Budget and Responsibility Accounting was rewritten to use the variable costing approach. Also, added coverage on traceable and untraceable costs.

ADDED more detailed coverage of overhead variances in Chapter 23. Flexible Budgets and Standard Costs.

ADDED new Chapter P: Partnerships. The streamlined partnership chapter covers all the basics, including partnership creation, adding a partner/removing a partner, allocating P&L, and liquidation. New examples were also written to retain consistency and match the rest of the text (Sheena Bright of Smart Touch creates a partnership).

UPDATED Full MyAccountingLab Coverage: Special Purpose Journals and Investments. The two online chapters have been posted in **MyAccountingLab**. The special purpose journals chapter covers the streamlined journalizing process using the continuing company, Smart Touch. The investments chapter covers classification and treatment of stock investments, also using Smart Touch.

These two chapters contain full **MyAccountingLab** coverage and supplements for instructors who wish to have it. These decisions have been widely supported by reviewers.

NEW and IMPROVED Chapter Openers. All of the chapter openers have been redesigned and rewritten. The financial chapter openers include a visual of a balance sheet, highlighting the specific section of the balance sheet that will be covered within the chapter. The managerial chapter openers include a visual of a smartphone device, complete with decision-making tools as apps. As students progress through these chapters, the decision being discussed is highlighted on the first page of the chapter. These visuals help set the stage while providing students with direction as they navigate through the material.

FOCUSED on Student Success. We've made it easy for students to identify what their focal point should be in every chapter:

- **NEW Key Takeaway Feature.** At the end of each main topic throughout the book, we've included a brief takeaway feature. This marginal feature hones in on the key point of that section so students will know exactly what they should have understood before moving on.
- **NEW Translation Guides.** We've included "translation guides" throughout the text, set off by a different font style/treatment, in which accounting terminology is translated into a language students can easily understand. In doing so, we aim to make accounting more approachable (for example: **Assets are resources that provide future economic benefits to a company. An asset is something you own that has value, like your iPod.**).
- **NEW Connect To Boxes.** We've included a marginal "Connect To" box in each chapter that focuses on topics such as IFRS, Ethics, Technology, and Accounting Information Systems. Each contains a subtitle so instructors can easily see what each box features.
- **IMPROVED Stop & Think Boxes.** We've refined many of the existing Stop & Think boxes, making them less technical.

EXTENSIVE REVISION of the End-of-Chapter Materials:

- **NEW End-of-Chapter Student Success Section.** We've added a new half-page, end-of-chapter "Student Success" section that does the following:
  - Lists hints on some common trouble spots/mistakes students make when taking a test on the chapter.
  - Tells students exactly where to go in the chapter and **MyAccountingLab** to get help related to a particular topic covered within that chapter.
- **IMPROVED End-of-Chapter Material.** We've improved the end-of-chapter exercises, while retaining the exercises often used in **MyAccountingLab**.
- **NEW End-of-Chapter Fraud Activity.** We've added a short end-of-chapter activity that asks students to look at a fraud issue related to the chapter.
- **NEW End-of-Chapter Communication Activity.** We've added a short end-of-chapter activity that asks students to restate key chapter content in their own words, encouraging them to learn and use chapter vocabulary.

ACCURACY. To ensure the level of accuracy instructors expect and require, accuracy checkers verified the in-chapter content, figures, and illustrations while additional accuracy checkers worked through the end-of-chapter material.

pearsonhighered.com/horngren

Students will have more "I Get It!" moments

Students understand (or "get it") right after the instructor does a problem in class. Once they leave the classroom, however, students often struggle to complete the homework on their own. This frustration can cause them to give up on the material altogether and fall behind in the course, resulting in an entire class falling behind as the instructor attempts to keep everyone on the same page.

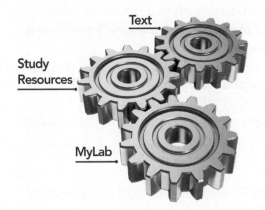

With the *Accounting, Ninth Edition* Student Learning System, all the features of the student textbook, study resources, and online homework system are designed to work together to provide students with the consistency and repetition that will keep both the instructor and students on track by providing more "I Get It!" moments inside and outside the classroom.

Replicating the Classroom Experience with Demo Doc Examples

The Demo Doc Examples, available in chapters 1 through 4 of the text, consist of entire problems, worked through step-by-step and narrated with the kind of comments that instructors would say in class. Demo Docs will aid students when they are trying to solve exercises and problems on their own, duplicating the classroom experience outside of class.

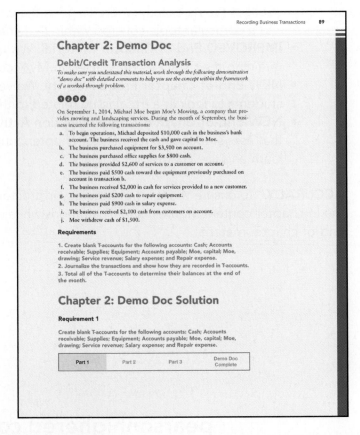

with *Accounting* and MyAccountingLab!

Consistency and Repetition Throughout the Learning Process

The concepts, materials, and practice problems are presented with clarity and consistency across all mediums—textbook, study resources, and online homework system. No matter which platform students use, they will continually experience the same look, feel, and language, minimizing confusion and ensuring clarity.

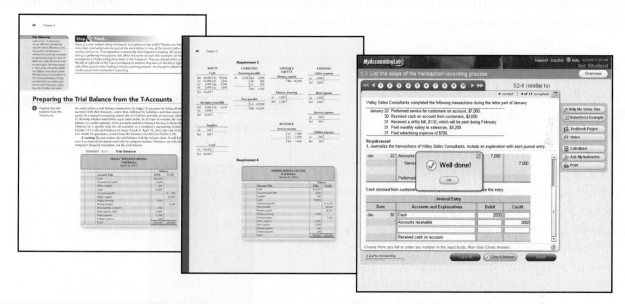

Experiencing the Power of Practice with MyAccountingLab: myaccountinglab.com

MyAccountingLab is an online homework system that gives students more "I Get It!" moments through the power of practice. With MyAccountingLab students can:

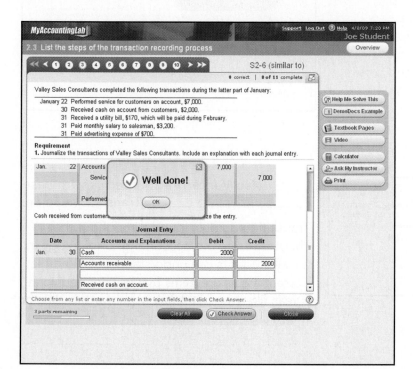

- work on the exact end-of-chapter material and/or similar problems assigned by the instructor.
- use the Study Plan for self-assessment and customized study outlines.
- use the Help Me Solve This tool for a step-by-step tutorial.
- watch a video to see additional information pertaining to the lecture.
- open the etext to the exact section of the book that will provide help on the specific problems.

Accounting...

With its tried-and-true framework and respected author team, Horngren/Harrison/Oliver's *Accounting* is the trusted choice for instructors and students of Introductory Accounting.

The ninth edition preserves the classic, solid foundation of the previous editions, while also including a modern and fresh teaching approach that helps students understand the complexities of accounting and achieve more "I Get It" moments.

NEW *Off to the right start:* Chapter Openers

Redesigned and rewritten, the chapter openers in this edition are focused on preparing students for the reading. The financial chapter openers include a visual of a balance sheet that highlights what will be covered within the chapter. The managerial chapter openers include a visual of a smartphone—complete with decision-making tools as apps—that visually displays the concepts and decision-making tools students will encounter.

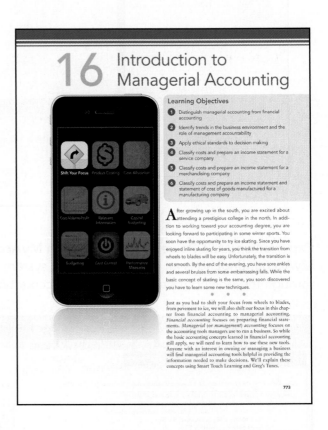

Current Assets

Current assets will be converted to cash, sold, or used up during the next 12 months, or within the business's operating cycle if the cycle is longer than a year. Current assets are items that will be used up in a year, like your notebook paper for this class or the change in your pocket. The operating cycle is the time span when

1. cash is used to acquire goods and services,

2. these goods and services are sold to customers, and

3. the business collects cash from customers.

NEW *Interpret the terms with ease:* Translation Guides

Translation guides, found throughout the chapters, translate accounting terminology in a way students can understand. For example, **Current assets are items that will be used up in a year, like your notebook paper for this class or the change in your pocket.**

The trusted choice for "I Get It" moments!

NEW *Link today's topics to the fundamentals:* **Connect To** _____

The Connect To marginal boxes in each chapter highlight hot topics such as IFRS, Ethics, and Accounting Information Systems as they pertain to the material being presented.

NEW *Highlight what matters:* **Key Takeaway**

At the end of each learning objective, the authors added a new marginal feature that emphasizes the key points covered within the section so students can see what they need to understand before reading further.

> **Connect To: Ethics**
>
> The classification of assets and liabilities as current or long-term affects many key ratios that outsiders use to evaluate the financial health of a company. Many times, the classification of a particular account is very clear—for example, a building is normally a long-term asset. But what if the company must demolish the existing building within six months due to some structural default? It would not be ethical to still show the building as a long-term asset.

IMPROVED *Put the concepts in context:* **Stop & Think Boxes**

Improved Stop & Think boxes relate accounting concepts to students' everyday lives by presenting them with relevant examples of the topic in practice.

Keep it consistent: **Consistent Examples**

Rather than learn about a new company each time an example is presented, this text provides two sets of company data that are carried through all of the in-chapter examples. As a result, students gain a sense of familiarity with the context of these examples and can focus their energy on learning the accounting principles in question.

Illustrate the concepts: **Decision Guidelines**

Decision Guidelines explain why the accounting concepts addressed in the chapter are important in a business setting. The left-hand side of the Decision Guidelines table explains the decision or action asked of the student in simple terms, while the right-hand side shows the accounting topics that will help facilitate those decisions.

Putting "I Get It" moments into practice!

NEW *Help where it's needed:* Destination Student Success

The new Destination Student Success sections at the end of each chapter list hints on some common mistakes in order to prevent students from falling into the same traps. These sections also show students exactly where to go within the chapter and in **MyAccountingLab** to get help related to a particular topic or learning objective.

● Destination: Student Success

Student Success Tips

The following are hints on some common trouble areas for students in this chapter:

- Commit to memory the normal balance of the six main account types. The normal balance is the side of the T-account where the account INCREASES. Assets, Drawing, and Expenses have normal debit balances. Liabilities, Equity, and Revenues have normal credit balances.
- Recall that debits are listed first in every journal entry.
- Remember debits ALWAYS EQUAL credits in every journal entry.
- Keep in mind that posting is just gathering all the journal entries made to an individual T-account so that you can determine the new balance in the account. Journal debit entries are posted on the left side of the T-account. Journal credit entries are posted on the right side of the T-account.
- The accounting equation MUST ALWAYS balance after each transaction is posted.
- The trial balance lists all accounts with a balance, ordered by assets, liabilities, equity, drawing, revenues, and expenses. Total debits should equal total credits on the trial balance.

Getting Help

If there's a learning objective from the chapter you aren't confident about, try using one or more of the following resources:

- Review the Chapter 2 Demo Doc located on page 89 of the textbook.
- Practice additional exercises or problems at the end of Chapter 2 that cover the specific learning objective that is challenging you.
- Watch the white board videos for Chapter 2 located at myaccountinglab.com under the Chapter Resources button.
- Go to myaccountinglab.com and select the Study Plan button. Choose Chapter 2 and work the questions covering that specific learning objective until you've mastered it.
- Work the Chapter 2 pre/post tests in myaccountinglab.com.
- Visit the learning resource center on your campus for tutoring.

NEW *Examine the potential for fraud:* End-of-Chapter Fraud Case

This edition now includes a new end-of-chapter activity that asks students to look at a fraud issue related to the material. This activity helps students make the connection between the concepts and this popular accounting topic.

● Fraud Case 2-1

Roy Akins was the accounting manager at Zelco, a tire manufacturer, and he played golf with Hugh Stallings, the CEO, who was something of a celebrity in the community. The CEO stood to earn a substantial bonus if Zelco increased net income by year-end. Roy was eager to get into Hugh's elite social circle; he boasted to Hugh that he knew some accounting tricks that could increase company income by simply revising a few journal entries for rental payments on storage units. At the end of the year, Roy changed the debits from "rent expense" to "prepaid rent" on several entries. Later, Hugh got his bonus, and the deviations were never discovered.

Requirements

1. How did the change in the journal entries affect the net income of the company at year-end?
2. Who gained and who lost as a result of these actions?

NEW *Speak accounting fluently:* End-of-Chapter Communication Activity

To help students increase their confidence, understanding, and communication of accounting terms, the end-of-chapter Communication Activity asks students to restate, in their own words, what they've learned within the chapter.

● Communication Activity 2-1

In 35 words or fewer, explain the difference between a debit and a credit and explain what the normal balance of the six account types is.

Master the material: Extensive Practice Opportunities

Five Book-Match Sets of Problems and Exercises (A, B, C, D, E):
EXERCISES: Students will have access to exercise set A within the text. Exercise set A along with alternative static exercise sets B, C, D, and E can be assigned by the instructor and completed by students in MyAccountingLab.

PROBLEMS: Students will have access to A and B problems within the text. Problem set A and B along with alternative static problem sets C, D, and E can be assigned by the instructor and completed by students in MyAccountingLab.

Continuing Exercise:
The unique Continuing Exercise takes a single company and adds transactions or questions in each chapter to the existing fact pattern. As students move through the text, they complete additional steps in this comprehensive exercise. Students are able to see the big picture and learn how the accounting topics build off one another. The Continuing Exercise is also available in MyAccountingLab.

Continuing Problem:
For more detailed and in-depth practice, a Continuing Problem is also available. Like the Continuing Exercise, the Continuing Problem takes a single company and adds transactions or questions in each chapter to the existing fact pattern. As students move through the text, they complete additional steps in this comprehensive problem. The Continuing Problem is also available in MyAccountingLab.

Unique Practice Set Within Chapters 1–8:
An in-text Practice Set is built into Chapters 1–8 of the student text. Students do not have to purchase any additional material for their practice sets, and instructors no longer have to create their own. Since the same authors of the textbook created the Practice Set, students will once again have consistency. The Practice Set is also available in MyAccountingLab.

MyAccountingLab®

End-of-Chapter Material Integrated with MyAccountingLab
myaccountinglab.com
Students need practice and repetition in order to successfully learn the fundamentals. All of the end-of-chapter problems and exercises in *Accounting* can be assigned and graded through MyAccountingLab. And learning goes one step further with MyAccountingLab's algorithmic versions of the questions that provide students with unlimited practice.

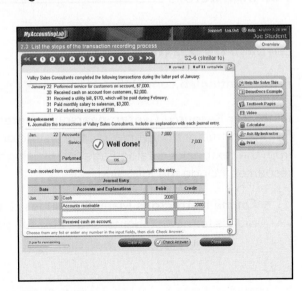

pearsonhighered.com/horngren

Student and Instructor Resources

For Students

MyAccountingLab®

myaccountinglab.com Online Homework and Assessment Manager
MyAccountingLab is Web-based tutorial and assessment software for accounting that gives students more "I Get It!" moments. MyAccountingLab provides students with a personalized interactive learning environment where they can complete their course assignments with immediate tutorial assistance, learn at their own pace, and measure their progress.

In addition to completing assignments and reviewing tutorial help, students have access to the following resources in **MyAccountingLab**:

- Pearson eText
- Data Files
- Videos
- Demo Docs

- Audio and Student PowerPoint® Presentations
- Working Papers in Both Excel and PDF
- MP3 Files with Chapter Objectives and Summaries
- Flash Cards

Student Resource Web site: pearsonhighered.com/horngren
The book's Web site contains the following:
- Data Files: Select end-of-chapter problems have been set up in different software applications, including Peachtree 2010, QuickBooks 2010, and Excel
- Excel Working Papers
- Online Chapter Materials (Special Purpose Journals and Investments)

For Instructors

MyAccountingLab®

myaccountinglab.com Online Homework and Assessment Manager

Instructor Resource Center: pearsonhighered.com/accounting
For the instructor's convenience, the instructor resources are available on CD or can be downloaded from the textbook's catalog page (pearsonhighered.com/horngren) and **MyAccountingLab**. Available resources include the following:

- **Online Instructor's Manual:** Includes chapter summaries, teaching tips provided by reviewers, pitfalls for new students, and "best of" practices from instructors across the country. And, to effectively implement the array of resources available, a Resource Roadmap is provided, giving a description and location of each resource, along with recommendations for classroom applications. Additional resources offered in the instructor's manual include the following:

- Introduction to the Instructor's Manual with a list of resources and a roadmap to help navigate what's available in MyAccountingLab.
- Instructor tips for teaching courses in multiple formats—traditional, hybrid, or online.
- "First Day of Class" student handout that includes tips for success in the course, as well as an additional document that shows students how to register and log on to MyAccountingLab.
- Sample syllabi for 10- and 16-week courses.
- Chapter overview and teaching outline that includes a brief synopsis and overview of each chapter.
- Key topics that walk instructors through what material to cover and what examples to use when addressing certain items within the chapter.
- Student chapter summary handout.
- Assignment grid that outlines all end-of-chapter exercises and problems, the topic being covered in that particular exercise or problem, estimated completion time, level of difficulty, and availability in Excel templates.
- Ten-minute quizzes that quickly assess students' understanding of the chapter material.

- **Instructor's Solutions Manual:** Contains solutions to all end-of-chapter questions, including short exercises, exercises, and problems.
- **TestBank:** Includes more than 3,000 questions and is formatted for use with WebCT, Blackboard, and CourseCompass™. Both objective-based questions and computational problems are available.
- **PowerPoint Presentations:** These presentations help facilitate classroom discussion by demonstrating where the numbers come from and what they mean to the concept at hand.
  - Instructor PowerPoint Presentations—complete with lecture notes
  - Student PowerPoint Presentations
  - Audio Narrated PowerPoint Presentations
  - Clicker Response System (CRS) PowerPoint Presentations
- **Working Papers and Solutions in Excel and PDF Format**
- **Image Library**
- **Data and Solution Files:** Select end-of-chapter problems have been set up in different software applications, including Peachtree 2010, QuickBooks 2010, and Excel. Corresponding solution files are also provided.

Acknowledgments

Acknowledgments for This Edition

The authors and editorial team thank Jodi McPherson for her vision and unwavering support over the past five years. Go SOX!

We would also like to extend a special thank you to the following individuals who were very helpful in the revision of this book:

Contributors:

Marcye Hampton, *University of Central Florida*
Brenda Mattison, *Tri-County Technical College*
Craig Reeder, *Florida Agricultural and Mechanical University*

Advisory Panel:

Lisa Banks, *Mott Community College*
Betty Christopher, *Mission College*
Tracy Corr, *Southeast Community College*
Anthony J. Dellarte, *Luzerne County Community College*
Robert Fahnestock, *University of West Florida*
Charles Fazzi, *Saint Vincent College*
Jaclyn Felder-Strauss, *Kaplan University*
Anita Feller, *University of Illinois at Urbana–Champaign*
Marina Grau, *Houston Community College*
Geoffrey Gurka, *Mesa State College of Colorado*
Geoffrey Heriot, *Greenville Technical College*
Patty Holmes, *Des Moines Area Community College*
Emil Koren, *Saint Leo University*
Suzanne Lay, *Mesa State College of Colorado*
Maria Leach, *Auburn University–Montgomery*

Dorinda Lynn, *Pensacola State College*
Brenda Mattison, *Tri-County Technical College*
Cheryl McKay, *Monroe County Community College*
Audrey Morrison, *Pensacola State College*
Tim Murphy, *Diablo Valley College*
Ed Napravnik, *Metropolitan Community College*
Tracie Nobles, *Austin Community College*
Jamie Payton, *Gadsden State Community College*
Craig Reeder, *Florida Agricultural and Mechanical University*
Carla Rich, *Pensacola State College*
Randy Rinke, *Mercyhurst College*
Dennis Roth, *West Virginia Northern Community College*
Linda Tarrago, *Hillsborough Community College*
Melanie Torborg, *Minnesota School of Business*
Andy Williams, *Edmonds Community College*

Accuracy Checkers:

Nabanita Bhattacharya, *Northwest Florida State College*
Ron Burris, *GEX Publishing Services*
David Doyon, *GEX Publishing Services*
Anita Hope, *Tarrant County College*
Peg Johnson, *Metropolitan Community College*

Dorinda Lynn, *Pensacola State College*
Cynthia Miller, *University of Kentucky*
Noriko Tilley, *Northwest Florida State College*
Greg Yost, *University of West Florida*

Reviewers:

Dave Alldredge, *Salt Lake Community College*
Lee Daniel, *Troy University*
Heidi Hansel, *Kirkwood Community College*
Paige Paulson, *Salt Lake Community College*
Michelle Powell-Dancy, *Holmes Community College–Ridgeland*

Joan Ryan, *Clackamas Community College*
Beverly Strachan, *Troy University*
Rick Turpin, *Troy University*
Susan Wright, *Dekalb Technical College*

Supplements Authors and Reviewers:

Natalie Allen, *Texas A&M University*
Helen Brubeck, *San Jose State University*
Colleen Chung, *Miami Dade College*
Wanda Edwards, *Troy State University*
Shirley Glass, *Macomb Community College*
Rob Hochschild, *Ivy Tech Community College*
Jamie McCracken, *Saint Mary-of-the-Woods College*
Brit McKay, *Georgia Southern University*
Jennie Mitchell, *Saint Mary-of-the-Woods College*

Cathy Nash, *Dekalb Technical College*
Craig Reeder, *Florida Agricultural and Mechanical University*
Rick Street, *Spokane Community College*
Allan Sheets, *International Business College*
John Stancil, *Florida Southern University College*
Noriko Tilley, *Northwest Florida State College*
Robin Turner, *Rowan-Cabarrus Community College*
Susan Wright, *Dekalb Technical College*
Greg Yost, *University of West Florida*

Acknowledgments for Previous Editions

Contributors:

Helen Brubeck, *San Jose State University*
Florence McGovern, *Bergen Community College*
Sherry Mills, *New Mexico State University*

Advisory Panel:

David Baglia, *Grove City College*
Joan Cezair, *Fayetteville State University*
Margaret Costello Lambert, *Oakland Community College*
Kathy Crusto-Way, *Tarrant County College*
Jim Ellis, *Bay State College–Boston*
Anita Ellzey, *Harford Community College*

Al Fagan, *University of Richmond*
Todd Jackson, *Northeastern State University*
Donnie Kristof-Nelson, *Edmonds Community College*
Cheryl McKay, *Monroe County Community College*
Mary Ann Swindlehurst, *Carroll Community College*
Andy Williams, *Edmonds Community College*

Reviewers:

Joseph Adamo, *Cazenovia College*
Audrey Agnello, *Niagara County Community College*
William Alexander, *Indian Hills Community College–Ottumwa*
Asokan Anandarajan, *New Jersey Institute of Technology*
Susan Anders, *St. Bonaventure University*
Joe Aubert, *Bemidji State University*
Melody Ashenfelter, *Southwestern Oklahoma State University*

Charles Baird, *University of Wisconsin–Stout*
Dan Bayak, *Northampton Community College*
Richard Bedwell, *Jones County Junior College*
Judy Beebe, *Western Oregon University*
Irene Bembenista, *Davenport University*
Margaret Berezewski, *Robert Morris College*
Lecia Berven, *Iowa Lakes Community College*
Charles Betts, *Delaware Technical and Community College*
Greg Bischoff, *Houston Community College*
Margaret Black, *San Jacinto College*
William Black, *Raritan Valley Community College*
David Bland, *Cape Fear Community College*
Allen Blay, *University of California–Riverside*
Susan Blizzard, *San Antonio College*
Michael Blue, *Bloomsburg University*
Dale Bolduc, *Intercoast College*
Linda Bolduc, *Mount Wachusett Community College*
Donald Bond, *Houston Community College*
John Boyd, *Oklahoma City Community College*
Suzanne Bradford, *Angelina College*
Thomas Branton, *Alvin Community College*
Jerold Braun, *Daytona Beach Community College*
Nat Briscoe, *Northwestern State University*
Julie Browning, *California Baptist University*
Carroll Buck, *San Jose State University*

Jane Calvert, *University of Central Oklahoma*
Vickie Campbell, *Cape Fear Community College*
David Candelaria, *Mount San Jacinto College*

Lee Cannell, *El Paso Community College*
Michelle Cannon, *Ivy Tech Community College*
Greg Carlton, *Davidson County Community College*
Kay Carnes, *Gonzaga University–Spokane*
Brian Carpenter, *University of Scranton*
Thomas Carr, *International College of Naples*
Lloyd Carroll, *Borough Manhattan Community College*
Stanley Carroll, *New York City College of Technology of CUNY*
Roy Carson, *Anne Arundel Community College*
Al Case, *Southern Oregon University*
Gerald Caton, *Yavapai College*
Bea Chiang, *The College of New Jersey*
Catherine Chiang, *North Carolina Central University*
Stephen Christian, *Jackson Community College*
Shifei Chung, *Rowan University of New Jersey*
Toni Clegg, *Palm Beach Atlantic University*
Lynn Clements, *Florida Southern College*
Doug Clouse, *Lakeland Community College*
Cynthia Coleman, *Sandhills Community College*
Christie Comunale, *Long Island University*
Sally Cook, *Texas Lutheran University*
Sue Counte, *St. Louis Community College*
Chris Crosby, *York Technical College*
Ted Crosby, *Montgomery County Community College*
Barbara Crouteau, *Santa Rosa Junior College*
Chris Cusatis, *Gwynedd-Mercy College*

Julie Dailey, *Central Virginia Community College*
DeeDee Daughtry, *Johnston Community College*
Judy Daulton, *Piedmont Technical College*
David L. Davis, *Tallahassee Community College*
Elaine Dessouki, *Virginia Wesleyan College*
Ken Duffe, *Brookdale Community College*

John Eagan, *Erie Community College*
Gene Elrod, *University of Texas–Arlington*
Beth Engle, *Montgomery County Community College*

Harlan Etheridge, *University of Louisiana*
Charles Evans, *Keiser College*

Charles Fazzi, *Saint Vincent College*
Calvin Fink, *Bethune Cookman College*
Phil Fink, *University of Toledo*
Carolyn Fitzmorris, *Hutchinson Community College*
Rebecca Floor, *Greenville Technical College*
Joseph Foley, *Assumption College*
Jeannie Folk, *College of DuPage*
David Forsyth, *Palomar College*

Shelly Gardner, *Augustana College*
Harold Gellis, *York College of CUNY*
Renee Goffinet, *Spokane Community College*
Saturnino (Nino) Gonzales, *El Paso Community College*
Janet Grange, *Chicago State University*
Marina Grau, *Houston Community College*
John Graves, *PCDI*
Gloria Grayless, *Sam Houston State University*
Barbara Gregorio, *Nassau Community College*
Tim Griffin, *Hillsborough Community College*
Judy Grotrian, *Peru State College*

Amy Haas, *Kingsborough Community College*
Betty Habershon, *Prince George's Community College*
Patrick Haggerty, *Lansing Community College*
Penny Hanes, *Mercyhurst College–Erie*
Phil Harder, *Robert Morris University*
Marc Haskell, *Fresno City College*
Clair Helms, *Hinds Community College*
Kathy Heltzel, *Luzerne County Community College*
Sueann Hely, *West Kentucky Community and Technical College*
Geoffrey Heriot, *Greenville Technical College*
Humberto M. Herrera, *Laredo Community College*
Chuck Heuser, *Brookdale Community College*
Matt Hightower, *Three Rivers Community College*

Merrily Hoffman, *San Jacinto College*
Mary Hollars, *Vincennes University*
Patty Holmes, *Des Moines Area Community College–Ankeny*
Bambi Hora, *University of Central Oklahoma*
Maggie Houston, *Wright State University*
William Huffman *Missouri Southern State College*
James Hurat, *National College of Business and Technology*
Larry Huus, *University of Minnesota*
Constance Hylton, *George Mason University*

Verne Ingram, *Red Rocks Community College*

Fred Jex, *Macomb Community College*
Peg Johnson, *Metropolitan Community College*
Becky Jones, *Baylor University*
Jeffrey Jones, *Community College of Southern Nevada*
Christine Jonick, *Gainesville State College*
Paul Juriga, *Richland Community College*

Lolita Keck, *Globe College*
Christopher Kelly, *Community College of Southern Nevada*
James Kelly, *Ft. Lauderdale City College*
Ashraf Khallaf, *University of Southern Indiana*
Randy Kidd, *Longview Community College*
Chula King, *University of West Florida*
Cody King, *Georgia Southwestern State University*
Susan Koepke, *Illinois Valley Community College*
Ken Koerber, *Bucks County Community College*
Dennis Kovach, *Community College of Allegheny County–Allegheny*

Lawrence Leaman, *University of Michigan*
Denise Leggett, *Middle Tennessee State University*
Pamela Legner, *College of DuPage*
Maria Lehoczky, *American Intercontinental University*
Bruce Leung, *City College of San Francisco*
Judy Lewis, *Angelo State University*
Bruce Lindsey, *Genesee Community College*
Elizabeth Lynn Locke, *Northern Virginia Community College*

Michelle Maggio, *Westfield State College*
Bridgette Mahan, *Harold Washington College*
Lori Major, *Luzerne County Community College*
James Makofske, *Fresno City College*
Ken Mark, *Kansas City Kansas Community College*
Ariel Markelevich, *Long Island University*
Hector Martinez, *San Antonio College*
John May, *Southwestern Oklahoma State University*
Nora McCarthy, *Wharton County Junior College*
Bruce McMurrey, *Community College of Denver*

Patrick McNabb, *Ferris State University*
Pam Meyer, *University of Louisiana*
John Miller, *Metropolitan Community College*
Barry Mishra, *University of California–Riverside*
Norma Montague, *Central Carolina Community College*
Tim Murphy, *Diablo Valley College*

Lisa Nash, *Vincennes University*
Lanny Nelms, *Gwinnet Technical College*
Jennifer Niece, *Assumption College*
Deborah Niemer, *Oakland Community College*
Tom Nohl, *Community College of Southern Nevada*
Pat Novak, *Southeast Community College*

Ron O'Brien, *Fayetteville Technical Community College*
Kathleen O'Donnell, *Onondaga Community College*
John Olsavsky, *SUNY at Fredonia*
Liz Ott, *Casper College*
Glenn Owen, *Marymount College*

Carol Pace, *Grayson County College*
Susan Pallas, *Southeast Community College*
Jeffrey Patterson, *Grove City College*
Kathy Pellegrino, *Westfield State College*
Susan Pope, *University of Akron*
Robert Porter, *Cape Fear Community College*
Michelle Powell, *Holmes Community College*
Cheryl Prachyl, *University of Texas–El Paso*
Debra Prendergast, *Northwestern Business College*
Darlene Pulliam, *West Texas A&M University–Canyon*
Karl Putnam, *University of Texas–El Paso*

Margaret Quarles, *Sam Houston State University*
Behnaz Quigley, *Marymount College*

Jim Racic, *Lakeland Community College*
Paulette Ratliff-Miller, *Arkansas State University*
Carla Rich, *Pensacola State College*
Denver Riffe, *National College of Business and Technology*
Michael Robinson, *Baylor University*
Stephen Rockwell, *University of Tulsa*
Patrick Rogan, *Cosumnes River College*
Dennis Roth, *West Virginia Northern Community College*
Karen Russom, *North Harris College*
J.T. Ryan, *Onondaga Community College*

Martin Sabo, *Community College of Denver*
Phillipe Sammour, *Eastern Michigan University*
Richard Savich, *California State University–San Bernardino*
Nancy Schendel, *Iowa Lakes Community College*
Sandra Scheuermann, *University of Louisiana*

Bunney Schmidt, *Keiser College*
Debbie Schmidt, *Cerritos College*
Robert Schoener, *New Mexico State University*
Tony Scott, *Norwalk Community College*
Linda Serres Sweeny, *Sam Houston State University*
Brandi Shay, *Southwestern Community College*
Alice Sineath, *Forsyth Technical Community College*
Lois Slutsky, *Broward Community College South*
Kimberly Smith, *County College of Morris*
Chuck Smith, *Iowa Western Community College*
Ken Snow, *Kaplan Education Centers*
John Stancil, *Florida Southern College*
Lawrence Steiner, *College of Marin*
Sally Stokes, *Wilmington College*
Thomas Stolberg, *Alfred State University*
Joan Stone, *University of Central Oklahoma*
John Stone, *Potomac State College*
Thomas Szczurek, *Delaware County Community College*

Kathy Terrell, *University of Central Oklahoma*
Cynthia Thompson, *Carl Sandburg College–Carthage*

Shafi Ullah, *Broward Community College South*

Peter Van Brunt, *SUNY College of Technology at Delhi*
Kathi Villani, *Queensborough Community College*
Audrey Voyles, *San Diego Miramar College*

Patricia Walczak, *Lansing Community College*
Kay Walker-Hauser, *Beaufort County Community College–Washington*
Scott Wallace, *Blue Mountain College*
Douglas Ward, *Southwestern Community College*
Jeffrey Waybright, *Spokane Community College*
Roberta Wheeler, *Northwest Florida State College*
Bill Whitley, *Athens State University*
Randall Whitmore, *San Jacinto College*
Vicki White, *Ivy Tech Community College*
Idalene Williams, *Metropolitan Community College*
Betsy Willis, *Baylor University*
Tom Wilson, *University of Louisiana*
Joe Woods, *University of Arkansas*
Patty Worsham, *Riverside Community College*
Gloria Worthy, *Southwest Tennessee Community College*

Shi-Mu (Simon) Yang, *Adelphi University*
Lynnette Yerbuy, *Salt Lake Community College*
Laura Young, *University of Central Arkansas*

Tony Zordan, *University of St.Francis*

1

Accounting and the Business Environment

> As you'll learn in this chapter, the accounting equation (Assets = Liabilities + Equity) IS the balance sheet.

SMART TOUCH LEARNING
Balance Sheet
May 31, 2013

Assets				Liabilities	
Current assets:				**Current liabilities:**	
Cash		$ 4,800		Accounts payable	$ 48,700
Accounts receivable		2,600		Salary payable	900
Inventory		30,500		Interest payable	100
Supplies		600		Unearned service revenue	400
Prepaid rent		2,000		Total current liabilities	50,100
Total current assets			$ 40,500	**Long-term liabilities:**	
Plant assets:				Notes payable	20,000
Furniture	$18,000			Total liabilities	70,100
Less: Accumulated depreciation—furniture	300	17,700			
Building	48,000				
Less: Accumulated depreciation—building	200	47,800		**Owner's Equity**	
Total plant assets			65,500	Bright, capital	35,900
Total assets			$106,000	Total liabilities and owner's equity	$106,000

Learning Objectives

1. Define accounting vocabulary

2. Define the users of financial information

3. Describe the accounting profession and the organizations that govern it

4. Identify the different types of business organizations

5. Delineate the distinguishing characteristics and organization of a proprietorship

6. Apply accounting concepts and principles

7. Describe the accounting equation, and define assets, liabilities, and equity

8. Use the accounting equation to analyze transactions

9. Prepare financial statements

10. Use financial statements to evaluate business performance

Have you ever dreamed of running your own business? If so, where would you begin? How much money would you need? How would you measure its success or failure? Or maybe you're looking to become a manager in an organization. How would you gather the information you need to make strategic decisions? Do you have dreams of retiring early? If so, how do you pick companies to invest in? How can you make smart investment decisions throughout your life? You don't have to be an accountant to make good decisions, but understanding accounting can help you answer these questions and many more.

In this chapter, we'll start our exploration into accounting by looking at two businesses: Smart Touch Learning and Greg's Tunes. We'll see how the owners of these two businesses—Sheena Bright of Smart Touch and Greg Moore of Greg's Tunes—started successful companies by treating people fairly, having realistic expectations, and capitalizing on their general business and accounting savvy. We'll also see how understanding financial statements—like the balance sheet shown on the previous page—is one of the first steps toward business success.

Accounting Vocabulary: The Language of Business

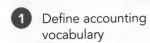 Define accounting vocabulary

You've heard the term *accounting*, but what exactly is it? **Accounting** is the information system that measures business activity, processes the data into reports, and communicates the results to decision makers. **Accounting is "the language of business."** The better you understand the language of business, the better you can manage your own business. For example, how will you decide whether to borrow money to start up a business? You need to consider your income and whether you will be able to pay back that loan. Understanding what income is and how it's calculated is an accounting concept.

A key product of accounting is a set of reports called financial statements. **Financial statements** report on a business in monetary terms. Is Smart Touch making a profit? Should Greg's Tunes expand? If Greg's Tunes expands, how will it get the funds needed to expand? Where is Smart Touch's cash coming from? Financial statements help managers and owners answer questions like these and many more. We'll discuss financial statements in detail later in the chapter. For now, let's turn our attention to the users of accounting information.

Key Takeaway

Accounting is the language of business. Financial statements report a company's activities in monetary terms.

Decision Makers: The Users of Accounting Information

2 Define the users of financial information

We can divide accounting into two fields—financial accounting and managerial accounting.

Financial accounting provides information for external decision makers, such as outside investors and lenders. **Financial accounting provides data for outsiders.**

Managerial accounting focuses on information for internal decision makers, such as the company's managers. **Managerial accounting provides data for insiders.**

Exhibit 1-1 illustrates the difference between financial accounting and managerial accounting. Regardless of whether they are external or internal to the company, all decision makers need information to make the best choices. The bigger the decision, the more information decision makers need. Let's look at some ways in which various people use accounting information to make important decisions.

Individuals

How much cash do you have? How much do you need to save each month to retire at a certain age or pay for your children's college education? Accounting can help you answer questions like these. By using accounting information, you can manage your money, evaluate a new job, and better decide whether you can afford to buy a new computer. Businesses need accounting information to make similar decisions.

EXHIBIT 1-1 | **Financial Accounting and Managerial Accounting**

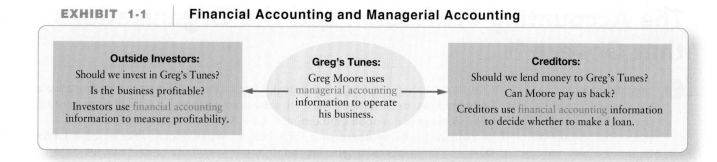

Businesses

Business owners use accounting information to set goals, to measure progress toward those goals, and to make adjustments when needed. The financial statements give owners the information they need to help make those decisions. For example, say Sheena Bright of Smart Touch wants to know whether her business is profitable enough to purchase another computer. Financial statements will help her make that decision.

Investors

Outside investors who have some ownership interest often provide the money to get a business going. For example, Smart Touch may need to raise cash for an expansion. Suppose you're considering investing in Smart Touch. How would you decide whether it is a good investment? In making this decision, you might try to predict the amount of income you would earn on the investment. Also, after making an investment, investors can use a company's financial statements to analyze how their investment is performing.

Every person has the opportunity to invest in their retirement through a company-sponsored retirement plan or IRA contributions. Which investments should you pick? Understanding a company's financial statements will help you decide. (Note that you can view the financial statements of large companies that report to the SEC by logging on to finance.yahoo.com, google.com/finance, or the Security and Exchange Commission's EDGAR database.)

Creditors

Any person or business lending money is a **creditor**. For example, suppose Smart Touch needs $200,000 to buy an office building. Before lending money to Smart Touch, a bank will evaluate the company's ability to make the loan payments by reviewing its financial statements. The same process will apply to you if you need to borrow money for a new car or a house. The bank will review accounting data to determine your ability to make the loan payments. What does your financial position tell the bank about your ability to pay the loan? Are you a good risk for the bank?

Taxing Authorities

Local, state, and federal governments levy taxes. Income tax is figured using accounting information. Good accounting records can help individuals and businesses take advantage of lawful deductions. Without good records, the IRS can disallow tax deductions, resulting in a higher tax bill plus interest and penalties.

Key Takeaway

Different users—including individuals, business owners, managers, investors, creditors, and tax authorities—review a company's financial statements for different reasons. Each user's goal will determine which pieces of the financial statements he or she will find most useful.

The Accounting Profession and the Organizations that Govern It

3 Describe the accounting profession and the organizations that govern it

What do businesses such as Smart Touch, Greg's Tunes, **Walmart,** or the **Coca-Cola Company** have in common? They all need accountants! That is why accounting opens so many doors upon graduation.

You've probably heard of a CPA before. What does it take to be a CPA? Although requirements vary between states, to be certified in a profession, one must meet the educational and/or experience requirements AND pass a qualifying exam. **Certified public accountants,** or **CPAs,** are licensed professional accountants who serve the general public. **Certified management accountants,** or **CMAs,** are certified professionals who work for a single company.

How much do accountants make? The average starting salary for a 2009 college graduate with a bachelor's degree in accounting was $48,334.[1] A graduate with a master's degree earns about 10% more to start, and CPAs earn another 10%.

Many accounting firms are organized as partnerships, and the partners are the owners. It usually takes 10 to 15 years to rise to the rank of partner. The partners of large accounting firms, such as **Ernst & Young,** earn from $150,000 to $500,000 per year. In private accounting, where accountants work for a single company, such as **Walmart,** the top position is called the chief financial officer (CFO), and a CFO earns about as much as a partner in an accounting firm.

Accountants get to the top of organizations as often as anyone else. Why? Because accountants must deal with every aspect of the company's business in order to record all of its activities. Accountants often have the broadest view of what is going on in the company.

As you move through this book, you will learn to account for everything that affects a business—all the revenue, all the expenses, all the cash, all the inventory, all the debts, and all the owner's accounts. Accounting requires you to consider everything, and that is why it is so valuable to an organization. Ultimately, accounting affects everyone, which is why it is important to you.

All professions have regulations. Let's look at the organizations that govern the accounting profession.

Governing Organizations

In the United States, the **Financial Accounting Standards Board (FASB),** a privately funded organization, formulates accounting standards. The FASB works with governmental regulatory agencies like the Securities and Exchange Commission (SEC). The SEC is the U.S. governmental agency that oversees U.S. financial markets. It also oversees those organizations that set standards (like the FASB). The FASB also works with congressionally created groups like the Public Companies Accounting Oversight Board (PCAOB) and private groups like the American Institute of Certified Public Accountants (AICPA) and the Institute of Management Accountants (IMA).

The guidelines for public information are called **generally accepted accounting principles (GAAP). GAAP is the main U.S. accounting rule book.** Some of these guidelines are described later in this chapter. Currently, the SEC has indicated that U.S. GAAP will move to converge with **international financial reporting standards (IFRS)** published by the **International Accounting Standards Board (IASB)** as early as 2012 for some companies. Whereas U.S. GAAP is more specific in its regulation, IFRS is

---

[1]http://www.employmentwebsites.org/salary-offers-college-class-2009-are-flat

less specific and based more on general principles, leaving more room for professional judgment. **IFRS is the international accounting rule book.**

Ethics in Accounting and Business

Ethical considerations affect accounting. Investors and creditors need relevant and reliable information about a company such as **Amazon.com** or **Walmart**. Companies want to be profitable and financially strong to attract investors, so there is a conflict of interest here. To provide reliable information, the SEC requires companies to have their financial statements audited by independent accountants. An **audit** is an examination of a company's financial records. The independent accountants then issue an opinion that states whether or not the financial statements give a fair picture of the company's financial situation.

The vast majority of accountants do their jobs professionally and ethically, but we never hear about them. Unfortunately, only those who cheat make the headlines. In recent years we have seen many accounting scandals.

In response to the **Enron** and **WorldCom** reporting scandals, the U.S. government took swift action. It passed the Sarbanes-Oxley Act, which made it a criminal offense to falsify financial statements. It also created a new watchdog agency, the PCAOB, to monitor the work of independent accountants who audit public companies. More recent scandals, such as the Bernie Madoff scandal, have further undermined the public's faith in financial reporting. This may result in more legislation for future reporting.

Standards of Professional Conduct

The AICPA's Code of Professional Conduct for Accountants provides guidance to CPAs in their work. Ethical standards are designed to produce relevant and reliable information for decision making. The preamble to the Code states the following:

> "[A] certified public accountant assumes an obligation of self-discipline above and beyond the requirements of laws and regulations ... [and] an unswerving commitment to honorable behavior... ."

The opening paragraph of the Standards of Ethical Conduct of the Institute of Management Accountants (IMA) states the following:

> "Management accountants have an obligation to the organizations they serve, their profession, the public, and themselves to maintain the highest standards of ethical conduct."

Most companies also set standards of ethical conduct for employees. For example, Greg's Tunes must comply with copyright laws in order to serve customers ethically. **Microsoft** has a highly developed set of business conduct guidelines. For example, **Microsoft** states that "it is not enough to intend to do things right, we must also do them in the right way."[2] A business's or an individual's reputation is often hard earned and can easily be lost. As one chief executive has stated, "Ethical practice is simply good business." Truth is always better than dishonesty—in accounting, in business, and in life.

> **Key Takeaway**
>
> Most U.S. businesses follow generally accepted accounting principles (GAAP). If the company is publicly traded, then it must also follow SEC guidelines. If the company operates internationally, then international financial reporting standards (IFRS) will apply. The goal is that, eventually, all public U.S. companies will report using IFRS rules.

Types of Business Organizations

A business can be organized as one of the following:

- Proprietorship
- Partnership

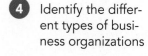

4   Identify the different types of business organizations

---
[2]Excerpt from http://www.microsoft.com/about/legal/en/us/Compliance/Buscond/Default.aspx

- Corporation
- Limited-liability partnership (LLP) and limited-liability company (LLC)
- Not-for-profit

Let's look at the differences among the five types of business organizations.

Proprietorships

A **proprietorship** has a single owner, called the proprietor, who often manages the business. Proprietorships tend to be small retail stores or professional businesses, such as attorneys and accountants. From an accounting perspective, every proprietorship is distinct from its owner: The accounting records of the proprietorship do *not* include the proprietor's personal records. However, from a legal perspective, the business *is* the proprietor. **A proprietorship has one owner called a proprietor.** Smart Touch Learning is a proprietorship.

Partnerships

A **partnership** joins two or more individuals as co-owners. Each owner is a partner and can commit the partnership in a binding contract. This is called **mutual agency**. Mutual agency means that one partner can make all partners mutually liable. Many retail stores and professional organizations of physicians, attorneys, and accountants are partnerships. Most partnerships are small or medium-sized, but some are gigantic, with thousands of partners. For accounting purposes, the partnership is a separate organization, distinct from the partners. **A partnership has two or more owners called partners.**

Corporations

A **corporation** is a business owned by **stockholders**, or **shareholders**. These are the people who own shares of stock in the business. **Stock** is a certificate representing ownership interest in a corporation. A business becomes a corporation when the state grants a **charter** to the company, and the state approves its articles of incorporation and the first stock share is issued. The **articles of incorporation** are the rules approved by the state that govern the management of the corporation. Unlike a proprietorship and a partnership, a corporation is a legal entity distinct from its owners. This legal distinction between corporations and traditional proprietorships and partnerships can be very important for the following reason: If a proprietorship or a partnership cannot pay its debts, lenders can take the owners' personal assets to satisfy the obligations. But if a corporation goes bankrupt, lenders *cannot* take the personal assets of the stockholders. The largest businesses in the United States and in other countries are corporations. The **Coca-Cola Company**, for example, has billions of shares of stock owned by many stockholders. **A corporation has one or more owners called shareholders.**

Limited-Liability Partnerships (LLPs) and Limited-Liability Companies (LLCs)

In a **limited-liability partnership**, each member/partner is liable (obligated) only for his or her own actions and those under his or her control. Similarly, a business can be organized as a **limited-liability company**. In an LLC, the business—and not the members of the LLC—is liable for the company's debts. This arrangement prevents an unethical partner from creating a large liability for the other partners, much like the protection a corporation has. Today most proprietorships and partnerships are organized as LLCs and LLPs. **An LLC has one or more owners called members.**

Not-for-Profits

A **not-for-profit** is an organization that has been approved by the Internal Revenue Service to operate for a religious, charitable, or educational purpose. A board, usually composed of volunteers, makes the decisions for the not-for-profit organization.

Board members have **fiduciary responsibility**, which is an ethical and legal obligation to perform their duties in a trustworthy manner. Their goal is to raise cash to fund their operations. Examples of not-for-profit organizations are the **United Way**, churches, and schools. **A not-for-profit has no owners.** Exhibit 1-2 summarizes the differences among the five types of business organization.

EXHIBIT 1-2 | **Comparison of the Five Forms of Business Organization**

	Proprietorship	Partnership	Corporation	LLP/LLC	Not-for-Profit
1. Owner(s)	Proprietor—only one owner	Partners—two or more owners	Stockholders—generally many owners	Members	None
2. Life of the organization	Limited by the owner's choice, or death	Limited by the owners' choice, or death	Indefinite	Indefinite	Indefinite
3. Personal liability of the owner(s) for the business's debts	Proprietor is personally liable	Partners are personally liable*	Stockholders are not personally liable	Members are not personally liable	Fiduciary liability of board members

*unless it is a limited-liability partnership (LLP)

Stop & Think...

How does a company pick the best type of organization? Deciding on the type of business organization that best meets a company's needs and objectives should be a well-thought-out decision. Small businesses should consult a CPA to consider the tax implications and an attorney to discuss the legal implications of the form of business.

Distinguishing Characteristics and Organization of a Proprietorship

There are several features that distinguish a proprietorship from other types of business organizations. Let's look at them now.

5 Delineate the distinguishing characteristics and organization of a proprietorship

Separate Legal Entity

As we noted earlier, a *corporation* is a business entity formed under state law. The state grants a charter (articles of incorporation), which is the document that gives the state's permission to form a corporation. This is called **authorization** because the state "authorizes" or approves the establishment of the corporate entity.

A proprietorship is a business entity that is not formally "created" by registering with a state agency. It is formed when one individual decides to create a business. It is an entity that exists apart from its owner. However, the proprietorship has many of the rights that a person has. For example, a proprietorship may buy, own, and sell property; enter into contracts; sue; and be sued. Items that the business owns (its assets) and those items that the business has to pay later (its liabilities) belong to the business.

The ownership interest of a proprietorship is recognized in the capital account, which is part of owner's equity. This is listed in the company's books as "Name of owner, capital." So, for example, Sheena Bright is the owner of Smart Touch. Her capital account in the accounting records of Smart Touch would be named Bright, capital.

No Continuous Life or Transferability of Ownership

The life of a proprietorship business is limited by either the owner's choice or the owner's death, whichever comes first. Thus, there is no transferability of ownership in a proprietorship.

Unlimited Liability of Owner

A proprietor has unlimited liability for the business's debts. General partners in partnerships have the same liability; however, stockholders in corporations have limited liability. This unlimited liability makes owning a proprietorship unattractive due to the owner's real fear of losing his or her personal wealth if the proprietorship fails.

Unification of Ownership and Management

The owners of a proprietorship also manage the business. This unification between owners and management is beneficial to the proprietorship and its sole owner because their goals are the same.

Conversely, the separation that exists between stockholders (owners of the corporation) and management in a corporation may create problems. Corporate officers may decide to run the business for their own benefit rather than for the benefit of the company. Stockholders may find it difficult to lodge an effective protest against management because of the distance between them and the top managers.

Business Taxation

Proprietorships are not separate taxable entities. The income earned by the business flows directly to the sole owner. The owner pays tax on the business income on his or her personal tax return. Additionally, the owner must pay self-employment tax for both the employee and employer portions (discussed in Chapter 10).

Government Regulation

Government regulation is an advantage for the proprietorship. There are no stockholders to notify nor are there articles of incorporation to file. Decisions can easily be made by the sole owner/manager.

Organization of a Corporation

As noted earlier, creation of a corporation begins when its organizers, called the incorporators, obtain a charter from the state. The charter includes the authorization for the corporation to issue a certain number of shares of stock, which represent the ownership in the corporation. The incorporators pay fees, sign the charter, and file the required documents with the state. Once the first share of stock is issued, the corporation comes into existence. The incorporators agree to a set of bylaws, which act as the constitution for governing the corporation. **Bylaws are the rule book that guides the corporation.**

The ultimate control of the corporation rests with the stockholders, who normally receive one vote for each share of stock they own. The stockholders elect the members of the board of directors, which sets policy for the corporation and appoints the officers. The board elects a chairperson, who usually is the most powerful person in the corporation. The board also designates the president, who as chief operating officer manages day-to-day operations. Most corporations also have vice-presidents in charge of sales, operations, accounting and finance, and other key areas. Exhibit 1-3 shows the authority structure in a corporation. In the next section, we'll cover the concepts and principles behind financial statements.

> **Key Takeaway**
>
> Proprietorships are formed when one person creates a business. One person owns the proprietorship. Although the proprietorship is a separate entity, it has no continuous life and the owner has unlimited liability for the business's debts. Proprietorships have a more difficult time raising capital but have the advantage of reduced regulation and less taxes than the corporate form of business.

EXHIBIT 1-3 | **Structure of a Corporation**

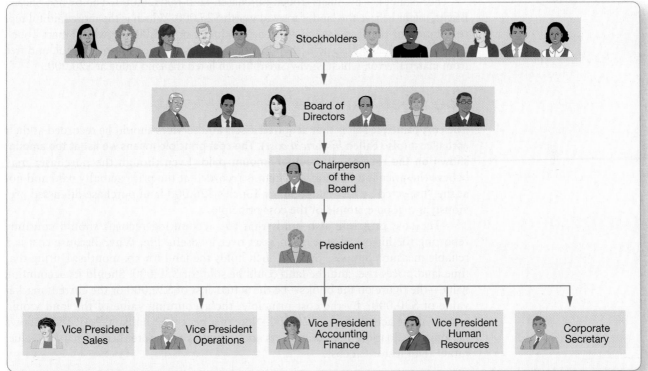

Accounting Concepts and Principles

As mentioned earlier in the chapter, the guidelines that govern accounting fall under GAAP, which stands for generally accepted accounting principles. GAAP rests on a conceptual framework. The primary objective of financial reporting is to provide information useful for making investment and lending decisions. To be useful, information must be relevant, reliable, and comparable. These basic accounting concepts and principles are part of the foundation for the financial reports that companies present.

6 Apply accounting concepts and principles

The Entity Concept

The most basic concept in accounting is that of the **entity**. An accounting entity is an organization that stands apart as a separate economic unit. We draw boundaries around each entity to keep its affairs distinct from those of other entities. **An entity refers to one business, separate from its owners.**

Consider Smart Touch. Assume Sheena Bright started the business by investing capital of $30,000. Following the entity concept, Smart Touch accounted for the $30,000 separately from Sheena's personal assets, such as her clothing and car. To mix the $30,000 of business cash with her personal assets would make it difficult to measure the success or failure of Smart Touch. Thus, *the entity concept applies to any economic unit that needs to be evaluated separately.*

The Faithful Representation Principle

Accounting information is based on the fact that the data faithfully represents the measurement or description of that data. This guideline is the **faithful representation principle.** Faithfully represented data are complete, neutral, and free from material error. For example, a promissory note outlines the details of a bank loan. This note is a faithful representation (evidence) of the loan.

For example, say Smart Touch purchased land for $20,000. The owner, Sheena Bright, might believe the land is instead worth $25,000. Which is the more faithful representation of the land's value—Sheena's estimate of $25,000 or what Smart Touch actually paid, $20,000? The $20,000 amount paid is more complete, neutral, and free from material error, which is why Smart Touch listed the land value at $20,000.

The Cost Principle

The **cost principle** states that acquired assets and services should be recorded at their actual cost (also called *historical cost*). **The cost principle means we list at the amount shown on the receipt—the actual amount paid.** Even though the purchaser may believe the price is a bargain, the item is recorded at the price actually paid and not at the "expected" cost. Again, Smart Touch's $20,000 land purchase discussed previously is a good example of the cost principle.

The cost principle also holds that the accounting records should continue reporting the historical cost of an asset over its useful life. Why? Because cost is a reliable measure. Suppose Smart Touch holds the land for six months. During that time land prices rise, and the land could be sold for $30,000. Should its accounting value—the figure on the books—be the actual cost of $20,000 or the current market value of $30,000? By the cost principle, the accounting value of the land would remain at the actual cost of $20,000. Note that generally, unlike GAAP, IFRS allows periodic revaluation of certain assets and liabilities to restate them to market value, rather than historical cost.

The Going-Concern Concept

Another reason for measuring assets at historical cost is the **going-concern concept.** This concept assumes that the entity will remain in operation for the foreseeable future. Under the going-concern concept, accountants assume that the business will remain in operation long enough to use existing resources for their intended purpose. **The going-concern principle assumes the business won't close soon.**

To understand the going-concern concept better, consider the alternative—which is to go out of business. A store that is closing intends to cease future operations. In that case, the relevant measure is current market value. But going out of business is the exception rather than the rule, which is why we use historical cost.

The Stable Monetary Unit Concept

In the United States, we record transactions in dollars because the dollar is the medium of exchange. The value of a dollar changes over time, and a rise in the price level is called inflation. During periods of inflation, a dollar will purchase less. But accountants assume that the dollar's purchasing power is stable. This assumption is the basis of the **stable monetary unit concept. The stable monetary unit concept means stable currency buying power.**

Now that we've reviewed some of the basic concepts/assumptions underlying financial statements, we'll cover the accounting equation.

The Accounting Equation

The basic tool of accounting is the **accounting equation**. It measures the resources of a business and the claims to those resources.

7 Describe the accounting equation, and define assets, liabilities, and equity

Assets and Liabilities

Assets are economic resources that are expected to benefit the business in the future. **Assets are something the business owns that has value.** Cash, merchandise inventory, furniture, and land are examples of assets.

Claims to those assets come from two sources. **Liabilities** are debts payable to outsiders who are known as creditors. **Liabilities are something the business owes.** For example, a creditor who has loaned money to Smart Touch has a claim to some of the business's assets until the business pays the debt. Many liabilities have the word *payable* in their titles. Examples include Accounts payable, Notes payable, and Salary payable.

The owner's claims to the assets of the business are called **equity** (also called **owner's, stockholders',** or **shareholders' equity,** depending on how the company is organized). **Equity equals what is owned (assets) minus what is owed (liabilities). It is the company's net worth.** These insider claims begin when an owner, such as Sheena Bright, invests assets in the business and receives capital.

The accounting equation shows how assets, liabilities, and owner's equity are related. Assets appear on the left side of the equation, and the liabilities and owner's equity appear on the right side. **The accounting equation is an equation—so the left side of the equation always equals the right side of the equation.**

Exhibit 1-4 diagrams how the two sides must always be equal (amounts are assumed for this illustration):

(Economic Resources)		(Claims to Economic Resources)
ASSETS	=	**LIABILITIES + EQUITY**
$5,000	=	$2,000 + $3,000

EXHIBIT 1-4 | **The Accounting Equation**

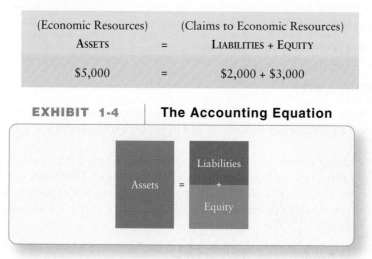

Equity

The equity of a sole proprietorship is called owner's equity. For a proprietorship, the accounting equation can be written as

$$\text{ASSETS} = \text{LIABILITIES} + \underbrace{\text{OWNER'S EQUITY}}$$
$$\text{ASSETS} = \text{LIABILITIES} + \qquad\text{CAPITAL}$$

- **Capital** is the net amount invested in the business by the owner. An owner can contribute cash or other net assets to the business and receive capital.
- Capital contains the amount earned by income-producing activities and kept (retained) for use in the business. Two types of events that affect capital are revenues and expenses. **Revenues** are increases in capital from delivering goods or services to customers. **Revenues are earnings.** For example, if Smart Touch provided e-learning services and earned $5,500 of revenue, the business's capital increased by $5,500.

There are relatively few types of revenue, including the following:

- **Sales revenue.** Greg's Tunes earns sales revenue by selling CDs to customers.
- **Service revenue.** Smart Touch earns service revenue by providing e-learning services.
- **Interest revenue.** Interest revenue is earned on bank deposits and on money lent out to others.
- **Dividend revenue.** Dividend revenue is earned on investments in the stock of other corporations.

Expenses are the decreases in capital that result from operations. **Expenses are incurred costs that you will have to pay for, either now or later.** For example, Smart Touch paid salaries of $1,200 to its employees and that is an expense that decreases capital. Expenses are the opposite of revenues.

Unfortunately, businesses have lots of expenses. Some common expenses are as follows:

- Store (or office) rent expense
- Salary expense for employees
- Advertising expense
- Utilities expense for water, electricity, and gas
- Insurance expense
- Supplies expense for supplies used up
- Interest expense on loans payable
- Property tax expense

Businesses strive for net income. When revenues exceed expenses, the result of operations is a profit or **net income.** When expenses exceed revenues, the result is a **net loss.**

After earning net income, the business may distribute cash or other assets to the owner, a third type of transaction that affects capital. **Drawings** are distributions of capital (usually of cash) to owners. Drawings are not expenses. An owner may or may not make withdrawals from the business. Exhibit 1-5 shows the components of capital.

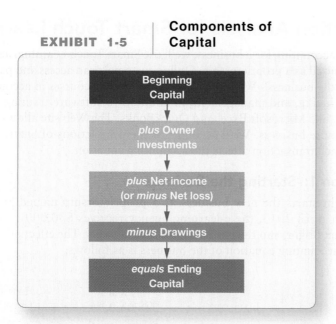

EXHIBIT 1-5 | **Components of Capital**

Beginning Capital

↓

plus Owner investments

↓

plus Net income (or *minus* Net loss)

↓

minus Drawings

↓

equals Ending Capital

The owners' equity of partnerships is similar. The main difference is there are separate capital accounts for each partner. For example, a partnership of Joan Pratt and Simon Nagle would have accounts for Pratt, capital and Nagle, capital. The owners' equity (or shareholders' or stockholders' equity) of a corporation is also different. Stockholders' equity has two components: Paid-in capital and Retained earnings. **Paid-in capital,** or **contributed capital,** is the amount invested in the corporation by its owners, the stockholders. The basic component of paid-in capital is stock, which the corporation issues to the stockholders as evidence of their ownership. **Common stock** represents the basic ownership of every corporation. **Retained earnings** of a corporation represent the net earnings retained by the corporation.

Stop & Think...

The accounting equation is important to a business, but it is also important to the individual. Consider your "personal" accounting equation. Are you content with your current net worth (equity) or do you want to increase it? Do you think your education will help you to increase your net worth?

Students enroll in education programs for many reasons. However, underneath all the reasons is a basic desire to increase net worth through knowledge, higher paying job skills, or a better understanding of business.

Accounting for Business Transactions

Accounting is based on actual transactions, not opinions or desires. A **transaction** is any event that affects the financial position of the business *and* can be measured reliably. **Transactions affect what the company owns, owes, or its net worth.** Many events affect a company, including economic booms and recessions. Accountants, however, do not record the effects of those events. An accountant records only those events that have dollar amounts that can be measured reliably, such as the purchase of a building, a sale of merchandise, and the payment of rent.

What are some of your personal transactions? You may have bought a car. Your purchase was a transaction. If you are making payments on an auto loan, your payments are also transactions. You need to record all your business transactions—just as Smart Touch does—in order to manage your business affairs.

 8 Use the accounting equation to analyze transactions

Transaction Analysis for Smart Touch Learning

To illustrate accounting for a business, we'll use Smart Touch Learning, an e-learning agency organized as a proprietorship. Online customers can access and pay for training through the business's Web site. The Web site offers courses in accounting, economics, marketing, and management, in addition to software training on specific applications, like Microsoft Excel and QuickBooks. The Web site allows the agency to transact more business. We'll account for the transactions of Smart Touch and show how each transaction affects the accounting equation.

Transaction 1: Starting the Business

Sheena Bright starts the new business as a proprietorship named Smart Touch Learning. In April 2013, the e-learning agency receives $30,000 cash from the owner, Sheena Bright, and the business gave capital to her. The effect of this transaction on the accounting equation of the business is as follows:

ASSETS		LIABILITIES	+	OWNER'S EQUITY (OE)	TYPE OF OE TRANSACTION
Cash	=			Bright, capital	
(1) +30,000				+30,000	*Owner investment*

For each transaction, the amount on the left side of the equation must equal the amount on the right side. The first transaction increases both the assets (in this case, Cash) and the owner's equity (Bright, capital) of the business. To the right of the transaction, we write "Owner investment" to keep track of the source of the equity.

BE SURE TO START ON THE RIGHT TRACK—Keep in mind that we are doing the accounting for Smart Touch Learning, the business. We are *not* accounting for Sheena Bright, the person.

View all transactions, and do all the accounting, from the perspective of the business—not from the viewpoint of the owner. This is the entity concept we reviewed earlier in the chapter.

Transaction 2: Purchase of Land

The business purchases land for an office location, paying cash of $20,000. This transaction affects the accounting equation of Smart Touch as follows:

	ASSETS			LIABILITIES	+	OWNER'S EQUITY
	Cash	+	Land			Bright, capital
(1)	30,000			=		30,000
(2)	−20,000		+20,000			
Bal	10,000		20,000			30,000
		30,000				30,000

The cash purchase of land increases one asset, Land, and decreases another asset, Cash. After the transaction is completed, the business has cash of $10,000, land of $20,000, no liabilities, and owner's equity of $30,000. Note that the total balances (abbreviated Bal) on both sides of the equation must always be equal—in this case $30,000.

Transaction 3: Purchase of Office Supplies

The e-learning agency buys office supplies on account (credit), agreeing to pay $500 within 30 days. The company will use the supplies in the future, so they are an asset to the business. This transaction increases both the assets and the liabilities of the business, as follows:

	ASSETS					LIABILITIES	+	OWNER'S EQUITY
	Cash	+	Office supplies	+	Land	Accounts payable	+	Bright, capital
Bal	10,000				20,000			30,000
(3)			+500			+500		
Bal	10,000		500		20,000	500		30,000
			30,500				30,500	

Office supplies is an asset, not an expense, because the supplies aren't used up now, but will be in the future. The liability created by purchasing "on account" is an **Account payable**, which is a short-term liability that will be paid in the future. A payable is always a liability.

Transaction 4: Earning of Service Revenue

Smart Touch earns service revenue by providing training services for clients. The business earns $5,500 of revenue and collects this amount in cash. The effect on the accounting equation is an increase in Cash and an increase in Bright, capital as follows:

	ASSETS				LIABILITIES	+ OWNER'S EQUITY	TYPE OF OE TRANSACTION
	Cash	+ supplies	+ Land		Accounts payable	+ Bright, capital	
		Office					
Bal	10,000	500	20,000	=	500	30,000	
(4)	+5,500					+5,500	*Service revenue*
Bal	15,500	500	20,000		500	35,500	
		36,000				36,000	

A revenue transaction grows the business, as shown by the increases in assets and owner's equity (Bright, capital).

Transaction 5: Earning of Service Revenue on Account

Smart Touch performs a service for clients who do not pay immediately. The business receives the clients' promise to pay $3,000 within one month. This promise is an asset, an **Account receivable**, because the agency expects to collect the cash in the future. In accounting, we say that Smart Touch performed this service *on account*. It is in performing the service (doing the work), not collecting the cash, that the company *earns* the revenue. As in transaction 4, increasing earnings increases Bright, capital. Smart Touch records the earning of $3,000 of revenue on account, as follows:

		ASSETS				LIABILITIES +	OWNER'S EQUITY	TYPE OF OE TRANSACTION
	Cash	+ Accounts receivable	+ Office supplies	+ Land	=	Accounts payable +	Bright, capital	
Bal	15,500		500	20,000		500	35,500	
(5)		+3,000					+3,000	*Service revenue*
Bal	15,500	3,000	500	20,000		500	38,500	
			39,000				39,000	

Transaction 6: Payment of Expenses

During the month, the business pays $3,300 in cash expenses: rent expense on a computer, $600; office rent, $1,100; employee salary, $1,200; and utilities, $400. The effects on the accounting equation are as follows:

		ASSETS				LIABILITIES +	OWNER'S EQUITY	TYPE OF OE TRANSACTION
	Cash	+ Accounts receivable	+ Office supplies	+ Land	=	Accounts payable +	Bright, capital	
Bal	15,500	3,000	500	20,000		500	38,500	
(6)	–600						–600	*Rent expense, computer*
(6)	–1,100						–1,100	*Rent expense, office*
(6)	–1,200						–1,200	*Salary expense*
(6)	–400						–400	*Utilities expense*
Bal	12,200	3,000	500	20,000		500	35,200	
			35,700				35,700	

Expenses have the opposite effect of revenues. Expenses shrink the business, as shown by the decreased balances of assets and owner's equity (Bright, capital).

Each expense can be recorded separately. The expenses are listed as one transaction here for simplicity. We could record the cash payment in a single amount for the sum of the four expenses: $3,300 ($600 + $1,100 + $1,200 + $400). However the expenses are recorded, the accounting equation must balance. (Notice that each side totals to $35,700.)

Transaction 7: Payment on Account

The business pays $300 to the store from which it purchased supplies in transaction 3. In accounting, we say that the business pays $300 *on account*. The effect on the accounting equation is a decrease in Cash and a decrease in Accounts payable, as shown here:

		ASSETS					LIABILITIES + OWNER'S EQUITY	
	Cash +	Accounts receivable +	Office supplies +	Land		=	Accounts payable +	Bright, capital
Bal	12,200	3,000	500	20,000			500	35,200
(7)	–300						–300	
Bal	11,900	3,000	500	20,000			200	35,200
		35,400					35,400	

The payment of cash on account has no effect on the amount of office supplies (asset) Smart Touch has nor on the amount of office supplies it uses (expense). Smart Touch was paying off a liability (accounts payable decreased $300), with cash (Cash decreased $300).

Transaction 8: Personal Transaction

Sheena Bright buys groceries at a cost of $200, paying cash from personal funds. This event is *not* a transaction of Smart Touch. It has no effect on the e-learning agency and, therefore, is not recorded by the business. It is a transaction of the Sheena Bright *personal* entity, not the e-learning agency. This transaction illustrates the *entity concept*.

Transaction 9: Collection on Account

In transaction 5, the business performed services for a client on account. The business now collects $1,000 from the client. We say that Smart Touch collects the cash *on account*. The business will record an increase in the asset Cash. Should it also record an increase in service revenue? No, because the business already recorded the revenue when it earned the revenue in transaction 5. The phrase "collect cash on account" means to record an increase in Cash and a decrease in Accounts receivable. Accounts receivable is decreased because the $1,000 that the business was to collect at some point in the future is being collected today. The effect on the accounting equation is as follows:

		ASSETS					LIABILITIES + OWNER'S EQUITY	
	Cash +	Accounts receivable +	Office supplies +	Land		=	Accounts payable +	Bright, capital
Bal	11,900	3,000	500	20,000			200	35,200
(9)	+1,000	–1,000						
Bal	12,900	2,000	500	20,000			200	35,200
		35,400					35,400	

Total assets are unchanged from the preceding total. Why? Because Smart Touch exchanged one asset (Cash) for another (Accounts receivable).

Transaction 10: Sale of Land

The business sells some land owned by the e-learning agency. The sale price of $9,000 is equal to the cost of the land, so Smart Touch didn't gain or lose anything extra from the land sale. The business receives $9,000 cash, and the effect on the accounting equation follows:

		ASSETS				LIABILITIES + OWNER'S EQUITY	
	Cash +	Accounts receivable +	Office supplies +	Land		Accounts payable +	Bright, capital
Bal	12,900	2,000	500	20,000	=	200	35,200
(10)	+9,000			−9,000			
Bal	21,900	2,000	500	11,000		200	35,200
		35,400				35,400	

Transaction 11: Owner Drawing of Cash

Sheena Bright withdraws $2,000 cash from the business. The effect on the accounting equation is:

		ASSETS				LIABILITIES +	OWNER'S EQUITY	TYPE OF OE TRANSACTION
	Cash +	Accounts receivable +	Office supplies +	Land		Accounts payable +	Bright, capital	
Bal	21,900	2,000	500	11,000	=	200	35,200	
(11)	−2,000						−2,000	*Owner withdrawal*
Bal	19,900	2,000	500	11,000		200	33,200	
		33,400				33,400		

The owner withdrawal decreases the business's Cash and owner's equity (Bright, capital). *Drawings do not represent an expense because they are not related to the earning of revenue. Therefore, drawings do not affect the business's net income or net loss.* The double underlines below each column indicate a final total after the last transaction.

Preparing the Financial Statements—The User Perspective of Accounting

 Prepare financial statements

We have now recorded Smart Touch's transactions, and they are summarized in Exhibit 1-6. Notice how total assets equals total liabilities plus owner's equity.

But a basic question remains: How will people actually use this information? The mass of data in Exhibit 1-6 will not tell a lender whether Smart Touch can pay off a loan. The data in the exhibit do not tell whether the business is profitable.

To address these important questions, we need financial statements. As noted earlier, *financial statements* are business documents that report on a business in

EXHIBIT 1-6 | **Analysis of Transactions, Smart Touch Learning**

PANEL A—Details of Transactions

1. The e-learning agency received $30,000 cash and gave capital to Sheena Bright.
2. Paid $20,000 cash for land.
3. Bought $500 of office supplies on account.
4. Received $5,500 cash from clients for service revenue earned.
5. Performed services for clients on account, $3,000.
6. Paid cash expenses: computer rent, $600; office rent, $1,100; employee salary, $1,200; utilities, $400.
7. Paid $300 on the account payable created in transaction 3.
8. Bright buys $200 of groceries. This is *not* a transaction of the business.
9. Collected $1,000 on the account receivable created in transaction 5.
10. Sold land for cash at its cost of $9,000.
11. Owner withdrew cash of $2,000.

PANEL B—Analysis of Transactions

		Assets				Liabilities +	Owner's Equity (OE)	Type of OE Transaction
	Cash +	Accounts receivable +	Office supplies +	Land		Accounts payable +	Bright, capital	
1.	+ 30,000						+ 30,000	Owner investment
Bal	30,000	0	0	0		0	30,000	
2.	− 20,000			+ 20,000				
Bal	10,000	0	0	20,000		0	30,000	
3.			+ 500			+ 500		
Bal	10,000	0	500	20,000		500	30,000	
4.	+ 5,500						+ 5,500	Service revenue
Bal	15,500	0	500	20,000		500	35,500	
5.		+ 3,000					+ 3,000	Service revenue
Bal	15,500	3,000	500	20,000		500	38,500	
6.	− 600				=		− 600	Rent expense, computer
6.	− 1,100						− 1,100	Rent expense, office
6.	− 1,200						− 1,200	Salary expense
6.	− 400						− 400	Utilities expense
Bal	12,200	3,000	500	20,000		500	35,200	
7.	− 300					− 300		
Bal	11,900	3,000	500	20,000		200	35,200	
8.	Not a transaction of the business							
9.	+ 1,000	− 1,000						
Bal	12,900	2,000	500	20,000		200	35,200	
10.	+ 9,000			− 9,000				
Bal	21,900	2,000	500	11,000		200	35,200	
11.	− 2,000						− 2,000	Owner withdrawal
Bal	19,900	2,000	500	11,000		200	33,200	

33,400   33,400

Connect To: Accounting Information Systems (AIS)

The accounting information system is the system that records the transactions for a company. It can be manual or computerized. Most businesses today use some sort of computerized system, which simplifies repetitive transactions. However, the system must be able to not only record transactions properly, but also comply with regulatory agencies, such as the SEC, GAAP, IFRS, and/or the PCAOB. Another way to say this is the AIS must be able to meet a variety of users' different reporting needs so those users can get the information they require.

monetary terms. People use financial statements to make business decisions. Consider the following examples:

- Sheena Bright wants to know whether the business is profitable. Is the business earning a net income, or is it experiencing a net loss? The **income statement** answers this question by reporting the net income or net loss of the business.
- The banker asks what the business did with any profits earned. Did Bright withdraw the earnings or did she keep the earnings in the training agency? The **statement of owner's equity** answers this question. Suppose the business needs $200,000 to buy an office building. The banker will want to know how much in assets the e-learning company has and how much it already owes. The **balance sheet** answers this question by reporting the business's assets and liabilities.
- The banker wants to know if the agency generates enough cash to pay its bills. The **statement of cash flows** answers this question by reporting cash receipts and cash payments and whether cash increased or decreased.
- Outside investors also use financial statements. Smart Touch may need to raise cash for an expansion. Suppose you are considering investing in the training agency. In making this decision, you would ask the same questions that Sheena Bright and the banker have been asking.

In summary, the main users of financial statements are

- business owners and managers,
- lenders, and
- outside investors.

Others also use the financial statements, but the three user groups listed above are paramount, and we will be referring to them throughout this book. Now let's examine the financial statements in detail.

The Financial Statements

After analyzing transactions, we want to see the overall results. The financial statements summarize the transaction data into a form that is useful for decision making. As we discussed the financial statements are the

- income statement,
- statement of owner's equity,
- balance sheet, and
- statement of cash flows.

Headings

Each financial statement (and every other financial document you'll probably see or use) has a heading that provides three pieces of data:

- Name of the business (such as Smart Touch Learning)
- Name of the financial statement (income statement, balance sheet, or other financial statement)
- Date or time period covered by the statement (April 30, 2013, for the balance sheet; month ended April 30, 2013, for the other statements)

Financial statements that show activity, like an income statement that covers a year that ended in December 2013, are dated "Year Ended December 31, 2013." A monthly income statement (or statement of owner's equity) for September 2013 shows "Month Ended September 30, 2013." A quarterly income statement (or statement of owner's equity) for the three months ending June 30, 2013, shows "Quarter Ended June 30, 2013." **The dateline describes the period covered by the statement.** Let's look at each of these financial statements in a bit more detail.

Income Statement

The income statement (also called the **statement of earnings** or **statement of operations**) presents a summary of a business entity's revenues and expenses for a period of time, such as a month, quarter, or year. The income statement is like a video—a moving picture of operations during the period. It displays one of the most important pieces of information about a business: Did the business make a profit? The income statement tells us whether the business enjoyed net income or suffered a net loss. Remember,

- **net income** means total revenues are greater than total expenses.
- **net loss** means total expenses are greater than total revenues.

Net income is good news, net loss is bad news. What was the result of Smart Touch's operations during April? Good news—the business earned net income of $5,200 (see the first part of Exhibit 1-7 on the next page).

Statement of Owner's Equity

The statement of owner's equity (shown in the first overlay of Exhibit 1-7) shows the changes in capital for a business entity during a time period, such as a month, quarter, or year.

Capital increases when the business has

- owner contributions of capital, or
- a net income (revenues exceed expenses).

Capital decreases when the business has

- a net loss (expenses exceed revenues), or
- owner withdrawals of cash or other assets.

What changes occurred in Smart Touch's capital during April? Capital increased by the $30,000 of capital contributed by Sheena Bright and by the amount of net income of $5,200. Capital decreased $2,000 for the drawing made by Sheena Bright (see Exhibit 1-7).

Balance Sheet

The balance sheet lists a business entity's assets, liabilities, and owner's equity as of a specific date, usually the end of a month, quarter, or year. The balance sheet is like a snapshot of the entity. It is also called the **statement of financial position** (see the second overlay showing the middle of Exhibit 1-7.) **The balance sheet mirrors the accounting equation.**

Statement of Cash Flows

The statement of cash flows reports the cash coming in (positive amounts) and the cash going out (negative amounts) during a period. Business activities result in a net cash inflow or a net cash outflow. The statement of cash flows reports the net increase or decrease in cash during the period and the ending cash balance. (See the final overlay of Exhibit 1-7.)

In the first part of this book, we focus on the

- income statement,
- statement of owner's equity, and
- balance sheet.

In Chapter 14 we cover the statement of cash flows in detail.

Key Takeaway

Financial statements are prepared from the ending balances of each account. Each financial statement shows a different view of the company's overall results.

EXHIBIT 1-7 | **Financial Statements of Smart Touch Learning**

SMART TOUCH LEARNING		
Income Statement		
Month Ended April 30, 2013		
Revenue:		
Service revenue		$8,500
Expenses:		
Salary expense	$1,200	
Rent expense, office	1,100	
Rent expense, computer	600	
Utilities expense	400	
Total expenses		3,300
Net income		$5,200

Using Financial Statements to Evaluate Business Performance

Exhibit 1-7 illustrates all four financial statements in the order that we prepare them. The data come from the transaction analysis in Exhibit 1-6 that covers the month of April 2013. Study the exhibit carefully. Then, observe the following in Exhibit 1-7:

10 Use financial statements to evaluate business performance

1. The *income statement* for the month ended April 30, 2013,
   a. reports April's revenues and expenses.
   b. lists expenses in order of largest to smallest expense.
   c. calculates and lists total expenses.
   d. reports *net income* of the period if total revenues exceed total expenses. If total expenses exceed total revenues, a *net loss* is reported instead.

2. The *statement of owner's equity* for the month ended April 30, 2013,
   a. opens with the capital balance at the beginning of the period (zero for a new entity).
   b. adds *owner contributions* made during the month.
   c. adds *net income* directly from the income statement (see arrow 1 in Exhibit 1-7).
   d. subtracts *drawings* (and net loss, if applicable). Parentheses indicate a subtraction.
   e. ends with the capital balance at the end of the period.

3. The *balance sheet* at April 30, 2013,
   a. reports all *assets*, all *liabilities*, and *owner's equity* at the end of the period.
   b. lists assets in the order of their liquidity (closeness to cash) with cash coming first because it is the most liquid asset.
   c. reports liabilities similarly. That is, the liability that must be paid first is listed first, usually Accounts payable.
   d. reports that total assets equal total liabilities plus total equity (the accounting equation).
   e. reports the ending capital balance, taken directly from the statement of owner's equity (see arrow 2).

4. The *statement of cash flows* for the month ended April 30, 2013,
   a. reports cash flows from three types of business activities (*operating*, *investing*, and *financing activities*) during the month. Each category of cash-flow activities includes both cash receipts (positive amounts), and cash payments (negative amounts denoted by parentheses).
   b. reports a net increase (or decrease) in cash during the month and ends with the cash balance at April 30, 2013. This is the amount of cash to report on the balance sheet (see arrow 3).

Each of the statements identified in Exhibit 1-7 provides different information about the company to the users of the financial statements.

- The income statement provides information about profitability for a particular period for the company. Recall that expenses are listed in this statement from largest to smallest. This ordering shows users which expenses are consuming the largest part of the revenues.

- The statement of owner's equity informs users about how much of the earnings were kept and reinvested in the company. Recall from Exhibit 1-7 that three main items appear in this statement that explain the change in the capital balance:

1. Owner contributions

2. Net income or net loss

3. Drawings by the owner

If the owner drawings were larger than income for the period, this could signal concern to financial statement users.

The balance sheet in Exhibit 1-7 provides valuable information to financial statement users about economic resources the company owns (assets) as well as debts the company owes (liabilities). Thus, the balance sheet presents the overall financial position of the company on a specific date. This allows decision makers to determine their opinion about the financial status of the company.

The cash flow statement is covered in detail in a later chapter in the textbook. Briefly, its purpose and value to users is to explain why the net income number on the income statement does not equal the change in the cash balance for the period.

As we conclude this chapter, we return to our opening question: Have you ever thought of having your own business? The Decision Guidelines feature on the next page shows how to make some of the decisions that you will face if you start a business. Decision Guidelines appear in each chapter.

Key Takeaway

Financial statements are prepared from the transaction analyses (summary of events) reported in each account (Exhibit 1-6) in the order shown in Exhibit 1-7. No one financial statement shows everything about a company. It is the financial statements AND the relationships the statements show that give users the overall picture for a specific company.

Decision Guidelines 1-1

MAJOR BUSINESS DECISIONS

Suppose you open a business to take photos at parties at your school. You hire a professional photographer and line up suppliers for party favors and photo albums. Here are some factors you must consider if you expect to be profitable.

Decision	Guidelines
• How to organize the business?	If a single owner—a *proprietorship*.
	If two or more owners, but not incorporated— a *partnership* or *limited liability company*.
	If the business issues stock to stockholders—a *corporation*.
	If the motives are religious, charitable, or educational—a *not-for-profit*.
• What to account for?	Account for the business, a separate entity apart from its owner (*entity concept*).
	Account for transactions and events that affect the business's accounting equation and can be measured reliably.
• How much to record for assets and liabilities?	U.S. GAAP—Actual historical amount (*cost principle*).
	IFRS—Market value.
• How to analyze a transaction?	The accounting equation:

$$\begin{array}{ccccc} (\text{own}) = & (\text{owe}) & + & (\text{net worth}) \\ \text{Assets} = & \text{Liabilities} & + & \text{Owner's Equity} \end{array}$$

Decision	Guidelines
• How to measure profits and losses?	Income statement:

$$\text{Revenues} - \text{Expenses} = \text{Net Income (or Net Loss)}$$

Decision	Guidelines
• Did owner's equity increase or decrease?	Statement of owner's equity:

$$\begin{array}{l} \text{Beginning capital} \\ + \text{ Owner investments} \\ + \text{ Net income (or } - \text{ Net loss)} \\ - \text{ Drawings} \\ \hline = \text{Ending capital} \end{array}$$

Decision	Guidelines
• Where does the business stand financially?	Balance sheet (accounting equation):

$$\text{Assets} = \text{Liabilities} + \text{Owner's Equity}$$

Summary Problem 1-1

Ron Smith opens an apartment-locator business near a college campus. The company will be named Campus Apartment Locators. During the first month of operations, July 2013, the business completes the following transactions:

a. Smith invests $35,000. The business receives $35,000 cash and gives capital to Smith.
b. Purchases $350 of office supplies on account.
c. Pays cash of $30,000 to acquire a lot next to the campus. Smith intends to use the land as a future building site for the business office.
d. Locates apartments for clients and receives cash of $1,900.
e. Pays $100 on the account payable he created in transaction b.
f. Pays $2,000 of personal funds for a vacation.
g. Pays cash expenses for office rent, $400, and utilities, $100.
h. Returns office supplies of $150 from transaction b.
i. Smith withdrew cash of $1,200.

Requirements

1. Analyze the preceding transactions in terms of their effects on the accounting equation of Campus Apartment Locators. Use Exhibit 1-6 as a guide, but show balances only after the last transaction.
2. Prepare the income statement, statement of owner's equity, and balance sheet of the business after recording the transactions. Use Exhibit 1-7 as a guide.

Solution

Requirement 1

Analysis of transactions

	ASSETS				LIABILITIES + OWNER'S EQUITY		TYPE OF OE TRANSACTION
	Cash	+	Office supplies	+ Land	Accounts payable +	Smith, capital	
(a)	+35,000					+35,000	*Owner investment*
(b)			+350		+350		
(c)	−30,000			+30,000			
(d)	+1,900					+1,900	*Service revenue*
(e)	−100				−100		
(f)	Not a transaction of the business						
(g)	−400					−400	*Rent expense*
	−100					−100	*Utilities expense*
(h)			−150		−150		
(i)	−1,200					−1,200	*Owner withdrawal*
Bal	5,100		200	30,000	100	35,200	
		35,300				35,300	

Requirement 2

Financial Statements of Campus Apartment Locators.

CAMPUS APARTMENT LOCATORS
Income Statement
Month Ended July 31, 2013

Revenue:		
Service revenue		$1,900
Expenses:		
Rent expense	$400	
Utilities expense	100	
Total expenses		500
Net income		$1,400

CAMPUS APARTMENT LOCATORS
Statement of Owner's Equity
Month Ended July 31, 2013

Smith, capital, July 1, 2013	$ 0
Owner investment	35,000
Net income for the month	1,400
	36,400
Drawing	(1,200)
Smith, capital, July 31, 2013	$35,200

CAMPUS APARTMENT LOCATORS
Balance Sheet
July 31, 2013

Assets		Liabilities	
Cash	$ 5,100	Accounts payable	$ 100
Office supplies	200		
Land	30,000		
		Owner's Equity	
		Smith, capital	35,200
Total assets	$35,300	Total liabilities and owner's equity	$35,300

Chapter 1: Demo Doc

Transaction Analysis Using Accounting Equation/Financial Statement Preparation

To make sure you understand this material, work through the following demonstration "demo doc" with detailed comments to help you see the concept within the framework of a worked-through problem.

7 8 9

On March 1, 2014, David Richardson started a painting business near a historical housing district. David was the sole proprietor of the company, which he named DR Painting. During March 2014, DR Painting engaged in the following transactions:

a. DR Painting received cash of $40,000 from David Richardson and gave capital to Richardson.
b. The business paid $20,000 cash to acquire a truck.
c. The business purchased supplies costing $1,800 on account.
d. The business painted a house for a client and received $3,000 cash.
e. The business painted a house for a client for $4,000. The client agreed to pay next week.
f. The business paid $800 cash toward the supplies purchased in transaction c.
g. The business paid employee salaries of $1,000 in cash.
h. Richardson withdrew cash of $1,500.
i. The business collected $2,600 from the client in transaction e.
j. David paid $100 cash for personal groceries.

Requirements

1. Analyze the preceding transactions in terms of their effects on the accounting equation of DR Painting. Use Exhibit 1-6 as a guide, but show balances only after the last transaction.

2. Prepare the income statement, statement of owner's equity, and balance sheet of the business after recording the transactions. Use Exhibit 1-7 in the text as a guide.

Chapter 1: Demo Doc Solution

Requirement 1

Analyze the preceding transactions in terms of their effects on the accounting equation of DR Painting. Use Exhibit 1-6 as a guide, but show balances only after the last transaction.

Part 1	Part 2	Part 3	Part 4	Demo Doc Complete

a. DR Painting received $40,000 cash from David Richardson and gave capital to Richardson.

The business is receiving cash from the owner, so this is a recordable transaction for DR Painting.

The business's Cash (an asset) is increased by $40,000 and Richardson, capital (owner's equity) is also increased by $40,000.

The effect of this transaction on the accounting equation is as follows:

	ASSETS	= LIABILITIES +	OWNER'S EQUITY (OE)	TYPE OF OE TRANSACTION
	Cash =		Richardson, capital	
a.	+40,000		+40,000	*Owner investment*
	40,000 =		40,000	

To record this in the table, we add $40,000 under Assets (Cash) and add $40,000 under Owner's Equity (Richardson, capital). To the right of the transaction, we write "Owner investment" to help us keep track of changes in the equity of the business. Before we move on, we should double-check to see that the left side of the equation equals the right side. It is important to remember that the equation must always balance after each transaction is recorded.

b. **The business paid $20,000 cash to acquire a truck.**

The Truck (an asset) is increased by $20,000, while Cash (an asset) decreases by $20,000.

The effect of this transaction on the accounting equation is as follows:

	ASSETS		= LIABILITIES +	OWNER'S EQUITY	TYPE OF OE TRANSACTION
	Cash +	Truck =		Richardson, capital	
Bal	40,000		=	40,000	
b.	−20,000	+20,000			
Bal	20,000	20,000 =		40,000	
		40,000 =	40,000		

Note that transactions do not have to affect both sides of the equation. However, the accounting equation *always* equals, so *both sides must always balance*. It helps to check that this is true after every transaction.

c. **The business purchased supplies costing $1,800 on account.**

The supplies are an asset that is increased by $1,800. However, the supplies were not paid for in cash, but instead *on account*. This relates to accounts *pay*able (because it will have to be *paid* later). Because we now owe *more* money that has to be paid later, it is an increase to Accounts payable (a liability) of $1,800.

The effect of this transaction on the accounting equation is as follows:

	ASSETS			= LIABILITIES +	OWNER'S EQUITY	TYPE OF OE TRANSACTION
	Cash +	Supplies +	Truck =	Accounts payable +	Richardson, capital	
Bal	20,000		20,000		40,000	
c.		+1,800		+1,800		
Bal	20,000	1,800	20,000 =	1,800	40,000	
			41,800 =	41,800		

Remember that the supplies will be recorded as an asset until the time that they are used by the business (the adjustment will be addressed in a later chapter). The obligation to pay the $1,800 will remain in Accounts payable until it is paid.

d. The business painted a house for a client and received cash of $3,000.

When the business paints houses, it means that it is doing work, or performing services for clients, which is the way that the business makes money. By performing services, the business is earning service revenues.

This means that there is an increase in Service revenue (which increases Richardson, capital) of $3,000. Because the clients paid in cash, there is also an increase in Cash (an asset) of $3,000.

Remember: Revenues *increase* net income, which increases owner's equity (Richardson, capital).

The effect of this transaction on the accounting equation is as follows:

		ASSETS		=	LIABILITIES	+	OWNER'S EQUITY	TYPE OF OE TRANSACTION
	Cash	+ Supplies	+ Truck	=	Accounts payable	+	Richardson, capital	
Bal	20,000	1,800	20,000	=	1,800		40,000	
d.	+3,000						+3,000	*Service revenue*
Bal	23,000	1,800	20,000	=	1,800		43,000	
			44,800	=	44,800			

Note that we write "Service revenue" to the right of the Richardson, capital column to record the type of transaction.

e. The business painted a house for a client for $4,000. The client agreed to pay next month.

This transaction is similar to transaction **d**, except that the business is not receiving the cash immediately. Does this mean that we should wait to record the revenue until the cash is received? No, DR Painting should recognize the revenue when the service is performed, regardless of whether it has received the cash.

Again, the business is performing services for clients, which means that it is earning service revenues. This results in an increase to Service revenue (Richardson, capital) of $4,000.

However, this time the client did not pay in cash but instead agreed to pay later. This is the same as charging the services *on account*. This is money that the business will *receive* in the future (when the customers eventually pay), so it is called accounts *receivable*. Accounts receivable (an asset) is increasing by $4,000. Accounts receivable represents amounts owed to the business and decreases when a customer pays.

The effect of this transaction on the accounting equation is as follows:

		ASSETS			=	LIABILITIES	+	OWNER'S EQUITY	TYPE OF OE TRANSACTION
	Cash	+ Accounts receivable	+ Supplies	+ Truck	=	Accounts payable	+	Richardson, capital	
Bal	23,000		1,800	20,000		1,800		43,000	
e.		+4,000						+4,000	*Service revenue*
Bal	23,000	4,000	1,800	20,000	=	1,800		47,000	
				48,800	=	48,800			

f. **The business paid $800 cash toward the supplies purchased in transaction c.**

Think of Accounts payable (a liability) as a list of companies to which the business will *pay* money at some point in the future. In this particular problem, the business owes money to the company from which it purchased supplies on account in transaction c. When the business *pays* the money in full, it can cross this company off of the list. Right now, the business is paying only *part* of the money owed.

This is a decrease to Accounts payable (a liability) of $800 and a decrease to Cash (an asset) of $800. Because the business is only paying part of the money it owes to the supply store, the balance of Accounts payable is $1,800 – $800 = $1,000.

You should note that this transaction does not affect Supplies because we are not buying more supplies. We are simply paying off a liability, not acquiring more assets or incurring a new expense.

The effect of this transaction on the accounting equation is as follows:

		ASSETS			=	LIABILITIES	+	OWNER'S EQUITY	TYPE OF OE TRANSACTION
	Cash	+ Accounts receivable	+ Supplies	+ Truck	=	Accounts payable	+	Richardson, capital	
Bal	23,000	4,000	1,800	20,000		1,800		47,000	
f.	–800					–800			
Bal	22,200	4,000	1,800	20,000	=	1,000		47,000	
				48,000	=	48,000			

g. **The business paid employee salaries of $1,000 cash.**

The work the employees have given to the business has *already been used*. By the end of March, DR Painting has had the employees working and painting for customers for the entire month. This means that the *benefit* of the work has already been received. This means that it is a salary *expense*. So, Salary expense would increase by $1,000, which is a decrease to owner's equity.

Remember: Expenses *decrease* net income, which decreases Richardson, capital.

The salaries were paid in cash, so Cash (an asset) is also decreased by $1,000.

The effect of this transaction on the accounting equation is as follows:

		ASSETS			=	LIABILITIES	+	OWNER'S EQUITY	TYPE OF OE TRANSACTION
	Cash	+ Accounts receivable	+ Supplies	+ Truck	=	Accounts payable	+	Richardson, capital	
Bal	22,200	4,000	1,800	20,000		1,000		47,000	
g.	–1,000							–1,000	Salary expense
Bal	21,200	4,000	1,800	20,000	=	1,000		46,000	
				47,000	=	47,000			

h. **Richardson withdrew cash of $1,500.**

When the business pays cash, it is a recordable transaction. In this case, there is a decrease of $1,500 to Cash (an asset). David is the owner of the proprietorship and is being given some of his value/ownership in cash. In other words, some of the *earnings* that were *retained* by the business are now being distributed to the owner. This results in a decrease of $1,500 to owner's equity, because Richardson, capital is decreasing.

You should note that *drawings are not an expense* because the cash is not used for operations. The cash drawings are for the owner's personal use rather than to earn revenue for the business.

The effect of this transaction on the accounting equation is as follows:

		ASSETS			= LIABILITIES +	OWNER'S EQUITY	TYPE OF OE TRANSACTION
	Cash +	Accounts receivable +	Supplies +	Truck =	Accounts payable +	Richardson, capital	
Bal	21,200	4,000	1,800	20,000	1,000	46,000	
h.	−1,500	_____	_____	_____	_____	−1,500	*Owner withdrawal*
Bal	19,700	4,000	1,800	20,000 =	1,000	44,500	
				45,500 =	45,500		

i. **The business collected $2,600 from the client in transaction e.**

Think of Accounts receivable (an asset) as a list of clients from whom the business will *receive* money at some point in the future. Later, when the business collects (*receives*) the cash in full from any particular customer, it can cross that customer off the list.

In transaction e, DR Painting performed services for a client on account. Now, DR is receiving part of that money. This is a collection that decreases Accounts receivable (an asset) by $2,600.

Because the cash is received, this is an increase to Cash (an asset) of $2,600.

The effect of this transaction on the accounting equation is as follows:

		ASSETS			= LIABILITIES +	OWNER'S EQUITY	TYPE OF OE TRANSACTION
	Cash +	Accounts receivable +	Supplies +	Truck =	Accounts payable +	Richardson, capital	
Bal	19,700	4,000	1,800	20,000	1,000	44,500	
i.	+2,600	−2,600	_____	_____	_____	_____	
Bal	22,300	1,400	1,800	20,000 =	1,000	44,500	
				45,500 =	45,500		

j. **David paid $100 cash for personal groceries.**

David is using $100 of *his own cash* for groceries. This is a *personal* expense for David's *personal* use that does not relate to the business and therefore is not a recordable transaction for the business. This transaction has no effect on the business's accounting equation. Had David used the *business's* cash to purchase groceries, *then* the business would record the transaction.

		ASSETS			= LIABILITIES	+	OWNER'S EQUITY (OE)	TYPE OF OE TRANSACTION
	Cash	+ Accounts receivable +	Supplies +	Truck	= Accounts payable	+	Richardson, capital	
a.	+$40,000						+40,000	Owner investment
b.	–$20,000			+$20,000				
c.			+$1,800		+$1,800			
d.	+$3,000						+$ 3,000	Service revenue
e.		+$4,000					+4,000	Service revenue
f.	–$800				–$800			
g.	–$1,000						–$ 1,000	Salary expense
h.	–$1,500						–$ 1,500	Owner withdrawal
i.	+$2,600	–$2,600						
j.	Not a transaction of business							
Bal	$22,300	$1,400	$1,800	$20,000	= $1,000		$44,500	
				$45,500	= $45,500			

Requirement 2

Prepare the income statement, statement of owner's equity, and balance sheet of the business after recording the transactions. Use Exhibit 1-7 in the text as a guide.

Part 1	**Part 2**	Part 3	Part 4	Demo Doc Complete

Income Statement

The income statement is the first statement that can be prepared because the other financial statements rely upon the net income number calculated on the income statement.

The income statement reports the profitability of the business. To prepare an income statement, begin with the proper heading. A proper heading includes the name of the company (DR Painting), the name of the statement (Income Statement), and the time period covered (Month Ended March 31, 2014). Notice that we are reporting income for a period of time, rather than a single date.

The income statement lists all revenues and expenses. It uses the following formula to calculate net income:

$$Revenues - Expenses = Net\ Income$$

First, you should list revenues. Second, list the expenses. Having trouble finding the revenues and expenses? Look in the equity column of the accounting equation. After you have listed and totaled the revenues and expenses, you subtract the total expenses from total revenues to determine net income or net loss. If you have a positive number, then you will record net income. A negative number indicates that expenses exceeded revenues, and you will record this as a net loss.

In the case of DR Painting, transactions **d** and **e** increased Service revenue (by $3,000 and $4,000, respectively). This means that total Service revenue for the month was $3,000 + $4,000 = $7,000.

The only expenses that were incurred were in transaction **g**, which resulted in a Salary expense of $1,000. On the income statement, these would be recorded as follows:

DR PAINTING Income Statement Month Ended March 31, 2014		
Revenue:		
Service revenue		$7,000
Expenses:		
Salary expense	$1,000	
Total expenses		1,000
Net income		$6,000

Note the result is a net income of $6,000 ($7,000 – $1,000 = $6,000). You will use this amount on the statement of owner's equity.

Part 1	Part 2	**Part 3**	Part 4	Demo Doc Complete

Statement of Owner's Equity

The statement of owner's equity shows the changes in the owner's capital for a period of time. To prepare a statement of owner's equity, begin with the proper heading. A proper heading includes the name of the company (DR Painting), the name of the statement (Statement of Owner's Equity), and the time period covered (Month Ended March 31, 2014). As with the income statement, we are reporting capital for a period of time, rather than a single date.

Net income is used on the statement of owner's equity to calculate the new balance in the owner's capital account. This calculation uses the following formula:

> **Beginning Capital**
> **+ Owner investment**
> **+ Net Income (or – Net Loss)**
> **– Drawing**
> **Ending Capital**

Start the body of the statement of owner's equity with the Richardson, capital account balance at the beginning of the period (March 1). In this case, because this is a new company, the beginning Richardson, capital is zero. Next, add the owner investment during March of $40,000. Then, add net income as reported on the income statement, $6,000. Following net income, you will add the amounts on the statement so far, $46,000. Then, list the drawing by the owner of $1,500 from transaction **h**, which reduces capital. Finally, total all amounts and compute the balance at the end of the period. The statement of owner's equity follows:

DR PAINTING Statement of Owner's Equity Month Ended March 31, 2014	
Richardson, capital, March 1, 2014	$ 0
Owner investment	40,000
Net income for the month	6,000
	46,000
Drawing	(1,500)
Richardson, capital, March 31, 2014	$ 44,500

Note the result is a balance of $44,500 ($40,000 + $6,000 − $1,500 = $44,500) for Richardson, capital. You will use this amount on the balance sheet.

Part 1	Part 2	Part 3	**Part 4**	Demo Doc Complete

Balance Sheet

The balance sheet reports the financial position of the business. To prepare a balance sheet, begin with the proper heading. A proper heading includes the name of the company (DR Painting), the name of the statement (Balance Sheet), and the specific date (March 31, 2014). Unlike the income statement and statement of owner's equity, we are reporting the financial position of the company for a specific date rather than a period of time.

The balance sheet is a listing of all assets, liabilities, and equity, with the accounting equation verified at the bottom.

To prepare the body of the statement, begin by listing assets. Then you will record liabilities and owner's equity. Notice that the balance sheet is organized in the same order as the accounting equation. You should note that the amount of Richardson, capital comes directly from the ending Richardson, capital on the statement of owner's equity. You should then total both sides to make sure that they are equal. If they are not equal, then you will need to look for an error.

In this case, assets include the cash balance of $22,300, accounts receivable of $1,400, $1,800 worth of supplies, and the truck's cost of $20,000, for a total of $45,500 in assets. Liabilities total $1,000, the balance of the Accounts payable account. The figures for assets and liabilities come directly from the accounting equation worksheet. From the statement of owner's equity, we have ending Richardson, capital of $44,500. This gives us a total for liabilities and equity of $1,000 + $44,500 = $45,500, confirming that assets = liabilities + equity.

DR PAINTING
Balance Sheet
March 31, 2014

Assets		Liabilities	
Cash	$22,300	Accounts payable	$ 1,000
Accounts receivable	1,400		
Supplies	1,800	**Owner's Equity**	
Truck	20,000	Richardson, capital	44,500
Total assets	$45,500	Total liabilities and owner's equity	$45,500

Part 1	Part 2	Part 3	Part 4	Demo Doc Complete

Review *Accounting and the Business Environment*

● Accounting Vocabulary

Account Payable (p. 15)
A liability backed by the general reputation and credit standing of the debtor.

Account Receivable (p. 15)
The right to receive cash in the future from customers to whom the business has sold goods or for whom the business has performed services.

Accounting (p. 2)
The information system that measures business activities, processes that information into reports, and communicates the results to decision makers.

Accounting Equation (p. 11)
The basic tool of accounting, measuring the resources of the business and the claims to those resources: Assets = Liabilities + Equity.

Articles of Incorporation (p. 6)
The rules approved by the state that govern the management of the corporation.

Asset (p. 11)
An economic resource that is expected to be of benefit in the future.

Audit (p. 5)
An examination of a company's financial records.

Authorization (p. 7)
The acceptance by the state of the Corporate by-laws.

Balance Sheet (p. 20)
An entity's assets, liabilities, and owner's equity as of a specific date. Also called the **statement of financial position**.

Capital (p. 12)
The net amount invested in the business by the owner.

Certified Management Accountant (CMA) (p. 4)
A certified accountant who works for a single company.

Certified Public Accountants (CPAs) (p. 4)
Licensed accountants who serve the general public rather than one particular company.

Charter (p. 6)
Document that gives the state's permission to form a corporation.

Common Stock (p. 13)
Represents the basic ownership of every corporation.

Contributed Capital (p. 13)
The amount invested in a corporation by its owners, the stockholders. Also called **paid-in capital**.

Corporation (p. 6)
A business owned by stockholders. A corporation begins when the state approves its articles of incorporation and the first share of stock is issued. It is a legal entity, an "artificial person," in the eyes of the law.

Cost Principle (p. 10)
A principle that states that acquired assets and services should be recorded at their actual cost.

Creditors (p. 3)
Those to whom a business owes money.

Drawing (p. 12)
Distributions of capital by a company to its owner.

Entity (p. 10)
An organization or a section of an organization that, for accounting purposes, stands apart from other organizations and individuals as a separate economic unit.

Equity (p. 11)
The claim of a company's owners to the assets of the business. Also called **owner's equity** for proprietorships and partnerships and called **shareholders' equity** or **stockholders' equity** for a corporation.

Expenses (p. 12)
Decrease in equity that occurs from using assets or increasing liabilities in the course of delivering goods or services to customers.

Faithful Representation Principle (p. 10)
Principle that asserts accounting information is based on the fact that the data faithfully represents the measurement or description of that data. Faithfully represented data are complete, neutral, and free from material error.

Fiduciary Responsibility (p. 7)
An ethical and legal obligation to perform a person's duties in a trustworthy manner.

Financial Accounting (p. 2)
The branch of accounting that focuses on information for people outside the firm.

Financial Accounting Standards Board (FASB) (p. 4)
The private organization that determines how accounting is practiced in the United States.

Financial Statements (p. 2)
Documents that report on a business in monetary amounts, providing information to help people make informed business decisions.

Generally Accepted Accounting Principles (GAAP) (p. 4)
Accounting guidelines, formulated by the Financial Accounting Standards Board, that govern how accountants measure, process, and communicate financial information.

Going-Concern Concept (p. 10)
This concept assumes that the entity will remain in operation for the foreseeable future.

Income Statement (p. 20)
Summary of an entity's revenues, expenses, and net income or net loss for a specific period. Also called the **statement of earnings** or the **statement of operations**.

International Accounting Standards Board (p. 4)
The organization that determines how accounting is practiced internationally.

International Financial Reporting Standards (IFRS) (p. 4)
Accounting guidelines, formulated by the International Accounting Standards Board, that govern how accountants measure, process, and communicate financial information.

Liabilities (p. 11)
Economic obligations (debts) payable to an individual or an organization outside the business.

Limited-Liability Company (p. 6)
Company in which each member is only liable for his or her own actions or those under his or her control.

Limited-Liability Partnership (p. 6)
Company in which each partner is only liable for his or her own actions or those under his or her control.

Managerial Accounting (p. 2)
The branch of accounting that focuses on information for internal decision makers of a business.

Mutual Agency (p. 6)
The ability of partners in a partnership to commit other partners and the business to a contract.

Net Income (p. 12)
Excess of total revenues over total expenses. Also called **net earnings** or **net profit**.

Net Loss (p. 12)
Excess of total expenses over total revenues.

Not-for-Profit (p. 6)
Organization that has been approved by the Internal Revenue Service to operate for a religious, charitable, or educational purpose.

Owner's Equity (p. 11)
The claim of a company's owners to the assets of the business. For a corporation, owner's equity is called **shareholders'** or **stockholders' equity**.

Paid-In Capital (p. 13)
The amount invested in a corporation by its owners, the stockholders. Also called **contributed capital**.

Partnership (p. 6)
A business with two or more owners and not organized as a corporation.

Proprietorship (p. 6)
A business with a single owner.

Retained Earnings (p. 13)
The amount earned over the life of a business by income-producing activities and kept (retained) for use in the business.

Revenue (p. 12)
Amounts earned by delivering goods or services to customers. Revenues increase capital.

Shareholder (p. 6)
A person who owns stock in a corporation. Also called a **stockholder**.

Shareholders' Equity (p. 11)
The claim of a corporation's owners to the assets of the business. Also called **stockholders' equity**.

Stable Monetary Unit Concept (p. 11)
The concept that says that accountants assume that the dollar's purchasing power is stable.

Statement of Cash Flows (p. 20)
Report of cash receipts and cash payments during a period.

Statement of Earnings (p. 21)
Summary of an entity's revenues, expenses, and net income or net loss for a specific period. Also called the **income statement** or the **statement of operations**.

Statement of Financial Position (p. 21)
An entity's assets, liabilities, and owner's equity as of a specific date. Also called the **balance sheet**.

Statement of Operations (p. 21)
Summary of an entity's revenues, expenses, and net income or net loss for a specific period. Also called the **income statement** or **statement of earnings**.

Statement of Owner's Equity (p. 20)
Summary of the changes in an owner's capital account during a specific period.

Stock (p. 6)
A certificate representing ownership interest in a corporation. The holders of stock are called **stockholders** or **shareholders**.

Stockholder (p. 6)
A person who owns stock in a corporation. Also called a **shareholder**.

Stockholders' Equity (p. 11)
The claim of a corporation's owners to the assets of the business. Also called **shareholders' equity**.

Transaction (p. 13)
An event that affects the financial position of a particular entity and can be measured and recorded reliably.

● Destination: Student Success

Student Success Tips

The following are hints on some common trouble areas for students in this chapter:

● The four financial statements are prepared in this order: Income statement, statement of owner's equity, balance sheet, statement of cash flows.

● The accounting equation contains the same accounts as the balance sheet: Assets = Liabilities + Equity.

● Business forms vary, but the goal of accounting is to provide information to users of financial information.

● The accounting concepts are guidelines that help us record business activities.

Getting Help

If there's a learning objective from the chapter you aren't confident about, try using one or more of the following resources:

● Review the Chapter 1 Demo Doc located on page 28 of the textbook.

● Practice additional exercises or problems at the end of Chapter 1 that cover the specific learning objective you are working on.

● Watch the white board videos for Chapter 1, located at myaccountinglab.com under the Chapter Resources button.

● Go to myaccountinglab.com and select the Study Plan button. Choose Chapter 1 and work the questions covering that specific learning objective until you've mastered it.

● Work the Chapter 1 pre/post tests in myaccountinglab.com.

● Consult the Check Figures for End of Chapter starters, exercises, and problems, located at myaccountinglab.com.

● Visit the learning resource center on your campus for tutoring.

• Quick Check

1. Generally accepted accounting principles (GAAP) are formulated by the
   a. Financial Accounting Standards Board (FASB).
   b. Securities and Exchange Commission (SEC).
   c. Institute of Management Accountants (IMA).
   d. American Institute of Certified Public Accountants (AICPA).

2. Which type of business organization is owned by one owner?
   a. Corporation
   c. Proprietorship
   b. Partnership
   d. Items a, b, and c are all correct.

3. Which accounting concept or principle specifically states that we should record transactions at amounts that can be verified?
   a. Faithful representation
   c. Entity concept
   b. Cost principle
   d. Going-concern concept

4. **Fossil** is famous for fashion wristwatches and leather goods. At the end of a recent year, **Fossil's** total assets added up to $363,000,000, and equity was $228,000,000. How much were **Fossil's** liabilities?
   a. Cannot determine from the data given
   c. $135,000,000
   b. $363,000,000
   d. $228,000,000

5. Assume that **Fossil** sold watches to a department store on account for $48,000. How would this transaction affect **Fossil's** accounting equation?
   a. Increase both assets and liabilities by $48,000
   b. Increase both assets and equity by $48,000
   c. Increase both liabilities and equity by $48,000
   d. No effect on the accounting equation because the effects cancel out

6. Accounting is the information system that
   a. measures business activity.
   b. communicates the results to decision makers.
   c. processes data into reports.
   d. All of the above

7. Which of the following is least likely to be a user of a business's financial information?
   a. Taxing authorities
   c. Creditors
   b. Customers
   d. Investors

8. Consider the overall effects on **Fossil** of selling watches on account for $64,000 and paying expenses totaling $25,000. What is **Fossil's** net income or net loss?
   a. Net income of $39,000
   b. Net loss of $39,000
   c. Net income of $64,000
   d. Cannot determine from the data given

9. The balance sheet reports
   a. financial position on a specific date.
   b. results of operations on a specific date.
   c. financial position for a specific period.
   d. results of operations for a specific period.

10. Which of the following characteristics best describes a corporation?

    a. Mutual agency   c. Limited liability of stockholders

    b. A board of investors   d. Not for profit

Answers are given after Apply Your Knowledge (p. 61).

Assess Your Progress

● Short Exercises

S1-1   **❶ Explaining revenues and expenses [5 min]**   *MyAccountingLab*

Sherman Lawn Service has been open for one year, and Hannah Sherman, the owner, wants to know whether the business earned a net income or a net loss for the year. First, she must identify the revenues earned and the expenses incurred during the year.

Requirements

    1. What are *revenues* and *expenses*?

    2. If revenues increase, what would be the effect, if any, on equity?

S1-2   **❷ Users of financial information [5 min]**

Suppose you are the manager of Greg's Tunes. The company needs a bank loan in order to purchase music equipment. In evaluating the loan request, the banker asks about the assets and liabilities of the business. In particular, the banker wants to know the amount of the business's owner's equity.

Requirements

    1. Is the banker considered an internal or external user of financial information?

    2. Which financial statement would provide the best information to answer the banker's questions?

S1-3   **❸ Organizations that govern CPAs [5–10 min]**

Suppose you are starting a business, Wholly Shirts, to imprint logos on T-shirts. In organizing the business and setting up its accounting records, you take your information to a CPA to prepare financial statements for the bank. You state to the CPA, "I really need to get this loan, so be sure you make my financial statements look great."

Requirement

    1. Name the organization that governs the majority of the guidelines that the CPA will use to prepare financial statements for Wholly Shirts.

S1-4   **❹ Types of business organizations [5–10 min]**

Chloe Michaels plans on opening Chloe Michaels Floral Designs. She is considering the various types of business organizations and wishes to organize her business with unlimited life and limited liability features. Additionally, Chloe wants the option to raise additional equity easily in the future.

Requirement

    1. Which type of business organization will meet Chloe's needs best?

S1-5 **⑤ Organizing a proprietorship [5–10 min]**

You begin No Limits Cell Service by investing $10,000 of your own money in a business bank account. You receive capital. Then the business borrows $5,000 cash by signing a note payable to Summit Bank.

Requirement

1. Identify the advantages and disadvantages of owning a proprietorship.

S1-6 **⑥ Applying accounting concepts and principles [5–10 min]**

Michael McNamee is the proprietor of a property management company near the campus of Pensacola State College. The business has cash of $8,000 and furniture that cost $9,000 and has a market value of $13,000. Debts include accounts payable of $6,000. Michael's personal home is valued at $400,000 and his personal bank account has a balance of $1,200.

Requirements

1. Consider the accounting principles discussed in the chapter and define the principle that best matches the situation:
   a. Michael's personal assets are not recorded on the property management company's balance sheet.
   b. Michael records furniture at its cost of $9,000, not its market value of $13,000.
   c. Michael does not make adjustments for inflation.
   d. The account payable of $6,000 is documented by a statement from the furniture company showing the business still owes $6,000 on the furniture. Michael's friend thinks he should only owe about $5,000. The account payable is recorded at $6,000.
2. How much equity is in the business?

S1-7 **⑦ Using the accounting equation [5 min]**

Turtle Creek Kennel earns service revenue by caring for the pets of customers. Turtle Creek's main expense is the salary paid to an employee.

Requirement

1. Write the accounting equation for the following transactions:
   a. Received $320 cash for service revenue earned.
   b. Paid $125 cash for salary expense.
   c. Earned $440 for service revenue, but the customer has not paid Turtle Creek Kennel yet.
   d. Received utility bill of $65, which will be paid next month.

S1-8 **⑧ Analyzing transactions [5 min]**

Monte Hall Gaming paid $26,000 cash to purchase land.

Requirement

1. Identify which accounts were affected by this transaction and the amount of the change.

S1-9   **⑧ Analyzing transactions [5 min]**
Getaway Travel recorded revenues of $2,800 earned on account by providing travel service for clients.

Requirements

1. How much are the business's cash and total assets after the transaction?
2. Name the business's asset which was increased as a result of the transaction.

S1-10   **⑧ Analyzing transactions [5 min]**
Bob Martin Deliveries collected cash on account from a client for whom the business had provided delivery services one month earlier.

Requirements

1. Why didn't the business record revenue when it collected the cash on account?
2. Write two accounting equations to show the effects of
   a. receiving cash of $500 for service revenue earned.
   b. receiving cash of $500 from a customer on account.

S1-11   **⑨ Prepare the balance sheet [10 min]**
Examine Exhibit 1-6. The exhibit summarizes the transactions of Smart Touch Learning for the month of April 2013. Suppose the business has completed only the first seven transactions and needs a bank loan on April 21. The vice president of the bank requires financial statements to support all loan requests.

Requirement

1. Prepare the balance sheet that the business would present to the banker *after completing the first seven transactions* on April 21, 2013. Exhibit 1-7 shows the format of the balance sheet.

S1-12   **⑨ Prepare the income statement [10 min]**
Elegant Arrangements has just completed operations for the year ended December 31, 2012. This is the third year of operations for the company. As the owner, you want to know how well the business performed during the year. To address this question, you have assembled the following data:

Insurance expense	$ 4,000	Salary expense	$42,000
Service revenue	74,000	Accounts payable	6,800
Supplies expense	1,100	Supplies	2,100
Rent expense	13,000	Rose, drawing	3,900

Requirement

1. Prepare the income statement of Elegant Arrangements for the year ended December 31, 2012.

Note: Short Exercise 1-13 should be attempted only after completing Short Exercise 1-12.

S1-13   **⑩ Evaluating business performance [10 min]**
Consider the facts presented in S1-12 for Elegant Arrangements.

Requirements

1. Review the income statement prepared in S1-12. Evaluate the results of 2012 operations for Elegant Arrangements. Was the year good or bad?
2. If the company's service revenue was 20% less than reported in S1-12, how will the net income (loss) change?
3. If the company's salary expense was 20% more than reported in S1-12, how will the net income (loss) change?

• Exercises

E1-14 ❶ ❺ ❻ **Using accounting vocabulary [10–15 min]**
Consider the following accounting terms and definitions:

TERMS:	DEFINITIONS:
1. Accounting Equation	A. An economic resource that is expected to be of benefit in the future
2. Asset	B. An economic obligation (a debt) payable to an individual or an organization outside the business
3. Balance Sheet	
4. Expense	C. Excess of total expenses over total revenues
5. Income Statement	D. Excess of total revenues over total expenses
6. Liability	E. The basic tool of accounting, stated as Assets = Liabilities + Equity
7. Net Income	F. Decrease in equity that occurs from using assets or increasing liabilities in the course of delivering goods or services to customers
8. Net Loss	
9. Revenue	G. Amounts earned by delivering goods or services to customers
10. Statement of Cash Flows	H. Report of cash receipts and cash payments during a period
11. Statement of Owner's Equity	I. Report of an entity's assets, liabilities, and equity as of a specific date
	J. Report of an entity's revenues, expenses and net income/net loss for the period
	K. Report that shows the changes in capital for a period of time

Requirement

1. Match the term to the correct definition.

E1-15 ❷ ❸ ❹ ❾ **Users of financial information; the accounting profession, types of business organizations, and preparing the financial statements [15–20 min]**
Evan O'Brien publishes a travel magazine. In need of cash, the business applies for a loan with National Bank. The bank requires borrowers to submit financial statements. With little knowledge of accounting, Evan O'Brien, the proprietor, does not know how to proceed.

Requirements

1. Explain how to prepare the balance sheet and the income statement.
2. Which organization is the privately funded body of accountants that defines pronouncements that guide how the financial statements will be prepared?
3. Indicate why a lender would require this information.
4. What type of organization is Evan O'Brien?
5. If Evan wanted to attract outside investors, which form of business would best enable that option?

E1-16 ❺ ❻ ❼ **Characteristics of a proprietorship, accounting concepts, and using the accounting equation [5–10 min]**
Select financial information for three companies follows:

	Assets	Liabilities	Owner's Equity
New Rock Gas	$?	$24,000	$50,000
DJ Video Rentals	75,000	?	32,000
Corner Grocery	100,000	53,000	?

Requirements

1. Compute the missing amount in the accounting equation for each entity.
2. List the main characteristics of a proprietorship.
3. Which accounting concept tells us that the previous three proprietorships will continue to exist in the future?

E1-17   ⑥ **Comparing U.S. GAAP to IFRS [5–10 min]**
Winged Wheel Garage purchased a parcel of land on January 3, 2012, for $50,000. Its market value at the end of 2012 was $55,000.

Requirements

1. Using the U.S. GAAP cost principle, at what value would the land be reported on the balance sheet as of January 3, 2012? What value would the land be reported at on the December 31, 2012, balance sheet?
2. Using IFRS, at what value would the land be reported on the balance sheet as of January 3, 2012? What value would the land be reported at on the December 31, 2012, balance sheet?

E1-18   ⑦⑧ **Using the accounting equation to analyze business transactions [5–10 min]**
Great City Builders balance sheet data at May 31, 2012, and June 30, 2012, follow:

	May 31, 2012	June 30, 2012
Total assets	$177,000	$213,000
Total liabilities	122,000	144,000

Requirement

1. Following are three situations about owner's investments and drawings of the business during June. For each situation, compute the amount of net income or net loss during June 2012.

   a. The owner invested $6,000 in the business and made no withdrawals.
   b. The owner made no investments. The owner withdrew cash of $10,000.
   c. The company owner made investments of $18,000 and withdrew cash of $20,000.

E1-19   ⑦⑧ **Using the accounting equation to analyze transactions [5–10 min]**
As the manager of a Papa Sam's restaurant, you must deal with a variety of business transactions.

Requirement

1. Give an example of a transaction that has each of the following effects on the accounting equation:

   a. Increase one asset and decrease another asset.
   b. Decrease an asset and decrease owner's equity.
   c. Decrease an asset and decrease a liability.
   d. Increase an asset and increase owner's equity.
   e. Increase an asset and increase a liability.

E1-20 **7** **8** **Using the accounting equation to analyze transactions [10–20 min]**

Requirement

1. Indicate the effects of the following business transactions on the accounting equation of a Viviani Video store. Transaction (a) is answered as a guide.

   a. Received cash of $8,000 and gave capital.
      Answer: Increase asset (Cash)
      Increase capital (Viviani, capital)
   b. Earned video rental revenue on account, $1,800.
   c. Purchased office furniture on account, $400.
   d. Received cash on account, $600.
   e. Paid cash on account, $100.
   f. Sold land for $15,000, which was the cost of the land.
   g. Rented videos and received cash of $300.
   h. Paid monthly office rent of $900.
   i. Paid $200 cash to purchase supplies that will be used in the future.

E1-21 **7** **8** **Using the accounting equation to analyze transactions [10–20 min]**
Caren Smith opened a medical practice. During July, the first month of operation, the business, titled Caren Smith, M.D., experienced the following events:

Jul 6	Smith invested $55,000 in the business by opening a bank account in the name of C. Smith, M.D. The business gave capital to Smith.
9	Paid $46,000 cash for land.
12	Purchased medical supplies for $1,800 on account.
15	Officially opened for business.
15–31	During the rest of the month, Smith treated patients and earned service revenue of $8,000, receiving cash.
29	Paid cash expenses: employees' salaries, $1,600; office rent, $900; utilities, $100.
30	Returned supplies purchased on the 12th for the cost of those supplies, $700.
31	Paid $1,100 on account.

Requirement

1. Analyze the effects of these events on the accounting equation of the medical practice of Caren Smith, M.D. Use a format similar to that of Exhibit 1-6, with headings for Cash; Medical supplies; Land; Accounts payable; and Smith, capital.

E1-22 **7** **8** **9** **Using the accounting equation to analyze transactions and calculate net income or net loss [10–15 min]**
The analysis of the first eight transactions of All-in-one Accounting Service follows. The owner made only one investment and there were no owner drawings.

	Cash	+	Accounts receivable	+	Equipment	=	Accounts payable	+	Larrison, capital
1	+ 31,000								+31,000
2			+ 3,800						+ 3,800
3					+ 13,400		+ 13,400		
4	+ 190		– 190						
5	– 410				+ 410				
6	– 8,000						– 8,000		
7	+ 790								+790
8	– 1,500								– 1,500

Requirements

1. Describe each transaction.
2. If these transactions fully describe the operations of All-in-one Accounting Service during the month, what was the amount of net income or net loss?

E1-23 ❼ ❿ **Using the accounting equation and evaluating business performance [10 min]**

Bob Auto Repairs started 2012 with total assets of $19,000 and total liabilities of $9,000. At the end of 2012, Bob's total assets stood at $27,000, and total liabilities were $13,000.

Requirements

1. Did the owner's equity of Bob Auto Repairs increase or decrease during 2012? By how much?
2. Identify three possible reasons for the change in owner's equity during the year.

E1-24 ❼ ❾ ❿ **Using the accounting equation, preparing financial statements, and evaluating business performance [10–15 min]**

The 2012 annual report of American Express Services (AES) reported revenue of $21,000,000,000. Total expenses for the year were $14,000,000,000. AES ended the year with total assets of $30,000,000,000, and it owed debts totaling $14,000,000,000. At year-end 2011, the business reported total assets of $23,000,000,000 and total liabilities of $14,000,000,000.

Requirements

1. Compute AES's net income for 2012.
2. Did AES's owner's equity increase or decrease during 2012? By how much?
3. Assume you are a creditor of AES. Would the company's 2012 performance be good or bad for you, as a creditor?

E1-25 ❼ ❾ ❿ **Using the accounting equation, preparing financial statements, and evaluating business performance [30–40 min]**

Compute the missing amount for Felix Company. You will need to work through total owner's equity.

Beginning:		Owner's Equity:	
Assets	$45,000	Owner investments	$ 0
Liabilities	29,000	Owner drawings	19,000
Ending:		Income Statement:	
Assets	$55,000	Revenues	$242,000
Liabilities	38,000	Expenses	?

Requirements

1. Did Felix earn a net income or suffer a net loss for the year? Compute the amount.
2. Would you consider Felix's performance for the year to be good or bad? Give your reason.

E1-26 **8** **Analyzing business transactions [10–15 min]**

Shane's Roasted Peanuts supplies snack foods. The business experienced the following events.

    a. Shane's Roasted Peanuts received cash from the owner and gave capital to Shane.

    b. Cash purchase of land for a building site.

    c. Paid cash on accounts payable.

    d. Purchased equipment; signed a note payable.

    e. Performed service for a customer on account.

    f. Employees worked for the week but will be paid next Tuesday.

    g. Received cash from a customer on account receivable.

    h. Borrowed money from the bank.

    i. Owner withdrew cash.

    j. Incurred utility expense on account.

Requirement

    1. State whether each event (1) increased, (2) decreased, or (3) had no effect on the *total assets* of the business. Identify any specific asset affected.

E1-27 **9** **10** **Preparing financial statements and evaluating business performance [10–20 min]**

The account balances of Wilson Towing Service at June 30, 2012, follow:

Equipment	$13,600	Service revenue	$11,200
Supplies	900	Accounts receivable	6,200
Note payable	6,900	Accounts payable	3,000
Rent expense	550	Wilson, capital, Jun 1, 2012	4,950
Cash	2,900	Salary expense	1,900
Wilson, drawing	0		

Requirements

    1. Prepare the balance sheet of the business at June 30, 2012.

    2. What does the balance sheet report—financial position or operating results?

    3. Which financial statement reports the other accounts listed for the business?

E1-28 **9** **10** **Preparing financial statements and evaluating business performance [10–15 min]**

The assets, liabilities, owner's equity, revenues, and expenses of Davis Design Studio have the following balances at December 31, 2012, the end of its first year of operation. During the year, the owner invested $15,000.

Note payable	$ 42,000	Office furniture	$ 49,000
Rent expense	23,000	Utilities expense	6,900
Cash	3,600	Accounts payable	3,200
Office supplies	4,500	Davis, capital	33,300
Salary expense	65,000	Service revenue	158,300
Salaries payable	2,200	Accounts receivable	8,600
Property tax expense	1,500	Supplies expense	4,200

Requirements

    1. Prepare the income statement of Davis Design Studio for the year ended December 31, 2012. What is the result of operations for 2012?

    2. What was the amount of the owner drawing during the year?

● Problems (Group A)

P1-29A ①②③④⑤⑥ Accounting vocabulary, financial statement users, accounting profession, types of business organizations, proprietorship characteristics, and accounting concepts [15–20 min]   *MyAccountingLab*

Consider the following terms and definitions:

TERMS:	DEFINITIONS:
1. Proprietorship	A. Feature that enables a corporation to raise more money than proprietorships and partnerships
2. Faithful representation	B. Holds that fair market value should not be used over actual costs
3. Partnership	C. Stands for Financial Accounting Standards Board
4. Stock	D. Owner is referred to as a proprietor
5. Limited liability	E. Asserts that data are complete, neutral, and free from material error
6. Limited Liability Company	F. Revenues of $70,000 and expenses of $85,000
7. Cost principle	G. Has unlimited liability
8. FASB	H. Represents ownership in a corporation
9. Net loss of $15,000	I. Type of entity that is designed to limit personal liability exposure
10. Creditors	J. Person or business lending money

Requirement

1. Match the terms with their correct definitions.

P1-30A ⑤⑥⑨ Proprietorship attributes, applying the entity concept, and preparing financial statements [20–25 min]

Andrea Scarlett is a realtor. She organized her business as a proprietorship, Andrea Scarlett, Realtor, by investing $19,000 cash. The business gave capital to her. Consider the following facts at September 30, 2012.

    a. The business owes $61,000 on a note payable for land that the business acquired for a total price of $83,000.

    b. The business spent $23,000 for a Zinka Banker real estate franchise, which entitles the business to represent itself as a Zinka Banker office. This franchise is a business asset.

    c. Scarlett owes $80,000 on a personal mortgage for her personal residence, which she acquired in 2012 for a total price of $160,000.

    d. Scarlett has $5,000 in her personal bank account, and the business has $9,000 in its bank account.

    e. Scarlett owes $4,000 on a personal charge account with Chico's.

    f. The office acquired business furniture for $15,000 on September 25. Of this amount, the business owes $2,000 on account at September 30.

    g. Office supplies on hand at the real estate office total $1,300.

Requirements

1. Scarlett was concerned about taxes. Which proprietorship feature limits Scarlett's business taxes?

2. Prepare the balance sheet of the real estate business of Andrea Scarlett, Realtor, at September 30, 2012.

3. Identify the personal items that would not be reported on the business records.

P1-31A ⑥⑦⑧⑨ Applying the entity concept, using the accounting equation for transaction analysis, and preparing financial statements [20–30 min]

Alex Shore practiced accounting with a partnership for five years. Recently he opened his own accounting firm, which he operates as a proprietorship. The name of the new entity is Alex Shore, CPA. Shore experienced the following events during the organizing phase of the new business and its first month of operations. Some of the events were personal and did not affect the business.

Feb	4	Shore received $27,000 cash from former accounting partners.*
	5	Deposited $50,000 in a new business bank account titled Alex Shore, CPA. The business gave capital to Shore.
	6	Paid $100 cash for letterhead stationery for the new office.
	7	Purchased office furniture for the office. The business will pay the account payable, $9,700, within three months.
	10	Shore sold personal investment in Amazing.com stock, which he had owned for several years, receiving $50,000 cash.*
	11	Shore deposited the $50,000 cash from sale of the Amazing.com stock in his personal bank account.*
	12	A representative of a large company telephoned Shore and told him of the company's intention to transfer its accounting business to Shore.
	18	Finished tax hearings on behalf of a client and submitted a bill for accounting services, $17,000. Shore expected to collect from this client within two weeks.
	25	Paid office rent, $1,500.
	28	Shore withdrew cash of $1,000.

*Personal transaction of Alex Shore.

Requirements

1. Analyze the effects of the events on the accounting equation of the proprietorship of Alex Shore, CPA. Use a format similar to Exhibit 1-6.
2. As of February 28, compute Alex Shore's
   a. total assets.
   b. total liabilities.
   c. total owner's equity.
   d. net income or net loss for February.

P1-32A ⑥⑦⑧⑨⑩ **Applying the entity concept, using the accounting equation for transaction analysis, preparing financial statements, and evaluating business performance [20–30 min]**

Angela Peters practiced law with a partnership for 10 years. Recently she opened her own law office, which she operates as a proprietorship. The name of the new entity is Angela Peters, Attorney. Peters experienced the following events during the organizing phase of the new business and its first month of operation. Some of the events were personal and did not affect the law practice. Others were business transactions and should be accounted for by the business.

Mar	1	Sold personal investment in eBay stock, which she had owned for several years, receiving $31,000 cash.
	2	Deposited the $31,000 cash from sales of the eBay stock in her personal bank account.
	3	Received $139,000 cash from former law partners.
	5	Deposited $89,000 cash in a new business bank account titled Angela Peters, Attorney. The business gave capital to Peters.
	7	Paid $400 cash for ink cartridges for the printer.
	9	Purchased computer for the law office, agreeing to pay the account, $9,300, within three months.
	23	Finished court hearings on behalf of a client and submitted a bill for legal services, $13,500, on account.
	30	Paid utilities, $1,200.
	31	Peters withdrew cash of $2,000.

Requirements

1. Analyze the effects of the preceding events on the accounting equation of the proprietorship of Angela Peters, Attorney. Use a format similar to Exhibit 1-6.
2. At March 31, compute the business's
   a. total assets.
   b. total liabilities.
   c. total owner's equity.
   d. net income or net loss for the month.

3. Evaluate Angela Peters, Attorney's first month of operations. Were the results good or bad?

P1-33A **7** **8** **Using the accounting equation for transaction analysis [20–25 min]**
Zelinsky Electronics was recently formed as a proprietorship. The balance of each item in the company's accounting equation is shown for October 1 and for each of the following business days.

	Cash	Accounts receivable	Supplies	Land	Accounts payable	Zelinsky, capital
Oct 1	$4,000	$7,300	$1,200	$12,800	$4,000	$21,300
4	9,000	7,300	1,200	12,800	4,000	26,300
9	5,000	7,300	1,200	16,800	4,000	26,300
13	5,000	7,300	1,600	16,800	4,400	26,300
16	3,500	7,300	1,600	16,800	2,900	26,300
19	4,800	6,000	1,600	16,800	2,900	26,300
22	9,800	6,000	1,600	16,800	2,900	31,300
25	9,200	6,000	1,600	16,800	2,300	31,300
27	8,400	6,000	2,400	16,800	2,300	31,300
30	2,700	6,000	2,400	16,800	2,300	25,600

Requirement

1. A single transaction took place on each day. Briefly describe the transaction that most likely occurred on each day, beginning with October 4. Indicate which accounts were increased or decreased and by what amounts. Assume that no revenue or expense transactions occurred during the month.

P1-34A **7** **8** **Using the accounting equation for transaction analysis [15–25 min]**
Matilda Crone owns and operates a public relations firm called Dance Fever. The following amounts summarize her business on August 31, 2012:

		Assets				=	Liabilities	+	Owner's equity
Date	Cash	+ Accounts receivable	+ Supplies	+ Land		=	Accounts payable	+	Crone, capital
Bal	2,300	1,800	0	14,000		=	8,000	+	10,100

During September 2012, the business completed the following transactions:

a. Gave capital to Crone and received cash of $13,000.
b. Performed service for a client and received cash of $900.
c. Paid off the beginning balance of accounts payable.
d. Purchased supplies from **OfficeMax** on account, $600.
e. Collected cash from a customer on account, $700.
f. Received cash of $1,600 and gave capital to owner.
g. Consulted for a new band and billed the client for services rendered, $5,500.
h. Recorded the following business expenses for the month:
    1. Paid office rent, $1,200.
    2. Paid advertising, $600.
i. Returned supplies to **OfficeMax** for $110 from item d, which was the cost of the supplies.
j. Crone withdrew cash of $2,000.

Requirement

1. Analyze the effects of the preceding transactions on the accounting equation of Dance Fever. Adapt the format to that of Exhibit 1-6.

P1-35A ⑨ ⑩ **Preparing financial statements and evaluating business performance [20–30 min]**

Presented here are the accounts of Gate City Answering Service for the year ended December 31, 2012.

Land	$ 8,000	Owner investment, 2012	$ 28,000
Note payable	32,000	Accounts payable	11,000
Property tax expense	2,600	Accounts receivable	1,000
Wayne, drawing	30,000	Advertising expense	15,000
Rent expense	13,000	Building	145,200
Salary expense	65,000	Cash	3,000
Salary payable	1,300	Equipment	16,000
Service revenue	192,000	Insurance expense	2,500
Supplies	10,000	Interest expense	7,000
Wayne, capital, 12/31/2011	54,000		

Requirements

1. Prepare Gate City Answering Service's income statement.
2. Prepare the statement of owner's equity.
3. Prepare the balance sheet.
4. Answer these questions about the company:
   a. Was the result of operations for the year a profit or a loss? How much?
   b. How much in total economic resources does the company have as it moves into the new year?
   c. How much does the company owe to creditors?
   d. What is the dollar amount of the owner's equity in the business at the end of the year?

P1-36A ⑨ **Preparing financial statements [20–30 min]**

Studio Photography works weddings and prom-type parties. The balance of Ansel, capital was $16,000 at December 31, 2011. At December 31, 2012, the business's accounting records show these balances:

Insurance expense	$ 8,000	Accounts receivable	$ 8,000
Cash	37,000	Note payable	12,000
Accounts payable	7,000	Ansel, capital, Dec 31, 2012	?
Advertising expense	3,000	Salary expense	25,000
Service revenue	80,000	Equipment	50,000
Ansel, drawing	13,000	Owner investment, 2012	29,000

Requirement

1. Prepare the following financial statements for Studio Photography for the year ended December 31, 2012:
   a. Income statement
   b. Statement of owner's equity
   c. Balance sheet

P1-37A ⑨ ⑩ **Preparing financial statements and evaluating business performance [20–30 min]**

The bookkeeper of Greener Landscaping prepared the company's balance sheet while the accountant was ill. The balance sheet contains numerous errors. In particular, the bookkeeper knew that the balance sheet should balance, so he plugged in the owner's equity amount needed to achieve this balance. The owner's equity is incorrect. All other amounts are right, but some are out of place.

GREENER LANDSCAPING				
Balance Sheet				
Month Ended November 30, 2012				
Assets		**Liabilities**		
Cash	$ 4,900	Accounts receivable	$ 2,200	
Office supplies	600	Tum, drawing	10,000	
Land	34,200	Service revenue	39,000	
Salary expense	2,800	Property tax expense	2,600	
Office furniture	6,100	Accounts payable	2,700	
Note payable	24,200			
Rent expense	300	**Owner's Equity**		
		Tum, capital	16,600	
Total assets	$ 73,100	Total liabilities	$ 73,100	

Requirements

1. Prepare a corrected balance sheet.
2. Consider the original balance sheet as presented and the corrected balance sheet you prepared for Requirement 1. Did total assets as presented in your corrected balance sheet increase, decrease, or stay the same from the original balance sheet? Why?

● Problems (Group B)

P1-38B ❶❷❸❹❺❻ Accounting vocabulary, financial statement users, accounting profession, types of business organizations, proprietorship characteristics, and accounting concepts [15–20 min]   *MyAccountingLab*
Consider the following terms and definitions:

TERMS:	DEFINITIONS:
1. Proprietorship	A. Feature that sets the maximum amount of financial loss by a stockholder to the cost of the investment
2. Faithful representation	B. Reason why accountants should not write up the value of equipment due to an increase in its fair value
3. Partnership	C. Is composed of accountants
4. Stock	D. An entity that has fewer than two owners
5. Limited liability	E. Principle that does not accept incomplete or bias data
6. Limited Liability Company	F. Revenues of $40,000 and expenses of $25,000
7. Cost principle	G. Possess mutual agency
8. FASB	H. The corporate charter specifies how much of this a corporation can sell
9. Net income of $15,000	I. Entity where the business, and not the proprietor, is liable for the company's debts
10. Business owners	J. Use accounting information to set goals, to measure progress toward those goals, and to make adjustments when needed

Requirement

1. Match the terms with their correct definitions.

P1-39B ❺❻❾ Proprietorship attributes, applying the entity concept, and preparing financial statements [20–25 min]
Sandy White is a realtor. She organized her business as a proprietorship, Sandy White, Realtor, by investing $27,000 cash.

The business gave capital to her. Consider the following facts at May 31, 2012:

a. The business owes $62,000 on a note payable for land that the business acquired for a total price of $80,000.

b. The business spent $26,000 for a Minko Banker real estate franchise, which entitles the business to represent itself as a Minko Banker office. This franchise is a business asset.

c. White owes $70,000 on a personal mortgage for her personal residence, which she acquired in 2012 for a total price of $130,000.

d. White has $4,000 in her personal bank account, and the business has $13,000 in its bank account.

e. White owes $3,000 on a personal charge account with **Chico's.**

f. The office acquired business furniture for $20,000 on May 25. Of this amount, the business owes $5,000 on account at May 31.

g. Office supplies on hand at the real estate office total $1,100.

Requirements

1. White was concerned about taxes. Which propriertorship feature limits White's business taxes?

2. Prepare the balance sheet of the real estate business of Sandy White, Realtor at May 31, 2012.

3. Identify the personal items that would not be reported on the business records.

P1-40B **6 7 8 9** **Applying the entity concept, using the accounting equation for transaction analysis, and preparing financial statements [20–30 min]**
Arron Woody practiced accounting with a partnership for five years. Recently he opened his own accounting firm, which he operates as a proprietorship. The name of the new entity is Arron Woody, CPA. Woody experienced the following events during the organizing phase of the new business and its first month of operations. Some of the events were personal and did not affect the business.

Feb	4	Woody received $31,000 cash from former accounting partners.*
	5	Deposited $40,000 in a new business bank account titled Arron Woody, CPA. The business gave capital to Woody.
	6	Paid $200 cash for letterhead stationery for the new office.
	7	Purchased office furniture for the office. The business will pay the account payable, $9,500, within three months.
	10	Woody sold personal investment in Amazing.com stock, which he had owned for several years, receiving $51,000 cash.*
	11	Woody deposited the $51,000 cash from sale of the Amazing.com stock in his personal bank account.*
	12	A representative of a large company telephoned Woody and told him of the company's intention to transfer its accounting business to Woody.
	18	Finished tax hearings on behalf of a client and submitted a bill for accounting services, $14,000. Woody expected to collect from this client within two weeks.
	25	Paid office rent, $1,900.
	28	Woody withdrew cash of $8,000.
*Personal transaction of Arron Woody.		

Requirements

1. Analyze the effects of the events on the accounting equation of the proprietorship of Arron Woody, CPA. Use a format similar to Exhibit 1-6.

2. As of February 28, compute Arron Woody's
    a. total assets.
    b. total liabilities.
    c. total owner's equity.
    d. net income or net loss for February.

P1-41B ⑥ ⑦ ⑧ ⑨ ⑩ **Applying the entity concept, using the accounting equation for transaction analysis, preparing financial statements, and evaluating business performance [20–30 min]**

Aimee Griffin practiced law with a partnership for 10 years. Recently she opened her own law office, which she operates as a proprietorship. The name of the new entity is Aimee Griffin, Attorney. Griffin experienced the following events during the organizing phase of the new business and its first month of operation. Some of the events were personal and did not affect the law practice. Others were business transactions and should be accounted for by the business.

Dec	1	Sold personal investment in **eBay** stock, which she had owned for several years, receiving $33,000 cash.
	2	Deposited the $33,000 cash from sales of the **eBay** stock in her personal bank account.
	3	Received $159,000 cash from former law partners.
	5	Deposited $109,000 cash in a new business bank account titled Aimee Griffin, Attorney. The business gave capital to Griffin.
	7	Paid $900 cash for ink cartridges for the printer.
	9	Purchased a computer for the law office, agreeing to pay the account, $9,200, within three months.
	23	Finished court hearings on behalf of a client and submitted a bill for legal services, $17,000, on account.
	30	Paid utilities, $1,900.
	31	Griffin withdrew cash of $5,000.

Requirements

1. Analyze the effects of the preceding events on the accounting equation of the propriertorship of Aimee Griffin, Attorney. Use a format similar to Exhibit 1-6.

2. At December 31, compute the business's
   a. total assets.
   b. total liabilities.
   c. total owner's equity.
   d. net income or net loss for the month.

3. Evaluate Aimee Griffin, Attorney's first month of operations. Were the results good or bad?

P1-42B ⑦ ⑧ **Using the accounting equation for transaction analysis [20–25 min]**

Alterri Mechanical was recently formed as a proprietorship. The balance of each item in the company's accounting equation is shown for November 1 and for each of the following business days:

		Cash	Accounts receivable	Supplies	Land	Accounts payable	Alterri, capital
Nov	1	$3,000	$7,300	$ 1,100	$12,000	$4,300	$19,100
	4	6,000	7,300	1,100	12,000	4,300	22,100
	9	3,000	7,300	1,100	15,000	4,300	22,100
	13	3,000	7,300	1,300	15,000	4,500	22,100
	16	1,300	7,300	1,300	15,000	2,800	22,100
	19	2,200	6,400	1,300	15,000	2,800	22,100
	22	10,200	6,400	1,300	15,000	2,800	30,100
	25	9,700	6,400	1,300	15,000	2,300	30,100
	27	9,100	6,400	1,900	15,000	2,300	30,100
	30	3,600	6,400	1,900	15,000	2,300	24,600

Requirement

1. A single transaction took place on each day. Briefly describe the transaction that most likely occurred on each day, beginning with November 4. Indicate which accounts were increased or decreased and by what amounts. Assume that no revenue or expense transactions occurred during the month.

P1-43B ⑦ ⑧ ⑨ ⑩ **Using the accounting equation for transaction analysis [60–75 min]**

Missy Crone owns and operates a public relations firm called Top 40. The following amounts summarize her business on August 31, 2012:

			Assets					=	Liabilities	+	Owner's equity
			Accounts						Accounts		Crone,
Date	Cash	+	receivable	+	Supplies	+	Land	=	payable	+	capital
Bal	2,100	+	2,000	+	0	+	10,000	=	6,000	+	8,100

During September 2012, the business completed the following transactions:

a. Gave capital to Crone and received cash of $10,000.
b. Performed service for a client and received cash of $1,000.
c. Paid off the beginning balance of accounts payable.
d. Purchased supplies from **OfficeMax** on account, $700.
e. Collected cash from a customer on account, $500.
f. Received cash of $1,900 and gave capital to owner.
g. Consulted for a new band and billed the client for services rendered, $5,800.
h. Recorded the following business expenses for the month:
   1. Paid office rent, $900.
   2. Paid advertising, $400.
i. Returned supplies to **OfficeMax** for $80 from item d, which was the cost of the supplies.
j. Crone withdrew cash of $2,700.

Requirement

1. Analyze the effects of the preceding transactions on the accounting equation of Top 40. Adapt the format to that of Exhibit 1-6.

P1-44B ⑨ ⑩ **Preparing financial statements and evaluating business performance [20–30 min]**

Presented here are the accounts of Quick and EZ Delivery for the year ended December 31, 2012.

Land	$ 7,000	Owner investment, 2012	$ 32,000
Note payable	30,000	Accounts payable	14,000
Property tax expense	2,900	Accounts receivable	1,700
Trott, drawing	32,000	Advertising expense	17,000
Rent expense	13,000	Building	137,900
Salary expense	69,000	Cash	6,000
Salary payable	500	Equipment	17,000
Service revenue	192,000	Insurance expense	2,000
Supplies	8,000	Interest expense	6,000
Trott, capital, 12/31/2011	51,000		

Requirements

1. Prepare Quick and EZ Delivery's income statement.
2. Prepare the statement of owner's equity.
3. Prepare the balance sheet.
4. Answer these questions about the company:
   a. Was the result of operations for the year a profit or a loss? How much?
   b. How much in total economic resources does the company have as it moves into the new year?
   c. How much does the company owe to creditors?
   d. What is the dollar amount of the owner's equity in the business at the end of the year?

P1-45B ⑨ **Preparing financial statements [20–30 min]**

Photo Gallery works weddings and prom-type parties. The balance of Leibovitz, capital was $17,000 at December 31, 2011. At December 31, 2012, the business's accounting records show these balances:

Insurance expense	$ 9,000	Accounts receivable	$ 6,000
Cash	26,000	Note payable	14,000
Accounts payable	4,000	Leibovitz, capital, Dec 31, 2012	?
Advertising expense	2,000	Salary expense	21,000
Service revenue	78,000	Equipment	70,000
Leibovitz, drawing	14,000	Owner investment, 2012	35,000

Requirement

1. Prepare the following financial statements for Photo Gallery for the year ended December 31, 2012:
   a. Income statement
   b. Statement of owner's equity
   c. Balance sheet

P1-46B ⑨ ⑩ **Preparing financial statements and evaluating business performance [20–30 min]**

The bookkeeper of Outdoor Life Landscaping prepared the company's balance sheet while the accountant was ill. The balance sheet contains numerous errors. In particular, the bookkeeper knew that the balance sheet should balance, so he plugged in the owner's equity amount needed to achieve this balance. The owner's equity is incorrect. All other amounts are right, but some are out of place.

OUTDOOR LIFE LANDSCAPING			
Balance Sheet			
Month Ended July 31, 2012			
Assets		**Liabilities**	
Cash	$ 5,000	Accounts receivable	$ 2,300
Office supplies	800	Kamp, drawing	8,000
Land	28,400	Service revenue	39,200
Salary expense	3,500	Property tax expense	2,000
Office furniture	5,200	Accounts payable	2,800
Note payable	26,400		
Rent expense	700	**Owner's Equity**	
		Kamp, capital	15,700
Total assets	$ 70,000	Total liabilities	$ 70,000

Requirements

1. Prepare a corrected balance sheet.
2. Consider the original balance sheet as presented and the corrected balance sheet you prepared for Requirement 1. Did total assets as presented in your corrected balance sheet increase, decrease, or stay the same from the original balance sheet? Why?

• Continuing Exercise

Exercise 1-47 is the first exercise in a sequence that begins an accounting cycle. The cycle is continued in Chapter 2 and completed in Chapter 5.

E1-47 ⑧ Analyzing transactions [10–15 min]

Lawlor Lawn Service began operations and completed the following transactions during May 2012:

May 1	Received $1,700 and gave capital to Lawlor. Deposited this amount in bank account titled Lawlor Lawn Service.
3	Purchased on account a mower, $1,200, and weed whacker, $240. The equipment is expected to remain in service for four years.
5	Purchased $30 of gas. Wrote check #1 from the new bank account.
6	Performed lawn services for client on account, $150.
8	Purchased $150 of fertilizer that will be used on future jobs. Wrote check #2 from the new bank account.
17	Completed landscaping job for client, received cash $800.
31	Received $100 on account from May 6 sale.

Requirement

1. Analyze the effects of Lawlor Lawn Service transactions on the accounting equation. Use the format of Exhibit 1-6, and include these headings: Cash; Accounts receivable; Lawn supplies; Equipment; Accounts payable; and Lawlor, capital.

In Chapter 2, we will account for these same transactions a different way—as the accounting is actually performed in practice.

• Continuing Problem

Problem 1-48 is the first problem in a sequence that begins an accounting cycle. The cycle is continued in Chapter 2 and completed in Chapter 5.

P1-48 ⑧ ⑨ Analyzing transactions and preparing financial statements [20–25 min]

Draper Consulting began operations and completed the following transactions during the first half of December:

Dec 2	Received $18,000 cash and gave capital to Draper.
2	Paid monthly office rent, $550.
3	Paid cash for a **Dell** computer, $1,800. This equipment is expected to remain in service for five years.
4	Purchased office furniture on account, $4,200. The furniture should last for five years.
5	Purchased supplies on account, $900.
9	Performed consulting service for a client on account, $1,500.
12	Paid utility expenses, $250.
18	Performed service for a client and received cash of $1,100.

Requirements

1. Analyze the effects of Draper Consulting's transactions on the accounting equation. Use the format of Exhibit 1-6, and include these headings: Cash; Accounts receivable; Supplies; Equipment; Furniture; Accounts payable; and Draper, capital.

2. Prepare the income statement of Draper Consulting for the month ended December 31, 2012.

3. Prepare the statement of owner's equity for the month ended December 31, 2012.

4. Prepare the balance sheet at December 31, 2012.

In Chapter 2, we will account for these same transactions a different way—as the accounting is actually performed in practice.

• Practice Set

8 **Analyzing transactions [10–15 min]** Consider the following transactional data for the first month of operations of Shine King Cleaning.   **MyAccountingLab**

Nov 1: Evan Hudson deposited $35,000 in the business account. Also on this date, Evan transferred his truck title, worth $8,000, to the business. Evan received capital in return.

Nov 2: Wrote a check for $2,000 to Pleasant Properties. In the "for" area of the the check, it states "November through February Rent." (Debit Prepaid rent)

Nov 3: Purchased business insurance policy for $2,400 for the term November 1, 2012, through October 31, 2013 and paid cash. (Debit Prepaid insurance)

Nov 4: Evan went to the Cleaning Supply Company and purchased $270 of cleaning supplies on account. The invoice is due 20 days from the date of purchase.

Nov 5: Purchased on account an industrial vacuum cleaner from Penny Purchase costing $1,000. The invoice is payable on or before November 25.

Nov 7: Purchased a computer and printer costing a total of $1,200. A check for the same amount to the computer store was written on the same date.

Nov 9: Performed cleaning services on account for Pierre's Wig Stand in the amount of $3,000.

Nov 10: Deposited Pierre's check for $100 in the bank.

Nov 15: Wrote check payable to Eric Ryder for $500 for contract labor.

Nov 16: Received $3,600 for 1-year contract beginning November 16 for cleaning services to be provided to the Sea Side Restaurant. Contract begins November 16, 2012, and ends November 15, 2013. (Credit Unearned service revenue)

Nov 17: Provided cleaning services for Tip Top Solutions for $800. Tip Top paid with a check.

Nov 18: Received water and electric bill for $175 with due date of December 4, 2012.

Nov 20: Borrowed $40,000 from bank with interest rate of 9% per year.

Nov 21: Deposited check from Pierre's Wig Stand for $900 paid on account.

Nov 25: Wrote check to Penny Purchase for invoice #1035 in the amount of $500.

Nov 29: Wrote check payable to St. Petersburg News for $100 for advertising.

Nov 30: Evan withdrew cash of $600.

Requirement

1. Prepare an analysis of the November activity using the format displayed in Exhibit 1-6 as a guide. Include the following headings: Cash; Accounts receivable, Supplies; Prepaid rent; Prepaid insurance; Truck; Equipment; Accounts payable; Unearned service revenue; Notes payable; and Hudson, capital.

Apply Your Knowledge

● Decision Cases

Decision Case 1-1 Let's examine a case using Greg's Tunes and another company, Sal's Silly Songs. It is now the end of the first year of operations, and both owners—Sally Siegman and Greg Moore—want to know how well they came out at the end of the year. Neither business kept complete accounting records and neither owner made any drawings. Moore and Siegman throw together the following data at year end:

Sal's Silly Songs:	
Total assets	$23,000
Siegman, capital	8,000
Total revenues	35,000
Total expenses	22,000
Greg's Tunes:	
Total liabilities	$10,000
Moore, capital	6,000
Total expenses	44,000
Net income	9,000

Working in the music business, Moore has forgotten all the accounting he learned in college. Siegman majored in English literature, so she never learned any accounting. To gain information for evaluating their businesses, they ask you several questions. For each answer, you must show your work to convince Moore and Siegman that you know what you are talking about.

1. Which business has more assets?
2. Which business owes more to creditors?
3. Which business has more owner's equity at the end of the year?
4. Which business brought in more revenue?
5. Which business is more profitable?
6. Which of the foregoing questions do you think is most important for evaluating these two businesses? Why? (Challenge)
7. Which business looks better from a financial standpoint? (Challenge)

Decision Case 1-2 Dave and Reba Guerrera saved all their married life to open a bed and breakfast (B&B) named Tres Amigos. They invested $100,000 of their own money and the company gave capital to them. The business then got a $100,000 bank loan for the $200,000 needed to get started. The company bought a run-down old Spanish colonial home in Tucson for $80,000. It cost another $50,000 to renovate. They found most of the furniture at antique shops and flea markets—total cost was $20,000. Kitchen equipment cost $10,000, and a **Dell** computer set cost $2,000.

Prior to the grand opening, the banker requests a report on their activities thus far. Tres Amigos' bank statement shows a cash balance of $38,000. Dave and Reba believe that the $38,000 represents net income for the period, and they feel pretty good about the results of their business. To better understand how well they are doing, they prepare the following income statement for presentation to the bank:

TRES AMIGOS BED AND BREAKFAST
Income Statement
Six Months Ended June 30, 2013

Revenues:		
	Investments by owner	$100,000
	Bank loan	100,000
	Total revenues	200,000
Expenses:		
	Cost of the house	$ 80,000
	Renovation to the house	50,000
	Furniture expense	20,000
	Kitchen equipment expense	10,000
	Computer expense	2,000
	Total expenses	162,000
Net income		38,000

1. Suppose you are the Guerreras' banker, and they have given you this income statement. Would you congratulate them on their net income? If so, explain why. If not, how would you advise them to measure the net income of the business? Does the amount of cash in the bank measure net income? Explain.

2. Prepare Tres Amigos' balance sheet from their data. There is no net income or loss yet.

● Ethical Issues

Ethical Issue 1-1 The board of directors of Xiaping Trading Company is meeting to discuss the past year's results before releasing financial statements to the bank. The discussion includes this exchange:

Wai Lee, company owner: "This has not been a good year! Revenue is down and expenses are way up. If we are not careful, we will report a loss for the third year in a row. I can temporarily transfer some land that I own into the company's name, and that will beef up our balance sheet. Brent, can you shave $500,000 from expenses? Then we can probably get the bank loan that we need."

Brent Ray, company chief accountant: "Wai Lee, you are asking too much. Generally accepted accounting principles are designed to keep this sort of thing from happening."

Requirements

1. What is the fundamental ethical issue in this situation?
2. How do the two suggestions of the company owner differ?

Ethical Issue 1-2 The tobacco companies have paid billions because of smoking-related illnesses. In particular, **Philip Morris**, a leading cigarette manufacturer, paid over $3,000,000,000 in one year.

Requirements

1. Suppose you are the chief financial officer (CFO) responsible for the financial statements of **Philip Morris**. What ethical issue would you face as you consider what to report in your company's annual report about the cash payments? What is the ethical course of action for you to take in this situation?

2. What are some of the negative consequences to **Philip Morris** for not telling the truth? What are some of the negative consequences to **Philip Morris** for telling the truth?

● Fraud Case 1-1

Exeter is a building contractor on the Gulf Coast. After losing a number of big lawsuits, it was facing its first annual net loss as the end of the year approached. The owner, Hank Snow, was under intense pressure from the company's creditors to report positive net income for the year. However, he knew that the controller, Alice Li, had arranged a short-term bank loan of $10,000 to cover a temporary shortfall of cash. He told Alice to record the incoming cash as "construction revenue" instead of a loan. That would nudge the company's income into positive territory for the year, and then, he said, the entry could be corrected in January when the loan was repaid.

Requirements

1. How would this action affect the year-end income statement? How would it affect the year-end balance sheet?
2. If you were one of the company's creditors, how would this fraudulent action affect you?

● Financial Statement Case 1-1

This and similar cases in later chapters focus on the financial statement of a real company—**Amazon.com, Inc.**, the Internet shopping leader. As you work each case, you will gain confidence in your ability to use the financial statements of real companies.

Refer to **Amazon.com's** financial statements in Appendix A at the end of the book.

Requirements

1. How much in cash (including cash equivalents) did **Amazon.com** have on December 31, 2009?
2. What were the company's total assets at December 31, 2009? At December 31, 2008?
3. Write the company's accounting equation at December 31, 2009, by filling in the dollar amounts:

$$\text{ASSETS} = \text{LIABILITIES} + \text{EQUITY}$$

4. Identify net sales (revenue) for the year ended December 31, 2009. How much did total revenue increase or decrease from 2008 to 2009?
5. How much net income or net loss did **Amazon** earn for 2009 and for 2008? Based on net income, was 2009 better or worse than 2008?

● Team Projects

Team Project 1-1 You are opening Quail Creek Pet Kennel. Your purpose is to earn a profit, and you organize as a proprietorship.

1. Make a detailed list of 10 factors you must consider to establish the business.
2. Identify 10 or more transactions that your business will undertake to open and operate the kennel.
3. Prepare the Quail Creek Pet Kennel income statement, statement of owner's equity, and balance sheet at the end of the first month of operations. Use made-up figures and include a complete heading for each financial statement. Date the balance sheet as of January 31, 20XX.
4. Discuss how you will evaluate the success of your business and how you will decide whether to continue its operation.

Team Project 1-2 You are promoting a rock concert in your area. Your purpose is to earn a profit, and you organize Concert Enterprises as a proprietorship.

Requirements

1. Make a detailed list of 10 factors you must consider to establish the business.

2. Describe 10 of the items your business must arrange in order to promote and stage the rock concert.

3. Prepare your business's income statement, statement of owner's equity, and balance sheet on June 30, 20XX, immediately after the rock concert. Use made-up amounts, and include a complete heading for each financial statement. For the income statement and the statement of owner's equity, assume the period is the three months ended June 30, 20XX.

4. Assume that you will continue to promote rock concerts if the venture is successful. If it is unsuccessful, you will terminate the business within three months after the concert. Discuss how you will evaluate the success of your venture and how you will decide whether to continue in business.

● Communication Activity 1-1

In 25 words or fewer, illustrate the accounting equation and explain each part of the accounting equation.

Quick Check Answers

1. *a* 2. *c* 3. *a* 4. *c* 5. *b* 6. *d* 7. *b* 8. *a* 9. *a* 10. *c*

For online homework, exercises, and problems that provide you immediate feedback, please visit myaccountinglab.com.

2

Recording Business Transactions

How do the activities of the company affect what it OWNS?

How do the activities of the company affect what it OWES?

SMART TOUCH LEARNING
Balance Sheet
May 31, 2013

Assets				Liabilities	
Current assets:				**Current liabilities:**	
Cash		$ 4,800		Accounts payable	$ 48,700
Accounts receivable		2,600		Salary payable	900
Inventory		30,500		Interest payable	100
Supplies		600		Unearned service revenue	400
Prepaid rent		2,000		Total current liabilities	50,100
Total current assets			$ 40,500	**Long-term liabilities:**	
Plant assets:				Notes payable	20,000
Furniture	$18,000			Total liabilities	70,100
Less: Accumulated depreciation—furniture	300	17,700			
Building	48,000			**Owner's Equity**	
Less: Accumulated depreciation—building	200	47,800			
Total plant assets			65,500	Bright, capital	35,900
Total assets			$106,000	Total liabilities and owner's equity	$106,000

How do the activities of the company affect its NET WORTH?

Learning Objectives

1 Explain accounts, journals, and ledgers as they relate to recording transactions and describe common accounts

2 Define debits, credits, and normal account balances, and use double-entry accounting and T-accounts

3 List the steps of the transaction recording process

4 Journalize and post sample transactions to the ledger

5 Prepare the trial balance from the T-accounts

After reading Chapter 1, you have a basic understanding of what financial statements are. But how do you create them for your business or the company you work for? How do large companies like **Microsoft** create their statements for investors? How does any business capture the financial events that occur so that it can create financial statements?

In Chapter 1, we saw how Sheena Bright of Smart Touch Learning recorded her company's business transactions in terms of the accounting equation. That procedure works well for a handful of transactions, but it's not very efficient if your business generates lots of transactions. In this chapter, we'll show you a more efficient way to capture business transactions. As you'll see, this chapter is a critical foundation for learning accounting.

The Account, the Journal, and the Ledger

The basic summary device of accounting is the account. An **account** is the detailed record of all the changes that have occurred in an individual asset, liability, or owner's equity (or stockholders' equity for a corporation) during a specified period. As we saw in Chapter 1, business transactions cause the changes.

Accountants record transactions first in a **journal**, which is the chronological record of transactions. Accountants then post (copy) the data to the book of accounts called the **ledger**. A list of all the ledger accounts and their balances is called a **trial balance**.

The following diagram summarizes the accounting process covered in this chapter. Take a moment to become familiar with these important terms. You will be using them over and over again.

 Explain accounts, journals, and ledgers as they relate to recording transactions and describe common accounts

- **Account**—the detailed record of all the changes that have occurred in a particular asset, liability, or owner's equity
- **Journal**—the chronological record of transactions
- **Ledger**—the book holding all the accounts with their balances
- **Trial balance**—the list of all the ledger accounts with their balances

Accounts are grouped in three broad categories, according to the accounting equation:

$$\text{Assets} = \text{Liabilities} + \text{Owner's Equity}$$

Assets

Assets are economic resources that will benefit the business in the future, **or simply, something the business owns that has value.** Most firms use the following asset accounts:

Cash

The Cash account is a record of the cash effects of transactions. Cash includes money, such as a bank balance, paper currency, coins, and checks. Cash is the most pressing need of start-up businesses, such as Smart Touch Learning and Greg's Tunes.

Accounts Receivable

Most businesses sell goods or services in exchange for a promise of future cash receipts. Such sales are made on credit ("on account"), and Accounts receivable is the account that holds these amounts. **Accounts receivable is the right to receive cash in the near future.** Most sales in the United States and in other developed countries are made on account.

Notes Receivable

A business may sell goods or services and receive a **note receivable** or *promissory note*. A note receivable is a written pledge that the customer will pay a fixed amount of money and interest by a certain date. **A note receivable is the right to receive cash and interest in the future.**

Prepaid Expenses

A business often pays certain expenses, such as rent and insurance, in advance. A **prepaid expense** is considered an asset because the prepayment provides a future benefit. **With a prepaid expense, the company pays for the expense before it is used.** Prepaid rent, Prepaid insurance, and Office supplies are separate prepaid expense accounts. Your college tuition that you paid at the beginning of the term is an asset to you.

Land

The Land account shows the cost of land a business holds for use in operations. Land held for sale is different. Its cost is an investment.

Building

The cost of buildings—an office or a warehouse—appears in the Buildings account. **Frito-Lay** and **The Coca-Cola Company** own buildings around the world where they make chips and drinks.

Equipment, Furniture, and Fixtures

A business has a separate asset account for each type of equipment—Computer equipment, Office equipment, and Store equipment, for example. The Furniture account shows the cost of this asset. Similarly, the Fixtures account shows the cost of light fixtures and shelving, for example.

Liabilities

Recall that a *liability* is a debt—that is, something you owe. A business generally has fewer liability accounts than asset accounts.

Accounts Payable

Accounts payable is the opposite of Accounts receivable. The promise to pay a debt arising from a credit purchase is an Account payable. Such a purchase is said to be made on account. **An account payable is an obligation to pay cash in the near future.** All companies, from Smart Touch and Greg's Tunes to **Coca-Cola** to **eBay**, have Accounts payable.

Notes Payable

Notes payable is the opposite of Notes receivable. A note payable is an obligation to pay, whereas a note receivable is a right to receive. Notes payable represents debts the business owes because it signed promissory notes to borrow money or to purchase something. **Notes payable is an obligation to pay cash and interest in the future.**

Accrued Liabilities

An **accrued liability** is a liability for which the business knows the amount owed, but the bill has not been paid. Taxes payable, Interest payable, and Salary payable are examples of accrued liability accounts.

Owner's Equity

The owner's claim to the assets of the business is called *owner's equity*. A company has separate accounts for the various elements of owner's equity.

Capital

The capital account represents the net investment of the owner in the business. It holds the accumulation of owner investment, withdrawals, and net income (loss) of the business over the life of the business. In other words, capital is the net worth invested in the business by the owner.

Drawing

The owner may withdraw cash or other assets at any time from the company. This represents a return of his or her capital investment, as well as a distribution of earnings from the company. **Owner drawings mean less earnings retained by the company for future growth.**

Revenues

The increase in equity created by delivering goods or services to customers is called *revenue*. **Revenues refer to earnings for work done or goods delivered by the company, regardless of when the cash is received.** The ledger contains as many revenue accounts as needed. Smart Touch, for example, needs a Service revenue account for amounts earned by providing e-learning services. If Smart Touch lends money to an outsider, it needs an Interest revenue account for the interest earned on the loan. If the business rents out a building to a tenant, it needs a Rent revenue account.

Expenses

Expenses use up assets or create liabilities in the course of operating a business. Expenses have the opposite effect of revenues. Expenses *decrease* equity. **Expenses are present or future payments of cash that are incurred to help the company earn revenues.** A business needs a separate account for each type of expense, such as Salary expense, Rent expense, Advertising expense, and Utilities expense. Businesses strive to minimize their expenses in order to maximize net income—whether that business is **General Electric**, Smart Touch, or Greg's Tunes.

Exhibit 2-1 shows how asset, liability, and owner's equity accounts can be grouped in the ledger.

Chart of Accounts

The ledger contains the accounts grouped under these headings:

- Assets, Liabilities, and Owner's Equity
- Revenues and Expenses

Companies use a **chart of accounts** to list all their accounts along with the account numbers. The chart of accounts for Smart Touch appears in Exhibit 2-2. Account numbers are just shorthand versions of the account names. One account number equals one account name—just like your Social Security number is unique to you.

Account numbers usually have two or more digits. Assets are often numbered beginning with 1, liabilities with 2, owner's equity with 3, revenues with 4, and expenses with 5. The second and third digits in an account number indicate where the account fits within the category. For example, if Sheena Bright is using three-digit

EXHIBIT 2-1 | The Ledger—Asset, Liability, and Owner's Equity Accounts

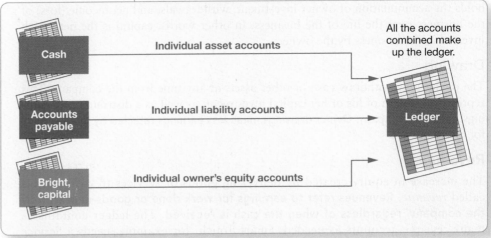

account numbers, Cash may be account number 101, the first asset account. Accounts receivable may be account number 111, the second asset. Accounts payable may be number 201, the first liability. When numbers are used, all accounts are numbered by this system. However, each company chooses its own account numbering system.

Notice in Exhibit 2-2 the gap in account numbers between 121 and 141. Sheena Bright of Smart Touch may need to add another asset account in the future. For example, she may start selling some type of inventory and want to use account number 131 for Inventory. So, the chart of accounts will change as the business evolves.

EXHIBIT 2-2 | Chart of Accounts— Smart Touch Learning

Balance Sheet Accounts

Assets	Liabilities	Owner's Equity
101 Cash	201 Accounts payable	301 Bright, capital
111 Accounts receivable	211 Salary payable	311 Bright, drawing
121 Notes receivable	221 Interest payable	
141 Supplies	231 Notes payable	
151 Furniture		
171 Building		
191 Land		

Income Statement Accounts
(Part of Owner's Equity)

Revenues	Expenses
401 Service revenue	501 Rent expense, computer
411 Interest revenue	502 Rent expense, office
	505 Salary expense
	510 Depreciation expense
	520 Utilities expense
	530 Advertising expense
	540 Supplies expense

Charts of accounts vary from business to business, though many account names are common to all companies' charts of accounts. For example, you will find Cash on every company's chart of accounts. **The chart of accounts contains the list of account names you might use to record a transaction to.**

Debits, Credits, and Double-Entry Accounting

As we saw in Chapter 1, accounting is based on transaction data, not on mere whim or opinion. Each business transaction has dual effects:

- The receiving side
- The giving side

For example, in the $30,000 cash receipt by Smart Touch in Chapter 1, the business

- received cash of $30,000.
- gave or issued $30,000 of capital to Bright.

Accounting uses the **double-entry system**, which means that we record the dual effects of each transaction. As a result, every transaction affects at least two accounts. It would be incomplete to record only the giving side, or only the receiving side, of a transaction.

Consider a cash purchase of supplies. What are the dual effects? A cash purchase of supplies

1. increases supplies (you received supplies).
2. decreases cash (you gave cash).

Similarly, a credit purchase of equipment (a purchase on account)

1. increases equipment (you received equipment).
2. increases accounts payable (you gave your promise to pay in the future).

2 Define debits, credits, and normal account balances, and use double-entry accounting and T-accounts

The T-Account

A shortened form of the general ledger account is called the **T-account** because it takes the form of the capital letter *T*. The vertical line divides the account into its left and right sides, with the title at the top. For example, the Cash account appears as follows.

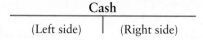

The left side of the account is called the **Debit** side, and the right side is called the **Credit** side. To become comfortable using these terms, remember the following:

Debits go on the left; credits go on the right. The terms *debit* and *credit* are deeply entrenched in business.[1] They are abbreviated as follows:

| DR = Debit | CR = Credit |

Increases and Decreases in the Accounts

The account category (asset, liability, equity) governs how we record increases and decreases. For any given account, increases are recorded on one side, and decreases are recorded on the opposite side. The following T-accounts provide a summary:

Assets		Liabilities and Owner's Equity	
Increase = Debit	Decrease = Credit	Decrease = Debit	Increase = Credit

These are the *rules of debit and credit*. **Whether an account is increased or decreased by a debit or a credit depends on the type of account.** Debits are not "good" or "bad." Neither are credits. Debits are not always increases or always decreases—neither are credits.

In a computerized accounting information system, the computer interprets debits and credits as increases or decreases, based on the account type. For example, a computer reads a debit to Cash as an increase, because it is an asset account. The computer reads a debit to Accounts payable as a decrease, because it is a liability account.

Exhibit 2-3 shows the relationship between the accounting equation and the rules of debit and credit.

EXHIBIT 2-3 | **The Accounting Equation and the Rules of Debit and Credit**

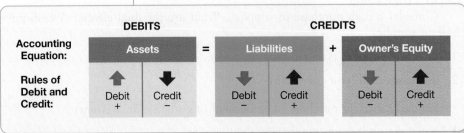

To illustrate the ideas diagrammed in Exhibit 2-3, let's look at the first transaction from Chapter 1 again. Smart Touch received $30,000 cash and gave capital to Bright. Which accounts of the business are affected?

The answer: The business's assets and equity would increase by $30,000, as the T-accounts show.

| ASSETS | = | LIABILITIES | + | OWNER'S EQUITY |

Cash			Bright, capital
Debit for increase, 30,000			Credit for increase, 30,000

---

[1]The words *debit* and *credit* abbreviate the Latin terms *debitum* and *creditum*. Luca Pacioli, the Italian monk who wrote about accounting in the fifteenth century, popularized these terms.

The amount remaining in an account is called its *balance*. The first transaction gives Cash a $30,000 debit balance and Bright, capital a $30,000 credit balance.

The second transaction is a $20,000 purchase of land. Exhibit 2-4 illustrates the accounting equation after Smart Touch Learning's first two transactions. After transaction 2, Cash has a $10,000 debit balance, Land has a debit balance of $20,000, and Bright, capital has a $30,000 credit balance.

We create accounts as needed. The process of creating a new account is called *opening the account*. For transaction 1, we opened the Cash account and the Bright, capital account. For transaction 2, we opened the Land account.

EXHIBIT 2-4   **The Accounting Equation After the First Two Transactions of Smart Touch Learning**

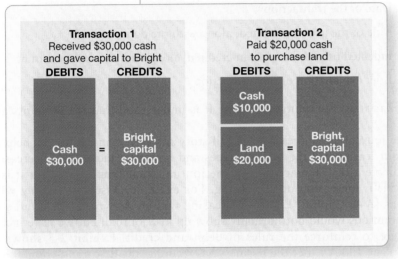

List the Steps of the Transaction Recording Process

In practice, accountants record transactions in a *journal*. The journalizing process has three steps:

3 List the steps of the transaction recording process

1. Identify each account affected and its type (asset, liability, or owner's equity).

2. Determine whether each account is increased or decreased. Use the rules of debit and credit.

3. Record the transaction in the journal, including a brief explanation. The debit side of the entry is entered first. The credit side is indented. Total debits should always equal total credits. This step is also called "making the journal entry" or "journalizing the transaction."

These steps are the same whether done by computer or manually.

Let's journalize the first transaction of Smart Touch—the receipt of $30,000 cash and investment of capital by Bright.

STEP 1: The accounts affected by the receipt of cash and issuance of stock are *Cash* and *Bright, capital*. Cash is an asset. Bright, capital is equity.

STEP 2: Both accounts increase by $30,000. Assets increase with debits. Therefore, we debit Cash because it is an asset. Equity increases in the business because capital investment by the owner increased. To increase equity, we credit. Therefore, we credit the Bright, capital account.

Step 3: The journal entry is as follows:

Journal				Page 1
Date	Accounts and Explanation		Debit	Credit
Apr 1[a]	Cash[b] (A+)		30,000[b]	
	Bright, capital[c] (Q+)			30,000[c]
	Owner investment.[d]			

Footnotes a, b, c, and d are explained as follows. The journal entry includes four parts:

a. Date of the transaction

b. Title of the account debited, along with the dollar amount

c. Indented title of the account credited, along with the dollar amount

d. Brief explanation of the transaction

Dollar signs are omitted because it is understood that the amounts are in dollars.

The journal entry presents the full story for each transaction. To help reinforce your learning of the account types and how they increase or decrease, we will indicate after each account in the journal what type of account it is and whether it is increasing or decreasing. For example, Assets increasing will be shown as (A+), Capital (Equity) increasing will be shown as (Q+), and so on. These notations would not normally show up in a journal, but we have included them here to reinforce the rules of debit and credit. Exhibit 2-5 shows how Journal Page 1 looks after the business has recorded the first transaction.

EXHIBIT 2-5 | **The Journal Page**

Journal				Page 1
Date	Accounts and Explanation		Debit	Credit
Apr 1	Cash (A+)		30,000	
	Bright, capital (Q+)			30,000
	Owner investment.			

Posting (Copying Information) from the Journal to the Ledger

Journalizing a transaction records the data only in the journal—but not in the ledger. The data must also be copied to the ledger. The process of copying from the journal to the ledger is called **posting**. We *post* from the journal to the ledger.

Debits in the journal are posted as debits in the ledger and credits as credits—no exceptions. The first transaction of Smart Touch is posted to the ledger in Exhibit 2-6.

EXHIBIT 2-6 | Making a Journal Entry and Posting to the Ledger in T-Account Form

Journal Entry:

		Accounts and Explanation	Debit	Credit
Apr 1		Cash (A+)	30,000	
		Bright, capital (Q+)		30,000
		Owner investment.		

Posting to the Ledger:

Cash	Bright, capital
30,000	30,000

Expanding the Rules of Debit and Credit: Revenues and Expenses

As we have noted, *revenues* are increases in equity that result from providing goods or services for customers. *Expenses* are decreases in equity that result from using up assets or increasing liabilities in the course of operations. **Revenues are earned. Expenses are incurred.** Therefore, we must expand the accounting equation to include revenues and expenses. There are several elements of owner's equity.

Exhibit 2-7 shows revenues and expenses under owner's equity because they directly affect equity.

EXHIBIT 2-7 | The Accounting Equation Includes Revenues and Expenses

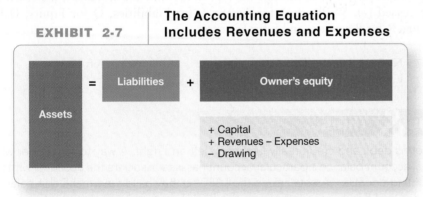

Assets = Liabilities + Owner's equity

+ Capital
+ Revenues − Expenses
− Drawing

We can now express the rules of debit and credit in complete form as shown in Exhibit 2-8. Note that the accounting equation now includes revenues and expenses.

EXHIBIT 2-8 | Complete Rules of Debit and Credit

Assets	=	Liabilities	+	Owner's equity			

Assets		=	Liabilities		+	Capital		+	Revenues		−	Expenses		−	Drawing	
DR	CR		DR	CR		DR	CR		DR	CR		DR	CR		DR	CR
+	−		−	+		−	+		−	+		+	−		+	−

The Normal Balance of an Account

An account's **normal balance** appears on the side—either debit or credit—where we record an *increase* (+) in the account's balance. For example, assets normally have a debit balance, so assets are *debit-balance accounts*. Liabilities and equity accounts normally have the opposite balance, so they are *credit-balance accounts*. Expenses and Drawing are equity accounts that have debit balances—unlike the other equity accounts. They have debit balances because they decrease equity. Revenues increase equity, so a revenue's normal balance is a credit. Notice in Exhibit 2-8 that all the + signs are bolded because + is the normal balance for all accounts.

As we have seen, owner's equity includes the following:

Capital—a credit-balance account

Drawing—a debit-balance account

Revenues—a credit balance account

Expenses—a debit balance account

An account with a normal debit balance may occasionally have a credit balance. That indicates a negative amount of the item. For example, Cash will have a credit balance if the business overdraws its bank account. Also, the liability Accounts payable—a credit balance account—could have a debit balance if the company overpays its accounts payable. In other cases, a non-normal account balance indicates an error. For example, a credit balance in Office supplies, Furniture, or Buildings is an error because negative amounts of these assets make no sense. In each journal entry, we will indicate the type of account and whether it increased (+) or decreased (−). We'll use A for Assets, L for Liabilities, Q for Equity, D for Drawing, R for Revenues, and E for Expenses.

> Normal Balance Tip: Assets, Expenses, and Drawing: left Debits.
> Liabilities, Equity, and Revenues: right Credits.

Stop & Think...

The terms debit and credit really just mean left and right. A way to remember what normal account balance a particular account has is to associate the accounts with the accounting equation. Assets are on the LEFT so they have a normal Debit balance. Liabilities and Equity accounts are on the RIGHT so they have a normal Credit balance. So think of debit as left and credit as right when remembering normal balance of accounts.

Now let's put your new learning into practice and account for the early transactions of Smart Touch.

Exhibit 2-9 summarizes the flow of data through the accounting system. In the pages that follow, we record Smart Touch's early transactions. Keep in mind that we are accounting for the e-learning business. We are *not* accounting for Sheena Bright's personal transactions because of the entity concept we learned in Chapter 1.

EXHIBIT 2-9 | **Flow of Accounting Data from the Journal to the Ledger**

Source Documents—The Origin of the Steps

Accounting data come from source documents, as shown in the second segment of Exhibit 2-9. In that exhibit, Smart Touch received $30,000 and gave capital to Sheena Bright. The *bank deposit ticket* is the document that shows the amount of cash received by the business, and the capital account shows the net investment of the owner, Sheena Bright. Based on these documents, Bright can determine how to record this transaction in the journal.

When the business buys supplies on account, the vendor sends Smart Touch an invoice requesting payment. The *purchase invoice* is the source document that tells the business how much and when to pay the vendor. The invoice shows what Smart Touch purchased and how much it cost—indicating to the business how to record the transaction.

Smart Touch may pay the account payable with a *bank check*, another source document. The check and the purchase invoice give the business the information it needs to record the cash payment accurately.

When Smart Touch provides education services for a client, the business e-mails a sales invoice to the client. Smart Touch's *sales invoice* is the source document that tells the business how much revenue to record.

There are many different types of source documents in business. In the transactions that follow, we illustrate some of the more common types of documents that Smart Touch uses in its business.

Key Takeaway

A transaction occurs and is recorded on a source document. Then, we identify the account names affected by the transaction and determine whether the accounts increased or decreased using the rules of debit and credit for the six main account types. We then record the transaction in the journal, listing the debits first. Debits must equal credits. We then post all transactions to the ledger (T-account).

Journalizing Transactions and Posting to the Ledger

Practice Journalizing with Specific Examples

4 Journalize and post sample transactions to the ledger

Transaction 1

Smart Touch received $30,000 cash on April 1 from Sheena Bright and gave her capital in the business. The business deposited the money in its bank account, as shown by the following deposit ticket:

—| DEPOSIT TICKET |—

Smart Touch Learning
281 Wave Ave
Niceville, FL 32578

DATE _____ *April 1* _____, 2013

CASH	CURRENCY		
	COIN		
LIST CHECKS SEPARATELY		30,000	00
TOTAL FROM OTHER SIDE			
TOTAL		30,000	00
LESS CASH RECEIVED			
NET DEPOSIT		30,000	00

VALPARAISO FIRST BANK
John Sims Pkwy
Valparaiso, FL

⑆122000661⑆1400⑈03857

The business increased cash, which is an asset, so we debit Cash. The business also increased owner's equity, so we credit Bright, capital.

Journal Entry	Apr 1	Cash (A+)		30,000	
		Bright, capital (Q+)			30,000
		Owner investment.			

Ledger Accounts	Cash	Bright, capital
	Apr 1 30,000	Apr 1 30,000

Transaction 2

On April 2, Smart Touch paid $20,000 cash for land. The purchase decreased cash. Therefore, we credit Cash. The asset, land, increased, so we debit the Land account.

Journal Entry	Apr 2	Land (A+)		20,000	
		Cash (A−)			20,000
		Paid cash for land.			

Ledger Accounts	Cash		Land
	Apr 1 30,000	Apr 2 20,000	Apr 2 20,000

Transaction 3

Smart Touch purchased $500 of office supplies on account on April 3, as shown on this purchase invoice.

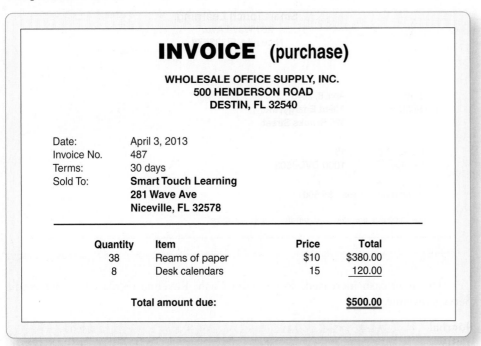

INVOICE (purchase)

WHOLESALE OFFICE SUPPLY, INC.
500 HENDERSON ROAD
DESTIN, FL 32540

Date:	April 3, 2013
Invoice No.	487
Terms:	30 days
Sold To:	**Smart Touch Learning**
	281 Wave Ave
	Niceville, FL 32578

Quantity	Item	Price	Total
38	Reams of paper	$10	$380.00
8	Desk calendars	15	120.00
	Total amount due:		**$500.00**

The supplies will benefit Smart Touch in future periods, so they are an asset to the company until they are used. (We will talk about accounting for using the supplies in Chapter 3.)

The asset office supplies increased, so we debit Office supplies. The liability accounts payable increased, so we credit Accounts payable.

Journal Entry	Apr 3	Office supplies (A+)		500	
		Accounts payable (L+)			500
		Purchased supplies on account.			

Ledger Accounts	Office supplies		Accounts payable	
	Apr 3	500		Apr 3	500

Transaction 4

On April 8, Smart Touch collected cash of $5,500 for service revenue that the business earned by providing e-learning services for clients. The source document is Smart Touch's sales invoice on the following page.

INVOICE (sale)

Smart Touch Learning
281 Wave Ave.
Niceville, FL 32578

Date:	April 8, 2013
Sold to:	**Allied Energy, Inc.**
	325 Brooks Street

Invoice No:	**15**
Service:	1000 DVD0503

Total amount due: $5,500

All accounts are due and payable within 30 days.

The asset cash increased, so we debit Cash. Revenue increased, so we credit Service revenue.

Journal Entry				
Apr 8	Cash (A+)		5,500	
	Service revenue (R+)			5,500
	Performed service and received cash.			

Ledger Accounts	Cash					Service revenue	
	Apr 1	30,000	Apr 2	20,000		Apr 8	5,500
	Apr 8	5,500					

In Chapter 1 we listed service revenue and expenses under Bright, capital. Here we record the revenues and the expenses directly in their own accounts. You will see in Chapter 4 how the revenue and expense accounts ultimately get into the Bright, capital account.

Transaction 5

On April 10, Smart Touch performed services for clients, for which the clients will pay the company later. The business earned $3,000 of service revenue on account.

This transaction increased Accounts receivable, so we debit this asset. Service revenue is increased with a credit.

Journal Entry				
Apr 10	Accounts receivable (A+)		3,000	
	Service revenue (R+)			3,000
	Performed service on account.			

Ledger Accounts	Accounts receivable		Service revenue	
	Apr 10	3,000	Apr 8	5,500
			Apr 10	3,000

Notice the differences and the similarities between transactions 4 and 5. In both transactions, Service revenue was increased (credited) because in both cases the company had earned revenue. However, in transaction 4, the company was paid at the time of service. In transaction 5, on the other hand, the company will receive cash later (Accounts receivable). This difference is key, because the amount of earnings is not determined by when the company receives cash. Earnings (Revenue) are recorded when the company does the work or provides the service.

Transaction 6

Smart Touch paid the following cash expenses on April 15: Rent expense on a computer, $600; Office rent, $1,000; Salary expense, $1,200; Utilities expense, $400. We need to debit each expense account to record its increase and credit Cash for the total decrease.

Journal Entry	Apr 15	Rent expense, computer (E+)	600	
		Rent expense, office (E+)	1,000	
		Salary expense (E+)	1,200	
		Utilities expense (E+)	400	
		Cash (A–)		3,200
		Paid cash expenses.		

Note: In practice, the business would record these expenses in four separate journal entries. Here we show them together to illustrate a **compound journal entry.** A compound journal entry (like transaction 6) has more than two accounts, but total debits still must equal total credits.

Ledger Accounts

	Cash				Rent expense, computer		Rent expense, office
Apr 1	30,000	Apr 2	20,000		Apr 15 600		Apr 15 1,000
Apr 8	5,500	Apr 15	3,200				

Salary expense	Utilities expense
Apr 15 1,200	Apr 15 400

Transaction 7

On April 21, Smart Touch paid $300 on the account payable created in transaction 3. The paid check is Smart Touch's source document, or proof, for this transaction.

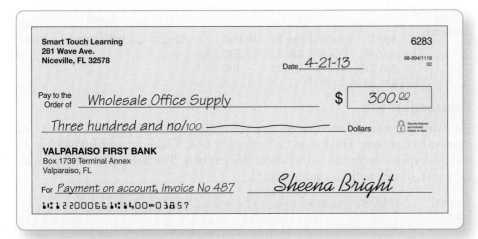

The payment decreased cash, so we credit Cash. The payment decreased Accounts payable, so we debit that liability.

Journal Entry	Apr 21	Accounts payable (L–)	300	
		Cash (A–)		300
		Paid cash on account.		

Ledger Accounts

	Cash				Accounts payable		
Apr 1	30,000	Apr 2	20,000		Apr 21 300	Apr 3	500
Apr 8	5,500	Apr 15	3,200				
		Apr 21	300				

Transaction 8

Sheena Bright remodeled her home with personal funds. This is not a transaction of the business, so there is no entry on the business's books (based on the entity concept).

Transaction 9

On April 22, Smart Touch collected $2,000 cash from the client in transaction 5. Cash is increased, so we debit Cash. Accounts receivable is decreased, so we credit Accounts receivable.

Journal Entry	Apr 22	Cash (A+)		2,000	
		Accounts receivable (A–)			2,000
		Received cash on account.			

Note: This transaction has no effect on revenue; the related revenue was recorded in transaction 5.

Ledger Accounts		Cash				Accounts receivable			
	Apr 1	30,000	Apr 2	20,000		Apr 10	3,000	Apr 22	2,000
	Apr 8	5,500	Apr 15	3,200					
	Apr 22	2,000	Apr 21	300					

Transaction 10

On April 24, Smart Touch sold a parcel of land owned by the business. The sale price, $9,000, equaled the cost. Cash increased, so we debit Cash. Land decreased, so we credit Land.

Journal Entry	Apr 24	Cash (A+)		9,000	
		Land (A–)			9,000
		Sold land at cost.			

Ledger Accounts		Cash				Land			
	Apr 1	30,000	Apr 2	20,000		Apr 2	20,000	Apr 24	9,000
	Apr 8	5,500	Apr 15	3,200					
	Apr 22	2,000	Apr 21	300					
	Apr 24	9,000							

Transaction 11

On April 30, Smart Touch received a telephone bill for $100 and will pay this expense next month. There is no cash payment now. This is an accrued liability. The Utilities expense increased, so we debit this expense. The liability accounts payable increased, so we credit Accounts payable.

Journal Entry	Apr 30	Utilities expense (E+)		100	
		Accounts payable (L+)			100
		Received utility bill.			

Ledger Accounts		Accounts payable				Utilities expense			
	Apr 21	300	Apr 3	500		Apr 15	400		
			Apr 30	100		Apr 30	100		

Transaction 12

Also on April 30, Bright withdrew cash of $2,000. The withdrawal decreased the entity's cash, so we credit Cash. The drawing also decreased total owner's equity. Decreases in equity that result from owner withdrawals are debited to the owner's drawing account, so we debit Bright, drawing.

Journal Entry	Apr 30	Bright, drawing (D+)	2,000	
		Cash (A–)		2,000
		Owner withdrawal.		

Connect To: Accounting Information Systems

The journals you've seen are called general journals because all types of transactions may be posted in them. There are also special purpose journals, used for posting large volumes of similar transactions. Special purpose journals are mostly used with computer software programs, such as QuickBooks and Peachtree. Many of the icons used in these software programs represent a specific type of transaction. For example, in QuickBooks, the Write Check icon is used to print checks. Refer to Transaction 7. It's the same kind of transaction: We wrote a check to pay a vendor. This would be called a "cash payments special purpose journal." In this chapter and in this text, we will focus on general journals only.

Ledger Accounts

Cash						Bright, drawing	
Apr 1	30,000	Apr 2	20,000			Apr 30	2,000
Apr 8	5,500	Apr 15	3,200				
Apr 22	2,000	Apr 21	300				
Apr 24	9,000	Apr 30	2,000				

Each journal entry posted to the ledger is keyed by date or by transaction number. In this way, any transaction can be traced back and forth between the journal and the ledger. This helps you locate any information you may need.

The Ledger Accounts After Posting

We next show the accounts of Smart Touch after posting. The accounts are grouped under their headings in Exhibit 2-10.

Each account has a balance. An account balance is the difference between the account's total debits and its total credits. For example, the $21,000 balance in the Cash account is the difference between the following:

- Total debits, $46,500 ($30,000 + $5,500 + $2,000 + $9,000)
- Total credits, $25,500 ($20,000 + $3,200 + $300 + $2,000)

We set a balance apart from the transaction amounts by a horizontal line. The final figure, below the horizontal line, is denoted as the balance (Bal).

EXHIBIT 2-10   **Smart Touch Learning's Ledger Accounts After Posting April's Transactions**

ASSETS

Cash

Apr 1	30,000	Apr 2	20,000
Apr 8	5,500	Apr 15	3,200
Apr 22	2,000	Apr 21	300
Apr 24	9,000	Apr 30	2,000
Bal	21,000		

Accounts receivable

Apr 10	3,000	Apr 22	2,000†
Bal	1,000		

Office supplies

Apr 3	500	
Bal	500	

Land

Apr 2	20,000	Apr 24	9,000
Bal	11,000		

LIABILITIES

Accounts payable

Apr 21	300	Apr 3	500
		Apr 30	100
		Bal	300

OWNER'S EQUITY

Bright, capital

		Apr 1	30,000
		Bal	30,000

Bright, drawing

Apr 30	2,000	
Bal	2,000	

REVENUE

Service revenue

		Apr 8	5,500
		Apr 10	3,000
		Bal	8,500

EXPENSES

Rent expense, computer

Apr 15	600	
Bal	600	

Rent expense, office

Apr 15	1,000†	
Bal	1,000	

Salary expense

Apr 15	1,200	
Bal	1,200	

Utilities expense

Apr 15	400	
Apr 30	100	
Bal	500†	

†These values are intentionally different than those presented in Chapter 1.

Key Takeaway

Let's review. A transaction occurs. We then identify the account names affected by the transaction and determine whether the accounts increased or decreased using the rules of debit and credit for the six main account types. We then record in the journal, listing the debits first. Debits must equal credits. We then post all transactions to the T-account (ledger). Finally, we determine the ending balance in each T-account, using the rules of debit and credit.

 **Stop & Think...**

Have you ever walked along the beach and gathered sea shells? Maybe you had more than one bucket and you put all the sand dollars in one, all the hermit crabs in another, and so on. That separation is essentially what happens in posting. All we are doing is gathering transactions that affect the same account (for example, all the transactions to Cash) and putting them in the T-account. They are placed either on the left or right side of the T-account based on whether they were on the left or right side of the journal entry. Posting is merely a sorting process—no change to debits or credits occurs from transaction to posting.

Preparing the Trial Balance from the T-Accounts

 Prepare the trial balance from the T-accounts

As noted earlier, a trial balance summarizes the ledger (T-accounts) by listing all the accounts with their balances—assets first, followed by liabilities, and then owner's equity. In a manual accounting system, the trial balance provides an accuracy check by showing whether total debits equal total credits. In all types of systems, the trial balance is a useful summary of the accounts and their balances because it shows the balances on a specific date for all accounts in a company's accounting system. Exhibit 2-11 is the trial balance of Smart Touch at April 30, 2013, the end of the first month of operations, created from the balances calculated in Exhibit 2-10.

A warning: Do not confuse the trial balance with the balance sheet. A trial balance is an internal document used only by company insiders. Outsiders see only the company's financial statements, not the trial balance.

EXHIBIT 2-11 | **Trial Balance**

SMART TOUCH LEARNING Trial Balance April 30, 2013		
Account Title	**Debit**	**Credit**
Cash	$21,000	
Accounts receivable	1,000	
Office supplies	500	
Land	11,000	
Accounts payable		$ 300
Bright, capital		30,000
Bright, drawing	2,000	
Service revenue		8,500
Rent expense, computer	600	
Rent expense, office	1,000	
Salary expense	1,200	
Utilities expense	500	
Total	$38,800	$38,800

Correcting Trial Balance Errors

Throughout the accounting process, total debits should always equal total credits. If they do not, there is an error. Computerized accounting systems eliminate many errors because most software will not let you make a journal entry that does not balance. But computers cannot *eliminate* all errors because humans can input the wrong data.

Balancing errors can be detected by computing the difference between total debits and total credits on the trial balance. Then perform one or more of the following actions:

1. Search the trial balance for a missing account. For example, suppose the accountant omitted Bright, drawing from the trial balance in Exhibit 2-11. Total debits would then be $36,800 ($38,800 – $2,000). Trace each account from the ledger to the trial balance, and you will locate the missing account.

2. Divide the difference between total debits and total credits by 2. A debit treated as a credit, or vice versa, doubles the amount of error. Suppose the accountant posted a $500 credit as a debit. Total debits contain the $500, and total credits omit the $500. The out-of-balance amount is $1,000. Dividing the difference by 2 identifies the $500 amount of the transaction. Then search the trial balance for a $500 transaction and trace it to the account affected.

3. Divide the out-of-balance amount by 9. If the result is evenly divisible by 9, the error may be a *slide* (example: writing $1,000 as $100 or writing $100 as $1,000) or a *transposition* (example: listing $1,200 as $2,100). Suppose, for example, that the accountant printed the $2,000 Bright, drawing as $20,000 on the trial balance. This is a slide-type error. Total debits would differ from total credits by $18,000 ($20,000 – $2,000 = $18,000). Dividing $18,000 by 9 yields $2,000, the correct amount of drawing. Trace $2,000 through the ledger until you reach the Bright, drawing account. You have then found the error.

Total debits can equal total credits on the trial balance; however, there still could be errors in individual account balances because an incorrect account might have been selected in an individual journal entry.

Details of Journals and Ledgers

In practice, the journal and the ledger provide details to create a "trail" through the records. Suppose a supplier bills us twice for an item that we purchased. To show we have already paid the bill, we must prove our payment. That requires us to use the journal and the ledger to get to the source document (cancelled check).

Details in the Journal

Exhibit 2-12 illustrates recording a transaction in a journal with these details:

- The *transaction date*, April 1, 2013
- The *accounts* debited and credited, along with their dollar amounts
- The *posting reference*, abbreviated Post. Ref.

EXHIBIT 2-12 | **Details of Journalizing and Posting**

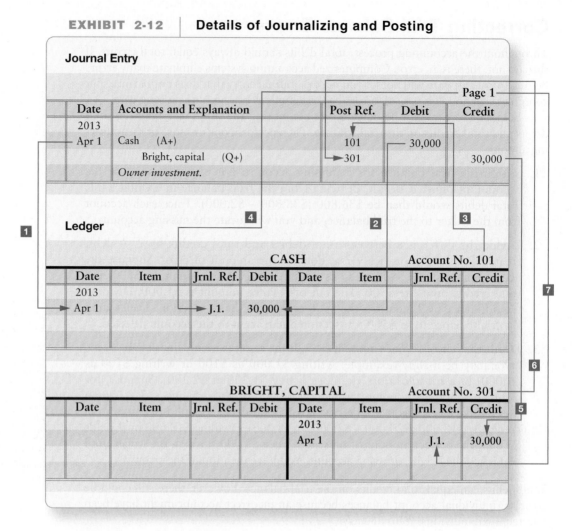

Details in the Ledger

As noted earlier, posting means copying information from the journal to the ledger. But how do we handle the details? Exhibit 2-12 illustrates the steps, denoted by arrows:

Arrow **1**—Post the transaction **date** from the journal to the ledger.

Arrow **2**—Post the debit, **$30,000**, from the journal as a debit to the Cash account in the ledger.

Arrow **3**—Post the account number (**101**) from the ledger back to the journal. This step shows that the debit has been posted to the ledger. **Post. Ref.** is the abbreviation for Posting Reference.

Arrow **4**—Post the page number from the journal to the ledger. **Jrnl. Ref.** means Journal Reference, and **J.1** refers to Journal Page **1**. This step shows where the data came from, in this case Journal Page 1. Arrows **5**, **6**, and **7** repeat steps 2, 3, and 4 to post the credit, **$30,000**, from the journal to the Bright, capital account in the ledger. Now the ledger accounts have correct amounts.

The Four-Column Account: An Alternative to the T-Account

The ledger accounts illustrated thus far appear as T-accounts, with the debits on the left and the credits on the right. The T-account clearly separates debits from credits and is used for teaching. Another account format has four amount columns, as illustrated in Exhibit 2-13.

EXHIBIT 2-13 | **Account in Four-Column Format**

CASH   Account No. 101

Date	Item	Jrnl. Ref.	Debit	Credit	Balance Debit	Credit
2013						
Apr 1		J.1	30,000		30,000	
Apr 2		J.1		20,000	10,000	
Apr 8		J.1	5,500		15,500	
Apr 15		J.1		3,200	12,300	
Apr 21		J.1		300	12,000	
Apr 22		J.1	2,000		14,000	
Apr 24		J.1	9,000		23,000	
Apr 30		J.1		2,000	21,000	

The first pair of Debit/Credit columns is for transaction amounts posted to the account from the journal, such as the $30,000 debit. The second pair of Debit/Credit columns shows the balance of the account as of each date. Because the four-column format provides more information, it is used more often in practice than the T-account. In Exhibit 2-13, Cash has a debit balance of $30,000 after the first transaction and a $10,000 balance after the second transaction. Notice that the balance after the last transaction on April 30 is $21,000, which is the same balance calculated in the T-account in Exhibit 2-10.

Key Takeaway

Once the ledger (T-account) balances are calculated, the ending balance for each account is transferred to the trial balance. Recall that the trial balance is a listing of all accounts and their balances on a specific date. Total debits must ALWAYS equal total credits on the trial balance. If they do not, then review the correcting trial balance errors section on page 81.

Decision Guidelines 2-1

ANALYZING AND RECORDING TRANSACTIONS

Suppose Greg Moore, the owner of Greg's Tunes, opens a small office and needs an accountant to keep his books. Moore interviews you for the job. The pay is good. Can you answer Moore's questions, which are outlined in the Decision Guidelines? If so, you may get the job.

Decision	Guidelines
• What determines if a transaction has occurred?	If the event affects the entity's financial position and can be recorded
• Where would a business record the transaction?	In the *journal*, the chronological record of transactions
• What does a business record for each transaction?	Increases and/or decreases in all the accounts affected by the transaction
• How do we record an increase/decrease in accounts?	Rules of debit and credit:

	Debit	Credit
Asset	+	−
Liability	−	+
Owner's Equity	−	+
Drawing	+	−
Revenue	−	+
Expense	+	−

Decision	Guidelines
• Where is all the information for each account's transactions and ending balance stored?	In the *ledger* (T-account), the record holding all the accounts
• What statement lists all the accounts and their balances for a business?	The *trial balance*

Summary Problem 2-1

The trial balance of Harper Service Center on March 1, 2014, lists the entity's assets, liabilities, and equity on that date.

		Balance	
	Account Title	Debit	Credit
	Cash	$26,000	
	Accounts receivable	4,500	
	Accounts payable		$ 2,000
	Harper, capital		28,500
	Total	$30,500	$30,500

During March, the business engaged in the following transactions:

a. Borrowed $45,000 from the bank and signed a note payable in the name of the business.
b. Paid cash of $40,000 to acquire land.
c. Performed service for a customer and received cash of $5,000.
d. Purchased supplies on account, $300.
e. Performed customer service and earned revenue on account, $2,600.
f. Paid $1,200 on account.
g. Paid the following cash expenses: salaries, $3,000; rent, $1,500; and interest, $400.
h. Received $3,100 on account.
i. Received a $200 utility bill that will be paid next week.
j. Harper withdrew cash of $1,800.

Requirements

1. Open the following accounts, with the balances indicated, in the ledger of Harper Service Center. Use the T-account format.

   - **Assets**—Cash, $26,000; Accounts receivable, $4,500; Supplies, no balance; Land, no balance
   - **Liabilities**—Accounts payable, $2,000; Note payable, no balance
   - **Owner's equity**—Harper, capital, $28,500; Harper, drawing, no balance
   - **Revenue**—Service revenue, no balance
   - **Expenses**—(none have balances) Salary expense, Rent expense, Utilities expense, Interest expense

2. Journalize each transaction. Key journal entries by transaction letter.
3. Post to the ledger.
4. Prepare the trial balance of Harper Service Center at March 31, 2014.

Solution

Requirement 1

ASSETS	LIABILITIES	OWNER'S EQUITY	EXPENSES

ASSETS

Cash
Bal 26,000	

LIABILITIES

Accounts payable
	Bal 2,000

OWNER'S EQUITY

Harper, capital
	Bal 28,500

EXPENSES

Salary expense

Accounts receivable
Bal 4,500	

Note payable

Harper, drawing

Rent expense

Supplies

Utilities expense

REVENUE

Land

Service revenue

Interest expense

Requirement 2

a. Journal Entry	Cash (A+)	45,000	
	Note payable (L+)		45,000
	Borrowed cash on note payable.		

b. Journal Entry	Land (A+)	40,000	
	Cash (A–)		40,000
	Purchased land.		

c. Journal Entry	Cash (A+)	5,000	
	Service revenue (R+)		5,000
	Performed service and received cash.		

d. Journal Entry	Supplies (A+)	300	
	Accounts payable (L+)		300
	Purchased supplies on account.		

e. Journal Entry	Accounts receivable (A+)	2,600	
	Service revenue (R+)		2,600
	Performed service on account.		

f. Journal Entry	Accounts payable (L–)	1,200	
	Cash (A–)		1,200
	Paid on account.		

g. Journal Entry	Salary expense (E+)	3,000	
	Rent expense (E+)	1,500	
	Interest expense (E+)	400	
	Cash (A–)		4,900
	Paid expenses.		

h. Journal Entry	Cash (A+)	3,100	
	Accounts receivable (A–)		3,100
	Received cash on account.		

i. Journal Entry	Utilities expense (E+)	200	
	Accounts payable (L+)		200
	Received utility bill.		

j. Journal Entry	Harper, drawing (D+)	1,800	
	Cash (A–)		1,800
	Owner withdrawal.		

Requirement 3

ASSETS

Cash

Bal	26,000	(b)	40,000
(a)	45,000	(f)	1,200
(c)	5,000	(g)	4,900
(h)	3,100	(j)	1,800
Bal	31,200		

Accounts receivable

Bal	4,500	(h)	3,100
(e)	2,600		
Bal	4,000		

Supplies

(d)	300		
Bal	300		

Land

(b)	40,000		
Bal	40,000		

LIABILITIES

Accounts payable

(f)	1,200	Bal	2,000
		(d)	300
		(i)	200
		Bal	1,300

Note payable

		(a)	45,000
		Bal	45,000

OWNER'S EQUITY

Harper, capital

		Bal	28,500

Harper, drawing

(j)	1,800		
Bal	1,800		

REVENUE

Service revenue

		(c)	5,000
		(e)	2,600
		Bal	7,600

EXPENSES

Salary expense

(g)	3,000		
Bal	3,000		

Rent expense

(g)	1,500		
Bal	1,500		

Interest expense

(g)	400		
Bal	400		

Utilities expense

(i)	200		
Bal	200		

Requirement 4

HARPER SERVICE CENTER
Trial Balance
March 31, 2014

Account Title	Balance Debit	Balance Credit
Cash	$31,200	
Accounts receivable	4,000	
Supplies	300	
Land	40,000	
Accounts payable		$ 1,300
Note payable		45,000
Harper, capital		28,500
Harper, drawing	1,800	
Service revenue		7,600
Salary expense	3,000	
Rent expense	1,500	
Interest expense	400	
Utilities expense	200	
Total	$82,400	$82,400

Chapter 2: Demo Doc

Debit/Credit Transaction Analysis

To make sure you understand this material, work through the following demonstration "demo doc" with detailed comments to help you see the concept within the framework of a worked-through problem.

① ② ③ ④

On September 1, 2014, Michael Moe began Moe's Mowing, a company that provides mowing and landscaping services. During the month of September, the business incurred the following transactions:

a. To begin operations, Michael deposited $10,000 cash in the business's bank account. The business received the cash and gave capital to Moe.

b. The business purchased equipment for $3,500 on account.

c. The business purchased office supplies for $800 cash.

d. The business provided $2,600 of services to a customer on account.

e. The business paid $500 cash toward the equipment previously purchased on account in transaction b.

f. The business received $2,000 in cash for services provided to a new customer.

g. The business paid $200 cash to repair equipment.

h. The business paid $900 cash in salary expense.

i. The business received $2,100 cash from customers on account.

j. Moe withdrew cash of $1,500.

Requirements

1. Create blank T-accounts for the following accounts: Cash; Accounts receivable; Supplies; Equipment; Accounts payable; Moe, capital; Moe, drawing; Service revenue; Salary expense; and Repair expense.

2. Journalize the transactions and show how they are recorded in T-accounts.

3. Total all of the T-accounts to determine their balances at the end of the month.

Chapter 2: Demo Doc Solution

Requirement 1

Create blank T-accounts for the following accounts: Cash; Accounts receivable; Supplies; Equipment; Accounts payable; Moe, capital; Moe, drawing; Service revenue; Salary expense; and Repair expense.

Part 1	Part 2	Part 3	Demo Doc Complete

Opening a T-account means drawing a blank account that looks like a capital "T" and putting the account title across the top. T-accounts give you a diagram of the additions and subtractions made to the accounts. For easy reference, they are usually organized into assets, liabilities, owner's equity, revenue, and expenses (in that order).

ASSETS   =   LIABILITIES   +   OWNER'S EQUITY

| Cash | Supplies | Accounts payable | Moe, capital |

| | | | Moe, drawing |

| | | | Service revenue |

| Accounts receivable | Equipment | | Salary expense |

| | | | Repair expense |

Requirement 2

Journalize the transactions and show how they are recorded in T-accounts.

| Part 1 | **Part 2** | Part 3 | Demo Doc Complete |

a. To begin operations, Moe deposited $10,000 cash in the business's bank account. The business received the cash and gave capital to Moe.

First, we must determine which accounts are affected.

The business received $10,000 cash from its owner (Michael Moe). In exchange, the business gave capital to Moe. So, the accounts involved are Cash and Moe, capital.

The next step is to determine what type of accounts these are. Cash is an asset and Moe, capital is part of equity.

Next, we must determine if these accounts increased or decreased. From *the business's* point of view, Cash (an asset) has increased. Moe, capital (equity) has also increased.

Now we must determine if these accounts should be debited or credited. According to the rules of debit and credit, an increase in assets is a debit, while an increase in equity is a credit.

So, Cash (an asset) increases, which is a debit. Moe, capital (equity) also increases, which is a credit.

The journal entry would be as follows:

a.	Cash (A+)	10,000	
	Moe, capital (Q+)		10,000
	Owner investment.		

Note that the total dollar amounts of debits will equal the total dollar amounts of credits.

Remember to use the transaction letters as references. This will help as we post this entry to the T-accounts.

Each T-account has two sides for recording debits and credits. To record the transaction to the T-account, simply transfer the amount of the debit(s) to the correct account(s) as a debit (left-side) entry, and transfer the amount of the credit(s) to the correct account(s) as a credit (right-side) entry.

For this transaction, there is a debit of $10,000 to cash. This means that $10,000 is entered on the left side of the Cash T-account. There is also a credit of $10,000 to Moe, capital. This means that $10,000 is entered on the right side of the Moe, capital account.

Cash	Moe, capital
a. 10,000	a. 10,000

b. **The business purchased equipment for $3,500 on account.**

The business received equipment in exchange for a promise to pay for the $3,500 cost at a future date. So the accounts involved in the transaction are Equipment and Accounts payable.

Equipment is an asset and Accounts payable is a liability.

The asset Equipment has increased. The liability Accounts payable has also increased.

Looking at Exhibit 2-8, an increase in assets (in this case, the increase in Equipment) is a debit, while an increase in liabilities (in this case, Accounts payable) is a credit.

The journal entry would be as follows:

b.	Equipment (A+)	3,500	
	Accounts payable (L+)		3,500
	Purchase of equipment on account.		

$3,500 is entered on the debit (left) side of the Equipment T-account. $3,500 is entered on the credit (right) side of the Accounts payable account.

Equipment	Accounts payable
b. 3,500	b. 3,500

c. **The business purchased office supplies for $800 cash.**

The business purchased supplies in exchange for $800 cash. So the accounts involved in the transaction are Supplies and Cash.

Supplies and Cash are both assets.

Supplies (an asset) has increased. Cash (an asset) has decreased.

Looking at Exhibit 2-8, an increase in assets is a debit, while a decrease in assets is a credit.

So the increase to Supplies (an asset) is a debit, while the decrease to Cash (an asset) is a credit.

The journal entry would be as follows:

c.	Supplies (A+)	800	
	Cash (A−)		800
	Purchase of supplies for cash.		

$800 is entered on the debit (left) side of the Supplies T-account. $800 is entered on the credit (right) side of the Cash account.

Cash				Supplies	
a. 10,000	c.	800	c.	800	

Notice the $10,000 already on the debit side of the Cash account. This is from transaction **a.**

d. **The business provided $2,600 of services to a customer on account.**

The business received promises from customers to send $2,600 cash next month in exchange for services rendered. So the accounts involved in the transaction are Accounts receivable and Service revenue.

Accounts receivable is an asset and Service revenue is revenue.

Accounts receivable (an asset) has increased. Service revenue (revenue) has also increased.

Looking at Exhibit 2-8, an increase in assets is a debit, while an increase in revenue is a credit.

So the increase to Accounts receivable (an asset) is a debit, while the increase to Service revenue (revenue) is a credit.

The journal entry is as follows:

d.	Accounts receivable (A+)	2,600	
	Service revenue (R+)		2,600
	Provided services on account.		

$2,600 is entered on the debit (left) side of the Accounts receivable T-account. $2,600 is entered on the credit (right) side of the Service revenue account.

Accounts receivable		Service revenue	
d. 2,600		d.	2,600

e. **The business paid $500 cash toward the equipment previously purchased on account in transaction b.**

The business paid *some* of the money that was owed on the purchase of equipment in transaction b. The accounts involved in the transaction are Accounts payable and Cash.

Accounts payable is a liability that has decreased. Cash is an asset that has also decreased.

Remember, the Accounts payable account is a list of creditors to whom the business will have to make payments in the future (a liability). When the business makes these payments to the creditors, the amount of this account decreases, because the business now owes less (in this case, it reduces from $3,500—in transaction **b**—to $3,000).

Looking at Exhibit 2-8, a decrease in liabilities is a debit, while a decrease in assets is a credit.

So Accounts payable (a liability) decreases, which is a debit. Cash (an asset) decreases, which is a credit.

e.	Accounts payable (L–)	500	
	Cash (A–)		500
	Partial payment on Accounts payable.		

$500 is entered on the debit (left) side of the Accounts payable T-account. $500 is entered on the credit (right) side of the Cash account.

	Cash				Accounts payable	
a.	10,000				b.	3,500
		c.	800	e.	500	
		e.	500			

Again notice the amounts already in the T-accounts from previous transactions. We can tell which transaction caused each amount to appear by looking at the reference letter next to each number.

f. **The business received $2,000 in cash for services provided to a new customer.**

The business received $2,000 cash in exchange for mowing and landscaping services rendered to clients. The accounts involved in the transaction are Cash and Service revenue.

Cash is an asset that has increased and Service revenue is revenue, which has also increased.

Looking at Exhibit 2-8, an increase in assets is a debit, while an increase in revenue is a credit.

So the increase to Cash (an asset) is a debit. The increase to Service revenue (revenue) is a credit.

f.	Cash (A+)	2,000	
	Service revenue (R+)		2,000
	Provided services for cash.		

$2,000 is entered on the debit (left) side of the Cash T-account. $2,000 is entered on the credit (right) side of the Service revenue account.

	Cash				Service revenue		
a.	10,000					d.	2,600
		c.	800			f.	2,000
		e.	500				
f.	2,000						

Notice how we keep adding onto the T-accounts. The values from previous transactions are already in place.

g.   The business paid $200 cash to repair equipment.

The business paid $200 cash to repair equipment. Because the benefit of the repairs has already been used, the repairs are recorded as Repair expense. Because the repairs were paid in cash, the Cash account is also involved.

Repair expense is an expense that has increased and Cash is an asset that has decreased.

Looking at Exhibit 2-8, an increase in expenses is a debit, while a decrease in an asset is a credit.

So Repair expense (an expense) increases, which is debit. Cash (an asset) decreases, which is a credit.

g.	Repair expense (E+)		200	
	Cash (A–)			200
	Payment for repairs.			

$200 is entered on the debit (left) side of the Repair expense T-account. $200 is entered on the credit (right) side of the Cash account.

	Cash				Repair expense	
a.	10,000			g.	200	
		c.	800			
		e.	500			
f.	2,000					
		g.	200			

h.   The business paid $900 cash for salary expense.

The business paid employees $900 in cash. Because the benefit of the employees' work has already been used, their salaries are recorded as Salary expense. Because the salaries were paid in cash, the Cash account is also involved.

Salary expense is an expense that has increased and Cash is an asset that has decreased.

Looking at Exhibit 2-8, an increase in expenses is a debit, while a decrease in an asset is a credit.

In this case, Salary expense (an expense) increases, which is a debit. Cash (an asset) decreases, which is a credit.

h.	Salary expense (E+)		900	
	Cash (A–)			900
	Payment of salary.			

$900 is entered on the debit (left) side of the Salary expense T-account. $900 is entered on the credit (right) side of the Cash account.

	Cash					Salary expense	
a.	10,000				h.	900	
		c.	800				
		e.	500				
f.	2,000						
		g.	200				
		h.	900				

i. **The business received $2,100 cash from customers on account.**

The business received $2,100 from customers for services previously provided in transaction d. The accounts involved in this transaction are Cash and Accounts receivable.

Cash and Accounts receivable are both assets.

The asset Cash has increased, and the asset Accounts receivable has decreased.

Remember, Accounts receivable is a list of customers from whom the business will receive money. When the business receives these payments from its customers, the amount of this account decreases, because the business now has less to receive in the future (in this case, it reduces from $2,600—in transaction d—to $500).

Looking at Exhibit 2-8, an increase in assets is a debit, while a decrease in assets is a credit.

So Cash (an asset) increases, which is a debit. Accounts receivable (an asset) decreases, which is a credit.

i.		Cash (A+)	2,100	
		Accounts receivable (A–)		2,100
		Receipt of payment from customer.		

$2,100 is entered on the debit (left) side of the Cash T-account. $2,100 is entered on the credit (right) side of the Accounts receivable account.

	Cash					Accounts receivable	
a.	10,000				d.	2,600	
		c.	800				i. 2,100
		e.	500				
f.	2,000						
		g.	200				
		h.	900				
i.	2,100						

j. **Moe withdrew cash of $1,500.**

Moe withdrew cash from the business. This caused Moe's ownership interest (equity) to decrease. The accounts involved in this transaction are Moe, drawing and Cash.

Moe, drawing has increased and Cash is an asset that has decreased.

Looking at Exhibit 2-8, an increase in drawing is a debit, while a decrease in an asset is a credit.

Remember that Drawing is a negative element of owner's equity. Therefore, when Drawing increases, owner's equity decreases. So in this case, Moe, drawing decreases equity with a debit. Cash (an asset) decreases with a credit.

j.		Moe, drawing (D+)	1,500	
		Cash (A–)		1,500
		Owner withdrawal.		

$1,500 is entered on the debit (left) side of the Moe, drawing T-account.
$1,500 is entered on the credit (right) side of the Cash account.

Cash				Moe, drawing	
a.	10,000			j.	1,500
		c.	800		
		e.	500		
f.	2.000				
		g.	200		
		h.	900		
i.	2,100				
		j.	1,500		

Now we will summarize all of the journal entries during the month:

Ref.	Accounts and Explanation	Debit	Credit
a.	Cash	10,000	
	Moe, capital		10,000
	Owner investment.		
b.	Equipment	3,500	
	Accounts payable		3,500
	Purchase of equipment on account.		
c.	Supplies	800	
	Cash		800
	Purchase of supplies for cash.		
d.	Accounts receivable	2,600	
	Service revenue		2,600
	Provided services on credit.		
e.	Accounts payable	500	
	Cash		500
	Partial payment on account.		
f.	Cash	2,000	
	Service revenue		2,000
	Provided services for cash.		
g.	Repair expense	200	
	Cash		200
	Payment for repairs.		
h.	Salary expense	900	
	Cash		900
	Payment of salary.		
i.	Cash	2,100	
	Accounts receivable		2,100
	Receipt of cash on account.		
j.	Moe, drawing	1,500	
	Cash		1,500
	Owner withdrawal.		

Requirement 3

Total all of the T-accounts to determine their balances at the end of the month.

Part 1	Part 2	**Part 3**	Demo Doc Complete

To compute the balance in a T-account (total the T-account), add up the numbers on the debit/left side of the account and (separately) the credit/right side of the account. The difference between the total debits and total credits is the account's balance, which is placed on the side of the larger number (that is, the side with a balance). This gives the balance in the T-account (the net total of both sides combined).

For example, for the Cash account, the numbers on the debit/left side total $10,000 + $2,000 + $2,100 = $14,100. The credit/right side = $800 + $500 + $200 + $900 + $1,500 = $3,900. The difference is $14,100 – $3,900 = $10,200. We put the $10,200 on the debit side because that was the side of the bigger number of $14,100. This is called a debit balance.

Following is an easy way to think of totaling T-accounts:

> Beginning balance in T-account
> + Increases to T-account
> – Decreases to T-account
> _____
> T-account balance (total)

T-accounts after posting all transactions and totaling each account:

| ASSETS | | = | LIABILITIES | + | OWNER'S EQUITY |

Cash

a.	10,000		
		c.	800
		e.	500
f.	2,000		
		g.	200
		h.	900
i.	2,100		
		j.	1,500
Bal	10,200		

Accounts receivable

d.	2,600		
		i.	2,100
Bal	500		

Supplies

c.	800	
Bal	800	

Equipment

b.	3,500	
Bal	3,500	

Accounts payable

		b.	3,500
e.	500		
		Bal	3,000

Moe, capital

		a.	10,000
		Bal	10,000

Moe, drawing

j.	1,500	
Bal	1,500	

Service revenue

		d.	2,600
		f.	2,000
		Bal	4,600

Salary expense

h.	900	
Bal	900	

Repair expense

g.	200	
Bal	200	

Part 1	Part 2	Part 3	**Demo Doc Complete**

Review *Recording Business Transactions*

• Accounting Vocabulary

Account (p. 63)
The detailed record of all the changes that have occurred in a particular asset, liability, or owner's equity (stockholders' equity) during a period. The basic summary device of accounting.

Accrued Liability (p. 64)
A liability for which the business knows the amount owed but the bill has not been paid.

Chart of Accounts (p. 65)
A list of all a company's accounts with their account numbers.

Compound Journal Entry (p. 77)
Same as a journal entry, except this entry is characterized by having multiple debits and/or multiple credits. The total debits still equal the total credits in the compound journal.

Credit (p. 67)
The right side of an account.

Debit (p. 67)
The left side of an account.

Double-Entry System (p. 67)
A system of accounting where every transaction affects at least two accounts.

Journal (p. 63)
The chronological accounting record of an entity's transactions.

Ledger (p. 63)
The record holding all the accounts and amounts.

Normal Balance (p. 72)
The balance that appears on the side of an account—debit or credit—where we record increases.

Note Receivable (p. 64)
A written promise for future collection of cash.

Notes Payable (p. 64)
Represents debts the business owes because it signed promissory notes to borrow money or to purchase something.

Posting (p. 70)
Copying amounts from the journal to the ledger.

Prepaid Expenses (p. 64)
Expenses paid in advance of their use.

T-account (p. 67)
Summary device that is shaped like a capital "T" with debits posted on the left side of the vertical line and credits on the right side of the vertical line. A "shorthand" version of a ledger.

Trial Balance (p. 63)
A list of all the ledger accounts with their balances at a point in time.

• Destination: Student Success

Student Success Tips

The following are hints on some common trouble areas for students in this chapter:

- Commit to memory the normal balance of the six main account types. The normal balance is the side of the T-account where the account INCREASES. Assets, Drawing, and Expenses have normal debit balances. Liabilities, Equity, and Revenues have normal credit balances.

- Recall that debits are listed first in every journal entry.

- Remember debits ALWAYS EQUAL credits in every journal entry.

- Keep in mind that posting is just gathering all the journal entries made to an individual T-account so that you can determine the new balance in the account. Journal debit entries are posted on the left side of the T-account. Journal credit entries are posted on the right side of the T-account.

- The accounting equation MUST ALWAYS balance after each transaction is posted.

- The trial balance lists all accounts with a balance, ordered by assets, liabilities, equity, drawing, revenues, and expenses. Total debits should equal total credits on the trial balance.

Getting Help

If there's a learning objective from the chapter you aren't confident about, try using one or more of the following resources:

- Review the Chapter 2 Demo Doc located on page 89 of the textbook.

- Practice additional exercises or problems at the end of Chapter 2 that cover the specific learning objective that is challenging you.

- Watch the white board videos for Chapter 2 located at myaccountinglab.com under the Chapter Resources button.

- Go to myaccountinglab.com and select the Study Plan button. Choose Chapter 2 and work the questions covering that specific learning objective until you've mastered it.

- Work the Chapter 2 pre/post tests in myaccountinglab.com.

- Visit the learning resource center on your campus for tutoring.

● Quick Check

1. Which sequence correctly summarizes the accounting process?

   a. Journalize transactions, post to the accounts, prepare a trial balance

   b. Journalize transactions, prepare a trial balance, post to the accounts

   c. Post to the accounts, journalize transactions, prepare a trial balance

   d. Prepare a trial balance, journalize transactions, post to the accounts

2. The left side of an account is used to record which of the following?

   a. Debit or credit, depending on the type of account

   b. Increases

   c. Credits

   d. Debits

3. Suppose Hunt Company has receivables of $65,000, furniture totaling $205,000, and cash of $52,000. The business has a $109,000 note payable and owes $81,000 on account. How much is Hunt's owner's equity?

   a. $28,000

   b. $132,000

   c. $190,000

   d. $322,000

4. Your business purchased supplies of $2,500 on account. The journal entry to record this transaction is as follows:

   a.
Supplies	2,500	
Accounts receivable		2,500

   b.
Supplies	2,500	
Accounts payable		2,500

   c.
Accounts payable	2,500	
Supplies		2,500

   d.
Inventory	2,500	
Accounts payable		2,500

5. Which journal entry records your payment for the supplies purchase described in Quick Check question 4?

   a.
Accounts payable	2,500	
Accounts receivable		2,500

   b.
Accounts payable	2,500	
Cash		2,500

   c.
Cash	2,500	
Accounts payable		2,500

   d.
Supplies	2,500	
Cash		2,500

Experience the Power of Practice!

As denoted by the logo, all of these questions, as well as additional practice materials, can be found in *MyAccountingLab*.

Please visit myaccountinglab.com

6. Posting a $2,500 purchase of supplies on account appears as follows:

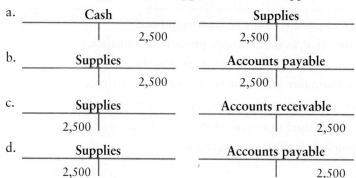

a.

Cash	
	2,500

Supplies	
2,500	

b.

Supplies	
	2,500

Accounts payable	
2,500	

c.

Supplies	
2,500	

Accounts receivable	
	2,500

d.

Supplies	
2,500	

Accounts payable	
	2,500

7. The detailed record of the changes in a particular asset, liability, or owner's equity is called

   a. an account.

   b. a journal.

   c. a ledger.

   d. a trial balance.

8. Pixel Copies recorded a cash collection on account by debiting Cash and crediting Accounts payable. What will the trial balance show for this error?

   a. Too much for cash

   b. Too much for liabilities

   c. Too much for expenses

   d. The trial balance will not balance

9. Timothy McGreggor, Attorney, began the year with total assets of $129,000, liabilities of $77,000, and owner's equity of $52,000. During the year the business earned revenue of $113,000 and paid expenses of $34,000. McGreggor also withdrew cash of $63,000. How much is the business's equity at year-end?

   a. $68,000

   b. $97,000

   c. $131,000

   d. $165,000

10. Michael Barry, Attorney, began the year with total assets of $126,000, liabilities of $74,000, and owner's equity of $52,000. During the year the business earned revenue of $110,000 and paid expenses of $33,000. Barry also withdrew cash of $69,000. How would Michael Barry record expenses paid of $33,000?

a.

Cash	33,000	
Expenses		33,000

b.

Accounts payable	33,000	
Cash		33,000

c.

Expenses	33,000	
Accounts payable		33,000

d.

Expenses	33,000	
Cash		33,000

Answers are given after Apply Your Knowledge (p. 129).

Assess Your Progress

● Short Exercises

S2-1 **1** **Using accounting vocabulary [10 min]**
Accounting has its own vocabulary and basic relationships.

Requirement

1. Match the accounting terms on the left with the corresponding definitions on the right.

——— 1. Posting	A. Using up assets in the course of operating a
——— 2. Receivable	business
——— 3. Debit	B. Book of accounts
——— 4. Journal	C. An asset
——— 5. Expense	D. Record of transactions
——— 6. Net income	E. Left side of an account
——— 7. Normal balance	F. Side of an account where increases are recorded
——— 8. Ledger	G. Copying data from the journal to the ledger
——— 9. Payable	H. Always a liability
——— 10. Equity	I. Revenues – Expenses = ————
	J. Assets – Liabilities = ————

S2-2 **2** **Explaining accounts and the rules of debit and credit [5 min]**
Margaret Alves is tutoring Timothy Johnson, who is taking introductory accounting. Margaret explains to Timothy that *debits* are used to record increases in accounts and *credits* record decreases. Timothy is confused and seeks your advice.

Requirements

1. When are debits increases? When are debits decreases?
2. When are credits increases? When are credits decreases?

S2-3 **2** **Normal account balances [5 min]**
The accounting equation includes three basic types of accounts: assets, liabilities, and owner's equity. In turn, owner's equity holds the following types: capital, drawing, revenues, and expenses.

Requirement

1. Identify which types of accounts have a normal debit balance and which types have a normal credit balance.

S2-4 **3** **Steps of the transaction recording process [5 min]**
Data Integrity Company performed $1,000 of services on account for a customer on January 5. The same customer paid $600 of the January 5 bill on January 28.

Requirement

1. Identify the three steps to record a transaction and perform the three steps to record the transactions for Data Integrity Company.

S2-5 **4** **Journalizing transactions [10 min]**
Ned Brown opened a medical practice in San Diego, California.

Jan 1	The business received $29,000 cash and gave capital to Brown.
2	Purchased medical supplies on account, $14,000.
2	Paid monthly office rent of $2,600.
3	Recorded $8,000 revenue for service rendered to patients on account.

Requirement

1. Record the preceding transactions in the journal of Ned Brown, M.D. Include an explanation with each entry.

S2-6 ④ **Journalizing transactions [10 min]**

Texas Sales Consultants completed the following transactions during the latter part of January:

Jan 22	Performed service for customers on account, $8,000.
30	Received cash on account from customers, $7,000.
31	Received a utility bill, $180, which will be paid during February.
31	Paid monthly salary to salesman, $2,000.
31	Paid advertising expense of $700.

Requirement

1. Journalize the transactions of Texas Sales Consultants. Include an explanation with each journal entry.

S2-7 ④ **Journalizing transactions and posting to T-accounts [10–15 min]**

Kenneth Dolkart Optical Dispensary purchased supplies on account for $3,400. Two weeks later, the business paid half on account.

Requirements

1. Journalize the two transactions for Kenneth Dolkart Optical Dispensary. Include an explanation for each entry.
2. Open the Accounts payable T-account and post to Accounts payable. Compute the balance, and denote it as *Bal.*

S2-8 ④ **Journalizing transactions and posting [10–15 min]**

Washington Law Firm performed legal services for a client who could not pay immediately. The business expected to collect the $16,000 the following month. Later, the business received $9,600 cash from the client.

Requirements

1. Record the two transactions for Washington Law Firm. Include an explanation for each transaction.
2. Open these T-accounts: Cash; Accounts receivable; Service revenue. Post to all three accounts. Compute each T-account's balance, and denote as *Bal.*
3. Answer these questions based on your analysis:
   a. How much did the business earn? Which account shows this amount?
   b. How much in total assets did the business acquire as a result of the two transactions? Identify each asset and show its balance.

Note: Short Exercise 2-9 should be used only after completing Short Exercise 2-5.

S2-9 ④⑤ **Posting, balancing T-accounts, and preparing a trial balance [10–15 min]**

Use the January transaction data for Ned Brown, M.D., given in Short Exercise 2-5.

Requirements

1. Open the following T-accounts: Cash; Accounts receivable; Medical supplies; Accounts payable; Brown, capital; Service revenue; and Rent expense.
2. After making the journal entries in Short Exercise 2-5, post to the T-accounts. No dates or posting references are required. Compute the balance of each account, and denote it as *Bal.*
3. Prepare the trial balance, complete with a proper heading, at January 3, 2012.

S2-10 ⑤ **Preparing a trial balance [10 min]**

Oakland Floor Coverings reported the following summarized data at December 31, 2012. Accounts appear in no particular order.

Revenues	$34,000	Other liabilities	$18,000
Equipment	45,000	Cash	12,000
Accounts payable	2,000	Expenses	19,000
Oakland, capital	22,000		

Requirement

1. Prepare the trial balance of Oakland Floor Coverings at December 31, 2012.

S2-11 ⑤ **Correcting a trial balance [10 min]**

Brenda Longval Travel Design prepared its trial balance. Suppose Longval made an error: She erroneously listed capital of $30,600 as a debit rather than a credit.

BRENDA LONGVAL TRAVEL DESIGN		
Trial Balance		
April 30, 2012		

	Balance	
Account Title	Debit	Credit
Cash	$ 18,000	
Accounts receivable	1,000	
Office supplies	500	
Land	14,000	
Accounts payable		$ 400
Longval, capital	30,600	
Longval, drawing	3,000	
Service revenue		8,800
Rent expense, computer	700	
Rent expense, office	900	
Salary expense	1,100	
Utilities expense	600	
Total		

Requirement

1. Compute the incorrect trial balance totals for debits and credits. Then show how to correct this error.

S2-12 ❺ **Correcting a trial balance [10 min]**

Review Francis Nangle Travel Design's trial balance. Assume that Nangle accidentally listed drawing as $300 instead of the correct amount of $3,000.

FRANCIS NANGLE TRAVEL DESIGN
Trial Balance
January 31, 2012

Account Title	Balance Debit	Balance Credit
Cash	$ 20,000	
Accounts receivable	1,000	
Office supplies	500	
Land	12,000	
Accounts payable		$ 100
Nangle, capital		31,000
Nangle, drawing	300	
Service revenue		8,700
Rent expense, computer	700	
Rent expense, office	1,200	
Salary expense	1,200	
Utilities expense	200	
Total		

Requirement

1. Compute the incorrect trial balance totals for debits and credits. Then show how to correct this error, which is called a *slide*.

● Exercises

E2-13 ❶ **Using accounting vocabulary [10 min]**

Review basic accounting definitions by completing the following crossword puzzle.

Down:
1. Right side of an account
4. The basic summary device of accounting
6. Book of accounts
7. An economic resource
8. Record of transactions
9. Normal balance of a revenue

Across:
2. Records a decrease in a liability
3. List of accounts with their balances
5. Another word for liability

E2-14 ❶ **Using accounting vocabulary [10–15 min]**

Sharpen your use of accounting terms by working this crossword puzzle.

Down:

1. Records a decrease in a liability
4. Bottom line of an income statement
7. Revenue – net income = _____

Across:

2. Amount collectible from a customer
3. Statement of financial position
5. Copy data from the journal to the ledger
6. Records a decrease in an asset

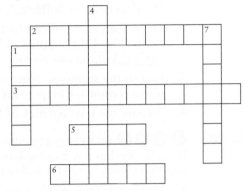

E2-15 ❶❷ **Using debits and credits with the accounting equation [10–15 min]**

Link Back to Chapter 1 (Accounting Equation). John's Cream Soda makes specialty soft drinks. At the end of 2012, John's had total assets of $390,000 and liabilities totaling $260,000.

Requirements

1. Write the company's accounting equation, and label each amount as a debit or a credit.

2. The business's total revenues for 2012 were $480,000, and total expenses for the year were $350,000. How much was the business's net income (or net loss) for 2012? Write the equation to compute the company's net income, and indicate which element is a debit and which is a credit. Does net income represent a net debit or a net credit?

E2-16 ❸❹ **Analyzing and journalizing transactions [10–15 min]**

The following transactions occurred for London Engineering:

Jul	2	Paid utilities expense of $400.
	5	Purchased equipment on account, $2,100.
	10	Performed service for a client on account, $2,000.
	12	Borrowed $7,000 cash, signing a note payable.
	19	Sold for $29,000 land that had cost this same amount.
	21	Purchased supplies for $800 and paid cash.
	27	Paid the liability from July 5.

Requirement

1. Identify and perform the three steps to record the previously described transactions.

E2-17 ❷❸❹❺ **Describing transactions, posting to T-accounts, and preparing a trial balance [20–30 min]**

The journal of Ward Technology Solutions includes the following entries for May, 2012:

May	1	The business received cash of $75,000 and gave capital to the owner.
	2	Purchased supplies of $500 on account.
	4	Paid $53,000 cash for a building.
	6	Performed service for customers and received cash, $2,600.
	9	Paid $400 on accounts payable.
	17	Performed service for customers on account, $2,500.
	23	Received $1,900 cash on account from a customer.
	31	Paid the following expenses: salary, $1,100; rent, $900.

Requirements

1. Describe each transaction. For example, the May 4 transaction description could be "Paid cash for building."

2. Open T-accounts using the following account numbers: Cash, 110; Accounts receivable, 120; Supplies, 130; Building, 140; Accounts payable, 210; Ward, capital, 310; Service revenue, 410; Rent expense, 510; Salary expense, 520.

3. Post to the accounts. Write dates and journal references (use account numbers) in the accounts. Compute the balance of each account after posting.

4. Prepare the trial balance of Ward Technology Solutions at May 31, 2012.

E2-18 ②③④⑤ **Analyzing accounting errors [20–30 min]**
Danielle Neylon has trouble keeping her debits and credits equal. During a recent month, Danielle made the following accounting errors:

a. In preparing the trial balance, Danielle omitted a $7,000 note payable.

b. Danielle posted a $90 utility expense as $900. The credit to Cash was correct.

c. In recording an $800 payment on account, Danielle debited Furniture instead of Accounts payable.

d. In journalizing a receipt of cash for service revenue, Danielle debited Cash for $1,200 instead of the correct amount of $120. The credit was correct.

e. Danielle recorded a $540 purchase of supplies on account by debiting Supplies and crediting Accounts payable for $450.

Requirements

1. For each of these errors, state whether total debits equal total credits on the trial balance.

2. Identify each account that has an incorrect balance, and indicate the amount and direction of the error (such as "Accounts receivable $500 too high").

Note: Exercise 2-19 should be used only after completing Exercise 2-16.

E2-19 ②④⑤ **Applying the rules of debit and credit, posting, and preparing a trial balance [15–25 min]**
Refer to the transactions of London Engineering in Exercise 2-16.

Requirements

1. Open the following T-accounts with their July 1 balances: Cash, debit balance $4,000; Accounts receivable $0; Equipment $0; Land, debit balance $29,000; Supplies $0; Accounts payable $0; Notes payable $0; London, capital, credit balance $33,000; Service revenue $0; Utilities expense $0.

2. Post the transactions of Exercise 2-16 to the T-accounts. Use the dates as posting references. Start with July 2.

3. Compute the July 31, 2012, balance for each account, and prove that total debits equal total credits by preparing a trial balance.

E2-20 ②③④⑤ **Journalizing transactions, posting, and preparing a trial balance [10 min]**
In December, 2012, the first five transactions of Adams' Lawn Care Company have been posted to the accounts as follows:

Cash				Supplies		Equipment		Building	
(1)	53,000	(3)	40,000	(2) 700		(5) 4,700		(3) 40,000	
(4)	50,000	(5)	4,700						

Accounts payable		Note payable		Adams, capital	
	(2) 700		(4) 50,000		(1) 53,000

Requirements

1. Prepare the journal entries that served as the sources for the five transactions. Include an explanation for each entry as illustrated on page 87.

2. Prepare the trial balance of Adams' Lawn Care Company at December 31, 2012.

E2-21 **④ Using actual business documents [10 min]**

Suppose your name is Thomas Sell, and Best Automotive repaired your car. You settled the bill as noted on the following invoice. To you this is a purchase invoice. To Best Automotive, it is a sales invoice.

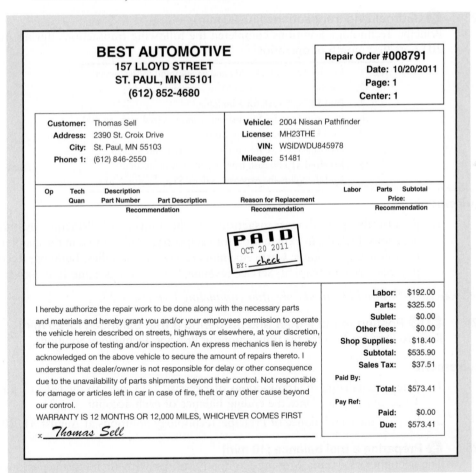

Requirements

1. Journalize your repair expense transaction.

2. Journalize Best Automotive's service revenue transaction.

E2-22   ④⑤ Recording transactions, using four-column ledger accounts, and preparing a trial balance [20–25 min]

The following transactions occurred during the month for Teresa Parker, CPA:

    a. Parker opened an accounting firm by investing $14,100 cash and office furniture valued at $5,200. The business issued $19,300 of capital to Parker.

    b. Paid monthly rent of $1,500.

    c. Purchased office supplies on account, $900.

    d. Paid employee's salary, $1,700.

    e. Paid $700 of the account payable created in transaction (c).

    f. Performed accounting service on account, $5,900.

    g. Owner withdrew cash of $6,700.

Requirements

1. Open the following four-column accounts of Teresa Parker, CPA: Cash; Accounts receivable; Office supplies; Office furniture; Accounts payable; Parker, capital; Parker, drawing; Service revenue; Salary expense; Rent expense.

2. Journalize the transactions and then post to the four-column accounts. Use the letters to identify the transactions. Keep a running balance in each account.

3. Prepare the trial balance at December 31, 2012.

E2-23   ④ Journalizing transactions [10–20 min]

Principe Technology Solutions completed the following transactions during August 2012, its first month of operations:

Aug	1	Received cash of $48,000 and gave capital to the owner.
	2	Purchased supplies of $500 on account.
	4	Paid $47,000 cash for a building.
	6	Performed service for customers and received cash, $4,400.
	9	Paid $200 on accounts payable.
	17	Performed service for customers on account, $2,200.
	23	Received $1,600 cash from a customer on account.
	31	Paid the following expenses: salary, $1,900; rent, $700.

Requirement

1. Record the preceding transactions in the journal of Principe Technology Solutions. Include an explanation for each entry, as illustrated in the chapter. Use the following accounts: Cash; Accounts receivable; Supplies; Building; Accounts payable; Principe, capital; Service revenue; Salary expense; and Rent expense.

Note: Exercise 2-24 should be used only after completing Exercise 2-23.

E2-24   ④⑤ Posting to the ledger and preparing a trial balance [15–20 min]

Refer to Exercise 2-23 for the transactions of Principe Technology Solutions.

Requirements

1. After journalizing the transactions of Exercise 2-23, post to the ledger using the T-account format. Date the ending balance of each account Aug 31.

2. Prepare the trial balance of Principe Technology Solutions at August 31, 2012.

E2-25   ⑤ Preparing a trial balance [10 min]

The accounts of Atkins Moving Company follow with their normal balances at August 31, 2012. The accounts are listed in no particular order.

Atkins, capital	$ 72,000	Trucks	$ 132,000
Insurance expense	600	Fuel expense	3,000
Accounts payable	4,000	Atkins, drawing	5,400
Service revenue	80,000	Utilities expense	500
Building	48,000	Accounts receivable	8,800
Supplies expense	400	Note payable	54,000
Cash	4,000	Supplies	300
Salary expense	7,000		

Requirement

1. Prepare Atkins' trial balance at August 31, 2012.

E2-26 ⑤ **Correcting errors in a trial balance [15–20 min]**

The following trial balance of Joy McDowell Tutoring Service at May 31, 2012, does not balance:

JOY MCDOWELL TUTORING SERVICE		
Trial Balance		
May 31, 2012		
Account	Debit	Credit
Cash	$ 3,000	
Accounts receivable	2,000	
Supplies	600	
Computer equipment	25,800	
Accounts payable		$ 11,400
McDowell, capital		11,600
Service revenue		9,800
Salary expense	1,700	
Rent expense	700	
Utilities expense	500	
Total	$ 34,300	$ 32,800

Investigation of the accounting records reveals that the bookkeeper:

a. Recorded a $500 cash revenue transaction by debiting Accounts receivable. The credit entry was correct.
b. Posted a $1,000 credit to Accounts payable as $100.
c. Did not record utilities expense or the related account payable in the amount of $400.
d. Understated McDowell, capital by $600.

Requirement

1. Prepare the corrected trial balance at May 31, 2012, complete with a heading; journal entries are not required.

● Problems (Group A)

P2-27A ① ② **Identifying common accounts and normal account balances [10–15 min]**   *MyAccountingLab*

Showtime Amusements Company owns movie theaters. Showtime engaged in the following business transactions in 2012:

Sep	1	Don Cougliato invested $370,000 personal cash in the business by depositing that amount in a bank account titled Showtime Amusements. The business gave capital to Cougliato.
	2	Paid $360,000 cash to purchase a theater building.
	5	Borrowed $260,000 from the bank. Cougliato signed a note payable to the bank in the name of Showtime.
	10	Purchased theater supplies on account, $1,400.
	15	Paid $1,200 on account.
	15	Paid property tax expense on theater building, $1,500.
	16	Paid employees' salaries $2,500, and rent on equipment $1,400. Make a single compound entry.
	28	Cougliato withdrew cash of $7,000.
	30	Received $21,000 cash from service revenue and deposited that amount in the bank.

Requirements

1. Create the list of accounts that Showtime Amusements will use to record these transactions.

2. Identify the account type and normal balance of each account identified in Requirement 1.

Note: Problem 2-27A must be completed before attempting Problem 2-28A.

P2-28A ③ ④ **Analyzing and journalizing transactions, posting, and preparing a trial balance [40–50 min]**
Review the facts given in P2-27A.

Requirements

1. Journalize each transaction of Showtime as shown for September 1. Explanations are not required.

Sep 1	Cash		370,000	
		Cougliato, capital		370,000

2. Post the transactions to the T-accounts, using transaction dates as posting references in the ledger accounts. Label the balance of each account *Bal*, as shown in the chapter.

P2-29A ② ③ ④ ⑤ **Analyzing and journalizing transactions, posting, and preparing a trial balance [45–60 min]**
Vernon Yung practices medicine under the business title Vernon Yung, M.D. During July, the medical practice completed the following transactions:

Jul	1	Yung deposited $68,000 cash in the business bank account. The business gave capital to Yung.
	5	Paid monthly rent on medical equipment, $560.
	9	Paid $16,000 cash to purchase land for an office site.
	10	Purchased supplies on account, $1,600.
	19	Borrowed $23,000 from the bank for business use. Yung signed a note payable to the bank in the name of the business.
	22	Paid $1,300 on account.
	31	Revenues earned during the month included $6,500 cash and $5,800 on account.
	31	Paid employees' salaries $2,500, office rent $1,100, and utilities $400. Make a single compound entry.
	31	Yung withdrew cash of $7,000.

The business uses the following accounts: Cash; Accounts receivable; Supplies; Land; Accounts payable; Notes payable; Yung, capital; Yung, drawing; Service revenue; Salary expense; Rent expense; and Utilities expense.

Requirements

1. Journalize each transaction, as shown for July 1. Explanations are not required.

Jul 1	Cash		68,000	
		Yung, capital		68,000

2. Post the transactions to the T-accounts, using transaction dates as posting references in the ledger accounts. Label the balance of each account *Bal*, as shown in the chapter.

3. Prepare the trial balance of Vernon Yung, M.D. at July 31, 2012.

P2-30A ③④⑤ **Journalizing transactions, posting to T-accounts, and preparing a trial balance [45–60 min]**

Doris Stewart started her practice as a design consultant on September 1, 2012. During the first month of operations, the business completed the following transactions:

Sep	1	Received $42,000 cash and gave capital to Stewart.
	4	Purchased supplies, $700, and furniture, $1,900, on account.
	6	Performed services for a law firm and received $1,400 cash.
	7	Paid $24,000 cash to acquire land for a future office site.
	10	Performed service for a hotel and received its promise to pay the $1,000 within one week.
	14	Paid for the furniture purchased September 4 on account.
	15	Paid secretary's bi-monthly salary, $490.
	17	Received cash on account, $400.
	20	Prepared a design for a school on account, $700.
	28	Received $2,100 cash for consulting with Plummer & Gorden.
	30	Paid secretary's bi-monthly salary, $490.
	30	Paid rent expense, $650.
	30	Stewart withdrew cash of $3,000.

Requirements

1. Open the following T-accounts: Cash; Accounts receivable; Supplies; Furniture; Land; Accounts payable; Stewart, capital; Stewart, drawing; Service revenue; Salary expense; and Rent expense.

2. Record each transaction in the journal, using the account titles given. Key each transaction by date. Explanations are not required.

3. Post the transactions to the T-accounts, using transaction dates as posting references in the ledger accounts. Label the balance of each account *Bal*, as shown in the chapter.

4. Prepare the trial balance of Doris Stewart, Designer, at September 30, 2012.

P2-31A ④⑤ **Journalizing transactions, posting to accounts in four-column format, and preparing a trial balance [45–60 min]**

Trevor Moore opened a law office on September 2, 2012. During the first month of operations, the business completed the following transactions:

Sep	2	Moore deposited $39,000 cash in the business bank account Trevor Moore, Attorney. The business gave capital to Moore.
	3	Purchased supplies, $600, and furniture, $2,000, on account.
	4	Performed legal service for a client and received cash, $1,300.
	7	Paid cash to acquire land for a future office site, $26,000.
	11	Prepared legal documents for a client on account, $700.
	15	Paid secretary's bi-monthly salary, $590.
	16	Paid for the supplies purchased September 3 on account.
	18	Received $2,400 cash for helping a client sell real estate.
	19	Defended a client in court and billed the client for $800.
	29	Received cash on account, $700.
	30	Paid secretary's bi-monthly salary, $590.
	30	Paid rent expense, $670.
	30	Moore withdrew cash of $2,400.

Requirements

1. Open the following T-accounts: Cash; Accounts receivable; Supplies; Furniture; Land; Accounts payable; Moore, capital; Moore, drawing; Service revenue; Salary expense; and Rent expense.

2. Record each transaction in the journal, using the account titles given. Key each transaction by date. Explanations are not required.

3. Post the transactions to T-accounts, using transaction dates as posting references in the ledger. Label the balance of each account *Bal*, as shown in the chapter.

4. Prepare the trial balance of Trevor Moore, Attorney, at September 30, 2012.

P2-32A ④⑤ **Journalizing transactions, posting to accounts in four-column format, and preparing a trial balance [45–60 min]**

The trial balance of Sam Mitchell, CPA, is dated January 31, 2012:

Account No.	Account	Debit	Credit
	SAM MITCHELL, CPA		
	Trial Balance		
	January 31, 2012		
11	Cash	$ 7,000	
12	Accounts receivable	10,500	
13	Supplies	600	
14	Land	17,000	
21	Accounts payable		$ 4,700
31	Mitchell, capital		30,400
32	Mitchell, drawing		
41	Service revenue		
51	Salary expense		
52	Rent expense		
	Total	$ 35,100	$ 35,100

During February, Mitchell or his business completed the following transactions:

Feb 4 Collected $4,000 cash from a client on account.

8 Performed tax services for a client on account, $4,600.

13 Paid business debt on account, $2,400.

18 Purchased office supplies on account, $900.

20 Mitchell withdrew cash of $2,200.

21 Mitchell paid for a deck for his private residence using personal funds, $8,000.

22 Received $2,300 cash for consulting work just completed.

27 Paid office rent, $500.

29 Paid employee salary, $1,600.

Requirements

1. Record the February transactions in the journal. Include an explanation for each entry.

2. Post the transactions to four-column accounts in the ledger, using dates, account numbers, journal references, and posting references. Open the ledger accounts listed in the trial balance, together with their balances at January 31.

3. Prepare the trial balance of Sam Mitchell, CPA, at February 29, 2012.

P2-33A ❹❺ **Journalizing transactions, posting to accounts in four-column format, and preparing a trial balance [45–60 min]**

The trial balance of Sharon Silver, Registered Dietician, at June 30, 2012, follows.

	SHARON SILVER, REGISTERED DIETICIAN		
	Trial Balance		
	June 30, 2012		
Account No.	Account	Debit	Credit
11	Cash	$ 7,000	
12	Accounts receivable	8,500	
13	Supplies	800	
14	Equipment	13,000	
21	Accounts payable		$ 4,800
31	Silver, capital		24,500
32	Silver, drawing		
41	Service revenue		
51	Salary expense		
52	Rent expense		
	Total	$ 29,300	$ 29,300

During July, Silver or her business completed the following transactions:

Jul	4	Collected $6,000 cash from a client on account.
	7	Performed a nutritional analysis for a hospital on account, $6,600.
	12	Silver used personal funds to pay for the renovation of her private residence, $55,000.
	16	Purchased supplies on account, $1,000.
	19	Silver withdrew cash of $2,300.
	20	Paid business debt on account, $2,500.
	24	Received $2,200 cash for consulting with Natural Foods.
	25	Paid rent, $500.
	31	Paid employee salary, $1,700.

Requirements

1. Record the July transactions in the business's journal. Include an explanation for each entry.
2. Post the transactions to four-column accounts in the ledger, using dates, account numbers, journal references, and posting references.
3. Prepare the trial balance of Sharon Silver, Registered Dietician, at July 31, 2012.

P2-34A ❹❺ **Recording transactions, using four-column accounts, posting, and preparing a trial balance [45–60 min]**

Maurey Wills started an environmental consulting company and during the first month of operations (February 2012), the business completed the following transactions:

a. Wills began the business with an investment of $48,000 cash and a building at $30,000. The business gave $78,000 of capital to Wills.

b. Purchased office supplies on account, $2,000.

c. Paid $14,000 for office furniture.

d. Paid employee's salary, $2,200.

e. Performed consulting services on account, $3,700.

f. Paid $900 of the account payable created in transaction (b).

g. Received a $600 bill for advertising expense that will be paid in the near future.

h. Performed consulting service for cash, $1,100.

i. Received cash on account, $1,100.

j. Paid the following cash expenses:
   (1) Rent on equipment, $1,000.
   (2) Utilities, $900.

k. Wills withdrew cash of $2,300.

Requirements

1. Open the following four-column accounts: Cash; Accounts receivable; Office supplies; Office furniture; Building; Accounts payable; Wills, capital; Wills, drawing; Service revenue; Salary expense; Rent expense; Advertising expense; and Utilities expense.

2. Record each transaction in the journal. Use the letters to identify the transactions.

3. Post to the accounts and keep a running balance for each account.

4. Prepare the trial balance of Wills Environmental Consulting Company at February 29, 2012.

P2-35A ② ⑤ **Correcting errors in a trial balance [15–25 min]**

The trial balance of Smart Tots Child Care does not balance.

SMART TOTS CHILD CARE		
Trial Balance		
August 31, 2012		
Account	Debit	Credit
Cash	$ 6,700	
Accounts receivable	7,000	
Supplies	700	
Equipment	87,000	
Accounts payable		$ 53,000
Tilley, capital		50,500
Tilley, drawing	2,400	
Service revenue		4,700
Salary expense	3,600	
Rent expense	500	
Total	$ 107,900	$ 108,200

The following errors are detected:

a. Cash is understated by $1,000.

b. A $4,000 debit to Accounts receivable was posted as a credit.

c. A $1,000 purchase of supplies on account was neither journalized nor posted.

d. Equipment's cost is $78,500, not $87,000.

e. Salary expense is overstated by $200.

Requirement

1. Prepare the corrected trial balance at August 31, 2012. Journal entries are not required.

P2-36A ② ⑤ **Correcting errors in a trial balance [15–25 min]**
The trial balance for Treasure Hunt Exploration Company does not balance.

TREASURE HUNT EXPLORATION COMPANY Trial Balance February 29, 2012		
Account	Debit	Credit
Cash	$ 6,300	
Accounts receivable	6,000	
Supplies	400	
Exploration equipment	22,300	
Computers	49,000	
Accounts payable		$ 2,800
Note payable		18,500
Jones, capital		50,000
Jones, drawing	4,000	
Service revenue		4,100
Salary expense	1,400	
Rent expense	800	
Advertising expense	900	
Utilities expense	800	
Total	$ 91,900	$ 75,400

The following errors were detected:

a. The cash balance is overstated by $5,000.
b. Rent expense of $340 was erroneously posted as a credit rather than a debit.
c. A $6,800 credit to Service revenue was not posted.
d. A $400 debit to Accounts receivable was posted as $40.
e. The balance of Utilities expense is understated by $70.
f. A $900 purchase of supplies on account was neither journalized nor posted.
g. Exploration equipment should be $16,490.

Requirement

1. Prepare the corrected trial balance at February 29, 2012. Journal entries are not required.

P2-37A ⑤ **Preparing financial statements from the trial balance [20–30 min]**
Link Back to Chapter 1 (Income Statement, Statement of Owner's Equity, Balance Sheet). Refer to Problem 2-28A. After completing the ledger in Problem 2-28A, prepare the following financial statements for Showtime Amusements Company:

Requirements

1. Income statement for the month ended September 30, 2012.
2. Statement of owner's equity for the month ended September 30, 2012. The beginning balance of capital was $0.
3. Balance sheet at September 30, 2012.

P2-38A ⑤ **Preparing financial statements from the trial balance [20–30 min]**
Link Back to Chapter 1 (Income Statement, Statement of Owner's Equity, Balance Sheet). Refer to Problem 2-29A. After completing the trial balance in Problem 2-29A, prepare the following financial statements for Vernon Yung, M.D.:

Requirements

1. Income statement for the month ended July 31, 2012.
2. Statement of owner's equity for the month ended July 31, 2012. The beginning balance of capital was $0.
3. Balance sheet at July 31, 2012.

P2-39A ⑤ **Preparing financial statements from the trial balance [20–30 min]**
Link Back to Chapter 1 (Income Statement, Statement of Owner's Equity, Balance Sheet). Refer to Problem 2-30A. After completing the trial balance in Problem 2-30A, prepare the following financial statements for Doris Stewart, Designer:

Requirements

1. Income statement for the month ended September 30, 2012.
2. Statement of owner's equity for the month ended September 30, 2012. The beginning balance of capital was $0.
3. Balance sheet at September 30, 2012.

P2-40A ⑤ **Preparing financial statements from the trial balance. [20–30 min]**
Link Back to Chapter 1 (Income Statement, Statement of Owner's Equity, Balance Sheet). Refer to Problem 2-31A. After completing the trial balance in Problem 2-31A, prepare the following financial statements for Trevor Moore, Attorney:

Requirements

1. Income statement for the month ended September 30, 2012.
2. Statement of owner's equity for the month ended September 30, 2012. The beginning balance of capital was $0.
3. Balance sheet at September 30, 2012.

P2-41A ⑤ **Preparing financial statements from the trial balance [20–30 min]**
Link Back to Chapter 1 (Income Statement, Statement of Owner's Equity, Balance Sheet). Refer to Problem 2-32A. After completing the trial balance in Problem 2-32A, prepare the following financial statements for Sam Mitchell, CPA:

Requirements

1. Income statement for the month ended February 29, 2012.
2. Statement of owner's equity for the month ended February 29, 2012. The beginning balance of capital was $0.
3. Balance sheet at February 29, 2012.

P2-42A ⑤ **Preparing financial statements from the trial balance [20–30 min]**
Link Back to Chapter 1 (Income Statement, Statement of Owner's Equity, Balance Sheet). Refer to Problem 2-33A. After completing the trial balance in Problem 2-33A, prepare the following financial statements for Sharon Silver, Registered Dietician:

Requirements

1. Income statement for the month ended July 31, 2012.
2. Statement of owner's equity for the month ended July 31, 2012. The beginning balance of capital was $0.
3. Balance sheet at July 31, 2012.

P2-43A ❺ **Preparing financial statements from the trial balance [20–30 min]**

Link Back to Chapter 1 (Income Statement, Statement of Owner's Equity, Balance Sheet). Refer to Problem 2-34A. After completing the trial balance in Problem 2-34A, prepare the following financial statements for Wills Environmental Consulting Company:

Requirements

1. Income statement for the month ended February 29, 2012.
2. Statement of owner's equity for the month ended February 29, 2012. The beginning balance of capital was $0.
3. Balance sheet at February 29, 2012.

● Problems (Group B)

P2-44B ❶ ❷ **Identifying common accounts and normal account balances [10–15 min]**   *MyAccountingLab*

Party Time Amusements Company owns movie theaters. Party Time engaged in the following business transactions in 2012:

Aug	1	Daniel Smith invested $400,000 personal cash in the business by depositing that amount in a bank account titled Party Time Amusements. The business gave capital to Smith.
	2	Paid $350,000 cash to purchase a theater building.
	5	Borrowed $200,000 from the bank. Smith signed a note payable to the bank in the name of Party Time.
	10	Purchased theater supplies on account, $1,300.
	15	Paid $1,000 on account.
	15	Paid property tax expense on theater building, $1,200.
	16	Paid employees' salaries $2,700, and rent on equipment $1,700. Make a single compound entry.
	28	Smith withdrew cash of $8,000.
	31	Received $25,000 cash from service revenue and deposited that amount in the bank.

Requirements

1. Create the list of accounts that Party Time Amusements will use to record these transactions.
2. Identify the account type and normal balance of each account identified in Requirement 1.

Note: Problem 2-44B must be completed before attempting Problem 2-45B.

P2-45B ❸ ❹ **Analyzing and journalizing transactions, posting, and preparing a trial balance [40–50 min]**

Review the facts given in P2-44B.

Requirements

1. Journalize each transaction of Party Time as shown for August 1. Explanations are not required.

Aug 1	Cash	400,000	
	Smith, capital		400,000

2. Post the transactions to the T-accounts, using transaction dates as posting references in the ledger accounts. Label the balance of each account *Bal*, as shown in the chapter.

P2-46B ③④⑤ **Analyzing and journalizing transactions, posting, and preparing a trial balance [45–60 min]**

Vince Rockford practices medicine under the business title Vince Rockford, M.D. During March, the medical practice completed the following transactions:

Mar 1	Rockford deposited $74,000 cash in the business bank account. The business gave capital to Rockford.	
5	Paid monthly rent on medical equipment, $560.	
9	Paid $24,000 cash to purchase land for an office site.	
10	Purchased supplies on account, $1,300.	
19	Borrowed $19,000 from the bank for business use. Rockford signed a note payable to the bank in the name of the business.	
22	Paid $900 on account.	
31	Revenues earned during the month included $7,100 cash and $4,700 on account.	
31	Paid employees' salaries $2,000, office rent $1,600, and utilities $320. Make a single compound entry.	
31	Rockford withdrew cash of $8,000.	

The business uses the following accounts: Cash; Accounts receivable; Supplies; Land; Accounts payable; Notes payable; Rockford, capital; Rockford, drawing; Service revenue; Salary expense; Rent expense; and Utilities expense.

Requirements

1. Journalize each transaction, as shown for March 1. Explanations are not required.

Mar 1	Cash	74,000	
	Rockford, capital		74,000

2. Post the transactions to the T-accounts, using transaction dates as posting references in the ledger accounts. Label the balance of each account *Bal*, as shown in the chapter.

3. Prepare the trial balance of Vince Rockford, M.D., at March 31, 2012.

P2-47B ④⑤ **Journalizing transactions, posting to T-accounts, and preparing a trial balance [45–60 min]**

Beth Yung started her practice as a design consultant on November 1, 2012. During the first month of operations, the business completed the following transactions:

Nov 1	Received $34,000 cash and issued capital to Yung.	
4	Purchased supplies, $500, and furniture, $1,900, on account.	
6	Performed services for a law firm and received $1,200 cash.	
7	Paid $25,000 cash to acquire land for a future office site.	
10	Performed service for a hotel and received its promise to pay the $1,200 within one week.	
14	Paid for the furniture purchased November 4 on account.	
15	Paid secretary's bi-monthly salary, $540.	
17	Received cash on account, $500.	
20	Prepared a design for a school on account, $800.	
28	Received $2,200 cash for consulting with Plummer & Gorden.	
30	Paid secretary's bi-monthly salary, $540.	
30	Paid rent expense, $830.	
30	Yung withdrew cash of $2,700.	

Requirements

1. Open the following T-accounts: Cash; Accounts receivable; Supplies; Furniture; Land; Accounts payable; Yung, capital; Yung, drawing; Service revenue; Salary expense; and Rent expense.

2. Record each transaction in the journal, using the account titles given. Key each transaction by date. Explanations are not required.

3. Post the transactions to the T-accounts, using transaction dates as posting references in the ledger accounts. Label the balance of each account *Bal*, as shown in the chapter.

4. Prepare the trial balance of Beth Yung, Designer, at November 30, 2012.

P2-48B ❹❺ **Journalizing transactions, posting to accounts in four-column format, and preparing a trial balance [45–60 min]**

Vince Smith opened a law office on April 2, 2012. During the first month of operations, the business completed the following transactions:

Apr	2	Smith deposited $32,000 cash in the business bank account Vince Smith, Attorney. The business gave Smith capital.
	3	Purchased supplies, $500, and furniture, $2,000, on account.
	4	Performed legal service for a client and received cash, $1,900.
	7	Paid cash to acquire land for a future office site, $24,000.
	11	Prepared legal documents for a client on account, $1,100.
	15	Paid secretary's bi-monthly salary, $460.
	16	Paid for the supplies purchased April 3 on account.
	18	Received $1,700 cash for helping a client sell real estate.
	19	Defended a client in court and billed the client for $700.
	29	Received cash on account, $800.
	30	Paid secretary's bi-monthly salary, $460.
	30	Paid rent expense, $730.
	30	Smith withdrew cash of $2,700.

Requirements

1. Open the following T-accounts: Cash; Accounts receivable; Supplies; Furniture; Land; Accounts payable; Smith, capital; Smith, drawing; Service revenue; Salary expense; and Rent expense.

2. Record each transaction in the journal, using the account titles given. Key each transaction by date. Explanations are not required.

3. Post the transactions to T-accounts, using transaction dates as posting references in the ledger. Label the balance of each account *Bal*, as shown in the chapter.

4. Prepare the trial balance of Vince Smith, Attorney, at April 30, 2012.

P2-49B ④ ⑤ **Journalizing transactions, posting to accounts in four-column format, and preparing a trial balance [45–60 min]**

The trial balance of John Hilton, CPA, is dated March 31, 2012:

	JOHN HILTON, CPA Trial Balance March 31, 2012		
Account No.	Account	Debit	Credit
11	Cash	$ 5,000	
12	Accounts receivable	8,100	
13	Supplies	800	
14	Land	14,000	
21	Accounts payable		$ 4,200
31	Hilton, capital		23,700
32	Hilton, drawing		
41	Service revenue		
51	Salary expense		
52	Rent expense		
	Total	$27,900	$27,900

During April, Hilton or his business completed the following transactions:

Apr	4	Collected $7,000 cash from a client on account.
	8	Performed tax services for a client on account, $5,000.
	13	Paid business debt on account, $2,500.
	18	Purchased office supplies on account, $600.
	20	Hilton withdrew cash of $2,300.
	21	Hilton paid for a deck for his private residence, using personal funds, $12,000.
	22	Received $2,100 cash for consulting work just completed.
	27	Paid office rent, $300.
	28	Paid employee salary, $1,300.

Requirements

1. Record the April transactions in the journal. Include an explanation for each entry.
2. Post the transactions to four-column accounts in the ledger, using dates, account numbers, journal references, and posting references. Open the ledger accounts listed in the trial balance, together with their balances at March 31.
3. Prepare the trial balance of John Hilton, CPA, at April 30, 2012.

P2-50B ④ ⑤ **Journalizing transactions, posting to accounts in four-column format, and preparing a trial balance [45–60 min]**

The trial balance of Shermana Peters, Registered Dietician, at June 30, 2012, follows:

	SHERMANA PETERS, REGISTERED DIETICIAN		
	Trial Balance		
	June 30, 2012		
Account No.	Account	Debit	Credit
11	Cash	$ 4,000	
12	Accounts receivable	7,600	
13	Supplies	600	
14	Equipment	16,000	
21	Accounts payable		$ 5,200
31	Peters, capital		23,000
32	Peters, drawing		
41	Service revenue		
51	Salary expense		
52	Rent expense		
	Total	$28,200	$28,200

During July, Peters or her business completed the following transactions:

Jul 4 Collected $7,000 cash from a client on account.
7 Performed a nutritional analysis for a hospital on account, $4,900.
12 Peters used personal funds to pay for the renovation of her private residence, $53,000.
16 Purchased supplies on account, $800.
19 Peters withdrew cash of $2,200.
20 Paid business debt on account, $2,300.
24 Received $2,100 cash for consulting with Bountiful Foods.
25 Paid rent, $300.
31 Paid employee salary, $1,500.

Requirements

1. Record the July transactions in the business's journal. Include an explanation for each entry.
2. Post the transactions to four-column accounts in the ledger, using dates, account numbers, journal references, and posting references.
3. Prepare the trial balance of Shermana Peters, Registered Dietician, at July 31, 2012.

P2-51B ④ ⑤ **Recording transactions, using four-column accounts, posting, and preparing a trial balance [45–60 min]**

Van Stubbs started an environmental consulting company and during the first month of operations (October 2012), the business completed the following transactions:

a. Stubbs began the business with an investment of $40,000 cash and a building at $26,000. The business gave $66,000 of capital to Stubbs.

b. Purchased office supplies on account, $2,400.

c. Paid $18,000 for office furniture.

d. Paid employee's salary, $1,900.

e. Performed consulting services on account, $3,600.

f. Paid $500 of the account payable created in transaction (b).

g. Received a $300 bill for advertising expense that will be paid in the near future.

h. Performed consulting service for cash, $800.

i. Received cash on account, $1,400.

j. Paid the following cash expenses:
   (1) Rent on equipment, $700.
   (2) Utilities, $500.

k. Stubbs withdrew cash of $2,400.

Requirements

1. Open the following four-column accounts: Cash; Accounts receivable; Office supplies; Office furniture; Building; Accounts payable; Stubbs, capital; Stubbs, drawing; Service revenue; Salary expense; Rent expense; Advertising expense; and Utilities expense.

2. Record each transaction in the journal. Use the letters to identify the transactions.

3. Post to the accounts and keep a running balance for each account.

4. Prepare the trial balance of Stubbs Environmental Consulting Company at October 31, 2012.

P2-52B ② ⑤ **Correcting errors in a trial balance [15–25 min]**

The trial balance of Building Blocks Child Care does not balance.

BUILDING BLOCKS CHILD CARE Trial Balance May 31, 2012		
Account	Debit	Credit
Cash	$ 6,300	
Accounts receivable	3,000	
Supplies	700	
Equipment	88,000	
Accounts payable		$ 57,000
Estella, capital		50,400
Estella, drawing	2,600	
Service revenue		4,700
Salary expense	3,200	
Rent expense	700	
Total	$ 104,500	$ 112,100

The following errors are detected:

a. Cash is understated by $4,000.

b. A $2,000 debit to Accounts receivable was posted as a credit.

c. A $1,200 purchase of supplies on account was neither journalized nor posted.

d. Equipment's cost is $87,700, not $88,000.

e. Salary expense is overstated by $100.

Requirement

1. Prepare the corrected trial balance at May 31, 2012. Journal entries are not required.

P2-53B ② ⑤ **Correcting errors in a trial balance [15–25 min]**

The trial balance for Treasure Hunt Exploration Company does not balance.

TREASURE HUNT EXPLORATION COMPANY Trial Balance July 31, 2012		
Account	Debit	Credit
Cash	$ 6,600	
Accounts receivable	9,000	
Supplies	200	
Exploration equipment	22,600	
Computers	46,000	
Accounts payable		$ 2,900
Note payable		18,900
Indiana, capital		50,100
Indiana, drawing	1,000	
Service revenue		4,900
Salary expense	1,800	
Rent expense	100	
Advertising expense	100	
Utilities expense	700	
Total	$ 88,100	$ 76,800

The following errors were detected:

- **a.** The cash balance is overstated by $1,000.
- **b.** Rent expense of $300 was erroneously posted as a credit rather than a debit.
- **c.** A $6,000 credit to Service revenue was not posted.
- **d.** A $500 debit to Accounts receivable was posted as $50.
- **e.** The balance of Utilities expense is understated by $90.
- **f.** A $600 purchase of supplies on account was neither journalized nor posted.
- **g.** Exploration equipment should be $17,160.

Requirement

1. Prepare the corrected trial balance at July 31, 2012. Journal entries are not required.

P2-54B ⑤ **Preparing financial statements from the trial balance [20–30 min]**

Link Back to Chapter 1 (Income Statement, Statement of Owner's Equity, Balance Sheet). Refer to Problem 2-45B. After completing the ledger in Problem 2-45B, prepare the following financial statements for Party Time Amusements Company:

Requirements

1. Income statement for the month ended August 31, 2012.

2. Statement of owner's equity for the month ended August 31, 2012. The beginning balance of capital was $0.

3. Balance sheet at August 31, 2012.

P2-55B ⑤ **Preparing financial statements from the trial balance [20–30 min]**

Link Back to Chapter 1 (Income Statement, Statement of Owner's Equity, Balance Sheet). Refer to Problem 2-46B. After completing the trial balance in Problem 2-46B, prepare the following financial statements for Vince Rockford, M.D.:

Requirements

1. Income statement for the month ended March 31, 2012.

2. Statement of owner's equity for the month ended March 31, 2012. The beginning balance of capital was $0.

3. Balance sheet at March 31, 2012.

P2-56B ⑤ **Preparing preparing financial statements from the trial balance. [20–30 min]**
Link Back to Chapter 1 (Income Statement, Statement of Owner's Equity, Balance Sheet). Refer to Problem 2-47B. After completing the trial balance in Problem 2-47B, prepare the following financial statements for Beth Yung, Designer:

Requirements

1. Income statement for the month ended November 30, 2012.

2. Statement of owner's equity for the month ended November 30, 2012. The beginning balance of capital was $0.

3. Balance sheet at November 30, 2012.

P2-57B ⑤ **Preparing financial statements from the trial balance. [20–30 min]**
Link Back to Chapter 1 (Income Statement, Statement of Owner's Equity, Balance Sheet). Refer to Problem 2-48B. After completing the trial balance in Problem 2-48B, prepare the following financial statements for Vince Smith, Attorney:

Requirements

1. Income statement for the month ended April 30, 2012.

2. Statement of owner's equity for the month ended April 30, 2012. The beginning balance of capital was $0.

3. Balance sheet at April 30, 2012.

P2-58B ⑤ **Preparing financial statements from the trial balance [20–30 min]**
Link Back to Chapter 1 (Income Statement, Statement of Owner's Equity, Balance Sheet). Refer to Problem 2-49B. After completing the trial balance in Problem 2-49B, prepare the following financial statements for John Hilton, CPA:

Requirements

1. Income statement for the month ended April 30, 2012.

2. Statement of owner's equity for the month ended April 30, 2012. The beginning balance of capital was $0.

3. Balance sheet at April 30, 2012.

P2-59B ⑤ **Preparing financial statements from the trial balance [20–30 min]**
Link Back to Chapter 1 (Income Statement, Statement of Owner's Equity, Balance Sheet). Refer to Problem 2-50B. After completing the trial balance in Problem 2-50B, prepare the following financial statements for Shermana Peters, Registered Dietician:

Requirements

1. Income statement for the month ended July 31, 2012.

2. Statement of owner's equity for the month ended July 31, 2012. The beginning balance of capital was 0.

3. Balance sheet at July 31, 2012.

P2-60B ⑤ **Preparing financial statements from the trial balance [20–30 min]**
Link Back to Chapter 1 (Income Statement, Statement of Owner's Equity, Balance Sheet). Refer to Problem 2-51B. After completing the trial balance in Problem 2-51B, prepare the following financial statements for Stubbs Environmental Consulting Company:

Requirements

1. Income statement for the month ended October 31, 2012.
2. Statement of owner's equity for the month ended October 31, 2012. The beginning balance of capital was $0.
3. Balance sheet at October 31, 2012.

● Continuing Exercise

② ③ ④ ⑤ **Journalizing transactions, posting to T-accounts, and preparing a trial balance [30–45 min]** Exercise 2-61 continues with the consulting business of Lawlor Lawn Service begun in Exercise 1-47. Here you will account for Lawlor Lawn Service's transactions as it is actually done in practice.

E2-61   Lawlor Lawn Service completed the following transactions during May:

May	1	Received $1,700 and gave capital to Lawlor. Opened bank account titled Lawlor Lawn Service.
	3	Purchased on account a mower, $1,200, and weed whacker, $240. The equipment is expected to remain in service for four years.
	5	Purchased $30 of gas. Wrote check #1 from the new bank account.
	6	Performed lawn services for client on account, $150.
	8	Purchased $150 of fertilizer supplies from the lawn store that will be used on future jobs. Wrote check #2 from the new bank account.
	17	Completed landscaping job for client, received cash $800.
	31	Received $100 on account from May 6 sale.

Requirements

1. Open T-accounts: Cash; Accounts receivable; Lawn supplies; Equipment; Accounts payable; Lawlor, capital; Lawlor, drawing; Service revenue; and Fuel expense.
2. Journalize the transactions. Explanations are not required.
3. Post to the T-accounts. Key all items by date, and denote an account balance as *Bal.* Formal posting references are not required.
4. Prepare a trial balance at May 31, 2012.

MyAccountingLab

● Continuing Problem

❷ ❸ ❹ ❺ **Journalizing transactions, posting to T-accounts, and preparing a trial balance [40–50 min]** Problem 2-62 continues with the consulting business of Carl Draper, begun in Problem 1-48. Here you will account for Draper Consulting's transactions as it is actually done in practice.

P2-62 Draper Consulting completed the following transactions during the first half of December, 2012:

Dec	2	Received $18,000 cash and gave capital to Draper.
	2	Paid monthly office rent, $550.
	3	Paid cash for a **Dell** computer, $1,800. This equipment is expected to remain in service for five years.
	4	Purchased office furniture on account, $4,200. The furniture should last for five years.
	5	Purchased supplies on account, $900.
	9	Performed consulting service for a client on account, $1,500.
	12	Paid utility expenses, $250.
	18	Performed service for a client and received cash of $1,100.

Requirements

1. Open T-accounts: Cash; Accounts receivable; Supplies; Equipment; Furniture; Accounts payable; Draper, capital; Draper, drawing; Service revenue; Rent expense; and Utilities expense.

2. Journalize the transactions. Explanations are not required.

3. Post to the T-accounts. Key all items by date, and denote an account balance as *Bal.* Formal posting references are not required.

4. Prepare a trial balance at December 18. In the Continuing Problem of Chapter 3, we will add transactions for the remainder of December and prepare a trial balance at December 31.

● Practice Set

②③④⑤ **Journalizing transactions, posting to T-accounts, and preparing a trial** **MyAccountingLab**
balance [45–60 min] Use the chart of accounts you created in Chapter 1 (and add accounts where necessary). All of the first month's activity for Shine King Cleaning is as follows.

Nov 1	Evan Hudson deposited $35,000 in the business account. Also on this date, Evan transferred his truck title, worth $8,000, to the business. Evan received $43,000 of capital.
2	Wrote a check for $2,000 to Pleasant Properties. In the "for" area of the check, it states "November through February Rent." (Debit Prepaid rent)
3	Purchased business insurance policy for $2,400 for the term November 1, 2012, through October 31, 2013, and paid cash. (Debit Prepaid insurance)
4	Evan went to the Cleaning Supply Company and purchased $270 of cleaning supplies on account. The invoice is due 20 days from the date of purchase.
5	Purchased on account an industrial vacuum cleaner from Penny Purchase costing $1,000. The invoice is payable on or before November 25.
7	Purchased a computer and printer costing a total of $1,200. A check for the same amount to the computer store was written on the same date.
9	Performed cleaning services on account for Pierre's Wig Stand in the amount of $3,000.
10	Deposited Pierre's check for $100 in the bank.
15	Wrote check payable to Eric Ryder for $500 for contract labor.
16	Received $3,600 for 1 year contract beginning November 16 for cleaning services to be provided to the Sea Side Restaurant. Contract begins November 16, 2012, and ends November 15, 2013. (Credit Unearned service revenue)
17	Provided cleaning services for Tip Top Solutions for $800. Tip Top paid with a check.
18	Received water and electric bill for $175 with due date of December 4, 2012.
20	Borrowed $40,000 from bank with interest at rate of 9% per year.
21	Deposited check from Pierre's Wig Stand for $900, with the notation "on account."
25	Wrote check to Penny Purchase for invoice #1035 in the amount of $500.
29	Wrote check payable to **St. Petersburg News** for $100 for advertising.
30	Hudson withdrew cash of $600.

Requirements

1. Journalize transactions as required from the activity data.
2. Post journal entries to T-accounts and calculate account balances.
3. Prepare the trial balance at November 30.

Apply Your Knowledge

● Decision Cases

Decision Case 2-1 You have been requested by a friend named Dean McChesney to advise him on the effects that certain transactions will have on his business. Time is short, so you cannot journalize the transactions. Instead, you must analyze the transactions without a journal. McChesney will continue the business only if he can expect to earn monthly net income of $6,000. The business completed the following transactions during June:

a. McChesney deposited $10,000 cash in a business bank account to start the company. The company gave capital to McChesney.

b. Paid $300 cash for supplies.

c. Incurred advertising expense on account, $700.

d. Paid the following cash expenses: secretary's salary, $1,400; office rent, $1,100.

e. Earned service revenue on account, $8,800.

f. Collected cash from customers on account, $1,200.

Requirements

1. Open the following T-accounts: Cash; Accounts receivable; Supplies; Accounts payable; McChesney, capital; Service revenue; Salary expense; Rent expense; and Advertising expense.

2. Post the transactions directly to the accounts without using a journal. Key each transaction by letter. Follow the format illustrated here for the first transaction.

Cash		McChesney, capital
(a) 10,000		(a) 10,000

3. Prepare a trial balance at June 30, 2014. List the largest expense first, the next largest second, and so on. The business name is A-Plus Travel Planners.

4. Compute the amount of net income or net loss for this first month of operations. Would you recommend that McChesney continue in business?

Decision Case 2-2 Answer the following questions. Consider each question separately.

Requirements

1. Explain the advantages of double-entry bookkeeping instead of recording transactions in terms of the accounting equation to a friend who is opening a used book store.

2. When you deposit money in your bank account, the bank credits your account. Is the bank misusing the word *credit* in this context? Why does the bank use the term *credit* to refer to your deposit, instead of *debit*?

• Ethical Issue 2-1

Better Days Ahead, a charitable organization, has a standing agreement with First National Bank. The agreement allows Better Days Ahead to overdraw its cash balance at the bank when donations are running low. In the past, Better Days Ahead managed funds wisely, and rarely used this privilege. Jacob Henson has recently become the president of Better Days. To expand operations, Henson acquired office equipment and spent large amounts on fundraising. During Henson's presidency, Better Days Ahead has maintained a negative bank balance of approximately $10,000.

Requirement

1. What is the ethical issue in this situation, if any? State why you approve or disapprove of Henson's management of Better Days Ahead's funds.

• Fraud Case 2-1

Roy Akins was the accounting manager at Zelco, a tire manufacturer, and he played golf with Hugh Stallings, the CEO, who was something of a celebrity in the community. The CEO stood to earn a substantial bonus if Zelco increased net income by year-end. Roy was eager to get into Hugh's elite social circle; he boasted to Hugh that he knew some accounting tricks that could increase company income by simply revising a few journal entries for rental payments on storage units. At the end of the year, Roy changed the debits from "rent expense" to "prepaid rent" on several entries. Later, Hugh got his bonus, and the deviations were never discovered.

Requirements

1. How did the change in the journal entries affect the net income of the company at year-end?

2. Who gained and who lost as a result of these actions?

● Financial Statement Case 2-1

This problem helps you develop skill in recording transactions by using a company's actual account titles. Refer to the **Amazon.com** financial statements in Appendix A. Note that large companies like **Amazon.com** use summary account titles in their financials, rather than listing each individual account by name. Assume that **Amazon.com** completed the following selected transactions during December 2009:

Dec	1	Earned sales revenue and collected cash, $60,000 ("Net sales").
	9	Borrowed $200,000 by signing a note payable ("Long-term debt").
	12	Purchased equipment on account, $10,000 ("Fixed assets").
	22	Paid half the account payable from December 12.
	28	Paid electricity bill for $3,000 ("General and administrative expense").
	31	Paid $100,000 of the note payable, plus interest expense of $1,000.

Requirement

1. Journalize these transactions, using the following account headings taken from the **Amazon.com** financial statements: Cash and cash equivalents, Equipment, Fixed assets, Accounts payable, Long-term debt, Net sales, General and administrative expense, and Interest expense. Explanations are not required.

● Team Project 2-1

Contact a local business and arrange with the owner to learn what accounts the business uses.

Requirements

1. Obtain a copy of the business's chart of accounts.

2. Prepare the company's financial statements for the most recent month, quarter, or year. (You may omit the statement of cash flows.) You may use either made-up account balances or balances supplied by the owner.

If the business has a large number of accounts within a category, combine related accounts and report a single amount on the financial statements. For example, the company may have several cash accounts. Combine all cash amounts and report a single Cash amount on the balance sheet.

　　You will probably encounter numerous accounts that you have not yet learned. Deal with these as best you can.

　　Keep in mind that the financial statements report the balances of the accounts listed in the company's chart of accounts, either by individual account or in summarized categories. Therefore, the financial statements must be consistent with the chart of accounts.

● Communication Activity 2-1

In 35 words or fewer, explain the difference between a debit and a credit and explain what the normal balance of the six account types is.

Quick Check Answers

1. *a* 2. *d* 3. *b* 4. *b* 5. *b* 6. *d* 7. *c* 8. *b* 9. *a* 10. *d*

For online homework, exercises, and problems that provide you immediate feedback, please visit myaccountinglab.com.

3

The Adjusting Process

Are these balances correctly showing everything the company OWNS?

Are these balances correctly showing everything the company OWES?

SMART TOUCH LEARNING
Balance Sheet
May 31, 2013

Assets				Liabilities	
Current assets:				Current liabilities:	
Cash		$ 4,800		Accounts payable	$ 48,700
Accounts receivable		2,600		Salary payable	900
Inventory		30,500		Interest payable	100
Supplies		600		Unearned service revenue	400
Prepaid rent		2,000		Total current liabilities	50,100
Total current assets			$ 40,500	Long-term liabilities:	
Plant assets:				Notes payable	20,000
Furniture	$18,000			Total liabilities	70,100
Less: Accumulated depreciation—furniture	300	17,700			
Building	48,000				
Less: Accumulated depreciation—building	200	47,800		Owner's Equity	
Total plant assets			65,500	Bright, capital	35,900
Total assets			$106,000	Total liabilities and owner's equity	$106,000

Learning Objectives

1. Differentiate between accrual and cash-basis accounting

2. Define and apply the accounting period concept, revenue recognition and matching principles, and time period concept

3. Explain why adjusting entries are needed

4. Journalize and post adjusting entries

5. Explain the purpose of and prepare an adjusted trial balance

6. Prepare the financial statements from the adjusted trial balance

7. Understand the alternate treatment of unearned revenues and prepaid expenses (see Appendix 3A, located at myaccountinglab.com)

If you're a business owner, manager, shareholder, or even an employee paid on commissions, you're anxious to see the final results of the period for your company. What is the company's net income or loss?

Chapter 1 introduced you to the accounting equation and the financial statements. In Chapter 2 you learned about T-accounts, debits, credits, and the trial balance. But have you captured all the transactions for a particular period? Not yet.

· · ·

In this chapter, we'll continue our exploration of the accounting cycle by learning how to update the accounts at the end of the period. This process is called *adjusting the books*, and it requires special journal entries called *adjusting journal entries*. For example, you'll see how at the end of a particular period, you must determine how many supplies you have used and how much you owe your employees and make adjusting entries to account for these amounts. These are just some of the adjusting entries you need to make before you can see the complete picture of how well your company performed—and determine commissions for salespeople and drawings for the owner.

We'll apply these principles to Smart Touch Learning for the month of May in this chapter, but these principles apply to giant companies such as **eBay** and **ExxonMobil** as well. They also apply to the business you may own or operate some day. Let's get started by comparing the accrual basis and cash basis of accounting.

Accrual Accounting Versus Cash-Basis Accounting

There are two ways to do accounting:

 Differentiate between accrual and cash-basis accounting

- **Accrual accounting** records the effect of each transaction as it occurs—that is, revenues are recorded when earned and expenses are recorded when incurred. Most businesses use the accrual basis as covered in this book.
- **Cash-basis accounting** records only cash receipts and cash payments. It ignores receivables, payables, and depreciation. Only very small businesses use the cash basis of accounting.

Suppose Smart Touch purchased $200 of office supplies on account on May 15, 2013, and paid the account in full on June 3, 2013. On the accrual basis, the business records this transaction as follows:

May 15	Office supplies (A+)	200	
	Accounts payable (L+)		200
	Purchased supplies on account.		
Jun 3	Accounts payable (L–)	200	
	Cash (A–)		200
	Paid on account.		

In contrast, cash-basis accounting ignores this transaction on May 15 because the business paid no cash. The cash basis records only cash receipts and cash payments. *In the cash basis,*

- cash receipts are treated as revenues.
- cash payments are treated as expenses.

Under the cash basis, Smart Touch would record each cash payment as an expense. So for our office supplies example, the company would recognize the cash basis expense on June 3, 2013, because that is the date that cash was paid. This is faulty accounting because the business acquired supplies, which are assets.

Now let's see how differently the accrual basis and the cash basis account for a revenue. Suppose Smart Touch performed service and earned revenue on May 20, 2013, but did not collect cash until June 5, 2013. Under the accrual basis, the business records $1,000 of revenue on account on May 20 as follows:

May 20	Accounts receivable (A+)		1,000	
	Service revenue (R+)			1,000
	Earned revenue on account.			
Jun 5	Cash (A+)		1,000	
	Accounts receivable (A–)			1,000
	Received cash on account.			

Under the cash basis, the business would record no revenue until the cash receipt, which in this case would be on June 5. As a result, cash-basis accounting never reports accounts receivable from customers. In this case, cash-basis accounting actually shows the revenue in the wrong accounting period (June). Revenue should be recorded when it is earned (May), and that is how the accrual basis operates.

Exhibit 3-1 illustrates the difference between the accrual basis and the cash basis for a florist. Keep in mind that the accrual basis is the preferred way to do accounting—and it's required by GAAP.

EXHIBIT 3-1 | Accrual Accounting Versus Cash-Basis Accounting

Key Takeaway

Cash-basis accounting and accrual accounting are different. Accrual accounting records revenues and expenses when they are EARNED/INCURRED. Cash-basis accounting records revenues and expenses when cash is RECEIVED or PAID.

Stop & Think...

Most of us think in terms of cash. Did our bank balance go up or down? This is in essence what the cash basis measures—changes in the cash balance. But consider your job. When do you actually earn your salary— when you go to work or when you get paid? When you go to work, you earn. That is when you accrue revenue under the accrual basis—not when you get paid by your employer.

Other Accounting Principles

 Define and apply the accounting period concept, revenue recognition and matching principles, and time period concept

We learned about some key accounting concepts in previous chapters. Now let's look at some additional accounting principles.

The Accounting Period Concept

Smart Touch will know with 100% certainty how well it has operated only if the company sells its assets, pays its liabilities, and gives any leftover cash to its owner(s). This process of going out of business is called **liquidation**. For obvious reasons, it is not practical to measure income this way. Because businesses need periodic reports on their affairs, accountants slice time into small segments and prepare financial statements for specific periods, such as a month, quarter, or year.

The basic accounting period is one year, and most businesses prepare annual financial statements. For most companies, the annual accounting period is the calendar year, from January 1 through December 31. Other companies use a *fiscal year*, which ends on a date other than December 31. The year-end date is usually the low point in business activity for the year. Retailers are a notable example. For instance, **Walmart** and **JCPenney** use a fiscal year that ends on January 31 because their business activity low point comes about a month after the holidays.

The Revenue Recognition Principle

The **revenue recognition principle** tells accountants

- *when* to record revenue—that is, when to make a journal entry for a revenue.
- the *amount* of revenue to record.

"Recording" something in accounting means making an entry in the journal. That is where the process starts.

When to Record Revenue

The revenue recognition principle says to record revenue when it has been earned—but not before. Revenue has been earned when the business has delivered a good or service to the customer. The company has done everything required by the sale agreement—that is, the earnings process is complete. **For you, revenue is earned when you go to work every day—not on the date you get paid.**

Exhibit 3-2 shows two situations that provide guidance on when to record revenue for Smart Touch. The first situation illustrates when *not* to record revenue—because the client merely states his plan. Situation 2 illustrates when revenue *should* be recorded—after the e-learning agency has performed a service for the client.

EXHIBIT 3-2 | **Recording Revenue: The Revenue Recognition Principle**

The Amount of Revenue to Record

Record revenue for the actual value of the item or service transferred to the customer. Suppose that in order to obtain a new client, Sheena Bright performs e-learning services for the cut-rate price of $100. Ordinarily, the business would have charged $200 for this service. How much revenue should the business record? Sheena Bright did not charge $200, so that is not the amount of revenue. Smart Touch charged only $100, so the business records $100 of revenue.

The Matching Principle

The **matching principle** guides accounting for expenses. Recall that expenses—such as salaries, rent, utilities, and advertising—are assets used up and liabilities incurred in order to earn revenue. The matching principle

1. measures all the expenses incurred during the period, and

2. matches the expenses against the revenues of the period.

To match expenses against revenues means to subtract expenses incurred during one month from revenues earned during that same month. The goal is to compute net income or net loss. Exhibit 3-3 illustrates the matching principle.

EXHIBIT 3-3 | **Recording Expenses: The Matching Principle**

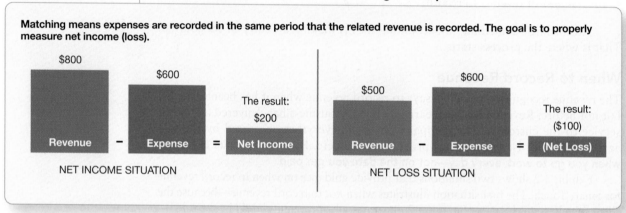

Matching means expenses are recorded in the same period that the related revenue is recorded. The goal is to properly measure net income (loss).

There is a natural link between some expenses and revenues. For example, Smart Touch pays a commission to the employee who sells the e-learning agency's services. Other expenses are not so easy to link to revenues. For example, Smart Touch Learning's monthly rent expense occurs regardless of the revenues earned that month. The matching principle tells us to identify those expenses with a particular period, such as a month or a year when the related revenue occurred. The business will record rent expense each month based on the rental agreement. Smart Touch also pays a monthly salary to its employee.

How does Smart Touch bring its accounts up-to-date for the financial statements? To address this question, accountants use the time-period concept.

The Time-Period Concept

Owners need periodic reports on their businesses. The **time-period concept** requires that information is reported at least annually. Often, companies report more than just annually. To measure income, companies update their accounts at the end of each period, usually monthly.

Let's look at Smart Touch for an example of an accrued expense. On May 31, the business recorded salary expense of $900 that it owed the employee at the end of the month. Smart Touch's accrual entry was as follows:

May 31	Salary expense (E+)	900	
	Salary payable (L+)		900
	Accrued salary expense.		

This entry assigns the salary expense to May because that was the month when the employee worked for the company. Without this entry, $900 of May's salary expense would be reported in the wrong period—June. May's expenses would also be understated, and May's net income would be overstated. The accrual entry also records the liability owed at May 31. Without this entry, total liabilities would be understated. The remainder of the chapter shows how to adjust the accounts and bring the books up-to-date.

Why We Adjust the Accounts

At the end of the period, the accountant prepares the financial statements. The end-of-period process begins with the trial balance, which you learned how to prepare in the previous chapter. Exhibit 3-4 is the trial balance of Smart Touch at May 31, 2013.

3 Explain why adjusting entries are needed

EXHIBIT 3-4 | **Unadjusted Trial Balance**

SMART TOUCH LEARNING Unadjusted Trial Balance May 31, 2013		
Account	Debit	Credit
Cash	$ 4,800	
Accounts receivable	2,200	
Supplies	700	
Prepaid rent	3,000	
Furniture	18,000	
Building	48,000	
Accounts payable		$18,200
Unearned service revenue		600
Notes payable		20,000
Bright, capital		33,200
Bright, drawing	1,000	
Service revenue		7,000
Salary expense	900	
Utilities expense	400	
Total	$79,000	$79,000

This *unadjusted trial balance* lists the revenues and expenses of the e-learning agency for May. But these amounts are incomplete because they omit various revenue and expense transactions. That is why the trial balance is *unadjusted*. Usually, however, we refer to it simply as the trial balance, without the label "unadjusted."

Accrual accounting requires adjusting entries at the end of the period. We must have correct balances for the financial statements. To see why, consider the Supplies account in Exhibit 3-4.

Smart Touch uses supplies during the month. This reduces the supplies on hand (an asset) and creates an expense (supplies expense). It is a waste of time to record supplies expense every time supplies are used. But by the end of the month, enough of the $700 of Supplies on the unadjusted trial balance (Exhibit 3-4) have probably been used that we need to adjust the Supplies account. This is an example of why we need to adjust some accounts at the end of the period.

Adjusting entries assign revenues to the period when they are earned and expenses to the period when they are incurred. Adjusting entries also update the asset and liability accounts. Adjustments are needed to properly measure two things:

1. net income (loss) on the income statement and

2. assets and liabilities on the balance sheet.

This end-of-period process is called *making the adjustments* or *adjusting the books*. Remember the following three facts about adjusting entries:

1. Adjusting entries never involve the Cash account.

2. Adjusting entries either
   a. increase revenue earned (Revenue credit) or
   b. increase an expense (Expense debit).

3. When information is provided about an adjustment to an account and the information is worded as "accrued" an amount for a particular account, you journalize the stated amount to the stated account in your adjusting entry. (This will be explained further in an example later in the chapter.)

Two Categories of Adjusting Entries

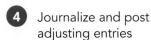

Journalize and post adjusting entries

The two basic categories of adjusting entries are *prepaids* and *accruals*. In a **prepaid** adjustment, the cash payment occurs before an expense is recorded or the cash receipt occurs before the revenue is earned. Prepaids are also called **deferrals** because the recognition of revenue or expense is deferred to a date after the cash is received or paid. **Accrual** adjustments are the opposite. An accrual records an expense before the cash payment or it records the revenue before the cash is received.

Adjusting entries fall into five types:

1. Prepaid expenses (prepaid)

2. Depreciation (prepaid)

3. Accrued expenses (accrual)

4. Accrued revenues (accrual)

5. Unearned revenues (prepaid)

The focus of this chapter is on learning how to account for these five types of adjusting entries.

Prepaid Expenses

Prepaid expenses are advance payments of expenses. **Prepaid expenses are always paid for before they are used up.** For example, **McDonald's**, the restaurant chain, makes prepayments for rent, insurance, and supplies. Prepaid expenses are considered assets rather than expenses. When the prepayment is used up, the used portion of the asset becomes an expense via an adjusting journal entry.

Prepaid Rent

Some landlords require tenants to pay rent in advance. This prepayment creates an asset for the renter. Suppose Smart Touch prepays three months' office rent of $3,000 ($1,000 per month × three months) on May 1, 2013. The entry to record the payment is as follows:

May 1	Prepaid rent ($1,000 × 3) (A+)	3,000	
	Cash (A–)		3,000
	Paid rent in advance.		

After posting, Prepaid rent has a $3,000 debit balance.

ASSETS

Prepaid rent

May 1	3,000

The trial balance at May 31, 2013, lists Prepaid rent with a debit balance of $3,000 (Exhibit 3-4). Throughout May, Prepaid rent maintains this balance. But $3,000 is *not* the amount of Prepaid rent for the balance sheet at May 31. Why?

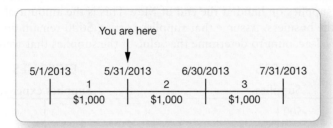

At May 31, Prepaid rent should be decreased for the amount that has been used up. The used-up portion is one month of the three months prepaid, or one-third of the prepayment. Recall that an asset that has expired is an *expense*. The adjusting entry transfers $1,000 ($3,000 × 1/3) from Prepaid rent to Rent expense. The adjusting entry is as follows:

a.	May 31	Rent expense ($3,000 × 1/3) (E+)	1,000	
		Prepaid rent (A–)		1,000
		To record rent expense.		

After posting, Prepaid rent and Rent expense show correct ending balances:

ASSETS				**EXPENSES**			
Prepaid rent				**Rent expense**			
May 1	3,000	May 31	1,000	May 31	1,000		
Bal	2,000			Bal	1,000		

Correct asset amount:		Total accounted for:		Correct expense amount:
$2,000	→	$3,000	←	$1,000

The Prepaid rent is an example of an asset that was overstated prior to posting the adjusting entry. Notice that the ending balance in Prepaid rent is now $2,000. Because Prepaid rent is an asset account for Smart Touch, it should contain only two more months of rent on May 31 (for June and July). $1,000 rent per month times two months equals the $2,000 Prepaid rent balance.

The same analysis applies to the prepayment of three months of insurance. The only difference is in the account titles. Prepaid insurance would be used instead of Prepaid rent, and Insurance expense would be used instead of Rent expense. In a computerized system, the adjusting entry can be programmed to recur automatically each accounting period.

Appendix 3A (located at myaccountinglab.com) shows an alternative treatment of prepaid expenses. The end result on the accounts is the same as illustrated here.

Supplies

Supplies are also accounted for as prepaid expenses. Let's look at an example. On May 2, Sheena Bright paid $500 for office supplies. On May 15, she spent another $200 on office supplies.

The May 31 trial balance, therefore, still lists Supplies with a $700 debit balance, as shown in Exhibit 3-4. But Smart Touch's May 31 balance sheet should *not* report supplies of $700. Why not?

During May, the e-learning agency used supplies to conduct business. The cost of the supplies used becomes *supplies expense*. To measure supplies expense, Bright counts the supplies on hand at the end of May. This is the amount of the asset still owned by the business. Assume that supplies costing $600 remain on May 31. Use the Supplies T-account to determine the value of the supplies that were used:

ASSETS				EXPENSES		
Supplies				**Supplies expense**		
May 2	500					
May 15	200	Supplies Used	???		???	
Bal	600			Bal	???	

So, we can solve for the supplies used as follows:

Beginning Supplies + Supplies Purchased − Supplies Used = Ending Supplies
$0 + (500 + 200) − Supplies Used = $600
Supplies Used = $100

The May 31 adjusting entry updates Supplies and records Supplies expense for May as follows:

b.	May 31	Supplies expense ($700 − $600) (E+)	100	
		Supplies (A−)		100
		To record supplies used.		

After posting the adjusting entry, the May 31 balance of Supplies is correctly reflected as $600 and the Supplies expense is correctly reflected as $100.

ASSETS				EXPENSES		
Supplies				**Supplies expense**		
May 2	500					
May 15	200	May 31	100	May 31	100	
Bal	600			Bal	100	

The Supplies account then enters June with a $600 balance, and the adjustment process is repeated each month. Supplies is another example of an asset that was overstated at $700 on the trial balance prior to posting the adjusting entry. The adjusting entry then left the correct balance of Supplies on May 31 of $600.

Depreciation

Plant assets are long-lived tangible assets used in the operation of a business. Examples include land, buildings, equipment, furniture, and automobiles. As a business uses the assets, their value and usefulness decline. The decline in usefulness of a plant asset is an expense, and accountants systematically spread the asset's cost over its useful life. The allocation of a plant asset's cost to expense is called **depreciation**.

You might pay cash for your car the day you buy it, but it's something you own that will last for years, so depreciation allocates the cost spent on the car over the time you use the car. Land is the exception. We record no depreciation for land, as its value typically does not decline with use.

Similarity to Prepaid Expenses

The concept of accounting for plant assets is the same as for a prepaid expense. The major difference is the length of time it takes for the asset to be used up. Prepaid expenses usually expire within a year, but plant assets remain useful for several years. Let's review an example for Smart Touch. On May 3, Smart Touch purchased furniture for $18,000 and made the following journal entry:

May 3	Furniture (A+)	18,000	
	Cash (A–)		18,000
	Purchased furniture.		

After posting, the Furniture account has an $18,000 balance:

ASSETS

Furniture
May 3 18,000	

Sheena Bright believes the furniture will remain useful for five years and then will be worthless. One way to compute depreciation is to divide the cost of the asset ($18,000) by its expected useful life (five years). So, the depreciation for each month is $300 ($18,000/5 years = $3,600/12 months = $300 per month). Depreciation expense for May is recorded by the following adjusting entry:

c.	May 31	Depreciation expense—furniture (E+)	300	
		Accumulated depreciation—furniture (CA+)		300
		To record depreciation on furniture.		

The Accumulated Depreciation Account

Notice that in the above adjusting entry for depreciation we credited Accumulated depreciation—furniture and NOT the asset account Furniture. Why? We need to keep the original cost of the furniture separate from the recovery (depreciation) of that cost because of the historical cost principle. Managers can then refer to the Furniture account to see how much the asset originally cost. This information may help decide how much to pay for new furniture. The **Accumulated depreciation** account is the sum of all the depreciation recorded for the asset, and that total increases (accumulates) over time.

Accumulated depreciation is a contra asset, which means that it is an asset account with a normal credit balance. **Contra means opposite.** A **contra account** has two main characteristics:

- A contra account is paired with and follows its related account.
- A contra account's normal balance (debit or credit) is the opposite of the balance of the related account.

For example, Accumulated depreciation—furniture is the contra account that follows the Furniture account on the balance sheet. The Furniture account has a debit balance, so Accumulated depreciation, a contra asset, has a credit balance.

A business may have a separate Accumulated depreciation account for each depreciable asset. If Smart Touch has both a Building and a Furniture account, it may have these two accounts: Accumulated depreciation—building, and Accumulated depreciation—furniture. However, small companies often have only one Accumulated depreciation account for all their assets.

After posting the depreciation, the accounts appear as follows:

	ASSETS		EXPENSES
NORMAL ASSET	CONTRA ASSET		

Furniture		Accumulated depreciation—furniture		Depreciation expense—furniture	
May 3 18,000			May 31 300	May 31 300	
Bal 18,000			Bal 300	Bal 300	

Book Value

The balance sheet reports both Furniture and Accumulated depreciation—furniture. Because it is a contra account, Accumulated depreciation—furniture is subtracted from Furniture. The resulting net amount (cost minus accumulated depreciation) of a plant asset is called its **book value**. For Smart Touch's furniture, the book value is as follows:

Book value of plant assets:	
Furniture	$18,000
Less: Accumulated depreciation—furniture	300
Book value of the furniture	$17,700

The book value represents costs invested in the asset that the business has not yet recovered (expensed).

Suppose the e-learning agency also owns a building that cost $48,000, with monthly depreciation of $200. The following adjusting entry would record depreciation for May:

d.	May 31	Depreciation expense—building (E+)		200	
		Accumulated depreciation—building (CA+)			200
		To record depreciation on building.			

The May 31 balance sheet would report plant assets as shown in Exhibit 3-5.

EXHIBIT 3-5 | **Plant Assets on the Balance Sheet of Smart Touch Learning (May 31)**

Plant Assets		
Furniture	$18,000	
Less: Accumulated depreciation—furniture	300	$17,700
Building	$48,000	
Less: Accumulated depreciation—building	200	47,800
Plant assets, net		$65,500

Accrued Expenses

Businesses often incur expenses before paying for them. The term **accrued expense** refers to an expense of this type. **An accrued expense hasn't been paid for yet.** Consider an employee's salary. The salary expense grows as the employee works, so the expense is said to *accrue*. Another accrued expense is interest expense on a note payable. Interest accrues as time passes on the note. An accrued expense always creates a liability.

Companies do not make weekly journal entries to accrue expenses. Instead, they wait until the end of the period. They make an adjusting entry to bring each expense (and the related liability) up-to-date for the financial statements.

Remember that prepaid expenses and accrued expenses are opposites.

> • A *prepaid expense* is paid first and expensed later.
>
> • An *accrued expense* is expensed first and paid later.

Next we'll see how to account for accrued expenses.

Accruing Salary Expense

Suppose Smart Touch pays its employee a monthly salary of $1,800—half on the 15th and half on the first day of the next month. Here is a calendar for May and June with the two paydays circled:

May 2013						
Sunday	Monday	Tuesday	Wednesday	Thursday	Friday	Saturday
Apr 28	29	30	May 1	2	3	4
5	6	7	8	9	10	11
12	13	14	⑮ Pay Day	16	17	18
19	20	21	22	23	24	25
26	27	28	29	30	31	Jun 1 Pay Day

During May, Sheena Bright paid the first half-month salary on Wednesday, May 15, and made this entry:

May 15	Salary expense (E+)	900	
	Cash (A–)		900
	To pay salary.		

After posting, Salary expense shows the following balance:

EXPENSES

Salary expense

May 15	900

The trial balance on May 31 (Exhibit 3-4) includes Salary expense, with a debit balance of $900. This is Smart Touch's salary expense for the first half of May. The second payment of $900 will occur on June 1; however, the expense was incurred in May, so the expense must be recorded in May. On May 31, Smart Touch makes the following adjusting entry:

e.	May 31	Salary expense (E+)	900	
		Salary payable (L+)		900
		To accrue salary expense.		

After posting, both Salary expense and Salary payable are up-to-date:

EXPENSES				LIABILITIES		
Salary expense				**Salary payable**		
May 15	900				May 31	900
May 31	900				Bal	900
Bal	1,800					

Salary expense shows a full month's salary, and Salary payable shows the liability owed at May 31. This is an example of a liability that was understated before the adjusting entry was made. It also is an example of the matching principle: We are recording May's salary expense in May so it will be reported on the same income statement period as May's revenues.

Accruing Interest Expense

Borrowing money creates a liability for a Note payable. If, on May 1, 2013, Smart Touch borrows $20,000 from the bank after signing a one-year note payable, the entry to record the note on May 1, 2013, is as follows:

	May 1	Cash (A+)		20,000	
		Note payable (L+)			20,000
		Borrowed money.			

Interest on this note is payable one year later, on May 1, 2014. On May 31, 2013, the company must make an adjusting entry to record the interest expense that has accrued for the month of May. Assume one month's interest expense on this note is $100. The May 31 adjusting entry to accrue interest expense is as follows:

f.	May 31	Interest expense (E+)		100	
		Interest payable (L+)			100
		To accrue interest expense.			

This is another example of a liability that was understated before the adjusting entry was made. After posting, Interest expense and Interest payable have the following balances:

EXPENSES				LIABILITIES		
Interest expense				**Interest payable**		
May 31	100				May 31	100
Bal	100				Bal	100

Accrued Revenues

As we have just seen, expenses can occur before a company makes a cash payment for them, which creates an accrued expense. Similarly, businesses can earn revenue before they receive the cash. This creates an **accrued revenue**, which is a revenue that has been earned but for which the cash has not yet been collected.

Assume that Smart Touch is hired on May 15 to perform e-learning services for the **University of West Florida**. Under this agreement, Smart Touch will earn $800 monthly. During May, Smart Touch will earn half a month's fee, $400, for work May 16 through May 31. On May 31, Smart Touch makes the following adjusting entry to accrue the revenue earned May 16 through May 31:

g.	May 31	Accounts receivable ($800 × 1/2) (A+)	400	
		Service revenue (R+)		400
		To accrue service revenue.		

The unadjusted trial balance in Exhibit 3-4 shows that Accounts receivable has an unadjusted balance of $2,200. Service revenue's unadjusted balance is $7,000 from the day-to-day May transactions recorded in the general journal. (Detailed entries for May transactions are not shown in the Accounts receivable or Service revenue T-accounts. Only adjusting entries are shown.) The adjusting entry updates both accounts.

	ASSETS			REVENUES	
	Accounts receivable			**Service revenue**	
	2,200				7,000
May 31	400			May 31	400
Bal	2,600			Bal	7,400

Without the adjustment, Smart Touch's financial statements would understate both an asset, Accounts receivable, and a revenue, Service revenue.

Now we turn to the final category of adjusting entries.

Unearned Revenues

Some businesses collect cash from customers in advance of performing work. Receiving cash before earning it creates a liability to perform work in the future called **unearned revenue**. The company owes a product or a service to the customer, or it owes the customer his or her money back. Only after completing the job will the business *earn* the revenue. Because of this delay, unearned revenue is also called **deferred revenue. Unearned revenue occurs when the company is paid cash before it does all the work to earn it.**

Suppose, for example, a law firm engages Smart Touch to provide e-learning services, agreeing to pay $600 in advance monthly, beginning immediately. Sheena Bright collects the first amount on May 21. Smart Touch records the cash receipt and a liability as follows:

	May 21	Cash (A+)	600	
		Unearned service revenue (L+)		600
		Collected revenue in advance.		

Now the liability account, Unearned service revenue, shows that Smart Touch owes $600 in services.

LIABILITIES
Unearned service revenue

	May 21	600

Unearned service revenue is a liability because the company owes a service to a client in the future.

The May 31 trial balance (Exhibit 3-4) lists Unearned service revenue with a $600 credit balance. During the last 10 days of the month—May 21 through May 31—Smart Touch will *earn* approximately one-third (10 days divided by

Connect To: Ethics

Many unethical schemes that are enacted to artificially inflate earnings or change accounts on the balance sheet are accomplished through adjusting journal entries. Remember that every journal entry will have some document that substantiates why the entry is being made, such as an invoice that supports how many supplies were purchased or a contract with a customer that supports what services are to be provided. "Supporting documents" for unethical entries often don't exist or are modified copies of real documents.

30 days) of the $600, or $200. Therefore, Smart Touch makes the following adjusting entry to record earning $200 of revenue:

h.	May 31	Unearned service revenue ($600 × 1/3) (L–)	200	
		Service revenue (R+)		200
		To record service revenue that was collected in advance.		

This adjusting entry shifts $200 from liability to revenue. Service revenue increases by $200, and Unearned service revenue decreases by $200. Now both accounts are up-to-date at May 31:

LIABILITIES

Unearned service revenue

May 31	200	May 21	600
		Bal	400

REVENUES

Service revenue

			7,000
		May 31	400
		May 31	200
		Bal	7,600

This is an example of a liability that was overstated prior to posting the adjusting journal entry. Remember this key point:

An unearned revenue is a liability account, not a revenue account.

An unearned revenue to one company is a prepaid expense to the company that paid in advance. Consider the law firm in the preceding example. The law firm had prepaid e-learning expense—an asset. Smart Touch had unearned service revenue—a liability.

Exhibit 3-6 summarizes the timing of prepaid and accrual adjustments. Study the exhibit from left to right, and then move down. Appendix 3A (available at myaccountinglab.com) shows an alternative treatment for unearned revenues.

Key Takeaway

Summary of the Adjusting Process

The adjusting process has two purposes:

1. to capture all transactions that should be reported in the period shown on the *income statement*. Every adjustment affects a *revenue* or an *expense*. AND

2. to update the *balance sheet* so that all accounts are properly valued. Every adjustment affects an *asset* or a *liability* (but NEVER the Cash account).

EXHIBIT 3-6 | **Prepaid and Accrual Adjustments**

ORIGINAL ENTRY	ADJUSTING ENTRY

PREPAIDS—Cash receipt or Cash payment occurs first.

	ORIGINAL ENTRY			ADJUSTING ENTRY		
Prepaid Expenses	Prepaid rent (A+)	XXX		Rent expense (E+)	XXX	
	Cash (A–)		XXX	Prepaid rent (A–)		XXX
	Pay for rent in advance and record an asset first.			*Adjust for rent used later.*		
Depreciation	Furniture (A+)	XXX		Depreciation expense—furniture (E+)	XXX	
	Cash (A–)		XXX	Accumulated depreciation—furniture (CA+)		XXX
	Pay for furniture in advance and record an asset first.			*Adjust for depreciation (use) of asset later.*		
Unearned Revenues	Cash (A+)	XXX		Unearned service revenue (L–)	XXX	
	Unearned service revenue (L+)		XXX	Service revenue (R+)		XXX
	Receive cash in advance and record a liability first.			*Adjust for revenue earned later.*		

ACCRUALS—Cash receipt or payment occurs later.

	ORIGINAL ENTRY			ADJUSTING ENTRY		
Accrued Expenses	Salary expense (E+)	XXX		Salary payable (L–)	XXX	
	Salary payable (L+)		XXX	Cash (A–)		XXX
	Accrue for expense incurred first.			*Pay cash later.*		
Accrued Revenues	Accounts receivable (A+)	XXX		Cash (A+)	XXX	
	Service revenue (R+)		XXX	Accounts receivable (A–)		XXX
	Accrue for revenue earned first.			*Receive cash later.*		

Source: The authors thank Darrel Davis and Alfonso Oddo for suggesting this exhibit.

Exhibit 3-7 on the following page summarizes the adjusting entries of Smart Touch at May 31. The adjustments are keyed by letter.

- Panel A gives the data for each adjustment.
- Panel B shows the adjusting entries.
- Panel C shows the account balances after posting.

Stop & Think...

Look at the eight adjusting entries in Exhibit 3-7 on the next page. Notice that only the last two adjusting entries, (g) and (h), increased revenues. Six of the eight adjusting entries increased expenses. So, when in doubt about an adjustment, most likely it will be an adjusting entry that increases (debits) an expense account. You can refer to the examples in the text and in the exhibit to confirm your adjusting entry.

EXHIBIT 3-7

Journalizing and Posting the Adjusting Entries of Smart Touch Learning, Inc.

PANEL A—Information for Adjustments at May 31, 2013

a. Prepaid rent expired, $1,000.
b. Supplies used, $100.
c. Depreciation on furniture, $300.
d. Depreciation on building, $200.
e. Accrued salary expense, $900.

f. Accrued interest on note, $100.
g. Accrued service revenue, $400.
h. Service revenue that was collected in advance and now has been earned, $200.

PANEL B—Adjusting Entries

	2013	Accounts and Explanations	Debit	Credit
a.	May 31	Rent expense (E+)	1,000	
		Prepaid rent (A–)		1,000
		To record rent expense.		
b.	May 31	Supplies expense (E+)	100	
		Supplies (A–)		100
		To record supplies used.		
c.	May 31	Depreciation expense—furniture (E+)	300	
		Accumulated depreciation—furniture (CA+)		300
		To record depreciation on furniture.		
d.	May 31	Depreciation expense—building (E+)	200	
		Accumulated depreciation—building (CA+)		200
		To record depreciation on building.		
e.	May 31	Salary expense (E+)	900	
		Salary payable (L+)		900
		To accrue salary expense.		
f.	May 31	Interest expense (E+)	100	
		Interest payable (L+)		100
		To accrue interest expense.		
g.	May 31	Accounts receivable (A+)	400	
		Service revenue (R+)		400
		To accrue service revenue.		
h.	May 31	Unearned service revenue (L–)	200	
		Service revenue (R+)		200
		To record service revenue that was collected in advance.		

EXHIBIT 3-7 | **Continued**

PANEL C—Ledger Accounts in T-account form

ASSETS	LIABILITIES	OWNER'S EQUITY	EXPENSES

ASSETS

Cash

Bal 4,800	

Accounts receivable

2,200	
(g) 400	
Bal 2,600	

Supplies

700	(b) 100
Bal 600	

Prepaid rent

3,000	(a) 1,000
Bal 2,000	

Furniture

Bal 18,000	

Building

Bal 48,000	

Accumulated depreciation—furniture

	(c) 300
	Bal 300

Accumulated depreciation—building

	(d) 200

LIABILITIES

Accounts payable

	Bal 18,200

Salary payable

	(e) 900
	Bal 900

Interest payable

	(f) 100
	Bal 100

Unearned service revenue

(h) 200	600
	Bal 400

Notes payable

	Bal 20,000

OWNER'S EQUITY

Bright, capital

	Bal 33,200

Bright, drawing

Bal 1,000	

REVENUE

Service revenue

	7,000
	(g) 400
	(h) 200
	Bal 7,600

EXPENSES

Rent expense

(a) 1,000	
Bal 1,000	

Salary expense

900	
(e) 900	
Bal 1,800	

Supplies expense

(b) 100	
Bal 100	

Depreciation expense—furniture

(c) 300	
Bal 300	

Depreciation expense—building

(d) 200	
Bal 200	

Interest expense

(f) 100	
Bal 100	

Utilities expense

Bal 400	

The Adjusted Trial Balance

This chapter began with the *unadjusted* trial balance (Exhibit 3-4). After the adjustments, the accounts appear as shown in Exhibit 3-7, Panel C. A useful step in preparing the financial statements is to list the accounts, along with their adjusted balances, on an **adjusted trial balance**. Exhibit 3-8 shows how to prepare the adjusted trial balance.

 5 Explain the purpose of and prepare an adjusted trial balance

EXHIBIT 3-8 | **Preparation of Adjusted Trial Balance**

	Trial Balance		Adjustments		Adjusted Trial Balance		
SMART TOUCH LEARNING Preparation of Adjusted Trial Balance May 31, 2013							
	Debit	Credit	Debit	Credit	Debit	Credit	
Cash	$ 4,800				$ 4,800		
Accounts receivable	2,200		(g) $ 400		2,600		
Supplies	700			(b) $ 100	600		
Prepaid rent	3,000			(a) 1,000	2,000		
Furniture	18,000				18,000		
Building	48,000				48,000		
Accumulated depreciation—furniture				(c) 300		$ 300	Balance Sheet *(Exhibit 3-11)*
Accumulated depreciation—building				(d) 200		200	
Accounts payable		$18,200				18,200	
Salary payable				(e) 900		900	
Interest payable				(f) 100		100	
Unearned service revenue		600	(h) 200			400	
Notes payable		20,000				20,000	
Bright, capital		33,200				33,200	Statement of Owner's Equity *(Exhibit 3-10)*
Bright, drawing	1,000				1,000		
Service revenue		7,000		(g) 400		7,600	
				(h) 200			
Rent expense			(a) 1,000		1,000		
Salary expense	900		(e) 900		1,800		Income Statement *(Exhibit 3-9)*
Supplies expense			(b) 100		100		
Depreciation expense—furniture			(c) 300		300		
Depreciation expense—building			(d) 200		200		
Interest expense			(f) 100		100		
Utilities expense	400				400		
	$79,000	$79,000	$3,200	$3,200	$80,900	$80,900	

Exhibit 3-8 is also a partial *worksheet*. We will cover the complete worksheet in Chapter 4. For now, simply note how clear this format is. The account titles and the trial balance are copied directly from the trial balance in Exhibit 3-4. The two Adjustments columns show the adjusting journal entries from Exhibit 3-7.

The Adjusted Trial Balance columns give the adjusted account balances. Each amount in these columns is computed by combining the trial balance amounts plus or minus the adjustments. For example, Accounts receivable starts with a debit balance of $2,200. Adding the $400 debit from adjustment (g) gives Accounts receivable an adjusted balance of $2,600. Supplies begins with a debit balance of $700. After the $100 credit adjustment, Supplies has a $600 balance. More than one entry may affect a single account. For example, Service revenue has two adjustments, (g) and (h), and both increased the Service revenue balance.

The Financial Statements

The May 2013 financial statements of Smart Touch are prepared from the adjusted trial balance in Exhibit 3-8. In the right margin of the exhibit, we see how the accounts are distributed to the financial statements. As always,

 6 Prepare the financial statements from the adjusted trial balance

- the income statement (Exhibit 3-9) reports revenues and expenses.
- the statement of owner's equity (Exhibit 3-10) shows why capital changed during the period.
- the balance sheet (Exhibit 3-11) reports assets, liabilities, and owner's equity.

Preparing the Statements

The financial statements should be prepared in the following order:

1. Income statement—to determine net income or net loss. The income statement should list expenses in descending order by amount, as shown in Exhibit 3-9.

2. Statement of owner's equity—which needs net income or net loss from the income statement for us to compute ending capital.

3. Balance sheet—which needs the amount of ending capital to achieve its balancing feature.

As you will recall from Chapter 1, all financial statements include the following elements:

Heading

- Name of the entity—such as Smart Touch Learning
- Title of the statement—income statement, statement of owner's equity, or balance sheet
- Date, or period, covered by the statement—May 31, 2013, or Month Ended May 31, 2013

Body of the statement

Relationships Among the Financial Statements

The arrows in Exhibits 3-9, 3-10, and 3-11 on the following page show how the financial statements relate to each other.

1. Net income from the income statement increases capital. A net loss decreases capital.

2. Ending capital from the statement of owner's equity goes to the balance sheet and makes total liabilities plus owner's equity equal total assets, satisfying the accounting equation.

To solidify your understanding of these relationships, trace Net income from the income statement to the statement of owner's equity. Then trace ending Bright, capital to the balance sheet. Note that these are the three main financial statements you learned about in the first chapter. They are always prepared in the order described previously: income statement, then statement of owner's equity, then balance sheet. Recall that we purposely omitted the statement of cash flows, which is covered in detail in a later chapter.

Key Takeaway

The financial statements must be prepared in order: income statement first, statement of owner's equity second, and balance sheet third. It is important for accountants to prepare accurate and complete financial statements because other people rely on the data to make decisions.

EXHIBIT 3-9

Preparing the Income Statement from the Adjusted Trial Balance

SMART TOUCH LEARNING Income Statement Month Ended May 31, 2013		
Revenue:		
Service revenue		$7,600
Expenses:		
Salary expense	$1,800	
Rent expense	1,000	
Utilities expense	400	
Depreciation expense—furniture	300	
Depreciation expense—building	200	
Interest expense	100	
Supplies expense	100	
Total expenses		3,900
Net income		$3,700

EXHIBIT 3-10

Preparing the Statement of Owner's Equity from the Adjusted Trial Balance

SMART TOUCH LEARNING Statement of Owner's Equity Month Ended May 31, 2013	
Bright, capital, May 1, 2013	$33,200
Net income	3,700
	36,900
Drawing	(1,000)
Bright, capital, May 31, 2013	$35,900

EXHIBIT 3-11

Preparing the Balance Sheet from the Adjusted Trial Balance

SMART TOUCH LEARNING Balance Sheet May 31, 2013					
Assets			**Liabilities**		
Cash		$ 4,800	Accounts payable		$18,200
Accounts receivable		2,600	Salary payable		900
Supplies		600	Interest payable		100
Prepaid rent		2,000	Unearned service revenue		400
Furniture	$18,000		Notes payable		20,000
Less: Accumulated depreciation— furniture	300	17,700	Total liabilities		39,600
Building	48,000				
Less: Accumulated depreciation— building	200	47,800	**Owner's Equity** Bright, capital		35,900
			Total liabilities		
Total assets		$75,500	and owner's equity		$75,500

Ethical Issues in Accrual Accounting

Business transactions or events can pose ethical challenges. Accountants must be honest in their work. Complete and accurate information can help people make wise decisions. Think about the following example.

Smart Touch has done well as a business and wishes to open another office. Assume the company needs to borrow $30,000.

Suppose the e-learning agency understated expenses in order to inflate net income on the income statement. A banker could be tricked into lending the company money. Then if the business could not repay the loan, the bank would lose—all because the banker relied on incorrect accounting information.

Accrual accounting provides opportunities for unethical behavior. For example, a dishonest businessperson could easily overlook depreciation expense at the end of the year. Failing to record depreciation would overstate net income and paint a more favorable picture of the company's financial position.

Decision Guidelines 3-1

ACCOUNTING BASIS AND THE ADJUSTING PROCESS

Take the role of Sheena Bright of Smart Touch Learning. Assume it is now the end of the first year, and Bright wants to know where the business stands financially. The Decision Guidelines give a map of the accounting process to help Bright manage the business.

Decision	Guidelines
• Which basis of accounting better measures business income?	*Accrual basis*, because it provides more complete reports of operating performance and financial position
• How does a company measure revenues?	Revenue recognition principle—Record revenues only after they are earned
• How does a company measure expenses?	Matching principle—Record expenses in the same time period that the related revenues are recorded to more accurately measure net income (loss)
• Where does a company start with the measurement of income at the end of the period?	Preparation of the adjusted trial balance
• How does a company update the accounts for the financial statements?	*Adjusting entries* at the end of the period
• What are the categories of adjusting entries?	Prepaid expenses Accrued revenues Depreciation Unearned revenues Accrued expenses

• How do the adjusting entries differ from other journal entries?	1. Adjusting entries are made only at the end of the period.
	2. Adjusting entries never affect the Cash account.
	3. All adjusting entries debit or credit
	   • at least one *income statement* account (a revenue or an expense), and
	   • at least one *balance sheet* account (an asset or a liability).

• Where are the accounts with their adjusted balances summarized?	*Adjusted trial balance*, which is used to prepare the financial statements

Summary Problem 3-1

The trial balance of Super Employment Services pertains to December 31, 2014, the end of Super's annual accounting period. Data needed for the adjusting entries include the following:

a. Supplies on hand at year-end, $200.
b. Depreciation on furniture, $2,000.
c. Depreciation on building, $1,000.
d. Salaries owed but not yet paid, $500.
e. Accrued service revenue, $1,300.
f. $3,000 of the unearned service revenue has been earned.

Requirements

1. Open the ledger accounts in T-account form with their unadjusted balances as shown for Accounts receivable:

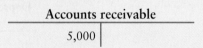

Accounts receivable
5,000 |

2. Journalize Super's adjusting entries at December 31, 2014. Key entries by letter, as in Exhibit 3-7.
3. Post the adjusting entries.
4. Write the trial balance on a worksheet, enter the adjusting entries, and prepare an adjusted trial balance, as shown in Exhibit 3-8.
5. Prepare the income statement, the statement of owner's equity, and the balance sheet. Draw arrows linking the three financial statements.

		SUPER EMPLOYMENT SERVICES Trial Balance December 31, 2014		
			Balance	
		Account Title	Debit	Credit
		Cash	$ 6,000	
		Accounts receivable	5,000	
		Supplies	1,000	
		Furniture	10,000	
		Accumulated depreciation—furniture		$ 4,000
		Building	50,000	
		Accumulated depreciation—building		30,000
		Accounts payable		2,000
		Salary payable		
		Unearned service revenue		8,000
		Mudge, capital		12,000
		Mudge, drawing	25,000	
		Service revenue		60,000
		Salary expense	16,000	
		Supplies expense		
		Depreciation expense—furniture		
		Depreciation expense—building		
		Advertising expense	3,000	
		Total	$116,000	$116,000

Solution

Requirements 1 and 3

ASSETS

Cash

Bal	6,000		

Accounts receivable

	5,000		
(e)	1,300		
Bal	6,300		

Supplies

	1,000	(a)	800
Bal	200		

Furniture

Bal	10,000		

Accumulated depreciation—furniture

			4,000
		(b)	2,000
		Bal	6,000

Building

Bal	50,000		

Accumulated depreciation—building

			30,000
		(c)	1,000
		Bal	31,000

LIABILITIES

Accounts payable

		Bal	2,000

Salary payable

		(d)	500
		Bal	500

Unearned service revenue

(f)	3,000		8,000
		Bal	5,000

OWNER'S EQUITY

Mudge, capital

		Bal	12,000

Mudge, drawing

Bal	25,000		

REVENUE

Service revenue

			60,000
		(e)	1,300
		(f)	3,000
		Bal	64,300

EXPENSES

Salary expense

	16,000		
(d)	500		
Bal	16,500		

Supplies expense

(a)	800		
Bal	800		

Depreciation expense—furniture

(b)	2,000		
Bal	2,000		

Depreciation expense—building

(c)	1,000		
Bal	1,000		

Advertising expense

Bal	3,000		

Requirement 2

	2014	Accounts and Explanations	Debit	Credit
a.	Dec 31	Supplies expense ($1,000 – $200) (E+)	800	
		Supplies (A–)		800
		To record supplies used.		
b.	Dec 31	Depreciation expense—furniture (E+)	2,000	
		Accumulated depreciation—furniture (CA+)		2,000
		To record depreciation expense on furniture.		
c.	Dec 31	Depreciation expense—building (E+)	1,000	
		Accumulated depreciation—building (CA+)		1,000
		To record depreciation expense on building.		
d.	Dec 31	Salary expense (E+)	500	
		Salary payable (L+)		500
		To accrue salary expense.		
e.	Dec 31	Accounts receivable (A+)	1,300	
		Service revenue (R+)		1,300
		To accrue service revenue.		
f.	Dec 31	Unearned service revenue (L–)	3,000	
		Service revenue (R+)		3,000
		To record service revenue earned that was collected in advance.		

Requirement 4

	SUPER EMPLOYMENT SERVICES Preparation of Adjusted Trial Balance December 31, 2014						
	Trial Balance		Adjustments		Adjusted Trial Balance	
Account Title	Debit	Credit	Debit	Credit	Debit	Credit
Cash	$ 6,000				$ 6,000	
Accounts receivable	5,000		(e) $1,300		6,300	
Supplies	1,000			(a) $ 800	200	
Furniture	10,000				10,000	
Accumulated depreciation—furniture		$ 4,000		(b) 2,000		$ 6,000
Building	50,000				50,000	
Accumulated depreciation—building		30,000		(c) 1,000		31,000
Accounts payable		2,000				2,000
Salary payable				(d) 500		500
Unearned service revenue		8,000	(f) 3,000			5,000
Mudge, capital		12,000				12,000
Mudge, drawing	25,000				25,000	
Service revenue		60,000		(e) 1,300 (f) 3,000		64,300
Salary expense	16,000		(d) 500		16,500	
Supplies expense			(a) 800		800	
Depreciation expense—furniture			(b) 2,000		2,000	
Depreciation expense—building			(c) 1,000		1,000	
Advertising expense	3,000				3,000	
Total	$116,000	$116,000	$8,600	$8,600	$120,800	$120,800

Requirement 5

SUPER EMPLOYMENT SERVICES
Income Statement
Year Ended December 31, 2014

Revenue:		
Service revenue		$64,300
Expenses:		
Salary expense	$16,500	
Advertising expense	3,000	
Depreciation expense—furniture	2,000	
Depreciation expense—building	1,000	
Supplies expense	800	
Total expenses		23,300
Net income		$41,000

SUPER EMPLOYMENT SERVICES
Statement of Owner's Equity
Year Ended December 31, 2014

Mudge, capital, January 1, 2014	$ 12,000
Net income	41,000
	53,000
Drawing	(25,000)
Mudge, capital, December 31, 2014	$ 28,000

SUPER EMPLOYMENT SERVICES
Balance Sheet
December 31, 2014

Assets			Liabilities	
Cash		$ 6,000	Accounts payable	$ 2,000
Accounts receivable		6,300	Salary payable	500
Supplies		200	Unearned service revenue	5,000
Furniture	$10,000		Total liabilities	7,500
Less: Accumulated depreciation— furniture	6,000	4,000		
Building	50,000			
Less: Accumulated depreciation—			**Owner's Equity**	
			Mudge, capital	28,000
building	31,000	19,000	Total liabilities and	
Total assets		$35,500	owner's equity	$35,500

Chapter 3: Demo Doc

Preparation of Adjusting Entries, Adjusted Trial Balance, and Financial Statements

To make sure you understand this material, work through the following demonstration "demo doc" with detailed comments to help you see the concept within the framework of a worked-through problem.

Cloud Break Consulting has the following information at June 30, 2014:

	CLOUD BREAK CONSULTING Unadjusted Trial Balance June 30, 2014		
	Account Title	**Debit**	**Credit**
	Cash	$131,000	
	Accounts receivable	104,000	
	Supplies	4,000	
	Prepaid rent	27,000	
	Land	45,000	
	Building	300,000	
	Accumulated depreciation—building		$155,000
	Accounts payable		159,000
	Unearned service revenue		40,000
	Moe, capital		102,000
	Moe, drawing	7,000	
	Service revenue		450,000
	Salary expense	255,000	
	Rent expense	25,000	
	Miscellaneous expense	8,000	
	Total	$906,000	$906,000

Cloud Break must make adjusting entries for the following items:

a. Supplies on hand at year-end, $1,000.

b. Nine months of rent ($27,000) were paid in advance on April 1, 2014.

c. Depreciation expense on the building of $12,000 has not been recorded.

d. Employees work Monday through Friday. The weekly payroll is $5,000 and is paid every Friday. June 30, 2014, is a Monday.

e. Service revenue of $15,000 must be accrued.

f. Cloud Break received $40,000 in advance for consulting services to be provided evenly from January 1, 2014, through August 31, 2014. None of the revenue from this client has been recorded.

Requirements

1. Open the ledger T-accounts with their unadjusted balances.

2. Journalize Cloud Break's adjusting entries at June 30, 2014, and post the entries to the T-accounts.

3. Total all of the T-accounts in the ledger.

4. Write the trial balance on a worksheet, enter the adjusting entries, and prepare an adjusted trial balance.

5. Prepare the income statement, the statement of owner's equity, and the balance sheet. Draw arrows linking the three financial statements.

Chapter 3: Demo Doc Solution

Requirement 1

Open the ledger T-accounts with their unadjusted balances.

Part 1	Part 2	Part 3	Part 4	Part 5	Demo Doc Complete

Remember from Chapter 2 that opening a T-account means drawing a blank account that looks like a capital "T" and putting the account title across the top. To help find the accounts later, they are usually organized into assets, liabilities, owner's equity, revenue, and expenses (in that order). If the account has a starting balance, it *must* be put in on the correct side.

Remember that debits are always on the left side of the T-account and credits are always on the right side. This is true for *every* account.

The correct side to enter each account's starting balance is the side of *increase* in the account. This is because we expect all accounts to have a *positive* balance (that is, more increases than decreases).

For assets, an increase is a debit, so we would expect all assets to have a debit balance. For liabilities and owner's equity, an increase is a credit, so we would expect all of these accounts to have a credit balance. By the same reasoning, we expect revenues to have credit balances, and expenses and dividends to have debit balances.

The unadjusted balances to be posted into the T-accounts are simply the amounts from the starting trial balance.

ASSETS

Cash
Bal 131,000

Accounts receivable
Bal 104,000

Supplies
Bal 4,000

Prepaid rent
Bal 27,000

Land
Bal 45,000

Building
Bal 300,000

Accumulated depreciation—building
Bal 155,000

LIABILITIES

Accounts payable
Bal 159,000

Unearned service revenue
Bal 40,000

OWNER'S EQUITY

Moe, capital
Bal 102,000

Moe, drawing
Bal 7,000

REVENUE

Service revenue
Bal 450,000

EXPENSES

Salary expense
Bal 255,000

Rent expense
Bal 25,000

Miscellaneous expense
Bal 8,000

Requirement 2

Journalize Cloud Break's adjusting entries at June 30, 2014, and post the entries to the T-accounts.

Part 1	**Part 2**	Part 3	Part 4	Part 5	Demo Doc Complete

a. **Supplies on hand at year-end, $1,000.**

On June 30, 2014, the unadjusted balance in supplies was $4,000. However, a count shows that only $1,000 of supplies actually remain on hand. The supplies that are no longer there have been used. When assets/benefits are used, an expense is created.

Cloud Break will need to make an adjusting journal entry to reflect the correct amount of supplies on the balance sheet.

Look at the Supplies T-account:

Supplies

Bal	4,000	X
Bal	1,000	

The supplies have decreased because they have been used up. The amount of the decrease is **X**.

$$X = \$4,000 - \$1,000$$
$$X = \$3,000$$

Three thousand dollars of Supplies expense must be recorded to show the value of supplies that have been used.

a.	Jun 30	Supplies expense ($4,000 – $1,000) (E+)		3,000	
		Supplies (A–)			3,000
		To record supplies used.			

After posting, Supplies and Supplies expense hold correct ending balances:

ASSETS				**EXPENSES**		
Supplies				**Supplies expense**		
Bal	4,000	a.	3,000	a.	3,000	
Bal	1,000			Bal	3,000	

b. **Nine months of rent ($27,000) were paid in advance on April 1, 2014.**

When something is prepaid, such as rent or insurance, it is a *future* benefit (an asset) because the business is now entitled to receive goods or services for the terms of the prepayment. Once those goods or services are received (in this case, once Cloud Break has occupied the building being rented), this becomes a *past* benefit, and therefore an expense.

Cloud Break prepaid $27,000 for nine months of rent on April 1. This means that Cloud Break pays $27,000/9 = $3,000 a month for rent. At June 30, Prepaid rent is adjusted for the amount of the asset that has been used up. Because Cloud Break has occupied the building being rented for three months, three months of the prepayment have been used. The amount of rent used is 3 × $3,000 = $9,000. Because that portion of the past benefit (asset) has expired, it becomes an expense (in this case, the adjusting entry transfers $9,000 from Prepaid rent to Rent expense).

This means that Rent expense must be increased (a debit) and Prepaid rent (an asset) must be decreased (a credit).

b.	Jun 30	Rent expense (E+)	9,000	
		Prepaid rent (A–)		9,000
		To record rent expense.		

ASSETS			EXPENSES		
Prepaid rent			**Rent expense**		
Bal	27,000		Bal	25,000	
		b. 9,000	b.	9,000	
Bal	18,000		Bal	34,000	

c. **Depreciation expense on the building of $12,000 has not been recorded.**

The cost principle compels us to keep the original cost of a plant asset in that asset account. Because there is $300,000 in the Building account, we know that this is the original cost of the building. We are told in the question that depreciation expense per year is $12,000.

The journal entry to record depreciation expense is *always* the same. It is only the *number* (dollar amount) in the entry that changes. There is always an increase to Depreciation expense (a debit) and an increase to the contra-asset account of Accumulated depreciation (a credit).

c.	Jun 30	Depreciation expense—building (E+)	12,000	
		Accumulated depreciation—building (CA+)		12,000
		To record depreciation on building.		

ASSETS				EXPENSES	
NORMAL ASSET		**CONTRA ASSET**			
Building		**Accumulated depreciation— building**		**Depreciation expense— building**	
Bal	300,000				
Bal	300,000	Bal	155,000		
		c.	12,000	c.	12,000
		Bal	167,000	Bal	12,000

The book value of the building is its original cost (the amount in the Building T-account) minus the accumulated depreciation on the building.

Book value of plant assets:	
Building	$ 300,000
Less: Accumulated depreciation	167,000
Book value of the building	$ 133,000

d. **Employees work Monday through Friday. The weekly payroll is $5,000 and is paid every Friday. June 30, 2014, is a Monday.**

Salary is an accrued expense. That is, it is a liability that incurs from an *expense* that has not been paid yet. Most employers pay their employees *after* the work has been done, so the work is a past benefit. So this expense (Salary expense, in this case) grows until payday.

Cloud Break's employees are paid $5,000 for five days of work. That means they earn $5,000/5 = $1,000 per day. By the end of the day on Monday, June 30, they have earned $1,000/day × 1 day = $1,000 of salary.

If the salaries have not been paid, then they are pay*able* (or in other words, they are *owed*) and must be recorded as some kind of payable account. You might be tempted to use accounts payable, but this account is usually reserved for *bills* received. But employees do not typically bill employers for their paychecks, they simply expect to be paid. The appropriate payable account for salaries is Salary payable.

There is an increase to the Salary expense (a debit) and an increase to the liability Salary payable (a credit) of $1,000.

d.	Jun 30	Salary expense (E+)	1,000	
		Salary payable (L+)		1,000
		To accrue salary expense.		

EXPENSES		LIABILITIES	
Salary expense		**Salary payable**	
Bal 255,000		d. 1,000	
d. 1,000			
Bal 256,000		Bal 1,000	

e. **Service revenue of $15,000 must be accrued.**

Accrued revenue is another way of saying "Accounts receivable" (or receipt in the future). When *accrued* revenue is recorded, it means that Accounts receivable is also recorded (that is, customers received goods or services from the business, but the business has not yet received the cash). The business is entitled to these receivables because the revenue has been earned.

Service revenue must be increased by $15,000 (a credit) and the Accounts receivable asset must be increased by $15,000 (a debit).

e.	Jun 30	Accounts receivable (A+)	15,000	
		Service revenue (R+)		15,000
		To accrue service revenue.		

ASSETS		REVENUES	
Accounts receivable		**Service revenue**	
104,000			450,000
e. 15,000		e.	15,000
Bal 119,000		Bal	465,000

f. **Cloud Break received $40,000 in advance for consulting services to be provided evenly from January 1, 2014, through August 31, 2014. None of the revenue from this client has been recorded.**

Cloud Break received cash in advance for work it had not yet performed for the client. By accepting the cash, Cloud Break also accepted the obligation to perform that work (or provide a refund if it did not). In accounting, an obligation is a liability. We call this liability "Unearned revenue" because it *will* be revenue (after the work is performed) but it is not revenue *yet*.

The $40,000 paid in advance is still in the unearned revenue account. However, some of the revenue has been earned as of June 30. Six months of the earnings period have passed (January 1 through June 30), so six months worth of the revenue has been earned.

The entire revenue earnings period is eight months (January 1 through August 31), so the revenue earned per month is $40,000/8 = $5,000. The six months of revenue that have been earned are 6 × $5,000 = $30,000.

So Unearned service revenue, a liability, must be decreased by $30,000 (a debit). Because that portion of the revenue is now earned, it can be recorded as Service revenue. Therefore, Service revenue is increased by $30,000 (a credit).

f.	Jun 30	Unearned service revenue (L–)	30,000	
		Service revenue (R+)		30,000
		To record the earning of service revenue collected in advance.		

The $30,000 has been shifted from "unearned revenue" to "earned" revenue.

LIABILITIES		REVENUES	
Unearned service revenue		**Service revenue**	

		Bal	40,000	Bal	450,000	
f.	30,000			e.	15,000	
				f.	30,000	
		Bal	10,000			
				Bal	495,000	

Now we will summarize all of the adjusting journal entries:

Ref.	Date	Accounts and Explanation	Debit	Credit
	2014			
a.	Jun 30	Supplies expense ($4,000 – $1,000) (E+)	3,000	
		Supplies (A–)		3,000
		To record supplies used.		
b.	30	Rent expense (E+)	9,000	
		Prepaid rent (A–)		9,000
		To record rent expense.		
c.	30	Depreciation expense—building (E+)	12,000	
		Accumulated depreciation—building (CA+)		12,000
		To record depreciation on building.		
d.	30	Salary expense (E+)	1,000	
		Salary payable (L+)		1,000
		To accrue salary expense.		
e.	30	Accounts receivable (A+)	15,000	
		Service revenue (R+)		15,000
		To accrue service revenue.		
f.	30	Unearned service revenue (L–)	30,000	
		Service revenue (R+)		30,000
		To record the earning of service revenue collected in advance.		

Requirement 3

Total all of the T-accounts in the ledger.

| Part 1 | Part 2 | **Part 3** | Part 4 | Part 5 | Demo Doc Complete |

After posting all of these entries and totaling all of the T-accounts, we have the following:

ASSETS

Cash

Bal 131,000	

Accounts receivable

Bal 104,000	
e. 15,000	
Bal 119,000	

Supplies

Bal 4,000	a. 3,000
Bal 1,000	

Prepaid rent

Bal 27,000	
	b. 9,000
Bal 18,000	

Land

Bal 45,000	

Building

Bal 300,000	

Accumulated depreciation—building

	155,000
	c. 12,000
	Bal 167,000

LIABILITIES

Accounts payable

	Bal 159,000

Salary payable

	d. 1,000
	Bal 1,000

Unearned service revenue

f. 30,000	40,000
	Bal 10,000

OWNER'S EQUITY

Moe, capital

	Bal 102,000

Moe, drawing

Bal 7,000	

REVENUE

Service revenue

	450,000
	e. 15,000
	f. 30,000
	Bal 495,000

EXPENSES

Salary expense

255,000	
d. 1,000	
Bal 256,000	

Supplies expense

a. 3,000	
Bal 3,000	

Rent expense

25,000	
b. 9,000	
Bal 34,000	

Depreciation expense—building

c. 12,000	
Bal 12,000	

Miscellaneous expense

Bal 8,000	

Requirement 4

Write the trial balance on a worksheet, enter the adjusting entries, and prepare an adjusted trial balance.

| Part 1 | Part 2 | Part 3 | **Part 4** | Part 5 | Demo Doc Complete |

First, we must copy the account titles and trial balance amounts directly from the trial balance (shown at the beginning of the question) into the Trial Balance section (columns). Place the amounts in the correct debit or credit column.

Next, we must record the adjusting journal entries in the correct debit or credit columns of the Adjustments section (columns) of the worksheet. Each entry should include a letter identifying the adjusting entry recorded.

Now calculate the new balances for each account by adding the debits and credits across. These should be the same balances that you calculated for the T-accounts in Requirement 3. Place these amounts into the Adjusted Trial Balance columns to give the adjusted account balances.

		Trial Balance		Adjustments		Adjusted Trial Balance	
CLOUD BREAK CONSULTING Preparation of Adjusted Trial Balance June 30, 2014							
Account Title		**Debit**	**Credit**	**Debit**	**Credit**	**Debit**	**Credit**
Cash		$131,000				$131,000	
Accounts receivable		104,000		(e) $15,000		119,000	
Supplies		4,000			(a) $ 3,000	1,000	
Prepaid rent		27,000			(b) 9,000	18,000	
Land		45,000				45,000	
Building		300,000				300,000	
Accumulated depreciation—building			$155,000		(c) 12,000		$167,000
Accounts payable			159,000				159,000
Salary payable					(d) 1,000		1,000
Unearned service revenue			40,000	(f) 30,000			10,000
Moe, capital			102,000				102,000
Moe, drawing		7,000				7,000	
Service revenue			450,000		(e) 15,000		
					(f) 30,000		495,000
Salary expense		255,000		(d) 1,000		256,000	
Supplies expense				(a) 3,000		3,000	
Rent expense		25,000		(b) 9,000		34,000	
Depreciation expense—building				(c) 12,000		12,000	
Miscellaneous expense		8,000				8,000	
Totals		$906,000	$906,000	$70,000	$70,000	$934,000	$934,000

Be sure that the debit and credit columns equal before moving on to the next section.

Requirement 5

Prepare the income statement, the statement of owner's equity, and the balance sheet. Draw arrows linking the three financial statements.

Part 1	Part 2	Part 3	Part 4	**Part 5**	Demo Doc Complete

The arrows in these statements show how the financial statements relate to each other. Follow the arrow that takes the ending balance of Moe, capital to the balance sheet.

1. Net income from the income statements is reported as an increase to Moe, capital on the statement of owner's equity. A net loss is recorded as a decrease to Moe, capital.

2. Ending Moe, capital from the statement of owner's equity is transferred to the balance sheet. The ending Moe, capital is the final balancing amount for the balance sheet.

CLOUD BREAK CONSULTING
Income Statement
Year Ended June 30, 2014

Revenue:		
Service revenue		$495,000
Expenses:		
Salary expense	$256,000	
Rent expense	34,000	
Depreciation expense—building	12,000	
Supplies expense	3,000	
Miscellaneous expense*	8,000	
Total expenses		313,000
Net income		$182,000

*Miscellaneous expense is always listed last, even if it is larger than other expenses.

CLOUD BREAK CONSULTING
Statement of Owner's Equity
Year Ended June 30, 2014

Moe, capital, July 1, 2013	$102,000
Net income	182,000
	284,000
Drawing	(7,000)
Moe, capital, June 30, 2014	$277,000

CLOUD BREAK CONSULTING
Balance Sheet
June 30, 2014

Assets			Liabilities	
Cash		$131,000	Accounts payable	$159,000
Accounts receivable		119,000	Salary payable	1,000
Supplies		1,000	Unearned service revenue	10,000
Prepaid rent		18,000	Total liabilities	$170,000
Land		45,000		
Building	$300,000			
Less: Accumulated			**Owner's Equity**	
depreciation	167,000	133,000	Moe, capital	277,000
			Total liabilities and	
Total assets		$447,000	owner's equity	$447,000

Part 1	Part 2	Part 3	Part 4	Part 5	**Demo Doc Complete**

Review *The Adjusting Process*

● Accounting Vocabulary

Accrual (p. 136)
The cash payment occurs after an expense is recorded or the cash is received after the revenue is earned.

Accrual-Basis Accounting (p. 131)
Accounting that records revenues when earned and expenses when incurred.

Accrued Expense (p. 140)
An expense that the business has incurred but not yet paid.

Accrued Revenue (p. 142)
A revenue that has been earned but for which the cash has not been collected yet.

Accumulated Depreciation (p. 139)
The sum of all depreciation expense recorded to date for an asset.

Adjusted Trial Balance (p. 147)
A list of all the accounts with their adjusted balances.

Adjusting Entries (p. 135)
Entries made at the end of the period to assign revenues to the period in which they are earned and expenses to the period in which they are incurred. Adjusting entries help measure the period's income and bring the related asset and liability accounts to correct balances for the financial statements.

Book Value (of a plant asset) (p. 140)
The asset's cost minus accumulated depreciation.

Cash-Basis Accounting (p. 131)
Accounting that records transactions only when cash is received or paid.

Contra Account (p. 139)
An account that always has a companion account and whose normal balance is opposite that of the companion account.

Deferral (p. 136)
The cash payment occurs before an expense is recorded or the cash is received before the revenue is earned. Also called a **prepaid**.

Deferred Revenue (p. 143)
A liability created when a business collects cash from customers in advance of doing work. Also called **unearned revenue**.

Depreciation (p. 138)
The allocation of a plant asset's cost over its useful life.

Liquidation (p. 132)
The process of going out of business by selling all the assets, paying all the liabilities, and giving any leftover cash to the owner(s).

Matching Principle (p. 134)
Guide to accounting for expenses. Identify all expenses incurred during the period, measure the expenses, and match them against the revenues earned during that same time period.

Plant Assets (p. 138)
Long-lived tangible assets—such as land, buildings, and equipment—used in the operation of a business.

Prepaid (p. 136)
The cash payment occurs before an expense is recorded or the cash is received before the revenue is earned. Also called a **deferral**.

Revenue Recognition Principle (p. 133)
The basis for recording revenues: tells accountants when to record revenue and the amount of revenue to record.

Time-Period Concept (p. 134)
Ensures that information is reported at least annually.

Unearned Revenue (p. 143)
A liability created when a business collects cash from customers in advance of doing work. Also called **deferred revenue**.

● Destination: Student Success

Student Success Tips

The following are hints on some common trouble areas for students in this chapter:

- Recall the difference between accrual accounting and cash-basis accounting: Accrual accounting records revenues and expenses when they are EARNED or INCURRED. Cash-basis accounting records revenues and expenses when cash is RECEIVED or PAID.

- Remember that debits = credits for every adjusting journal entry.

- The amount of the adjusting journal entry will ALWAYS affect either a revenue account (credit) or an expense account (debit). The adjustment amount in the adjusting journal entry will equal the additional EARNINGS for a revenue account or the additional INCURRENCE of EXPENSE for an expense account.

- Adjusting entries NEVER affect the Cash account.

- Trial balance amount +/– the Adjustment amount = the Adjusted trial balance amount. Use the rules of debit/credit to determine whether the adjustment is a + or –.

Getting Help

If there's a learning objective from the chapter you aren't confident about, try using one or more of the following resources:

- Practice additional exercises or problems at the end of Chapter 3 that cover the specific learning objective that is challenging you.

- Watch the white board videos for Chapter 3 located at myaccountinglab.com under the Chapter Resources button.

- Review the Chapter 3 Demo Doc located on page 157 of the textbook.

- Go to myaccountinglab.com and select the Study Plan button. Choose Chapter 3 and work the questions covering that specific learning objective until you've mastered it.

- Work the Chapter 3 pre/post tests in myaccountinglab.com.

- Visit the learning resource center on your campus for tutoring.

● Quick Check

1. What are the distinctive features of accrual accounting and cash-basis accounting?
   a. Accrual accounting records only receivables, payables, and depreciation.
   b. Accrual accounting is superior because it provides more information.
   c. Cash-basis accounting records all transactions.
   d. All the above are true.

2. The revenue recognition principle says
   a. divide time into annual periods to measure revenue properly.
   b. record revenue only after you have earned it.
   c. measure revenues and expenses in order to compute net income.
   d. record revenue after you receive cash.

3. Adjusting the accounts is the process of
   a. subtracting expenses from revenues to measure net income.
   b. recording transactions as they occur during the period.
   c. updating the accounts at the end of the period.
   d. zeroing out account balances to prepare for the next period.

4. Which types of adjusting entries are natural opposites?
   a. Net income and net loss
   b. Expenses and revenues
   c. Prepaids and accruals
   d. Prepaids and depreciation

5. Assume that the weekly payroll of In the Woods Camping Supplies is $300. December 31, end of the year, falls on Tuesday, and In the Woods will pay its employee on Friday for the full week. What adjusting entry will In the Woods make on Tuesday, December 31? (Use five days as a full work week.)

   a.

Salary expense	120	
Salary payable		120

   b.

Salary payable	300	
Salary expense		300

   c.

Salary expense	180	
Cash		180

   d. No adjustment is needed because the company will pay the payroll on Friday.

6. Get Fit Now gains a client who prepays $540 for a package of six physical training sessions. Get Fit Now collects the $540 in advance and will provide the training later. After four training sessions, what should Get Fit Now report on its income statement?
   a. Service revenue of $360
   b. Service revenue of $540
   c. Unearned service revenue of $360
   d. Cash of $180

7. Assume you prepay Get Fit Now for a package of six physical training sessions. Which type of account should you have in your records?
   a. Accrued revenue
   b. Accrued expense
   c. Prepaid expense
   d. Unearned revenue

8. Unearned revenue is always
   a. owner's equity because you collected the cash in advance.
   b. revenue.
   c. a liability.
   d. an asset.

9. The adjusted trial balance shows
   a. amounts that may be out of balance.
   b. amounts ready for the financial statements.
   c. assets, liabilities, and owner's equity only.
   d. revenues and expenses only.

10. Accounting data flow from the
    a. income statement to the statement of owner's equity.
    b. statement of owner's equity to the balance sheet.
    c. balance sheet to the income statement.
    d. Both a and b are correct.

Answers are given after Apply Your Knowledge (p. 197).

Assess Your Progress

● Short Exercises

MyAccountingLab

S3-1 ❶ **Comparing accrual and cash-basis accounting [5 min]**
Suppose you work summers house-sitting for people while they are away on vacation. Some of your customers pay you immediately after you finish a job. Some customers ask you to send them a bill. It is now June 30 and you have collected $900 from cash-paying customers. Your remaining customers owe you $1,300.

Requirements

1. How much service revenue would you have under the
   a. cash basis?
   b. accrual basis?

2. Which method of accounting provides more information about your house-sitting business?

S3-2 ❶ **Comparing accrual and cash-basis accounting [5 min]**
The Johnny Flowers Law Firm uses a client database. Suppose Johnny Flowers paid $2,900 for a computer.

Requirements

1. Describe how the business should account for the $2,900 expenditure under
   a. the cash basis.
   b. the accrual basis.

2. State why the accrual basis is more realistic for this situation.

S3-3 ❷ **Applying the revenue recognition principle [5 min]**
Northwest Magazine sells subscriptions for $36 for 12 issues. The company collects cash in advance and then mails out the magazines to subscribers each month.

Requirement

1. Apply the revenue recognition principle to determine
   a. when *Northwest Magazine* should record revenue for this situation.
   b. the amount of revenue *Northwest Magazine* should record for three issues.

S3-4 ❷ **Applying the matching principle [5 min]**
Suppose on January 1 you prepaid apartment rent of $5,700 for the full year.

Requirement

1. At July 31, what are your two account balances for this situation?

S3-5   ❸ **Identifying types of adjusting entries [5 min]**
A select list of transactions for Anuradha's Goals follows:

Apr	1	Paid six months of rent, $4,800.
	10	Received $1,200 from customer for six-month service contract that began April 1.
	15	Purchased computer for $1,000.
	18	Purchased $300 of office supplies on account.
	30	Work performed but not yet billed to customer, $500.
	30	Employees earned $600 in salary that will be paid May 2.

Requirement

1. For each transaction, identify what type of adjusting entry would be needed.

S3-6   ❹ **Journalizing adjusting entries [5 min]**
On April 1 your company prepaid six months of rent, $4,800.

Requirements

1. Prepare the journal entry for the April 1 payment.
2. Prepare the adjusting entry required at April 30.
3. Post to the two accounts involved and show their balances at April 30.

S3-7   ❹ **Posting adjusting entries [5 min]**
On May 1 your company paid cash of $54,000 for computers that are expected to remain useful for three years. At the end of three years, the value of the computers is expected to be zero, so depreciation is $18,000 per year.

Requirements

1. Post the purchase of May 1 and the depreciation on May 31 to T-accounts for the following accounts: Computer equipment, Accumulated depreciation—computer equipment, and Depreciation expense—computer equipment. Show their balances at May 31. (Assume that the journal entries have been completed.)
2. What is the computer equipment's book value on May 31?

S3-8   ❹ **Accruing interest expense and posting to T-accounts [10 min]**
Thompson Travel borrowed $68,000 on October 1, 2012, by signing a one-year note payable to Metro One Bank. Thompson's interest expense for the remainder of the fiscal year (October through December) is $884.

Requirements

1. Make the adjusting entry to accrue interest expense at December 31, 2012. Date the entry and include its explanation.
2. Post to the T-accounts of the two accounts affected by the adjustment.

S3-9   ❹ **Accounting for unearned revenues [5–10 min]**
Metro Magazine collects cash from subscribers in advance and then mails the magazines to subscribers over a one-year period.

Requirements

1. Journalize the entry to record the original receipt of $170,000 cash.
2. Journalize the adjusting entry that *Metro Magazine* makes to record the earning of $12,000 of subscription revenue that was collected in advance. Include an explanation for the entry.

S3-10 ⑤ **Preparing an adjusted trial balance [10 min]**

Famous Cut Hair Stylists has begun the preparation of its adjusted trial balance as follows:

	Trial Balance		Adjustments		Adjusted Trial Balance	
FAMOUS CUT HAIR STYLISTS Preparation of Adjusted Trial Balance December 31, 2012						
Account	Debit	Credit	Debit	Credit	Debit	Credit
Cash	$ 800					
Supplies	900					
Equipment	19,100					
Accumulated depreciation		$ 1,000				
Accounts payable		200				
Interest payable						
Note payable		2,500				
Fabio, capital		7,400				
Service revenue		14,800				
Rent expense	4,500					
Supplies expense						
Depreciation expense						
Interest expense	600					
Total	$25,900	$25,900				

Year-end data include the following:

    a. Supplies on hand, $300.
    b. Depreciation, $1,000.
    c. Accrued interest expense, $600.

Requirement

    1. Complete Famous Cut's adjusted trial balance. Key each adjustment by letter.

Note: Short Exercises 3-11 and 3-12 should be used only after completing Short Exercise 3-10.

S3-11 ⑥ **Preparing an income statement [10–15 min]**

Refer to the data in Short Exercise 3-10.

Requirement

    1. Compute Famous Cut's net income for the year ended December 31, 2012.

S3-12 ⑥ **Preparing a balance sheet [5 min]**

Refer to the data in Short Exercise 3-10.

Requirement

    1. Compute Famous Cut's total assets at December 31, 2012.

● Exercises

E3-13 ❶❷ **Comparing accrual and cash-basis accounting, and applying the revenue recognition principle [5–10 min]**

Momentous Occasions is a photography business that shoots videos at college parties. The freshman class pays $100 in advance on March 3 just to guarantee your services for its party to be held April 2. The sophomore class promises a minimum of $280 for filming its formal dance, and actually pays cash of $410 on February 28 at the party.

Requirement

1. Answer the following questions about the correct way to account for revenue under the accrual basis.
   a. Considering the $100 paid by the freshman class, on what date was revenue earned? Did the earnings occur on the same date cash was received?
   b. Considering the $410 paid by the sophomore class, on what date was revenue earned? Did the earnings occur on the same date cash was received?

E3-14 ❶❹❻ **Comparing accrual and cash-basis accounting, preparing adjusting entries, and preparing income statements [15-25 min]**

Sweet Catering completed the following selected transactions during May, 2012:

May	1	Prepaid rent for three months, $1,500.
	5	Paid electricity expenses, $400.
	9	Received cash for meals served to customers, $2,600.
	14	Paid cash for kitchen equipment, $2,400.
	23	Served a banquet on account, $3,000.
	31	Made the adjusting entry for rent (from May 1).
	31	Accrued salary expense, $1,400.
	31	Recorded depreciation for May on kitchen equipment, $40.

Requirements

1. Prepare journal entries for each transaction.
2. Using the journal entries as a guide, show whether each transaction would be handled as a revenue or an expense using both the cash and accrual basis by completing the following table.

	Amount of Revenue (Expense) for May	
Date	Cash-Basis Amount of Revenue (Expense)	Accrual-Basis Amount of Revenue (Expense)

3. After completing the table, calculate the amount of net income or net loss for Sweet Catering under the accrual and cash basis for May.
4. Considering your results from Requirement 3, which method gives the best picture of the true earnings of Sweet Catering? Why?

E3-15 ❷ **Applying the time-period concept [5–10 min]**

Consider the following situations:

a. Business receives $2,000 on January 1 for 10-month service contract for the period January 1 through October 31.
b. Total salary for all employees is $3,000 per month. Employees are paid on the 1st and 15th of the month.
c. Work performed but not yet billed to customers for the month is $900.
d. The company pays interest on its $10,000, 6% note payable of $50 on the first day of each month.

Requirement

1. Assume the company records adjusting entries monthly. Calculate the amount of each adjustment needed, if any, as of February 28.

E3-16 **2 4** **Applying accounting principles and preparing journal entries for prepaid rent [10–15 min]**

Consider the facts presented in the following table for Tropical View:

	Situation			
	A	**B**	**C**	**D**
Beginning Prepaid rent..................................	$ 1,200	$ 900	$ 200	$ 700
Payments for Prepaid rent during the year.......................................	1,400	b	1,800	d
Total amount to account for	2,600	1,400	?	?
Subtract: Ending Prepaid rent.......................	600	500	c	400
Rent expense...	$ a	$ 900	$1,900	$1,100

Requirements

1. Complete the table by filling in the missing values.
2. Prepare one journal entry for each situation, if required, for the missing amounts (a–d). Label the journal entries by letter.

E3-17 **3 4** **Categorizing and journalizing adjusting entries [10–15 min]**

Consider the following independent situations at December 31, 2014.

a. On August 1, a business collected $3,300 rent in advance, debiting Cash and crediting Unearned rent revenue. The tenant was paying one year's rent in advance. At December 31, the business must account for the amount of rent it has earned.

b. Salary expense is $1,700 per day—Monday through Friday—and the business pays employees each Friday. This year December 31 falls on a Thursday.

c. The unadjusted balance of the Supplies account is $3,500. Supplies on hand total $1,700.

d. Equipment depreciation was $300.

e. On March 1, when the business prepaid $600 for a two-year insurance policy, the business debited Prepaid insurance and credited Cash.

Requirements

1. For each situation, indicate which category of adjustment is described.
2. Journalize the adjusting entry needed on December 31 for each situation. Use the letters to label the journal entries.

E3-18 **4** **Recording adjustments in T-accounts and calculating ending balances [10–20 min]**

The accounting records of Maura Grayson Architect include the following selected, unadjusted balances at March 31: Accounts receivable, $1,400; Supplies, $1,100; Salary payable, $0; Unearned service revenue, $600; Service revenue, $4,200; Salary expense, $1,300; Supplies expense, $0. The data developed for the March 31 adjusting entries are as follows:

a. Service revenue accrued, $900.
b. Unearned service revenue that has been earned, $200.
c. Supplies on hand, $600.
d. Salary owed to employee, $400.

Requirement

1. Open a T-account for each account and record the adjustments directly in the T-accounts, keying each adjustment by letter. Show each account's adjusted balance. Journal entries are not required.

E3-19 ④⑤ **Preparing adjusting entries and preparing an adjusted trial balance [10–15 min]**

First Class Maids Company, the cleaning service, started the preparation of its adjusted trial balance as follows:

	Trial Balance	
FIRST CLASS MAIDS COMPANY Preparation of Adjusted Trial Balance December 31, 2012		
Account	**Debit**	**Credit**
Cash	$ 700	
Supplies	3,000	
Prepaid insurance	800	
Equipment	29,000	
Accumulated depreciation		$ 7,000
Accounts payable		2,800
Salary payable		
Unearned service revenue		500
Molly, capital		7,200
Molly, drawing	3,000	
Service revenue		25,000
Salary expense	6,000	
Supplies expense		
Depreciation expense		
Insurance expense		
Total	$42,500	$42,500

During the 12 months ended December 31, 2012, First Class Maids

a. used supplies of $1,800.
b. used up prepaid insurance of $620.
c. used up $460 of the equipment through depreciation.
d. accrued salary expense of $310 that First Class Maids hasn't paid yet.
e. earned $360 of the unearned service revenue.

Requirement

1. Prepare an adjusted trial balance. Use Exhibit 3-8 as a guide. Key each adjustment by letter.

Note: Exercise 3-20 should be used only in conjunction with Exercise 3-19.

E3-20 ④⑤ **Using an adjusted trial balance to prepare adjusting journal entries [10 min]**

Refer to the data in Exercise 3-19.

Requirement

1. Journalize the five adjustments, all dated December 31, 2012. Explanations are not required.

E3-21   ④⑤ **Using the adjusted trial balance to determine the adjusting journal entries [10–15 min]**

The adjusted trial balance of Jobs–4–U Employment Service follows but is incomplete.

	Trial Balance		Adjusted Trial Balance	
JOBS–4–U EMPLOYMENT SERVICE				
Adjusted Trial Balance				
April 30, 2012				
Account	**Debit**	**Credit**	**Debit**	**Credit**
Cash	$ 900		$ 900	
Accounts receivable	4,100		5,600	
Supplies	1,000		500	
Equipment	32,500		32,500	
Accumulated depreciation		$14,400		$15,400
Salary payable				1,200
Yost, capital		23,300		23,300
Yost, drawing	4,800		4,800	
Service revenue		9,100		10,600
Salary expense	2,500		3,700	
Rent expense	1,000		1,000	
Depreciation expense			1,000	
Supplies expense			500	
Total	$46,800	$46,800	$50,500	$50,500

Requirements

1. Calculate and enter the adjustment amounts directly in the missing Adjustments columns.

2. Prepare each adjusting journal entry calculated in Requirement 1. Date the entries and include explanations.

E3-22   ④⑥ **Journalizing adjusting entries and analyzing their effect on the income statement [5–10 min]**

The following data at January 31, 2013 is given for EBM.

a. Depreciation, $500.
b. Prepaid rent expired, $600.
c. Interest expense accrued, $300.
d. Employee salaries owed for Monday through Thursday of a five-day workweek; weekly payroll, $13,000.
e. Unearned service revenue earned, $1,300.

Requirements

1. Journalize the adjusting entries needed on January 31, 2013.

2. Suppose the adjustments made in Requirement 1 were not made. Compute the overall overstatement or understatement of net income as a result of the omission of these adjustments.

E3-23 **④ ⑥** **Using adjusting journal entries and computing financial statement amounts [10–20 min]**

The adjusted trial balances of Superior International at August 31, 2012, and August 31, 2011, include the following amounts:

	2012	2011
Supplies	$ 2,400	$ 1,200
Salary payable	2,500	4,100
Unearned service revenue	12,100	17,100

Analysis of the accounts at August 31, 2012, reveals the following transactions for the fiscal year ending in 2012:

Cash payments for supplies	$ 6,100
Cash payments for salaries	47,300
Cash receipts in advance for service revenue	83,200

Requirement

1. Compute the amount of Supplies expense, Salary expense, and Service revenue to report on the Superior International income statement for 2012.

Note: Exercise 3-24 should be used only in conjunction with Exercise 3-19.

E3-24 **⑤ ⑥** **Using an adjusted trial balance to prepare financial statements [10 min]**

Refer to the data in Exercise 3-19.

Requirements

1. Compute First Class Maids Company's net income for the period ended December 31, 2012.
2. Compute First Class Maids Company's total assets at December 31, 2012.

Note: Exercise 3-25 should be used only after completing Exercise 3-21.

E3-25 **⑥** **Preparing the financial statements [20 min]**

Refer to the adjusted trial balance in Exercise 3-21 for the month ended April 30, 2012.

Requirements

1. Prepare the income statement.
2. Prepare the statement of owner's equity.
3. Prepare the balance sheet.

E3-26 **6** **Preparing the income statement [15 min]**

The accountant for Reva Stewart, CPA, has posted adjusting entries (a) through (e) to the accounts at December 31, 2012. Selected balance sheet accounts and all the revenues and expenses of the entity follow in T-account form.

Accounts receivable			Supplies	
22,700		1,200	(a)	600
(e) 800				

Acc. depr.—equipment			Acc. depr.—building	
	5,000			30,000
(b)	1,900		(c)	5,000

Salary payable			Service revenue	
(d)	900			105,700
			(e)	800

Salary expense			Supplies expense	
28,200		(a)	600	
(d) 900				

Depreciation expense—equip.		Depreciation expense—bldg.	
(b)	1,900	(c)	5,000

Requirements

1. Prepare the income statement of Reva Stewart, CPA, for the year ended December 31, 2012.

2. Were 2012 operations successful?

E3-27 **6** **Preparing the statement of owner's equity [10-15 min]**

Rolling Hill Interiors began the year with Hill, capital of $20,000. On July 12, Dana Hill, the owner, invested $14,000 cash. The income statement for the year ended December 31, 2012, reported net income of $63,000. During this fiscal year, Hill withdrew cash of $6,000 each month.

Requirement

1. Prepare Rolling Hill Interiors' statement of owner's equity for the year ended December 31, 2012.

● Problems (Group A)

P3-28A ❶ **Comparing accrual and cash-basis accounting [15–25 min]**

Schaad's Stews completed the following transactions during June, 2012:

Jun	1	Prepaid rent for June through September, $3,600.
	2	Purchased computer for cash, $900.
	3	Performed catering services on account, $2,300.
	5	Paid Internet service provider invoice, $100.
	6	Catered wedding event for customer and received cash, $1,500.
	8	Purchased $150 of supplies on account.
	10	Collected $1,200 on account.
	14	Paid account payable from June 8.
	15	Paid salary expense, $1,200.
	30	Recorded adjusting entry for rent (see June 1).
	30	Recorded $25 depreciation on computer.
	30	There are $40 of supplies still on hand.

Requirement

1. Show whether each transaction would be handled as a revenue or an expense, using both the cash and accrual basis, by completing the following table.

	Amount of Revenue (Expense) for June	
Date	Cash-Basis Amount of Revenue (Expense)	Accrual-Basis Amount of Revenue (Expense)
Jun 1		

P3-29A ❷ **Applying the revenue principle [10–20 min]**

Crum's Cookies uses the accrual method of accounting and properly records transactions on the date they occur. Descriptions of customer transactions follow:

a. Received $3,000 cash from customer for six months of service beginning April 1, 2012.

b. Catered event for customer on April 28. Customer paid Crum's invoice of $600 on May 10.

c. Scheduled catering event to be held June 3. Customer paid Crum's a $500 deposit on May 25.

d. Catered customer's wedding on May 3. Customer paid Crum's an $800 deposit on April 15 and the balance due of $1,000 on May 3.

e. The company provided catering to a local church's annual celebration service on May 15. The church paid the $800 fee to Crum's on the same day.

f. The company provides food to the local homeless shelter two Saturdays each month. The cost of each event to the shelter is $280. The shelter paid Crum $1,120 on May 25 for April and May's events.

g. On April 1, Crum's entered into an annual service contract with an oil company to cater the customer's monthly staff events. The contract's total amount was $4,000, but Crum's offered a 2.5% discount since the customer paid the entire year in advance at the signing of the contract. The first event was held in April.

h. Crum's signed contract for $1,000 on May 5 to cater X-treme sports events to be held June 15, June 27, October 1, and November 15.

Requirement

1. Calculate the amount of revenue earned during May, 2012 for Crum's Cookies for each transaction.

P3-30A ③ **Explain why an adjusting entry is needed and calculate the amount of the adjustment [15–25 min]**

Descriptions of transactions and how they were recorded follow for October, 2012 for Ausley Acoustics.

a. Received $1,500 cash from customer for three months of service beginning October 1, 2012, and ending December 31, 2012. The company recorded a $1,500 debit to Cash and a $1,500 credit to Unearned service revenue.

b. Employees are paid $1,000 every Friday for the five-day work week. October 31, 2012, is on Wednesday.

c. The company pays $240 on October 1 for their six-month auto insurance policy. The company recorded a $240 debit to Prepaid insurance and a $240 credit to Cash.

d. The company purchased office furniture for $6,300 on January 2, 2012. The company recorded a $6,300 debit to Office furniture and a $6,300 credit to Accounts payable. Annual depreciation for the furniture is $900.

e. The company began October with $50 of supplies on hand. On October 10, the company purchased supplies on account of $100. The company recorded a $100 debit to Supplies and a $100 credit to Accounts payable. The company used $120 of supplies during October.

f. The company received its electric bill on October 30 for $125 but did not pay it until November 10. On November 10, it recorded a $125 debit to Utilities expense and a $125 credit to Cash.

g. The company paid November's rent on October 30 of $800. On October 30, the company recorded an $800 debit to Rent expense and an $800 credit to Cash.

Requirement

1. Indicate if an adjusting entry is needed for each item on October 31 and why the entry is needed (i.e., an asset or liability account is over/understated). Indicate which specific account on the balance sheet is misstated. Finally, indicate the correct balance that should appear in the balance sheet account after the adjustment is made. Use the following table guide. Item a is completed as an example:

Item	Adjustment needed?	Asset/ Liability	Over-/ Understated?	Balance sheet account	Correct balance on October 31
a.	Yes	Liability	Overstated	Unearned service revenue	$1,000

P3-31A ① ④ ⑥ **Comparing accrual and cash-basis accounting, preparing adjusting entries, and preparing income statements [15–25 min]**

Charlotte's Golf School completed the following transactions during March, 2012:

Mar	1	Prepaid insurance for March through May, $600.
	4	Performed services (gave golf lessons) on account, $2,500.
	5	Purchased equipment on account, $1,600.
	8	Paid property tax expense, $100.
	11	Purchased office equipment for cash, $1,500.
	19	Performed services and received cash, $900.
	24	Collected $400 on account.
	26	Paid account payable from March 5.
	29	Paid salary expense, $1,000.
	31	Recorded adjusting entry for March insurance expense (see March 1).
	31	Debited unearned revenue and credited revenue in an adjusting entry, $1,200.

Requirements

1. Prepare journal entries for each transaction.

2. Using the journal entries as a guide, show whether each transaction would be handled as a revenue or an expense, using both the cash and accrual basis, by completing the following table.

	Amount of Revenue (Expense) for March	
Date	Cash-Basis Amount of Revenue (Expense)	Accrual-Basis Amount of Revenue (Expense)
Mar 1		

3. After completing the table, calculate the amount of net income or net loss for the company under the accrual and cash basis for March.

4. Considering your results from Requirement 3, which method gives the best picture of the true earnings of Charlotte's Golf School? Why?

P3-32A ④ **Journalizing adjusting entries [15–25 min]**
Laughter Landscaping has the following independent cases at the end of the year on December 31, 2014.

a. Each Friday, Laughter pays employees for the current week's work. The amount of the weekly payroll is $7,000 for a five-day workweek. This year December 31 falls on a Wednesday.

b. Details of Prepaid insurance are shown in the account:

Prepaid insurance

Jan 1	$4,500	

Laughter prepays a full year's insurance each year on January 1. Record insurance expense for the year ended December 31.

c. The beginning balance of Supplies was $4,000. During the year, Laughter purchased supplies for $5,200, and at December 31 the supplies on hand total $2,400.

d. Laughter designed a landscape plan, and the client paid Laughter $7,000 at the start of the project. Laughter recorded this amount as Unearned service revenue. The job will take several months to complete, and Laughter estimates that the company has earned 60% of the total revenue during the current year.

e. Depreciation for the current year includes Equipment, $3,700; and Trucks, $1,300. Make a compound entry.

Requirement

1. Journalize the adjusting entry needed on December 31, 2014, for each of the previous items affecting Laughter Landscaping.

P3-33A ❹ **Analyzing and journalizing adjustments [15–20 min]**

Galant Theater Production Company's unadjusted and adjusted trial balances at December 31, 2012, follow.

	Trial Balance		Adjusted Trial Balance	
GALANT THEATER PRODUCTION COMPANY				
Adjusted Trial Balance				
December 31, 2012				
Account	**Debit**	**Credit**	**Debit**	**Credit**
Cash	$ 3,900		$ 3,900	
Accounts receivable	6,100		6,900	
Supplies	1,700		300	
Prepaid insurance	2,700		2,100	
Equipment	25,000		25,000	
Accumulated depreciation		$ 8,800		$ 13,200
Accounts payable		4,000		4,000
Salary payable				300
Galant, capital		20,300		20,300
Galant, drawing	30,500		30,500	
Service revenue		71,000		71,800
Depreciation expense			4,400	
Supplies expense			1,400	
Utilities expense	4,700		4,700	
Salary expense	29,500		29,800	
Insurance expense			600	
Total	$ 104,100	$ 104,100	$ 109,600	$ 109,600

Requirement

1. Journalize the adjusting entries that account for the differences between the two trial balances.

P3-34A ④⑤ **Journalizing and posting adjustments to the T-accounts and preparing an adjusted trial balance [45–60 min]**

The trial balance of Arlington Air Purification System at December 31, 2012, and the data needed for the month-end adjustments follow.

Account	Debit	Credit
ARLINGTON AIR PURIFICATION SYSTEM		
Trial Balance		
December 31, 2012		
Cash	$ 7,700	
Accounts receivable	19,200	
Prepaid rent	2,400	
Supplies	1,300	
Equipment	19,900	
Accumulated depreciation		$ 4,300
Accounts payable		3,600
Salary payable		
Unearned service revenue		2,600
Able, capital		39,500
Able, drawing	9,500	
Service revenue		15,400
Salary expense	3,500	
Rent expense		
Depreciation expense		
Advertising expense	1,900	
Supplies expense		
Total	$ 65,400	$ 65,400

Adjustment data at December 31 follow:

a. Unearned service revenue still unearned, $1,100.
b. Prepaid rent still in force, $500.
c. Supplies used during the month, $600.
d. Depreciation for the month, $900.
e. Accrued advertising expense, $900. (Credit Accounts payable)
f. Accrued salary expense, $1,100.

Requirements

1. Journalize the adjusting entries.
2. The unadjusted balances have been entered for you in the general ledger accounts. Post the adjusting entries to the ledger accounts.
3. Prepare the adjusted trial balance.
4. How will Arlington Air Purification System use the adjusted trial balance?

P3-35A ④⑤⑥ **Preparing and posting adjusting journal entries; preparing an adjusted trial balance and financial statements [45–60 min]**

The trial balance of Lexington Inn Company at December 31, 2012, and the data needed for the month-end adjustments follow.

LEXINGTON INN COMPANY		
Trial Balance		
December 31, 2012		
Account	Debit	Credit
Cash	$ 12,100	
Accounts receivable	14,300	
Prepaid insurance	2,300	
Supplies	1,100	
Building	411,000	
Accumulated depreciation		$312,500
Accounts payable		1,950
Salary payable		
Unearned service revenue		2,400
Calvasina, capital		114,740
Calvasina, drawing	2,860	
Service revenue		15,600
Salary expense	2,700	
Insurance expense		
Depreciation expense		
Advertising expense	830	
Supplies expense		
Total	$447,190	$447,190

Adjustment data at December 31 follow:

a. Prepaid insurance still in force, $700.
b. Supplies used during the month, $500.
c. Depreciation for the month, $1,600.
d. Accrued salary expense, $400.
e. Unearned service revenue still unearned, $1,400.

Requirements

1. Journalize the adjusting entries.
2. The unadjusted balances have been entered for you in the general ledger accounts. Post the adjusting entries to the ledger accounts.
3. Prepare the adjusted trial balance.
4. Prepare the income statement, statement of owner's equity, and balance sheet for the business for the month ended December 31, 2012.

P3-36A ⑤ ⑥ **Prepare an adjusted trial balance and financial statements. [45–60 min]**
Consider the unadjusted trial balance of Reliable Limo Service Company at June 30, 2012, and the related month-end adjustment data.

RELIABLE LIMO SERVICE COMPANY Trial Balance June 30, 2012		
	Balance	
Account	Debit	Credit
Cash	$ 6,900	
Accounts receivable	1,100	
Prepaid rent	3,500	
Supplies	1,100	
Automobile	77,000	
Accumulated depreciation		$ 3,400
Accounts payable		3,300
Salary payable		
Wake, capital		80,000
Wake, drawing	4,400	
Service revenue		9,600
Salary expense	1,500	
Rent expense		
Fuel expense	800	
Depreciation expense		
Supplies expense		
Total	$96,300	$96,300

Adjustment data at June 30 follow:

    a. Accrued service revenue at June 30, $1,500.
    b. One-fifth of the prepaid rent expired during the month.
    c. Supplies on hand at June 30, $700.
    d. Depreciation on automobile for the month, $1,400.
    e. Accrued salary expense at June 30 for one day only. The five-day weekly payroll is $1,500.

Requirements

1. Write the trial balance on a worksheet, using Exhibit 3-8 as an example, and prepare the adjusted trial balance of Reliable Limo Service Company at June 30, 2012. Key each adjusting entry by letter.

2. Prepare the income statement and the statement of owner's equity for the month ended June 30, 2012, and the balance sheet at that date.

P3-37A ⑥ **Preparing financial statements from an adjusted trial balance. [20–30 min]**
The adjusted trial balance of Party Piano Tuning Service at fiscal year end May 31, 2012, follows.

PARTY PIANO TUNING SERVICE Adjusted Trial Balance May 31, 2012		
	Balance	
Account Title	Debit	Credit
Cash	$ 12,600	
Accounts receivable	10,800	
Supplies	1,900	
Equipment	25,900	
Accumulated depreciation		$ 12,500
Accounts payable		3,300
Unearned service revenue		4,700
Salary payable		800
Note payable		14,000
Lindros, capital		13,600
Lindros, drawing	38,000	
Service revenue		65,000
Depreciation expense	5,600	
Salary expense	9,600	
Utilities expense	3,900	
Insurance expense	3,700	
Supplies expense	1,900	
Total	$113,900	$113,900

Requirements

1. Prepare Party's 2012 income statement.
2. Prepare the statement of owner's equity for the year.
3. Prepare the year-end balance sheet.
4. Which financial statement reports Party's results of operations? Were the 2012 operations successful? Cite specifics from the financial statements to support your evaluation.
5. Which statement reports the company's financial position?

• Problems (Group B)

P3-38B ❶ **Comparing accrual and cash-basis accounting [15–25 min]**

MyAccountingLab

Smith's Stews completed the following transactions during April 2012:

Apr 1	Prepaid rent for April through July, $4,800.
2	Purchased computer for cash, $3,600.
3	Performed catering services on account, $3,400.
5	Paid Internet service provider invoice, $225.
6	Catered wedding event for customer and received cash, $2,000.
8	Purchased $130 of supplies on account.
10	Collected $1,900 on account.
14	Paid account payable from April 8.
15	Paid salary expense, $1,000.
30	Recorded adjusting entry for rent (see April 1).
30	Recorded $100 depreciation on computer.
30	There are $35 of supplies still on hand.

Requirement

1. Show whether each transaction would be handled as a revenue or an expense, using both the cash and accrual basis, by completing the table.

	Amount of Revenue (Expense) for April	
Date	Cash-Basis Amount of Revenue (Expense)	Accrual-Basis Amount of Revenue (Expense)
Apr 1		

P3-39B ❷ **Applying the revenue principle [10–20 min]**

Nibble's Cookies uses the accrual method of accounting and properly records transactions on the date they occur. Descriptions of customer transactions follows:

a. Received $4,800 cash from customer for six months of service beginning January 1, 2012.

b. Catered event for customer on January 28. Customer paid Nibble's invoice of $800 on February 10.

c. Scheduled catering event to be held June 3. Customer paid Nibble's a $750 deposit on February 25.

d. Catered customer's wedding on February 3. Customer paid Nibble's a $600 deposit on January 15 and the balance due of $1,500 on February 3.

e. The company provided catering to a local church's annual celebration service on February 15. The church paid the $900 fee to Nibble's on the same day.

f. The company provides food to the local homeless shelter two Saturdays each month. The cost of each event to the shelter is $260. The shelter paid Nibble's $1,040 on February 25 for January and February's events.

g. On December 1, 2011, Nibble's entered into an annual service contract with an oil company to cater the customer's monthly staff events. The contract total amount was $8,000, but Nibble's offered a 1% discount since the customer paid the entire year in advance at the signing of the contract. The first event was held in December of last year.

h. Nibble's signed contract for $1,600 on February 5 to cater X-treme sports events to be held June 15, June 27, October 1, and November 15.

Requirement

1. Calculate the amount of revenue earned during February 2012 for Nibble's Cookies for each transaction.

P3-40B ❸ **Explain why an adjusting entry is needed and calculate the amount of the adjustment [15–25 min]**

Descriptions of transactions and how they were recorded follows for October 2012 for Ashley Acoustics.

a. Received $3,600 cash from customer for three months of service beginning October 1, 2012 and ending December 31, 2012. The company recorded a $3,600 debit to Cash and a $3,600 credit to Unearned service revenue.

b. Employees are paid $1,500 every Friday for the five-day work week. October 31, 2012 is on Wednesday.

c. The company pays $420 on October 1 for their six-month auto insurance policy. The company recorded a $420 debit to Prepaid insurance and a $420 credit to Cash.

d. The company purchased office furniture for $6,000 on January 2, 2012. The company recorded a $6,000 debit to Office furniture and a $6,000 credit to Accounts payable. Annual depreciation for the furniture is $1,200.

e. The company began October with $55 of supplies on hand. On October 10 the company purchased supplies on account of $115. The company recorded a $115 debit to Supplies and a $115 credit to Accounts payable. The company used $80 of supplies during October.

f. The company received their electric bill on October 30 for $205, but did not pay it until November 10. On November 10 they recorded a $205 debit to Utilities expense and a $205 credit to Cash.

g. The company paid November's rent on October 30 of $550. On October 30 the company recorded a $550 debit to Rent expense and a $550 credit to Cash.

Requirement

1. Indicate if an adjusting entry is needed for each item on October 31 and why the entry is needed (i.e., an asset or liability account is over/understated). Indicate which specific account on the balance sheet is misstated. Finally, indicate the correct balance that should appear in the balance sheet account after the adjustment is made. Use the table guide below. Item a is completed as an example:

Item	Adjustment needed?	Asset/ Liability	Over-/ Understated?	Balance sheet account	Correct balance on October 31
a.	Yes	Liability	Overstated	Unearned service revenue	$2,400

P3-41B ❶❹❻ **Comparing accrual and cash-basis accounting, preparing adjusting entries, and preparing income statements [15–25 min]**

Carolina's Golf School completed the following transactions during October 2012:

Oct	1	Prepaid insurance for October through December, $900.
	4	Performed services (gave golf lessons) on account, $2,400.
	5	Purchased equipment on account, $1,500.
	8	Paid property tax expense, $200.
	11	Purchased office equipment for cash, $1,000.
	19	Performed services and received cash, $700.
	24	Collected $500 on account.
	26	Paid account payable from October 5.
	29	Paid salary expense, $1,400.
	31	Recorded adjusting entry for October insurance expense (see October 1).
	31	Debited unearned revenue and credited revenue in an adjusting entry, $1,100.

Requirements

1. Prepare journal entries for each transaction.

2. Using the journal entries as a guide, show whether each transaction would be handled as a revenue or an expense, using both the cash and accrual basis, by completing the following table:

	Amount of Revenue (Expense) for October	
Date	Cash-Basis Amount of Revenue (Expense)	Accrual-Basis Amount of Revenue (Expense)
Oct 1		

3. After completing the table, calculate the amount of net income or net loss for the company under the accrual and cash basis for October.

4. Considering your results from Requirement 3, which method gives the best picture of the true earnings of Carolina's Golf School? Why?

P3-42B ④ **Journalizing adjusting entries [15–25 min]**
Lindsey Landscaping has the following independent cases at the end of the year on December 31, 2014.

a. Each Friday, Lindsey pays employees for the current week's work. The amount of the weekly payroll is $6,500 for a five-day workweek. This year December 31 falls on a Wednesday.

b. Details of Prepaid insurance are shown in the account:

Prepaid insurance

Jan   1 $5,500

Lindsey prepays a full year's insurance each year on January 1. Record insurance expense for the year ended December 31.

c. The beginning balance of Supplies was $4,200. During the year, Lindsey purchased supplies for $5,100, and at December 31, the supplies on hand total $2,400.

d. Lindsey designed a landscape plan, and the client paid Lindsey $9,000 at the start of the project. Lindsey recorded this amount as Unearned service revenue. The job will take several months to complete, and Lindsey estimates that the company has earned 70% of the total revenue during the current year.

e. Depreciation for the current year includes Equipment, $3,600; and Trucks, $1,400. Make a compound entry.

Requirement

1. Journalize the adjusting entry needed on December 31, 2014, for each of the previous items affecting Lindsey Landscaping.

P3-43B ④ **Analyzing and journalizing adjustments [15–20 min]**
Showtime Theater Production Company's unadjusted and adjusted trial balances at December 31, 2012, follow.

SHOWTIME THEATER PRODUCTION COMPANY
Adjusted Trial Balance
December 31, 2012

Account	Trial Balance Debit	Trial Balance Credit	Adjusted Trial Balance Debit	Adjusted Trial Balance Credit
Cash	$ 3,500		$ 3,500	
Accounts receivable	6,000		6,900	
Supplies	1,300		500	
Prepaid insurance	2,100		1,300	
Equipment	23,000		23,000	
Accumulated depreciation		$ 8,100		$ 11,600
Accounts payable		5,000		5,000
Salary payable				500
Webber, capital		21,100		21,100
Webber, drawing	28,500		28,500	
Service revenue		59,600		60,500
Depreciation expense			3,500	
Supplies expense			800	
Utilities expense	5,400		5,400	
Salary expense	24,000		24,500	
Insurance expense			800	
Total	$ 93,800	$ 93,800	$ 98,700	$ 98,700

Requirement

1. Journalize the adjusting entries that account for the differences between the two trial balances.

P3-44B ❹❺ **Journalizing and posting adjustments to the T-accounts, and preparing an adjusted trial balance [45–60 min]**

The trial balance of Canton Air Purification System at December 31, 2012, and the data needed for the month-end adjustments follow.

CANTON AIR PURIFICATION SYSTEM Trial Balance December 31, 2012		
Account	Debit	Credit
Cash	$ 7,200	
Accounts receivable	19,400	
Prepaid rent	2,200	
Supplies	1,600	
Equipment	20,000	
Accumulated depreciation		$ 3,700
Accounts payable		3,400
Salary payable		
Unearned service revenue		2,600
Canton, capital		39,000
Canton, drawing	9,600	
Service revenue		15,900
Salary expense	3,300	
Rent expense		
Depreciation expense		
Advertising expense	1,300	
Supplies expense		
Total	$ 64,600	$ 64,600

Adjustment data at December 31 follow:

a. Unearned service revenue still unearned, $1,800.
b. Prepaid rent still in force, $600.
c. Supplies used during the month, $400.
d. Depreciation for the month, $700.
e. Accrued advertising expense, $900. (Credit Accounts payable)
f. Accrued salary expense, $800.

Requirements

1. Journalize the adjusting entries.
2. The unadjusted balances have been entered for you in the general ledger accounts. Post the adjusting entries to the ledger accounts.
3. Prepare the adjusted trial balance.
4. How will Canton Air Purification System use the adjusted trial balance?

P3-45B ④⑤⑥ **Preparing and posting adjusting journal entries; preparing an adjusted trial balance and financial statements. [45–60 min]**

The trial balance of Concord Bed and Breakfast Company at December 31, 2012, and the data needed for the month-end adjustments follow.

CONCORD BED AND BREAKFAST COMPANY		
Trial Balance		
December 31, 2012		
Account	Debit	Credit
Cash	$ 12,000	
Accounts receivable	14,400	
Prepaid insurance	2,800	
Supplies	1,400	
Building	435,000	
Accumulated depreciation		$310,500
Accounts payable		1,930
Salary payable		
Unearned service revenue		3,000
Wagner, capital		141,060
Wagner, drawing	2,940	
Service revenue		15,700
Salary expense	2,800	
Insurance expense		
Depreciation expense		
Advertising expense	850	
Supplies expense		
Total	$472,190	$472,190

Adjustment data at December 31 follow:

- a. Prepaid insurance still in force, $900.
- b. Supplies used during the month, $500.
- c. Depreciation for the month, $1,000.
- d. Accrued salary expense, $300.
- e. Unearned service revenue still unearned, $1,500.

Requirements

1. Journalize the adjusting entries.
2. The unadjusted balances have been entered for you in the general ledger accounts. Post the adjusting entries to the ledger accounts.
3. Prepare the adjusted trial balance.
4. Prepare the income statement, statement of owner's equity, and balance sheet for the business for the month ended December 31, 2012.

P3-46B ⑤ ⑥ **Prepare an adjusted trial balance and financial statements [45–60 min]**

Consider the unadjusted trial balance of Star Limo Service Company at September 30, 2012, and the related month-end adjustment data.

STAR LIMO SERVICE COMPANY Trial Balance September 30, 2012		
	Balance	
Account	**Debit**	**Credit**
Cash	$ 6,800	
Accounts receivable	1,400	
Prepaid rent	5,000	
Supplies	1,200	
Automobile	72,000	
Accumulated depreciation		$ 3,800
Accounts payable		3,600
Salary payable		
Simmons, capital		75,000
Simmons, drawing	3,700	
Service revenue		9,700
Salary expense	1,400	
Rent expense		
Fuel expense	600	
Depreciation expense		
Supplies expense		
Total	$92,100	$92,100

Adjustment data at September 30 follow:

a. Accrued service revenue at September 30, $1,800.
b. One-fifth of the prepaid rent expired during the month.
c. Supplies on hand at September 30, $800.
d. Depreciation on automobile for the month, $1,000.
e. Accrued salary expense at September 30 for one day only. The five-day weekly payroll is $1,200.

Requirements

1. Write the trial balance on a worksheet, using Exhibit 3-8 as an example, and prepare the adjusted trial balance of Star Limo Service at September 30, 2012. Key each adjusting entry by letter.

2. Prepare the income statement and the statement of owner's equity for the month ended September 30, 2012, and the balance sheet at that date.

P3-47B ⑥ **Preparing financial statements from an adjusted trial balance [20–30 min]**

The adjusted trial balance of A Plus Events Piano Tuning Service at fiscal year end October 31, 2012, follows.

	A PLUS EVENTS PIANO TUNING SERVICE Adjusted Trial Balance October 31, 2012		
		Balance	
	Account Title	Debit	Credit
	Cash	$ 12,300	
	Accounts receivable	10,700	
	Supplies	1,800	
	Equipment	25,800	
	Accumulated depreciation		$ 12,300
	Accounts payable		3,300
	Unearned service revenue		4,600
	Salary payable		700
	Note payable		15,000
	Bach, capital		9,000
	Bach, drawing	36,000	
	Service revenue		66,000
	Depreciation expense	5,500	
	Salary expense	9,600	
	Utilities expense	4,100	
	Insurance expense	3,700	
	Supplies expense	1,400	
	Total	$110,900	$110,900

Requirements

1. Prepare A Plus's 2012 income statement.
2. Prepare the statement of owner's equity for the year.
3. Prepare the year-end balance sheet.
4. Which financial statement reports A Plus's results of operations? Were 2012 operations successful? Cite specifics from the financial statements to support your evaluation.
5. Which statement reports the company's financial position?

● Continuing Exercise

E3-48 ④⑤ **Preparing adjusting entries and preparing an adjusted trial balance [20–30 min]**

This exercise continues the Lawlor Lawn Service situation from Exercise 2-61 of Chapter 2. Start from the trial balance and the posted T-accounts that Lawlor Lawn Service prepared at May 31, 2012.

MyAccountingLab

Requirements

1. Open these additional T-accounts: Accumulated depreciation—equipment; Depreciation expense—equipment; Supplies expense.
2. Mindy Lawlor determines there are $40 in Lawn supplies left at May 31, 2012. Depreciation on the equipment was $30 for the month. Journalize any required adjusting journal entries.

3. Post to the T-accounts, keying all items by date.
4. Prepare the adjusted trial balance, as illustrated in Exhibit 3-8.

● Continuing Problem

MyAccountingLab **P3-49** **❹ ❺ ❻ Preparing adjusting entries; preparing an adjusted trial balance; and preparing financial statements from an adjusted trial balance [40–50 min]**
This problem continues the Draper Consulting situation from Problem 2-62 of Chapter 2. Start from the trial balance and the posted T-accounts that Draper Consulting prepared at December 18, 2012, as follows:

			Balance	
	Account Title		**Debit**	**Credit**
	Cash		$ 16,500	
	Accounts receivable		1,500	
	Supplies		900	
	Equipment		1,800	
	Accumulated depreciation—equipment			
	Furniture		4,200	
	Accumulated depreciation—furniture			
	Accounts payable			$ 5,100
	Salary payable			
	Unearned service revenue			
	Draper, capital			18,000
	Draper, drawing			
	Service revenue			2,600
	Rent expense		550	
	Utilities expense		250	
	Salary expense			
	Depreciation expense—equipment			
	Depreciation expense—furniture			
	Supplies expense			
	Total		$25,700	$25,700

DRAPER CONSULTING
Trial Balance
December 18, 2012

Later in December, the business completed these transactions, as follows:

Dec 21	Received $1,400 in advance for client service to be performed evenly over the next 30 days.
21	Hired a secretary to be paid $2,055 on the 20th day of each month. The secretary begins work immediately.
26	Paid $450 on account.
28	Collected $300 on account.
30	Draper withdrew cash of $1,400.

Requirements

1. Open these additional T-accounts: Accumulated depreciation—equipment; Accumulated depreciation—furniture; Salary payable; Unearned service revenue; Salary expense; Depreciation expense—equipment; Depreciation expense—furniture; Supplies expense.

2. Journalize the transactions of December 21–30.

3. Post to the T-accounts, keying all items by date.

4. Prepare a trial balance at December 31. Also set up columns for the adjustments and for the adjusted trial balance, as illustrated in Exhibit 3-8.

5. At December 31, the business gathers the following information for the adjusting entries:

    a. Accrued service revenue, $550.
    b. Earned $700 of the service revenue collected in advance on December 21.
    c. Supplies on hand, $200.
    d. Depreciation expense—equipment, $30; furniture, $70.
    e. Accrued $685 expense for secretary's salary.

    On your worksheet, make these adjustments directly in the adjustments columns, and complete the adjusted trial balance at December 31. Throughout the book, to avoid rounding errors, we base adjusting entries on 30-day months and 360-day years.

6. Journalize and post the adjusting entries. In the T-accounts, denote each adjusting amount as *Adj* and an account balance as *Bal*.

7. Prepare the income statement and the statement of owner's equity of Draper Consulting for the month ended December 31, 2012, and prepare the balance sheet at that date.

● Practice Set

④ ⑤ Preparing adjusting entries and preparing an adjusted trial balance [20–30 min]   *MyAccountingLab*

Using the trial balance prepared in Chapter 2, consider the following adjustment data gathered by Evan:

a. Evan prepared an inventory of supplies and found there were $50 of supplies in the cabinet on November 30.
b. One month's combined depreciation on all assets was estimated to be $170.

Requirements

1. Using the data provided from the trial balance, the previous adjustment information, and the information from Chapter 2, prepare all required adjusting journal entries for November.

2. Prepare an adjusted trial balance as of November 30 for Shine King Cleaning.

Apply Your Knowledge

● Decision Cases

Decision Case 3-1 Lee Nicholas has been the owner and has operated World.com Advertising since its beginning 10 years ago. The company has prospered. Recently, Nicholas mentioned that he would sell the business for the right price.

Assume that you are interested in buying World.com Advertising. You obtain the most recent monthly trial balance, which follows. Revenues and expenses vary little from month to month, and January is a typical month. The trial balance shown is a preliminary or unadjusted trial balance. The controller informs you that the necessary accrual adjustments should include revenues of $3,800 and expenses of $1,100. Also, if you were to buy World.com Advertising, you would hire a manager so you could devote your time to other duties. Assume that this person would require a monthly salary of $5,000.

WORLD.COM ADVERTISING
Trial Balance
January 31, 2015

Account Title	Balance Debit	Balance Credit
Cash	$ 9,700	
Accounts receivable	14,100	
Prepaid expenses	2,600	
Building	221,300	
Accumulated depreciation		$ 68,600
Accounts payable		13,000
Salary payable		
Unearned service revenue		56,700
Nicholas, capital		110,400
Nicholas, drawing	9,000	
Service revenue		12,300
Rent expense		
Salary expense	3,400	
Utilities expense	900	
Depreciation expense		
Supplies expense		
Total	$261,000	$261,000

Requirements

1. Assume that the most you would pay for the business is 20 times the monthly net income *you could expect to earn* from it. Compute this possible price.

2. Nicholas states the least he will take for the business is an amount equal to the business's owner's equity balance on January 31. Compute this amount.

3. Under these conditions, how much should you offer Nicholas? Give your reason.

Decision Case 3-2 One year ago, Tyler Stasney founded Swift Classified Ads. Stasney remembers that you took an accounting course while in college and comes to you for advice. He wishes to know how much net income his business earned during the past year in order to decide whether to keep the company going. His accounting records consist of the T-accounts from his ledger, which were prepared by an accountant who moved to another city. The ledger at December 31 follows. The accounts have *not* been adjusted.

Stasney indicates that at year-end, customers owe him $1,600 for accrued service revenue. These revenues have not been recorded. During the year, Stasney collected $4,000 service revenue in advance from customers, but he earned only $900 of that amount. Rent expense for the year was $2,400, and he used up $1,700 of the supplies. Stasney determines that depreciation on his equipment was $5,000 for the year. At December 31, he owes his employee $1,200 accrued salary.

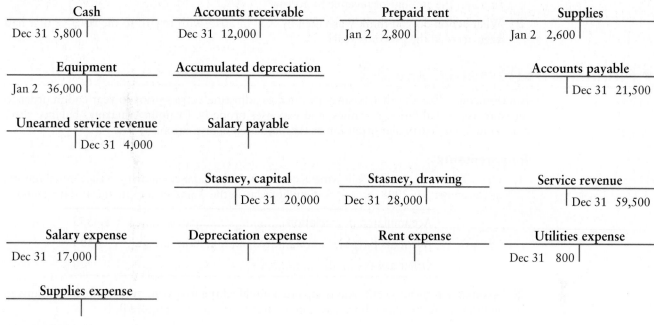

Cash		Accounts receivable		Prepaid rent		Supplies	
Dec 31 5,800		Dec 31 12,000		Jan 2 2,800		Jan 2 2,600	

Equipment		Accumulated depreciation				Accounts payable	
Jan 2 36,000							Dec 31 21,500

Unearned service revenue		Salary payable					
	Dec 31 4,000						

		Stasney, capital		Stasney, drawing		Service revenue	
			Dec 31 20,000	Dec 31 28,000			Dec 31 59,500

Salary expense		Depreciation expense		Rent expense		Utilities expense	
Dec 31 17,000						Dec 31 800	

Supplies expense	

Requirement

1. Help Stasney compute his net income for the year. Advise him whether to continue operating Swift Classified Ads.

● Ethical Issue 3-1

The net income of Steinbach & Sons, a department store, decreased sharply during 2014. Mort Steinbach, manager of the store, anticipates the need for a bank loan in 2015. Late in 2014, Steinbach instructs the store's accountant to record a $2,000 sale of furniture to the Steinbach family, even though the goods will not be shipped from the manufacturer until January 2015. Steinbach also tells the accountant *not* to make the following December 31, 2014, adjusting entries:

Salaries owed to employees	$900
Prepaid insurance that has expired	400

Requirements

1. Compute the overall effects of these transactions on the store's reported income for 2014.
2. Why is Steinbach taking this action? Is his action ethical? Give your reason, identifying the parties helped and the parties harmed by Steinbach's action. (Challenge)
3. As a personal friend, what advice would you give the accountant? (Challenge)

● Fraud Case 3-1

XM, Ltd., was a small engineering firm that built hi-tech robotic devices for electronics manufacturers. One very complex device was partially completed at the end of 2014. Barb McLauren, head engineer and owner, knew the experimental technology was a failure and XM would not be able to complete the $20,000,000 contract next year. However, she was getting ready to sell the company and retire in January. She told the controller that the device was 80% complete at year-end, and on track for successful completion the following spring; the controller accrued 80% of the contract revenue in December 2014. McLauren sold the company in January 2015 and retired. By mid-year, it became apparent that XM would not be able to complete the project successfully, and the new owner would never recoup his investment.

Requirements

1. For complex, hi-tech contracts, how does a company determine the percentage of completion and the amount of revenue to accrue?

2. What action do you think was taken by XM in 2015 with regard to the revenue that had been accrued the previous year?

● Financial Statement Case 3-1

Amazon.com—like all other businesses—makes adjusting entries prior to year-end in order to measure assets, liabilities, revenues, and expenses properly. Examine **Amazon**'s balance sheet and Note 3. Pay particular attention to Accumulated depreciation.

Requirements

1. Open T-accounts for the following accounts with the balances shown on the annual reports at December 31, 2008 (amounts in millions, as in the **Amazon.com** financial statements):

Accumulated depreciation	$ 555
Accounts payable	3,594
Other assets	720

2. Assume that during 2009 **Amazon.com** completed the following transactions (amounts in millions). Journalize each transaction (explanations are not required).

---

a. Recorded depreciation expense, $70. (In order to simplify this exercise, the amount shown here is not the same as the actual amount disclosed in Note 3 of the annual report.)

b. Paid the December 31, 2008, balance of accounts payable.

c. Purchased inventory on account, $5,605.

d. Purchased other assets for cash of $754.

---

3. Post to the three T-accounts. Then the balance of each account should agree with the corresponding amount reported in **Amazon**'s December 31, 2009, balance sheet. Check to make sure they do agree with **Amazon**'s actual balances. You can find Accumulated depreciation in Note 3.

● Team Project 3-1

It's Just Lunch is a nationwide service company that arranges lunch dates for clients. **It's Just Lunch** collects cash up front for a package of dates. Suppose your group is opening an **It's Just Lunch** office in your area. You must make some important decisions—where to locate, how to advertise, and so on—and you must also make some accounting decisions. For example, what will be the end of your business's accounting year? How often will you need financial statements to evaluate operating performance and financial position? Will you use the cash basis or the accrual basis? When will you account for the revenue that the business earns? How will you account for the expenses?

Requirements

Write a report (or prepare an oral presentation, as directed by your professor) to address the following considerations:

1. Will you use the cash basis or the accrual basis of accounting? Give a complete explanation of your reasoning.

2. How often do you want financial statements? Why? Discuss how you will use each financial statement.

3. What kind of revenue will you earn? When will you record it as revenue?

4. Prepare a made-up income statement for **It's Just Lunch** for the year ended December 31, 2015. List all the business's expenses, starting with the most important (largest dollar amount) and working through to the least important (smallest dollar amount). Merely list the accounts. Dollar amounts are not required.

● Communication Activity 3-1

In 25 words or fewer, explain adjusting journal entries.

Quick Check Answers

1. *b* 2. *b* 3. *c* 4. *c* 5. *a* 6. *a* 7. *c* 8. *c* 9. *b* 10. *d*

For online homework, exercises, and problems that provide you immediate feedback, please visit myaccountinglab.com.

4

Completing the Accounting Cycle

All accounts not on the balance sheet reset to zero at the end of a period, and update the capital balance.

SMART TOUCH LEARNING
Balance Sheet
May 31, 2013

Assets				Liabilities		
Current assets:				Current liabilities:		
Cash		$ 4,800		Accounts payable		$ 48,700
Accounts receivable		2,600		Salary payable		900
Inventory		30,500		Interest payable		100
Supplies		600		Unearned service revenue		400
Prepaid rent		2,000		Total current liabilities		50,100
Total current assets			$ 40,500	Long-term liabilities:		
Plant assets:				Notes payable		20,000
Furniture	$18,000			Total liabilities		70,100
Less: Accumulated depreciation—furniture	300	17,700				
Building	48,000					
Less: Accumulated depreciation—building	200	47,800		**Owner's Equity**		
Total plant assets			65,500	**Bright, capital**		**35,900**
Total assets			$106,000	Total liabilities and owner's equity		$106,000

Learning Objectives

1. Prepare an accounting worksheet

2. Use the worksheet to prepare financial statements

3. Close the revenue, expense, and drawing accounts

4. Prepare the post-closing trial balance

5. Classify assets and liabilities as current or long-term

6. Describe the effect of various transactions on the current ratio and the debt ratio

7. Understand reversing entries (see Appendix 4A, located at myaccountinglab.com)

What do football, baseball, basketball, hockey, soccer, and accounting have in common? They all have a player in each position and each game starts with a score of zero.

Sheena Bright and Greg Moore have operated Smart Touch Learning and Greg's Tunes, respectively, for a month. They took in revenue, incurred expenses, and earned net income during the first month. It is time to look ahead to the next period.

Should Smart Touch or Greg's Tunes start month 2 with the net income that the business earned last month? No, just like a game, both companies must start from zero in order to measure their business performance in the second month. Therefore, they must set their accounting scoreboard back to zero.

This process of getting back to zero is called *closing the books*, and it is the last step in the accounting cycle. The **accounting cycle** is the process by which companies produce their financial statements.

●   ●   ●

This chapter completes the accounting cycle by showing how to close the books. It begins with the *adjusted trial balance*, which you learned about in Chapter 3. In this chapter we'll learn how to prepare a more complete version of an adjusted trial balance document called the *worksheet*. Worksheets help by summarizing lots of data in one place.

The accounting cycle starts with the beginning asset, liability, and owner's equity account balances left over from the preceding period. Exhibit 4-1 outlines the complete accounting cycle of Smart Touch and every other business. Start with item 1 and move clockwise.

EXHIBIT 4-1   The Accounting Cycle

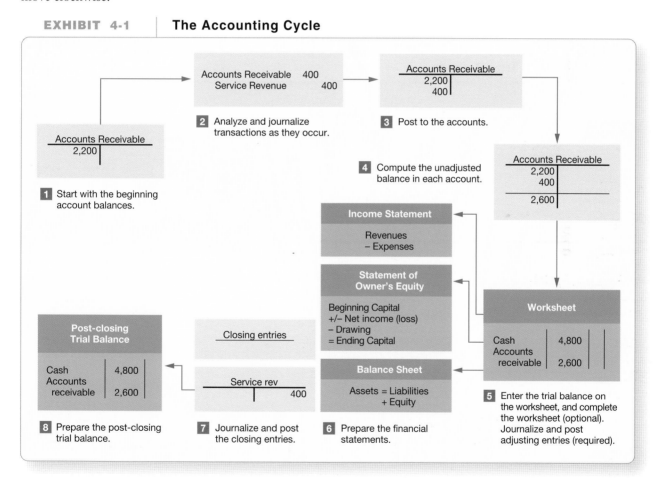

Accounting takes place at two different times:

• During the period—Journalizing transactions, posting to the accounts
• End of the period—Adjusting the accounts, preparing the financial statements, and closing the accounts

The end-of-period work also readies the accounts for the next period. In Chapters 3 and 4, we cover the end-of-period accounting for service businesses such as Greg's Tunes and Smart Touch. Chapter 5 shows how a merchandising entity such as **Walmart** or **Sports Academy** adjusts and closes its books.

The Worksheet

 Prepare an accounting worksheet

Accountants often use a **worksheet**—a document with several columns—to summarize data for the financial statements. The worksheet is not a journal, a ledger, or a financial statement. It is merely a summary device that helps identify the accounts that need adjustment. An Excel spreadsheet works well for preparing a worksheet. Note that the worksheet is an internal document. It is not meant to be given to outsiders.

Exhibits 4-2 though 4-6 illustrate the development of a typical worksheet for Smart Touch. The heading at the top displays the following information:

- Name of the business (Smart Touch Learning)
- Title of the document (Worksheet)
- Period covered by the worksheet (Month Ended May 31, 2013)

A step-by-step description of the worksheet follows, with all amounts given in Exhibits 4-2 though 4-6. Simply turn the acetate pages to follow from exhibit to exhibit.

1. **Enter the account titles and their unadjusted balances in the Trial Balance columns of the worksheet, and total the amounts.** (See Exhibit 4-2.) The data

EXHIBIT 4-2 | **Trial Balance**

SMART TOUCH LEARNING
Worksheet
Month Ended May 31, 2013

	Trial Balance		Adjustments		Adj. Trial Balance		Income Statement		Balance Sheet	
	Debit	Credit	Debit	Credit	Debit	Credit	Debit	Credit	Debit	Credit
Cash	$ 4,800									
Accounts receivable	2,200									
Supplies	700									
Prepaid rent	3,000									
Furniture	18,000									
Building	48,000									
Accumulated depreciation—furniture										
Accumulated depreciation—building										
Accounts payable		$18,200								
Salary payable										
Interest payable										
Unearned service revenue		600								
Notes payable		20,000								
Bright, capital		33,200								
Bright, drawing	1,000									
Service revenue		7,000								
Rent expense										
Salary expense	900									
Supplies expense										
Depreciation expense—furniture										
Depreciation expense—building										
Interest expense										
Utilities expense	400									
	$79,000	$79,000								

come from the ledger accounts before any adjustments. Accounts are listed in proper order (Cash first, Accounts receivable second, and so on). Total debits must equal total credits. Note that these two columns of the worksheet are the same as the trial balance from Chapter 3.

2. **Enter the adjusting entries in the Adjustments columns, and total the amounts.** Exhibit 4-3 includes the May adjusting entries that we made in Chapter 3. The adjusting entries, letters a–h from Exhibit 3-8, are posted into the adjustments column of the worksheet.

3. **Compute each account's adjusted balance by combining the trial balance and adjustment figures. Enter each account's adjusted amount in the Adjusted Trial Balance columns.** Exhibit 4-4 shows the worksheet with the adjusted trial balance completed. For example, Cash is up-to-date, so it receives no adjustment. Accounts receivable's adjusted balance of $2,600 is computed by adding the $400 adjustment to the unadjusted amount of $2,200. For Supplies we subtract the $100 credit adjustment from the unadjusted debit balance of $700. Note that an account may receive more than one adjustment. For example, Service revenue has two adjustments. The adjusted balance of $7,600 is computed by taking the unadjusted balance of $7,000 and adding the adjustment credits of $400 and $200 to arrive at the $7,600 adjusted balance. As on the trial balance, total debits must equal total credits on the adjusted trial balance. Notice how the three completed column sets of Exhibit 4-4 look exactly like Exhibit 3-8.

4. **Draw an imaginary line above the first revenue account (in this case, Service revenue). Every account above that line (assets, liabilities, and equity accounts) is copied from the Adjusted Trial Balance to the Balance Sheet columns. Every account below the line (revenues and expenses) is copied from the Adjusted Trial Balance to the Income Statement columns.** Each account's balance should appear in only one column, as shown in Exhibit 4-5.

   First, total the *income statement columns*, as follows:

   Income Statement

   ■ Debits (Dr.) ⟶ Total expenses = $3,900   Difference = $3,700, a net income
   ■ Credits (Cr.) ⟶ Total revenues = $7,600   because total credits (revenues) exceed total debits (expenses)

   Then total the *balance sheet* columns:

   Balance Sheet

   ■ Debits (Dr.) ⟶ Total assets and drawing   = $77,000   Difference = $3,700,
   ■ Credits (Cr.) ⟶ Total liabilities, owner's equity,   a net income because
                 and accumulated depreciation = $73,300   total debits are greater

5. **On the income statement, compute net income or net loss as total revenues minus total expenses. Enter net income (loss) as the balancing amount on the income statement. Also enter net income (loss) as the balancing amount on the balance sheet. Then total the financial statement columns.** Exhibit 4-6 presents the completed worksheet.

Revenue (total **credits** on the income statement).............................	$ 7,600
Expenses (total **debits** on the income statement).............................	(3,900)
Net income..	$ 3,700

Net Income

Net income of $3,700 is entered as the balancing amount in the debit column of the income statement. This brings total debits up to total credits on the income statement. Net income is also entered as the balancing amount in the credit column of the balance sheet. Net income brings the balance sheet into balance. Note that the difference in these columns is the same: Net income.

Net Loss

If expenses exceed revenues, the result is a net loss. In that event, print Net loss on the worksheet next to the result. The net loss amount should be entered in the *credit* column of the income statement (to balance out) and in the *debit* column of the balance sheet (to balance out). After completion, total debits should equal total credits in both the Income Statement columns and in the Balance Sheet columns.

Now practice what you have learned by working Summary Problem 4-1.

Key Takeaway

The worksheet is a tool that puts the whole accounting process in one place. Remember that debits = credits in the first three columns. Columns 4 and 5 (Income Statement and Balance Sheet) debits do not equal credits until you post the net income or net loss for the period.

Summary Problem 4-1

The trial balance of Super Employment Services, at December 31, 2014, follows.

SUPER EMPLOYMENT SERVICES Trial Balance December 31, 2014		
	Balance	
Account Title	**Debit**	**Credit**
Cash	$ 6,000	
Accounts receivable	5,000	
Supplies	1,000	
Furniture	10,000	
Accumulated depreciation—furniture		$ 4,000
Building	50,000	
Accumulated depreciation—building		30,000
Accounts payable		2,000
Salary payable		
Unearned service revenue		8,000
Mudge, capital		12,000
Mudge, drawing	25,000	
Service revenue		60,000
Salary expense	16,000	
Supplies expense		
Depreciation expense—furniture		
Depreciation expense—building		
Advertising expense	3,000	
Total	$116,000	$116,000

Data needed for the adjusting entries include the following:

    a. Supplies on hand at year-end, $200.

    b. Depreciation on furniture, $2,000.

    c. Depreciation on building, $1,000.

    d. Salaries owed but not yet paid, $500.

    e. Accrued service revenue, $1,300.

    f. $3,000 of the unearned service revenue was earned during 2014.

Requirement

1. Prepare the worksheet of Super Employment Services for the year ended December 31, 2014. Key each adjusting entry by the letter corresponding to the data given.

Solution

SUPER EMPLOYMENT SERVICES
Worksheet
Year Ended December 31, 2014

Account Title	Trial Balance Dr.	Trial Balance Cr.	Adjustments Dr.	Adjustments Cr.	Adjusted Trial Balance Dr.	Adjusted Trial Balance Cr.	Income Statement Dr.	Income Statement Cr.	Balance Sheet Dr.	Balance Sheet Cr.
Cash	$ 6,000				$ 6,000				$ 6,000	
Accounts receivable	5,000		(e) $1,300		6,300				6,300	
Supplies	1,000			(a) $ 800	200				200	
Furniture	10,000				10,000				10,000	
Accumulated depreciation— furniture		$ 4,000		(b) 2,000		$ 6,000				$ 6,000
Building	50,000				50,000				50,000	
Accumulated depreciation—building		30,000		(c) 1,000		31,000				31,000
Accounts payable		2,000				2,000				2,000
Salary payable				(d) 500		500				500
Unearned service revenue		8,000	(f) 3,000			5,000				5,000
Mudge, capital		12,000				12,000				12,000
Mudge, drawing	25,000				25,000				25,000	
Service revenue		60,000		(e) 1,300						
				(f) 3,000		64,300		$64,300		
Salary expense	16,000		(d) 500		16,500		$16,500			
Supplies expense			(a) 800		800		800			
Depreciation expense—furniture			(b) 2,000		2,000		2,000			
Depreciation expense—building			(c) 1,000		1,000		1,000			
Advertising expense	3,000				3,000		3,000			
	$116,000	$116,000	$8,600	$8,600	$120,800	$120,800	$23,300	$64,300	$97,500	$56,500
Net income							41,000			41,000
							$64,300	$64,300	$97,500	$97,500

Completing the Accounting Cycle

 Use the worksheet to prepare financial statements

The worksheet helps accountants make the adjusting entries, prepare the financial statements, and close the accounts. First, let's prepare the financial statements. We'll start by returning to the running example of Smart Touch Learning, whose financial statements are given in Exhibit 4-7 on the following page. Notice that these are identical to the financial statements prepared in Chapter 3 (Exhibits 3-9 though 3-11).

Preparing the Financial Statements from a Worksheet

The worksheet shows the amount of net income or net loss for the period, but it is an internal document. We still must prepare the financial statements for external decision makers. Exhibit 4-7 on the next page shows the May financial statements for Smart Touch (based on data from the worksheet in Exhibit 4-6). We can prepare the business's financial statements immediately after completing the worksheet.

Stop & Think...

Look at the formal financial statements in Exhibit 4-7 and the worksheet financial statement columns in Exhibit 4-6. The income number is the same on both sheets, so why do we need to do both a worksheet and a formal document, such as an income statement? The answer is the worksheet will be used mainly by internal decision makers, whereas the formal financial statements will be used by external decision makers.

Recording the Adjusting Entries from a Worksheet

Adjusting the accounts requires journalizing entries and posting to the accounts. We learned how to prepare adjusting journal entries in Chapter 3. The adjustments that are journalized after they are entered on the worksheet are *exactly* the same adjusting journal entries. Panel A of Exhibit 4-8 on page 206 repeats Smart Touch's adjusting entries that we journalized in Chapter 3. Panel B shows the revenue and the expense accounts after all adjustments have been posted. Only the revenue and expense accounts are presented here to focus on the closing process.

EXHIBIT 4-7 | **Financial Statements**

SMART TOUCH LEARNING
Income Statement
Month Ended May 31, 2013

Revenue:			
Service revenue			$7,600
Expenses:			
Salary expense		$1,800	
Rent expense		1,000	
Utilities expense		400	
Depreciation expense—furniture		300	
Depreciation expense—building		200	
Interest expense		100	
Supplies expense		100	
Total expenses			3,900
Net income			$3,700

SMART TOUCH LEARNING
Statement of Owner's Equity
Month Ended May 31, 2013

Bright, capital, May 1, 2013	$ 33,200
Net income	3,700
	36,900
Drawing	(1,000)
Bright, capital, May 31, 2013	$ 35,900

SMART TOUCH LEARNING
Balance Sheet
May 31, 2013

Assets			Liabilities	
Cash		$ 4,800	Accounts payable	$18,200
Accounts receivable		2,600	Salary payable	900
Supplies		600	Interest payable	100
Prepaid rent		2,000	Unearned service revenue	400
Furniture	$18,000		Notes payable	20,000
Less: Accumulated			Total liabilities	39,600
depreciation—				
furniture	300	17,700		
Building	48,000			
Less: Accumulated				
depreciation—			**Owner's Equity**	
building	200	47,800	Bright, capital	35,900
			Total liabilities	
Total assets		$75,500	and owner's equity	$75,500

EXHIBIT 4-8 | **Journalizing and Posting the Adjusting Entries of Smart Touch Learning**

PANEL A—Adjusting Entries

a.		Rent expense (E+)	1,000	
		Prepaid rent (A−)		1,000
		To record rent expense.		
b.		Supplies expense (E+)	100	
		Supplies (A−)		100
		To record supplies used.		
c.		Depreciation expense—furniture (E+)	300	
		Accumulated depreciation—furniture (CA+)		300
		To record depreciation on furniture.		
d.		Depreciation expense—building (E+)	200	
		Accumulated depreciation—building (CA+)		200
		To record depreciation on building.		
e.		Salary expense (E+)	900	
		Salary payable (L+)		900
		To accrue salary expense.		
f.		Interest expense (E+)	100	
		Interest payable (L+)		100
		To accrue interest expense.		
g.		Accounts receivable (A+)	400	
		Service revenue (R+)		400
		To accrue service revenue.		
h.		Unearned service revenue (L−)	200	
		Service revenue (R+)		200
		To record service revenue that was collected in advance.		

PANEL B—Ledger Accounts

REVENUES

Service revenue

		7,000	
	(g)	400	
	(h)	200	
	Bal	7,600	

EXPENSES

Rent expense

(a)	1,000		
Bal	1,000		

Salary expense

	900		
(e)	900		
Bal	1,800		

Supplies expense

(b)	100		
Bal	100		

Depreciation expense— furniture

(c)	300		
Bal	300		

Depreciation expense— building

(d)	200		
Bal	200		

Interest expense

(f)	100		
Bal	100		

Utilities expense

Bal	400		

Accountants can use the worksheet to prepare monthly statements (as in Exhibit 4-7) without journalizing and posting the adjusting entries. A big advantage of the worksheet is that a small business can see the complete results of a period on one page. Many small companies journalize and post the adjusting entries only at the end of the year.

Now we are ready to move to the last step—closing the accounts.

Closing the Accounts

Closing the accounts occurs at the end of the period. Closing consists of journalizing and posting the closing entries in order to get the accounts ready for the next period. The closing process zeroes out all the revenues and all the expenses in order to measure each period's net income separately from all other periods. It also updates the Capital account balance. The last step in the closing process zeroes out drawing.

 Close the revenue, expense, and drawing accounts

Stop & Think...

Have you ever closed an account at a bank? How much was left in your account when you closed it? You needed to take all the money out, right? Well it's the same theory behind closing journal entries—after closing, we leave a zero balance in all revenue, expense, and drawing accounts.

Recall that the income statement reports net income for a specific period. For example, the business's net income for 2013 relates exclusively to 2013. At December 31, 2013, Smart Touch closes its revenue and expense accounts for the year. For this reason, revenues and expenses are called **temporary accounts** (also known as **nominal accounts**). For example, Smart Touch's balance of Service revenue at May 31, 2013, is $7,600. This balance relates exclusively to May and must be zeroed out before Smart Touch records revenue for June. Similarly, the various expense account balances are for May only and must also be zeroed out at the end of the month.

The Bright, drawing account is also temporary and must be closed at the end of the period because it measures the owner drawing for only that one period. All temporary accounts (drawing, revenues, and expenses) are closed (zeroed).

By contrast, the **permanent accounts** (also known as **real accounts**)—the assets, liabilities, and capital—are not closed at the end of the period. Another way to remember which accounts are permanent is to recall that all accounts on the balance sheet are permanent accounts because they are part of the accounting equation.

Closing entries transfer the revenue, expense, and drawing balances to the Capital account to ready the company's books for the next period.

As an intermediate step, the revenues and the expenses may be transferred first to an account titled **Income summary**. The Income summary account *summarizes* the net income (or net loss) for the period by collecting the sum of all the expenses (a debit) and the sum of all the revenues (a credit). **The Income summary account is like a temporary "holding tank" that shows the amount of net income or net loss of the current period.** Its balance—net income or net loss—is then transferred (closed) to the Capital account (the final account in the closing process). Exhibit 4-9 summarizes the closing process.

EXHIBIT 4-9 | **The Closing Process**

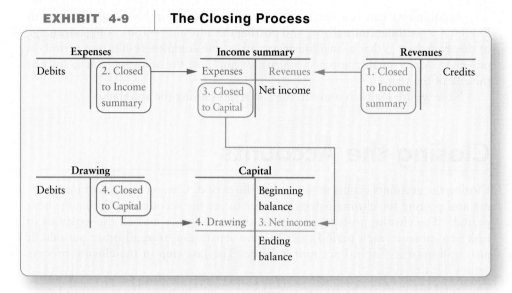

Closing Temporary Accounts

As we stated previously, all temporary accounts are closed (zeroed out) during the closing process. **Temporary accounts are not permanent. Only the accounting equation accounts (the balance sheet accounts) are permanent.** The four steps in closing the books follow (and are illustrated in Exhibit 4-10).

STEP 1: Make the revenue accounts equal zero via the Income summary account. This closing entry transfers total revenues to the *credit* side of the Income summary account.

STEP 2: Make expense accounts equal zero via the Income summary account. This closing entry transfers total expenses to the *debit* side of the Income summary account.

The Income summary account now holds the net income or net loss of the period. The Income summary T-account is presented next:

Income summary			
Closing Entry 2	Expenses	Closing Entry 1	Revenues
Expenses > Revenues	Net Loss	Revenues > Expenses	Net Income

STEP 3: Make the Income summary account equal zero via the Capital account. This closing entry transfers net income (or net loss) to the Capital account.

STEP 4: Make the Drawing account equal zero via the Capital account. This entry transfers the drawing to the *debit* side of the Capital account.

These steps are best illustrated with an example. Suppose Smart Touch closes its books at the end of May. Exhibit 4-10 on the following page shows the complete closing process for Smart Touch's training agency. Panel A gives the closing entries, and Panel B shows the accounts after posting. After the closing entries, Bright, capital ends with a balance of $35,900. Trace this balance to the statement of owner's equity and then to the balance sheet in Exhibit 4-7.

Key Takeaway

Closing the accounts is just like starting a new baseball game. The score is 0-0. All temporary account balances are zero after closing.

EXHIBIT 4-10 | **Journalizing and Posting the Closing Entries**

PANEL A—Journalizing

Closing Entries

	Date	Accounts	Debit	Credit
1	May 31	Service revenue (R–)	7,600	
		Income summary		7,600
2	31	Income summary	3,900	
		Rent expense (E–)		1,000
		Salary expense (E–)		1,800
		Supplies expense (E–)		100
		Depreciation expense—furniture (E–)		300
		Depreciation expense—building (E–)		200
		Interest expense (E–)		100
		Utilities expense (E–)		400
3	31	Income summary ($7,600 − $3,900)	3,700	
		Bright, capital (Q+)		3,700
4	31	Bright, capital (Q–)	1,000	
		Bright, drawing (D–)		1,000

PANEL B—Posting

Rent expense

Adj	1,000		
Bal	1,000	Clo 2	1,000
Bal	0		

Salary expense

	900		
Adj	900		
Bal	1,800	Clo 2	1,800
Bal	0		

Supplies expense

Adj	100		
Bal	100	Clo 2	100
Bal	0		

Depreciation expense—furniture

Adj	300		
Bal	300	Clo 2	300
Bal	0		

Depreciation expense—building

Adj	200		
Bal	200	Clo 2	200
Bal	0		

Interest expense

Adj	100		
Bal	100	Clo 2	100
Bal	0		

Utilities expense

Bal	400	Clo 2	400
Bal	0		

2 Income summary

Clo 2	3,900	Clo 1	7,600
Clo 3	3,700	Bal	3,700
		Bal	0

1

Service revenue

			7,000
		Adj	400
		Adj	200
Clo 1	7,600	Bal	7,600
		Bal	0

Bright, drawing

Bal	1,000	Clo 4	1,000
Bal	0		

4 Bright, capital

Clo 4	1,000		33,200
		Clo 3	3,700
		Bal	35,900

3

Adj = Amount posted from an adjusting entry
Clo = Amount posted from a closing entry
Bal = Balance

Post-Closing Trial Balance

 Prepare the post-
closing trial balance

The accounting cycle can end with a **post-closing trial balance** (see Exhibit 4-11). This optional step lists the accounts and their adjusted balances after closing.

EXHIBIT 4-11	Post-Closing Trial Balance

SMART TOUCH LEARNING
Post-Closing Trial Balance
May 31, 2013

	Debit	Credit
Cash	$ 4,800	
Accounts receivable	2,600	
Supplies	600	
Prepaid rent	2,000	
Furniture	18,000	
Building	48,000	
Accumulated depreciation—furniture		$ 300
Accumulated depreciation—building		200
Accounts payable		18,200
Salary payable		900
Interest payable		100
Unearned service revenue		400
Notes payable		20,000
Bright, capital		35,900
Total	$ 76,000	$ 76,000

Key Takeaway

In summary, the post-closing trial balance contains the same accounts that the balance sheet contains—assets, liabilities, and capital.

Only assets, liabilities, and capital accounts appear on the post-closing trial balance. No temporary accounts—revenues, expenses, or drawing—are included because they have been closed (their balances are zero). The ledger is now up-to-date and ready for the next period.

Classifying Assets and Liabilities

 Classify assets and liabilities as current or long-term

Assets and liabilities are classified as either *current* or *long-term* to show their relative liquidity. **Liquidity** measures how quickly and easily an account can be converted to cash, because cash is the most liquid asset. Accounts receivable are relatively liquid because receivables are collected quickly. Supplies are less liquid, and furniture and buildings are even less so because they take longer to convert to cash. A classified balance sheet lists assets in the order of their liquidity.

Assets

Owners need to know what they own. The balance sheet lists assets in liquidity order. Balance sheets report two asset categories: *current assets* and *long-term assets*.

Current Assets

Current assets will be converted to cash, sold, or used up during the next 12 months, or within the business's operating cycle if the cycle is longer than a year. **Current assets are items that will be used up in a year, like your notebook paper for this class or the change in your pocket.** The **operating cycle** is the time span when

1. cash is used to acquire goods and services,

2. these goods and services are sold to customers, and

3. the business collects cash from customers.

For most businesses, the operating cycle is a few months. Cash, Accounts receivable, Supplies, and Prepaid expenses are current assets. Merchandising entities such as **Lowes** and **Coca-Cola** have another current asset: inventory. Inventory shows the cost of the goods the company holds for sale to customers, like tools at **Lowes** or cans of soda for **Coca-Cola**.

Long-Term Assets

Long-term assets are all the assets that will not be converted to cash within the business's operating cycle. **Long-term assets can be used for more than a year, like your car or computer.** One category of long-term assets is plant assets (also called fixed assets or property, plant, and equipment). Land, Buildings, Furniture, and Equipment are plant assets. Of these, Smart Touch has Furniture and a Building.

Other categories of long-term assets include Long-Term Investments and Other Assets (a catchall category). We will discuss these categories in later chapters.

Liabilities

Owners need to know when they must pay each liability. The balance sheet lists liabilities in the order in which they must be paid. Balance sheets report two liability categories: *current liabilities* and *long-term liabilities*.

Current Liabilities

Current liabilities must be paid either with cash or with goods and services within one year, or within the entity's operating cycle if the cycle is longer than a year. **Your cell phone bill is a current liability because you have to pay it every month.** Accounts payable, Notes payable due within one year, Salary payable, Interest payable, and Unearned revenue are all current liabilities.

Long-Term Liabilities

All liabilities that do not need to be paid within the entity's operating cycle are classified as **long-term liabilities. When you buy a car, you often sign up for several years of car payments, making it a long-term liability.** Many notes payable are long-term, such as a mortgage on a building.

The Classified Balance Sheet

So far we have presented the *unclassified* balance sheet of Smart Touch. We are now ready for the balance sheet that is actually used in practice—called a **classified balance sheet.** Exhibit 4-12 presents Smart Touch's classified balance sheet using the data from Exhibit 4-7 on page 205.

Smart Touch classifies each asset and each liability as either current or long-term. Notice that the Total assets of $75,500 is the same as the Total assets on the unclassified balance sheet in Exhibit 4-7.

Connect To: Ethics

The classification of assets and liabilities as current or long-term affects many key ratios that outsiders use to evaluate the financial health of a company. Many times, the classification of a particular account is very clear—for example, a building is normally a long-term asset. But what if the company must demolish the existing building within six months due to some structural default? It would not be ethical to still show the building as a long-term asset.

EXHIBIT 4-12 | **Classified Balance Sheet in Account Form**

SMART TOUCH LEARNING
Balance Sheet
May 31, 2013

Assets				Liabilities	
Current assets:				Current liabilities:	
Cash		$ 4,800		Accounts payable	$18,200
Accounts receivable		2,600		Salary payable	900
Supplies		600		Interest payable	100
Prepaid rent		2,000		Unearned service revenue	400
Total current assets			$10,000	Total current liabilities	19,600
Plant assets:				Long-term liabilities:	
Furniture	$18,000			Notes payable	20,000
Less: Accumulated depreciation—furniture	300	17,700		Total liabilities	39,600
Building	48,000				
Less: Accumulated depreciation—building	200	47,800		**Owner's Equity**	
Total plant assets			65,500	Bright, capital	35,900
Total assets			$75,500	Total liabilities and owner's equity	$75,500

Balance Sheet Forms

Key Takeaway

Classification means dividing assets and liabilities between those that will last less than a year (current) and those that will last longer than a year (long-term). The classified balance sheet still represents the accounting equation and must balance (Assets = Liabilities + Equity).

Smart Touch's balance sheet in Exhibit 4-12 lists the assets on the left and the liabilities and the equity on the right in an arrangement known as the *account form*. The balance sheet of Smart Touch in Exhibit 4-13 lists the assets at the top and the liabilities and owner's equity below in an arrangement known as the *report form*. Although either form is acceptable, the report form is more popular.

	Classified Balance Sheet
EXHIBIT 4-13	**in Report Form**

SMART TOUCH LEARNING
Balance Sheet
May 31, 2013

Assets			
Current assets:			
Cash		$ 4,800	
Accounts receivable		2,600	
Supplies		600	
Prepaid rent		2,000	
Total current assets			$10,000
Plant assets:			
Furniture	$18,000		
Less: Accumulated depreciation—furniture	300	17,700	
Building	48,000		
Less: Accumulated depreciation—building	200	47,800	
Total plant assets			65,500
Total assets			$75,500
Liabilities			
Current liabilities:			
Accounts payable			$18,200
Salary payable			900
Interest payable			100
Unearned service revenue			400
Total current liabilities			19,600
Long-term liabilities			
Notes payable			20,000
Total liabilities			39,600
Owner's Equity			
Bright, capital			35,900
Total owner's equity			35,900
Total liabilities and owner's equity			$75,500

Accounting Ratios

Accounting is designed to provide information that business owners, managers, and lenders then use to make decisions. A bank considering lending money to a business must predict whether that business can repay the loan. If Smart Touch already has a lot of debt, repayment is less certain than if it does not owe much money. To measure the business's financial position, decision makers use financial ratios that they compute from the company's financial statements. Two of the most widely used decision aids in business are the current ratio and the debt ratio.

6 Describe the effect of various transactions on the current ratio and the debt ratio

Current Ratio

The **current ratio** measures a company's ability to pay its current liabilities with its current assets. This ratio is computed as follows:

$$\text{Current ratio} = \frac{\text{Total current assets}}{\text{Total current liabilities}}$$

A company prefers to have a high current ratio because that means it has plenty of current assets to pay its current liabilities. A current ratio that has increased from the prior period indicates improvement in a company's ability to pay its current debts. A current ratio that has decreased from the prior period signals deterioration in the company's ability to pay its current liabilities. **Your personal current ratio is your checking account balance (your current assets) divided by your monthly bills (your current liabilities).**

A Rule of Thumb: A strong current ratio is 1.50, which indicates that the company has $1.50 in current assets for every $1.00 in current liabilities. A current ratio of 1.00 is considered low and somewhat risky.

Debt Ratio

The **debt ratio** measures an organization's overall ability to pay its total liabilities (debt). The debt ratio is computed as follows:

$$\text{Debt ratio} = \frac{\text{Total liabilities}}{\text{Total assets}}$$

The debt ratio indicates the proportion of a company's assets that are financed with debt. A *low* debt ratio is safer than a high debt ratio. Why? Because a company with low liabilities usually has low required payments and is less likely to get into financial difficulty. **Your personal debt ratio is everything you owe divided by everything you own.**

A Rule of Thumb: A debt ratio below 0.60, or 60%, is considered safe for most businesses, as it indicates that the company owes only $0.60 for every $1.00 in total assets. A debt ratio above 0.80, or 80%, borders on high risk.

Now study the Decision Guidelines feature, which summarizes what you have learned in this chapter.

Key Takeaway

The current ratio measures liquidity within one year by comparing current assets to current liabilities. The debt ratio measures the ability to pay liabilities in the long term by comparing all liabilities to all assets. The different ratios give different views of a company's financial health.

Decision Guidelines 4-1

COMPLETING THE ACCOUNTING CYCLE

Suppose you own Greg's Tunes or Smart Touch Learning. How can you measure the success of your business? The Decision Guidelines describe the accounting process you will use to provide the information for any accounting decisions you need to make.

Decision	Guidelines
• What document summarizes the effects of all the entity's transactions and adjustments throughout the period?	The *worksheet* with columns for • Trial balance • Adjustments • Adjusted trial balance • Income statement • Balance sheet
• What is the last *major* step in the accounting cycle?	*Closing entries for the temporary accounts:* • Revenues • Expenses } Income statement accounts • Drawing
• Why close out the revenues, expenses, and drawing accounts?	Because these *temporary accounts* have balances that relate only to one accounting period and *do not* carry over to the next period
• Which accounts do *not* get closed out?	*Permanent (balance sheet) accounts:* • Assets • Liabilities • Capital The balances of these accounts *do* carry over to the next period.
• How do businesses classify their assets and liabilities for reporting on the balance sheet?	*Current* (within one year, or the entity's operating cycle if longer than a year), or *Long-term* (not current)
• How do Greg Moore and Sheena Bright evaluate their companies?	There are many ways, such as the company's net income (or net loss) on the income statement and the trend of net income from year to year. Another way to evaluate a company is based on the company's *financial ratios.* Two key ratios are the current ratio and the debt ratio:

$$\text{Current ratio} = \frac{\text{Total current assets}}{\text{Total current liabilities}}$$

The *current ratio* measures the company's ability to pay current liabilities with current assets.

$$\text{Debt ratio} = \frac{\text{Total liabilities}}{\text{Total assets}}$$

The *debt ratio* measures the company's overall ability to pay liabilities. The debt ratio shows the proportion of the company's assets that are financed with debt.

Summary Problem 4-2

Refer to the data in Summary Problem 4-1 (Super Employment Services).

Requirements

1. Journalize and post the adjusting entries. (Before posting to the accounts, enter into each account its balance as shown in the trial balance. For example, enter the $5,000 balance in the Accounts receivable account before posting its adjusting entry.) Key adjusting entries by *letter*, as shown in the worksheet solution to Summary Problem 4-1. You can take the adjusting entries straight from the worksheet in the chapter.

2. Journalize and post the closing entries. (Each account should carry its balance as shown in the adjusted trial balance.) To distinguish closing entries from adjusting entries, key the closing entries by *number*. Draw arrows to illustrate the flow of data, as shown in Exhibit 4-10. Indicate the balance of the Mudge, capital account after the closing entries are posted.

3. Prepare the income statement for the year ended December 31, 2014.

4. Prepare the statement of owner's equity for the year ended December 31, 2014. Draw an arrow linking the income statement to the statement of owner's equity.

5. Prepare the classified balance sheet at December 31, 2014. Use the account form. All liabilities are current. Draw an arrow linking the statement of owner's equity to the balance sheet.

Solution

Requirement 1

		Adjusting Entries		
a.	Dec 31	Supplies expense (E+)	800	
		Supplies (A–)		800
b.	31	Depreciation expense—furniture (E+)	2,000	
		Accumulated depreciation—furniture (CA+)		2,000
c.	31	Depreciation expense—building (E+)	1,000	
		Accumulated depreciation—building (CA+)		1,000
d.	31	Salary expense (E+)	500	
		Salary payable (L+)		500
e.	31	Accounts receivable (A+)	1,300	
		Service revenue (R+)		1,300
f.	31	Unearned service revenue (L–)	3,000	
		Service revenue (R+)		3,000

Accounts receivable

	5,000		
(e)	1,300		
Bal	6,300		

Supplies

	1,000	(a)	800
Bal	200		

Accumulated depreciation—furniture

			4,000
		(b)	2,000
		Bal	6,000

Accumulated depreciation—building

			30,000
		(c)	1,000
		Bal	31,000

Salary payable

		(d)	500
		Bal	500

Unearned service revenue

(f)	3,000		8,000
		Bal	5,000

Service revenue

			60,000
		(e)	1,300
		(f)	3,000
		Bal	64,300

Salary expense

	16,000		
(d)	500		
Bal	16,500		

Supplies expense

(a)	800		
Bal	800		

Depreciation expense—furniture

(b)	2,000		
Bal	2,000		

Depreciation expense—building

(c)	1,000		
Bal	1,000		

Requirement 2

Closing Entries					
1.	Dec 31	Service revenue	(R–)	64,300	
		Income summary			64,300
2.	31	Income summary		23,300	
		Salary expense	(E–)		16,500
		Supplies expense	(E–)		800
		Depreciation expense—furniture	(E–)		2,000
		Depreciation expense—building	(E–)		1,000
		Advertising expense	(E–)		3,000
3.	31	Income summary ($64,300 – $23,300)		41,000	
		Mudge, capital	(Q+)		41,000
4.	31	Mudge, capital	(Q–)	25,000	
		Mudge, drawing	(D–)		25,000

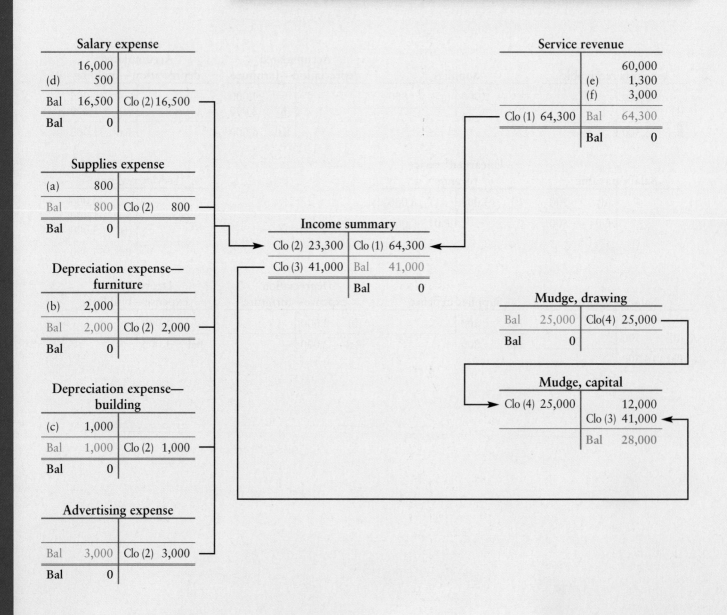

Salary expense

	16,000		
(d)	500		
Bal	16,500	Clo (2)	16,500
Bal	0		

Supplies expense

(a)	800		
Bal	800	Clo (2)	800
Bal	0		

Depreciation expense—furniture

(b)	2,000		
Bal	2,000	Clo (2)	2,000
Bal	0		

Depreciation expense—building

(c)	1,000		
Bal	1,000	Clo (2)	1,000
Bal	0		

Advertising expense

Bal	3,000	Clo (2)	3,000
Bal	0		

Income summary

Clo (2)	23,300	Clo (1)	64,300
Clo (3)	41,000	Bal	41,000
		Bal	0

Service revenue

			60,000
		(e)	1,300
		(f)	3,000
Clo (1)	64,300	Bal	64,300
		Bal	0

Mudge, drawing

Bal	25,000	Clo(4)	25,000
Bal	0		

Mudge, capital

Clo (4)	25,000		12,000
		Clo (3)	41,000
		Bal	28,000

Requirement 3

SUPER EMPLOYMENT SERVICES		
Income Statement		
Year Ended December 31, 2014		
Revenue:		
Service revenue		$64,300
Expenses:		
Salary expense	$16,500	
Advertising expense	3,000	
Depreciation expense—furniture	2,000	
Depreciation expense—building	1,000	
Supplies expense	800	
Total expenses		23,300
Net income		$41,000

Requirement 4

SUPER EMPLOYMENT SERVICES	
Statement of Owner's Equity	
Year Ended December 31, 2014	
Mudge, capital, January 1, 2014	$ 12,000
Net income	41,000
	53,000
Drawing	(25,000)
Mudge, capital, December 31, 2014	$ 28,000

Requirement 5

SUPER EMPLOYMENT SERVICES						
Balance Sheet						
December 31, 2014						
Assets				**Liabilities**		
Current assets:				Current liabilities:		
Cash		$ 6,000		Accounts payable		$ 2,000
Accounts receivable		6,300		Salary payable		500
Supplies		200		Unearned service		
Total current assets		12,500		revenue		5,000
Long-term assets:				Total current liabilities		7,500
Furniture	$10,000					
Less: Accumulated depreciation—furniture	6,000	4,000				
Building	50,000			**Owner's Equity**		
Less: Accumulated depreciation—building	31,000	19,000		Mudge, capital		28,000
Total assets		$35,500		Total liabilities and owner's equity		$35,500

Chapter 4: Demo Doc

Accounting Worksheets and Closing Entries

To make sure you understand this material, work through the following demonstration "demo doc" with detailed comments to help you see the concept within the framework of a worked-through problem.

This question continues on from the Cloud Break Consulting Demo Doc in Chapter 3.

Use the data from the adjusted trial balance of Cloud Break Consulting at June 30, 2014:

CLOUD BREAK CONSULTING Adjusted Trial Balance June 30, 2014		
Account Title	**Debit**	**Credit**
Cash	$131,000	
Accounts receivable	119,000	
Supplies	1,000	
Prepaid rent	18,000	
Land	45,000	
Building	300,000	
Accumulated depreciation—building		$167,000
Accounts payable		159,000
Salary payable		1,000
Unearned service revenue		10,000
Moe, capital		102,000
Moe, drawing	7,000	
Service revenue		495,000
Salary expense	256,000	
Supplies expense	3,000	
Rent expense	34,000	
Depreciation expense—building	12,000	
Miscellaneous expense	8,000	
Totals	$934,000	$934,000

Requirements

1. **Prepare Cloud Break's accounting worksheet showing the adjusted trial balance, the income statement accounts, and the balance sheet accounts.**
2. **Journalize and post Cloud Break's closing entries.**

Chapter 4: Demo Doc Solution

Requirement 1

Prepare Cloud Break's accounting worksheet showing the adjusted trial balance, the income statement accounts, and the balance sheet accounts.

Part 1	Part 2	Part 3	Part 4	Part 5	Demo Doc Complete

The accounting worksheet is very similar to the adjusted trial balance; however, the worksheet has additional debit and credit columns for the income statement and balance sheet.

CLOUD BREAK CONSULTING
Worksheet
Month Ended June 30, 2014

Account Title	Adjusted Trial Balance Debit	Credit	Income Statement Debit	Credit	Balance Sheet Debit	Credit
Cash	$131,000					
Accounts receivable	119,000					
Supplies	1,000					
Prepaid rent	18,000					
Land	45,000					
Building	300,000					
Accumulated depreciation—building		$167,000				
Accounts payable		159,000				
Salary payable		1,000				
Unearned service revenue		10,000				
Moe, capital		102,000				
Moe, drawing	7,000					
Service revenue		495,000				
Salary expense	256,000					
Supplies expense	3,000					
Rent expense	34,000					
Depreciation expense—building	12,000					
Miscellaneous expense	8,000					
	$934,000	$934,000				

The accounts that belong on the income statement are put into the income statement columns and all other accounts are put into the balance sheet columns.

The income statement lists revenues and expenses. So Cloud Break's revenues (Service revenue) and expenses (Salary expense, Supplies expense, Rent expense, Depreciation expense—building, and Miscellaneous expense) are copied over to the income statement columns.

	Adjusted Trial Balance		Income Statement		Balance Sheet	
CLOUD BREAK CONSULTING **Worksheet** Month Ended June 30, 2014						
Account Title	Debit	Credit	Debit	Credit	Debit	Credit
Cash	$131,000					
Accounts receivable	119,000					
Supplies	1,000					
Prepaid rent	18,000					
Land	45,000					
Building	300,000					
Accumulated depreciation—building		$167,000				
Accounts payable		159,000				
Salary payable		1,000				
Unearned service revenue		10,000				
Moe, capital		102,000				
Moe, drawing	7,000					
Service revenue		495,000		$495,000		
Salary expense	256,000		$256,000			
Supplies expense	3,000		3,000			
Rent expense	34,000		34,000			
Depreciation expense—building	12,000		12,000			
Miscellaneous expense	8,000		8,000			
	$934,000	$934,000	$313,000	$495,000		
Net income			182,000			
			$495,000	$495,000		

Net income is calculated by subtracting the expenses from the revenues, $495,000 − $313,000 = $182,000. Notice that this is the same as net income from the income statement prepared in the Chapter 3 Demo Doc.

The other accounts (assets, liabilities, equity, and drawing) are now copied over to the balance sheet columns.

	Adjusted Trial Balance		Income Statement		Balance Sheet	
Account Title	**Debit**	**Credit**	**Debit**	**Credit**	**Debit**	**Credit**
Cash	$131,000				$131,000	
Accounts receivable	119,000				119,000	
Supplies	1,000				1,000	
Prepaid rent	18,000				18,000	
Land	45,000				45,000	
Building	300,000				300,000	
Accumulated depreciation—building		$167,000				$167,000
Accounts payable		159,000				159,000
Salary payable		1,000				1,000
Unearned service revenue		10,000				10,000
Moe, capital		102,000				102,000
Moe, drawing	7,000				7,000	
Service revenue		495,000		$495,000		
Salary expense	256,000		$256,000			
Supplies expense	3,000		3,000			
Rent expense	34,000		34,000			
Depreciation expense—building	12,000		12,000			
Miscellaneous expense	8,000		8,000			
	$934,000	$934,000	$313,000	$495,000	$621,000	$439,000
Net income			182,000			182,000
			$495,000	$495,000	$621,000	$621,000

CLOUD BREAK CONSULTING
Worksheet
Month Ended June 30, 2014

Net income is added to the credit side of the balance sheet to make total credits equal total debits. This is because net income increases Moe, capital (and therefore equity) as seen in Requirement 2 of this Demo Doc (where the closing entries are journalized).

Requirement 2

Journalize and post Cloud Break's closing entries.

Part 1	**Part 2**	Part 3	Part 4	Part 5	Demo Doc Complete

We prepare closing entries to (1) clear out the revenue, expense, and drawing accounts to a zero balance in order to get them ready for the next period—that is, they must begin the next period empty so that we can evaluate each period's earnings separately from other periods. We also need to (2) update the Moe, capital account by transferring net income (or net loss) and drawing into it.

The Capital balance is calculated each year using the following formula:

> Beginning capital
> + Net income (or – Net loss)
> – Drawing
> = Ending capital

You can see this in the Capital T-account as well:

Capital	
	Beginning capital
	Net income
Drawing	
	Ending capital

This formula is the key to preparing the closing entries. We will use this formula, but we will do it *inside* the Capital T-account.

From the adjusted trial balance, we know that beginning Moe, capital is $102,000. The first component of the formula is already in the T-account.

The next component is net income, which is *not* yet in the Moe, capital account. There is no T-account with net income in it, but we can *create* one.

We will create a new T-account called *Income summary*. We will place in the Income summary account all the components of net income and come out with the net income number at the bottom. Remember:

> Revenues – Expenses = Net income (or Net loss)

This means that we need to get all of the revenues and expenses into the Income summary account.

Look at the Service revenue T-account:

Service revenue	
	Bal 495,000

In order to clear out all the income statement accounts so that they are empty to begin the next year, the first step is to debit each revenue account for the amount of its credit balance. Service revenue has a *credit* balance of $495,000, so to bring that to zero, we need to *debit* Service revenue for $495,000.

This means that we have part of our first closing entry:

1.	Service revenue (R–)	495,000	
	???		495,000

What is the credit side of this entry? The reason we were looking at Service revenue to begin with was to help calculate net income using the Income summary account. So the other side of the entry must go to the Income summary account:

1.	Service revenue	(R–)	495,000	
	Income summary			495,000

Part 1	Part 2	**Part 3**	Part 4	Part 5	Demo Doc Complete

The second step is to *credit* each expense account for the amount of its *debit* balance to bring each expense account to zero. In this case, we have five different expenses:

	Salary expense			Supplies expense
Bal	256,000		Bal	3,000

	Rent expense			Depreciation expense—building
Bal	34,000		Bal	12,000

	Miscellaneous expense
Bal	8,000

The sum of all the expenses will go to the debit side of the Income summary account:

2.	Income summary		313,000	
	Salary expense	(E–)		256,000
	Supplies expense	(E–)		3,000
	Rent expense	(E–)		34,000
	Depreciation expense—building	(E–)		12,000
	Miscellaneous expense	(E–)		8,000

Part 1	Part 2	Part 3	**Part 4**	Part 5	Demo Doc Complete

Now look at the Income summary account:

	Income summary		
		1.	495,000
2.	313,000		
		Bal	182,000

Remember that the credit of $495,000 is from the first closing entry prepared at the beginning of this requirement.

The purpose of creating the Income summary was to get the net income number into a single account. Notice that the Income summary balance is the same net income number that appears on the income statement and in the accounting worksheet in Requirement 1.

Income summary now has a *credit* balance of $182,000. The third step in the closing process is to transfer net income to the Moe, capital account. To zero out the Income summary account, we must *debit* the Income summary for $182,000:

3.	Income summary	182,000	
	???		182,000

What is the credit side of this entry? It is the Moe, capital account. The reason we created the (temporary) Income summary account was to help calculate the net income or net loss for the Moe, capital account. So the credit side of the entry must go to Moe, capital:

3.	Income summary	182,000	
	Moe, capital (Q+)		182,000

This entry adds the net income to Moe, capital. Notice that it also brings the Income summary account to a zero balance.

Part 1	Part 2	Part 3	Part 4	**Part 5**	Demo Doc Complete

The last component of the capital formula is drawing. There is already a Moe, drawing account:

Moe, drawing

Bal	7,000	

The final step in the closing process is to transfer Moe, drawing to the debit side of the Moe, capital account. The Moe, drawing account has a *debit* balance of $7,000, so to bring that to zero, we need to *credit* Moe, drawing by $7,000. The balancing debit will go to Moe, capital:

4.	Moe, capital (Q–)	7,000	
	Moe, drawing (D–)		7,000

This entry subtracts Moe, drawing from the Moe, capital account.
Moe, capital now holds the following data:

Moe, capital

				102,000	Beginning capital
			3.	182,000	Net income
Drawing	4.	7,000			
			Bal	277,000	Ending capital

The formula to update Moe, capital has now been re-created inside the Moe, capital T-account.

The following accounts are included in the closing process:

	Service revenue		
			495,000
1.	495,000		
		Bal	0

	Salary expense		
	256,000		
		2.	256,000
Bal	0		

	Supplies expense		
	3,000		
		2.	3,000
Bal	0		

	Rent expense		
	34,000		
		2.	34,000
Bal	0		

	Depreciation expense—building		
	12,000		
		2.	12,000
Bal	0		

	Miscellaneous expense		
	8,000		
		2.	8,000
Bal	0		

	Income summary		
		1.	495,000
2.	313,000		
		Bal	182,000
3.	182,000		
		Bal	0

	Moe, drawing		
	7,000		
		4.	7,000
Bal	0		

	Moe, capital		
			102,000
		3.	182,000
4.	7,000		
		Bal	277,000

Notice that all the temporary accounts (the revenues, the expenses, Drawing, and Income summary) now have a zero balance.

Part 1	Part 2	Part 3	Part 4	Part 5	**Demo Doc Complete**

Review *Completing the Accounting Cycle*

● Accounting Vocabulary

Accounting Cycle (p. 199)
Process by which companies produce their financial statements for a specific period.

Classified Balance Sheet (p. 211)
A balance sheet that classifies each asset and each liability as either current or long-term.

Closing the Accounts (p. 207)
Step in the accounting cycle at the end of the period. Closing the accounts consists of journalizing and posting the closing entries to set the balances of the revenue, expense, and drawing accounts to zero for the next period.

Closing Entries (p. 207)
Entries that transfer the revenue, expense, and drawing balances to the Capital account.

Current Assets (p. 211)
Assets that are expected to be converted to cash, sold, or used up during the next 12 months, or within the business's normal operating cycle if the cycle is longer than a year.

Current Liabilities (p. 211)
Debts due to be paid with cash or with goods and services within one year, or within the entity's operating cycle if the cycle is longer than a year.

Current Ratio (p. 214)
Current assets divided by current liabilities. This ratio measures the company's ability to pay current liabilities from current assets.

Debt Ratio (p. 214)
Total liabilities divided by total assets. This ratio reveals the proportion of a company's assets that it has financed with debt.

Income Summary (p. 207)
A temporary "holding tank" account into which revenues and expenses are transferred prior to their final transfer to the Capital account.

Liquidity (p. 210)
Measure of how quickly an item can be converted to cash.

Long-Term Assets (p. 211)
Any assets that will NOT be converted to cash or used up within the business's operating cycle, or one year, whichever is greater.

Long-Term Liabilities (p. 211)
Liabilities that are not current.

Nominal Accounts (p. 207)
The revenue and expense accounts that relate to a particular accounting period and are closed at the end of that period. For a company, the Drawing account is also temporary. Also called **temporary accounts**.

Operating Cycle (p. 211)
Time span during which cash is paid for goods and services, which are then sold to customers from whom the business collects cash.

Permanent Accounts (p. 207)
Accounts that are *not* closed at the end of the period—the asset, liability, and capital accounts. Also called **real accounts**.

Post-Closing Trial Balance (p. 210)
List of the accounts and their balances at the end of the period after journalizing and posting the closing entries. This last step of the accounting cycle ensures that the ledger is in balance to start the next accounting period. It should include only balance sheet accounts.

Real Accounts (p. 207)
Accounts that are not closed at the end of the period—the assets, liabilities, and capital accounts. Also called **permanent accounts**.

Reversing Entries (online Appendix 4A)
Special journal entries that ease the burden of accounting for transactions in the next period.

Temporary Accounts (p. 207)
The revenue and expense accounts that relate to a particular accounting period and are closed at the end of that period. For a company, the Drawing account is also temporary. Also called **nominal accounts**.

Worksheet (p. 200)
An internal columnar document designed to help move data from the trial balance to their financial statements.

● Destination: Student Success

Student Success Tips

The following are hints on some common trouble areas for students in this chapter:

● Be sure you remember the four closing entries, paying special attention to which accounts are closed. (TIP: Make temporary accounts = zero.)

● Practice the 5-column worksheets. Remember that debits = credits in the first 3 columns. Debits from columns 4 and 5 (Income Statement and Balance Sheet) do not equal credits until you post the net income or net loss for the period. (TIP: Total Debits from Column 3 = Column 4 Debits + Column 5 Debits.)

● Recall the classification difference between current (normally, 1 year or less) and long term (more than a year). (TIP: If it lasts more than a year, it's long term.)

Getting Help

If there's a learning objective from the chapter you aren't confident about, try using one or more of the following resources:

● Practice additional exercises or problems at the end of Chapter 4 that cover the specific learning objective that is challenging you.

● Watch the white board tips and/or videos for Chapter 4 located at myaccountinglab.com under the Chapter Resources button.

● Review the Chapter 4 Demo Doc located on page 220 of the textbook.

● Go to myaccountinglab.com and select the Study Plan button. Choose Chapter 4 and work the questions covering that specific learning objective until you've mastered it.

● Destination: Student Success *(Continued)*

Student Success Tips

- Remember the formulas for the current ratio and debt ratio. (TIP: The current ratio usually should be greater than 1; the debt ratio should be less than 1.)

Getting Help

- Work the Chapter 4 pre/post tests in myaccountinglab.com.

- Consult the Check Figures for End of Chapter starters, exercises, and problems—located at myaccountinglab.com.

- Visit the learning resource center on your campus for tutoring.

● Quick Check

1. Consider the steps in the accounting cycle in Exhibit 4-1. Which part of the accounting cycle provides information to help a business decide whether to expand its operations?

   a. Post-closing trial balance   c. Closing entries

   b. Adjusting entries   d. Financial statements

2. Which columns of the accounting worksheet show unadjusted amounts?

   a. Adjustments   c. Income Statement

   b. Trial Balance   d. Balance Sheet

3. Which of the following accounts may appear on a post-closing trial balance?

   a. Cash, Salary payable, and Capital

   b. Cash, Salary payable, and Service revenue

   c. Cash, Service revenue, and Salary expense

   d. Cash, Salary payable, and Salary expense

4. Which situation indicates a net loss within the Income Statement columns of the worksheet?

   a. Total credits exceed total debits   c. Total debits equal total credits

   b. Total debits exceed total credits   d. None of the above

5. Supplies has a $10,000 unadjusted balance on your trial balance. At year-end you count supplies of $6,000. What adjustment will appear on your worksheet?

   a.
Supplies	4,000	
Supplies expense		4,000

   b.
Supplies expense	6,000	
Supplies		6,000

   c.
Supplies expense	4,000	
Supplies		4,000

   d. No adjustment is needed because the Supplies account already has a correct balance.

6. Which of the following accounts is *not* closed?

   a. Depreciation expense   c. Service revenue

   b. Drawing   d. Accumulated depreciation

7. What do closing entries accomplish?

   a. Zero out the revenues, expenses, and drawing

   b. Transfer revenues, expenses, and drawing to the Capital account

   c. Bring the Capital account to its correct ending balance

   d. All of the above

Experience the Power of Practice!

As denoted by the logo, all of these questions, as well as additional practice materials, can be found in

MyAccountingLab.

Please visit myaccountinglab.com

8. Which of the following is *not* a closing entry?

a.
Capital	XXX	
Drawing		XXX

b.
Service revenue	XXX	
Income summary		XXX

c.
Salary payable	XXX	
Income summary		XXX

d.
Income summary	XXX	
Rent expense		XXX

9. Assets and liabilities are listed on the balance sheet in order of their

   a. purchase date.   c. liquidity.

   b. adjustments.   d. balance.

10. Clean Water Softener Systems has cash of $600, receivables of $900, and supplies of $400. Clean owes $500 on accounts payable and salary payable of $200. Clean's current ratio is

   a. 2.71   c. 0.63

   b. 2.50   d. 0.37

Answers are given after Apply Your Knowledge (p. 253).

Assess Your Progress

● Short Exercises

MyAccountingLab   **S4-1**   **①** **Explaining worksheet items [10 min]**
Link Back to Chapter 3 (Adjusting Entries). Consider the following adjusting entries:

		Journal Entry		
	Date	Accounts and Explanations	Debit	Credit
a.	Apr 30	Rent expense	900	
		Prepaid rent		900
b.	30	Unearned service revenue	350	
		Service revenue		350
c.	30	Supplies expense	200	
		Supplies		200
d.	30	Salary expense	850	
		Salary payable		850
e.	30	Depreciation expense—furniture	450	
		Accumulated depreciation—furniture		450

Requirement

1. State one reason why each of the previous adjusting entries were made.

   Example: The explanation for journal entry a could be some of the Prepaid rent has expired. Another correct explanation would be the asset account Prepaid rent was overstated. A third correct explanation would be that Rent expense incurred was understated.

S4-2 ❶ **Explaining worksheet items [10–15 min]**

Link Back to Chapters 2 and 3 (Definitions of Accounts). Consider the following list of accounts:

a. Accounts receivable   f. Accounts payable
b. Supplies   g. Unearned service revenue
c. Prepaid rent   h. Service revenue
d. Furniture   i. Rent expense
e. Accumulated depreciation—
    furniture

Requirement

1. Explain what a normal balance in each account means. For example, if the account is "Cash," the explanation would be "the balance of cash on a specific date."

S4-3 ❷ **Using the worksheet to prepare financial statements [5–10 min]**

Answer the following questions:

Requirements

1. What type of normal balance does the Capital account have—debit or credit?
2. Which type of income statement account has the same type of balance as the Capital account?
3. Which type of income statement account has the opposite type of balance as the Capital account?
4. What do we call the difference between total debits and total credits on the income statement? Into what account is the difference figure closed at the end of the period?

S4-4 ❸ **Journalizing closing entries [10–15 min]**

It is December 31 and time for you to close the books for Brett Tilman Enterprises.

Requirement

1. Journalize the closing entries for Brett Tilman Enterprises:

a. Service revenue, $20,600.
b. Make a single closing entry for all the expenses: Salary, $7,200; Rent, $4,500; Advertising, $3,400.
c. Income summary.
d. Drawing, $3,800.

S4-5 ❸ **Posting closing entries directly to T-accounts [5 min]**

It is December 31 and time for your business to close the books. The following balances appear on the books of Sarah Simon Enterprises:

a. Drawing, $8,500.
b. Service revenue, $23,700.
c. Expense account balances: Salary, $6,100; Rent, $4,000; Advertising, $3,300.

Requirements

1. Set up each T-account given and insert its adjusted balance as given (denote as *Bal*) at December 31. Also set up a T-account for Simon, capital, $26,100, and for Income summary.
2. Post the closing entries to the accounts, denoting posted amounts as *Clo*.
3. Compute the ending balance of Simon, capital.

S4-6 ③ **Making closing entries [5 min]**

Brown Insurance Agency reported the following items at November 30, 2012:

Sales and marketing expense	$2,100	Cash	$1,100
Other assets	700	Service revenue	5,500
Depreciation expense	800	Accounts payable	500
Long-term liabilities	600	Accounts receivable	900

Requirement

1. Journalize Brown's closing entries, as needed for these accounts.

S4-7 ③ **Posting closing entries [5 min]**

Patel Insurance Agency reported the following items at September 30:

Sales and marketing expense	$1,600	Cash	$1,300
Other assets	700	Service revenue	4,000
Depreciation expense	900	Patel, capital	500
Long-term liabilities	600	Accounts receivable	900

Requirement

1. Prepare T-accounts for Patel Insurance Agency. Insert the account balances prior to closing. Post the closing entries to the affected T-accounts, and show each account's ending balance after closing. Also show the Income summary T-account. Denote a balance as *Bal* and a closing entry amount as *Clo*.

S4-8 ④ **Preparing a post-closing trial balance [10 min]**

After closing its accounts at July 31, 2012, Goodrow Electric Company had the following account balances:

Long-term liabilities	$ 800	Equipment	$ 4,500
Land	1,200	Cash	100
Accounts receivable	1,600	Service revenue	0
Total expenses	0	Goodrow, capital	3,000
Accounts payable	1,100	Supplies	200
Unearned service revenue	1,400	Accumulated depreciation	1,300
Goodrow, drawing	0		

Requirement

1. Prepare Goodrow's post-closing trial balance at July 31, 2012.

S4-9 ⑤ **Classifying assets and liabilities as current or long-term [5 min]**

Jet Fast Printing reported the following:

Buildings	$4,200	Service revenue	$1,115
Accounts payable	600	Cash	400
Total expenses	1,200	Receivables	700
Accumulated depreciation	3,000	Interest expense	110
Accrued liabilities (such as Salary payable)	400	Equipment	1,100
Prepaid expenses	300		

Requirements

1. Identify the assets (including contra assets) and liabilities.
2. Classify each asset and each liability as current or long-term.

S4-10 ⑤ **Classifying assets and liabilities as current or long-term [10 min]**
Link Back to Chapter 3 (Book Value). Examine Jet Fast Printing's account balances in Short Exercise 4-9.

Requirement

1. Identify or compute the following amounts for Jet Fast Printing:
   a. Total current assets
   b. Total current liabilities
   c. Book value of plant assets
   d. Total long-term liabilities

S4-11 ⑥ **Computing the current and debt ratios [10–15 min]**
Heart of Texas Telecom has these account balances at December 31, 2012:

Note payable, long-term	$ 7,800	Accounts payable	$ 3,700
Prepaid rent	2,300	Accounts receivable	5,700
Salary payable	3,000	Cash	3,500
Service revenue	29,400	Depreciation expense	6,000
Supplies	500	Equipment	15,000

Requirements

1. Compute Heart of Texas Telecom's current ratio and debt ratio.
2. How much in *current* assets does Heart of Texas Telecom have for every dollar of *current* liabilities that it owes?

● Exercises

E4-12 ① **Preparing a worksheet [30–40 min]**
Data for the unadjusted trial balance of Mexican Riviera Tanning Salon at March 31, 2012, follow.

Cash	$ 13,000	Service revenue	$ 89,900
Equipment	66,500	Salary expense	42,200
Accumulated depreciation	18,500	Depreciation expense	
Accounts payable	3,200	Supplies expense	
Supplies	1,400	Neeland, drawing	
Neeland, capital	11,500		

Adjusting data for March 2012 are:

a. Accrued service revenue, $2,600.   c. Accrued salary expense, $1,700.
b. Supplies used in operations, $400.   d. Depreciation expense, $4,100.

Les Neeland, the owner, has received an offer to sell the company. He needs to know the net income for the month covered by these data.

Requirements

1. Prepare the worksheet for Mexican Riviera Tanning Salon.
2. How much was the net income/net loss for March?

E4-13 ❶ **Preparing a worksheet and using it to calculate net income [20–30 min]**

The trial balance of Telegraphic Link at November 30, follows:

	Balance	
TELEGRAPHIC LINK Trial Balance November 30, 2012		
Account	**Debit**	**Credit**
Cash	$ 4,000	
Accounts receivable	3,200	
Prepaid rent	1,900	
Supplies	3,000	
Equipment	34,800	
Accumulated depreciation		$ 1,600
Accounts payable		5,400
Salary payable		
Thomas, capital		35,700
Thomas, drawing	2,100	
Service revenue		8,600
Depreciation expense		
Salary expense	1,700	
Rent expense		
Utilities expense	600	
Supplies expense		
Total	$51,300	$51,300

Additional information at November 30, 2012:

a. Accrued service revenue, $600.
b. Depreciation, $300.
c. Accrued salary expense, $800.
d. Prepaid rent expired, $500.
e. Supplies used, $100.

Requirements

1. Complete Telegraphic Link's worksheet for the month ended November 30, 2012.
2. How much was net income for November?

Note: Exercise 4-14 should be used only after completing Exercise 4-13.

E4-14 ❷ **Preparing financial statements from the completed worksheet [15–20 min]**

Use your answer from E4-13.

Requirement

1. Prepare Telegraphic Link's balance sheet as of November 30, 2012.

Note: Exercise 4-15 should be used only after completing Exercise 4-13.

E4-15 ❸ **Journalizing adjusting and closing entries [15–20 min]**

Use your answer from E4-13.

Requirement

1. Journalize Telegraphic Link's adjusting and closing entries at November 30, 2012.

Note: Exercise 4-16 should be used only after completing Exercise 4-13 and 4-15.

E4-16 ③ **Using the worksheet, and posting adjusting and closing entries [20–30 min]**
Consider the entries prepared in Exercise 4-15.

Requirements

1. Set up T-accounts for those accounts affected by the adjusting and closing entries in Exercise 4-15.

2. Post the adjusting and closing entries to the accounts; denote adjustment amounts by *Adj*, closing amounts by *Clo*, and balances by *Bal*. Double underline the accounts with zero balances after you close them, and show the ending balance in each account.

E4-17 ③ **Preparing adjusting and closing entries [20 min]**
Link Back to Chapter 3 (Adjusting Entries). Todd McKinney Magic Show's accounting records include the following account balances as of December 31:

	2011	2012
Prepaid rent	$ 200	$ 3,100
Unearned service revenue	1,000	500

During 2012, the business recorded the following:

a. Prepaid annual rent of $8,000.
b. Made the year-end adjustment to record rent expense of $5,100 for the year.
c. Collected $4,400 cash in advance for service revenue to be earned later.
d. Made the year-end adjustment to record the earning of $4,900 service revenue that had been collected in advance.

Requirements

1. Set up T-accounts for Prepaid rent, Rent expense, Unearned service revenue, and Service revenue. Insert beginning and ending balances for Prepaid rent and Unearned service revenue.

2. Journalize the adjusting entries a–d, and post to the accounts. Explanations are not required.

3. What is the balance in Service revenue after adjusting?

4. What is the balance in Rent expense after adjusting?

5. Journalize any required closing entries.

E4-18 ③ **Preparing closing entries from a partial worksheet [15–25 min]**
The adjusted trial balance from the January worksheet of Silver Sign Company follows:

	SILVER SIGN COMPANY		
	Partial Worksheet		
	Month Ended January 31, 2012		
		Adjusted Trial Balance	
Account	Debit	Credit	
Cash	$14,300		
Supplies	2,400		
Prepaid rent	1,400		
Equipment	45,000		
Accumulated depreciation		$ 6,100	
Accounts payable		4,500	
Salary payable		300	
Unearned service revenue		4,500	
Note payable, long-term		5,300	
Silver, capital		32,600	
Silver, drawing	800		
Service revenue		16,800	
Salary expense	3,600		
Rent expense	1,400		
Depreciation expense	400		
Supplies expense	200		
Utilities expense	600		
Total	$70,100	$70,100	

Requirements

1. Journalize Silver's closing entries at January 31.
2. How much net income or net loss did Silver earn for January? How can you tell?

E4-19 ③ **Preparing a statement of owner's equity [5–10 min]**
Selected accounts of Guitars by Peter for the year ended December 31, 2012, follow:

Peter, capital				Peter, drawing				Income summary			
Clo	31,000	Jan 1	152,000	Mar 31	10,000			Clo	100,000	Clo	220,000
		Clo	120,000	Jun 30	7,000			Clo	120,000	Bal	120,000
		Bal	241,000	Sep 30	8,000						
				Dec 31	6,000						
				Bal	31,000	Clo	31,000				

Requirement

1. Prepare the company's statement of owner's equity for the year.

E4-20 ③ **Identifying and journalizing closing entries [15 min]**

Gunther recorded the following transactions and year-end adjustments during 2012:

Journal Entry		
Accounts and Explanations	Debit	Credit
Prepaid rent	8,000	
Cash		8,000
Prepaid the annual rent.		
Rent expense	5,100	
Prepaid rent		5,100
Adjustment to record rent expense for the year.		
Cash	4,200	
Unearned service revenue		4,200
Collected cash in advance of service revenue to be earned.		
Unearned service revenue	4,700	
Service revenue		4,700
Adjustment to record revenue earned.		

Requirements

1. Assuming that there were no other service revenue and rent expense transactions during 2012, journalize Gunther's closing entries at the end of 2012.

2. Open T-accounts for Service revenue and Rent expense. Post the closing entries to these accounts. What are their balances after closing?

E4-21 ③ **Identifying and journalizing closing entries [10–15 min]**

The accountant for Klein Photography has posted adjusting entries (a)–(e) to the following selected accounts at December 31, 2012.

Accounts receivable		Supplies	
46,000		5,000	(b) 2,400
(a) 2,000			

Accumulated depr.—furniture		Accumulated depr.—building	
	8,000		30,000
	(c) 800		(d) 6,200

Salary payable		Klein, capital	
	(e) 700		47,000

Klein, drawing		Service revenue	
57,000			108,000
			(a) 2,000

Salary expense		Supplies expense	
25,400		(b) 2,400	
(e) 700			

Depreciation expense—furniture		Depreciation expense—building	
(c) 800		(d) 6,200	

Requirements

1. Journalize Klein Photography's closing entries at December 31, 2012.
2. Determine Klein Photography's ending Klein, capital balance at December 31, 2012.

Note: Exercise 4-22 should be prepared only after completing Exercises 4-13 through 4-16.

E4-22 ❹ **Preparing a post-closing trial balance [10–15 min]**
Review your answers from Exercises 4-13 through 4-16.

Requirement

1. Prepare the post-closing trial balance of Telegraphic Link at November 30, 2012.

E4-23 ❺❻ **Preparing a classified balance sheet, and calculating the current and debt ratios [15–20 min]**
The adjusted trial balance amounts from the August worksheet of Brian O'Brion Dance Studio Company follow:

BRIAN O'BRION DANCE STUDIO COMPANY		
Partial Worksheet		
Month Ended August 31, 2012		
	Adjusted Trial Balance	
Account	Debit	Credit
Cash	$15,800	
Supplies	2,000	
Prepaid rent	900	
Equipment	49,000	
Accumulated depreciation		$ 5,500
Accounts payable		4,500
Salary payable		500
Unearned service revenue		5,100
Long-term note payable		4,400
O'Brion, capital		36,500
O'Brion, drawing	1,100	
Service revenue		18,100
Salary expense	3,000	
Rent expense	1,500	
Depreciation expense	300	
Supplies expense	400	
Utilities expense	600	
Total	$74,600	$74,600

Requirements

1. Prepare the classified balance sheet of Brian O'Brion Dance Studio Company at August 31, 2012. Use the report form. You must compute the ending balance of O'Brion, capital.
2. Compute O'Brion's current ratio and debt ratio at August 31, 2012. One year ago, the current ratio was 1.49 and the debt ratio was 0.29. Indicate whether O'Brion's ability to pay current and total debts has improved, deteriorated, or remained the same during the current year.

Problems (Group A)

P4-24A ① ② Preparing a worksheet and the financial statements [40–50 min]
The trial balance and adjustment data of Myla's Motors at November 30, 2012, follow:

	MYLA'S MOTORS Trial Balance November 30, 2012		
		Balance	
Account		**Debit**	**Credit**
Cash		$ 4,300	
Accounts receivable		26,600	
Supplies		500	
Prepaid insurance		1,700	
Equipment		53,500	
Accumulated depreciation			$36,400
Accounts payable			13,400
Wages payable			
Unearned service revenue			8,000
Myla, capital			19,700
Myla, drawing		3,800	
Service revenue			16,000
Depreciation expense			
Wage expense		1,600	
Insurance expense			
Utilities expense		1,500	
Supplies expense			
Total		$93,500	$93,500

Additional data at November 30, 2012:

a. Depreciation on equipment, $1,100.
b. Accrued wage expense, $600.
c. Supplies on hand, $200.
d. Prepaid insurance expired during November, $200.
e. Unearned service revenue earned during November, $4,000.
f. Accrued service revenue, $800.

Requirements

1. Complete Myla's worksheet for November. Key adjusting entries by letter.
2. Prepare the income statement, the statement of owner's equity, and the classified balance sheet in account form for the month ended November 30, 2012.

P4-25A ① ② ③ **Preparing a worksheet, financial statements, and closing entries [50–60 min]**

The trial balance of Fugazy Investment Advisers at December 31, 2012, follows:

FUGAZY INVESTMENT ADVISERS		
Trial Balance		
December 31, 2012		
	Bala	nce
Account	**Debit**	**Credit**
Cash	$ 32,000	
Accounts receivable	46,000	
Supplies	3,000	
Equipment	25,000	
Accumulated depreciation		$ 11,000
Accounts payable		15,000
Salary payable		
Unearned service revenue		2,000
Note payable, long-term		39,000
Fugazy, capital		38,000
Fugazy, drawing	50,000	
Service revenue		97,000
Salary expense	32,000	
Supplies expense		
Depreciation expense		
Interest expense	3,000	
Rent expense	9,000	
Insurance expense	2,000	
Total	$202,000	$202,000

Adjustment data at December 31, 2012:

    a. Unearned service revenue earned during the year, $500.
    b. Supplies on hand, $1,000.
    c. Depreciation for the year, $6,000.
    d. Accrued salary expense, $1,000.
    e. Accrued service revenue, $4,000.

Requirements

1. Enter the account data in the Trial Balance columns of a worksheet, and complete the worksheet through the Adjusted Trial Balance. Key each adjusting entry by the letter corresponding to the data given. Leave a blank line under Service revenue.

2. Prepare the income statement, the statement of owner's equity, and the classified balance sheet in account format.

3. Prepare closing journal entries from the worksheet.

4. Did the company have a good or a bad year during 2012? Give the reason for your answer.

P4-26A ① ② ③ ④ ⑤ ⑥ **Completing the accounting cycle [120–150 min]**
The trial balance of Wolfe Anvils at October 31, 2012, and the data for the month-end adjustments follow:

WOLFE ANVILS		
Trial Balance		
October 31, 2012		

	Balance	
Account	**Debit**	**Credit**
Cash	$ 4,300	
Accounts receivable	15,000	
Prepaid rent	2,700	
Supplies	1,600	
Equipment	31,200	
Accumulated depreciation		$ 3,000
Accounts payable		6,900
Salary payable		
Unearned service revenue		5,400
Wolfe, capital		26,600
Wolfe, drawing	3,500	
Service revenue		18,900
Salary expense	2,500	
Rent expense		
Depreciation expense		
Supplies expense		
Total	$60,800	$60,800

Adjustment data:

a. Unearned service revenue still unearned at October 31, $1,200.
b. Prepaid rent still in force at October 31, $2,500.
c. Supplies used during the month, $1,000.
d. Depreciation for the month, $300.
e. Accrued salary expense at October 31, $200.

Requirements

1. Prepare adjusting journal entries.
2. Enter the trial balance on a worksheet and complete the worksheet through the Adjusted Trial Balance of Wolfe Anvils for the month ended October 31, 2012.
3. Prepare the income statement, the statement of owner's equity, and the classified balance sheet in report form.
4. Using the worksheet data that you prepared, journalize the closing entries and post the adjusting and closing entries to T-accounts. Use dates and show the ending balance of each account.
5. Prepare a post-closing trial balance.
6. Calculate the current and debt ratios for the company.

P4-27A ① ② ③ ④ ⑤ ⑥ **Completing the accounting cycle [120–150 min]**
The trial balance of Racer Internet at March 31, 2012, follows:

	Balance	
RACER INTERNET		
Trial Balance		
March 31, 2012		
Account	**Debit**	**Credit**
Cash	$ 4,300	
Accounts receivable	15,100	
Prepaid rent	2,300	
Supplies	1,000	
Equipment	30,600	
Accumulated depreciation		$ 3,900
Accounts payable		6,400
Salary payable		
Unearned service revenue		9,800
Racer, capital		23,000
Racer, drawing	4,100	
Service revenue		17,300
Salary expense	3,000	
Rent expense		
Depreciation expense		
Supplies expense		
Total	$60,400	$60,400

Adjusting data at March 31, 2012:

    a. Unearned service revenue still unearned, $500.
    b. Prepaid rent still in force, $2,000.
    c. Supplies used during the month, $800.
    d. Depreciation for the month, $400.
    e. Accrued salary expense, $600.

Requirements

1. Journalize adjusting journal entries.
2. Enter the trial balance on a worksheet and complete the worksheet of Racer Internet.
3. Prepare the income statement, statement of owner's equity, and classified balance sheet in report form.
4. Using the worksheet data that you prepared, journalize the closing entries, and post the adjusting and closing entries to T-accounts. Use dates and show the ending balance of each account.
5. Prepare a post-closing trial balance.
6. Calculate the current and debt ratios for the company.

P4-28A ❸ **Journalizing adjusting and closing entries [45–60 min]**

The *unadjusted* trial balance and adjustment data of Elias Real Estate Appraisal Company at June 30, 2012, follow:

ELIAS REAL ESTATE APPRAISAL COMPANY		
Unadjusted Trial Balance		
June 30, 2012		
Account Title	Debit	Credit
Cash	$ 4,900	
Accounts receivable	4,000	
Supplies	3,000	
Prepaid insurance	2,200	
Building	74,400	
Accumulated depreciation		$ 18,800
Land	13,600	
Accounts payable		19,500
Interest payable		8,800
Salary payable		1,300
Elias, capital		30,800
Elias, drawing	27,900	
Service revenue		97,900
Salary expense	32,400	
Depreciation expense	0	
Insurance expense	4,200	
Utilities expense	4,000	
Supplies expense	6,500	
Total	$ 177,100	$ 177,100

Adjustment data at June 30, 2012:

    a. Prepaid insurance expired, $300.
    b. Accrued service revenue, $1,300.
    c. Accrued salary expense, $900.
    d. Depreciation for the year, $8,500.
    e. Supplies used during the year, $600.

Requirements

1. Open T-accounts for Elias, capital and all the accounts that follow on the trial balance. Insert their unadjusted balances. Also open a T-account for Income summary, which has a zero balance.

2. Journalize the adjusting entries and post to the accounts that you opened. Show the balance of each revenue account and each expense account.

3. Journalize the closing entries and post to the accounts that you opened. Draw double underlines under each account balance that you close to zero.

4. Compute the ending balance of Elias, capital.

P4-29A ⑤ ⑥ **Preparing a classified balance sheet in report form, and using the current and debt ratios to evaluate a company [30–40 min]**
Selected accounts of Blume Irrigation System at December 31, 2012, follow:

Insurance expense	$ 900	Accounts payable	$24,700
Note payable, long-term	2,800	Accounts receivable	43,100
Other assets	2,200	Accumulated depreciation—building	24,000
Building	55,800	Blume, capital, December 31, 2011	52,000
Prepaid insurance	4,000	Accumulated depreciation—equipment	7,900
Salary expense	16,300	Cash	11,000
Salary payable	3,900	Interest payable	400
Service revenue	74,800	Blume, drawing	2,000
Supplies	3,300	Equipment	23,000
Unearned service revenue	1,600	Depreciation expense	30,500

Requirements

1. Prepare the company's classified balance sheet in report form at December 31, 2012.
2. Compute the company's current ratio and debt ratio at December 31, 2012. At December 31, 2011, the current ratio was 1.81 and the debt ratio was 0.34. Did the company's ability to pay debts improve or deteriorate, or did it remain the same during 2012?

● Problems (Group B)

MyAccountingLab

P4-30B ① ② **Preparing a worksheet and the financial statements [40–50 min]**
The trial balance and adjustment data of Brooke's Motors at September 30, 2012, follow:

BROOKE'S MOTORS		
Trial Balance		
September 30, 2012		

	Balance	
Account	Debit	Credit
Cash	$ 4,200	
Accounts receivable	26,500	
Supplies	800	
Prepaid insurance	1,800	
Equipment	53,500	
Accumulated depreciation		$36,300
Accounts payable		13,300
Wages payable		
Unearned service revenue		8,500
Brooke, capital		19,000
Brooke, drawing	3,500	
Service revenue		16,500
Depreciation expense		
Wage expense	2,100	
Insurance expense		
Utilities expense	1,200	
Supplies expense		
Total	$93,600	$93,600

Additional data at September 30, 2012:

    a. Depreciation on equipment, $1,100.
    b. Accrued wage expense, $500.
    c. Supplies on hand, $700.
    d. Prepaid insurance expired during September, $200.
    e. Unearned service revenue earned during September, $4,500.
    f. Accrued service revenue, $900.

Requirements

1. Complete Brooke's worksheet for September. Key adjusting entries by letter.

2. Prepare the income statement, the statement of owner's equity, and the classified balance sheet in account form for the month ended September 30, 2012.

P4-31B ❶❷❸ **Preparing a worksheet, financial statements, and closing entries [50–60 min]**

The trial balance of Giambi Investment Advisers at December 31, 2012, follows:

GIAMBI INVESTMENT ADVISERS Trial Balance December 31, 2012		
	Balance	
Account	**Debit**	**Credit**
Cash	$ 28,000	
Accounts receivable	50,000	
Supplies	8,000	
Equipment	26,000	
Accumulated depreciation		$ 16,000
Accounts payable		14,000
Salary payable		
Unearned service revenue		1,000
Note payable, long-term		44,000
Giambi, capital		40,000
Giambi, drawing	50,000	
Service revenue		97,000
Salary expense	32,000	
Supplies expense		
Depreciation expense		
Interest expense	7,000	
Rent expense	7,000	
Insurance expense	4,000	
Total	$212,000	$212,000

Adjustment data at December 31, 2012:

    a. Unearned service revenue earned during the year, $500.
    b. Supplies on hand, $5,000.
    c. Depreciation for the year, $8,000.
    d. Accrued salary expense, $1,000.
    e. Accrued service revenue, $3,000.

Requirements

1. Enter the account data in the Trial Balance columns of a worksheet, and complete the worksheet through the Adjusted Trial Balance. Key each adjusting entry by the letter corresponding to the data given. Leave a blank line under Service revenue.

2. Prepare the income statement, the statement of owner's equity, and the classified balance sheet in account format.

3. Prepare closing journal entries from the worksheet.

4. Did the company have a good or a bad year during 2012? Give the reason for your answer.

P4-32B ① ② ③ ④ ⑤ ⑥ **Completing the accounting cycle [120–150 min]**
The trial balance of Leopard Anvils at January 31, 2012, and the data for the month-end adjustments follow:

LEOPARD ANVILS Trial Balance January 31, 2012		
	Balance	
Account	Debit	Credit
Cash	$ 4,400	
Accounts receivable	14,800	
Prepaid rent	2,300	
Supplies	1,200	
Equipment	30,100	
Accumulated depreciation		$ 4,600
Accounts payable		7,500
Salary payable		
Unearned service revenue		4,900
Leopard, capital		25,700
Leopard, drawing	4,800	
Service revenue		17,400
Salary expense	2,500	
Rent expense		
Depreciation expense		
Supplies expense		
Total	$60,100	$60,100

Adjustment data:

a. Unearned service revenue still unearned at January 31, $400.
b. Prepaid rent still in force at January 31, $1,800.
c. Supplies used during the month, $1,100.
d. Depreciation for the month, $400.
e. Accrued salary expense at January 31, $500.

Requirements

1. Prepare adjusting journal entries.

2. Enter the trial balance on a worksheet and complete the worksheet through the Adjusted Trial Balance of Leopard Anvils for the month ended January 31, 2012.

3. Prepare the income statement, the statement of owner's equity, and the classified balance sheet in report form.

4. Using the worksheet data that you prepared, journalize and post the adjusting and closing entries to T-accounts. Use dates and show the ending balance of each account.

5. Prepare a post-closing trial balance.

6. Calculate the current and debt ratios for the company.

P4-33B ① ② ③ ④ ⑤ ⑥ **Completing the accounting cycle [120–150 min]**
The trial balance of Road Runner Internet at July 31, 2012, follows:

ROAD RUNNER INTERNET Trial Balance July 31, 2012		
	Balance	
Account	Debit	Credit
Cash	$ 4,200	
Accounts receivable	14,600	
Prepaid rent	2,000	
Supplies	1,600	
Equipment	30,900	
Accumulated depreciation		$ 3,900
Accounts payable		6,700
Salary payable		
Unearned service revenue		5,400
Runner, capital		25,800
Runner, drawing	3,200	
Service revenue		17,700
Salary expense	3,000	
Rent expense		
Depreciation expense		
Supplies expense		
Total	$59,500	$59,500

Adjusting data at July 31, 2012:

    a. Unearned service revenue still unearned, $1,200.
    b. Prepaid rent still in force at July 31, $1,900.
    c. Supplies used during the month, $800.
    d. Depreciation for the month, $300.
    e. Accrued salary expense at July 31, $500.

Requirements

1. Journalize adjusting journal entries.

2. Enter the trial balance on a worksheet and complete the worksheet for Road Runner Internet.

3. Prepare the income statement, statement of owner's equity, and classified balance sheet in report form.

4. Using the worksheet data that you prepared, journalize the closing entries and post the adjusting and closing entries to T-accounts. Use dates and show the ending balance of each account.

5. Prepare a post-closing trial balance.

6. Calculate the current and debt ratios for the company.

P4-34B ③ **Journalizing adjusting and closing entries [45–60 min]**

The *unadjusted* trial balance and adjustment data of Smith Real Estate Appraisal Company at June 30, 2012, follow:

SMITH REAL ESTATE APPRAISAL COMPANY Unadjusted Trial Balance June 30, 2012		
Account Title	Debit	Credit
Cash	$ 4,600	
Accounts receivable	3,500	
Supplies	3,000	
Prepaid insurance	2,100	
Building	74,700	
Accumulated depreciation		$ 18,600
Land	14,000	
Accounts payable		18,900
Interest payable		8,000
Salary payable		600
Smith, capital		33,000
Smith, drawing	27,000	
Service revenue		97,500
Salary expense	32,100	
Depreciation expense	0	
Insurance expense	5,100	
Utilities expense	3,600	
Supplies expense	6,900	
Total	$ 176,600	$ 176,600

Adjustment data at June 30, 2012:

    a. Prepaid insurance expired, $400.
    b. Accrued service revenue, $1,100.
    c. Accrued salary expense, $700.
    d. Depreciation for the year, $8,500.
    e. Supplies used during the year, $100.

Requirements

1. Open T-accounts for Smith, capital and all the accounts that follow on the trial balance. Insert their unadjusted balances. Also open a T-account for Income summary, which has a zero balance.
2. Journalize the adjusting entries and post to the accounts that you opened. Show the balance of each revenue account and each expense account.
3. Journalize the closing entries and post to the accounts that you opened. Draw double underlines under each account balance that you close to zero.
4. Compute the ending balance of Smith, capital.

P4-35B ❺❻ **Preparing a classified balance sheet in report form, and using the current and debt ratios to evaluate a company [30–40 min]**

Selected accounts of Browne Irrigation Systems at December 31, 2012, follow:

Insurance expense	$ 500	Accounts payable	$22,300
Note payable, long-term	4,200	Accounts receivable	43,600
Other assets	2,000	Accumulated depreciation—building	24,200
Building	58,200	Browne, capital, December 31, 2011	54,000
Prepaid insurance	4,800	Accumulated depreciation—equipment	6,900
Salary expense	17,700	Cash	6,500
Salary payable	2,800	Interest payable	400
Service revenue	73,000	Browne, drawing	5,000
Supplies	3,300	Equipment	23,000
Unearned service revenue	1,800	Depreciation expense	25,000

Requirements

1. Prepare the company's classified balance sheet in report form at December 31, 2012.
2. Compute the company's current ratio and debt ratio at December 31, 2012. At December 31, 2011, the current ratio was 1.83 and the debt ratio was 0.39. Did the company's ability to pay debts improve or deteriorate, or did it remain the same during 2012?

● Continuing Exercise

E4-36 This exercise continues the Lawlor Lawn Service situation from Exercise 3-48 of Chapter 3. Start from the posted T-accounts and the *adjusted* trial balance for Lawlor Lawn Service prepared for the company at May 31, 2012:

MyAccountingLab

Requirements

1. Complete the accounting worksheet at May 31, 2012.
2. Journalize and post the closing entries at May 31, 2012. Denote each closing amount as *Clo* and an account balance as *Bal*.

● Continuing Problem

This problem continues the Draper Consulting situation from Problem 3-49 of Chapter 3.

P4-37 Start from the posted T-accounts and the *adjusted* trial balance that Draper Consulting prepared for the company at December 31:

		DRAPER CONSULTING		
		Adjusted Trial Balance		
		December 31, 2012		
			Balance	
		Account Title	Debit	Credit
		Cash	$16,350	
		Accounts receivable	1,750	
		Supplies	200	
		Equipment	1,800	
		Accumulated depreciation—equipment		$ 30
		Furniture	4,200	
		Accumulated depreciation—furniture		70
		Accounts payable		4,650
		Salary payable		685
		Unearned service revenue		700
		Draper, capital		18,000
		Draper, drawing	1,400	
		Service revenue		3,850
		Rent expense	550	
		Utilities expense	250	
		Salary expense	685	
		Depreciation expense—equipment	30	
		Depreciation expense—furniture	70	
		Supplies expense	700	
		Total	$27,985	$27,985

Requirements

1. Complete the accounting worksheet at December 31.
2. Journalize and post the closing entries at December 31. Denote each closing amount as *Clo* and an account balance as *Bal*.
3. Prepare a classified balance sheet at December 31.

● Practice Set

Refer to the Practice Set data provided in Chapters 1, 2, and 3.

Requirements

1. Prepare an accounting worksheet.
2. Prepare an income statement, statement of owner's equity, and balance sheet using the report format.
3. Prepare closing entries for the month.
4. Prepare a post-closing trial balance.

Apply Your Knowledge

● Decision Case 4-1

One year ago, Ralph Collins founded Collins Consignment Sales Company, and the business has prospered. Collins comes to you for advice. He wishes to know how much net income the business earned during the past year. The accounting records consist of the T-accounts in the ledger, which were prepared by an accountant who has moved. The accounts at December 31 follow:

Cash	Accounts receivable	Prepaid rent	Supplies
Dec 31 Bal 5,800	Dec 31 Bal 12,300	Jan 2 2,800	Jan 2 2,600

Equipment	Accumulated depreciation		Accounts payable
Jan 2 52,000			Dec 31 Bal 18,500

Salary payable	Unearned service revenue	Collins, capital	Collins, drawing
	Dec 31 Bal 4,100	Jan 2 40,000	Dec 31 Bal 50,000

Service revenue		Salary expense	Depreciation expense
Dec 31 Bal 80,700		Dec 31 Bal 17,000	

Advertising expense	Utilities expense	Supplies expense	
	Dec 31 Bal 800		

Collins indicates that, at year-end, customers owe him $1,000 accrued service revenue, which he expects to collect early next year. These revenues have not been recorded. During the year, he collected $4,100 service revenue in advance from customers, but the business has earned only $800 of that amount. During the year he has incurred $2,400 of advertising expense, but he has not yet paid for it. In addition, he has used up $2,100 of the supplies. Collins determines that depreciation on equipment was $7,000 for the year. At December 31, he owes his employee $1,200 accrued salary. The owner made no capital investments during the year.

Collins expresses concern that drawing during the year might have exceeded the business's net income. To get a loan to expand the business, Collins must show the bank that the business's owner's equity has grown from its original $40,000 balance. Has it? You and Collins agree that you will meet again in one week.

Requirement

1. Prepare the financial statement that helps address the first issue concerning Collins. Can he expect to get the loan? Give your reason(s).

● Ethical Issue 4-1

Link Back to Chapter 3 (Revenue Principle). Grant Film Productions wishes to expand and has borrowed $100,000. As a condition for making this loan, the bank requires that the business maintain a current ratio of at least 1.50.

Business has been good but not great. Expansion costs have brought the current ratio down to 1.40 on December 15. Rita Grant, owner of the business, is considering what might happen if she reports a current ratio of 1.40 to the bank. One course of action for Grant is to record in December $10,000 of revenue that the business will earn in January of next year. The contract for this job has been signed.

Requirements

1. Journalize the revenue transaction, and indicate how recording this revenue in December would affect the current ratio.
2. Discuss whether it is ethical to record the revenue transaction in December. Identify the accounting principle relevant to this situation, and give the reasons underlying your conclusion.

Fraud Case 4-1

Arthur Chen, a newly minted CPA, was on his second audit job in the Midwest with a new client called Parson Farm Products. He was looking through the last four years of financials, and doing a few ratios, when he noticed something odd. The current ratio went from 1.9 in 2007 down to 0.3 in 2008, despite the fact that 2008 had record income. He decided to sample a few transactions from December 2008. He found that many of Parson's customers had returned products to the company because of substandard quality. Chen discovered that the company was clearing the receivables (i.e., crediting accounts receivable) but "stashing" the debits in an obscure long-term asset account called "grain reserves" to keep the company's income "in the black" (i.e., positive income).

Requirements

1. How did the fraudulent accounting just described affect the current ratio? (Hint: Think about Cash.)
2. Can you think of any reasons why someone in the company would want to take this kind of action?

Financial Statement Case 4-1

This case, based on the balance sheet of **Amazon.com** in Appendix A at the end of the book, will familiarize you with some of the assets and liabilities of that company. Use the **Amazon.com** balance sheet to answer the following questions.

Requirements

1. Which balance sheet format does **Amazon.com** use?
2. Name the company's largest current asset and largest current liability at December 31, 2009.
3. Compute **Amazon's** current ratios at December 31, 2009 and 2008. Did the current ratio improve, worsen, or hold steady during 2009?
4. Under what category does **Amazon** report furniture, fixtures, and equipment?
5. What was the cost of the company's fixed assets at December 31, 2009? What was the amount of accumulated depreciation? What was the book value of the fixed assets? See Note 3 for the data.

Team Project 4-1

Kathy Wintz formed a lawn service business as a summer job. To start the business on May 1, she deposited $1,000 in a new bank account in the name of the business. The $1,000 consisted of a $600 loan from Bank One to her company, Wintz Lawn Service, and $400 of her own money. The company gave $400 of capital to Wintz. Wintz rented lawn equipment, purchased supplies, and hired other students to mow and trim customers' lawns.

At the end of each month, Wintz mailed bills to the customers. On August 31, she was ready to dissolve the business and return to college. Because she was so busy, she kept few records other than the checkbook and a list of receivables from customers.

At August 31, the business's checkbook shows a balance of $2,000, and customers still owe $750. During the summer, the business collected $5,500 from customers. The business checkbook lists payments for supplies totaling $400, and it still has gasoline, weed eater cord, and other supplies that cost a total of $50. The business paid employees $1,800 and still owes them $300 for the final week of the summer.

Wintz rented some equipment from Ludwig's Machine Shop. On May 1, the business signed a six-month rental agreement on mowers and paid $600 for the full rental period in advance. Ludwig's will refund the unused portion of the prepayment if the equipment is returned in good shape. In order to get the refund, Wintz has kept the mowers in excellent condition. In fact, the business had to pay $300 to repair a mower.

To transport employees and equipment to jobs, Wintz used a trailer that the business bought for $300. The business estimates that the summer's work used up one-third of the trailer's service potential. The business checkbook lists a payment of $500 for cash withdrawals during the summer. The business paid the loan back during August. (For simplicity, ignore any interest expense associated with the loan.)

Requirements

1. Prepare the income statement and the statement of owner's equity of Wintz Lawn Service for the four months May through August.

2. Prepare the classified balance sheet of Wintz Lawn Service at August 31.

3. Was Wintz's summer work successful? Give the reason for your answer.

● Communication Activity 4-1

In 25 words or fewer, explain the rationale for closing the temporary accounts.

Quick Check Answers

1. *d* 2. *b* 3. *a* 4. *b* 5. *c* 6. *d* 7. *d* 8. *c* 9. *c* 10. *a*

For online homework, exercises, and problems that provide you immediate feedback, please visit myaccountinglab.com.

Comprehensive Problem for Chapters 1–4

Journalizing, Posting, Worksheet, Adjusting, Closing, and the Financial Statements

Matthews Delivery Service completed the following transactions during its first month of operations for January 2012:

a. Matthews Delivery Service began operations by receiving $6,000 cash and a truck valued at $11,000. The business gave Matthews capital to aquire these assets.

b. Paid $300 cash for supplies.

c. Prepaid insurance, $700.

d. Performed delivery services for a customer and received $800 cash.

e. Completed a large delivery job, billed the customer $1,500, and received a promise to collect the $1,500 within one week.

f. Paid employee salary, $700.

g. Received $12,000 cash for performing delivery services.

h. Collected $600 in advance for delivery service to be performed later.

i. Collected $1,500 cash from a customer on account.

j. Purchased fuel for the truck, paying $200 with a company credit card. (Credit Accounts payable)

k. Performed delivery services on account, $900.

l. Paid office rent, $600. This rent is not paid in advance.

m. Paid $200 on account.

n. Owner withdrew cash of $2,100.

Requirements

1. Record each transaction in the journal. Key each transaction by its letter. Explanations are not required.

2. Post the transactions that you recorded in Requirement 1 in the T-accounts.

Cash	Service revenue
Accounts receivable	Salary expense
Supplies	Depreciation expense
Prepaid insurance	Insurance expense
Delivery truck	Fuel expense
Accumulated depreciation	Rent expense
Accounts payable	Supplies expense
Salary payable	
Unearned service revenue	
Matthews, capital	
Matthews, drawing	
Income summary	

3. Enter the trial balance in the worksheet for the month ended January 31, 2012. Complete the worksheet using the adjustment data given at January 31.
    a. Accrued salary expense, $700.
    b. Depreciation expense, $60.
    c. Prepaid insurance expired, $250.
    d. Supplies on hand, $200.
    e. Unearned service revenue earned during January, $500.

4. Prepare Matthews Delivery Service's income statement and statement of owner's equity for the month ended January 31, 2012, and the classified balance sheet on that date. On the income statement, list expenses in decreasing order by amount—that is, the largest expense first, the smallest expense last.

5. Journalize and post the adjusting entries beginning with a.

6. Journalize and post the closing entries.

7. Prepare a post-closing trial balance at January 31, 2012.

5

Merchandising Operations

Does the company update inventory perpetually or only at the end of a period?

SMART TOUCH LEARNING
Balance Sheet
May 31, 2013

Assets				Liabilities	
Current assets:				Current liabilities:	
Cash		$ 4,800		Accounts payable	$ 48,700
Accounts receivable		2,600		Salary payable	900
Inventory		**30,500**		Interest payable	100
Supplies		600		Unearned service revenue	400
Prepaid rent		2,000		Total current liabilities	50,100
Total current assets			$ 40,500	Long-term liabilities:	
Plant assets:				Notes payable	20,000
Furniture	$18,000			Total liabilities	70,100
Less: Accumulated depreciation—furniture	300	17,700			
Building	48,000				
Less: Accumulated depreciation—building	200	47,800		Owner's Equity	
Total plant assets			65,500	Bright, capital	35,900
Total assets			$106,000	Total liabilities and owner's equity	$106,000

Learning Objectives

1 Describe and illustrate merchandising operations and the two types of inventory systems

2 Account for the purchase of inventory using a perpetual system

3 Account for the sale of inventory using a perpetual system

4 Adjust and close the accounts of a merchandising business

5 Prepare a merchandiser's financial statements

6 Use gross profit percentage, inventory turnover, and days in inventory to evaluate a business

7 Account for the sale of inventory using a periodic system (Appendix 5A)

8 Prepare worksheets for a merchandiser (see Appendix 5B, located at myaccountinglab.com)

So what kind of business do you think you want to own, manage, or invest in? A business that offers a service or a business that sells a product?

Chapters 1–4 discussed Smart Touch Learning and Greg's Tunes. Smart Touch and Greg's Tunes are similar. Both are proprietorships, and they follow similar accounting procedures. However, Greg Moore's music business differs from Sheena Bright's e-learning service in one important way: Bright provides a service for customers, whereas Moore sells both services and products—event music services and CDs. Businesses that sell a product are called **merchandisers** because they sell merchandise, or goods, to customers.

• • •

In this chapter, we'll introduce accounting for merchandisers, showing how to account for the purchase and sale of inventory, the additional current asset that merchandisers have. **Inventory** is defined as the merchandise that a company holds for sale to customers. For example, Greg's Tunes must hold some CD inventory in order to operate. **Walmart** carries food inventory in addition to clothing, housewares, and school supplies. A **Honda** dealer holds inventories of automobiles and auto parts.

In this chapter, Smart Touch has decided to discontinue its service business and instead plans to sell tutorial CDs and DVDs that it purchases from a vendor. With its change in business strategy, Smart Touch is now considered a merchandiser. By continuing the same company with a different business strategy in the examples, we will give you a basis for comparison between service and merchandising businesses. We'll also cover examples using Greg's Tunes. Let's get started by looking at some basics of merchandising operations.

What Are Merchandising Operations?

1 Describe and illustrate merchandising operations and the two types of inventory systems

Merchandising consists of buying and selling products rather than services. Exhibit 5-1 shows how a service entity's financial statements (on the left) differ from a merchandiser's financial statements (on the right). As you can see, merchandisers have some new balance sheet and income statement items.

	Financial Statements of a Service
EXHIBIT 5-1	**Company and a Merchandising Company**

SERVICE CO.* Balance Sheet—Partial June 30, 2013			MERCHANDISING CO.** Balance Sheet—Partial June 30, 2013		
Assets			**Assets**		
Current assets:			Current assets:		
Cash		$X	Cash		$X
Short-term investments		X	Short-term investments		X
Accounts receivable, net		X	Accounts receivable, net		X
Prepaid insurance		X	Inventory		X
			Prepaid insurance		X

*Such as Smart Touch before it changed to a merchandising operation.

**Such as Greg's Tunes

SERVICE CO. Income Statement Year Ended June 30, 2013			MERCHANDISING CO. Income Statement Year Ended June 30, 2013		
Service revenue		$XXX	Sales revenue		$X,XXX
Operating expenses:			Cost of goods sold		X
Salary expense		X	Gross profit		$ XXX
Depreciation expense		X	Operating expenses:		
Rent expense		X	Salary expense		X
Net income		$ X	Depreciation expense		X
			Rent expense		X
			Net income		$ X

Balance Sheet:
- Inventory, an asset

Income Statement:
- Sales revenue (or simply, Sales)
- Cost of goods sold, an expense

We'll define these new items later in the chapter. Notice we now show the expenses heading as Operating expenses. These are the same expenses you've been learning about in previous chapters. The heading just categorizes the expenses as operating rather than *all* expenses. For now, let's examine the operating cycle of a merchandising business.

The Operating Cycle of a Merchandising Business

The operating cycle of a merchandiser is as follows (see Exhibit 5-2):

1. It begins when the company purchases inventory from a **vendor**.

2. The company then sells the inventory to a **customer**.

3. Finally, the company collects cash from customers.

EXHIBIT 5-2 | **Operating Cycle of a Merchandiser**

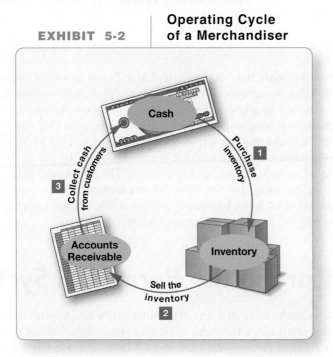

Now let's see how companies account for their inventory. We begin with journal entries. Then we post to the ledger accounts and, finally, prepare the financial statements.

Inventory Systems: Perpetual and Periodic

There are two main types of inventory accounting systems:

- Periodic system
- Perpetual system

The **periodic inventory system** is normally used for relatively inexpensive goods. A small, local store without optical-scanning cash registers does not keep a running record of every loaf of bread and every key chain that it sells. Instead, the business physically counts its inventory periodically to determine the quantities on hand.

Restaurants and small retail stores often use the periodic system. Appendix 5A covers the periodic system, which is becoming less and less popular with the use of computers.

The **perpetual inventory system** keeps a running *computerized* record of inventory—that is, the number of inventory units and the dollar amounts are perpetually (constantly) updated. This system achieves better control over the inventory. A modern perpetual inventory system records the following:

- Units purchased and cost amount
- Units sold and sales and cost amounts
- The quantity of inventory on hand and its cost

In this system, inventory and purchasing systems are integrated with accounts receivable and sales. For example, **Target**'s computers use bar codes to keep up-to-the-minute records and show the current inventory at any time.

Bar code

In a perpetual system, the "cash register" at a **Target** store is a computer terminal that records sales and updates inventory records. Bar codes such as the one illustrated here are scanned by a laser. The bar coding represents inventory and cost data that keep track of each unique inventory item. However, note that even in a perpetual system, the business must count inventory at least once a year. The physical count captures inventory transactions that are not recorded by the electronic system (such as misplaced, stolen, or damaged inventory). The count establishes the correct amount of ending inventory for the financial statements and also serves as a check on the perpetual records. Most businesses use bar codes and computerized cash registers, which is why we cover the perpetual system.

Accounting for Inventory in the Perpetual System

 Account for the purchase of inventory using a perpetual system

As noted previously, the cycle of a merchandising entity begins with the purchase of inventory. In this section, we trace the steps that Smart Touch takes to account for inventory. Smart Touch plans to sell CDs and DVDs that it purchases from **RCA**.

1. **RCA**, the vendor, ships the CD and DVD inventory to Smart Touch and sends an invoice the same day. The **invoice** is the seller's (**RCA**'s) request for payment from the buyer (Smart Touch). An invoice is also called a *bill*. Exhibit 5-3 is the bill that Smart Touch receives from **RCA**.

2. After the inventory is received, Smart Touch pays **RCA**.

Purchase of Inventory

Here we use the actual invoice in Exhibit 5-3 to illustrate the purchasing process. Suppose Smart Touch receives the goods on June 3, 2013. Smart Touch records this purchase on account as follows:

Jun 3	Inventory	(A+)		700	
	Accounts payable	(L+)			700
	Purchased inventory on account.				

The Inventory account, an asset, is used only for goods purchased that Smart Touch owns and intends to resell to customers. Supplies, equipment, and other assets are recorded in their own accounts. Recall that Inventory is an asset until it is sold. We record the Inventory at its *gross value* (total invoice amount before discount) using the *gross method*. An alternative method, the *net method*, will be discussed in future accounting courses.

Purchase Discounts

Many businesses offer customers a discount for early payment. This is called a **purchase discount**. RCA's **credit terms** of "3/15, NET 30 DAYS" mean that Smart Touch can deduct 3% from the total bill (excluding freight charges, if any) if the company pays within 15 days of the invoice date. Otherwise, the full amount—NET—is due in 30 days. These credit terms can also be expressed as "3/15, n/30."

EXHIBIT 5-3 | **Purchase Invoice**

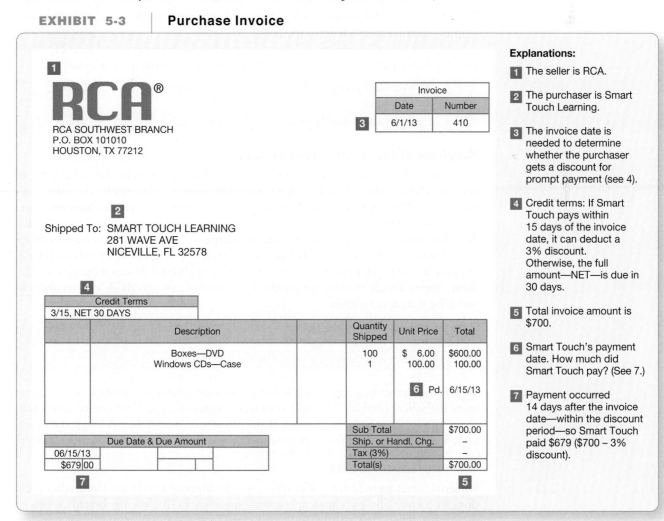

Terms of "n/30" mean that no discount is offered and payment is due 30 days after the invoice date. Most credit terms express the discount, the discount time period, and the final due date. Occasionally, the credit terms are expressed as *eom*, which means payment is due at the end of the current month.

If Smart Touch pays within the discount period, the cash payment entry would be as follows:

Jun 15	Accounts payable (L–)	700	
	Cash ($700 × 0.97) (A–)		679
	Inventory ($700 × 0.03) (A–)		21
	Paid within discount period.		

The discount is credited to Inventory because the discount for early payment decreases the actual cost paid for Inventory, as shown in the T-account:

Inventory

Jun 3	700	Jun 15	21
Bal	679		

Notice that the balance in the Inventory account, $679, is exactly what was paid for the Inventory on June 15, 2013.

What if Smart Touch pays this invoice after the discount period on June 24, 2013? Smart Touch must pay the full $700. In that case, the payment entry is as follows:

Jun 24	Accounts payable (L–)	700	
	Cash (A–)		700
	Paid after discount period.		

Purchase Returns and Allowances

Businesses allow customers to return merchandise that is defective, damaged, or otherwise unsuitable. This is called a **purchase return**. Alternately, the seller may deduct an allowance from the amount the buyer owes. **Purchase allowances** are granted to the purchaser as an incentive to keep goods that are not "as ordered." Together, **purchase returns and allowances** decrease the buyer's cost of the inventory.

Assume that Smart Touch has not yet paid the original **RCA** bill of June 3. Suppose a case of CDs purchased on that invoice (Exhibit 5-3) was damaged in shipment. Smart Touch returns the goods (CDs, in this case) to **RCA** and records the purchase return as follows:

Jun 4	Accounts payable (L–)	100	
	Inventory (A–)		100
	Returned inventory to seller (vendor).		

The exact same entry is made for a purchase allowance granted to the buyer from the seller (vendor). The only difference between a purchase return and a purchase allowance is that, in the case of the allowance, Smart Touch keeps the inventory. See Exhibit 5-4 on the next page for a copy of the purchase allowance granted.

Transportation Costs

Someone must pay the transportation cost of shipping inventory from seller (vendor) to buyer. The purchase agreement specifies FOB (**free on board**) terms to determine when title to the good transfers to the purchaser and who pays the freight. Exhibit 5-5 shows that

- **FOB shipping point** means the buyer takes ownership (title) to the goods at the shipping point. In this case, the buyer (owner of the goods at the shipping point) also pays the freight.

- **FOB destination** means the buyer takes ownership (title) to the goods at the delivery destination point. In this case, the seller (owner of the goods while in transit) usually pays the freight.

  Freight costs are either freight in or freight out.

- **Freight in** is the transportation cost to ship goods INTO the purchaser's warehouse; thus, it is freight on *purchased goods*.
- **Freight out** is the transportation cost to ship goods OUT of the warehouse and to the customer; thus, it is freight on *goods sold*.

EXHIBIT 5-4 | **Purchase Allowance**

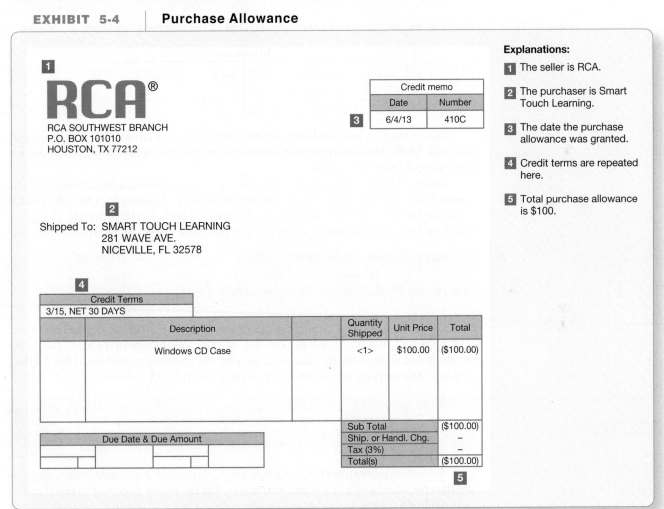

EXHIBIT 5-5 | **FOB Terms Determine Who Pays the Freight**

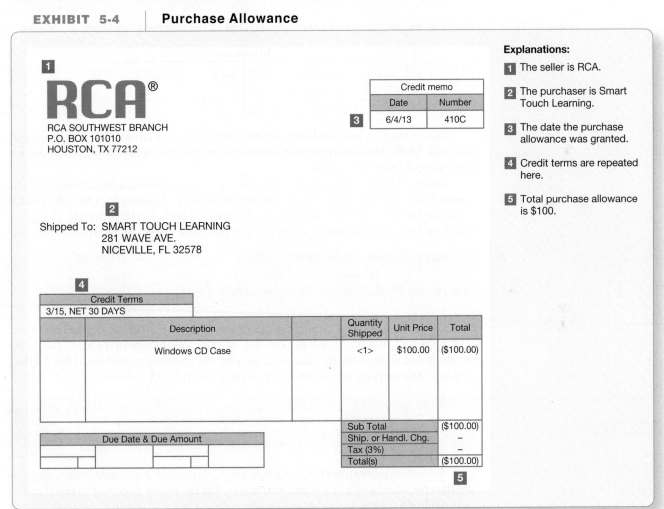

Freight In   FOB shipping point is most common. The buyer owns the goods while they are in transit, so the buyer pays the freight. Because paying the freight is a cost that must be paid to acquire the inventory, freight in becomes part of the cost of inventory. As a result, freight in costs are debited to the Inventory account. Suppose Smart Touch pays a $60 freight charge on June 3 and makes the following entry:

Jun 3	Inventory (A+)	60	
	Cash (A–)		60
	Paid a freight bill.		

The freight charge increases the net cost of the inventory to $660, as follows:

		Inventory			
Jun 3	Purchase	700	Jun 4	Return	100
Jun 3	Freight in	60			
Bal	Net cost	660			

Discounts are computed only on the merchandise purchased from the seller, in this case $600. Discounts are not computed on the transportation costs, because there is no discount on freight.

Under FOB shipping point, the seller sometimes prepays the transportation cost as a convenience and lists this cost on the invoice. Assume, for example, Greg's Tunes makes a $5,000 purchase of goods, coupled with a related freight charge of $400, on June 20 on terms of 3/5, n/30. The purchase would be recorded as follows:

Jun 20	Inventory ($5,000 + $400) (A+)	5,400	
	Accounts payable (L+)		5,400
	Purchased inventory on account, including freight.		

If Greg's Tunes pays within the discount period, the discount will be computed only on the $5,000 merchandise cost, not on the total invoice of $5,400. The $400 freight is not eligible for the discount. So, the 3% discount would be $150 ($5,000 × 0.03). The entry to record the early payment on June 25 follows:

Jun 25	Accounts payable (L–)	5,400	
	Inventory ($5,000 × 0.03) (A–)		150
	Cash (A–)		5,250

After posting both entries to Greg's Tunes' Inventory T-account below, you can see that the cost Greg's Tunes has invested in this Inventory purchase is equal to the cost paid of $5,250:

		Inventory			
Jun 20	Purchase	5,400	Jun 25	Discount	150
Bal	Net cost	5,250			

Freight Out   As noted previously, a freight out expense is one in which the seller pays freight charges to ship goods to customers. Freight out is a delivery expense to the seller. Delivery expense is an operating expense and is debited to the Delivery expense account. **Operating expenses** are expenses (other than Cost of goods sold) that occur in the entity's major line of business. Assume Greg's Tunes paid **UPS** $100 to ship goods to a customer on June 23. The entry to record that payment is as follows:

Jun 23	Delivery expense (E+)	100	
	Cash (A–)		100

Summary of Purchase Returns and Allowances, Discounts, and Transportation Costs

Suppose Smart Touch buys $35,000 of inventory, returns $700 of the goods, and takes a 2% early payment discount. Smart Touch also pays $2,100 of freight in. The following summary shows Smart Touch's net cost of this inventory. All amounts are assumed for this illustration.

Purchases of inventory									Net cost of inventory
Inventory	−	Purchase returns and allowances	−	Purchase discounts*	+	Freight in	=		Inventory
$35,000	−	$700	−	$686	+	$2,100	=		$35,714

*Purchase discount of $686 = [Purchases $35,000 − Purchase returns $700] × 0.02 discount]

Inventory			
Purchases of inventory	35,000	Purchase returns & allow.	700
Freight in	2,100	Purchase discount	686*
Bal	35,714		

Key Takeaway

All purchase transactions are between the company and a vendor. In a perpetual system, every transaction that affects the quantity or price of inventory is either debited or credited to the asset, Inventory, based on the rules of debit and credit. Increases debit Inventory (increase in quantity or cost per unit). Decreases credit Inventory (decrease in quantity or cost per unit).

Sale of Inventory

After a company buys inventory, the next step is to sell the goods. We shift now to the selling side and follow Smart Touch through a sequence of selling transactions.

The amount a business earns from selling merchandise inventory is called **Sales revenue (Sales)**. At the time of the sale, two entries must be recorded in the perpetual system: One entry records the sale and the cash (or receivable) at the time of the sale. The second entry records Cost of goods sold (debit the expense) and reduces the Inventory (credit the asset). **Cost of goods sold (COGS)** is the cost of inventory that has been sold to customers. Cost of goods sold (also known as **Cost of sales** or COS) is the merchandiser's major expense.

After making a sale on account, Smart Touch may experience any of the following:

- *A sales return:* The customer may return goods to Smart Touch, asking for a refund or credit to the customer's account.
- *A sales allowance:* Smart Touch may grant a sales allowance to entice the customer to accept non-standard goods. This allowance will reduce the future cash collected from the customer.
- *A sales discount:* If the customer pays within the discount period—under terms such as 2/10, n/30—Smart Touch collects the discounted amount.
- *Freight out:* Smart Touch may have to pay delivery expense to transport the goods to the buyer.

Let's begin with a cash sale.

Cash Sale

Sales of retailers, such as Smart Touch and Greg's Tunes, are often made for cash. Suppose Smart Touch made a $3,000 cash sale on June 9, 2013, to a customer and issued the sales invoice in Exhibit 5-6. **To the seller, a sales invoice is a bill showing what amount the customer must pay.**

3 Account for the sale of inventory using a perpetual system

EXHIBIT 5-6 | **Sales Invoice**

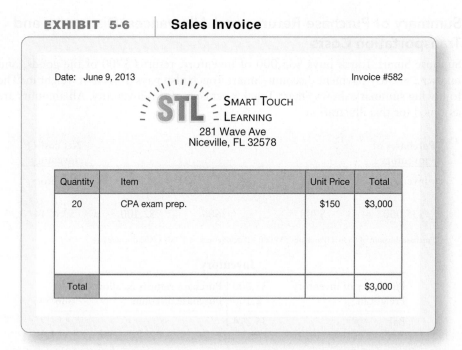

Cash sales of $3,000 are recorded by debiting Cash and crediting Sales revenue as follows:

1	Jun 9	Cash (A+)		3,000	
		Sales revenue (R+)			3,000
		Cash sale.			

Smart Touch sold goods. Therefore, a second journal entry must also be made to decrease the Inventory balance. Suppose these goods cost Smart Touch $1,900. The second journal entry will transfer the $1,900 from the Inventory account to the Cost of goods sold account, as follows:

2	Jun 9	Cost of goods sold (E+)		1,900	
		Inventory (A–)			1,900
		Recorded the cost of goods sold.			

The Cost of goods sold account keeps a current balance throughout the period in a perpetual inventory system. In this example, Cost of goods sold is $1,900 (the cost to Smart Touch) rather than $3,000, the selling price (retail) of the goods. **Cost of goods sold is always based on the company's cost, not the retail price.**

	Inventory					Cost of goods sold	
Bal	35,714	2 Cost of sales	1,900	←→	2 Jun 9	1,900	

The computer automatically records the Cost of goods sold entry in a perpetual inventory system. The cashier scans the bar code on the product and the computer performs this task.

Sale on Account

Most sales in the United States are made on account (on credit). Now let's assume that Smart Touch made a $5,000 sale on account on terms of n/10 (no discount offered) for goods that cost $2,900. The entries to record the sale and cost of goods sold follow:

1	Jun 11	Accounts receivable (A+)	5,000	
		Sales revenue (R+)		5,000
		Sale on account.		

2	Jun 11	Cost of goods sold (E+)	2,900	
		Inventory (A–)		2,900
		Recorded the cost of goods sold.		

When Smart Touch receives the cash, it records the cash receipt on account as follows:

	Jun 19	Cash (A+)	5,000	
		Accounts receivable (A–)		5,000
		Collection on account.		

Sales Discounts and Sales Returns and Allowances

We saw that purchase returns and allowances and purchase discounts decrease the cost of inventory purchases. In the same way, **sales returns and allowances** and **sales discounts** decrease the net amount of revenue earned on sales. Sales returns and allowances and Sales discounts are contra accounts to Sales revenue. Recall that a contra account has the opposite normal balance of its companion account. So, Sales returns and allowances and Sales discounts both are contra revenue accounts and have normal debit balances.

Companies maintain separate accounts for Sales discounts and Sales returns and allowances so they can track these items separately. **Net sales revenue** is calculated as Net sales revenue = Sales revenue – Sales returns and allowances – Sales discounts. **Sales made to customers – Sales returned by customers (or allowances granted to customers) – Discounts given to customers who paid early = Net sales.**

Sales revenue	–	Sales returns and allowances	–	Sales discounts	=	Net sales revenue[1]

Now let's examine a sequence of Greg's Tunes sale transactions. Assume Greg's Tunes is selling to a customer. On July 7, 2014, Greg's Tunes sells CDs for $7,200 on credit terms of 2/10, n/30. These goods cost Greg's Tunes $4,700. Greg's Tunes' entries to record this credit sale and the related cost of goods sold follow:

1	Jul 7	Accounts receivable (A+)	7,200	
		Sales revenue (R+)		7,200
		Sale on account.		

2	7	Cost of goods sold (E+)	4,700	
		Inventory (A–)		4,700
		Recorded cost of goods sold.		

---

[1]Often abbreviated as Net sales.

Sales Returns Assume that on July 12, 2014, the customer returns $600 of the goods. Greg's Tunes, the seller, records the sales return as follows:

1	Jul 12	Sales returns and allowances (CR+)	600	
		Accounts receivable (A−)		600
		Received returned goods.		

Accounts receivable decreases because Greg's Tunes will not collect cash for the returned goods.

Greg's Tunes receives the returned merchandise and updates its inventory records. Greg's Tunes must also decrease Cost of goods sold as follows (the returned goods cost $400):

2	Jul 12	Inventory (A+)	400	
		Cost of goods sold (E−)		400
		Placed goods back in inventory.		

Sales Allowances Suppose on July 15 Greg's Tunes grants a $100 sales allowance for goods damaged in transit. A sales allowance is recorded as follows:

1	Jul 15	Sales returns and allowances (CR+)	100	
		Accounts receivable (A−)		100
		Granted a sales allowance for damaged goods.		

There is no second entry to adjust inventory for a sales allowance because the seller receives no returned goods from the customer.

After these entries are posted, Accounts receivable has a $6,500 debit balance, as follows:

Accounts receivable

Jul 7	Sale	7,200	Jul 12	Return	600
			15	Allowance	100
Bal		6,500			

Sales Discounts On July 17, the last day of the discount period, Greg's Tunes collects this receivable. Assuming no freight is included in the invoice, the company's cash receipt is $6,370 [$6,500 − ($6,500 × 0.02)], and the collection entry is as follows:

Jul 17	Cash (A+)	6,370	
	Sales discounts ($6,500 × 0.02) (CR+)	130	
	Accounts receivable (A−)		6,500
	Cash collection within the discount period.		

Now, Greg's Tunes' Accounts receivable balance is zero:

Accounts receivable

Jul 7	Sale	7,200	Jul 12	Return	600
			15	Allowance	100
			17	Collection	6,500
Bal		0			

Notice that all selling transactions utilize accounts beginning with "S," such as Sales revenue, Sales returns and allowances, and Sales discounts.

Net Sales Revenue, Cost of Goods Sold, and Gross Profit

Net sales revenue, cost of goods sold, and gross profit are key elements of profitability. Net sales revenue minus Cost of goods sold is called **Gross profit,** or **Gross margin.** You can also think of gross profit as the mark-up on the inventory.

Gross profit is the extra amount the company received from the customer over what the company paid to the vendor.

$$\text{Net sales revenue} - \text{Cost of goods sold} = \text{Gross profit}$$

Gross profit, along with net income, is a measure of business success. A sufficiently high gross profit is vital to a merchandiser.

The following example will clarify the nature of gross profit. Suppose Greg's Tunes' cost to purchase a CD is $15 and it sells the same CD for $20. Greg's Tunes' gross profit for each CD is $5, computed as follows:

Sales revenue earned by selling one CD	$ 20
Cost of goods sold for the CD (what the CD cost)	15
Gross profit on the sale of one CD	$ 5

The gross profit reported on Greg's Tunes' income statement is the sum of the gross profits on the CDs and all the other products the company sold during the year. The gross profit must cover the company's operating expenses for the company to survive.

Summary Problem 5-1 puts into practice what you have learned in the first half of this chapter.

Summary Problem 5-1

Suppose Heat Miser Air Conditioner Company engaged in the following transactions during June of the current year:

Jun	3	Purchased inventory on credit terms of 1/10 net eom (end of month), $1,600.
	9	Returned 40% of the inventory purchased on June 3. It was defective.
	12	Sold goods for cash, $920 (cost, $550).
	15	Purchased goods for $5,000. Credit terms were 3/15, net 30.
	16	Paid a $260 freight bill on goods purchased.
	18	Sold inventory for $2,000 on credit terms of 2/10, n/30 (cost, $1,180).
	22	Received returned goods from the customer of the June 18 sale, $800 (cost, $480).
	24	Borrowed money from the bank to take advantage of the discount offered on the June 15 purchase. Signed a note payable to the bank for the net amount, $4,850.
	24	Paid supplier for goods purchased on June 15.
	28	Received cash in full settlement of the account from the customer who purchased inventory on June 18.
	29	Paid the amount owed on account from the purchase of June 3.

Requirements

1. Journalize the preceding transactions. Explanations are not required.
2. Set up T-accounts and post the journal entries to show the ending balances in the Inventory and the Cost of goods sold accounts only.

3. Assume that the note payable signed on June 24 requires the payment of $90 interest expense. Was borrowing funds to take the cash discount a wise or unwise decision? What was the net savings or cost of the decision?

Solution

Requirement 1

Jun 3	Inventory (A+)		1,600	
	Accounts payable (L+)			1,600
9	Accounts payable ($1,600 × 0.40) (L–)		640	
	Inventory (A–)			640
12	Cash (A+)		920	
	Sales revenue (R+)			920
12	Cost of goods sold (E+)		550	
	Inventory (A–)			550
15	Inventory (A+)		5,000	
	Accounts payable (L+)			5,000
16	Inventory (A+)		260	
	Cash (A–)			260
18	Accounts receivable (A+)		2,000	
	Sales revenue (R+)			2,000
18	Cost of goods sold (E+)		1,180	
	Inventory (A–)			1,180
22	Sales returns and allowances (CR+)		800	
	Accounts receivable (A–)			800
22	Inventory (A+)		480	
	Cost of goods sold (E–)			480
24	Cash (A+)		4,850	
	Note payable (L+)			4,850
24	Accounts payable (L–)		5,000	
	Inventory ($5,000 × 0.03) (A–)			150
	Cash ($5,000 × 0.97) (A–)			4,850
28	Cash [($2,000 – $800) × 0.98] (A+)		1,176	
	Sales discounts [($2,000 – $800) × 0.02] (CR+)		24	
	Accounts receivable ($2,000 – $800) (A–)			1,200
29	Accounts payable ($1,600 – $640) (L–)		960	
	Cash (A–)			960

Requirement 2

Inventory					Cost of goods sold			
Jun 3	1,600	Jun 9	640		Jun 12	550	Jun 22	480
15	5,000	12	550		18	1,180		
16	260	18	1,180					
22	480	24	150		Bal	1,250		
Bal	4,820							

Requirement 3

Heat Miser's decision to borrow funds was wise because the $150 discount received exceeded the interest paid of $90. Thus, Heat Miser Air Conditioner Company was $60 better off.

Adjusting and Closing the Accounts of a Merchandiser

A merchandiser adjusts and closes accounts the same way a service entity does. If a worksheet is used, the trial balance is entered, and the worksheet is completed to determine net income or net loss.

 4 Adjust and close the accounts of a merchandising business

Adjusting Inventory Based on a Physical Count

The Inventory account should stay current at all times in a perpetual inventory system. However, the actual amount of inventory on hand may differ from what the books show. Theft, damage, and errors occur. For this reason, businesses take a physical count of inventory *at least* once a year. The most common time to count inventory is at the end of the fiscal year. The business then adjusts the Inventory account based on the physical count.

Greg's Tunes' Inventory account shows an unadjusted balance of $40,500.

Inventory

Dec 31 40,500	

With no shrinkage—due to theft or error—the business should have inventory costing $40,500. But on December 31, Greg's Tunes counts the inventory on hand, and the total cost comes to only $40,200.

Inventory balance before adjustment	–	Actual inventory on hand	=	Adjusting entry to inventory
$40,500	–	$40,200	=	Credit of $300

Greg's Tunes records this adjusting entry for inventory shrinkage:

Dec 31	Cost of goods sold (E+)	300	
	Inventory ($40,500 – $40,200) (A–)		300
	Adjustment for inventory shrinkage.		

This entry brings Inventory to its correct balance.

Inventory

Dec 31 Bal	40,500	Dec 31 Adj 300
Dec 31 Adj Bal	40,200	

Other adjustments, plus a complete merchandising worksheet, are covered in Appendix 5B, located at myaccountinglab.com.

Stop & Think...

Consider the amount of goods a company has available for sale. At the end of the period, the total spent for those items can only appear in two accounts: Inventory (asset) or Cost of goods sold (expense). So what happens to the goods that are missing or damaged? This is considered a cost of doing business and those values are "buried" in the Cost of goods sold amount, rather than shown in a separate account in the ledger.

Closing the Accounts of a Merchandiser

Exhibit 5-7 presents Greg's Tunes' closing entries for December, which are similar to those you learned in Chapter 4, except for the new accounts (highlighted in color). **Closing still means to zero out all accounts that aren't on the balance sheet.** *All amounts are assumed* for this illustration.

EXHIBIT 5-7	**Closing Entries for a Merchandiser—Amounts Assumed**

Journal

	Date	Accounts	Debit	Credit
1.	Dec 31	Sales revenue (R–)	169,300	
		Sales discounts (CR–)		1,400
		Sales returns and allowances (CR–)		2,000
		Income summary		165,900
2.	31	Income summary	112,800	
		Cost of goods sold (E–)		90,800
		Wage expense (E–)		10,200
		Rent expense (E–)		8,400
		Depreciation expense (E–)		600
		Insurance expense (E–)		1,000
		Supplies expense (E–)		500
		Interest expense (E–)		1,300
3.	31	Income summary ($165,900 – $112,800)	53,100	
		Moore, capital (Q+)		53,100
4.	31	Moore, capital (Q–)	54,100	
		Moore, drawing (D–)		54,100

Income summary

Clo 2	112,800	Clo 1	165,900
		Bal	53,100
Clo 3	53,100		
		Bal	0

Moore, capital

Clo 4	54,100	Bal	25,900
		Clo 3	53,100
		Bal	24,900

Dividends

Bal	54,100		
		Clo 4	54,100
Bal	0		

The four-step closing process for a merchandising company follows:

STEP 1: Make the revenue and contra revenue accounts equal zero via the Income summary account. This closing entry transfers the difference of total revenues ($169,300) and contra revenues ($1,400 + $2,000) to the *credit* side of the Income summary account, $165,900.

STEP 2: Make expense accounts equal zero via the Income summary account. This closing entry transfers total expenses to the *debit* side of the Income summary account, $112,800.

The Income summary account now holds the net income or net loss of the period. See the following Income summary T-account to illustrate.

Income summary

Closing entry 2	Expenses	Closing entry 1	Revenues
	Net loss if Debit balance		Net income if Credit balance

STEP 3: Make the Income summary account equal zero via the Capital account. This closing entry transfers net income (or net loss) to Capital.

STEP 4: Make the Drawing account equal zero via the Capital account. This entry transfers the drawing to the *debit* side of Capital.

> **Key Takeaway**
>
> Closing entries are made at the end of a period to all accounts that are temporary (not on the balance sheet). To close an account means to make the balance zero.

Preparing a Merchandiser's Financial Statements

Exhibit 5-8 on the next page shows Greg's Tunes' financial statements for 2014.

5 Prepare a merchandiser's financial statements

Income Statement The income statement begins with Sales, Cost of goods sold, and Gross profit. Then come the operating expenses, which are those expenses other than Cost of goods sold. **Operating expenses are all the normal expenses incurred to run the business other than COGS.**

Both merchandisers and service companies report operating expenses in two categories:

- **Selling expenses** are expenses related to marketing and selling the company's products. These include sales salaries, sales commissions, advertising, depreciation, store rent, utilities on store buildings, property taxes on store buildings, and delivery expense.

- **General expenses** include expenses *not* related to marketing the company's products. These include office expenses, such as the salaries of the executives and office employees; depreciation; rent, other than on stores (for example, rent on the administrative office); utilities, other than on stores (for example, utilities on the administrative office); and property taxes on the administrative office building.

Gross profit minus Operating expenses equals **Operating income** or **Income from operations. Operating income measures the results of the entity's major ongoing activities (normal operations).**

The last section of Greg's Tunes' income statement is **Other revenue and expense.** This category reports revenues and expenses that fall outside Greg's Tunes' main, day-to day, regular operations. Examples include interest revenue, interest expense, and gains and losses on the sale of plant assets. These examples have nothing to do with Greg's Tunes' "normal" business of selling CDs. As a result, they are classified as "other" items.

The bottom line of the income statement is net income:

> **Net income = Total revenues and gains − Total expenses and losses**

We often hear the term *bottom line* to refer to a final result. The bottom line is net income on the income statement.

Statement of Owner's Equity A merchandiser's statement of owner's equity looks exactly like that of a service business.

EXHIBIT 5-8 | **Financial Statements—Amounts Assumed**

GREG'S TUNES
Income Statement
Year Ended December 31, 2014

Sales revenue		$169,300
Less: Sales returns and allowances	$2,000	
Sales discounts	1,400	3,400
Net sales revenue		$165,900
Cost of goods sold		90,800
Gross profit		$ 75,100
Operating expenses:		
Selling expenses:		
Wage expense	$10,200	
General expenses:		
Rent expense	8,400	
Insurance expense	1,000	
Depreciation expense	600	
Supplies expense	500	20,700
Operating income		$ 54,400
Other revenue and (expense):		
Interest expense		(1,300)
Net income		$ 53,100

GREG'S TUNES
Statement of Owner's Equity
Year Ended December 31, 2014

Moore, capital, Dec 31, 2013	$ 25,900
Net income	53,100
	79,000
Drawing	(54,100)
Moore, capital, Dec 31, 2014	$ 24,900

GREG'S TUNES
Balance Sheet
December 31, 2014

Assets			Liabilities	
Current assets:			Current liabilities:	
Cash		$ 2,800	Accounts payable	$39,500
Accounts receivable		4,600	Unearned sales revenue	700
Inventory		40,200	Wages payable	400
Prepaid insurance		200	Total current liabilities	40,600
Supplies		100	Long-term liabilities:	
Total current assets		47,900	Note payable	12,600
Plant assets:			Total liabilities	53,200
Furniture	$33,200		**Owner's Equity**	
Less: Accumulated			Moore, capital	24,900
depreciation	3,000	30,200	Total liabilities and	
Total assets		$78,100	owner's equity	$78,100

Balance Sheet For a merchandiser, the balance sheet is the same as for a service business, except merchandisers have an additional current asset, Inventory. Service businesses have no inventory.

Income Statement Formats: Multi-Step and Single-Step

As we saw in Chapter 4, the balance sheet appears in two formats:

- The report format (assets at top, owner's equity at bottom)
- The account format (assets at left, liabilities and owner's equity at right)

There are also two formats for the income statement:

- The multi-step format
- The single-step format

A **multi-step income statement** lists several important subtotals. In addition to net income (the bottom line), it also reports subtotals for gross profit and income from operations. The income statements presented thus far in this chapter have been multi-step, and multi-step format is more popular. The multi-step income statement for Greg's Tunes appears in Exhibit 5-8 (on the previous page).

The **single-step income statement** is the income statement format you first learned about in Chapter 1. It groups all revenues together and all expenses together without calculating other subtotals. Many companies use this format. The single-step format clearly distinguishes revenues from expenses and works well for service entities because they have no gross profit to report. Exhibit 5-9 shows a single-step income statement for Greg's Tunes.

EXHIBIT 5-9 | **Single-Step Income Statement**

GREG'S TUNES
Income Statement
Year Ended December 31, 2014

Revenues:		
Sales revenue		$169,300
Less: Sales returns and allowances	$ 2,000	
Less: Sales discounts	1,400	3,400
Net sales revenue		$165,900
Expenses:		
Cost of goods sold	$90,800	
Wage expense	10,200	
Rent expense	8,400	
Interest expense	1,300	
Insurance expense	1,000	
Depreciation expense	600	
Supplies expenses	500	
Total expenses		$112,800
Net income		$ 53,100

Three Ratios for Decision Making

6 Use gross profit percentage, inventory turnover, and days in inventory to evaluate a business

Inventory is the most important asset for a merchandiser. Merchandisers use several ratios to evaluate their operations, among them the *gross profit percentage*, the *rate of inventory turnover*, and *days in inventory*.

The Gross Profit Percentage

Gross profit (gross margin) is net sales minus the cost of goods sold. Merchandisers strive to increase the **gross profit percentage** (also called the **gross margin percentage**), which is computed as follows:

> **For Greg's Tunes**
> **(Values from Exhibit 5-8)**
>
> $$\text{Gross profit percentage} = \frac{\text{Gross profit}}{\text{Net sales revenue}}$$
>
> $$= \frac{\$75,100}{\$165,900} = 0.453 = 45.3\%$$

The gross profit percentage is one of the most carefully watched measures of profitability. A small increase from last year to this year may signal an important rise in income. Conversely, a small decrease from last year to this year may signal trouble.

The Rate of Inventory Turnover

Owners and managers strive to sell inventory quickly because the inventory generates no profit until it is sold. Further, fast-selling inventory is less likely to become obsolete (worthless). The faster the inventory sells, the larger the income. Additionally, larger inventories mean more storage costs, more risk of loss, and higher insurance premiums. Therefore, companies try to manage their inventory levels such that they have just enough inventory to meet customer demand without investing large amounts of money in inventory sitting on the shelves gathering dust. **Inventory turnover** measures how rapidly inventory is sold. It is computed as follows:

> **For Greg's Tunes**
> **(Values from Exhibit 5-8)**
>
> $$\frac{\text{Inventory}}{\text{turnover}} = \frac{\text{Cost of goods sold}}{\text{Average inventory}} = \frac{\text{Cost of goods sold}}{(\text{Beginning inventory*} + \text{Ending inventory})/2}$$
>
> $$= \frac{\$90,800}{(\$38,600^* + \$40,200)/2} = 2.3 \text{ times per year}$$

*Ending inventory from the preceding period. Amount assumed for this illustration.

A high turnover rate is desirable, and an increase in the turnover rate usually means higher profits.

Days in Inventory

Another key measure is the **number of days in inventory** ratio. This measures the average number of days inventory is held by the company and is calculated as follows:

$$\text{Days in inventory} = \frac{365 \text{ days}}{\text{Inventory turnover ratio}}$$

$$= \frac{365 \text{ days}}{2.3 \text{ times}}$$

$$= 159 \text{ days (rounded)}$$

As stated earlier, companies try to manage their inventory levels such that they have just enough inventory to meet customer demand without investing large amounts of money in inventory. It appears Greg's Tunes has nearly a five-month supply of inventory, which seems excessive. More investigation is needed, but it is likely Greg's could reduce its inventory investment and still serve its customers well.

Key Takeaway

Ratios serve as an alternate way to measure how well a company is managing its various assets.

Decision Guidelines 5-1

MERCHANDISING OPERATIONS AND THE ACCOUNTING CYCLE

Merchandising companies like **Walmart** are very different than service companies, like the international CPA firm **Ernst & Young**. How do these two types of businesses differ? How are they similar? The Decision Guidelines answer these questions.

Decision	Guidelines
• How do merchandisers differ from service entities?	• Merchandisers buy and sell *merchandise inventory*. • Service entities perform a *service*.

• How do a merchandiser's financial statements differ from the statements of a service business?

Balance Sheet:

Merchandiser has *Inventory*, an asset.   Service business has *no* inventory.

Income Statement:

Merchandiser

Sales revenue	$XXX
– Cost of goods sold	X
= Gross profit	XX
– Operating expenses	X
= Net income	$ X

Service Business

Service revenue	$XX
– Operating expenses	X
= Net income	$ X

Statement of Owner's Equity: No difference

Decision	Guidelines
• What are the different inventory systems used?	• The *periodic inventory system* shows the correct balances of inventory and cost of goods sold only after a physical count of the inventory has taken place, which occurs at least once each year. • The *perpetual inventory system* is a computerized inventory system that perpetually shows the amount of inventory on hand (the asset) and the cost of goods sold (the expense).

• What are the options for formatting the merchandiser's income statement?

Single-Step Format

Revenues: Sales revenue		$ XXX
Other revenues		X
Total revenues		$XXXX
Expenses: Cost of goods sold		X
Operating expenses		X
Other expenses		X
Total expenses		$ XXX
Net income		$ X

Decision	Guidelines
	Multi-Step Format

Sales revenue...........................	$XXX
– Cost of goods sold...............	X
= Gross profit.........................	$ XX
– Operating expenses	X
= Operating income.................	$ X
+ Other revenues....................	X
– Other expenses....................	(X)
= Net income..........................	$ X

Decision	Guidelines
• How can merchandisers evaluate their business operations?	Three key ratios

Gross profit percentage

$$\text{Gross profit percentage} = \frac{\text{Gross profit}}{\text{Net sales revenue}}$$

$$\text{Inventory} - \frac{\text{Purchase returns}}{\text{and allowances}} - \frac{\text{Purchase}}{\text{discounts}} = \frac{\text{Net}}{\text{inventory}}$$

$$\text{Inventory turnover* } = \frac{\text{Cost of goods sold}}{\text{Average inventory}}$$

*In most cases—the higher, the better.

$$\text{Days in inventory} = \frac{365 \text{ days}}{\text{Inventory turnover ratio}}$$

Summary Problem 5-2

The adjusted trial balance of King Cornelius Company follows:

KING CORNELIUS COMPANY Adjusted Trial Balance December 31, 2014		
Account	**Debit**	**Credit**
Cash	$ 5,600	
Accounts receivable	37,100	
Inventory	25,800	
Supplies	1,300	
Prepaid rent	1,000	
Furniture	26,500	
Accumulated depreciation		$ 23,800
Accounts payable		6,300
Salary payable		2,000
Interest payable		600
Unearned sales revenue		2,400
Note payable, long-term		35,000
Cornelius, capital		22,200
Cornelius, drawing	48,000	
Sales revenue		244,000
Interest revenue		2,000
Sales discounts	10,000	
Sales returns and allowances	8,000	
Cost of goods sold	81,000	
Salary expense	72,700	
Rent expense	7,700	
Depreciation expense	2,700	
Utilities expense	5,800	
Supplies expense	2,200	
Interest expense	2,900	
Total	$338,300	$338,300

Requirements

1. Journalize the closing entries at December 31. Post to the Income summary account as an accuracy check on net income. Recall that the credit balance closed out of Income summary should equal net income as computed on the income statement. Also post to Cornelius, capital, whose balance should agree with the amount reported on the balance sheet.
2. Prepare the company's multi-step income statement, statement of owner's equity, and balance sheet in account form. Draw arrows linking the statements. Note: King Cornelius doesn't separate its operating expenses as either selling or general.
3. Compute the inventory turnover and days in inventory for 2014. Inventory at December 31, 2013, was $21,000. Turnover for 2013 was 3.0 times. Would you expect King Cornelius Company to be more profitable or less profitable in 2014 than in 2013? Why?

Requirement 1

	Closing Entries			
	Date	Accounts	Debit	Credit
	2014			
1	Dec 31	Sales revenue (R–)	244,000	
		Interest revenue (R–)	2,000	
		Sales returns and allowances (CR–)		8,000
		Income summary		228,000
		Sales discounts (CR–)		10,000
2	Dec 31	Income summary	175,000	
		Cost of goods sold (E–)		81,000
		Salary expense (E–)		72,700
		Rent expense (E–)		7,700
		Depreciation expense (E–)		2,700
		Utilities expense (E–)		5,800
		Supplies expense (E–)		2,200
		Interest expense (E–)		2,900
3	Dec 31	Income summary ($228,000 – $175,000)	53,000	
		Cornelius, capital (Q+)		53,000
4	Dec 31	Cornelius, capital (Q–)	48,000	
		Cornelius, drawing (D–)		48,000

Income summary			
Clo 2	175,000	Clo 1	228,000
Clo 3	53,000	Bal	53,000
		Bal	0

Cornelius, capital			
			22,200
Clo 4	48,000	Clo 3	53,000
		Bal	27,200

Requirement 2

KING CORNELIUS COMPANY
Income Statement
Year Ended December 31, 2014

Sales revenue:			$244,000
Less: Sales discounts		$10,000	
Sales returns and allowances		8,000	18,000
Net sales revenue			$226,000
Cost of goods sold			81,000
Gross profit			$145,000
Operating expenses:			
Salary expense		$72,700	
Rent expense		7,700	
Utilities expense		5,800	
Interest expense		2,900	
Depreciation expense		2,700	
Supplies expense		2,200	94,000
Operating income			$ 51,000
Other revenue and (expense):			
Interest revenue			2,000
Net income			$ 53,000

KING CORNELIUS COMPANY
Statement of Owner's Equity
Year Ended December 31, 2014

Cornelius, capital, Dec 31, 2013	$ 22,200
Net income	53,000
	75,200
Drawing	(48,000)
Cornelius, capital, Dec 31, 2014	$ 27,200

KING CORNELIUS COMPANY
Balance Sheet
December 31, 2014

Assets			Liabilities	
Current:			Current:	
Cash		$ 5,600	Accounts payable	$ 6,300
Accounts receivable		37,100	Salary payable	2,000
Inventory		25,800	Interest payable	600
Supplies		1,300	Unearned sales revenue	2,400
Prepaid rent		1,000	Total current liabilities	11,300
Total current assets		70,800	Long-term:	
Plant:			Note payable	35,000
Furniture	$26,500		Total liabilities	46,300
Less: Accumulated			**Owner's Equity**	
depreciation	23,800	2,700	Cornelius, capital	27,200
			Total liabilities and	
Total assets		$73,500	owner's equity	$73,500

Requirement 3

$$\frac{\text{Inventory}}{\text{turnover}} = \frac{\text{Cost of goods sold}}{\text{Average inventory}}$$

$$= \frac{\$81,000}{(\$21,000 + \$25,800)/2} = 3.5 \text{ times (rounded)}$$

The increase in the rate of inventory turnover from 3.0 to 3.5 suggests higher profits.

$$\text{Days in inventory} = \frac{365 \text{ days}}{\text{Inventory turnover ratio}}$$

$$= \frac{365 \text{ days}}{3.5}$$

$$= 105 \text{ days (rounded)}$$

The days in inventory turnover of 105 suggests the company has almost three and a half months inventory on hand. The company should investigate further to determine if it can reduce the amount of inventory on hand and still supply its customers well.

Review *Merchandising Operations*

● Accounting Vocabulary

Cost of Goods Sold (COGS) (p. 263)
The cost of the inventory that the business has sold to customers. Also called **cost of sales**.

Cost of Sales (p. 263)
The cost of the inventory that the business has sold to customers. Also called **cost of goods sold**.

Credit Terms (p. 259)
The terms of purchase or sale as stated on the invoice. A common example is 2/10, n/30.

Customer (p. 257)
The individual or business that buys goods from a seller.

Free On Board (FOB) (p. 260)
The purchase agreement specifies FOB terms to indicate who pays the freight. FOB terms also determine when title to the goods transfer to the purchaser.

FOB Destination (p. 261)
Situation in which the buyer takes ownership (title) at the delivery destination point and the seller pays the freight.

FOB Shipping Point (p. 260)
Situation in which the buyer takes ownership (title) to the goods at the shipping point and the buyer pays the freight.

Freight In (p. 261)
The transportation cost to ship goods INTO the warehouse; therefore, it is freight on purchased goods.

Freight Out (p. 261)
The transportation cost to ship goods OUT of the warehouse; therefore, it is freight on goods sold to a customer.

General Expenses (p. 271)
Expenses incurred that are not related to marketing the company's products.

Gross Margin (p. 266)
Excess of net sales revenue over cost of goods sold. Also called **gross profit**.

Gross Margin Percentage (p. 274)
Gross profit divided by net sales revenue. A measure of profitability. Also called **gross profit percentage**.

Gross Profit (p. 266)
Excess of net sales revenue over cost of goods sold. Also called **gross margin**.

Gross Profit Percentage (p. 274)
Gross profit divided by net sales revenue. A measure of profitability. Also called **gross margin percentage**.

Income from Operations (p. 271)
Gross profit minus operating expenses. Also called **operating income**.

Inventory (p. 256)
All the goods that the company owns and expects to sell to customers in the normal course of operations.

Inventory Turnover (p. 274)
Ratio of cost of goods sold divided by average inventory. Measures the number of times a company sells its average level of inventory during a period.

Invoice (p. 258)
A seller's request for cash from the purchaser.

Merchandisers (p. 256)
Businesses that sell merchandise, or goods, to customers.

Merchandising (p. 256)
Consists of buying and selling products rather than services.

Multi-Step Income Statement (p. 273)
Format that contains subtotals to highlight significant relationships. In addition to net income, it reports gross profit and operating income.

Net Purchases (p. 304)
Purchases less purchase discounts and purchase returns and allowances.

Net Sales Revenue (p. 265)
Sales revenue less sales discounts and sales returns and allowances.

Number of Days in Inventory (p. 275)
Ratio that measures the average number of days that inventory is held by a company.

Operating Expenses (p. 262)
Expenses, other than cost of goods sold, that are incurred in the entity's major line of business. Examples include rent, depreciation, salaries, wages, utilities, and supplies expense.

Operating Income (p. 271)
Gross profit minus operating expenses. Also called **income from operations**.

Other Revenue and Expense (p. 271)
Revenue or expense that is outside the normal day-to-day operations of a business, such as a gain or loss on the sale of plant assets.

Periodic Inventory System (p. 257)
A system in which the business does not keep a continuous record of inventory on hand. At the end of the period, the business takes a physical count of on-hand inventory and uses this information to prepare the financial statements.

Perpetual Inventory System (p. 258)
The computerized accounting inventory system in which the business keeps a constant/running record of inventory and cost of goods sold.

Purchase Allowances (p. 260)
An amount granted to the purchaser as an incentive to keep goods that are not "as ordered."

Purchase Discount (p. 259)
A discount that businesses offer to purchasers as an incentive for early payment.

Purchase Returns (p. 260)
A situation in which businesses allow purchasers to return merchandise that is defective, damaged, or otherwise unsuitable.

Sales (p. 263)
The amount that a merchandiser earns from selling its inventory. Short name for **Sales revenue**.

Sales Discount (p. 265)
Reduction in the amount of cash received from a customer for early payment. Offered by the seller as an incentive for the purchasers to pay early. A contra account to Sales revenue.

Sales Returns and Allowances (p. 265)
Decreases in the seller's receivable from a customer's return of merchandise or from granting the customer an allowance from the amount owed to the seller. A contra account to Sales revenue.

Sales Revenue (p. 263)
The amount that a merchandiser earns from selling its inventory. Also called **Sales**.

Selling Expenses (p. 271)
Expenses related to marketing and selling the company's products.

Single-Step Income Statement (p. 273)
Format that groups all revenues together and then lists and deducts all expenses together without calculating any subtotals.

Vendor (p. 257)
The individual or business from whom a company purchases goods. A merchandising company mainly purchases inventory from vendors.

Looking for the Demo Docs for Chapter 5? You can find them online at myaccountinglab.com or in the Study Guide.

● Destination: Student Success

Student Success Tips

The following are hints on some common trouble areas for students in this chapter:

● Remember that transactions with customers use selling accounts (Sales, Sales discounts, Sales returns and allowances).

● Perpetual inventory purchasing transactions with vendors use the Inventory account, whether its quantity or cost per unit is increasing or decreasing.

● The four closing entries you learned in Chapter 4 are the same for a merchandiser, you just have more accounts to close. (TIP: Make temporary accounts = zero).

● Discounts, whether sales or purchases, are calculated for early payment ONLY on the cost of goods. No discount is given for freight charges.

● Remember that bottom line net income (loss) is the same whether you prepare a multi-step or a single-step income statement. The difference is that there are more subtotals on the multi-step statement.

● Remember the formulas for gross profit percentage, inventory turnover, and days in inventory. (TIP: Gross profit is a % of net sales; inventory turnover is how many TIMES the average inventory was sold during the year, and the days in inventory ratio represents how many days of inventory you have in the warehouse to meet future sales needs.)

Getting Help

If there's a learning objective from the chapter you aren't confident about, try using one or more of the following resources:

● Practice additional exercises or problems at the end of Chapter 5 that cover the specific learning objective that is challenging you.

● Watch the white board videos for Chapter 5, located at myaccountinglab.com under the Chapter Resources button.

● Go to myaccountinglab.com and select the Study Plan button. Choose Chapter 5 and work the questions covering that specific learning objective until you've mastered it.

● Work the Chapter 5 pre/post tests in myaccountinglab.com.

● Visit the learning resource center on your campus for tutoring.

● Quick Check

Experience the Power of Practice!

As denoted by the logo, all of these questions, as well as additional practice materials, can be found in **MyAccountingLab**.

Please visit myaccountinglab.com

1. Which account does a merchandiser use that a service company does not use?
   a. Cost of goods sold
   b. Inventory
   c. Sales revenue
   d. All of the above

2. The two main inventory accounting systems are the
   a. perpetual and periodic.
   b. purchase and sale.
   c. returns and allowances.
   d. cash and accrual.

3. The journal entry for the purchase of inventory on account is

a.
Inventory...............................	XXX	
Accounts receivable		XXX

b.
Accounts payable	XXX	
Inventory.................................		XXX

c.
Inventory...............................	XXX	
Accounts payable.......................		XXX

d.
Inventory...............................	XXX	
Cash		XXX

4. JC Manufacturing purchased inventory for $5,300 and also paid a $260 freight bill. JC Manufacturing returned 45% of the goods to the seller and later took a 2% purchase discount. What is JC Manufacturing's final cost of the inventory that it kept? (Round your answer to the nearest whole number.)

a. $2,997
b. $2,337
c. $3,117
d. $2,857

5. Suppose Austin Sound had sales of $300,000 and sales returns of $45,000. Cost of goods sold was $152,000. How much gross profit did Austin Sound report?

a. $148,000
b. $103,000
c. $255,000
d. $88,000

6. Suppose Dave's Discount's Inventory account showed a balance of $8,000 before the year-end adjustments. The physical count of goods on hand totaled $7,400. To adjust the accounts, Dave Marshall would make the following entry:

a.
Cost of goods sold..........................	600	
Inventory.................................		600

b.
Inventory..	600	
Accounts receivable		600

c.
Accounts payable	600	
Inventory.................................		600

d.
Inventory..	600	
Cost of goods sold		600

7. Which account in question 6 would Dave Marshall close at the end of the year?

a. Cost of goods sold
b. Inventory
c. Accounts receivable
d. Accounts payable

8. The final closing entry for a proprietorship is

a.

Sales revenue......................................	XXX
Income summary	XXX

b.

Capital...	XXX
Drawing....................................	XXX

c.

Drawing...	XXX
Capital....................................	XXX

d.

Income summary.............................	XXX
Expenses.....................................	XXX

9. Which subtotals appear on a multi-step income statement but do not appear on a single-step income statement?

a. Gross profit and Income from operations

b. Operating expenses and Net income

c. Cost of goods sold and Net income

d. Net sales and Cost of goods sold

10. Assume Juniper Natural Dyes made net Sales of $90,000, and Cost of goods sold totaled $58,000. Average inventory was $17,000. What was Juniper Natural Dyes' gross profit percentage for this period? (Round your answer to the nearest whole percent.)

a. 36%   c. 64%

b. 3.4 times   d. 17%

Answers are given after Apply Your Knowledge (page 302).

Assess Your Progress

● Short Exercises

MyAccountingLab

S5-1 ❶ **Comparing periodic and perpetual inventory systems [10 min]**
You may have shopped at a Billy's store. Suppose Billy's purchased T-shirts on January 1 on account for $15,900. Credit terms are 2/15, n/30. Billy's paid within the discount period on January 8. Billy's sold the goods on February 5.

Requirements

1. If Billy's uses a periodic inventory system, in which month will the purchase of inventory be recorded as an expense? How much will the net expense be?

2. If Billy's uses the perpetual inventory system, in which month will the purchase of inventory be recorded as an expense? How much will the net expense be?

S5-2 ❷ **Analyzing purchase transactions—perpetual inventory [5–10 min]**
Suppose KC Toys buys $185,800 worth of MegoBlock toys on credit terms of 2/10, n/30. Some of the goods are damaged in shipment, so KC Toys returns $18,530 of the merchandise to MegoBlock.

Requirement

1. How much must KC Toys pay MegoBlock
   a. after the discount period?
   b. within the discount period?

Note: Short Exercise 5-3 should be used only after completing Short Exercise 5-2.

S5-3   **②** **Journalizing purchase transactions—perpetual inventory [10 min]**
Refer to the KC Toys facts in Short Exercise 5-2.

Requirements

1. Journalize the following transactions. Explanations are not required.
   a. Purchase of the goods on July 8, 2012.
   b. Return of the damaged goods on July 12, 2012.
   c. Payment on July 15, 2012.
2. In the final analysis, how much did the inventory cost KC Toys?

S5-4   **②** **Journalizing purchase transactions—perpetual inventory [5–10 min]**
Suppose a Bubba store purchases $61,000 of women's sportswear on account from Tomas on July 1, 2012. Credit terms are 2/10, net 45. Bubba pays electronically, and Tomas receives the money on July 10, 2012.

Requirements

1. Journalize Bubba's transactions for July 1, 2012, and July 10, 2012.
2. What was Bubba's net cost of this inventory?

Note: Short Exercise 5-5 covers this same situation for the seller.

S5-5   **③** **Journalizing sales transactions—perpetual inventory [10 min]**
Consider the facts in the Short Exercise 5-4 as they apply to the seller, Tomas. The goods cost Tomas $32,000.

Requirement

1. Journalize Tomas's transactions for July 1, 2012, and July 10, 2012.

S5-6   **③** **Journalizing sales transactions—perpetual inventory [10 min]**
Suppose Piranha.com sells 2,500 books on account for $15 each (cost of these books is $22,500) on October 10, 2012. One hundred of these books (cost $900) were damaged in shipment, so Piranha.com later received the damaged goods as sales returns on October 13, 2012. Then the customer paid the balance on October 22, 2012. Credit terms offered to the customer were 2/15, net 60.

Requirement

1. Journalize Piranha.com's October 2012 transactions.

Note: Short Exercise 5-7 should be used only after completing Short Exercise 5-6.

S5-7   **③** **Calculating net sales and gross profit—perpetual inventory [5 min]**
Use the data in Short Exercise 5-6 for Piranha.com.

Requirements

1. Calculate net sales revenue for October 2012.
2. Calculate gross profit for October 2012.

S5-8   **④** **Adjusting inventory for shrinkage [5 min]**
Rich's Furniture's Inventory account at year-end appeared as follows:

Inventory	
Unadjusted balance 63,000	

The physical count of inventory came up with a total of $61,900.

Requirement

1. Journalize the adjusting entry.

S5-9 ❹ **Journalizing closing entries—perpetual inventory [5–10 min]**
Rockwell RV Center's accounting records include the following accounts at December 31, 2012:

Cost of goods sold	$385,000	Accumulated depreciation	$ 39,000
Accounts payable	17,000	Cash	43,000
Rent expense	21,000	Sales revenue	696,000
Building	108,000	Depreciation expense	12,000
Rockwell, capital	208,800	Rockwell, drawing	61,000
Inventory	261,000	Sales discounts	9,000

Requirement

1. Journalize the required closing entries for Rockwell RV Center for December 31, 2012.

S5-10 ❺ **Preparing a merchandiser's income statement [5–10 min]**
Carolina Communications reported the following figures in its financial statements:

Cash	$ 3,800	Cost of goods sold	$ 18,000
Total operating expenses	3,500	Equipment, net	10,200
Accounts payable	4,100	Accrued liabilities	1,700
Total owner's equity	4,200	Net sales revenue	28,000
Long–term notes payable	700	Accounts receivable	2,700
Inventory	500		

Requirement

1. Prepare the business's multi-step income statement for the year ended July 31, 2012.

Note: Short Exercise 5-11 should be used only after completing Short Exercise 5-10.

S5-11 ❺ **Preparing a merchandiser's balance sheet [10 min]**
Review the data in Short Exercise 5-10.

Requirement

1. Prepare Carolina Communications' classified balance sheet at July 31, 2012. Use the report format.

Note: Short Exercise 5-12 should be used only after completing Short Exercises 5-10 and 5-11.

S5-12 ❻ **Computing the gross profit percentage, the rate of inventory turnover, and days in inventory [10 min]**
Refer to the Carolina Communications data in Short Exercises 5-10 and 5-11.

Requirement

1. Calculate the gross profit percentage, rate of inventory turnover, and days in inventory ratios for 2012. One year earlier, at July 31, 2011, Carolina's inventory balance was $425.

● Exercises

E5-13   **①** **Describing periodic and perpetual inventory systems [10–15 min]**

The following characteristics may be related to either periodic inventory or perpetual inventory systems or both.

A.	Purchases of inventory are journalized to an asset account at the time of purchase.
B.	Purchases of inventory are journalized to an expense account at the time of purchase.
C.	Inventory records are constantly updated.
D.	Sales made require a second entry to be journalized to record cost of goods sold.
E.	Bar code scanners that record sales transactions are most often associated with this inventory system.
F.	A physical count of goods on hand at year end is required.

Requirement

1. Identify each characteristic as one of the following:
   a. Periodic inventory
   b. Perpetual inventory
   c. Both periodic and perpetual inventory
   d. Neither periodic nor perpetual inventory

E5-14   **②** **Journalizing purchase transactions from an invoice—perpetual inventory [10–15 min]**

As the proprietor of Kingston Tires, you received the following invoice from a supplier:

FIELDS DISTRIBUTION, INC.
7290 S. Prospect Street
Ravenna, OH 44266

Invoice date: September 23, 2012

Sold to: Kingston Tires   **Payment terms:** 1/10, n/30
6678 Diamond Avenue
Ravenna, OH 44266

Description	Quantity Shipped	Price	Amount
D39–X4 Radials....................................	4	$38.12	$152.48
M223 Belted-bias...................................	10	42.84	428.40
Q92 Truck tires..	6	58.12	348.72
Total...			$929.60

Due date:	Amount:
October 3, 2012	$920.30
October 4 through October 22, 2012	$929.60

Requirements

1. Journalize the transaction required on September 23, 2012.

2. Journalize the return on September 28, 2012, of the D39–X4 Radials, which were ordered by mistake.

3. Journalize the payment on October 1, 2012, to Fields Distribution, Inc.

E5-15 ❷ **Journalizing purchase transactions—perpetual system [10–15 min]**

On June 30, 2012, Hayes Jewelers purchased inventory of $5,800 on account from Slater Diamonds, a jewelry importer. Terms were 3/15, net 45. The same day Hayes paid freight charges of $400. Upon receiving the goods, Hayes checked the order and found $800 of unsuitable merchandise, which was returned to Slater on July 4. Then, on July 14, Hayes paid the invoice.

Requirement

1. Journalize all necessary transactions for Hayes Jewelers. Explanations are not required.

E5-16 ❷ ❸ **Computing inventory and cost of goods sold amounts [10–15 min]**

Consider the following incomplete table of merchandiser's profit data:

	Sales	Sales Discounts	Net Sales	Cost of Goods Sold	Gross Profit
$	89,500	$ 1,560	$ 87,940	$ 60,200	(a)
	103,600	(b)	99,220	(c)	$ 34,020
	66,200	2,000	(d)	40,500	(e)
	(f)	2,980	(g)	75,800	36,720

Requirement

1. Calculate the missing table values to complete the table.

E5-17 ❷ ❸ **Journalizing purchase and sales transactions—perpetual system [15–20 min]**

The following transactions occurred during February 2012, for Soul Art Gift Shop:

Feb 3	Purchased $2,700 of inventory on account under terms of 4/10, n/eom (end of month) and FOB shipping point.
7	Returned $400 of defective merchandise purchased on February 3.
9	Paid freight bill of $110 on February 3 purchase.
10	Sold inventory on account for $4,350. Payment terms were 2/15, n/30. These goods cost the company $2,300.
12	Paid amount owed on credit purchase of February 3, less the return and the discount.
16	Granted a sales allowance of $500 on the February 10 sale.
23	Received cash from February 10 customer in full settlement of her debt, less the allowance and the discount.

Requirement

1. Journalize the February transactions for Soul Art Gift Shop. No explanations are required.

E5-18 ❸ **Journalizing sales transactions—perpetual system [10–15 min]**

Refer to the facts presented in Exercise 5-15.

Requirement

1. Journalize the transactions of the seller, Slater Diamonds. Slater's cost of goods sold was 45% of the sales price. Explanations are not required.

E5-19 ❹ **Journalizing adjusting and closing entries, and computing gross profit [10–15 min]**

Emerson St. Paul Book Shop's accounts at June 30, 2012, included the following unadjusted balances:

Inventory	$ 5,400
Cost of goods sold	40,300
Sales revenue	85,300
Sales discounts	1,400
Sales returns and allowances	2,000

The physical count of inventory on hand on June 30, 2012, was $5,000.

Requirements

1. Journalize the adjustment for inventory shrinkage.
2. Journalize the closing entries for June 2012.
3. Compute the gross profit.

E5-20   **4 Making closing entries [15–20 min]**

Howe Audio Equipment's accounting records carried the following selected accounts at April 30, 2012:

Inventory	$ 5,900	Selling expense	$ 7,300
Interest revenue	40	Sales revenue	38,400
Accounts payable	1,000	Interest expense	30
Cost of goods sold	26,900	Accounts receivable	600
Other expense	1,700	General and administrative expense	900
Howe, drawing	300	Howe, capital	8,730

Requirements

1. Journalize the closing entries at April 30, 2012.
2. Set up T-accounts for Income summary and Howe, capital. Post the closing entries to the T-accounts and calculate their ending balances.

E5-21   **4 Journalizing closing entries [10–15 min]**

The trial balance and adjustments columns of the worksheet of Budget Business Systems at March 31, 2012, follow:

BUDGET BUSINESS SYSTEMS
Worksheet
Year Ended March 31, 2012

Account	Trial Balance Debit	Trial Balance Credit	Adjustments Debit	Adjustments Credit
Cash	$ 2,400			
Accounts receivable	8,900		(a)$ 2,500	
Inventory	36,500			(b)$ 4,800
Supplies	13,700			(c) 7,300
Equipment	42,500			
Accumulated depreciation		$ 11,600		(d) 2,300
Accounts payable		9,200		
Salary payable				(e) 1,000
Note payable, long-term		7,900		
Bitzes, capital		34,000		
Bitzes, drawing	43,000			
Sales revenue		232,000		(a) 2,500
Sales discounts	2,500			
Cost of goods sold	111,500		(b) 4,800	
Selling expense	21,100		(c) 5,100	
			(e) 1,000	
General expense	10,300		(c) 2,200	
			(d) 2,300	
Interest expense	2,300			
Total	$294,700	$294,700	$17,900	$17,900

Requirements

1. Compute the adjusted balance for each account that must be closed.
2. Journalize the required closing entries at March 31, 2012.
3. How much was Budget's net income or net loss?

E5-22 ④ ⑤ **Preparing a merchandiser's multi-step income statement to evaluate the business [10–15 min]**
Review the data in Exercise 5-21.

Requirement

1. Prepare Budget's *multi-step* income statement.

E5-23 ⑤ **Preparing a single-step income statement. [10–15 min]**
Review the data given in Exercise 5-21.

Requirement

1. Prepare Budget's *single-step* income statement.

E5-24 ⑥ **Calculating inventory turnover and the gross profit percentage to evaluate the business [10–15 min]**
Review the data in Exercise 5-21.

Requirements

1. Compute the rate of inventory turnover for the fiscal year ended March 31, 2012, assuming $22,000 in average inventory.
2. The inventory turnover rate for the fiscal year ended March 31, 2011, was 3.8 times. Did the inventory turnover rate improve or deteriorate from 2011 to 2012?
3. Calculate the gross profit percentage.
4. The gross profit percentage for the fiscal year ended March 31, 2011, was 62%. Did the gross profit percentage improve or deteriorate during the fiscal year ended March 31, 2012?

E5-25 ⑥ **Calculating gross profit percentage and inventory turnover to evaluate a business [10 min]**
LanWan Software earned sales revenue of $65,000,000 in 2012. Cost of goods sold was $39,000,000, and net income reached $9,000,000, the company's highest ever. Total current assets included inventory of $3,000,000 at December 31, 2012. Inventory was $5,000,000 on December 31, 2011.

Requirement

1. Compute the company's gross profit percentage and rate of inventory turnover for 2012.

● Problems (Group A)

P5-26A ① ② ③ **Journalizing purchase and sale transactions [10–15 min]**
Consider the following transactions that occurred in May 2012 for High Roller.

May 1	Purchased $3,000 of inventory from P&M, terms 1/10, n/20.
3	Sold $3,500 of goods to Frames R Us, Inc., terms 2/10, n/eom. *(Cost $2,240).
5	Frames R Us, returned $300 of goods (Cost $198).
11	Paid P&M.
13	Received payment from Frames R Us.

Requirements

1. What type of inventory system is High Roller using—periodic or perpetual?
2. Which transaction date helped you decide?
3. Journalize May transactions for High Roller. No explanations are required.

P5-27A ❷ ❸ **Journalizing purchase and sale transactions—perpetual inventory [20–25 min]**

Consider the following transactions that occurred in September 2012 for Aquamarines.

Sep	3	Purchased inventory on terms 1/15, n/eom, $5,000.
	4	Purchased inventory for cash of $1,700.
	6	Returned $500 of inventory from September 4 purchase.
	8	Sold goods on terms of 2/15, n/35 of $6,000 that cost $2,640.
	10	Paid for goods purchased September 3.
	12	Received goods from September 8 sale of $400 that cost $160.
	23	Received payment from September 8 customer.
	25	Sold goods to Smithsons for $1,100 that cost $400. Terms of n/30 were offered. As a courtesy to Smithsons, $75 of freight was added to the invoice for which cash was paid directly to **UPS** by Aquamarines.
	29	Received payment from Smithsons.

Requirement

1. Journalize September transactions for Aquamarines. No explanations are required.

P5-28A ❷ ❸ **Journalizing purchase and sale transactions—perpetual system [15–20 min]**

The following transactions occurred between Belvidere Pharmaceuticals and D & S, the pharmacy chain, during July of the current year:

Jul	6	D & S purchased $12,000 of merchandise from Belvidere on credit terms of 3/10, n/30, FOB shipping point. Separately, D & S paid a $200 bill for freight in. These goods cost Belvidere $3,600.
	10	D & S returned $3,000 of the merchandise purchased on July 6. Belvidere accounted for the sales return and placed the goods back in inventory (Belvidere's cost, $1,200).
	15	D & S paid $6,000 of the invoice amount owed to Belvidere for the July 6 purchase, less the discount.
	27	D & S paid the remaining amount owed to Belvidere for the July 6 purchase.

Requirements

1. Journalize these transactions on the books of D & S.
2. Journalize these transactions on the books of Belvidere Pharmaceuticals.

P5-29A ❷❸ Journalizing purchase and sale transactions—perpetual inventory [20–25 min]

Thelma's Amusements completed the following transactions during November 2012:

Nov	1	Purchased supplies for cash, $700.
	4	Purchased inventory on credit terms of 3/10, n/eom, $9,600.
	8	Returned half the inventory purchased on November 4. It was not the inventory ordered.
	10	Sold goods for cash, $1,200 (cost, $700).
	13	Sold inventory on credit terms of 2/15, n/45, $9,900 (cost, $5,300).
	14	Paid the amount owed on account from November 4, less the return (November 8) and the discount.
	17	Received defective inventory as a sales return from the November 13 sale, $600. Thelma's cost of the inventory received was $450.
	18	Purchased inventory of $4,100 on account. Payment terms were 2/10, net 30.
	26	Paid the net amount owed for the November 18 purchase.
	28	Received cash in full settlement of the account from the customer who purchased inventory on November 13, less the return and the discount.
	29	Purchased inventory for cash, $12,000, plus freight charges of $200.

Requirement

1. Journalize the transactions on the books of Thelma's Amusements.

P5-30A ❹❺ Preparing financial statements and preparing closing entries [35–45 min]

Alto Publishers Company's selected accounts as of November 30, 2012, follow:

Selling expenses	$ 18,100	Inventory	$ 44,000
Furniture	37,300	Cash	36,100
Sales returns and allowances	3,000	Note payable	21,700
Salary payable	1,400	Accumulated depreciation	23,100
Alto, capital	29,400	Cost of goods sold	53,000
Sales revenue	114,200	Sales discounts	2,400
Accounts payable	13,400	General expenses	9,300

Requirements

1. Prepare the multi-step income statement, statement of owner's equity, and balance sheet for the first year of operations.
2. Prepare closing entries for the first year of operations.

P5-31A ④⑤⑥ **Making closing entries, preparing financial statements, and computing gross profit percentage, inventory turnover, and days in inventory [20–30 min]**

The adjusted trial balance of Big Papi Music Company at June 30, 2012, follows:

BIG PAPI MUSIC COMPANY Adjusted Trial Balance June 30, 2012		
Account	Debit	Credit
Cash	$ 3,600	
Accounts receivable	38,800	
Inventory	17,200	
Supplies	200	
Furniture	40,000	
Accumulated depreciation		$ 8,400
Accounts payable		13,300
Salary payable		1,200
Unearned sales revenue		6,700
Note payable, long–term		15,000
Papi, capital		36,000
Papi, drawing	40,500	
Sales revenue		180,000
Sales returns	5,000	
Cost of goods sold	82,500	
Selling expense	19,200	
General expense	12,000	
Interest expense	1,600	
Total	$ 260,600	$ 260,600

Requirements

1. Journalize Big Papi's closing entries.
2. Prepare Big Papi's single-step income statement for the year.
3. Compute the gross profit percentage, the rate of inventory turnover, and the days in inventory for the fiscal year ending June 30, 2012. Inventory on hand one year ago, at June 30, 2011, was $12,200.
4. For the year ended June 30, 2011, Big Papi's gross profit percentage was 50%, and inventory turnover was 4.9 times. Did the results for the year ended June 30, 2012, suggest improvement or deterioration in profitability over last year?

P5-32A ⑤ **Preparing a multi-step income statement and a classified balance sheet [30–40 min]**

← *Link Back to Chapter 4 (Classified Balance Sheet).* The accounts of Taylor Electronics Company are listed along with their balances before closing for the month ended March 31, 2012.

Interest revenue	$ 200	Accounts payable	$ 16,700
Inventory	45,100	Accounts receivable	33,600
Note payable, long–term	46,000	Accumulated depreciation	37,700
Salary payable	2,700	Taylor, capital, Feb 29	54,100
Sales discounts	2,900	Taylor, drawing	20,000
Sales returns and allowances	7,500	Cash	8,000
Sales revenue	297,000	Cost of goods sold	162,300
Selling expense	38,200	Equipment	129,100
Supplies	6,000	General expenses	16,700
Unearned sales revenue	13,800	Interest payable	1,200

Requirements

1. Prepare Taylor Electronics' *multi-step* income statement.
2. Prepare Taylor Electronics' statement of owner's equity.
3. Prepare Taylor Electronics' classified balance sheet in *report form*.

P5-33A ⑤⑥ **Preparing a multi-step income statement and calculating gross profit percentage [15–25 min]**
The records of Grade A Steak Company list the following selected accounts for the quarter ended April 30, 2012:

Interest revenue	$ 800	Accounts payable	$ 17,000
Inventory	45,100	Accounts receivable	33,500
Note payable, long–term	47,000	Accumulated depreciation	37,600
Salary payable	2,400	Angus, capital, Jan 31	53,300
Sales discounts	2,000	Angus, drawing	20,000
Sales returns and allowances	7,500	Cash	7,600
Sales revenue	296,100	Cost of goods sold	162,100
Selling expense	38,300	Equipment	130,600
Supplies	5,700	General expenses	16,300
Unearned sales revenue	13,300	Interest payable	1,200

Requirements

1. Prepare a multi-step income statement.
2. M. Davidson, manager of the company, strives to earn gross profit percentage of at least 50% and net income percentage of 20%. Did Grade A achieve these goals? Show your calculations.

● Problems (Group B)

MyAccountingLab   **P5-34B** ①②③ **Journalizing purchase and sale transactions [10–15 min]**
Consider the following transactions that occurred in January 2012 for 5th Grader.

Jan 1	Purchased $5,000 of inventory from M&P, terms 1/10, n/20.
3	Sold $1,000 of goods to Display Town, Inc., terms 2/10, n/eom *(Cost $700).
5	Display Town, Inc., returned $300 of goods (Cost $183).
11	Paid M&P.
13	Received payment from Display Town, Inc.

Requirements

1. What type of inventory system is 5th Grader using—periodic or perpetual?
2. Which transaction date helped you decide?
3. Journalize January transactions for 5th Grader. No explanations are required.

P5-35B ② ③ **Journalizing purchase and sale transactions—perpetual inventory [20–25 min]**

Consider the following transactions that occurred in February 2012 for Gems.

Feb	3	Purchased inventory on terms 1/5, n/eom, $2,000.
	4	Purchased inventory for cash of $1,600.
	6	Returned $600 of inventory from February 4 purchase.
	8	Sold goods on terms of 2/15, n/35 of $7,000 that cost $3,500.
	10	Paid for goods purchased on February 3.
	12	Received goods from February 8 sale of $500 that cost $190.
	23	Received payment from February 8 customer.
	25	Sold goods to Farms for $900 that cost $350. Terms of n/30 were offered. As a courtesy to Farms, $75 of freight was added to the invoice for which cash was paid directly to **UPS** by Gems.
	29	Received payment from Farms.

Requirement

1. Journalize February transactions for Gems. No explanations are required.

P5-36B ② ③ **Journalizing purchase and sale transactions—perpetual system [15–20 min]**

The following transactions occurred between East Pharmaceuticals and E & M, the pharmacy chain, during August of the current year:

Aug	6	E & M purchased $11,000 of merchandise from East on credit terms of 3/10, n/30, FOB shipping point. Separately, E & M paid a $250 bill for freight in. These goods cost East $3,300.
	10	E & M returned $2,750 of the merchandise purchased on August 6. East accounted for the sales return and placed the goods back in inventory (East's cost, $1,100).
	15	E & M paid $5,500 of the invoice amount owed to East for the August 6 purchase less the discount.
	27	E & M paid the remaining amount owed to East for the August 6 purchase.

Requirements

1. Journalize these transactions on the books of E & M.
2. Journalize these transactions on the books of East Pharmaceuticals.

P5-37B ② ③ **Journalizing purchase and sale transactions—perpetual inventory [20–25 min]**

Trisha's Amusements completed the following transactions during January 2012:

Jan	1	Purchased supplies for cash, $740.
	4	Purchased inventory on credit terms of 3/10, n/eom, $9,400.
	8	Returned half the inventory purchased on January 4. It was not the inventory ordered.
	10	Sold goods for cash, $1,700 (cost, $1,200).
	13	Sold inventory on credit terms of 2/15, n/45, $9,300 (cost, $4,700).
	14	Paid the amount owed on account from January 4, less the return (January 8) and the discount.
	17	Received defective inventory as a sales return from the January 13 sale, $700. Trisha's cost of the inventory received was $550.
	18	Purchased inventory of $3,300 on account. Payment terms were 2/10, net 30.
	26	Paid the net amount owed for the January 18 purchase.
	28	Received cash in full settlement of the account from the customer who purchased inventory on January 13, less the return and the discount.
	29	Purchased inventory for cash, $13,000, plus freight charges of $200.

Requirement

1. Journalize the transactions on the books of Trisha's Amusements.

P5-38B **4 5** **Preparing financial statements and preparing closing entries [35–45 min]**
Aspen Publishers Company's selected accounts as of November 30, 2012, follow:

Selling expenses	$ 18,900	Inventory	$ 42,000
Furniture	36,900	Cash	36,200
Sales returns and allowances	2,600	Note payable	21,800
Salary payable	1,100	Accumulated depreciation	22,800
Aspen, capital	27,800	Cost of goods sold	54,000
Sales revenue	114,300	Sales discounts	1,800
Accounts payable	13,600	General expenses	9,000

Requirements

1. Prepare the multi-step income statement, statement of owner's equity, and balance sheet for its first year of operations.
2. Prepare closing entries for the first year of operations.

P5-39B **4 5 6** **Making closing entries, preparing financial statements, and computing gross profit percentage, inventory turnover, and days in inventory [20–30 min]**
The adjusted trial balance of Daddy's Music Company at April 30, 2012, follows:

DADDY'S MUSIC COMPANY		
Adjusted Trial Balance		
April 30, 2012		
Account	Debit	Credit
Cash	$ 4,300	
Accounts receivable	38,200	
Inventory	17,800	
Supplies	600	
Furniture	39,400	
Accumulated depreciation		$ 9,000
Accounts payable		13,600
Salary payable		1,200
Unearned sales revenue		6,600
Note payable, long–term		14,000
Otousan, capital		40,100
Otousan, drawing	40,000	
Sales revenue		180,000
Sales returns	8,000	
Cost of goods sold	81,800	
Selling expense	19,200	
General expense	14,000	
Interest expense	1,200	
Total	$ 264,500	$ 264,500

Requirements

1. Journalize Daddy's closing entries.
2. Prepare Daddy's single-step income statement for the year.
3. Compute the gross profit percentage, the rate of inventory turnover, and the days in inventory for the fiscal year ending April 30, 2012. Inventory on hand one year ago, at April 30, 2011, was $13,000.

4. For the year ended April 30, 2011, Daddy's gross profit percentage was 50%, and inventory turnover was 4.9 times. Did the results for the year ended April 30, 2012, suggest improvement or deterioration in profitability over last year?

P5-40B ⑤ **Preparing a multi-step income statement and a classified balance sheet [30–40 min]**

← *Link Back to Chapter 4 (Classified Balance Sheet).* The accounts of Smith Electronics Company are listed along with their balances before closing for the month ended October 31, 2012.

Interest revenue	$ 500	Accounts payable	$ 16,900
Inventory	45,400	Accounts receivable	33,900
Note payable, long–term	47,000	Accumulated depreciation	38,100
Salary payable	3,400	Smith, capital, Sep 30	52,500
Sales discounts	2,700	Smith, drawing	19,000
Sales returns and allowances	8,100	Cash	7,600
Sales revenue	296,500	Cost of goods sold	162,100
Selling expense	37,500	Equipment	130,900
Supplies	6,300	General expenses	16,200
Unearned sales revenue	13,800	Interest payable	1,000

Requirements

1. Prepare Smith Electronics' *multi-step* income statement.
2. Prepare Smith Electronics' statement of owner's equity.
3. Prepare Smith Electronics' classified balance sheet in *report form*.

P5-41B ⑤ ⑥ **Preparing a multi-step income statement and calculating gross profit percentage [15–25 min]**

The records of Hill Tower Steak Company list the following selected accounts for the quarter ended September 30, 2012:

Interest revenue	$ 400	Accounts payable	$ 16,500
Inventory	45,700	Accounts receivable	33,900
Note payable, long–term	42,000	Accumulated depreciation	37,500
Salary payable	3,400	Holstein, capital, Jun 30	52,900
Sales discounts	2,200	Holstein, drawing	18,500
Sales returns and allowances	8,400	Cash	8,100
Sales revenue	296,700	Cost of goods sold	162,400
Selling expense	37,500	Equipment	125,000
Supplies	6,000	General expenses	16,100
Unearned sales revenue	13,200	Interest payable	1,200

Requirements

1. Prepare a multi-step income statement.
2. M. Davidson, manager of the company, strives to earn gross profit percentage of at least 50% and net income percentage of 20%. Did Hill Tower achieve these goals? Show your calculations.

● Continuing Exercise

MyAccountingLab **E5-42** ❷ ❸ ❹ ❺ **Journalizing purchase and sale transactions—perpetual inventory; making closing entries, and preparing financial statements [30–40 min]**

This exercise continues the Lawlor Lawn Service situation from Exercise 4-36 of Chapter 4. Lawlor Lawn Service has also begun selling plants that it purchases from a wholesaler. During June, Lawlor Lawn Service completed the following transactions:

Jun	2	Completed lawn service and received cash of $800.
	5	Purchased 110 plants on account for inventory, $304, plus freight in of $15.
	15	Sold 60 plants on account, $600 (cost $174).
	17	Consulted with a client on landscaping design for a fee of $250 on account.
	20	Purchased 120 plants on account for inventory, $384.
	21	Paid on account, $400.
	25	Sold 110 plants for cash, $990 (cost $337).
	30	Recorded the following adjusting entries:
		Depreciation $30
		Physical count of plant inventory, 30 plants (cost $96)

Requirements

1. Open the following selected T-accounts in the ledger: Cash; Accounts receivable; Lawn supplies; Plant inventory; Equipment; Accumulated depreciation—equipment; Accounts payable; Salary payable; Lawlor, capital; Lawlor, drawing; Income summary; Service revenue; Sales revenue; Cost of goods sold; Salary expense; Rent expense; Utilities expense; Depreciation expense—equipment; and Supplies expense.

2. Journalize and post the June transactions. Key all items by date. Compute each account balance, and denote the balance as *Bal*.

3. Journalize and post the closing entries. Denote each closing amount as *Clo*. After posting all closing entries, prove the equality of debits and credits in the ledger.

4. Prepare the June income statement of Lawlor Lawn Service. Use the single-step format.

● Continuing Problem

MyAccountingLab **P5-43** ❷ ❸ ❹ ❺ **Journalizing purchase and sale transactions—perpetual inventory; making closing entries, and preparing financial statements [30–40 min]**

This problem continues the Draper Consulting situation from Problem 4-37 of Chapter 4. Draper performs systems consulting. Draper has also begun selling accounting software. During January, Draper Consulting completed the following transactions:

Jan	2	Completed a consulting engagement and received cash of $7,800.
	2	Prepaid three months office rent, $1,650.
	7	Purchased 80 units software inventory on account, $1,680, plus freight in, $80.
	18	Sold 40 software units on account, $3,500 (cost $880).
	19	Consulted with a client for a fee of $1,000 on account.
	20	Paid employee salary, $2,055.
	21	Paid on account, $1,760.
	22	Purchased 240 units software inventory on account, $6,240.
	24	Paid utilities, $250.
	28	Sold 120 units software for cash, $4,680 (cost $2,960).
	31	Recorded the following adjusting entries:
		Accrued salary expense, $685
		Depreciation, $100 (Equipment, $30; Furniture, $70)
		Expiration of prepaid rent, $550
		Physical count of inventory, 145 units, $3,770

Requirements

1. Open the following selected T-accounts in the ledger: Cash; Accounts receivable; Software inventory; Prepaid rent; Accumulated depreciation—equipment; Accumulated depreciation—furniture; Accounts payable; Salary payable; Draper, capital; Draper, drawing; Income summary, Service revenue; Sales revenue; Cost of goods sold; Salary expense; Rent expense; Utilities expense; Depreciation expense—equipment; and Depreciation expense—furniture.

2. Journalize and post the January transactions. Key all items by date. Compute each account balance, and denote the balance as *Bal.*

3. Journalize and post the closing entries. Denote each closing amount as *Clo.* After posting all closing entries, prove the equality of debits and credits in the ledger.

4. Prepare the January income statement of Draper Consulting. Use the single-step format.

● Practice Set

This problem continues the Shine King Cleaning practice set begun in Chapter 1 and continued through Chapters 2, 3, and 4.

MyAccountingLab

P5-44 ② ③ ④ ⑤ **Journalizing purchase and sale transactions—perpetual inventory; making closing entries, and preparing financial statements [30–40 min]**

Shine King Cleaning has decided that, in addition to providing cleaning services, it will sell cleaning products. During December 2012, Shine King completed the following transactions:

Dec	2	Purchased 600 units of inventory for $3,600 from Sparkle, Co., on terms, 3/10, n/20.
	5	Purchased 400 units of inventory from Borax on terms 4/5, n/30. The total invoice was for $3,200, which included a $200 freight charge.
	7	Returned 100 units of inventory to Sparkle from the December 2 purchase (cost $600).
	9	Paid Borax.
	11	Sold 350 units of goods to Happy Maids for $4,900 on terms 5/10, n/30. Shine King's cost of the goods was $2,100.
	12	Paid Sparkle.
	15	Received 30 units with a retail price of $420 of goods back from customer Happy Maids. The goods cost Shine King $180.
	21	Received payment from Happy Maids, settling the amount due in full.
	28	Sold 200 units of goods to Bridget, Inc., for cash of $3,000 (cost $1,144).
	29	Paid cash for Utilities of $350.
	30	Paid cash for Sales commission expense of $225.
	31	Recorded the following adjusting entries:
		Physical count of Inventory on December 31 showed 330 units of goods on hand, $2,541
		Depreciation, $170
		Accrued salary expense of $700
		Prepared all other adjustments necessary for December

Requirements

1. Add any needed accounts to Shine King's existing chart of accounts.

2. Journalize and post the December transactions. Key all items by date. Compute each account balance, and denote the balance as *Bal.*

3. Journalize and post the adjusting entries. Denote each adjusting amount as *Adj.* After posting all adjusting entries, prove the equality of debits and credits in the ledger.

4. Prepare the December multi-step income statement, statement of owner's equity, and balance sheet for the company.

5. Journalize the December closing entries for the company.

Apply Your Knowledge

• Decision Cases

Decision Case 5-1 ← *Link Back to Chapter 4* (*Classified Balance Sheet, Current Ratio, and Debt Ratio*). Jan Lorange is the owner of Poppa Rollo's Pizza, which has prospered during its second year of operation. In order to help her decide whether to open another pizzeria, Lorange has prepared the current income statement of the business. Lorange read in an industry trade journal that a successful two-year-old pizzeria meets the following criteria:

a. Gross profit percentage is at least 60%.

b. Net income is at least $90,000.

Lorange believes the business meets both criteria. She intends to go ahead with the expansion plan and asks your advice on preparing the income statement in accordance with generally accepted accounting principles. When you point out that the statement includes errors, Lorange assures you that all amounts are correct. But some items are listed in the wrong place.

Requirement

1. Prepare a multi-step income statement and make a recommendation about whether Lorange should undertake the expansion.

POPPA ROLLO'S PIZZA Income Statement Year Ended December 31, 2014	
Sales revenue	$195,000
Gain on sale of land	24,600
Total revenue	219,600
Cost of goods sold	85,200
Gross profit	134,400
Operating expenses:	
Salary expense	35,600
Interest expense	6,000
Depreciation expense	4,800
Utilities expense	3,700
Total operating expense	50,100
Income from operations	84,300
Other revenue:	
Sales returns	10,700
Net income	$ 95,000

Decision Case 5-2 Bill Hildebrand opened Party-Time T-Shirts to sell T-shirts for parties at his college. The company completed the first year of operations, and the owner is generally pleased with operating results as shown by the following income statement:

PARTY-TIME T-SHIRTS Income Statement Year Ended December 31, 2011	
Net sales revenue	$350,000
Cost of goods sold	210,000
Gross margin	$140,000
Operating expenses:	
Selling expense	40,000
General expense	25,000
Net income	$ 75,000

Hildebrand is considering how to expand the business. He proposes two ways to increase profits to $100,000 during 2012.

a. Hildebrand believes he should advertise more heavily. He believes additional advertising costing $20,000 will increase net sales by 30% and leave general expense unchanged. Assume that Cost of goods sold will remain at the same percentage of net sales as in 2011, so if net sales increases in 2012, Cost of goods sold will increase proportionately.

b. Hildebrand proposes selling higher-margin merchandise, such as party dresses, in addition to the existing product line. An importer can supply a minimum of 1,000 dresses for $40 each; Party-Time can mark these dresses up 100% and sell them for $80. Hildebrand realizes he will have to advertise the new merchandise, and this advertising will cost $5,000. Party-Time can expect to sell only 80% of these dresses during the coming year.

Requirement

1. Help Hildebrand determine which plan to pursue. Prepare a single-step income statement for 2012 to show the expected net income under each plan.

● Ethical Issue 5-1

Dobbs Wholesale Antiques makes all sales under terms of FOB shipping point. The company usually ships inventory to customers approximately one week after receiving the order. For orders received late in December, Kathy Dobbs, the owner, decides when to ship the goods. If profits are already at an acceptable level, Dobbs delays shipment until January. If profits for the current year are lagging behind expectations, Dobbs ships the goods during December.

Requirements

1. Under Dobbs' FOB policy, when should the company record a sale?
2. Do you approve or disapprove of Dobbs' manner of deciding when to ship goods to customers and record the sales revenue? If you approve, give your reason. If you disapprove, identify a better way to decide when to ship goods. (There is no accounting rule against Dobbs' practice.)

● Fraud Case 5-1

Rae Philippe was a warehouse manager for Atkins Oilfield Supply, a business that operated across eight Western states. She was an old pro and had known most of the other warehouse managers for many years. Around December each year, auditors would come to do a physical count of the inventory at each warehouse. Recently, Rae's brother started his own drilling company, and persuaded Rae to "loan" him 80 joints of 5-inch drill pipe to use for his first well. He promised to have it back to Rae by December, but the well encountered problems and the pipe was still in the ground. Rae knew the auditors were on the way, so she called her friend Andy, who ran another Atkins warehouse. "Send me over 80 joints of 5-inch pipe tomorrow and I'll get them back to you ASAP" said Rae. When the auditors came, all the pipe on the books was accounted for, and they filed a "no-exception" report.

Requirements

1. Is there anything the company or the auditors could do in future to detect this kind of fraudulent practice?
2. How would this kind of action impact the financial performance of the company?

● Financial Statement Case 5-1

This case uses both the income statement (statement of operations) and the balance sheet of **Amazon.com** in Appendix A at the end of the book. It will help you understand the closing process of a business.

Requirements

1. Journalize **Amazon.com**'s closing entries for the revenues and expenses of 2009. Show all amounts in millions as in the **Amazon** financial statements. You may be unfamiliar with certain revenues and expenses, but treat each item on the income statement as either a revenue or an expense. For example, Net sales is the first revenue item. Other items you may be unfamiliar with are as follows: "Other operating expense (income), net" is shown in parentheses, so it should be treated as revenue. "Interest Income" should be treated as revenue. Although the amount shown for "Interest expense" is in parentheses, you may ignore those parentheses for this purpose and treat it similar to other expenses. "Other income (expense), net" is shown as a positive number, so it should be treated as revenue. The "provision for income taxes" should be treated as an expense. "Equity method investment activity, net of tax" is shown in parentheses, so it should be shown as an expense. In your closing entries, ignore all subtotals such as Gross profit, Total operating expenses, Income from operations, Total non-operating income (expense), and Net income (loss).

2. Create a T-account for the Income summary, post to that account, and then close the Income summary. (Note: Use the Retained earnings account to replace the Capital account in your entries.) How much was closed to Retained earnings? How is the amount that was closed to Retained earnings labeled on the income statement?

● Team Project 5-1

With a small team of classmates, visit one or more merchandising businesses in your area. Interview a responsible manager of the company to learn about its inventory policies and accounting system. Obtain answers to the following questions, write a report, and be prepared to make a presentation to the class if your instructor so directs.

Requirements

1. What merchandise inventory does the business sell?
2. From whom does the business buy its inventory? Is the relationship with the supplier new or longstanding?
3. What are the FOB terms on inventory purchases? Who pays the freight, the buyer or the seller? Is freight a significant amount? What percentage of total inventory cost is the freight?
4. What are the credit terms on inventory purchases—2/10, n/30, or other? Does the business pay early to get purchase discounts? If so, why? If not, why not?
5. How does the business actually pay its suppliers? Does it mail a check or pay electronically? What is the actual payment procedure?
6. Which type of inventory accounting system does the business use—perpetual or periodic? Is this system computerized?
7. How often does the business take a physical count of its inventory? When during the year is the count taken? Describe the count procedures followed by the company.
8. Does the manager use the gross profit percentage and the rate of inventory turnover to evaluate the business? If not, show the manager how to use these ratios in decision making.
9. Ask any other questions your group considers appropriate.

● Communication Activity 5-1

In 30 words or fewer, explain the difference between a sales discount and a purchase discount.

Quick Check Answers

1. *d* 2. *a* 3. *c* 4. *c* 5. *b* 6. *a* 7. *a* 8. *b* 9. *a* 10. *a*

For online homework, exercises, and problems that provide you immediate feedback, please visit myaccountinglab.com.

Accounting for Merchandise in a Periodic Inventory System

Some smaller businesses find it too expensive to invest in a perpetual inventory system. These businesses use a periodic system.

7 Account for the sale of inventory using a periodic system

Recording the Purchase of Inventory

All inventory systems use the Inventory account. But in a periodic system, purchases, purchase discounts, purchase returns and allowances, and transportation costs are recorded in separate accounts. Let's account for Smart Touch's purchase of the **RCA** goods in Exhibit 5A-1.

EXHIBIT 5A-1 | **Purchase Invoice**

1

RCA®

RCA SOUTHWEST BRANCH
P.O. BOX 101010
HOUSTON, TX 77212

Invoice	
Date	Number
3 6/1/13	410

2

Shipped To: SMART TOUCH LEARNING
281 WAVE AVE
NICEVILLE, FL 32578

4

Credit Terms
3/15, NET 30 DAYS

Description	Quantity Shipped	Unit Price	Total
Boxes—DVD	100	$ 6.00	$600.00
Windows CDs—Case	1	100.00	100.00
	6 Pd.	6/15/13	

Due Date & Due Amount			
06/15/13			
$679 00			
7			

Sub Total	$700.00
Ship. or Handl. Chg.	–
Tax (3%)	–
Total(s)	$700.00

5

Explanations:

1 The seller is RCA.

2 The purchaser is Smart Touch Learning.

3 The invoice date is needed to determine whether the purchaser gets a discount for prompt payment (see 4).

4 Credit terms: If Smart Touch pays within 15 days of the invoice date, it can deduct a 3% discount. Otherwise, the full amount—NET—is due in 30 days.

5 Total invoice amount is $700.

6 Smart Touch's payment date. How much did Smart Touch pay? (See 7.)

7 Payment occurred 14 days after the invoice date—within the discount period—so Smart Touch paid $679 ($700 – 3% discount).

Recording Purchases and Purchase Discounts

The following entries record the purchase and payment on account within the discount period. Smart Touch received the goods on June 3 and paid within the discount period.

Jun 3	Purchases (E+)	700	
	Accounts payable (L+)		700
	Purchased inventory on account.		
Jun 15	Accounts payable (L−)	700	
	Cash ($700 × 0.97) (A−)		679
	Purchase discounts ($700 × 0.03) (CE+)		21
	Paid within discount period.		

Recording Purchase Returns and Allowances

Suppose that, prior to payment, Smart Touch returned to **RCA** goods costing $100 and also received from **RCA** a purchase allowance of $10. Smart Touch would record these transactions as follows:

Jun 4	Accounts payable (L−)	100	
	Purchase returns and allowances (CE+)		100
	Returned inventory to seller (vendor).		
4	Accounts payable (L−)	10	
	Purchase returns and allowances (CE+)		10
	Received a purchase allowance.		

During the period, the business records the cost of all inventory bought in the Purchases account. The balance of Purchases is a *gross* amount because it does not include subtractions for discounts, returns, or allowances. **Net purchases** is the remainder after subtracting the contra accounts from Purchases:

> **Purchases** (*debit*)
> − **Purchase discounts** (*credit*)
> − **Purchase returns and allowances** (*credit*)
> = **Net purchases** (a *debit* subtotal, not a separate account)

Recording Transportation Costs

Under the periodic system, costs to transport purchased inventory from seller to buyer are debited to a separate Freight in account, as shown for a $60 freight bill:

Jun 3	Freight in (E+)	60	
	Cash (A−)		60
	Paid a freight bill.		

Recording the Sale of Inventory

Recording sales is streamlined in the periodic system. With no running record of inventory to maintain, we can record a $3,000 sale as follows:

Jun 9	Accounts receivable (A+)	3,000	
	Sales revenue (R+)		3,000
	Sale on account.		

There is no accompanying entry to Inventory and Cost of goods sold in the periodic system.

Accounting for sales discounts and sales returns and allowances is the same as in a perpetual inventory system, except that there are no entries to Inventory or Cost of goods sold.

Cost of goods sold (also called *cost of sales*) is the largest single expense of most businesses that sell merchandise, such as Smart Touch and **Gap, Inc.** It is the cost of the inventory the business has sold to customers. In a periodic system, cost of goods sold must be computed as shown in Exhibit 5A-2.

Cost of Goods Sold in a Periodic Inventory System

The amount of cost of goods sold is the same regardless of the inventory system—perpetual or periodic. As we have seen under the perpetual system, cost of goods sold is simply the sum of the amounts posted to that account.

Cost of goods sold is computed differently under the periodic system. At the end of each period, the company combines a number of accounts to compute cost of goods sold for the period. Exhibit 5A-2 shows how to make the computation.

EXHIBIT 5A-2 | **Measuring Cost of Goods Sold in the Periodic Inventory System**

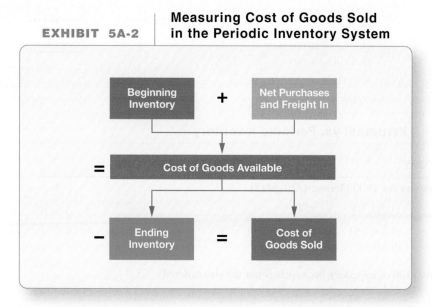

Here is Greg's Tunes' computation of cost of goods sold for 2014:

Cost of goods sold:		
Beginning inventory		$ 38,600
Purchases	$91,400	
Less: Purchase discounts	3,000	
Purchase returns and allowances	1,200	
Net purchases		87,200
Freight in		5,200
Cost of goods available		131,000
Less: Ending inventory		40,200
Cost of goods sold		$ 90,800

Cost of goods sold is reported as the first expense on the merchandiser's income statement, immediately following net sales on a multi-step statement.

Exhibit 5A-3 summarizes this appendix by showing Greg's Tunes' net sales revenue, cost of goods sold, and gross profit on the income statement for the periodic system. (All amounts are assumed.)

Exhibit 5A-4 on page 306 is intended to provide a side-by-side comparison of periodic and perpetual inventory journal entries for the same company's transactions.

EXHIBIT 5A-3

EXHIBIT 5A-3 | **Partial Income Statement Periodic Inventory System**

GREG'S TUNES
Income Statement
Year Ended December 31, 2014

Sales revenue			$169,300
Less: Sales returns and allowances			2,000
Sales discounts			1,400
Net sales revenue			$165,900
Cost of goods sold:			
Beginning inventory		$ 38,600	
Purchases	$91,400		
Less: Purchase discounts	3,000		
Purchase returns and allowances	1,200		
Net purchases		87,200	
Freight in		5,200	
Cost of goods available		$131,000	
Less: Ending inventory		40,200	
Cost of goods sold			90,800
Gross profit			$ 75,100

EXHIBIT 5A-4 | **Perpetual vs. Periodic Inventory**

PERPETUAL INVENTORY   **PERIODIC INVENTORY**

Jan 1: Purchase of Inventory for $500 (Terms: 1/10, n/15)

	DR	CR		DR	CR
Inventory (A+)	500		Purchases (E+)	500	
Accounts payable (L+)		500	Accounts payable (L+)		500

Jan 4: Purchaser returns $100 of inventory because it is not the size ordered

	DR	CR		DR	CR
Accounts payable (L–)	100		Accounts payable (L–)	100	
Inventory (A–)		100	Purchase returns & allowances (CE+)		100

Jan 10: Purchaser pays balance taking advantage of terms

	DR	CR		DR	CR
Accounts payable (L–)	400		Accounts payable (L–)	400	
Inventory (400 × 0.01) (A–)		4	Purchase discounts (CE+)		4
Cash (A–)		396	Cash (A–)		396

Jan 12: Purchaser pays freight bill of $15 to UPS for shipping of Jan 1 purchase

	DR	CR		DR	CR
Inventory (A+)	15		Freight in (E+)	15	
Cash (A–)		15	Cash (A–)		15

Note that the net COST of all goods acquired is the same.

1) Perpetual: Inventory (500DR – 100CR – 4CR + 15DR = 411)
2) Periodic: Purchases 500DR – Purchase Returns 100CR – Purchase Discounts 4CR + Freight In 15DR = 411

Appendix 5A Assignments

● Short Exercises

S5A-1 ❼ **Computing cost of goods sold in a periodic inventory system [5 min]**
G Wholesale Company began the year with inventory of $6,000. During the year, G purchased $97,000 of goods and returned $6,200 due to damage. G also paid freight charges of $1,500 on inventory purchases. At year-end, G's adjusted inventory balance stood at $17,300. G uses the periodic inventory system.

Requirement

1. Compute G's cost of goods sold for the year.

Experience the Power of Practice!

As denoted by the logo, all of these questions, as well as additional practice materials, can be found in

MyAccountingLab.

Please visit myaccountinglab.com

● Exercises

MyAccountingLab

E5A-2 ❼ **Journalizing periodic transactions [10–15 min]**
On April 30, Fire & Ice Jewelers purchased inventory of $7,200 on account from Ruby Jewels, a jewelry importer. Terms were 3/15, net 45. On receiving the goods, Fire & Ice checked the order and found $600 of unsuitable merchandise. Therefore, Fire & Ice returned $600 of merchandise to Ruby on May 4.

On May 14, Fire & Ice paid the net amount owed from April 30, less the return.

Requirement

1. Journalize indicated transactions of Ruby Jewels. Use the periodic inventory system. Explanations are not required.

E5A-3 ❼ **Journalizing periodic transactions [10–15 min]**
Refer to the business situation in Exercise 5A-2.

Requirement

1. Journalize the transactions of Fire & Ice Jewelers. Use the periodic inventory system. Explanations are not required.

E5A-4 ❼ **Cost of goods sold in a periodic system [10–15 min]**
Delta Electric uses the periodic inventory system. Delta reported the following selected amounts at May 31, 2012:

Inventory, May 31, 2011	$ 16,000	Freight in	$ 4,000
Inventory, May 31, 2012	23,000	Sales revenue	174,000
Purchases (of inventory)	84,000	Sales discounts	6,000
Purchase discounts	3,000	Sales returns	17,000
Purchase returns	9,000	Owner's equity	47,000

Requirement

1. Compute Delta's
   a. Net sales revenue.
   b. Cost of goods sold.
   c. Gross profit.

● Problem (Group A)

MyAccountingLab **P5A-5A** ❼ **Journalizing periodic transactions [10–15 min]**

Assume that the following transactions occurred between Brighton Medical Supply and a Best drug store during April of the current year.

Apr	6	Best purchased $5,800 of merchandise from Brighton Medical Supply on credit terms of 2/10, n/30, FOB shipping point. Separately, Best paid freight in of $150.
	10	Best returned $900 of the merchandise to Brighton.
	15	Best paid $2,900 of the invoice amount owed to Brighton for the April 6 purchase, less the discount.
	27	Best paid the remaining amount owed to Brighton for the April 6 purchase.

Requirement

1. Journalize these transactions, first on the books of the Best drug store and second on the books of Brighton Medical Supply. Use the periodic inventory system.

● Problem (Group B)

MyAccountingLab **P5A-6B** ❼ **Journalizing periodic transactions [10–15 min]**

Assume that the following transactions occurred between Springfield Medical Supply and a Brookston drug store during September of the current year.

Sep	6	Brookston purchased $6,300 of merchandise from Springfield Medical Supply on credit terms of 2/10, n/30, FOB shipping point. Separately, Brookston paid freight in of $500.
	10	Brookston returned $700 of the merchandise to Springfield.
	15	Brookston paid $3,150 of the invoice amount owed to Springfield for the September 6 purchase, less the discount.
	27	Brookston paid the remaining amount owed to Springfield for the September 6 purchase.

Requirement

1. Journalize these transactions, first on the books of the Brookston drug store and second on the books of Springfield Medical Supply. Use the periodic inventory system.

Comprehensive Problem for Chapters 1–5

Completing a Merchandiser's Accounting Cycle

The end-of-month trial balance of St. Paul Technology at January 31, 2012, follows:

ST. PAUL TECHNOLOGY Trial Balance January 31, 2012		
Account	Debit	Credit
Cash	$ 16,260	
Accounts receivable	18,930	
Inventory	65,000	
Supplies	2,580	
Building	188,090	
Accumulated depreciation—building		$ 35,300
Furniture	44,800	
Accumulated depreciation—furniture		5,500
Accounts payable		27,900
Salary payable		
Unearned sales revenue		6,480
Note payable, long-term		85,000
Tarsus, capital		152,190
Tarsus, drawing	9,100	
Sales revenue		179,930
Sales discounts	7,100	
Sales returns and allowances	8,080	
Cost of goods sold	101,900	
Selling expense	21,380	
General expense	9,080	
Total	$492,300	$492,300

Additional data at January 31, 2012:

a. Supplies consumed during the month, $1,400. Half is selling expense, and the other half is general expense.

b. Depreciation for the month: building, $3,800; furniture, $4,600. One-fourth of depreciation is selling expense, and three-fourths is general expense.

c. Unearned sales revenue earned during January, $4,420.

d. Accrued salaries, a general expense, $1,100.

e. Inventory on hand, $63,460. St. Paul uses the perpetual inventory system.

Requirements

1. Using four-column accounts, open the accounts listed on the trial balance, inserting their unadjusted balances. Date the balances of the following accounts January 1: Supplies; Building; Accumulated depreciation—building; Furniture; Accumulated depreciation—furniture; Unearned sales revenue; and Tarsus, capital. Date the balance of Tarsus, drawing, January 31. Also open the Income summary account.

2. Enter the trial balance on a worksheet, and complete the worksheet for the month ended January 31, 2012. St. Paul Technology groups all operating expenses under two accounts, Selling expense and General expense. Leave two blank lines under Selling expense and three blank lines under General expense.

3. Prepare the company's *multi-step* income statement and statement of owner's equity for the month ended January 31, 2012. Also prepare the balance sheet at that date in *report* form.

4. Journalize the adjusting and closing entries at January 31.

5. Post the adjusting and closing entries.

6

Merchandise Inventory

Inventory represents the cost of goods that are still on the shelf.

SMART TOUCH LEARNING
Balance Sheet
May 31, 2013

Assets					Liabilities	
Current assets:					Current liabilities:	
Cash		$ 4,800			Accounts payable	$ 48,700
Accounts receivable		2,600			Salary payable	900
Inventory		**30,500**			Interest payable	100
Supplies		600			Unearned service revenue	400
Prepaid rent		2,000			Total current liabilities	50,100
Total current assets			$ 40,500		Long-term liabilities:	
Plant assets:					Notes payable	20,000
Furniture	$18,000				Total liabilities	70,100
Less: Accumulated depreciation—furniture	300	17,700				
Building	48,000					
Less: Accumulated depreciation—building	200	47,800			Owner's Equity	
Total plant assets			65,500		Bright, capital	35,900
Total assets			$106,000		Total liabilities and owner's equity	$106,000

Learning Objectives

1 Define accounting principles related to inventory

2 Define inventory costing methods

3 Account for perpetual inventory using the three most common costing methods

4 Compare the effects of the three most common inventory costing methods

5 Apply the lower-of-cost-or-market rule to inventory

6 Measure the effects of inventory errors

7 Estimate ending inventory by the gross profit method

8 Account for periodic inventory using the three most common costing methods (Appendix 6A)

Think about major retailers, like **Target**. What if you were the manager of one division for **Target** or the owner of your own retail company—how would you decide on the sales price for your products? What information would you need to set a price that appeals to your customers but also makes the company a profit?

Having detailed information about the cost of the product would certainly help you. You'd need to know if every shipment of the product cost the same per unit or whether the price changes. Knowing this information will also help you determine the *inventory costing method* that works best for your company.

Chapter 5 introduced accounting for merchandise inventory. It showed how Smart Touch Learning, an e-learning company, recorded the purchase and sale of its inventory. The current chapter completes the accounting for merchandise inventory.

Smart Touch may select from several different methods to account for its inventory. Inventory is one of the first areas in which you must pick the accounting method you will use. In this chapter we use Smart Touch to illustrate the different inventory costing methods.

● ● ●

First let's review how merchandise inventory affects a company. Exhibit 6-1 gives a partial balance sheet and income statement for Smart Touch. Inventories, cost of goods sold, and gross profit are highlighted. These amounts (I, C, and P) are left blank to indicate that throughout the chapter we will be computing them using various inventory accounting methods.

The remainder of the chapter explores how to compute these amounts in Exhibit 6-1:

- Ending inventory (I) on the balance sheet
- Cost of goods sold (C) and gross profit (P) on the income statement

EXHIBIT 6-1 | **Merchandising Sections of the Financial Statements**

SMART TOUCH LEARNING
Balance Sheet—Partial
July 31, 2013

Assets	
Current assets:	
Cash	$ 6,000
Short-term investments	3,000
Accounts receivable	12,000
Inventories	I
Prepaid expenses	4,000

SMART TOUCH LEARNING
Income Statement—Partial
Year Ended July 31, 2013

Net sales		$80,000
Cost of goods sold		C
Gross profit		$ P

We turn now to the accounting principles affecting inventories.

Accounting Principles and Inventories

Several accounting principles affect inventories. Among them are consistency, disclosure, materiality, and accounting conservatism.

1 Define accounting principles related to inventory

Consistency Principle

The **consistency principle** states that businesses should use the same accounting methods from period to period. Consistency helps investors compare a company's financial statements from one period to the next.

Suppose you are analyzing a company's net income over a two-year period. The company switched to a different inventory method from the method it had been using. Its net income increased dramatically but only as a result of the change in inventory method. If you did not know about the change, you might believe that the company's income really increased. Therefore, companies must report any changes in the accounting methods they use. Investors need this information to make wise decisions about the company.

Disclosure Principle

The **disclosure principle** holds that a company should report enough information for outsiders to make wise decisions about the company. In short, the company should report *relevant*, *reliable*, and *comparable* information about itself. This includes disclosing the method being used to account for inventories. **All major accounting decisions are described in the footnotes to the financial statements.** Suppose a banker is comparing two companies—one using inventory method A and the other using inventory method B. The B company reports higher net income but only because of the inventory method it selected. Without knowledge of these accounting methods, the banker could lend money to the wrong business.

Materiality Concept

The **materiality concept** states that a company must perform strictly proper accounting *only* for significant items. **Information is significant—or, in accounting terms, *material*—when it would cause someone to change a decision.** The materiality concept frees accountants from having to report every last item in strict accordance with GAAP. For example, $1,000 is material to a small business with annual sales of $100,000. However, $1,000 isn't material to a large company like **Apple**.

Accounting Conservatism

Conservatism in accounting means exercising caution in reporting items in the financial statements. Conservatism says,

- "Anticipate no gains, but provide for all probable losses."
- "If in doubt, record an asset at the lowest reasonable amount and a liability at the highest reasonable amount."
- "When there's a question, record an expense rather than an asset."
- "When you are faced with a decision between two options, you must choose the option that undervalues, rather than overvalues, your business."

The goal of conservatism is to report realistic figures.

Key Takeaway

The accounting principles are the foundations that guide how we record transactions.

Inventory Costing Methods

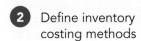 Define inventory costing methods

As we saw in Chapter 5,

$$\text{Ending inventory} = \begin{matrix}\text{Number of units}\\\text{on hand}\end{matrix} \times \text{Unit cost}$$

$$\text{Cost of goods sold} = \begin{matrix}\text{Number of units}\\\text{sold}\end{matrix} \times \text{Unit cost}$$

Companies determine the number of units from perpetual inventory records backed up by a physical count. The cost of each unit of inventory is as follows:

$$\text{Cost per unit} = \text{Purchase price} - \text{Purchase discounts} - \text{Purchase returns} + \text{Freight in}$$

Exhibit 6-2 gives the inventory data for DVD0503 (Basic Excel Training DVD) for Smart Touch.

EXHIBIT 6-2 | **Perpetual Inventory Record—Showing Cost**

Item: DVD0503

Date	Quantity Purchased	Quantity Sold	Cost per Unit	Quantity on Hand
FIFO → Jul 1			40	2
5	6		45	8
15		4		4
LIFO → 26	9		47	13
31		10		3
Totals	15	14	N/A	3

In this exhibit, Smart Touch began July with 2 DVD0503s in inventory. It had 3 DVD0503s at the end of July. The company plans on selling each DVD for $80 to its customers.

Measuring inventory cost is easy when prices do not change. But unit cost does change often. Looking at Exhibit 6-2, you can see that Smart Touch's cost per unit did change each time it made a purchase. The July 1 beginning inventory cost $40 each, the purchases made July 5 cost $45 each, and the purchases made July 26 cost $47 each. How many of the DVD0503s that were sold cost $40? How many cost $45? To compute ending inventory and cost of goods sold, Smart Touch must assign a unit cost to each item. The four costing methods we'll illustrate that GAAP allows are as follows:

1. Specific unit cost
2. First-in, first-out (FIFO) cost
3. Last-in, first-out (LIFO) cost
4. Average cost

A company can use any of these methods to account for its inventory.

The **specific-unit-cost method** is also called the **specific-identification method**. This method uses the specific cost of each unit of inventory to determine ending inventory and to determine cost of goods sold. **In the specific-unit-cost method, the company knows exactly which item was sold and exactly what the item cost.** This costing method is best for businesses that sell unique, easily identified inventory items, such as automobiles (identified by the vehicle identification number [VIN]), jewels (a specific diamond ring), and real estate (identified by address). For instance, a **Chevrolet** dealer may have two Camaro vehicles with *exactly* the same colors, interior, and options package. Assume one of the Camaros was purchased by the dealership on January 5 for $16,000 and the other was purchased on March 8 for $19,000. The dealer would determine the cost of each of the identical vehicles sold based on the vehicle identification number. If the dealer sells the model whose VIN is on the March 8 invoice, the cost of goods sold is $19,000. Suppose the other Camaro is the only unit left in inventory at the end of the period. In that case, ending inventory would be $16,000—the cost of the January 5 vehicle.

Amazon.com uses the specific-unit-cost method to account for its inventory. But very few other companies use this method, so we'll shift our focus to the more popular inventory costing methods.

- Under the **FIFO (First-In, First-Out) inventory costing method**, the cost of goods sold is based on the oldest purchases—that is, the First In is the First Out of the warehouse (sold). In Exhibit 6-2, this is illustrated by the Cost of goods sold coming from the *first* goods purchased, which are from the July 1 beginning inventory. FIFO costing is consistent with the physical movement of inventory (for most companies). **That is, under the FIFO method, companies sell their oldest inventory first.**

- LIFO is the opposite of FIFO. Under the **LIFO (Last-In, First-Out) inventory costing method**, ending inventory comes from the oldest costs (first purchases) of the period. The cost of goods sold is based on the most recent purchases (new costs)—that is, the Last In is the First Out of the warehouse (sold). This is illustrated by the Cost of goods sold coming from the *last* goods in the warehouse—the July 26 purchase in Exhibit 6-2. **Under the LIFO method, companies sell their newest inventory first.**

- Under the **average-cost inventory costing method**, the business computes a new average cost per unit after each purchase. Ending inventory and cost of goods sold are then based on the same average cost per unit. So, cost per unit sold falls somewhere between the low cost of $40 and the highest cost of $47 in Exhibit 6-2. **Under the average-cost method, an average price is calculated and applied to all goods.**

Stop & Think...

Think about going to the grocery store to buy a gallon of milk. Which gallon is in front of the milk cooler: the older milk or the newer milk? The older milk is in front. That's FIFO. Now visualize reaching all the way to the back of the cooler to get the newer milk. That's LIFO.

Now let's see how Smart Touch would compute inventory amounts under FIFO, LIFO, and average costing for all of July. We use the transaction data from Exhibit 6-2 for all the illustrations. Keep in mind the cost paid to purchase goods is the same under all inventory costing methods. The difference is where we divide up the dollars between the asset Inventory and the expense, COGS, on the income statement.

In the body of the chapter, we show inventory costing in a perpetual system. Appendix 6A shows inventory costing in a periodic system.

Key Takeaway

Inventory costing methods include specific-unit-cost, FIFO, LIFO, and average cost. Specific unit identifies the specific cost of each unit of inventory that is in ending inventory and each item that is in cost of goods sold. Under FIFO, the cost of goods sold is based on the oldest purchases. Under LIFO, the cost of goods sold is based on the newest purchases. Under the average-cost method, the business computes a new average cost per unit after each purchase. Keep in mind the cost paid to purchase goods is the same under all inventory costing methods. The difference is where we divide up the dollars between the asset, Inventory, and the expense, COGS, on the income statement.

Inventory Accounting in a Perpetual System

3 Account for perpetual inventory using the three most common costing methods

The different inventory costing methods produce different amounts for

- ending inventory, and
- cost of goods sold.

For each calculation, we'll use the information in Exhibit 6-2 about Smart Touch's purchases of DVD0503. Recall that Smart Touch sold the units to customers for $80 each.

First-In, First-Out (FIFO) Method

Assume that Smart Touch uses the FIFO method to account for its inventory. Under FIFO, the first costs incurred by Smart Touch are the first costs assigned to cost of goods sold. FIFO leaves in ending inventory the last—the newest—costs. This is illustrated in the FIFO inventory record in Exhibit 6-3.

EXHIBIT 6-3 | **Perpetual Inventory Record: FIFO**

DVD0503	Purchases			Cost of Goods Sold			Inventory on Hand		
Date	Quantity	Unit Cost	Total Cost	Quantity	Unit Cost	Total Cost	Quantity	Unit Cost	Total Cost
Jul 1							2	$40	$80
5	6	$45	$270				2	40	80
							6	45	270
15				2	$40	$ 80			
				2	45	90	4	45	180
26	9	47	423				4	45	180
							9	47	423
31				4	45	180			
				6	47	282	3	47	141
31	15		$693	14		$632	3		$141

Smart Touch began July with 2 DVD0503s that cost $40 each. After the July 5 purchase, the inventory on hand consists of 8 units.

$$
\text{8 units on hand}
\begin{cases}
2 @ \$40 & = \$\ 80 \\
6 @ \$45 & = \ \underline{270}
\end{cases}
$$
$$
\text{Inventory on hand} = \$350
$$

On July 15, Smart Touch sold 4 units. Under FIFO, the first 2 units sold had the oldest cost ($40 per unit). The next 2 units sold cost $45 each. That leaves 4 units in inventory on July 15 at $45 each. The remainder of the inventory record follows the same pattern. Consider the sale on July 31 of 10 units. The oldest cost is from July 5 (4 units @ $45). The next oldest cost is from the July 26 purchase at $47 each (6 units @ $47). This leaves 3 units in inventory on July 31 at $47 each.

The FIFO monthly summary at July 31 is as follows:

- Cost of goods sold: 14 units that cost a total of $632
- Ending inventory: 3 units that cost a total of $141

Notice the total cost of goods sold of $632 plus the total ending inventory of $141 equals the total cost of goods available for sale during July $773 [(2 @ $40) + (6 @ $45) + (9 @ $47)]. Smart Touch measures cost of goods sold and inventory in this manner to prepare its financial statements.

Journal Entries Under FIFO

The journal entries under FIFO follow the data in Exhibit 6-3. For example, on July 5, Smart Touch purchased $270 of inventory and made the first journal entry. On July 15, Smart Touch sold 4 DVD0503s for the sale price of $80 each. Smart Touch recorded the sale, $320, and the cost of goods sold, $170 (figured in Exhibit 6-3 as 2 @ $40 + 2 @ $45). The remaining journal entries (July 26 and 31) follow the inventory data in Exhibit 6-3.

The amounts unique to FIFO are shown in blue for emphasis. All other amounts are the same for all three inventory methods.

FIFO Journal Entries (All purchases and sales on account) The sales price of a DVD0503 is $80		
Jul 5	Inventory (6 × $45) (A+)	270	
	Accounts payable (L+)		270
	Purchased inventory on account.		
15	Accounts receivable (4 × $80) (A+)	320	
	Sales revenue (R+)		320
	Sale on account.		
15	Cost of goods sold (2 @ $40 + 2 @ $45) (E+)	170	
	Inventory (A–)		170
	Cost of goods sold.		
26	Inventory (9 × $47) (A+)	423	
	Accounts payable (L+)		423
	Purchased inventory on account.		
31	Accounts receivable (10 × $80) (A+)	800	
	Sales revenue (R+)		800
	Sale on account.		
31	Cost of goods sold (4 @ $45 + 6 @ $47) (E+)	462	
	Inventory (A–)		462
	Cost of goods sold.		

Last-In, First-Out (LIFO) Method

Exhibit 6-4 gives a perpetual inventory record for the LIFO method.

EXHIBIT 6-4 | **Perpetual Inventory Record: LIFO**

DVD0503

Date	Purchases Quantity	Unit Cost	Total Cost	COGS Quantity	Unit Cost	Total Cost	Inventory Quantity	Unit Cost	Total Cost
Jul 1							2	$40	$80
5	6	$45	$270				2	40	80
							6	45	270
15				4	$45	$180	2	40	80
							2	45	90
26	9	47	423				2	40	80
							2	45	90
							9	47	423
31				9	47	423			
				1	45	45	2	40	80
							1	45	45
31	15		$693	14		$648	3		$125

Again, Smart Touch had 2 DVD0503s at the beginning. After the purchase on July 5, Smart Touch holds 8 units of inventory (2 @ $40 plus 6 @ $45). On July 15, Smart Touch sells 4 units. Under LIFO, the cost of goods sold always comes from the most recent purchase. That leaves 4 DVD0503s in inventory on July 15.

4 units on hand:
- 2 @ $40 = $ 80
- 2 @ $45 = 90
- Inventory on hand = $170

The purchase of 9 units on July 26 adds a new $47 layer to inventory. Now inventory holds 13 units.

13 units on hand:
- 2 @ $40 = $ 80
- 2 @ $45 = 90
- 9 @ $47 = 423
- Inventory on hand = $593

Then the sale of 10 units on July 31 peels back units in LIFO order. The LIFO monthly summary at July 31 is as follows:

- Cost of goods sold: 14 units that cost a total of $648
- Ending inventory: 3 units that cost a total of $125

Under LIFO, Smart Touch could measure cost of goods sold and inventory in this manner to prepare its financial statements.

Connect To: IFRS

The LIFO method, although permitted by U.S. GAAP, is not permitted under IFRS. Companies currently utilizing LIFO will have to change inventory methods when they convert to IFRS reporting standards.

Journal Entries Under LIFO

The journal entries under LIFO follow the data in Exhibit 6-4. On July 5, Smart Touch purchased inventory of $270. The July 15 sale brought in sales revenue (4 units @ $80 = $320) and cost of goods sold ($180). The July 26 and 31 entries also come from the data in Exhibit 6-4. Amounts unique to LIFO are shown in blue.

LIFO Journal Entries (All purchases and sales on account)		
The sales price of a DVD0503 is $80		
Jul 5	Inventory (6 × $45) (A+)	270
	Accounts payable (L+)		270
	Purchased inventory on account.		
15	Accounts receivable (4 × $80) (A+)	320
	Sales revenue (R+)		320
	Sale on account.		
15	Cost of goods sold (4 @ $45) (E+)	180
	Inventory (A−)		180
	Cost of goods sold.		
26	Inventory (9 × $47) (A+)	423
	Accounts payable (L+)		423
	Purchased inventory on account.		
31	Accounts receivable (10 × $80) (A+)	800
	Sales revenue (R+)		800
	Sale on account.		
31	Cost of goods sold (9 @ $47 + 1 @ $45) (E+)	468
	Inventory (A−)		468
	Cost of goods sold.		

Average-Cost Method

Suppose Smart Touch uses the average-cost method to account for its inventory of DVD0503s. Exhibit 6-5 shows a perpetual inventory record for the average-cost method. We round average unit cost to the nearest cent and total cost to the nearest dollar.

EXHIBIT 6-5 | **Perpetual Inventory Record:** Average Cost

DVD0503									
	Purchases			Cost of Goods Sold			Inventory on Hand		
Date	Quantity	Unit Cost	Total Cost	Quantity	Unit Cost	Total Cost	Quantity	Unit Cost	Total Cost
Jul 1							2	$40.00	$ 80
5	6	$45	$270				8	43.75	350
15				4	$43.75	$175	4	43.75	175
26	9	47	423				13	46.00	598
31				10	46.00	460	3	46.00	138
31	15		$693	14		$635	3		$138

As noted previously, after each purchase, Smart Touch computes a new average cost per unit. For example, on July 5, the new average unit cost is as follows:

	Total cost of inventory on hand		Number of units on hand		Average cost per unit
Jul 5	$80 + $270 = $350	÷	8 units	=	$43.75

The goods sold on July 15 are then costed out at $43.75 per unit. On July 26 when the next purchase is made, the new average unit cost is as follows:

	Total cost of inventory on hand		Number of units on hand		Average cost per unit
Jul 26	(4 @ $43.75) + (9 @ $47)	÷	4 + 9	=	?
	175 + 423 or $598	÷	13	=	$46.00

The average-cost summary at July 31 is as follows:

- Cost of goods sold: 14 units that cost a total of $635
- Ending inventory: 3 units that cost a total of $138

Under the average-cost method, Smart Touch could use these amounts to prepare its financial statements.

Journal Entries Under Average Costing

The journal entries under average costing follow the data in Exhibit 6-5. On July 5, Smart Touch purchased $270 of inventory and made the first journal entry. On July 15, Smart Touch sold 4 DVD0503s for $80 each. Smart Touch recorded the sale ($320) and the cost of goods sold ($175). The remaining journal entries (July 26 and 31) follow the data in Exhibit 6-5. Amounts unique to the average-cost method are shown in blue.

Average Cost Journal Entries (All purchases and sales on account) The sales price of a DVD0503 is $80			
Jul 5	Inventory (6 × $45) (A+)	270	
	Accounts payable (L+)		270
	Purchased inventory on account.		
15	Accounts receivable (4 × $80) (A+)	320	
	Sales revenue (R+)		320
	Sale on account.		
15	Cost of goods sold (4 @ $43.75) (E+)	175	
	Inventory (A–)		175
	Cost of goods sold.		
26	Inventory (9 × $47) (A+)	423	
	Accounts payable (L+)		423
	Purchased inventory on account.		
31	Accounts receivable (10 × $80) (A+)	800	
	Sales revenue (R+)		800
	Sale on account.		
31	Cost of goods sold (10 @ $46.00) (E+)	460	
	Inventory (A–)		460
	Cost of goods sold.		

Key Takeaway

The inventory costing method dictates which purchases are deemed sold (COGS). The sales price to the customer (Sales revenue) is the same regardless of which costing method is used to record COGS. Only the amounts in the COGS journal entries differ among the three costing methods.

Comparing FIFO, LIFO, and Average Cost

Exhibit 6-6 shows that FIFO is the most popular inventory costing method, LIFO is the next most popular, and average cost ranks third.

4 Compare the effects of the three most common inventory costing methods

EXHIBIT 6-6 **Use of the Various Inventory Costing Methods**

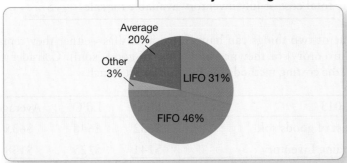

What leads Smart Touch to select the FIFO method, **General Electric** to use LIFO, and **Fossil** (the watch company) to use average cost? The different methods have different benefits.

Exhibit 6-7 summarizes the results for the three inventory costing methods for Smart Touch. It shows sales revenue, cost of goods sold, and gross profit for FIFO, LIFO, and average cost.

EXHIBIT 6-7 **Comparative Results for FIFO, LIFO, and Average Cost**

	FIFO	LIFO	Average
Sales revenue	$1,120	$1,120	$1,120
Cost of goods sold (From Exhibits 6-3, 6-4, and 6-5)	632	648	635
Gross profit	$ 488	$ 472	$ 485

Exhibit 6-7 shows that FIFO produces the lowest cost of goods sold and the highest gross profit for Smart Touch. Because operating expenses will be the same, regardless of which inventory method a company uses, net income is also the highest under FIFO when inventory costs are rising. Many companies prefer high income in order to attract investors and borrow on good terms. FIFO offers this benefit in a period of rising prices.

LIFO results in the highest cost of goods sold and the lowest gross profit. Lower profits means lower taxable income; thus, LIFO lets companies pay the lowest income taxes when inventory costs are rising. Low tax payments conserve cash, and that is the main benefit of LIFO. The downside of LIFO is that the company reports low net income.

The average-cost method generates amounts that fall between the extremes of FIFO and LIFO. Companies that seek a "middle-ground" solution, therefore, use the average-cost method for inventory.

Consider again the purchases made by Smart Touch during July. Smart Touch had total inventory in July as follows:

Jul	1	2 @ $40	$ 80
	5	6 @ $45	$270
	26	9 @ $47	$423
		Total cost of July inventory available for sale	$773

Only one of two things can happen to the DVDs—either they remain in the warehouse (Inventory) or they are sold (Cost of goods sold). Consider the results from each of the costing methods for July for Smart Touch.

Jul 2013	FIFO	LIFO	Average
Cost of goods sold	$632	$648	$635
+ Ending Inventory	$141	$125	$138
= Cost of goods available for sale	$773	$773	$773

The sum of cost of goods sold plus inventory equals the **cost of goods available for sale**, $773 for each costing method. Verifying that COGS plus Ending inventory equals Cost of good available for sale is a good way to verify your final calculation results.

Summary Problem 6-1

Fossil specializes in designer watches and leather goods. Assume **Fossil** began June holding 10 wristwatches that cost $50 each. During June, **Fossil** bought and sold inventory as follows:

Jun	3	Sold 8 units for $100 each
	16	Purchased 10 units @ $56 each
	23	Sold 8 units for $100 each

Requirements

1. Prepare a perpetual inventory record for **Fossil** using FIFO, LIFO, and Average cost.
2. Journalize all of **Fossil's** inventory transactions for June under all three costing methods.
3. Show the computation of gross profit for each method.
4. Which method maximizes net income? Which method minimizes income taxes?

Solution

1. Perpetual inventory records:

FIFO

Wristwatches

Date	Purchases Quantity	Purchases Unit Cost	Purchases Total Cost	Cost of Goods Sold Quantity	Cost of Goods Sold Unit Cost	Cost of Goods Sold Total Cost	Inventory on Hand Quantity	Inventory on Hand Unit Cost	Inventory on Hand Total Cost
Jun 1							10	$50	$500
3				8	$50	$400	2	50	100
16	10	$56	$560				2	50	100
							10	56	560
23				2	50	100			
				6	56	336	4	56	224
30	10		$560	16		$836	4		$224

LIFO

Wristwatches

Date	Purchases Quantity	Purchases Unit Cost	Purchases Total Cost	Cost of Goods Sold Quantity	Cost of Goods Sold Unit Cost	Cost of Goods Sold Total Cost	Inventory on Hand Quantity	Inventory on Hand Unit Cost	Inventory on Hand Total Cost
Jun 1							10	$50	$500
3				8	$50	$400	2	50	100
16	10	$56	$560				2	50	100
							10	56	560
23				8	56	448	2	50	100
							2	56	112
30	10		$560	16		$848	4		$212

AVERAGE COST

Wristwatches

Date	Purchases Quantity	Purchases Unit Cost	Purchases Total Cost	Cost of Goods Sold Quantity	Cost of Goods Sold Unit Cost	Cost of Goods Sold Total Cost	Inventory on Hand Quantity	Inventory on Hand Unit Cost	Inventory on Hand Total Cost
Jun 1							10	$50.00	$500
3				8	$50.00	$400	2	50.00	100
16	10	$56	$560				12	55.00	660
23				8	55.00	440	4	55.00	220
30	10		$560	16		$840	4		$220

2. Journal entries:

			FIFO		LIFO		Average	
Jun 3	Accounts receivable	(A+)	800		800		800	
	Sales revenue	(R+)		800		800		800
3	Cost of goods sold	(E+)	400		400		400	
	Inventory	(A−)		400		400		400
16	Inventory	(A+)	560		560		560	
	Accounts payable	(L+)		560		560		560
23	Accounts receivable	(A+)	800		800		800	
	Sales revenue	(R+)		800		800		800
23	Cost of goods sold	(E+)	436		448		440	
	Inventory	(A−)		436		448		440

3. Gross profit:

	FIFO	LIFO	Average
Sales revenue ($800 + $800).........................	$1,600	$1,600	$1,600
Cost of goods sold ($400 + $436)	836		
($400 + $448)		848	
($400 + $440)			840
Gross profit..	$ 764	$ 752	$ 760

4. FIFO maximizes net income.
LIFO minimizes income taxes.

Lower-of-Cost-or-Market Rule

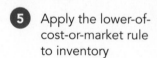

5 Apply the lower-of-cost-or-market rule to inventory

In addition to the FIFO, LIFO, and average costing methods, accountants face other inventory issues, such as the **lower-of-cost-or-market rule** (abbreviated as **LCM**). LCM shows accounting conservatism in action and requires that inventory be reported in the financial statements at whichever is lower—

- the historical cost of the inventory, or
- the market value of the inventory.

For inventories, market value generally means the current replacement cost (that is, the cost to replace the inventory on hand). If the replacement cost of inventory is less than its historical cost, the business must adjust the inventory value. By adjusting the inventory down (crediting Inventory), the balance sheet value of the asset, Inventory, is at its correct value (market) rather than its overstated value (cost). If the inventory market is greater than cost, then we don't adjust the inventory account because of the conservatism principle.

Suppose Smart Touch paid $3,000 for its CD01 inventory. By July 31, the inventory can now be replaced for $2,200, and the decline in value appears permanent. Market value is below cost, and the entry to write down the inventory to LCM is as follows:

Cost of goods sold (cost, $3,000 − market, $2,200)	(E+)		800	
Inventory	(A−)			800
To write inventory down to market value.				

In this case, Smart Touch's balance sheet would report this inventory as follows:

Balance Sheet	
Current assets:	
Inventory...	$2,200

Companies often disclose LCM in notes to their financial statements, as shown here for Smart Touch:

> NOTE 2: STATEMENT OF SIGNIFICANT ACCOUNTING POLICIES
>
> *Inventories.* Inventories are carried at the *lower of cost or market*. Cost is determined using the first-in, first-out method.

Key Takeaway

If the cost of inventory is declining, an adjustment must be made to lower the Inventory account to the lower value (market). If market is greater than cost, no adjustment is made to the Inventory account.

Effects of Inventory Errors

Businesses count their inventory at the end of the period. For the financial statements to be accurate, it is important to get a correct count of ending inventory. This can be difficult for a company with widespread operations.

An error in ending inventory creates a whole string of errors in other related accounts. To illustrate, suppose Smart Touch accidentally reported $5,000 more ending inventory than it actually had. In that case, ending inventory would be overstated by $5,000 on the balance sheet. The following shows how an overstatement of ending inventory affects cost of goods sold, gross profit, and net income:

6 Measure the effects of inventory errors

		Ending Inventory Overstated $5,000
Sales revenue		Correct
Cost of goods sold:		
	Beginning inventory	Correct
	Net purchases	Correct
	Cost of goods available	Correct
	Ending inventory	ERROR: Overstated $5,000
	Cost of goods sold	Understated $5,000
Gross profit		Overstated $5,000
Operating expenses		Correct
Net income		Overstated $5,000

Understating the ending inventory—reporting the inventory too low—has the opposite effect. If Smart Touch understated the inventory by $1,200, the effect would be as shown here:

		Ending Inventory Understated $1,200
Sales revenue		Correct
Cost of goods sold:		
	Beginning inventory	Correct
	Net purchases	Correct
	Cost of goods available	Correct
	Ending inventory	ERROR: Understated $1,200
	Cost of goods sold	Overstated $1,200
Gross profit		Understated $1,200
Operating expenses		Correct
Net income		Understated $1,200

Recall that one period's ending inventory becomes the next period's beginning inventory. As a result, an error in ending inventory carries over into the next period. Exhibit 6-8 illustrates the effect of an inventory error, assuming all other items on the income statement are unchanged for the three periods. Period 1's ending inventory is overstated by $5,000; Period 1's ending inventory should be $10,000. The error carries over to Period 2. Period 3 is correct. In fact, both Period 1 and Period 2 should look like Period 3.

EXHIBIT 6-8 | **Inventory Errors: An Example Using Periodic Inventory**

SAMPLE COMPANY
Income Statement
For the years ended Period 1, 2, and 3

	Period 1 Ending Inventory Overstated by $5,000		Period 2 Beginning Inventory Overstated by $5,000		Period 3 Correct	
Sales revenue		$100,000		$100,000		$100,000
Cost of goods sold:						
Beginning inventory	$ 10,000		$ 15,000		$ 10,000	
Net purchases	50,000		50,000		50,000	
Cost of goods available	$ 60,000		$ 65,000		$ 60,000	
Ending inventory	(15,000)		(10,000)		(10,000)	
Cost of goods sold		45,000		55,000		50,000
Gross profit		$ 55,000		$ 45,000		$ 50,000

The correct gross profit is $50,000 for each period. $100,000

Source: The authors thank Carl High for this example.

Ending inventory is *subtracted* to compute cost of goods sold in one period and the same amount is *added* as beginning inventory in the next period. Therefore, an inventory error cancels out after two periods. The overstatement of cost of goods sold in Period 2 counterbalances the understatement for Period 1. Thus, total gross profit for the two periods combined is correct. These effects are summarized in Exhibit 6-9.

EXHIBIT 6-9 | **Effects of Inventory Errors**

SAMPLE COMPANY
Income Statement
For the years ended Period 1 and 2

	Period 1		Period 2	
	Cost of Goods Sold	Gross Profit and Net Income	Cost of Goods Sold	Gross Profit and Net Income
Period 1 Ending inventory *overstated*	Understated	Overstated	Overstated	Understated
Period 1 Ending inventory *understated*	Overstated	Understated	Understated	Overstated

Estimating Ending Inventory

7 Estimate ending inventory by the gross profit method

Often a business must *estimate* the value of its ending inventory. When this happens, the business will only have partial records showing its beginning inventory and records from vendors showing their net purchases. The following shows the basic periodic calculation for inventory (from Appendix 5A), which is useful when a company needs to estimate ending inventory.

Beginning inventory
+ Net purchases
—————————
= Cost of goods available
– Ending inventory
—————————
= Cost of goods sold

Recall that cost of goods available for sale is either deemed sold (COGS) or in Ending inventory. Since COGS plus Ending inventory equals cost of goods available for sale, we can rearrange them as follows:

Beginning inventory
+ Net purchases
—————————
= Cost of goods available
– Cost of goods sold (Sales – Gross profit = COGS)
—————————
= Ending inventory

Suppose Smart Touch suffers a natural catastrophe and all its inventory is destroyed. To collect insurance, the company must estimate the cost of the inventory destroyed. Using its normal *gross profit percent* (that is, gross profit divided by net sales revenue), Smart Touch can estimate cost of goods sold. Then it needs to subtract cost of goods sold from goods available to estimate ending inventory. Exhibit 6-10 illustrates the **gross profit method** (amounts assumed for this illustration):

EXHIBIT 6-10	Gross Profit Method of Estimating Inventory (amounts assumed)		
Beginning inventory			$ 14,000
Net purchases			66,000
Cost of goods available			$ 80,000
Estimated cost of goods sold:			
Sales revenue		$100,000	
Less: Estimated gross profit of 40%		40,000	
Estimated cost of goods sold			(60,000)
Estimated cost of *ending inventory*			$ 20,000

Ethical Issues

No area of accounting has a deeper ethical dimension than inventory. Companies whose profits are lagging can be tempted to "cook the books." An increase in reported income will make the business look more successful than it really is.

There are two main schemes for cooking the books. The easiest way is to overstate ending inventory. In Exhibit 6-9, we saw how an inventory error affects net income.

The second way to cook the books involves sales. **Datapoint Corporation** and **MiniScribe**, both computer-related companies, were charged with creating fictitious sales to boost reported profits. By increasing sales without having a corresponding cost of goods sold, the profits were overstated.

Datapoint is alleged to have hired drivers to transport its inventory around the city so that the goods could not be counted. **Datapoint**'s plan seemed to create the impression that the inventory must have been sold. The scheme broke down when the trucks returned the goods to **Datapoint**. The sales returns were much too high to be realistic, and the sales proved to be phony.

MiniScribe is alleged to have cooked its books by shipping boxes of bricks labeled as computer parts. The scheme boomeranged when **MiniScribe** had to record the sales returns. In virtually every area, accounting imposes a discipline that brings out the facts sooner or later. This is one reason why maintaining good controls over inventory is very important for a merchandiser. Good controls insure that inventory purchases and sales are properly authorized and accounted for by the accounting system.

Key Takeaway

Because the total spent to acquire goods available for sale is allocated to only the Inventory or the COGS account, if Inventory is incorrectly stated due to an error, COGS is also incorrectly stated. When discovered, errors must be disclosed and corrected in the affected financial statements.

Decision Guidelines 6-1

GUIDELINES FOR INVENTORY MANAGEMENT

Assume you are starting a business to sell school supplies to your college friends. You will need to stock jump drives, notebooks, and other inventory items. To manage the business, you will also need some accounting records. Here are some of the decisions you will face.

Decision	Guidelines	System or Method
• Which inventory system to use?	• Expensive merchandise	Perpetual system
	• Cannot control inventory by visual inspection	Perpetual system
	• Can control inventory by visual inspection	Periodic system
• Which costing method to use?	• Unique and/or high dollar inventory items	Specific unit cost
	• The most current cost of ending inventory	FIFO
	• Maximizes reported income when costs are rising	FIFO
	• The most current costs are measured as cost of goods sold	LIFO
	• Minimizes income tax when costs are rising	LIFO
	• Middle-of-the-road approach for income tax and net income	Average-cost method
• How to estimate the cost of ending inventory?	• The cost-of-goods-sold model provides the framework	Gross profit method

Summary Problem 6-2

Suppose Greg's Tunes has the following inventory records for July 2013:
Operating expense for July was $1,900.

Date	Item	Quantity	Unit Cost	Sale Price
Jul 1	Beginning inventory	100 units	$ 8	
10	Purchase.............................	60 units	9	
15	Sale	70 units		$20
21	Purchase.............................	100 units	10	
30	Sale	90 units		25

Requirement

1. Prepare the July income statement in multi-step format. Show amounts for
   FIFO, LIFO, and Average cost. Label the bottom line "Operating income."
   Show your computations using periodic inventory, using the income statement
   on page 326 as your guide to compute cost of goods sold.

Solution

	GREG'S TUNES					
	Income Statement for Computer Parts					
	Month Ended July 31, 2013					
	FIFO		**LIFO**		**Average Cost**	
Sales revenue		$3,650		$3,650		$3,650
Cost of goods sold:						
Beginning inventory	$ 800		$ 800		$ 800	
Net purchases	1,540		1,540		1,540	
Cost of goods available	$ 2,340		$2,340		$2,340	
Ending inventory	(1,000)		(800)		(900)	
Cost of goods sold		1,340		1,540		1,440
Gross profit		$2,310		$2,110		$2,210
Operating expenses		1,900		1,900		1,900
Operating income		$ 410		$ 210		$ 310

Computations

Sales revenue:	(70 × $20) + (90 × $25)	= $3,650
Beginning inventory:	100 × $8	= $800
Purchases:	(60 × $9) + (100 × $10)	= $1,540
Ending inventory:		
FIFO	100* × $10	= $1,000
LIFO	100 × $8	= $800
Average cost:	100 × $9~	= $900

* Number of units in ending inventory = 100 + 60 − 70 + 100 − 90 = 100
~ Average cost per unit = $2,340/(100 + 60+ 100) total available units or $9.00 periodic average cost per unit

Review *Merchandise Inventory*

● Accounting Vocabulary

Average-Cost Inventory Costing Method (p. 315)
Inventory costing method based on the average cost of inventory during the period. Average cost is determined by dividing the cost of goods available for sale by the number of units available.

Conservatism (p. 313)
Reporting the least favorable figures in the financial statements.

Consistency Principle (p. 313)
A business should use the same accounting methods and procedures from period to period.

Cost of Goods Available for Sale (p. 322)
The total cost spent on inventory that was available to be sold during a period.

Disclosure Principle (p. 313)
A business's financial statements must report enough information for outsiders to make knowledgeable decisions about the company.

First-In, First-Out (FIFO) Inventory Costing Method (p. 315)
Inventory costing method in which the first costs into inventory are the first costs out to cost of goods sold. Ending inventory is based on the costs of the most recent purchases.

Gross Profit Method (p. 327)
A way to estimate inventory on the basis of the cost-of-goods-sold model: Beginning inventory + Net purchases = Cost of goods available for sale. Cost of goods available for sale – Cost of goods sold = Ending inventory.

Last-In, First-Out (LIFO) Inventory Costing Method (p. 315)
Inventory costing method in which the last costs into inventory are the first costs out to cost of goods sold. The method leaves the oldest costs—those of beginning inventory and the earliest purchases of the period—in ending inventory.

Lower-of-Cost-or-Market (LCM) Rule (p. 324)
Rule that inventory should be reported in the financial statements at whichever is lower—its historical cost or its market value.

Materiality Concept (p. 313)
A company must perform strictly proper accounting only for items that are significant to the business's financial situations.

Specific-Identification Method (p. 315)
Inventory costing method based on the specific cost of particular units of inventory. Also called the **specific-unit-cost method**.

Specific-Unit-Cost Method (p. 315)
Inventory costing method based on the specific cost of particular units of inventory. Also called the **specific-identification method**.

● Destination Student Success

Student Success Tips

The following are hints on some common trouble areas for students in this chapter:

● Remember that the total cost of goods available for sale is split into Inventory and COGS.

● Recall the inventory costing methods: Specific-unit-cost, FIFO (first-in, first-out/sold), LIFO (last-in, first-out/sold), and average-cost (average price).

● FIFO periodic and FIFO perpetual calculations ALWAYS result in the same COGS and Inventory amounts. This is not necessarily true with LIFO or with average cost; therefore, you must calculate both periodic and perpetual LIFO and average cost.

● The lower-of-cost-or-market (LCM) rule means the lowest amount goes to the Inventory account.

● Since Cost of goods available for sale dollars can only go to either the Inventory account or the COGS account, if inventory is overstated, COGS will be understated. If inventory is understated, COGS will be overstated.

● Remember the formulas for gross profit percentage you learned in the previous chapter. These can be used to help estimate ending inventory. (For example: Sales, 100% – COGS, 70% = GP, 30%).

Getting Help

If there's a learning objective from the chapter you aren't confident about, try using one or more of the following resources:

● Use examples you have at your house to help you get the inventory costing methods down. (Try using three cans of soup. Mark each with a date, say the 1st, 15th, and 30th of the month and a price of $1, $2, and $3, respectively. Practice visualizing the sale and calculating Inventory/COGS.)

● Practice additional exercises or problems at the end of Chapter 6 that cover the specific learning objective that is challenging you.

● Watch the white board videos for Chapter 6 located at myaccountinglab.com under the Chapter Resources button.

● Go to myaccountinglab.com and select the Study Plan button. Choose Chapter 6 and work the questions covering that specific learning objective until you've mastered it.

● Work the Chapter 6 pre/post tests in myaccountinglab.com.

● Visit the learning resource center on your campus for tutoring.

● Quick Check

1. T. J. Jackson had inventory that cost $1,300. The market value of the inventory is $750. Normal profit is $325. At what value should Jackson show on the balance sheet for inventory?

    a. $1,625

    b. $1,075

    c. $750

    d. $1,300

2. Which inventory costing method assigns to ending inventory the newest—the most recent—costs incurred during the period?

    a. First-in, first-out (FIFO)

    b. Average-cost

    c. Specific-unit-cost

    d. Last-in, first-out (LIFO)

3. Assume Nile.com began April with 14 units of inventory that cost a total of $266. During April, Nile purchased and sold goods as follows:

Apr	8	Purchase	42 units @ $20
	14	Sale	35 units @ $40
	22	Purchase	28 units @ $22
	27	Sale	42 units @ $40

    Under the FIFO inventory method, how much is Nile's cost of goods sold for the sale on April 14?

    a. $1,106

    b. $686

    c. $1,400

    d. $700

4. Under the FIFO method, Nile.com's journal entry (entries) on April 14 is (are):

    a.
Accounts receivable	686	
Inventory		686

    b.
Cost of goods sold	686	
Inventory		686

    c.
Accounts receivable	1,400	
Sales revenue		1,400

    d. Both b and c are correct.

5. After the purchase on April 22, what is Nile's cost of the inventory on hand? Nile.com uses FIFO.

    a. $1,022

    b. $1,036

    c. $616

    d. $1,722

6. Which inventory costing method results in the lowest net income during a period of rising inventory costs?

    a. Average-cost

    b. Specific-unit-cost

    c. First-in, first-out (FIFO)

    d. Last-in, first-out (LIFO)

7. Suppose Nile.com used the average-cost method and the perpetual inventory system. Use the Nile.com data in question 3 to compute the average unit cost of the company's inventory on hand at April 8. Round unit cost to the nearest cent.

   a. $21.00

   b. $19.75

   c. $19.50

   d. Cannot be determined from the data given

8. Which of the following is most closely linked to accounting conservatism?

   a. Lower-of-cost-or-market rule

   b. Materiality concept

   c. Disclosure principle

   d. Consistency principle

9. At December 31, 2012, Stevenson Company overstated ending inventory by $36,000. How does this error affect cost of goods sold and net income for 2012?

   a. Overstates cost of goods sold and understates net income

   b. Understates cost of goods sold and overstates net income

   c. Leaves both cost of goods sold and net income correct because the errors cancel each other

   d. Overstates both cost of goods sold and net income

10. Suppose Supreme Clothing suffered a hurricane loss and needs to estimate the cost of the goods destroyed. Beginning inventory was $94,000, net purchases totaled $564,000, and sales came to $940,000. Supreme's normal gross profit percentage is 55%. Use the gross profit method to estimate the cost of the inventory lost in the hurricane.

    a. $658,000

    b. $235,000

    c. $517,000

    d. $141,000

Answers are given after Apply Your Knowledge (p. 348).

Assess Your Progress

● Short Exercises

S6-1   **1** **Inventory accounting principles [5 min]**
Davidson Hardware used the FIFO inventory method in 2012. Davidson plans to continue using the FIFO method in future years.

Requirement

1. Which inventory principle is most relevant to Davidson's decision?

S6-2   **2** **Inventory methods [5 min]**
Davidson Hardware does not expect prices to change dramatically and wants to use a method that averages price changes.

Requirements

1. Which inventory method would best meet Davidson's goal?

2. What if Davidson wanted to expense out the newer purchases of goods instead? Which inventory method would best meet that need?

S6-3   **❸ Perpetual inventory record—FIFO [10 min]**

Mountain Cycles uses the FIFO inventory method. Mountain started August with 12 bicycles that cost $42 each. On August 16, Mountain bought 40 bicycles at $68 each. On August 31, Mountain sold 36 bicycles.

Requirement

1. Prepare Mountain's perpetual inventory record.

S6-4   **❸ Perpetual inventory record—LIFO [10 min]**

Review the facts on Mountain Cycles in Short Exercise 6-3.

Requirement

1. Prepare a perpetual inventory record for the LIFO method.

S6-5   **❸ Perpetual inventory record—average cost [10 min]**

Review the facts on Mountain Cycles in Short Exercise 6-3.

Requirement

1. Prepare a perpetual inventory record for the average-cost method.

S6-6   **❸ Journalizing inventory transactions—FIFO [5–10 min]**

Use the Mountain Cycles data in Short Exercise 6-3.

Requirements

1. Journalize the August 16 purchase of inventory on account.
2. Journalize the August 31 sale of inventory on account. Mountain sold each bicycle for $84.
3. Journalize the Cost of goods sold under FIFO on August 31.

S6-7   **❸ Journalizing inventory transactions—LIFO [5–10 min]**

Use the Mountain Cycles data in Short Exercise 6-4.

Requirements

1. Journalize the August 16 purchase of inventory on account.
2. Journalize the August 31 sale of inventory on account. Mountain sold each bicycle for $84.
3. Journalize the Cost of goods sold under LIFO on August 31.

S6-8   **❸ Journalizing inventory transactions—average cost [5–10 min]**

Use the Mountain Cycles data in Short Exercise 6-5.

Requirements

1. Journalize the August 16 purchase of inventory on account.
2. Journalize the August 31 sale of inventory on account. Mountain sold each bicycle for $84.
3. Journalize the Cost of goods sold under average cost on August 31.

S6-9   **❹ Comparing Cost of goods sold under FIFO, LIFO, and average cost [5–10 min]**

Refer to Short Exercises 6-3 through 6-8. After completing those exercises, answer the following questions:

Requirements

1. Which method of inventory accounting produced the lowest cost of goods sold?
2. Which method of inventory accounting produced the highest cost of goods sold?
3. If prices had been declining instead of rising, which inventory method would have produced the highest cost of goods sold?

S6-10 ⑤ **Applying the lower-of-cost-or-market rule [5–10 min]**

Refer to Short Exercises 6-3 through 6-9. At August 31, the accountant for Mountain Cycles determines that the current replacement cost of each bike is $40.

Requirements

1. Assuming inventory was calculated using the FIFO method, make any adjusting entry needed to apply the lower-of-cost-or-market rule. Inventory would be reported on the balance sheet at what value on August 31?

2. Assuming inventory was calculated using the LIFO method, make any adjusting entry needed to apply the lower-of-cost-or-market rule. Inventory would be reported on the balance sheet at what value on August 31?

3. Assuming inventory was calculated using the average-cost method, make any adjusting entry needed to apply the lower-of-cost-or-market rule. Inventory would be reported on the balance sheet at what value on August 31?

S6-11 ⑤ **Applying the lower-of-cost-or-market rule [5–10 min]**

Assume that a Rocket Burger restaurant has the following perpetual inventory record for hamburger patties:

Hamburger Patties			
Date	Purchases	Cost of Goods Sold	Inventory on Hand
Feb 9	$ 470		$ 470
22		$ 280	190
28	210		400

Requirements

1. At February 28, the accountant for the restaurant determines that the current replacement cost of the ending inventory is $447. Make any adjusting entry needed to apply the lower-of-cost-or-market rule. Inventory would be reported on the balance sheet at what value on February 28?

2. Inventory would be reported on the balance sheet at what value if Rocket uses the average-cost method?

S6-12 ⑥ **Effect of an inventory error—one year only [5 min]**

California Pool Supplies' inventory data for the year ended December 31, 2012, follow:

Sales revenue	$ 60,000
Cost of goods sold:	
Beginning inventory	$ 4,200
Net purchases	26,600
Cost of goods available	$ 30,800
Ending inventory	(6,200)
Cost of goods sold	$ 24,600
Gross profit	$ 35,400

Assume that the ending inventory was accidentally overstated by $2,400.

Requirement

1. What are the correct amounts for cost of goods sold and gross profit?

S6-13 ⑥ **Next year's effect of an inventory error [5–10 min]**

Refer back to the California Pool Supplies' inventory data in Short Exercise 6-12.

Requirement

1. How would the inventory error affect California Pool Supplies' cost of goods sold and gross profit for the year ended December 31, 2013, if the error is not corrected in 2012?

S6-14   **7** **Estimating ending inventory by the gross profit method [10 min]**
Glass Company began the year with inventory of $42,450 and purchased $263,000 of goods during the year. Sales for the year are $501,000, and Glass's gross profit percentage is 55% of sales.

Requirement

1. Compute the estimated cost of ending inventory by the gross profit method.

● Exercises

E6-15   **1** **2** **Accounting principles related to inventory and inventory costing methods defined [15–20 min]**   *MyAccountingLab*
Review inventory accounting definitions and principles.

Requirement

1. Complete the crossword puzzle using the following clues:

Down:

1. Treats the oldest inventory purchases as the first units sold.
3. Identifies exactly which inventory item was sold. Usually used for higher cost inventory. (Two words)
6. Principle whose foundation is to exercise caution in reporting financial statement items.
7. Business should use the same accounting methods from period to period.

Across:

2. Requires that a company report enough information for outsiders to make decisions.
4. Calculates an average cost based on the purchases made and the units acquired. (Two words)
5. Treats the most recent/newest purchases as the first units sold.
8. Principle that states significant items must conform to GAAP.

E6-16 ❷ **Inventory methods [10–15 min]**

Express Lane, a regional convenience store chain, maintains milk inventory by the gallon. The first month's milk purchases and sales at its Freeport, FL, location follows:

Nov 2	1 gallon @ $2.00 each
6	2 gallons @ $2.10 each
13	2 gallons @ $2.20 each
14	The store sold 4 gallons of milk to a customer.

Requirement

1. Describe which costs would be sold and which costs would remain in inventory. Then, identify the amount that would be reported in inventory on November 15 using
   a. FIFO.
   b. LIFO.
   c. average cost.

E6-17 ❸ **Measuring and journalizing inventory and cost of goods sold in a perpetual system—FIFO [20–25 min]**

Golf Haven carries an inventory of putters and other golf clubs. Golf Haven uses the FIFO method and a perpetual inventory system. The sales price of each putter is $128. Company records indicate the following for a particular line of Golf Haven's putters:

Date	Item	Quantity	Unit Cost
Nov 1	Balance	17	$68
6	Sale	7	
8	Purchase	20	$74
17	Sale	20	
30	Sale	4	

Requirements

1. Prepare a perpetual inventory record for the putters. Then determine the amounts Golf Haven should report for ending inventory and cost of goods sold using the FIFO method.
2. Journalize Golf Haven's inventory transactions using the FIFO method.

E6-18 ❸ **Measuring ending inventory and cost of goods sold in a perpetual system—LIFO [20–25 min]**

Refer to the Golf Haven inventory data in Exercise 6-17. Assume that Golf Haven uses the perpetual LIFO cost method.

Requirements

1. Prepare Golf Haven's perpetual inventory record for the putters on the LIFO basis. Then identify the cost of ending inventory and cost of goods sold for the month.
2. Journalize Golf Haven's inventory transactions using the perpetual LIFO method.

E6-19 ❸ **Measuring ending inventory and cost of goods sold in a perpetual system—average cost [20–25 min]**

Refer to the Golf Haven inventory data in Exercise 6-17. Assume that Golf Haven uses the average-cost method.

Requirements

1. Prepare Golf Haven's perpetual inventory record for the putters on the average-cost basis. Round average cost per unit to the nearest cent and all other amounts to the nearest dollar. Then identify the cost of ending inventory and cost of goods sold for the month.
2. Journalize Golf Haven's inventory transactions using the perpetual average-cost method.

E6-20 ❸ **Journalizing perpetual inventory transactions—cost of sales given [10–15 min]**

Accounting records for Josh's Shopping Bags yield the following data for the year ended May 31, 2012:

Inventory, May 31, 2011	$ 8,000
Purchases of inventory (on account)	46,000
Sales of inventory – 81% on account; 19% for cash (cost $38,000) ...	76,000
Inventory, May 31, 2012	?

Requirements

1. Journalize the inventory transactions for the company using the data given.
2. Report ending inventory on the balance sheet, and sales, cost of goods sold, and gross profit on the income statement.

E6-21 ❹ **Comparing amounts for ending inventory—perpetual inventory—FIFO and LIFO [5–10 min]**

Assume that a Models and More store bought and sold a line of dolls during December as follows:

Beginning inventory	13	units @	$	11
Sale	9	units		
Purchase	17	units @	$	13
Sale	13	units		

Models and More uses the perpetual inventory system.

Requirements

1. Compute the cost of ending inventory using FIFO.
2. Compute the cost of ending inventory using LIFO.
3. Which method results in a higher cost of ending inventory?

E6-22 ❹ **Comparing cost of goods sold in a perpetual system—FIFO and LIFO [15–20 min]**

Review the data in Exercise 6-21.

Requirements

1. Compute the cost of goods sold under FIFO.
2. Compute the cost of goods sold under LIFO.
3. Which method results in the higher cost of goods sold?

E6-23 ❹ **Comparing cost of goods sold in a perpetual system—FIFO, LIFO, and average-cost methods [15–20 min]**

Assume that a JR Tire Store completed the following perpetual inventory transactions for a line of tires:

Beginning inventory	16	tires @	$	65
Purchase	10	tires @	$	78
Sale	12	tires @	$	90

Requirements

1. Compute cost of goods sold and gross profit using FIFO.
2. Compute cost of goods sold and gross profit using LIFO.
3. Compute cost of goods sold and gross profit using average-cost. (Round average cost per unit to the nearest cent and all other amounts to the nearest dollar.)
4. Which method results in the largest gross profit and why?

E6-24   **⑤ Applying the lower-of-cost-or-market rule to inventories [5 min]**
Eagle Resources, which uses the FIFO method, has the following account balances at May 31, 2012, prior to releasing the financial statements for the year:

	Inventory		Cost of goods sold		Sales revenue	
Beg Bal	12,500					
End Bal	13,000		Bal 69,000		Bal 118,000	

Eagle has determined that the replacement cost (current market value) of the May 31, 2012, ending inventory is $12,800.

Requirements

1. Prepare any adjusting journal entry required from the information given.
2. What value would Eagle report on the balance sheet at May 31, 2012, for inventory?

E6-25   **⑤ Applying the lower-of-cost-or-market rule to inventories [5 min]**
Naturally Good Foods reports inventory at the lower of average cost or market. Prior to releasing its March 2012 financial statements, Naturally's *preliminary* income statement, before the year-end adjustments, appears as follows:

NATURALLY GOOD FOODS	
Income Statement—Partial	
For the year ended March 31, 2012	
Sales revenue	$ 117,000
Cost of goods sold	45,000
Gross profit	$ 72,000

Naturally has determined that the replacement cost of ending inventory is $17,000. Cost is $18,000.

Requirements

1. Journalize the adjusting entry for inventory, if any is required.
2. Prepare a revised income statement to show how Naturally Good Foods should report sales, cost of goods sold, and gross profit.

E6-26   **⑥ Measuring the effect of an inventory error [10–15 min]**
Grandma Kate Bakery reported sales revenue of $52,000 and cost of goods sold of $22,000.

Requirement

1. Compute Grandma Kate's correct gross profit if the company made either of the following independent accounting errors. Show your work.
   a. Ending inventory is overstated by $6,000.
   b. Ending inventory is understated by $6,000.

E6-27 ⑥ **Correcting an inventory error—two years [15–20 min]**

Great Foods Grocery reported the following comparative income statement for the years ended June 30, 2012 and 2011:

GREAT FOODS GROCERY Income Statements Years Ended June 30, 2012 and 2011				
	2012		**2011**	
Sales revenue		$ 139,000		$ 120,000
Cost of goods sold:				
Beginning inventory	$13,000		$12,000	
Net purchases	76,000		70,000	
Cost of goods available	$89,000		$82,000	
Ending inventory	(17,000)		(13,000)	
Cost of goods sold		72,000		69,000
Gross profit		$ 67,000		$ 51,000
Operating expenses		23,000		18,000
Net income		$ 44,000		$ 33,000

During 2012, Great Foods discovered that ending 2011 inventory was overstated by $4,500.

Requirements

1. Prepare corrected income statements for the two years.

2. State whether each year's net income—before your corrections—is understated or overstated and indicate the amount of the understatement or overstatement.

E6-28 ⑦ **Estimating ending inventory by the gross profit method [10–15 min]**

Deluxe Auto Parts holds inventory all over the world. Assume that the records for one auto part show the following:

Beginning inventory	$ 220,000
Net purchases	800,000
Net sales	1,100,000
Gross profit rate	45%

Suppose this inventory, stored in the United States, was lost in a fire.

Requirement

1. Estimate the amount of the loss to Deluxe Auto Parts. Use the gross profit method.

E6-29 ⑦ **Estimating ending inventory by the gross profit method [10–15 min]**

R K Landscaping and Nursery began November with inventory of $46,800. During November, R K made net purchases of $33,900 and had net sales of $61,800. For the past several years, R K's gross profit has been 45% of sales.

Requirement

1. Use the gross profit method to estimate the cost of the ending inventory for November.

Problems (Group A)

P6-30A ❶ ❺ **Accounting principles for inventory and applying the lower-of-cost-or-market rule [15–20 min]**

Some of M and T Electronics' merchandise is gathering dust. It is now December 31, 2012, and the current replacement cost of the ending inventory is $20,000 below the business's cost of the goods, which was $100,000. Before any adjustments at the end of the period, the company's Cost of goods sold account has a balance of $410,000.

Requirements

1. Journalize any required entries.
2. At what amount should the company report for Inventory on the balance sheet?
3. At what amount should the company report for Cost of goods sold?
4. Which accounting principle or concept is most relevant to this situation?

P6-31A ❷ ❸ **Accounting for inventory using the perpetual system—LIFO, and journalizing inventory transactions [30–40 min]**

Fit World began January with an inventory of 80 crates of vitamins that cost a total of $4,000. During the month, Fit World purchased and sold merchandise on account as follows:

Purchase 1	140 crates	@ $ 55
Sale 1	160 crates	@ $ 100
Purchase 2	160 crates	@ $ 60
Sale 2	170 crates	@ $ 110

Fit World uses the LIFO method.
Cash payments on account totaled $5,000. Operating expenses for the month were $3,300, with two-thirds paid in cash, and the rest accrued as Accounts payable.

Requirements

1. Which inventory method most likely mimics the physical flow of Fit World's inventory?
2. Prepare a perpetual inventory record, using LIFO cost, for this merchandise.
3. Journalize all transactions using LIFO.

P6-32A ❸ ❹ **Accounting for results on income for inventory using the LIFO cost method [20–30 min]**

Refer to the Fit World situation in Problem 6-31A.

Requirement

1. Using the results from the LIFO costing method calculations in Problem 6-31A, prepare a multi-step income statement for Fit World for the month ended January 31, 2012.

P6-33A ❸ ❹ **Accounting for inventory using the perpetual system—FIFO, LIFO, and average cost, and comparing FIFO, LIFO, and average cost [20–25 min]**

Decorative Steel began August with 55 units of iron inventory that cost $35 each. During August, the company completed the following inventory transactions:

	Units	Unit Cost	Unit Sale Price
Aug 3 Sale	45		$83
8 Purchase	75	$52	
21 Sale	70		$85
30 Purchase	10	$55	

Requirements

1. Prepare a perpetual inventory record for the inventory using FIFO.
2. Prepare a perpetual inventory record for the inventory using LIFO.
3. Prepare a perpetual inventory record for the inventory using average cost.
4. Determine the company's cost of goods sold for August using FIFO, LIFO, and average cost.
5. Compute gross profit for August using FIFO, LIFO, and average cost.

P6-34A ❺ **Applying the lower-of-cost-or-market rule to inventories [5 min]**
Richmond Sporting Goods, which uses the FIFO method, has the following account balances at August 31, 2012, prior to releasing the financial statements for the year:

Inventory	Cost of goods sold	Sales revenue
Bal 14,500	Bal 67,000	Bal 117,000

Richmond has determined that the replacement cost (current market value) of the August 31, 2012, ending inventory is $13,500.

Requirements

1. Prepare any adjusting journal entry required from the information given.
2. What value would Richmond report on the balance sheet at August 31, 2012, for inventory?

P6-35A ❻ **Correcting inventory errors over a three-year period [15–20 min]**
Evergreen Carpets' books show the following data. In early 2013, auditors found that the ending inventory for 2010 was understated by $6,000 and that the ending inventory for 2012 was overstated by $7,000. The ending inventory at December 31, 2011, was correct.

	2012		2011		2010	
Net sales revenue		$210,000		$162,000		$169,000
Cost of goods sold:						
Beginning inventory	$ 20,000		$ 27,000		$ 41,000	
Net purchases	140,000		108,000		98,000	
Cost of goods available ...	$160,000		$135,000		$139,000	
Ending inventory	(29,000)		(20,000)		(27,000)	
Cost of goods sold		131,000		115,000		112,000
Gross profit		$ 79,000		$ 47,000		$ 57,000
Operating expenses		53,000		18,000		24,000
Net income		$ 26,000		$ 29,000		$ 33,000

Requirements

1. Prepare corrected income statements for the three years.
2. State whether each year's net income—before your corrections—is understated or overstated and indicate the amount of the understatement or overstatement.

P6-36A ❼ **Estimating ending inventory by the gross profit method and preparing the income statement [25–30 min]**
Halloween Costumes estimates its inventory by the gross profit method. The gross profit has averaged 30% of net sales. The company's inventory records reveal the following data:

Inventory, May 1	$ 270,000
Transactions during May:	
Purchases	7,520,000
Purchase discounts..........	146,000
Purchase returns..............	37,000
Sales.................................	8,719,000
Sales returns....................	27,000

Requirements

1. Estimate the May 31 inventory, using the gross profit method.
2. Prepare the May income statement through gross profit for Halloween Costumes.

● Problems (Group B)

MyAccountingLab

P6-37B ❶ ❺ **Accounting principles for inventory and applying the lower-of-cost-or-market rule [15–20 min]**

Some of P and Y Electronics' merchandise is gathering dust. It is now December 31, 2012, and the current replacement cost of the ending inventory is $30,000 below the business's cost of the goods, which was $95,000. Before any adjustments at the end of the period, the company's Cost of goods sold account has a balance of $415,000.

Requirements

1. Journalize any required entries.
2. What amount should the company report for Inventory on the balance sheet?
3. What amount should the company report for Cost of goods sold?
4. Which accounting principle or concept is most relevant to this situation?

P6-38B ❷ ❸ **Accounting for inventory using the perpetual system—LIFO and journalizing inventory transactions [30–40 min]**

Health World began January with an inventory of 50 crates of vitamins that cost a total of $1,000. During the month, Health World purchased and sold merchandise on account as follows:

Purchase 1	100 crates	@ $ 25
Sale 1	130 crates	@ $ 40
Purchase 2	90 crates	@ $ 30
Sale 2	100 crates	@ $ 50

Health World uses the LIFO method.

Cash payments on account totaled $5,500. Operating expenses for the month were $3,000, with two-thirds paid in cash and the rest accrued as Accounts payable.

Requirements

1. Which inventory method most likely mimics the physical flow of Health World's inventory?
2. Prepare a perpetual inventory record, using LIFO cost, for this merchandise.
3. Journalize all transactions using LIFO.

P6-39B ❸ ❹ **Accounting for results on income for inventory using the LIFO cost method [20–30 min]**

Refer to the Health World situation in Problem 6-38B.

Requirement

1. Using the results from the LIFO costing method calculations in Problem 6-38B, prepare a multi-step income statement for Health World for the month ended January 31, 2012.

P6-40B ❸❹ Accounting for inventory using the perpetual system—FIFO, LIFO, and average cost; comparing FIFO, LIFO, and average cost [20–25 min]

Ornamental Iron Works began January with 45 units of iron inventory that cost $24 each. During January, the company completed the following inventory transactions:

	Units	Unit Cost	Unit Sale Price
Jan 3 Sale	35		$51
8 Purchase	70	$32	
21 Sale	65		$73
30 Purchase	25	$47	

Requirements

1. Prepare a perpetual inventory record for the inventory using FIFO.
2. Prepare a perpetual inventory record for the inventory using LIFO.
3. Prepare a perpetual inventory record for the inventory using average cost.
4. Determine the company's cost of goods sold for January using FIFO, LIFO, and average cost.
5. Compute gross profit for January using FIFO, LIFO, and average cost.

P6-41B ❺ Applying the lower-of-cost-or-market rule to inventories [5 min]

Rocky Bayou Golf Clubs, which uses the FIFO method, has the following account balances at July 31, 2012, prior to releasing the financial statements for the year:

Inventory	Cost of goods sold	Sales revenue
Bal 13,500	Bal 68,000	Bal 119,000

Rocky Bayou has determined that the replacement cost (current market value) of the July 31, 2012, ending inventory is $13,000.

Requirements

1. Prepare any adjusting journal entry required from the information given.
2. What value would Rocky Bayou report on the balance sheet at July 31, 2012, for inventory?

P6-42B ❻ Correcting inventory errors over a three-year period [15–20 min]

Peaceful Carpets' books show the following data. In early 2013, auditors found that the ending inventory for 2010 was understated by $4,000 and that the ending inventory for 2012 was overstated by $5,000. The ending inventory at December 31, 2011, was correct.

	2012	2011	2010
Net sales revenue	$201,000	$161,000	$176,000
Cost of goods sold:			
Beginning inventory	$ 22,000	$ 25,000	$ 38,000
Net purchases	130,000	104,000	92,000
Cost of goods available	$152,000	$129,000	$130,000
Ending inventory	(31,000)	(22,000)	(25,000)
Cost of goods sold	121,000	107,000	105,000
Gross profit	$ 80,000	$ 54,000	$ 71,000
Operating expenses	56,000	26,000	35,000
Net income	$ 24,000	$ 28,000	$ 36,000

Requirements

1. Prepare corrected income statements for the three years.
2. State whether each year's net income—before your corrections—is understated or overstated and indicate the amount of the understatement or overstatement.

P6-43B ❼ **Estimating ending inventory by the gross profit method and preparing the income statement [25–30 min]**

Kids Costumes estimates its inventory by the gross profit method. The gross profit has averaged 39% of net sales. The company's inventory records reveal the following data:

Inventory, July 1	$ 268,000
Transactions during July:	
Purchases.........................	7,661,000
Purchase discounts..........	171,000
Purchase returns..............	32,000
Sales...............................	8,788,000
Sales returns....................	35,000

Requirements

1. Estimate the July 31 inventory using the gross profit method.
2. Prepare the July income statement through gross profit for Kids Costumes.

● Continuing Exercise

E6-44 ❸ **Accounting for inventory using the perpetual system—FIFO [25–30 min]**

This exercise continues the Lawlor Lawn Service situation from Exercise 5-42 in Chapter 5. Consider the June transactions for Lawlor Lawn Service that were presented in Chapter 5. (Cost data has been removed from the sale transactions):

Jun	2	Completed lawn service and received cash of $800.
	5	Purchased 110 plants on account for inventory, $304, plus freight in of $15.
	15	Sold 60 plants on account, $600.
	17	Consulted with a client on landscaping design for a fee of $250 on account.
	20	Purchased 120 plants on account for inventory, $384.
	21	Paid on account, $400.
	25	Sold 110 plants for cash, $990.
	30	Recorded the following adjusting entries: Depreciation, $30. Physical count of plant inventory, 30 plants.

Requirements

1. Prepare perpetual inventory records for June for Lawlor using the FIFO method. (Note: You must figure cost on the 15th, 25th, and 30th.)

2. Journalize and post the June transactions using the perpetual inventory record created in Requirement 1. Key all items by date. Compute each account balance, and denote the balance as *Bal*.

3. Journalize and post the adjusting entries. Denote each adjusting amount as *Adj*. After posting all adjusting entries, prove the equality of debits and credits in the ledger.

● Continuing Problem

P6-45 ❸ **Accounting for inventory using the perpetual system—LIFO [30–40 min]**   *MyAccountingLab*
This problem continues the Draper Consulting situation from Problem 5-43 in Chapter 5. Consider the January transactions for Draper Consulting that were presented in Chapter 5. (Cost data has been removed from the sale transactions.)

Jan	2	Completed a consulting engagement and received cash of $7,800.
	2	Prepaid three months' office rent, $1,650.
	7	Purchased 80 units software inventory on account, $1,680, plus freight in, $80.
	18	Sold 40 software units on account, $3,500.
	19	Consulted with a client for a fee of $1,000 on account.
	20	Paid employee salary, $2,055.
	21	Paid on account, $1,760.
	22	Purchased 240 units software inventory on account, $6,240.
	24	Paid utilities, $250.
	28	Sold 120 units of software for cash, $4,680.
	31	Recorded the following adjusting entries:
		Accrued salary expense, $685.
		Depreciation, $100 (Equipment, $30; Furniture, $70).
		Expiration of prepaid rent, $550.
		Physical count of inventory, 145 units.

Requirements

1. Prepare perpetual inventory records for January for Draper using the LIFO perpetual method. (Note: You must figure cost on the 18th, 28th, and 31st.)

2. Journalize and post the January transactions using the perpetual inventory record created in requirement 1. Key all items by date. Compute each account balance, and denote the balance as *Bal.*

3. Journalize and post the adjusting entries. Denote each adjusting amount as *Adj.* After posting all adjusting entries, prove the equality of debits and credits in the ledger.

● Practice Set

This problem continues the Shine King Cleaning problem begun in Chapter 1 and continued   *MyAccountingLab*
through Chapter 5.

P6-46 ❸ **Accounting for inventory using the perpetual system—FIFO [30–40 min]**
Consider the December transactions for Shine King Cleaning that were presented in Chapter 5. (Cost data has been removed from the sale transactions.)

Dec	2	Purchased 600 units of inventory, $3,600, from Sparkle, Co., on terms, 3/10, n/20.
	5	Purchased 400 units of inventory from Borax on terms 4/5, n/30. The total invoice was for $3,200, which included a $200 freight charge.
	7	Returned 100 units of inventory to Sparkle from the December 2 purchase.
	9	Paid Borax.
	11	Sold 350 units of goods to Happy Maids for $4,900 on terms 5/10, n/30.
	12	Paid Sparkle.
	15	Received 30 units with a retail price of $420 of goods back from customer Happy Maids.
	21	Received payment from Happy Maids, settling the amount due in full.
	28	Sold 200 units of goods to Bridget, Inc., for cash of $3,000.
	29	Paid cash for Utilities of $350.
	30	Paid cash for Sales commission expense of $225.
	31	Recorded these adjusting entries: Physical count of Inventory on December 31 revealed 330 units of goods on hand. Depreciation, $170. Accrued salary expense of $700. Prepared all other adjustments necessary for December.

Requirements

1. Prepare perpetual inventory records for December for Shine King using the FIFO method. (Note: You must figure cost on the 11th, 28th, and 31st.)

2. Journalize and post the December transactions using the perpetual inventory record created in Requirement 1. Key all items by date. Compute each account balance, and denote the balance as *Bal*.

3. Journalize and post the adjusting entries. Denote each adjusting amount as *Adj*. After posting all adjusting entries, prove the equality of debits and credits in the ledger.

Apply Your Knowledge

● Decision Cases

Decision Case 6-1 Assume you are opening a **Bed Bath & Beyond** store. To finance the business, you need a $500,000 loan, and your banker requires a set of forecasted financial statements. Assume you are preparing the statements and must make some decisions about how to do the accounting for the business.

Requirements

Answer the following questions (refer to Chapter 5 if necessary):

1. Which type of inventory system will you use? Perpetual or Periodic? Give your reason.

2. Show how to compute net purchases (see the vocabulary list in Chapter 5 for the definition of "net purchases") and net sales. How will you treat the cost of freight in?

3. How often do you plan to do a physical count of inventory on hand? What will the physical count accomplish?

4. Inventory costs are rising. Which inventory costing method would have the effect of
    a. maximizing net income?
    b. paying the least amount of income tax?

Decision Case 6-2 Suppose you manage Campbell Appliance. The store's summarized financial statements for 2012, the most recent year, follow:

CAMPBELL APPLIANCE
Income Statement
Year Ended December 31, 2012

Sales	$800,000
Cost of goods sold	660,000
Gross profit	$140,000
Operating expenses	100,000
Net income	$ 40,000

CAMPBELL APPLIANCE
Balance Sheet
December 31, 2012

Assets		Liabilities and Equity	
Cash	$ 30,000	Accounts payable	$ 35,000
Inventories	75,000	Note payable	280,000
Land and buildings, net	360,000	Total liabilities	$315,000
		Owner's equity	150,000
Total assets	$465,000	Total liabilities and equity	$465,000

Assume that you need to double net income. To accomplish your goal, it will be very difficult to raise the prices you charge because there is a **Best Buy** nearby. Also, you have little control over your cost of goods sold because the appliance manufacturers set the price you must pay.

Requirement

1. Identify several strategies for doubling net income. (Challenge)

● Ethical Issue 6-1

During 2012, Crop-Paper-Scissors, a craft store, changed to the LIFO method of accounting for inventory. Suppose that during 2013, Crop-Paper-Scissors switches back to the FIFO method and the following year switches back to LIFO again.

Requirements

1. What would you think of a company's ethics if it changed accounting methods every year?
2. What accounting principle would changing methods every year violate?
3. Who can be harmed when a company changes its accounting methods too often? How?

● Fraud Case 6-1

Ever since he was a kid, Carl Montague wanted to be a pro football player. When that didn't work out, he found another way to channel his natural competitive spirit: He bought a small auto parts store in Kentucky that was deep in red ink (negative earnings). At the end of the year, he created "ghost" inventory by recording fake inventory purchases. He offset these transactions by "adjustments" to Cost of goods sold, thereby boosting profit and strengthening the balance sheet. Fortified with great financials, he got bank loans that allowed him to build up a regional chain of stores, buy a local sports franchise, and take on the lifestyle of a celebrity. When the economy in the region tanked, he could no longer cover his losses with new debt or equity infusions, and the whole empire fell like a house of cards.

Requirements

1. Name several parties that could have been hurt by the actions of Carl Montague.
2. What kind of adjustment to Cost of goods sold (debit or credit) would have the effect of boosting earnings?

● Financial Statement Case 6-1

The notes are an important part of a company's financial statements, giving valuable details that would clutter the tabular data presented in the statements. This case will help you learn to use a company's inventory notes. Refer to the **Amazon.com** financial statements and related notes in Appendix A at the end of the book, and answer the following questions:

Requirements

1. How much was the **Amazon** merchandise inventory at December 31, 2009? At December 31, 2008?
2. Which cost method does **Amazon** use for inventories? How does **Amazon** value its inventories? See Note 1.
3. By rearranging the cost-of-goods-sold formula, you can compute purchases, which are not reported in the **Amazon** statements. How much were **Amazon**'s inventory purchases during 2009?

● Team Project 6-1

Link Back to Chapter 5 (Gross Profit Percentage and Inventory Turnover). Obtain the annual reports of as many companies as you have team members—one company per team member. Most companies post their financial statements on their Web sites.

Requirements

1. Identify the inventory method used by each company.
2. Compute each company's gross profit percentage and rate of inventory turnover for the most recent two years.
3. For the industries of the companies you are analyzing, obtain the industry averages for gross profit percentage and inventory turnover from Robert Morris Associates, *Annual Statement Studies*; Dun and Bradstreet, *Industry Norms and Key Business Ratios*; or Leo Troy, *Almanac of Business and Industrial Financial Ratios*.
4. How well does each of your companies compare to the average for its industry? What insight about your companies can you glean from these ratios?

● Communication Activity 6-1

In 50 words or fewer, explain the difference in calculating COGS using the FIFO, LIFO, and average-cost methods.

Quick Check Answers

1. *c* 2. *a* 3. b 4. *d* 5. b 6. *d* 7. *b* 8. *a* 9. b 10. *b*

For online homework, exercises, and problems that provide you immediate feedback, please visit myaccountinglab.com.

Accounting for Inventory in a Periodic System

We described the periodic inventory system briefly in Chapter 5 and in Appendix 5A. Accounting is simpler in a periodic system because the company keeps no daily running record of inventory on hand. The only way to determine the ending inventory and cost of goods sold in a periodic system is to count the goods—usually at the end of the year. The periodic system works well for a small business in which the inventory can be controlled by visual inspection—that is, the inventory usually is not large in size or dollar amount.

This appendix illustrates how the periodic system works. The accounting in a periodic system is similar to a perpetual system, except for the following aspects:

8 Account for periodic inventory using the three most common costing methods

1. The periodic system uses four additional accounts:

   • **Purchases**—this account holds the cost of inventory as it is purchased. Purchases carries a debit balance and is an expense account.

   • **Purchase discounts**—this contra account carries a credit balance. Discounts for early payment of purchases are recorded here.

   • **Purchase returns and allowances**—this contra account carries a credit balance. Items purchased but returned to the vendor are recorded in this account. Allowances granted by a vendor are also recorded in this account.

   • **Freight in**—this account holds the transportation cost paid on inventory purchases. It carries a debit balance and is an expense account.

   In the perpetual system, all these costs go into the Inventory account.

2. The end-of-period entries are more extensive in the periodic system because we must close out the beginning inventory balance and set up the cost of the ending inventory. This appendix illustrates the closing process for the periodic system.

3. Cost of goods sold in a periodic system is computed by the following formula (using assumed amounts for this illustration):

Beginning inventory (ending inventory from the preceding period)	$ 5,000
Net purchases (often abbreviated as Purchases)	20,000*
Cost of goods available	25,000
Ending inventory (on hand at the end of the current period)	(7,000)
Cost of goods sold	$18,000

*Net purchases is determined as follows (all amounts assumed):	
Purchases	$21,000
Purchase discounts	(2,000)
Purchase returns and allowances	(5,000)
Freight in	6,000
Net purchases	$20,000

Inventory Costing in the Periodic System

The various inventory costing methods (FIFO, LIFO, and average) in a periodic inventory system follow the pattern illustrated earlier for the perpetual system. To show how the periodic system works, we use the same Smart Touch Learning data that we used for the perpetual system, as follows:

SMART TOUCH LEARNING DVD0503

			Number of Units	Unit Cost
Jul	1	Beginning inventory	2	$40
	5	Purchase	6	45
	26	Purchase	9	47
	31	Ending inventory	3	?

We use these data to illustrate FIFO, LIFO, and average cost.

For all three inventory costing methods, cost of goods available is always the sum of beginning inventory plus net purchases:

Beginning inventory (2 units @ $40)	$ 80
Net purchases (6 units @ $45) + (9 units @ $47)........................	693
Cost of goods available (17 units)	$773

The different methods—FIFO, LIFO, and average cost—compute different amounts for ending inventory and cost of goods sold. In other words, the $773 invested in cost of goods available for sale will be either on the balance sheet in Inventory, or expensed on the income statement, Cost of goods sold.

First-In, First-Out (FIFO) Method

Under FIFO, the ending inventory comes from the newest—the most recent—purchases, which cost $47 per unit. FIFO is illustrated in the box that follows on the next page. Notice that the FIFO periodic Cost of goods sold is $632, exactly the same amount as we got using the FIFO perpetual system. Periodic and perpetual are *always* the same for FIFO because FIFO sells oldest inventory acquisitions first. Therefore, it does not matter when FIFO is calculated; the first purchase will always be the same whether we calculate cost of goods sold on the sale date (Perpetual) or at the end of the period (Periodic).

Last-In, First-Out (LIFO) Method

Under LIFO, the ending inventory comes from the oldest cost of the period—in this case the beginning inventory of two units that cost $40 per unit, plus the first purchase at $45. LIFO is also illustrated in the box that follows on the next page.

Average-Cost Method

In the average-cost method, we compute a single average cost per unit for the entire period:

Cost of goods available	÷	Number of units available	=	Average cost per unit
$773	÷	17 units	=	$45.47

Then apply this average cost to compute ending inventory and cost of goods sold, as shown in the far right column:

	FIFO	LIFO	Average
Cost of goods available	$773	$773	$773
Ending inventory			
FIFO (3 units @ $47)............................	(141)		
LIFO (2 units @ $40			
1 unit @ $45).............................		(125)	
Average (3 units @ $45.47)			(136)
Cost of goods sold...	$632	$648	$637

Comparing the Perpetual and Periodic Inventory Systems

Exhibit 6A-1 provides a side-by-side comparison of the perpetual and the periodic inventory systems.

EXHIBIT 6A-1 | **Comparing the Perpetual and Periodic Inventory Systems**

JOURNAL ENTRIES

Perpetual System			Periodic System		
Inventory (A+)	$570,000		Purchases (E+)	$570,000	
Accounts payable (L+)		570,000	Accounts payable (L+)		$570,000
Purchased inventory on account.			*Purchased inventory on account.*		
Accounts payable (L–)	20,000		Accounts payable (L–)	20,000	
Inventory (A–)		20,000	Purchase returns and allowances (CE+)		20,000
Returned damaged goods to seller.			*Returned damaged goods to seller.*		
Accounts receivable (A+)	900,000		Accounts receivable (A+)	900,000	
Sales revenue (R+)		900,000	Sales revenue (R+)		900,000
Sale on account.			*Sale on account.*		
Cost of goods sold (E+)	530,000		No entry for cost of goods sold.		
Inventory (A–)		530,000			
Cost of goods sold.					

CLOSING ENTRIES (End of the Period)

			1. Cost of goods sold (E+)	$100,000	
			Inventory (beginning) (A–)		$100,000
			Transfer beginning inventory to COGS.		
			2. Inventory (ending) (A+)	120,000	
			Cost of goods sold (E–)		120,000
			Record ending inventory physical count.		
			3. Cost of goods sold (E+)	550,000	
			Purchase returns and allowances (CE–)	20,000	
			Purchases (E–)		570,000
			Transfer net purchases to COGS.		
1.	Income summary	530,000	4. Income summary	530,000	
	Cost of goods sold (E–)		530,000	Cost of goods sold (E–)		530,000
	Close Cost of goods sold.			*Close Cost of goods sold.*		
				($100,000 – $120,000 + $550,000 = $530,000)	

EXHIBIT 6A-1 | **Continued**

LEDGER T-ACCOUNTS

Perpetual System		Periodic System	

Inventory		Cost of goods sold	
Beg Bal 100,000	20,000	Bal 530,000	Clo 530,000
570,000	530,000		
End Bal 120,000			

Inventory		Cost of goods sold	
Beg Bal 100,000	Clo 1 100,000	Clo 1 100,000	Clo 2 120,000
Clo 2 120,000		Clo 3 550,000	Clo 4 530,000
End Bal 120,000			

REPORTING IN THE FINANCIAL STATEMENTS

Perpetual System		Periodic System	

Income Statement

Sales revenue....................................	$900,000
Cost of goods sold............................	530,000
Gross profit..	$370,000

Income Statement

Sales revenue...		$900,000
Cost of goods sold:		
Beginning inventory...........................	$ 100,000*	
Purchases........................	$570,000	
Less: Purchase returns		
and allowances.......	20,000	550,000
Cost of goods available.........................		$ 650,000
Less: Ending inventory..........................		120,000
Cost of goods sold...		530,000
Gross profit..		$370,000

Balance Sheet—Partial

Current assets:

Cash...	$ XXX
Accounts receivable.........................	XXX
Inventory..	120,000

Balance Sheet—Partial

Current assets:

Cash...	$ XXX
Accounts receivable.........................	XXX
Inventory..	120,000

Appendix 6A Assignments

• Exercises

E6A-1 ⑧ **Computing periodic inventory amounts [10–15 min]**

The periodic inventory records of Synergy Prosthetics indicate the following at July 31:

Jul	1	Beginning inventory ...	6	units @	$60
	8	Purchase	5	units @	$67
	15	Purchase	10	units @	$70
	26	Purchase	5	units @	$85

At July 31, Synergy counts two units of inventory on hand.

Requirement

1. Compute ending inventory and cost of goods sold, using each of the following methods:
   a. Average cost (round average unit cost to the nearest cent)
   b. First-in, first-out
   c. Last-in, first-out

E6A-2 ⑧ **Journalizing periodic inventory transactions [10–15 min]**
Halton Prosthetics uses the periodic inventory system and had the following transactions:

    a. Purchase of inventory on account, $2,000
    b. Sale of inventory on account for $3,100
    c. Closing entries:
      (1) Beginning inventory, $480
      (2) Ending inventory at FIFO cost, $670
      (3) Purchases, $2,000
      (4) Cost of goods sold at FIFO cost, $1,810

Requirement

1. Journalize the transactions for the company.

E6A-3 ⑧ **Computing periodic inventory amounts [10–15 min]**
Consider the data of the following companies:

Company	Net sales	Beginning inventory	Net purchases	Ending inventory	Cost of goods sold	Gross profit
Red	$ 101,000	$ 22,000	$ 65,000	$ 17,000	(a) $	31,000
Yellow	(b)	25,000	95,000	(c)	96,000	40,000
Orange	93,000	(d)	52,000	22,000	62,000	(e)
Green	86,000	12,000	(f)	5,000	(g)	49,000

Requirements

1. Supply the missing amounts in the preceeding table.
2. Prepare the income statement for Red Company, which uses the periodic inventory system. Include a complete heading and show the full computation of cost of goods sold. Red's operating expenses for the year were $11,000.

● Problem (Group A)

P6A-4A ⑧ **Computing periodic inventory amounts [15–20 min]**
A Tomorrows Electronic Center began October with 90 units of inventory that cost $70 each. During October, the store made the following purchases:

Oct	3	. . . .	20 @ $75
	12	. . . .	40 @ $78
	18	. . . .	60 @ $84

Tomorrows uses the periodic inventory system, and the physical count at October 31 indicates that 110 units of inventory are on hand.

Requirements

1. Determine the ending inventory and cost of goods sold amounts for the October financial statements using the average cost, FIFO, and LIFO methods.
2. Sales revenue for October totaled $26,000. Compute Tomorrows' gross profit for October using each method.
3. Which method will result in the lowest income taxes for Tomorrows? Why? Which method will result in the highest net income for Tomorrows? Why?

MyAccountingLab

• Problem (Group B)

P6A-5B ⑧ **Computing periodic inventory amounts [15–20 min]**

Easy Use Electronic Center began October with 80 units of inventory that cost $57 each. During October, the store made the following purchases:

Oct	3	. . . .	10 @ $65
	12	. . . .	30 @ $70
	18	. . . .	70 @ $72

Easy Use uses the periodic inventory system, and the physical count at October 31 indicates that 115 units of inventory are on hand.

Requirements

1. Determine the ending inventory and cost of goods sold amounts for the October financial statements using the average cost, FIFO, and LIFO methods.

2. Sales revenue for October totaled $22,000. Compute Easy Use's gross profit for October using each method.

3. Which method will result in the lowest income taxes for Easy Use? Why? Which method will result in the highest net income for Easy Use? Why?

7

Internal Control and Cash

Assets are listed in order of liquidity. How are you protecting the assets of the company so that your hard work is not lost?

SMART TOUCH LEARNING
Balance Sheet
May 31, 2013

Assets				Liabilities	
Current assets:				Current liabilities:	
Cash		$ 4,800		Accounts payable	$ 48,700
Accounts receivable		2,600		Salary payable	900
Inventory		30,500		Interest payable	100
Supplies		600		Unearned service revenue	400
Prepaid rent		2,000		Total current liabilities	50,100
Total current assets			$ 40,500	Long-term liabilities:	
Plant assets:				Notes payable	20,000
Furniture	$18,000			Total liabilities	70,100
Less: Accumulated depreciation—furniture	300	17,700			
Building	48,000				
Less: Accumulated depreciation—building	200	47,800		Owner's Equity	
Total plant assets			65,500	Bright, capital	35,900
Total assets			$106,000	Total liabilities and owner's equity	$106,000

Learning Objectives

1. Define internal control

2. Explain the Sarbanes-Oxley Act

3. List and describe the components of internal control and control procedures

4. Explain control procedures unique to e-commerce

5. Demonstrate the use of a bank account as a control device

6. Prepare a bank reconciliation and journalize the related entries

7. Apply internal controls to cash receipts

8. Apply internal controls to cash payments

9. Explain and journalize petty cash transactions

10. Identify ethical dilemmas in an internal control situation

You've worked hard to make your company successful—so hard in fact that the company is expanding. As companies expand, authority and control must be given to other employees. Delegating control doesn't mean you can't protect your business's assets or still have your vision for the company executed. So how do you protect all the business has worked for?

In the preceding chapter, Smart Touch Learning sold training DVDs. The training DVDs were a big hit, so Smart Touch plans to expand the business. Recognizing she can't perform all the business's tasks anymore, Sheena Bright's brother, Andrew, has agreed to join Smart Touch as the marketing director. He can sell the training materials around neighboring colleges and help develop an online marketing plan for new DVDs. In addition, he will also be doing the company's accounting.

With boxes of DVDs crammed into every corner, Smart Touch's current office space is getting outgrown. Sheena will need to rent warehouse space or buy another building. Expansion will bring a new set of challenges:

- How will Sheena safeguard Smart Touch's assets?
- How will she ensure that Andrew follows policies that are best for the business?

● ● ●

This chapter presents a framework for dealing with these issues. It also shows how to account for cash, the most liquid of all assets.

Internal Control

1 Define internal control

A key responsibility of a business manager is to control operations. Owners set goals, hire managers to lead the way, and hire employees to carry out the business plan. **Internal control** is the organizational plan and all the related measures designed to accomplish the following:

1. **Safeguard assets.** A company must protect its assets; otherwise it is throwing away resources. If you fail to safeguard your cash, the most liquid of assets, it will quickly slip away.

2. **Encourage employees to follow company policy.** Everyone in an organization needs to work toward the same goals. With Sheena's brother, Andrew, operating part of Smart Touch, it is important for the business to identify policies to help meet the company's goals. These policies are also important for the company to ensure that all customers are treated similarly, and that results can be measured effectively.

3. **Promote operational efficiency.** Businesses cannot afford to waste resources. Sheena and Andrew work hard to make sales for Smart Touch and do not want to waste any of the benefits. If Smart Touch can buy a particular training DVD for $3, why pay $4? Promoting operational efficiency reduces expenses and increases business profits.

4. **Ensure accurate, reliable accounting records.** Accurate, reliable accounting records are essential. Without reliable records, managers cannot tell which part of the business is profitable and which part needs improvement. Smart Touch could be losing money on every DVD sold and not realize it—unless it keeps good records for the cost of its products.

Stop & Think...

Internal controls do not only apply to "big business." We do things every day that mirror the four internal control measures defined previously. Consider your car, for example. You always lock the doors and you buy gas at the station with the lowest price per gallon. How do these personal acts relate to an internal control plan? Locking the door is an example of safeguarding assets. Finding the lowest price per gallon for gas is an example of operational efficiency.

Key Takeaway

Internal control systems are the rules and boundaries that help protect what the company owns, ensure that the company is operating efficiently within those rules, and ensure that the accounting reports accurately show transactions that have occurred.

How critical are internal controls? They are so important that the U.S. Congress passed a law requiring **public companies**—those that sell their stock to the general public—to maintain a system of internal controls.

The Sarbanes-Oxley Act (SOX)

2 Explain the Sarbanes-Oxley Act

The **Enron** and **WorldCom** accounting scandals rocked the United States in the early years of this millenium. **Enron** overstated profits and went out of business almost overnight. **WorldCom** (now part of **Verizon**) reported expenses as assets and overstated both profits and assets. The same accounting firm, **Arthur Andersen**, had audited both companies' financial statements. **Arthur Andersen** voluntarily closed its doors in 2002 after nearly 90 years in public accounting.

As the scandals unfolded, many people asked, "How could this happen? Where were the auditors?" To address public concern, Congress passed the **Sarbanes-Oxley Act**, abbreviated as SOX. SOX revamped corporate governance in the United States and affected the accounting profession. Here are some of the SOX provisions:

1. Public companies must issue an **internal control report**, which is a report by management describing its responsibility for and the adequacy of internal controls over financial reporting. Additionally, an outside auditor must evaluate the client's internal controls and report on the internal controls as part of the audit report.

2. A new body, the Public Company Accounting Oversight Board (PCAOB), oversees the work of auditors of public companies.

3. Accounting firms are not allowed to audit a public client and also provide certain consulting services for the same client.

4. Stiff penalties await violators—25 years in prison for securities fraud and 20 years for an executive making false sworn statements.

In 2005, the former chief executive of **WorldCom** was convicted of securities fraud and sentenced to 25 years in prison. The top executives of **Enron** were also sent to prison. You can see that internal controls and related matters can have serious consequences.

Exhibit 7-1 diagrams the shield that internal controls provide for an organization. Protected by the wall, people do business securely. How does a business achieve good internal control? The next section identifies the components of internal control.

> **Key Takeaway**
>
> The Sarbanes-Oxley Act changed the rules for auditors, limiting what services they can perform in addition to the audit and requiring the evaluation of internal controls. SOX also created the PCAOB to watch over the work of public company auditors.

EXHIBIT 7-1 | **The Shield of Internal Control**

The Components of Internal Control

3 List and describe the components of internal control and control procedures

A business can achieve its internal control objectives by applying five components. (TIP: You can remember the five components by using the acronym MICER.)

- Monitoring of controls
- Information system

- Control procedures
- Control Environment
- Risk assessment

Monitoring of Controls

Companies hire auditors to monitor their controls. **Internal auditors** are employees of the business who ensure that the company's employees are following company policies and that operations are running efficiently. Internal auditors also determine whether the company is following legal requirements to monitor internal controls to safeguard assets. **An internal auditor is an employee of the company he or she is auditing.** **External auditors** are outside accountants who are completely independent of the business. They evaluate the controls to ensure that the financial statements are presented fairly in accordance with the generally accepted accounting principles (GAAP) and they may suggest improvements to help the business. **An external auditor is an independent evaluator of a company's financial information.**

Information System

As we have seen, the information system is critical. Controls must be in place within the information system to ensure that only authorized users have access to various parts of the accounting information system. Additionally, controls must be in place to insure adequate approvals for recorded transactions are in place. The decision makers need accurate information to keep track of assets and measure profits and losses.

Control Procedures

Control procedures are designed to ensure that the business's goals are achieved. The next section discusses internal control procedures.

Control Environment

The control environment is the "tone at the top" of the business. It starts with the owner or CEO and the top managers. They must behave honorably to set a good example for company employees. Each must demonstrate the importance of internal controls if he or she expects the employees to take the controls seriously. Former executives of **Enron** and **WorldCom** failed to establish a good control environment and went to prison as a result.

Risk Assessment

A company must identify its risks. For example, **Kraft Foods** faces the risk that its food products may harm people, **American Airlines** planes may crash, **Sony** faces copyright infringement risks, and all companies face the risk of bankruptcy. Companies facing difficulties might be tempted to falsify the financial statements to make themselves look better than they really are. As part of the internal control system, the company's business risk, as well as risk over individual accounts, must be assessed. The higher the risk, the more controls must be in place to safeguard the company's assets.

Internal Control Procedures

Whether the business is Smart Touch, **Microsoft**, or a **BP** gas station, all companies need the following internal control procedures:

Competent, Reliable, and Ethical Personnel

Employees should be competent, reliable, and ethical. Paying good salaries will attract high-quality employees. Employees should also be trained to do the job and their work should be adequately supervised.

Assignment of Responsibilities

In a business with good internal controls, no duty is overlooked. Each employee has certain responsibilities. At Smart Touch, Sheena Bright is the owner. Suppose she writes the checks in order to control cash payments. She lets Andrew, her brother, do the accounting. In a large company, the person in charge of writing checks is called the **treasurer**. The chief accounting officer is called the **controller**. Clearly assigned responsibilities create job accountability, thus ensuring all important tasks get done.

Separation of Duties

Smart management divides responsibility between two or more people. **Separation of duties** limits fraud and promotes the accuracy of the accounting records. Separation of duties can be divided into two parts:

1. **Separate operations from accounting.** Accounting should be completely separate from the operating departments, such as production and sales. What would happen if sales personnel recorded the company's revenue? Sales figures could be inflated, and then top managers would not know how much the company actually sold.

2. **Separate the custody of assets from accounting.** Accountants must not handle cash, and cashiers must not have access to the accounting records. If one employee has both duties, the employee could steal cash and conceal the theft in the accounting records. The treasurer of a company handles cash, and the controller accounts for the cash. Neither person has both responsibilities.

Audits

To assess their accounting records, most companies perform both internal and external audits. As noted earlier, an audit is an examination by an auditor of the company's financial statements and accounting system. Internal audits are performed by employees of the company. External audits are performed by independent auditors who are NOT employees of the company. To evaluate the accounting system, auditors must examine the internal controls. As part of the evaluation, auditors will review the internal control system and test controls to ensure the controls are working properly. For example, a control might require authorization by a manager for payments over $50. An auditor would check a sample of payments greater than $50 to determine if all were properly authorized by a manager.

Documents

Documents provide the details of business transactions. Documents include invoices and orders and may be paper or electronic. Documents should be pre-numbered to prevent theft and inefficiency. A gap in the numbered sequence draws attention.

For example, for Smart Touch, a key document is the customer invoice. The manager can compare the total sales on the invoices with the amount of cash received and deposited into the bank account.

Electronic Devices

Accounting systems are relying less on paper documents and more on electronic documents and digital storage devices. For example, retailers such as **Target** and **Macy's** control inventory by attaching an electronic sensor to merchandise. The cashier removes the sensor. If a customer tries to leave the store with the sensor attached, an alarm sounds. According to Checkpoint Systems, these devices reduce theft by as much as 50%.

Other Controls

The types of other controls are as endless as the types of businesses that exist. Some examples of other common controls are

- fireproof vaults to store important documents;
- burglar alarms, fire alarms, and security cameras; and
- loss-prevention specialists who train company employees to spot suspicious activity.

As another control, fidelity bonds are purchased for employees who handle cash. The bond is an insurance policy that reimburses the company for any losses due to employee theft. Mandatory vacations and job rotation improve internal control. These controls also improve morale by giving employees a broad view of the business.

Internal Controls for E-Commerce

 4 Explain control procedures unique to e-commerce

E-commerce creates its own unique types of risks. Hackers may gain access to confidential information, such as account numbers and passwords, or may introduce computer viruses, Trojans, or phishing expeditions.

Stolen Account Numbers or Passwords

Suppose you buy CDs from Greg's Tunes' online store. To make the purchase, you must create an online account with a password for the site. When you submit your purchase, your credit card number must travel through the Internet, potentially exposing it, your account, and password information. Additionally, wireless (Wi-Fi) networks are creating new security hazards. Accessing unsecured Wi-Fi networks exposes the computer and consequently the company's data to the potential for network attacks and viruses.

For example, in 2008, **Heartland Payment Systems**, a provider of credit and debit card processing services, had its network security system breached. Over 100 million cards were potentially compromised. Heartland reported expenses related to the breach of $139.4 million and insurance recoveries related to the breach of only $30.7 million through March 31, 2010.

Computer Viruses and Trojans

A **computer virus** is a malicious program that (a) enters program code without consent and (b) performs destructive actions. A **Trojan** hides inside a legitimate program and works like a virus. Both can destroy or alter data, make bogus calculations, and infect files. (This, of course, is a risk to any business using the Internet.) Most firms have found a virus at some point in time in their system.

Suppose an individual plants a virus into your school's computer that changes all the grades for students for a semester. This type of virus or Trojan could undermine not only a grade, but a school's reputation, to say the least.

Phishing Expeditions

Thieves phish by creating bogus Web sites, such as AOL4Free.com. The neat-sounding Web site attracts lots of visitors, and the thieves obtain account numbers and passwords from unsuspecting people who use the bogus site. They then use the data for illicit purposes.

Security Measures

To address the risks posed by e-commerce, companies have devised a number of security measures. One technique for protecting customer data is encryption. **Encryption** rearranges plain-text messages by a mathematical process. **The encrypted message cannot be read by those who do not know the code.** An accounting encryption example uses check-sum digits for account numbers. Each account number has its last digit equal to the sum of the previous digits. For example, consider customer number 2237, where 2 + 2 + 3 = 7. Any account number failing this test triggers an error message.

Another technique for protecting data is firewalls. **Firewalls** limit access into a local network. Members can access the network but nonmembers cannot. Usually several firewalls are built into the system. **Think of a firewall as a fortress with multiple walls protecting the king's chamber in the center.** At the point of entry, passwords, PINs (personal identification numbers), and signatures are used. More sophisticated firewalls are used deeper in the network. The PIN security starts with Firewall 3 and works toward the network through two additional PIN-secured firewalls.

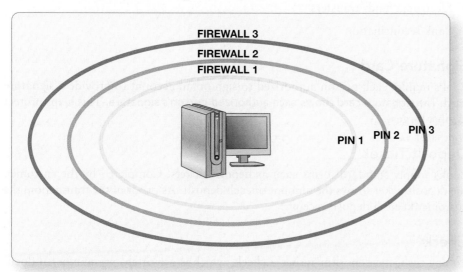

The Limitations of Internal Control—Costs and Benefits

Unfortunately, most internal controls can be overcome. **Collusion**—two or more people working together—can beat internal controls. For example, consider the following scenario with Galaxy Theater. Ralph and Lana, employees of Galaxy Theater, can design a scheme in which Ralph, the ticket seller, sells tickets and pockets the cash from 10 customers. Lana, the ticket taker, admits 10 customers to the theater without taking their tickets. Ralph and Lana split the cash. Ralph and Lana have colluded to circumvent controls, resulting in Galaxy Theater losing revenues. To prevent this situation, the manager must take additional steps, such as matching the number of people in the theater against the number of ticket stubs retained, which takes time away from the manager's other duties. It is difficult and costly to plan controls that can prevent collusion.

The stricter the internal control system, the more it costs. A complex system of internal control can strangle the business with red tape. How tight should the controls be? Internal controls must always be judged in light of their costs versus their benefits. Following is an example of a good cost/benefit relationship: A security guard at a **Walmart** store costs about $28,000 a year. On average, each guard prevents about $50,000 of theft. The net savings to **Walmart** is $22,000. An example of a bad cost/benefit relationship would be paying the same security guard $28,000 a year to guard a $1,000 cash drawer. The net cost exceeds the benefit by $27,000.

Key Takeaway

Internal control for e-commerce changes constantly as technology continues to advance and new threats to online security appear. Protecting the company's computer systems and thus the company's electronic assets from these threats is a top priority when designing a company's internal control system.

The Bank Account as a Control Device

 Demonstrate the use of a bank account as a control device

Cash is the most liquid asset because it is the medium of exchange. Cash is easy to conceal and relatively easy to steal. As a result, most businesses create specific controls for cash.

Keeping cash in a **bank account** helps control cash because banks have established practices for safeguarding customers' money. The controls of a bank account include the following:

- Signature card
- Deposit ticket
- Check
- Bank statement
- Electronic funds transfers
- Bank reconciliation

Signature Card

Banks require each person authorized to sign on an account to provide a **signature card. The signature card shows each authorized person's signature.** This helps protect against forgery.

Deposit Ticket

Banks supply standard forms such as **deposit tickets.** Completed by the customer, the deposit ticket shows the amount of each deposit. As proof of the transaction, the customer keeps a deposit receipt.

Check

To pay cash, the depositor writes a **check**, which is a written, pre-numbered document that tells the bank to pay the designated party a specified amount. There are three parties to a check:

- The **maker**, who signs the check
- The **payee**, to whom the check is paid
- The bank, on which the check is drawn

Exhibit 7-2 shows a check drawn by Smart Touch, the maker. The check has two parts, the check itself and the **remittance advice** below. This optional attachment tells the payee the reason for the payment.

Bank Statement

Banks send monthly statements to customers. A **bank statement** reports what the bank did with the customer's cash. The statement shows the account's beginning and ending balances, cash receipts, and payments. Included with the statement are physical or scanned copies of the maker's **canceled checks** (or the actual paid checks). Exhibit 7-3 is the April 2013 bank statement of Smart Touch.

Electronic Funds Transfer

Electronic funds transfer (EFT) moves cash by electronic communication. It is cheaper to pay without having to mail a check, so many people pay their mortgage, rent, and insurance by EFT. Debit card transactions and direct deposits are EFTs.

EXHIBIT 7-2 | **Check with Remittance Advice**

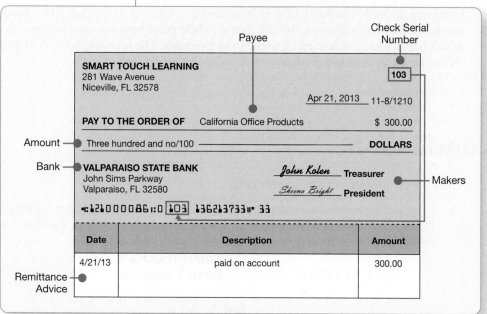

Payee

Check Serial Number

SMART TOUCH LEARNING
281 Wave Avenue
Niceville, FL 32578

Apr 21, 2013   11-8/1210

PAY TO THE ORDER OF   California Office Products $ 300.00

Amount → Three hundred and no/100 ——————————— **DOLLARS**

Bank → VALPARAISO STATE BANK
John Sims Parkway
Valparaiso, FL 32580

John Kolen Treasurer
Sheena Bright President

← Makers

⑂121000086⑂:0 103 136213733⑂ 33

Date	Description	Amount
4/21/13	paid on account	300.00

Remittance Advice

EXHIBIT 7-3 | **Bank Statement**

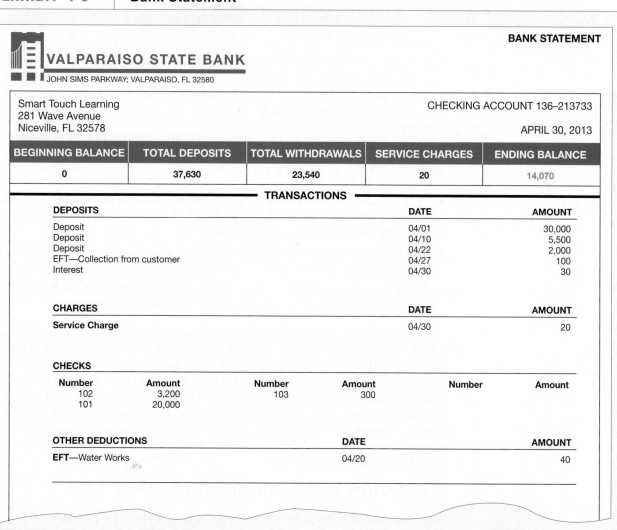

BANK STATEMENT

VALPARAISO STATE BANK

JOHN SIMS PARKWAY; VALPARAISO, FL 32580

Smart Touch Learning
281 Wave Avenue
Niceville, FL 32578

CHECKING ACCOUNT 136–213733

APRIL 30, 2013

BEGINNING BALANCE	TOTAL DEPOSITS	TOTAL WITHDRAWALS	SERVICE CHARGES	ENDING BALANCE
0	37,630	23,540	20	14,070

TRANSACTIONS

DEPOSITS	DATE	AMOUNT
Deposit	04/01	30,000
Deposit	04/10	5,500
Deposit	04/22	2,000
EFT—Collection from customer	04/27	100
Interest	04/30	30

CHARGES	DATE	AMOUNT
Service Charge	04/30	20

CHECKS

Number	Amount	Number	Amount	Number	Amount
102	3,200	103	300		
101	20,000				

OTHER DEDUCTIONS	DATE	AMOUNT
EFT—Water Works	04/20	40

Bank Reconciliation

Preparing a bank reconciliation is considered a control over cash. The **bank reconciliation** reconciles on a specific date the differences between cash on the company's books and cash according to the bank's records. The preparation of the bank reconciliation is discussed in detail in the following section.

The Bank Reconciliation

 6 Prepare a bank reconciliation and journalize the related entries

There are two records of a business's cash:

1. The Cash account in the company's general ledger. April's T-account for Smart Touch, originally presented in Chapter 2, is reproduced below. Exhibit 7-4 shows that Smart Touch's ending cash balance is $21,000.

EXHIBIT 7-4	Smart Touch's Cash T-account

Cash			
Apr 1	30,000	Apr 2	20,000
Apr 8	5,500	Apr 15	3,200
Apr 22	2,000	Apr 21	300
Apr 24	9,000	Apr 30	2,000
Bal Apr 30	21,000		

2. The bank statement, which shows the cash receipts and payments transacted through the bank. In Exhibit 7-3, however, the bank shows an ending balance of $14,070 for Smart Touch.

The books and the bank statement usually show different cash balances. Differences arise because of a time lag in recording transactions, called **timing differences**. Three examples of timing differences follow:

- When a business writes a check, it immediately deducts the amount in its checkbook. But the bank does not subtract the check from the company's account until the bank pays the check a few days later.
- Likewise, a company immediately adds the cash receipt for all its deposits. But it may take a day or two for the bank to add deposits to the company's balance.
- EFT payments and cash receipts are often recorded by the bank before a company learns of them. (We will discuss this in more detail later.)

To ensure accurate cash records, a company must update its checkbook (or check register) either online or after the company receives its bank statement. The result of this updating process creates a bank reconciliation. The bank reconciliation explains all differences between the company's cash records and the bank's records of the company's balance. The person who prepares the bank reconciliation should have no other cash duties. This means the reconciler should not be a person who has access to cash or has duties requiring journalizing cash transactions. Otherwise, he or she could steal cash and manipulate the reconciliation to conceal the theft.

Preparing the Bank Reconciliation

Here are the items that appear on a bank reconciliation. They all cause differences between the bank balance and the book balance. (We call a checkbook record [or check register] the "Books.")

Bank Side of the Reconciliation

The bank side contains items not yet recorded by the bank, but recorded by the company or errors made by the bank. These items include the following:

1. **Deposits in transit** (outstanding deposits). These deposits have been recorded and have already been added to the company's book balance, but the bank has not yet recorded them. **Deposits in transit are deposits the company made that haven't yet cleared the bank.** These are shown as "Add deposits in transit" on the bank side because when the bank does record these deposits, it will increase the bank balance.

2. **Outstanding checks.** These checks have been recorded and have already been deducted from the company's book balance, but the bank has not yet paid (deducted) them. **Outstanding checks are checks the company wrote that haven't yet cleared the bank.** They are shown as "Less outstanding checks" on the bank side because when the bank does record the checks, it will decrease the bank balance.

3. **Bank errors.** Bank errors are posting errors made by the bank that either incorrectly increase or decrease the bank balance. All bank errors are corrected on the Bank side of the reconciliation by reversing the effect of the errors.

Book Side of the Reconciliation

The book side contains items not yet recorded by the company on its books but that are recorded by the bank, or errors made by the company. Items to show on the *Book* side include the following:

1. **Bank collections.** Bank collections are cash receipts the bank has received and recorded for a company's account but that the company has not recorded yet on its books. An example of a bank collection would be if a business has its customers pay directly to its bank. This is called a **lock-box system**. This system helps to reduce theft. Another example is a bank's collecting of a note receivable for a business. A bank collection (which increases the bank balance) that appears on the bank statement will show as "Add bank collections" on the book side of the reconciliation because it represents cash receipts not yet recorded by the company.

2. **Electronic funds transfers.** The bank may receive or pay cash on a company's behalf. An EFT may be a cash receipt or a cash payment. These will either show up on the book side of the reconciliation as "Add EFT" for receipts not yet added to the company's books or "Less EFT" for payments not yet deducted on the company's books.

3. **Service charge.** This cash payment is the bank's fee for processing a company's transactions. This will show as "Less service charges" on the book side of the reconciliation because it represents a cash payment not yet subtracted from the company's cash balance.

4. **Interest revenue on a checking account.** A business will earn interest if it keeps enough cash in its account. The bank statement tells the company of this cash receipt. This will show as "Add interest revenue" on the book side of the reconciliation because it represents cash receipts not yet added in the company's cash balance.

5. **Nonsufficient funds (NSF) checks.** These are earlier cash receipts that have turned out to be worthless. NSF checks (sometimes called *hot checks* or *bad checks*) are treated as subtractions on a company's bank reconciliation. **NSF checks are customer checks the company has received and deposited for which the customer doesn't have enough money in his or her bank account to cover.** NSF checks will show as "Less NSF checks" on the book side of the reconciliation.

6. **The cost of printed checks.** This cash payment is handled like a service charge. This cost is subtracted on the book side of the reconciliation because it represents a cash payment not yet subtracted from the company's cash balance.

7. **Book errors.** Book errors are errors made on the books of the company that either incorrectly increase or decrease the cash balance in the company's general ledger. All book errors are corrected on the book side of the reconciliation by reversing the effect of the errors.

Bank Reconciliation Illustrated

The bank statement in Exhibit 7-3 shows that the April 30 bank balance of Smart Touch is $14,070 (upper-right corner). However, the company's Cash account has a balance of $21,000, as shown in Exhibit 7-4. This situation calls for a bank reconciliation to explain the differences. Exhibit 7-5, Panel A, lists the reconciling items for your easy reference, and Panel B shows the completed reconciliation.

EXHIBIT 7-5 | **Bank Reconciliation**

PANEL A—Reconciling Items

Bank side:

1. Deposit in transit, Apr 24, $9,000.
2. Outstanding check no. 104, $2,000.

Book side:

3. EFT receipt from customer, $100.
4. Interest revenue earned on bank balance, $30.
5. Bank service charge, $20.
6. EFT payment of water bill, $40.

PANEL B—Bank Reconciliation

SMART TOUCH LEARNING
Bank Reconciliation
April 30, 2013

BANK			BOOK		
Balance, April 30, 2013		$14,070	Balance, April 30, 3013		$21,000
ADD:			ADD:		
1. Deposit in transit		9,000	3. EFT receipt from customer		100
		$23,070	4. Interest revenue earned on bank balance		30
					$21,130
LESS:			LESS:		
2. Outstanding checks			5. Service charge	$20	
No. 104	$2,000	2,000	6. EFT payment of water bill	40	60
Adjusted bank balance, April 30, 2013		$21,070	Adjusted book balance, April 30, 2013		$21,070

These amounts should agree.

SUMMARY OF THE VARIOUS RECONCILING ITEMS:

BANK BALANCE—ALWAYS

- *Add* deposits in transit.
- *Subtract* outstanding checks.
- *Add* or *subtract* corrections of bank errors.

BOOK BALANCE—ALWAYS

- *Add* bank collections, interest revenue, and EFT receipts.
- *Subtract* service charges, NSF checks, and EFT payments.
- *Add* or *subtract* corrections of book errors.

Stop & Think...

Although we all have our own personal methods for balancing our check book, some are more formal than others. The bank reconciliation in Exhibit 7-5 is mirrored on the back page of each statement you receive from the bank every month. Take a look at your most recent bank statement and see how similar parts of it look to the bank statement in Exhibit 7-3.

Journalizing Transactions from the Reconciliation

The bank reconciliation is an accountant's tool separate from the journals and ledgers. It does *not* account for transactions in the journal. To get the transactions into the accounts, we must make journal entries and post to the ledger. All items on the Book side of the bank reconciliation require journal entries. We make no entries on the Bank side because we do not have access to the bank's general ledger.

The bank reconciliation in Exhibit 7-5 requires Smart Touch to make journal entries to bring the Cash account up-to-date. Numbers in the journal entries in Exhibit 7-6 correspond to the reconciling items listed in Exhibit 7-5, Panel A, and to the Book side of the reconciliation in Panel B. Note: We chose to list each item in a separate journal entry here, but one compound entry could be made instead of the four separate entries illustrated in Exhibit 7-6.

EXHIBIT 7-6 | **Entries from Bank Reconciliation**

	2013			
3	Apr 30	Cash (A+)	100	
		Accounts receivable (A–)		100
		To record account receivable collected by bank.		
4	30	Cash (A+)	30	
		Interest revenue (R+)		30
		To record interest earned on bank balance.		
5	30	Miscellaneous expense (or Bank service charge expense) (E+)	20	
		Cash (A–)		20
		To record bank service charges incurred.		
6	30	Utilities expense (E+)	40	
		Cash (A–)		40
		To record payment of water bill by EFT.		

After posting the entries from Exhibit 7-6, the cash T-account will then appear as follows:

Cash

Apr 1	30,000	Apr 2	20,000
Apr 8	5,500	Apr 15	3,200
Apr 22	2,000	Apr 21	300
Apr 24	9,000	Apr 30	2,000
Bal Apr 30 before bank recon.	21,000		
AJE 3	100	AJE 5	20
AJE 4	30	AJE 6	40
Bal Apr 30 after posting bank reconciliation entries	21,070		

Stop & Think...

How do we "journalize" transactions from our personal bank reconciliation? For most of us, the answer is we write them down in our checkbook ledger. That is our personal "journal" of bank transactions.

Online Banking

Online banking allows a company to pay its bills and view its bank account electronically—the company does not have to wait until the end of the month to get a bank statement. With online banking, the company can reconcile transactions at any time and keep its account current whenever the company wishes. Exhibit 7-7 shows a page from the account history of Greg's Tunes' bank account.

EXHIBIT 7-7 | **Online Banking—Account History (like a Bank Statement)**

**Account History for Greg's Tunes # 5401-632-9
as of Close of Business 07/27/2017**

Account Details

Current Balance $5,306.43

Date ↓	Description	Withdrawals	Deposits	Balance
07/27/17	DEPOSIT		1,170.35	$ 5,306.43
07/26/17	26 DAYS-INTEREST		2.26	$ 4,136.08
07/24/17	Check #6130 View Image	500.00		$ 4,133.82
07/23/17	EFT PYMT VERIZON	61.15		$ 4,633.82
07/22/17	EFT PYMT AMEX PAYMENT	3,172.85		$ 4,694.97
07/15/17	Check #6123 View Image	830.00		$ 7,867.82
07/13/17	Check #6124 View Image	150.00		$ 8,697.82
07/11/17	ATM 4900 SANGER AVE	200.00		$ 8,847.82
07/09/17	Check #6119 View Image	30.00		$ 9,047.82
07/05/17	Check #6125 View Image	2,500.00		$ 9,077.82
07/04/17	ATM 4900 SANGER AVE	100.00		$11,577.82
07/01/17	DEPOSIT		9,026.37	$11,677.82

FDIC EQUAL HOUSING LENDER   E-Mail

The transaction history—like a bank statement—lists deposits, checks, EFT payments, ATM withdrawals, and interest earned on your bank balance. More and more banks today make it much easier to do the reconciliations. They not only have running daily balances available on the history, but they also have various icons that allow the company to reconcile to the checkbook online, pay bills online, and set up automatic payments for its bills. In addition, banks promote a paperless/green approach with electronic notification of bank statements and/or transactions and secure online delivery of the same. Banks also offer integration of the company's accounts to Excel and other popular financial packages like **QuickBooks** and **Peachtree**. The result: Paper statements and checks are becoming obsolete.

Key Takeaway

The bank statement, whether online or in paper form, identifies transactions that need to be recorded in the Cash account. The reconciliation is a control over cash.

Summary Problem 7-1

The cash account of Baylor Associates at February 28, 2014, follows.

	Cash			
Feb 1	Bal 3,995	Feb 3	400	
6	800	12	3,100	
15	1,800	19	1,100	
23	1,100	25	500	
28	2,400	27	900	
Feb 28	Bal 4,095			

Baylor Associates received the following bank statement on February 28, 2014:

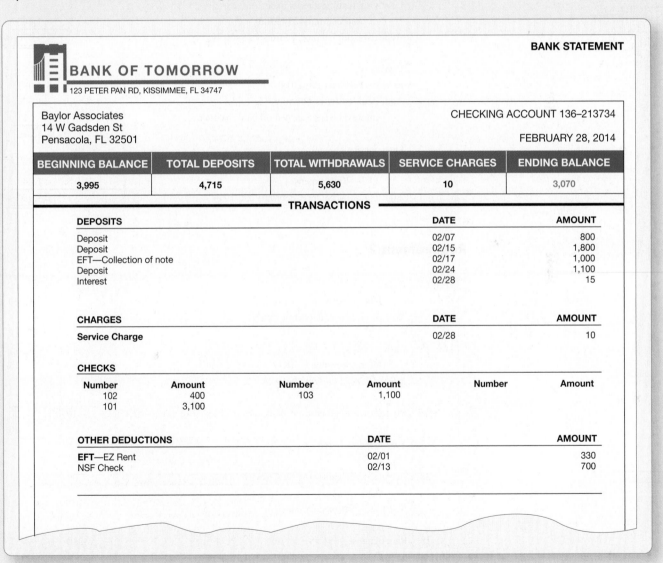

BANK STATEMENT				

BANK OF TOMORROW
123 PETER PAN RD, KISSIMMEE, FL 34747

Baylor Associates
14 W Gadsden St
Pensacola, FL 32501

CHECKING ACCOUNT 136–213734

FEBRUARY 28, 2014

BEGINNING BALANCE	TOTAL DEPOSITS	TOTAL WITHDRAWALS	SERVICE CHARGES	ENDING BALANCE
3,995	4,715	5,630	10	3,070

TRANSACTIONS

DEPOSITS	DATE	AMOUNT
Deposit	02/07	800
Deposit	02/15	1,800
EFT—Collection of note	02/17	1,000
Deposit	02/24	1,100
Interest	02/28	15

CHARGES	DATE	AMOUNT
Service Charge	02/28	10

CHECKS

Number	Amount	Number	Amount	Number	Amount
102	400	103	1,100		
101	3,100				

OTHER DEDUCTIONS	DATE	AMOUNT
EFT—EZ Rent	02/01	330
NSF Check	02/13	700

Additional data:
Baylor deposits all cash receipts in the bank and makes all payments by check.

Requirements

1. Prepare the bank reconciliation of Baylor Associates at February 28, 2014.
2. Journalize the entries based on the bank reconciliation.

Solution

Requirement 1

BAYLOR ASSOCIATES
Bank Reconciliation
February 28, 2014

Bank:			
Balance, February 28, 2014			$ 3,070
Add: Deposit of February 28 in transit			2,400
			$ 5,470
Less: Outstanding checks issued on February 25 ($500)			
and February 27 ($900)			1,400
Adjusted bank balance, February 28, 2014			$ 4,070
Books:			
Balance, February 28, 2014			$ 4,095
Add: Bank collection of note receivable			1,000
Interest revenue earned on bank balance			15
			$ 5,110
Less: Service charge		$ 10	
NSF check		700	
EFT—Rent expense		330	1,040
Adjusted book balance, February 28, 2014			$ 4,070

Requirement 2

Feb 28	Cash (A+)		1,000	
	Note receivable (A–)			1,000
	Note receivable collected by bank.			
28	Cash (A+)		15	
	Interest revenue (R+)			15
	Interest earned on bank balance.			
28	Miscellaneous expense (or Bank service charge expense) (E+)		10	
	Cash (A–)			10
	Bank service charge.			
28	Accounts receivable—M. E. Crown (A+)		700	
	Cash (A–)			700
	NSF check returned by bank.			
28	Rent expense (E+)		330	
	Cash (A–)			330
	Monthly rent expense.			

Internal Control over Cash Receipts

All cash receipts should be deposited for safekeeping in the bank—quickly. Companies receive cash over the counter and through the mail. Each source of cash has its own security measures.

7 Apply internal controls to cash receipts

Cash Receipts over the Counter

Exhibit 7-8 illustrates a cash receipt over the counter in a store. The point-of-sale terminal (cash register) provides control over the cash receipts. Consider a **Target** store. For each transaction, **Target** issues a receipt to ensure that each sale is recorded. The cash drawer opens when the clerk enters a transaction, and the machine (cash register) records it. At the end of the day, a manager proves the cash by comparing the cash in the drawer against the machine's record of sales. This step helps prevent theft by the clerk.

EXHIBIT 7-8 | **Cash Receipts over the Counter**

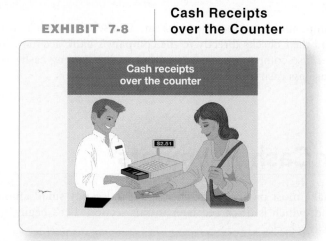

At the end of the day—or several times a day if business is brisk—the cashier deposits the cash in the bank. The machine tape then goes to the accounting department to record the journal entry to record cash receipts and sales revenue. These measures, coupled with oversight by a manager, discourage theft.

Cash Receipts by Mail

Many companies receive cash by mail. Exhibit 7-9 shows how companies control cash received by mail. All incoming mail is opened by a mailroom employee. The mailroom then sends all customer checks to the treasurer, who has the cashier deposit the money in the bank. The remittance advices go to the accounting department (or bookkeeper) for journal entries to Cash and customer accounts. As a final control, the controller compares the following records for the day:

- Bank deposit amount from the treasurer
- Debit to Cash from the accounting department

The debit to Cash should equal the amount deposited in the bank. All cash receipts are safe in the bank, and the company books are up-to-date.

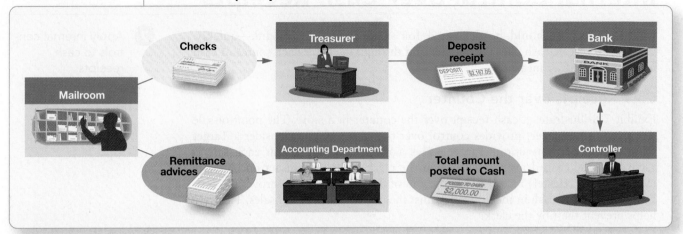

EXHIBIT 7-9 | Cash Receipts by Mail

Many companies use a lock-box system, as discussed earlier in the chapter. Customers send their checks directly to the company's bank account. Internal control is tight because company personnel never touch incoming cash. The lock-box system puts business cash to work immediately.

Internal Control over Cash Payments

 Apply internal controls to cash payments

Companies make most payments by check. They also pay small amounts from a petty cash fund, which is discussed later in this section. Let's begin by discussing cash payments by check.

Controls over Payment by Check

As we have seen, companies need a good separation of duties between operations and writing checks for cash payments. Payment by check is an important internal control for the following reasons:

- The check provides a record of the payment.
- The check must be signed by an authorized official.
- Before signing the check, the official reviews the invoice or other evidence supporting the payment.

Controls over Purchase and Payment

To illustrate the internal control over cash payments by check, suppose Smart Touch buys its inventory from **Sony**. The purchasing and payment process follows these steps, as shown in Exhibit 7-10.

Start with the box for Smart Touch on the left side.

STEP 1: Smart Touch e-mails a *purchase order* to **Sony** that states, "Please send us 1,000 DVD-Rs."

STEP 2: **Sony** ships the goods and e-mails an *invoice* back to Smart Touch.

STEP 3: Smart Touch receives the *inventory* and prepares a *receiving report*.

STEP 4: After approving all documents, Smart Touch sends a *check* to **Sony**.

For good internal control, the purchasing agent should neither receive the goods nor approve the payment. If these duties are not separated, a purchasing agent could buy

EXHIBIT 7-10 | **Cash Payments by Check**

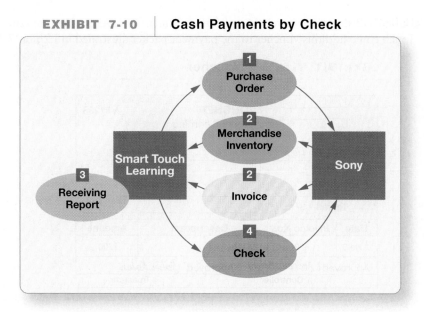

goods and have them shipped to his or her home. Or a purchasing agent could spend too much on purchases, approve the payment, and split the excess with the supplier.

Exhibit 7-11 shows Smart Touch's payment packet of documents. These may be electronic or paper versions of the documents. Before signing the check, the controller or the treasurer should examine the packet to prove that all the documents agree. Only then does the company know

1. it received the goods ordered.

2. it is paying only for the goods received.

EXHIBIT 7-11 | **Payment Packet**

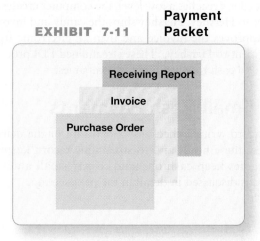

After payment, the check signer punches a hole through the paper payment packet. Dishonest people have been known to run a bill through twice for payment. This hole confirms the bill has been paid. Alternately, the package can be stamped "paid." Electronically, paid invoices are automatically marked "paid" by most accounting systems.

The Voucher System

Many companies use the voucher system for internal control over cash payments. A **voucher** is a sequentially numbered document authorizing a cash payment.

The voucher system uses (1) vouchers, (2) a voucher register (similar to a purchases journal discussed in an online chapter), and (3) a check register (similar to a cash payments journal, also discussed in the online chapter). All expenditures must be approved before payment. This approval takes the form of a voucher.

Exhibit 7-12 illustrates a voucher of Smart Touch. To enhance internal control, Smart Touch could add this voucher to the payment packet illustrated in Exhibit 7-11.

EXHIBIT 7-12 | **Voucher**

VOUCHER			V#1238
Smart Touch Learning			

Payee   RCA

Due Date   June 3
Terms   3/15, n/30

Date	Invoice No.	Description	Amount
June 3	620	DVD-Rs	$700

Approved   *Andrew Bright*   Approved   *John Kolen*
            Controller   Treasurer

Streamlined Procedures

Technology is streamlining payment procedures. **Evaluated Receipts Settlement (ERS)** compresses the payment approval process into a single step: Compare the receiving report to the purchase order. If those documents match, then Smart Touch got the DVD-Rs it ordered. In that case Smart Touch pays **RCA**, the vendor.

An even more streamlined process bypasses paper documents altogether. In **Electronic Data Interchange (EDI)**, **Walmart**'s computers communicate directly with the computers of suppliers like **Hanes** textiles and **Hershey Foods**. When **Walmart**'s inventory of **Hershey** candy reaches a low level, the computer creates and sends an electronic purchase order to **Hershey**. **Hershey** ships the candy and invoices to **Walmart**. A **Walmart** manager approves the invoice and then an electronic fund transfer (EFT) sends **Walmart**'s payment to **Hershey**. These streamlined EDI procedures are used for both cash payments and cash receipts in many companies.

Controlling Small Cash Payments

It is not cost-effective to write a check for a taxi fare or the delivery of a package across town. To meet these needs and to streamline record keeping for small cash transactions, companies keep cash on hand to pay small amounts. This fund is called **petty cash** and is discussed in detail in the next section.

Key Takeaway

Internal controls are designed to insure that ALL cash payments are made timely for actual bills of the company.

The Petty Cash Fund

9 Explain and journalize petty cash transactions

We have already established that cash is the most liquid of assets. Petty cash is more liquid than cash in the bank because none of the bank controls are in place. Therefore, petty cash needs controls such as the following:

- Designate a **custodian of the petty cash fund**. The custodian is the individual assigned responsibility for the petty cash fund.
- Designate a specific amount of cash to be kept in the petty cash fund.
- Support all petty cash fund payments with a **petty cash ticket**. These tickets are sequentially numbered. The petty cash ticket serves as an authorization voucher and explanation. **Petty cash is like the cash in your wallet and you are the fund custodian.**

Setting Up the Petty Cash Fund

The petty cash fund is opened when the company writes a check for the designated amount. The company makes the check payable to Petty cash. On August 1, 2013, Smart Touch creates a petty cash fund of $200. The custodian cashes a $200 check and places the money in the fund. The journal entry is as follows:

Aug 1	Petty cash (A+)	200	
	Cash in bank (A–)		200
	To open the petty cash fund.		

For each petty cash payment, the custodian prepares a petty cash ticket like the one in Exhibit 7-13.

EXHIBIT 7-13 | **Petty Cash Ticket**

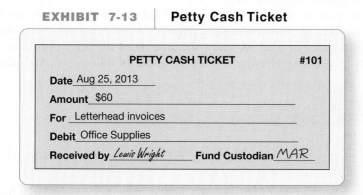

Signatures (or initials) identify the recipient of the cash and the fund custodian. The custodian keeps the petty cash tickets in the fund box. The sum of the cash plus the total of the petty cash tickets should equal the fund balance, $200, at all times.

Maintaining the Petty cash account at its designated balance is the nature of an **imprest system**. The imprest system requires that, at any point in time, the petty cash box contains cash and receipts that total the amount of the imprest balance. This clearly identifies the amount of cash for which the custodian is responsible, and it is the system's main internal control feature. Payments deplete the fund, so periodically the fund must be replenished.

Replenishing the Petty Cash Fund

On August 31 the petty cash fund holds

- $118 in petty cash, and
- $80 in petty cash tickets (ticket #101 for $60 for office supplies and ticket #102 for $20 for a delivery).

You can see $2 is missing:

Fund balance...	$200
Cash on hand.......................................	$118
Petty cash tickets..................................	80
Total accounted for..............................	$198
Amount of cash missing	$ 2

To replenish the petty cash fund, you need to bring the cash on hand up to $200. The company writes a check, payable to Petty cash, for $82 ($200 imprest balance – $118 petty cash on hand). The fund custodian cashes this check and puts $82 back in the fund. Now the fund holds $200 cash as it should.

The petty cash tickets tell you what to debit and the check amount tells you what to credit, as shown in this entry to replenish the fund:

	2013			
	Aug 31	Office supplies (A+)	60	
		Delivery expense (E+)	20	
		Cash short & over (E+)	2	
		Cash (A–)		82

Missing petty cash funds are either debited or credited to a new account, Cash short & over. In this case, $2 was missing, so we debit Cash short & over for the missing petty cash. Another way to look at this is that we needed another $2 debit to make the journal entry balance.

At times the sum of cash in the petty cash fund plus the tickets may exceed the fund balance. Consider the previous example. Assume the petty cash ticket #102 for delivery was for $30 instead of $20. We know the amount of the petty cash tickets and the amount of the check to replenish the funds. Consider the following partial journal entry:

	2013			
	Aug 31	Office supplies (A+)	60	
		Delivery expenses (E+)	30	
		Cash (A–)		82

We know the total debits are $90 ($60 + $30). We know the check to replenish the fund was still $82 (credit to cash) because the fund balance should total $200 and there was $118 in the petty cash box. For this situation, we need an $8 credit to make the journal entry balance, a gain, which is credited to Cash short & over, as follows (using assumed amounts):

	2013			
	Aug 31	Office supplies (A+)	60	
		Delivery expenses (E+)	30	
		Cash short & over (E–)		8
		Cash (A–)		82

Over time the Cash short & over account should net out to a zero balance.

The Petty cash account keeps its $200 balance at all times. Petty cash is debited only when the fund is started (see the August 1 entry) or when its amount is changed. If the business raises the fund amount from $200 to $250, this would require a check to be cashed for $50 and the debit would be to Petty cash.

Stop & Think...

We are all custodians of a petty cash fund—the cash in our wallets. Sometimes we are good trackers of our petty cash, keeping receipts and tracking where the cash goes. Sometimes we are not, as in "Gee, I just got $50 from the ATM and now I have only $5—where did my money go?" Sometimes we increase our petty cash imprest balance ("I need to get out an extra $200 for my trip to Raleigh."). Sometimes we decrease our petty cash imprest balance ("I am going to put $30 of the $60 in my wallet back in the bank so I don't spend it.").

Key Takeaway

Because petty cash is so liquid, the main control over petty cash is establishing ONE individual who has control and responsibility for the petty cash fund.

Ethics and Accounting

President Theodore Roosevelt said, "To educate a person in mind and not in morals is to educate a menace to society." Roosevelt knew unethical behavior does not work. Sooner or later it comes back to haunt you. Moreover, ethical behavior wins out in the long run because it is the right thing to do. **Ethics** in business is really a system of values, analyzing right from wrong.

10 Identify ethical dilemmas in an internal control situation

Corporate and Professional Codes of Ethics

Most companies have a code of ethics to encourage employees to behave ethically. But codes of ethics are not enough by themselves. Owners and managers must set a high ethical tone, as we saw in the earlier section in this chapter on Control Environment. The owner or CEO must make it clear the company will not tolerate unethical conduct.

As professionals, accountants are expected to maintain higher standards than society in general. Their ability to do business depends entirely on their reputation. Most independent accountants are members of the American Institute of Certified Public Accountants and must abide by the AICPA Code of Professional Conduct. Rule 102 of the Code requires members to maintain objectivity and integrity, to be free of conflicts of interest, and to not knowingly misrepresent facts or subordinate their judgment to others.[1] Accountants who are members of the Institute of Management Accountants are bound by the Statement of Ethical Professional Practice, which requires integrity and credibility as part of its standards.

Ethical Issues in Accounting

In many situations, the ethical choice is obvious. For example, stealing cash is both unethical and illegal. In other cases, the choices are more difficult. But in every instance, ethical judgments boil down to a personal decision: What should I do in a given situation? Let's consider two ethical issues in accounting.

Situation 1

Grant Jacobs is preparing the income tax return of a client who has earned more income than expected. On January 2, the client pays for advertising and asks Jacobs to backdate the expense to the preceding year. Backdating the deduction would lower the client's immediate tax payments. After all, there is a difference of only two days between December 31 and January 2. This client is important to Jacobs. What should he do?

> Jacobs should refuse the request because the transaction took place in January of the new year.

If Jacobs backdated the transaction in the accounting records, what control device could prove he behaved unethically? An IRS audit could prove the expense occurred in January rather than in December. Falsifying IRS documents is both unethical and illegal and is subject to severe preparer penalties. Jacobs should establish controls in the company's accounting system to prevent such actions from occurring or to detect such actions if they occur.

---

[1]http://www.aicpa.org/Research/Standards/CodeofConduct/Pages/et_102.aspx

Situation 2

Chris Morris's software company owes $40,000 to **Bank of America**. The loan agreement requires Morris's company to maintain a current ratio (current assets divided by current liabilities) of 1.50 or higher. At present, the company's current ratio is 1.40. At this level, Morris is in violation of her loan agreement. She can increase the current ratio to 1.53 by paying off some current liabilities right before year-end. Is it ethical to do so?

> Yes, because paying the bills early is a real business transaction.

Morris should be aware that paying off the liabilities is only a delaying tactic. It will hold off the bank for now, but the current ratio must remain above 1.50 in order to keep from violating the agreement in the future. If Morris's software company has internal control policies requiring authorization for early payments to vendors and Morris did not receive proper authorization before paying the bills early, then Morris would have circumvented internal controls established for cash payments.

Situation 3

Dudley Dorite, CPA, the lead auditor of Nimron Corporation, thinks Nimron may be understating the liabilities on its balance sheet. Nimron's transactions are very complex, and outsiders may never figure this out. Dorite asks his CPA firm's audit standards committee how he should handle the situation. The CPA firm's audit standards committee replies, "Require Nimron to report all its liabilities." Nimron is Dorite's most important client, and Nimron is pressuring him to certify the liabilities. Dorite can rationalize that Nimron's reported amounts are okay. What should he do? To make his decision, Dorite consults the framework outlined in the following Decision Guidelines 7-1 feature.

Key Takeaway

Internal controls should be designed to remove the opportunity for individuals to act unethically.

Decision Guidelines 7-1

FRAMEWORK FOR MAKING ETHICAL JUDGMENTS

Weighing tough ethical judgments requires a decision framework. Answering these four questions will guide you through tough decisions. Let's apply them to Dorite's situation.

Decision	Guidelines
• What is the ethical issue?	1. *Identify the ethical issue.* Dorite's ethical dilemma is to decide what he should do with the information he has uncovered.
• What are Dorite's options?	2. *Specify the alternatives.* For Dorite, the alternatives include (a) going along with Nimron's liabilities as reported or (b) forcing Nimron to report higher amounts of liabilities.
• What are the possible consequences?	3. *Assess the possible outcomes.* a. If Dorite certifies Nimron's present level of liabilities—and if no one ever objects—Dorite will keep this valuable client. But if Nimron's actual liabilities turn out to be higher than reported, Nimron investors may lose money and take Dorite to court, which would damage his reputation as an auditor and hurt his firm. b. If Dorite follows his company policy, he must force Nimron to increase its reported liabilities, which may anger the company. Nimron may fire Dorite as its auditor, costing him some business in the short run, but Dorite will save his reputation.
• What should he do?	4. *Make the decision.* In the end Dorite went along with Nimron and certified the company's liabilities. To do so, Dorite had to ignore internal control flaws that allowed Nimron to underreport its liabilities. Further, he did not disclose the flaws in the audit report's evaluation of Nimron's internal controls. He also went directly against his firm's policies and GAAP. Nimron later admitted understating its liabilities, Dorite had to retract his audit opinion, and the firm for which Dorite worked collapsed quickly. Dorite should have followed company policy. Rarely is one person smarter than a team of experts. Furthermore, it is never worthwhile to act unethically, as Dorite did.

Summary Problem 7-2

Misler Company established a $300 petty cash fund on January 12, 2012. Karen Misler (KM) is the fund custodian. At the end of the month, the petty cash fund contains the following:

a. **Cash: $163**
b. **Petty cash tickets, as follows:**

No.	Amount	Issued to	Signed by	Account Debited
44	$14	B. Jarvis	B. Jarvis and KM	Office supplies
45	39	S. Bell	S. Bell	Delivery expense
47	43	R. Tate	R. Tate and KM	—
48	33	L. Blair	L. Blair and KM	Travel expense

Requirements

1. Identify three internal control weaknesses revealed in the given data.
2. Journalize the following transactions:
   a. Establishment of the petty cash fund on January 12, 2012.
   b. Replenishment of the fund on January 31, 2012. Assume petty cash ticket no. 47 was issued for the purchase of office supplies.
3. What is the balance in the Petty cash account immediately before replenishment? Immediately after replenishment?

Solution

Requirement 1

The three internal control weaknesses are as follows:

1. Petty cash ticket no. 46 is missing. There is no indication of what happened to this ticket. The company should investigate.
2. The petty cash custodian (KM) did not sign petty cash ticket no. 45. This omission may have been an oversight on her part. However, it raises the question of whether she authorized the payment. Both the fund custodian and the recipient of cash should sign the petty cash ticket.
3. Petty cash ticket no. 47 does not indicate which account to debit on the actual ticket. If Tate could not remember where the $43 went, then the accountant will not know what account should be debited.

Requirement 2

Petty cash journal entries:

a. Entry to establish the petty cash fund:

a	Jan 12	Petty cash (A+)	300	
		Cash in bank (A–)		300

b. Entry to replenish the fund:

b	Jan 31	Office supplies ($14 + $43) (A+)	57	
		Delivery expense (E+)	39	
		Travel expense (E+)	33	
		Cash short & over (E+)	8	
		Cash in bank (A–)		137

Requirement 3

The balance in Petty cash is *always* its specified balance, in this case $300.

Review *Internal Control and Cash*

● Accounting Vocabulary

Bank Account (p. 362)
Helps control cash because banks have established practices for safeguarding customers' money.

Bank Collections (p. 365)
Collection of money by the bank on behalf of a depositor.

Bank Errors (p. 366)
Posting errors made by the bank that either incorrectly increase or decrease the bank balance.

Bank Reconciliation (p. 364)
Document explaining the reasons for the difference between a depositor's cash records and the depositor's cash balance in its bank account.

Bank Statement (p. 362)
Document the bank uses to report what it did with the depositor's cash. Shows the bank account beginning and ending balance and lists the month's cash transactions conducted through the bank.

Book Errors (p. 365)
Posting errors made in the company's general ledger that either incorrectly increase or decrease the book balance.

Canceled Checks (p. 362)
Physical or scanned copies of the maker's paid checks.

Check (p. 362)
Document that instructs a bank to pay the designated person or business a specified amount of money.

Collusion (p. 361)
Two or more people working together to circumvent internal controls and defraud a company.

Computer Virus (p. 360)
A malicious program that (a) reproduces itself, (b) enters program code without consent, and (c) performs destructive actions.

Controller (p. 359)
The chief accounting officer of a company.

Custodian of the Petty Cash Fund (p. 374)
The individual assigned responsibility for the petty cash fund.

Deposit Tickets (p. 362)
Completed by the customer; show the amount of each deposit.

Deposits in Transit (p. 365)
A deposit recorded by the company but not yet by its bank.

Electronic Data Interchange (EDI) (p. 374)
Streamlined process that bypasses paper documents altogether. Computers of customers communicate directly with the computers of suppliers to automate routine business transactions.

Electronic Funds Transfer (EFT) (p. 362)
System that transfers cash by electronic communication rather than by paper documents.

Encryption (p. 361)
Rearranging plain-text messages by a mathematical process—the primary method of achieving security in e-commerce.

Ethics (p. 377)
A system of values analyzing right from wrong.

Evaluated Receipts Settlement (ERS) (p. 374)
Compresses the payment approval process into a single step: Compare the receiving report to the purchase order.

External Auditors (p. 358)
Outside accountants completely independent of the business who monitor the controls to ensure that the financial statements are presented fairly in accordance with GAAP.

Firewalls (p. 361)
Devices that enable members of a local network to access the Internet, while keeping nonmembers out of the network.

Imprest System (p. 375)
A way to account for petty cash by maintaining a constant balance in the petty cash account, supported by the fund (cash plus payment tickets) totaling the same amount.

Internal Auditors (p. 358)
Employees of the business who ensure that the company's employees are following company policies, meeting legal requirements, and that operations are running efficiently.

Internal Control (p. 356)
Organizational plan and all the related measures adopted by an entity to safeguard assets, encourage employees to follow company policy, promote operational efficiency, and ensure accurate and reliable accounting records.

Internal Control Report (p. 357)
A report by management describing its responsibility for and the adequacy of internal controls over financial reporting.

Lock-Box System (p. 365)
A system in which customers pay their accounts directly to a business's bank.

Maker (p. 362)
On a check, the person who signs it.

Nonsufficient Funds (NSF) Check (p. 365)
A "hot" check; one for which the maker's bank account has insufficient money to pay the check.

Outstanding Checks (p. 365)
Checks issued by the company and recorded on its books but not yet paid by its bank.

Payee (p. 362)
On a check, the person to whom the check is paid.

Petty Cash (p. 374)
Fund containing a small amount of cash that is used to pay for minor expenditures.

Petty Cash Ticket (p. 374)
Supports all petty cash fund payments. The petty cash ticket serves as an authorization voucher and explanation of the expenditure.

Public Companies (p. 356)
Companies that sell their stock to the general public.

Remittance Advice (p. 362)
An optional attachment to a check that tells the payee the reason for the payment.

Sarbanes-Oxley Act (p. 357)
An act passed by Congress, abbreviated as SOX. SOX revamped corporate governance in the United States and affected the accounting profession.

Separation of Duties (p. 359)
Dividing responsibility between two or more people.

Service Charge (p. 365)
A cash payment that is the bank's fee for processing transactions.

Signature Card (p. 362)
A card that shows each authorized person's signature for a bank account.

Timing Difference (p. 364)
Differences that arise between the balance on the bank statement and the balance on the books because of a time lag in recording transactions.

Treasurer (p. 359)
In a large company, the person in charge of writing checks.

Trojan (p. 360)
A malicious computer program that hides inside a legitimate program and works like a virus.

Voucher (p. 373)
Sequentially numbered document authorizing a cash payment.

● Destination: Student Success

Student Success Tips

The following are hints on some common trouble areas for students in this chapter:

● Remember that the benefit obtained from the control should outweigh the cost of the control.

● Recall that each adjusting item only affects one side of the bank reconciliation.

● The bank reconciliation is a control tool. Keep in mind that the adjusted bank balance should equal the adjusted book balance on the completed bank reconciliation.

● Recall that the petty cash fund receipts plus petty cash should equal the imprest petty cash balance. The fund custodian is responsible for the petty cash fund.

Getting Help

If there's a learning objective from the chapter you aren't confident about, try using one or more of the following resources:

● Balance your personal checking account using the bank reconciliation form on the back of your monthly bank statement.

● Practice additional exercises or problems at the end of Chapter 7 that cover the specific learning objective that is challenging you.

● Watch the white board videos for Chapter 7 located at myaccountinglab.com under the Chapter Resources button.

● Go to myaccountinglab.com and select the Study Plan button. Choose Chapter 7 and work the questions covering that specific learning objective until you've mastered it.

● Work the Chapter 7 pre/post tests in myaccountinglab.com.

● Visit the learning resource center on your campus for tutoring.

● Quick Check

Experience the Power of Practice!

As denoted by the logo, all of these questions, as well as additional practice materials, can be found in **MyAccountingLab**.

Please visit myaccountinglab.com

1. Which of the following is *not* part of the definition of internal control?
   a. Separation of duties
   b. Safeguard assets
   c. Encourage employees to follow company policy
   d. Promote operational efficiency

2. The Sarbanes-Oxley Act
   a. created the Private Company Accounting Board.
   b. allows accountants to audit and to perform any type of consulting work for a public company.
   c. stipulates that violators of the act may serve 20 years in prison for securities fraud.
   d. requires that an outside auditor must evaluate a public company's internal controls.

3. Michelle Darby receives cash from customers. Her other assigned job is to post the collections to customer accounts receivable. Her company has weak
   a. assignment of responsibilities.
   b. ethics.
   c. computer controls.
   d. separation of duties.

4. Encryption

   a. avoids the need for separation of duties.

   b. creates firewalls to protect data.

   c. cannot be broken by hackers.

   d. rearranges messages by a special process.

5. The document that explains all differences between the company's cash records and the bank's figures is called a(n)

   a. bank collection.

   b. electronic fund transfer.

   c. bank statement.

   d. bank reconciliation.

6. Ethics for AICPA members is governed by

   a. generally accepted accounting principles.

   b. the AICPA Code of Professional Conduct.

   c. the CPA's ethical guide.

   d. Standards of Ethical Conduct for Management Accountants.

7. Payment by check is an important internal control over cash payments because

   a. the check must be signed by an authorized official.

   b. before signing the check, the official reviews the invoice supporting the payment.

   c. Both a and b

   d. None of the above

8. Sahara Company's Cash account shows an ending balance of $650. The bank statement shows a $29 service charge and an NSF check for $150. A $240 deposit is in transit, and outstanding checks total $420. What is Sahara's adjusted cash balance?

   a. $291

   b. $829

   c. $471

   d. $470

9. The petty cash fund had an initial imprest balance of $100. It currently has $20 and petty cash tickets totaling $75 for office supplies. The entry to replenish the fund would contain

   a. a credit to Cash short & over for $5.

   b. a credit to Petty cash for $80.

   c. a debit to Cash short & over for $5.

   d. a debit to Petty cash for $80.

10. Separation of duties is important for internal control of

   a. cash receipts.

   b. cash payments.

   c. Neither of the above

   d. Both a and b

Answers are given after Apply Your Knowledge (p. 403).

Assess Your Progress

● Short Exercises

MyAccountingLab

S7-1 **❶ Definition of internal control [5 min]**

Internal controls are designed to safeguard assets, encourage employees to follow company policies, promote operational efficiency, and ensure accurate accounting records.

Requirements

1. Which objective is most important?
2. Which must the internal controls accomplish for the business to survive? Give your reason.

S7-2 **❷ Sarbanes-Oxley Act [5 min]**

The Sarbanes-Oxley Act affects public companies.

Requirement

1. How does the Sarbanes-Oxley Act relate to internal controls? Be specific.

S7-3 **❸ Characteristics of internal control [5–10 min]**

Separation of duties is a key internal control.

Requirement

1. Explain in your own words why separation of duties is often described as the cornerstone of internal control for safeguarding assets. Describe what can happen if the same person has custody of an asset and also accounts for the asset.

S7-4 **❹ Pitfalls of e-commerce [5 min]**

Shannon's account at Commerce Bank has a balance of $1,200. Shannon's account number is 1236.

Requirement

1. Assuming the bank uses encryption for customer account numbers and the last digit is a check figure, show the mathematical formula the bank used to generate the last digit in Shannon's account. (Hint: you may use +, –, ×, and ÷)

S7-5 **❺ Bank account controls [5–10 min]**

Answer the following questions about the controls in bank accounts:

Requirements

1. Which bank control protects against forgery?
2. Which bank control reports what the bank did with the customer's cash each period?
3. Which bank control confirms the amount of money put into the bank?

S7-6 **❻ Preparing a bank reconciliation [10 min]**

The Cash account of First on Alert Security Systems reported a balance of $2,470 at December 31, 2012. There were outstanding checks totaling $700 and a December 31 deposit in transit of $100. The bank statement, which came from Park Cities Bank, listed the December 31 balance of $3,700. Included in the bank balance was a collection of $640 on account from Brendan Ballou, a First on Alert customer who pays the bank directly. The bank statement also shows a $30 service charge and $20 of interest revenue that First on Alert earned on its bank balance.

Requirement

1. Prepare First on Alert's bank reconciliation at December 31.

Note: Short Exercise 7-7 should be used only after completing Short Exercise 7-6.

S7-7 ⑥ **Recording transactions from a bank reconciliation [5 min]**
Review your results from preparing First on Alert Security Systems' bank reconciliation in Short Exercise 7-6.

Requirement

1. Journalize the company's transactions that arise from the bank reconciliation. Include an explanation with each entry.

S7-8 ⑦ **Control over cash receipts [5 mins]**
Sandra Kristof sells furniture for McKinney Furniture Company. Kristof is having financial problems and takes $650 that she received from a customer. She rang up the sale through the cash register.

Requirement

1. What will alert Megan McKinney, the controller, that something is wrong?

S7-9 ⑦ **Control over cash receipts by mail [5–10 min]**
Review the internal controls over cash receipts by mail presented in the chapter.

Requirement

1. Exactly what is accomplished by the final step in the process, performed by the controller?

S7-10 ⑧ **Internal control over cash payments by check [5 min]**
A purchasing agent for Franklin Office Supplies receives the goods that he purchases and also approves payment for the goods.

Requirements

1. How could this purchasing agent cheat his company?
2. How could Franklin avoid this internal control weakness?

S7-11 ⑨ **Petty cash [10 min]**
The following petty cash transactions of Grayson Gaming Supplies occurred in March:

Mar	1	Established a petty cash fund with a $150 balance.
	31	The petty cash fund has $14 in cash and $148 in petty cash tickets that were issued to pay for Office supplies ($58) and Entertainment expense ($90). Replenished the fund with $136 of cash and recorded the expenses.

Requirement

1. Prepare journal entries without explanations.

S7-12 ⑩ **Making an ethical judgment [5 min]**
Shelby Emerson, an accountant for England Limited, discovers that her supervisor, Percy Halifax, made several errors last year. Overall, the errors overstated the company's net income by 18%. It is not clear whether the errors were deliberate or accidental.

Requirement

1. What should Emerson do?

• Exercises

E7-13   ① ② ③ **Understanding Sarbanes-Oxley and identifying internal control strengths and weaknesses [10–15 min]**

The following situations suggest a strength or a weakness in internal control.

    a. Top managers delegate all internal control procedures to the accounting department.

    b. The accounting department (or bookkeeper) orders merchandise and approves invoices for payment.

    c. Cash received over the counter is controlled by the sales clerk, who rings up the sale and places the cash in the register. The sales clerk matches the total recorded by the register to each day's cash sales.

    d. The employee who signs checks need not examine the payment packet because he is confident the amounts are correct.

Requirements

1. Define internal control.

2. The system of internal control must be tested by external auditors. What law or rule requires this testing?

3. Identify each item as either a strength or a weakness in internal control and give the reason for your answer.

E7-14   ③ **Identifying internal controls [10 min]**

Consider the following situations.

    a. While reviewing the records of Quality Pharmacy, you find that the same employee orders merchandise and approves invoices for payment.

    b. Business is slow at Amazing Amusement Park on Tuesday, Wednesday, and Thursday nights. To reduce expenses, the owner decides not to use a ticket taker on those nights. The ticket seller (cashier) is told to keep the tickets as a record of the number sold.

    c. The same trusted employee has served as cashier for 12 years.

    d. When business is brisk, Quickie Mart deposits cash in the bank several times during the day. The manager at one store wants to reduce the time employees spend delivering cash to the bank, so he starts a new policy. Cash will build up over weekends, and the total will be deposited on Monday.

    e. Grocery stores such as Convenience Market and Natural Foods purchase most merchandise from a few suppliers. At another grocery store, the manager decides to reduce paperwork. He eliminates the requirement that the receiving department prepare a receiving report listing the goods actually received from the supplier.

Requirement

1. Consider each situation separately. Identify the missing internal control procedure from these characteristics:
   - Assignment of responsibilities
   - Separation of duties
   - Audits
   - Electronic controls
   - Other controls (specify)

E7-15   ④ **E-commerce control procedures [10–15 min]**

The following situations suggest a strength or a weakness in e-commerce internal controls.

    a. Netproducts sells merchandise over the Internet. Customers input their credit card information for payment.

    b. Netproducts maintains employee information on the company intranet. Employees can retrieve information about annual leave, payroll deposits, and benefits from any computer using their login information.

    c. Netproducts maintains trend information about its customers, products, and pricing on the company's intranet.

    d. Tax identification numbers for all vendors are maintained in Netproducts' database.

Requirement

1. Identify the control that will best protect the company.

E7-16 ❺ **Using a bank reconciliation as a control device [10 min]**
Lynn Cavender owns Cavender's Boot City. She fears that a trusted employee has been stealing from the company. This employee receives cash from customers and also prepares the monthly bank reconciliation. To check up on the employee, Cavender prepares her own bank reconciliation, as shown. This reconciliation is both complete and accurate, based on the available data.

CAVENDER'S BOOT CITY				
Bank Reconciliation				
January 31, 2012				
Bank			**Books**	
Balance, January 31	$ 1,500	Balance, January 31		$ 1,050
Add: Deposit in transit	410	Add: Bank collection		790
		Interest revenue		15
Less: Outstanding checks	1,080	Less: Service charge		20
Adjusted bank balance	$ 830	Adjusted book balance		$ 1,835

Requirements

1. How is the preparation of a bank reconciliation considered to be a control device?
2. Which side of the reconciliation shows the true cash balance?
3. What is Cavender's true cash balance?
4. Does it appear that the employee has stolen from the company?
5. If so, how much? Explain your answer.

E7-17 ❻ **Classifying bank reconciliation items [5 min]**
The following items could appear on a bank reconciliation:

a. Outstanding checks, $670.
b. Deposits in transit, $1,500.
c. NSF check from customer, #548 for $175.
d. Bank collection of our note receivable of $800, and interest of $80.
e. Interest earned on bank balance, $20.
f. Service charge, $10.
g. Book error: We credited Cash for $200. The correct amount was $2,000.
h. Bank error: The bank decreased our account by $350 for a check written by another customer.

Requirement

1. Classify each item as (1) an addition to the book balance, (2) a subtraction from the book balance, (3) an addition to the bank balance, or (4) a subtraction from the bank balance.

E7-18 ❻ **Preparing a bank reconciliation [10–20 min]**
D. J. Harrison's checkbook lists the following:

Date	Check No.	Item	Check	Deposit	Balance
Nov 1					$ 540
4	622	Java Joe's	$ 15		525
9		Dividends received		$ 130	655
13	623	Skip's Market	55		600
14	624	Fill-N-Go	75		525
18	625	Cash	60		465
26	626	Fernwood Golf Course	85		380
28	627	Upstate Realty, Co.	265		115
30		Paycheck		1,210	1,325

Harrison's November bank statement shows the following:

Balance		$ 540	
Deposits		130	
Debit Checks:	No.	Amount	
	622 . . . . . . $	15	
	623	55	
	624	115 *	
	625	60	(245)
Other charges:			
Printed checks		$ 35	
Service charge		20	(55)
Balance		$ 370	

*This is the correct amount for check number 624.

Requirements

1. Prepare Harrison's bank reconciliation at November 30, 2012.
2. How much cash does Harrison actually have on November 30, 2012?

E7-19 ❻ **Preparing a bank reconciliation [20–25 min]**

Brett Knight operates four bowling alleys. He just received the October 31 bank statement from City National Bank, and the statement shows an ending balance of $905. Listed on the statement are an EFT rent collection of $410, a service charge of $10, NSF checks totaling $70, and a $30 charge for printed checks. In reviewing his cash records, Knight identified outstanding checks totaling $450 and a deposit in transit of $1,775. During October, he recorded a $310 check by debiting Salary expense and crediting Cash for $31. His Cash account shows an October 31 balance of $2,209.

Requirements

1. Prepare the bank reconciliation at October 31.
2. Journalize any transactions required from the bank reconciliation.

E7-20 ❼ **Evaluating internal control over cash receipts [10 min]**

When you check out at a **Target** store, the cash register displays the amount of the sale. It also shows the cash received and any change returned to you. Suppose the register also produces a customer receipt but keeps no internal record of the transactions. At the end of the day, the clerk counts the cash in the register and gives it to the cashier for deposit in the company bank account.

Requirements

1. Identify the internal control weakness over cash receipts.
2. What could you do to correct the weakness?

E7-21 ❽ **Evaluating internal control over cash payments [10 min]**

Gary's Great Cars purchases high-performance auto parts from a Nebraska vendor. Dave Simon, the accountant for Gary's, verifies receipt of merchandise and then prepares, signs, and mails the check to the vendor.

Requirements

1. Identify the internal control weakness over cash payments.
2. What could you do to correct the weakness?

E7-22 ⑨ **Accounting for petty cash [10–15 min]**

Karen's Dance Studio created a $370 imprest petty cash fund. During the month, the fund custodian authorized and signed petty cash tickets as follows:

Petty Cash Ticket No.	Item	Account Debited	Amount
1	Delivery of programs to customers	Delivery expense	$ 25
2	Mail package	Postage expense	15
3	Newsletter	Supplies expense	35
4	Key to closet	Miscellaneous expense	55
5	Computer jump drive	Supplies expense	80

Requirement

1. Make the general journal entries to
   a. create the petty cash fund and
   b. record its replenishment. Cash in the fund totals $147, so $13 is missing. Include explanations.

E7-23 ⑨ **Control over petty cash [10 min]**

Hangin' Out Night Club maintains an imprest petty cash fund of $100, which is under the control of Sandra Morgan. At March 31, the fund holds $9 cash and petty cash tickets for office supplies, $77, and delivery expense, $20.

Requirements

1. Explain how an *imprest* petty cash system works.
2. Journalize establishment of the petty cash fund on March 1 and replenishment of the fund on March 31.
3. Prepare a T-account for Petty cash, and post to the account. What is Petty cash's balance at all times?

E7-24 ⑩ **Evaluating the ethics of conduct by leaders [15–20 min]**

AIG, which received more than $170,000,000 in taxpayer bailout money from the U.S. Treasury, planned to pay $165,000,000 in bonuses to its executives in 2009.

Requirement

1. Suppose you were one of those executives slated to receive a large bonus. Apply the ethical judgment framework outlined in the Decision Guidelines 7-1 to decide whether you would accept or reject the bonus.

• Problems (Group A)

P7-25A ❶ ❷ ❸ ❹ Internal control, components, procedures, and laws [20–25 min]

TERMS:	DEFINITIONS:
1. Internal control	A. What internal and external auditors do.
2. Control procedures	B. Part of internal control that ensures resources are not wasted.
3. Firewalls	C. Law passed by congress to address public concerns following the Enron and WorldCom scandals.
4. Encryption	D. Should be pre-numbered to prevent theft and inefficiency.
5. Control environment	E. Limits access to a local network.
6. Information system	F. Example: The person who opens the bank statement should not also be the person who is reconciling cash.
7. Separation of duties	
8. Monitoring of controls	G. Identification of uncertainties that may arise due to a company's products, services, or operations.
9. Documents	H. May be internal and external.
10. Audits	I. Without a sufficient one of these, information cannot properly be gathered and summarized.
11. Operational efficiency	J. The organizational plan and all the related measures that safeguard assets, encourage employees to follow company policy, promote operational efficiency, and insure accurate and reliable accounting data.
12. Risk assessment	
13. Sarbanes-Oxley Act	
	K. Component of internal control that helps ensure business goals are achieved.
	L. Rearranges data by a mathematical process.
	M. To establish one, a company's owner/CEO and top managers must behave honorably to set a good example for employees.

Requirement

1. Match the terms with their definitions.

P7-26A ❸ ❺ ❼ ❽ Correcting internal control weakness [10–20 min]

Each of the following situations has an internal control weakness.

a. Upside – Down Applications develops custom programs to customer's specifications. Recently, development of a new program stopped while the programmers redesigned Upside – Down's accounting system. Upside – Down's accountants could have performed this task.

b. Norma Rottler has been your trusted employee for 24 years. She performs all cash-handling and accounting duties. Ms. Rottler just purchased a new Lexus and a new home in an expensive suburb. As owner of the company, you wonder how she can afford these luxuries because you pay her only $30,000 a year and she has no source of outside income.

c. Izzie Hardwoods, a private company, falsified sales and inventory figures in order to get an important loan. The loan went through, but Izzie later went bankrupt and could not repay the bank.

d. The office supply company where Pet Grooming Goods purchases sales receipts recently notified Pet Grooming Goods that its documents were not prenumbered. Howard Mustro, the owner, replied that he never uses receipt numbers.

e. Discount stores such as Cusco make most of their sales for cash, with the remainder in credit-card sales. To reduce expenses, one store manager ceases purchasing fidelity bonds on the cashiers.

f. Cornelius' Corndogs keeps all cash receipts in an empty bread box for a week, because he likes to go to the bank on Tuesdays when Joann is working.

Requirements

1. Identify the missing internal control characteristics in each situation.
2. Identify the possible problem caused by each control weakness.
3. Propose a solution to each internal control problem.

P7-27A ⑥ **Preparing a bank reconciliation and journal entries [20–25 min]**

The December cash records of Dunlap Insurance follow:

Cash Receipts		Cash Payments	
Date	Cash Debit	Check No.	Cash Credit
Dec 4	$ 4,170	1416	$ 860
9	510	1417	130
14	530	1418	650
17	2,180	1419	1,490
31	1,850	1420	1,440
		1421	900
		1422	630

Dunlap's Cash account shows a balance of $16,740 at December 31. On December 31, Dunlap Insurance received the following bank statement:

Bank Statement for December				
Beginning balance			$	13,600
Deposits and other Credits:				
Dec	1	EFT	$ 300	
	5		4,170	
	10		510	
	15		530	
	18		2,180	
	22	BC	1,400	9,090
Checks and other Debits:				
Dec	8	NSF	$ 1,000	
	11 (check no. 1416)		860	
	19	EFT	700	
	22 (check no. 1417)		130	
	29 (check no. 1418)		650	
	31 (check no. 1419)		1,940	
	31	SC	60	(5,340)
Ending balance			$	17,350

Explanations: BC–bank collection; EFT–electronic funds transfer; NSF–nonsufficient funds checks; SC–service charge

Additional data for the bank reconciliation follows:

a. The EFT credit was a receipt of rent. The EFT debit was an insurance payment.

b. The NSF check was received from a customer.

c. The $1,400 bank collection was for a note receivable.

d. The correct amount of check 1419 for rent expense is $1,940. Dunlap's controller mistakenly recorded the check for $1,490.

Requirements

1. Prepare the bank reconciliation of Dunlap Insurance at December 31, 2012.

2. Journalize any required entries from the bank reconciliation.

P7-28A ⑥ **Preparing a bank reconciliation and journal entries [20 min]**

The August 31 bank statement of Winchester's Healthcare has just arrived from United Bank. To prepare the bank reconciliation, you gather the following data:

    a. The August 31 bank balance is $4,870.

    b. The bank statement includes two charges for NSF checks from customers. One is for $400 (#1), and the other for $110 (#2).

    c. The following Winchester checks are outstanding at August 31:

Check No.	Amount
237	$ 50
288	170
291	520
294	580
295	50
296	140

    d. Winchester collects from a few customers by EFT. The August bank statement lists a $1,300 EFT deposit for a collection on account.

    e. The bank statement includes two special deposits that Winchester hasn't recorded yet: $970, for dividend revenue, and $80, the interest revenue Winchester earned on its bank balance during August.

    f. The bank statement lists a $30 subtraction for the bank service charge.

    g. On August 31, the Winchester treasurer deposited $350, but this deposit does not appear on the bank statement.

    h. The bank statement includes a $1,000 deduction for a check drawn by Multi-State Freight Company. Winchester notified the bank of this bank error.

    i. Winchester's Cash account shows a balance of $2,900 on August 31.

Requirements

1. Prepare the bank reconciliation for Winchester's Healthcare at August 31, 2012.
2. Journalize any required entries from the bank reconciliation. Include an explanation for each entry.

P7-29A ⑦ **Identifying internal control weakness in cash receipts [10–15 min]**

Brother Productions makes all sales on credit. Cash receipts arrive by mail. Justin Broaddus in the mailroom opens envelopes and separates the checks from the accompanying remittance advices. Broaddus forwards the checks to another employee, who makes the daily bank deposit but has no access to the accounting records. Broaddus sends the remittance advices, which show cash received, to the accounting department for entry in the accounts. Broaddus's only other duty is to grant sales allowances to customers. (A *sales allowance* decreases the amount receivable.) When Broaddus receives a customer check for $375 less a $60 allowance, he records the sales allowance and forwards the document to the accounting department.

Requirements

1. Identify the internal control weakness in this situation.
2. Who should record sales allowances?
3. What is the amount that should be shown in the ledger for cash receipts?

P7-30A 🟢 **Accounting for petty cash transactions [20–30 min]**

On June 1, Bash Salad Dressings creates a petty cash fund with an imprest balance of $450. During June, Al Franklin, the fund custodian, signs the following petty cash tickets:

Petty Cash Ticket Number	Item	Amount
101	Office supplies	$ 15
102	Cab fare for executive	10
103	Delivery of package across town	20
104	Dinner money for city manager to entertain the mayor	35
105	Inventory	65

On June 30, prior to replenishment, the fund contains these tickets plus cash of $310. The accounts affected by petty cash payments are Office supplies expense, Travel expense, Delivery expense, Entertainment expense, and Inventory.

Requirements

1. Explain the characteristics and the internal control features of an imprest fund.
2. On June 30, how much cash should the petty cash fund hold before it is replenished?
3. Journalize all required entries to create the fund and replenish it. Include explanations.
4. Make the July 1 entry to increase the fund balance to $475. Include an explanation, and briefly describe what the custodian does.

P7-31A 🟢 **Accounting for petty cash transactions [20–30 min]**

Suppose that on June 1, Rockin' Gyrations, a disc jockey service, creates a petty cash fund with an imprest balance of $500. During June, Michael Martell, fund custodian, signs the following petty cash tickets:

Petty Cash Ticket Number	Item	Amount
1	Postage for package received	$ 20
2	Decorations and refreshments for office party	25
3	Two boxes of stationery	35
4	Printer cartridges	15
5	Dinner money for sales manager entertaining a customer	75

On June 30, prior to replenishment, the fund contains these tickets plus cash of $325. The accounts affected by petty cash payments are Office supplies expense, Entertainment expense, and Postage expense.

Requirements

1. On June 30, how much cash should this petty cash fund hold before it is replenished?
2. Journalize all required entries to (a) create the fund and (b) replenish it. Include explanations.
3. Make the entry on July 1 to increase the fund balance to $550. Include an explanation.

P7-32A 🔟 **Making an ethical judgment [15–30 min]**

North Bank has a loan receivable from Westminster Dance Company. Westminster is late making payments to the bank, and Kevin McHale, a North Bank vice president, is helping Westminster restructure its debt. McHale learns that Westminster is depending on landing a $1,500,000 contract from Envy Theater, another North Bank client. McHale also serves as Envy's loan officer at the bank. In this capacity, he is aware that Envy is considering declaring bankruptcy. McHale has been a great help to Westminster, and Westminster's owner is counting on him to carry the company through this difficult restructuring. To help the bank collect on this large loan, McHale has a strong motivation to help Westminster survive.

Requirements

1. Identify the ethical issue that McHale is facing. Specify the two main alternatives available to McHale.
2. Identify the possible consequences of McHale identifying Envy's financial position to Westminster Dance Company.
3. Identify the correct ethical decision McHale must make based on the two alternatives identified in Requirement 2.

● Problems (Group B)

MyAccountingLab **P7-33B** ① ② ③ ④ **Internal control, components, procedures, and laws [20–25 min]**

TERMS:	DEFINITIONS:
1. Collusion	A. The "tone at the top" of the business.
2. Controller	B. Control procedure that divides responsibility between two or more people.
3. Lock-box system	C. Outside accountants completely independent of the business who monitor the controls to ensure that the financial statements are presented fairly in accordance with GAAP.
4. Firewalls	
5. Encryption	D. After using this process, messages cannot be read by those who do not know the code.
6. Control environment	E. Two or more people working together to circumvent internal controls and defraud a company.
7. Documents	F. The chief accounting officer of a company.
8. Internal control	G. The organizational plan and all related measures that promote operational efficiency.
9. External auditors	H. Prevents nonmembers from accessing the network but allows members to access the network.
10. Timing difference	I. Without a sufficient one of these, information cannot properly be gathered and summarized.
11. Information system	J. These should be pre-numbered to prevent theft and inefficiency.
12. Separation of duties	K. A system in which customers pay their accounts directly to a business's bank.
	L. Differences that arise between the balance on the bank statement and the balance on the books because of a time lag in recording transactions.

Requirement

1. Match the terms with their definitions.

P7-34B ③ ⑤ ⑦ ⑧ **Correcting internal control weakness [10–20 min]**

Each of the following situations has an internal control weakness:

a. Soft Wizzard Applications sells accounting software. Recently, development of a new program stopped while the programmers redesigned Soft Wizzard's accounting system. Soft Wizzard's accountants could have performed this task.

b. Rita Johnson has been your trusted employee for 30 years. She performs all credit functions, including credit authorization. Ms. Johnson just purchased a new Lexus and a new home in an expensive suburb. As owner of the company, you wonder how she can afford these luxuries because you pay her only $27,500 a year and she has no source of outside income.

c. Wong Hardwoods, a private company, falsified sales discount and net profit figures in order to get an important loan. The loan went through, but Wong later went bankrupt and could not repay the bank.

d. The office supply company where Retail Display Goods purchases customer invoices recently notified Retail Display Goods that its documents were not pre-numbered. Adrian Monet, the owner, replied that he never uses the customer invoice numbers.

e. Discount stores such as Wallman make most of their sales for cash, with the remainder in credit-card sales. To reduce expenses and increase efficiency, the store manager stops rotating clerks among different job stations.

f. Kayleigh's Keys keeps all cash receipts in an old hat box for a month because Kayleigh likes to "see" her earnings.

Requirements

1. Identify the missing internal control characteristic in each situation.
2. Identify the possible problem caused by each control weakness.
3. Propose a solution to each internal control problem.

P7-35B ⑥ **Preparing a bank reconciliation and journal entries [20–25 min]**

The May cash records of Dickson Insurance follow:

Cash Receipts		Cash Payments		
Date	Cash Debit	Check No.	Cash Credit	
May 4	$ 4,150	1416	$	850
9	540	1417		160
14	560	1418		670
17	2,190	1419		1,690
31	1,870	1420		1,450
		1421		1,200
		1422		640

Dickson's Cash account shows a balance of $16,650 at May 31. On May 31, Dickson received the following bank statement:

Bank Statement for May				
Beginning balance				$ 14,000
Deposits and other Credits:				
May	1	EFT	$ 200	
	5		4,150	
	10		540	
	15		560	
	18		2,190	
	22	BC	1,700	9,340
Checks and other Debits:				
May	8	NSF	$ 700	
	11 (check no. 1416)		850	
	19	EFT	400	
	22 (check no. 1417)		160	
	29 (check no. 1418)		670	
	31 (check no. 1419)		1,960	
	31	SC	10	(4,750)
Ending balance				$ 18,590

Explanations: BC–bank collection; EFT–electronic funds transfer; NSF–nonsufficient funds checks; SC–service charge

Additional data for the bank reconciliation follow:

a. The EFT deposit was a receipt of rent. The EFT debit was an insurance payment.
b. The NSF check was received from a customer.
c. The $1,700 bank collection was for a note receivable.
d. The correct amount of check number 1419 for rent expense is $1,960. Dickson's controller mistakenly recorded the check for $1,690.

Requirements

1. Prepare the bank reconciliation of Dickson Insurance at May 31, 2012.
2. Journalize any required entries from the bank reconciliation.

P7-36B ⑥ **Preparing a bank reconciliation and journal entries [20 min]**

The October 31 bank statement of White's Healthcare has just arrived from State Bank. To prepare the bank reconciliation, you gather the following data:

    a. The October 31 bank balance is $5,170.

    b. The bank statement includes two charges for NSF checks from customers. One is for $420 (#1), and the other is for $120 (#2).

    c. The following White checks are outstanding at October 31:

Check No.	Amount
237	$ 90
288	150
291	580
294	590
295	10
296	150

    d. White collects from a few customers by EFT. The October bank statement lists a $1,400 EFT deposit for a collection on account.

    e. The bank statement includes two special deposits that White hasn't recorded yet: $1,050, for dividend revenue, and $50, the interest revenue White earned on its bank balance during October.

    f. The bank statement lists a $70 subtraction for the bank service charge.

    g. On October 31, the White treasurer deposited $290, but this deposit does not appear on the bank statement.

    h. The bank statement includes a $700 deduction for a check drawn by Multi-State Freight Company. White notified the bank of this bank error.

    i. White's Cash account shows a balance of $2,700 on October 31.

Requirements

    1. Prepare the bank reconciliation for White's Healthcare at October 31, 2012.

    2. Journalize any required entries from the bank reconciliation. Include an explanation for each entry.

P7-37B ⑦ **Identifying internal control weakness in cash receipts [10–15 min]**

Rocking Chair Productions makes all sales on credit. Cash receipts arrive by mail. Larry Padgitt in the mailroom opens envelopes and separates the checks from the accompanying remittance advices. Padgitt forwards the checks to another employee, who makes the daily bank deposit, but has no access to the accounting records. Padgitt sends the remittance advices, which show cash received, to the accounting department for entry in the accounts. Padgitt's only other duty is to grant sales allowances to customers. (A *sales allowance* decreases the amount receivable.) When Padgitt receives a customer check for $300 less a $40 sales allowance, he records the sales allowance and forwards the document to the accounting department.

Requirements

    1. Identify the internal control weakness in this situation.

    2. Who should record sales allowances?

    3. What is the amount that should be shown in the ledger for cash receipts?

P7-38B   ⑨ **Accounting for petty cash transactions [20–30 min]**

On September 1, Cool Salad Dressings creates a petty cash fund with an imprest balance of $250. During September, Michael Martell, the fund custodian, signs the following petty cash tickets:

Petty Cash Ticket Number	Item	Amount
101	Office supplies	$ 30
102	Cab fare for executive	20
103	Delivery of package across town	35
104	Dinner money for city manager to entertain the mayor	25
105	Inventory	80

On September 30, prior to replenishment, the fund contains these tickets plus cash of $65. The accounts affected by petty cash payments are Office supplies expense, Travel expense, Delivery expense, Entertainment expense, and Inventory.

Requirements

1. Explain the characteristics and the internal control features of an imprest fund.
2. On September 30, how much cash should the petty cash fund hold before it is replenished?
3. Journalize all required entries to create the fund and replenish it. Include explanations.
4. Make the October 1 entry to increase the fund balance to $300. Include an explanation, and briefly describe what the custodian does.

P7-39B   ⑨ **Accounting for petty cash transactions [20–30 min]**

Suppose that on September 1, Bash Gyrations, a disc jockey service, creates a petty cash fund with an imprest balance of $250. During September, Ruth Mangan, fund custodian, signs the following petty cash tickets:

Petty Cash Ticket Number	Item	Amount
1	Postage for package received	$ 30
2	Decorations and refreshments for office party	10
3	Two boxes of stationery	25
4	Printer cartridges	35
5	Dinner money for sales manager entertaining a customer	65

On September 30, prior to replenishment, the fund contains these tickets plus cash of $80. The accounts affected by petty cash payments are Office supplies expense, Entertainment expense, and Postage expense.

Requirements

1. On September 30, how much cash should this petty cash fund hold before it is replenished?
2. Journalize all required entries to (a) create the fund and (b) replenish it. Include explanations.
3. Make the entry on October 1 to increase the fund balance to $325. Include an explanation.

P7-40B ⑩ **Making an ethical judgment [15–30 min]**

Citizenship Bank has a loan receivable from Therot Recording Company. Therot is late making payments to the bank, and Robert Phelps, a Citizenship Bank vice president, is helping Therot restructure its debt. Phelps learns that Therot is depending on landing a $1,000,000 contract from Starstruck Theater, another Citizenship Bank client. Phelps also serves as Starstruck's loan officer at the bank. In this capacity, he is aware that Starstruck is considering declaring bankruptcy. Phelps has been a great help to Therot, and Therot's owner is counting on him to carry the company through this difficult restructuring. To help the bank collect on this large loan, Phelps has a strong motivation to help Therot survive.

Requirements

1. Identify the ethical issue that Phelps is facing. Specify the two main alternatives available to Phelps.
2. Identify the possible consequences of Phelps identifying Starstruck's financial position to Therot Recording Company.
3. Identify the correct ethical decision Phelps must make based on the two alternatives identified in Requirement 2.

● Continuing Exercise

E7-41 ⑨ **Accounting for petty cash transactions [20–30 min]**

This exercise continues the Lawlor Lawn Service situation from Exercise 6-44 of Chapter 6. During June, Lawlor Lawn Service decided that it needed a petty cash fund. Lawlor started the fund by cashing a check from her business bank account for $200. At the end of June, Lawlor had $123 in the petty cash fund. She also had three receipts, as shown:

    a. Receipt for $45 from the lawn supply store for Lawn Supplies

    b. Receipt for $11 from the gas station for fuel

    c. Receipt for $17 for lunch with a potential client

Requirements

1. Journalize the entry to establish the Petty cash fund.
2. Journalize any entries to replenish the fund at the end of June. Add any new accounts to the chart for Lawlor that may be necessary.

● Continuing Problem

P7-42 ⑥ **Preparing a bank reconciliation and journal entries [20–25 min]**

This problem continues the Draper Consulting situation from Problem 6-45 of Chapter 6. Draper performs systems consulting. Draper's February Cash from its general ledger is as follows:

Cash				
Jan 31 Bal	23,115	ck207	4,300	Feb 1
Feb 6	2,930	ck208	825	Feb 14
Feb 13	2,800	ck209	1,455	Feb 14
Feb 20	4,800	ck210	190	Feb 28
Feb 27	3,690	ck211	550	Feb 28
Feb 28 Unadj Bal	30,015			

Draper's bank statement dated February 28, 2013, follows:

Bank Statement for February 2013		
Beginning Balance, January 31, 2013		$23,510
Deposits and other Credits:		
Feb 1	$ 700	
Feb 8	2,930	
Feb 14	2,800	
Feb 20 EFT Hip Hop Hats-a customer	400	
Feb 22	4,800	
Feb 28 Interest credit	22	11,652
Checks and other Debits:		
Feb 2 EFT to Paper Products	$ 9	
Feb 2 ck#206	1,095	
Feb 18 ck#207	4,300	
Feb 19 ck#209	1,455	
Feb 28 EFT to The Cable Co.	85	
Feb 28 ck#208	825	
Bank Service Charge	18	(7,787)
Ending Balance, February 28, 2013		$27,375

Requirements

1. Prepare the February bank reconciliation.
2. Journalize and post any transactions required from the bank reconciliation. Key all items by date. Compute each account balance, and denote the balance as *Bal.*

● Practice Set

MyAccountingLab This problem continues the Shine King Cleaning problem begun in Chapter 1 and continued through Chapters 2–6.

P7-43 ❻ **Preparing a bank reconciliation and journal entries [20–25 min]**
Consider the November 2012 transactions for Shine King Cleaning that were presented in Chapter 2. The bank statement dated November 30, 2012, for Shine King follows.

Bank Statement for November 2012		
Beginning Balance, October 31, 2012		$ 0
Deposits and other Credits:		
Nov 2	$35,000	
Nov 10	100	
Nov 18	4,400	
Nov 21	40,000	
Nov 29 EFT Pierre's Wig Stand	600	
Nov 30 Interest credit	16	80,116
Checks and other Debits:		
Nov 2 EFT to Check Art	$ 30	
Nov 5 ck#101	2,000	
Nov 9 ck#103	1,200	
Nov 9 ck#102	2,400	
Nov 26 ck#105	500	
Nov 28 EFT to Calpine Energy	145	
Nov 28 ck#106	100	
Bank Service Charge	18	(6,393)
Ending Balance, November 30, 2012		$73,723

Requirements

1. Prepare the bank reconciliation.
2. Journalize any required entries from the bank reconciliation.

Apply Your Knowledge

● Decision Cases

Decision Case 7-1 Research the Sarbanes-Oxley Act on the Internet.

Requirement

1. Surf around for information on internal control, write a report of your findings, and present it to your class (if required by your instructor).

Decision Case 7-2 This case is based on an actual situation. Centennial Construction Company, headquartered in Dallas, Texas, built a Rodeway Motel 35 miles north of Dallas. The construction foreman, whose name was Slim Chance, hired the 40 workers needed to complete the project. Slim had the construction workers fill out the necessary tax forms, and he sent their documents to the home office.

Work on the motel began on April 1 and ended September 1. Each week, Slim filled out a time card of hours worked by each employee during the week. Slim faxed the time sheets to the home office, which prepared the payroll checks on Friday morning. Slim drove to the home office on Friday, picked up the payroll checks, and returned to the construction site. At 5 PM on Friday, Slim distributed payroll checks to the workers.

Requirements

1. Describe in detail the main internal control weakness in this situation. Specify what negative result(s) could occur because of the internal control weakness.
2. Describe what you would do to correct the internal control weakness.

Decision Case 7-3 San Diego Harbor Tours has poor internal control over cash. Ben Johnson, the owner, suspects the cashier of stealing. Here are some details of company cash at September 30:

a. The Cash account in the ledger shows a balance of $6,450.
b. The September 30 bank statement shows a balance of $4,300. The bank statement lists a $200 bank collection, a $10 service charge, and a $40 NSF check.
c. At September 30, the following checks are outstanding:

Amount
$100
300
600
200

d. There is a $3,000 deposit in transit at September 30.
e. The cashier handles all incoming cash and makes bank deposits. He also writes checks and reconciles the monthly bank statement.

Johnson asks you to determine whether the cashier has stolen cash from the business and, if so, how much.

Requirements

1. Perform your own bank reconciliation using the format illustrated in the chapter. There are no bank or book errors.
2. Explain how Johnson can improve his internal controls.

Ethical Issue 7-1

Mel O'Conner owns rental properties in Michigan. Each property has a manager who collects rent, arranges for repairs, and runs advertisements in the local newspaper. The property managers transfer cash to O'Conner monthly and prepare their own bank reconciliations. The manager in Lansing has been stealing from the company. To cover the theft, he understates the amount of the outstanding checks on the monthly bank reconciliation. As a result, each monthly bank reconciliation appears to balance. However, the balance sheet reports more cash than O'Conner actually has in the bank. O'Conner is currently putting his entire business up for sale. In negotiating the sale of the business, O'Conner is showing the balance sheet to prospective buyers.

Requirements

1. Identify who, other than O'Conner, could be harmed by this theft. In what ways could they be harmed?
2. Discuss the role accounting plays in this situation.

Fraud Case 7-1

Levon Helm was a kind of one-man mortgage broker. He would drive around Tennessee looking for homes that had second mortgages, and if the criteria were favorable, he would offer to buy the second mortgage for "cash on the barrelhead." Helm bought low and sold high, making sizable profits. Being a small operation, he employed one person, Cindy Patterson, who did all his bookkeeping. Patterson was an old family friend, and he trusted her so implicitly that he never checked up on the ledgers or the bank reconciliations. At some point, Patterson started "borrowing" from the business and concealing her transactions by booking phony expenses. She intended to pay it back someday, but she got used to the extra cash and couldn't stop. By the time the scam was discovered, she had drained the company of funds that it owed to many of its creditors. The company went bankrupt, Patterson did some jail time, and Helm lost everything.

Requirements

1. What was the key control weakness in this case?
2. Many small businesses cannot afford to hire enough people for adequate separation of duties. What can they do to compensate for this?

Financial Statement Case 7-1

Study the audit opinion (labeled Report of Ernst & Young LLP) of **Amazon.com** and the **Amazon** financial statements given in Appendix A at the end of this book. Answer the following questions about the company.

Requirements

1. What is the name of **Amazon**'s outside auditing firm (independent registered public accounting firm)? What office of this firm signed the audit report? How long after the **Amazon** year-end did the auditors issue their opinion?
2. Who bears primary responsibility for the financial statements? How can you tell?
3. Does it appear that the **Amazon** internal controls are adequate? How can you tell?
4. What standard of auditing did the outside auditors use in examining the **Amazon** financial statements? By what accounting standards were the statements evaluated?
5. By how much did **Amazon**'s cash balance (including cash equivalents) change during 2009? What were the beginning and ending cash balances?

• Team Project 7-1

You are promoting a rock concert in your area. Each member of your team will invest $10,000 of his or her hard-earned money in this venture. It is April 1 and the concert is scheduled for June 30. Your promotional activities begin immediately, and ticket sales start on May 1. You expect to sell all the business's assets, pay all the liabilities, and distribute all remaining cash to the group members by July 31.

Requirement

1. Write an internal control manual that will help safeguard the assets of the business. The starting point of the manual is to assign responsibilities among the group members. Authorize individuals, including group members and any outsiders that you need to hire, to perform specific jobs. Separate duties among the group and any employees.

• Communication Activity 7-1

In 75 words or fewer, explain why there may be a difference between the bank statement ending cash balance and the ending balance in the Cash account. Give at least two examples each of adjustments to the bank balance and to the book balance.

Quick Check Answers

1. *a* 2. *d* 3. *d* 4. *d* 5. *d* 6. *b* 7. *c* 8. *c* 9. *c* 10. *d*

For online homework, exercises, and problems that provide you immediate feedback, please visit myaccountinglab.com.

8 Receivables

The amount of cash expected to be collected in the near future.

SMART TOUCH LEARNING
Balance Sheet
May 31, 2013

Assets				Liabilities	
Current assets:				Current liabilities:	
Cash		$ 4,800		Accounts payable	$ 48,700
Accounts receivable		2,600		Salary payable	900
Inventory		30,500		Interest payable	100
Supplies		600		Unearned service revenue	400
Prepaid rent		2,000		Total current liabilities	50,100
Total current assets			$ 40,500	Long-term liabilities:	
Plant assets:				Notes payable	20,000
Furniture	$18,000			Total liabilities	70,100
Less: Accumulated depreciation—furniture	300	17,700			
Building	48,000				
Less: Accumulated depreciation—building	200	47,800		Owner's Equity	
Total plant assets			65,500	Bright, capital	35,900
Total assets			$106,000	Total liabilities and owner's equity	$106,000

Learning Objectives

1 Define and explain common types of receivables and review internal controls for receivables

2 Use the allowance method to account for uncollectibles

3 Understand the direct write-off method for uncollectibles

4 Journalize credit-card and debit-card sales

5 Account for notes receivable

6 Report receivables on the balance sheet and evaluate a company using the acid-test ratio, days' sales in receivables, and the accounts receivable turnover ratio

7 Discount a note receivable (see Appendix 8A)

Smart Touch Learning is doing well—so well in fact that Sheena's alma mater, The University of West Florida, has ordered 50 Microsoft Outlook training DVDs. This is great news, but there is a hitch. The college cannot pay Sheena immediately. It usually takes around 30 days to clear the paperwork and cut a check. Can Smart Touch wait 30 days to get the money? If it can't wait, the company may lose the sale.

Greg's Tunes is also expanding and accepting sales on credit as well as credit and debit cards from its customers. Greg's Tunes also must determine whether the change will help Greg's to expand, even though its cash receipts will be different.

Most businesses face this situation. There are both advantages and disadvantages to extending credit to customers. In the case of both companies, the pluses outweigh the minuses, so Smart Touch and Greg's Tunes will accept these terms of payment.

The main advantage of selling on credit (selling on account) is expanding the business's customer base, which is a way to increase sales. The disadvantages are that the company has to wait to receive cash and some customers may never pay, which means that the company may never collect some of the receivables.

●   ●   ●

This chapter focuses on accounting for receivables.

Receivables: An Introduction

You have a **receivable** when you sell goods or services to another party on credit. The receivable is the seller's claim for the amount of the transaction. You also have a receivable when you loan money to another party. **So a receivable is the right to receive cash in the future from a current transaction.** It is something the business owns; therefore, it is an asset. *Each* receivable transaction involves two parties:

 Define and explain common types of receivables and review internal controls for receivables

- The creditor, who gets a receivable (an asset). **The creditor will collect cash from the customer.**
- The **debtor**, who takes on an obligation/payable (a liability). **The debtor will pay cash later.**

Types of Receivables

The two major types of receivables are

- accounts receivable, and
- notes receivable.

Accounts receivable, also called **trade receivables**, are amounts to be collected from customers from sales made on credit. Accounts receivable serves as a control account because it summarizes the total of all the individual customer receivables. A **control account** is an account in the general ledger that summarizes related **subsidiary accounts**. So, for example, Accounts receivable is a control account and Brown is a customer who has an accounts receivable subsidiary account. A **subsidiary ledger** is a ledger that contains the details, for example by customer or vendor, of individual account balances. The sum of all related subsidiary ledger accounts will equal the control account. Companies also keep a ledger of each receivable from each customer. This customer subsidiary ledger contains the details for each individual customer that are summarized in the Accounts receivable control ledger. **The subsidiary ledger is the list of all the individual amounts** owed by customers that totals the amount shown in Accounts receivable (the control account) on the balance sheet. This is illustrated as follows:

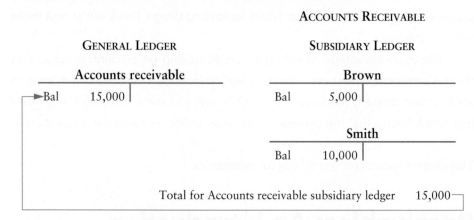

ACCOUNTS RECEIVABLE

| GENERAL LEDGER | SUBSIDIARY LEDGER |

Accounts receivable

→Bal   15,000 |

Brown

Bal   5,000 |

Smith

Bal   10,000 |

Total for Accounts receivable subsidiary ledger   15,000

The control account, Accounts receivable, shows a balance of $15,000. The individual customer accounts in the subsidiary ledger (Brown $5,000 + Smith $10,000) add up to a total of $15,000.

Notes receivable are usually longer in term than accounts receivable. **Notes receivable represent the right to receive a certain amount of cash in the future from a customer or other party.** The debtor of a note promises to pay the creditor a definite sum at a future date—called the **maturity date. The maturity date is the date the debt must be completely paid off.** A written document known as a **promissory note** serves as the evidence of the indebtedness and is signed by both the creditor and the debtor. Notes receivable due within one year or less are current assets. Notes due beyond one year are long-term assets.

Other receivables make up a miscellaneous category that includes any other type of cash that is receivable in the future. Common examples include loans to employees and interest receivable. These other receivables may be either long-term or current assets, depending on whether they are due within one year or less.

Internal Control over Receivables

Businesses that sell on credit receive cash (check payments) by mail or online payments (EFT), so internal control over collections is important. As we discussed in the previous chapter, a critical element of internal control is the separation of cash-handling and cash-accounting duties.

Most large companies also have a credit department to evaluate customers' credit applications. **Evaluating credit applications means the customer's credit is reviewed to determine whether the customer meets the company's credit approval standards. Then the customer is either approved to charge the purchase with the vendor or the customer gets declined to charge the purchase.** The extension of credit is a balancing act. The company does not want to lose sales to good customers, but it also wants to avoid receivables that will never be collected. For good internal control over cash collections from receivables, the credit department should have no access to cash. Additionally, those who handle cash should not be in a position to grant credit to customers. For example, if a credit department employee also handles cash, the company would have no separation of duties. The employee could pocket money received from a customer. He or she could then label the customer's account as uncollectible, and the company would write off the account receivable, as discussed in the next section. The company would stop billing that customer, and the employee may have covered his or her theft. For this reason, separation of duties is important.

Key Takeaway

The two main differences between accounts receivable and notes receivable are that 1) accounts receivable are usually collected in a short time, such as within 30 days; and 2) notes receivable are usually longer in term and have a signed, interest-bearing document to support the note. Since receivables ultimately result in cash collections for the company, good internal controls should be in place.

Accounting for Uncollectibles (Bad Debts)

As we discussed earlier, selling on credit (on account) creates an account receivable. The creation of this account receivable is really the first step in the process. However, if the company sells only for cash, it has no accounts receivable and, therefore, no bad debts from unreceived customer accounts. The examples in this chapter assume that the company making the sale is also going to handle collecting its own sales. Another option the company has is to hire a third party collection agency to collect receivables on the company's behalf for a fee. Let's say that Greg's Tunes sells $5,000 in services to customer Brown on account and also sells $10,000 of inventory to customer Smith on account on August 8, 2014. The revenue is recorded (ignore COGS) as follows:

	2014			
1a	Aug 8	Accounts receivable—Brown (A+)	5,000	
		Service revenue (R+)		5,000
		Performed service on account.		

1a	Aug 8	Accounts receivable—Smith (A+)	10,000	
		Sales revenue (R+)		10,000
		Sold goods on account.		

The business collects cash from both customers on August 29—$4,000 from Brown and $8,000 from Smith. Collecting cash is the second step in the process and Greg's makes the following entry:

2	Aug 29	Cash (A+)	12,000	
		Accounts receivable—Smith (A–)		8,000
		Accounts receivable—Brown (A–)		4,000
		Collected cash on account.		

Selling on credit brings both a benefit and a cost.

- **The benefit:** Increase revenues and profits by making sales to a wider range of customers.
- **The cost:** Some customers do not pay, and that creates an expense called **uncollectible account expense, doubtful account expense,** or **bad debt expense.** All three account names mean the same thing. **A bad debt expense arises when a customer did not pay his or her account balance.**

There are two methods of accounting for uncollectible receivables:

- the allowance method,
- or, in certain limited cases, the direct write-off method.

We begin with the allowance method because it is the method preferred by GAAP and IFRS.

The Allowance Method

Most companies use the allowance method to measure bad debts. The **allowance method** is based on the matching principle; thus, the key concept is to record uncollectible accounts expense in the same period as the sales revenue. The offset to the expense is a contra account called **Allowance for uncollectible accounts** or the

 2 Use the allowance method to account for uncollectibles

Allowance for doubtful accounts. The Allowance account reduces Accounts receivable. The business does not wait to see which customers will not pay. Instead, it records a bad debt expense based on estimates developed from past experience and uses the allowance for uncollectible accounts to house the pool of "unknown" bad debtors.

Estimating Uncollectibles

So, how are uncollectible receivables estimated? Companies use their past experience as well as considering the economy, the industry they operate in, and other variables. In short, they make an educated guess, called an estimate. There are two basic ways to estimate uncollectibles:

- Percent-of-sales
- Aging-of-accounts-receivable

Both approaches are part of the allowance method, and both normally require a journal entry.

Percent-of-Sales Method

The **percent-of-sales method** computes uncollectible account expense as a percentage of net credit sales. This method is also called the **income-statement approach** because it focuses on the amount of expense. Let's go back to our Greg's Tunes receivables for August. The accounts have the following balances:

Accounts receivable		Allowance for uncollectible accounts	
3,000			0

Interpretation: Accounts receivable reports the amount that customers owe you. If you were to collect from all customers, you would receive $3,000. Allowance for uncollectible accounts should report the amount of the receivables that you *never* expect to collect. At this point, Greg's Tunes thinks all receivables are collectible ($0 balance in Allowance).

How the Percent-of-Sales Method Works

Based on prior experience, Greg's uncollectible account expense is normally 2% of net credit sales, which totaled $15,000 for August. The journal entry records the following at August 31, 2014:

	2014			
1b	Aug 31	Uncollectible account expense ($15,000 × 0.02) (E+)	300	
		Allowance for uncollectible accounts (CA+)		300
		Recorded uncollectible expense for the period.		

After posting, the accounts are ready for the balance sheet.

Accounts receivable		Allowance for uncollectible accounts		
3,000				0
			Aug 31	300
			End Bal	300

Accounts receivable, net $2,700

Now the allowance for uncollectible accounts is realistic. **Net realizable value** is the net value that the company expects to collect from its receivables (Accounts receivable – Allowance for uncollectible accounts). The balance sheet will report accounts receivable at the net amount of $2,700 on August 31, 2014. The income statement will report uncollectible account expense for August of $300.

Aging-of-Accounts Method

The other approach for estimating uncollectible receivables is the **aging-of-accounts method**. This method is also called the **balance-sheet approach** because it focuses on the actual age of the accounts receivable and determines a target allowance balance from that age. Assume it is now December 31, 2014, and Greg's Tunes has recorded the remainder of the year's activity in the accounts such that the accounts now have the following balances *before the year-end adjustments:*

Accounts receivable		Allowance for uncollectible accounts
2,800		150

In the aging approach, you group individual accounts (Broxson, Andrews, etc.) according to how long they have been outstanding. The computer can sort customer accounts by age. Exhibit 8-1 shows how Greg's Tunes groups its accounts receivable. This is called an aging schedule.

EXHIBIT 8-1   **Aging the Accounts Receivable of Greg's Tunes**

Customer Name	1–30 Days	31–60 Days	61–90 Days	Over 90 Days	Total Balance
Broxson	$ 500				$ 500
Phi Chi Fraternity	1,300				1,300
Andrews		80			80
Jones		120			120
Other accounts	60		340	$400	800
Totals	$1,860	$200	$340	$400	$2,800 A
Estimated percentage uncollectible	× 1%	× 2%	× 5%	× 90%	
Allowance for Uncollectible Accounts balance	+ $ 19*	+ $ 4	+ $ 17	+ $360	= $ 400 B

*Value is rounded

Interpretation: Customers owe you $2,800 **A**, but you expect not to collect $400 **B** of this amount. Notice that the percentage uncollectible increases as a customer account gets older.

Stop & Think...

Have you ever loaned money to a friend? If so, you have had a receivable. The more that time passes from when you loaned that friend money, the less likely you are to receive your cash back. This is the premise of the aging method in Exhibit 8-1. Another way to say this is that the older accounts have a HIGHER percentage of uncollectibility.

How the Aging Method Works

The aging method tells you what the credit balance of the allowance account needs to be—the target allowance balance—$400 in this case. So, place the target balance into the Allowance T-account as follows:

Accounts receivable		Allowance for uncollectible accounts	
2,800			150
			$400 Target Balance

Then consider the account information:

$150 Credit balance plus/minus adjustment = $400 Credit Target Balance

The Allowance account needs $250 more in Credit. To adjust the allowance, make the following entry at year end:

	2014				
4	Dec 31	Uncollectible account expense (E+)		250	
		Allowance for uncollectible accounts ($400 – $150) (CA+)			250
		Adjusted the allowance account.			

After posting, the accounts are up-to-date and ready for the balance sheet.

Accounts receivable		Allowance for uncollectible accounts		
2,800				150
			Adj	250
			End Bal	400

Accounts receivable, net $2,400

Report Accounts receivable at net realizable value of $2,400 because that is the amount Greg's Tunes expects to collect in cash in the future.

Using Percent-of-Sales and Aging Methods Together

In practice, companies use the percent-of-sales and the aging-of-accounts methods together.

- For *interim statements* (monthly or quarterly), companies use the percent-of-sales method because it is easier.
- At the end of the year, companies use the aging method to ensure that Accounts receivable is reported at *net realizable value*.
- Using the two methods together provides good measures of both the expense and the asset. Exhibit 8-2 summarizes and compares the two methods.

EXHIBIT 8-2	Comparing the Percent-of-Sales and Aging Methods

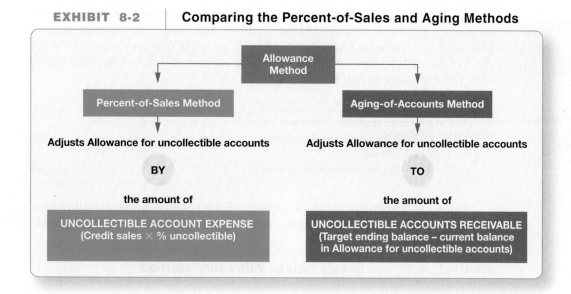

Identifying and Writing Off Uncollectible Accounts

Early in 2015, Greg's Tunes collects most of its accounts receivable and records the cash receipts as follows (amount assumed):

	2015			
2	Jan 5	Cash (A+)	2,000	
		Accounts receivable (various customers) (A–)		2,000
		Collected on account.		

Suppose that, after repeated attempts, Greg's accountant finally decides on January 10, 2015, that the company cannot collect a total of $200 from customers Andrews and Jones (from Exhibit 8-1). At the time these bad debts are identified, the entry is made to write off the receivables from these customers, as follows:

	2015			
3	Jan 10	Allowance for uncollectible accounts (CA–)	200	
		Accounts receivable—Andrews (A–)		80
		Accounts receivable—Jones (A–)		120
		Wrote off uncollectible accounts.		

Recovery of Accounts Previously Written Off— Allowance Method

When an account receivable is written off as uncollectible, the receivable does not die: The customer still owes the money. However, the company stops pursuing collection and writes off the account as uncollectible. Some companies turn delinquent receivables over to an attorney or other collection agency to recover some of the cash for the company.

Recall that Greg's Tunes wrote off the $80 receivable from customer Andrews on January 10, 2015. It is now March 4, 2015, and Greg's unexpectedly receives $80 cash from Andrews. To account for this recovery, the company must reverse the effect of the earlier write-off to the Allowance account and record the cash collection. The entries are as follows:

	2015			
5	Mar 4	Accounts receivable—Andrews (A+)	80	
		Allowance for uncollectible accounts (CA+)		80
		Cash (A+)	80	
		Accounts receivable—Andrews (A–)		80

Exhibit 8-3 summarizes the entries we have covered using the allowance method of accounting for uncollectible accounts and the entries we have made for Greg's Tunes:

EXHIBIT 8-3 | **Greg's Tunes—Allowance Method**

PANEL A—Transactions

1a) Make sales on account.
1b) Establish a pool for future potential uncollectibility (2%).
2) Collect cash on account.
3) Identify a bad debt.
4) Adjust allowance account to reflect adjustments to the estimate.
5) Recover previously written off account.

PANEL B—Journal Entries

1a	Aug 8, 2014	Accounts receivable—Brown (A+)	5,000	
		Service revenue (R+)		5,000
		Accounts receivable—Smith (A+)	10,000	
		Sales revenue (R+)		10,000
1b	Aug 31, 2014	Uncollectible account expense (E+)	300	
		Allowance for uncollectible accounts (CA+)		300
		(15,000 credit sales × 0.02)		
2	Aug 29, 2014	Cash (A+)	12,000	
		Accounts receivable—Smith (A–)		8,000
		Accounts receivable—Brown (A–)		4,000
3	Jan 10, 2015	Allowance for uncollectible accounts (CA–)	200	
		Accounts receivable—Andrews (A–)		80
		Accounts receivable—Jones (A–)		120
4	Dec 31, 2014	Uncollectible account expense (E+)	250	
		Allowance for uncollectible accounts (CA+)		250
5	Mar 4, 2015	Accounts receivable—Andrews (A+)	80	
		Allowance for uncollectible accounts (CA+)		80
		Cash (A+)	80	
		Accounts receivable—Andrews (A–)		80

The Direct Write-Off Method

3 Understand the direct write-off method for uncollectibles

There is another way to account for uncollectible receivables that is primarily used by small, non-public companies. It is called the **direct write-off method**. Under the direct write-off method, you do not use the Allowance for uncollectible accounts account to record the expense based on an estimate. Instead, you wait until you determine that you will never collect from a specific customer. Then you write off the customer's account receivable by debiting Uncollectible account expense and crediting the customer's Account receivable. Although this method is required for tax purposes, it generally does not create a result in which the credit sales are matching in the same periods as the subsequent uncollectible accounts (bad debts). For example, let's reconsider Greg's Tunes' identified bad debts from January 10, 2015. The entry under the direct write-off method would be as follows:

	2015				
3	Jan 10	Uncollectible account expense (E+)		200	
		Accounts receivable—Andrews (A–)			80
		Accounts receivable—Jones (A–)			120
		Wrote off a bad account.			

The direct write-off method is defective for two reasons:

1. It does not set up an Allowance for uncollectible accounts account. As a result, the direct write-off method always reports accounts receivables at their full amount. Thus, assets are overstated on the balance sheet.

2. It does not match Uncollectible account expense against revenue very well. In this example, Greg's Tunes made the sales to Andrews and Jones in 2014 and journalized Sales revenue on August 31 of that year. However, Greg's wrote off the bad debts by recording the Uncollectible account expense on January 10, 2015, a different year. As a result, Greg's Tunes *overstates* net income in 2014 and *understates* net income in 2015.

The direct write-off method is acceptable only when uncollectible receivables are very low. It works well for small companies, but it also works for retailers such as **Walmart**, **McDonald's**, and **Gap** because those companies carry almost no receivables.

Recovery of Accounts Previously Written Off— Direct Write-Off Method

As with the allowance method, under the direct write-off method, an account receivable that is written off as uncollectible does not die: The customer still owes the money. However, the accounting between the two methods differs slightly. Recall that Greg's Tunes wrote off the $80 receivable from customer Andrews on January 10, 2015. It is now March 4, 2015, and the company unexpectedly receives $80 from Andrews. To account for this recovery, the company must reverse the effect of the earlier write-off to the Uncollectible account expense account and record the cash collection. The entries are as follows:

5	Mar 4	Accounts receivable—Andrews (A+)		80	
		Uncollectible account expense (E–)			80
		Cash (A+)		80	
		Accounts receivable—Andrews (A–)			80

Exhibit 8-4 summarizes the entries that would be made using the direct write-off method of accounting for uncollectible accounts and the entries we have made for Greg's Tunes.

EXHIBIT 8-4 | **Greg's Tunes—Direct Write-Off Method**

PANEL A—Transactions

1a) Make sales on account.
1b) N/A
2) Collect cash on account.
3) Identify a bad debt.
4) N/A
5) Recover previously written off account.

PANEL B—Journal Entries

1a	Aug 8, 2014	Accounts receivable—Brown	(A+)	5,000	
		Service revenue	(R+)		5,000
		Accounts receivable—Smith	(A+)	10,000	
		Sales revenue	(R+)		10,000
1b	Aug 31, 2014	no entry			
2	Aug 29, 2014	Cash	(A+)	12,000	
		Accounts receivable—Smith	(A−)		8,000
		Accounts receivable—Brown	(A−)		4,000
3	Jan 10, 2015	Uncollectible account expense	(E+)	200	
		Accounts receivable—Andrews	(A−)		80
		Accounts receivable—Jones	(A−)		120
4	Dec 31, 2014	no entry			
5	Mar 4, 2015	Accounts receivable—Andrews	(A+)	80	
		Uncollectible account expense	(E−)		80
		Cash	(A+)	80	
		Accounts receivable—Andrews	(A−)		80

Key Takeaway

There is no Allowance for uncollectible accounts account or estimates used for the direct write-off method. The expense is journalized at the time the company determines a customer cannot pay. The downside to this method is Accounts receivable is shown at 100% on the balance sheet, indicating to financial statement users that all the receivables will likely turn into cash collections in the future.

Compare Exhibit 8-4, using the direct write-off method, and Exhibit 8-3, using the allowance method. The entries that differ between the two methods are highlighted in blue.

Credit-Card and Debit-Card Sales

 Journalize credit-card and debit-card sales

So far we've discussed how to account for revenue transactions that are on account. Now let's look at two alternative forms of payment—by credit card and debit card—and how companies account for these transactions.

Credit-Card Sales

Credit card sales are an alternative form of receiving payment from a customer. By accepting credit cards, businesses are able to attract more customers. There are two main types of credit cards:

1. credit cards that are issued by a financial institution (bank or credit union). These are usually issued under the **Visa** and **Mastercard** name.

2. credit cards that are issued by a credit card company. Common examples of this type include **American Express** and **Discover** cards.

Credit cards offer the customer the convenience of buying something without having to pay cash immediately.

Retailers also benefit. They do not have to check each customer's credit rating or worry about keeping accounts receivable records or even collecting from the customer. The card issuer has the responsibility of collecting from the customer. Thus, instead of collecting cash from the customer, the seller will receive cash from the card issuer. There is almost always a fee to the seller to cover the processing costs.

Debit-Card Sales

Another means by which businesses attract customers is by accepting debit card payments. From the seller's viewpoint, debit cards have almost the same benefits as credit cards. The main difference between credit and debit cards is in how and when the customer must pay the card issuer.

Credit-/Debit-Card Sales

Companies like Greg's Tunes or **Target** hire a third-party processor to process credit and debit card transactions. Transactions are usually entered into an electronic terminal (card scanner) that the company either purchases or rents from the processor. The fees the card processor charges the company for its processing services vary depending on the type of card and the specific agreement the company has with the card processor. The processor agreement specifies how fees are paid to the processor. Following are two common methods of deposits of proceeds:

- NET: The total sale less the processing fee assessed equals the net amount of cash deposited by the processor, usually within a few days of the sale date.
- GROSS: The total sale is deposited daily within a few days of the actual sale date. The processing fees for all transactions processed for the month are deducted from the company's bank account by the processor, often on the last day of the month.

Proceeds from credit and debit card transactions are usually deposited within a few business days. Therefore, credit and debit card sales are journalized similar to cash sales.

Suppose you and your family have dinner at a **Good Eats** restaurant on February 25. You pay the bill—$50—with a **Discover® Card**.

Good Eats entry to record the $50 sale, assuming the card processor assesses a 4% discount and nets the deposit, is as follows:

Feb 25	Cash (A+)	48	
	Card discount expense ($50 × 0.04) (E+)	2	
	Sales revenue (R+)		50
	Recorded credit-card sales, net of fee.		

The same entry assuming the processor uses the gross method on the sale date would be as follows:

Feb 25	Cash (A+)		50	
	Sales revenue (R+)			50
	Recorded credit-card sales.			

At the end of February, the processor would collect the fees assessed for the month. (Note: We assume only the one card sale for this month.)

Feb 28	Card discount expense ($50 × 0.02) (E+)		2	
	Cash (A–)			2
	Recorded fees assessed by card processor.			

Summary Problem 8-1

Monarch Map Company's balance sheet at December 31, 2011, reported the following:

Accounts receivable..	$60,000
Less: Allowance for uncollectible accounts........	2,000

Requirements

1. How much of the receivable did Monarch expect to collect? Stated differently, what was the net realizable value of these receivables?
2. Journalize, without explanations, 2012 entries for Monarch:
   a. Total credit sales for 2012 were $80,000; 3% of sales were estimated to be uncollectible. Monarch received cash payments on account during 2012 of $74,300.
   b. Accounts receivable identified to be uncollectible totaled $2,700.
   c. December 31, 2012, aging of receivables indicates that $2,200 of the receivables is uncollectible (target balance).
3. Post the transactions to the Accounts receivable and the Allowance for uncollectible accounts T-accounts. Calculate and report Monarch's receivables and related allowance on the December 31, 2012 balance sheet. What is the net realizable value of receivables at December 31, 2012? How much is the uncollectible account expense for 2012?
4. What if the beginning balance in the Allowance for uncollectible accounts had instead been $200 credit? Journalize the entry or (entries) that would change. What would be the ending balance in the Allowance for uncollectible accounts after posting the entries? What would be the balance in Accounts receivable?

Solution

Requirement 1

Net realizable value of receivables ($60,000 – $2,000)............	$58,000

Requirement 2

a.		Accounts receivable (A+)	80,000	
		Sales revenue (R+)		80,000
		Uncollectible account expense (80,000 × 0.03) (E+)	2,400	
		Allowance for uncollectible accounts (CA+)		2,400
		Cash (A+)	74,300	
		Accounts receivable (A–)		74,300
b.		Allowance for uncollectible accounts (CA–)	2,700	
		Accounts receivable (A–)		2,700
c.		Uncollectible account expense ($2,200 – $1,700) (E+)	500	
		Allowance for uncollectible accounts (CA+)		500

Accounts receivable

Dec 31, 2011 Bal	60,000		
a.	80,000	74,300	a.
		2,700	b.
Dec 31, 2012 Bal	63,000		

Allowance for uncollectible accounts

		Dec 31, 2011 Bal	2,000
2012 Write-offs Adj b.	2,700	2012 Expense Adj a.	2,400
		Bal before Adj	1,700
		Dec 31, 2012 Adj c.	500
		Dec 31, 2012 Bal	2,200

Requirement 3

Accounts receivable	$63,000
Less: Allowance for uncollectible accounts	2,200
Accounts receivable, net	$60,800
Uncollectible account expense for 2012 ($2,400 + $500)	$ 2,900

Requirement 4

a.		Accounts receivable (A+)	80,000	
		Sales revenue (R+)		80,000
		Cash (A+)	74,300	
		Accounts receivable (A–)		74,300
		Uncollectible account expense (80,000 × 0.03) (E+)	2,400	
		Allowance for uncollectible accounts (CA+)		2,400
b.		Allowance for uncollectible accounts (CA–)	2,700	
		Accounts receivable (A–)		2,700
c.		Uncollectible account expense ($100 + $2,000) (E+)	2,300	
		Allowance for uncollectible accounts (CA+)		2,300

Accounts receivable

Dec 31, 2011 Bal	60,000		
a.	80,000	74,300	a.
		2,700	b.
Dec 31, 2012 Bal	63,000		

Allowance for uncollectible accounts

		Dec 31, 2011 Bal	200
2012 Write-offs Adj b.	2,700	2012 Expense Adj a.	2,400
Bal Before Adj	100		
		Dec 31, 2012 Adj c.	2,300
		Dec 31, 2012 Bal	2,200

Accounts receivable...	$63,000
Less: Allowance for uncollectible accounts.................................	2,200
Accounts receivable, net..	$60,800
Uncollectible account expense for 2012 ($2,400 + $2,300).........	$ 4,700

Notes Receivable

 Account for notes receivable

Notes receivable are more formal than accounts receivable. The debtor signs a promissory note as evidence of the transaction. Before launching into the accounting, let's define the special terms used for notes receivable:

- **Promissory note:** A written promise to pay a specified amount of money at a particular future date.
- **Maker of the note (debtor):** The entity that signs the note and promises to pay the required amount; the maker of the note is the *debtor.* **The debtor is the company that must pay the money back.**
- **Payee of the note (creditor):** The entity to whom the maker promises future payment; the payee of the note is the *creditor.* **The creditor is the company that loans the money.**
- **Principal:** The amount loaned out by the payee and borrowed by the maker of the note.
- **Interest:** The revenue to the payee for loaning money. Interest is expense to the debtor and revenue to the creditor.
- **Interest period:** The period of time during which interest is computed. It extends from the original date of the note to the maturity date. Also called the **note term.**
- **Interest rate:** The percentage rate of interest specified by the note. Interest rates are almost always stated for a period of one year. **A 9% note means that the amount of interest for *one year* is 9% of the note's principal.**
- **Maturity date:** As stated earlier, this is the date when final payment of the note is due. Also called the **due date.**
- **Maturity value:** The sum of the principal plus interest due at maturity. **Maturity value is the total amount that will be paid back.**

Exhibit 8-5 illustrates a promissory note. Study it carefully.

EXHIBIT 8-5 | **A Promissory Note**

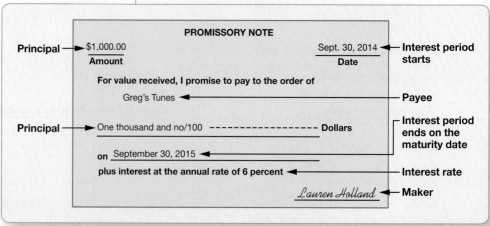

In Exhibit 8-5, we can see Greg's Tunes is lending Lauren Holland $1,000 on September 30, 2014, for one year at an annual interest rate of 6%.

Identifying Maturity Date

Some notes specify the maturity date. For example, September 30, 2015, is the maturity date of the note shown in Exhibit 8-5. Other notes state the period of the note in days or months. When the period is given in months, the note's maturity date falls on the same day of the month as the date the note was issued. For example, a six-month note dated February 16, 2014, would mature on August 16, 2014.

When the period is given in days, the maturity date is determined by counting the actual days from the date of issue. A 180-day note dated February 16, 2014, matures on August 15, 2014, as shown here:

Month	Number of Days	Cumulative Total
Feb 2014	28 – 16 = 12	12
Mar 2014	31	43
Apr 2014	30	73
May 2014	31	104
Jun 2014	30	134
Jul 2014	31	165
Aug 2014	15	180

In counting the days remaining for a note, remember to

- count the maturity date.
- omit the date the note was issued.

Computing Interest on a Note

The formula for computing the interest is as follows:

	Interest			Amount of
Principal ×	rate	× Time	=	interest

In the formula, **time (period)** represents the portion of a year that interest has accrued on the note. It may be expressed as a fraction of a year in months (x/12) or a fraction of a year in days (x/360 or x/365). Using the data in Exhibit 8-5, Greg's Tunes computes interest revenue for one year as follows:

	Interest			Amount of
Principal ×	rate	× Time	=	interest
$1,000	0.06	12/12		$60

The maturity value of the note is $1,060 ($1,000 principal + $60 interest). The time element is 12/12 or 1 because the note's term is one year.

When the term of a note is stated in months, we compute the interest based on the 12-month year. Interest on a $2,000 note at 10% for nine months is computed as follows:

	Interest			Amount of
Principal ×	rate	× Time	=	interest
$2,000	0.10	9/12		$150

When the interest period is stated in days, we sometimes compute interest based on a 360-day year rather than on a 365-day year.[1] The interest on a $5,000 note at 12% for 60 days can be computed as follows:

Principal	×	Interest rate	×	Time	=	Amount of interest
$5,000		0.12		60/360		$100

Keep in mind that interest rates are stated as an annual rate. Therefore, the time in the interest formula should also be expressed in terms of a fraction of the year.

Accruing Interest Revenue

Some notes receivable may be outstanding at the end of an accounting period. The interest revenue earned on the note up to year-end is part of that year's earnings. Recall that interest revenue is earned over time, not just when cash is received. Because of the matching principle, we want to record the earnings from the note in the year in which they were earned.

Now, we continue with Greg's Tunes' note receivable from Exhibit 8-5. Greg's Tunes' accounting period ends December 31.

- How much of the total interest revenue does Greg's Tunes earn in 2014 (from September 30 through December 31)?

$$\$1{,}000 \times 0.06 \times 3/12 = \$15.00$$

Greg's Tunes makes the following adjusting entry at December 31, 2014:

2014			
Dec 31	Interest receivable ($1,000 × 0.06 × 3/12) (A+)	15	
	Interest revenue (R+)		15
	Accrued interest revenue.		

- How much interest revenue does Greg's Tunes earn in 2015 (for January 1 through September 30)?

$$\$1{,}000 \times 0.06 \times 9/12 = \$45.00$$

On the note's maturity date, Greg's Tunes makes the following entry:

2015			
Sep 30	Cash [$1,000 + ($1,000 × 0.06)] (A+)	1,060	
	Notes receivable—L. Holland (A−)		1,000
	Interest receivable ($1,000 × 0.06 × 3/12) (A−)		15
	Interest revenue ($1,000 × 0.06 × 9/12) (R+)		45
	Collected note receivable plus interest.		

Earlier we determined that total interest on the note was $60 ($1,000 × 0.06 × 12/12). These entries assign the correct amount of interest to each year:

- $15 for 2014 + $45 for 2015 = $60 total interest

---

[1]A 360-day year eliminates some rounding.

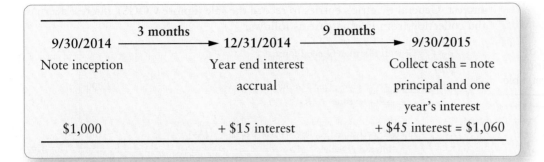

Stop & Think...

Why do we calculate interest on notes if we aren't getting paid yet? Think about any debts you may have. Does the interest continue to accrue until the point you pay off the debt? Yes, it does. The same is true for interest you receive from the bank on your savings account. The interest continues to accrue on your account until the bank deposits the cash in your bank account at the end of the month. This is the same reason companies accrue interest on the notes: The customers owe the interest to the company as soon as time expires on the note. This is the revenue recognition principle you learned about in Chapter 1.

Consider the loan agreement shown in Exhibit 8-5. Lauren Holland signs the note, and Greg's Tunes gives Holland $1,000 cash. At maturity, Holland pays Greg's Tunes $1,060 ($1,000 principal plus $60 interest). Greg's Tunes' entries are summarized as shown:

Loan Out Money

		Greg's Tunes' General Journal		
2014				
Sep 30		Notes receivable—L. Holland (A+)	1,000	
		Cash (A–)		1,000
Dec 31		Interest receivable ($1,000 × 0.06 × 3/12) (A+)	15	
		Interest revenue (R+)		15
2015				
Sep 30		Cash [$1,000 + ($1,000 × 0.06 × 12/12)] (A+)	1,060	
		Notes receivable—L. Holland (A–)		1,000
		Interest receivable (A–)		15
		Interest revenue ($1,000 × 0.06 × 9/12) (R+)		45

Some companies sell merchandise in exchange for notes receivable. Assume that on July 1, 2014, **General Electric** sells household appliances for $2,000 to Dorman Builders. Dorman signs a nine-month promissory note at 10% annual interest. **General Electric**'s entries to record the sale (ignore COGS), interest accrual, and collection from Dorman are as follows:

Sale on a Note Receivable

		General Electric's General Journal		
2014				
Jul 1		Notes receivable—Dorman Builders (A+)	2,000	
		Sales revenue (R+)		2,000
Dec 31		Interest receivable ($2,000 × 0.10 × 6/12) (A+)	100	
		Interest revenue (R+)		100
2015				
Apr 1		Cash [$2,000 + ($2,000 × 0.10 × 9/12)] (A+)	2,150	
		Notes receivable—Dorman Builders (A–)		2,000
		Interest receivable (A–)		100
		Interest revenue ($2,000 × 0.10 × 3/12) (R+)		50

A company may accept a note receivable from a trade customer who fails to pay an account receivable. The customer signs a promissory note and gives it to the creditor. Suppose Sports Club cannot pay Blanding Services. Blanding may accept a 60-day, $5,000 note receivable, with 12% interest, from Sports Club on November 19, 2014. Blanding's entries are as follows:

Converting Accounts receivable to Notes receivable

		Blanding Services' General Journal		
2014				
Nov 19		Notes receivable—Sports Club (A+)	5,000	
		Accounts receivable—Sports Club (A–)		5,000
Dec 31		Interest receivable ($5,000 × 0.12 × 42/360) (A+)	70	
		Interest revenue (R+)		70
2015				
Jan 18		Cash [$5,000 + ($5,000 × 0.12 × 60/360)] (A+)	5,100	
		Notes receivable—Sports Club (A–)		5,000
		Interest receivable (A–)		70
		Interest revenue ($5,000 × 0.12 × 18/360) (R+)		30

A company holding a note may need cash before the note matures. A procedure for selling the note to receive cash immediately, called discounting a note receivable, appears in Appendix 8A.

Dishonored Notes Receivable

If the maker of a note does not pay at maturity, the maker **dishonors** (**defaults on**) the note. Because the note has expired, it is no longer in force. But the debtor still owes the payee. The payee can transfer the note receivable amount to Accounts receivable. Suppose Rubinstein Jewelers has a six-month, 10% note receivable for $1,200 from Mark Adair that was signed on March 3, 2014, and Adair defaults. Rubinstein Jewelers will record the default on September 3, 2014, as follows:

2014				
Sep 3		Accounts receivable—M. Adair (A+)	1,260	
		Notes receivable—M. Adair (A–)		1,200
		Interest revenue ($1,200 × 0.10 × 6/12) (R+)		60
		Recorded a dishonored note receivable.		

Rubinstein will then bill Adair for the account receivable.

Computers and Receivables

Accounting for receivables by a company like **Mars** requires thousands of postings for credit sales and cash collections. Manual accounting cannot keep up. However, Accounts receivable can be computerized. At **Mars** the order entry, shipping, and billing departments work together, as shown in Exhibit 8-6.

EXHIBIT 8-6 | **Order Entry, Shipping, and Billing Working Together at Mars**

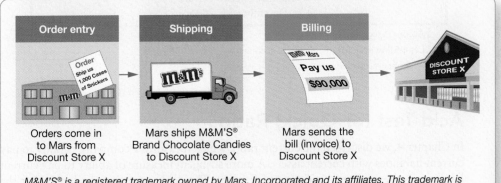

Orders come in to Mars from Discount Store X

Mars ships M&M'S® Brand Chocolate Candies to Discount Store X

Mars sends the bill (invoice) to Discount Store X

M&M'S® is a registered trademark owned by Mars, Incorporated and its affiliates. This trademark is used with permission. Mars, Incorporated is not associated with Pearson Prentice Hall. M&M'S® images printed with permission of Mars, Incorporated. © Mars, Inc. 2009.

Using Accounting Information for Decision Making

As discussed earlier in the text, the balance sheet lists assets in order of liquidity (closeness to cash). The partial balance sheet of Greg's Tunes shown in Exhibit 8-7 provides an example of this. Focus on the current assets at December 31, 2014. Balance-sheet data become more useful by showing the relationships among assets, liabilities, and revenues. Let's examine three important ratios.

6 Report receivables on the balance sheet and evaluate a company using the acid-test ratio, days' sales in receivables, and the accounts receivable turnover ratio

EXHIBIT 8-7 | **Greg's Tunes Balance Sheet**

GREG'S TUNES Balance Sheet—Partial December 31, 2015 and 2014		
Assets	December 31, 2015	2014
Current assets:		
Cash	$ 800	$ 400
Short-term investments	1,500	300
Accounts receivable, net of allowance for uncollectible accounts of $400 in 2015 and $300 in 2014	2,400	2,600
Interest receivable	0	15
Inventory	800	600
Notes receivable	0	1,000
Total current assets	5,500	4,915
Liabilities		
Current liabilities:		
Total current liabilities	$4,400	$2,900

Notice that Accounts receivable appear in the Current assets section of the balance sheet, net of the allowance for uncollectible accounts. This is the most common method of presentation. Interest receivable is also listed as a current asset, since we expect to collect it in less than a year. Finally, Notes receivable is also listed as a current asset since the note term was one year.

A company could also choose an alternate presentation for the Accounts receivable and Allowance for uncollectible accounts as shown below:

Greg's Tunes Balance Sheet—Partial December 31, 2015	
Accounts receivable	$2,800
Less: Allowance for uncollectible accounts	400
Accounts receivable, net	$2,400

Acid-Test (or Quick) Ratio

In Chapter 4, we discussed the current ratio, which measures a company's ability to pay current liabilities with current assets. A more stringent measure of ability to pay current liabilities is the **acid-test ratio** (or **quick ratio**). The acid-test ratio reveals whether the entity could pay all its current liabilities if they were to become due immediately.

For Greg's Tunes (Exhibit 8-7)

$$\text{Acid-test ratio} = \frac{\text{Cash} + \text{Short-term investments} + \text{Net current receivables}}{\text{Total current liabilities}}$$

$$= \frac{\$800 + \$1,500 + \$2,400}{\$4,400} = 1.07 \text{ (rounded)}$$

The higher the acid-test ratio, the more able the business is to pay its current liabilities. Greg's acid-test ratio of 1.07 means that the business has $1.07 of quick assets to pay each $1 of current liabilities. This is a strong position.

What is an acceptable acid-test ratio? That depends on the industry. **Walmart** operates smoothly with an acid-test ratio of less than 0.20. Several things make this possible: **Walmart** collects cash rapidly and has almost no receivables. The acid-test ratios for most department stores are about 0.80, while travel agencies average 1.10. In general, an acid-test ratio of 1.00 is considered safe.

Days' Sales in Receivables

After making a credit sale, the next step is to collect the receivable. **Days' sales in receivables**, also called the **collection period**, indicates how many days it takes to collect the average level of receivables. **The number of days in average accounts receivable should be close to the number of days customers are allowed to pay.** The shorter the collection period, the more quickly the organization can use its cash. The longer the collection period, the less cash is available for operations. Days' sales in receivables can be computed in two steps, as follows:[2]*

$$\underline{\text{For Greg's Tunes (Exhibit 8-7)}}$$

1. One day's sales = $\dfrac{\text{Net sales}}{\text{(or Total revenues)}} \Big/ 365 \text{ days}$

$= \dfrac{\$22,600^*}{365} = \$62 \text{ per day (rounded)}$

*From Greg's 2015 income statement, which is not reproduced here.

2. Days' sales in receivables $= \dfrac{\text{Average net accounts receivable}}{\text{One day's sales}}$

$= \dfrac{\left(\text{Beginning net accounts receivable} + \text{Ending net accounts receivable}\right)/2}{\text{One day's sales}}$

$= \dfrac{(\$2,400 + \$2,600)/2}{\$62} = 40 \text{ days (rounded)}$

On average, it takes Greg's Tunes 40 days to collect its accounts receivable. The length of the collection period depends on the credit terms of the sale. For example, sales on net 30 terms should be collected within approximately 30 days. When there is a discount, such as 2/10, net 30, the collection period may be shorter. Credit terms of net 45 result in a longer collection period.

Accounts Receivable Turnover Ratio

The **accounts receivable turnover ratio** measures the number of times the company sells and collects the average receivables balance in a year. The higher the ratio, the faster the cash collections. Greg's Tunes' accounts receivable turnover ratio, presented below, indicates a relatively slow turnover at only a little over nine times a year.

$$\text{Accounts receivable turnover} = \dfrac{\text{Net credit sales}}{\text{Average net accounts receivable}}$$

$$= \dfrac{22,600}{(2,400 + 2,600/2)} = 9.04 \text{ times}$$

*From Greg's 2015 income statement, which is not reproduced here.

Investors and creditors do not evaluate a company on the basis of one or two ratios. Instead, they analyze all the information available. Then they stand back and ask, "What is our overall impression of this company?" We present all the financial ratios in Chapter 15. By the time you get to that point of your study, you will have an overall view of the company.

---

[2]Days' sales in receivables can also be computed in this one step:

$$\text{Days' sales in receivables} = \dfrac{\text{Average net accounts receivables}}{\text{Net sales}} \times 365$$

> **Key Takeaway**
>
> Accounts receivable, net of allowance is listed in the Current asset section of the balance sheet. Notes receivable is listed as current ONLY if the note will be collected in one year or less. Ratios serve as benchmarks to see how well a company is managing its receivables.

Decision Guidelines 8-1

ACCOUNTING FOR RECEIVABLES

The Decision Guidelines feature summarizes some key decisions for receivables. Accounting for receivables is the same for Greg's Tunes as for a large company like **Mars**. Suppose you decide that Greg's will sell on account, as most other companies do. How should you account for your receivables? These guidelines show the way.

Decision	Guidelines
ACCOUNTS RECEIVABLE	
• How much of our receivables will we collect?	Less than the full amount of the receivables because we cannot collect from some customers

• How do we report receivables at their net realizable value?	• Use the *allowance method* to account for uncollectible receivables. Set up the contra account, Allowance for uncollectible accounts.
	 • Estimate uncollectibles by the
	    • *percent-of-sales method (income-statement approach).*
	    • *aging-of-accounts method (balance sheet approach).*
	 • Write off uncollectible receivables as they prove uncollectible.
	
	 Net accounts receivable = Accounts receivable – Allowance for uncollectible accounts

• Is there a simpler way to account for uncollectible receivables?	Yes, but it is unacceptable for most companies. The *direct write-off method* uses no Allowance for uncollectible accounts account. It simply debits Uncollectible accounts expense and credits a customer's Accounts receivable to remove the receivable when it has proved uncollectible. This method is acceptable only when uncollectibles are insignificant.
NOTES RECEIVABLE	
• What two other accounts are related to notes receivable?	Notes receivable are related to • interest revenue, and • interest receivable (interest revenue earned but not yet collected).
• How do we compute the interest on a note receivable?	Amount of interest = Principal × Interest rate × Time
• How do we report receivables on the balance sheet?	Accounts (or Notes) receivable $XXX Less: Allowance for uncollectible accounts X Accounts (or notes) receivable, net $ XX
• How can we use receivables to evaluate a company's financial position?	$$\text{Acid-test ratio} = \frac{\text{Cash + Short-term investments + Net current receivables}}{\text{Total current liabilities}}$$ $$\text{Days' sales in receivables} = \frac{\text{Average net accounts receivable}}{\text{One day's sales}}$$ $$\text{Accounts receivable turnover} = \frac{\text{Net credit sales}}{\text{Average net accounts receivable}}$$

Summary Problem 8-2

Suppose First Fidelity Bank engaged in the following transactions:

2013	
Apr 1	Loaned out $8,000 to Bland, Co. Received a six-month, 10% note.
Oct 1	Collected the Bland note at maturity.
Dec 1	Loaned $6,000 to Flores, Inc., on a 180-day, 12% note.
Dec 31	Accrued interest revenue on the Flores note.
2014	
May 30	Collected the Flores note at maturity.

First Fidelity's accounting period ends on December 31.

Requirement

Explanations are not needed. Use a 360-day year to compute interest.

1. Journalize the 2013 and 2014 transactions on First Fidelity's books.

Solution

Requirement 1

2013			
Apr 1	Note receivable—Bland, Co. (A+)	8,000	
	Cash (A–)		8,000
Oct 1	Cash ($8,000 + $400) (A+)	8,400	
	Notes receivable—Bland, Co. (A–)		8,000
	Interest revenue ($8,000 × 0.10 × 6/12) (R+)		400
2013			
Dec 1	Notes receivable—Flores, Inc. (A+)	6,000	
	Cash (A–)		6,000
31	Interest receivable (A+)	60	
	Interest revenue ($6,000 × 0.12 × 30/360) (R+)		60
2014			
May 30	Cash [$6,000 + ($6,000 × 0.12 × 180/360) (A+)	6,360	
	Notes receivable—Flores, Inc. (A–)		6,000
	Interest receivable (A–)		60
	Interest revenue ($6,000 × 0.12 × 150/360) (R+)		300

Review *Receivables*

● Accounting Vocabulary

Accounts Receivable Turnover Ratio (p. 425)
A ratio that measures the number of times the company sells and collects the average receivables balance in a year.

Acid-Test Ratio (p. 424)
Ratio of the sum of cash plus short-term investments plus net current receivables to total current liabilities. Tells whether the entity could pay all its current liabilities if they came due immediately. Also called the **quick ratio**.

Aging-of-Accounts Method (p. 409)
A way to estimate bad debts by analyzing individual accounts receivable according to the length of time they have been receivable from the customer. Also called the **balance-sheet approach**.

Allowance for Doubtful Accounts (p. 408)
A contra account, related to accounts receivable, that holds the estimated amount of collection losses. Also called **allowance for uncollectible accounts**.

Allowance for Uncollectible Accounts (p. 407)
A contra account, related to accounts receivable, that holds the estimated amount of collection losses. Also called **allowance for doubtful accounts**.

Allowance Method (p. 407)
A method of recording collection losses on the basis of estimates instead of waiting to see which customers the company will not collect from.

Bad Debt Expense (p. 407)
Cost to the seller of extending credit. Arises from the failure to collect from credit customers. Also called **doubtful account expense** or **uncollectible account expense**.

Balance-Sheet Approach (p. 409)
A way to estimate bad debts by analyzing individual accounts receivable according to the length of time they have been receivable from the customer. Also called the **aging-of-accounts method**.

Collection Period (p. 424)
Ratio of average net accounts receivable to one day's sales. Tells how many days' sales it takes to collect the average level of receivables. Also called the **days' sales in receivables**.

Control Account (p. 405)
An account in the general ledger that summarizes related subsidiary accounts.

Days' Sales in Receivables (p. 424)
Ratio of average net accounts receivable to one day's sales. Tells how many days' sales it takes to collect the average level of receivables. Also called the **collection period**.

Debtor (p. 405)
The party to a credit transaction who makes a purchase and takes on an obligation/payable.

Default on a Note (p. 422)
Failure of a note's maker to pay a note receivable at maturity. Also called **dishonor of a note**.

Direct Write-Off Method (p. 413)
A method of accounting for uncollectible receivables in which the company waits until the credit department decides that a customer's account receivable is uncollectible and then debits Uncollectible account expense and credits the customer's Account receivable.

Discounting a Note Receivable (p. 450)
Selling a note receivable before its maturity date.

Dishonor of a Note (p. 422)
Failure of a note's maker to pay a note receivable at maturity. Also called **default on a note**.

Doubtful Account Expense (p. 407)
Cost to the seller of extending credit. Arises from the failure to collect from credit customers. Also called **uncollectible account expense** or **bad debt expense**.

Due Date (p. 418)
The date when final payment of the note is due. Also called the **maturity date**.

Income-Statement Approach (p. 408)
A method of estimating uncollectible receivables that calculates uncollectible-account expense. Also called the **percent-of-sales method**.

Interest (p. 418)
The revenue to the payee for loaning money—the expense to the debtor.

Interest Period (p. 418)
The period of time during which interest is computed. It extends from the original date of the note to the maturity date. Also called the **note term**, or simply **time period**.

Interest Rate (p. 418)
The percentage rate of interest specified by the note. Interest rates are almost always stated for a period of one year.

Maturity Date (p. 406)
The date when final payment of the note is due. Also called the **due date**.

Maturity Value (p. 418)
The sum of the principal plus interest due at maturity.

Net Realizable Value (p. 409)
Net value that a company expects to collect from its receivables. (Accounts receivable – Allowance for uncollectible accounts)

Note Term (p. 418)
The period of time during which interest is computed. It extends from the original date of the note to the maturity date. Also called the **interest period**, or simply **time period**.

Percent-of-Sales Method (p. 408)
A method of estimating uncollectible receivables that calculates uncollectible account expense. Also called the **income-statement approach**.

Principal (p. 418)
The amount loaned out by the payee and borrowed by the maker of the note.

Promissory Note (p. 406)
A written promise to pay a specified amount of money at a particular future date.

Quick Ratio (p. 424)
Ratio of the sum of cash plus short-term investments plus net current receivables to total current liabilities. Tells whether the entity could pay all its current liabilities if they came due immediately. Also called the **acid-test ratio.**

Receivable (p. 405)
Monetary claim against a business or an individual.

Subsidiary Accounts (p. 405)
Contains the details by individual account that are summarized in the control account.

Subsidiary Ledger (p. 405)
A ledger that contains the details, for example by customer or vendor, of individual account balances. The sum of all related subsidiary ledger accounts will equal the control account.

Time (Period) (p. 419)
The period of time during which interest is computed. It extends from the original date of the note to the maturity date. Also called the **note term** or **interest period.**

Trade Receivables (p. 405)
Amounts to be collected from customers from sales made on credit. Also called **Accounts receivable.**

Uncollectible Account Expense (p. 407)
Cost to the seller of extending credit. Arises from the failure to collect from credit customers. Also called **doubtful account expense** or **bad debt expense.**

● Destination: Student Success

Student Success Tips

The following are hints on some common trouble areas for students in this chapter:

- Recall that the main difference between the allowance method and the direct write-off method is MATCHING. The allowance method records the expense in the same period as the sale. The direct write-off method records the expense when the identification occurs, usually several months later than the sale.

- Remember that there are two ways illustrated in the chapter to calculate/adjust the amount that is in the allowance for uncollectible accounts: **percentage of sales** and the **target balance through aging-of-accounts method.**

- Keep in mind that when a business accepts credit cards and debit cards as payment for sales, the card issuer assesses a fee based on a small percentage of the sale. This fee is called Card discount expense, and it reduces the amount of cash the company receives from the sale.

- The formula for calculating interest is Principal × Interest Rate × Time. Interest must be calculated as time goes by on the note.

- When counting the number of days, don't count the day the note was made when determining how many days have passed. Also, consider using the knuckle trick to help you recall the number of days in each month (Make two fists and put them together: knuckles have 31 days, joints between your knuckles don't.)

Getting Help

If there's a learning objective from the chapter you aren't confident about, try using one or more of the following resources:

- Review Exhibits 8-3 and 8-4 to recall the difference between the allowance method and the direct write-off method.

- Practice additional exercises or problems at the end of Chapter 8 that cover the specific learning objective that is challenging you.

- Watch the white board videos for Chapter 8 located at myaccountinglab.com under the Chapter Resources button.

- Go to myaccountinglab.com and select the Study Plan button. Choose Chapter 8 and work the questions covering that specific learning objective until you've mastered it.

- Work the Chapter 8 pre/post tests in myaccountinglab.com.

- Visit the learning resource center on your campus for tutoring.

● Quick Check

1. With good internal controls, the person who handles cash can also
   a. account for cash payments.
   b. account for cash receipts from customers.
   c. issue credits to customers for sales returns.
   d. None of the above

2. "Bad debts" are the same as
   a. doubtful accounts.
   b. uncollectible accounts.
   c. Neither of the above
   d. Both a and b.

3. When recording credit- or debit-card sales using the net method,

   a. cash received equals sales.

   b. cash received equals sales minus the fee assessed by the card processing company.

   c. cash received equals sales plus the fee assessed by the card processing company.

   d. cash isn't received by the seller until the customer pays his or her credit card statement.

4. Your company uses the allowance method to account for uncollectible receivables. At the beginning of the year, Allowance for uncollectible accounts had a credit balance of $1,000. During the year you recorded Uncollectible account expense of $2,700 and wrote off bad receivables of $2,100. What is your year-end balance in Allowance for uncollectible accounts?

   a. $1,600   c. $3,700

   b. $4,800   d. $600

5. Your ending balance of Accounts receivable is $19,500. Use the data in the preceding question to compute the net realizable value of Accounts receivable at year-end.

   a. $16,800   c. $17,400

   b. $19,500   d. $17,900

6. What is wrong with the direct write-off method of accounting for uncollectibles?

   a. The direct write-off method overstates assets on the balance sheet.

   b. The direct write-off method does not match expenses against revenue very well.

   c. The direct write-off method does not set up an allowance for uncollectibles.

   d. All of the above

7. At January 31, you have a $8,400 note receivable from a customer. Interest of 10% has accrued for 10 months on the note. What will your financial statements report for this situation?

   a. The balance sheet will report the note receivable of $8,400.

   b. The balance sheet will report the note receivable of $8,400 and interest receivable of $700.

   c. Nothing, because you have not received the cash yet.

   d. The income statement will report a note receivable of $8,400.

8. Return to the data in the preceding question. What will the income statement report for this situation?

   a. Nothing, because you have not received the cash yet

   b. Note receivable of $8,400

   c. Interest revenue of $700

   d. Both b and c

9. At year-end, your company has cash of $11,600, receivables of $48,900, inventory of $37,900, and prepaid expenses totaling $5,100. Liabilities of $55,900 must be paid next year. What is your acid-test ratio?

   a. 1.08

   b. 0.21

   c. 1.76

   d. Cannot be determined from the data given

10. Return to the data in the preceding question. A year ago receivables stood at $67,400, and sales for the current year totaled $807,800. How many days did it take you to collect your average level of receivables?

   a. 49   c. 29

   b. 35   d. 26

Answers are given after Apply Your Knowledge (p. 449).

Assess Your Progress

● Short Exercises

S8-1   **❶ Different types of receivables [5 min]**
Consider accounts receivable and notes receivable.

Requirement

     1.   What is the difference between accounts receivable and notes receivable?

S8-2   **❶ Internal control over the collection of receivables [5 min]**
Consider internal control over receivables collections.

Requirement

     1.   What job must be withheld from a company's credit department in order to safe-guard its cash? If the credit department does perform this job, what can a credit department employee do to hurt the company?

S8-3   **❷ Applying the allowance method (percentage of sales) to account for uncollectibles [5 min]**
During its first year of operations, Spring Garden Plans earned revenue of $322,000 on account. Industry experience suggests that bad debts will amount to 2% of revenues. At December 31, 2012, accounts receivable total $36,000. The company uses the allowance method to account for uncollectibles.

Requirements

     1.   Journalize Spring's sales and uncollectible account expense using the percent-of-sales method.

     2.   Show how to report accounts receivable on the balance sheet at December 31, 2012. Use the long reporting format illustrated in the chapter.

S8-4   **❷ Applying the allowance method (percentage of sales) to account for uncollectibles [5–10 min]**
The Accounts receivable balance for Winter Retreats at December 31, 2011, was $18,000. During 2012, Winter completed the following transactions:

       a.   Sales revenue on account, $447,000 (ignore cost of goods sold).
       b.   Collections on account, $424,000.
       c.   Write-offs of uncollectibles, $5,900.
       d.   Uncollectible account expense, 2% of credit sales.

Requirement

     1.   Journalize Winter's 2012 transactions.

S8-5   **❷ Applying the allowance method (aging of accounts) to account for uncollectibles [10 min]**
Summer and Sandcastles Resort had the following balances at December 31, 2012, before the year-end adjustments:

Accounts receivable		Allowance for uncollectible accounts	
78,000			1,900

The aging of accounts receivable yields the following data:

	Age of Accounts receivable		
	0–60 Days	Over 60 Days	Total Receivables
Accounts receivable . . .	$75,000	$3,000	$78,000
Percent uncollectible . . .	× 4%	× 24%	

Requirements

1. Journalize Summer's entry to adjust the allowance account to its correct balance at December 31, 2012.

2. Prepare a T-account to compute the ending balance of Allowance for uncollectible accounts.

S8-6 ③ **Applying the direct write-off method to account for uncollectibles [10 min]**
Sherman Peterson is an attorney in Los Angeles. Peterson uses the direct write-off method to account for uncollectible receivables.

At January 31, 2012, Peterson's accounts receivable totaled $15,000. During February, he earned revenue of $18,000 on account and collected $19,000 on account. He also wrote off uncollectible receivables of $1,800 on February 29, 2012.

Requirements

1. Use the direct write-off method to journalize Peterson's write-off of the uncollectible receivables.

2. What is Peterson's balance of Accounts receivable at February 29, 2012? Does Peterson expect to collect the total amount?

S8-7 ③ **Collecting a receivable previously written off—direct write-off method [5–10 min]**
Gate City Cycles had trouble collecting its account receivable from Sue Ann Noel. On June 19, 2012, Gate City finally wrote off Noel's $700 account receivable. Gate City turned the account over to an attorney, who hounded Noel for the rest of the year. On December 31, Noel sent a $700 check to Gate City Cycles with a note that said, "Here's your money. Please call off your bloodhound!"

Requirement

1. Journalize the entries required for Gate City Cycles, assuming Gate City uses the direct write-off method.

S8-8 ④ **Recording credit-card and debit-card sales [5 min]**
Restaurants do a large volume of business by credit and debit cards. Suppose Chocolate Passion restaurant had these transactions on January 28, 2012:

National Express credit-card sales	$ 9,300
ValueCard debit-card sales	9,000

Suppose Chocolate Passion's processor charges a 3% fee and deposits sales net of the fee.

Requirement

1. Journalize these sale transactions for the restaurant.

S8-9 ⑤ **Computing interest amounts on notes receivable [10 min]**
A table of notes receivable for 2012 follows:

	Principal	Interest Rate	Interest Period During 2012
Note 1	$ 30,000	8%	4 months
Note 2	10,000	11%	45 days
Note 3	19,000	10%	75 days
Note 4	100,000	7%	10 months

Requirement

1. For each of the notes receivable, compute the amount of interest revenue earned during 2012. Use a 360-day year, and round to the nearest dollar.

S8-10   ⑤ **Accounting for a note receivable [5–10 min]**
Lakeland Bank & Trust Company lent $110,000 to Samantha Michael on a 90-day, 9% note.

Requirement

1. Journalize the following transactions for the bank (explanations are not required):

   a. Lending the money on June 6.
   b. Collecting the principal and interest at maturity. Specify the date. For the computation of interest, use a 360-day year.

S8-11   ⑥ **Reporting receivables and other accounts in the financial statements [10–15 min]**
Northend Medical Center included the following selected items in its financial statements:

Allowance for doubtful accounts	$ 150	Service revenue	$ 14,700
Cash	1,010	Other assets	380
Accounts receivable	2,590	Cost of services sold and other expenses	12,400
Accounts payable	900	Notes payable	3,490

Requirements

1. How much net income did Northend earn for the month?
2. Show two ways Northend can report receivables on its classified balance sheet.

S8-12   ⑥ **Using the acid-test ratio and days' sales in receivables to evaluate a company [10–15 min]**
Southside Clothiers reported the following selected items at September 30, 2012 (last year's—2011—amounts also given as needed):

Accounts payable	$ 320,000	Accounts receivable, net:	
Cash	260,000	September 30, 2012	$ 270,000
Inventories		September 30, 2011	170,000
September 30, 2012	290,000	Cost of goods sold	1,150,000
September 30, 2011	200,000	Short–term investments	140,000
Net sales revenue	2,920,000	Other current assets	120,000
Long–term assets	420,000	Other current liabilities	180,000
Long–term liabilities	130,000		

Requirement

1. Compute Southside's (a) acid-test ratio, (b) days' sales in average receivables for 2012, and (c) accounts receivable turnover ratio. Evaluate each ratio value as strong or weak. Southside sells on terms of net 30.

● Exercises

E8-13   ① **Common receivables terms [10–15 min]**   *MyAccountingLab*

TERMS:	DEFINITIONS:
1. Account receivable	A. Transaction results in a liability for this party
2. Promissory note	B. Transaction results in a receivable for this party
3. Borrower	C. The debtor promises to pay the creditor a definite sum at a future date usually with interest
4. Note receivable	
5. Maturity date	D. Amounts to be collected from customers from sales made on credit
6. Creditor	E. Serves as evidence of the indebtedness and includes the terms of the debt
	F. The date a note is due to be paid in full

Requirement

1. Match the terms with their correct definition.

E8-14 ❶ **Identifying and correcting internal control weakness [10 min]**

Suppose The Right Rig Dealership is opening a regional office in Omaha. Cary Regal, the office manager, is designing the internal control system. Regal proposes the following procedures for credit checks on new customers, sales on account, cash collections, and write-offs of uncollectible receivables:

- The credit department runs a credit check on all customers who apply for credit. When an account proves uncollectible, the credit department authorizes the write-off of the account receivable.
- Cash receipts come into the credit department, which separates the cash received from the customer remittance slips. The credit department lists all cash receipts by customer name and amount of cash received.
- The cash goes to the treasurer for deposit in the bank. The remittance slips go to the accounting department for posting to customer accounts.
- The controller compares the daily deposit slip to the total amount posted to customer accounts. Both amounts must agree.

Requirement

1. Recall the components of internal control you learned in Chapter 7. Identify the internal control weakness in this situation, and propose a way to correct it.

E8-15 ❷❻ **Accounting for uncollectible accounts using the allowance method and reporting receivables on the balance sheet [15–30 min]**

At December 31, 2012, the Accounts receivable balance of GPS Technology is $190,000. The Allowance for doubtful accounts has an $8,600 credit balance. GPS Technology prepares the following aging schedule for its accounts receivable:

| | Age of Accounts | | | |
	1–30 Days	31–60 Days	61–90 Days	Over 90 Days
Accounts receivable				
$190,000	$80,000	$60,000	$40,000	$10,000
Estimated percent uncollectible	0.4 %	5.0 %	6.0 %	50.0 %

Requirements

1. Journalize the year-end adjusting entry for doubtful accounts on the basis of the aging schedule. Show the T-account for the Allowance for uncollectible accounts at December 31, 2012.

2. Show how GPS Technology will report its net Accounts receivable on its December 31, 2012 balance sheet.

E8-16 ❷❻ **Accounting for uncollectible accounts using the allowance method and reporting receivables on the balance sheet [15–20 min]**

At September 30, 2012, Windy Mountain Flagpoles had Accounts receivable of $34,000 and Allowance for uncollectible accounts had a credit balance of $3,000. During October 2012, Windy Mountain Flagpoles recorded the following:

- Sales of $189,000 ($165,000 on account; $24,000 for cash).
- Collections on account, $133,000.
- Uncollectible account expense, estimated as 1% of credit sales.
- Write-offs of uncollectible receivables, $2,800.

Requirements

1. Journalize sales, collections, uncollectible account expense using the allowance method (percent-of-sales method), and write-offs of uncollectibles during October 2012.

2. Prepare T-accounts to show the ending balances in Accounts receivable and Allowance for uncollectible accounts. Compute *net* accounts receivable at October 31. How much does Windy Mountain expect to collect?

3. Show how Windy Mountain Flagpoles will report net Accounts receivable on its October 31, 2012 balance sheet.

E8-17 ❸❻ **Accounting for uncollectible accounts using the direct write-off method and reporting receivables on the balance sheet [10–15 min]**
Refer to the facts presented in Exercise 8-16.

Requirements

1. Journalize sales, collections, uncollectible account expense using the direct write-off method, and write-offs of uncollectibles during October 2012.

2. Show how Accounts receivable would be reported for Windy Mountain Flagpoles on its October 31, 2012 balance sheet under the direct write-off method.

E8-18 ❸❻ **Journalizing transactions using the direct-write off method and reporting receivables on the balance sheet [10–20 min]**
High Performance Cell Phones sold $23,000 of merchandise to Anthony Trucking Company on account. Anthony fell on hard times and paid only $8,000 of the account receivable. After repeated attempts to collect, High Performance finally wrote off its accounts receivable from Anthony. Six months later High Performance received Anthony's check for $15,000 with a note apologizing for the late payment.

Requirements

1. Journalize for High Performance:

   a. Sale on account, $23,000. (Ignore cost of goods sold.)
   b. Collection of $8,000 on account.
   c. Write-off of the remaining portion of Anthony's account receivable. High Performance uses the direct write-off method for uncollectibles.
   d. Reinstatement of Anthony's account receivable.
   e. Collection in full from Anthony, $15,000.

2. Show how High Performance would report receivables on its balance sheet after all entries have been posted.

E8-19 ❹❺ **Journalizing card sales, note receivable transactions, and accruing interest [10–15 min]**
Marathon Running Shoes reports the following:

2012	
May 4	Recorded Estate credit-card sales of $107,000, net of processor fee of 3%.
Sep 1	Loaned $17,000 to Jean Porter, an executive with the company, on a one-year, 15% note.
Dec 31	Accrued interest revenue on the Porter note.
2013	
Sep 1	Collected the maturity value of the Porter note.

Requirement

1. Journalize all entries required for Marathon Running Shoes.

E8-20 ❺ **Computing note receivable amounts [15–25 min]**
On September 30, 2012, Synergy Bank loaned $88,000 to Kendall Kelsing on a one-year, 12% note.

Requirements

1. Journalize all entries for Synergy Bank related to the note for 2012 and 2013.

2. Which party has a
   a. note receivable?
   b. note payable?
   c. interest revenue?
   d. interest expense?

3. How much in total would Kelsing pay the bank if she pays off the note early on April 30, 2013?

E8-21 ⑤ **Journalizing note receivable transactions [10–15 min]**
The following selected transactions occurred during 2012 for Caspian Importers. The company ends its accounting year on April 30, 2012:

Feb	1	Loaned $14,000 cash to Brett Dowling on a one-year, 8% note.
Apr	6	Sold goods to Putt Masters, receiving a 90-day, 6% note for $9,000.
	30	Made a single entry to accrue interest revenue on both notes.

Requirement

1. Journalize all required entries from February 1 through April 30, 2012. Use a 360-day year for interest computations.

E8-22 ⑤ **Journalizing note receivable transactions [10 min]**
Hot Heat Steam Cleaning performs services on account. When a customer account becomes four months old, Hot Heat converts the account to a note receivable. During 2012, the company completed the following transactions:

Apr 28	Performed service on account for Sinclair Club, $18,000.
Sep 1	Received an $18,000, 60-day, 9% note from Sinclair Club in satisfaction of its past-due account receivable.
Oct 31	Collected the Sinclair Club note at maturity.

Requirement

1. Record the transactions in Hot Heat's journal.

E8-23 ⑥ **Evaluating ratio data [15–20 min]**
Algonquin Carpets reported the following amounts in its 2013 financial statements. The 2012 figures are given for comparison.

		2013		2012
Current assets:				
Cash		$ 4,000		$ 10,000
Short-term investments		20,000		9,000
Accounts receivable	$ 63,000		$ 76,000	
Less: Allowance for uncollectibles ..	6,000	57,000	5,000	71,000
Inventory		195,000		191,000
Prepaid insurance		4,000		4,000
Total current assets		$ 280,000		$ 285,000
Total current liabilities		$ 104,000		$ 106,000
Net sales (all on account)		$ 732,000		$ 735,000

Requirements

1. Calculate Algonquin's acid-test ratio for 2013. Determine whether Algonquin's acid-test ratio improved or deteriorated from 2012 to 2013. How does Algonquin's acid-test ratio compare with the industry average of 0.80?

2. Calculate the days' sales in receivables for 2013. How do the results compare with Algonquin's credit terms of net 30?

3. Calculate Algonquin's accounts receivable turnover ratio. How does Algonquin's ratio compare to the industry average accounts receivable turnover of 10?

E8-24 ⑥ **Collection period for receivables [10–15 min]**

Contemporary Media Sign Company sells on account. Recently, Contemporary reported the following figures:

	2012	2011
Net sales	$ 572,000	$ 600,000
Receivables at end of year	38,700	46,100

Requirements

1. Compute Contemporary's average collection period on receivables during 2012.

2. Suppose Contemporary's normal credit terms for a sale on account are "2/10, net 30." How well does Contemporary's collection period compare to the company's credit terms? Is this good or bad for Contemporary?

● Problems (Group A)

P8-25A ① **Explaining common types of receivables and designing internal controls for receivables [20–30 min]**

MyAccountingLab

Organizational Kings performs organizational consulting services on account, so virtually all cash receipts arrive in the mail. Average daily cash receipts are $36,000. Katie Stykle, the owner, has just returned from a meeting with new ideas for the business. Among other things, Stykle plans to institute stronger internal controls over cash receipts from customers.

Requirements

1. What types of receivables are most likely to be collected by Organizational Kings?

2. List the following procedures in the correct order.

   a. Another person, such as the owner or the manager, compares the amount of the bank deposit to the total of the customer credits posted by the accountant. This gives some assurance that the day's cash receipts went into the bank and that the same amount was posted to customer accounts.

   b. The person who handles cash should not prepare the bank reconciliation.

   c. An employee with no access to the accounting records deposits the cash in the bank immediately.

   d. The remittance slips go to the accountant, who uses them for posting credits to the customer accounts.

   e. Someone other than the accountant opens the mail. This person separates customer checks from the accompanying remittance slips.

P8-26A ② ③ ⑥ **Accounting for uncollectible accounts using the allowance and direct write-off methods, and reporting receivables on the balance sheet [20–30 min]**

On August 31, 2012, Daisy Floral Supply had a $155,000 debit balance in Accounts receivable and a $6,200 credit balance in Allowance for uncollectible accounts. During September, Daisy made

- sales on account, $590,000.
- collections on account, $627,000.
- write-offs of uncollectible receivables, $7,000.

Requirements

1. Journalize all September entries using the *allowance* method. Uncollectible account expense was estimated at 3% of credit sales. Show all September activity in Accounts receivable, Allowance for uncollectible accounts, and Uncollectible account expense (post to these T-accounts).

2. Using the same facts, assume instead that Daisy used the direct write-off method to account for uncollectible receivables. Journalize all September entries using the *direct write-off* method. Post to Accounts receivable and Uncollectible account expense and show their balances at September 30, 2012.

3. What amount of uncollectible account expense would Daisy report on its September income statement under each of the two methods? Which amount better matches expense with revenue? Give your reason.

4. What amount of *net* accounts receivable would Daisy report on its September 30, 2012 balance sheet under each of the two methods? Which amount is more realistic? Give your reason.

P8-27A ②⑥ **Accounting for uncollectible accounts using the allowance method, and reporting receivables on the balance sheet [25–35 min]**
At September 30, 2012, the accounts of Mountain Terrace Medical Center (MTMC) include the following:

Accounts receivable	$ 145,000
Allowance for uncollectible accounts (credit balance) ...	3,500

During the last quarter of 2012, MTMC completed the following selected transactions:

Dec 28	Wrote off accounts receivable as uncollectible: Regan, Co., $1,300; Owen Mac, $900; and Rain, Inc., $700.
Dec 31	Recorded uncollectible account expense based on the aging of accounts receivable, as follows:

	Age of Accounts			
	1–30	31–60	61–90	Over 90
Accounts receivable	Days	Days	Days	Days
$165,000	$97,000	$ 37,000	$ 14,000	$ 17,000
Estimated percent				
uncollectible	0.3%	3%	30%	35%

Requirements

1. Journalize the transactions.
2. Open the Allowance for uncollectible accounts T-account, and post entries affecting that account. Keep a running balance.
3. Show how Mountain Terrace Medical Center should report net accounts receivable on its December 31, 2012 balance sheet. Use the three line reporting format.

P8-28A ②⑥ **Accounting for uncollectible accounts using the allowance method (percentage of sales), and reporting receivables on the balance sheet [20–30 min]**
Quality Watches completed the following selected transactions during 2012 and 2013:

2012

Dec 31   Estimated that uncollectible account expense for the year was 2% of credit sales of $450,000 and recorded that amount as expense. Use the allowance method.

31   Made the closing entry for uncollectible account expense.

2013

Jan 17   Sold inventory to Malcom Monet, $700, on account. Ignore cost of goods sold.

Jun 29   Wrote off Malcom Monet's account as uncollectible after repeated efforts to collect from him.

Aug 6   Received $700 from Malcom Monet, along with a letter apologizing for being so late. Reinstated Monet's account in full and recorded the cash receipt.

Dec 31   Made a compound entry to write off the following accounts as uncollectible: Brian Kemper, $1,600; May Milford, $1,000; and Ronald Richter, $400.

31   Estimated that uncollectible account expense for the year was 2% on credit sales of $460,000 and recorded the expense.

31   Made the closing entry for uncollectible account expense.

Requirements

1. Open T-accounts for Allowance for uncollectible accounts and Uncollectible account expense. Keep running balances, assuming all accounts begin with a zero balance.

2. Record the transactions in the general journal, and post to the two T-accounts.

3. Assume the December 31, 2013, balance of Accounts receivable is $135,000. Show how net Accounts receivable would be reported on the balance sheet at that date. Use the three line format of reporting the net accounts receivable.

P8-29A ② ④ ⑤ **Accounting for uncollectible accounts (aging of accounts method), card sales, notes receivable, and accrued interest revenue [20–30 min]**

Relaxing Recliner Chairs completed the following selected transactions:

2011

Jul 1   Sold inventory to Great – Mart, receiving a $45,000, nine-month, 12% note. Ignore cost of goods sold.

Oct 31   Recorded credit- and debit-card sales for the period of $21,000.

Nov 3   Card processor drafted company's checking account for processing fee of $410.

Dec 31   Made an adjusting entry to accrue interest on the Great – Mart note.

31   Made an adjusting entry to record uncollectible account expense based on an aging of accounts receivable. The aging schedule shows that $15,200 of accounts receivable will not be collected. Prior to this adjustment, the credit balance in Allowance for uncollectible accounts is $11,600.

2012

Apr 1   Collected the maturity value of the Great – Mart note.

Jun 23   Sold merchandise to Ambiance, Corp., receiving a 60-day, 9% note for $13,000. Ignore cost of goods sold.

Aug 22   Ambiance, Corp., dishonored its note (failed to pay) at maturity; we converted the maturity value of the note to an account receivable.

Nov 16   Loaned $21,000 cash to Creed, Inc., receiving a 90-day, 8% note.

Dec 5   Collected in full on account from Ambiance, Corp.

31   Accrued the interest on the Creed, Inc., note.

Requirement

1. Record the transactions in the journal of Relaxing Recliner Chairs. Explanations are not required. (For notes stated in days, use a 360-day year. Round to the nearest dollar.)

P8-30A 🅢 **Accounting for notes receivable and accruing interest [35–45 min]**
Kelly Realty loaned money and received the following notes during 2012.

Note	Date	Principal Amount	Interest Rate	Term
(1)	Aug 1	$ 24,000	17%	1 year
(2)	Nov 30	18,000	6%	6 months
(3)	Dec 19	12,000	12%	30 days

Requirements

For each note, compute interest using a 360-day year. Explanations are not required.

1. Determine the due date and maturity value of each note.
2. Journalize the entry to record the inception of each of the three notes and also journalize a single adjusting entry at December 31, 2012, the fiscal year end, to record accrued interest revenue on all three notes.
3. Journalize the collection of principal and interest at maturity of all three notes.

P8-31A 🅢 **Accounting for notes receivable, dishonored notes, and accrued interest revenue [20–30 min]**
Consider the following transactions for Jo Jo Music.

2011	
Dec 6	Received a $7,000, 90-day, 12% note on account from Dark Star Music.
31	Made an adjusting entry to accrue interest on the Dark Star Music note.
31	Made a closing entry for interest revenue.
2012	
Mar 4	Collected the maturity value of the Dark Star Music note.
Jun 30	Loaned $11,000 cash to Love Joy Music, receiving a six-month, 11% note.
Oct 2	Received a $2,400, 60-day, 11% note for a sale to Voice Publishing. Ignore cost of goods sold.
Dec 1	Voice Publishing dishonored its note at maturity; wrote off the note as uncollectible, debiting Allowance for uncollectible accounts.
30	Collected the maturity value of the Love Joy Music note.

Requirement

1. Journalize all transactions for Jo Jo Music. Round all amounts to the nearest dollar. (For notes stated in days, use a 360-day year.)

P8-32A ⑥ **Using ratio data to evaluate a company's financial position [20–30 min]**

The comparative financial statements of Lakeland Cosmetic Supply for 2012, 2011, and 2010 include the data shown here:

	2012	2011	2010
Balance sheet—partial			
Current assets:			
Cash	$ 90,000	$ 70,000	$ 30,000
Short-term investments	145,000	175,000	125,000
Receivables, net	290,000	260,000	250,000
Inventories	370,000	335,000	325,000
Prepaid expenses	60,000	15,000	50,000
Total current assets	$ 955,000	$ 855,000	$ 780,000
Total current liabilities	$ 560,000	$ 600,000	$ 690,000
Income statement—partial			
Sales revenue (all on account) . . .	$5,860,000	$5,140,000	$4,200,000

Requirements

1. Compute these ratios for 2012 and 2011:
   a. Acid-test ratio
   b. Days' sales in receivables
   c. Accounts receivable turnover

2. Considering each ratio individually, which ratios improved from 2011 to 2012 and which ratios deteriorated? Is the trend favorable or unfavorable for the company?

● Problems (Group B)

P8-33B ① **Explaining common types of receivables and designing internal controls for receivables [20–30 min]**   *MyAccountingLab*

Tutor Tots performs tutoring services on account, so virtually all cash receipts arrive by mail and are then placed in the petty cash box for a week. Average daily cash receipts are $24,000. Jennifer Swanson, the owner, has just returned from a meeting with new ideas for the business. Among other things, Swanson plans to institute stronger internal controls over cash receipts from customers.

Requirements

1. What types of receivables are most likely to be collected by Tutor Tots?

2. List the following procedures in the correct order.

   a. Another person, such as the owner or the manager, compares the amount of the bank deposit to the total of the customer credits posted by the accountant. This gives some assurance that the day's cash receipts went into the bank and that the same amount was posted to customer accounts.
   b. The person who handles cash should not prepare the bank reconciliation.
   c. An employee with no access to the accounting records deposits the cash in the bank immediately.
   d. The remittance slips go to the accountant, who uses them for posting credits to the customer accounts.
   e. Someone other than the accountant opens the mail. This person separates customer checks from the accompanying remittance slips.

P8-34B ② ③ ⑥ **Accounting for uncollectible accounts using the allowance and direct write-off methods, and reporting receivables on the balance sheet [20–30 min]**

On October 31, 2012, Blossom Floral Supply had a $180,000 debit balance in Accounts receivable and a $7,200 credit balance in Allowance for uncollectible accounts. During November, Blossom made

- sales on account, $560,000.
- collections on account, $598,000.
- write-offs of uncollectible receivables, $9,000.

Requirements

1. Journalize all November entries using the *allowance* method. Uncollectible account expense was estimated at 1% of credit sales. Show all November activity in Accounts receivable, Allowance for uncollectible accounts, and Uncollectible account expense (post to these T-accounts).

2. Using the same facts, assume instead that Blossom used the direct write-off method to account for uncollectible receivables. Journalize all November entries using the *direct write-off* method. Post to Accounts receivable and Uncollectible account expense and show their balances at November 30, 2012.

3. What amount of uncollectible account expense would Blossom report on its November income statement under each of the two methods? Which amount better matches expense with revenue? Give your reason.

4. What amount of *net* accounts receivable would Blossom report on its November 30, 2012 balance sheet under each of the two methods? Which amount is more realistic? Give your reason.

P8-35B ❷ ❻ **Accounting for uncollectible accounts using the allowance method, and reporting receivables on the balance sheet [25–35 min]**
At September 30, 2012, the accounts of Park Terrace Medical Center (PTMC) include the following:

Accounts receivable	$ 141,000
Allowance for uncollectible accounts (credit balance) ...	3,400

During the last quarter of 2012, PTMC completed the following selected transactions:

Dec 28	Wrote off accounts receivable as uncollectible: Red Co., $1,600; Jacob Weiss, $1,300; and Star, Inc., $300.
Dec 31	Recorded uncollectible account expense based on the aging of accounts receivable, as follows:

	Age of Accounts			
Accounts receivable	1–30 Days	31–60 Days	61–90 Days	Over 90 Days
$161,000	$99,000	$ 42,000	$ 15,000	$ 5,000
Estimated percent uncollectible	0.2%	2%	20%	25%

Requirements

1. Journalize the transactions.

2. Open the Allowance for uncollectible accounts T-account, and post entries affecting that account. Keep a running balance.

3. Show how Park Terrace Medical Center should report net Accounts receivable on its December 31, 2012 balance sheet. Use the three line reporting format.

P8-36B ❷ ❻ **Accounting for uncollectible accounts using the allowance method (percentage of sales), and reporting receivables on the balance sheet [20–30 min]**
Beta Watches completed the following selected transactions during 2011 and 2012:

2011

Dec 31   Estimated that uncollectible account expense for the year was 3% of credit sales of $440,000 and recorded that amount as expense. Use the allowance method.

    31   Made the closing entry for uncollectible account expense.

2012

Jan 17   Sold inventory to Manny Vasquez, $800, on account. Ignore cost of goods sold.

Jun 29   Wrote off Manny Vasquez's account as uncollectible after repeated efforts to collect from him.

Aug 6   Received $800 from Manny Vasquez, along with a letter apologizing for being so late. Reinstated Vasquez's account in full and recorded the cash receipt.

Dec 31   Made a compound entry to write off the following accounts as uncollectible: Bill Kappy, $1,400; Mike Venture, $1,100; and Russell Reeves, $200.

    31   Estimated that uncollectible account expense for the year was 3% on credit sales of $470,000 and recorded the expense.

    31   Made the closing entry for uncollectible account expense.

Requirements

1. Open T-accounts for Allowance for uncollectible accounts and Uncollectible account expense. Keep running balances, assuming all accounts begin with a zero balance.

2. Record the transactions in the general journal, and post to the two T-accounts.

3. Assume the December 31, 2012, balance of Accounts receivable is $139,000. Show how net Accounts receivable would be reported on the balance sheet at that date. Use the three line format of reporting the net accounts receivable.

P8-37B   ② ④ ⑤   **Accounting for uncollectible accounts (aging of accounts method), card sales, notes receivable, and accrued interest revenue [20–30 min]**

Sleepy Recliner Chairs completed the following selected transactions:

2011

Jul 1   Sold inventory to Go – Mart, receiving a $37,000, nine-month, 8% note. Ignore cost of goods sold.

Oct 31   Recorded credit- and debit-card sales for the period of $19,000.

Nov 3   Card processor drafted company's checking account for processing fee of $420.

Dec 31   Made an adjusting entry to accrue interest on the Go – Mart note.

    31   Made an adjusting entry to record uncollectible account expense based on an aging of accounts receivable. The aging schedule shows that $14,100 of accounts receivable will not be collected. Prior to this adjustment, the credit balance in Allowance for uncollectible accounts is $10,200.

2012

Apr 1   Collected the maturity value of the Go – Mart note.

Jun 23   Sold merchandise to Appeal, Corp., receiving a 60-day, 12% note for $7,000. Ignore cost of goods sold.

Aug 22   Appeal, Corp., dishonored its note (failed to pay) at maturity; we converted the maturity value of the note to an account receivable.

Nov 16   Loaned $23,000 cash to Creed, Inc., receiving a 90-day, 16% note.

Dec 5   Collected in full on account from Appeal, Corp.

    31   Accrued the interest on the Creed, Inc., note.

Requirement

1. Record the transactions in the journal of Sleepy Recliner Chairs. Explanations are not required. (For notes stated in days, use a 360-day year. Round to the nearest dollar.)

P8-38B ⑤ **Accounting for notes receivable and accruing interest [35–45 min]**
Christie Realty loaned money and received the following notes during 2012.

Note	Date	Principal Amount	Interest Rate	Term
(1)	Jun 1	$ 12,000	10%	1 year
(2)	Sep 30	20,000	9%	6 months
(3)	Oct 19	10,000	12%	30 days

Requirements

For each note, compute interest using a 360-day year. Explanations are not required.

1. Determine the due date and maturity value of each note.

2. Journalize the entry to record the inception of each of the three notes and also journalize a single adjusting entry at October 31, 2012, the fiscal year end, to record accrued interest revenue on all three notes.

3. Journalize the collection of principal and interest at maturity of all three notes.

P8-39B ⑤ **Accounting for notes receivable, dishonored notes, and accrued interest revenue [20–30 min]**
Consider the following transactions for Rural Beginnings.

2011	
Dec 6	Received a $4,000, 90-day, 9% note on account from AM Publishing.
31	Made an adjusting entry to accrue interest on the AM Publishing note.
31	Made a closing entry for interest revenue.

2012	
Mar 4	Collected the maturity value of the AM Publishing note.
Jun 30	Loaned $15,000 cash to Johnathon's Publishing, receiving a six-month, 8% note.
Oct 2	Received a $2,000, 60-day, 8% note for a sale to Ying Yang Music. Ignore cost of goods sold.
Dec 1	Ying Yang Music dishonored its note at maturity; wrote off the note as uncollectible, debiting Allowance for uncollectible accounts.
30	Collected the maturity value of the Johnathon's Publishing note.

Requirement

1. Journalize all transactions for Rural Beginnings. Round all amounts to the nearest dollar. (For notes stated in days, use a 360-day year.)

P8-40B ⑥ **Using ratio data to evaluate a company's financial position [20–30 min]**

The comparative financial statements of Perfection Cosmetic Supply for 2012, 2011, and 2010 include the data that follow:

	2012	2011	2010
Balance sheet—partial			
Current assets:			
Cash	$ 60,000	$ 50,000	$ 60,000
Short-term investments	155,000	155,000	120,000
Receivables, net	300,000	240,000	260,000
Inventories	355,000	320,000	320,000
Prepaid expenses	75,000	25,000	55,000
Total current assets	$ 945,000	$ 790,000	$ 815,000
Total current liabilities	$ 590,000	$ 580,000	$ 680,000
Income statement—partial			
Sales revenue (all on account)	$5,830,000	$5,110,000	$4,210,000

Requirements

1. Compute these ratios for 2012 and 2011:
   a. Acid-test ratio
   b. Days' sales in receivables
   c. Accounts receivable turnover

2. Considering each ratio individually, which ratios improved from 2011 to 2012 and which ratios deteriorated? Is the trend favorable or unfavorable for the company?

● Continuing Exercise

E8-41 ③ **Applying the direct write-off method to account for uncollectibles [10 min]**   *MyAccountingLab*

This exercise continues the Lawlor Lawn Service situation from Exercise 7-41 of Chapter 7. Lawlor reviewed the receivables list from the June transactions (from Chapter 6). Lawlor identified on July 31 that Johnson was not going to pay his receivable from June 15. Lawlor uses the direct write-off method to account for uncollectible accounts.

Requirement

1. Journalize the entry to record Johnson's uncollectible account.

● Continuing Problem

P8-42 ② **Accounting for uncollectible accounts using the allowance method [15–20 min]**   *MyAccountingLab*

This problem continues the Draper Consulting situation from Problem 7-42 of Chapter 7. Draper reviewed the receivables list from the January transactions (from Chapter 6). Draper identified on February 15 that a customer was not going to pay his receivable of $200 from December 9. Draper uses the allowance method for receivables, estimating uncollectibles to be 5% of January credit sales.

Requirements

1. Journalize the entry to record and establish the allowance using the percentage method for January credit sales.

2. Journalize the entry to record the identification of the customer's bad debt.

Practice Set

This problem continues the Shine King Cleaning problem begun in Chapter 1 and continued through Chapters 2–7.

P8-43 ② ⑥ **Accounting for uncollectible accounts using the allowance and reporting accounts receivable on the balance sheet method [25–30 min]**
Consider the following January transactions for Shine King Cleaning:

Jan	1	Performed cleaning services for Debbie's D-list for $8,000 on terms 3/10, n/20.
	3	Shine King decides to adopt the allowance method. Uncollectible account expense is estimated at 2% of credit sales.
	10	Borrowed money from North Spot Bank, $10,000, 7% for 180 days.
	12	After discussions with Pierre's Wig Stand, Shine King has determined that $225 of the receivable owed will not be collected. Write off this portion of the receivable.
	15	Sold goods to Watertown for $4,000 on terms 4/10, n/30. Cost of goods sold was $600.
	15	Recorded uncollectible account expense estimate for Watertown sale.
	28	Sold goods to Bridget, Inc., for cash of $1,200 (cost $280).
	28	Collected from Pierre's Wig Stand $225 of receivable previously written off. Reinstated the remaining balance of Pierre's receivable.
	29	Paid cash for utilities of $350.
	31	Created an aging schedule for Shine King for accounts receivable. Shine King determined that accounts 1–20 days old were 2% uncollectible and accounts over 20 days old were 15% uncollectible. Prepared an aging schedule and adjusted the Allowance for uncollectible accounts to the aging schedule.
	31	Shine King prepared all other adjusting entries necessary for January.

Requirements

1. Prepare all required journal entries and post them to Shine King's ledger.
2. Reconcile the Accounts receivable control account to the Accounts receivable subsidiary ledger.

Apply Your Knowledge

Decision Cases

Decision Case 8-1 Weddings on Demand sells on account and manages its own receivables. Average experience for the past three years has been as follows:

	Total
Sales	$350,000
Cost of goods sold	210,000
Bad debt expense	4,000
Other expenses	61,000

Unhappy with the amount of bad debt expense she has been experiencing, Aledia Sanchez, owner of Weddings on Demand, is considering a major change in her business. Her plan would be to stop selling on account altogether but accept either cash, credit, or debit cards from her customers. Her market research indicates that if she does so, her sales will increase by 10% (i.e., from $350,000 to $385,000), of which $200,000 will be credit or debit card sales, and the rest will be cash sales. With a 10% increase in sales, there will also be a 10% increase in Cost of goods sold. If she adopts this plan, she will no longer have bad debt expense, but she will have to pay a fee on debit/credit card transactions of 2% of sales. She also believes this plan will allow her to save $5,000 per year in other operating expenses.

Requirement

1. Should Sanchez start accepting debit and credit cards? Show the computations of net income under her present arrangement and under the plan. (Challenge)

Decision Case 8-2 Pauline's Pottery has always used the direct write-off method to account for uncollectibles. The company's revenues, bad-debt write offs, and year-end receivables for the most recent year follow:

Year	Revenues	Write-Offs	Receivables at Year-End
2011	$150,000	$3,900	$14,000

The business is applying for a bank loan, and the loan officer requires figures based on the allowance method of accounting for bad debts. In the past, bad debts have run about 4% of revenues.

Requirements

Pauline must give the banker the following information:

1. How much more or less would net income be for 2011 if Pauline's Pottery were to use the allowance method for bad debts? Please use the percentage-of-sales method.

2. How much of the receivables balance at the end of 2011 does Pauline's Pottery actually expect to collect? (Disregard beginning account balances for the purpose of this question.)

3. Compute these amounts, and then explain for Pauline's Pottery why net income is more or less using the allowance method versus the direct write-off method for uncollectibles.

● Ethical Issue 8-1

E-Z Loan, Co., makes loans to high-risk borrowers. E-Z borrows from its bank and then lends money to people with bad credit. The bank requires E-Z Loan to submit quarterly financial statements in order to keep its line of credit. E-Z's main asset is Notes receivable. Therefore, Uncollectible note expense and Allowance for uncollectible notes are important accounts.

Slade McMurphy, the owner of E-Z Loan, wants net income to increase in a smooth pattern, rather than increase in some periods and decrease in others. To report smoothly increasing net income, McMurphy underestimates Uncollectible note expense in some periods. In other periods, McMurphy overestimates the expense. He reasons that over time the income overstatements roughly offset the income understatements.

Requirement

1. Is McMurphy's practice of smoothing income ethical? Why or why not?

● Fraud Case 8-1

Dylan worked for a propane gas distributor as an accounting clerk in a small Midwestern town. Last winter, his brother Mike lost his job at the machine plant. By January, temperatures were sub-zero, and Mike had run out of money. Dylan saw that Mike's account was overdue, and he knew Mike needed another delivery to heat his home. He decided to credit Mike's account and debit the balance to the parts inventory, because he knew the parts manager, the owner's son, was incompetent and would never notice the extra entry. Months went by, and Dylan repeated the process until an auditor ran across the charges by chance. When the owner fired Dylan, he said "if you had only come to me and told me about Mike's situation, we could have worked something out."

Requirements

1. What can a business like this do to prevent employee fraud of this kind?

2. What effect would Dylan's actions have on the balance sheet? The income statement?

3. How much discretion does a business have with regard to accommodating hardship situations? (Challenge)

● Financial Statement Case 8-1

Use **Amazon.com**'s balance sheet and the Note 1 data on "Allowance for doubtful accounts" in Appendix A at the end of this book.

Requirements

1. Do accounts receivable appear to be an important asset for **Amazon.com**?

2. Assume that all of "Accounts receivable, Net, and Other" is accounts receivable. Further assume that gross receivables at December 31, 2009, were $908 million. Answer the following questions based on these data, plus what is reported on the balance sheet.
   a. How much did customers owe **Amazon.com** at December 31, 2009?
   b. How much did **Amazon.com** expect to collect from customers after December 31, 2008?
   c. Of the total receivable amount at December 31, 2009, how much did **Amazon.com** expect *not* to collect?

3. Compute **Amazon.com**'s acid-test ratio at the end of 2009. Marketable securities are short-term investments. Disregard deferred tax assets. If all the current liabilities came due immediately, could **Amazon** pay them?

● Team Project 8-1

Bob Davidson and Sheila Thornton worked for several years as sales representatives for **Xerox Corporation**. During this time, they became close friends as they acquired expertise with the company's full range of copier equipment. Now they see an opportunity to put their experience to work and fulfill lifelong desires to establish their own business. Rolltide College, located in their city, is expanding, and there is no copy center within five miles of the campus. Business in the area is booming, and the population in this section of the city is growing.

Davidson and Thornton want to open a copy center, similar to a **FedEx Office**, near the campus. A small shopping center across the street from the college has a vacancy that would fit their needs. Davidson and Thornton each have $20,000 to invest in the business, and they forecast the need for $30,000 to renovate the store. **Xerox Corporation** will lease two large copiers to them at a total monthly rental of $4,000. With enough cash to see them through the first six months of operation, they are confident they can make the business succeed. The two work very well together, and both have excellent credit ratings. Davidson and Thornton must borrow $40,000 to amass a total startup capital of $80,000, which will allow them to start the business, advertise its opening, and keep it running for its first six months.

Assume the role of Davidson and Thornton, the partners who will own Rolltide Copy Center.

Requirements

1. As a group, visit a copy center to familiarize yourselves with its operations. If possible, interview the manager or another employee. Then write a loan request that Davidson and Thornton will submit to a bank with the intent of borrowing $40,000 to be paid back over three years. The loan will be a personal loan to the partnership of Davidson and Thornton, not to Rolltide Copy Center. The request should specify all the details of Davidson and Thornton's plan that will motivate the bank to grant the loan. Include a budgeted income statement for the first six months of the copy center's operation.

2. As a group, interview a loan officer in a bank. Have the loan officer evaluate your loan request. Write a report, or make a presentation to your class—as directed by your instructor—to reveal the loan officer's decision.

• Communication Activity 8-1

In 50 words or fewer, explain the difference between the percentage-of-sales method and the aging method for calculating the journal entry to adjust the allowance for uncollectible accounts.

Quick Check Answers

1. *d* 2. *d* 3. *b* 4. *a* 5. *d* 6. *d* 7. *b* 8. *c* 9. *a* 10. *d*

For online homework, exercises, and problems that provide you immediate feedback, please visit myaccountinglab.com.

Appendix 8A

Discounting a Note Receivable

7 Discount a note receivable

A payee of a note receivable may need cash before the maturity date of the note. When this occurs, the payee may sell the note, a practice called **discounting a note receivable**. The price to be received for the note is determined by present-value concepts. But the transaction between the seller and the buyer of the note can take any form agreeable to the two parties. Here we illustrate one procedure used for discounting short-term notes receivable. To receive cash immediately, the seller accepts a lower price than the note's maturity value.

To illustrate discounting a note receivable, recall that earlier in the chapter, Greg's Tunes loaned $1,000 to L. Holland on September 30, 2014. Greg's Tunes took a note receivable from Holland. The maturity date of the one-year, 6% Holland note is September 30, 2015. Suppose Greg's Tunes discounts the Holland note at First City Bank on November 30, 2014, when the note is two months old. The bank applies a 12% annual interest rate to determine the discounted value of the note. The bank will use a discount rate that is higher than the note's interest rate in order to earn some interest on the transaction. The discounted value, called the *proceeds*, is the amount Greg's Tunes receives from the bank. The proceeds can be computed in five steps, as shown in Exhibit 8A-1.

EXHIBIT 8A-1 | **Discounting (Selling) a Note Receivable**

Step	Computation		
1. Compute the original amount of interest on the note receivable.	$1,000 × 0.06 × 12/12	=	$ 60
2. Maturity value of the note = Principal + Interest	$1,000 + $60	=	$1,060
3. Determine the period (number of days, months, or years) the *bank* will hold the note (the discount period).	Dec 1, 2014 to Sep 30, 2015	=	10 months
4. Compute the bank's discount on the note. This is the bank's interest revenue from holding the note.	$1,060 × 0.12 × 10/12	=	$ 106
5. Seller's proceeds from discounting the note receivable = Maturity value of the note – Bank's discount on the note.	$1,060 – $106	=	$ 954

The authors thank Doug Hamilton for suggesting this exhibit.

Greg's Tunes' entry to record discounting (selling) the note on November 30, 2014, is as follows:

2014			
Nov 30	Cash (A+)	954	
	Interest expense (E+)	46	
	Note receivable—L. Holland (A–)		1,000
	Discounted a note receivable.		

When the proceeds from discounting a note receivable are less than the principal amount of the note, the payee records a debit to Interest expense for the amount of the difference. When the proceeds from discounting the note are more than the note principal, the payee records a credit to Interest revenue. For example, assume Greg's Tunes discounts the note receivable for cash proceeds of $1,020. The entry to record this discounting transaction is as follows:

2014			
Nov 30	Cash (A+)	1,020	
	Note receivable—L. Holland (A–)		1,000
	Interest revenue (R+)		20
	Discounted a note receivable.		

Appendix 8A Assignments

● Exercise

E8A-1 ⑦ **Journalizing notes receivable transactions [10–15 min]**
Big Ted Toys sells on account. When a customer account becomes three months old, Big Ted converts the account to a note receivable and immediately discounts the note to a bank. During 2012, Big Ted completed the following transactions:

Aug 29	Sold goods on account to V. Mayer, $3,000.
Dec 1	Received a $3,000, 60-day, 11% note from Mayer in satisfaction of his past-due account receivable.
1	Sold the Mayer note by discounting it to a bank for $2,600.

Requirement
1. Record the transactions in Big Ted's journal.

Experience the Power of Practice!

As denoted by the logo, all of these questions, as well as additional practice materials, can be found in

MyAccountingLab.

Please visit myaccountinglab.com

● Problem (Group A)

P8A-2A ⑦ **Journalizing notes receivable transactions [15–20 min]**
A company received the following notes during 2012. The notes were discounted on the dates and at the rates indicated:

Note	Date	Principal Amount	Interest Rate	Term	Date Discounted	Discount Rate
(1)	Jun 1	$ 13,000	10%	120 days	Aug 15	13%
(2)	Aug 19	10,000	9%	90 days	Aug 30	11%
(3)	Jul 15	4,000	7%	6 months	Oct 15	9%

Requirements
Identify each note by number, compute interest using a 360-day year, and round all interest amounts to the nearest dollar. Explanations are not required.
1. Determine the due date and maturity value of each note.
2. Determine the discount and proceeds from the sale (discounting) of each note.
3. Journalize the discounting of notes (1) and (2).

● Problem (Group B)

P8A-3B ⑦ **Journalizing notes receivable transactions [15–20 min]**
A company received the following notes during 2012. The notes were discounted on the dates and at the rates indicated:

Note	Date	Principal Amount	Interest Rate	Term	Date Discounted	Discount Rate
(1)	Jul 1	$ 12,000	13%	120 days	Sep 10	16%
(2)	Jun 19	11,000	8%	90 days	Jun 20	10%
(3)	Jul 15	8,000	6%	6 months	Oct 15	8%

Requirements
Identify each note by number, compute interest using a 360-day year, and round all interest amounts to the nearest dollar. Explanations are not required.
1. Determine the due date and maturity value of each note.
2. Determine the discount and proceeds from the sale (discounting) of each note.
3. Journalize the discounting of notes (1) and (2).

9

Plant Assets and Intangibles

How do we determine what value to report for our assets?

SMART TOUCH LEARNING
Balance Sheet
May 31, 2013

Assets				Liabilities	
Current assets:				Current liabilities:	
Cash		$ 4,800		Accounts payable	$ 48,700
Accounts receivable		2,600		Salary payable	900
Inventory		30,500		Interest payable	100
Supplies		600		Unearned service revenue	400
Prepaid rent		2,000		Total current liabilities	50,100
Total current assets			$ 40,500	Long-term liabilities:	
Plant assets:				Notes payable	20,000
Furniture	$18,000			Total liabilities	70,100
Less: Accumulated depreciation—furniture	300	17,700			
Building	48,000				
Less: Accumulated depreciation—building	200	47,800		**Owner's Equity**	
Total plant assets			65,500	Bright, capital	35,900
Total assets			$106,000	Total liabilities and owner's equity	$106,000

Learning Objectives

1. Measure the cost of a plant asset
2. Account for depreciation
3. Record the disposal of an asset by sale or trade
4. Account for natural resources
5. Account for intangible assets
6. Describe ethical issues related to plant assets

You've been working at your business now for a few months. Things are going great—sales are increasing every month. Until now, you've been handling the paperwork manually, but you need a better way to keep up with it all. You're considering buying several laptop computers, a server, and computerized software. The total cost of the system, including installation, will be $20,000. This will help you operate the business more efficiently, but what about the cost of the system? Do you expense it all or set up asset accounts for each of the assets? How long do you think each component will last before you need to upgrade your computers? How do you recover/match the cost of the system to the revenue you earn?

The computer system you plan to buy for your business is one type of plant asset. Other types include land, buildings, equipment, and furniture. Often, plant assets are referred to as Property, Plant, and Equipment. Plant assets have some special characteristics. For example, you hold them for use in the business—not to sell as inventory. Also,

* plant assets are relatively expensive.
* the full cost invested in plant assets can be a challenge to determine because of the difficulty of tracking installation, shipping, and other costs related to the asset.
* plant assets usually last several years and, as a result, should be allocated over the years they are expected to be used.
* plant assets may be sold or traded in. Accounting for the disposal of a plant asset is important because the disposal may create a gain or loss that must be reported on the income statement.

As you can see, plant assets pose some accounting challenges.

Generally, plant assets can be classified into three main categories:

1. **Real or tangible assets.** This includes assets whose physical characteristics define their utility or usefulness, such as buildings, desks, and equipment.
2. **Natural resources.** This includes assets that come from the ground and can ultimately be used up. For example, oil, diamonds, and coal are all natural resource assets.
3. **Intangible assets.** This includes assets whose value is not derived from their physicality. For example, software programs on a CD are intangible assets. The "physical" CD is not the value—the knowledge/programs on the CD really represent the asset.

● ● ●

Exhibit 9-1 shows which expense applies to each category of plant asset.

In this chapter, we will conclude our coverage of assets, except for investments. After completing this chapter, you should understand the various plant assets of a business and how to account for them. Along the way, we'll look at how both Smart Touch Learning and Greg's Tunes account for their plant assets.

EXHIBIT 9-1 | **Plant Assets and Their Related Expenses**

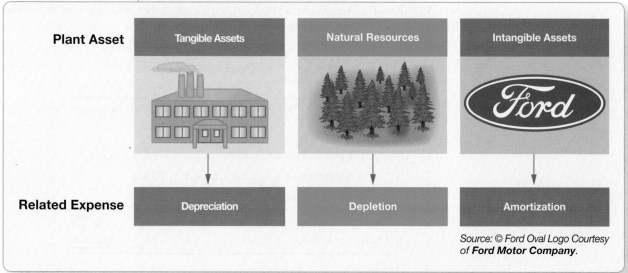

Source: © Ford Oval Logo Courtesy of **Ford Motor Company**.

Measuring the Cost of a Plant Asset

 Measure the cost of a plant asset

The *cost principle* says to carry an asset at its historical cost—the amount paid for the asset. The rule for measuring cost is as follows:

Cost of an asset = Sum of all the costs incurred to bring the asset to its intended purpose, net of all discounts

The *cost of a plant asset* is its purchase price plus taxes, purchase commissions, and all other amounts paid to ready the asset for its intended use. In Chapter 6, we applied this principle to inventory. These costs vary, so let's discuss each asset individually.

Land and Land Improvements

The cost of land is not depreciated. It includes the following costs paid by the purchaser:

- Purchase price
- Brokerage commission
- Survey and legal fees
- Property taxes in arrears
- Taxes assessed to transfer the ownership (title) on the land
- Cost of clearing the land and removing unwanted buildings

The cost of land does *not* include the following costs:

- Fencing
- Paving
- Sprinkler systems
- Lighting
- Signs

These separate plant assets—called **land improvements**—are subject to depreciation.

Suppose Smart Touch needs property and purchases land for $50,000 with a note payable for the same amount. Smart Touch also pays cash as follows: $4,000 in property taxes in arrears, $2,000 in transfer taxes, $5,000 to remove an old building, and a $1,000 survey fee. What is the company's cost of this land? Exhibit 9-2 shows all the costs incurred to bring the land to its intended use:

EXHIBIT 9-2   **Measuring the Cost of Land**

Purchase price of land......................		$50,000
Add related costs:		
Property taxes in arrears...........	$4,000	
Transfer taxes...........................	2,000	
Removal of building................	5,000	
Survey fee	1,000	12,000
Total cost of land............................		$62,000

The entry to record the purchase of the land on August 1, 2013, follows:

2013			
Aug 1	Land (A+)	62,000	
	Note payable (L+)		50,000
	Cash (A–)		12,000

We would say that Smart Touch *capitalized* the cost of the land at $62,000. **Capitalized** means that an asset account was debited (increased) because the company acquired an asset. So, for our land example, Smart Touch debited the Land account for $62,000, the capitalized cost of the asset.

Suppose Smart Touch then pays $20,000 for fences, paving, lighting, landscaping, and signs on August 15, 2013. The following entry records the cost of these land improvements:

2013			
Aug 15	Land improvements (A+)	20,000	
	Cash (A–)		20,000

Land and land improvements are two entirely separate assets. Recall that land is not depreciated. However, the cost of land improvements *is* depreciated over that asset's useful life.

Buildings

The cost of a building depends on whether the company is constructing the building itself or is buying an existing one. These costs include the following:

Constructing a Building

- Architectural fees
- Building permits
- Contractor charges
- Payments for material, labor, and overhead
- Capitalized interest cost, if self-constructed

Purchasing an Existing Building

- Purchase price
- Costs to renovate the building to ready the building for use, which may include any of the charges listed under "Constructing a Building"

Machinery and Equipment

The cost of machinery and equipment includes its

- purchase price (less any discounts),
- transportation charges,
- insurance while in transit,
- sales tax and other taxes,
- purchase commission,
- installation costs, and
- the cost of testing the asset before it is used.

After the asset is up and running, the company no longer debits the cost of insurance, taxes, ordinary repairs, and maintenance to the Equipment account. From that point on, insurance, taxes, repairs, and maintenance costs are recorded as expenses.

There are many different kinds of equipment. Smart Touch has CD/DVD burning equipment. **Delta** has airplanes, and **Office Depot** has copiers. Most businesses have computer equipment.

Furniture and Fixtures

Furniture and fixtures include desks, chairs, file cabinets, display racks, shelving, and so forth. The cost of furniture and fixtures includes the basic cost of each asset (less any discounts), plus all other costs to ready the asset for its intended use. For example, for a desk, this may include the costs to ship the desk to the business and the cost paid to a laborer to assemble the desk.

A Lump-Sum (Basket) Purchase of Assets

A company may pay a single price for several assets as a group—a "basket purchase." For example, Smart Touch may pay a single price for land and a building. For accounting, the company must identify the cost of each asset, as shown in the following diagram. The total cost paid (100%) is divided among the assets according to their relative sales or market values. This is called the **relative-sales-value method**.

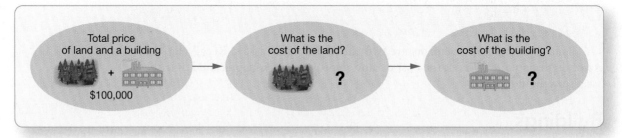

Suppose Smart Touch paid a combined purchase price of $100,000 on August 1, 2013, for the land and building. An appraisal performed a month before the purchase indicates that the land's market (sales) value is $30,000 and the building's market (sales) value is $90,000. It is clear that Smart Touch got a good deal, paying less than fair market value, which is $120,000 for the combined assets. But how will Smart Touch allocate the $100,000 paid for both assets?

First, figure the ratio of each asset's market value to the total for both assets combined. The total appraised value is $120,000.

Land Market Value	+	Building Market Value	=	Total Market Value
$30,000	+	$90,000	=	$120,000

The land makes up 25% of the total market value, and the building 75%, as follows:

Asset	Market (Sales) Value	Percentage of Total Value		×	Total Purchase Price	=	Cost of Each Asset
Land	$ 30,000	$30,000/$120,000 =	25%	×	$100,000	=	$ 25,000
Building	90,000	$90,000/$120,000 =	75%	×	100,000	=	75,000
Total	$120,000		100%				$100,000

For Smart Touch, the land cost $25,000 and the building cost $75,000. Suppose Smart Touch paid by signing a note payable. The entry to record the purchase of the land and building is as follows:

2013				
Aug 1	Land (A+)		25,000	
	Building (A+)		75,000	
		Notes payable (L+)		100,000

Capital Expenditures

Accountants divide spending made on plant assets into two categories:

- Capital expenditures
- Expenses

Capital expenditures are debited to an asset account because they

- increase the asset's capacity or efficiency, or
- extend the asset's useful life.

Examples of capital expenditures include the purchase price plus all the other costs to bring an asset to its intended use, as discussed in the preceding sections. Also, an **extraordinary repair** is a capital expenditure because it extends the asset's capacity or useful life. An example of an extraordinary repair would be spending $3,000 to rebuild the engine on a five-year-old truck. This extraordinary repair would extend the asset's life past the normal expected life. As a result, its cost would be debited to the asset account for the truck as follows:

Truck (A+)		3,000	
Cash (A–)			3,000
To record cost of rebuilding the truck's engine.			

Expenses incurred to maintain the asset in working order, such as repair or maintenance expense, are *not* debited to an asset account. Examples include the costs of maintaining equipment, such as repairing the air conditioner on a truck, changing the oil filter, and replacing its tires. These **ordinary repairs** are debited to Repairs and maintenance expense, as shown in the following example, when the tires were replaced for $500:

Repairs and maintenance expense (E+)		500	
Cash (A–)			500
To record the cost of tires for the truck.			

Exhibit 9-3 shows some (a) capital expenditures and (b) expenses for a delivery truck.

EXHIBIT 9-3 | **Delivery Truck Expenditures—Capital Expenditure or Expense?**

CAPITAL EXPENDITURE: Debit an Asset Account	EXPENSE: Debit Repairs and maintenance expense
Extraordinary repairs:	*Ordinary repairs:*
Major engine or transmission overhaul	Repair of transmission or engine
Modification for new use	Oil change, lubrication, and so on
Addition to storage capacity	Replacement of tires or windshield
Increase the life of the asset	Paint job

Treating a capital expenditure as an expense, or vice versa, creates an accounting error. Suppose Greg's Tunes replaces the engine in the truck. This would be an extraordinary repair because it increases the truck's life. If the company expenses the cost by debiting Repair and maintenance expense rather than capitalizing it (debiting the asset), the company would be making an accounting error. This error

- overstates Repair and maintenance expenses.
- understates net income.
- understates owner's equity.
- understates the Equipment account (asset) on the balance sheet.

Incorrectly capitalizing an expense creates the opposite error. Assume a minor repair, such as replacing the water pump on the truck, was incorrectly debited to the Asset account. The error would result in expenses being understated and net income being overstated. Additionally, the balance sheet would overstate the truck assets by the amount of the repair bill.

Key Takeaway

All costs spent to ready an asset to perform its intended function are capitalized (debited to the asset account). All repairs that neither extend the asset's life nor improve its efficiency are expensed.

Depreciation

 Account for depreciation

As we learned in an earlier chapter, *depreciation* is the allocation of a plant asset's cost to expense over its useful life. **Depreciation distributes the asset's cost over the time (life) the asset is used.** Depreciation matches the expense against the revenue generated from using the asset to measure net income. Exhibit 9-4 illustrates this matching of revenues and depreciation expense for a $40,000 truck (numbers assumed).

EXHIBIT 9-4 | **Depreciation—Matching Expense with Revenue**

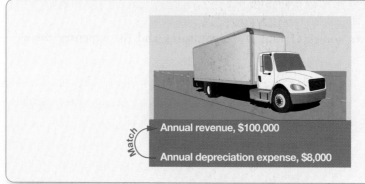

Match

Annual revenue, $100,000

Annual depreciation expense, $8,000

Causes of Depreciation

All assets, except land, wear out as they are used. Greg's delivery truck can only go so many miles before it is worn out. As the truck is driven, this use is part of what causes depreciation. Additionally, physical factors, like age and weather, can cause depreciation of assets.

Some assets, such as computers and software, may become *obsolete* before they wear out. An asset is **obsolete** when a newer asset can perform the job more efficiently. As a result, an asset's useful life may be shorter than its physical life. In all cases, the asset's cost is depreciated over its useful life.

Now that we have discussed causes of depreciation, let's itemize what depreciation is *not*.

1. *Depreciation is not a process of valuation.* Businesses do not record depreciation based on changes in the asset's market (sales) value. **Depreciation is recapturing the cost invested in the asset.**

2. *Depreciation does not mean that the business sets aside cash to replace an asset when it is used up.* Depreciation has nothing to do with cash.

Measuring Depreciation

Depreciation of a plant asset is based on three main factors:

1. Capitalized cost

2. Estimated useful life

3. Estimated residual value

Capitalized cost is a known cost and, as mentioned earlier in this chapter, includes all items spent for the asset to perform its intended function. The other two factors are estimates.

Estimated useful life is the length of the service period expected from the asset. **The estimated useful life is how long the company expects it can use the asset.** Useful life may be expressed in years, units, output, or miles. For each asset, the goal is to define the estimated useful life with the measure (years, units, etc.) that best mimics the asset's decline or use. For example, a building's life is stated in years, a truck's in the number of miles it can drive, and a copier's in the number of copies it can make.

Estimated residual value—also called **salvage value**—is the asset's expected cash value at the end of its useful life. A delivery truck's useful life may be 100,000 miles. When the truck has been driven that distance, the company will sell or scrap it. The expected cash receipt at the end of the truck's life is the truck's estimated residual value. Estimated residual value is *not* depreciated because you expect to receive this amount at the end. Cost minus estimated residual value is called **depreciable cost.**

> Depreciable cost = Cost – Estimated residual value

Depreciation Methods

There are many depreciation methods for plant assets, but three are used most commonly:

- Straight-line
- Units-of-production
- Declining-balance

These methods work differently in *how* they derive the yearly depreciation amount, but they all result in the same total depreciation over the total life of the asset. Exhibit 9-5 gives the data we will use for a truck that Greg's Tunes purchases and places in service on January 1, 2011.

EXHIBIT 9-5 | **Data for Recording Depreciation on a Truck**

Data Item	Amount
Cost of truck	$41,000
Estimated residual value..	(1,000)
Depreciable cost...	$40,000
Estimated useful life—Years..	5 years
Estimated useful life—Units	100,000 mi.

Straight-Line Method

The **straight-line (SL) method** allocates an equal amount of depreciation to each year. Greg's Tunes might want to use this method for the truck if it thinks time is the best indicator of the truck's depreciation. The equation for SL depreciation, applied to the Greg's Tunes' truck, is as follows:

$$\text{Straight-line depreciation} = (\text{Cost} - \text{Residual value}) \times \frac{1}{\text{life}} \times \frac{\#}{12}$$

$$= (41,000 - 1,000) \times \frac{1}{5} \times \frac{12}{12}$$

$$= \$8,000 \text{ per year}$$

represents the number of months used in a year

Since the asset was placed in service on the first day of the year, the entry to record each year's depreciation is as follows:

Dec 31	Depreciation expense—truck (E+)	8,000	
	Accumulated depreciation—truck (CA+)		8,000

A straight-line depreciation schedule for this truck is shown in Exhibit 9-6.

EXHIBIT 9-6 | **Straight-Line Depreciation for a Truck**

Date	Asset Cost	Depreciation for the Year			Accumulated Depreciation	Book Value
		Depreciable Cost	Depreciation Rate	Depreciation Expense		
1-1-2011	$41,000					$41,000
12-31-2011		($41,000–$1,000)	$\times \frac{1}{5} \times \frac{12}{12}$	= $8,000	$ 8,000	33,000
12-31-2012		($41,000–$1,000)	$\times \frac{1}{5} \times \frac{12}{12}$	= 8,000	16,000	25,000
12-31-2013		($41,000–$1,000)	$\times \frac{1}{5} \times \frac{12}{12}$	= 8,000	24,000	17,000
12-31-2014		($41,000–$1,000)	$\times \frac{1}{5} \times \frac{12}{12}$	= 8,000	32,000	9,000
12-31-2015		($41,000–$1,000)	$\times \frac{1}{5} \times \frac{12}{12}$	= 8,000	40,000	1,000 ← Residual value

The final column shows the asset's *book value*, which is cost less accumulated depreciation.

As an asset is used, accumulated depreciation increases and book value decreases. (See the Accumulated Depreciation and Book Value columns in Exhibit 9-6.) At the end of its estimated useful life, the asset is said to be **fully depreciated**. An asset's final book value is called its residual value ($1,000 in this example).

Units-of-Production (UOP) Method

The **units-of-production (UOP) method** allocates a fixed amount of depreciation to each unit of output. **UOP depreciates by units rather than by years.** As we noted above, a unit of output can be miles, units, hours, or output, depending on which unit type best defines the asset's use.

$$\text{Units-of-production depreciation per unit of output} = (\text{Cost} - \text{Residual value}) \times \frac{1}{\text{life in units}}$$

$$= (41,000 - 1,000) \times \frac{1}{100,000}$$

$$= \$0.40 \text{ per mile}$$

The truck in our example is estimated to be driven 20,000 miles the first year, 30,000 the second, 25,000 the third, 15,000 the fourth, and 10,000 during the fifth (for a total of 100,000 miles). The UOP depreciation for each period varies with the number of units (miles, in the case of the truck) the asset produces. Units-of-production for Greg's Tunes' truck is illustrated in Exhibit 9-7. Greg's Tunes might want to use UOP depreciation for the truck if it thinks miles is the best measure of the truck's depreciation.

EXHIBIT 9-7 | **Units-of-Production Depreciation for a Truck**

Date	Asset Cost	Depreciation for the Year			Accumulated Depreciation	Book Value
		Depreciation Per Unit	Number of Units	Depreciation Expense		
1-1-2011	$41,000					$41,000
12-31-2011		$0.40* ×	20,000 =	$ 8,000	$ 8,000	33,000
12-31-2012		0.40 ×	30,000 =	12,000	20,000	21,000
12-31-2013		0.40 ×	25,000 =	10,000	30,000	11,000
12-31-2014		0.40 ×	15,000 =	6,000	36,000	5,000
12-31-2015		0.40 ×	10,000 =	4,000	40,000	1,000 ← Residual value

* see previous page for $0.40 per mile calculation

Double-Declining-Balance Method

An **accelerated depreciation method** writes off more depreciation near the start of an asset's life than straight-line does. The main accelerated method of depreciation is the **double-declining-balance (DDB) method**. Greg's Tunes might want to use this method for its tax return preparation so it could recover more depreciation in the earlier years of the truck's use (life) and pay less taxes. The DDB method multiplies decreasing book value by a constant percentage that is twice the straight-line rate. DDB amounts can be computed using the following formula:

$$\text{Double-declining balance depreciation} = (\text{Cost} - \text{Accumulated depreciation}) \times \frac{2}{\text{life}} \times \frac{\#}{12}$$

For the first year of the truck, the calculation would be as shown:

$$\text{DDB, year 1} = (41,000 - 0) \times \frac{2}{5} \times \frac{12}{12} \text{ or } \$16,400$$

In year 2, the amount of depreciation would decline because the asset has accumulated some depreciation (the $16,400 for the first year). For the second year of the truck, therefore, the calculation would be as shown:

$$\text{DDB, year 2} = (41,000 - 16,400) \times \frac{2}{5} \times \frac{12}{12} \text{ or } \$9,840$$

Note that **residual value is not included in the formula. Residual value is ignored until the last year.**

Final-year depreciation is calculated as the amount needed to bring the asset to its residual value. In the case of the truck, Residual value was given at $1,000. In the DDB schedule in Exhibit 9-8 notice that, after year 4 (12-31-2014), the truck's book value is $5,314. By definition, the truck is to last five years, which ends on 12-31-2015. Also by definition, at the end of the asset's life, its value should equal the residual value. Therefore, in the final-year, depreciation is book value, $5,314, less the $1,000 residual value, or $4,314 in depreciation expense.

Connect To: Taxes

The Modified Accelerated Cost Recovery System (MACRS) is the name for the IRS's version of DDB depreciation. The main difference between the IRS MACRS and DDB is in portion of the year part of the formula $(\frac{\#}{12})$. The IRS utilizes different conventions (for example, half-year or mid-quarter) to calculate the depreciation expense.

EXHIBIT 9-8	Double-Declining-Balance Depreciation for a Truck

Date	Asset Cost	Depreciation for the Year			Accumulated Depreciation	Book Value
		Depreciable Cost	DDB Rate	Depreciation Expense		
1-1-2011	$41,000					$41,000
12-31-2011		$41,000 ×	$\frac{2}{5} \times \frac{12}{12}$ =	$16,400	$16,400	24,600
12-31-2012		24,600 ×	$\frac{2}{5} \times \frac{12}{12}$ =	9,840	26,240	14,760
12-31-2013		14,760 ×	$\frac{2}{5} \times \frac{12}{12}$ =	5,904	32,144	8,856
12-31-2014		8,856 ×	$\frac{2}{5} \times \frac{12}{12}$ =	3,542	35,686	5,314
12-31-2015			=	4,314*	40,000	1,000 ← Residual value

*Last-year depreciation is the "plug figure" needed to reduce book value to the residual amount ($5,314 − $1,000 = $4,314).

SWITCHOVER TO STRAIGHT-LINE Some companies change to the straight-line method during the next-to-last year of the asset's life when the amount of depreciation calculated using the straight-line method is greater than the amount of depreciation calculated using the double-declining balance method. Let's use this plan to compute annual depreciation for 2014 and 2015. In Exhibit 9-8, at the end of 2013,

Book value = $8,856
Depreciable cost = $7,856 ($8,856 − $1,000)
Straight-line depreciation for 2014 and 2015 = $3,928 ($7,856 ÷ 2 years remaining)

So Greg's Tunes might switch to straight-line in year 2014 because depreciation expense would be $3,928 instead of only $3,542 using double-declining balance.

Comparing Depreciation Methods

Let's compare the depreciation methods. Annual amounts vary, but total accumulated depreciation is $40,000 for all three methods.

	AMOUNT OF DEPRECIATION PER YEAR		
			Accelerated Method
Year	Straight-Line	Units-of-Production	Double-Declining-Balance (No Switch to Straight-Line)
1	$ 8,000	$ 8,000	$16,400
2	8,000	12,000	9,840
3	8,000	10,000	5,904
4	8,000	6,000	3,542
5	8,000	4,000	4,314
Total Accumulated Depreciation	$40,000	$40,000	$40,000

Deciding which method is best depends on the asset. A business should match an asset's expense against the revenue that the asset produces. The following are some guidelines:

Straight-Line

For an asset that generates revenue evenly over time, the straight-line method follows the matching principle. Each period shows an equal amount of depreciation. For example, the straight-line method would be appropriate for depreciating a building.

Units-of-Production

The UOP method works best for an asset that depreciates due to wear and tear rather than obsolescence. More use causes greater depreciation. For example, UOP would be appropriate for depleting natural resources, like oil or coal. UOP is also appropriate for vehicles (miles) and machinery (machine hours).

Double-Declining-Balance

The accelerated method (DDB) works best for assets that produce more revenue in their early years. Higher depreciation in the early years is matched against the greater revenue. For example, DDB would be appropriate for depreciating computers.

Exhibit 9-9 shows the three methods in one graph for additional comparison.

EXHIBIT 9-9 | **Annual Depreciation by Method**

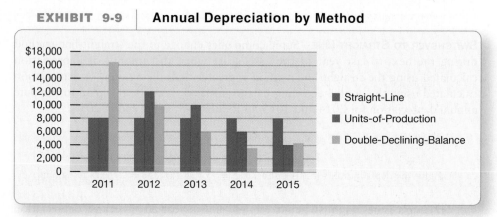

Accounting for Partial-Year Depreciation on Assets

Refer to Exhibit 9-5 on page 460, which provides data for Greg's Tunes' truck. What would happen if Greg's places the truck in service on July 1, 2011, instead of January 1, 2011? Would the depreciation for any of the methods change? Yes, but only the methods that utilize #/12 (number of months of the year) in the formula, which means only straight-line and double-declining balance would change. Units-of-production does not consider years in its formula; thus, that calculation remains the same. The revised straight-line calculation under the altered in-service date of July 1, 2011 is as follows:

$$\text{Straight-line depreciation} = (\text{Cost} - \text{Residual value}) \times \frac{1}{\text{life}} \times \frac{\#}{12}$$

$$= (41,000 - 1,000) \times \frac{1}{5} \times \frac{6}{12}$$

$$= \$4,000 \text{ (Jul 1 - Dec 31)}$$

Since we used the asset for six months of the year, we only record 6/12 of straight-line depreciation expense, or $4,000, in 2011. What about double-declining-balance? The revised calculation considering the altered in-service date of July 1, 2011, is as follows:

$$\text{Double-declining-balance depreciation} = (\text{Cost} - \text{Accumulated depreciation}) \times \frac{2}{\text{life}} \times \frac{\#}{12}$$

$$= (41,000 - 0) \qquad \times \frac{2}{5} \times \frac{6}{12}$$

$$= \$8,200$$

Again, since we used the asset for six months of the year, we only record 6/12 of double-declining-balance depreciation expense, or $8,200, in 2011.

Stop & Think...

Think about your car. What best allocates its use? Is it the age of the car, or is it how many miles you drive per year? How many miles you drive would probably be the best measure. That is how companies should pick depreciation methods—they should figure out what is the best measure to allocate the asset's cost with its use and then pick a depreciation method that mirrors that use.

Other Issues in Accounting for Plant Assets

There are a few additional issues to keep in mind when accounting for plant assets.

Changing the Useful Life of a Depreciable Asset

Estimating the useful life of a plant asset poses a challenge. As the asset is used, the business may change its estimated useful life. For example, Greg's Tunes may find that its truck lasts eight years instead of five. This is a change in estimate. Accounting changes like this are common because they are estimates and, as a result, are not based on perfect foresight. When a company makes an accounting change, generally accepted accounting principles require the business to disclose the nature, reason, and effect of the accounting change.

For a change in either estimated asset life or residual value, the asset's remaining depreciable book value is spread over the asset's remaining life. Suppose Greg's Tunes used the truck purchased on January 1, 2011, for two full years. Under the straight-line method, accumulated depreciation would be $16,000. (Refer to Exhibit 9-6.)

$$\text{Straight-line depreciation for 2 years} = (\$41,000 - \$1,000) \times \frac{1}{5} \times \frac{12}{12}$$

$$= \$8,000 \text{ per year} \times 2 \text{ years}$$

$$= \$16,000$$

Remaining depreciable book value (cost *less* accumulated depreciation *less* residual value) is $24,000 ($41,000 – $16,000 – $1,000). Suppose Greg's Tunes believes the truck will remain useful for six more years (for a total of eight years). At the start of 2013, the company would re-compute depreciation as follows:

Remaining Depreciable Book Value	÷	(New) Estimated Useful Life Remaining	=	(New) Annual Depreciation, 2013–2018
$24,000	÷	6 years	=	$4,000

In years 2013–2018, the yearly depreciation entry based on the new useful life would be as follows:

Dec 31	Depreciation expense—truck	(E+)		4,000	
	Accumulated depreciation—truck	(CA+)			4,000

Revised straight-line depreciation is computed very much like straight-line depreciation, except the accumulated depreciation taken to date is accounted for in the following formula:

$$\text{Revised SL depreciation} = (\text{Cost} - \boxed{\text{Accumulated depreciation}} - \text{New residual value}) \times \frac{1}{\text{new remaining life}} \times \frac{\#}{12}$$

Asset Impairments

Another consideration for assets held and used by the business is that the asset's value or usefulness could significantly decline, outside of normal depreciation. There are many factors that could cause this decline—for example, the asset's physical condition has deteriorated more rapidly than anticipated. (These factors are covered in FASB Codification section 360-10-35.)

Intangible assets with indefinite lives, such as goodwill (discussed later in the chapter), must be tested annually for **impairment**. Tangible assets, such as trucks or equipment, don't have to be tested annually. Rather, tangible assets are tested for impairment when some event happens in which their value might be impaired. For simplification and as an example, assume that a measurable decline has occurred on a forklift for which a company originally paid $100,000 and has recorded accumulated depreciation to date of $40,000. The forklift has **net book value** of $60,000, but its value after impairment is only $50,000. We record the impairment as follows:

Loss on impairment (E+)	10,000	
Accumulated depreciation (CA–)	40,000	
Forklift (A–)		50,000
To record the impairment.		

Using Fully Depreciated Assets

As explained earlier in the chapter, a fully depreciated asset is one that has reached the end of its *estimated* useful life. No more depreciation is recorded for the asset. If the asset is no longer useful, it is disposed of. If the asset is still useful, the company may continue using it. The asset account and its accumulated depreciation remain on the books, but no additional depreciation is recorded. In short, the asset never goes below residual value.

> **Key Takeaway**
>
> Depreciation recovers the cost invested in an asset over the asset's useful life. In this section we illustrated three methods: straight-line, UOP, and double-declining-balance. Although the three methods allocate the cost differently, when the asset's life is over, the net book value is always equal to the asset's residual value. Asset impairments also can reduce the value recorded on the books for the asset. Impairments recognize decline in an asset's value for issues other than normal depreciation.

Summary Problem 9-1

Latté On Demand purchased a coffee drink machine on January 1, 2011, for $44,000. Expected useful life is 10 years or 100,000 drinks. In 2011, 3,000 drinks were sold and in 2012, 14,000 drinks were sold. Residual value is $4,000. Under three depreciation methods, annual depreciation and total accumulated depreciation at the end of 2011 and 2012 are as follows:

	Method A		Method B		Method C	
Year	Annual Depreciation Expense	Accumulated Depreciation	Annual Depreciation Expense	Accumulated Depreciation	Annual Depreciation Expense	Accumulated Depreciation
2011	$1,200	$1,200	$8,800	$ 8,800	$4,000	$4,000
2012	5,600	6,800	7,040	15,840	4,000	8,000

Requirements

1. Identify the depreciation method used in each instance, and show the equation and computation for each method. (Round to the nearest dollar.)
2. Assume use of the same method through 2013. Compute depreciation expense, accumulated depreciation, and net book value for 2011–2013 under each method, assuming 12,000 drinks were sold in 2013.

Solution

Requirement 1

Method A: Units-of-Production

$$\text{Depreciation per unit} = \frac{\$44,000 - \$4,000}{100,000 \text{ units}} = \$0.40/\text{drink}$$

2011: $\$0.40 \times 3,000 \text{ units} = \$1,200$
2012: $\$0.40 \times 14,000 \text{ units} = \$5,600$

Method B: Double-Declining-Balance

2011: $(\$44,000 - 0) \times \frac{2}{10} \times \frac{12}{12} = \$8,800$

2012: $(\$44,000 - \$8,800) \times \frac{2}{10} \times \frac{12}{12} = \$7,040$

Method C: Straight-Line

Each year: $(\$44,000 - \$4,000) \times \frac{1}{10} \times \frac{12}{12} = \$4,000$

Requirement 2

Method A: Unit-of-Production

Year	Annual Depreciation Expense	Accumulated Depreciation	Book Value
Start			$44,000
2011	$1,200	$ 1,200	42,800
2012	5,600	6,800	37,200
2013	4,800	11,600	32,400

Method B: Double-Declining-Balance

Year	Annual Depreciation Expense	Accumulated Depreciation	Book Value
Start			$44,000
2011	$8,800	$ 8,800	35,200
2012	7,040	15,840	28,160
2013	5,632	21,472	22,528

Method C: Straight-Line

Year	Annual Depreciation Expense	Accumulated Depreciation	Book Value
Start			$44,000
2011	$4,000	$ 4,000	40,000
2012	4,000	8,000	36,000
2013	4,000	12,000	32,000

Annual Depreciation Expense for the 3rd year; 2013:

Units-of-production	$0.40 \times 12,000$ units $= \$4,800$
Double-declining-balance	$(\$44,000 - \$15,840) \times \frac{2}{10} \times \frac{12}{12} = \$5,632$
Straight-line	$(\$44,000 - \$4,000) \times \frac{1}{10} \times \frac{12}{12} = \$4,000$

Disposing of a Plant Asset

 Record the disposal of an asset by sale or trade

Eventually, an asset wears out or becomes obsolete. The owner then has two choices:

- Trade the asset for non-like property. This choice includes selling or scrapping the asset, or trading for an asset that is not similar in functionality. Examples include selling a truck for cash, scrapping a truck for no cash, or trading a truck for equipment. All are non-like property exchanges and a gain or loss on the transaction must be recognized by the company.

- Trade the asset for another asset that has similar functionality. This is called a **non-monetary** or **like-kind exchange**. The basic principle for like-kind exchanges is to value the asset received at its fair value, if it is more clearly evident. Fair value is either the fair value of the asset(s) given up OR the fair value of the asset(s) received plus/minus any cash received/paid in the transaction. An example of a non-monetary asset exchange would be trading a **Ford** truck for a **Toyota** truck.

Regardless of the type of exchange (like or non-like kind property), the four steps for journalizing disposals or trades are similar and are as follows:

1. Bring the depreciation up to date.

2. Remove the old, disposed of asset from the books.
   a. Make the Asset account equal zero by crediting the asset for its original cost.
   b. Make the Accumulated depreciation account for the asset equal zero by debiting it for all the depreciation taken to date on the asset.

3. Record the value of any cash (or other accounts) paid (or received) for the asset. For example, if cash is given, credit Cash. If cash is received, debit Cash. If a note payable was signed, credit Notes payable.

4. Finally, determine the difference between the total debits and total credits made in the journal entry.
   a. If the asset was traded for a like-kind asset and the fair value of neither asset is determinable, the net difference in debits and credits will be recorded as a debit to the new asset account.

b. If the asset was traded in a non-like kind manner or the fair value of either the asset received or given up is known, then the net difference will represent gain or loss on the disposal (or sale) of the disposed asset. Record the gain or loss to the income statement as follows:

- If the total debits > total credits—a credit entry will be made to make the journal entry balance. The credit represents a Gain on sale (or disposal) of an asset.
- If the total debits < total credits—a debit entry will be made to make the journal entry balance. The debit represents a Loss on sale (or disposal) of an asset.
- If total debits = total credits—there is no Gain or Loss on sale (or disposal) of the asset.

To apply this, let's consider the truck Greg's Tunes purchased on January 1, 2011. Assume the business recorded depreciation using the straight-line method through December 31, 2012. According to Exhibit 9-6 presented earlier in the chapter, Greg's Tunes' historical cost of the truck was $41,000, $1,000 was the estimated residual value, and $16,000 has been recorded in total accumulated depreciation through 12-31-2012.

Truck		Accumulated depreciation—truck	
41,000			16,000

Before we consider any transactions, the T-accounts would appear as follows:

To illustrate accounting for disposal of an asset, let's consider the five options that Greg's Tunes has to dispose of the truck. All options are assumed to take place on March 31, 2013. Separate exhibits illustrate each of the five options.

1. Situation A – The truck is in an accident and is totaled. The truck is completely worthless and must be scrapped for $0. There are no insurance proceeds from the accident.

2. Situation B – Greg's Tunes sells the truck to Bob's Burger House for $10,000 cash.

3. Situation C – Greg's Tunes sells the truck to Harry's Hot Dogs. Harry's gives Greg's $20,000 cash and a piece of equipment worth $5,000 for the truck.

4. Situation D – Greg's Tunes trades the old truck in for a new **Toyota** truck. The fair market value of the **Toyota** truck is $32,000.

5. Situation E – Greg's Tunes trades the old truck and $3,000 in cash for a **Toyota** truck. The fair value of neither the old or the new truck is known.

Situation A—Scrap the Truck

If assets are junked before they are fully depreciated, there is a loss equal to the asset's book value. Let's apply the four steps for disposal outlined previously to demonstrate this:

STEP 1: Bring the depreciation up to date. Depreciation has not been taken on the truck since December 31, 2012. It is now March 31, 2013, so three months have passed and we need to record three months of depreciation. The problem stated earlier that Greg's is using the straight-line method, so we calculate depreciation for the three months and journalize.

STEP 2: Remove the old, disposed of asset from the books. To remove the asset, we must zero out both the asset and Accumulated depreciation accounts. (Note that the entry is incomplete at this point because we must record what we have received, if anything, in the next step.)

STEP 3: Then, record the value of any cash (or other accounts) paid or received. Since Greg's Tunes received $0 for the scrapped truck, there is nothing to add to our disposal entry we are building from step 2.

STEP 4: Finally, determine the difference between the total debits and total credits made in the journal entry. Total Debits are $18,000, and total Credits are $41,000. Credits > Debits, so we must record a Debit for the difference, or $23,000 ($41,000 – $18,000). This is a loss on disposal because we received nothing for the truck that had net book value (Cost – Accumulated depreciation) of $23,000.

Step 1	2013	Depreciation expense (E+)	2,000	
	Mar 31	Accumulated depreciation (CA+)		2,000
		[(41,000 Cost – 1,000 Residual Value) × 1/5 yr × 3/12]		
Steps 2, 3, 4		Accumulated depreciation (16,000 + 2,000) (CA–)	18,000	
		Loss on disposal of truck (E+)	23,000	
		Truck (A–)		41,000

Situation B—Sell the Truck for $10,000

Selling the truck for cash is a non-like kind exchange, as cash does not have the same utility that a truck does. Considering the same facts for Greg's Tunes, let's apply the four steps for disposal outlined previously to demonstrate this situation:

STEP 1: Bring the depreciation up to date. This is identical to what we journalized in Situation A.

STEP 2: Remove the old, disposed of asset from the books. To remove the asset, we must zero out both the asset and Accumulated depreciation accounts (note that this entry is incomplete at this point).

STEP 3: Then, record the value of any cash (or other accounts) paid or received. Since Greg's received $10,000 for the truck, we must add that Cash to our entry.

STEP 4: Finally, determine the difference between the total debits and total credits made in the journal entry. Total Debits are $28,000 ($10,000 + $18,000), and total Credits are $41,000. Credits > Debits, so we must record a Debit for the difference, or $13,000 ($41,000 – $28,000). This is a loss on sale.

Step 1	2013	Depreciation expense (E+)	2,000	
	Mar 31	Accumulated depreciation (CA+)		2,000
		[(41,000 Cost – 1,000 Residual Value) × 1/5 yr × 3/12]		
Steps 2, 3, 4		Cash (A+)	10,000	
		Accumulated depreciation (16,000 + 2,000) (CA–)	18,000	
		Loss on sale of truck (E+)	13,000	
		Truck (A–)		41,000

Situation C—Sell the Truck for $20,000 Cash and $5,000 Equipment

Selling the truck for cash and other equipment is still considered a non-like kind exchange, as neither cash nor equipment has the same utility that a truck does. Considering the same facts for Greg's Tunes, let's apply the four steps for disposal outlined previously to demonstrate this situation:

STEP 1: Bring the depreciation up to date. This is identical to what we journalized in Situations A and B.

STEP 2: Remove the old, disposed of asset from the books. To remove the asset, we must zero out both the asset and Accumulated depreciation accounts (note that this entry is incomplete at this point).

STEP 3: Then, record the value of any cash (or other accounts) paid or received. Since Greg's received $20,000 in Cash and $5,000 in Equipment, we must add both the Cash and Equipment to our incomplete entry.

STEP 4: Finally, determine the difference between the total debits and total credits made in the journal entry. Total Debits are $43,000 ($20,000 + $5,000 + $18,000), and total Credits are $41,000. Debits > Credits, so we must record a Credit for the difference, or $2,000 ($43,000 – $41,000). This is a gain on sale.

Step 1	2013	Depreciation expense (E+)	2,000	
	Mar 31	Accumulated depreciation (CA+)		2,000
		[(41,000 Cost – 1,000 Residual Value) × 1/5 yr × 3/12]		
Steps 2, 3, 4		Cash (A+)	20,000	
		Equipment (A+)	5,000	
		Accumulated depreciation (16,000 + 2,000) (CA–)	18,000	
		Gain on sale of truck (R+)		2,000
		Truck (A–)		41,000

Situation D—Trade the Truck for a Toyota Truck

This is considered a non-monetary/like-kind exchange, as Greg's Tunes is trading a truck for another truck—they both have the same basic utility. Considering the same facts for Greg's Tunes, let's apply the four steps for disposal outlined previously to demonstrate this situation:

STEP 1: Bring the depreciation up to date. This is identical to what we journalized in Situations A through C.

STEP 2: Remove the old, disposed of asset from the books. To remove the asset, we must zero out both the asset and Accumulated depreciation accounts (note that this entry is incomplete at this point).

STEP 3: Record the value of any cash (or other accounts) paid or received. Greg did not receive cash. He received a new **Toyota** truck. Since the value of the new **Toyota** truck is known to be $32,000, we must record the new **Toyota** truck at its fair value of $32,000.

STEP 4: Finally, determine the difference between the total debits and total credits made in the journal entry. Total Debits are $50,000 ($18,000 + $32,000), and total Credits are $41,000. Credits > Debits, so we must record a Credit for the difference, or $9,000 ($50,000 – $41,000). This is a gain on sale.

Step 1	2013	Depreciation expense (E+)	2,000	
	Mar 31	Accumulated depreciation (CA+)		2,000
		[(41,000 Cost – 1,000 Residual Value) × 1/5 yr × 3/12]		
Steps 2, 3, 4		Accumulated depreciation (16,000 + 2,000) (CA–)	18,000	
		Truck (**Toyota**) (A+)	32,000	
		Truck (A–)		41,000
		Gain on exchange of truck (R+)		9,000

Situation E—Trade the Truck and $3,000 Cash for a Toyota Truck

This is considered a like-kind exchange, as Greg's Tunes is trading a truck for another truck. Considering the same facts for Greg's Tunes, let's apply the four steps for disposal outlined previously to demonstrate this situation:

STEP 1: Bring the depreciation up to date. This is identical to what we journalized in Situations A through D.

STEP 2: Remove the old, disposed of asset from the books. To remove the asset, we must zero out both the asset and Accumulated depreciation accounts (note that this entry is incomplete at this point).

STEP 3: Record the value of any cash (or other accounts) paid or received. Greg did not receive cash, but he did pay cash of $3,000, so we need to record the credit to Cash of $3,000. He received a **Toyota** truck. Since it is a non-monetary/like-kind exchange and neither the old or new truck's fair value is known, there is no gain or loss, so we do not have to calculate the step 4 gain. We take the difference in the debits and credits (as done previously in step 4), and the difference is recorded to the new truck. Total Debits are $18,000, and total Credits are $44,000 ($41,000 + $3,000). The difference, $26,000, is recorded to the new **Toyota** truck.

STEP 4: This step does not apply because it's a like-kind exchange and the value of the new truck is based on the value of what assets were given up; thus, debits equal credits and no gain or loss is recognized.

Step 1	2013	Depreciation expense (E+)	2,000	
	Mar 31	Accumulated depreciation (CA+)		2,000
		[(41,000 Cost – 1,000 Residual Value) × 1/5 yr × 3/12]		
Steps 2, 3, 4		Accumulated depreciation (16,000 + 2,000) (CA–)	18,000	
		Truck (Toyota) (A+)	26,000	
		Truck (A–)		41,000
		Cash (A–)		3,000

Accounting for Natural Resources

 Account for natural resources

Natural resources are plant assets that come from the earth. Natural resources are like inventories in the ground or on top of the ground. Examples include iron ore, oil, natural gas, diamonds, coal, and timber. Natural resources are expensed through *depletion*. **Depletion expense** is that portion of the cost of natural resources that is used up in a particular period. **It's called depletion because the company is depleting (using up) a natural resource such that at some point in time, there is nothing left to dig out of the ground.** Depletion expense is computed by the units-of-production formula:

$$\text{Depletion expense (UOP)} = (\text{Cost} - \text{Residual value}) \times \frac{1}{\substack{\text{Estimated total units} \\ \text{of natural resources}}} \times \text{Number of units removed}$$

An oil well may cost $700,000,000 and hold 70,000,000 barrels of oil. Natural resources usually have no residual value. The depletion rate, as a result, would be $10 per barrel [($700,000,000 − 0) × 1/70,000,000 barrels]. If 3,000 barrels are extracted during the month, then depletion expense for that month is $30,000 (3,000 barrels × $10 per barrel). The depletion entry at the end of the month is as follows:

| Depletion expense (3,000 barrels × $10)   (E+) | 30,000 | |
| Accumulated depletion—oil   (CA+) | | 30,000 |

If 4,500 barrels are removed next month, depletion expense is $45,000 (4,500 barrels × $10 per barrel).

Accumulated depletion is a contra account similar to Accumulated depreciation. Natural resources can be reported on the balance sheet as shown for oil in the following example:

Property, Plant, and Equipment:		
Land..		$ 40,000,000
Buildings...	$ 80,000,000	
Equipment...	20,000,000	
	100,000,000	
Less: Accumulated depreciation	30,000,000	70,000,000
Oil...	$700,000,000	
Less: Accumulated depletion	75,000	699,925,000
Property, plant, and equipment, net		$809,925,000

Accounting for Intangible Assets

As we saw earlier, *intangible assets* have no physical form. Instead, these assets convey special rights from patents, copyrights, trademarks, and other creative works.

5 Account for intangible assets

In our technology-driven economy, intangibles are very important. The intellectual capital of **Microsoft** or **Intel** is difficult to measure. However, when one company buys another, we get a glimpse of the value of the intellectual capital of the acquired company. For example in 2000, **America Online (AOL)** acquired **Time Warner. AOL** said it would give $146 billion for **Time Warner**'s net tangible assets of only $9 billion. Why so much for so little? Because **Time Warner**'s intangible assets were worth billions. Intangibles can account for most of a company's market value, so companies must value their intangibles just as they value inventory and equipment.

A **patent** is an intangible asset that is a federal government grant conveying an exclusive 20-year right to produce and sell an invention. The invention may be a process or a product—for example, the Dolby noise-reduction process or a prescription drug formula. The acquisition cost of a patent is debited to the Patents account. The intangible is expensed through **amortization**, the systematic reduction of the asset's carrying value on the books. Amortization applies to intangibles exactly as depreciation applies to equipment and depletion to oil and timber.

Amortization is computed over the asset's estimated useful life—usually by the straight-line method. Obsolescence is the most common reason an intangible's useful life gets shortened from its expected length. Amortization expense for an intangible asset can be credited directly to the asset instead of using an accumulated amortization account. The residual value of most intangibles is zero.

Some intangibles have indefinite lives. For them, the company records no systematic amortization each period. Instead, it accounts for any decrease in the value of the intangible as an impairment of goodwill (to be discussed later in the chapter).

Specific Intangibles

As noted earlier, patents, copyrights, and trademarks are intangible assets. Accounting for their purchase and their decline in value for each is the same. We will illustrate the accounting by using a patent.

Patents

Like any other asset, a patent may be purchased. Suppose Greg's Tunes pays $200,000 to acquire a patent on January 1, 2011. Greg's Tunes believes this patent's useful life is only five years because it is likely that a new, more efficient process will be developed within that time. Amortization expense is therefore $40,000 per year ($200,000/5 years). Acquisition and amortization entries for this patent are as follows:

2011				
Jan 1	Patents (A+)		200,000	
	Cash (A–)			200,000
	To acquire a patent.			
Dec 31	Amortization expense—patents ($200,000/5) (E+)		40,000	
	Patents (A–)			40,000
	To amortize the cost of a patent.			

At the end of the first year, Greg's Tunes will report this patent at $160,000 ($200,000 minus first-year amortization of $40,000), the next year at $120,000, and so forth. Each year for five years the value of the patent will be reduced until the end of its five-year life, at which point its net book value will be $0.

Copyrights

A **copyright** is the exclusive right to reproduce and sell a book, musical composition, film, or other work of art or intellectual property. Copyrights also protect computer software programs, such as **Microsoft Windows**™ and the **Excel** spreadsheet software. Issued by the federal government, a copyright extends 70 years beyond the author's life.

A company may pay a large sum to purchase an existing copyright. For example, the publisher **Simon & Schuster** may pay $1 million for the copyright on a popular novel because it thinks it will be able to profit from selling the novel. Most copyrights have short, useful lives.

Trademarks and Brand Names

Trademarks and **brand names** (also known as **trade names**) are assets that represent distinctive products or services, such as the **Nike** "swoosh" or the **NASCAR** number 3 for Dale Earnhardt. Legally protected slogans include **Chevrolet**'s "Like a Rock" and **Avis Rent A Car**'s "We try harder." The cost of a trademark or trade name is amortized over its useful life.

Franchises and Licenses

Franchises and **licenses** are privileges granted by a private business or a government to sell goods or services under specified conditions. The **Dallas Cowboys** football organization is a franchise granted by the **National Football League**. **McDonald's** and **Subway** are well-known business franchises. The acquisition cost of a franchise or license is amortized over its useful life.

Goodwill

Goodwill in accounting has a different meaning from the everyday phrase "goodwill among men." In accounting, **goodwill** is the excess of the cost to purchase another company over the market value of its net assets (assets minus liabilities). **Goodwill is the value paid above the net worth of the company's assets and liabilities.**

Suppose **Walmart** acquired **Monterrey Company** in Mexico on January 1, 2011. The sum of the market values of **Monterrey**'s assets was $9 million and its liabilities totaled $1 million, so **Monterrey**'s net assets totaled $8 million. Suppose **Walmart** paid $10 million to purchase **Monterrey Company**. In this case, **Walmart** paid $2 million above the value of **Monterrey**'s net assets. Therefore, that $2 million is considered goodwill and is computed as follows:

Purchase price to acquire Monterrey Company..........		$10,000,000
Market value of Monterrey Company's assets............	$9,000,000	
Less: Monterrey Company's liabilities........................	1,000,000	
Market value of Monterrey Company's net assets......		8,000,000
Excess, called *goodwill*..		$ 2,000,000

Walmart's entry to record the purchase of **Monterrey**, including the goodwill that **Walmart** purchased, would be as follows:

2011			
Jan 1	Assets (Cash, Receivables, Inventories, Plant assets,		
	all at market value) (A+)	9,000,000	
	Goodwill (A+)	2,000,000	
	Liabilities (L+)		1,000,000
	Cash (A–)		10,000,000
	Purchased Monterrey Company.		

Goodwill has some special features:

1. Goodwill is recorded only by an acquiring company when it purchases another company and pays more for that company than the value of the assets acquired. (As in our entry above where **Walmart** purchased **Monterrey** for $2 million more than the value of **Monterrey**'s net assets.) An outstanding reputation may create goodwill, but that company never records goodwill for its own business.

2. According to generally accepted accounting principles (GAAP), goodwill is *not* amortized. Instead, the acquiring company measures the current value of its goodwill each year. If the goodwill has increased in value, there is nothing to record. But if goodwill's value has decreased, then the company records a loss and writes the goodwill down. For example, suppose **Walmart**'s goodwill—which we talked about with its purchase of **Monterrey**—is worth only $1,500,000 on December 31, 2011. In that case, **Walmart** would make the following entry:

2011			
Dec 31	Loss on impairment of goodwill (E+)	500,000	
	Goodwill ($2,000,000 – $1,500,000) (A–)		500,000
	Recorded impairment loss on goodwill.		

Walmart would then report this goodwill at its reduced current value of $1,500,000.

Accounting for Research and Development Costs

Research and development (R&D) costs are the lifeblood of companies such as **Procter & Gamble, General Electric, Intel,** and **Boeing.** In general, companies do not report R&D assets on their balance sheets because GAAP requires companies to expense R&D costs as they are incurred.

Ethical Issues

 6 Describe ethical issues related to plant assets

The main ethical issue in accounting for plant assets is whether to capitalize or expense a cost. In this area, company opinions vary greatly. On the one hand, companies want to save on taxes. This motivates them to expense all costs and decrease taxable income. On the other hand, they want to look as good as possible to investors, with high net income and sufficient assets.

In most cases, a cost that is capitalized or expensed for tax purposes must be treated the same way in the financial statements. What, then, is the ethical path? Accountants should follow the general guidelines for capitalizing a cost:

> *Capitalize all costs that provide a future benefit.*
> *Expense all other costs.*

Many companies have gotten into trouble by capitalizing costs that were really expenses. They made their financial statements look better than the facts warranted. **WorldCom** committed this type of accounting fraud, and its former top executives are now in prison as a result. There are very few cases of companies getting into trouble by following the general guidelines, or even by erring on the side of accounting conservatism. Following the guidelines works.

Decision Guidelines 9-1

ACCOUNTING FOR PLANT ASSETS AND RELATED EXPENSES

The Decision Guidelines summarize key decisions a company makes in accounting for plant assets. Suppose you buy a **Starbucks** or a **Curves International** franchise and invest in related equipment. You have some decisions to make about how to account for the franchise and the equipment. The Decision Guidelines will help you maximize your cash flow and properly account for the business.

Decision	Guidelines
• Capitalize or expense a cost?	General rule: Capitalize all costs that provide *future benefit*.
	Expense all costs that provide *no future benefit*.
• Capitalize or expense:	
• Cost associated with a new asset?	Capitalize all costs that bring the asset to its intended use.
• Cost associated with an existing asset?	Capitalize only those costs that add to the asset's usefulness or extend its useful life. Expense all other costs as repairs or maintenance.
• Which depreciation method to use:	
• For financial reporting?	Use the method that best matches depreciation expense against the revenues produced by the asset.
• For tax purposes?	Generally, use the method that reduces taxes the most.
• How do you calculate depreciation using the:	
• straight-line method?	$(\text{Cost} - \text{Residual value}) \times \dfrac{1}{\text{life}} \times \dfrac{\#}{12}$
• units-of-production method?	$(\text{Cost} - \text{Residual value}) \times \dfrac{1}{\text{life in units}}$
• double-declining-balance method?	$(\text{Cost} - \text{Accumulated depreciation}) \times \dfrac{2}{\text{life}} \times \dfrac{\#}{12}$
• When do we recognize gains/losses on asset sales?	Recognize gain or loss when the asset is sold, destroyed, traded for a non-like kind asset, or traded in an exchange where the fair value of either the asset given up or acquired is known.
• When do we NOT recognize gains/losses on asset sales?	Do not recognize gains/losses when the asset is traded and neither the fair value of the asset given up nor the fair value of the asset acquired is known.

Summary Problem 9-2

The following figures appear in the Answers to Summary Problem 9-1, Requirement 2.

	Method B: Double-Declining-Balance			Method C: Straight-Line		
Year	Annual Depreciation Expense	Accumulated Depreciation	Book Value	Annual Depreciation Expense	Accumulated Depreciation	Book Value
Start			$44,000			$44,000
2011	$8,800	$ 8,800	35,200	$4,000	$ 4,000	40,000
2012	7,040	15,840	28,160	4,000	8,000	36,000
2013	5,632	21,472	22,528	4,000	12,000	32,000

Latté On Demand purchased a coffee machine on January 1, 2011. Management has depreciated the equipment by using the double-declining-balance method. On July 1, 2013, the company sold the equipment for $27,000 cash.

Requirement

1. Record Latté On Demand's depreciation for 2013 and the sale of the equipment on July 1, 2013.

Solution

Record depreciation to date of sale and the sale of the Latté On Demand equipment:

2013			
Jul 1	Depreciation expense ($5,632 × 6/12) (E+)	2,816	
	Accumulated depreciation (CA+)		2,816
	To update depreciation.		
Jul 1	Cash (A+)	27,000	
	Accumulated depreciation ($15,840 + $2,816) (CA–)	18,656	
	Equipment (A–)		44,000
	Gain on sale of equipment (R+)		1,656
	To record the sale of equipment.		

Review *Plant Assets and Intangibles*

● Accounting Vocabulary

Accelerated Depreciation Method (p. 462)
A depreciation method that writes off more of the asset's cost near the start of its useful life than the straight-line method does.

Amortization (p. 473)
Systematic reduction of the asset's carrying value on the books. Expense that applies to intangibles in the same way depreciation applies to plant assets and depletion to natural resources.

Brand Names (p. 474)
Assets that represent distinctive identifications of a product or service. Also called **trade names**.

Capital Expenditures (p. 457)
Expenditures that increase the capacity or efficiency of an asset or extend its useful life. Capital expenditures are debited to an asset account.

Capitalized (p. 455)
A company acquires land, building, or other assets and capitalizes the cost by debiting (increasing) an asset account.

Copyright (p. 474)
Exclusive right to reproduce and sell a book, musical composition, film, other work of art, or intellectual property. Issued by the federal government, copyrights extend 70 years beyond the author's life.

Depletion Expense (p. 472)
Portion of a natural resource's cost used up in a particular period. Computed in the same way as units-of-production depreciation.

Depreciable Cost (p. 459)
The cost of a plant asset minus its estimated residual value.

Double-Declining-Balance (DDB) Method (p. 462)
An accelerated depreciation method that computes annual depreciation by multiplying the asset's decreasing book value by a constant percent that is two times the straight-line rate.

Estimated Residual Value (p. 459)
Expected cash value of an asset at the end of its useful life. Also called **salvage value**.

Estimated Useful Life (p. 459)
Length of the service period expected from an asset. May be expressed in years, units of output, miles, or another measure.

Extraordinary Repair (p. 457)
Repair work that generates a capital expenditure because it extends the asset's life past the normal expected life.

Franchises (p. 474)
Privileges granted by a private business or a government to sell a product or service under specified conditions.

Fully Depreciated Asset (p. 461)
An asset that has reached the end of its estimated useful life. No more depreciation is recorded for the asset.

Goodwill (p. 474)
Excess of the cost of an acquired company over the sum of the market values of its net assets (assets minus liabilities).

Impairment (p. 466)
A decline in asset value, outside of normal depreciation. Recorded as a loss in the period that the decline is identified.

Intangible Assets (p. 453)
Assets with no physical form. Valuable because of the special rights they carry. Examples are patents and copyrights.

Land Improvements (p. 454)
Depreciable improvements to land, such as fencing, sprinklers, paving, signs, and lighting.

Licenses (p. 474)
Privileges granted by a private business or a government to sell a product or service under specified conditions.

Like-Kind Exchange (p. 468)
Trading an asset for another asset that has similar functionality. The asset received is valued at either 1) fair value of the asset given up or 2) fair value of the asset received plus/minus cash received/paid. Also called a **non-monetary exchange**.

Natural Resources (p. 472)
Plant assets that come from the earth. Natural resources are like inventories in the ground (oil) or on top of the ground (timber).

Net Book Value (p. 466)
Original cost of the asset less total accumulated depreciation taken on the asset.

Non-Monetary Exchange (p. 468)
Trading an asset for another asset that has similar functionality. The asset received is valued at either 1) fair value of the asset given up or 2) fair value of the asset received plus/minus cash received/paid. Also called a **like-kind exchange**.

Obsolete (p. 459)
An asset is considered obsolete when a newer asset can perform the job more efficiently than the old.

Ordinary Repairs (p. 457)
Repair work that is debited to an expense account.

Patent (p. 473)
An intangible asset that is a federal government grant conveying an exclusive 20-year right to produce and sell a process or formula.

Real Assets (p. 453)
Assets with physical form. Examples include a truck or building. Also called **tangible assets**.

Relative-Sales-Value Method (p. 456)
Method of allocating the total cost (100%) of multiple assets purchased at one time. Total cost is divided among the assets according to their relative sales/market values.

Salvage Value (p. 459)
Expected cash value of an asset at the end of its useful life. Also called **estimated residual value**.

Straight-Line (SL) Method (p. 460)
Depreciation method in which an equal amount of depreciation expense is assigned to each year of asset use.

Tangible Assets (p. 453)
Assets with physical form. Examples include a truck or building. Also called **real assets**.

Trade Names (p. 474)
Assets that represent distinctive identifications of a product or service. Also called **brand names**.

Trademarks (p. 474)
Assets that represent distinctive identifications of a product or service.

Units-of-Production (UOP) Method (p. 461)
Depreciation method by which a fixed amount of depreciation is assigned to each unit of output produced by an asset.

● Destination: Student Success

Student Success Tips

The following are hints on some common trouble areas for students in this chapter:

- Recall that everything spent to make the asset perform its intended function is part of the capitalized cost of the asset (asset on the balance sheet).

- If a cost expended increases the asset's life or efficiency, then it's part of the asset cost (debit asset account). If it doesn't, then the cost expended is a Repair or maintenance expense.

- Review the three methods illustrated for calculating depreciation, depletion, and amortization: straight-line, UOP, and double-declining-balance.

- Keep in mind that when an asset is sold or traded, the original cost and the accumulated depreciation for that asset must both be removed from the books.

- Remember that the #/12 part of the depreciation formula is used to account for how many months out of the year the asset was used. If the asset was used the entire year, that ratio is 12/12.

Getting Help

If there's a learning objective from the chapter you aren't confident about, try using one or more of the following resources:

- Review the Summary Problems in the chapter as they provide examples of how to calculate depreciation and asset disposals.

- Practice additional exercises or problems at the end of Chapter 9 that cover the specific learning objective that is challenging you.

- Watch the white board videos for Chapter 9 located at myaccountinglab.com under the Chapter Resources button.

- Go to myaccountinglab.com and select the Study Plan button. Choose Chapter 9 and work the questions covering that specific learning objective until you've mastered it.

- Work the Chapter 9 pre/post tests in myaccountinglab.com.

- Visit the learning resource center on your campus for tutoring.

● Quick Check

Experience the Power of Practice!

As denoted by the logo, all of these questions, as well as additional practice materials, can be found in

MyAccountingLab.

Please visit myaccountinglab.com

1. Which cost is *not* recorded as part of the cost of a building?
   a. Real estate commission paid to buy the building
   b. Construction materials and labor
   c. Concrete for the building's foundation
   d. Annual building maintenance

2. Unlimited Airline bought four used Canada Tran airplanes. Each plane was worth $33,000,000, but the owner sold the combination for $124,000,000. How much is Unlimited Airline's cost of each plane?
   a. $124,000,000
   b. $31,000,000
   c. $132,000,000
   d. $33,000,000

3. How should you record a capital expenditure?
   a. Debit a liability
   b. Debit capital
   c. Debit an expense
   d. Debit an asset

4. Which method almost always produces the most depreciation in the first year?
   a. Units-of-production
   b. Straight-line
   c. Double-declining-balance
   d. All produce the same total depreciation

5. A Celty Airline jet costs $28,000,000 and is expected to fly 200,000,000 miles during its 10-year life. Residual value is expected to be zero because the plane was used when acquired. If the plane travels 54,000,000 miles the first year, how much depreciation should Celty Airline record under the units-of-production method?

   a. $2,800,000

   c. $5,600,000

   b. $7,560,000

   d. Cannot be determined from the data given

6. Which depreciation method would you generally prefer to use for income tax purposes? Why?

   a. Double-declining-balance because it gives the most total depreciation over the asset's life

   b. Straight-line because it is simplest

   c. Double-declining-balance because it gives the fastest tax deductions for depreciation

   d. Units-of-production because it best tracks the asset's use

7. A copy machine costs $45,000 when new and has accumulated depreciation of $44,000. Suppose Print and Photo Center junks this machine, receiving nothing. What is the result of the disposal transaction?

   a. No gain or loss

   c. Loss of $1,000

   b. Gain of $1,000

   d. Loss of $45,000

8. Suppose Print and Photo Center in the preceding question sold the machine for $1,000. What is the result of this disposal transaction?

   a. Loss of $44,000

   c. Loss of $1,000

   b. Gain of $1,000

   d. No gain or loss

9. Which method is used to compute depletion?

   a. Double-declining-balance method

   c. Depletion method

   b. Straight-line method

   d. Units-of-production method

10. Which intangible asset is recorded only as part of the acquisition of another company?

    a. Patent

    c. Copyright

    b. Goodwill

    d. Franchise

Answers are given after Apply Your Knowledge (p. 495).

Assess Your Progress

● Short Exercises

S9-1   **❶ Measuring plant asset cost [5 min]**

This chapter lists the costs included for the acquisition of land. First is the purchase price, which is obviously included in the cost of the land. The reasons for including the other costs are not so obvious. For example, removing a building looks more like an expense.

Requirements

1. State why the costs listed in the chapter are included as part of the cost of the land.

2. After the land is ready for use, will these costs be capitalized or expensed?

S9-2   **①** **Lump-sum asset purchase [10 min]**

Rural Tech Support pays $130,000 for a group purchase of land, building, and equipment. At the time of your acquisition, the land has a market value of $70,000, the building $56,000, and the equipment $14,000.

Requirement

1. Journalize the lump-sum purchase of the three assets for a total cost of $130,000. You sign a note payable for this amount.

S9-3   **②** **Computing first-year depreciation and book value [10 min]**

At the beginning of the year, Alaska Freight Airlines purchased a used airplane for $43,000,000. Alaska Freight Airlines expects the plane to remain useful for five years (4,000,000 miles) and to have a residual value of $7,000,000. The company expects the plane to be flown 1,400,000 miles the first year.

Requirements

1. Compute Alaska Freight Airlines' *first-year* depreciation on the plane using the following methods:
    a. Straight-line
    b. Units-of-production
    c. Double-declining-balance

2. Show the airplane's book value at the end of the first year under the straight-line method.

S9-4   **②** **Computing second-year depreciation and accumulated depreciation [10–15 min]**

At the beginning of 2012, Air Canada purchased a used airplane at a cost of $46,000,000. Air Canada expects the plane to remain useful for eight years (5,000,000 miles) and to have a residual value of $6,000,000. Air Canada expects the plane to be flown 1,300,000 miles the first year and 1,000,000 miles the second year.

Requirements

1. Compute *second-year (2013)* depreciation on the plane using the following methods:
    a. Straight-line
    b. Units-of-production
    c. Double-declining-balance

2. Calculate the balance in Accumulated depreciation at the end of the second year using the straight-line method of depreciation.

S9-5   **②** **Selecting the best depreciation method for tax purposes [10 min]**

This exercise uses the Alaska Freight Airlines data from Short Exercise 9-3. Alaska Freight Airlines is deciding which depreciation method to use for income tax purposes.

Requirements

1. Which depreciation method offers the tax advantage for the first year? Describe the nature of the tax advantage.

2. How much extra depreciation will Alaska Freight Airlines get to deduct for the first year as compared with the straight-line method?

S9-6   **②** **Partial year depreciation [5–10 min]**

On July 31, 2012, Logan Services purchased a **Xerox** copy machine for $40,400. Logan Services expects the machine to last for four years and to have a residual value of $2,000.

Requirement

1. Compute depreciation on the machine for the year ended December 31, 2012, using the straight-line method.

S9-7 **②** **Change in the estimated life of an asset [10 min]**

Assume that Alpha Communications paid $75,000 for equipment with a 15-year life and zero expected residual value. After using the equipment for six years, the company determines that the asset will remain useful for only five more years.

Requirements

1. Record depreciation on the equipment for year 7 by the straight-line method.
2. What is accumulated depreciation at the end of year 7?

S9-8 **③** **Sale of asset at gain or loss [10 min]**

Global Positioning Net purchased equipment on January 1, 2012, for $36,000. Global Positioning Net expected the equipment to last for four years and to have a residual value of $4,000. Suppose Global Positioning Net sold the equipment for $26,000 on December 31, 2013, after using the equipment for two full years. Assume depreciation for 2013 has been recorded.

Requirement

1. Journalize the sale of the equipment, assuming straight-line depreciation was used.

S9-9 **③** **Like-kind exchange [5–10 min]**

Brown's Salvage Company purchased a computer for $2,600, debiting Computer equipment. During 2012 and 2013, Brown's Salvage Company recorded total depreciation of $2,000 on the computer. On January 1, 2014, Brown's Salvage Company traded in the computer for a new one, paying $2,500 cash. The fair value of the new computer is $3,100.

Requirement

1. Journalize Brown's Salvage Company's exchange of computers.

S9-10 **④** **Accounting for depletion of natural resources [5–10 min]**

TexAm Petroleum holds huge reserves of oil and gas assets. Assume that at the end of 2012, TexAm Petroleum's cost of oil and gas reserves totaled $72,000,000,000, representing 8,000,000,000 barrels of oil and gas.

Requirements

1. Which depreciation method does TexAm Petroleum use to compute depletion?
2. Suppose TexAm Petroleum removed 400,000,000 barrels of oil during 2013. Journalize depletion expense for 2013.

S9-11 **⑤** **Accounting for goodwill [10 min]**

When one media company buys another, goodwill is often the most costly asset. TMC Advertising paid $170,000 to acquire *Seacoast Report*, a weekly advertising paper. At the time of the acquisition, *Seacoast Report*'s balance sheet reported total assets of $130,000 and liabilities of $70,000. The fair market value of *Seacoast Report*'s assets was $100,000.

Requirements

1. How much goodwill did TMC Advertising purchase as part of the acquisition of *Seacoast Report*?
2. Journalize TMC Advertising's acquisition of *Seacoast Report*.

S9-12   6 Ethics—capitalizing vs. expensing assets [5 min]

Harrington Precision Parts repaired one of its Boeing 737 aircrafts at a cost of $150,000. Harrington Precision Parts erroneously capitalized this cost as part of the cost of the plane.

Requirements

1. How will this accounting error affect Harrington Precision Parts' net income? Ignore depreciation.

2. Should the company correct the error or can it ignore the error to report more favorable earnings results?

● Exercises

E9-13   1 Determining the cost of assets [5–10 min]

Ogden Furniture purchased land, paying $70,000 cash plus a $300,000 note payable. In addition, Ogden paid delinquent property tax of $2,500, title insurance costing $2,000, and $8,000 to level the land and remove an unwanted building. The company then constructed an office building at a cost of $700,000. It also paid $55,000 for a fence around the property, $18,000 for a sign near the entrance, and $10,000 for special lighting of the grounds.

Requirements

1. Determine the cost of the land, land improvements, and building.

2. Which of these assets will Ogden depreciate?

E9-14   1 Lump-sum purchase of assets [10–15 min]

Deadwood Properties bought three lots in a subdivision for a lump-sum price. An independent appraiser valued the lots as follows:

Lot	Appraised Value
1	$ 70,500
2	235,000
3	164,500

Deadwood paid $210,000 in cash.

Requirement

1. Record the purchase in the journal, identifying each lot's cost in a separate Land account. Round decimals to two places, and use your computed percentages throughout.

E9-15   1 Distinguishing capital expenditures from expenses [5–10 min]

Consider the following expenditures:

a. Purchase price.
b. Ordinary recurring repairs to keep the machinery in good working order.
c. Lubrication before machinery is placed in service.
d. Periodic lubrication after machinery is placed in service.
e. Major overhaul to extend useful life by three years.
f. Sales tax paid on the purchase price.
g. Transportation and insurance while machinery is in transit from seller to buyer.
h. Installation.
i. Training of personnel for initial operation of the machinery.
j. Income tax paid on income earned from the sale of products manufactured by the machinery.

Requirement

1. Classify each of the expenditures as a capital expenditure or an expense related to machinery.

E9-16 ❷ **Explaining the concept of depreciation [10–15 min]**

Joe Yusakae just slept through the class in which Professor Ogilvie explained the concept of depreciation. Because the next test is scheduled for Friday, Yusakae telephones Dan Danielson to get his notes from the lecture. Danielson's notes are concise: "Depreciation—Sounds like Greek to me." Yusakae next tries Sara Visaj, who says she thinks depreciation is what happens when an asset wears out. Andrew Greyson is confident that depreciation is the process of creating a cash fund to replace an asset at the end of its useful life.

Requirement

1. Explain the concept of depreciation for Yusakae. Evaluate the explanations of Visaj and Greyson. Be specific.

E9-17 ❷ **Computing depreciation—three methods [10–15 min]**

Papa's Fried Chicken bought equipment on January 2, 2012, for $39,000. The equipment was expected to remain in service for four years and to perform 11,000 fry jobs. At the end of the equipment's useful life, Papa's estimates that its residual value will be $6,000. The equipment performed 1,100 jobs the first year, 3,300 the second year, 4,400 the third, and 2,200 the fourth year.

Requirements

1. Prepare a schedule of *depreciation expense* per year for the equipment under the three depreciation methods. After two years under double-declining-balance depreciation, the company switched to the straight-line method. Show your computations. *Note: Three depreciation schedules must be prepared.*
2. Which method tracks the wear and tear on the equipment most closely?

E9-18 ❷ **Selecting the best depreciation method for tax purposes—partial year [15–20 min]**

Tumble Gymnastics Center, whose fiscal year ends December 31, paid $110,000 for fitness equipment on April 1, 2012, that is expected to have a 10-year life. The expected residual value is $50,000.

Requirement

1. Select the appropriate depreciation method for income tax purposes. Then determine the extra amount of depreciation that Tumble can deduct by using the selected method, versus straight-line, through December 2013.

E9-19 ❷ **Changing an asset's useful life [10–15 min]**

Everyday Hardware Consultants purchased a building for $540,000 and depreciated it on a straight-line basis over a 40-year period. The estimated residual value is $96,000. After using the building for 15 years, Everyday realized that wear and tear on the building would wear it out before 40 years. Starting with the 16th year, Everyday began depreciating the building over a revised total life of 25 years.

Requirement

1. Journalize depreciation on the building for years 15 and 16.

E9-20 ❷ ❸ **Partial year depreciation and sale of an asset [10–15 min]**

On January 2, 2012, Repeat Clothing Consignments purchased showroom fixtures for $11,000 cash, expecting the fixtures to remain in service for five years. Repeat has depreciated the fixtures on a double-declining-balance basis, with zero residual value. On October 31, 2013, Repeat sold the fixtures for $6,200 cash.

Requirement

1. Record both depreciation for 2013 and sale of the fixtures on October 31, 2013.

E9-21 ③ **Trade in asset—two situations [10–15 min]**

Community Bank recently traded in office fixtures. Here are the facts:

Old fixtures:	New fixtures:
• Cost, $96,000.	• Cash paid, $103,000, plus the old fixtures.
• Accumulated depreciation, $65,000.	

Requirements

1. Record Community Bank's trade-in of old fixtures for new ones.

2. Now let's change one fact and see a different outcome. Community Bank feels compelled to do business with Mountain Furniture, a bank customer, even though the bank can get the fixtures elsewhere at a better price. Community Bank is aware that the new fixtures' market value is only $127,000. Now record the trade-in.

E9-22 ② ③ **Measuring asset cost, UOP depreciation, and asset trade [10–15 min]**

Safety Trucking Company uses the units-of-production (UOP) depreciation method because UOP best measures wear and tear on the trucks. Consider these facts about one **Mack** truck in the company's fleet.

When acquired in 2010, the rig cost $450,000 and was expected to remain in service for 10 years or 1,000,000 miles. Estimated residual value was $150,000. The truck was driven 82,000 miles in 2010, 122,000 miles in 2011, and 162,000 miles in 2012. After 45,000 miles in 2013, the company traded in the **Mack** truck for a less-expensive **Freightliner**. Safety also paid cash of $22,000. Fair value of the **Mack** truck was equal to its net book value on the date of the trade.

Requirement

1. Determine Safety's cost of the new truck. Journal entries are not required.

E9-23 ④ **Natural resource depletion [10–15 min]**

Sierra Mountain Mining paid $448,500 for the right to extract mineral assets from a 500,000-ton deposit. In addition to the purchase price, Sierra also paid a $500 filing fee, a $1,000 license fee to the state of Nevada, and $60,000 for a geological survey of the property. Because Sierra purchased the rights to the minerals only, it expects the asset to have zero residual value. During the first year, Sierra removed 50,000 tons of the minerals.

Requirement

1. Make journal entries to record (a) purchase of the minerals (debit Mineral asset), (b) payment of fees and other costs, and (c) depletion for the first year.

E9-24 ⑤ **Acquisition of patent, amortization, and change in useful life [10–15 min]**

Miracle Printers (MP) manufactures printers. Assume that MP recently paid $600,000 for a patent on a new laser printer. Although it gives legal protection for 20 years, the patent is expected to provide a competitive advantage for only eight years.

Requirements

1. Assuming the straight-line method of amortization, make journal entries to record (a) the purchase of the patent and (b) amortization for year 1.

2. After using the patent for four years, MP learns at an industry trade show that another company is designing a more efficient printer. On the basis of this new

information, MP decides, starting with year 5, to amortize the remaining cost of the patent over two remaining years, giving the patent a total useful life of six years. Record amortization for year 5.

E9-25   **⑤ Measuring and recording goodwill [10–15 min]**

Potters has acquired several other companies. Assume that Potters purchased Kittery for $6,000,000 cash. The book value of Kittery's assets is $12,000,000 (market value, $15,000,000), and it has liabilities of $11,000,000.

Requirements

1. Compute the cost of the goodwill purchased by Potters.
2. Record the purchase of Kittery by Potters.

E9-26   **⑥ Ethics [10–15 min]**

Furniture.com uses automated shipping equipment. Assume that early in year 1, Furniture purchased equipment at a cost of $400,000. Management expects the equipment to remain in service for five years, with zero residual value. Furniture uses straight-line depreciation. Furniture's CEO informs the controller to expense the entire cost of the equipment at the time of purchase because Furniture's profits are too high.

Requirements

1. Compute the overstatement or understatement in the following items immediately after purchasing the equipment:
   a. Equipment
   b. Net income
2. Is there an ethical violation? What should the controller do?

● Problems (Group A)

P9-27A   **① ② Capitalized asset cost and partial year depreciation [20–25 min]**   *MyAccountingLab*

Drive and Fly, near an airport, incurred the following costs to acquire land, make land improvements, and construct and furnish a small building:

a.	Purchase price of three acres of land	$ 80,000
b.	Delinquent real estate taxes on the land to be paid by Drive and Fly	5,600
c.	Additional dirt and earthmoving	9,000
d.	Title insurance on the land acquisition	3,200
e.	Fence around the boundary of the property	9,100
f.	Building permit for the building	500
g.	Architect's fee for the design of the building	20,700
h.	Signs near the front of the property	9,000
i.	Materials used to construct the building	215,000
j.	Labor to construct the building	173,000
k.	Interest cost on construction loan for the building	9,500
l.	Parking lots on the property	29,000
m.	Lights for the parking lots	11,300
n.	Salary of construction supervisor (80% to building; 20% to parking lot and concrete walks)	80,000
o.	Furniture	11,600
p.	Transportation of furniture from seller to the building	2,200
q.	Landscaping (shrubs)	6,300

Drive and Fly depreciates land improvements over 20 years, buildings over 40 years, and furniture over 10 years, all on a straight-line basis with zero residual value.

Requirements

1. Set up columns for Land, Land improvements, Building, and Furniture. Show how to account for each cost by listing the cost under the correct account. Determine the total cost of each asset.

2. All construction was complete and the assets were placed in service on July 1. Record partial-year depreciation for the year ended December 31.

P9-28A ❶ ❷ **Capitalized asset cost and first year depreciation, and identifying depreciation results that meet management objectives [30–40 min]**

On January 3, 2012, Trusty Delivery Service purchased a truck at a cost of $90,000. Before placing the truck in service, Trusty spent $3,000 painting it, $1,500 replacing tires, and $4,500 overhauling the engine. The truck should remain in service for five years and have a residual value of $9,000. The truck's annual mileage is expected to be 22,500 miles in each of the first four years and 10,000 miles in the fifth year—100,000 miles in total. In deciding which depreciation method to use, Mikail Johnson, the general manager, requests a depreciation schedule for each of the depreciation methods (straight-line, units-of-production, and double-declining-balance).

Requirements

1. Prepare a depreciation schedule for each depreciation method, showing asset cost, depreciation expense, accumulated depreciation, and asset book value.

2. Trusty prepares financial statements using the depreciation method that reports the highest net income in the early years of asset use. For income tax purposes, the company uses the depreciation method that minimizes income taxes in the early years. Consider the first year that Trusty uses the truck. Identify the depreciation methods that meet the general manager's objectives, assuming the income tax authorities permit the use of any of the methods.

P9-29A ❷ ❸ **Lump sum asset purchases, partial year depreciation, and impairments [20–25 min]**

Gretta Chung Associates surveys American eating habits. The company's accounts include Land, Buildings, Office equipment, and Communication equipment, with a separate accumulated depreciation account for each asset. During 2012 and 2013, Gretta Chung completed the following transactions:

2012 Jan 1	Traded in old office equipment with book value of $40,000 (cost of $132,000 and accumulated depreciation of $92,000) for new equipment. Chung also paid $80,000 in cash. Fair value of the new equipment is $119,000.
Apr 1	Acquired land and communication equipment in a group purchase. Total cost was $270,000 paid in cash. An independent appraisal valued the land at $212,625 and the communication equipment at $70,875.
Sep 1	Sold a building that cost $555,000 (accumulated depreciation of $255,000 through December 31 of the preceding year). Chung received $370,000 cash from the sale of the building. Depreciation is computed on a straight-line basis. The building has a 40-year useful life and a residual value of $75,000.
Dec 31	Recorded depreciation as follows: Communication equipment is depreciated by the straight-line method over a five-year life with zero residual value. Office equipment is depreciated using the double-declining-balance method over five years with $2,000 residual value.
2013 Jan 1	The company identified that the communication equipment suffered significant decline in value. The fair value of the communication equipment was determined to be $55,000.

Requirement

1. Record the transactions in the journal of Gretta Chung Associates.

P9-30A ❹ **Natural resource accounting [15–20 min]**

McCabe Oil Company has an account titled Oil and gas properties. McCabe paid $6,200,000 for oil reserves holding an estimated 500,000 barrels of oil. Assume the company paid $510,000 for additional geological tests of the property and $490,000 to prepare for drilling. During the first year, McCabe removed 90,000 barrels of oil, which it sold on account for $39 per barrel. Operating expenses totaled $850,000, all paid in cash.

Requirement

1. Record all of McCabe's transactions, including depletion for the first year.

P9-31A ❺ **Accounting for intangibles [20–25 min]**

Midland Telecom provides communication services in Iowa, Nebraska, the Dakotas, and Montana. Midland purchased goodwill as part of the acquisition of Shipley Wireless Company, which had the following figures:

Book value of assets	$	750,000
Market value of assets		1,000,000
Liabilities		530,000

Requirements

1. Journalize the entry to record Midland's purchase of Shipley Wireless for $320,000 cash plus a $480,000 note payable.
2. What special asset does Midland's acquisition of Shipley Wireless identify? How should Midland Telecom account for this asset after acquiring Shipley Wireless? Explain in detail.

P9-32A ❻ **Ethics [10–20 min]**

On May 31, 2012, Express Delivery, the overnight shipper, had total assets of $21,000,000,000 and total liabilities of $13,000,000,000. Included among the assets were property, plant, and equipment with a cost of $17,000,000,000 and accumulated depreciation of $10,000,000,000. During the year ended May 31, 2012, Express Delivery earned total revenues of $28,000,000,000 and had total expenses of $25,000,000,000, of which $8,000,000,000 was depreciation expenses. The CFO and the controller are concerned that the results of 2012 will make investors unhappy. Additionally, both hold stock options to purchase shares at a reduced price, so they would like to see the market price continue to grow. They decide to "extend" the life of assets so that depreciation will be reduced to $5,000,000,000 for 2012.

Requirements

1. What is the change to net income due to their decision?
2. What appears to be their motivation for the change in asset lives? Is this ethical? Explain.

Problems (Group B)

MyAccountingLab   **P9-33B** ❶ ❷ **Capitalized asset cost and partial year depreciation [20–25 min]**

Best Parking, near an airport, incurred the following costs to acquire land, make land improvements, and construct and furnish a small building:

a.	Purchase price of three acres of land	$ 89,000
b.	Delinquent real estate taxes on the land to be paid by Best Parking	6,000
c.	Additional dirt and earthmoving	8,000
d.	Title insurance on the land acquisition	3,600
e.	Fence around the boundary of the property	9,100
f.	Building permit for the building	800
g.	Architect's fee for the design of the building	20,200
h.	Signs near the front of the property	9,400
i.	Materials used to construct the building	212,000
j.	Labor to construct the building	172,000
k.	Interest cost on construction loan for the building	9,300
l.	Parking lots on the property	28,900
m.	Lights for the parking lots	10,100
n.	Salary of construction supervisor (75% to building; 25% to parking lot and concrete walks)	40,000
o.	Furniture	11,500
p.	Transportation of furniture from seller to the building	2,000
q.	Landscaping (shrubs)	6,900

Best Parking depreciates land improvements over 25 years, buildings over 50 years, and furniture over 12 years, all on a straight-line basis with zero residual value.

Requirements

1. Set up columns for Land, Land improvements, Building, and Furniture. Show how to account for each cost by listing the cost under the correct account. Determine the total cost of each asset.

2. All construction was complete and the assets were placed in service on July 1. Record partial-year depreciation for the year ended December 31.

P9-34B ❶ ❷ **Capitalized asset cost and first year depreciation, and identifying depreciation results that meet management objectives [30–40 min]**

On January 8, 2012, Speedway Delivery Service purchased a truck at a cost of $65,000. Before placing the truck in service, Speedway spent $4,000 painting it, $2,500 replacing tires, and $8,000 overhauling the engine. The truck should remain in service for five years and have a residual value of $6,000. The truck's annual mileage is expected to be 22,000 miles in each of the first four years and 12,000 miles in the fifth year—100,000 miles in total. In deciding which depreciation method to use, David Greer, the general manager, requests a depreciation schedule for each of the depreciation methods (straight-line, units-of-production, and double-declining-balance).

Requirements

1. Prepare a depreciation schedule for each depreciation method, showing asset cost, depreciation expense, accumulated depreciation, and asset book value.

2. Speedway prepares financial statements using the depreciation method that reports the highest net income in the early years of asset use. For income tax

purposes, the company uses the depreciation method that minimizes income taxes in the early years. Consider the first year that Speedway uses the truck. Identify the depreciation methods that meet the general manager's objectives, assuming the income tax authorities permit the use of any of the methods.

P9-35B ❷❸ **Lump sum asset purchases, partial year depreciation, and impairments [20–25 min]**

Hilda Carr Associates surveys American eating habits. The company's accounts include Land, Buildings, Office equipment, and Communication equipment, with a separate accumulated depreciation account for each asset. During 2012 and 2013, Hilda Carr completed the following transactions:

2012 Jan 1	Traded in old office equipment with book value of $43,000 (cost of $140,000 and accumulated depreciation of $97,000) for new equipment. Carr also paid $83,000 in cash. Fair value of the new equipment is $119,000.
Apr 1	Acquired land and communication equipment in a group purchase. Total cost was $430,000 paid in cash. An independent appraisal valued the land at $338,625 and the communication equipment at $112,875.
Sep 1	Sold a building that cost $560,400 (accumulated depreciation of $260,000 through December 31 of the preceding year). Carr received $390,000 cash from the sale of the building. Depreciation is computed on a straight-line basis. The building has a 40-year useful life and a residual value of $90,000.
Dec 31	Recorded depreciation as follows:
	Communication equipment is depreciated by the straight-line method over a five-year life with zero residual value.
	Office equipment is depreciated using the double-declining-balance over five years with $1,000 residual value.
2013 Jan 1	The company identified that the communication equipment suffered significant decline in value. The fair value of the communication equipment was determined to be $75,000.

Requirement

1. Record the transactions in the journal of Hilda Carr Associates.

P9-36B ❹ **Natural resource accounting [15–20 min]**

Garrison Oil Company has an account titled Oil and gas properties. Garrison paid $6,400,000 for oil reserves holding an estimated 500,000 barrels of oil. Assume the company paid $530,000 for additional geological tests of the property and $460,000 to prepare for drilling. During the first year, Garrison removed 82,000 barrels of oil, which it sold on account for $32 per barrel. Operating expenses totaled $830,000, all paid in cash.

Requirement

1. Record all of Garrison's transactions, including depletion for the first year.

P9-37B ❺ **Accounting for intangibles [20–25 min]**

Heartland Telecom provides communication services in Iowa, Nebraska, the Dakotas, and Montana. Heartland purchased goodwill as part of the acquisition of Shurburn Wireless Company, which had the following figures:

Book value of assets	$	800,000
Market value of assets		900,000
Liabilities		540,000

Requirements

1.   Journalize the entry to record Heartland's purchase of Shurburn Wireless for $360,000 cash plus a $540,000 note payable.

2.   What special asset does Heartland's acquisition of Shurburn Wireless identify? How should Heartland Telecom account for this asset after acquiring Shurburn Wireless? Explain in detail.

P9-38B   ❻ **Ethics [10–20 min]**
On May 31, 2012, Overnight It, the overnight shipper, had total assets of $22,000,000,000 and total liabilities of $10,000,000,000. Included among the assets were property, plant, and equipment with a cost of $15,000,000,000 and accumulated depreciation of $8,000,000,000. During the year ended May 31, 2012, Overnight It earned total revenues of $36,000,000,000 and had total expenses of $34,000,000,000, of which $5,000,000,000 was depreciation expenses. The CFO and the controller are concerned that the results of 2012 will make investors unhappy. Additionally, both hold stock options to purchase shares at a reduced price, so they would like to see the market price continue to grow. They decide to "extend" the life of assets so that depreciation will be reduced to $3,000,000,000 for 2012.

Requirements

1.   What is the change to net income due to their decision?

2.   What appears to be their motivation for the change in asset lives? Is this ethical? Explain.

● Continuing Exercise

E9-39   ❷ **Calculating and journalizing partial year depreciation [10–15 min]**
This problem continues the Lawlor Lawn Service situation from Problem 8-41 of Chapter 8. Refer to the Chapter 2 data for Exercise 2-61. In Chapter 2, we learned that Lawlor Lawn Service had purchased a lawn mower, $1,200, and weed whacker, $240, on May 3, 2012 and that they were expected to last four years.

Requirements

1.   Calculate the amount of depreciation for each asset for the year ended December 31, 2012, assuming both assets are using straight-line depreciation.

2.   Record the entry for the partial year's depreciation. Date it December 31, 2012.

● Continuing Problem

P9-40   ❷ **Calculating and journalizing partial year depreciation [10–15 min]**
This problem continues the Draper Consulting situation from Problem 8-42 of Chapter 8. Refer to Problem 2-62 of Chapter 2. In Chapter 2, we learned that Draper Consulting had purchased a **Dell** computer, $1,800, and office furniture, $4,200 on December 3 and 4, respectively, and that they were expected to last five years.

Requirements

1.   Calculate the amount of depreciation for each asset for the year ended December 31, 2012, assuming both assets are using straight-line depreciation.

2.   Record the entry for the one month's depreciation. Date it December 31, 2012.

Apply Your Knowledge

• Decision Case 9-1

Suppose you are an investment advisor, and you are looking at two companies to recommend to your clients, Shelly's Seashell Enterprises and Jeremy Feigenbaum Systems. The two companies are virtually identical, and both began operations at the beginning of the current year. During the year, each company purchased inventory as follows:

Jan	4	10,000 units at $4 = $	40,000
Apr	6	5,000 units at 5 =	25,000
Aug	9	7,000 units at 6 =	42,000
Nov	27	10,000 units at 7 =	70,000
Totals		32,000	$177,000

During the first year, both companies sold 25,000 units of inventory.

In early January, both companies purchased equipment costing $143,000, with a 10-year estimated useful life and a $20,000 residual value. Shelly uses the inventory and depreciation methods that maximize reported income (FIFO and straight-line). By contrast, Feigenbaum uses the inventory and depreciation methods that minimize income taxes (LIFO and double-declining-balance). Both companies' trial balances at December 31, 2013, included the following:

Sales revenue.............................	$270,000
Operating expenses..................	80,700

Requirements

1. Prepare both companies' income statements. (Disregard income tax expense.)
2. Write an investment letter to address the following questions for your clients: Which company appears to be more profitable? Which company has more cash to invest in new projects? Which company would you prefer to invest in? Why?

• Ethical Issue 9-1

Western Bank & Trust purchased land and a building for the lump sum of $3,000,000. To get the maximum tax deduction, Western allocated 90% of the purchase price to the building and only 10% to the land. A more realistic allocation would have been 70% to the building and 30% to the land.

Requirements

1. Explain the tax advantage of allocating too much to the building and too little to the land.
2. Was Western's allocation ethical? If so, state why. If not, why not? Identify who was harmed.

● Fraud Case 9-1

Jim Reed manages a fleet of utility trucks for a rural county government. He's been in his job 30 years, and he knows where the angles are. He makes sure that when new trucks are purchased, the salvage value is set as low as possible. Then, when they become fully depreciated, they are sold off by the county at salvage value. Jim makes sure his buddies in the construction business are first in line for the bargain sales, and they make sure he gets a little something back. Recently, a new county commissioner was elected with vows to cut expenses for the taxpayers. Unlike other commissioners, this man has a business degree, and he is coming to visit Jim tomorrow.

Requirements

1. When a business sells a fully depreciated asset for its salvage value, is a gain or loss recognized?
2. How do businesses determine what salvage values to use for their various assets? Are there "hard and fast" rules for salvage values?
3. How would an organization prevent the kind of fraud depicted here?

● Financial Statement Case 9-1

Refer to the **Amazon.com** financial statements, including Notes 1 and 3, in Appendix A at the end of this book. Answer the following questions.

Requirements

1. Which depreciation method does **Amazon** use for reporting in the financial statements? What type of depreciation method does the company probably use for income tax purposes? Why is this method preferable for tax purposes?
2. Depreciation expense is embedded in the operating expense amounts listed on the income statement. Note 3 gives the amount of depreciation expense. What was the amount of depreciation for 2009? Record **Amazon**'s depreciation expense for 2009.
3. The statement of cash flows reports the purchases of fixed assets. How much were **Amazon**'s fixed asset purchases during 2009? Journalize the company's purchases of assets for cash, as reflected in the cash flow report.

● Team Project 9-1

Visit a local business.

Requirements

1. List all its plant assets.
2. If possible, interview the manager. Gain as much information as you can about the business's plant assets. For example, try to determine the assets' costs, the depreciation method the company is using, and the estimated useful life of each asset category. If an interview is impossible, then develop your own estimates of the assets' costs, useful lives, and book values, assuming an appropriate depreciation method.
3. Determine whether the business has any intangible assets. If so, list them and learn as much as possible about their nature, cost, and estimated useful lives.
4. Write a detailed report of your findings and be prepared to present it to the class.

● Communication Activity 9-1

In 25 words or fewer, explain the depreciable cost used for each of the three methods. Your explanation should identify which methods calculate depreciable base the same way.

Quick Check Answers

1. *d* 2. *b* 3. *d* 4. *c* 5. *b* 6. *c* 7. *c* 8. *d* 9. *d* 10. *b*

For online homework, exercises, and problems that provide you immediate feedback, please visit myaccountinglab.com.

10 Current Liabilities and Payroll

SMART TOUCH LEARNING
Balance Sheet
May 31, 2013

Assets				Liabilities		
Current assets:				Current liabilities:		
Cash		$ 4,800		Accounts payable		$ 48,700
Accounts receivable		2,600		Salary payable		900
Inventory		30,500		Interest payable		100
Supplies		600		Unearned service revenue		400
Prepaid rent		2,000		**Total current liabilities**		**50,100**
Total current assets			$ 40,500	Long-term liabilities:		
Plant assets:				Notes payable		20,000
Furniture	$18,000			Total liabilities		70,100
Less: Accumulated depreciation—furniture	300	17,700				
Building	48,000					
Less: Accumulated depreciation—building	200	47,800		Owner's Equity		
Total plant assets			65,500	Bright, capital		35,900
Total assets			$106,000	Total liabilities and owner's equity		$106,000

Learning Objectives

1 Account for current liabilities of known amount

2 Account for current liabilities that must be estimated

3 Calculate payroll and payroll tax amounts

4 Journalize basic payroll transactions

Up to this point, we've been focusing on all the assets a business owns. But what about the bills a business owes? As a business owner or manager, you have to know what you owe (your liabilities) and what date you have to pay them. Why? To be sure you have cash on hand to pay these bills. In this chapter, we'll focus on some common current liabilities a business may owe. As with other chapters, we'll continue to focus on Smart Touch Learning and see how it manages its current liabilities.

• • •

Current Liabilities of Known Amount

The amounts of most liabilities are known. Recall that current liabilities are those debts due to be paid within one year, or within the entity's operating cycle if that cycle is longer than a year. Let's begin with current liabilities of a known amount.

 1 Account for current liabilities of known amount

Accounts Payable

Amounts owed for products or services purchased on account are *accounts payable*. Since these are due on average in 30 days, they are current liabilities. We have seen many accounts payable illustrations in preceding chapters. Consider the balance sheet for May 31, 2013, prepared in Chapter 4 for Smart Touch Learning and reproduced as follows:

EXHIBIT 10-1	Classified Balance Sheet in Account Form (Reproduced from Exhibit 4-12)

SMART TOUCH LEARNING
Balance Sheet
May 31, 2013

Assets				Liabilities	
Current assets:				Current liabilities:	
Cash		$ 4,800		Accounts payable	$18,200
Accounts receivable		2,600		Salary payable	900
Supplies		600		Interest payable	100
Prepaid rent		2,000		Unearned service revenue	400
Total current assets			$10,000	Total current liabilities	19,600
Plant assets:				Long-term liabilities:	
Furniture	$18,000			Notes payable	20,000
Less: Accumulated depreciation—furniture	300	17,700		Total liabilities	39,600
Building	48,000				
Less: Accumulated depreciation—building	200	47,800		**Owner's Equity**	
Total plant assets			65,500	Bright, capital	35,900
Total assets			$75,500	Total liabilities and owner's equity	$75,500

Notice that the balance on May 31, 2013, for Accounts payable is $18,200. As we learned in Chapter 5, one of Smart Touch's common transactions is the credit purchase of inventory. With accounts payable and inventory systems integrated, Smart Touch records the purchase of inventory on account, using the perpetual system. A reproduction of the Chapter 5 entry that Smart Touch made on June 3 to purchase $700 of inventory on account follows:

Jun 3	Inventory (A+)	700	
	Accounts payable (L+)		700
	Purchase on account.		

Then, when Smart Touch paid the liability and took advantage of the purchase discount on June 15, the entry was as follows:

Jun 15	Accounts payable (L–)	700	
	Cash (A–)		679
	Inventory (A–)		21
	Paid on account within discount period.		

Keep in mind that Smart Touch purchased more inventory in other transactions in June.

Short-Term Notes Payable

Short-term notes payable are a common form of financing. Short-term notes payable are promissory notes that must be paid within one year. Consider how the entry on June 3 would change if Smart Touch had purchased the inventory with a 10%, one-year note payable. The modified June 3 purchase entry follows:

2013			
Jun 3	Inventory (A+)	700	
	Short-term notes payable (L+)		700
	Purchased inventory on a one-year, 10% note.		

A *

At year-end it is necessary to accrue interest expense for the seven months from June to December (do not adjust interest for the three days in June) as follows:

2013			
Dec 31	Interest expense ($700 × 0.10 × 7/12) (E+)	41	
	Interest payable (L+)		41
	Accrued interest expense at year-end.		

B

The interest accrual at December 31, 2013, allocated $41 of the interest on this note to 2013. During 2014, the interest on this note for the five remaining months is $29, as shown in the following entry for the payment of the note in 2014:

2014			
Jun 3	Short-term notes payable (L–)	700	
	Interest payable (L–)	41	
	Interest expense ($700 × 0.10 × 5/12) (E+)	29	
	Cash (A–)		770
	Paid note and interest at maturity.		

Sales Tax Payable

Most states assess sales tax on retail sales. Retailers collect the sales tax in addition to the price of the item sold. Sales tax payable is a current liability because the retailer must pay the state in less than a year. **Sales tax collected is owed to the state.** Let's apply this to Smart Touch.

Suppose December's taxable sales for Smart Touch totaled $10,000. Smart Touch collected an additional 6% sales tax, which would equal $600 ($10,000 × 0.06). Smart Touch would record that month's sales as follows:

2013			
Dec 31	Cash ($10,000 × 1.06) (A+)	10,600	
	Sales revenue (R+)		10,000
	Sales tax payable ($10,000 × 0.06) (L+)		600
	To record cash sales and the related sales tax.		

C

As noted above, Sales tax payable is a current liability. Notice how it shows as an obligation (credit balance) in the Sales tax payable T-account, just after the sale.

---

*The red colored boxes throughout the chapter reference Exhibit 11-5 in Chapter 11 on page 547.

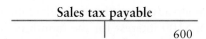

Sales tax payable

		600

Companies forward the sales tax to the state at regular intervals. They normally submit it monthly, but they could file it at other intervals, depending on the state and the amount of the tax. To pay the tax, the company debits Sales tax payable and credits Cash.

2014			
Jan 20	Sales tax payable (L–)	600	
	Cash (A–)		600

Current Portion of Long-Term Notes Payable

Most long-term notes payable are paid in installments. The **current portion of notes payable** (also called **current maturity**) is the principal amount that will be paid within one year—a current liability. **The current portion of notes payable is equal to this year's principal payments.** The remaining portion is long-term. Let's consider the $20,000 notes payable that Smart Touch signed on May 1, 2013 (refer to Exhibit 10-1). The note bears interest at 6%. If the note will be paid over four years with payments of $5,000 plus interest due each May 1, what portion of the note is current? The portion that must be paid within one year, $5,000, is current. At the inception of the note, the company recorded the entire note as long term. A second entry to the account for the $5,000 principal that is current will need to be made on May 1, 2013.

2013			
May 1	Cash (A+)	20,000	
	Long-term notes payable (L+)		20,000
May 1	Long-term notes payable (L–)	5,000	
	Current portion of long-term notes payable (L+)		5,000

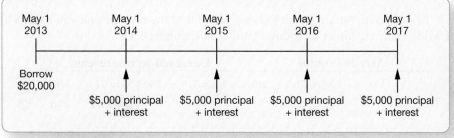

Notice that the reclassification entry on May 1 does not change the total amount of debt. It only reclassifies $5,000 of the total debt from long-term to current. Interest would still accrue (see the next section). We focus on the current portion classification in this chapter. In Chapter 11, we'll focus on the long-term portion and the yearly payments on the note.

Accrued Liabilities

In Chapter 3, we learned that an accrued expense is any expense that has been incurred but has not yet been paid. When an expense is accrued (debited), it often has a related unpaid bill, or an accrued liability (credited). Accrued liabilities typically occur with the passage of time, such as interest on a note payable.

Refer to Exhibit 10-1, Smart Touch's May 31, 2013, balance sheet. Like most other companies, Smart Touch has accrued liabilities for salaries payable and interest payable. Smart Touch has already accrued one month of interest on the $20,000 note (20,000 × 6% × 1/12); $100 interest for the month of May 2013, as shown in Exhibit 10-1. Now, at December 31, Smart Touch still needs to accrue interest from May 31 to December 31, or seven more month's interest on the $20,000 note:

Dec 31	Interest expense (20,000 × 6% × 7/12) (E+)	700	
	Interest payable (L+)		700

B

Unearned Revenues

Unearned revenue is also called *deferred revenue*. Unearned revenue arises when a business has received cash in advance of performing work and, therefore, has an obligation to provide goods or services to the customer in the future. **If you receive cash before you do the work, you owe the work (unearned service revenue).** Let's consider an example using Smart Touch's May 31, 2013, balance sheet.

Smart Touch received $600 in advance on May 21 for a month's work beginning on that date. On May 31, because it received cash before earning the revenue, Smart Touch has a liability to perform 20 more days of work for the client. The liability is called Unearned service revenue. The entry made by Smart Touch on May 21, 2013, follows:

2013			
May 21	Cash (A+)	600	
	Unearned service revenue (L+)		600

During May, Smart Touch delivered one-third of the work and earned $200 ($600 × 1/3) of the revenue. The May 31, 2013, adjusting entry made by Smart Touch decreased the liability and increased the revenue as follows:

2013			
May 31	Unearned service revenue (L–)	200	
	Service revenue (R+)		200

At this point, Smart Touch has earned $200 of the revenue and still owes $400 of work to the customer, as follows (and as in Exhibit 10-1):

Service revenue			Unearned service revenue			
	May 31	200	May 31	200	May 21	600
					Bal	400

F

Current Liabilities that Must Be Estimated

2 Account for current liabilities that must be estimated

A business may know that a liability exists, but not know the exact amount. The business cannot simply ignore the liability. It must report it on the balance sheet. A prime example is Estimated warranty payable, which is common for manufacturing companies like **Dell** and **Sony**.

Estimated Warranty Payable

Many companies guarantee their products against defects under **warranty** agreements. Both 90-day and one-year warranties are common.

The matching principle says to record the *Warranty expense* in the same period that the company records the revenue related to that warranty. The expense, therefore, is incurred when the company makes a sale, not when the company pays the warranty claims. At the time of the sale, the company does not know the exact amount of warranty expense, but can estimate it.

Assume that Smart Touch made sales on account of $50,000 subject to product warranties on June 10, 2013. Smart Touch estimates that 3% of its products may require warranty repairs. The company would record the sales and the estimated warranty expense in the same period, as follows:

2013			
Jun 10	Accounts receivable (A+)	50,000	
	Sales revenue (R+)		50,000
	Sales on account.		
Jun 10	COGS (E+)	21,000	
	Inventory (A–)		21,000
	To record cost of inventory sold.		
Jun 10	Warranty expense ($50,000 × 0.03) (E+)	1,500	
	Estimated warranty payable (L+)		1,500
	To accrue warranty payable.		

Assume that some of Smart Touch's customers make claims that must be honored through the warranty offered by the company. The warranty payments total $800 and are made on June 27, 2013. Smart Touch repairs the defective goods and makes the following journal entry:

2013			
Jun 27	Estimated warranty payable (L–)	800	
	Cash (A–)		800
	To pay warranty claims.		

Smart Touch's expense on the income statement is $1,500, the estimated amount, not the $800 actually paid. After paying for these warranties, Smart Touch's liability account has a credit balance of $700. This $700 balance represents warranty claims Smart Touch expects to pay in the future based on its estimates; therefore, the $700 is a liability to Smart Touch.

Estimated warranty payable

800		1,500
	Bal	700

Contingent Liabilities

A **contingent liability** is a potential, rather than an actual, liability because it depends on a *future* event. **Some event must happen (the contingency) for a contingent liability to have to be paid.** For example, suppose Smart Touch is sued because of alleged patent infringement on one of its learning DVDs. Smart Touch, therefore, faces a contingent liability, which may or may not become an actual liability. If the outcome of this lawsuit is unfavorable, it could hurt Smart Touch by increasing its liabilities. Therefore, it would be unethical to withhold knowledge of the lawsuit from investors and creditors.

Another contingent liability arises when you *co-sign a note payable* for another entity. An example of this would occur if Greg's Tunes were to co-sign Smart Touch's note payable. The company co-signing (Greg's Tunes) has a contingent liability until the note comes due and is paid by the other entity (Smart Touch). If the other company (Smart Touch) pays off the note, the contingent liability vanishes (for Greg's Tunes). If not, the co-signing company (Greg's Tunes) must pay the debt for the other entity (Smart Touch).

Connect To: Ethics

Accounting for liabilities poses an ethical challenge. Businesses like to show high levels of net income because that makes them look successful. As a result, owners and managers may be tempted to overlook some expenses and liabilities at the end of the accounting period. For example, a company can fail to accrue warranty expense. This will cause total expenses to be understated, net income to be overstated, and total liabilities to be understated. Contingent liabilities also pose an ethical challenge. Because contingencies are potential, rather than actual, liabilities, they are easier to overlook. But a contingency can turn into an actual liability and can significantly change the company's financial position. Successful people do not play games with their accounting. Falsifying financial statements can land a person in prison.

As shown in Exhibit 10-2, the accounting profession divides contingent liabilities into three categories—remote, reasonably possible, and probable—based on the likelihood of an actual loss.

EXHIBIT 10-2 | **Contingent Liabilities: Three Categories**

Likelihood of an Actual Loss	How to Report the Contingency
Remote	Do not disclose. *Example:* A frivolous lawsuit.
Reasonably possible	Describe the situation in a note to the financial statements. *Example:* The company is the defendant in a significant lawsuit and the outcome is unknown.
Probable, and the amount of the loss can be reasonably estimated	Record an expense and an actual liability, based on estimated amounts. *Example:* Warranty expense, as illustrated in the preceding section.

Codification Section: 450-20-55

Stop and review what you have learned by studying the Decision Guidelines on the next page.

Stop & Think...

Do you ever guess how much money you will need to pay your tuition each semester? If you do, you are making an informal sort of accounting estimate. Estimations can be formal or informal, but we all make accounting estimates. The key to why we estimate is so that we can accurately measure income. In the case of estimating your tuition, it might be just so you are sure you have enough cash on hand to pay it. Journalizing an estimate, such as for your tuition, is an example of an accrued liability.

Decision Guidelines 10-1

ACCOUNTING FOR CURRENT LIABILITIES

Suppose you are in charge of accounting for a large construction company. The company needs to borrow $10,000 for materials for an upcoming construction job. The bank wants to see the company's balance sheet. These Decision Guidelines will help you report current liabilities accurately.

Decision	Guidelines
• What are the two main issues in accounting for current liabilities?	• *Recording* the liability in the journal • *Reporting* the liability on the balance sheet
• What are the two basic categories of current liabilities?	• Current liabilities of *known amount*: Accounts payable — Accrued liabilities (interest payable, rent payable) Short-term notes payable — Salary, wages, commission, and bonus payable Sales tax payable — Unearned revenues Current portion of long-term notes payable • Current liabilities that *must be estimated*: Estimated warranty payable Estimated lawsuit losses where the likelihood of an actual loss is probable and the amount of the loss can be reasonably estimated

Summary Problem 10-1

Answer each question independently.

Requirements

1. A **Wendy's** restaurant made cash sales of $4,000 subject to a 5% sales tax. Record the sales and the related sales tax. Also record **Wendy's** payment of the tax to the state of South Carolina.

2. At December 31, 2011, Chastains' Hair Salons reported the following liabilities:

Current Liabilities	
Portion of long-term note payable due within one year.................	$ 10,000
Interest payable ($210,000 × 0.06 × 6/12)..................................	6,300
Total current liabilities...	$ 16,300
Long-Term Liabilities	
Long-term note payable	$200,000
Total liabilities	$216,300

Chastains' Hair Salons signed a $210,000, 21-year, 6% note on July 1, 2011. The note payments of $10,000 plus interest are due June 30 each year.

    Show how Chastains' Hair Salons would report its liabilities on the year-end balance sheet one year later—December 31, 2012.

3. How does a contingent liability differ from an actual liability? When would a contingent liability be journalized?

Solution

Requirement 1

Cash ($4,000 × 1.05) (A+)		4,200	
Sales revenue (R+)			4,000
Sales tax payable ($4,000 × 0.05) (L+)			200
To record cash sales and sales tax.			
Sales tax payable (L–)		200	
Cash (A–)			200
To pay sales tax.			

Requirement 2

Chastains' Hair Salons' balance sheet at December 31, 2012, is as follows:

Current Liabilities	
Portion of long-term note payable due within one year.................	$ 10,000
Interest payable ($200,000 × 0.06 × 6/12)..................................	6,000
Total current liabilities...	$ 16,000
Long-Term Liabilities	
Long-term note payable	$190,000
Total liabilities	$206,000

Requirement 3

A contingent liability is a *potential*, rather than an actual, liability because it depends on a future event. Some event must happen (the contingency) for a contingent liability to have to be paid. Contingent liabilities are journalized when the likelihood of an actual loss is *probable*, and the amount of the loss can be reasonably estimated.

Accounting for Payroll

Payroll, also called **employee compensation**, also creates accrued expenses. For service organizations—such as CPA firms and travel agencies—payroll is *the* major expense. Labor cost is so important that most businesses develop a special payroll system. There are numerous ways to label an employee's pay:

> **3** Calculate payroll and payroll tax amounts

- *Salary* is pay stated at an annual, monthly, or weekly rate, such as $62,400 per year, $5,200 per month, or $1,200 per week.
- *Wages* are pay amounts stated at an hourly rate, such as $10 per hour.
- *Commission* is pay stated as a percentage of a sale amount, such as a 5% commission on a sale. A realtor who earns 5% commission, for example, earns $5,000 on a $100,000 sale of real estate.
- *Bonus* is pay over and above base salary (or wage or commission). A bonus is usually paid for exceptional performance—in a single amount after year-end.
- *Benefits* are extra compensation—items that are not paid directly to the employee. Benefits cover health, life, and disability insurance. The employer pays the insurance company, which then provides coverage for the employee. Another type of benefit, retirement, sets aside money for the employee for his or her future retirement.

Businesses pay employees at a base rate for a set period—called *straight time*. For additional hours—*overtime*—the employee may get a higher pay rate, depending on the job classification and wage and hour laws.

Assume Ryan Oliver was hired as an accountant for Smart Touch. His pay is as follows:

- Ryan earns wages of $600 per week for straight time (40 hours), so his hourly pay rate is $15 ($600/40).
- The company pays *time-and-a-half* for overtime. That rate is 150% (1.5 times) the straight-time pay rate. Thus, Ryan earns $22.50 per hour of overtime ($15.00 × 1.5 = $22.50).
- For working 42 hours during a week, he earns gross pay of $645, computed as follows:

Straight-time pay for 40 hours	$600
Overtime pay for 2 overtime hours: 2 × $22.50	45
Gross pay	$645

Gross Pay and Net (Take-Home) Pay

Two pay amounts are important for accounting purposes:

- **Gross pay** is the total amount of salary, wages, commissions, and bonuses earned by the employee during a pay period, before taxes or any other deductions. Gross pay is an expense to the employer. In the preceding example, Ryan Oliver's gross pay was $645.

- **Net pay** is the amount the employee gets to keep. **Net pay is also called take-home pay.** Take-home pay equals gross pay minus all deductions. The employer either writes a paycheck to each employee for his or her take-home pay or direct deposits the employee's take home pay into the employee's bank account.

Payroll Withholding Deductions

The federal government and most states require employers to deduct taxes from employee paychecks. Insurance companies and investment companies may also get some of the employee's gross pay. Amounts withheld from paychecks are called *withholding deductions*. Payroll withholding deductions are the difference between gross pay and take-home pay. These deductions are withheld from paychecks and sent directly to the government, to insurance companies, or to other entities. Payroll withholding deductions fall into two categories:

- *Required deductions*, such as employee federal and state income tax and Social Security tax. Employees pay their income tax and Social Security tax through payroll deductions.
- *Optional deductions*, including insurance premiums, retirement plan contributions, charitable contributions, and other amounts that are withheld at the employee's request.

After being withheld, payroll deductions become the liability of the employer, who then pays the outside party—taxes to the government and contributions to charitable organizations, for example.

Required Withholding for Employee Income Tax

United States law requires companies to withhold income tax from employee paychecks. The income tax deducted from gross pay is called **withheld income tax**. The amount withheld depends on the employee's gross pay and on the number of *withholding allowances* he or she claims.

An employee files Form W-4 with his or her employer to indicate the number of allowances claimed for income-tax withholding. Each allowance lowers the amount of tax withheld:

- An unmarried taxpayer usually claims one allowance.
- A childless married couple usually claims two allowances.
- A married couple with one child usually claims three allowances, and so on.

Exhibit 10-3 shows a W-4 for Ryan Oliver, who claims married with three allowances (line 5).

Required Withholding for Employee Social Security (FICA) Tax

The **Federal Insurance Contributions Act (FICA)**, also known as the Social Security Act, created the Social Security Tax. The Social Security program provides retirement, disability, and medical benefits. The law requires employers to withhold **Social Security (FICA) tax** from employees' paychecks. The FICA tax has two components:

1. Old age, survivors, and disability insurance (OASDI)

2. Health insurance (Medicare)

The amount of tax withheld varies from year to year because the wage base is subject to OASDI tax changes each year. For 2010, the OASDI tax applies to the first $106,800 of employee earnings in a year. The taxable amount of earnings is adjusted annually. The OASDI tax rate is 6.2%. Therefore, the maximum OASDI tax that an employee paid in 2010 was $6,622 ($106,800 $\times$ 0.062).

EXHIBIT 10-3 | **W-4 for Ryan Oliver (2010 form was the latest form released by the IRS at the time of printing)**

Form **W-4**	**Employee's Withholding Allowance Certificate**	OMB No. 1545-0074
Department of the Treasury Internal Revenue Service	▶ Whether you are entitled to claim a certain number of allowances or exemption from withholding is subject to review by the IRS. Your employer may be required to send a copy of this form to the IRS.	2010

1 Type or print your first name and middle initial.	Last name	2 Your social security number
Ryan G.	Oliver	123 ː 45 ː 6789

Home address (number and street or rural route)	3 ☐ Single ☑ Married ☐ Married, but withhold at higher Single rate.
305 Lost Key Drive	**Note.** If married, but legally separated, or spouse is a nonresident alien, check the "Single" box.
City or town, state, and ZIP code	4 If your last name differs from that shown on your social security card,
Pensacola, FL 32526	check here. You must call 1-800-772-1213 for a replacement card. ▶ ☐

5	Total number of allowances you are claiming (from line **H** above **or** from the applicable worksheet on page 2)	5	3
6	Additional amount, if any, you want withheld from each paycheck	6	$
7	I claim exemption from withholding for 2010, and I certify that I meet **both** of the following conditions for exemption.		
	• Last year I had a right to a refund of **all** federal income tax withheld because I had **no** tax liability **and**		
	• This year I expect a refund of **all** federal income tax withheld because I expect to have **no** tax liability.		
	If you meet both conditions, write "Exempt" here . . . . ▶	7	

Under penalties of perjury, I declare that I have examined this certificate and to the best of my knowledge and belief, it is true, correct, and complete.

Employee's signature
(Form is not valid unless you sign it.) ▶ *Ryan D Oliver*　　　　Date ▶ 1/1/2013

8 Employer's name and address (Employer: Complete lines 8 and 10 only if sending to the IRS.)	9 Office code (optional)	10 Employer identification number (EIN)
Smart Touch Learning; 281 Wave Ave; Niceville, FL 32578	20	1234567

For Privacy Act and Paperwork Reduction Act Notice, see page 2.	Cat. No. 10220Q	Form **W-4** (2010)

The Medicare portion of the FICA tax applies to all employee earnings—that means that there is no maximum tax. This tax rate is 1.45%. Therefore, an employee pays a combined FICA tax rate of 7.65% (6.2% + 1.45%) of the first $106,800 of annual earnings ($106,800 is the 2010 rate as it was the most current wage cap at the time of printing), plus 1.45% of earnings above $106,800.

To make your calculations easier to compute, assume that the 2012 FICA tax rate is 7.65%. The wage limit for Social Security (6.2%) is only on the first $106,800 of employee earnings each year. For Medicare, there is no wage limit. (Use these numbers when you complete this chapter's assignments.)

Assume that James Kolen, another employee of Smart Touch, earned $99,800 prior to December. Kolen's salary for December is $10,000.

- How much of Kolen's December salary is subject to FICA tax? Only $7,000 is subject to Social Security tax—from $99,800 up to the $106,800 maximum. All $10,000 is subject to Medicare tax.

- How much FICA tax will be withheld from Kolen's December paycheck? The computation follows:

	OASDI (Social Security)	HI (Medicare)
Employee earnings subject to the tax in one year	$106,800	No max
Employee earnings prior to the current month	− 99,800	
Current pay subject to OASDI portion of FICA tax	$ 7,000	$ 10,000
FICA tax rate	× 0.062	× 0.0145
FICA tax to be withheld from the current paycheck..................	$ 434	$ 145
Total OASDI & HI tax (434 + 145)...		$ 579

Optional Withholding Deductions

As a convenience to employees, some companies withhold payroll deductions and then pay designated organizations according to employee instructions. Insurance premiums, retirement savings, union dues, and gifts to charities are examples.

The following table summarizes James Kolen's final pay period on December 31. Employee income tax is assumed to be 20% of gross pay. The FICA tax of $579 was calculated on the previous page. The insurance and contribution amounts are assumed.

Gross pay		$10,000
Withholding deductions:		
Employee income tax (20%)	$2,000	
Employee FICA tax	579	
Employee co-pay for health insurance	180	
Employee contribution to United Way	20	
Total withholdings		2,779
Net (take-home) pay		$ 7,221

Employer Payroll Taxes

In addition to income tax and FICA tax, which are withheld from employee paychecks, *employers* must pay at least three payroll taxes. These taxes do *not* come out of employee paychecks:

1. Employer FICA tax

2. State unemployment compensation tax

3. Federal unemployment compensation tax

Employer FICA Tax

In addition to the FICA tax withheld from the employee's paycheck, the employer must pay an equal amount into the program. The Social Security system is funded by equal contributions from employer and employee.

State and Federal Unemployment Compensation Taxes

State and federal **unemployment compensation taxes** finance workers' compensation for people laid off from work. In recent years, employers have paid a combined tax of 6.2% on the first $7,000 of each employee's annual earnings for unemployment tax. The proportion paid to the state depends on the individual state, but for many it is 5.4% to the state plus 0.8% to the federal government. For this payroll tax, the employer uses two liability accounts:

- Federal unemployment tax payable (FUTA payable)
- State unemployment tax payable (SUTA payable)

Exhibit 10-4 shows a typical distribution of payroll costs for an employee who earns a weekly salary of $1,000. All amounts are assumed.

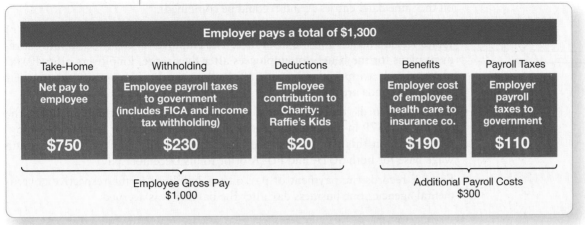

| EXHIBIT 10-4 | **Typical Breakdown of Payroll Costs for One Employee** |

Journalizing Payroll Transactions

Exhibit 10-5A summarizes an employer's entries for a monthly payroll of $10,000. All amounts are assumed, based on James Kolen's December salary.

4 Journalize basic payroll transactions

| EXHIBIT 10-5A | **Payroll Accounting by the Employer—James Kolen's Paydate December 31, 2013** |

	2013				
a.	Dec 31	Salary expense (E+)	10,000		
		Salary payable (L+)		10,000	
		To record salary expense.			
b.	Dec 31	Salary payable (L–)	10,000		
		Employee income tax payable (L+)		2,000	**H** *
		FICA tax payable (L+)		579	**I**
		Payable to health insurance (L+)		180	**J**
		Payable to United Way (L+)		20	**K**
		Cash (take-home pay) (A–)		7,221	
		To record payment of salaries.			
c.	Dec 31	Health insurance expense (E+)	800		
		Life insurance expense (E+)	200		
		Retirement plan expense (E+)	500		
		Employee benefits payable (L+)		1,500	**L**
		To record employee benefits payable by the employer.			
d.	Dec 31	Payroll tax expense (E+)**	579		
		FICA tax payable (L+)		579	**I**
		To record employer's payroll taxes.			
	2014				
e.	Jan 2	Employee income tax payable (L–)	2,000		
		FICA tax payable (L–) ($579 + $579)	1,158		
		Cash (A–) ($2,000 + $1,158)		3,158	
		To record payment of payroll taxes to the government.			

*The red colored boxes throughout the chapter reference Exhibit 11-5 in Chapter 11 on page 547.
**No FUTA or SUTA tax is due in December because James is over the maximum wage base.

- Entry A records the salary expense accrual and the liability based on gross pay.
- Entry B records the payment of salaries. Gross salary is $10,000, and net (take-home) pay is $7,221. There is a payable to United Way of $20 because James Kolen

specified this charitable deduction. (Note entries A and B often occur on different days but are shown here as December 31. If the salary expense and payment occur on the same date, entries A and B could be combined).

- Entry C records *benefits* paid by the employer. This company pays for part of James Kolen's health and life insurance. The employer also pays cash into retirement plans for the benefit of employees after they retire. Employers offer 401(k) plans, which are popular because they allow workers to specify where their retirement funds are invested.

- Entry D records the employer's *payroll tax expense*, which includes the employer's $579 in matching FICA tax. There are no state or federal unemployment taxes on this payroll because James had already reached the maximum wage base for both SUTA and FUTA prior to his December pay.

- Entry E records the payment of payroll tax liabilities to the respective governmental agencies one business day after the liability was accrued.

What if the paydate for James Kolen were January 6, 2014, instead of December 31, 2013—would James's pay change? What about the employer's taxes—would they change? Exhibit 10-5B shows the changes, highlighted in blue:

EXHIBIT 10-5B | **Payroll Accounting by the Employer—James Kolen's Paydate January 6, 2014**

a.	2013 Dec 31	Salary expense (E+)	10,000	
		Salary payable (L+)		10,000
		To record salary expense.		
b.	2014 Jan 6	Salary payable (L–)	10,000	
		Employee income tax payable (L+)		2,000
		FICA tax payable (L+) (10,000^ × 7.65%)		765
		Payable to health insurance (L+)		180
		Payable to United Way (L+)		20
		Cash (take home pay) (A–)		7,035
		To record payment of salaries.		
c.	2013 Dec 31	Health insurance expense (E+)	800	
		Life insurance expense (E+)	200	
		Retirement plan expense (E+)	500	
		Employee benefits payable (L+)		1,500
		To record employee benefits payable by the employer.		
d.	2014 Jan 6	Payroll tax expense (E+) ($765 + $378 + $56)	1,199	
		FICA tax payable (L+) (10,000^ × 7.65%)		765
		State unemployment tax payable (L+) (7,000* × 5.4%)		378
		Federal unemployment tax payable (L+) (7,000* × 0.8%)		56
		To record employer's payroll taxes.		
e.	Jan 7	Employee income tax payable (L–)	2,000	
		FICA tax payable (L–) ($765 + $765)	1,530	
		State unemployment tax payable (L–)	378	
		Federal unemployment tax payable (L–)	56	
		Cash (A–) ($2,000 + $1,530 + $378 + $56)		3,964
		To record payment of payroll taxes to the government.		

^All $10,000 of James's wages would be subject to FICA tax because James's 2014 year-to-date wages would be less than the Social Security max wage limit of $106,800.

*James's 2014 year-to-date wages of $10,000 on January 6 would be greater than the annual unemployment maximum taxable wage base of $7,000. So, only $7,000 of James's $10,000 gross pay would be subject to federal and state unemployment taxes.

Internal Control over Payroll

There are two main controls for payroll:

- Controls for efficiency
- Controls to safeguard payroll disbursements

Controls for Efficiency

Reconciling the bank account can be time-consuming because there may be many outstanding paychecks. To limit the outstanding checks, a company may use two payroll bank accounts. It pays the payroll from one account one month and from the other account the next month. This way the company can reconcile each account every other month, and that decreases accounting expense. Alternatively, the company may require direct deposits for employees' pay.

Payroll transactions are ideal for computer processing. The payroll data are stored in a file, and the computer makes the calculations, prints paychecks, and updates all records electronically.

Controls to Safeguard Payroll Disbursements

The owner of a small business can monitor his or her payroll by personal contact with employees. Large companies cannot. A particular risk is that a paycheck may be written to a fictitious person and cashed by a dishonest employee. To guard against this, large businesses adopt strict internal controls for payrolls.

Hiring and firing employees should be separated from accounting and from passing out paychecks. Photo IDs ensure that only actual employees are paid. Employees clock in at the start and clock out at the end of the workday to prove their attendance and hours worked.

As we saw in Chapter 7, the foundation of internal control is the separation of duties. This is why companies have separate departments for the following payroll functions:

- The Human Resources Department hires and fires workers.
- The Payroll Department maintains employee earnings records.
- The Accounting Department records all transactions.
- The Treasurer (or bursar) distributes paychecks to employees.

Now let's summarize the accounting for payroll by examining the Decision Guidelines on the next page.

Key Takeaway

Recording payroll amounts requires five basic journal entries. The first entry records the gross payroll expense and liability. The second entry records the payment of net pay and the accrual of all employee-paid payroll liabilities. The third entry records employee benefits. The fourth journal entry records the employer payroll liabilities. The last journal entry records the payment of taxes to the taxing authorities. These payroll liabilities are all current liabilities of the company. Internal controls over payroll focus on operational efficiency and insuring the payroll disbursements are valid and accurate.

Decision Guidelines 10-2

ACCOUNTING FOR PAYROLL

What decisions must Smart Touch on the next page (or any another company) make to account for payroll?

Decision	Guidelines
• What records will Smart Touch keep in its payroll system to determine how much income tax to withhold from an employee's pay?	Employee's Withholding Allowance Certificate, Form W-4

• How does Smart Touch determine an employee's take-home pay?	*Gross pay* (Total amount earned by the employee)
	– *Payroll withholding deductions*:
	  a. Withheld income tax
	  b. Withheld FICA tax—equal amount also paid by employer
	  c. Optional withholding deductions (insurance, retirement, charitable contributions, union dues)
	= *Net (take-home) pay*

• What is Smart Touch's total payroll expense?	Total payroll expense = Gross pay
	+ *Employer paid benefits*
	  a. Insurance (health, life, and disability)
	  b. Retirement benefits
	+ *Employer payroll taxes*
	  a. Employer FICA tax—equal amount also paid by employee
	  b. Employer state and federal unemployment taxes

• Where will Smart Touch report payroll costs?	• Payroll expenses on the income statement • Payroll liabilities on the balance sheet

Summary Problem 10-2

Rags-to-Riches, a clothing resale store, employs one salesperson, Dee Hunter. Hunter's straight-time wage is $400 per week, with time-and-a-half pay for hours above 40. Rags-to-Riches withholds income tax (10%) and FICA tax (7.65%) from Hunter's pay. Rags-to-Riches also pays payroll taxes for FICA (7.65%) and state and federal unemployment (5.4% and 0.8%, respectively). In addition, Rags-to-Riches contributes 6% of Hunter's gross pay into her retirement plan.

During the week ended December 26, Hunter worked 50 hours. Prior to this week, she had earned $2,000.

Requirements

(Round all amounts to the nearest dollar.)

1. Compute Hunter's gross pay and net (take-home) pay for the week.
2. Record the payroll entries that Rags-to-Riches would make for each of the following:
   a. Hunter's gross pay, including overtime
   b. Expense for employee benefits
   c. Employer payroll taxes
   d. Payment of net pay to Hunter
   e. Payment for employee benefits
   f. Payment of all payroll taxes
3. How much was Rags-to-Riches' total payroll expense for the week?

Solution

Requirement 1

Gross pay:	Straight-time pay for 40 hours		$400
	Overtime pay:		
	Rate per hour ($400/40 × 1.5)	$15	
	Hours (50 – 40)	10	150
	Gross pay		$550
Net pay:	Gross pay		$550
	Less: Withheld income tax ($550 × 0.10)	$55	
	Withheld FICA tax ($550 × 0.0765)	42	97
	Net pay		$453

Requirement 2

a.	Wages expense (E+)	550	
	Wages payable (L+)		550
b.	Retirement-plan expense ($550 × 0.06) (E+)	33	
	Employee benefits payable (L+)		33
c.	Payroll tax expense (E+)	76	
	FICA tax payable ($550 × 0.0765) (L+)		42
	State unemployment tax payable ($550 × 0.054) (L+)		30
	Federal unemployment tax payable ($550 × 0.008) (L+)		4
d.	Wages payable (L–)	550	
	Employee income tax payable (L+)		55
	FICA tax payable (L+)		42
	Cash (A–)		453
e.	Employee benefits payable (L–)	33	
	Cash (A–)		33
f.	Employee income tax payable (L–)	55	
	FICA tax payable ($42 × 2) (L–)	84	
	State unemployment tax payable (L–)	30	
	Federal unemployment tax payable (L–)	4	
	Cash (A–)		173

Requirement 3

Rags-to-Riches incurred *total payroll expense* of $659 (gross pay of $550 + payroll taxes of $76 + benefits of $33). See entries (a) through (c).

Review *Current Liabilities and Payroll*

• Accounting Vocabulary

Contingent Liability (p. 501)
A potential liability that depends on some future event.

Current Maturity (p. 499)
Amount of the principal that is payable within one year. Also called **current portion of notes payable**.

Current Portion of Notes Payable (p. 499)
Amount of the principal that is payable within one year. Also called **current maturity**.

Employee Compensation (p. 505)
A major expense. Also called **payroll**.

Federal Insurance Contributions Act (FICA) Tax (p. 506)
Federal Insurance Contributions Act (FICA) tax, which is withheld from employees' pay and matched by the employer. Also called **Social Security tax**.

Gross Pay (p. 505)
Total amount of salary, wages, commissions, or any other employee compensation before taxes and other deductions.

Net (Take-Home) Pay (p. 506)
Gross pay minus all deductions. The amount of compensation that the employee actually takes home.

Payroll (p. 505)
A major expense. Also called **employee compensation**.

Short-Term Note Payable (p. 498)
Promissory note payable due within one year—a common form of financing.

Social Security (FICA) Tax (p. 506)
Federal Insurance Contributions Act (FICA) tax, which is withheld from employees' pay and matched by the employer. Also called **FICA tax**.

Unemployment Compensation Tax (p. 508)
Payroll tax paid by employers to the government, which uses the money to pay unemployment benefits to people who are out of work.

Warranties (p. 500)
Product guarantees.

Withheld Income Tax (p. 506)
Income tax deducted from employees' gross pay.

• Destination: Student Success

Student Success Tips

The following are hints on some common trouble areas for students in this chapter:

- Keep in mind that current is defined as one year or the operating cycle, whichever is less. So current liabilities will be paid in one year or less.

- Recall the formula for interest is Principal x Rate x Time. Interest expense accrues on the liability as the amount of time passes on the note.

- Remember the cash received from a taxable sale is split between the sales revenue earned and the liability to the state for the sales tax collected.

- Recall the current portion of long-term notes is only the portion of principal that is due currently (in a year or less).

- Remember that unearned revenue results when the company is paid by a customer BEFORE the company does the work (earnings); therefore, it is a liability—the company owes the work or it must pay the money back.

- Consider that contingent means dependent on some future event. So, contingent liabilities are potential liabilities that depend on the future event's outcome.

- Recall in calculating payroll, some taxes the employee pays (federal income tax withholding), some taxes the employer pays (unemployment taxes), and some taxes both employee and employer must pay (Social Security and Medicare).

Getting Help

If there's a learning objective from the chapter you aren't confident about, try using one or more of the following resources:

- Review Exhibit 10-4 for a depiction of total payroll costs.

- Review the Summary Problems in the chapter to reinforce your understanding of current liabilities and payroll.

- Practice additional exercises or problems at the end of Chapter 10 that cover the specific learning objective that is challenging you.

- Watch the white board videos for Chapter 10, located at myaccountinglab.com under the Chapter Resources button.

- Go to myaccountinglab.com and select the Study Plan button. Choose Chapter 10 and work the questions covering that specific learning objective until you've mastered it.

- Work the Chapter 10 pre/post tests in myaccountinglab.com.

- Visit the learning resource center on your campus for tutoring.

● Quick Check

1. Known liabilities of estimated amounts are

   a. ignored. (Record them when paid.)

   b. reported on the balance sheet.

   c. contingent liabilities.

   d. reported only in the notes to the financial statements.

2. On January 1, 2012, you borrowed $18,000 on a five-year, 5% note payable. At December 31, 2013, you should *record*

   a. interest payable of $900.

   b. note receivable of $18,000.

   c. cash payment of $18,000.

   d. nothing. (The note is already on the books.)

3. Your company sells $180,000 of goods and you collect sales tax of 8%. What current liability does the sale create?

   a. Sales tax payable of $14,400

   b. Sales revenue of $194,400

   c. Unearned revenue of $14,400

   d. None; you collected cash up front.

4. Wells Electric (WE) owed Estimated warranty payable of $1,200 at the end of 2011. During 2012, WE made sales of $120,000 and expects product warranties to cost the company 3% of the sales. During 2012, WE paid $2,300 for warranties. What is WE's Estimated warranty payable at the end of 2012?

   a. $2,300

   b. $2,500

   c. $3,600

   d. $4,800

5. At December 31, your company owes employees for three days of the five-day workweek. The total payroll for the week is $7,800. What journal entry should you make at December 31?

   a. Nothing because you will pay the employees on Friday.

   b.
   | Salary expense | 7,800 | |
   | Salary payable | | 7,800 |

   c.
   | Salary payable | 4,680 | |
   | Salary expense | | 4,680 |

   d.
   | Salary expense | 4,680 | |
   | Salary payable | | 4,680 |

6. Swell Company has a lawsuit pending from a customer claiming damages of $100,000. Swell's attorney advises that the likelihood the customer will win is remote. GAAP requires at a minimum that this contingent liability be

   a. disclosed in the footnotes.

   b. disclosed in the footnotes, with ranges of potential loss.

   c. booked, as well as disclosed in the footnotes.

   d. No disclosure is required.

7. An employee has year-to-date earnings of $105,000. The employee's gross pay for the next pay period is $5,000. If the FICA wage base is $106,800, how much FICA tax will be withheld from the employee's pay?

   a. $184.10

   b. $382.50

   c. $310.00

   d. $137.70

8. The employer is responsible for which of the following payroll taxes?

   a. 6.2% Social Security

   b. 1.45% Medicare tax

   c. Federal and state unemployment taxes

   d. All of the above

9. Jade Larson Antiques owes $20,000 on a truck purchased for use in the business. The company makes principal payments of $5,000 each year plus interest at 8%. Which of the following is true?

   a. After the first payment is made, the company owes $15,000 plus three year's interest.

   b. After the first payment, $15,000 would be shown as a long-term liability.

   c. After the first payment is made, $5,000 would be shown as the current portion due on the long-term note.

   d. Just before the last payment is made, $5,000 will appear as a long-term liability on the balance sheet.

10. Sydney Park Fitness Gym has Unearned revenue of $10,000, Salaries payable of $15,000, and Allowance for uncollectible accounts of $5,000. What amount would Sydney report as Total current liabilities?

    a. $30,000

    b. $25,000

    c. $20,000

    d. $15,000

Answers are given after Apply Your Knowledge (p. 528).

Assess Your Progress

● Short Exercises

S10-1   **❶ Accounting for a note payable [10 min]**

On December 31, 2012, Edgmont purchased $10,000 of inventory on a one-year, 10% note payable. Edgmont uses a perpetual inventory system.

Requirements

1. Journalize the company's accrual of interest expense on June 30, 2013, its fiscal year-end.

2. Journalize the company's payment of the note plus interest on December 31, 2013.

S10-2   **❷ Accounting for warranty expense and warranty payable [10 min]**

Trekster Corrector guarantees its snowmobiles for three years. Company experience indicates that warranty costs will add up to 4% of sales.

Assume that the Trekster dealer in Colorado Springs made sales totaling $533,000 during 2012. The company received cash for 30% of the sales and notes receivable for the remainder. Warranty payments totaled $17,000 during 2012.

Requirements

1. Record the sales, warranty expense, and warranty payments for the company.
2. Post to the Estimated warranty payable T-account. At the end of 2012, how much in Estimated warranty payable does the company owe?

S10-3 ❷ **Interpreting an actual company's contingent liabilities [5–10 min]**
Farley Motors, a motorcycle manufacturer, included the following note (adapted) in its annual report:

> Notes to Consolidated Financial Statements
>
> *7 Commitments and Contingencies (Adapted)*
>
> The Company self-insures its product liability losses in the United States up to $3,000,000.
>
> Catastrophic coverage is maintained for individual claims in excess of $3,000,000 up to $25,000,000.

Requirements

1. Why are these *contingent* (versus actual) liabilities?
2. How can a contingent liability become an actual liability for Farley Motors? What are the limits to the company's product liabilities in the United States?

S10-4 ❸ **Computing an employee's total pay [10 min]**
Gloria Traxell is paid $800 for a 40-hour workweek and time-and-a-half for hours above 40.

Requirements

1. Compute Traxell's gross pay for working 48 hours during the first week of February. Carry amounts to the nearest cent.
2. Traxell is single, and her income tax withholding is 10% of total pay. Traxell's only payroll deductions are payroll taxes. Compute Traxell's net (take-home) pay for the week. Use a 7.65% FICA tax rate, and carry amounts to the nearest cent.

Note: Short Exercise 10-5 should be used only after completing Short Exercise 10-4.

S10-5 ❸ **Computing the payroll expense of an employer [10 min]**
Return to the Gloria Traxell payroll situation in Short Exercise 10-4. Traxell's employer, College of San Bernardino, pays all the standard payroll taxes plus benefits for the employee retirement plan (5% of total pay), health insurance ($113 per employee per month), and disability insurance ($8 per employee per month).

Requirement

1. Compute College of San Bernardino's total expense of employing Gloria Traxell for the 48 hours that she worked during the first week of February. Carry amounts to the nearest cent.

S10-6 ❸ **Computing payroll amounts considering Social Security tax ceilings [10 min]**
Suppose you work for MRK, the accounting firm, all year and earn a monthly salary of $5,700. There is no overtime pay. Your withheld income taxes consume 15% of gross pay. In addition to payroll taxes, you elect to contribute 5% monthly to your retirement plan. MRK also deducts $150 monthly for your co-pay of the health insurance premium.

Requirement

1. Compute your net pay for November. Use 7.65% FICA tax rate and assume the 2010 FICA wage ceiling of $106,800 applies.

Note: Short Exercise 10-7 should be used only after completing Short Exercises 10-4 and 10-5.

S10-7 🔵**4** **Journalizing payroll [10 min]**
Consult your solutions for Short Exercises 10-4 and 10-5.

Requirements

1. Journalize salary expense and payment for College of San Bernardino related to the employment of Gloria Traxell.
2. Journalize benefits expense for College of San Bernardino related to the employment of Gloria Traxell.
3. Journalize employer payroll taxes for College of San Bernardino related to the employment of Gloria Traxell.

● Exercises

E10-8 🔵**1** **Recording sales tax [5–15 min]**
Consider the following transactions of Pearl Software:

Mar 31	Recorded cash sales of $180,000, plus sales tax of 8% collected for the state of Texas.
Apr 6	Sent March sales tax to the state.

Requirement

1. Journalize the transactions for the company.

E10-9 🔵**1** **Recording note payable transactions [5–10 min]**
Consider the following note payable transactions of Creative Video Productions.

2012	
May 1	Purchased equipment costing $17,000 by issuing a one-year, 6% note payable.
Dec 31	Accrued interest on the note payable.
2013	
May 1	Paid the note payable at maturity.

Requirement

1. Journalize the transactions for the company.

E10-10 🔵**1** **Recording and reporting current liabilities [10–15 min]**
TransWorld Publishing completed the following transactions during 2012:

Oct 1	Sold a six-month subscription, collecting cash of $330, plus sales tax of 9%.
Nov 15	Remitted (paid) the sales tax to the state of Tennessee.
Dec 31	Made the necessary adjustment at year-end to record the amount of subscription revenue earned during the year.

Requirement

1. Journalize the transactions (explanations are not required).

E10-11 🔵**1** **Journalizing current liabilities [15 min]**
Edmund O'Mally Associates reported short-term notes payable and salary payable as follows:

	2012	2011
Current liabilities—Partial:		
Short-term notes payable	$ 16,400	$ 15,600
Salary payable	3,400	3,100

During 2012, O'Mally paid off both current liabilities that were left over from 2011, borrowed money on short-term notes payable, and accrued salary expense.

Requirement

1. Journalize all four of these transactions for O'Mally during 2012.

E10-12 ❷ **Accounting for warranty expense and warranty payable [5–15 min]**

The accounting records of Clay Ceramics included the following at January 1, 2012:

	Estimated warranty payable	
	Beginning balance	4,000

In the past, Clay's warranty expense has been 8% of sales. During 2012, Clay made sales of $136,000 and paid $7,000 to satisfy warranty claims.

Requirements

1. Journalize Clay's warranty expense and warranty payments during 2012. Explanations are not required.

2. What balance of Estimated warranty payable will Clay report on its balance sheet at December 31, 2012?

E10-13 ❸ ❹ **Computing and recording gross and net pay [10–15 min]**

Henry Striker manages a Frosty Boy drive-in. His straight-time pay is $10 per hour, with time-and-a-half for hours in excess of 40 per week. Striker's payroll deductions include withheld income tax of 8%, FICA tax of 7.65%, and a weekly deduction of $5 for a charitable contribution to the United Fund. Striker worked 52 hours during the week.

Requirements

1. Compute Striker's gross pay and net pay for the week. Carry amounts to the nearest cent.

2. Journalize Frosty Boy's wage expense accrual for Striker's work. An explanation is not required.

3. Journalize the subsequent payment of wages to Striker.

E10-14 ❹ **Recording a payroll [10–15 min]**

Ricardo's Mexican Restaurants incurred salary expense of $65,000 for 2012. The payroll expense includes employer FICA tax of 7.65%, in addition to state unemployment tax of 5.4% and federal unemployment tax of 0.8%. Of the total salaries, $17,000 is subject to unemployment tax. Also, the company provides the following benefits for employees: health insurance (cost to the company, $2,060), life insurance (cost to the company, $350), and retirement benefits (cost to the company, 7% of salary expense).

Requirement

1. Journalize Ricardo's expenses for employee benefits and for payroll taxes. Explanations are not required.

● Problems (Group A)

P10-15A ❶ ❷ Journalizing liability transactions [30–40 min]

The following transactions of Denver Pharmacies occurred during 2011 and 2012:

2011		
Jan	9	Purchased computer equipment at a cost of $9,000, signing a six-month, 6% note payable for that amount.
	29	Recorded the week's sales of $64,000, three-fourths on credit, and one-fourth for cash. Sales amounts are subject to a 6% state sales tax.
Feb	5	Sent the last week's sales tax to the state.
	28	Borrowed $204,000 on a four-year, 10% note payable that calls for $51,000 annual installment payments plus interest. Record the current and long-term portions of the note payable in two separate accounts.
Jul	9	Paid the six-month, 6% note, plus interest, at maturity.
Aug	31	Purchased inventory for $12,000, signing a six-month, 9% note payable.
Dec	31	Accrued warranty expense, which is estimated at 2% of sales of $603,000.
	31	Accrued interest on all outstanding notes payable. Make a separate interest accrual for each note payable.
2012		
Feb	28	Paid the first installment and interest for one year on the four-year note payable.
	29	Paid off the 9% note plus interest at maturity.

Requirement

1. Journalize the transactions in Denver's general journal. Explanations are not required.

P10-16A ❷ Journalizing liability transactions [20–25 min]

The following transactions of Brooks Garrett occurred during 2012:

Apr 30	Garrett is party to a patent infringement lawsuit of $200,000. Garrett's attorney is certain it is remote that Garrett will lose this lawsuit.
Jun 30	Estimated warranty expense at 2% of sales of $400,000.
Jul 28	Warranty claims paid in the amount of $6,000.
Sep 30	Garrett is party to a lawsuit for copyright violation of $100,000. Garrett's attorney advises that it is probable Garrett will lose this lawsuit.
Dec 31	Garrett estimates warranty expense on sales for the second half of the year of $500,000 at 2%.

Requirements

1. Journalize required transactions, if any, in Garrett's general journal. Explanations are not required.
2. What is the balance in Estimated warranty payable?

P10-17A ❶ ❸ Journalizing and posting liabilities [35–45 min]

The general ledger of Speedy Ship at June 30, 2012, the end of the company's fiscal year, includes the following account balances before adjusting entries.

Accounts payable	$ 114,000
Current portion of notes payable	
Interest payable	
Salary payable	
Employee payroll taxes payable	970
Employer payroll taxes payable	
Unearned rent revenue	6,900
Long–term note payable	210,000

The additional data needed to develop the adjusting entries at June 30 are as follows:

a. The long-term debt is payable in annual installments of $42,000, with the next installment due on July 31. On that date, Speedy Ship will also pay one year's interest at 8%. Interest was last paid on July 31 of the preceding year. Make the adjusting entry to shift the current installment of the long-term note payable to a current liability. Also accrue interest expense at year end.

b. Gross salaries for the last payroll of the fiscal year were $4,300.

c. Employer payroll taxes owed are $850.

d. On February 1, the company collected one year's rent of $6,900 in advance.

Requirements

1. Using the four-column ledger format, open the listed accounts and insert the unadjusted June 30 balances.

2. Journalize and post the June 30 adjusting entries to the accounts that you opened. Key adjusting entries by letter.

3. Prepare the current liabilities section of the balance sheet at June 30, 2012.

P10-18A ③ ④ Computing and journalizing payroll amounts [25–35 min]

Louis Welch is general manager of United Tanning Salons. During 2012, Welch worked for the company all year at a $6,200 monthly salary. He also earned a year-end bonus equal to 10% of his salary.

Welch's federal income tax withheld during 2012 was $850 per month, plus $924 on his bonus check. State income tax withheld came to $70 per month, plus $40 on the bonus. The FICA tax withheld was 7.65% of the first $106,800 in annual earnings. Welch authorized the following payroll deductions: Charity Fund contribution of 1% of total earnings and life insurance of $5 per month.

United incurred payroll tax expense on Welch for FICA tax of 7.65% of the first $106,800 in annual earnings. The company also paid state unemployment tax of 5.4% and federal unemployment tax of 0.8% on the first $7,000 in annual earnings. In addition, United provides Welch with health insurance at a cost of $150 per month. During 2012, United paid $4,000 into Welch's retirement plan.

Requirements

1. Compute Welch's gross pay, payroll deductions, and net pay for the full year 2012. Round all amounts to the nearest dollar.

2. Compute United's total 2012 payroll expense for Welch.

3. Make the journal entry to record United's expense for Welch's total earnings for the year, his payroll deductions, and net pay. Debit Salary expense and Bonus expense as appropriate. Credit liability accounts for the payroll deductions and Cash for net pay. An explanation is not required.

Problems (Group B)

P10-19B ❶ ❷ **Journalizing liability transactions [30–40 min]**

The following transactions of Plymouth Pharmacies occurred during 2011 and 2012:

2011		
Jan	9	Purchased computer equipment at a cost of $7,000, signing a six-month, 9% note payable for that amount.
	29	Recorded the week's sales of $67,000, three-fourths on credit, and one-fourth for cash. Sales amounts are subject to a 6% state sales tax.
Feb	5	Sent the last week's sales tax to the state.
	28	Borrowed $210,000 on a four-year, 8% note payable that calls for $52,500 annual installment payments plus interest. Record the current and long-term portions of the note payable in two separate accounts.
Jul	9	Paid the six-month, 9% note, plus interest, at maturity.
Aug	31	Purchased inventory for $6,000, signing a six-month, 11% note payable.
Dec	31	Accrued warranty expense, which is estimated at 4% of sales of $608,000.
	31	Accrued interest on all outstanding notes payable. Make a separate interest accrual for each note payable.
2012		
Feb	28	Paid the first installment and interest for one year on the four-year note payable.
	29	Paid off the 11% note plus interest at maturity.

Requirement

1. Journalize the transactions in Plymouth's general journal. Explanations are not required.

P10-20B ❷ **Journalizing liability transactions [20–25 min]**

The following transactions of Dunn Miles occurred during 2012:

Apr 30	Miles is party to a patent infringement lawsuit of $230,000. Miles's attorney is certain it is remote that Miles will lose this lawsuit.
Jun 30	Estimated warranty expense at 3% of sales of $430,000.
Jul 28	Warranty claims paid in the amount of $6,400.
Sep 30	Miles is party to a lawsuit for copyright violation of $130,000. Miles's attorney advises that it is probable Miles will lose this lawsuit.
Dec 31	Miles estimates warranty expense on sales for the second half of the year of $510,000 at 3%.

Requirements

1. Journalize required transactions, if any, in Miles's general journal. Explanations are not required.
2. What is the balance in Estimated warranty payable?

P10-21B ❶ ❸ **Journalizing and posting liabilities [35–45 min]**

The general ledger of Pack-N-Ship at June 30, 2012, the end of the company's fiscal year, includes the following account balances before adjusting entries.

Accounts payable	$ 111,000
Current portion of notes payable	
Interest payable	
Salary payable	
Employee payroll taxes payable	960
Employer payroll taxes payable	
Unearned rent revenue	6,300
Long–term note payable	220,000

The additional data needed to develop the adjusting entries at June 30 are as follows:

a. The long-term debt is payable in annual installments of $44,000, with the next installment due on July 31. On that date, Pack-N-Ship will also pay one year's interest at 10%. Interest was last paid on July 31 of the preceding year. Make the adjusting entry to shift the current installment of the long-term note payable to a current liability. Also accrue interest expense at year end.

b. Gross salaries for the last payroll of the fiscal year were $4,900.

c. Employer payroll taxes owed are $810.

d. On February 1, the company collected one year's rent of $6,300 in advance.

Requirements

1. Using the four-column ledger format, open the listed accounts and insert the unadjusted June 30 balances.

2. Journalize and post the June 30 adjusting entries to the accounts that you opened. Key adjusting entries by letter.

3. Prepare the current liabilities section of the balance sheet at June 30, 2012.

P10-22B ③ ④ **Computing and journalizing payroll amounts [25–35 min]**

Lenny Worthington is general manager of Crossroad Tanning Salons. During 2012, Worthington worked for the company all year at a $6,100 monthly salary. He also earned a year-end bonus equal to 5% of his salary.

Worthington's federal income tax withheld during 2012 was $810 per month, plus $928 on his bonus check. State income tax withheld came to $80 per month, plus $60 on the bonus. The FICA tax withheld was 7.65% of the first $106,800 in annual earnings. Worthington authorized the following payroll deductions: United Fund contribution of 1% of total earnings and life insurance of $15 per month.

Crossroad incurred payroll tax expense on Worthington for FICA tax of 7.65% of the first $106,800 in annual earnings. The company also paid state unemployment tax of 5.4% and federal unemployment tax of 0.8% on the first $7,000 in annual earnings. In addition, Crossroad provides Worthington with health insurance at a cost of $110 per month. During 2012, Crossroad paid $7,000 into Worthington's retirement plan.

Requirements

1. Compute Worthington's gross pay, payroll deductions, and net pay for the full year 2012. Round all amounts to the nearest dollar.

2. Compute Crossroad's total 2012 payroll expense for Worthington.

3. Make the journal entry to record Crossroad's expense for Worthington's total earnings for the year, his payroll deductions, and net pay. Debit Salary expense and Bonus expense as appropriate. Credit liability accounts for the payroll deductions and Cash for net pay. An explanation is not required.

● Continuing Exercise

E10-23 ③ ④ **Computing and journalizing payroll amounts [25–35 min]**

This exercise continues the Lawlor Lawn Service situation from Exercise 9-39 of Chapter 9. Refer to the Chapter 2 data for Exercise 2-61. Lawlor Lawn Service is considering hiring its first "real" employee. The employee will earn $900 weekly and will have $81 in federal income tax and $33 for health insurance withheld, in addition to 7.65% FICA, each week. Assume the employee will pay no state or other taxes. The employer must pay 7.65% FICA tax, federal unemployment tax of 0.8% of the first $7,000 in pay, and state unemployment tax of 5.4% of the first $7,000 in pay.

Requirements

1. Calculate the amount of the employee's weekly net pay.
2. Journalize the entries to accrue the weekly payroll on July 31, 2012, to record the employer's payroll taxes associated with the payroll, and to pay the payroll on August 4, 2012.

● Continuing Problem

P10-24   ❶ Accounting for liabilities of a known amount [15–20 min]
This problem continues the Draper Consulting situation from Problem 9-40 of Chapter 9. Refer to Problem 2-62 of Chapter 2. Draper Consulting believes the company will need to borrow $300,000 in order to expand operations. Draper consults the bank and secures a 10%, five-year note on March 1, 2013. Draper must pay the bank principal in 5 equal installments plus interest annually on March 1.

Requirements

1. Record the $300,000 note payable on March 1, 2013.
2. Record the entry to accrue interest due on the note at December 31, 2013.
3. Record the entry Draper would make to record the payment to the bank on March 1, 2014.

Apply Your Knowledge

● Decision Cases

Decision Case 10-1 Golden Bear Construction operates throughout California. The owner, Gaylan Beavers, employs 15 work crews. Construction supervisors report directly to Beavers, and the supervisors are trusted employees. The home office staff consists of an accountant and an office manager.

Because employee turnover is high in the construction industry, supervisors hire and fire their own crews. Supervisors notify the office of all personnel changes. Also, supervisors forward to the office the employee W-4 forms. Each Thursday, the supervisors submit weekly time sheets for their crews, and the accountant prepares the payroll. At noon on Friday, the supervisors come to the office to get paychecks for distribution to the workers at 5 PM.

The company accountant prepares the payroll, including the paychecks. Beavers signs all paychecks. To verify that each construction worker is a bona fide employee, the accountant matches the employee's endorsement signature on the back of the canceled paycheck with the signature on that employee's W-4 form.

Requirements

1. Identify one way that a supervisor can defraud Golden Bear Construction under the present system.
2. Discuss a control feature that the company can use to *safeguard* against the fraud you identified in Requirement 1.

Decision Case 10-2 Sell-Soft is the defendant in numerous lawsuits claiming unfair trade practices. Sell-Soft has strong incentives not to disclose these contingent liabilities. However, GAAP requires that companies report their contingent liabilities.

Requirements

1. Why would a company prefer *not* to disclose its contingent liabilities?
2. Describe how a bank could be harmed if a company seeking a loan did not disclose its contingent liabilities.
3. What ethical tightrope must companies walk when they report contingent liabilities?

• Ethical Issue 10-1

Many small businesses have to squeeze down costs any way they can just to survive. One way many businesses do this is by hiring workers as "independent contractors" rather than as regular employees. Unlike rules for regular employees, a business does not have to pay Social Security (FICA) taxes and unemployment insurance payments for independent contractors. Similarly, they do not have to withhold federal income taxes or the employee's share of FICA taxes. The IRS has a "20 factor test" that determines whether a worker should be considered an employee or a contractor, but many businesses ignore those rules or interpret them loosely in their favor. When workers are treated as independent contractors, they do not get a W-2 form at tax time (they get a 1099 instead), they do not have any income taxes withheld, and they find themselves subject to "self-employment" taxes, by which they bear the brunt of both the employee and the employer's share of FICA taxes.

Requirements

1. When a business abuses this issue, how is the independent contractor hurt?
2. If a business takes an aggressive position—that is, interprets the law in a very slanted way—is there an ethical issue involved? Who is hurt?

• Fraud Case 10-1

Sara Chung knew the construction contractors in her area well. She was the purchasing manager at the power plant, a business that was the major employer in the region. Whenever a repair or maintenance job came up, Sara's friends would inflate the invoice by 10%. The invoice would then be passed through the accounts payable department, where the clerk was supposed to review and verify the charges before processing the payment. The accounts payable clerk, Valerie Judson, was happy to have a job and didn't want anything to jeopardize it. She knew the deal, but kept her mouth shut. Sara's contractor friends would always "kick back" the 10% extra to Sara under the table. One day Valerie had a heart attack and went into the hospital. The company hired a new accounts payable clerk, Spencer Finn. He had worked construction in his college days and suspected something was fishy, but he couldn't prove it. He did, however, wish to protect himself in case the fraud came to light.

Requirements

1. How could an auditor detect fraud of this sort?
2. What can a business do to prevent this kind of fraudulent activity?
3. What should the new accountant do to protect himself?

● Financial Statement Case 10-1

Details about a company's liabilities appear in a number of places in the annual report. Use **Amazon.com**'s financial statements, including Note 1, to answer the following questions. **Amazon**'s financial statements are in Appendix A at the end of this book.

Requirements

1. Give the breakdown of **Amazon**'s current liabilities at December 31, 2009. Give the January 2010 entry to record the payment of accrued expenses and other current liabilities that **Amazon** owed at December 31, 2009. (Please assume the entire balance of this item represents accrued expenses.)

2. At December 31, 2009, how much did **Amazon** report for unearned revenue that **Amazon** had collected in advance? Which account on the balance sheet reports this liability?

● Team Project 10-1

In recent years, the airline industry has dominated headlines. Consumers are shopping **Priceline.com** and other Internet sites for the lowest rates. The airlines have also lured customers with frequent-flyer programs, which award free flights to passengers who accumulate specified miles of travel. Unredeemed frequent-flyer mileage represents a liability that airlines must report on their balance sheets, usually as Air traffic liability.

Southwest Airlines, a profitable, no-frills carrier based in Dallas, has been rated near the top of the industry. **Southwest** controls costs by flying to smaller, less-expensive airports; using only one model of aircraft; serving no meals; increasing staff efficiency; and having a shorter turnaround time on the ground between flights. The fact that most of the cities served by **Southwest** have predictable weather maximizes its on-time arrival record.

Requirements

With a partner or group, lead your class in a discussion of the following questions, or write a report as directed by your instructor.

1. Frequent-flyer programs have grown into significant obligations for airlines. Why should a liability be recorded for those programs? Discuss how you might calculate the amount of this liability. Can you think of other industries that offer incentives that create a similar liability?

2. One of **Southwest Airlines**' strategies for success is shortening stops at airport gates between flights. The company's chairman has stated, "What [you] produce is lower fares for the customers because you generate more revenue from the same fixed cost in that airplane." Look up **fixed cost** in the Glindex of this book. What are some of the "fixed costs" of an airline? How can better utilization of assets improve a company's profits?

● Communication Activity 10-1

In 30 words or fewer, explain how to report the total owed on a long-term note.

Quick Check Answers

1. *b* 2. *a* 3. *a* 4. *b* 5. *d* 6. *d* 7. *a* 8. *d* 9. *c* 10. *b*

For online homework, exercises, and problems that provide you immediate feedback, please visit myaccountinglab.com.

11 Long-Term Liabilities, Bonds Payable, and Classification of Liabilities on the Balance Sheet

> These are debts that will be paid in full more than one year from the balance sheet date.

SMART TOUCH LEARNING
Balance Sheet
May 31, 2013

Assets				Liabilities	
Current assets:				Current liabilities:	
Cash		$ 4,800		Accounts payable	$ 48,700
Accounts receivable		2,600		Salary payable	900
Inventory		30,500		Interest payable	100
Supplies		600		Unearned service revenue	400
Prepaid rent		2,000		Total current liabilities	50,100
Total current assets			$ 40,500	**Long-term liabilities:**	
Plant assets:				Notes payable	20,000
Furniture	$18,000			Total liabilities	70,100
Less: Accumulated depreciation—furniture	300	17,700			
Building	48,000				
Less: Accumulated depreciation—building	200	47,800		Owner's Equity	
Total plant assets			65,500	Bright, capital	35,900
Total assets			$106,000	Total liabilities and owner's equity	$106,000

Learning Objectives

1. Journalize transactions for long-term notes payable and mortgages payable

2. Describe bonds payable

3. Measure interest expense on bonds using the straight-line amortization method

4. Report liabilities on the balance sheet

5. Use the time value of money: present value of a bond and effective-interest amortization (see Appendix 11A)

6. Retire bonds payable (see Appendix 11B)

Most companies have several types of liabilities. In the previous chapter, we learned about *current liabilities*, debts that must be paid within one year or within the company's operating cycle if it is longer than a year. In this chapter, we'll focus on obligations due beyond that period. These are *long-term liabilities*. Lastly, we show how Smart Touch Learning's liabilities appear on the balance sheet.

Long-Term Notes Payable and Mortgages Payable

1 Journalize transactions for long-term notes payable and mortgages payable

Both long-term notes payable and mortgages payable are common long-term liabilities. First we'll discuss long-term notes payable, continuing with Smart Touch's $20,000 note payable from the previous chapter.

Long-Term Notes Payable

We learned about the current portion of long-term notes payable in the previous chapter. Now, we focus on the long-term portion of the notes payable and the payments made according to the note.

Recall that most long-term notes payable are paid in installments. The *current portion of notes payable* is the principal amount that will be paid within one year—a current liability. The remaining portion is long-term. Consider the $20,000 note payable that Smart Touch signed on May 1, 2013 (refer to Exhibit 10-1 in Chapter 10). The note will be paid over four years with payments of $5,000 plus interest due each May 1. Remember that the amount due May 1, 2014, $5,000, is current. We recorded the inception of the note on May 1, 2013, and the May 1, 2013, reclassification of the current portion of the note as follows:

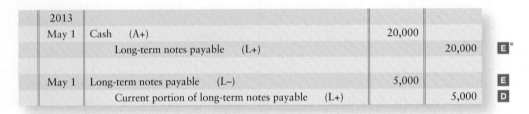

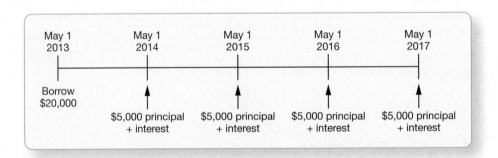

Notice that the reclassification entry on May 1 does not change the total amount of debt. It only reclassifies $5,000 of the total debt from long-term to current.

So, on December 31, 2013, Smart Touch still owes the total $20,000 on the note signed May 1, 2013. But what about interest owed? Remember that Smart Touch also recorded adjustments in May for one month's interest of $100 and in December for seven months interest of $700, or eight months total interest ($20,000 × 6% × 8/12 = $800) for the $800 interest accrued on the note as of December 31, 2013.

*The red colored boxes throughout Chapters 10 and 11 reference Exhibit 11-5.

So consider now that it's May 1, 2014, and Smart Touch must make its first installment payment of $5,000 principal + interest on the note. What's happened since December 31, 2013, the last time Smart Touch recorded any entries related to the note? First, four months have gone by, so Smart Touch has incurred four months of interest expense. But how much will Smart Touch need to pay? The note stated it must pay $5,000 in principal and a year's interest, based on the amount still owed on the note. What about the interest accrued in 2013? That $800 for eight month's interest accrued in 2013 (interest payable) will be paid when Smart Touch pays the full year of interest to the bank on May 1, 2014. So the entry follows:

2014			
May 1	Interest expense ($20,000 × 0.06 × 4/12) (E+)	400	
	Interest payable (L–)	800	
	Long-term notes payable (L–)	5,000	
	Cash (A–)		6,200

Notice the entry debited the Long-term notes payable account—not the Current portion of long-term notes payable. Why? Because each year, $5,000 of the note balance becomes due (is current). When we make payments on the note, we just reduce the long-term notes payable (one entry), rather than making the payment and then doing another reclassification entry, like we did on May 1, 2013.

So after the May 1, 2014, entry, how much does Smart Touch owe? Let's review the T-accounts:

Interest payable			Current portion of long-term notes payable	
	100 May 31, 2013			5,000 May 1, 2013
	700 Dec 31, 2013			
	41 Dec 31, 2013			5,000 Bal May 1, 2014
May 1, 2014 800				
	41 Bal May 31, 2014			

Long-term notes payable	
May 1, 2013 5,000	20,000 May 1, 2013
May 1, 2014 5,000	
	10,000 Bal May 1, 2014

Smart Touch owes $15,000 ($20,000 original note amount minus the $5,000 principal paid on May 1, 2014). How much of the $15,000 notes payable is long-term? As you can see from the T-accounts, $10,000 is long-term and $5,000 is current. What about the $41 in interest payable? That is the balance of interest due on the short-term note from Chapter 10 that will be paid on June 3, 2014.

Next, we'll discuss mortgages payable.

Mortgages Payable

Mortgages payable are long-term debts that are backed with a security interest in specific property. The mortgage will state that the borrower promises to transfer the legal title to specific assets if the mortgage isn't paid on schedule. This is very similar to the long-term notes payable we just covered. **The main difference is the mortgage payable is secured with specific assets, whereas long-term notes are not secured with specific assets.** Like long-term notes payable, the total mortgage payable amount will have a portion due within one year (current) and a portion that is due more than one year from a specific date.

Commonly, mortgages will specify a monthly payment of principal and interest to the lender (usually a bank). The most common type of mortgage is on property—for example, a mortgage on your home. Let's review an example of their treatment.

Assume on December 31, 2012, that Smart Touch purchases land and a building for $150,000, paying $49,925 in cash and signing a $100,075, 6%, 30-year mortgage payable that requires $600 monthly payments, which includes principal and interest beginning January 31, 2013. Recall from Chapter 9 that the $150,000 purchase price is allocated based on the land and building's relative fair market (sales) values. Smart Touch determined that $40,000 of the purchase price was allocated to the land and $110,000 of the purchase price was allocated to the building. So the entry to record this acquisition is as follows:

2012				
Dec 31	Building (A+)		110,000	
	Land (A+)		40,000	
	Mortgage payable (L+)			100,075
	Cash (A–)			49,925

The principal portion of the total mortgage payable that is due within one year is current. To figure the amount of each payment to apply to the mortgage payable and how much is interest expense, we create an **amortization schedule**. An amortization schedule details each loan payment's allocation between principal and interest. Smart Touch's loan will be amortized monthly by the lender/bank. A partial amortization schedule for 2013 and 2014 is shown in Exhibit 11-1.

EXHIBIT 11-1	Partial Amortization Schedule for Monthly Mortgage

Payment #	Date	Payment	Interest Expense (Principal × 6% × 1/12)	Principal	Mortgage Balance
Loan	1/1/2013				100,075.00
1	1/31/2013	600.00	500.38	99.62	99,975.38
2	2/28/2013	600.00	499.88	100.12	99,875.26
3	3/31/2013	600.00	499.38	100.62	99,774.64
4	4/30/2013	600.00	498.87	101.13	99,673.51
5	5/31/2013	600.00	498.37	101.63	99,571.88
6	6/30/2013	600.00	497.86	102.14	99,469.74
7	7/31/2013	600.00	497.35	102.65	99,367.09
8	8/31/2013	600.00	496.84	103.16	99,263.93
9	9/30/2013	600.00	496.32	103.68	99,160.25
10	10/31/2013	600.00	495.80	104.20	99,056.05
11	11/30/2013	600.00	495.28	104.72	98,951.33
12	12/31/2013	600.00	494.76	105.24	98,846.09
	2013 totals	7,200.00	5,971.09	1,228.91	
13	1/31/2014	600.00	494.23	105.77	98,740.32
14	2/28/2014	600.00	493.70	106.30	98,634.02
15	3/31/2014	600.00	493.17	106.83	98,527.19
16	4/30/2014	600.00	492.64	107.36	98,419.83
17	5/31/2014	600.00	492.10	107.90	98,311.93
18	6/30/2014	600.00	491.56	108.44	98,203.49
19	7/31/2014	600.00	491.02	108.98	98,094.51
20	8/31/2014	600.00	490.47	109.53	97,984.98
21	9/30/2014	600.00	489.92	110.08	97,874.90
22	10/31/2014	600.00	489.37	110.63	97,764.27
23	11/30/2014	600.00	488.82	111.18	97,653.09
24	12/31/2014	600.00	488.27	111.73	97,541.36
	2014 totals	7,200.00	5,895.27	1,304.73	

We can confirm the interest calculations provided in the amortization table by using the interest formula we learned in Chapter 8 (Principal × Rate × Time). So, for the first payment on 1/31/2013, the interest is calculated as $100,075.00 × 6% × 1/12 or $500.38 in interest expense. The principal of $99.62 is the difference between the monthly payment of $600.00 minus the interest expense of $500.38 ($600.00 – $500.38 = $99.62). The $99.62 reduces the mortgage payable from $100,075.00 to $99,975.38 ($100,075.00 – $99.62 = $99,975.38). So after reviewing the amortization schedule, Smart Touch would reclassify the portion of the $100,075 mortgage balance that is current as follows:

2012				
Dec 31	Mortgage payable (L–)		1,228.91	
	Current portion of mortgage payable (L+)			1,228.91

Smart Touch adjusts the current portion of the mortgage payable each year-end on December 31 rather than monthly, since the change to the account is not material from month to month. In the interim, principal payments are posted against the

Mortgage payable account. The entry to record Smart Touch's first mortgage payment is as follows:

	2013			
	Jan 31	Interest expense ($100,075 × 0.06 × 1/12) (E+)	500.38	
		Mortgage payable ($600.00 – $500.38) (L–)	99.62	
		Cash (A–)		600.00

The balances at December 31, 2013, after Smart Touch makes 12 timely mortgage payments of $600 each are as follows:

Current portion of mortgage payable			Mortgage payable		
	1,228.91 12/31/2012 reclass	12/31/2012 reclass	1,228.91	100,075.00 12/31/2012	
		1/31/2013 payment	99.62		
		2/28/2013 payment	100.12		
		3/31/2013 payment	100.62		
	1,228.91 12/31/2013 Bal	4/30/2013 payment	101.13		
		5/31/2013 payment	101.63		
		6/30/2013 payment	102.14		
		7/31/2013 payment	102.65		
		8/31/2013 payment	103.16		
		9/30/2013 payment	103.68		
		10/31/2013 payment	104.20		
		11/30/2013 payment	104.72		
		12/31/2013 payment	105.24		
				97,617.18 12/31/2013 Bal	

However, these balances aren't correct yet. Smart Touch still needs to make the annual adjusting entry for the current portion of the mortgage payable. Refer to the amortization schedule in Exhibit 11-1. What part of the principal will be due within one year of 12/31/2013? $1,304.73, which is the total of principal payments that will be made during 2014. So Smart Touch needs to adjust the Current portion of mortgage payable account so the ending balance reflects $1304.73. The adjustment follows:

	2013			
	Dec 31	Mortgage payable ($1,304.73 – $1,228.91) (L–)	75.82	
		Current portion of mortgage payable (L+)		75.82

After posting the adjustments, the T-accounts would have the correct balances, as shown next:

Current portion of mortgage payable		
	1,228.91	12/31/2012 reclass
	1,228.91	12/31/2013 Bal
	75.82	AJE
	1,304.73 N	12/31/2013 Adj. Bal

Mortgage payable			
12/31/2012 reclass	1,228.91	100,075	12/31/12
1/31/2013 payment	99.62		
2/28/2013 payment	100.12		
3/31/2013 payment	100.62		
4/30/2013 payment	101.13		
5/31/2013 payment	101.63		
6/30/2013 payment	102.14		
7/31/2013 payment	102.65		
8/31/2013 payment	103.16		
9/30/2013 payment	103.68		
10/31/2013 payment	104.20		
11/30/2013 payment	104.72		
12/31/2013 payment	105.24		
		97,617.18	12/31/2013 Bal
AJE	75.82		
		97,541.36 O	12/31/2013 Adj. Bal

The total of the adjusted balance of the Current portion of mortgage payable account plus the adjusted balance of the Mortgage payable account equals the total due on the mortgage at December 31, 2013 ($1,304.73 + $97,541.36 = $98,846.09).

If Smart Touch pays the $600 monthly payments on time every month for 30 years, Smart Touch will have made total payments of $216,000 ($600 × 12 payments a year × 30 years). Recall the original loan amount was $100,075. What's the difference? It's interest of $115,925 ($216,000 – $100,075 = $115,925).

What if Smart Touch decides to pay double payments every month? Assume there is no penalty in the loan agreement for Smart Touch to pay extra. That is, Smart Touch will choose to pay $1,200 a month, rather than the bank required minimum payment of $600 per month. How much of the extra payment goes toward paying off the mortgage payable? ALL OF IT! Smart Touch would be able to pay the loan in FULL in less than eight years!

Bonds: An Introduction

Large companies such as **Best Buy** and **Google** need large amounts of money to finance their operations. They may borrow long-term from banks and/or issue bonds payable to the public to raise the money. **Bonds payable** are groups of long-term liabilities issued to multiple lenders, called bondholders, usually in increments of $1,000. **For example, a company could borrow $100,000 from one lender (the bank) or the company could issue 100 bonds payable, each at $1,000 from 100 different lenders.** By issuing bonds payable, **Best Buy** can borrow millions of dollars from thousands of investors rather than depending on a loan from one single bank or lender. Each investor can buy a specified amount of **Best Buy** bonds.

Each bondholder gets a bond certificate that shows the name of the company that borrowed the money, exactly like a note payable. The certificate states the *principal*, which is the amount of the bond issue. The bond's principal amount is also called *maturity value*, *face value*, or *par value*. The company must then pay each bondholder the principal amount at a specific future date, called the *maturity date*. In Chapter 10, we saw how to account for short-term notes payable. There are many similarities between the accounting for short-term notes payable and long-term notes payable.

2 Describe bonds payable

People buy (invest in) bonds to earn interest. The bond certificate states the interest rate that the company will pay and the dates the interest is due, generally semi-annually (twice a year). Exhibit 11-2 shows a bond certificate issued by Smart Touch. Review the following bond fundamentals in Exhibit 11-2:

- **Principal amount** (also called *maturity value*, *face value*, or **par value**): The amount the borrower must pay back to the bondholders on the maturity date.
- **Maturity date:** The date on which the borrower must pay the principal amount to the bondholders. **The maturity date is the date the principal is paid off.**
- **Stated interest rate** (also called *face rate*, *coupon rate*, or *nominal rate*): The annual rate of interest that the borrower pays the bondholders. **The stated interest rate is the interest rate that cash payments to bondholders are based on.**

Types of Bonds

There are various types of bonds, including the following:

- **Term bonds** all mature at the same specified time. For example, $100,000 of term bonds may all mature five years from today.
- **Serial bonds** mature in installments at regular intervals. For example, a $500,000, five-year serial bond may mature in $100,000 annual installments over a five-year period.
- **Secured bonds** give the bondholder the right to take specified assets of the issuer if the issuer fails to pay principal or interest. A mortgage on a house is an example of a secured bond.
- **Debentures** are unsecured bonds that are not backed by assets. They are backed only by the goodwill of the bond issuer.

EXHIBIT 11-2 | **Bond Certificate**

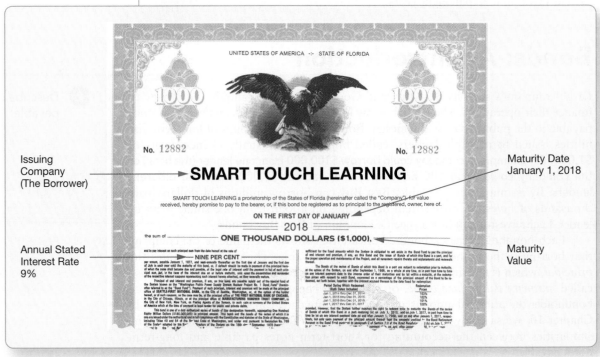

Bond Prices

A bond can be issued at any price agreed upon by the issuer and the bondholders. A bond can be issued at

- **face (or par or maturity) value.** Example: A $1,000 bond issued for $1,000. A bond issued at face value (maturity value or par value) has no discount or premium.
- a **discount (or bond discount)**, a price below maturity (par) value. Example: A $1,000 bond issued for $980. The discount is $20 ($1,000 – $980).
- a **premium (or bond premium)**, a price above maturity (par) value. Example: A $1,000 bond issued for $1,015. The premium is $15 ($1,015 – $1,000).

The issue price of a bond does not affect the required payment at maturity. In all of the preceding cases, the company must pay the maturity value of the bonds at the maturity date stated on the face of the bond.

As a bond approaches maturity, its market price moves toward maturity value. On the maturity date, the market value of a bond exactly equals the maturity value because the company pays that amount to retire the bond.

After a bond is issued, investors may buy and sell it through the bond market just as they buy and sell stocks through the stock market. The most famous bond market is the New York Exchange, which lists several thousand bonds.

Bond prices are quoted as a percentage of maturity value. For example,

- a $1,000 bond quoted at 100 is bought or sold for 100% of maturity value, ($1,000. × 1.00).
- a $1,000 bond quoted at 88.375 is bought or sold for 88.375% of maturity value, $883.75 ($1,000 × .88375).
- a $1,000 bond quoted at 101.5 is bought or sold for 101.5% of maturity value, $1,015 ($1,000 × 1.015).

The issue price of a bond determines the amount of cash the company receives when it issues the bond. In all cases, the company must pay the bond's maturity value to retire it at the maturity date.

Exhibit 11-3 shows example price information for the bonds of Smart Touch. On this particular day, 12 of Smart Touch's 9% bonds maturing in 2018 (indicated by 18) were traded. The bonds' highest price on this day was $795 ($1,000 × 0.795). The lowest price of the day was $784.50 ($1,000 × 0.7845). The closing price (last sale of the day) was $795.

EXHIBIT 11-3	**Bond Price Information for Smart Touch Learning (SMT)**

Bonds	Volume	High	Low	Close
SMT 9% of 18	12	79.5	78.45	79.5

Present Value

Money earns income over time, a fact called the **time value of money**. Appendix 11A covers the time value of money in detail.

Let's see how the time value of money affects bond prices. Assume that a $1,000 bond reaches maturity three years from now and carries no interest. Would you pay $1,000 to purchase this bond? No, because paying $1,000 today to receive $1,000 later yields no income on your investment. How much would you pay today in order to receive $1,000 in three years? The answer is some amount less than $1,000. Suppose $750 is a fair price. By investing $750 now to receive $1,000 later, you will earn $250 over the three years. The diagram that follows illustrates the relationship between a bond's price (present value) and its maturity amount (future value).

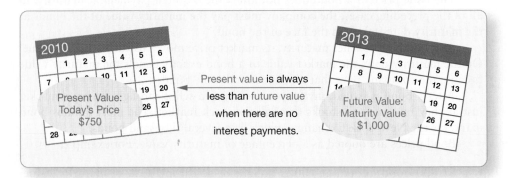

The amount that a person would invest *at the present time* is called the **present value**. The present value is the bond's market price. In our example, $750 is the present value (market price of the bond), and the $1,000 maturity value to be received in three years is the future amount. We show how to compute present value in Appendix 11A.

Bond Interest Rates

Bonds are sold at their market price (issue price on the date the bonds are first sold), which is the present value of the interest payments the bondholder will receive while holding the bond plus the bond principal paid at the end of the bond's life. Two interest rates work together to set the price of a bond:

- The stated interest rate determines the amount of cash interest the borrower pays each year. The stated interest rate is printed on the bond and *does not change* from year to year. For example, Smart Touch's 9% bonds payable have a stated interest rate of 9% (see Exhibit 11-2). Therefore, Smart Touch pays $90 of interest annually on each $1,000 bond. The dollar amount of interest paid is not affected by the issue or selling price of the bond.

- The **market interest rate** (also known as the **effective interest rate**) is the rate that investors demand to earn for loaning their money. The market interest rate *varies* constantly. A company may issue bonds with a stated interest rate that differs from the market interest rate, due to the time gap between the time the bonds were printed (engraved) showing the stated rate and the actual issuance of the bonds.

Smart Touch may issue its 9% bonds when the market rate has risen to 10%. Will the Smart Touch bonds attract investors in this market? No, because investors can earn 10% on other bonds. Therefore, investors will purchase Smart Touch bonds only at a price *less* than maturity value. The difference between the lower price and the bonds' maturity value is a *discount* that will allow the investor to earn 10%, even though Smart Touch's interest checks will be paid at the stated rate of 9%. The difference between what is paid for the bond (less than $1,000) and the bond principal of $1,000 is the interest rate difference between 9% and 10% over the life of the bond.

On the other hand, if the market interest rate is 8%, Smart Touch's 9% bonds will be so attractive that investors will pay more than maturity value for them because investors will receive more in interest payments. The difference between the higher price and maturity value is a *premium*. Exhibit 11-4 shows how the stated interest rate and the market interest rate work together to determine the price of a bond.

EXHIBIT 11-4	**Interaction of the Stated Interest Rate and the Market Interest Rate to Determine the Price of a Bond**	

Example: Bond with a Stated Interest Rate of 9%

Bond's Stated Interest Rate		Market Interest Rate		Issue Price of Bonds Payable
9%	=	9%	→	Maturity value of the bond
9%	<	10%	→	Discount (price below maturity value)
9%	>	8%	→	Premium (price above maturity value)

Accounting for Bonds Payable: Straight-Line Method

The basic journal entry to record the issuance of bonds payable debits Cash and credits Bonds payable. As noted previously, a company may issue bonds, a long-term liability:

- at *maturity (face or par)* value.
- at a *discount*.
- at a *premium*.

We begin with the simplest case—issuing bonds payable at maturity (face or par) value.

③ Measure interest expense on bonds using the straight-line amortization method

Issuing Bonds Payable at Maturity (Par) Value

Smart Touch has $100,000 of 9% bonds payable that mature in five years. Smart Touch issues these bonds at maturity (par) value on January 1, 2013. The issuance entry is as follows:

2013			
Jan 1	Cash (A+)	100,000	
	Bonds payable (L+)		100,000
	Issued bonds.		

Smart Touch, the borrower, makes this one-time journal entry to record the receipt of cash and issuance of bonds payable. Interest payments occur each June 30 and December 31. Smart Touch's first semiannual interest payment is journalized as follows:

2013			
Jun 30	Interest expense ($100,000 × 0.09 × 6/12) (E+)	4,500	
	Cash (A–)		4,500
	Paid semiannual interest.		

Each semiannual interest payment follows this same pattern.

At maturity, Smart Touch will record payment of the bonds as follows:

2018			
Jan 1	Bonds payable (L–)	100,000	
	Cash (A–)		100,000
	Paid off bonds at maturity.		

Now let's see how to issue bonds payable at a discount. This is one of the most common situations.

Issuing Bonds Payable at a Discount

We know that market conditions may force a company such as Smart Touch to accept a discounted price for its bonds. Suppose Smart Touch issues $100,000 of its 9%, five-year bonds that pay interest semiannually when the market interest rate is 10%. The market price of the bonds drops to 96.149, which means 96.149% of par value. Smart Touch receives $96,149 ($100,000 × 0.96149) at issuance and makes the following journal entry:

2013			
Jan 1	Cash ($100,000 × 0.96149) (A+)	96,149	
	Discount on bonds payable (CL+)	3,851	
	Bonds payable (L+)		100,000
	Issued bonds at a discount.		

After posting, the bond accounts have the following balances:

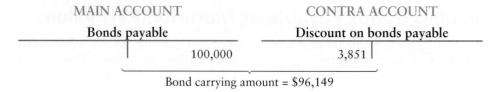

MAIN ACCOUNT	CONTRA ACCOUNT
Bonds payable	**Discount on bonds payable**
100,000	3,851

Bond carrying amount = $96,149

Discount on bonds payable is a contra account to Bonds payable. Bonds payable *minus* the discount gives the **carrying amount of the bonds** (known as carrying value). Smart Touch would report these bonds payable on the balance sheet as follows immediately after issuance:

Long-term liabilities:		
Bonds payable	$100,000	
Less: Discount on bonds payable.....	3,851	$96,149

Interest Expense on Bonds Payable Issued at a Discount

In this case, we see that a bond's stated interest rate may differ from the market interest rate. The market rate was 10% when Smart Touch issued its 9% bonds. This 1% interest-rate difference created the $3,851 discount on the bonds. Smart Touch needed to offer this discount because investors were willing to pay only $96,149 for a $100,000, 9% bond when they could earn 10% on other bonds.

Smart Touch borrowed $96,149 but still must pay $100,000 when the bonds mature five years later. What happens to the $3,851 discount? The discount is additional interest expense to Smart Touch. The discount raises Smart Touch's true interest expense on the bonds to the market interest rate of 10%. The discount becomes interest expense for Smart Touch through the process called *amortization*, the gradual reduction of an item over time.

Straight-Line Amortization of Bond Discount

We can amortize a bond discount by dividing it into equal amounts for each interest period. This method is called *straight-line amortization* and it works very much like the straight-line depreciation method we discussed in the Plant Assets chapter. In our example, the initial discount is $3,851, and there are 10 semiannual interest periods during the bonds' five-year life.

Therefore, 1/5 years × 6/12 of the year or 1/10 of the $3,851 bond discount ($385, rounded) is amortized each interest period. Smart Touch's first semiannual interest entry is as follows:

2013				
Jun 30	Interest expense (E+)		4,885	
	Cash ($100,000 × 0.09 × 6/12) (A–)			4,500
	Discount on bonds payable ($3,851 × 1/5 yrs × 6/12) (CL–)			385
	Paid semiannual interest and amortized discount.			

Interest expense of $4,885 for each six-month period is the sum of

- the stated interest ($4,500, which is paid in cash),
- *plus* the amortization of discount, $385.

This same entry would be made again on December 31, 2013. So, the bond discount balance would be $3,851 – $385 (from June 30 entry) – $385 (from December 31 entry) = $3,081 balance in the Discount on bonds payable account on December 31, 2013. So what would be the balance shown on the December 31, 2013, balance sheet for Bonds payable?

Long-term liabilities:		
Bonds payable	$100,000	
Less: Discount on bonds payable.....	3,081	$96,919 **M**

Discount on bonds payable has a debit balance. Therefore we credit the Discount on bonds payable account to amortize (reduce) its balance. Ten amortization entries will decrease the Discount to zero (with rounding). Then the carrying amount of the bonds payable will be $100,000 at maturity—$100,000 in Bonds payable minus $0 in Discount on bonds payable.

Finally, the entry to pay off the bonds at maturity is as follows:

2018			
Jan 1	Bonds payable (L–)	100,000	
	Cash (A–)		100,000
	Paid off bonds at maturity.		

Now you're ready to review Decision Guidelines 11-1.

Decision Guidelines 11-1

LONG-TERM LIABILITIES—PART A

If a company has borrowed some money by issuing bonds payable, how can we determine what type of bonds the company issued? How much cash will the company pay each interest period? How much cash must the company pay at maturity? The Decision Guidelines address these and other questions.

Decision	Guidelines
• When will you pay off the bonds? • At maturity?	Types of bonds: • Term bonds

• Are the bonds secured?
     • Yes
     • No
	
	 • Mortgage (secured) bonds
	 • Debenture (unsecured) bonds

• How are bond prices
     • quoted?
 	
     • determined?
	
	 • As a percentage of maturity value (Example: A $500,000 bond priced at $510,000 would be quoted at 102 ($510,000 / $500,000 = 1.02))
	 • Present value of the future maturity value of the bond *plus* present value of the future interest payments (see Appendix 11A)

• What are the two interest rates used for bonds?	• The *stated interest rate* determines the amount of cash interest the borrower pays. This interest rate does *not* change. • The *market interest rate* is the rate that investors demand to earn for loaning their money. This interest rate determines the bonds' market prices and varies constantly.

• What causes a bond to be priced at
     • maturity (face or par) value?
 	
     • a discount?
 	
     • a premium?
	• The *stated* interest rate on the bond *equals* the *market* interest rate.
	 • The *stated* interest rate on the bond is *less than* the *market* interest rate.
	 • The *stated* interest rate on the bond is *greater than* the *market* interest rate.

• How do we report bonds payable on the balance sheet?	Maturity (face or par) value $\begin{cases} \text{– Discount on bonds payable} \\ \quad\quad\quad\quad \text{or} \\ \text{+ Premium on bonds payable} \end{cases}$

• What is the relationship between interest expense and interest payments when bonds are issued at
     • maturity (face or par) value?
     • a discount?
     • a premium?
	
	 • Interest expense *equals* the interest payment.
	 • Interest expense is *greater than* the interest payment.
	 • Interest expense is *less than* the interest payment.

Issuing Bonds Payable at a Premium

The issuance of bonds payable at a premium is rare.

To illustrate a bond premium, let's change the Smart Touch example. Assume that the market interest rate is 8% when Smart Touch issues its 9%, five-year bonds. These 9% bonds are attractive in an 8% market, and investors will pay a premium to acquire them. Assume the bonds are priced at 104.1 (104.1% of maturity value). In that case, Smart Touch receives $104,100 cash upon issuance. Smart Touch's entry to borrow money and issue these bonds is as follows:

2013				
Jan 1	Cash ($100,000 × 1.041) (A+)	104,100		
	Bonds payable (L+)		100,000	
	Premium on bonds payable (AL+)		4,100	
	Issued bonds at a premium.			

After posting, the bond accounts have the following balances:

MAIN ACCOUNT	ADJUNCT ACCOUNT
Bonds payable	**Premium on bonds payable**
100,000	4,100

Bond carrying amount $104,100

The Bonds payable account and the Premium on bonds payable account each carries a credit balance. The Premium is an adjunct account to Bonds payable. **Adjunct accounts** are related accounts that have the same normal balance and which are reported together on the balance sheet. Adjunct accounts work similar to contra accounts—the only difference is that the adjunct account has the same balance as the main account, whereas the contra account has the opposite balance of its main account. Therefore, we add the Premium on bonds payable to Bonds payable to determine bond carrying amount. Smart Touch would report these bonds payable as follows immediately after issuance:

Long-term liabilities:		
Bonds payable	$100,000	
Add: Premium on bonds payable	4,100	$104,100

Interest Expense on Bonds Payable Issued at a Premium

The 1% difference between the bonds' 9% stated interest rate and the 8% market rate creates the $4,100 premium ($104,100 – $100,000 face). Smart Touch borrows $104,100 but must pay back only $100,000 at maturity. The premium is like a saving of interest expense to Smart Touch. The premium cuts Smart Touch's cost of borrowing and reduces interest expense to 8%, the market rate. The amortization of bond premium decreases interest expense over the life of the bonds.

Straight-Line Amortization of Bond Premium

In our example, the beginning premium is $4,100 and there are 10 semiannual interest periods during the bonds' five-year life. Therefore, 1/5 years × 6/12 months or 1/10 of the $4,100 ($410) of bond premium is amortized each interest period. Smart Touch's first semiannual interest entry is as follows:

2013				
Jun 30	Interest expense (E+)		4,090	
	Premium on bonds payable ($4,100 × 1/5 yrs × 6/12) (AL–)		410	
	Cash ($100,000 × 0.09 × 6/12) (A–)			4,500
	Paid semiannual interest and amortized premium.			

Interest expense of $4,090 is

- the stated interest ($4,500, which is paid in cash)
- *minus* the amortization of the premium of $410.

At June 30, 2013, immediately after amortizing the bond premium, the bonds have the following carrying amount:

$$\$103,690 \ [\$100,000 + (\$4,100 - \$410)]$$

At December 31, 2013, the bonds' carrying amount will be as follows:

$$\$103,280 \ [\$100,000 + (\$4,100 - \$410 - \$410)]$$

At maturity on January 1, 2018, the bond premium will have been fully amortized (it will have a zero balance), and the bonds' carrying amount will be $100,000 (the amount in the Bonds payable account).

Stop & Think...

If companies could change the stated interest rate on the bonds to equal market it would be easier, would it not? Then there would be no need for discounts or premiums. That sounds great but, in reality, the market is constantly changing and reacting to many things that ultimately affect the required rate of return for investors (market interest rate). The discount or premium still allows the company to raise capital, just a different amount of capital than the principal amount of the bonds. Remember that the discount or premium is really just the value today of the interest difference.

Adjusting Entries for Bonds Payable

Companies may issue bonds payable when they need cash. The interest payments dates rarely are set on December 31, so interest expense must be accrued at year-end. The accrual entry records the interest expense and amortizes any bond discount or premium.

Suppose Smart Touch issued $100,000 of 8%, 10-year bonds at a $2,000 discount on October 1, 2013. The interest payments occur on March 31 and September 30 each year. On December 31, Smart Touch accrues interest and amortizes bond discount for three months (October, November, and December) as follows:

2013				
Dec 31	Interest expense (E+)		2,050	
	Interest payable ($100,000 × 0.08 × 3/12) (L+)			2,000
	Discount on bonds payable ($2,000 × 1/10 × 3/12) (CL–)			50
	Accrued interest and amortized discount.			

Interest payable is credited for three months (October, November, and December). Discount on bonds payable must also be amortized for these three months.

The next semiannual interest payment occurs on March 31, 2014, and Smart Touch makes the following journal entry:

2014			
Mar 31	Interest payable (from Dec 31) (L–)	2,000	
	Interest expense (E+)	2,050	
	Cash ($100,000 × 0.08 × 6/12) (A–)		4,000
	Discount on bonds payable ($2,000 × 1/10 × 3/12) (CL–)		50
	Paid interest and amortized discount.		

Amortization of a bond premium is similar except that Premium on bonds payable is debited.

Issuing Bonds Payable Between Interest Dates

In most of the examples we have seen thus far, Smart Touch issued bonds payable right after an interest date, such as January 1. Companies can also issue bonds between interest dates. If they do so, however, they must account for the accrued interest.

Assume that Smart Touch has $100,000 of 6% bonds payable that are dated January 1. That means the interest starts accruing on January 1.

Suppose Smart Touch issues these bonds on April 1 when the market rate of interest is also 6% (no discount or premium). How should we account for the interest for January, February, and March? At issuance on April 1, Smart Touch collects three months' accrued interest from the bondholder and records the issuance of bonds payable as follows:

2013			
Apr 1	Cash (A+)	101,500	
	Bonds payable (L+)		100,000
	Interest payable ($100,000 × 0.06 × 3/12) (L+)		1,500
	Issued bonds three months after the planned issuance date of		
	the bonds.		

Companies cannot split interest payments. They pay in either six-month or annual amounts as stated on the bond certificate.

On the next interest date, Smart Touch will pay six months' interest to whomever owns the bonds at that time. But Smart Touch will have interest expense only for the three months the bonds have been outstanding (April, May, and June). To allocate interest expense to the correct months, Smart Touch makes the following entry on June 30 for the customary six-month interest payment:

2013			
Jun 30	Interest payable (from April 1) (L–)	1,500	
	Interest expense (for April, May, June) (E+)	1,500	
	Cash ($100,000 × 0.06 × 6/12) (A–)		3,000
	Paid interest.		

Reporting Liabilities on the Balance Sheet

 Report liabilities on the balance sheet

At the end of each period, a company reports all of its current and long-term liabilities on the balance sheet. As we have seen throughout, there are two categories of liabilities, current and long-term. Smart Touch's liabilities portion of its balance sheet from data within Chapters 10 and 11 is shown in Exhibit 11-5. The red blocked letters correspond to the matching letters on several figures within chapters 10 and 11 to help you visualize where the numbers on the balance sheet came from.

EXHIBIT 11-5 | **Liabilities Portion of Balance Sheet**

SMART TOUCH LEARNING Balance Sheet—partial December 31, 2013		
Liabilities		
Current liabilities:*		
Accounts payable	$ 17,000	*Value assumed
Employee income tax payable	2,000	H
FICA tax payable (579 + 579)	1,158	I
Payable to health insurance	180	J
Payable to United Way	20	K
Employee benefits payable	1,500	L
Interest payable (41 + 100 + 700)	841	B
Sales tax payable	600	C
Unearned service revenue	400	F
Estimated warranty payable	700	G
Short-term notes payable	700	A
Current portion mortgage payable	1,305	N
Current portion of long-term notes payable	5,000	D
Total current liabilities	$ 31,404	
Long-term liabilities:		
Long-term notes payable	15,000	E
Mortgage payable	97,541	O
Bonds payable, net of discount, $3,081	96,919	M
Total long-term liabilities	$209,460	
Total liabilities	$240,864	

*Current liabilities values are from Chapter 10. All amounts rounded to the nearest dollar.

The balance sheet presentation of bonds payable uses the discount bond example on page 542 of the chapter. The presentation of bonds payable issued at a premium is shown in the Premium section of this chapter.

Now we'll wrap up the chapter with Decision Guidelines 11-2.

Key Takeaway

Current liabilities are those liabilities due in a year of the balance sheet date or the business operating cycle, whichever is longer. Long-term liabilities are those liabilities due over a year from the balance sheet date.

Decision Guidelines 11-2

LONG-TERM LIABILITIES—PART B

Suppose Greg's Tunes needs $50 million to purchase manufacturing facilities and equipment. Greg's Tunes issues bonds payable to finance the purchase and now must account for the bonds payable. The Decision Guidelines outline some of the issues Greg's Tunes must consider.

Decision	Guidelines
• What happens to the bonds' carrying amount when bonds payable are issued at • maturity (face or par) value? • a premium? • a discount?	• Carrying amount *stays* at maturity (face or par) value • Carrying amount *decreases* gradually to maturity value • Carrying amount *increases* gradually to maturity value
• How do we account for the retirement of bonds payable?	**At maturity date:**

At maturity date:

| Bonds payable........... | Maturity value | |
| Cash .... | | Maturity value |

Before maturity date (Covered in Appendix 11B) (assume a discount on the bonds and a gain on retirement):

Bonds payable..............	Maturity value	
Discount on bonds payable		Balance
Cash		Amount paid
Gain on retirement of bonds payable...		Excess

Summary Problem 11-1

West Virginia Power Company has 8%, 10-year bonds payable that mature on June 30, 2023. The bonds are issued on June 30, 2013, and West Virginia Power pays interest each June 30 and December 31.

Requirements

1. Will the bonds be issued at face value, at a premium, or at a discount if the market interest rate on the date of issuance is 7%? If the market interest rate is 10%?
2. West Virginia Power issued $100,000 of the bonds at 87.548. Round all calculations to the nearest dollar.
   a. Record issuance of the bonds on June 30, 2013.
   b. Record the payment of interest and amortization of the discount on December 31, 2013. Use the straight-line amortization method.
   c. Compute the bonds' carrying amount at December 31, 2013.
   d. Record the payment of interest and amortization of discount on June 30, 2014.

Solution

Requirement 1

Market Interest Rate	Bond Price for an 8% Bond
7%	Premium
10%	Discount

Requirement 2

	2013			
a.	Jun 30	Cash ($100,000 × 0.87548) (A+)	87,548	
		Discount on bonds payable (CL+)	12,452	
		Bonds payable (L+)		100,000
		Issued bonds at a discount.		
b.	Dec 31	Interest expense (E+)	4,623	
		Cash ($100,000 × 0.08 × 6/12) (A–)		4,000
		Discount on bonds payable ($12,452 × 1/10 yrs. × 6/12) (CL–)		623
		Paid semiannual interest and amortized discount.		
c.		Bond carrying amount at Dec 31, 2013:		
		$88,171 [$100,000 – ($12,452 – $623)]		
	2014			
d.	Jun 30	Interest expense (E+)	4,623	
		Cash ($100,000 × 0.08 × 6/12) (A–)		4,000
		Discount on bonds payable ($12,452 × 1/10 yrs. × 6/12) (CL–)		623
		Paid semiannual interest and amortized discount.		

Review *Long-Term Liabilities, Bonds Payable, and Classification of Liabilities on the Balance Sheet*

● Accounting Vocabulary

Adjunct Account (p. 544)
An account that is directly related to another account. Adjunct accounts have the same normal balance and are reported together on the balance sheet.

Amortization Schedule (p. 532)
A schedule that details each loan payment's allocation between principal and interest.

Bond Discount (p. 537)
Excess of a bond's maturity value over its issue price. Also called a **discount (on a bond)**.

Bond Premium (p. 537)
Excess of a bond's issue price over its maturity value. Also called a **premium**.

Bonds Payable (p. 535)
Groups of notes payable issued to multiple lenders called bondholders, usually in increments of $1,000 per bond.

Callable Bonds (p. 577)
Bonds that the issuer may call and pay off at a specified price whenever the issuer wants.

Carrying Amount of Bonds (p. 541)
Bond maturity value *minus* the discount account current balance or *plus* the premium account current balance.

Debentures (p. 536)
Unsecured bonds backed only by the goodwill of the bond issuer.

Discount (on a Bond) (p. 537)
Excess of a bond's maturity value over its issue price. Also called a **bond discount**.

Effective Interest Method (p. 569)
Method of amortizing bond premium or discount that uses the present-value concepts covered in Appendix 11A.

Effective Interest Rate (p. 538)
Interest rate that investors demand in order to loan their money. Also called the **market interest rate**.

Face Value (p. 537)
The amount a borrower must pay back to the bondholders on the maturity date. Also called **par value, principal amount**, or **maturity value**.

Market Interest Rate (p. 538)
Interest rate that investors demand in order to loan their money. Also called the **effective interest rate**.

Mortgage Payable (p. 532)
Long-term debts that are backed with a security interest in specific property. The mortgage will state that the borrower promises to transfer the legal title to specific assets if the mortgage isn't paid on schedule.

Par Value (p. 537)
The amount a borrower must pay back to the bondholders on the maturity date. Also called **face value, principal amount**, or **maturity value**.

Premium (p. 537)
Excess of a bond's issue price over its maturity value. Also called **bond premium**.

Present Value (p. 538)
Amount a person would invest now to receive a greater amount in the future.

Secured Bonds (p. 536)
Bonds that give bondholders the right to take specified assets of the issuer if the issuer fails to pay principal or interest.

Serial Bonds (p. 536)
Bonds that mature in installments at regular intervals.

Stated Interest Rate (p. 536)
Interest rate that determines the amount of cash interest the borrower pays and the investor receives each year.

Term Bonds (p. 536)
Bonds that all mature at the same time.

Time Value of Money (p. 538)
Recognition that money earns income over time.

● Destination: Student Success

Student Success Tips

The following are hints on some common trouble areas for students in this chapter:

- Keep in mind that long-term is defined as more than one year or the operating cycle, whichever is longer.

- Recall the formula for interest is Principal × Rate × Time. Interest accrues as time passes on the note.

- Recall the long-term portion of long-term notes is only the portion of principal that is due in one year or longer.

- Recall part of each mortgage payment is principal and part is interest.

Getting Help

If there's a learning objective from the chapter you aren't confident about, try using one or more of the following resources:

- Review the Decision Guidelines in the chapter.

- Review Summary Problem 11-1 in the chapter to reinforce your understanding of bonds payable.

- Practice additional exercises or problems at the end of Chapter 11 that cover the specific learning objective that is challenging you.

- Watch the white board videos for Chapter 11, located at myaccountinglab.com under the Chapter Resources button.

● Destination: Student Success *(Continued)*

Student Success Tips

- Remember that bond prices are stated in terms of 100. So a bond issue price of 101 really means 101% of maturity value.

- If bonds are issued at a discount, interest expense is larger than the cash paid to bondholders. If bonds are issued at a premium, interest expense is less than the cash paid to bondholders.

Getting Help

- Go to myaccountinglab.com and select the Study Plan button. Choose Chapter 11 and work the questions covering that specific learning objective until you've mastered it.

- Work the Chapter 11 pre/post tests in myaccountinglab.com.

- Visit the learning resource center on your campus for tutoring.

● Quick Check

1. A five-year, $100,000, 6% note payable was issued on December 31, 2010. The note requires principal payments of $20,000 plus interest due each year beginning December 31, 2011. On December 31, 2012, immediately after the note payment, the balance sheet would show
   a. $60,000 in Long-term notes payable.
   b. $6,000 in Interest payable.
   c. $20,000 in Current portion of long-term notes payable and $6,000 in Interest payable.
   d. $40,000 in Long-term notes payable.

2. Sassy's trial balance shows $200,000 face value of bonds with a discount balance of $2,000. The bonds mature in 10 years. How will the bonds be presented on the balance sheet?
   a. Bonds payable $198,000 (net of $2,000 discount) will be listed as a long-term liability.
   b. Bonds payable $200,000 will be listed as a long-term liability. A $2,000 discount on bonds payable will be listed as a contra current liability.
   c. Bonds payable $200,000 will be listed as a long-term liability.
   d. Bonds payable $200,000 will be listed as a long-term liability. A $2,000 discount on bonds payable will be listed as a current liability.

3. Bonds payable with face value of $400,000 and term of 10 years were issued on January 1, 2012, for $410,000. On the maturity date, what amount will the company pay to bondholders?
   a. $400,000
   b. $410,000
   c. $390,000
   d. $10,000

4. Patterson Company issued $200,000 of 4% serial bonds at face value on December 31, 2012. Half of the bonds mature January 1, 2015, while the other half of the bonds mature January 1, 2020. On December 31, 2014, the balance sheet will show which of the following?
   a. Bonds payable of $200,000 will be listed as a long-term liability.
   b. Bonds payable of $100,000 will be listed as a long-term liability. Bonds payable of $100,000 will be listed as a current liability.
   c. Bonds payable of $200,000 will be listed as a current liability.
   d. Bonds payable of $208,000 will be listed as a long-term liability.

Experience the Power of Practice!

As denoted by the logo, all of these questions, as well as additional practice materials, can be found in

MyAccountingLab.

Please visit myaccountinglab.com

5. Which of the following is the correct journal entry to record the issuance of a $100,000 face value bond at 95?

a.

Cash	100,000	
Discount on bonds payable		5,000
Bonds payable		95,000

b.

Cash	95,000	
Bonds payable		95,000

c.

Bonds payable	95,000	
Cash		95,000

d.

Cash	95,000	
Discount on bonds payable	5,000	
Bonds payable		100,000

6. A $200,000 bond priced at 101.5 can be bought or sold for

a. $200,000 plus interest.

b. $203,000.

c. $3,000.

d. $197,000.

7. Flipco signed a 10-year note payable on January 1, 2014, of $800,000. The note requires annual principal payments each December 31 of $80,000 plus interest at 5%. The entry to record the annual payment on December 31, 2015 includes

a. a debit to Interest expense for $36,000.

b. a debit to Interest expense for $40,000.

c. a credit to Long-term notes payable for $80,000.

d. a credit to Cash of $120,000.

8. Daniels's bonds payable carry a stated interest rate of 5%, and the market rate of interest is 7%. The price of the Daniels bonds will be at

a. par value.

b. a premium.

c. maturity value.

d. a discount.

9. Alan Smith Antiques issued its 7%, 20-year bonds payable at a price of $846,720 (maturity value is $900,000). The company uses the straight-line amortization method for the bonds. Interest expense for each year is

a. $65,664.

b. $60,336.

c. $63,000.

d. $59,270.

10. Nicholas Smith Fitness Gym has $700,000 of 20-year bonds payable outstanding. These bonds had a discount of $56,000 at issuance, which was 10 years ago. The company uses the straight-line amortization method. The carrying amount of these bonds payable is

a. $672,000.

b. $644,000.

c. $700,000.

d. $728,000.

Answers are given after Apply Your Knowledge (p. 564).

Assess Your Progress

● Short Exercises

S11-1 **①** **Accounting for a long-term note payable [10-15 min]**

On January 1, 2014, LeMay-Finn signed a $200,000, five-year, 6% note. The loan required LeMay-Finn to make payments on December 31 of $40,000 principal plus interest.

Requirements

1. Journalize the issuance of the note on January 1, 2014.
2. Journalize the reclassification of the current portion of the note payable.
3. Journalize the first note payment on December 31, 2014.

S11-2 **①** **Accounting for mortgages payable [10–20 min]**

Ethan purchased a building valued at $250,000 and land valued at $50,000 on January 1, 2013. Ethan paid $20,000 cash and signed a 20-year, 6% mortgage payable for the balance. The amortization schedule shows that Ethan will pay $7,475 in principal the first year. Ethan plans on adjusting the current portion of the mortgage at year-end each December 31.

Requirements

1. Journalize the January 1, 2013 purchase.
2. Journalize the reclassification of the current portion of the mortgage.
3. Journalize the first monthly payment of $2,006 on January 31, 2013. (Round to the nearest dollar.).

S11-3 **②** **Determining bond prices [5 min]**

Bond prices depend on the market rate of interest, stated rate of interest, and time.

Requirement

1. Determine whether the following bonds payable will be issued at maturity value, at a premium, or at a discount:

    a. The market interest rate is 6%. Boise issues bonds payable with a stated rate of 5 3/4%.
    b. Dallas issued 8% bonds payable when the market rate was 7 1/4%.
    c. Cleveland's Cables issued 7% bonds when the market interest rate was 7%.
    d. Atlanta's Travel issued bonds payable that pay stated interest of 7 1/2%. At issuance, the market interest rate was 9 1/4%.

S11-4 **②** **Pricing bonds [5 min]**

Bond prices depend on the market rate of interest, stated rate of interest, and time.

Requirements

1. Compute the price of the following 7% bonds of United Telecom.

    a. $500,000 issued at 76.75.
    b. $500,000 issued at 104.75.
    c. $500,000 issued at 95.75.
    d. $500,000 issued at 104.25.

2. Which bond will United Telecom have to pay the most to retire the bond at maturity? Explain your answer.

S11-5 ❸ **Journalizing bond transactions [10 min]**

Vernon issued a $110,000, 6.5%, 15-year bond payable.

Requirement

1. Journalize the following transactions for Vernon and include an explanation for each entry:

    a. Issuance of the bond payable at par on January 1, 2012.
    b. Payment of semiannual cash interest on July 1, 2012.
    c. Payment of the bond payable at maturity. (Give the date.)

S11-6 ❸ **Determining bond amounts [5 min]**

Superb Drive-Ins borrowed money by issuing $6,000,000 of 4% bonds payable at 97.5.

Requirements

1. How much cash did Superb receive when it issued the bonds payable?
2. How much must Superb pay back at maturity?
3. How much cash interest will Superb pay each six months?

S11-7 ❸ **Journalizing bond transactions [10 min]**

Origin issued a $40,000, 5%, 10-year bond payable at a price of 90 on January 1, 2012.

Requirements

1. Journalize the issuance of the bond payable on January 1, 2012.
2. Journalize the payment of semiannual interest and amortization of the bond discount or premium on July 1, 2012, using the straight-line method to amortize the bond discount or premium.

S11-8 ❸ **Journalizing bond transactions [10 min]**

Worthington Mutual Insurance Company issued a $50,000, 5%, 10-year bond payable at a price of 108 on January 1, 2012.

Requirements

1. Journalize the issuance of the bond payable on January 1, 2012.
2. Journalize the payment of semiannual interest and amortization of the bond discount or premium on July 1, 2012, using the straight-line method to amortize the bond discount or premium.

S11-9 ❸ **Journalizing bond transactions [10 min]**

Clarity Communication issued $42,000 of 8%, 10-year bonds payable on October 1, 2012, at par value. Clarity's accounting year ends on December 31.

Requirements

1. Journalize the issuance of the bonds on October 1, 2012.
2. Journalize the accrual of interest expense on December 31, 2012.
3. Journalize the payment of the first semiannual interest amount on April 1, 2013.

S11-10 ③ **Journalizing bond transactions—issuance between interest payment dates [10 min]**

Silk Realty issued $300,000 of 8%, 10-year bonds payable at par value on May 1, 2012, four months after the bond's original issue date of January 1, 2012.

Requirements

1. Journalize the issuance of the bonds payable on May 1, 2012.
2. Journalize the payment of the first semiannual interest amount on July 1, 2012.

S11-11 ④ **Preparing the liabilities section of the balance sheet [5 min]**

Luxury Suites Hotels includes the following selected accounts in its general ledger at December 31, 2012:

Note payable, long-term	$ 125,000	Accounts payable	$ 34,000
Bonds payable	325,000	Discount on bonds payable	9,750
Interest payable (due next year)	1,200	Salary payable	2,800
Estimated warranty payable	1,800	Sales tax payable	800

Requirement

1. Prepare the liabilities section of Luxury Suites' balance sheet at December 31, 2012. Report a total for current liabilities.

S11-12 ④ **Preparing the liabilities section of the balance sheet [10–15 min]**

Blue Socks' account balances at June 30, 2014, include the following:

Data Table			
Cash	$ 138,000	Salary payable	$ 6,500
Long-term notes payable	117,000	Building, net of depreciation	780,000
Accounts payable	13,200	Interest payable (due next year)	2,400
Current portion of long-term notes payable	8,000	FICA taxes payable	1,900
Blue, capital	500,000	Accounts receivable	145,000
Premium on bonds payable	12,000	Bonds payable (Maturity date 12/31/2020)	400,000
Sales taxes payable	4,000	Blue, drawing	2,000

Requirement

1. Prepare the liabilities section of Blue Socks' balance sheet at June 30, 2014.

● Exercises

E11-13 ① **Accounting for long-term note payable transactions [15–20 min]**

MyAccountingLab

Consider the following note payable transactions of Tube Video Productions.

2014	
Mar 1	Purchased equipment costing $80,000 by issuing an eight-year, 12% note payable. The note requires annual principal payments of $10,000 plus interest each March 1.
Mar 1	Recorded current portion of the note in the journal.
Dec 31	Accrued interest on the note payable.
2015	
Mar 1	Paid the first installment on the note.
Dec 31	Accrued interest on the note payable.

Requirements

1. Journalize the transactions for the company.
2. Considering the given transactions only, what are Tube Video Productions' total liabilities on December 31, 2015?

E11-14 ➊ **Recording mortgage payable entries from an amortization schedule [10–15 min]**

Kaiser Company's partial amortization schedule follows:

Payment #	Date	Payment	Interest Expense (Principal × 6% × 1/12)	Principal	Mortgage Balance
Loan	1/1/2013				500,000.00
1	1/31/2013	3,597.30	2,500.00	1,097.30	498,902.70
2	2/28/2013	3,597.30	2,494.51	1,102.79	497,799.91
3	3/31/2013	3,597.30	2,489.00	1,108.30	496,691.61
4	4/30/2013	3,597.30	2,483.46	1,113.84	495,577.77
5	5/31/2013	3,597.30	2,477.89	1,119.41	494,458.36
6	6/30/2013	3,597.30	2,472.29	1,125.01	493,333.35
7	7/31/2013	3,597.30	2,466.67	1,130.63	492,202.72
8	8/31/2013	3,597.30	2,461.01	1,136.29	491,066.43
9	9/30/2013	3,597.30	2,455.33	1,141.97	489,924.46
10	10/31/2013	3,597.30	2,449.62	1,147.68	488,776.78
11	11/30/2013	3,597.30	2,443.88	1,153.42	487,623.36
12	12/31/2013	3,597.30	2,438.12	1,159.18	486,464.18
	2013 totals	43,167.60	29,631.78	13,535.82	

Requirements

1. Journalize the note issuance and the reclassification of the current portion on January 1, 2013 (explanations are not required).
2. Journalize the first payment on January 31, 2013 (do not round).
3. Journalize the second payment on February 28, 2013 (do not round).

E11-15 ➋ **Determining bond prices [5–10 min]**

Adams is planning to issue $520,000 of 6%, five-year bonds payable to borrow for a major expansion. The owner, Shane Adams, asks your advice on some related matters.

Requirements

1. Answer the following questions:

   a. At what type of bond price will Adams have total interest expense equal to the cash interest payments?
   b. Under which type of bond price will Adams' total interest expense be greater than the cash interest payments?
   c. If the market interest rate is 7%, what type of bond price can Adams expect for the bonds?

2. Compute the price of the bonds if the bonds sell for 93.
3. How much will Adams pay in interest each year? How much will Adams' interest expense be for the first year, assuming the straight-line method is used?

E11-16 ➌ **Journalizing bond issuance and interest payments [10 min]**

On June 30, Dogwood Limited issues 8%, 20-year bonds payable with a maturity value of $130,000. The bonds sell at 94 and pay interest on June 30 and December 31. Dogwood amortizes bond discount by the straight-line method.

Requirements

1. Journalize the issuance of the bonds on June 30.
2. Journalize the semiannual interest payment and amortization of bond discount on December 31.

E11-17   ❸ Journalizing bond issuance and interest payments [10-20 min]

On May 1, 2012, Noah Unlimited issues 9%, 20-year bonds payable with a maturity value of $200,000. The bonds sell at 103 and pay interest on May 1 and November 1. Noah Unlimited amortizes bond premium by the straight-line method.

Requirements

1. Journalize the issuance of the bonds on May 1, 2012.
2. Journalize the semiannual interest payment and amortization of bond premium on November 1, 2012.
3. Journalize the interest accrual needed on December 31, 2012.
4. Journalize the interest payment on May 1, 2013.

E11-18   ❸ Journalizing bond transactions [15–20 min]

Clark issued $50,000 of 10-year, 9% bonds payable on January 1, 2012. Clark pays interest each January 1 and July 1 and amortizes discount or premium by the straight-line method. The company can issue its bonds payable under various conditions.

Requirements

1. Journalize Clark's issuance of the bonds and first semiannual interest payment assuming the bonds were issued at par value. Explanations are not required.
2. Journalize Clark's issuance of the bonds and first semiannual interest payment assuming the bonds were issued at a price of 95. Explanations are not required.
3. Journalize Clark's issuance of the bonds and first semiannual interest payment assuming the bonds were issued at a price of 106. Explanations are not required.
4. Which bond price results in the most interest expense for Clark? Explain in detail.

E11-19   ❸ Journalizing bond transactions—year-end interest accrual [10 min]

Filmore Homebuilders issued $250,000 of 8%, 10-year bonds at par on September 30, 2012. Filmore pays semiannual interest on March 31 and September 30.

Requirements

1. Journalize the issuance of the bonds payable on September 30, 2012.
2. Journalize the accrual of interest on December 31, 2012.
3. Journalize the payment of semiannual interest on March 31, 2013.

Note: Exercise 11-20 should be used only after completing Exercise 11-19.

E11-20   ❹ Reporting current and long-term liabilities [5–15 min]

Review your responses to Exercise 11-19. On March 31, 2013, Filmore's accountant states that the company owes $15,000 in employee salaries and $17,000 in Accounts payable. Further, the company has Unearned rent revenue of $12,000 representing rent through September 30, 2013. Finally, Filmore has a mortgage on its office building of $140,000, of which $10,000 is due in the next year.

Requirement

1. Report Filmore Homebuilders' liabilities on its classified balance sheet as of March 31, 2013. List the liabilities in descending order (largest to smallest), and calculate subtotals for each classification.

E11-21   ❹ Reporting current and long-term liabilities [5–15 min]

Medical Dispensary borrowed $390,000 on January 2, 2012, by issuing a 10% serial bond payable that must be paid in three equal annual installments plus interest for the year. The first payment of principal and interest comes due January 2, 2013.

Requirement

1. Insert the appropriate amounts to show how Medical Dispensary should report its current and long-term liabilities.

	December 31		
	2012	2013	2014
Current liabilities:			
Bonds payable..	$_____	$_____	$_____
Interest payable...	_____	_____	_____
Long–term liabilities:			
Bonds payable..	_____	_____	_____

E11-22 ❹ **Reporting liabilities [10 min]**

At December 31, MediSharp Precision Instruments owes $50,000 on accounts payable, salary payable of $16,000, and income tax payable of $8,000. MediSharp also has $280,000 of bonds payable that were issued at face value that require payment of a $35,000 installment next year and the remainder in later years. The bonds payable require an annual interest payment of $4,000, and MediSharp still owes this interest for the current year.

Requirement

1. Report MediSharp's liabilities on its classified balance sheet. List the current liabilities in descending order (largest first, and so on), and show the total of current liabilities.

● Problems (Group A)

P11-23A ❶❹ **Journalizing liability transactions and reporting them on the balance sheet [30–40 min]**

The following transactions of Emergency Pharmacies occurred during 2014 and 2015:

2014

Mar	1	Borrowed $360,000 from Lessburg Bank. The six-year, 10% note requires payments due annually, on March 1. Each payment consists of $60,000 principal plus one year's interest.
Mar	1	Reclassified current portion of Lessburg Bank note.
Dec	1	Mortgaged the warehouse for $200,000 cash with Saputo Bank. The mortgage requires monthly payments of $4,000. The interest rate on the note is 9% and accrues monthly. The first payment is due on January 1, 2015.
Dec	1	Reclassified current portion of the Saputo Bank note for the principal due in 2015 of $31,505.
Dec	31	Recorded interest accrued on the Saputo Bank note.
Dec	31	Recorded interest accrued on the Lessburg Bank note.

2015

Jan	1	Paid Saputo Bank monthly mortgage payment.
Feb	1	Paid Saputo Bank monthly mortgage payment.
Mar	1	Paid Saputo Bank monthly mortgage payment.
Mar	1	Paid first installment on note due to Lessburg Bank.

Requirements

1. Journalize the transactions in Emergency Pharmacies' general journal. Round all answers to the nearest dollar. Explanations are not required.

2. Assume Emergency Pharmacies only adjusts the current portion of long-term notes on the last day of each year, December 31. Prepare the liabilities section of the balance sheet for Emergency Pharmacies on March 1, 2015.

P11-24A ② ③ **Analyzing and journalizing bond transactions [30–40 min]**

On March 1, 2012, Mechanics Credit Union (MCU) issued 7%, 20-year bonds payable with maturity value of $300,000. The bonds pay interest on February 28 and August 31. MCU amortizes bond premium and discount by the straight-line method.

Requirements

1. If the market interest rate is 6% when MCU issues its bonds, will the bonds be priced at maturity (par) value, at a premium, or at a discount? Explain.

2. If the market interest rate is 8% when MCU issues its bonds, will the bonds be priced at par, at a premium, or at a discount? Explain.

3. The issue price of the bonds is 95. Journalize the following bond transactions:

   a. Issuance of the bonds on March 1, 2012.
   b. Payment of interest and amortization of discount on August 31, 2012.
   c. Accrual of interest and amortization of discount on December 31, 2012.
   d. Payment of interest and amortization of discount on February 28, 2013.

P11-25A ② ③ ④ **Analyzing, journalizing, and reporting bond transactions [30 min]**

Billy's Hamburgers issued 5%, 10-year bonds payable at 90 on December 31, 2010. At December 31, 2012, Billy reported the bonds payable as follows:

Long-term debt:				
Bonds payable ...	$	400,000		
Less: Discount ...		32,000	$	368,000

Billy uses the straight-line amortization method and pays semiannual interest each June 30 and December 31.

Requirements

1. Answer the following questions about Billy's bonds payable:

   a. What is the maturity value of the bonds?
   b. What is the carrying amount of the bonds at December 31, 2012?
   c. What is the annual cash interest payment on the bonds?
   d. How much interest expense should the company record each year?

2. Record the June 30, 2013, semiannual interest payment and amortization of discount.

3. What will be the carrying amount of the bonds at December 31, 2013?

P11-26A ③ ④ **Journalizing and reporting bond transactions [20–25 min]**

The owner of Delta Health Spa authorizes the issuance of $600,000 of 5%, 10-year bonds payable. The semiannual interest dates are May 31 and November 30. The bonds are issued on July 31, 2012, at par plus accrued interest.

Requirements

1. Journalize the following transactions (Round your answers to the nearest whole dollar.):

   a. Issuance of the bonds on July 31, 2012.
   b. Payment of interest on November 30, 2012.
   c. Accrual of interest on December 31, 2012.
   d. Payment of interest on May 31, 2013.

2. Report interest payable and bonds payable as they would appear on the Delta balance sheet at December 31, 2012.

P11-27A ④ **Report liabilities on the balance sheet [10–15 min]**

The accounting records of Route Maker Wireless include the following:

Accounts payable	$ 76,000	Salary payable	$ 9,500
Mortgage note payable, long-term	80,000	Bonds payable, current installment	30,000
Interest payable	19,000	Premium on all bonds payable	
Bonds payable, long-term	164,000	(all long-term)	11,000
Rory, capital	175,000	Unearned service revenue	3,000

Requirement

1. Report these liabilities on the Route Maker Wireless balance sheet, including headings and totals for current liabilities and long-term liabilities.

• Problems (Group B)

MyAccountingLab

P11-28B ① ④ **Journalizing liability transactions and reporting them on the balance sheet [30–40 min]**

The following transactions of Johnson Pharmacies occurred during 2014 and 2015:

2014		
Mar	1	Borrowed $100,000 from Naples Bank. The five-year, 15% note requires payments due annually, on March 1. Each payment consists of $20,000 principal plus one year's interest.
Mar	1	Reclassified current portion of the Naples Bank note.
Dec	1	Mortgaged the warehouse for $400,000 cash with Sage Bank. The mortgage requires monthly payments of $8,000. The interest rate on the note is 7% and accrues monthly. The first payment is due on January 1, 2015.
Dec	1	Reclassified current portion of the Sage Bank note for the principal due in 2015 of $70,634.
Dec	31	Recorded interest accrued on the Sage Bank note.
Dec	31	Recorded interest accrued on the Naples Bank note.
2015		
Jan	1	Paid Sage Bank monthly mortgage payment.
Feb	1	Paid Sage Bank monthly mortgage payment.
Mar	1	Paid Sage Bank monthly mortgage payment.
Mar	1	Paid first installment on note due to Naples Bank.

Requirement

1. Journalize the transactions in Johnson Pharmacies' general journal. Round all answers to the nearest dollar. Explanations are not required.

2. Assume Johnson Pharmacies only adjusts the current portion of long-term notes on the last day of each year, December 31. Prepare the liabilities section of the balance sheet for Johnson Pharmacies on March 1, 2015.

P11-29B ② ③ **Analyzing and journalizing bond transactions [30–40 min]**

On March 1, 2012, Professors Credit Union (PCU) issued 6%, 20-year bonds payable with maturity value of $500,000. The bonds pay interest on February 28 and August 31. PCU amortizes bond premium and discount by the straight-line method.

Requirements

1. If the market interest rate is 5% when PCU issues its bonds, will the bonds be priced at maturity (par) value, at a premium, or at a discount? Explain.

2. If the market interest rate is 7% when PCU issues its bonds, will the bonds be priced at par, at a premium, or at a discount? Explain.

3. The issue price of the bonds is 97. Journalize the following bond transactions:

   a. Issuance of the bonds on March 1, 2012.
   b. Payment of interest and amortization of discount on August 31, 2012.
   c. Accrual of interest and amortization of discount on December 31, 2012.
   d. Payment of interest and amortization of discount on February 28, 2013.

P11-30B ② ③ ④ **Analyzing, journalizing, and reporting bond transactions [30 min]**
Danny's Hamburgers issued 9%, 10-year bonds payable at 85 on December 31, 2010. At December 31, 2012, Danny reported the bonds payable as follows:

Long-term debt:		
Bonds payable . . .	$ 700,000	
Less: Discount . . .	84,000	$ 616,000

Danny uses the straight-line amortization method and pays semiannual interest each June 30 and December 31.

Requirements

1. Answer the following questions about Danny's bonds payable:

   a. What is the maturity value of the bonds?
   b. What is the carrying amount of the bonds at December 31, 2012?
   c. What is the annual cash interest payment on the bonds?
   d. How much interest expense should the company record each year?

2. Record the June 30, 2013, semiannual interest payment and amortization of discount.
3. What will be the carrying amount of the bonds at December 31, 2013?

P11-31B ② ③ ④ **Journalizing and reporting bond transactions [20–25 min]**
The owner of Theta Health Spa authorizes the issuance of $450,000 of 10%, 10-year bonds payable. The semiannual interest dates are May 31 and November 30. The bonds are issued on July 31, 2012, at par plus accrued interest.

Requirements

1. Journalize the following transactions:

   a. Issuance of the bonds on July 31, 2012.
   b. Payment of interest on November 30, 2012.
   c. Accrual of interest on December 31, 2012.
   d. Payment of interest on May 31, 2013.

2. Report interest payable and bonds payable as they would appear on the Theta balance sheet at December 31, 2012.

P11-32B ④ **Reporting liabilities on the balance sheet. [10–15 min]**
The accounting records of Compass Point Wireless include the following:

Accounts payable	$ 75,000	Salary payable	$ 7,500
Mortgage note payable, long-term	72,000	Bonds payable, current installment	17,000
Interest payable	17,000	Premium on all bonds payable	
Bonds payable, long-term	163,000	(all long-term)	12,000
West, capital	170,000	Unearned service revenue	3,200

Requirement

1. Report these liabilities on the Compass Point Wireless balance sheet, including headings and totals for current liabilities and long-term liabilities.

● Continuing Exercise

E11-33 **1** **4** **Journalize transactions for long-term notes payable and reporting liabilities on the balance sheet. [15–20 min]**
This exercise continues the Lawlor Lawn Service situation from Exercise 10-23 of Chapter 10. Assume that Lawlor also owes $120,000 on a 10-year, 6% mortgage that was issued on August 1, 2012. Monthly payments of $1,000 of principal plus interest will be made on the first day of each month, beginning on September 1, 2012.

Requirements

1. Journalize the entry for the note issuance on August 1, 2012; the reclassification of the current portion of the note payable; the first payment on September 1, 2012; and any adjusting entries needed at September 30, 2012.

2. Considering only this note, prepare the liabilities section of the balance sheet for Lawlor Lawn Service as of September 30, 2012.

3. Journalize the October 1, 2012 note payment.

4. Beginning in Chapter 12, E12-44, Lawlor incorporates by issuing 170 shares of common stock to Lawlor in exchange for the balance in Lawlor, capital.

● Continuing Problem

P11-34 **2** **3** **Describe bonds and journalize transactions for bonds payable using the straight-line method. [20–30 min]**
This problem continues the Draper Consulting situation from Problem 10-24 of Chapter 10. Draper Consulting is considering raising additional capital. Draper plans to raise the capital by issuing $400,000 of 8%, seven-year bonds on March 1, 2012. The bonds pay interest semiannually on March 1 and September 1. On March 1, 2012, the market rate of interest required by similar bonds by investors is 10%.

Requirements

1. Will Draper's bonds issue at par, a premium, or a discount?

2. Calculate and record the cash received on the bond issue date.

3. Journalize the first interest payment on September 1 and amortize the premium or discount using the straight-line interest method.

4. Journalize the entry required, if any, on December 31 related to the bonds.

5. Beginning in Chapter 12, P12-45, Draper incorporates by issuing 100 shares of common stock to Draper in exchange for the balance in Draper, capital.

Apply Your Knowledge

● Decision Case 11-1

The following questions are not related.

Requirements

1. Duncan Brooks needs to borrow $500,000 to open new stores. Brooks can borrow $500,000 by issuing 5%, 10-year bonds at a price of 96. How much will Brooks actually receive in cash under this arrangement? How much must Brooks pay back at maturity? How will Brooks account for the difference between the cash received on the issue date and the amount paid back?

2. Brooks prefers to borrow for longer periods when interest rates are low and for shorter periods when interest rates are high. Why is this a good business strategy?

● Ethical Issue 11-1

Raffie's Kids, a non-profit organization that provides aid to victims of domestic violence, low-income families, and special-needs children has a 30-year, 5% mortgage on the existing building. The mortgage requires monthly payments of $3,000. Raffie's bookkeeper is preparing financial statements for the board and in doing so, lists the mortgage balance of $287,000 under current liabilities because the board hopes to be able to pay the mortgage off in full next year. $20,000 of the mortgage principal will be paid next year if Raffie's pays according to the mortgage agreement.

Requirement

1. The board members call you, their trusted CPA, to advise them on how Raffie's Kids should report the mortgage on its balance sheet. Provide your recommendation and discuss the reason for your recommendation.

● Fraud Case 11-1

Bill and Edna had been married two years, and had just reached the point where they had enough savings to start investing. Bill's uncle Dave told them that he had recently inherited some very rare railroad bonds from his grandmother's estate. He wanted to help Bill and Edna get a start in the world, and would sell them 50 of the bonds at $100 each. The bonds were dated 1873, beautifully engraved, showing a face value of $1,000 each. Uncle Dave pointed out that "United States of America" was printed prominently at the top, and that the U.S. government had established a "sinking fund" to retire the old railroad bonds. All Bill and Edna needed to do was hold on to them until the government contacted them, and they would eventually get the full $1,000 for each bond. Bill and Edna were overjoyed.....until a year later when they saw the exact same bonds for sale at a coin and stamp shop priced as "collectors items" for $9.95 each!

Requirements

1. If a company goes bankrupt, what happens to the bonds they issued, and the investors who bought the bonds?
2. When investing in bonds, how do you tell if it is a legitimate transaction?
3. Is there a way to determine the relative risk of corporate bonds?

● Financial Statement Case 11-1

Details about a company's liabilities appear in a number of places in the annual report. Use **Amazon.com**'s financial statements, including Notes 1 and 5, to answer the following questions. **Amazon**'s financial statements are in Appendix A at the end of this book.

Requirements

1. How much was **Amazon**'s long-term debt at December 31, 2009? Of this amount, how much was due within one year? How much was payable beyond one year in the future?
2. Journalize in a single entry **Amazon**'s interest expense for 2009. **Amazon** paid cash of $32 million for interest.

• Team Project 11-1

Each member of the team should select a large corporation and go to its Web site. Surf around until you find the company's balance sheet. Often the appropriate tab is labeled as one of the following:

- Investor Relations
- About the Company
- Financial Reports
- 10-K Report

From the company's balance sheet, scroll down until you find the liabilities.

Requirements

1. List all the company's liabilities—both current and long-term—along with each amount.
2. Read the company's notes to the financial statements and include any details that help you identify the amount of a liability.
3. Compute the company's current ratio and debt ratio.
4. Bring your findings to your team meeting, compare your results with those of your team members, and prepare either a written report or an oral report, as directed by your instructor.

• Communication Activity 11-1

In 50 words or fewer, explain why a bond would sell for more than the bond's maturity value on the bond issuance date.

Quick Check Answers

1. *d* 2. *a* 3. *a* 4. *b* 5. *d* 6. *b* 7. *a* 8. *d* 9. *a* 10. *a*

For online homework, exercises, and problems that provide you immediate feedback, please visit myaccountinglab.com.

Appendix 11A

The Time Value of Money: Present Value of a Bond and Effective-Interest Amortization

The term *time value of money* refers to the fact that money earns interest over time. Interest is the cost of using money. To borrowers, interest is the expense of using someone else's money. To lenders, interest is the revenue earned from lending. In this appendix, we focus on the borrower, who owes money on the bonds payable.

5 Use the time value of money: present value of a bond and effective-interest amortization

Present Value

Often a person knows a future amount, such as the maturity value of a bond, and needs to know the bond's present value. The present value of the bond measures its price and tells an investor how much to pay for the bond today.

Present Value of $1

Suppose an investment promises you $5,000 at the *end* of one year. How much would you pay *now* to acquire this investment? You would be willing to pay the present value of the $5,000 future amount.

Present value depends on three factors:

1. The amount to be received in the future
2. The time span between your investment and your future receipt
3. The interest rate

Computing a present value is called *discounting* because the present value is *always less* than the future value.

In our example, the future receipt is $5,000. The investment period is one year. Assume that you require an annual interest rate of 10% on your investment. You can compute the present value of $5,000 at 10% (0.10) for one year, as follows:

$$\frac{\text{Future value}}{(1 + \text{Interest rate})} = \frac{\$5,000}{1.10} = \$4,545$$

So, the present value of $5,000 to be received one year from now is $4,545.

The following diagram demonstrates the relationship between present value and future value.

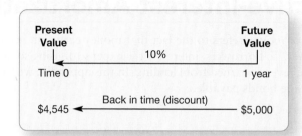

If the $5,000 is to be received two years from now, the calculation is as follows:

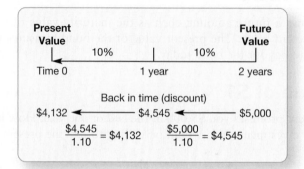

So, the present value of $5,000 to be received two years from now is $4,132.

Present-Value of $1

We have shown how to compute a present value. But that computation is burdensome for an investment that spans many years. Present-value tables ease our work. Let's reexamine our examples of present value by using Appendix B, Table B-1, Present Value of $1.

For the 10% investment for one year, we find the junction in the 10% column and across from 1 in the Period column. The figure 0.909 is computed as follows: 1/1.10 = 0.909. This work has been done for us and all the present values are given in the table. The heading in Appendix B, Table B-1 states Present Value of $1. To figure present value for $5,000, we multiply $5,000 by 0.909. The result is $4,545, which matches the result we obtained earlier.

For the two-year investment, we read down the 10% column and across the Period 2 row. We multiply 0.826 (computed as 0.909/1.10 = 0.826) by $5,000 and get $4,130, which confirms our earlier computation of $4,132 (the difference is due to rounding in the present-value table). Using Table B-1, we can compute the present value of any single future amount.

Present Value of Annuity of $1

Let's return to the investment example that provided a single future receipt ($5,000 at the end of two years). Annuity investments provide multiple receipts of an equal amount at equal time intervals.

Consider an investment that promises *annual* cash receipts of $10,000 to be received at the end of each of three years. Assume that you demand a 12% return on your investment. What is the investment's present value? The present value determines how much you would pay today to acquire the investment. The investment spans three periods, and you would pay the sum of three present values. The computation follows:

Year	Annual Cash Receipt	×	Present Value of $1 at 12% (Appendix B, Table B-1)	=	Present Value of Annual Cash Receipt
1	$10,000	×	0.893	=	$ 8,930
2	10,000	×	0.797	=	7,970
3	10,000	×	0.712	=	7,120
	Total present value of investment			=	$24,020

The present value of this annuity is $24,020. By paying $24,020 today, you will receive $10,000 at the end of each of the three years while earning 12% on your investment.

The example illustrates repetitive computations of the three future amounts using the Present Value of $1 table from Appendix B, Table B-1. One way to ease the computational burden is to add the three present values of $1 (0.893 + 0.797 + 0.712) and multiply their sum (2.402) by the annual cash receipt ($10,000) to obtain the present value of the annuity ($10,000 × 2.402 = $24,020).

An easier approach is to use a present value of an annuity table. Appendix B, Table B-2 shows the present value of an annuity of $1 to be received at the end of each period for a given number of periods.

The present value of a three-period annuity at 12% is 2.402 (the junction of the Period 3 row and the 12% column). So, $10,000 received annually at the end of each of three years, discounted at 12%, is $24,020 ($10,000 × 2.402), which is the present value.

Present Value of Bonds Payable

The present value of a bond—its market price—is the sum of

- the present value of the principal amount to be received at maturity, a single amount (present value of $1),
- *plus* the present value of the future stated interest amounts, an annuity because it occurs in equal amounts over equal time periods (present value of annuity of $1).

Discount Price

Let's compute the present value of the 9%, five-year bonds of Smart Touch. The maturity value of the bonds is $100,000 and they pay (9% × 6/12) or 4.5% stated interest semiannually. At issuance, the annual market interest rate is 10% (5% semiannually). Therefore, the market interest rate for each of the 10 semiannual periods is 5%. We use 5% to compute the present value (PV) of the maturity and the present value (PV) of the stated interest. The market price of these bonds is $96,149, computed as follows:

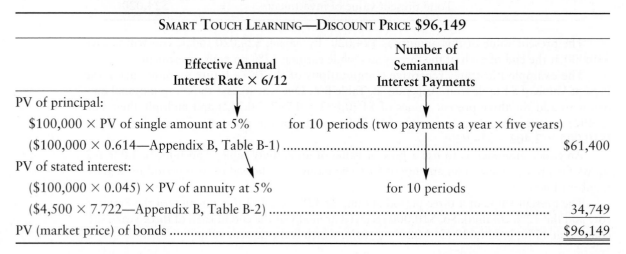

SMART TOUCH LEARNING—DISCOUNT PRICE $96,149		
	Effective Annual Interest Rate × 6/12	Number of Semiannual Interest Payments
PV of principal:		
$100,000 × PV of single amount at 5%	for 10 periods (two payments a year × five years)	
($100,000 × 0.614—Appendix B, Table B-1)		$61,400
PV of stated interest:		
($100,000 × 0.045) × PV of annuity at 5%	for 10 periods	
($4,500 × 7.722—Appendix B, Table B-2)		34,749
PV (market price) of bonds		$96,149

The market price of the Smart Touch bonds shows a discount because the stated interest rate on the bonds (9%) is less than the market interest rate (10%). We discuss these bonds in more detail in the next section of this appendix.

Premium Price

Let's consider a premium price for the Smart Touch bonds. Now suppose the market interest rate is 8% at issuance (4% for each of the 10 semiannual periods). We would compute the market price of these bonds as follows:

SMART TOUCH LEARNING—PREMIUM PRICE $104,100		
	Effective Annual Interest Rate × 6/12	Number of Semiannual Interest Payments
PV of principal:		
$100,000 × PV of single amount at 4%	for 10 periods	$ 67,600
($100,000 × 0.676—Appendix B, Table B-1)		
PV of stated interest:		
($100,000 × 0.045) × PV of annuity at 4%	for 10 periods	
($4,500 × 8.111—Appendix B, Table B-2)		36,500
PV (market price) of bonds		$104,100

The market price of the Smart Touch bonds shows a premium because the stated interest rate on the bonds (9%) is higher than the market interest rate (8%). We discuss accounting for these bonds in the next section.

Effective-Interest Method of Amortization

We began this chapter with straight-line amortization to introduce the concept of amortizing bonds. A more precise way of amortizing bonds is used in practice, and it is called the **effective-interest method**. This appendix explains the present value concepts used to amortize bond discounts and premiums using the effective-interest method.

Generally accepted accounting principles require that interest expense be measured using the *effective-interest method* unless the straight-line amounts are similar. In that case, either method is permitted. Total interest expense over the life of the bonds is the same under both methods; however, interest expense each year is different between the two methods. Let's look at how the effective-interest method works.

Effective-Interest Amortization for a Bond Discount

Assume that Smart Touch issues $100,000 of 9% bonds at a time when the market rate of interest is 10%. These bonds mature in five years and pay interest semiannually, so there are 10 semi-annual interest payments. As we just saw, the issue price of the bonds is $96,149, and the discount on these bonds is $3,851 ($100,000 – $96,149). Exhibit 11A-1 shows how to measure interest expense by the effective-interest method. (You will need an amortization table to account for bonds by the effective-interest method.)

The *accounts* debited and credited under the effective-interest method and the straight-line method are the same. Only the *amounts* differ.

Exhibit 11A-1 gives the amounts for all the bond transactions of Smart Touch. Begin with the issuance of the bonds payable on January 1, 2013, and the first interest payment on June 30. Entries follow, using amounts from the respective lines of Exhibit 11A-1.

EXHIBIT 11A-1 | **Effective-Interest Amortization of a Bond Discount**

PANEL A—Bond Data

Maturity value—$100,000

Stated interest rate—9%

Interest paid—semiannually, $4,500 ($100,000 × .09 × 6/12)

Market interest rate at time of issue—10% annually

Issue price—$96,149 on January 1, 2013

PANEL B—Amortization Table

	A	B	C	D	E
End of Semiannual Interest Period	Interest *Payment* (9% × 6/12) × Maturity Value	Interest *Expense* (10% × 6/12) × Bond Carrying Amount	Discount Amortization (B – A)	Discount Balance (D – C)	Bond Carrying Amount ($100,000 – D)
Jan 1, 2013				$3,851	$ 96,149
Jun 30, 2013	$4,500	$4,807	$307	3,544	96,456
Dec 31, 2013	4,500	4,823	323	3,221	96,779
Jun 30, 2014	4,500	4,839	339	2,882	97,118
Dec 31, 2014	4,500	4,856	356	2,526	97,474
Jun 30, 2015	4,500	4,874	374	2,152	97,848
Dec 31, 2015	4,500	4,892	392	1,760	98,240
Jun 30, 2016	4,500	4,912	412	1,348	98,652
Dec 31, 2016	4,500	4,933	433	915	99,085
Jun 30, 2017	4,500	4,954	454	461	99,539
Dec 31, 2017	4,500	4,961*	461	0	100,000

*Adjusted for effect of rounding.

Notes
- *Column A* The interest payments are constant.
- *Column B* The interest expense each period is the preceding bond carrying amount multiplied by the market interest rate.
- *Column C* The excess of interest expense (B) over interest payment (A) is the discount amortization.
- *Column D* The discount decreases by the amount of amortization for the period (C).
- *Column E* The bonds' carrying amount increases from $96,149 at issuance to $100,000 at maturity.

	2013			
	Jan 1	Cash (column E) (A+)	96,149	
		Discount on bonds payable (column D) (CL+)	3,851	
		Bonds payable (maturity value) (L+)		100,000
		Issued bonds at a discount.		

	2013			
	Jun 30	Interest expense (column B) (E+)	4,807	
		Discount on bonds payable (column C) (CL–)		307
		Cash (column A) (A–)		4,500
		Paid semiannual interest and amortized discount.		

Effective-Interest Amortization of a Bond Premium

Smart Touch may issue its bonds payable at a premium. Assume that Smart Touch issues $100,000 of five-year, 9% bonds when the market interest rate is 8%. The bonds' issue price is $104,100, and the premium is $4,100.

Exhibit 11A-2 provides the data for all the bond transactions of Smart Touch.

EXHIBIT 11A-2 | **Effective-Interest Amortization of a Bond Premium**

PANEL A—Bond Data

Maturity value—$100,000

Stated interest rate—9%

Interest paid—semiannually, $4,500 ($100,000 × .09 × 6/12)

Market interest rate at time of issue—8% annually, 4% semiannually

Issue price—$104,100 on January 1, 2013

PANEL B—Amortization Table

	A	B	C	D	E
End of Semiannual Interest Period	Interest *Payment* (9% × 6/12 × Maturity Value)	Interest *Expense* (8% × 6/12 × Bond Carrying Amount)	Premium Amortization (A – B)	Premium Balance (D – C)	Bond Carrying Amount ($100,000 + D)
Jan 1, 2013				$4,100	$104,100
Jun 30, 2013	$4,500	$4,164	$336	3,764	103,764
Dec 31, 2013	4,500	4,151	349	3,415	103,415
Jun 30, 2014	4,500	4,137	363	3,052	103,052
Dec 31, 2014	4,500	4,122	378	2,674	102,674
Jun 30, 2015	4,500	4,107	393	2,281	102,281
Dec 31, 2015	4,500	4,091	409	1,872	101,872
Jun 30, 2016	4,500	4,075	425	1,447	101,447
Dec 31, 2016	4,500	4,058	442	1,005	101,005
Jun 30, 2017	4,500	4,040	460	545	100,545
Dec 31, 2017	4,500	3,955*	545	0	100,000

*Adjusted for effect of rounding.

Notes
• *Column A* The interest payments are constant.
• *Column B* The interest expense each period is the preceding bond carrying amount multiplied by the market interest rate.
• *Column C* The excess of interest payment (A) over interest expense (B) is the premium amortization.
• *Column D* The premium balance decreases by the amount of amortization for the period.
• *Column E* The bonds' carrying amount decreases from $104,100 at issuance to $100,000 at maturity.

Let's begin with the issuance of the bonds on January 1, 2013, and the first interest payment on June 30. These entries follow:

2013			
Jan 1	Cash (column E) (A+)	104,100	
	Bonds payable (maturity value) (L+)		100,000
	Premium on bonds payable (column D) (AL+)		4,100
	Issued bonds at a premium.		

	2013			
	Jun 30	Interest expense (column B) (E+)	4,164	
		Premium on bonds payable (column C) (AL–)	336	
		Cash (column A) (A–)		4,500
		Paid semiannual interest and amortized premium.		

Appendix 11A Assignments

● Problems (Group A)

P11A-1A ⑤ Calculating present value [15–25 min]

Flexon needs new manufacturing equipment. Two companies can provide similar equipment but under different payment plans:

> Plan A: SVL offers to let Flexon pay $55,000 each year for six years. The payments include interest at 14% per year.
>
> Plan B: Easternhouse will let Flexon make a single payment of $525,000 at the end of six years. This payment includes both principal and interest at 14%.

Requirements

1. Calculate the present value of Plan A.
2. Calculate the present value of Plan B.
3. Flexon will purchase the equipment that costs the least, as measured by present value. Which equipment should Flexon select? Why?

P11A-2A ⑤ Calculating the value of bonds when stated rate and market rate are different [40–50 min]

Interest rates determine the present value of future amounts.

Requirements

1. Determine the present value of seven-year bonds payable with maturity value of $91,000 and stated interest rate of 14%, paid semiannually. The market rate of interest is 14% at issuance.
2. Same bonds payable as in Requirement 1, but the market interest rate is 16%.
3. Same bonds payable as in Requirement 1, but the market interest rate is 12%.

Note: Problem 11A-2A must be completed before attempting Problem 11A-3A.

P11A-3A ⑤ Journalizing bond transactions [20–30 min]

Consider your answers from Requirements 1–3 of Problem 11A-2A.

Requirement

1. Journalize issuance of the bond and the first semiannual interest payment under each of the three assumptions in Problem 11A-2A. The company amortizes bond premium and discount by the effective-interest method. Explanations are not required.

P11A-4A ⑤ Calculating and recording bonds when stated rate and market rate are different [15–20 min]

TVX issued $800,000 of 5%, 10-year bonds payable at a price of 92.595 on March 31, 2012. The market interest rate at the date of issuance was 6%, and the bonds pay interest semiannually.

Requirements

1. How much cash did the company receive upon issuance of the bonds payable?

2. Prepare an effective-interest amortization table for the bond discount through the first two interest payments. Use Exhibit 11A-1 as a guide, and round amounts to the nearest dollar.

3. Journalize the issuance of the bonds on March 31, 2012, and on September 30, 2012, payment of the first semiannual interest amount and amortization of the bond discount. Explanations are not required.

P11A-5A ⑤ Calculating and recording bonds when stated rate and market rate are different [15–20 min]

Nicholas Rausch issued $300,000 of 11%, 10-year bonds payable at a price of 106.2410 on March 31, 2012. The market interest rate at the date of issuance was 10%, and the bonds pay interest semiannually.

Requirements

1. How much cash did the company receive upon issuance of the bonds payable?

2. Prepare an effective-interest amortization table for the bond premium, through the first two interest payments. Use Exhibit 11A-2 as a guide, and round amounts to the nearest dollar.

3. Journalize the issuance of the bonds on May 31, 2012, and, on November 30, 2012, payment of the first semiannual interest amount and amortization of the bond premium. Explanations are not required.

P11A-6A ⑤ Calculating and recording bonds when stated rate and market rate are different [20–25 min]

Relaxation is authorized to issue 14%, 10-year bonds payable. On January 2, 2012, when the market interest rate is 16%, the company issues $500,000 of the bonds and receives cash of $451,130. Relaxation amortizes bond discount by the effective-interest method. Interest dates are January 2 and July 2.

Requirements

1. Prepare an amortization table for the first two semiannual interest periods. Follow the format of Exhibit 11A-1.

2. Journalize the issuance of the bonds payable and the first semiannual interest payment on July 2.

P11A-7A ⑤ Calculating and recording bonds when stated rate and market rate are different [15–20 min]

On January 1, 2012, Ginsberg issued $400,000 of 7.375%, five-year bonds payable when the market interest rate was 8%. Ginsberg pays interest annually at year-end. The issue price of the bonds was $390,018.

Requirement

1. Create a spreadsheet model to measure interest and bond discount amortization based on the table.

1	A	B	C	D	E	F
2						Bond
3		Interest	Interest	Discount	Discount	Carrying
4	Date	Payment	Expense	Amortization	Balance	Amount
5	1-1-12				$☐	390,018
6	12-31-12	$☐	$☐	$☐		☐
7	12-31-13					
8	12-31-14					
9	12-31-15					
10	12-31-16					
		400,000*7.375	+F5*.08	+C6–B6	400,000–F5	+F5+D6

P11A-8A ⑤ Calculating and recording bonds when stated rate and market rate are different [30–40 min]

On December 31, 2012, when the market interest rate is 10%, O'Brien Realty issues $800,000 of 7.25%, 10-year bonds payable. The bonds pay interest semiannually.

Requirements

1. Determine the present value of the bonds at issuance.
2. Assume that the bonds are issued at the price computed in Requirement 1. Prepare an effective-interest method amortization table for the first two semian-nual interest periods.
3. Using the amortization table prepared in Requirement 2, journalize issuance of the bonds and the first two interest payments.

● Problems (Group B)

MyAccountingLab

P11A-9B ⑤ Calculating present value [15–25 min]

Exacto needs new manufacturing equipment. Two companies can provide similar equipment but under different payment plans:

Plan A: NKS offers to let Exacto pay $65,000 each year for six years. The payments
include interest at 10% per year.

Plan B: Westernhome will let Exacto make a single payment of $50,000 at the end of six
years. This payment includes both principal and interest at 10%.

Requirements

1. Calculate the present value of Plan A.
2. Calculate the present value of Plan B.
3. Exacto will purchase the equipment that costs the least, as measured by present value. Which equipment should Exacto select? Why?

P11A-10B ⑤ Calculating the value of bonds when stated rate and market rate are different [40–50 min]

Interest rates determine the present value of future amounts.

Requirements

1. Determine the present value of seven-year bonds payable with maturity value of $83,000 and stated interest rate of 12%, paid semiannually. The market rate of interest is 12% at issuance.
2. Same bonds payable as in Requirement 1, but the market interest rate is 14%.
3. Same bonds payable as in Requirement 1, but the market interest rate is 10%.

Note: Problem 11A-10B must be completed before attempting Problem 11A-11B.

P11A-11B ⑤ Journalizing bond transactions [20–30 min]

Consider your answers from Requirements 1–3 of Problem 11A-10B.

Requirement

1. Journalize issuance of the bond and the first semiannual interest payment under each of the three assumptions in Problem 11A-10B. The company amortizes bond premium and discount by the effective-interest method. Explanations are not required.

P11A-12B ⑤ **Calculating and recording bonds when stated rate and market rate are different [15–20 min]**

MIRAX issued $500,000 of 7%, 10-year bonds payable at a price of 93.165 on March 31, 2012. The market interest rate at the date of issuance was 8%, and the bonds pay interest semiannually.

Requirements

1. How much cash did the company receive upon issuance of the bonds payable?
2. Prepare an effective-interest amortization table for the bond discount, through the first two interest payments. Use Exhibit 11A-1 as a guide, and round amounts to the nearest dollar.
3. Journalize the issuance of the bonds on March 31, 2012, and on September 30, 2012, payment of the first semiannual interest amount and amortization of the bond discount. Explanations are not required.

P11A-13B ⑤ **Calculating and recording bonds when stated rate and market rate are different [15–20 min]**

Ben Norton issued $700,000 of 5%, 10-year bonds payable at a price of 108.1776 on March 31, 2012. The market interest rate at the date of issuance was 4%, and the bonds pay interest semiannually.

Requirements

1. How much cash did the company receive upon issuance of the bonds payable?
2. Prepare an effective-interest amortization table for the bond premium, through the first two interest payments. Use Exhibit 11A-2 as a guide, and round amounts to the nearest dollar.
3. Journalize the issuance of the bonds on May 31, 2012, and, on November 30, 2012, payment of the first semiannual interest amount and amortization of the bond premium. Explanations are not required.

P11A-14B ⑤ **Calculating and recording bonds when stated rate and market rate are different [20–25 min]**

Soothing is authorized to issue 11%, 10-year bonds payable. On January 2, 2012, when the market interest rate is 12%, the company issues $600,000 of the bonds and receives cash of $565,710. Soothing amortizes bond discount by the effective-interest method. Interest dates are January 2 and July 2.

Requirements

1. Prepare an amortization table for the first two semiannual interest periods. Follow the format of Exhibit 11A-1.
2. Journalize the issuance of the bonds payable and the first semiannual interest payment on July 2.

P11A-15B ⑤ **Calculating and recording bonds when stated rate and market rate are different [15–20 min]**

On January 1, 2012, Trikel issued $600,000 of 8.375%, five-year bonds payable when the market interest rate was 10%. Trikel pays interest annually at year-end. The issue price of the bonds was $563,040.

Requirement

1. Create a spreadsheet model to measure interest and bond discount amortization based on the following table:

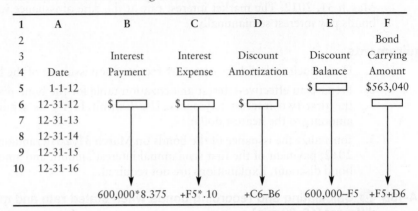

1	A	B	C	D	E	F
2						Bond
3		Interest	Interest	Discount	Discount	Carrying
4	Date	Payment	Expense	Amortization	Balance	Amount
5	1-1-12				$ ☐	$563,040
6	12-31-12	$ ☐	$ ☐	$ ☐		☐
7	12-31-13					
8	12-31-14					
9	12-31-15					
10	12-31-16					
		600,000*8.375	+F5*.10	+C6–B6	600,000–F5	+F5+D6

P11A-16B ⑤ Calculating and recording bonds when stated rate and market rate are different [30–40 min]

On December 31, 2012, when the market interest rate is 8%, Benson Realty issues $300,000 of 5.25%, 10-year bonds payable. The bonds pay interest semiannually.

Requirements

1. Determine the present value of the bonds at issuance.
2. Assume that the bonds are issued at the price computed in Requirement 1. Prepare an effective-interest method amortization table for the first two semi-annual interest installments.
3. Using the amortization table prepared in Requirement 2, journalize issuance of the bonds and the first two interest payments.

Retiring Bonds Payable

Normally, companies wait until maturity to pay off, or *retire*, their bonds payable. The basic retirement entry debits Bonds payable and credits Cash, as we saw in the chapter. But companies sometimes retire their bonds prior to maturity. The main reason for retiring bonds early is to relieve the pressure of paying the interest payments.

⑥ Retire bonds payable

Some bonds are **callable**, which means the company may *call*, or pay off, the bonds at a specified price. The call price is usually 100 or a few percentage points above maturity value, perhaps 101 or 102 to provide an incentive to the bond holder. Callable bonds give the issuer the flexibility to pay off the bonds when it benefits the company. An alternative to calling the bonds is to purchase them in the open market at their current market price. Whether the bonds are called or purchased in the open market, the journal entry is the same.

Suppose on December 31, 2013, Smart Touch has $100,000 of bonds payable outstanding with a remaining discount balance of $3,081 (the original discount of $3,851 [$100,000 − $96,149] less the straight-line amortization of $385 in June and less the amortization of $385 in December).

Lower interest rates have convinced management to pay off these bonds now. These bonds are callable at 100. If the market price of the bonds is 95, should Smart Touch call the bonds at 100 or purchase them in the open market at 95? The market price is lower than the call price, so Smart Touch should buy the bonds on the open market at their market price. Retiring the bonds on December 31, 2013, at 95 results in a gain of $1,919, computed as follows:

Maturity value of bonds being retired	$100,000
Less: Discount	3,081
Carrying amount of bonds payable	$ 96,919
Market price ($100,000 × 0.95) paid to retire the bonds	95,000
Gain on retirement of bonds payable	$ 1,919

The following entry records retirement of the bonds, immediately after an interest date:

2013			
Dec 31	Bonds payable (L−)	100,000	
	Discount on bonds payable (CL−)		3,081
	Cash ($100,000 × 0.95) (A−)		95,000
	Gain on retirement of bonds payable (R+)		1,919
	Retired bonds payable.		

After posting, the bond accounts have zero balances.

Bonds payable			Discount on bonds payable			
Retirement 100,000	Prior		Jan 1	3,851	Jun 30 Amort.	385
	balance 100,000				Dec 30 Amort.	385
					Retirement	3,081
	0			0		

The journal entry removes the bonds from the books and records a gain on retirement. Any existing premium would be removed with a debit. If Smart Touch retired only half of these bonds, it would remove only half the discount or premium.

When retiring bonds before maturity, follow these steps:

1. Record partial-period amortization of discount or premium if the retirement date does not fall on an interest payment date.

2. Write off the portion of Discount or Premium that relates to the bonds being retired.

3. Credit a gain or debit a loss on retirement.

Appendix 11B Assignments

● Short Exercises

S11B-1 ⑥ **Retiring bonds payable [10 min]**
On January 1, 2012, Platz issued $200,000 of 9%, five-year bonds payable at 106. Platz has extra cash and wishes to retire the bonds payable on January 1, 2013, immediately after making the second semiannual interest payment. To retire the bonds, Platz pays the market price of 96. Platz uses the straight-line amortization method.

Requirements

1. What is Platz's carrying amount of the bonds payable on the retirement date?
2. How much cash must Platz pay to retire the bonds payable?
3. Compute Platz's gain or loss on the retirement of the bonds payable.

S11B-2 ⑥ **Retiring bonds payable [5–10 min]**
Oldcity has $1,750,000 of callable bonds payable outstanding, with a bond premium of $35,000 on May 31, 2012, immediately after an interest payment. Oldcity decides to retire the bonds when the call price is 105 and the market price is 103.

Requirements

1. What is Oldcity's carrying amount of its callable bonds payable prior to the retirement?
2. Journalize Oldcity's retirement of the bonds payable. No explanation is required.

● Exercises

E11B-3 ⑥ **Retiring bonds payable [15–20 min]**
Virtuoso Transportation issued $400,000 of 7% bonds payable at 90 on October 1, 2012. These bonds are callable at 100 and mature on October 1, 2020. Virtuoso pays interest each April 1 and October 1. On October 1, 2017, when the bonds' market price is 97, Virtuoso retires the bonds in the most economical way available.

Requirement

1. Record the payment of the interest and amortization of bond discount at October 1, 2017, and the retirement of the bonds on that date. Virtuoso uses the straight-line amortization method.

E11B-4 ⑥ **Retiring bonds payable [15–20 min]**
Worldview Magazine issued $300,000 of 15-year, 5% callable bonds payable on July 31, 2012, at a price of 96. On July 31, 2015, Worldview called the bonds at a price of 101.

Requirements

1. Without making journal entries, compute the carrying amount of the bonds payable at July 31, 2015. The company uses the straight-line method to amortize bond discount.

2. Assume all amortization has been recorded properly. Journalize the retirement of the bonds on July 31, 2015. No explanation is required.

E11B-5 ❻ **Retiring bonds payable [10–15 min]**

Villain Industries reported the following at September 30:

Long-term liabilities:		
Callable bonds payable	$ 250,000	
Less: Discount on bonds payable ..	15,000 $	235,000

Requirements

1. Journalize retirement of half of the bonds on October 1 at the market price of 93.

2. Journalize retirement of the remaining half of the bonds on October 1 at the call price of 101.

Comprehensive Problem for Chapters 7–11

Comparing Two Businesses

Suppose you created a software package, sold the business, and now are ready to invest in a resort property. Several locations look promising: Monterrey, California; Durango, Colorado; and Mackinac Island, Michigan. Each place has its appeal, but Durango wins out. Two small resorts are available in Durango. The property owners provide the following data:

GOLD RUSH RESORTS & MOUNTAIN HIDEAWAY Balance Sheets December 31, 2013		
	Gold Rush Resorts	**Mountain Hideaway**
Cash	$ 31,000	$ 63,000
Accounts receivable	20,000	18,000
Inventory	64,000	70,000
Land	270,000	669,000
Buildings	1,200,000	1,500,000
Accumulated depreciation—buildings	(20,000)	(100,000)
Furniture	750,000	900,000
Accumulated depreciation—furniture	(75,000)	(180,000)
Total assets	$2,240,000	$2,940,000
Total liabilities	$1,300,000	$1,000,000
Owner's equity	940,000	1,940,000
Total liabilities and owner's equity	$2,240,000	$2,940,000

Income: Income statements for the last year report net income of $500,000 for Gold Rush Resorts and $400,000 for Mountain Hideaway.

Inventories: Gold Rush Resorts uses the FIFO inventory method, and Mountain Hideaway uses LIFO. If Gold Rush had used LIFO, its ending inventory would have been $7,000 lower.

Plant Assets: Gold Rush Resorts uses the straight-line depreciation method and an estimated useful life of 40 years for buildings and 10 years for furniture. Estimated residual values are $400,000 for buildings and $0 for furniture. Gold Rush's buildings are one-year old. Annual depreciation expense for the buildings is $20,000 and $75,000 per year on the furniture.

Mountain Hideaway uses the double-declining-balance method and depreciates buildings over 30 years. The furniture, also one-year old, is being depreciated over 10 years. First year depreciation expense for the buildings is $100,000 and $180,000 for the furniture.

Accounts Receivable: Gold Rush Resorts uses the direct write-off method for uncollectible receivables. Mountain Hideaway uses the allowance method. The Gold Rush owner estimates that $2,000 of the company's receivables are doubtful. Mountain Hideaway receivables are already reported at net realizable value.

Requirements

1. To compare the two resorts, convert Gold Rush Resorts' net income to the accounting methods and the estimated useful lives used by Mountain Hideaway.

2. Compare the two resorts' net incomes after you have revised Gold Rush's figures. Which resort looked better at the outset? Which looks better when they are placed on equal footing?

12 Corporations: Paid-In Capital and the Balance Sheet

				This represents the net worth of the corporation

SMART TOUCH LEARNING, INC.
Balance Sheet
May 31, 2013

Assets				Liabilities	
Current assets:				Current liabilities:	
Cash		$ 4,800		Accounts payable	$ 48,700
Accounts receivable		2,600		Salary payable	900
Inventory		30,500		Interest payable	100
Supplies		600		Unearned service revenue	400
Prepaid rent		2,000		Total current liabilities:	50,100
Total current assets			$ 40,500	Long-term liabilities:	
Plant assets:				Notes payable	20,000
Furniture	$18,000			Total liabilities	70,100
Less: Accumulated depreciation—furniture	300	17,700			
Building	48,000			**Stockholders' Equity**	
Less: Accumulated depreciation—building	200	47,800		Common stock	30,000
Total plant assets			65,500	Retained earnings	5,900
				Total stockholders' equity	**35,900**
Total assets			$106,000	Total liabilities and stockholders' equity	$106,000

Learning Objectives

1. Review the characteristics of a corporation

2. Describe the two sources of stockholders' equity and the classes of stock

3. Journalize the issuance of stock and prepare the stockholders' equity section of a corporation balance sheet

4. Illustrate Retained earnings transactions

5. Account for cash dividends

6. Use different stock values in decision making

7. Evaluate return on assets and return on stockholders' equity

8. Account for the income tax of a corporation

9. Compare issuing bonds to issuing stocks (Appendix 12A)

It is 6 AM and the Smart Touch Learning team has pulled an all-nighter putting together a big order. In her sleep-deprived state, Sheena Bright, President of Smart Touch, decides that the company needs to raise capital for expansion. How will the company do it? The same way other large companies like **Google** or **IHOP** do—issue stock.

We reviewed corporation basics in Chapter 1. Now, let's review corporations with Smart Touch as the focus company.

Corporations: An Overview

 1 Review the characteristics of a corporation

Corporations dominate business activity in the United States. Proprietorships and partnerships are more numerous, but corporations do much more business and are larger. Most well-known companies, such as **Intel** and **Nike**, are corporations. Their full names include *Corporation* or *Incorporated* (abbreviated *Corp.* and *Inc.*) to show that they are corporations—for example, **Intel Corporation** and **Nike, Inc.** What makes the corporate form of organization so attractive? Several things. To review the characteristics of corporations, Exhibit 12-1 summarizes their advantages and disadvantages, which we discussed in Chapter 1.

EXHIBIT 12-1 | **Corporations: Advantages and Disadvantages**

Advantages	Disadvantages
1. Corporations can raise more money than a proprietorship or partnership.	1. Ownership and management are often separated.
2. A corporation has a continuous life.	2. Double taxation.
3. The transfer of corporate ownership is easy.	3. Government regulation is expensive.
4. There is no mutual agency among the stockholders.	4. Start-up costs are higher than other business forms.
5. Stockholders have limited liability.	

The state authorizes in the bylaws of a corporation the maximum shares of a stock class the corporation may issue, which is called **authorization of stock. Authorization is the state's permission for the corporation to operate.** A corporation issues **stock certificates** to the stockholders when they buy the stock. The stock certificate represents the individual's ownership of the corporation's capital, so it is called **capital stock.** The basic unit of stock is a **share.** A share represents a portion of ownership in the corporation. A corporation may issue a physical stock certificate for any number of shares. Today, many corporations issue the stocks electronically rather than "printing" a paper certificate. Exhibit 12-2 shows a stock certificate for 288 shares of Smart Touch common stock owned by Courtney Edwards. The certificate shows the following:

- Company name
- Stockholder name
- Number of shares owned by the stockholder

Stock that is held by the stockholders is said to be **outstanding stock.** The outstanding stock of a corporation represents 100% of its ownership. **Outstanding stock equals issued stock minus stock repurchased by the corporation.**

EXHIBIT 12-2 | **Stock Certificate**

- Company's name
- Stockholder's name
- Number of shares held by the stockholder

Stockholders' Equity Basics

Recall that a corporation's owners' equity is called stockholders' equity. State laws require corporations to report their sources of capital because some of the capital must be maintained by the company. The two basic sources we described in Chapter 1 are as follows:

2 Describe the two sources of stockholders' equity and the classes of stock

- Paid-in capital (also called contributed capital) represents amounts received from the stockholders. Common stock is the main source of paid-in capital. **Paid-in capital is *externally* generated capital and results from transactions with outsiders.**
- Retained earnings is capital earned by profitable operations. **Retained earnings is *internally* generated capital because it results from corporate decisions to RETAIN net income to use in future operations or for expansion.**

Exhibit 12-3 outlines a summarized version of the stockholders' equity of Smart Touch before the first share of stock is issued:

EXHIBIT 12-3 | **Stockholders' Equity of Smart Touch Learning**

Stockholders' Equity	
Paid-in capital:	
Common stock $1 par; 20,000,000 shares authorized; 0 shares issued	$0
Retained earnings	0
Total stockholders' equity	$0

Stop & Think...

Consider a small corporation that gains authorization by the state. When does the company become an actual corporation? Well, the state may have approved the corporation, but until the corporation actually issues at least one share of stock, the corporation has no owners. So it is the first issuance that solidifies the corporation's existence.

Stockholders' Rights

A stockholder has four basic rights, unless a right is withheld by contract:

1. **Vote.** Stockholders participate in management by voting on corporate matters. This is the only way in which a stockholder can help to manage the corporation. Normally, each share of common stock carries one vote.

2. **Dividends.** Stockholders receive a proportionate part of any dividend that is declared and paid. Each share of stock receives an equal dividend so, for example, a shareholder who owns 1% of the total shares in the company receives 1% of any dividend.

3. **Liquidation.** Stockholders receive their proportionate share of any assets remaining after the corporation pays its debts and liquidates (goes out of business).

4. **Preemption.** Stockholders can maintain their proportionate ownership in the corporation. Suppose you own 5% of a corporation's stock. If the corporation issues 100,000 new shares of stock, it must offer you the opportunity to buy 5% (5,000) of the new shares. This right, however, is usually withheld by contract for most corporations.

Classes of Stock

Corporations can issue different classes of stock. The stock of a corporation may be either

- **common** or **preferred.**
- **par** or **no-par.**

Common Stock and Preferred Stock

Recall that every corporation issues *common stock*, which represents the basic ownership of the corporation. The real "owners" of the corporation are the common stockholders. Some companies issue Class A common stock, which carries the right to vote. They may also issue Class B common stock, which may be non-voting. There must be at least one voting "class" of stock. However, there is no limit as to the number or types of classes of stock that a corporation may issue. Each class of stock has a separate account in the company's ledger.

Preferred stock gives its owners certain advantages over common stock. Most notably, preferred stockholders receive dividends before the common stockholders. They also receive assets before common stockholders if the corporation liquidates. When dividends are declared, corporations pay a fixed dividend on preferred stock. The amount of the preferred dividend is printed on the face of the preferred stock certificate. Investors usually buy preferred stock to earn those fixed dividends. With these advantages, preferred stockholders take less investment risk than common stockholders.

Owners of preferred stock also have the four basic stockholder rights, unless a right is withheld. The right to vote, however, is usually withheld from preferred stock. Companies may issue different series of preferred stock (Series A and Series B, for example). Each series is recorded in a separate account. Preferred stock is more rare than you might think. Many corporations have authorization for preferred stock, but few actually issue the preferred shares. For an example, refer to the **Amazon.com** report in Appendix A.

Par Value, Stated Value, and No-Par Stock

Stock may carry a par value or it may be no-par stock. **Par value** is an arbitrary amount assigned by a company to a share of its stock. Most companies set par value low to avoid issuing their stock below par.

The par value of **IHOP**'s common stock is $0.01 (1 cent) per share. **Deere & Co.**, which makes John Deere tractors, and **Whirlpool**, the appliance company, have common stock with a par value of $1 per share. Par value of preferred stock may be higher per share than common stock par values. Par value is arbitrary and is assigned when the organizers file the corporate charter with the state. There is no real "reason" for why par values vary. It is a choice made by the organizers of the corporation. Smart Touch's common stock has $1 par value. Companies maintain some minimum amount of stockholders' equity for the protection of creditors (often through retaining earnings), and this minimum represents the corporation's legal capital. However, the concepts of par and legal capital have been virtually eliminated entirely by the Model Business Corporation Act. Accountants still use the outdated concepts of par and legal capital because many corporations' stocks were issued prior to the adoption of the provisions of the Model Business Corporation Act, which is why we are still guided by these terms in our recording of stock issuances.

No-par stock does not have par value. **Pfizer**, the pharmaceutical company, has preferred stock with no par value. But some no-par stock has a **stated value**, an arbitrary amount similar to par-value. Usually the state the company incorporates in will determine whether a stock may be par or stated value stock. As far as accounting for it goes, par is treated the same as stated value. Next we'll review some stock issuance examples to further illustrate this idea.

> **Key Takeaway**
>
> Stock types include common and preferred, par or no-par. Attributes such as voting rights, dividends proportionate to ownership percentage, liquidation preferences, and the right to maintain the same percentage of ownership (preemption) may apply. All these factors, as well as others, affect the risk inherent in the stock.

Issuing Stock

Corporations such as **Intel** and **Nike** need huge quantities of money. They cannot finance all their operations through borrowing, so they raise capital by issuing stock. A company can sell its stock directly to stockholders or it can use the services of an **underwriter**, such as the brokerage firms **Merrill Lynch** and **Morgan Stanley**. An underwriter usually agrees to buy all the stock it cannot sell to its clients.

The price that the corporation receives from issuing stock is called the **issue price**. Usually, the issue price exceeds par value because par value is normally set quite low. In the following sections, we use Smart Touch to show how to account for the issuance of stock.

 3 Journalize the issuance of stock and prepare the stockholders' equity section of a corporation balance sheet

Issuing Common Stock

Stocks of public companies are bought and sold on a stock exchange, such as the New York Stock Exchange (NYSE). The *Wall Street Journal* is the most popular medium for advertising initial public offerings of stock. The ads are called *tombstones* due to their heavy black borders and heavy black print. Exhibit 12-4 demonstrates what Smart Touch's tombstone would look like.

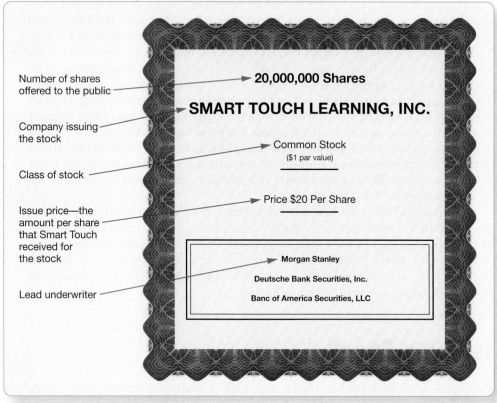

EXHIBIT 12-4 **Announcement of Public Offering of Smart Touch Learning Stock**

Smart Touch's tombstone shows that the company hoped to raise approximately $200,000,000 of capital (10,000,000 shares × $20 per share).

Issuing Common Stock at Par

Suppose Smart Touch's common stock carried a par value of $1 per share. The stock issuance entry of one million shares at par value on January 1 would be as follows:

Jan 1	Cash (1,000,000 × $1) (A+)	1,000,000	
	Common stock (Q+)		1,000,000
	Issued common stock at par.		

Issuing Common Stock at a Premium

As stated above, most corporations set par value low and issue common stock for a price above par. The amount above par is called a **premium**. Assume Smart Touch sells an additional one million shares for $20 a share on January 2. The $19 difference between the issue price ($20) and par value ($1) is a premium.

A premium on the sale of stock is not a gain, income, or profit for the corporation because the company is dealing with its own stock. This situation illustrates one of the fundamentals of accounting:

A company can have no income statement reported profit or loss when buying or selling its own stocks.

So, the premium is another type of paid-in capital account called "Paid-in capital in excess of par." It is also called **additional paid-in capital**.

With a par value of $1, Smart Touch's entry to record the issuance of its stock at $20 per share on January 2 is as follows:

Jan 2	Cash (1,000,000 shares × $20 issue price) (A+)	20,000,000	
	Common stock (1,000,000 shares × $1 par value) (Q+)		1,000,000
	Paid-in capital in excess of par—		
	common [1,000,000 shares × ($20 – $1)] (Q+)		19,000,000
	Issued common stock at a premium.		

Smart Touch would report stockholders' equity on its balance sheet after the January 1 and January 2 stock issuance as follows, assuming that its charter authorizes 20,000,000 shares of common stock and also assuming the balance of retained earnings is $9,000,000.

SMART TOUCH LEARNING, INC.
Stockholders' Equity
January 2, 2013

Paid-in capital:	
Common stock; $1 par; 20,000,000 shares authorized,	
2,000,000* shares issued	$ 2,000,000
Paid-in capital in excess of par	19,000,000
Total paid-in capital	$21,000,000
Retained earnings	9,000,000
Total stockholders' equity	$30,000,000

*1,000,000 shares issued Jan 1 (page 586) + 1,000,000 shares issued Jan 2

The balance of the Common stock account is calculated as follows:

Number of shares issued	×	Par value per share	=	Common stock account balance
2,000,000	×	$1	=	$2,000,000

Paid-in capital in excess of par is the total amount received from issuing the common stock minus its par value. For Smart Touch, this amount was recorded in the January 2 sale:

Paid-in capital in excess of par—common

	$19,000,000

Altogether, total paid-in capital is the sum of the following:

Common stock	+	Paid-in capital in excess of par	=	Total paid-in capital
$2,000,000	+	$19,000,000	=	$21,000,000

Issuing No-Par Stock

When a company issues no-par stock, it debits the asset received and credits the stock account. **For no-par stock there can be no paid-in capital in excess of par, because there is no par to be in excess of.**

Assume that, instead of $1 par value, Smart Touch's common stock were no-par. How would that change the recording of the issuance of 1,000,000 shares for $1 on

January 1 and 1,000,000 shares for $20 on January 2? The stock-issuance entries would be as follows:

Jan 1	Cash (1,000,000 × $1) (A+)	1,000,000	
	Common stock (Q+)		1,000,000
Jan 2	Cash (1,000,000 × $20) (A+)	20,000,000	
	Common stock (Q+)		20,000,000
	Issued no-par common stock.		

Regardless of the stock's price, Cash is debited and Common stock is credited for the cash received. So, although the total equity of $21,000,000 remains the same, the Common stock account differs between par, $2,000,000, and no-par, $21,000,000, stock.

Let's consider how the stockholders' equity section of the balance sheet would change:

SMART TOUCH LEARNING, INC.
Stockholders' Equity
January 2, 2013

Paid-in capital:	
Common stock; no par; 20,000,000 shares authorized, 2,000,000 shares issued	$21,000,000
Retained earnings	9,000,000
Total stockholders' equity	$30,000,000

Issuing No-Par Stock with a Stated Value

Accounting for no-par stock with a stated value is almost identical to accounting for par-value stock. The only difference is that no-par stock with a stated value uses an account titled Paid-in capital in excess of *stated* value to record amounts received above the stated value.

Issuing Stock for Assets Other Than Cash

A corporation may issue stock for assets other than cash. It records the assets received at their current market value and credits the stock accounts accordingly. The asset received's prior book value is irrelevant. Now let's reconsider the January 2 entry for Smart Touch. Assume that, instead of cash, Smart Touch received a building worth $20,000,000 in exchange for the 1,000,000 shares of its $1 par common stock on January 2. How would the entry change?

Jan 2	Building (A+)	20,000,000	
	Common stock (1,000,000 × $1) (Q+)		1,000,000
	Paid-in capital in excess of par—		
	common (20,000,000 – 1,000,000) (Q+)		19,000,000
	Issued common stock in exchange for a building.		

As you can see, the only change is in the asset received, the building.

Issuing Preferred Stock

Accounting for preferred stock follows the pattern illustrated for issuing common stock. Assume that Smart Touch has authorization from the state to issue 2,000 shares of preferred stock. Smart Touch decides to issue 1,000 shares of its $50 par, 6% preferred stock on January 3 at par value. The issuance entry would be as follows:

Jan 3	Cash (A+)	50,000	
	Preferred stock (1,000 shares × $50 par) (Q+)		50,000
	Issued preferred stock.		

Most preferred stock is issued at par value. Therefore, Paid-in capital in excess of par for preferred stock is rare. Assume, however, that Smart Touch issues another 1,000 shares of preferred stock on January 4 for $55. The issuance entry would be as follows:

Jan 4	Cash (1,000 shares × $55 issue price) (A+)	55,000	
	Preferred stock (1,000 shares × $50 par) (Q+)		50,000
	Paid-in capital in excess of par—		
	preferred (55,000 – 50,000) (Q+)		5,000

Review of Accounting for Paid-In Capital

Let's review the first half of this chapter by showing the stockholders' equity section of Smart Touch's balance sheet in Exhibit 12-5, assuming both stocks were par value.

EXHIBIT 12-5 | **Part of Smart Touch Learning's Balance Sheet**

SMART TOUCH LEARNING, INC.
Stockholders' Equity
January 4, 2013

Paid-in capital:	
Preferred stock, 6%, $50 par, 2,000 shares authorized,	
2,000 shares issued	$ 100,000
Paid-in capital in excess of par—preferred	5,000
Common stock, $1 par, 20,000,000 shares authorized,	
2,000,000 shares issued	2,000,000
Paid-in capital in excess of par—common	19,000,000
Total paid-in capital	$21,105,000
Retained earnings	9,000,000
Total stockholders' equity	$30,105,000

Observe the order of the stockholders' equity accounts:

- Preferred stock, at par value
- Paid-in capital in excess of par on preferred stock issuances
- Common stock at par value
- Paid-in capital in excess of par on common stock issuances
- Retained earnings (after all of the paid-in capital accounts)

The following Decision Guidelines will help to solidify your understanding of stockholders' equity.

Key Takeaway

Companies may issue their stock in exchange for cash or other assets. The issuance entry always involves a credit to the stock account, whether common or preferred. The amount credited to the stock account depends on whether the stock is par value stock or no-par value stock. If the stock has a par value, the number of shares issued multiplied by the par value is recorded in the stock account. The premium received, if any, is credited to Paid-in capital in excess of par. If the stock has no par, then the total amount received goes to the stock account. Stockholders' equity always lists paid-in capital first and within that listing, preferred stock amounts are listed before common stock amounts.

Decision Guidelines 12-1

THE STOCKHOLDERS' EQUITY OF A CORPORATION

Suppose your company is considering raising capital by issuing stock. Your company isn't sure what type of stock it should issue. You know you have to at least issue common shares, but you aren't sure of your other choices. The following guidelines are relevant to the company's decision.

Decision	Guidelines
• What are the two main segments of stockholders' equity?	• Paid-in capital • Retained earnings
• Which is more permanent, paid-in capital or retained earnings?	Paid-in capital is more permanent because corporations can use retained earnings for dividends, which decreases the size of the company's equity.

• How are paid-in capital and retained earnings
  • similar?
 	
  • different?
	• Both represent stockholders' equity (ownership/net worth) of the corporation.
	• Paid-in capital and retained earnings come from different sources:
	   a. *Paid-in capital* comes from the stockholders (outside the company).
	   b. *Retained earnings* comes from profitable operations (inside the company).

• What are the main categories of paid-in capital?	• Preferred stock, plus paid-in capital in excess of par, preferred (or just Preferred stock if no par) • Common stock, plus paid-in capital in excess of par, common (or just Common stock if no par)

Summary Problem 12-1

Delphian Corporation has two classes of common stock. The company's balance sheet includes the following:

DELPHIAN CORPORATION Stockholders' Equity December 31, 2013	
Paid-in capital:	
Class A common stock, voting, $1 par value,	
authorized and issued 1,200,000 shares	$ 1,200,000
Paid-in capital in excess of par—Class A common	2,000,000
Class B common stock, nonvoting, no par value,	
authorized and issued 11,000,000 shares	55,000,000
	58,200,000
Retained earnings	800,000,000
Total stockholders' equity	$858,200,000

Requirements

1. Journalize the issuance of the Class A common stock.
2. Journalize the issuance of the Class B common stock.
3. What is the total paid-in capital of the company?
4. What was the average issue price of each share of Class B common stock?

Solution

1.	Cash (A+)	3,200,000	
	Common stock—Class A (Q+)		1,200,000
	Paid-in capital in excess of par—Class A Common (Q+)		2,000,000
	To record issuance of Class A common stock.		
2.	Cash (A+)	55,000,000	
	Common stock—Class B (Q+)		55,000,000
	To record issuance of Class B common stock.		

3. Total paid-in capital is $58,200,000
     ($1,200,000 + $2,000,000 + $55,000,000).

4. Average issue price of each share of Class B
     common stock = $5 ($55,000,000/11,000,000 shares)

Retained Earnings

4 Illustrate Retained earnings transactions

Recall that corporations close their revenues and expenses into the Income summary account. Then, they close net income from the Income summary account to the Retained earnings account. Assume Smart Touch's sales revenue was $500,000 and expenses totaled $400,000 for December. The closing entries would be as follows:

①	Dec 31	Sales revenue (R–)	500,000	
		Income summary		500,000
		To close sales revenue.		
②	31	Income summary	400,000	
		Expenses (detailed) (E–)		400,000
		To close expenses.		

Now, the Income summary holds revenues, expenses, and net income.

Income summary

② Expenses	400,000	① Revenues	500,000
		Balance (net income)	100,000

Finally, the Income summary's balance is closed to Retained earnings.

③	Dec 31	Income summary	100,000	
		Retained earnings (Q+)		100,000
		To close net income to Retained earnings.		

This closing entry completes the closing process. The Income summary is zeroed out, and Retained earnings now holds net income, as follows:

Income summary

② Expenses	400,000	① Revenues	500,000
③ Closing	100,000		
			0

Retained earnings

	③ Closing (net income)	100,000

If Smart Touch's expenses had been $560,000 instead of $400,000, the company would have had a $60,000 net *loss*, and Income summary would have a debit balance, as follows:

Income summary

Expenses	560,000	Revenues	500,000
Net loss	60,000		

To close this $60,000 loss, the final closing entry credits Income summary and debits Retained earnings as follows:

	Dec 31	Retained earnings (Q–)	60,000	
		Income summary		60,000
		To close net loss to Retained earnings.		

The accounts now have their final balances.

Income summary					Retained earnings		
② Expenses	560,000	① Revenues	500,000		③ Closing (net loss)	60,000	
		③ Closing	60,000				
			0				

A Retained Earnings Deficit

A loss may cause a debit balance in Retained earnings. This condition—called a Retained earnings **deficit**—is reported as a negative amount in stockholders' equity. Reconsider the stockholders' equity presented for Smart Touch, assuming the Retained earnings balance just shown:

> **Key Takeaway**
>
> The steps of the closing process are the same as those you learned in Chapter 4. Net income increases Retained earnings. Net loss decreases Retained earnings.

Smart Touch Learning's Balance Sheet—Retained Earnings Deficit Stockholders' Equity December 31, 2013	
Paid-in capital:	
Preferred stock, 6%, $50 par, 2,000 shares authorized, 2,000 shares issued	$ 100,000
Paid-in capital in excess of par—preferred	5,000
Common stock, $1 par, 20,000,000 shares authorized, 2,000,000 shares issued	2,000,000
Paid-in capital in excess of par—common	19,000,000
Total paid-in capital	$21,105,000
Retained earnings	(60,000)
Total stockholders' equity	$21,045,000

Now let's look at how to account for cash dividends.

Accounting for Cash Dividends

As discussed in Chapter 1, a profitable corporation may distribute cash to stockholders in the form of *dividends*. Cash dividends cause a decrease in both assets and equity (Retained earnings). Most states prohibit using paid-in capital for dividends. Accountants, therefore, use the term **legal capital** to refer to the portion of stockholders' equity that cannot be used for dividends. Corporations declare cash dividends from Retained earnings and then pay with cash.

5 Account for cash dividends

Dividend Dates

A corporation declares a dividend before paying it. Three dividend dates are relevant:

1. **Declaration date.** On the declaration date—say, May 1—the board of directors announces the intention to pay the dividend. **The declaration of a cash dividend creates an obligation (liability) for the corporation.**

2. **Date of record** (or *record date*). Those stockholders holding the stock at the end of business on the date of record—a week or two after declaration, say, May 15—will receive the dividend check. **Date of record is the date the corporation records which stockholders get dividend checks.**

3. **Payment date.** Payment of the dividend usually follows the record date by a week or two—say, May 30. **The payment date means "The check's in the mail."**

Declaring and Paying Dividends

The cash dividend rate on *preferred stock* is often expressed as a percentage of the preferred-stock par value, such as 6%. But sometimes cash dividends on preferred stock are expressed as a flat dollar amount per share, such as $3 per share. Therefore, preferred dividends are computed two ways, depending on how the preferred-stock cash-dividend rate is stated on the preferred stock certificate. Let's look at the two ways to compute preferred dividends using Smart Touch's 2,000 outstanding shares of 6%, $50 par preferred stock. (Smart Touch's flat rate instead of 6% could be stated as $3 per share.)

1. Outstanding shares × par value × preferred dividend rate% = preferred dividend			
2,000 shares	× $50 par × 6%		= $6,000
2. Outstanding shares ×		flat dividend rate	= preferred dividend
2,000 shares	×	$3 per share	= $6,000

Recall that cash dividends on *common stock* are computed the second way, because those cash dividends are not expressed as a percentage.

To account for the declaration of a cash dividend, we debit Retained earnings and credit Dividends payable on the date of declaration. For Smart Touch's preferred dividend, the entry is as follows:[1]

May 1	Retained earnings (Q–)	6,000	
	Dividends payable, preferred (L+)		6,000
	Declared a cash dividend.		

Note: There is no journal entry on the date of record as the date of record is the cutoff point to determine who owned the stock and thus whose name is on the dividend check. To pay the dividend on the payment date, we debit Dividends payable and credit Cash.

May 30	Dividends payable, preferred (L–)	6,000	
	Cash (A–)		6,000
	Paid the cash dividend.		

---

[1]Some accountants debit a Dividends account, which is later closed to Retained earnings. But most small businesses debit Retained earnings directly, as shown here.

Dividends payable is a current liability. When a company has issued both preferred and common stock, the preferred stockholders get their dividends first. The common stockholders receive dividends only if the total dividend is large enough to satisfy the preferred requirement. In other words, the common stockholders get the leftovers.

Dividing Dividends Between Preferred and Common

Smart Touch has 2,000 shares of $50, 6% preferred stock outstanding and 2,000,000 shares of $1 par common stock outstanding. We calculated earlier that Smart Touch's annual preferred dividend was $6,000. So, total declared dividends must exceed $6,000 for the common stockholders to get anything. Exhibit 12-6 shows the division of dividends between preferred and common for two situations.

EXHIBIT 12-6	Dividing a Dividend Between Preferred Stock and Common Stock

Case A: Total dividend of $5,000:

Preferred dividend (the full $5,000 goes to preferred
    because the annual preferred dividend is $6,000)...................... $ 5,000

Common dividend (none because the total dividend
    did not cover the preferred dividend for the year)...................... 0

Total dividend .... $ 5,000

Case B: Total dividend of $50,000:

Preferred dividend (2,000 shares × $50 par × 6%) .... $ 6,000

Common dividend ($50,000 − $6,000) 44,000

Total dividend $50,000

If the year's dividend is equal to or less than the annual preferred amount (Case A), the preferred stockholders will receive the entire dividend, and the common stockholders get nothing that year. But, if Smart Touch's dividend is large enough to cover the preferred dividend (Case B), the preferred stockholders get their regular dividend of $6,000, and the common stockholders get the remainder of $44,000.

Dividends on Cumulative and Noncumulative Preferred

Preferred stock can be either

- cumulative or
- noncumulative.

Most preferred stock is cumulative. As a result, preferred is assumed to be cumulative unless it is specifically designated as noncumulative. Let's see how this plays out.

A corporation may fail to pay the preferred dividend if, for example, it does not have cash to fund the dividend. This is called *passing the dividend*, and the dividends are said to be in **arrears. Cumulative preferred stock** shareholders must receive all dividends in arrears before the common stockholders get any dividend.

The preferred stock of Smart Touch is cumulative. How do we know this? Because cumulative is the "default" for preferred stock and because the stock is not labeled as noncumulative.

Suppose Smart Touch passed the 2013 preferred dividend of $6,000. Before paying any common dividend in 2014, Smart Touch must first pay preferred dividends of

$6,000 for 2013 and $6,000 for 2014, a total of $12,000. Assume that in 2014, Smart Touch declares a $50,000 total dividend. How much of this dividend goes to preferred? How much goes to common? The allocation of this $50,000 dividend is as follows:

Total dividend	$50,000
Preferred gets	
2013: 2,000 shares × $50 par × 6%	$6,000
2014: 2,000 shares × $50 par × 6%	6,000
Total to preferred..	$12,000
Common gets the remainder	$38,000

Smart Touch's entry to record the declaration of this dividend on September 6, 2014 is as follows:

	2014				
	Sep 6	Retained earnings (Q–)		50,000	
		Dividends payable, preferred (L+)			12,000
		Dividends payable, common (L+)			38,000
		Declared a cash dividend.			

If the preferred stock is *noncumulative*, the corporation is not required to pay any dividends in arrears. Keep in mind that this is a risk that the investor bears when investing in noncumulative preferred stock. Suppose Smart Touch's preferred stock was noncumulative and the company passed the 2013 dividend. The preferred stockholders would lose the 2013 dividend of $6,000 forever. Then, before paying any common dividends in 2014, Smart Touch would have to pay only the 2014 preferred dividend of $6,000, which would leave $44,000 for the common stockholders.

Dividends in arrears are *not* a liability. A liability for dividends arises only after the board of directors *declares* the dividend. But a corporation reports cumulative preferred dividends in arrears in notes to the financial statements. This shows the common stockholders how big the declared dividend will need to be for them to get any dividends.

Stop & Think...

Think about a big holiday dinner, such as Thanksgiving, when a lot of people are there and you usually have a lot of food. Do you have that one family member who always seems to be in the dinner line first? That person is like the preferred stockholders in a corporation—they always are the first class of stockholders in line to get whatever is being "served" by the corporation, whether it is dividends or liquidation. Common stockholders get the leftovers the day after a holiday. Sometimes the leftovers are really good and there are a lot of them, and sometimes there is nothing left.

Different Values of Stock

6 Use different stock values in decision making

There are several different stock values in addition to par value and issue price. Market value, liquidation value, and book value are all used for decision making.

Market Value

Market value, or *market price*, is the price at which a person can buy or sell a share of stock. The corporation's net income and general economic conditions affect market value. The Internet and most newspapers report the current market prices of stocks. Log on to any company's Web site to track its stock price, which usually changes daily. *In almost all cases, stockholders are more concerned about the market value of a stock than about any other value.* The current market price will dictate whether a stockholder can sell at a gain or loss, which is why stockholders are most concerned about market value.

Liquidation Value

Liquidation value is the amount that is guaranteed to the preferred stockholders in the event a company liquidates (goes out of business). If a liquidation value exists, it will be printed on the face of the preferred stock certificate. Note that this value only has meaning to a decision-maker if the corporation liquidates.

Book Value

Book value per share of stock is the amount of stockholders' equity on the company's books for each share of its stock. If the company has both preferred and common stock outstanding, owners of preferred stock have first claim to the equity—just like they have first claim to the dividends. Therefore, we subtract preferred equity from total equity to compute book value per share of common stock. The preferred equity is as follows:

Book value attributred to preferred stock + Any preferred dividends that are in arrears, if cumulative

1. Book value attributed to preferred stock is either
   a. the number of outstanding preferred shares × liquidation value per share, OR
   b. the book value of preferred equity (the Preferred stock account balance)

2. PLUS any dividends that are in arrears, if the preferred stock is cumulative.

The common stockholders, once again, get whatever is left over in stockholders' equity. Exhibit 12-7 gives a model for calculating book value per share for each class of stock.

EXHIBIT 12-7 | **Calculating Book Value per Share**

Book Value (BV) attributed to Preferred stock (P/S):

1) Liquidation value × outstanding shares, OR 2) Preferred stock account balance	A
Dividends in Arrears on outstanding preferred shares, if cumulative	B
Total BV attributed to P/S	A + B
Outstanding preferred shares	C
Book Value per share on Preferred stock	(A + B)/C

Book Value (BV) attributed to Common stock (C/S):

Total Stockholders' equity	D
Book Value attributed to P/S (figured above)	(A + B)
Total BV attributed to C/S (leftovers)	D − (A + B)
Outstanding common shares	E
Book Value per share on Common stock	{D − (A + B)}/E

To illustrate, let's apply the calculation to Smart Touch's stockholders' equity presented earlier in Exhibit 12-5, assuming that preferred dividends are in arrears for one year. The results are presented in Exhibit 12-8.

EXHIBIT 12-8	Calculating Book Value per Share for Smart Touch Learning

Book Value (BV) attributed to Preferred stock (P/S):

1) Liquidation value × outstanding shares, OR 2) Preferred stock account balance	$ 100,000
Dividends in Arrears on outstanding preferred shares, if cumulative (2,000 shares × $50 par × 6% × 1 year)	$ 6,000
Total BV attributed to P/S ($100,000 + $6,000)	$ 106,000
Outstanding preferred shares	2,000
Book Value per share on Preferred stock ($106,000 / 2,000 shares)	$ 53.00

Book Value (BV) attributed to Common stock (C/S):

Total Stockholders' equity (from Exhibit 12-5)	$30,105,000
Book Value attributed to P/S (figured above)	$ (106,000)
Total BV attributed to C/S (leftovers)	$29,999,000
Outstanding common shares	2,000,000
Book Value per share on Common stock ($29,999,000 / 2,000,000 shares)*	$ 15.00

*Result rounded to the nearest penny

Book value may figure into the price to pay for a closely held company, whose stock is not publicly traded. In addition, a company may buy out a stockholder by paying the book value of the person's stock. Book value may also be considered in takeover bids for companies, especially if the book value is much greater than the market value per share.

Some investors compare the book value of a stock with its market value. The idea is that a stock selling below book value is a good buy. But the book value/market value relationship is far from clear. Other investors believe that a stock selling below book value means the company must be having problems.

Evaluating Operations

 Evaluate return on assets and return on stockholders' equity

Investors are constantly comparing companies' profits. To compare companies, we need some standard profitability measures. Two important ratios to use for comparison are return on assets and return on common stockholders' equity.

Rate of Return on Total Assets

The **rate of return on total assets**, or simply **return on assets**, measures a company's success in using assets to earn income. Two groups invest money to finance a corporation:

- Stockholders
- Creditors

Net income and interest expense are the returns to these two groups. The stockholders earn the corporation's net income, and interest is the return to the creditors.

The sum of net income plus interest expense is the numerator of the return-on-assets ratio. The corporation incurs interest because it borrowed money. Interest expense is added back to determine the real return on the assets employed regardless of the corporation's financing choices (debt or equity). The denominator is average total assets. Net income and interest expense are taken from the income statement. Average total assets comes from the beginning and ending balance sheets.

Let's assume Smart Touch has the following data for 2014:

Net income	$33,000,000
Interest expense	$22,000,000
Total assets, 12/31/2014	$843,000,000
Total assets, 12/31/2013	$822,000,000
Preferred dividends	$6,000,000

Return on assets is computed as follows:

$$\frac{\text{Rate of return}}{\text{on total assets}} = \frac{\text{Net income} + \text{Interest expense}}{\text{Average total assets}}$$

$$= \frac{\$33,000,000 + \$22,000,000}{(\$843,000,000 + \$822,000,000) \, / \, 2} = \frac{\$55,000,000}{\$832,500,000} = 0.066$$

Smart Touch has returned $0.066 for each $1 invested in the company's average assets. What is a good rate of return on total assets? There is no single answer because rates of return vary widely by industry. In most industries, a 10% return on assets is considered good. Smart Touch's 6.6% return on assets would not be considered good if the industry average is 10%.

Rate of Return on Common Stockholders' Equity

Rate of return on common stockholders' equity, often shortened to **return on equity**, shows the relationship between net income available to the common stockholders and their average common equity invested in the company. The numerator is net income minus preferred dividends. Preferred dividends are subtracted because the preferred stockholders have first claim to any dividends. The denominator is *average common stockholders' equity*—total equity minus preferred equity. Let's return to Smart Touch's data for 2014. Assume Smart Touch's common equity was $280,000,000 in 2013 and $300,000,000 in 2014. Smart Touch's rate of return on common stockholders' equity for 2014 is computed as follows:

$$\frac{\text{Rate of return on common}}{\text{stockholders' equity}} = \frac{\text{Net income} - \text{Preferred dividends}}{\text{Average common stockholders' equity}}$$

$$= \frac{\$33,000,000 - \$6,000,000}{(\$280,000,000 + \$300,000,000) \, / \, 2} = \frac{\$27,000,000}{\$290,000,000} = 0.093$$

Smart Touch has returned $0.093 for each $1 of the average invested by the common stockholders. Smart Touch's rates of return carry both bad news and good news.

- The bad news is that these rates of return are low. Most companies strive for return on equity of 15% or higher. Smart Touch's 9.3% is disappointing.
- The good news is that return on equity exceeds return on assets. That means Smart Touch is earning more for its stockholders than it is paying for interest expense, and that is a healthy sign.

If return on assets ever exceeds return on equity, the company is in trouble. Why? Because the company's interest expense is greater than its return on equity. In that case, no wise investor would buy the company's stock. Return on assets should always be significantly lower than return on equity.

Key Takeaway

Return on assets and return on equity ratios are both measures of how a company is performing. Return on assets measures earnings based on average total assets employed. Return on equity measures earnings for the common stockholders based on average common equity invested.

Accounting for Income Taxes by Corporations

 8 Account for the income tax of a corporation

Corporations pay income tax just as individuals do, but not at the same rates. At this writing, the federal tax rate on most corporate income is 35%. Most states also levy a corporate income tax, so most corporations pay a combined federal and state income tax rate of approximately 40%.

To account for income tax, a corporation measures two income tax amounts:

> Income tax expense = Income before tax on the income statement × Income tax rate

> Income tax payable = Taxable income from the IRS filed tax return × Income tax rate

The income statement and the income tax return are entirely separate documents. You have been studying the income statement throughout this course, but the tax return is new. It reports taxes to the Internal Revenue Service (IRS).

For most companies, income tax expense and income tax payable differ. The most important difference occurs when a corporation uses straight-line depreciation for the income statement and accelerated depreciation for the tax return (to save tax dollars).

Continuing with the Smart Touch illustration, Smart Touch's 2014 figures are as follows:

- Income before income tax of $33,000,000 (This comes from the income statement, which is not presented here.)
- Taxable income of $20,000,000 (This comes from the tax return, which is not presented here.)

Smart Touch will record income tax for 2014 as follows (assume an income tax rate of 40%):

2014			
Dec 31	Income tax expense ($33,000,000 × 0.40) (E+)	13,200,000	
	Income tax payable ($20,000,000 × 0.40) (L+)		8,000,000
	Deferred tax liability (L+)		5,200,000
	Recorded income tax for the year.		

Smart Touch will pay the $8,000,000 of Income tax payable to the IRS and the applicable states within a few months. The difference between Income tax expense and Income tax payable is the Deferred tax liability of $5,200,000. It is a liability because Income tax expense (the amount of expense incurred in 2014) is greater than Income tax payable (the amount Smart Touch has to pay to the IRS when it files its 2014 tax return). It is deferred because Smart Touch will have to pay the 5,200,000 difference in future years on its tax return. The Deferred tax liability account is long-term because it is related to a long-term depreciable asset.

Next, the Decision Guidelines will review some items an investor would consider when purchasing stock.

Decision Guidelines 12-2

DIVIDENDS, STOCK VALUES, EVALUATING OPERATIONS, AND CORPORATE INCOME TAX

Suppose you are considering buying some **IHOP** stock. You are naturally interested in how well the company is doing. Does **IHOP** pay dividends? What are **IHOP**'s stock values? What are the rates of return on **IHOP**'s assets and equity? The Decision Guidelines will help you evaluate the company.

Decision	Guidelines
Dividends	
• When does a company declare a cash dividend?	• The company must have enough Retained earnings to declare the dividend.
	• The company must have enough cash to pay the dividend.
• What happens with a dividend?	• The **IHOP** board of directors declares the dividend. At that point, the dividend becomes a liability for **IHOP**.
	• The stockholder that owns the stock on the date of record will receive the dividend.
	• Payment of the dividend occurs later.
• Who receives the dividend?	• Preferred stockholders get their dividends first. Preferred dividends have a specified rate.
	• Common stockholders receive any remainder.
Stock Values	
• How much should investors pay for a stock?	Its market value
• How is book value used in decision making?	Can measure the value of a stock that is not traded on a stock exchange
Evaluating Operations	
• How can you evaluate the operations of a corporation?	Two measures:
	• Rate of return on total assets (return on assets)
	• Rate of return on common stockholders' equity (return on equity) For a healthy company, return on equity should exceed return on assets by a wide margin.
Accounting for Income Tax	
• What are the three main tax general ledger accounts used in accounting for income taxes?	• Income tax expense, a debit for the amount of income tax expense incurred in the period
	• Income tax payable, a current liability credited for the amount of income tax that must be paid in one year or less
	• Deferred taxes: If Income tax expense > Income tax payable, difference is credited to Deferred tax liability. If Income tax expense < Income tax payable, difference is debited to Deferred tax liability to reduce the liability (or a deferred tax asset if there is no balance in the Deferred tax liability account).
• How to measure	
• income tax expense?	Income before income tax (from the income statement) 3 Income tax rate
• income tax payable?	Taxable income (from the income tax return filed with the Internal Revenue Service) × Income tax rate
• deferred tax asset/liability?	Difference between income tax expense and income tax payable

Summary Problem 12-2

Use the following accounts and related balances to prepare the classified balance sheet of Fiesta, Inc., at September 30, 2014. Compute the book value per share of Fiesta's common stock. Preferred dividends are $5,000 in arrears because Fiesta has not declared the current-year dividend.

Common stock, $1 par, 50,000 shares authorized, 20,000 shares issued	$20,000	Inventory	$ 85,000
Salary payable	3,000	Long-term note payable	70,000
Preferred stock, $2.50, no-par, 10,000 shares authorized, 2,000 shares issued	50,000	Property, plant, and equipment, net	205,000
Accounts payable	20,000	Accounts receivable, net	25,000
Retained earnings	80,000	Cash	15,000
Paid-in capital in excess of par—common	75,000	Income tax payable	12,000

Solution

FIESTA, INC.
Balance Sheet
September 30, 2014

Assets		Liabilities		
Current:		**Current:**		
Cash	$ 15,000	Accounts payable		$ 20,000
Accounts receivable, net	25,000	Salary payable		3,000
Inventory	85,000	Income tax payable		12,000
Total current assets	$125,000	Total current liabilities		$ 35,000
Property, plant, and equipment, net	205,000	Long-term note payable		70,000
		Total liabilities		$105,000
		Stockholders' Equity		
		Preferred stock, $2.50, no-par, 10,000 shares authorized, 2,000 shares issued	$ 50,000	
		Common stock, $1 par, 50,000 shares authorized, 20,000 shares issued	20,000	
		Paid-in capital in excess of par—common	75,000	
		Total paid-in capital	$145,000	
		Retained earnings	80,000	
		Total stockholders' equity		225,000
Total assets	$330,000	Total liabilities and stockholders' equity		$330,000

Book Value (BV) attributed to Preferred stock (P/S):

1) Liquidation value × outstanding shares, OR 2) Preferred stock	$ 50,000
Dividends in Arrears on outstanding preferred shares	5,000
Total BV attributed to P/S	$ 55,000
Outstanding preferred shares	2,000
Book Value per share on Preferred stock	$ 27.50

Book Value (BV) attributed to Common stock (C/S):

Total Stockholders' equity	$225,000
Book Value attributed to P/S (figured above)	55,000
Total BV attributed to C/S (leftovers)	$170,000
Outstanding common shares	20,000
Book Value per share on Common stock	$ 8.50

Review *Corporations: Paid-In Capital and the Balance Sheet*

● Accounting Vocabulary

Additional Paid-In Capital (p. 586)
The paid-in capital in excess of par plus other accounts combined for reporting on the balance sheet. Also called *Paid-in capital in excess of par*.

Arrears (p. 595)
A preferred stock dividend is in arrears if the cumulative dividend has not been paid for the year.

Authorization of Stock (p. 582)
Provision in a corporate charter that gives the state's permission for the corporation to issue—that is, to sell—a certain maximum number of shares of stock.

Book Value per Share of Stock (p. 597)
Amount of owners' equity on the company's books for each share of its stock.

Capital Stock (p. 582)
Represents the individual's ownership of the corporation's capital.

Cumulative Preferred Stock (p. 595)
Preferred stock whose owners must receive all dividends in arrears before the corporation pays dividends to the common stockholders.

Deficit (p. 593)
Debit balance in the Retained earnings account.

Issue Price (p. 585)
The price the stock initially sells for the first time it is sold.

Legal Capital (p. 593)
The portion of stockholders' equity that cannot be used for dividends.

Liquidation Value (p. 597)
The amount guaranteed to the preferred shareholders in the event a company liquidates.

Market Value (p. 596)
Price for which a person could buy or sell a share of stock.

No Par Stock (p. 585)
No arbitrary amount (par) is assigned by a company to a share of its stock.

Outstanding Stock (p. 582)
Issued stock in the hands of stockholders.

Par Value (p. 584)
Arbitrary amount assigned by a company to a share of its stock.

Preferred Stock (p. 584)
Stock that gives its owners certain advantages over common stockholders, such as the right to receive dividends before the common stockholders and the right to receive assets before the common stockholders if the corporation liquidates.

Premium (p. 586)
The amount above par at which a stock is issued.

Rate of Return on Common Stockholders' Equity (p. 599)
Net income minus preferred dividends, divided by average common stockholders' equity. A measure of profitability. Also called **return on equity**.

Rate of Return on Total Assets (p. 598)
The sum of net income plus interest expense divided by average total assets. Measures the success a company has in using its assets to earn income for those financing the business. Also called **return on assets**.

Return on Assets (p. 598)
The sum of net income plus interest expense divided by average total assets. Measures the success a company has in using its assets to earn income for those financing the business. Also called **rate of return on total assets**.

Return on Equity (p. 599)
Net income minus preferred dividends, divided by average common stockholders' equity. A measure of profitability. Also called **rate of return on common stockholders' equity**.

Share (p. 582)
Portions into which the owners' equity of a corporation is divided.

Stated Value (p. 585)
An arbitrary amount that accountants treat as though it were par value.

Stock Certificate (p. 582)
Paper evidencing ownership in a corporation.

Underwriter (p. 585)
A firm, such as **Morgan Stanley**, that usually agrees to buy all the stock a company wants to issue if the firm cannot sell all of the stock to its clients.

● Destination: Student Success

Student Success Tips

The following are hints on some common trouble areas for students in this chapter:

● Keep in mind that par is treated the same as stated value stock. No-par is treated the same as no stated value stock.

● When journalizing stock issuances, credit the common or preferred stock account for either par (stated) value, if it exists, or the full value received, if it's no-par (no stated value) stock. If it's a par value stock, the extra amount received above par goes to the Paid-in capital in excess of par account.

Getting Help

If there's a learning objective from the chapter you aren't confident about, try using one or more of the following resources:

● Review the Decision Guidelines in the chapter.

● Review Summary Problems 12-1 and 12-2 in the chapter to reinforce your understanding of stocks.

● Review Exhibit 12-7, the guide to calculating book value per share.

● Practice additional exercises or problems at the end of Chapter 12 that cover the specific learning objective that is challenging you.

● Destination: Student Success (Continued)

Student Success Tips

- The order of preparation for the stockholders' equity section is the same as the order of liquidation: preferred stock is first, common stock is second, and retained earnings are last.

- Review the cash dividend dates. Remember the date of declaration is when the corporation journalizes (credits) the liability.

- Review the difference between market value, liquidation value, and book value per share.

- Remember that income tax expense and income tax payable are usually not equal. The difference between the amounts is journalized to either a deferred tax asset (debit) or a deferred tax liability (credit).

Getting Help

- Watch the white board videos for Chapter 12 located at myaccountinglab.com under the Chapter Resources button.

- Go to myaccountinglab.com and select the Study Plan button. Choose Chapter 12 and work the questions covering that specific learning objective until you've mastered it.

- Work the Chapter 12 pre/post tests in myaccountinglab.com.

- Visit the learning resource center on your campus for tutoring.

● Quick Check

1. Which characteristic of a corporation is most attractive?
   a. Double taxation
   b. Limited liability
   c. Mutual agency
   d. Items a, b, and c are all correct

2. Which corporate characteristic is a disadvantage?
   a. Mutual agency
   b. Double taxation
   c. Limited liability
   d. None are disadvantages

3. The two basic sources of corporate capital are
   a. assets and equity.
   b. preferred and common.
   c. Retained earnings and Dividends.
   d. paid-in capital and Retained earnings.

4. The amount of equity attributed per common share is called
   a. market value per share.
   b. liquidation value per share.
   c. book value per share.
   d. par value per share.

5. Suppose Value Home and Garden Imports issued 400,000 shares of $0.10 par common stock at $4 per share. Which journal entry correctly records the issuance of this stock?

   a.

Common stock	1,600,000	
Cash		40,000
Paid-in capital in excess of par—common		1,560,000

   b.

Common stock	1,600,000	
Cash		1,600,000

   c.

Cash	1,600,000	
Common stock		40,000
Paid-in capital in excess of par—common		1,560,000

   d.

Cash	1,600,000	
Common stock		1,600,000

6. Suppose Yummy Treats Bakery issues common stock to purchase a building. Yummy Treats Bakery should record the building at

   a. the par value of the stock given.

   b. its book value.

   c. its market value.

   d. a value assigned by the board of directors.

7. Jackson Health Foods has 8,000 shares of $2 par common stock outstanding, which was issued at $15 per share. Jackson also has a deficit balance in Retained earnings of $86,000. How much is Jackson's total stockholders' equity?

   a. $16,000   c. $206,000

   b. $120,000   d. $34,000

8. Winston Corporation has 9,000 shares of 4%, $10 par preferred stock, and 47,000 shares of common stock outstanding. Winston declared no dividends in 2011. In 2012, Winston declares a total dividend of $54,000. How much of the dividends go to the common stockholders?

   a. $54,000   c. $46,800

   b. $50,400   d. None; it all goes to preferred.

9. Dale Corporation has the following data:

Net income	$ 24,000	Average total assets	$ 300,000
Interest expense	9,000	Average common equity	100,000
Preferred dividends	12,000		

   Dale's return on assets is

   a. 5%.   c. 11%.

   b. 12%.   d. 8%.

10. A corporation's income tax payable is computed as

    a. Net income × Income tax rate.

    b. Income before tax × Income tax rate.

    c. Taxable income × Income tax rate.

    d. Return on equity × Income tax rate.

Answers are given after Apply Your Knowledge (p. 622).

Assess Your Progress

● Short Exercises

S12-1   ❶ Corporation characteristics [5 min]

Due to the recent beef recalls, Southern Steakhouse is considering incorporating. Bill, the owner, wants to protect his personal assets in the event the restaurant is sued.

Requirement

   1. Which advantage of incorporating is most applicable?

MyAccountingLab

S12-2 ② **Sources of stockholders' equity [5 min]**

Stockholders' equity may arise from several sources.

Requirements

1. Identify the two primary sources of stockholders' equity.
2. Which source would be considered to be "internally" generated?

S12-3 ③ **Issuing stock [5 min]**

California Corporation has two classes of stock: Common, $2 par; and Preferred, $10 par.

Requirement

1. Journalize California's issuance of
   a. 2,000 shares of common stock for $11 per share.
   b. 2,000 shares of preferred stock for a total of $20,000.

S12-4 ③ **Effect of a stock issuance [5-10 min]**

Brawndo issued common stock and received $29,000,000. The par value of the Brawndo stock was only $34,000.

Requirements

1. Is the excess amount of $28,966,000 a profit to Brawndo?
2. Journalize the entry to record the stock issuance.

S12-5 ③ **Issuing stock and interpreting stockholders' equity [5–10 min]**

Scifilink.com issued stock beginning in 2012 and reported the following on its balance sheet at December 31, 2012:

Common stock, $ 2.00 par value	
Authorized: 6,000 shares	
Issued: 4,000 shares	$ 8,000
Paid-in capital in excess of par	4,000
Retained earnings	26,500

Requirement

1. Journalize the company's issuance of the stock for cash.

S12-6 ③ **Preparing the stockholders' equity section of the balance sheet [5 min]**

Mountainview Corporation reported the following accounts:

Cost of goods sold	$ 60,500	Accounts payable	$ 6,500
Paid-in capital in excess of par	90,000	Retained earnings	18,000
Common stock, $ 3 par value,		Unearned revenue	5,300
60,000 shares issued	180,000	Total assets	?
Cash	22,500	Long-term note payable	7,700

Requirements

1. Prepare the stockholders' equity section of Mountainview's balance sheet.
2. What was the average selling price of each common share?

S12-7 ④ **Closing entries [5–10 min]**

The data for Amanda's Tax Service, Inc., for the year ended August 31, 2012, follow:

Cost of goods sold	$ 62,000	Sales revenue	$ 125,000
Dividends	14,000	Operating expenses	44,000
Interest revenue	1,800	Retained earnings	24,000

Requirements

1. Journalize the required closing entries for the year.
2. What is the balance in Retained earnings after the closing entries are posted?

S12-8 ④⑤ **Accounting for cash dividends [10 min]**

Frenchvanilla Company earned net income of $75,000 during the year ended December 31, 2012. On December 15, Frenchvanilla declared the annual cash dividend on its 5% preferred stock (par value, $115,000) and a $0.50 per share cash dividend on its common stock (55,000 shares). Frenchvanilla then paid the dividends on January 4, 2013.

Requirement

1. Journalize for Frenchvanilla:
   a. Declaring the cash dividends on December 15, 2012.
   b. Paying the cash dividends on January 4, 2013.

S12-9 ⑤ **Dividing cash dividends between preferred and common stock [5–10 min]**

Precious Metal Trust has the following stockholders' equity:

Paid-in capital:	
Preferred stock, 5%, $15 par, 7,000 shares authorized, 5,500 shares issued	$ 82,500
Common stock, $0.30 par, 1,200,000 shares authorized and issued	360,000
Paid-in capital in excess of par—common	400,000
Total paid-in capital	$ 842,500
Retained earnings	260,000
Total stockholders' equity	$1,102,500

Requirements

1. Is Precious Metal's preferred stock cumulative or noncumulative? How can you tell?
2. Precious Metal declares cash dividends of $25,000 for 2010. How much of the dividends goes to preferred? How much goes to common?
3. Precious Metal passed the preferred dividend in 2011 and 2012. In 2013 the company declares cash dividends of $35,000. How much of the dividend goes to preferred? How much goes to common?

S12-10 ⑥ **Book value per share of common stock [5–10 min]**

Bronze Tint Trust has the following stockholders' equity:

Paid-in capital:	
Preferred stock, 5%, $10 par, 6,000 shares authorized, 4,500 shares issued	$ 45,000
Common stock, $0.20 par, 1,200,000 shares authorized and issued	240,000
Paid-in capital in excess of par—common	400,000
Total paid-in capital	$ 685,000
Retained earnings	255,000
Total stockholders' equity	$ 940,000

Bronze Tint has not declared preferred dividends for five years (including the current year).

Requirement

1. Compute the book value per share of Bronze Tint's preferred and common stock.

S12-11 ⑦ **Computing return on assets and return on equity [5–10 min]**

Godhi's 2012 financial statements reported the following items—with 2011 figures given for comparison:

GODHI Balance Sheet		
	2012	**2011**
Total assets	$ 33,538	$ 29,562
Total liabilities	17,100	14,962
Total stockholders' equity (all common)	16,438	14,600
Total liabilities and equity	$ 33,538	$ 29,562

GODHI Income Statement	
Net sales	$ 21,960
Cost of goods sold	7,900
Gross profit	$ 14,060
Selling, administrative, and general expenses	8,600
Interest expense	210
All other expenses	1,360
Net income	$ 3,890

Requirement

1. Compute Godhi's rate of return on total assets and rate of return on common stockholders' equity for 2012. Do these rates of return look high or low?

S12-12 ⑧ **Accounting for income tax [5–10 min]**

Hoxey Flowers had income before income tax of $70,000 and taxable income of $60,000 for 2012, the company's first year of operations. The income tax rate is 30%.

Requirements

1. Make the entry to record Hoxey's income taxes for 2012.
2. Show what Hoxey's will report on its 2012 income statement, starting with income before income tax.

• Exercises

E12-13 ❶ **Advantages and disadvantages of a corporation [5–10 min]**   *MyAccountingLab*
Following is a list of advantages and disadvantages of the corporate form of business.

    1. Ownership and management are separated.

    2. Has continuous life.

    3. Transfer of ownership is easy.

    4. Stockholders' liability is limited.

    5. Double taxation.

    6. Can raise more money than a partnership or proprietorship.

    7. Government regulation is expensive.

Requirement

    1. Identify each quality as either an advantage or a disadvantage.

E12-14 ❷ **Paid-in capital for a corporation [10 min]**
Alley Corporation recently organized. The company issued common stock to an inventor in exchange for a patent with a market value of $56,000. In addition, Alley received cash both for 2,000 shares of its $10 par preferred stock at par value and for 9,000 shares of its no-par common stock at $45 per share.

Requirement

    1. Without making journal entries, determine the total *paid-in capital* created by these transactions.

E12-15 ❸ **Issuing stock [10–15 min]**
Susie Systems completed the following stock issuance transactions:

May 19	Issued 2,000 shares of $1 par common stock for cash of $9.50 per share.
Jun 3	Sold 300 shares of $3, no-par preferred stock for $15,000 cash.
11	Received equipment with market value of $78,000. Issued 3,000 shares of the $1 par common stock in exchange.

Requirements

    1. Journalize the transactions. Explanations are not required.

    2. How much paid-in capital did these transactions generate for Susie Systems?

E12-16 ❸ **Recording issuance of no-par stock [5–10 min]**
Dates, Corp., issued 4,000 shares of no-par common stock for $9 per share.

Requirements

    1. Record issuance of the stock if the stock
        a. is true no-par stock and
        b. has stated value of $2 per share.

    2. Which type of stock results in more total paid-in capital?

E12-17 ❸ **Issuing stock and preparing the stockholders' equity section of the balance sheet [15–20 min]**

The charter for KCAS-TV, Inc., authorizes the company to issue 100,000 shares of $4, no-par preferred stock and 500,000 shares of common stock with $1 par value. During its start-up phase, KCAS completed the following transactions:

Sep 6	Issued 275 shares of common stock to the promoters who organized the corporation, receiving cash of $8,250.
12	Issued 400 shares of preferred stock for cash of $20,000.
14	Issued 1,600 shares of common stock in exchange for land valued at $18,000.
30	Closed net income of $32,000 into Retained earnings.

Requirements

1. Record the transactions in the general journal.
2. Prepare the stockholders' equity section of the KCAS-TV balance sheet at September 30, 2012.

E12-18 ❸ **Stockholders' equity section of the balance sheet [10–15 min]**

The charter of Evergreen Capital Corporation authorizes the issuance of 900 shares of preferred stock and 1,250 shares of common stock. During a two-month period, Evergreen completed these stock-issuance transactions:

Mar 23	Issued 230 shares of $4 par common stock for cash of $15 per share.
Apr 12	Received inventory valued at $23,000 and equipment with a market value of $20,000 for 320 shares of the $4 par common stock.
17	Issued 900 shares of 5%, $20 par preferred stock for $20 per share.

Requirements

1. Record the transactions in the general journal.
2. Prepare the stockholders' equity section of the Evergreen balance sheet for the transactions given in this exercise. Retained earnings has a balance of $79,000.

E12-19 ❹ **Calculating retained earnings [10–15 min]**

Oulette Publishing Company has the following selected account balances at June 30, 2012.

Inventory	$ 112,000	Common stock, no par with $0.50	
Machinery and equipment	108,000	stated value, 900 shares	
Dividends	8,000	authorized and issued	$ 450
Depreciation expense	9,000	Accumulated depreciation	61,000
Rent expense	19,000	Salary expense	85,000
Utilities expense	5,000	Retained earnings, June 30, 2011	114,000
Cost of goods sold	81,000	Sales revenue	240,000

Requirements

1. Journalize all required closing entries for the year.
2. Calculate the balance in Retained earnings at June 30, 2012. Use a T-account to show your calculations.

E12-20 ⑤ **Dividing dividends between preferred and common stock [10–15 min]**
Northern Communications has the following stockholders' equity:

NORTHERN COMMUNICATIONS	
Stockholders' Equity	
Paid-in Capital:	
Preferred stock, 6%, $11 par, 150,000 shares authorized	
20,000 shares issued and outstanding	$ 220,000
Common stock, $3 par, 575,000 shares authorized	
400,000 shares issued and outstanding	1,200,000
Paid-in capital in excess of par—common	1,000,000
Total paid-in capital	2,420,000
Retained earnings	190,000
Total stockholders' equity	$2,610,000

Requirements

1. First, determine whether preferred stock is cumulative or noncumulative.
2. Compute the amount of dividends to preferred and to common for 2011 and 2012 if total dividends are $12,200 in 2011 and $55,000 in 2012.
3. What is the average price at which each preferred share sold for? What is the average price at which each common share sold for?

E12-21 ⑤ **Computing dividends on preferred and common stock [15–20 min]**
The following elements of stockholders' equity are adapted from the balance sheet of Sandler Marketing, Corp.

SANDLER MARKETING, CORP.	
Stockholders' Equity	
Preferred stock, 7% cumulative, $2 par,	
75,000 shares authorized, issued and outstanding	$ 150,000
Common stock, $0.10 par, 10,250,000 shares authorized,	
9,500,000 shares issued and outstanding	950,000

Sandler paid no preferred dividends in 2011.

Requirement

1. Compute the dividends to the preferred and common shareholders for 2012 if total dividends are $195,000.

E12-22 ⑥ **Book value per share of common stock [0–15 min]**
The balance sheet of Mark Todd Wireless, Inc., reported the following:

Preferred stock, 9%, $20 par, 1,300 shares authorized, issued and outstanding	$ 26,000
Common stock, no-par value, 12,000 shares authorized, 5,300 shares issued	200,000
Retained earnings	50,000
Total stockholders' equity	$ 276,000

Assume that Todd has paid preferred dividends for the current year and all prior years (no dividends in arrears).

Requirement

1. Compute the book value per share of the common stock.

E12-23 ⑥ **Book value per share of common stock, and preferred dividends in arrears [10–15 min]**

The balance sheet of Moe Taylor, Inc., reported the following:

Preferred stock, 7%, $30 par, 1,000 shares authorized, issued and outstanding	$ 30,000
Common stock, no-par value, 11,000 shares authorized, 5,600 shares issued	226,000
Retained earnings	80,000
Total stockholders' equity	$ 336,000

Requirement

1. Compute the book value per share of Taylor's preferred and common stock if three years' preferred dividends (including dividends for the current year) are in arrears.

E12-24 ⑦ **Evaluating profitability [10–15 min]**

Lofty Exploration Company reported these figures for 2012 and 2011:

	2012	2011
Income Statement—partial:		
Interest expense	12,400,000	17,400,000
Net Income	17,900,000	19,100,000

	2012	2011
Balance Sheet—partial:		
Total assets	$ 328,000,000	$ 318,000,000
Preferred stock, $2, no-par, 150,000 shares authorized, issued and outstanding	$ 2,400,000	$ 2,400,000
Common stockholders' equity	178,000,000	171,000,000
Retained earnings	4,000,000	3,000,000
Total stockholders' equity	$ 184,400,000	$ 176,400,000

Requirements

1. Compute rate of return on total assets and rate of return on common stockholders' equity for 2012.
2. Do these rates of return suggest strength or weakness? Give your reason.

E12-25 ⑧ **Accounting for corporate income tax [10–15 min]**

The income statement of Jennifer's Cards, Inc., reported income before income tax of $400,000,000 during a recent year. Assume Jennifer's taxable income for the year was $342,000,000. The company's income tax rate was 35.0%.

Requirements

1. Journalize Jennifer's entry to record income tax expense for the year.
2. Show how Jennifer's would report income tax expense on its income statement and income tax liabilities on its balance sheet. Complete the income statement, starting with income before tax. For the balance sheet, assume all beginning balances were zero.

● Problems (Group A)

MyAccountingLab

P12-26A ① ③ **Organizing a corporation and issuing stock [10–20 min]**

Jay and Mike are opening a paint store. There are no competing paint stores in the area. Their fundamental decision is how to organize the business. They anticipate profits of $300,000 the first year, with the ability to sell franchises in the future. Although they have enough to start the business now as a partnership, cash flow will be an issue as they grow. They feel the corporate form of operation will be best for the long term. They seek your advice.

Requirements

1. What is the main advantage they gain by selecting a corporate form of business now?
2. Would you recommend they initially issue preferred or common stock? Why?
3. If they decide to issue $2 par common stock and anticipate an initial market price of $30 per share, how many shares will they need to issue to raise $1,800,000?

P12-27A ② ③ ⑤ **Sources of equity, stock issuance, and dividends [15–20 min]**

Terrific Comfort Specialists, Inc., reported the following stockholders' equity on its balance sheet at June 30, 2012:

TERRIFIC COMFORT SPECIALISTS, INC. Stockholders' Equity June 30, 2012	
Paid-in Capital:	
Preferred stock, 5%, ? par, 650,000 shares authorized, 280,000 shares issued	$ 1,400,000
Common stock, par value $1 per share, 5,000,000 shares authorized, 1,350,000 shares issued and outstanding	1,350,000
Paid in capital in excess of par—common	2,400,000
Total paid-in capital	5,150,000
Retained earnings	12,300,000
Total stockholders' equity	$ 17,450,000

Requirements

1. Identify the different issues of stock that Terrific has outstanding.
2. What is the par value per share of Terrific's preferred stock?
3. Make two summary journal entries to record issuance of all the Terrific stock for cash. Explanations are not required.
4. No preferred dividends are in arrears. Journalize the declaration of a $600,000 dividend at June 30, 2012. Use separate Dividends payable accounts for preferred and common. An explanation is not required.

P12-28A ② ⑤ ⑥ **Analyzing the stockholders' equity section of the balance sheet [15–20 min]**

The balance sheet of Buzzcraft, Inc., reported the following:

Preferred stock, $7 par, 5%, 1,000 shares authorized and issued	$ 7,000
Common stock, $1.50 par value, 43,000 shares authorized; 11,000 shares issued	16,500
Paid-in capital in excess of par—common	224,000
Total paid-in capital	247,500
Retained earnings	80,000
Total stockholders' equity	$ 327,500

Preferred dividends are in arrears for two years, including the current year. On the balance sheet date, the market value of the Buzzcraft common stock was $28 per share.

Requirements

1. Is the preferred stock cumulative or noncumulative? How can you tell?
2. What is the total paid-in capital of the company?
3. What was the total market value of the common stock?
4. Compute the book value per share of the common stock.

P12-29A ③ **Journalizing corporate transactions and preparing the stockholders' equity section of the balance sheet [20–25 min]**

B-Mobile Wireless needed additional capital to expand, so the business incorporated. The charter from the state of Georgia authorizes B-Mobile to issue 70,000 shares of 5%, $100-par preferred stock, and 110,000 shares of no-par common stock. B-Mobile completed the following transactions:

Oct 2	Issued 19,000 shares of common stock for equipment with a market value of $110,000.
6	Issued 800 shares of preferred stock to acquire a patent with a market value of $80,000.
9	Issued 15,000 shares of common stock for cash of $90,000.

Requirements

1. Record the transactions in the general journal.
2. Prepare the stockholders' equity section of the B-Mobile balance sheet at October 31. The ending balance of Retained earnings is $92,000.

P12-30A ③ **Issuing stock and preparing the stockholders' equity section of the balance sheet [15–20 min]**

Lincoln-Priest, Inc., was organized in 2011. At December 31, 2011, the Lincoln-Priest balance sheet reported the following stockholders' equity:

LINCOLN-PRIEST, INC.		
Stockholders' Equity		
December 31, 2011		
Paid-in Capital:		
Preferred stock, 7%, $40 par, 110,000 shares authorized, none issued	$	0
Common stock, $1 par, 520,000 shares authorized, 61,000 shares issued and outstanding		61,000
Paid-in capital in excess of par—common		41,000
Total paid-in capital		102,000
Retained earnings		29,000
Total stockholders' equity		$ 131,000

Requirements

1. During 2012, the company completed the following selected transactions. Journalize each transaction. Explanations are not required.
   a. Issued for cash 1,300 shares of preferred stock at par value.
   b. Issued for cash 2,400 shares of common stock at a price of $5 per share.
   c. Net income for the year was $74,000, and the company declared no dividends. Make the closing entry for net income.
2. Prepare the stockholders' equity section of the Lincoln-Priest balance sheet at December 31, 2012.

P12-31A ③ ④ **Stockholders' equity section of the balance sheet and Retained earnings [20–25 min]**

The following summaries for Miller Service, Inc., and Griffin, Co., provide the information needed to prepare the stockholders' equity section of each company's balance sheet. The two companies are independent.

* *Miller Service, Inc.*: Miller is authorized to issue 46,000 shares of $1 par common stock. All the stock was issued at $12 per share. The company incurred net losses of $44,000 in 2009 and $10,000 in 2010. It earned net income of $29,000 in 2011 and $181,000 in 2012. The company declared no dividends during the four-year period.

* *Griffin, Co.*: Griffin's charter authorizes the issuance of 30,000 shares of 6%, $12 par preferred stock and 520,000 shares of no-par common stock. Griffin issued 1,100 shares of the preferred stock at $12 per share. It issued 110,000 shares of the common stock for $220,000. The company's retained earnings balance at the beginning of 2012 was $140,000. Net income for 2012 was $90,000, and the company declared the specified preferred dividend for 2012. Preferred dividends for 2011 were in arrears.

Requirement

1. For each company, prepare the stockholders' equity section of its balance sheet at December 31, 2012. Show the computation of all amounts. Entries are not required.

P12-32A ⑤ **Computing dividends on preferred and common stock [15–20 min]**

Fashonista Skincare has 10,000 shares of 3%, $20 par value preferred stock and 90,000 shares of $2 par common stock outstanding. During a three-year period, Fashionista declared and paid cash dividends as follows: 2010, $3,000; 2011, $13,000; and 2012, $17,000.

Requirements

1. Compute the total dividends to preferred and to common for each of the three years if
   a. preferred is noncumulative.
   b. preferred is cumulative.

2. For requirement 1.b., journalize the declaration of the 2012 dividends on December 22, 2012, and payment on January 14, 2013. Use separate Dividends payable accounts for preferred and common.

P12-33A ③ ⑦ **Preparing a corporate balance sheet and measuring profitability [40–50 min]**

The following accounts and December 31, 2012, balances of New Jersey Optical Corporation are arranged in no particular order.

Retained earnings	$ 151,500	Common stock, $4 par	
Inventory	103,000	125,000 shares authorized,	
Property, plant, and equipment, net	285,000	24,000 shares issued	$ 96,000
Prepaid expenses	13,000	Dividends payable	4,000
Goodwill	64,000	Paid-in capital in excess of par—common	140,000
Accrued liabilities payable	17,000	Accounts payable	32,000
Long-term note payable	101,000	Preferred stock, 5%, $13 par,	
Accounts receivable, net	107,000	50,000 shares authorized,	
Cash	41,000	5,500 shares issued	71,500

Total assets, Dec 31, 2011	$	501,000
Common equity, Dec 31, 2011		307,000
Net income, 2012		47,000
Interest expense, 2012		3,000

Requirements

1. Prepare the company's classified balance sheet in account format at December 31, 2012.

2. Compute New Jersey Optical's rate of return on total assets and rate of return on common stockholders' equity for the year ended December 31, 2012.

3. Do these rates of return suggest strength or weakness? Give your reasoning.

P12-34A ⑧ **Computing and recording a corporation's income tax [15–20 min]**

The accounting records of Rhyme Redwood Corporation provide income statement data for 2012.

Total revenue	$	940,000
Total expenses		750,000
Income before tax	$	190,000

Total expenses include depreciation of $50,000 computed on the straight-line method. In calculating taxable income on the tax return, Rhyme Redwood uses the modified accelerated cost recovery system (MACRS). MACRS depreciation was $80,000 for 2012. The corporate income tax rate is 34%.

Requirements

1. Compute taxable income for the year. For this computation, substitute MACRS depreciation in place of straight-line depreciation.
2. Journalize the corporation's income tax for 2012.
3. Show how to report the two income tax liabilities on Rhyme's classified balance sheet.

● Problems (Group B)

MyAccountingLab

P12-35B ① ③ **Organizing a corporation and issuing stock [10–20 min]**

Ben and Eric are opening a comic book store. There are no competing comic book stores in the area. Their fundamental decision is how to organize the business. They anticipate profits of $350,000 the first year, with the ability to sell franchises in the future. Although they have enough to start the business now as a partnership, cash flow will be an issue as they grow. They feel the corporate form of operation will be best for the long term. They seek your advice.

Requirements

1. What is the main advantage they gain by selecting a corporate form of business now?
2. Would you recommend they initially issue preferred or common stock? Why?
3. If they decide to issue $1 par common stock and anticipate an initial market price of $80 per share, how many shares will they need to issue to raise $4,000,000?

P12-36B ② ③ ⑤ **Sources of equity, stock issuance, and dividends [15–20 min]**

Tree Comfort Specialists, Inc., reported the following stockholders' equity on its balance sheet at April 30, 2012.

TREE COMFORT SPECIALISTS, INC.		
Stockholders' Equity		
April 30, 2012		
Paid-in Capital:		
Preferred stock, 6%, ? par, 675,000 shares authorized, 240,000 shares issued	$	1,200,000
Common stock, par value $1 per share, 9,000,000 shares authorized,		
1,330,000 shares issued and outstanding		1,330,000
Paid-in capital in excess of par—common		2,600,000
Total paid-in capital		5,130,000
Retained earnings		11,900,000
Total stockholders' equity	$	17,030,000

Requirements

1. Identify the different issues of stock that Tree has outstanding.
2. What is the par value per share of Tree's preferred stock?
3. Make two summary journal entries to record issuance of all the Tree stock for cash. Explanations are not required.
4. No preferred dividends are in arrears. Journalize the declaration of a $300,000 dividend at April 30, 2012. Use separate Dividends payable accounts for preferred and common. An explanation is not required.

P12-37B ❷❺❻ **Analyzing the stockholders' equity section of the balance sheet [15–20 min]**

The balance sheet of Ballcraft, Inc., reported the following:

Preferred stock, $8 par, 5%,	
4,000 shares authorized and issued	$ 32,000
Common stock, $2.50 par value, 41,000 shares authorized;	
16,000 shares issued	40,000
Paid-in capital in excess of par—common	225,000
Total paid-in capital	297,000
Retained earnings	40,000
Total stockholders' equity	$ 337,000

Preferred dividends are in arrears for two years, including the current year. On the balance sheet date, the market value of the Ballcraft common stock was $31 per share.

Requirements

1. Is the preferred stock cumulative or noncumulative? How can you tell?
2. What is the total paid-in capital of the company?
3. What was the total market value of the common stock?
4. Compute the book value per share of the common stock.

P12-38B ❸ **Journalizing corporate transactions and preparing the stockholders' equity section of the balance sheet [20–25 min]**

Cell Wireless needed additional capital to expand, so the business incorporated. The charter from the state of Georgia authorizes Cell to issue 40,000 shares of 10%, $50 par preferred stock and 100,000 shares of no-par common stock. Cell completed the following transactions:

Jan 2	Issued 21,000 shares of common stock for equipment with a market value of $140,000.
6	Issued 600 shares of preferred stock to acquire a patent with a market value of $30,000.
9	Issued 11,000 shares of common stock for cash of $66,000.

Requirements

1. Record the transactions in the general journal.
2. Prepare the stockholders' equity section of the Cell balance sheet at January 31. The ending balance of Retained earnings is $93,000.

P12-39B ③ **Issuing stock and preparing the stockholders' equity section of the balance sheet [15–20 min]**

Lurvey-Priest, Inc., was organized in 2011. At December 31, 2011, the Lurvey-Priest balance sheet reported the following stockholders' equity:

LURVEY-PRIEST, INC.		
Stockholders' Equity		
December 31, 2011		
Paid-in Capital:		
Preferred stock, 4%, $55 par, 140,000 shares authorized, none issued	$	0
Common stock, $2 par, 540,000 shares authorized, 62,000 shares issued and outstanding		124,000
Paid-in capital in excess of par—common		42,000
Total paid-in capital		$ 166,000
Retained earnings		28,000
Total stockholders' equity		$ 194,000

Requirements

1. During 2012, the company completed the following selected transactions. Journalize each transaction. Explanations are not required.
   a. Issued for cash 1,500 shares of preferred stock at par value.
   b. Issued for cash 2,000 shares of common stock at a price of $7 per share.
   c. Net income for the year was $78,000, and the company declared no dividends. Make the closing entry for net income.

2. Prepare the stockholders' equity section of the Lurvey-Priest balance sheet at December 31, 2012.

P12-40B ③ ④ **Stockholders' equity section of the balance sheet [20–25 min]**

The following summaries for Maryland Service, Inc., and Grapone, Co., provide the information needed to prepare the stockholders' equity section of each company's balance sheet. The two companies are independent.

* *Maryland Service, Inc.*: Maryland is authorized to issue 44,000 shares of $1 par common stock. All the stock was issued at $11 per share. The company incurred net losses of $47,000 in 2009 and $15,000 in 2010. It earned net income of $32,000 in 2011 and $178,000 in 2012. The company declared no dividends during the four-year period.

* *Grapone, Co.*: Grapone's charter authorizes the issuance of 70,000 shares of 5%, $14 par preferred stock and 470,000 shares of no-par common stock. Grapone issued 1,400 shares of the preferred stock at $14 per share. It issued 130,000 shares of the common stock for $260,000. The company's retained earnings balance at the beginning of 2012 was $60,000. Net income for 2012 was $98,000, and the company declared the specified preferred dividend for 2012. Preferred dividends for 2011 were in arrears.

Requirement

1. For each company, prepare the stockholders' equity section of its balance sheet at December 31, 2012. Show the computation of all amounts. Entries are not required.

P12-41B ⑤ **Computing dividends on preferred and common stock [15–20 min]**

Mode Skincare has 10,000 shares of 5%, $10 par value preferred stock, and 110,000 shares of $1.50 par common stock outstanding. During a three-year period, Mode declared and paid cash dividends as follows: 2010, $4,000; 2011, $10,000; and 2012, $20,000.

Requirements

1. Compute the total dividends to preferred and to common for each of the three years if
   a. preferred is noncumulative.
   b. preferred is cumulative.

2. For requirement 1.b., journalize the declaration of the 2012 dividends on December 22, 2012, and payment on January 14, 2013. Use separate Dividends payable accounts for preferred and common.

P12-42B ❸ ❼ **Preparing a corporate balance sheet, and measuring profitability [40–50 min]**

The following accounts and December 31, 2012, balances of Georgia Optical Corporation are arranged in no particular order.

Retained earnings	$ 99,000	Common stock, $4 par	
Inventory	106,000	125,000 shares authorized,	
Property, plant, and equipment, net	277,000	25,000 shares issued	$ 100,000
Prepaid expenses	14,000	Dividends payable	6,000
Goodwill	61,000	Paid-in capital in excess of par—common	160,000
Accrued liabilities payable	15,000	Accounts payable	33,000
Long-term note payable	103,000	Preferred stock, 5%, $14 par,	
Accounts receivable, net	107,000	50,000 shares authorized,	
Cash	49,000	7,000 shares issued	98,000

Total assets, Dec 31, 2011	$	505,000
Common equity, Dec 31, 2011		305,000
Net income, 2012		45,000
Interest expense, 2012		3,500

Requirements

1. Prepare the company's classified balance sheet in account format at December 31, 2012.
2. Compute Georgia Optical's rate of return on total assets and rate of return on common stockholders' equity for the year ended December 31, 2012.
3. Do these rates of return suggest strength or weakness? Give your reasoning.

P12-43B ❽ **Computing and recording a corporation's income tax [15–20 min]**

The accounting records of Reflection Glass Corporation provide income statement data for 2012.

Total revenue	$	910,000
Total expenses		670,000
Income before tax	$	240,000

Total expenses include depreciation of $54,000 computed on the straight-line method. In calculating taxable income on the tax return, Reflection Glass uses the modified accelerated cost recovery system (MACRS). MACRS depreciation was $75,000 for 2012. The corporate income tax rate is 36%.

Requirements

1. Compute taxable income for the year. For this computation, substitute MACRS depreciation in place of straight-line depreciation.
2. Journalize the corporation's income tax for 2012.
3. Show how to report the two income tax liabilities on Reflection's classified balance sheet.

● Continuing Exercise

E12-44 ❷ ❺ **Sources of equity and journalizing cash dividends [10–15 min]**   *MyAccountingLab*

This exercise continues the Lawlor Lawn Service, Inc., situation from Exercise 11-33 of Chapter 11. On September 18, Lawlor Lawn Service declared a dividend of $2,000 to all common shareholders of record on September 23 to be paid on October 1.

Requirements

1. Journalize the entries related to the dividends.
2. On September 30, on what financial statement would the dividend balance appear? Why?

• Continuing Problem

P12-45 ❷❸❻ **Sources of equity, journalizing stock issuance, and calculating book value per share [20–25 min]**

This problem continues the Draper Consulting, Inc., situation from Problem 11-34 of Chapter 11. After issuing the bonds in Chapter 11, Draper decides to raise additional capital for the planned business expansion by issuing 20,000 additional no par common shares for $40,000 and by issuing 3,000, 6%, $80 par preferred shares at $100 per share.

Requirements

1. Assuming total stockholders' equity is $18,165 and includes 100 shares of common stock and 0 shares of preferred stock issued and outstanding immediately before the previously described transactions, journalize the entry related to the issuances of both common and preferred shares.

2. Calculate book value per preferred and book value per common share after the issuance.

Apply Your Knowledge

• Decision Cases

Decision Case 12-1 Lena Kay and Kathy Lauder have a patent on a new line of cosmetics. They need additional capital to market the products, and they plan to incorporate the business. They are considering the capital structure for the corporation. Their primary goal is to raise as much capital as possible without giving up control of the business. Kay and Lauder plan to invest the patent (an intangible asset, which will be transferred to the company's ownership in lieu of cash) in the company and receive 100,000 shares of the corporation's common stock. They have been offered $100,000 for the patent, which provides an indication of the "fair value" of the patent.

The corporation's plans for a charter include an authorization to issue 5,000 shares of preferred stock and 500,000 shares of $1 par common stock. Kay and Lauder are uncertain about the most desirable features for the preferred stock. Prior to incorporating, they are discussing their plans with two investment groups. The corporation can obtain capital from outside investors under either of the following plans:

- **Plan 1.** Group 1 will invest $150,000 to acquire 1,500 shares of 6%, $100 par nonvoting, noncumulative preferred stock.
- **Plan 2.** Group 2 will invest $100,000 to acquire 1,000 shares of $5, no-par preferred stock and $70,000 to acquire 70,000 shares of common stock. Each preferred share receives 50 votes on matters that come before the stockholders.

Requirements

Assume that the corporation has been chartered (approved) by the state.

1. Journalize the issuance of common stock to Kay and Lauder. Explanations are not required.
2. Journalize the issuance of stock to the outsiders under both plans. Explanations are not required.
3. Net income for the first year is $180,000 and total dividends are $30,000. Prepare the stockholders' equity section of the corporation's balance sheet under both plans.
4. Recommend one of the plans to Kay and Lauder. Give your reasons.

Decision Case 12-2 Answering the following questions will enhance your understanding of the capital stock of corporations. Consider each question independently of the others.

Requirements

1. Why are capital stock and retained earnings shown separately in the shareholders' equity section of the balance sheet?

2. Preferred shares have advantages with respect to dividends and corporate liquidation. Why might investors buy common stock when preferred stock is available?

3. Manuel Chavez, major shareholder of MC, Inc., proposes to sell some land he owns to the company for common shares in MC. What problem does MC face in recording the transaction?

● Ethical Issue 12-1

Note: This case is based on an actual situation.

Stan Sewell paid $50,000 for a franchise that entitled him to market software programs in the countries of the European Union. Sewell intended to sell individual franchises for the major language groups of Western Europe—German, French, English, Spanish, and Italian. Naturally, investors considering buying a franchise from Sewell asked to see the financial statements of his business.

Believing the value of the franchise to be $500,000, Sewell sought to capitalize his own franchise at $500,000. The law firm of St. Charles & LaDue helped Sewell form a corporation chartered to issue 500,000 shares of common stock with par value of $1 per share. Attorneys suggested the following chain of transactions:

a. Sewell's cousin, Bob, borrows $500,000 from a bank and purchases the franchise from Sewell.

b. Sewell pays the corporation $500,000 to acquire all its stock.

c. The corporation buys the franchise from Cousin Bob.

d. Cousin Bob repays the $500,000 loan to the bank.

In the final analysis, Cousin Bob is debt-free and out of the picture. Sewell owns all the corporation's stock, and the corporation owns the franchise. The corporation's balance sheet lists a franchise acquired at a cost of $500,000. This balance sheet is Sewell's most valuable marketing tool.

Requirements

1. What is unethical about this situation?

2. Who can be harmed? How can they be harmed? What role does accounting play?

● Fraud Case 12-1

Elaine Jackson just had a visit from her cousin Phil. He wanted to apologize. Last year he had regaled her with stories about a small company he had discovered that had just invented a high-tech converter to allow cars to run on water. It was still all hush-hush. The stock was trading for just one penny a share. He had put all his savings into it, and he wanted to share the tip with her. She ponied up $8,000 that she had been saving for two years. Later, when her money was long gone, she realized she had been the victim of a classic "pump and dump" scheme whereby unscrupulous promoters bought up "penny stocks," started a rumor about big profits, and when enough suckers bought in and the stock price shot up, the promoters bailed out and made a profit. Phil had just gotten out of prison and he felt terrible about what he had done. Elaine had learned an expensive lesson.

Requirements

1. Does the current market price of a share of stock give any indication of the value or success of a company?

2. What sort of information should an investor look for before deciding to invest in stock of a company?

● Financial Statement Case 12-1

The **Amazon.com** financial statements appear in Appendix A at the end of this book. Answer the following questions about **Amazon's** stock. The Accumulated Deficit account is Retained earnings with a negative (debit) balance.

Requirements

1. How much of **Amazon's** preferred stock was outstanding at December 31, 2009? How can you tell?

2. Examine **Amazon's** balance sheet. Which stockholders' equity account increased the most during 2009? What caused this increase? The Consolidated Statements of Stockholders' Equity helps to answer this question.

3. Use par value and the number of shares to show how to compute the balances in **Amazon's** Common stock account at the end of both 2009 and 2008, as shown in the balance sheet.

4. Would it be meaningful to compute **Amazon's** return on equity? Explain your answer.

● Team Project 12-1

Competitive pressures are the norm in business. **Lexus** automobiles (made in Japan) have cut into the sales of **Mercedes Benz** (a German company), **General Motors'** **Cadillac** Division, and **Ford's** **Lincoln** Division. **Dell**, **Gateway** (now owned by **Acer, Inc.**), and **Compaq** computers (now owned by **Hewlett-Packard**) have siphoned business away from **IBM**. Foreign steelmakers have reduced the once-massive U.S. steel industry to a fraction of its former size.

Indeed, corporate downsizing has occurred on a massive scale. During the past few years, companies mentioned here have pared down their plant and equipment, laid off employees, or restructured operations.

Requirements

1. Identify all the stakeholders of a corporation and the stake each group has in the company. A *stakeholder* is a person or a group who has an interest (that is, a stake) in the success of the organization.

2. Identify several areas of deficiency that may indicate a corporation's need for downsizing. How can downsizing help to solve this problem? Discuss how each measure can indicate the need for downsizing.

3. Debate the downsizing issue. One group of students takes the perspective of the company and its stockholders, and another group of students takes the perspective of other stakeholders of the company.

● Communication Activity 12-1

In 50 words or fewer, explain the difference between par and no-par stocks.

Quick Check Answers

1. *b* 2. *b* 3. *d* 4. *c* 5. *c* 6. *c* 7. *d* 8. *c* 9. *c* 10. *c*

For online homework, exercises, and problems that provide you immediate feedback, please visit myaccountinglab.com.

13 Corporations: Effects on Retained Earnings and the Income Statement

What else may affect retained earnings?

SMART TOUCH LEARNING, INC.
Balance Sheet
May 31, 2013

Assets				Liabilities	
Current assets:				Current liabilities:	
Cash		$ 4,800		Accounts payable	$ 48,700
Accounts receivable		2,600		Salary payable	900
Inventory		30,500		Interest payable	100
Supplies		600		Unearned service revenue	400
Prepaid rent		2,000		Total current liabilities	50,100
Total current assets			$ 40,500	Long-term liabilities:	
Plant assets:				Notes payable	20,000
Furniture	$18,000			Total liabilities	70,100
Less: Accumulated depreciation—furniture	300	17,700			
Building	48,000			**Stockholders' Equity**	
Less: Accumulated depreciation—building	200	47,800		Common stock	30,000
Total plant assets			65,500	**Retained earnings**	**5,900**
				Total stockholders' equity	35,900
Total assets			$106,000	Total liabilities and stockholders' equity	$106,000

Learning Objectives

1. Account for stock dividends

2. Account for stock splits

3. Account for treasury stock

4. Report restrictions on retained earnings

5. Complete a corporate income statement including earnings per share

How can a corporation reward its stockholders and employees without using up the corporation's cash? Corporations can do so by creatively using their own stocks. This chapter takes corporate equity a few steps further, as follows:

Chapter 12 Covered	Chapter 13 Covers
Paid-in capital	Stock dividends
Issuing stock	Stock splits
Retained earnings	Buying back a corporation's
Cash dividends	stock (treasury stock)
Corporate balance sheet	Corporate income statement

Chapter 13 completes our discussion of corporate equity. We'll continue following Smart Touch Learning and begin with *stock dividends* and *stock splits*—terms you have probably heard. Now, we'll see what these terms mean.

Stock Dividends

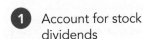

We have seen that the owners' equity of a corporation is called *stockholders' equity* or *shareholders' equity*. Paid-in capital and retained earnings make up stockholders' equity. We studied paid-in capital and retained earnings in Chapter 12. Now we'll focus on stock dividends.

A **stock dividend** is a distribution of a corporation's own stock to its shareholders. Unlike cash dividends, stock dividends do not give any of the corporation's assets, like cash, to the shareholders. Stock dividends

- affect *only* stockholders' equity accounts (including Retained earnings, Common stock, and Paid-in capital in excess of par—common stock).
- have *no* effect on total stockholders' equity.
- have *no* effect on assets or liabilities.

As Exhibit 13-1 shows, a stock dividend decreases Retained earnings and increases Paid-in capital, as it is a transfer *from* Retained earnings *to* Paid-in capital—specifically to Common stock and Paid-in capital in excess of par—common stock. **Total stockholders' equity is unchanged by a stock dividend.**

EXHIBIT 13-1 | **Effects of a Stock Dividend**

Retained earnings

Paid-in capital

Total Stockholders' equity is unchanged.

The corporation distributes stock dividends to stockholders in proportion to the number of shares the stockholders already own. Suppose you own 1,000 shares of Smart Touch's common stock. If Smart Touch distributes a 10% stock dividend, you would receive 100 (1,000 × 0.10) additional shares. You would now own 1,100 shares of the stock. All other Smart Touch stockholders also receive additional shares equal to 10% of their stock holdings; so you are all in the same relative position after the stock dividend as you were before. **With a stock dividend, the total number of shares issued and outstanding increases, but the percentage of total ownership of individual stockholders stays the same.**

Why Issue Stock Dividends?

A company issues stock dividends for several reasons:

1. **To continue dividends but conserve cash.** A company may wish to continue the distribution of dividends to keep stockholders happy, but may need to keep its cash for operations. A stock dividend is a way to do so without using corporate cash.

2. **To reduce the market price per share of its stock.** Depending on its size, a stock dividend may cause the company's market price per share to fall because of the increased supply of the stock. Suppose that a share of Smart Touch's stock was traded at $50 recently. Doubling the shares issued and outstanding by issuing a stock dividend would likely cause Smart Touch's stock market price per share to drop to $25 per share. One objective behind a stock dividend might be to make the stock less expensive and, therefore, more available and attractive to investors.

3. **To reward investors.** Investors often feel like they have received something of value when they get a stock dividend.

Recording Stock Dividends

As with a cash dividend, there are three dates for a stock dividend:

- Declaration date
- Record date
- Distribution (payment) date

The board of directors announces the stock dividend on the declaration date. The date of record and the distribution date then follow. The declaration of a stock dividend does *not* create a liability because the corporation is not obligated to pay assets. (Recall that a liability is a claim on *assets*.) With a stock dividend, the corporation has declared its intention to distribute its stock. Assume that Smart Touch has the following stockholders' equity prior to a stock dividend (from Chapter 12, Exhibit 12-5):

SMART TOUCH LEARNING, INC. Stockholders' Equity January 4, 2013	
Paid-in capital:	
Preferred stock, 6%, $50 par, 2,000 shares authorized, 2,000 shares issued	$ 100,000
Paid-in capital in excess of par—preferred	5,000
Common stock, $1 par, 20,000,000 shares authorized, 2,000,000 shares issued	2,000,000
Paid-in capital in excess of par—common	19,000,000
Total paid-in capital	$21,105,000
Retained earnings	9,000,000
Total stockholders' equity	$30,105,000

The entry to record a stock dividend depends on the size of the dividend. Generally accepted accounting principles (GAAP) distinguish between

- a **small stock dividend** (less than 20%–25% of issued and outstanding stock), and
- a **large stock dividend** (greater than 20%–25% of issued and outstanding stock).

Stock dividends between 20% and 25% are rare but subject to determination of their "small or large" status based on the individual corporation's facts and circumstances.

SMALL STOCK DIVIDENDS—LESS THAN 20%–25%   Small stock dividends are accounted for at the stock's market value. Here is how the various accounts are affected:

- Retained earnings* is debited for the market value of the dividend shares.
- Common stock is credited for the dividend stock's par value.
- Paid-in capital in excess of par is credited for the excess.

---

*As an alternative, a company could choose to debit a contra-equity account, Stock dividends. This account is a temporary account and would ultimately be closed to Retained earnings at year end.

Assume, for example, that Smart Touch distributes a 5% common stock dividend when the market value of Smart Touch common stock is $50 per share. The entry below illustrates the accounting for this 5% stock dividend on the distribution date.[1]

Feb 1	Retained earnings (2,000,000 shares × 0.05 × $50 market value)	(Q–)	5,000,000	
	Common stock (2,000,000 shares × 0.05 × $1 par) (Q+)			100,000
	Paid-in capital in excess of par—common (Q+)			4,900,000
	Issued 5% stock dividend.			

Remember that a stock dividend does not affect assets, liabilities, or *total* stockholders' equity. A stock dividend merely rearranges the balances in the stockholders' equity accounts, leaving total stockholders' equity unchanged. Exhibit 13-2 shows what Smart Touch's stockholders' equity looks like after the 5% common stock dividend.

EXHIBIT 13-2 | **Smart Touch Learning, Inc.'s Stockholders' Equity After 5% Common Stock Dividend**

SMART TOUCH LEARNING, INC. Stockholders' Equity February 1, 2013	
Paid-in capital:	
Preferred stock, 6%, $50 par, 2,000 shares authorized, 2,000 shares issued	$ 100,000
Paid-in capital in excess of par—preferred	5,000
Common stock, $1 par, 20,000,000 shares authorized, 2,100,000 shares issued	2,100,000
Paid-in capital in excess of par—common	23,900,000
Total paid-in capital	$26,105,000
Retained earnings	4,000,000
Total stockholders' equity	$30,105,000

Note that total stockholders' equity stays at $30,105,000. Total paid-in capital increased $5,000,000 and Retained earnings decreased $5,000,000.

LARGE STOCK DIVIDENDS—GREATER THAN 20%–25% Large stock dividends are rare, but when they are declared, they are normally accounted for at the stock's par value instead of the stock's market value. Par value is used because the larger number of issued and outstanding shares will reduce market price per share, making market price per share an invalid measurement of the stock dividend value. Assume, for example, that Smart Touch distributes a second common stock dividend of 50% when the market value of Smart Touch common stock is $50 per share. The entry to record the large stock dividend on the distribution date is as follows:

Feb 2	Retained earnings (2,100,000 shares × 50% × $1 par)	(Q–)	1,050,000	
	Common stock (Q+)			1,050,000
	Issued 50% stock dividend.			

---

[1]A stock dividend can be recorded with two journal entries—for (1) the declaration and (2) the stock distribution. But most companies record stock dividends with a single entry on the date of distribution, as we illustrate here.

The effect on the stockholders' equity after the 50% common stock dividend is illustrated in Exhibit 13-3:

EXHIBIT 13-3	Smart Touch Learning, Inc.'s Stockholders' Equity After 50% Common Stock Dividend

SMART TOUCH LEARNING, INC. Stockholders' Equity February 2, 2013	
Paid-in capital:	
Preferred stock, 6%, $50 par, 2,000 shares authorized, 2,000 shares issued	$ 100,000
Paid-in capital in excess of par—preferred	5,000
Common stock, $1 par, 20,000,000 shares authorized, 3,150,000 shares issued	3,150,000
Paid-in capital in excess of par—common	23,900,000
Total paid-in capital	$27,155,000
Retained earnings	2,950,000
Total stockholders' equity	$30,105,000

Notice that the large stock dividend also does not change total stockholders' equity of $30,105,000. Total paid-in capital increased $1,050,000 and Retained earnings decreased $1,050,000.

Stop & Think...

Have you ever mixed up a pitcher of **Koolaid**? If you have, you know the package instructions tell you the exact amount of water to add. If you add a little more water, your **Koolaid** will still taste pretty close to the expected flavor; but if you add an extra cup, it's going to taste watered-down. Stock dividends theory is similar to this. Add a bunch of extra stocks (more than 20–25%) and the market price per share is going to get watered down (decrease).

Key Takeaway

Stock dividends are either small (less than 20%–25%) or large (greater than 20%–25%). Small stock dividends are valued at the stock's fair market value. Large stock dividends are valued at par. Stock dividends have NO effect on total stockholders' equity but do increase paid-in capital and decrease Retained earnings.

Stock Splits

A **stock split** is fundamentally different from a stock dividend. A stock split increases the number of issued and outstanding shares of stock. A stock split also decreases par value per share, whereas stock dividends do not affect par value per share or the number of authorized shares. For example, if Smart Touch splits its common stock 2 for 1, the number of issued and outstanding shares is doubled and par value per share is cut in half. A stock split also decreases the market price per share of the stock. **A 2-for-1 stock split of a $2 par stock with a $20 market price per share will result in two shares of $1 par value with $10 market value per share.**

The market price of a share of Smart Touch common stock has been approximately $50 per share. Assume that Smart Touch wishes to decrease the market price to approximately $25 per share. The company can make the market price drop to around $25 by effecting a 2-for-1 split of its common stock. A 2-for-1 stock split means that Smart Touch will have twice as many shares of stock issued and outstanding after the split as it did before, and each share's par value is cut in half. Consider Smart Touch's balance sheet from Exhibit 13-3. It shows 3,150,000 shares issued and outstanding of $1 par common stock before the split. Exhibit 13-4 on the next page shows the before and after of how a 2-for-1 split affects Smart Touch's stockholders' equity.

2 Account for stock splits

EXHIBIT 13-4	Smart Touch Learning, Inc.'s Stockholders' Equity Before and After 2-for-1 Common Stock Split

Panel A—Before 2-for-1 common stock split SMART TOUCH LEARNING, INC. Stockholders' Equity—Before February 2, 2013		Panel B—After 2-for-1 common stock split SMART TOUCH LEARNING, INC. Stockholders' Equity—After February 3, 2013	
Paid-in capital:		Paid-in capital:	
Preferred stock, 6%, $50 par, 2,000 shares authorized, 2,000 shares issued	$ 100,000	Preferred stock, 6%, $50 par, 2,000 shares authorized, 2,000 shares issued	$ 100,000
Paid-in capital in excess of par—preferred	5,000	Paid-in capital in excess of par—preferred	5,000
Common stock, $1 par, 20,000,000 shares authorized, 3,150,000 shares issued	3,150,000	Common stock, $0.50 par, 20,000,000 shares authorized, 6,300,000 shares issued	3,150,000
Paid-in capital in excess of par—common	23,900,000	Paid-in capital in excess of par—common	23,900,000
Total paid-in capital	$27,155,000	Total paid-in capital	$27,155,000
Retained earnings	2,950,000	Retained earnings	2,950,000
Total stockholders' equity	$30,105,000	Total stockholders' equity	$30,105,000

Study the exhibit and you will see that a 2-for-1 stock split does the following:

- Cuts par value per share in half
- Doubles the number of shares of stock issued and outstanding
- Leaves all account balances and total stockholders' equity unchanged

Because the stock split does not affect any account balances, no formal journal entry is needed. Instead, the split is recorded in a **memorandum entry**, a journal entry that "notes" a significant event, but which has no debit or credit amount. The following is an example of a memorandum entry:

Feb 3	Split the common stock 2 for 1			
	OLD:	3,150,000 shares issued and outstanding, $1 par		
	NEW:	6,300,000 shares issued and outstanding, $0.50 par		

After the 2-for-1 common stock split, the stockholders' equity section will appear as shown in Exhibit 13-4, Panel B.

Stop & Think...

Take a dollar out of your pocket. If you were to exchange that dollar for four quarters, you would still have a dollar. Getting change for a dollar is just like a stock split. You have more pieces of paper (stock), but your total market value and ownership percentage in the company remain the same.

Stock Dividends and Stock Splits Compared

Stock dividends and stock splits have some similarities and some differences. Exhibit 13-5 on the next page summarizes their effects on stockholders' equity. For completeness, it also includes cash dividends.

		Effects of Cash Dividends, Common Stock Dividends, and Common
EXHIBIT 13-5		**Stock Splits on Account Balances**

Event	Common stock	Paid-in capital in excess of par	Retained earnings	Total Stockholders' equity
Cash dividend	No effect	No effect	Decrease	Decrease
Stock dividend	Increase	Increase	Decrease	No effect
Stock split	No effect	No effect	No effect	No effect

Treasury Stock

A company's own stock that it has previously issued and later reacquired is called **treasury stock**.[2] In effect, the corporation holds the stock in its treasury. A corporation, such as Smart Touch, may purchase treasury stock for several reasons:

3 Account for treasury stock

1. Management wants to increase net assets by buying low and selling high.

2. Management wants to support the company's stock price.

3. Management wants to avoid a takeover by an outside party by reducing the number of outstanding shares that have voting rights.

4. Management wants to reward valued employees with stock.

Treasury Stock Basics

Here are the basics of accounting for treasury stock:

- The Treasury stock account has a normal debit balance, which is the opposite of the other stockholders' equity accounts. Therefore, *Treasury stock is a contra-equity account.*

- Treasury stock is recorded at cost (what the company paid to reacquire the shares), without reference to par value.

- The Treasury stock account is reported beneath Retained earnings on the balance sheet as a reduction to total stockholders' equity.

Treasury stock decreases the company's stock that is outstanding—held by outsiders (the stockholders). Outstanding stock is computed as follows:

> Issued stock – Treasury stock = Outstanding stock

Only outstanding shares have voting rights and receive cash or stock dividends. Treasury stock does not carry a vote, and it gets no cash or stock dividends. Now we'll illustrate how to account for treasury stock, continuing with Smart Touch.

Purchase of Treasury Stock

After the stock split, discussed earlier in the chapter, Smart Touch had the stockholders' equity before purchasing treasury stock shown in Exhibit 13-4, Panel B.

Assume that on March 31, Smart Touch purchased 1,000 shares of previously issued common stock, paying $5 per share. To record the purchase, the company debits Treasury stock and credits Cash as follows:

---

[2]We illustrate the *cost* method of accounting for treasury stock because it is used most widely. Intermediate accounting courses also cover an alternative method.

	Mar 31	Treasury stock (1,000 × $5) (CQ+)		5,000	
		Cash (A–)			5,000
		Purchased treasury stock.			

Treasury stock

Mar 31	5,000	

Sale of Treasury Stock

Companies buy their treasury stock and eventually resell or retire it. A company may resell treasury stock at, above, or below its cost (what the company paid for the shares).

Sale at Cost

If treasury stock is sold for cost—the same price the corporation paid for it—then there is no difference between cost and sale price to journalize. Assume Smart Touch resells 100 of the treasury shares on April 1 for $5 each. The entry follows:

	Apr 1	Cash (100 shares × $5 mkt) (A+)	500	
		Treasury stock (100 shares × $5 cost) (CQ–)		500

Sale Above Cost

If treasury stock is resold for more than cost, the difference is credited to a new stockholders' equity account, Paid-in capital from treasury stock transactions. This excess is additional paid-in capital because it came from the company's stockholders. It has no effect on net income. Suppose Smart Touch resold 200 of its treasury shares for $6 per share on April 2 (recall that cost was $5 per share). The entry to resell treasury stock for a price above cost is as follows:

	Apr 2	Cash (200 shares × $6 mkt) (A+)		1,200	
		Paid-in capital from treasury stock transactions (Q+)			200
		Treasury stock (200 shares × $5 cost) (CQ–)			1,000

Paid-in capital from treasury stock transactions is reported with the other paid-in capital accounts on the balance sheet, beneath Common stock and Paid-in capital in excess of par.

Sale Below Cost

The resale price of treasury stock can be less than cost. The shortfall is debited first to Paid-in capital from treasury stock transactions. If this account's balance is too small, Retained earnings is debited for the remaining amount. To illustrate, assume Smart Touch had two additional treasury stock sales. First, on April 3, Smart Touch resold 200 treasury shares for $4.30 each. The entry to record the resale is as follows:

	Apr 3	Cash (200 shares × $4.30 mkt) (A+)		860	
		Paid-in capital from treasury stock transactions (Q–)		140	
		Treasury stock (200 shares × $5 cost) (CQ–)			1,000

The total loss on the sale of the treasury shares is $140. Smart Touch had previous gains of $200 from the April 2 sale of treasury stock, so there was enough Paid-in capital from treasury stock transactions to cover the loss.

Now what happens if Smart Touch resells an additional 200 treasury shares for $4.50 each on April 4?

Apr 4	Cash (200 shares × $4.50 mkt) (A+)	900	
	Paid-in capital from treasury stock transactions (Q–)	60	
	Retained earnings (1,000 – 900 – 60) (Q–)	40	
	Treasury stock (200 shares × $5 cost) (CQ–)		1,000

The total loss on the sale is $100 [($4.50 sales price per share minus $5 cost per share) × 200 shares]. Only $60 remains in Paid-in capital from the treasury stock transactions account to absorb the loss. The remainder, $100 − $60 or $40 in loss, is debited to Retained earnings.

So, what is left in stockholders' equity for Smart Touch after the treasury stock transactions? First, we'll post the treasury stock activity to the affected accounts:

	Treasury stock				Paid-in capital from treasury stock transactions			Retained earnings		
Mar 31	5,000					Apr 2	200			2,950,000
		Apr 1	500	Apr 3	140			Apr 4	40	
		Apr 2	1,000	Apr 4	60					2,949,960
		Apr 3	1,000							
		Apr 4	1,000				0			
	1,500									

Now, we can show the revised stockholders' equity for Smart Touch in Exhibit 13-6:

EXHIBIT 13-6   **Smart Touch Learning, Inc.'s Stockholders' Equity After Treasury Stock Transactions**

SMART TOUCH LEARNING, INC.
Stockholders' Equity
April 4, 2013

Paid-in capital:	
Preferred stock, 6%, $50 par, 2,000 shares authorized, 2,000 shares issued	$ 100,000
Paid-in capital in excess of par—preferred	5,000
Common stock, $0.50 par, 20,000,000 shares authorized, 6,300,000 shares issued	3,150,000
Paid-in capital in excess of par—common	23,900,000
Total paid-in capital	$27,155,000
Retained earnings	2,949,960
Treasury stock at cost (300 shares @ $5)	(1,500)
Total stockholders' equity	$30,103,460

So, how many common shares are outstanding on April 4? 6,300,000 common shares previously issued minus 300 treasury shares equals 6,299,700 outstanding common shares.

Retirement of Stock

Not all companies repurchase their previously issued stock to hold it in the treasury. A corporation may retire its stock by canceling the stock certificates. Retired stock cannot be reissued.

Retirements of preferred stock are common as companies seek to avoid paying the preferred dividends. To repurchase previously issued stock for retirement, we debit the stock account—for example, Preferred stock—and credit Cash. That removes the retired stock from the company's books, which reduces total assets and total stockholders' equity.

Key Takeaway

Treasury stock occurs when a company repurchases previously issued shares. Treasury stock is a contra-equity account; therefore, increases in Treasury stock decrease total stockholders' equity. Treasury stock purchases are recorded at cost, not par. All gains/losses on treasury stock sales are reported in the stockholders' equity accounts.

Restrictions on Retained Earnings

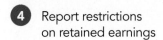 Report restrictions on retained earnings

Cash dividends and treasury stock purchases require a cash payment. These outlays leave fewer resources to pay liabilities. For example, a bank may agree to loan $500,000 to Smart Touch only if Smart Touch maintains a minimum level of stockholders' equity by limiting both its payment of cash dividends and its purchases of treasury stock.

Limits on Cash Dividends and Treasury Stock Purchases

To ensure that a corporation maintains a minimum level of stockholders' equity, lenders may restrict both cash dividend payments and treasury stock purchases. The restriction often focuses on the balance of retained earnings. Companies usually report their retained earnings restrictions in notes to the financial statements. The following disclosure by Smart Touch is typical:

Note F—Long-Term Debt The Smart Touch Learning Company's loan agreements with Valparaiso Bank restrict cash dividends and treasury stock purchases. Under the most restrictive of these provisions, retained earnings of $1,000,000 were unrestricted at December 31, 2013.

With this restriction, the maximum cash dividend that Smart Touch can pay is $1,000,000, the amount of unrestricted retained earnings.

Appropriations of Retained Earnings

Appropriations of retained earnings are retained earnings restrictions recorded by formal journal entries. A corporation may *appropriate*—that is, segregate in a separate account—a portion of retained earnings for a specific use (such as contingencies). For example, the board of directors may appropriate part of retained earnings for expansion. Appropriated retained earnings can be reported as shown in the bottom box of Exhibit 13-7 for an example company.

EXHIBIT 13-7	**Formats for Reporting Stockholders' Equity with Appropriations of Retained Earnings—Example Company**

SAMPLE COMPANY A
Stockholders' Equity
December 31, 2014

Teaching Format		Real-World Format	
Stockholders' equity		Stockholders' equity	
Paid-in capital:			
Preferred stock, 8%, $10 par,		Preferred stock, 8%, $10 par,	
30,000 shares authorized and issued	$ 300,000	30,000 shares authorized and issued	$ 300,000
Common stock, $1 par,		Common stock, $1 par,	
100,000 shares authorized,		100,000 shares authorized, 60,000 shares issued	60,000
60,000 shares issued	60,000	Additional paid-in capital	2,170,000
Paid-in capital in excess of par—common	2,150,000	Retained earnings (Note 7)	1,500,000
Paid-in capital from treasury stock transactions	20,000	Treasury stock, common	
Total paid-in capital	$2,530,000	(1,000 shares at cost)	(30,000)
Retained earnings appropriated		Total stockholders' equity	$4,000,000
for contingencies	500,000		
Retained earnings—unappropriated	1,000,000	*Note 7—Restriction on Retained earnings.*	
Total retained earnings	$1,500,000	At December 31, 2014, $500,000 of Retained	
Treasury stock, common		earnings is restricted for contingencies.	
(1,000 shares at cost)	(30,000)	Accordingly, dividends are limited to a	
Total stockholders' equity	$4,000,000	maximum of $1,000,000.	

Variations in Reporting Stockholders' Equity

Companies can report their stockholders' equity in ways that differ from our examples. They assume that investors understand the details. One of the most important skills you will learn in this course is how to read the financial statements of real companies. In Exhibit 13-7, we present a side-by-side comparison of a teaching format and the format you are likely to encounter in annual reports published by public companies. Note the following points in the real-world format:

1. The heading Paid-in capital does not appear. It is commonly understood that Preferred stock, Common stock, and Additional paid-in capital (Paid-in capital in excess of par) are elements of paid-in capital.

2. For presentation in the financial statements, all additional paid-in capital accounts are combined and reported as a single amount labeled Additional paid-in capital. It follows Common stock in the real-world format.

Retained earnings restrictions and appropriations are rare. Most companies disclose retained earnings restrictions and appropriations in the notes to the financial statements, as shown for Smart Touch on the previous page and in the real-world format of Exhibit 13-7.

You can review the first half of the chapter by studying the Decision Guidelines on the next page.

Key Takeaway

Restrictions on retained earnings most often arise from loan restrictions. These restrictions usually require companies to maintain minimum levels of retained earnings, thereby restricting amounts available for cash dividends and treasury stock purchases. Restrictions must be disclosed in the footnotes to the financial statements.

Decision Guidelines 13-1

ACCOUNTING FOR COMMON STOCK DIVIDENDS, COMMON STOCK SPLITS, TREASURY STOCK TRANSACTIONS, AND RETAINED EARNINGS

Retained earnings, stock dividends, stock splits, and treasury stock can affect a corporation's equity. The Decision Guidelines will help you understand their effects.

Decision	Guidelines

How should a company record:

- Distribution of a small stock dividend (less than 20%–25%)?

- Distribution of a large stock dividend (more than 20%–25%)?

Retained earnings	Market value	
Common stock		Par value
Paid-in capital in excess of par		Excess
Retained earnings	Par value	
Common stock		Par value

- Stock split?

Memorandum only describing the split.

What are the effects of stock dividends and stock splits on:	Effect of Common Stock Dividend	Effects of Common Stock Split
• Number of shares issued?	Increase	Increase
• Number of shares outstanding?	Increase	Increase
• Par value per share?	No effect	Decrease
• Total assets, total liabilities, and total stockholders' equity?	No effect	No effect
• Common stock (total par value)?	Increase	No effect
• Retained earnings?	Decrease	No effect

How to record:

1. Purchase of treasury stock

1.			
	Treasury stock (CQ+)	Cost	
	Cash (A–)		Cost

2. Sale of treasury stock: at cost (Amount received = Cost)

2.			
	Cash (A+)	Amount Received	
	Treasury stock (CQ–)		Cost

3. Sale of stock: above cost

3.			
	Cash (A+)	Amount Received	
	Paid-in capital from treasury stock transactions (Q+)		Amt Rec'd – Cost
	Treasury stock (CQ–)		Cost

4. Sale of treasury stock: below cost

4.			
	Cash (A+)	Amount Received	
	Paid-in capital from treasury stock transactions (Q–)	Up to Balance in Account	
	Retained earnings (Q–)	Excess	
	Treasury stock (CQ–)		Cost

What are the effects of the repurchase of previously issued stock and the resale of treasury stock on:	Effects of Purchase	Effects of Sale
• Total assets?	Decrease total assets by full amount of payment	Increase total assets by full amount of cash receipt
• Total stockholders' equity?	Decrease total stockholders' equity by full amount of payment	Increase total stockholders' equity by full amount of cash receipt

Summary Problem 13-1

Simplicity Graphics, creator of magazine designs, reported shareholders' equity as follows:

SIMPLICITY GRAPHICS Shareholders' Equity December 31, 2013	
Paid-in capital:	
Preferred stock, $10 par, 10,000 shares authorized, 0 issued	$ —
Common stock, $1 par value, 30,000 shares authorized,	
15,000 shares issued	15,000
Paid-in capital in excess of par—common	45,000
Total paid-in capital	$ 60,000
Retained earnings	90,000
Treasury stock, common, at cost (2,000 common shares)	(16,000)
Total stockholders' equity	$134,000

Requirements

1. What was the average issue price per share of the common stock?
2. Journalize the issuance of 1,000 shares of common stock at $4 per share. Use Simplicity's account titles.
3. How many shares of Simplicity's common stock are outstanding after Requirement 2?
4. How many shares of common stock would be issued after Simplicity split its common stock 3 for 1?
5. Using Simplicity account titles, journalize the distribution of a 10% common stock dividend when the market price of Simplicity common stock is $5 per share. Simplicity distributes the common stock dividend on the shares outstanding, which were computed in Requirement 3.
6. Journalize the following treasury stock transactions, which occur in the order given:
   a. Simplicity repurchases 500 shares of its previously issued common stock at $8 per share.
   b. Simplicity resells 100 shares of treasury stock for $9 per share.
   c. Simplicity resells 200 shares of treasury stock for $6 per share.

Solution

1		Average issue price of common stock was $4 per share		
		[($15,000 + $45,000)/15,000 shares] = $4 per share		
2		Cash (1,000 × $4) (A+)	4,000	
		Common stock (1,000 × $1) (Q+)		1,000
		Paid-in capital in excess of par—common (Q+)		3,000
		Issued common stock.		
3		Shares outstanding = 14,000 (16,000 shares issued minus		
		2,000 shares of treasury stock)		
4		Shares issued after a 3-for-1 stock split = 48,000		
		(16,000 issued shares × 3)		
5		Retained earnings (14,000 × .10 × $5) (Q–)	7,000	
		Common stock (14,000 × .10 × $1) (Q+)		1,400
		Paid-in capital in excess of par—common (Q+)		5,600
		Distributed a 10% common stock dividend.		
6	a.	Treasury stock (500 × $8) (CQ+)	4,000	
		Cash (A–)		4,000
		Purchased treasury stock.		
	b.	Cash (100 × $9) (A+)	900	
		Treasury stock (100 × $8) (CQ–)		800
		Paid-in capital from treasury stock transactions (Q+)		100
		Sold treasury stock.		
	c.	Cash (200 × $6) (A+)	1,200	
		Paid-in capital from treasury stock transactions (Q–)	100	
		Retained earnings (Q–)	300	
		Treasury stock (200 × $8) (CQ–)		1,600
		Sold treasury stock.		

The Corporate Income Statement

5 Complete a corporate income statement including earnings per share

The stockholders' equity of a corporation is more complex than the capital of a proprietorship or a partnership. Also, a corporation's income statement includes some unique items that do not often apply to a smaller business. Most of the income statements you will see belong to corporations. Why not proprietorships or partnerships? Because they are privately held, proprietorships and partnerships do not have to publish their financial statements. But public corporations do have to publish their financial statements, so we turn now to the corporate income statement.

Suppose you are considering investing in the stock of **IHOP**, **Nike**, or **Intel**. You would examine these companies' income statements. Of particular interest is the amount of net income they can expect to earn year after year. To understand net income, let's examine Exhibit 13-8, the income statement of Greg's Tunes. New items are in color for emphasis.

EXHIBIT 13-8 | **Income Statement in Multi-Step Format**

GREG'S TUNES, INC.
Income Statement
Year Ended December 31, 2013

Continuing Operations	Net sales revenue	$500,000
	Cost of goods sold	240,000
	Gross profit	$260,000
	Operating expenses (detailed)	181,000
	Operating income	$ 79,000
	Other gains (losses):	
	Gain on sale of machinery	11,000
	Income from continuing operations before income tax	$ 90,000
	Income tax expense	36,000
	Income from continuing operations	$ 54,000
Special Items	Discontinued operations, income of $35,000,	
	less income tax of $14,000	21,000
	Income before extraordinary item	$ 75,000
	Extraordinary flood loss, $20,000,	
	less income tax saving of $8,000	(12,000)
	Net income	$ 63,000
Earnings Per Share	Earnings per share of common stock	
	(20,000 shares outstanding):	
	Income from continuing operations	$ 2.70
	Income from discontinued operations	1.05
	Income before extraordinary item	$ 3.75
	Extraordinary loss	(0.60)
	Net income	$ 3.15

Continuing Operations

In Exhibit 13-8, the first section reports continuing operations. This part of the business should continue from period to period. Income from continuing operations, therefore, helps investors make predictions about future earnings. We may use this information to predict that Greg's Tunes, Inc., may earn approximately $54,000 next year.

The continuing operations of Greg's Tunes include two items that need explanation:

- Greg's Tunes had a gain on the sale of machinery, which is outside the company's core business of selling music products. This is why the gain is reported in the "other" category—separately from Greg's gross profit.
- Income tax expense of $36,000 is subtracted to arrive at income from continuing operations. Greg's Tunes' income tax rate is 40% ($90,000 × 0.40 = $36,000).

Special Items

After continuing operations, an income statement may include two distinctly different gains and losses:

- Discontinued operations
- Extraordinary items

Discontinued Operations

Most corporations engage in several lines of business. For example, **IHOP** is best known for its restaurants. But at one time **IHOP** owned **Golden Oaks Retirement Homes, United Rent-Alls**, and even a business college. **General Motors** is best known for its automobiles, but it also has a financing company (**GMAC**) and insurance foreign subsidiary company (**GMLAAM** and **GMAP**).

Each identifiable division of a company is called a **segment of the business**. **GMAC** is the financing segment of **General Motors**. A company may sell a segment of its business. For example, **IHOP** sold its retirement homes, **United Rent-Alls**, and its business college. These were discontinued operations for **IHOP**.

Financial analysts are always keeping tabs on companies they follow. They predict companies' net income, and most analysts do not include the results of discontinued operations because the discontinued segments will not be around in the future. The income statement reports information on the segments that have been sold under the heading Discontinued operations. In our example, income from discontinued operations of $35,000 is taxed at 40% and is reported as shown in Exhibit 13-8. A loss on discontinued operations is reported similarly, but with a subtraction for the income tax *savings* on the loss (the tax savings reduces the loss).

Gains and losses on the sale of plant assets are *not* reported as discontinued operations. Instead, they are reported as "Other gains (losses)" among continuing operations, because companies dispose of old plant assets and equipment all the time.

Extraordinary Gains and Losses (Extraordinary Items)

Extraordinary gains and losses, also called **extraordinary items**, are both unusual and infrequent. GAAP defines infrequent as an event that is not expected to recur in the foreseeable future, considering the environment in which the company operates. Losses from natural disasters (floods, earthquakes, and tornadoes) and the taking of company assets by a foreign government (expropriation) are generally considered to be extraordinary items. They are reported separately from continuing operations because of their infrequent and unusual nature.

Extraordinary items are reported along with their income tax effect. During 2013, Greg's Tunes lost $20,000 of inventory in a flood. This flood loss reduced both Greg's Tunes' income and its income tax. The tax effect decreases the net amount of Greg's Tunes' loss the same way income tax reduces net income. An extraordinary loss can be reported along with its tax effect, as follows:

Extraordinary flood loss......................................	$(20,000)
Less: Income tax saving......................................	8,000
Extraordinary flood loss, net of tax...................	$(12,000)

Trace this item to the income statement in Exhibit 13-8. An extraordinary gain is reported the same as a loss—net of the income tax effect. The following items do *not* qualify as extraordinary:

- Gains and losses on the sale of plant assets
- Losses due to lawsuits
- Losses due to employee labor strikes
- Natural disasters that occur frequently in the area (such as hurricanes in Florida)

These gains and losses fall outside the business's central operations, so they are reported on the income statement as other gains and losses, but they aren't extraordinary. One example for Greg's Tunes is the gain on sale of machinery reported in the Other gains (losses) section, as part of income from continuing operations in Exhibit 13-8.

Earnings per Share

The final segment of a corporate income statement reports the company's earnings per share, abbreviated as EPS. EPS is the most widely used of all business statistics. **Earnings per share (EPS)** reports the amount of net income (loss) for each share of the company's *outstanding common stock*. Recall that,

> Issued stock – Treasury stock = Outstanding stock

For example, Greg's Tunes has issued 25,000 shares of its common stock and holds 5,000 shares as treasury stock. Greg's Tunes, therefore, has 20,000 shares of common stock outstanding, and so we use the 20,000 outstanding common shares to compute EPS. EPS is a key measure of success in business. EPS is computed as follows:

$$\text{Earnings per share} = \frac{\text{Net income (loss) – Preferred dividends}}{\text{Average number of common shares outstanding}}$$

Corporations report a separate EPS figure for each element of income. Greg's Tunes' has no preferred stock, so preferred dividends are zero. Greg's EPS calculations follow:

Earnings per share of common stock (no preferred stock)	
(20,000 shares outstanding):	
Income from continuing operations ($54,000/20,000)..................	$ 2.70
Income from discontinued operations ($21,000/20,000)	1.05
Income before extraordinary item ($75,000/20,000)	$ 3.75
Extraordinary loss ($12,000/20,000)..	(0.60)
Net income ($63,000/20,000)	$ 3.15

The final section of Exhibit 13-8 reports the EPS figures for Greg's Tunes.

Effect of Preferred Dividends on Earnings per Share

Preferred dividends also affect EPS. Remember that EPS is earnings per share of outstanding *common* stock. Remember also that dividends on outstanding preferred stock are paid first. Therefore, preferred dividends must be subtracted from income to compute EPS.

Suppose Greg's Tunes had 10,000 shares of preferred stock outstanding, each share paying a $1.00 dividend. The annual preferred dividend would be $10,000 (10,000 shares × $1.00). The $10,000 preferred dividend is subtracted from each of the income subtotals (lines 1, 3, and 5), resulting in the following EPS computations for Greg's Tunes:

	Earnings per share of common stock (20,000 common shares outstanding and 10,000 preferred shares outstanding):	
1	Income from continuing operations ($54,000 – $10,000)/20,000.....	$ 2.20
2	Income from discontinued operations ($21,000/20,000)	1.05
3	Income before extraordinary item ($75,000 – $10,000)/20,000	$ 3.25
4	Extraordinary loss ($12,000/20,000)..	(0.60)
5	Net income ($63,000 – $10,000)/20,000.......................................	$ 2.65

Statement of Retained Earnings

The statement of retained earnings reports how the company moved from its beginning balance of Retained earnings to its ending balance during the period. Exhibit 13-9 shows the statement of retained earnings of Greg's Tunes for 2013.

EXHIBIT 13-9 | **Statement of Retained Earnings**

GREG'S TUNES, INC. Statement of Retained Earnings Year Ended December 31, 2013	
Retained earnings, December 31, 2012	$130,000
Net income for 2013	63,000
	$193,000
Dividends for 2013	(53,000)
Retained earnings, December 31, 2013	$140,000

Corporate dividends appear where drawings would appear if we were talking about sole proprietorships or partnerships. Greg's Tunes' net income comes from the income statement in Exhibit 13-8. All other data are assumed.

Combined Statement of Income and Retained Earnings

Companies can report income and retained earnings on a single statement. Exhibit 13-10 illustrates how Greg's Tunes would combine its income statement and its statement of retained earnings.

EXHIBIT 13-10 | **Combined Statement of Income and Retained Earnings**

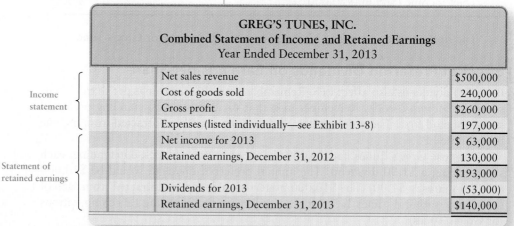

	GREG'S TUNES, INC. Combined Statement of Income and Retained Earnings Year Ended December 31, 2013	
Income statement	Net sales revenue	$500,000
	Cost of goods sold	240,000
	Gross profit	$260,000
	Expenses (listed individually—see Exhibit 13-8)	197,000
Statement of retained earnings	Net income for 2013	$ 63,000
	Retained earnings, December 31, 2012	130,000
		$193,000
	Dividends for 2013	(53,000)
	Retained earnings, December 31, 2013	$140,000

Prior-Period Adjustments

A company may make an accounting error. After the books are closed, Retained earnings holds the error, and its balance is wrong until corrected. Corrections to Retained earnings for errors of an earlier period are called **prior-period adjustments**. The prior-period adjustment either increases or decreases the beginning balance of the Retained earnings account and appears on the statement of retained earnings.

Because of the multiple new accounting pronouncements, in recent years there have been more prior-period adjustments than in the 20 previous years combined. Many companies have restated their net income to correct accounting errors. To illustrate, assume Greg's Tunes recorded $30,000 of salary expense for 2012. The correct amount of salary expense was $40,000. This error:

- understated salary expense by $10,000, and
- overstated net income by $10,000.

In 2013 Greg's paid the extra $10,000 in salaries owed for the prior year. Greg's prior-period adjustment decreased Retained earnings as shown in Exhibit 13-11:

EXHIBIT 13-11 | **Error Correction**

GREG'S TUNES, INC. Statement of Retained Earnings Year Ended December 31, 2013	
Retained earnings, December 31, 2012, as originally reported	$140,000
Prior-period adjustment—to correct error in 2012	(10,000)
Retained earnings, December 31, 2012, as adjusted	$130,000
Net income for 2013	63,000
	$193,000
Dividends for 2013	(53,000)
Retained earnings, December 31, 2013	$140,000

Reporting Comprehensive Income

As we have seen, all companies report net income or net loss on the income statement. However, there is another income figure. **Comprehensive income** is the company's change in total stockholders' equity from all sources other than its owners. Comprehensive income includes net income plus some specific gains and losses, as follows:

- Unrealized gains or losses on certain investments
- Foreign-currency translation adjustments
- Gains (losses) from post-retirement benefit plans
- Deferred gains (losses) from derivatives

The calculation of these items will be explained in future accounting courses. For now, you need to know that these items do not enter into the determination of net income but instead are reported as other comprehensive income. For example, assume that Greg's had unrealized gains of $1,000 from investments in 2013. Comprehensive income for 2013 for Greg's would be as shown in Exhibit 13-12.

EXHIBIT 13-12 | **Reporting Comprehensive Income**

GREG'S TUNES, INC. Statement of Income and Comprehensive Income Year Ended December 31, 2013	
Revenues	$500,000
Expenses (summarized)	437,000
Net income	$ 63,000
Other comprehensive income:	
Unrealized gain on investments	1,000
Comprehensive income	$ 64,000

Earnings per share apply only to net income and its components, as discussed earlier. Earnings per share are *not* reported for other comprehensive income.

Decision Guidelines 13-2

ANALYZING A CORPORATE INCOME STATEMENT

Three years out of college, you have saved $5,000 and are ready to start investing. Where do you start? You might begin by analyzing the income statements of **IHOP**, **Nike**, and **Intel**. These Decision Guidelines will help you analyze a corporate income statement.

Decision	Guidelines	
• What are the main sections of the income statement? See Exhibit 13-8 for an example.	Continuing operations	• Continuing operations, including other gains and losses and less income tax expense
	Special items	• Discontinued operations—gain or loss—less the income tax effect
		• Extraordinary gain or loss, less the income tax effect
		• Net income (or net loss)
		• Other comprehensive income (Exhibit 13-12)
• What earnings-per-share (EPS) figures must a corporation report?	Earnings per share	• Earnings per share—applies only to net income (or net loss), not to other comprehensive income
	Separate EPS figures for:	• Income (loss) from continuing operations
		• Discontinued operations
		• Income (loss) before extraordinary item
		• Extraordinary gain or loss
		• Net income (or net loss)
• How is EPS for net income computed?		

$$EPS = \frac{\text{Net income (loss)} - \text{Preferred dividends}}{\text{Average number of common shares outstanding}}$$

Summary Problem 13-2

The following information was taken from the ledger of Calenergy Corporation at December 31, 2014.

Common stock, no-par,		Discontinued operations,	
45,000 shares issued	$180,000	income	$20,000
Sales revenue	620,000	Prior-period adjustment—	
Extraordinary gain	26,000	credit to Retained earnings	5,000
Loss due to lawsuit	11,000	Gain on sale of plant assets	21,000
General expenses	62,000	Income tax expense (saving):	
Preferred stock 8%	50,000	Continuing operations	32,000
Selling expenses	108,000	Discontinued operations	8,000
Retained earnings, beginning,		Extraordinary gain	10,000
as originally reported	103,000	Treasury stock, common	
Dividends	14,000	(5,000 shares)	25,000
Cost of goods sold	380,000		

Requirement

1. Prepare a multi-step income statement and a statement of retained earnings for Calenergy Corporation for the year ended December 31, 2014. Include the EPS presentation and show your computations. Calenergy had no changes in its stock accounts during the year.

Solution

CALENERGY CORPORATION Income Statement Year Ended December 31, 2014		
Sales revenue		$620,000
Cost of goods sold		380,000
Gross profit		$240,000
Operating expenses:		
Selling expenses	$108,000	
General expenses	62,000	170,000
Operating income		$ 70,000
Other gains (losses):		
Gain on sale of plant assets	$ 21,000	
Loss due to lawsuit	(11,000)	10,000
Income from continuing operations before income tax		$ 80,000
Income tax expense		32,000
Income from continuing operations		$ 48,000
Discontinued operations, income of $20,000,		
less income tax of $8,000		12,000
Income before extraordinary item		$ 60,000
Extraordinary gain, $26,000, less income tax, $10,000		16,000
Net income		$ 76,000
Earnings per share:		
Income from continuing operations		
[($48,000 − $4,000) / 40,000 shares]		$ 1.10
Income from discontinued operations		
($12,000 / 40,000 shares)		0.30
Income before extraordinary item		
[($60,000 − $4,000) / 40,000 shares]		$ 1.40
Extraordinary gain ($16,000 / 40,000 shares)		0.40
Net income [($76,000 − $4,000) / 40,000 shares]		$ 1.80

$$\text{EPS} = \frac{\text{Income} - \text{Preferred dividends}}{\text{Average common shares outstanding}}$$

CALENERGY CORPORATION Statement of Retained Earnings Year Ended December 31, 2014	
Retained earnings balance, Dec 31, 2013, as originally reported	$103,000
Prior-period adjustment—credit	5,000
Retained earnings balance, Dec 31, 2013, as adjusted	$108,000
Net income	76,000
	$184,000
Dividends	(14,000)
Retained earnings balance, Dec 31, 2014	$170,000

Review *Corporations: Effects on Retained Earnings and the Income Statement*

● Accounting Vocabulary

Appropriation of Retained Earnings (p. 632)
Restriction of a portion of retained earnings that is recorded by a formal journal entry.

Comprehensive Income (p. 641)
Company's change in total stockholders' equity from all sources other than its owners.

Earnings per Share (EPS) (p. 639)
Amount of a company's net income for each share of its outstanding common stock.

Extraordinary Gains and Losses (p. 638)
A gain or loss that is both unusual for the company and infrequent. Also called **extraordinary items**.

Extraordinary Item (p. 638)
A gain or loss that is both unusual for the company and infrequent. Also called **extraordinary gain and loss**.

Large Stock Dividend (p. 625)
A stock dividend greater than 20%–25% of the issued stock.

Memorandum Entry (p. 628)
A journal entry that "notes" a significant event, but has no debit or credit amount.

Prior-Period Adjustment (p. 640)
A correction to retained earnings for an error of an earlier period.

Segment of the Business (p. 638)
One of various separate divisions of a company.

Small Stock Dividend (p. 625)
A stock dividend of less than 20%–25% of the issued stock.

Stock Dividend (p. 624)
A distribution by a corporation of its own stock to its shareholders.

Stock Split (p. 627)
An increase in the number of issued and outstanding shares of stock coupled with a proportionate reduction in the par value of the stock.

Treasury Stock (p. 629)
A corporation's own stock that it has previously issued and later reacquired.

● Destination: Student Success

Student Success Tips

The following are hints on some common trouble areas for students in this chapter:

- Recall that stock dividends are considered small and recorded at market value if the dividend is less than 20%–25%.

- Keep in mind that stock splits divide the shares' par, book, and market values. Stock splits do not change authorized shares.

- Recall that treasury stock is a contra-equity account, recorded at cost. Future sales of treasury shares, whether at a price greater or less than the cost, do not impact net income.

- Remember, retained earnings restrictions arise mostly from lender restrictions and must be disclosed in the footnotes to the financial statements.

- Review the expanded income statement for information about special items (those not included in continuing operations; e.g. discontinued operations and extraordinary items) and earnings per share.

Getting Help

If there's a learning objective from the chapter you aren't confident about, try using one or more of the following resources:

- Review the Decision Guidelines in the chapter.

- Review Summary Problems 13-1 and 13-2 in the chapter to reinforce your understanding of stock dividends, stock splits, and the expanded income statement.

- Review Exhibit 13-8, the guide to the expanded income statement and earnings per share disclosures.

- Practice additional exercises or problems at the end of Chapter 13 that cover the specific learning objective that is challenging you.

- Watch the white board videos for Chapter 13 located at myaccountinglab.com under the Chapter Resources button.

- Go to myaccountinglab.com and select the Study Plan button. Choose Chapter 13 and work the questions covering that specific learning objective until you've mastered it.

- Work the Chapter 13 pre/post tests in myaccountinglab.com.

- Visit the learning resource center on your campus for tutoring.

● Quick Check

1. A stock dividend
   a. decreases Common stock.
   b. has no effect on total equity.
   c. increases Retained earnings.
   d. Items a, b, and c are correct

2. In a small stock dividend,
   a. Paid-in capital in excess of par is debited for the difference between the debits to Retained earnings and to Common stock.
   b. Retained earnings is debited for the market value of the shares issued.
   c. Common stock is debited for the par value of the shares issued.
   d. Net income is always decreased.

3. Stock splits
   a. decrease par value per share.
   b. increase the number of shares of stock issued.
   c. Both a and b
   d. None of the above

4. A company's own stock that it has issued and repurchased is called
   a. outstanding stock.
   b. dividend stock.
   c. issued stock.
   d. treasury stock.

5. Assume that a company paid $6 per share to purchase 1,100 of its $3 par common as treasury stock. The purchase of treasury stock
   a. increased total equity by $3,300.
   b. decreased total equity by $3,300.
   c. decreased total equity by $6,600.
   d. increased total equity by $6,600.

6. Assume that the bank requires ABC, Co., to maintain at least $125,000 in Retained earnings. The $125,000 would be shown as
   a. a ratio of the $125,000 restriction divided by total Retained earnings.
   b. a current liability.
   c. a restriction to Retained earnings.
   d. a long-term liability.

7. Greg's Tunes in Exhibit 13-8 is most likely to earn net income of $x next year. How much is $x?
   a. $54,000
   b. $79,000
   c. $63,000
   d. $90,000

8. Which of the following events would be an extraordinary loss?
   a. Loss on the sale of equipment
   b. Loss on discontinued operations
   c. Loss due to an earthquake
   d. All of the above are extraordinary items.

9. What is the most widely followed statistic in business?
   a. Retained earnings
   b. Gross profit
   c. Earnings per share
   d. Dividends

10. Earnings per share is *not* computed for
    a. net income.
    b. comprehensive income.
    c. extraordinary items.
    d. discontinued operations.

Answers are given after Apply Your Knowledge (p. 660).

Assess Your Progress

● Short Exercises

S13-1 **1** **Recording a small stock dividend [5–10 min]**
Supreme Water Sports has 12,000 shares of $2 par common stock outstanding. Supreme distributes a 5% stock dividend when the market value of its stock is $22 per share.

Requirements

1. Journalize Supreme's distribution of the stock dividend on August 31. An explanation is not required.
2. What is the overall effect of the stock dividend on Supreme's total assets?
3. What is the overall effect on total stockholders' equity?

S13-2 **1** **Comparing and contrasting cash and stock dividends [5–10 min]**
Compare and contrast the accounting for cash dividends and stock dividends.

Requirement

1. In the space provided, insert either "Cash dividends," "Stock dividends," or "Both cash dividends and stock dividends" to complete each of the following statements:
   a. _____ decrease Retained earnings.
   b. _____ has(have) no effect on a liability.
   c. _____ increase paid-in capital by the same amount that they decrease Retained earnings.
   d. _____ decrease both total assets and total stockholders' equity, resulting in a decrease in the size of the company.

S13-3 **1** **Accounting for a stock dividend [5–10 min]**
Yummy, Inc., had 310,000 shares of $1 par common stock issued and outstanding as of December 1, 2012. The company is authorized to issue 1,400,000 common shares. On December 15, 2012, Yummy declared and distributed a 5% stock dividend when the market value for Yummy's common stock was $3.

Requirements

1. Journalize the stock dividend.
2. How many shares of common stock are outstanding after the dividend?

Note: Short Exercise 13-4 should be used only after completing Short Exercise 13-3.

S13-4 **1** **Accounting for a stock dividend [5–10 min]**
Return to the Yummy, Inc., data in Short Exercise 13-3. Assume instead that the December 15, 2012 stock dividend was 45%.

Requirements

1. Journalize the stock dividend.
2. How many shares of common stock are outstanding after the dividend?

S13-5 ❷ **Accounting for a stock split [5–10 min]**

Decorator Plus Imports recently reported the following stockholders' equity (adapted except par value per share):

Paid-in capital:	
Common stock, $1 par, 480,000,000 shares authorized, 114,000,000 shares issued	$ 114,000,000
Paid-in capital in excess of par	140,000,000
Total paid-in capital	$ 254,000,000
Retained earnings	650,000,000
Total stockholders' equity	$ 904,000,000

Suppose Decorator Plus split its common stock 2 for 1 in order to decrease the market price per share of its stock. The company's stock was trading at $20 per share immediately before the split.

Requirements

1. Prepare the stockholders' equity section of Decorator Plus Imports' balance sheet after the stock split.

2. Were the account balances changed or unchanged after the stock split?

S13-6 ❸ **Accounting for the purchase and sale of treasury stock [10 min]**

Discount Center Furniture, Inc., completed the following treasury stock transactions:

a. Purchased 1,400 shares of the company's $1 par common stock as treasury stock, paying cash of $5 per share.

b. Sold 400 shares of the treasury stock for cash of $8 per share.

Requirements

1. Journalize these transactions. Explanations are not required.

2. Show how Discount Center will report treasury stock on its December 31, 2012 balance sheet after completing the two transactions. In reporting the treasury stock, report only on the Treasury stock account. You may ignore all other accounts.

S13-7 ❹ **Interpreting a restriction on retained earnings [5 min]**

JP Corporation reported the following stockholders' equity:

Paid-in capital:	
Preferred stock, $1.50, no-par, 18,000 shares authorized, 0 issued	
Common stock, $1 par, 483,000 shares authorized, 150,000 shares issued	$150,000
Paid-in capital in excess of par—common	336,000
Total paid-in capital	$486,000
Retained earnings	506,000
Treasury stock, 5,000 shares at cost	(35,000)
Total stockholders' equity	$957,000

Requirements

1. JP Corporation's agreement with its bank lender restricts JP's dividend payments for the cost of treasury stock the company holds. How much is the maximum amount of dividends JP can declare?

2. Why would a bank lender restrict a corporation's dividend payments and treasury stock purchases?

S13-8   ⑤ **Preparing a corporate income statement [10–15 min]**

RAR Corporation's accounting records include the following items, listed in no particular order, at December 31, 2012:

Other gains (losses)	$ (15,000)	Extraordinary loss	$ 7,000
Net sales revenue	177,000	Cost of goods sold	73,000
Gain on discontinued operations	12,000	Operating expenses	55,000
Accounts receivable	21,000		

Income tax of 30% applies to all items.

Requirement

1. Prepare RAR's income statement for the year ended December 31, 2012. Omit earnings per share.

Note: Short Exercise 13-9 should be used only after completing Short Exercise 13-8.

S13-9   ⑤ **Reporting earnings per share [10–15 min]**

Return to the RAR data in Short Exercise 13-8. RAR had 13,500 shares of common stock outstanding during 2012. RAR declared and paid preferred dividends of $3,000 during 2012.

Requirement

1. Show how RAR reported EPS data on its 2012 income statement.

Note: Short Exercise 13-10 should be used only after completing Short Exercise 13-8.

S13-10   ⑤ **Reporting comprehensive income [5–10 min]**

Use the RAR data in Short Exercise 13-8. In addition, RAR had unrealized gains of $4,500 on investments during 2012.

Requirements

1. Start with RAR's net income from Short Exercise 13-8 and show how the company could report other comprehensive income on its 2012 income statement.
2. Should RAR report earnings per share for other comprehensive income?

S13-11   ⑤ **Reporting a prior-period adjustment [10 min]**

Wells Research Service, Inc., (WRSI) ended 2011 with retained earnings of $73,000. During 2012, WRSI earned net income of $93,000 and declared dividends of $26,000. Also during 2012, WRSI got a $20,000 tax refund from the Internal Revenue Service. A tax audit revealed that WRSI paid too much income tax back in 2010.

Requirement

1. Prepare WRSI's statement of retained earnings for the year ended December 31, 2012, to report the prior-period adjustment.

● Exercises

E13-12   ① **Journalizing a stock dividend and reporting stockholders' equity [10–15 min]**   *MyAccountingLab*

The stockholders' equity of Pondside Occupational Therapy, Inc., on December 31, 2011, follows:

STOCKHOLDERS' EQUITY	
Paid-in capital:	
Common stock, $1 par, 1,250 shares authorized,	
530 issued	$ 530
Paid–in capital in excess of par—common	2,120
Total paid-in capital	2,650
Retained earnings..	121,000
Total stockholders' equity	$ 123,650

On April 30, 2012, the market price of Pondside's common stock was $11 per share and the company distributed a 10% stock dividend.

Requirements

1.   Journalize the distribution of the stock dividend.

2.   Prepare the stockholders' equity section of the balance sheet after the stock dividend.

E13-13 ❶ **Journalizing cash and stock dividends [10–15 min]**

Painting Schools, Inc., is authorized to issue 200,000 shares of $1 par common stock. The company issued 77,000 shares at $3 per share. When the market price of common stock was $5 per share, Painting distributed a 10% stock dividend. Later, Painting declared and paid a $0.25 per share cash dividend.

Requirements

1.   Journalize the distribution of the stock dividend.

2.   Journalize both the declaration and the payment of the cash dividend.

E13-14 ❶❷❸ **Effect of stock dividends, stock splits, and treasury stock transactions [10–15 min]**

Many types of transactions may affect stockholders' equity.

Requirement

1.   Identify the effects of the following transactions on total stockholders' equity. Each transaction is independent.

a.   A 10% stock dividend. Before the dividend, 520,000 shares of $1 par common stock were outstanding; market value was $3 at the time of the dividend.

b.   A 2-for-1 stock split. Prior to the split, 65,000 shares of $4 par common stock were outstanding.

c.   Purchase of 1,000 shares of treasury stock (par value at $0.50) at $3 per share.

d.   Sale of 900 shares of $0.50 par treasury stock for $5 per share. Cost of the treasury stock was $3 per share.

E13-15 ❷ **Reporting stockholders' equity after a stock split [10–15 min]**

Snake Golf Club, Corp., had the following stockholders' equity at December 31, 2011:

STOCKHOLDERS' EQUITY		
Paid-in capital:		
Common stock, $1.00 par, 650 shares authorized,		
290 issued	$	290
Paid-in capital in excess of par—common		580
Total paid-in capital		870
Retained earnings		2,900
Total stockholders' equity	$	3,770

On June 30, 2012, Snake split its common stock 2 for 1.

Requirements

1.   Make the memorandum entry to record the stock split.

2.   Prepare the stockholders' equity section of the balance sheet immediately after the split.

E13-16 ❸ **Journalizing treasury stock transactions [10–15 min]**

Stock transactions for Careful Driving School, Inc., follow:

Mar 4	Issued 22,000 shares of $1 par common stock at $18 per share.
May 22	Purchased 1,400 shares of treasury stock—common at $11 per share.
Sep 22	Sold 500 shares of treasury stock—common at $24 per share.

Requirement

1.   Journalize the transactions.

E13-17 ❸ **Journalizing treasury stock transactions and reporting stockholders' equity [10–15 min]**

Southern Amusements Corporation had the following stockholders' equity on November 30:

STOCKHOLDERS' EQUITY		
Paid-in capital:		
Common stock, $5 par, 1,300 shares authorized,		
900 shares issued	$	4,500
Paid-in capital in excess of par—common		13,500
Total paid-in capital		18,000
Retained earnings		57,000
Total stockholders' equity	$	75,000

On December 30, Southern purchased 275 shares of treasury stock at $14 per share.

Requirements

1. Journalize the purchase of the treasury stock.
2. Prepare the stockholders' equity section of the balance sheet at December 31.
3. How many shares of common stock are outstanding after the purchase of treasury stock?

E13-18 ❹ **Reporting a retained earnings restriction [10–15 min]**

The agreement under which Rapid Copy issued its long-term debt requires the restriction of $150,000 of the company's retained earnings balance. Total retained earnings is $550,000 and common stock, no-par, has a balance of $110,000.

Requirement

1. Report stockholders' equity on Rapid's balance sheet, assuming the following:
   a. Rapid discloses the restriction in a note. Write the note.
   b. Rapid appropriates retained earnings in the amount of the restriction and includes no note in its statements.

E13-19 ❺ **Preparing a multi-step income statement [10–15 min]**

Click Photographic Supplies, Inc.'s accounting records include the following for 2012:

Income tax saving—extraordinary loss	$ 8,000	Sales revenue		$ 480,000
Income tax saving—loss		Operating expenses		
on discontinued operations	14,000	(including income taxes)		130,000
Extraordinary loss	20,000	Cost of goods sold		205,000
		Loss on discontinued operations		35,000

Requirement

1. Prepare Click's multi-step income statement for 2012. Omit earnings per share.

E13-20 ❺ **Computing EPS [5–10 min]**

Altar, Corp., earned net income of $118,000 for 2012. Altar's books include the following figures:

Preferred stock, 3%, $50 par, 1,000 shares issued		
and outstanding	$	50,000
Common stock, $2 par, 53,000 issued		106,000
Paid-in capital in excess of par—common		460,000
Treasury stock, common, 1,200 at cost		24,000

Requirement

1. Compute Altar's EPS for the year.

E13-21 ⑤ **Computing EPS [10–15 min]**

Franco Academy Surplus had 10,000 shares of common stock and 7,000 shares of 5%, $10 par preferred stock outstanding through December 31, 2012. Income from continuing operations for 2012 was $125,000, and loss on discontinued operations (net of income tax saving) was $5,000. Franco also had an extraordinary gain (net of tax) of $25,000.

Requirement

1. Compute Franco's EPS amounts for 2012, starting with income from continuing operations.

E13-22 ⑤ **Preparing a statement of retained earnings [10 min]**

Annie May Bakery, Inc., reported a prior-period adjustment in 2012. An accounting error caused net income of prior years to be overstated by $10,000. Retained earnings at December 31, 2011, as previously reported, stood at $47,000. Net income for 2012 was $71,000, and dividends were $29,000.

Requirement

1. Prepare the company's statement of retained earnings for the year ended December 31, 2012.

E13-23 ⑤ **Preparing a combined statement of income and retained earnings [10 min]**

During 2012, St. Bernard, Corp., earned income from continuing operations of $139,000. The company also sold a segment of the business (discontinued operations) at a loss of $37,000 and had an extraordinary gain of $11,000. At year-end, St. Bernard had an unrealized loss on investments of $5,000.

Requirements

1. Compute St. Bernard's net income and comprehensive income for 2012. All amounts are net of income taxes.

2. What final EPS figure should St. Bernard report for 2012? What is the correct title of this calculation? What is the amount of this calculation? St. Bernard had 30,000 shares of common stock (and no preferred stock) outstanding.

● Problems (Group A)

MyAccountingLab

P13-24A ① ② ③ **Journalizing stockholders' equity transactions [20–25 min]**

Summerborn Manufacturing, Co., completed the following transactions during 2012:

Jan 16	Declared a cash dividend on the 5%, $100 par preferred stock (900 shares outstanding). Declared a $0.30 per share dividend on the 80,000 shares of common stock outstanding. The date of record is January 31, and the payment due date is February 15.
Feb 15	Paid the cash dividends.
Jun 10	Split common stock 2 for 1. Before the split, Summerborn had 80,000 shares of $6 par common stock outstanding.
Jul 30	Distributed a 50% stock dividend on the common stock. The market value of the common stock was $9 per share.
Oct 26	Purchased 1,000 shares of treasury stock at $13 per share.
Nov 8	Sold 500 shares of treasury stock for $15 per share.
Nov 30	Sold 300 shares of treasury stock for $8 per share.

Requirement

1. Record the transactions in Summerborn's general journal.

P13-25A ① ③ **Journalizing dividend and treasury stock transactions, and preparing stockholders' equity [10–30 min]**

The balance sheet of Lennox Health Foods, at December 31, 2011, reported 120,000 shares of no-par common stock authorized, with 25,000 shares issued and a

Common stock balance of $190,000. Retained earnings had a balance of $115,000. During 2012, the company completed the following selected transactions:

Mar 15	Purchased 9,000 shares of treasury stock at $8 per share.
Apr 30	Distributed a 10% stock dividend on the *outstanding* shares of common stock. The market value of common stock was $9 per share.
Dec 31	Earned net income of $110,000 during the year. Closed net income to Retained earnings.

Requirements

1. Record the transactions in the general journal. Explanations are not required.
2. Prepare the stockholders' equity section of Lennox Health Foods' balance sheet at December 31, 2012.

P13-26A 1 3 **Journalizing dividend and treasury stock transactions, preparing a statement of retained earnings, and preparing stockholders' equity [30–45 min]**
The balance sheet of Goldstein Management Consulting, Inc., at December 31, 2011, reported the following stockholders' equity:

Paid-in capital:	
Common stock, $10 par, 200,000 shares authorized,	
15,000 shares issued	$ 150,000
Paid-in capital in excess of par—common	310,000
Total paid-in capital	460,000
Retained earnings	162,000
Total stockholders' equity	$ 622,000

During 2012, Goldstein completed the following selected transactions:

Feb 6	Distributed a 5% stock dividend on the common stock. The market value of Goldstein's stock was $21 per share.
Jul 29	Purchased 2,300 shares of treasury stock at $21 per share.
Nov 27	Declared a $0.10 per share cash dividend on the 13,450 shares of common stock outstanding. The date of record is December 17, 2012, and the payment date is January 7, 2013.
Dec 31	Closed the $81,000 net income to Retained earnings.

Requirements

1. Record the transactions in the general journal.
2. Prepare a retained earnings statement for the year ended December 31, 2012.
3. Prepare the stockholders' equity section of the balance sheet at December 31, 2012.

P13-27A 4 5 **Computing EPS and reporting a retained earnings restriction [20–25 min]**
The capital structure of Blacksmith, Inc., at December 31, 2011, included 18,000 shares of $1 preferred stock and 38,000 shares of common stock. Common stock outstanding during 2012 totaled 38,000 shares. Income from continuing operations during 2012 was $108,000. The company discontinued a segment of the business at a gain of $26,000 and also had an extraordinary gain of $12,000. The Blacksmith board of directors restricts $99,000 of retained earnings for contingencies. Retained earnings at December 31, 2011, was $99,000, and the company declared preferred dividends of $18,000 during 2012.

Requirements

1. Compute Blacksmith's earnings per share for 2012. Start with income from continuing operations. All income and loss amounts are net of income tax.
2. Show two ways of reporting Blacksmith's retained earnings restriction.

P13-28A ⑤ **Preparing a detailed income statement [25–35 min]**

The following information was taken from the records of Clarkson Motorsports, Inc., at November 30, 2012:

Selling expenses	$ 125,000	Common stock, $10 par, 21,000	
General expenses	134,000	shares authorized and issued	$ 210,000
Income from discontinued operations	5,000	Preferred stock, $4, no-par	
Retained earnings, beginning	90,000	6,000 shares issued	240,000
Cost of goods sold	430,000	Income tax expense:	
Treasury stock, common		Continuing operations	70,000
(1,000 shares)	11,000	Income from discontinued	
Net sales revenue	834,000	operations	2,000

Requirement

1. Prepare a multi-step income statement for Clarkson Motorsports for the fiscal year ended November 30, 2012. Include earnings per share.

P13-29A ⑤ **Preparing a corrected combined statement of income and retained earnings [25–35 min]**

Jim Heller, accountant for Complete Home Finance, was injured in a boating accident. Another employee prepared the accompanying income statement for the year ended December 31, 2012.

COMPLETE HOME FINANCE		
Income Statement		
Year ended December 31, 2012		
Revenue and gains:		
Sales		$ 362,000
Paid-in capital in excess of par—common		93,000
Total revenues and gains		455,000
Expenses and losses:		
Cost of goods sold	102,000	
Selling expenses	70,000	
General expenses	63,500	
Sales returns	12,000	
Sales discounts	5,500	
Dividends	17,000	
Income tax expense	34,000	
Total expenses and losses		304,000
Income from operations		$ 151,000
Other gains and losses		
Gain on discontinued operations		4,500
Net income		$ 155,500
Earnings per share		$ 3.11

The individual *amounts* listed on the income statement are correct. However, some accounts are reported incorrectly, and two items do not belong on the income statement at all. Also, income tax has *not* been applied to all appropriate figures. The income tax rate on discontinued operations was 40%. Complete Home Finance issued 55,000 shares of common stock in 2012 and held 5,000 shares as treasury stock during 2012. Retained earnings at December 31, 2011, was $167,000.

Requirement

1. Prepare a corrected combined statement of income and retained earnings for the fiscal year ended December 31, 2012, including earnings per share. Prepare the income statement in single-step format.

● Problems (Group B)

P13-30B **①②③** **Journalizing stockholders' equity transactions [20–25 min]**   *MyAccountingLab*

Dearborn Manufacturing, Co., completed the following transactions during 2012:

Jan 16	Declared a cash dividend on the 6%, $95 par preferred stock (1,000 shares outstanding). Declared a $0.55 per share dividend on the 90,000 shares of common stock outstanding. The date of record is January 31, and the payment due date is February 15.
Feb 15	Paid the cash dividends.
Jun 10	Split common stock 2 for 1. Before the split, Dearborn had 90,000 shares of $10 par common stock outstanding.
Jul 30	Distributed a 30% stock dividend on the common stock. The market value of the common stock was $12 per share.
Oct 26	Purchased 3,000 shares of treasury stock at $10 per share.
Nov 8	Sold 1,500 shares of treasury stock for $11 per share.
Nov 30	Sold 700 shares of treasury stock for $7 per share.

Requirement

1. Record the transactions in Dearborn's general journal.

P13-31B **①③** **Journalizing dividend and treasury stock transactions, and preparing stockholders' equity [10–30 min]**

The balance sheet of Franklin Foods, at December 31, 2011, reported 110,000 shares of no-par common stock authorized, with 30,000 shares issued and a Common stock balance of $180,000. Retained earnings had a balance of $120,000. During 2012, the company completed the following selected transactions:

Mar 15	Purchased 8,000 shares of treasury stock at $6 per share.
Apr 30	Distributed a 5% stock dividend on the *outstanding* shares of common stock. The market value of common stock was $8 per share.
Dec 31	Earned net income of $109,000 during the year. Closed net income to Retained earnings.

Requirements

1. Record the transactions in the general journal. Explanations are not required.
2. Prepare the stockholders' equity section of Franklin Foods' balance sheet at December 31, 2012.

P13-32B **①③** **Journalizing dividend and treasury stock transactions, preparing a statement of retained earnings, and preparing stockholders' equity [30–45 min]**

The balance sheet of MacMillan Management Consulting, Inc., at December 31, 2011, reported the following stockholders' equity:

Paid-in capital:	
Common stock, $12 par, 100,000 shares authorized, 20,000 shares issued	$ 240,000
Paid-in capital in excess of par—common	330,000
Total paid-in capital	570,000
Retained earnings	159,000
Total stockholders' equity	$ 729,000

During 2012, MacMillan completed the following selected transactions:

Feb	6	Distributed a 15% stock dividend on the common stock. The market value of MacMillan's stock was $26 per share.
Jul	29	Purchased 1,800 shares of treasury stock at $26 per share.
Nov	27	Declared a $0.30 per share cash dividend on the 21,200 shares of common stock outstanding. The date of record is December 17, 2012, and the payment date is January 7, 2013.
Dec	31	Closed the $82,000 net income to Retained earnings.

Requirements

1. Record the transactions in the general journal.
2. Prepare the retained earnings statement for the year ended December 31, 2012.
3. Prepare the stockholders' equity section of the balance sheet at December 31, 2012.

P13-33B ④ ⑤ Computing EPS and reporting a retained earnings restriction [20–25 min]
The capital structure of Hillstride, Inc., at December 31, 2011, included 26,000 shares of $2 preferred stock and 42,000 shares of common stock. Common stock outstanding during 2012 totaled 42,000 shares. Income from continuing operations during 2012 was $118,000. The company discontinued a segment of the business at a gain of $28,000 and also had an extraordinary gain of $18,000. The Hillstride board of directors restricts $97,000 of retained earnings for contingencies. Retained earnings at December 31, 2011, was $97,000, and the company declared preferred dividends of $52,000 during 2012.

Requirements

1. Compute Hillstride's earnings per share for 2012. Start with income from continuing operations. Income and loss amounts are net of income tax.
2. Show two ways of reporting Hillstride's retained earnings restriction.

P13-34B ⑤ Preparing a detailed income statement [25–35 min]
The following information was taken from the records of Daughtry Motorsports, Inc., at November 30, 2012:

Selling expenses	$ 120,000	Common stock, $10 par, 21,300	
General expenses	128,000	shares authorized and issued	$ 213,000
Income from discontinued operations	4,000	Preferred stock, $5, no-par	
Retained earnings, beginning	86,000	3,000 shares issued	150,000
Cost of goods sold	434,000	Income tax expense:	69,000
Treasury stock, common		Continuing operations	
(1,300 shares)	14,300	Income from discontinued	
Net sales revenue	839,000	operations	1,600

Requirement

1. Prepare a multi-step income statement for Daughtry Motorsports for the fiscal year ended November 30, 2012. Include earnings per share.

P13-35B ⑤ Preparing a corrected combined statement of income and retained earnings [25–35 min]
Jeff Halstrom, accountant for Home Bank Finance, was injured in a boating accident. Another employee prepared the following income statement for the year ended December 31, 2012:

HOME BANK FINANCE		
Income Statement		
Year ended December 31, 2012		
Revenue and gains:		
Sales		$ 364,000
Paid-in capital in excess of par—common		92,000
Total revenues and gains		456,000
Expenses and losses:		
Cost of goods sold	108,000	
Selling expenses	62,000	
General expenses	61,500	
Sales returns	14,000	
Sales discounts	8,500	
Dividends	13,000	
Income tax expense	33,000	
Total expenses and losses		300,000
Income from operations		$ 156,000
Other gains and losses		
Gain on discontinued operations		5,500
Net income		$ 161,500
Earnings per share		$ 3.23

The individual *amounts* listed on the income statement are correct. However, some accounts are reported incorrectly, and two items do not belong on the income statement at all. Also, income tax has *not* been applied to all appropriate figures. The income tax rate on discontinued operations is 30%. Home Bank Finance issued 54,000 shares of common stock in 2012 and held 4,000 shares as treasury stock during 2012. Retained earnings at December 31, 2011, was $164,000.

Requirement

1. Prepare a corrected combined statement of income and retained earnings for the fiscal year ended December 31, 2012. Prepare the income statement in single-step format.

● Continuing Exercise

E13-36 **❶ Journalizing stock dividends [10–15 min]**

MyAccountingLab

This exercise continues the Lawlor Lawn Service, Inc., situation from Exercise 12-44 of Chapter 12. On October 15, Lawlor Lawn Service declares and distributes a 10% stock dividend to all common shareholders of record on October 15 when the market price per common share is $5. Lawlor has 100 shares of common stock outstanding on the date of record.

Requirements

1. Is this a small or large stock dividend?
2. Journalize the entries related to the dividend.

• Continuing Problem

P13-37   **❸ Accounting for the purchase and sale of treasury stock [10–15 min]**
This problem continues the Draper Consulting, Inc., situation from Problem 12-45 of Chapter 12. In October, Draper has the following transactions related to its common shares:

Oct 1	Draper repurchased 200 of its common shares for $50 per share.
Oct 10	Draper reissued 90 of its treasury common shares for $65 per share.
Oct 20	Draper reissued 100 of its treasury common shares for $60 per share.

Requirements

1. Journalize the entry related to the transactions.
2. Calculate the balance in the T-accounts affected by the transactions.

Apply Your Knowledge

• Decision Cases

Decision Case 13-1 Valley Mills Construction, Inc., had the following stockholders' equity on June 30, 2013:

Common stock, no-par, 100,000 shares issued	$250,000
Retained earnings...	190,000
Total stockholders' equity	$440,000

In the past, Valley Mills has paid an annual cash dividend of $0.25 per share. Despite the large retained earnings balance, the board of directors wished to conserve cash for expansion. The board delayed the payment of cash dividends and in July distributed a 10% stock dividend. During August, the company's cash position improved. The board then declared and paid a cash dividend of $0.25 per share in September.

Suppose you owned 1,000 shares of Valley Mills common stock, acquired three years ago, prior to the 10% stock dividend. The market price of the stock was $22 per share before any of these dividends.

Requirements

1. What amount of cash dividends did you receive last year—before the stock dividend? What amount of cash dividends will you receive after the stock dividend?
2. How does the stock dividend affect your proportionate ownership in Valley Mills Construction? Explain.
3. Immediately after the stock dividend was distributed, the market value of Valley Mills stock decreased from $22 per share to $20 per share. Does this decrease represent a loss to you? Explain.

Decision Case 13-2 The following accounting issues have arisen at T-Shirts Plus, Inc.:

Requirements

1. Corporations sometimes purchase their own stock. When asked why they do so, T-Shirts Plus management responds that the stock is undervalued. What advantage would T-Shirts Plus gain by buying and selling its own undervalued stock?
2. T-Shirts Plus earned a significant profit in the year ended December 31, 2012, because land that it held was purchased by the State of Nebraska for a new highway. The company proposes to treat the sale of land as operating revenue. Why do you think the company is proposing this plan? Is this disclosure appropriate?

3. The treasurer of T-Shirts Plus wants to report a large loss as an extraordinary item because the company produced too much product and cannot sell it. (Under the rules of the lower of cost or market, this situation, in which the net realizable value of inventory is less than the book value, would trigger a write-down of inventory.) Why do you think the treasurer wants to report the loss as extraordinary? Would that be acceptable?

● Ethical Issue 13-1

Bobby's Bagels just landed a contract to open 100 new stores in shopping malls across the country. The new business should triple the company's profits. Prior to disclosing the new contract to the public, top managers of the company quietly bought most of Bobby's Bagels stock for themselves. After the discovery was announced, Bobby's Bagels stock price shot up from $7 to $52.

Requirements

1. Did Bobby's Bagels managers behave ethically? Explain your answer.
2. Who was helped and who was harmed by management's action?

● Fraud Case 13-1

The following is a true case. **General Electric (GE)**, like many other large corporations, is scrutinized by financial analysts who develop quarterly forecast EPS figures for the company. The companies are under intense pressure to meet or exceed these EPS forecasts. But when earnings fall short, some companies resort to accounting tricks. A few years ago, **GE** found itself facing this problem. In one case, it "sold" six locomotive engines to a financial institution at year-end with the idea that the financial institution would resell them to **GE**'s regular railroad customers in the first quarter of the following year. **GE** booked the revenue at year-end, which helped it hit its forecast EPS numbers. Later, upon investigation by the SEC, the transaction was found to be a "sham," or phony transaction, because the financial institutions were not taking over full ownership of the engines. In early 2009, **GE** was fined $50,000,000 for misrepresenting its financial results.

Requirements

1. What are the criteria for recording a sale of goods?
2. Why do company managers feel pressure to meet or exceed EPS forecasts of outside analysts?

● Financial Statement Case 13-1

Use the **Amazon.com** financial statements in Appendix A at the end of this book to answer the following questions.

Requirements

1. Show how **Amazon** computed basic earnings per share of $2.08 for 2009. (Ignore diluted earnings per share of $2.04.)
2. Prepare a T-account to show the beginning and ending balances and all activity in Retained earnings (Accumulated Deficit) for 2009.
3. How much in cash dividends did **Amazon** pay out during 2009, if any? Explain your answer.
4. How much treasury stock did **Amazon** have at December 31, 2009? Explain.

• Team Project 13-1

Obtain the annual reports (or annual report data) of five well-known companies. You can get the reports either from the companies' Web sites, your college library, or by mailing a request directly to the company (allow two weeks for delivery). Or you can visit the Web and search the SEC EDGAR database, which includes the financial reports of most well-known companies.

Requirements

1. After selecting five companies, examine their income statements to search for the following items:
   a. Income from continuing operations
   b. Discontinued operations
   c. Extraordinary gains and losses
   d. Net income or net loss
   e. Earnings per share data

2. Study the companies' balance sheets to see
   a. what classes of stock each company has issued.
   b. which item carries a larger balance—the Common stock account or Paid-in capital in excess of par (also labeled Additional paid-in capital).
   c. the percentage of each company's total stockholders' equity made up of retained earnings.
   d. whether the company has Treasury stock. If so, how many shares and how much is the cost?

3. Examine each company's statement of stockholders' equity for evidence of
   a. cash dividends.
   b. stock dividends. (Some companies use the term *stock split* to refer to a large stock dividend.)
   c. treasury stock purchases and sales.

4. As directed by your instructor, either write a report or present your findings to your class. You may not be able to understand *everything* you find, but neither can the Wall Street analysts! You will be amazed at how much you have learned.

• Communication Activity 13-1

In 100 words or fewer, explain the difference between stock dividends and stock splits. Include the effect on stock values.

Quick Check Answers

1. *b* 2. *b* 3. *c* . 4. *d* 5. *c* 6. *c* 7. *a* 8. *c* 9. *c* 10. *b*

For online homework, exercises, and problems that provide you immediate feedback, please visit myaccountinglab.com.

14

The Statement of Cash Flows

How do we explain the change in the cash balance?

SMART TOUCH LEARNING, INC.
Balance Sheet
May 31, 2013

Assets				Liabilities	
Current assets:				Current liabilities:	
Cash		**$4,800**		Accounts payable	$ 48,700
Accounts receivable		2,600		Salary payable	900
Inventory		30,500		Interest payable	100
Supplies		600		Unearned service revenue	400
Prepaid rent		2,000		Total current liabilities	50,100
Total current assets			$ 40,500	Long-term liabilities:	
Plant assets:				Notes payable	20,000
Furniture	$18,000			Total liabilities	70,100
Less: Accumulated depreciation—furniture	300	17,700			
Building	48,000			**Stockholders' Equity**	
Less: Accumulated depreciation—building	200	47,800		Common stock	30,000
Total plant assets			65,500	Retained earnings	5,900
				Total stockholders' equity	35,900
Total assets			$106,000	Total liabilities and stockholders' equity	$106,000

Learning Objectives

1 Identify the purposes of the statement of cash flows

2 Distinguish among operating, investing, and financing cash flows

3 Prepare the statement of cash flows by the indirect method

4 Identify noncash investing and financing activities

5 Analyze cash flows

6 Prepare the statement of cash flows by the direct method (Appendix 14A)

7 Prepare the indirect statement of cash flows using a spreadsheet (Appendix 14B)

Why is cash so important? You can probably answer that question from your own experience: It takes cash to pay the bills. You have some income and you have expenses; and these events generate cash receipts and payments.

Businesses, including Smart Touch Learning, Inc., and Greg's Tunes, Inc., work the same way. Net income is a good thing, but Smart Touch and Greg's both need enough cash to pay the bills and run their operations.

• • •

This chapter covers cash flows—cash receipts and cash payments. We will see how to prepare the statement of cash flows (or cash flow statement), starting with the format used by the vast majority of non-public companies; it is called the *indirect method*. Chapter Appendix 14A covers the alternate format of the statement of cash flows, the *direct method*. The cash flow statement is required by GAAP.

Chapter Appendix 14B shows how to use a spreadsheet to prepare the statement of cash flows. This appendix presents the indirect-method spreadsheet only. The focus companies throughout the chapter once again are Smart Touch and Greg's Tunes.

Introduction: The Statement of Cash Flows

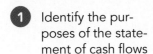

1 Identify the purposes of the statement of cash flows

The balance sheet reports financial position. When a comparative balance sheet for two periods is presented, it shows whether cash increased or decreased. For example, Smart Touch's comparative balance sheet reported the following:

	2014	2013	Increase (Decrease)
Cash..........	$22,000	$42,000	$(20,000)

Smart Touch's cash decreased by $20,000 during 2014. But the balance sheet does not show *why* cash decreased. We need the cash flow statement for that. The statement of cash flows reports **cash flows**—cash receipts and cash payments. It

- shows where cash came from (receipts) and how cash was spent (payments).
- reports why cash increased or decreased during the period.
- covers a span of time and is dated the same as the income statement—"Year Ended December 31, 2014," for example.

The statement of cash flows explains why net income as reported on the income statement does not equal the change in the cash balance. **In essence, the cash flow statement is the communicating link between the accrual based income statement and the cash reported on the balance sheet.** Exhibit 14-1 illustrates the relationships among the balance sheet, the income statement, and the statement of cash flows.

EXHIBIT 14-1 | **Timing of the Financial Statements**

December 31, 2013 (a point in time)	For the Year Ended December 31, 2014 (a period of time)	December 31, 2014 (a point in time)
Balance Sheet	Income Statement / Statement of Stockholders' Equity / Statement of Cash Flows	Balance Sheet

How do people use cash flow information? The statement of cash flows helps

1. **predict future cash flows.** Past cash receipts and payments help predict future cash flows.

2. **evaluate management decisions.** Wise investment decisions help the business prosper, while unwise decisions cause the business to have problems. Investors and creditors use cash flow information to evaluate managers' decisions.

3. **predict ability to pay debts and dividends.** Lenders want to know whether they will collect on their loans. Stockholders want dividends on their investments. The statement of cash flows helps make these predictions.

Cash Equivalents

On a statement of cash flows, *Cash* means more than cash on hand and cash in the bank. *Cash* includes **cash equivalents,** which are highly liquid investments that can be converted into cash in three months or less. **As the name implies, cash equivalents are so close to cash that they are treated as "equals."** Examples of cash equivalents are money-market accounts and investments in U.S. government securities. Throughout this chapter, the term *cash* refers to both cash and cash equivalents.

Operating, Investing, and Financing Activities

There are three basic types of cash flow activities, and the statement of cash flows has a section for each:

- Operating activities
- Investing activities
- Financing activities

2 Distinguish among operating, investing, and financing cash flows

Each section reports cash flows coming into the company and cash flows going out of the company based on these three divisions.

Operating Activities

- Is the most important category of cash flows because it reflects the day-to-day operations that determine the future of an organization
- Generate revenues, expenses, gains, and losses
- Affect net income on the income statement
- Affect current assets and current liabilities on the balance sheet

Investing Activities

- Increase and decrease long-term assets, such as computers, software, land, buildings, and equipment
- Include purchases and sales of these assets, plus long-term loans receivable from others (non-trade) and collections of those loans
- Include purchases and sales of long-term investments

Financing Activities

- Increase and decrease long-term liabilities and equity
- Include issuing stock, paying dividends, and buying and selling treasury stock
- Include borrowing money and paying off loans

Exhibit 14-2 shows the relationship between operating, investing, and financing cash flows and the various parts of the balance sheet.

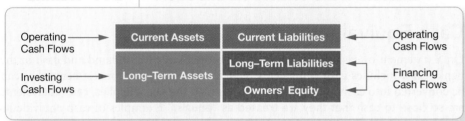

EXHIBIT 14-2 | **Operating, Investing, and Financing Cash Flows and the Balance-Sheet Accounts**

As you can see, operating cash flows affect the current accounts. Investing cash flows affect the long-term assets. Financing cash flows affect long-term liabilities and owners' equity.

Two Formats for Operating Activities

There are two ways to format operating activities on the statement of cash flows:

- The **indirect method** starts with net income and adjusts it to net cash provided by operating activities.
- The **direct method** restates the income statement in terms of cash. The direct method shows all the cash receipts and all the cash payments from operating activities.

    The indirect and direct methods

- use different computations but produce the same amount of cash flow from operations.
- present investing activities and financing activities in exactly the same format. Only the *operating activities* section is presented differently between the two methods.

    We will begin with the indirect method because most companies use it. To focus on the direct method, go to Appendix 14A.

Preparing the Statement of Cash Flows by the Indirect Method

 Prepare the statement of cash flows by the indirect method

To prepare the statement of cash flows, you need the income statement and both the current year's and the prior year's balance sheets. Consider Smart Touch's financial statements on page 667. To prepare the statement of cash flows by the indirect method, we follow Steps 1–4:

STEP 1: Lay out the statement format as shown in Exhibit 14-3. Steps 2–4 will complete the statement of cash flows.

Key Takeaway
Operating activities reflect the day-to-day business operations. Operating activities affect current assets and current liabilities. Investing activities report purchase and sales of long-term assets, such as buildings and long-term (non-trade) loans receivable. Financing activities reflect the capitalization of the business and include increases and decreases in long-term liability and equity accounts, paying dividends, and treasury stock transactions. Only the operating activities section is presented differently between the indirect and direct methods.

EXHIBIT 14-3   **Format of the Statement of Cash Flows: Indirect Method**

SMART TOUCH LEARNING, INC. Statement of Cash Flows Year Ended December 31, 2014		
± Cash flows from operating activities:		
Net income		
Adjustments to reconcile net income to net cash provided by		
operating activities:		
+ Depreciation / amortization expense		
+ Loss on sale of long-term assets		
− Gain on sale of long-term assets		
− Increases in current assets other than cash		
+ Decreases in current assets other than cash		
+ Increases in current liabilities		
− Decreases in current liabilities		
Net cash provided by (used for) operating activities		
± Cash flows from investing activities:		
+ Cash receipts from sales of long-term (plant) assets (investments,		
land, building, equipment, and so on)		
− Acquisition of long-term (plant) assets		
Net cash provided by (used for) investing activities		
± Cash flows from financing activities:		
+ Cash receipts from issuance of stock		
+ Cash receipts from sale of treasury stock		
− Purchase of treasury stock		
+ Cash receipts from issuance of notes or bonds payable (borrowing)		
− Payment of notes or bonds payable		
− Payment of dividends		
Net cash provided by (used for) financing activities		
= Net increase (decrease) in cash during the year		
+ Cash at December 31, 2013		
= Cash at December 31, 2014		

STEP 2: Compute the change in cash from the comparative balance sheet. The change in cash is the "key reconciling figure" for the statement of cash flows. Exhibit 14-5 is the comparative balance sheet of Smart Touch, where the top line shows that cash decreased by $20,000 during 2014.

STEP 3: Take net income, depreciation, and any gains or losses from the income statement. Exhibit 14-6 gives the 2014 income statement of Smart Touch, with the relevant items highlighted.

STEP 4: Complete the statement of cash flows using data from the income statement and the comparative balance sheet. The statement is complete only after you have explained all the year-to-year changes in all the accounts on the balance sheet.

Let's apply these steps to show the operating activities of Smart Touch. Exhibit 14-4 depicts the statement of cash flows. All lettered items are tied to either a balance sheet or income statement item. That makes it easy to trace the data from one statement to the other.

EXHIBIT 14-4 | **Indirect Method Statement of Cash Flows**

	SMART TOUCH LEARNING, INC. Statement of Cash Flows Year Ended December 31, 2014		
	Cash flows from operating activities:		
A	Net income		$ 40,000
	Adjustments to reconcile net income to net cash provided by operating activities:		
B	Depreciation	$ 20,000	
C	Gain on sale of plant assets	(10,000)	
	Increase in accounts receivable	(17,000)	
	Decrease in inventory	2,000	
D	Increase in accounts payable	40,000	
	Decrease in accrued liabilities	(5,000)	30,000
	Net cash provided by operating activities		$ 70,000
	Cash flows from investing activities:		
E	Acquisition of plant assets	$(310,000)	
F	Cash receipt from sale of plant asset	50,000	
	Net cash used for investing activities		(260,000)
	Cash flows from financing activities:		
I	Cash receipt from issuance of common stock	$ 120,000	
G	Cash receipt from issuance of notes payable	90,000	
H	Payment of notes payable	(10,000)	
J	Purchase of treasury stock	(20,000)	
K	Payment of dividends	(10,000)	
	Net cash provided by financing activities		170,000
L	Net decrease in cash		$ (20,000)
L	Cash balance, December 31, 2013		42,000
L	Cash balance, December 31, 2014		$ 22,000

Cash Flows from Operating Activities

Operating cash flows begin with net income, taken from the income statement.

A Net Income

The statement of cash flows—indirect method—begins with net income (or net loss) because revenues and expenses, which affect net income, produce cash receipts and cash payments. Revenues bring in cash receipts, and expenses must be paid. But net income as shown on the income statement is accrual based and the cash flows (cash basis net income) do not always equal the accrual basis revenues and expenses. For example, sales *on account* generate revenues that increase net income, but the company has not yet collected cash from those sales. Accrued expenses decrease net income, but the company has not paid cash *if the expenses are accrued*.

To go from net income to cash flow from operations, we must make some adjustments to net income on the statement of cash flows. These additions and subtractions follow net income and are labeled *Adjustments to reconcile net income to net cash provided by operating activities*.

EXHIBIT 14-5 | **Comparative Balance Sheet**

SMART TOUCH LEARNING, INC.
Comparative Balance Sheet
December 31, 2014 and 2013

	2014	2013	Increase (Decrease)	
Assets				
Current:				
Cash	$ 22,000	$ 42,000	$ (20,000)	L
Accounts receivable	90,000	73,000	17,000	D
Inventory	143,000	145,000	(2,000)	
Plant assets, net	460,000	210,000	250,000	E/F
Total assets	$715,000	$470,000	$245,000	
Liabilities				
Current:			—	
Accounts payable	$ 90,000	$ 50,000	$ 40,000	D
Accrued liabilities	5,000	10,000	(5,000)	
Long-term notes payable	160,000	80,000	80,000	G/H
Stockholders' Equity				
Common stock	370,000	250,000	120,000	I
Retained earnings	110,000	80,000	30,000	A/K
Treasury stock	(20,000)	0	(20,000)	J
Total liabilities and stockholders' equity	$715,000	$470,000	$245,000	

EXHIBIT 14-6 | **Income Statement**

SMART TOUCH LEARNING, INC.
Income Statement
Year Ended December 31, 2014

	Revenues and gains:		
	Sales revenue	$286,000	
	Interest revenue	12,000	
	Dividend revenue	9,000	
C	Gain on sale of plant assets	10,000	
	Total revenues and gains		$317,000
	Expenses:		
	Cost of goods sold	$156,000	
	Salary and wage expense	56,000	
B	Depreciation expense	20,000	
	Other operating expense	16,000	
	Interest expense	15,000	
	Income tax expense	14,000	
	Total expenses		277,000
A	Net income		$ 40,000

B Depreciation, Depletion, and Amortization Expenses

These expenses are added back to net income to reconcile from net income to cash flow from operations. Let's see why this occurs. Depreciation is recorded as follows:

Depreciation expense (E+)	20,000	
Accumulated depreciation (CA+)		20,000

You can see that depreciation does not affect cash because there is no Cash account in the journal entry. **Depreciation is a noncash expense.** However, depreciation, like all the other expenses, decreases net income. Therefore, to go from net income to cash flows, we must remove depreciation by adding it back to net income.

Example: Suppose you had only two transactions during the period:

- $40,000 cash sale
- Depreciation expense of $20,000

Accrual basis net income is $20,000 ($40,000 – $20,000), but cash flow from operations is $40,000. To reconcile from net income, $20,000, to cash flow from operations, $40,000, add back depreciation, $20,000. We would also add back any depletion and amortization expenses because they are noncash expenses, similar to depreciation.

C Gains and Losses on the Sale of Assets

Sales of long-term assets such as land and buildings are investing activities, and these sales usually create a gain or a loss. The gain or loss is included in net income, which is already in the operating section of the cash flow statement. The gain or loss must be removed from net income on the statement of cash flows so the total cash from the sale of the asset can be shown in the investing section.

Exhibit 14-4 includes an adjustment for a gain. During 2014, Smart Touch sold equipment, and there was a gain of $10,000 on the sale. The gain was included in the calculation of net income on the income statement, so the gain must be removed from operating cash flows. The gain made net income bigger, so it is subtracted in the operating section. On the other hand, a loss on the sale of plant assets would make net income smaller, so it would be added back to net income.

D Changes in the Current Assets and the Current Liabilities

Most current assets and current liabilities result from operating activities. For example,

- accounts receivable result from sales,
- inventory relates to cost of goods sold, and so on.

Changes in the current accounts create adjustments to net income on the cash flow statement, as follows:

↑ Current assets   ↓ Cash

1. **An increase in a current asset other than cash causes a decrease in cash.** If Accounts receivable, Inventory, or Prepaid expenses increased, then cash decreased. Therefore, we subtract the increase in the current asset from net income to get cash flow from operations. For example, Smart Touch's Accounts receivable went up by $17,000. That increase in the current asset shows as a decrease in cash on the cash flow statement (Exhibit 14-4).

↓ Current assets   ↑ Cash

2. **A decrease in a current asset other than cash causes an increase in cash.** Smart Touch's Inventory decreased by $2,000. What caused the decrease? Smart Touch must have sold some inventory and collected cash. Therefore, we add the decrease in Inventory of $2,000 in the cash flow statement (Exhibit 14-4).

3. **A decrease in a current liability causes a decrease in cash.** The payment of a current liability decreases cash. Therefore, we subtract decreases in current liabilities from net income to get cash flow from operations. Smart Touch's Accrued liabilities went down $5,000. That change shows up as a $5,000 decrease in cash flows in Exhibit 14-4.

↓ **Current liabilities**   ↓ **Cash**

4. **An increase in a current liability causes an increase in cash.** Smart Touch's Accounts payable increased by $40,000. This means that cash was not spent at the time the expense was incurred, but rather it will be paid at a later time—resulting in a liability. Accordingly, even though net income was reduced by the expense, cash was not reduced. However, cash will be reduced later when Smart Touch pays off its liability. Therefore, an increase in a current liability is *added* to net income in the statement of cash flows in Exhibit 14-4.

↑ **Current liabilities**   ↑ **Cash**

Evaluating Cash Flows from Operating Activities

During 2014, Smart Touch's operations provided net cash flow of $70,000. This amount exceeds net income (due to the adjustments discussed in sections **B**, **C**, and **D**). However, to fully evaluate a company's cash flows, we must also examine its investing and financing activities. Exhibit 14-4 shows the completed operating activities section.

Stop & Think...

The operating activities represent the core of the day-to-day results of any business. Remember when we learned the difference between accrual and cash basis accounting? All the operating activities section represents is a cash basis income statement. With the indirect method, we indirectly back into cash basis—that is, we start with accrual basis net income from the income statement and adjust it back to cash basis "operating" cash flows (cash basis net income).

Cash Flows from Investing Activities

Investing activities affect long-term assets, such as Plant assets and Investments. These are shown for Smart Touch in Exhibit 14-5. Now, let's see how to compute the investing cash flows. A summary table follows in Exhibit 14-7.

EXHIBIT 14-7 | **Computing Cash Flows from Investing Activities**

Cash Receipts

From sale of plant assets	Beginning plant assets (net)	+	Acquisition	−	Depreciation expense	−	Book value of assets sold	=	Ending plant assets (net)

$$\text{Cash receipt} = \text{Book value of assets sold} \begin{cases} + & \text{Gain on sale} \\ \text{or} & \\ - & \text{Loss on sale} \end{cases}$$

Cash Payments

For acquisition of plant assets	Beginning plant assets (net)	+	Acquisition	−	Depreciation expense	−	Book value of assets sold	=	Ending plant assets (net)

Computing Acquisitions and Sales of Plant Assets

Companies keep a separate account for each asset, but for computing investing cash flows, it is helpful to combine all the plant assets into a single Plant assets account. We subtract accumulated depreciation from the assets' cost in order to work with a single net figure for plant assets, such as Plant assets, net—$460,000. This simplifies the computations. Recall that Asset cost minus accumulated depreciation equals the book value of the asset. **So the Plant assets, net account holds the book value of plant assets.**

To illustrate, observe that Smart Touch's

- balance sheet reports plant assets, net of depreciation, of $460,000 at the end of 2014 and $210,000 at the end of 2013 (Exhibit 14-5).
- income statement shows depreciation expense of $20,000 and a $10,000 gain on sale of plant assets (Exhibit 14-6).

Also, assume that Smart Touch's acquisitions of plant assets during 2014 totaled $310,000. **E**

This gives us an incomplete T-account as follows:

Plant assets, net

12/31/13 Bal	210,000		
		Depreciation (from Inc Stmt) 20,000	**B**
E Acquisitions	310,000	Cost of sold assets (COSA)	?
12/31/14 Bal	460,000		

We also know that Smart Touch sold some older plant assets because there was a gain on sale of assets reported on the income statement. We don't care about the gain itself, we need to know the amount of cash received from the sale. Remember, we are looking for cash movement. How much cash did the business receive from the sale of plant assets? First, let's look at the cost of the sold assets. This will be the missing value in our Plant assets, net T-account.

12/31/13 Bal + Acquisitions – Depreciation – COSA? = 12/31/14 Bal
210,000 + 310,000 – 20,000 – COSA? = 460,000
500,000 – COSA? = 460,000
COSA = 40,000

So our completed T-account is as follows:

Plant assets, net

12/31/13 Bal	210,000		
		Depreciation (from Inc Stmt) 20,000	**B**
E Acquisitions	310,000	Cost of sold assets (COSA) 40,000	
12/31/14 Bal	460,000		

Cash received from selling plant assets can be computed by using the journal entry approach:

Cash (A+) **F**	?????	
Gain on sale of plant assets (from the income statement) (R+) **C**		10,000
Plant assets, net (from the T-account—COSA) (A–)		40,000

The $40,000 book-value comes from the Plant assets (Net) account on the balance sheet. The gain or loss comes from the income statement. The missing amount must be the cash received from the sale.

So, we compute the cash receipt from the sale as follows:

Cash = $10,000 Gain + $40,000 COSA (Plant assets, net)
Cash = $50,000 **F**

The cash receipt from the sale of plant assets of $50,000 is shown as item **F** in the investing activities section of the statement of cash flows (see Exhibit 14-4). Exhibit 14-7 (shown previously on page 669) summarizes the computation of the investing cash flows. Items we computed are shown in color.

Cash Flows from Financing Activities

Financing activities affect the liability and owners' equity accounts, such as Long-term notes payable, Bonds payable, Common stock, and Retained earnings. These are shown for Smart Touch in Exhibit 14-5. A summary follows in Exhibit 14-8.

EXHIBIT 14-8 | **Computing Cash Flows from Financing Activities**

Cash Receipts

| From issuance of notes payable | Beginning notes payable | + | Cash receipt from issuance of notes payable | − | Cash payment of notes payable | = | Ending notes payable |

| From issuance of stock | Beginning stock | + | Cash receipt from issuance of new stock | | | = | Ending stock |

Cash Payments

| Of notes payable | Beginning notes payable | + | Cash receipt from issuance of notes payable | − | Cash payment of notes payable | = | Ending notes payable |

| To purchase treasury stock | Beginning treasury stock | + | Cost of treasury stock purchased | | | = | Ending treasury stock |

| Of dividends | Beginning retained earnings | + | Net income | − | Dividends declared | = | Ending retained earnings |

Computing Issuances and Payments of Long-Term Notes Payable

The beginning and ending balances of Notes payable or Bonds payable are taken from the balance sheet. If either the amount of new issuances or payments is known, the other amount can be computed. For Smart Touch, new issuances of notes payable is known to be $90,000 (shown as item **G** in Exhibit 14-4). The computation of note payments uses the balance sheet amounts from the Long-term notes payable account in Exhibit 14-5 to create the following incomplete T-account:

Long-term notes payable

	12/31/13 Bal	80,000
Note payments ?	New notes issued	90,000 **G**
	12/31/14 Bal	160,000

Then, solve for the missing payments value:

12/31/13 Bal + New Notes Issued − Payments? = 12/31/14 Bal
80,000 + 90,000 − Payments? = 160,000
170,000 − Payments? = 160,000
Payments = 10,000

Complete the T-account:

Long-term notes payable

H Note payments	10,000	12/31/13 Bal	80,000	
		New notes issued	90,000	**G**
		12/31/14 Bal	160,000	

The payment of $10,000 is an outflow of cash, as shown on the statement of cash flows. (See item **H** in Exhibit 14-4).

Computing Issuances of Stock and Purchases of Treasury Stock

Cash flows for these financing activities can be determined by analyzing the stock accounts. For example, the amount of a new issuance of common stock is determined by analyzing the Common stock account. Using data from Exhibit 14-5, the incomplete Common stock T-account is as follows:

Common stock

		12/31/13 Bal	250,000
Retirements	?	Issuance	?
		12/31/14 Bal	370,000

We would have to be told if there were any stock retirements. Since there were no retirements, we know the balance change must be represented by new stock issuances.

Solving for the missing value is completed as follows:

$$12/31/13 \text{ Bal} + \text{Issuance of Stock?} - \text{Retirements?} = 12/31/14 \text{ Bal}$$
$$250,000 \quad + \text{Issuance of Stock?} - \quad 0 \quad = 370,000$$
$$\text{Issuance of Stock} = 120,000$$

The completed T-account for Common stock is as follows:

Common stock

		12/31/13 Bal	250,000	
Retirements	0	Issuance	120,000	**I**
		12/31/14 Bal	370,000	

Therefore, the new stock issuance shows as $120,000 positive cash flows in the financing activities section of the statement (item **I** in Exhibit 14-4).

The last item that changed on Smart Touch's balance sheet was Treasury stock. The incomplete T-account balances from the Treasury stock account on the balance sheet show the following:

Treasury stock

12/31/13 Bal	0		
Purchases	?	Sales	?
12/31/14 Bal	20,000		

Since we were not told that any treasury stock was sold, we must assume that 100% of the account change represents new acquisitions of treasury stock. Solving for the amount, the equation follows:

$$12/31/13 \text{ Bal} + \text{Purchases?} - \text{Sales?} = 12/31/14 \text{ Bal}$$
$$0 + \text{Purchases?} - 0 = 20,000$$
$$\text{Purchases} = 20,000$$

Completing the T-account, we have the following:

Treasury stock

	12/31/13 Bal	0		
J	Purchases	20,000	Sales	0
	12/31/14 Bal	20,000		

So, $20,000 is shown as a cash outflow in the financing section of the cash flow statement for purchase of treasury stock (item J in Exhibit 14-4).

Computing Dividend Payments

The amount of dividend payments can be computed by analyzing the Retained earnings account. First we input the balances from the balance sheet:

Retained earnings

		12/31/13 Bal	80,000
Net loss	?	Net income	?
Dividend declarations	?		
		12/31/14 Bal	110,000

Retained earnings increases when companies earn net income. Retained earnings decreases when companies have a net loss and when they declare dividends. We know that Smart Touch earned net income of $40,000 from the income statement in Exhibit 14-6.

Retained earnings

		12/31/13 Bal	80,000	
Net loss	?	Net income	40,000	A
Dividend declarations	?			
		12/31/14 Bal	110,000	

Smart Touch can't have both net income and net loss for the same period; therefore, the missing value must be the amount of dividends Smart Touch declared. Solving for the dividends follows:

$$12/31/13 \text{ Bal} + \text{Net income} - \text{Dividends declared} = 12/31/14 \text{ Bal}$$
$$80,000 + 40,000 - \text{Dividends declared} = 110,000$$
$$120,000 - \text{Dividends declared} = 110,000$$
$$\text{Dividends declared} = 10,000$$

So our final Retained earnings T-account shows the following:

Retained earnings

		12/31/13 Bal	80,000	
		Net income	40,000	A
K	Dividend declarations 10,000			
		12/31/14 Bal	110,000	

Connect To: IFRS

Under GAAP, interest or dividends received and interest paid are all reported as operating activities. Dividends paid are reported as a financing activity under GAAP. Under IFRS rules, interest and dividends received and paid may be classified as either operating, investing, or financing cash flows, provided that they are classified consistently from period to period.

A stock dividend has *no* effect on Cash and is *not* reported on the financing section of the cash flow statement. If there were stock dividends, they would be reported in the noncash transactions section, discussed later in the chapter. Smart Touch had no stock dividends—only cash dividends. Exhibit 14-8 (shown previously on page 671) summarizes the computation of cash flows from financing activities, highlighted in color.

Net Change in Cash and Cash Balances L

The next line of the cash flow statement (underneath Net cash provided by financing activities in Exhibit 14-4) represents the total change in cash for the period. In the case of Smart Touch, it is the net decrease in cash balances of $20,000 for the year. The decrease in cash of $20,000 is also represented by the following:

Net cash provided by Operating activities	−	Net cash used for Investing activities	+	Net cash provided by Financing activities		Net decrease in Cash
70,000	−	260,000	+	170,000	=	(20,000)

Next, the beginning cash from December 31, 2013, is listed at $42,000. The net decrease of $20,000 is subtracted from beginning cash of $42,000, which equals the ending cash balance on December 31, 2014, of $22,000. **This is the key to the statement of cash flows—it explains why the cash balance for Smart Touch decreased by $20,000, even though the company reported net income for the year.**

Stop & Think...

Most of you probably have a checking or savings account. Think about how the balance changes from month to month. It does not always change because you have earned revenues or incurred expenses (operating). Sometimes it changes because you buy a long-lasting asset, such as a computer (investing). Sometimes it changes because you make a principal payment on your car loan (financing). It is the same with business; business bank accounts do not change only because they earn revenue or incur expenses (operating). The cash flow statement explains all the reasons that cash changed (operating, investing, and financing).

Noncash Investing and Financing Activities

 Identify noncash investing and financing activities

Companies make investments that do not require cash. They also obtain financing other than cash. Such transactions are called noncash investing and financing activities and appear in a separate part of the cash flow statement. Our Smart Touch example did not include transactions of this type because the company did not have any noncash transactions during the year. So, to illustrate them, let's consider the three noncash transactions for Greg's Tunes. How would they be reported? First, we gather the noncash activities for the company:

1   Acquired $300,000 building by issuing stock

2   Acquired $70,000 land by issuing note payable

3   Paid $100,000 note payable by issuing common stock

Now, we consider each transaction individually.

1. Greg's Tunes issued common stock of $300,000 to acquire a building. The journal entry to record the purchase would be as follows:

Building (A+)	300,000	
Common stock (Q+)		300,000

This transaction would not be reported on the cash flow statement because no cash was paid. But the building and the common stock are important. The purchase of the building is an investing activity. The issuance of common stock is a financing activity. Taken together, this transaction is a *noncash investing and financing activity*.

2. The second transaction listed indicates that Greg's Tunes acquired $70,000 of land by issuing a note. The journal entry to record the purchase would be as follows:

Land (A+)	70,000	
Notes payable (L+)		70,000

This transaction would not be reported on the cash flow statement because no cash was paid. But the land and the notes payable are important. The purchase of the land is an investing activity. The issuance of the note is a financing activity. Taken together, this transaction is a *noncash investing and financing activity*.

3. The third transaction listed indicates that Greg's Tunes exchanged $100,000 of debt by issuing common stock. The journal entry to record the transaction would be as follows:

Notes payable (L–)	100,000	
Common stock (Q+)		100,000

This transaction would not be reported on the cash flow statement because no cash was paid. But the notes payable and the stock issuance are important. The payment on the note and the issuance of the common stock are both financing activities. Taken together, this transaction, even though it is two financing transactions, is reported in the *noncash investing and financing activities*.

Noncash investing and financing activities are reported in a separate part of the statement of cash flows. Exhibit 14-9 illustrates noncash investing and financing activities for Greg's Tunes. This information either follows the cash flow statement or can be disclosed in a note.

> **Key Takeaway**
>
> Companies make investments that do not require cash. They also obtain financing other than cash. Such transactions are called noncash investing and financing activities and appear in a separate part of the cash flow statement.

EXHIBIT 14-9 | **Noncash Investing and Financing Activities**

GREG'S TUNES Statement of Cash Flows—partial Year Ended December 31, 2014		
Noncash investing and financing activities:		
Acquisition of building by issuing common stock		$300,000
Acquisition of land by issuing note payable		70,000
Payment of note payable by issuing common stock		100,000
Total noncash investing and financing activities		$470,000

Measuring Cash Adequacy: Free Cash Flow

 5 Analyze cash flows

Throughout this chapter we have focused on cash flows from operating, investing, and financing activities. Some investors want to know how much cash a company can "free up" for new opportunities. **Free cash flow** is the amount of cash available from operations after paying for planned investments in long-term assets and after paying cash dividends to shareholders. Free cash flow can be computed as follows:

$$
\text{Free cash flow} = \begin{matrix} \text{Net cash provided} \\ \text{by operating} \\ \text{activities} \end{matrix} - \begin{matrix} \text{Cash payments planned} \\ \text{for investments in} \\ \text{long-term assets} \end{matrix} - \text{Cash dividends}
$$

Many companies use free cash flow to manage their operations. Suppose Greg's Tunes expects net cash provided by operations of $200,000. Assume Greg's Tunes plans to spend $160,000 to modernize its production facilities and pays $15,000 in cash dividends. In this case, Greg's Tunes' free cash flow would be $25,000 ($200,000 − $160,000 − $15,000). If a good investment opportunity comes along, Greg's Tunes should have $25,000 cash available to invest.

The Decision Guidelines on the next page will put into practice what you have learned about the statement of cash flows prepared by the indirect method.

Key Takeaway

Free cash flow measures the amount of cash available from normal operations after paying for planned investments in long-term assets and after paying cash dividends to shareholders.

Decision Guidelines 14-1

USING CASH FLOW AND RELATED INFORMATION TO EVALUATE INVESTMENTS

Ann Browning is a private investor. Through the years, she has devised some guidelines for evaluating investments. Here are some of her guidelines.

Question	Financial Statement	What to Look For
• Where is most of the company's cash coming from?	Statement of cash flows	Operating activities → Good sign Investing activities → Bad sign Financing activities → Okay sign
• Do high sales and profits translate into more cash?	Statement of cash flows	Usually, but cash flows from *operating* activities must be the main source of cash for long-term success.
• If sales and profits are low, how is the company generating cash?	Statement of cash flows	If *investing* activities are generating the cash, the business may be in trouble because it is selling off its long-term assets. If *financing* activities are generating the cash, that cannot go on forever. Sooner or later, investors will demand cash flow from operating activities.
• Is the cash balance large enough to provide for expansion?	Balance sheet	The cash balance should be growing over time. If not, the company may be in trouble.
• Can the business pay its debts?	Income statement	Does the trend indicate increasing net income?
	Statement of cash flows	Are cash flows from operating activities the main source of cash?
	Balance sheet	Are the current ratio and debt ratio adequate?

Summary Problem 14-1

The Adams Corporation reported the following income statement and comparative balance sheet for 2014 and 2013, along with transaction data for 2014:

ADAMS CORPORATION
Income Statement
Year Ended December 31, 2014

Sales revenue		$662,000
Cost of goods sold		560,000
Gross profit		$102,000
Operating expenses:		
Salary expense	$46,000	
Depreciation expense	10,000	
Rent expense	2,000	
Total operating expenses		58,000
Income from operations		$ 44,000
Other items:		
Loss on sale of equipment		(2,000)
Income before income tax		$ 42,000
Income tax expense		16,000
Net income		$ 26,000

ADAMS CORPORATION
Balance Sheet
December 31, 2014 and 2013

Assets	2014	2013	Liabilities	2014	2013
Current:			Current:		
Cash and cash equivalents	$ 22,000	$ 3,000	Accounts payable	$ 35,000	$ 26,000
Accounts receivable	22,000	23,000	Accrued liabilities	7,000	9,000
Inventory	35,000	34,000	Income tax payable	10,000	10,000
Total current assets	$ 79,000	$ 60,000	Total current liabilities	$ 52,000	$ 45,000
Equipment, net	126,000	72,000	Bonds payable	84,000	53,000
			Stockholders' Equity		
			Common stock	52,000	20,000
			Retained earnings	27,000	19,000
			Treasury stock	(10,000)	(5,000)
Total assets	$205,000	$132,000	Total liabilities and stockholders' equity	$205,000	$132,000

Transaction Data for 2014:

Purchase of equipment	$140,000
Payment of dividends	18,000
Issuance of common stock to retire bonds payable	13,000
Issuance of bonds payable to borrow cash	44,000
Cash receipt from issuance of common stock	19,000
Cash receipt from sale of equipment (book value, $76,000)	74,000
Purchase of treasury stock	5,000

Requirement

1. Prepare Adams Corporation's statement of cash flows for the year ended December 31, 2014. Format operating cash flows by the indirect method. Follow the four steps outlined below.

   STEP 1. Lay out the format of the statement of cash flows.

   STEP 2. From the comparative balance sheet, compute the change in cash during the year.

   STEP 3. From the income statement, take net income, depreciation, and the loss on sale of equipment to the statement of cash flows.

   STEP 4. Complete the statement of cash flows. Account for the year-to-year change in each balance sheet account. Prepare a T-account to show the transaction activity in each long-term balance-sheet account.

Solution

ADAMS CORPORATION Statement of Cash Flows Year Ended December 31, 2014		
Cash flows from operating activities:		
Net income		$26,000
Adjustments to reconcile net income to net cash		
provided by operating activities:		
Depreciation	$ 10,000	
Loss on sale of equipment	2,000	
Decrease in accounts receivable	1,000	
Increase in inventory	(1,000)	
Increase in accounts payable	9,000	
Decrease in accrued liabilities	(2,000)	19,000
Net cash provided by operating activities		$45,000
Cash flows from investing activities:		
Purchase of equipment	$(140,000)	
Sale of equipment	74,000	
Net cash used for investing activities		(66,000)
Cash flows from financing activities:		
Issuance of common stock	$ 19,000	
Payment of dividends	(18,000)	
Issuance of bonds payable	44,000	
Purchase of treasury stock	(5,000)	
Net cash provided by financing activities		40,000
Net increase in cash		$19,000
Cash balance, December 31, 2013		3,000
Cash balance, December 31, 2014		$22,000
Noncash investing and financing activities:		
Issuance of common stock to retire bonds payable		$13,000
Total noncash investing and financing activities		$13,000

Relevant T-accounts:

Equipment, net		
12/31/13 Bal 72,000		
140,000	10,000	
	76,000	
12/31/14 Bal 126,000		

Bonds payable		
	12/31/13 Bal	53,000
13,000		44,000
	12/31/14 Bal	84,000

Common stock		
	12/31/13 Bal	20,000
		13,000
		19,000
	12/31/14 Bal	52,000

Retained earnings		
	12/31/13 Bal	19,000
18,000		26,000
	12/31/14 Bal	27,000

Treasury stock		
12/31/13 Bal	5,000	
	5,000	
12/31/14 Bal	10,000	

Review *The Statement of Cash Flows*

● Accounting Vocabulary

Cash Equivalents (p. 663)
Highly liquid short-term investments that can be readily converted into cash in three months or less.

Cash Flows (p. 662)
Cash receipts and cash payments.

Direct Method (p. 664)
Format of the operating activities section of the statement of cash flows; lists the major categories of operating cash receipts and cash payments.

Financing Activities (p. 664)
Activities that obtain the cash needed to launch and sustain the business; a section of the statement of cash flows.

Free Cash Flow (p. 676)
The amount of cash available from operations after paying for planned investments in long-term assets and after paying dividends to shareholders.

Indirect Method (p. 664)
Format of the operating activities section of the statement of cash flows; starts with net income and reconciles to net cash provided by operating activities.

Investing Activities (p. 663)
Activities that increase or decrease long-term assets; a section of the statement of cash flows.

Operating Activities (p. 663)
Activities that create revenue or expense in the entity's major line of business; a section of the statement of cash flows. Operating activities affect the income statement.

● Destination: Student Success

Student Success Tips

The following are hints on some common trouble areas for students in this chapter:

● Keep in mind the cash flow statement explains why the change in the cash balance is not the same as the net income or net loss for the period.

● Recall that the cash flow statement has four sections: operating, investing, financing, and noncash transactions.

● Keep in mind the cash flow statement may be prepared using the indirect method or the direct method. The indirect method is the most commonly used method.

● Remember that Cash is an asset, so changes in other asset accounts have the opposite effect on cash (when other asset account increases, cash decreases). Changes in liability and equity accounts have the same effect on cash (when liability or equity account increases, cash increases).

Getting Help

If there's a learning objective from the chapter you aren't confident about, try using one or more of the following resources:

● Review the indirect method statement template in Exhibit 14-3.

● Review the Decision Guidelines in the chapter.

● Review Summary Problem 14-1 in the chapter to reinforce your understanding of the indirect cash flow statement.

● Practice additional exercises or problems at the end of Chapter 14 that cover the specific learning objective that is challenging you.

● Watch the white board videos for Chapter 14, located at myaccountinglab.com under the Chapter Resources button.

● Go to myaccountinglab.com and select the Study Plan button. Choose Chapter 14 and work the questions covering that specific learning objective until you've mastered it.

● Work the Chapter 14 pre/post tests in myaccountinglab.com.

● Visit the learning resource center on your campus for tutoring.

• Quick Check

1. The purposes of the cash flow statement are to
   a. evaluate management decisions.
   b. determine ability to pay liabilities and dividends.
   c. predict future cash flows.
   d. All of the above

2. The main categories of cash flow activities are
   a. direct and indirect.
   b. current and long-term.
   c. noncash investing and financing.
   d. operating, investing, and financing.

3. Operating activities are most closely related to
   a. long-term assets.
   b. current assets and current liabilities.
   c. long-term liabilities and owners' equity.
   d. dividends and treasury stock.

4. Which item does *not* appear on a statement of cash flows prepared by the indirect method?
   a. Collections from customers
   b. Depreciation
   c. Net income
   d. Gain on sale of land

5. Leather Shop earned net income of $57,000 after deducting depreciation of $5,000 and all other expenses. Current assets decreased by $4,000, and current liabilities increased by $8,000. How much was Leather Shop's cash provided by operating activities (indirect method)?
   a. $40,000
   b. $66,000
   c. $48,000
   d. $74,000

6. The Plant assets account of Star Media shows the following:

Plant assets, net

Beg	80,000	Depr	34,000
Purchase	428,000	Sale	42,000
End	432,000		

Star Media sold plant assets at an $11,000 loss. Where on the statement of cash flows should Star Media report the sale of plant assets? How much should the business report for the sale?
   a. Financing cash flows—cash receipt of $42,000
   b. Investing cash flows—cash receipt of $53,000
   c. Investing cash flows—cash receipt of $31,000
   d. Investing cash flows—cash receipt of $42,000

7. Mountain Water, Corp., issued common stock of $28,000 to pay off long-term notes payable of $28,000. In what section(s) would these transaction be recorded?

   a. Financing activities payment of note ($28,000)

   b. Financing activities cash receipt $28,000

   c. Noncash investing and financing activities $28,000

   d. Both a and b are correct

8. Holmes, Inc., expects cash flow from operating activities to be $160,000, and the company plans purchases of equipment of $83,000 and repurchases of stock of $24,000. What is Holmes' free cash flow?

   a. $53,000

   b. $160,000

   c. $77,000

   d. $83,000

9. **(Appendix 14A: Direct Method)** Maxwell Furniture Center had accounts receivable of $20,000 at the beginning of the year and $54,000 at year-end. Revenue for the year totaled $116,000. How much cash did the business collect from customers?

   a. $150,000

   b. $62,000

   c. $116,000

   d. $82,000

10. **(Appendix 14A: Direct Method)** Magic Toys Company had operating expense of $48,000. At the beginning of the year, Magic Toys owed $10,000 on accrued liabilities. At year-end, accrued liabilities were $5,000. How much cash did Magic Toys pay for operating expenses?

    a. $38,000

    b. $53,000

    c. $48,000

    d. $43,000

Answers are given after Apply Your Knowledge (p. 700).

Assess Your Progress

● Short Exercises

S14-1   **❶ Purposes of the statement of cash flows [10 min]**   MyAccountingLab
           Financial statements all have a goal. The cash flow statement does as well.

Requirement

   1. Describe how the statement of cash flows helps investors and creditors perform each of the following functions:
      a. Predict future cash flows.
      b. Evaluate management decisions.
      c. Predict the ability to make debt payments to lenders and to pay dividends to stockholders.

S14-2 ② Classifying cash flow items [10 min]

Cash flow items must be categorized into one of four categories: financing, investing, noncash, or operating.

Requirement

1. Answer the following questions about the statement of cash flows:
   a. List the categories of cash flows in the order they appear in the statement of cash flows.
   b. What is the "key reconciling figure" for the statement of cash flows? Where do you get this figure?
   c. What is the first dollar amount reported on the indirect method statement of cash flows?

S14-3 ③ Classifying items on the indirect statement of cash flows [10 min]

Destiny Corporation is preparing its statement of cash flows by the *indirect* method. Destiny has the following items for you to consider in preparing the statement:

_____ a. Increase in accounts payable   _____ g. Depreciation expense

_____ b. Payment of dividends   _____ h. Increase in inventory

_____ c. Decrease in accrued liabilities   _____ i. Decrease in accounts receivable

_____ d. Issuance of common stock   _____ j. Purchase of equipment

_____ e. Gain on sale of building

_____ f. Loss on sale of land

Requirement

1. Identify each item as a(n)
   • Operating activity—addition to net income (O+), or subtraction from net income (O–)
   • Investing activity—addition to cash flow (I+), or subtraction from cash flow (I–)
   • Financing activity—addition to cash flow (F+), or subtraction from cash flow (F–)
   • Activity that is not used to prepare the indirect cash flow statement (N)

S14-4 ③ Computing cash flows from operating activities—indirect method [10 min]

OMD Equipment, Inc., reported the following data for 2012:

Income statement	
Net income	$ 44,000
Depreciation	8,000
Balance sheet	
Increase in Accounts receivable	7,000
Decrease in Accounts payable	4,000

Requirement

1. Compute OMD's net cash provided by operating activities—indirect method.

S14-5 ③ Computing cash flows from operating activities—indirect method [10 min]

One Way Cellular accountants have assembled the following data for the year ended September 30, 2012:

Cash receipt from sale of land	$ 34,000	Net income	$ 55,000
Depreciation expense	20,000	Purchase of equipment	39,000
Payment of dividends	6,100	Decrease in current liabilities	19,000
Cash receipt from issuance of		Increase in current assets	
common stock	30,000	other than cash	14,000

Requirement

1. Prepare the *operating* activities section using the indirect method for One Way Cellular's statement of cash flows for the year ended September 30, 2012.

Note: Short Exercise 14-6 should be used only after completing Short Exercise 14-5.

S14-6 ❸ **Computing cash flows—indirect method [15 min]**

Use the data in Short Exercise 14-5 to complete this exercise.

Requirement

1. Prepare One Way Cellular's statement of cash flows using the indirect method for the year ended September 30, 2012. Stop after determining the net increase (or decrease) in cash.

S14-7 ❸ **Computing investing and financing cash flows [10 min]**

Kyler Media Corporation had the following income statement and balance sheet for 2012:

KYLER MEDIA CORPORATION Income Statement Year Ended December 31, 2012		
Service revenue	$	80,000
Depreciation expense		5,600
Other expenses		49,000
Net income	$	25,400

KYLER MEDIA CORPORATION Comparative Balance Sheet December 31, 2012 and 2011					
Assets	2012	2011	Liabilities	2012	2011
Current:			Current:		
Cash	$ 4,800	$ 3,800	Accounts payable	$ 9,000	$ 4,000
Accounts receivable	9,600	4,100	Long-term notes payable	9,000	15,000
Equipment, net	78,000	67,000	**Stockholders' Equity**		
			Common stock	22,000	17,000
			Retained earnings	52,400	38,900
Total assets	$ 92,400	$ 74,900	Total liabilities and stockholders' equity	$ 92,400	$ 74,900

Requirement

1. Compute for Kyler Media Corporation during 2012 the
   a. acquisition of equipment. The business sold no equipment during the year.
   b. payment of a long-term note payable. During the year, the business issued a $5,300 note payable.

Note: Short Exercise 14-8 should be used only after completing Short Exercise 14-7.

S14-8 ❸ **Preparing the statement of cash flows—indirect method [15–20 min]**

Use the Kyler Media Corporation data in Short Exercise 14-7 and the results you calculated from the requirements.

Requirement

1. Prepare Kyler Media's statement of cash flows—indirect method—for the year ended December 31, 2012.

S14-9 ❸ ❹ **Computing the change in cash; identifying noncash transactions [5 min]**
Judy's Makeup Shops earned net income of $22,000, which included depreciation of $14,000. Judy's acquired a $119,000 building by borrowing $119,000 on a long-term note payable.

Requirements

1. How much did Judy's cash balance increase or decrease during the year?
2. Were there any noncash transactions for the company? If so, show how they would be reported in the statement of cash flows.

S14-10 ❺ **Computing free cash flow [5 min]**
Cooper Lopez Company expects the following for 2012:

- Net cash provided by operating activities of $158,000.
- Net cash provided by financing activities of $60,000.
- Net cash used for investing activities of $80,000 (no sales of long-term assets).
- Cash dividends paid to shareholders was $10,000.

Requirement

1. How much free cash flow does Lopez expect for 2012?

• Exercises

MyAccountingLab

E14-11 ❶ **Predicting future cash flows [10 min]**
Anderson's Armoires reported net loss for the year of $25,000; however, it reported an increase in cash balance of $50,000. The CFO states, "Anderson's Armoires would have shown a profit were it not for the depreciation expense recorded this year."

Requirements

1. Can the CFO be right? Why?
2. Based on the information provided, what would you predict future cash flows to be?

E14-12 ❷ **Classifying cash flow items [10 min]**
Consider the following transactions:

    a. Purchased equipment for $130,000 cash.
    b. Issued $14 par preferred stock for cash.
    c. Cash received from sales to customers of $35,000.
    d. Cash paid to vendors, $17,000.
    e. Sold building for $19,000 gain for cash.
    f. Purchased common treasury shares for $28,000.
    g. Paid a notes payable with 1,250 of the company's common shares.

Requirement

1. Identify the category of the statement of cash flows in which each transaction would be reported.

E14-13 ❸ **Classifying items on the indirect statement of cash flows [5–10 min]**
The cash flow statement categorizes like transactions for optimal reporting.

Requirement

1. Identify each of the following transactions as one of the following:
   - Operating activity (O)
   - Investing activity (I)
   - Financing activity (F)
   - Noncash investing and financing activity (NIF)
   - Transaction that is not reported on the statement of cash flows (N)

For each cash flow, indicate whether the item increases (+) or decreases (–) cash. The *indirect* method is used to report cash flows from operating activities.

_____	a. Loss on sale of land.	_____	i. Cash sale of land.
_____	b. Acquisition of equipment by issuance of note payable.	_____	j. Issuance of long-term note payable to borrow cash.
_____	c. Payment of long-term debt.	_____	k. Depreciation.
_____	d. Acquisition of building by issuance of common stock.	_____	l. Purchase of treasury stock.
_____	e. Increase in salary payable.	_____	m. Issuance of common stock.
_____	f. Decrease in inventory.	_____	n. Increase in accounts payable.
_____	g. Increase in prepaid expenses.	_____	o. Net income.
_____	h. Decrease in accrued liabilities.	_____	p. Payment of cash dividend.

E14-14 ③ **Classifying transactions on the statement of cash flows—indirect method [5–10 min]**
Consider the following transactions:

a. Cash	72,000		g. Land	22,000	
Common stock		72,000	Cash		22,000
b. Treasury stock	16,500		h. Cash	9,600	
Cash		16,500	Equipment		9,600
c. Cash	88,000		i. Bonds payable	51,000	
Sales revenue		88,000	Cash		51,000
d. Land	103,000		j. Building	137,000	
Cash		103,000	Note payable, long-term		137,000
e. Depreciation expense	6,800		k. Loss on disposal of equipment	1,800	
Accumulated depreciation		6,800	Equipment, net		1,800
f. Dividends payable	19,500				
Cash		19,500			

Requirement

1. Indicate whether each transaction would result in an operating activity, an investing activity, or a financing activity for an indirect method statement of cash flows and the accompanying schedule of noncash investing and financing activities.

E14-15 ③ **Computing operating acitivites cash flow—indirect method [10–15 min]**
The records of McKnight Color Engraving reveal the following:

Net income	$ 38,000	Depreciation	$ 4,000
Sales revenue	51,000	Decrease in current liabilities	28,000
Loss on sale of land	5,000	Increase in current assets	
Acquisition of land	39,000	other than cash	14,000

Requirements

1. Compute cash flows from operating activities by the indirect method.
2. Evaluate the operating cash flow of McKnight Color Engraving. Give the reason for your evaluation.

E14-16 ❸ **Computing operating activities cash flow—indirect method [15–20 min]**

The accounting records of DVD Sales, Inc., include the following accounts:

Cash			Accounts receivable			Inventory		
Jul 1	5,500		Jul 1	21,000		Jul 1	22,000	
	????			????			????	
Jul 31	3,000		Jul 31	17,000		Jul 31	25,500	

Accounts payable			Accumulated depr.—equipment			Retained earnings		
		Jul 1	14,500		Jul 1	55,000		
			????		Depr	3,000		
				Dividend	19,000	Jul 1	65,000	
						Net Inc	65,000	
		Jul 31	19,500		Jul 31	58,000	Jul 31	111,000

Requirement

1. Compute DVD's net cash provided by (used for) operating activities during July. Use the indirect method.

E14-17 ❸ **Preparing the statement of cash flows—indirect method [20–30 min]**

The income statement of Minerals Plus, Inc., follows:

MINERALS PLUS, INC.		
Income Statement		
Year Ended September 30, 2012		
Revenues:		
Service revenue		$ 235,000
Expenses:		
Cost of goods sold	$ 97,000	
Salary expense	57,000	
Depreciation expense	26,000	
Income tax expense	4,000	184,000
Net income		$ 51,000

Additional data follow:

a. Acquisition of plant assets is $118,000. Of this amount, $100,000 is paid in cash and $18,000 by signing a note payable.

b. Cash receipt from sale of land totals $28,000. There was no gain or loss.

c. Cash receipts from issuance of common stock total $29,000.

d. Payment of note payable is $18,000.

e. Payment of dividends is $8,000.

f. From the balance sheet:

	September 30,	
	2012	2011
Current Assets:		
Cash	$ 30,000	$ 8,000
Accounts receivable	41,000	59,000
Inventory	97,000	93,000
Current Liabilities:		
Accounts payable	$ 30,000	$ 17,000
Accrued liabilities	11,000	24,000

Requirement

1. Prepare Minerals Plus's statement of cash flows for the year ended September 30, 2012, using the indirect method. Include a separate section for noncash investing and financing activities.

E14-18   ③ **Computing operating activities cash flow—indirect method [10–15 min]**
Consider the following facts for Espresso Place:

a. Beginning and ending Retained earnings are $44,000 and $70,000, respectively. Net income for the period is $61,000.

b. Beginning and ending Plant assets, net, are $104,000 and $109,000, respectively. Depreciation for the period is $17,000, and acquisitions of new plant assets total $28,000. Plant assets were sold at a $5,000 gain.

Requirements

1. How much are cash dividends?

2. What was the amount of the cash receipt from the sale of plant assets?

E14-19   ③ **Computing the cash effect of acquiring assets [10 min]**
McKnight Exercise Equipment, Inc., reported the following financial statements for 2012:

MCKNIGHT EXERCISE EQUIPMENT, INC.		
Income Statement		
Year Ended December 31, 2012		
Sales revenue		$ 714,000
Cost of goods sold	$ 347,000	
Depreciation expense	52,000	
Other expenses	205,000	
Total expenses		604,000
Net income		$ 110,000

	MCKNIGHT EXERCISE EQUIPMENT, INC.					
	Comparative Balance Sheet					
	December 31, 2012 and 2011					

Assets	2012	2011	Liabilities	2012	2011
Current:			Current:		
Cash	$ 19,000	$ 18,000	Accounts payable	$ 73,000	$ 72,000
Accounts receivable	54,000	49,000	Salary payable	2,000	5,000
Inventory	81,000	89,000	Long-term notes payable	59,000	66,000
Long-term investments	95,000	77,000	**Stockholders' Equity**		
Plant assets, net	221,000	183,000	Common stock	47,000	34,000
			Retained earnings	289,000	239,000
			Total liabilities and		
Total assets	$470,000	$416,000	stockholders' equity	$470,000	$416,000

Requirement

1. Compute the amount of McKnight Exercise's acquisition of plant assets. McKnight Exercise sold no plant assets.

E14-20 ❸ **Computing the cash effect of transactions [15 min]**
Use the McKnight Exercise Equipment data in Exercise 14-19.

Requirement

1. Compute the following:

a. New borrowing or payment of long-term notes payable, with McKnight Exercise having only one long-term note payable transaction during the year.

b. Issuance of common stock, with McKnight Exercise having only one common stock transaction during the year.

c. Payment of cash dividends.

Note: Exercise 14-21 should be used only after completing Exercises 14-19 and 14-20.

E14-21 ❸ **Computing the cash effect of transactions [15 min]**
Use the McKnight Exercise Equipment data in Exercises 14-19 and 14-20.

Requirement

1. Prepare the company's statement of cash flows—indirect method—for the year ended December 31, 2012.

E14-22 ❹ **Identifying and reporting noncash transactions [15 min]**
Dirtbikes, Inc., identified the following selected transactions that occurred during 2012:

a. Issued 1,250 shares of $2 par common stock for cash of $26,000.
b. Issued 5,500 shares of $2 par common stock for a building valued at $101,000.
c. Purchased new company truck with FMV of $28,000. Financed it 100% with a long-term note.
d. Paid short-term notes of $23,000 by issuing 2,400 shares of $2 par common stock.
e. Paid long-term note of $10,500 to Bank of Tallahassee. Issued new long-term note of $21,000 to Bank of Trust.

Requirement

1. Identify any noncash transactions that occurred during the year and show how they would be reported in the noncash section of the cash flow statement.

E14-23 ⑤ **Analyzing free cash flow [15 min]**

Use the McKnight Exercise Equipment data in Exercises 14-19 and 14-20. McKnight plans to purchase a truck for $29,000 and a forklift for $121,000 next year.

Requirement

1. Calculate the amount of free cash flow McKnight has for 2012.

● Problems (Group A)

P14-24A ① ② ③ **Purpose of the statement and preparing the statement of cash flows—indirect method [40–50 min]**   *MyAccountingLab*

Classic Reserve Rare Coins (CRRC) was formed on January 1, 2012. Additional data for the year follows:

---

a. On January 1, 2012, CRRC issued common stock for $425,000.

b. Early in January, CRRC made the following cash payments:
   1. For store fixtures, $54,000.
   2. For inventory, $270,000.
   3. For rent expense on a store building, $10,000.

c. Later in the year, CRRC purchased inventory on account for $243,000. Before year-end, CRRC paid $163,000 of this account payable.

d. During 2012, CRRC sold 2,100 units of inventory for $350 each. Before year-end, the company collected 80% of this amount. Cost of goods sold for the year was $260,000, and ending inventory totaled $253,000.

e. The store employs three people. The combined annual payroll is $94,000, of which CRRC still owes $4,000 at year-end.

f. At the end of the year, CRRC paid income tax of $23,000.

g. Late in 2012, CRRC paid cash dividends of $41,000.

h. For equipment, CRRC uses the straight-line depreciation method, over five years, with zero residual value.

Requirements

1. What is the purpose of the cash flow statement?
2. Prepare CRRC's income statement for the year ended December 31, 2012. Use the single-step format, with all revenues listed together and all expenses listed together.
3. Prepare CRRC's balance sheet at December 31, 2012.
4. Prepare CRRC's statement of cash flows using the indirect method for the year ended December 31, 2012.

P14-25A ③ **Preparing the statement of cash flows—indirect method [35–45 min]**

Accountants for Johnson, Inc., have assembled the following data for the year ended December 31, 2012:

	December 31,	
	2012	2011
Current Accounts:		
Current assets:		
Cash and cash equivalents	$ 92,100	$ 17,000
Accounts receivable	64,500	69,200
Inventories	87,000	80,000
Current liabilities:		
Accounts payable	57,900	56,200
Income tax payable	14,400	17,100

Transaction Data for 2012:

Issuance of common stock		Payment of note payable	$48,100
for cash	$ 40,000	Payment of cash dividends	54,000
Depreciation expense	25,000	Issuance of note payable	
Purchase of equipment	75,000	to borrow cash	67,000
Acquisition of land by issuing		Gain on sale of building	5,500
long-term note payable	122,000	Net income	70,500
Cost basis of building sold	53,000		

Requirement

1. Prepare Johnson's statement of cash flows using the *indirect* method. Include an accompanying schedule of noncash investing and financing activities.

P14-26A ③ ⑤ **Preparing the statement of cash flows—indirect method, evaluating cash flows, and measuring free cash flows [35–45 min]**

The comparative balance sheet of Jackson Educational Supply at December 31, 2012, reported the following:

	December 31,	
	2012	2011
Current assets:		
Cash and cash equivalents	$ 88,200	$ 22,500
Accounts receivable	14,400	21,700
Inventories	63,600	60,400
Current liabilities:		
Accounts payable	28,600	27,100
Accrued liabilities	10,600	11,200

Jackson's transactions during 2012 included the following:

Payment of cash dividend	$ 17,200	Depreciation expense	$ 16,700
Purchase of equipment	54,400	Purchase of building	100,000
Issuance of long-term note payable		Net income	59,600
to borrow cash	50,000	Issuance of common stock for cash	106,000

Requirements

1. Prepare the statement of cash flows of Jackson Educational Supply for the year ended December 31, 2012. Use the *indirect* method to report cash flows from operating activities.

2. Evaluate Jackson's cash flows for the year. Mention all three categories of cash flows and give the reason for your evaluation.

3. If Jackson plans similar activity for 2013, what is its expected free cash flow?

P14-27A ③ ④ **Preparing the statement of cash flows—indirect method with noncash transactions [35-45 min]**

The 2012 comparative balance sheet and income statement of Rolling Hills, Inc., follow:

ROLLING HILLS, INC. Comparative Balance Sheet December 31, 2012 and 2011			
	2012	**2011**	**Increase (Decrease)**
Current assets:			
Cash and cash equivalents	$ 26,400	$ 15,900	$ 10,500
Accounts receivable	26,700	25,500	1,200
Inventories	79,800	91,700	(11,900)
Plant assets:			
Land	34,600	11,000	23,600
Equipment, net	103,900	89,700	14,200
Total assets	$ 271,400	$ 233,800	$ 37,600
Current liabilities:			
Accounts payable	$ 35,500	$ 30,600	$ 4,900
Accrued liabilities	28,600	30,700	(2,100)
Long-term liabilities:			
Notes payable	78,000	101,000	(23,000)
Stockholders' equity:			
Common stock	88,800	64,900	23,900
Retained earnings	40,500	6,600	33,900
Total liabilities and stockholders' equity	$ 271,400	$ 233,800	$ 37,600

ROLLING HILLS, INC. Income Statement Year Ended December 31, 2012		
Revenues:		
Sales revenue		$ 436,000
Interest revenue		8,000
Total revenues		444,000
Expenses:		
Cost of goods sold	$ 202,200	
Salary expense	78,400	
Depreciation expense	14,400	
Other operating expense	10,200	
Interest expense	21,900	
Income tax expense	19,100	
Total expenses		346,200
Net income		$ 97,800

Additionally, Rolling Hills purchased land of $23,600 by financing it 100% with long-term notes payable during 2012. During the year, there were no sales of land or equipment, no additional issuances of notes payable, no retirements of stock, and no treasury stock transactions.

Requirements

1. Prepare the 2012 statement of cash flows, formatting operating activities by the *indirect* method.
2. How will what you learned in this problem help you evaluate an investment?

• Problems (Group B)

MyAccountingLab **P14-28B** ❶ ❷ ❸ **Purpose of the statement and preparing the statement of cash flows—indirect method [40–50 min]**

National Reserve Rare Coins (NRRC) was formed on January 1, 2012. Additional data for the year follows:

---

a. On January 1, 2012, NRRC issued common stock for $525,000.

b. Early in January, NRRC made the following cash payments:
   1. For store fixtures, $55,000.
   2. For inventory, $320,000.
   3. For rent expense on a store building, $17,000.

c. Later in the year, NRRC purchased inventory on account for $244,000. Before year-end, NRRC paid $164,000 of this account payable.

d. During 2012, NRRC sold 2,500 units of inventory for $400 each. Before year end, the company collected 85% of this amount. Cost of goods sold for the year was $320,000, and ending inventory totaled $244,000.

e. The store employs three people. The combined annual payroll is $80,000, of which NRRC still owes $3,000 at year-end.

f. At the end of the year, NRRC paid income tax of $20,000.

g. Late in 2012, NRRC paid cash dividends of $39,000.

h. For equipment, NRRC uses the straight-line depreciation method, over five years, with zero residual value.

Requirements

1. What is the purpose of the cash flow statement?

2. Prepare NRRC's income statement for the year ended December 31, 2012. Use the single-step format, with all revenues listed together and all expenses listed together.

3. Prepare NRRC's balance sheet at December 31, 2012.

4. Prepare NRRC's statement of cash flows using the *indirect* method for the year ended December 31, 2012.

P14-29B ❸ **Preparing the statement of cash flows—indirect method [35–45 min]**

Accountants for Smithson, Inc., have assembled the following data for the year ended December 31, 2012:

	December 31,	
	2012	2011
Current Accounts:		
Current assets:		
Cash and cash equivalents	$ 106,100	$ 26,000
Accounts receivable	64,300	68,900
Inventories	80,000	75,000
Current liabilities:		
Accounts payable	57,700	56,100
Income tax payable	14,500	17,000

Transaction Data for 2012:			
Issuance of common stock		Payment of note payable	$46,100
for cash .... $ 45,000		Payment of cash dividends	52,000
Depreciation expense	18,000	Issuance of note payable	
Purchase of equipment	70,000	to borrow cash	68,000
Acquisition of land by issuing		Gain on sale of building	3,500
long-term note payable ...	113,000	Net income	68,500
		Cost basis of building sold	$50,000

Requirement

1. Prepare Smithson's statement of cash flows using the *indirect* method. Include an accompanying schedule of noncash investing and financing activities.

P14-30B ③ ⑤ **Preparing the statement of cash flows—indirect method, evaluating cash flows, and measuring free cash flows [35–45 min]**

The comparative balance sheet of Morgensen Educational Supply at December 31, 2012, reported the following:

	December 31,	
	2012	2011
Current assets:		
Cash and cash equivalents	$ 89,600	$ 24,500
Accounts receivable	14,500	21,900
Inventories	62,800	60,000
Current liabilities:		
Accounts payable	30,100	27,600
Accrued liabilities	11,100	11,600

Morgensen's transactions during 2012 included the following:

Payment of cash dividend	$ 14,200	Depreciation expense	$ 17,300
Purchase of equipment	55,200	Purchase of building	103,000
Issuance of long-term note payable		Net income	57,600
to borrow cash	45,000	Issuance of common stock for cash	111,000

Requirements

1. Prepare the statement of cash flows of Morgensen Educational Supply for the year ended December 31, 2012. Use the *indirect* method to report cash flows from operating activities.

2. Evaluate Morgensen's cash flows for the year. Mention all three categories of cash flows and give the reason for your evaluation.

3. If Morgensen plans similar activity for 2013, what is its expected free cash flow?

P14-31B ③ ④ **Preparing the statement of cash flows—indirect method with noncash transactions [35–45 min]**

The 2012 comparative balance sheet and income statement of All Wired, Inc., follow:

ALL WIRED, INC. Comparative Balance Sheet December 31, 2012 and 2011			
	2012	2011	Increase (Decrease)
Current assets:			
Cash and cash equivalents	$ 26,700	$ 15,600	$ 11,100
Accounts receivable	26,500	25,300	1,200
Inventories	79,900	91,900	(12,000)
Plant assets:			
Land	35,500	11,000	24,500
Equipment, net	102,900	90,700	12,200
Total assets	$ 271,500	$ 234,500	$ 37,000
Current liabilities:			
Accounts payable	$ 35,600	$ 30,500	$ 5,100
Accrued liabilities	28,900	30,600	(1,700)
Long-term liabilities:			
Notes payable	77,000	103,000	(26,000)
Stockholders' equity:			
Common stock	88,200	64,300	23,900
Retained earnings	41,800	6,100	35,700
Total liabilities and stockholders' equity	$ 271,500	$ 234,500	$ 37,000

ALL WIRED, INC.

Income Statement

Year Ended December 31, 2012

Revenues:		
Sales revenue		$ 438,000
Interest revenue		8,500
Total revenues		446,500
Expenses:		
Cost of goods sold	$ 209,200	
Salary expense	72,400	
Depreciation expense	14,500	
Other operating expense	10,000	
Interest expense	21,500	
Income tax expense	19,400	
Total expenses		347,000
Net income		$ 99,500

Additionally, All Wired purchased land of $24,500 by financing it 100% with long-term notes payable during 2012. During the year, there were no sales of land or equipment, no additional issuances of notes payable, no retirements of stock, and no treasury stock transactions.

Requirements

1. Prepare the 2012 statement of cash flows, formatting operating activities by the *indirect* method.

2. How will what you learned in this problem help you evaluate an investment?

● Continuing Exercise

MyAccountingLab **E14-32** ❸ **Preparing the statement of cash flows—indirect method [25–35 min]**
This exercise continues the Lawlor Lawn Service, Inc., situation from Exercise 13-36 of Chapter 13. Refer to the comparative balance sheet for Lawlor Lawn Service.

LAWLOR LAWN SERVICE, INC.

Comparative Balance Sheet

May 31, 2013 and 2012

Assets	2013	2012
Cash	$ 17,420	$ 2,420
Accounts receivable	2,550	50
Lawn supplies	150	40
Equipment	1,440	1,440
Accumulated depreciation	(360)	(30)
Building	120,000	0
Accumulated depreciation	(2,500)	—
Total Assets	$138,700	$ 3,920
Liabilities		
Accounts payable	$ 440	$ 1,440
Interest payable	555	0
Current portion of mortgage payable	12,000	0
Mortgage payable	99,000	0
Total liabilities	$111,995	$ 1,440
Stockholders' Equity		
Common stock	2,700	1,700
Retained earnings	24,005	780
Total liabilities and stockholders' equity	$138,700	$ 3,920

Requirement

1. Prepare the statement of cash flows using the *indirect* method. Assume no dividends were declared or paid during the year.

● Continuing Problem

P14-33   ❸ Preparing the statement of cash flows—indirect method [25–35 min]

MyAccountingLab

This problem continues the Draper Consulting, Inc., situation from Problem 13-37 of Chapter 13. Refer to the comparative balance sheet for Draper Consulting.

DRAPER CONSULTING, INC. Comparative Balance Sheet December 31, 2013 and 2012		
Assets	2013	2012
Cash	$ 514,936	$ 16,350
Accounts receivable	37,500	1,750
Supplies	2,200	200
Equipment	16,000	1,800
Furniture	5,700	4,200
Building	125,000	0
Accumulated depreciation	(2,753)	(100)
Total assets	$ 698,583	$ 24,200
Liabilities		
Accounts payable	$ 10,000	$ 4,650
Salary payable	4,100	685
Unearned service revenue	0	700
Interest payable	10,667	0
Notes payable	40,000	0
Bonds payable	400,000	0
Discount on bonds payable	(36,184)	0
Stockholders' Equity		
Common stock	130,000	18,000
Retained earnings	140,000	165
Total liabilities and stockholders' equity	$ 698,583	$ 24,200

Requirement

1. Prepare the statement of cash flows using the indirect method.

Apply Your Knowledge

● Decision Cases

Decision Case 14-1 The 2014 comparative income statement and the 2014 comparative balance sheet of Golf America, Inc., have just been distributed at a meeting of the company's board of directors. The members of the board of directors raise a fundamental question: Why is the cash balance so low? This question is especially hard to understand because 2014 showed record profits. As the controller of the company, you must answer the question.

GOLF AMERICA, INC.
Comparative Income Statement
Years Ended December 31, 2014 and 2013

		2014	2013
Revenues and gains:			
	Sales revenue	$444	$310
	Gain on sale of equipment (sale price, $33)	0	18
	Total revenues and gains	$444	$328
Expenses and losses:			
	Cost of goods sold	$221	$162
	Salary expense	48	28
	Depreciation expense	46	22
	Interest expense	13	20
	Amortization expense on patent	11	11
	Loss on sale of land (sale price, $61)	0	35
	Total expenses and losses	$339	$278
Net income		$105	$ 50

GOLF AMERICA, INC.
Comparative Balance Sheet
December 31, 2014 and 2013

	2014	2013
Assets		
Cash	$ 25	$ 63
Accounts receivable, net	72	61
Inventories	194	181
Long-term investments	31	0
Property, plant, and equipment, net	125	61
Patents	177	188
Totals	$624	$554
Liabilities and Stockholders' Equity		
Accounts payable	$ 63	$ 56
Accrued liabilities	12	17
Notes payable, long-term	179	264
Total liabilities	$254	$337
Common stock	$149	$ 61
Retained earnings	221	156
Total stockholders' equity	$370	$217
Total liabilities and stockholders' equity	$624	$554

Requirements

1. Prepare a statement of cash flows for 2014 in the format that best shows the relationship between net income and operating cash flow. The company sold no plant assets or long-term investments and issued no notes payable during 2014. There were *no* noncash investing and financing transactions during the year. Show all amounts in thousands.

2. Considering net income and the company's cash flows during 2014, was it a good year or a bad year? Give your reasons.

Decision Case 14-2 Theater by Design and **Showcase Cinemas** are asking you to recommend their stock to your clients. Because Theater by Design and **Showcase** earn about the same net income and have similar financial positions, your decision depends on their cash flow statements, summarized as follows:

	Theater by Design		Showcase Cinemas	
Net cash provided by operating activities		$ 30,000		$ 70,000
Cash provided by (used for) investing activities:				
Purchase of plant assets	$(20,000)		$(100,000)	
Sale of plant assets	40,000	20,000	10,000	(90,000)
Cash provided by (used for) financing activities:				
Issuance of common stock		—		30,000
Paying off long-term debt		(40,000)		—
Net increase in cash		$ 10,000		$ 10,000

Requirement

1. Based on their cash flows, which company looks better? Give your reasons.

● Ethical Issue 14-1

Moss Exports is having a bad year. Net income is only $60,000. Also, two important overseas customers are falling behind in their payments to Moss, and Moss's accounts receivable are ballooning. The company desperately needs a loan. The Moss Exports board of directors is considering ways to put the best face on the company's financial statements. Moss's bank closely examines cash flow from operations. Daniel Peavey, Moss's controller, suggests reclassifying the receivables from the slow-paying clients as long-term. He explains to the board that removing the $80,000 rise in accounts receivable from current assets will increase net cash provided by operations. This approach may help Moss get the loan.

Requirements

1. Using only the amounts given, compute net cash provided by operations, both without and with the reclassification of the receivables. Which reporting makes Moss look better?

2. Under what condition would the reclassification of the receivables be ethical? Unethical?

● Fraud Case 14-1

Frank Lou had recently been promoted to construction manager at a development firm. He was responsible for dealing with contractors who were bidding on a multi-million dollar excavation job for the new high-rise. Times were tough, several contractors had gone under recently, and the ones left standing were viciously competitive. That morning, four bids were sitting on Frank's desk. The deadline was midnight, and the bids would be opened the next morning. The first bidder, Bo Freely, was a tough but personable character that Frank had known for years. Frank had lunch with him today, and after a few beers, Bo hinted that if Frank "inadvertently" mentioned the amount of the lowest bid, he'd receive a "birthday card" with a gift of cash. After lunch, Frank carefully unsealed the bids and noticed that another firm had underbid Bo's company by a small margin. Frank took Bo's bid envelope, wrote the low bid amount in pencil on it, and carried it downstairs where Bo's son William was waiting. Later that afternoon, a new bid came in from Bo's company. The next day, Bo's company got the job, and Frank got a birthday card in his mailbox.

Requirements

1. Was Frank's company hurt in any way by this fraudulent action?

2. How could this action hurt Frank?

3. How can a business protect against this kind of fraud?

Financial Statement Case 14-1

Use the **Amazon.com** statement of cash flows, along with the company's other financial statements at the end of this book, to answer the following questions.

Requirements

1. Which method does **Amazon** use to report net cash flows from *operating* activities? How can you tell?

2. **Amazon** earned net income during 2009. Did operations *provide* cash or *use* cash during 2009? Give the amount. How did operating cash during 2009 compare with 2008?

3. Evaluate 2009 in terms of net income, cash flows, balance sheet position, and overall results. Be specific.

Team Projects

Team Project 14-1 Each member of the team should obtain the annual report of a different company. Select companies in different industries. Evaluate each company's trend of cash flows for the most recent two years. In your evaluation of the companies' cash flows, you may use any other information that is publicly available: for example, the other financial statements (income statement, balance sheet, statement of stockholders' equity, and the related notes) and news stories from magazines and newspapers. Rank the companies' cash flows from best to worst and write a two-page report on your findings.

Team Project 14-2 Select a company and obtain its annual report, including all the financial statements. Focus on the statement of cash flows and, in particular, the cash flows from operating activities. Specify whether the company uses the *direct* method or the *indirect* method to report operating cash flows.

Communication Activity 14-1

In 60 words or fewer, explain the difference between operating, investing, and financing activities.

Quick Check Answers

1. d 2. d 3. b 4. a 5. d 6. c 7. c 8. c 9. d 10. b

For online homework, exercises, and problems that provide you immediate feedback, please visit myaccountinglab.com.

Preparing the Statement of Cash Flows by the Direct Method

The Financial Accounting Standards Board (FASB) prefers the direct method of reporting cash flows from operating activities. The direct method provides clearer information about the sources and uses of cash than does the indirect method. However, very few non-public companies use the direct method because it takes more computations than the indirect method. Investing and financing cash flows are exactly the same presentation under both direct and indirect methods. Since only the preparation of the operating section differs, it is all we discuss in this appendix.

To illustrate how the operating section of the statement of cash flows differs for the direct method, we will be using the Smart Touch Learning data we used within the main chapter. The steps to prepare the statement of cash flows by the direct method are as follows:

6 Prepare the statement of cash flows by the direct method

STEP 1: Lay out the operating section format of the statement of cash flows by the direct method, as shown in Exhibit 14A-1.

EXHIBIT 14A-1 | **Format of the Statement of Cash Flows: Direct Method**

SMART TOUCH LEARNING, INC.
Statement of Cash Flows
Year Ended December 31, 2014

± Cash flows from operating activities:
   Receipts:
      Collections from customers
      Interest received
      Dividends received on investments
        Total cash receipts
   Payments:
      To suppliers
      To employees
      For interest and income tax
        Total cash payments
   Net cash provided by (used for) operating activities
± Cash flows from investing activities:
   + Cash receipts from sales of long-term (plant) assets (investments, land, building, equipment, and so on)
   – Acquisitions of long-term (plant) assets
   Net cash provided by (used for) investing activities
± Cash flows from financing activities:
   + Cash receipts from issuance of stock
   + Cash receipts from sale of treasury stock
   – Purchase of treasury stock
   + Cash receipts from issuance of notes or bonds payable (borrowing)
   – Payment of notes or bonds payable
   – Payment of dividends
   Net cash provided by (used for) financing activities
= Net increase (decrease) in cash during the year
   + Cash at December 31, 2013
   = Cash at December 31, 2014

STEP 2: Use the comparative balance sheet to determine the increase or decrease in cash during the period. The change in cash is the "reconciling key figure" for the statement of cash flows. Smart Touch's comparative balance sheet shows that cash decreased by $20,000 during 2014. (See Exhibit 14A-2.)

EXHIBIT 14A-2 | Comparative Balance Sheet

SMART TOUCH LEARNING, INC.
Comparative Balance Sheet
December 31, 2014 and 2013

	2014	2013	Increase (Decrease)
Assets			
Current:			
Cash	$ 22,000	$ 42,000	$ (20,000)
Accounts receivable	90,000	73,000	17,000
Inventory	143,000	145,000	(2,000)
Plant assets, net	460,000	210,000	250,000
Total assets	$715,000	$470,000	$245,000
Liabilities			
Current:			
Accounts payable	$ 90,000	$ 50,000	$ 40,000
Accrued liabilities	5,000	10,000	(5,000)
Long-term notes payable	160,000	80,000	80,000
Stockholders' Equity			
Common stock	370,000	250,000	120,000
Retained earnings	110,000	80,000	30,000
Treasury stock	(20,000)	0	(20,000)
Total liabilities and stockholders' equity	$715,000	$470,000	$245,000

Operating { Accounts receivable, Inventory

Investing { Plant assets, net

Operating { Accounts payable, Accrued liabilities

Financing { Long-term notes payable

Net income—Operating
Dividends—Financing { Common stock, Retained earnings

EXHIBIT 14A-3 | Income Statement

SMART TOUCH LEARNING, INC.
Income Statement
Year Ended December 31, 2014

Revenues and gains:		
Sales revenue	$ 286,000	
Interest revenue	12,000	
Dividend revenue	9,000	
Gain on sale of plant assets	10,000	
Total revenues and gains		$317,000
Expenses:		
Cost of goods sold	$156,000	
Salary and wage expense	56,000	
Depreciation expense	20,000	
Other operating expense	16,000	
Interest expense	15,000	
Income tax expense	14,000	
Total expenses		277,000
Net income		$ 40,000

STEP 3: Use the available data to prepare the statement of cash flows. In the case of Smart Touch, there was no additional data outside of the balance sheet and income statement data in Exhibit 14A-3 that affected the operating activities section.

The statement of cash flows reports only transactions with cash effects. Exhibit 14A-4 shows Smart Touch's completed direct method statement of cash flows for 2014.

EXHIBIT 14A-4 | **Statement of Cash Flows—Direct Method**

SMART TOUCH LEARNING, INC.
Statement of Cash Flows
Year Ended December 31, 2014

	Cash flows from operating activities:		
	Receipts:		
	Collections from customers	$ 269,000	
	Interest received	12,000	
	Dividends received	9,000	
	Total cash receipts		$ 290,000
	Payments:		
	To suppliers	$(135,000)	
	To employees	(56,000)	
	For interest	(15,000)	
	For income tax	(14,000)	
	Total cash payments		(220,000)
	Net cash provided by operating activities		70,000
	Cash flows from investing activities:		
E	Acquisition of plant assets	$(310,000)	
F	Cash receipts from sale of plant assets	50,000	
	Net cash used for investing activities		(260,000)
	Cash flows from financing activities:		
I	Cash receipts from issuance of common stock	$ 120,000	
G	Cash receipts from issuance of notes payable	90,000	
H	Payment of notes payable	(10,000)	
J	Purchase of treasury stock	(20,000)	
K	Payment of dividends	(10,000)	
	Net cash provided by financing activities		170,000
L	**Net decrease in cash**		$ (20,000)
L	Cash balance, December 31, 2013		42,000
L	Cash balance, December 31, 2014		$ 22,000

*Letters denote same values as in Exhibit 14-4

Next, we will explain how we calculated each number.

Cash Flows from Operating Activities

In the indirect method, we start with net income and then adjust it to "cash-basis" through a series of adjusting items. When calculating the direct method, we take each line item of the income statement and convert it from accrual to cash basis. So, in essence, the operating activities section of the direct-method cash flows statement is really just a cash-basis income statement. We can do this using the T-account method or we can modify the account change chart used earlier in the chapter as seen in Exhibit 14A-5 on the following page.

EXHIBIT 14A-5

EXHIBIT 14A-5 | **Direct Method: How Changes in Account Balances Affect Cash Receipts and Cash Payments**

Asset ↑ Cash Flow ↓ Cash Receipts ↓ or Cash Payments ↑
Asset ↓ Cash Flow ↑ Cash Receipts ↑ or Cash Payments ↓
Liability ↑ Cash Flow ↑ Cash Receipts ↑ or Cash Payments ↓
Liability ↓ Cash Flow ↓ Cash Receipts ↓ or Cash Payments ↑
Equity ↑ Cash Flow ↑ Cash Receipts ↑ or Cash Payments ↓
Equity ↓ Cash Flow ↓ Cash Receipts ↓ or Cash Payments ↑

Notice that we have added the Cash Receipts and Cash Payments to the charts shown on page 668 and 669. An increase in Cash (indicated by ↑) is either going to arise from increasing cash receipts or decreasing cash payments (indicated by ↓). Now let's apply this information to Smart Touch.

Cash Collections from Customers

The first item on the income statement is Sales revenue. Sales revenue represents the total of all sales, whether for cash or on account. The balance sheet account related to Sales revenue is Accounts receivable. Accounts receivable went from $73,000 at 12/31/13 to $90,000 at 12/31/14, an increase of $17,000. Applying our chart appears as follows:

Sales revenue − Increase in Accounts receivable = Cash collections from customers
$286,000 − $17,000 = $269,000
Asset ↑ Cash Flow ↓ Cash Receipts ↓ or Cash Payments ↑

So, the cash Smart Touch received from customers is $269,000. This is the first item in the operating activities section of the direct-method cash flow statement. You can verify this by looking at Exhibit 14A-4 on page 703.

Cash Receipts of Interest

The second item on the income statement is interest revenue. The balance sheet account related to Interest revenue is Interest receivable. Since there is no Interest receivable account on the balance sheet, the interest revenue must have all been received in cash. So, the cash flow statement shows interest received of $12,000 in Exhibit 14A-4 on page 703.

Cash Receipts of Dividends

Dividend revenue is the third item reported on the income statement. The balance sheet account related to Dividend revenue is Dividends receivable. As with the interest, there is no Dividends receivable account on the balance sheet. Therefore, the dividend revenue must have all been received in cash. So, the cash flow statement shows cash received from dividends of $9,000 in Exhibit 14A-4 on page 703.

Gain on Sale of Plant Assets

The next item on the income statement is the gain on sale of plant assets. However, the cash received from the sale of the assets is reported in the investing section, not the operating section. As noted earlier, there is no difference in the investing section between the indirect method and direct method of the statement of cash flows.

Payments to Suppliers

Payments to suppliers include all payments for

- inventory and
- operating expenses except employee compensation, interest, and income taxes.

Suppliers are those entities that provide the business with its inventory and essential services. The accounts related to supplier payments for inventory are Cost of goods sold, Inventory, and Accounts payable. Cost of goods sold on the income statement was $156,000. Inventory decreased from $145,000 at 12/31/13 to $143,000 at 12/31/14. Accounts payable increased from $50,000 at 12/31/13 to $90,000 at 12/31/14. Applying our formula, we can calculate cash paid for inventory as follows:

Cost of goods sold – Decrease in Inventory – Increase in Accounts payable = Cash paid for Inventory

| $156,000 | – | $2,000 | – | $40,000 | = | $114,000 |

Asset ↓ Cash Flow ↑ **Cash Receipts** ↑ or Cash Payments ↓ Liability ↑ Cash Flow ↑ **Cash Receipts** ↑ or Cash Payments ↓

The accounts related to supplier payments for operating expenses are Other operating expenses and Accrued liabilities. Other operating expenses on the income statement were $16,000. Accrued liabilities decreased from $10,000 at 12/31/13 to $5,000 at 12/31/14. Applying our formula, we can calculate cash paid for operating expenses as follows:

Other operating expenses + Decrease in Accrued liabilities = Cash paid for operating expenses

| $16,000 | + | $5,000 | = | $21,000 |

Liability ↓ Cash Flow ↓ **Cash Receipts** ↓ or Cash Payments ↑

Adding them together, we get total cash paid to suppliers of $135,000. (Confirm in Exhibit 14A-4 on page 703.)

Cash paid for Inventory + Cash paid for operating expenses = Cash paid to suppliers

| $114,000 | + | $21,000 | = | $135,000 |

Payments to Employees

This category includes payments for salaries, wages, and other forms of employee compensation. Accrued amounts are not cash flows because they have not yet been paid. The accounts related to employee payments are salary and wage expense from the income statement and Salary and wage payable from the balance sheet. Since there is not a Salary payable account on the balance sheet, the Salary and wage expense account must represent all amounts paid in cash to employees. So, the cash flow statement shows cash payments to employees of $56,000 in Exhibit 14A-4 on page 703.

Depreciation, Depletion, and Amortization Expense

These expenses are *not* reported on the direct method statement of cash flows because they do not affect cash.

Payments for Interest Expense

These cash payments are reported separately from the other expenses. The accounts related to interest payments are Interest expense from the income statement and Interest payable from the balance sheet. Since there is no Interest payable account on the balance sheet, the Interest expense account from the income statement must represent all amounts paid in cash for interest. So, the cash flow statement shows cash payments for interest of $15,000 in Exhibit 14A-4 on page 703.

Payments for Income Tax Expense

Like interest expense, these cash payments are reported separately from the other expenses. The accounts related to income tax payments are Income tax expense from the income statement and Income tax payable from the balance sheet. Since there is no Income tax payable account on the balance sheet, the Income tax expense account from the income statement must represent all amounts paid in cash for income tax. So, the cash flow statement shows cash payments for income tax of $14,000 in Exhibit 14A-4 on page 703.

Net Cash Provided by Operating Activities

To calculate net cash provided by operating activities using the direct method, we add all the cash receipts and cash payments described previously and find the difference. For Smart Touch, total Cash receipts were $290,000. Total Cash payments were $220,000. So, net cash provided by operating activities is $70,000. If you refer back to the indirect-method cash flow statement shown in Exhibit 14-4 on page 666, you will find that it showed the same $70,000 for net cash provided by operating activities—only the method by which it was calculated was different.

The remainder of Smart Touch's cash flow statement is exactly the same as what we calculated using the indirect method. (See Exhibit 14-4 on page 666.)

Summary Problem 14A-1

Assume that **Berkshire Hathaway** is considering buying Granite Shoals Corporation. Granite Shoals reported the following comparative balance sheet and income statement for 2014:

GRANITE SHOALS CORPORATION Balance Sheet December 31, 2014 and 2013			
	2014	**2013**	**Increase (Decrease)**
Cash	$ 19,000	$ 3,000	$16,000
Accounts receivable	22,000	23,000	(1,000)
Inventory	34,000	31,000	3,000
Prepaid expenses	1,000	3,000	(2,000)
Equipment (net)	90,000	79,000	11,000
Intangible assets	9,000	9,000	—
Total assets	$175,000	$148,000	$27,000
Accounts payable	$ 14,000	$ 9,000	$ 5,000
Accrued liabilities	16,000	19,000	(3,000)
Income tax payable	14,000	12,000	2,000
Long-term note payable	45,000	50,000	(5,000)
Common stock	31,000	20,000	11,000
Retained earnings	64,000	40,000	24,000
Treasury stock	(9,000)	(2,000)	(7,000)
Total liabilities and stockholders' equity	$175,000	$148,000	$27,000

GRANITE SHOALS CORPORATION
Income Statement
Year Ended December 31, 2014

Sales revenue	$190,000
Gain on sale of equipment	6,000
Total revenue and gains	$196,000
Cost of goods sold	$ 85,000
Depreciation expense	19,000
Other operating expenses	36,000
Total expenses	$140,000
Income before income tax	$ 56,000
Income tax expense	18,000
Net income	$ 38,000

Requirements

1. Compute the following cash flow amounts for 2014:
   a. Collections from customers
   b. Payments for inventory
   c. Payments for other operating expenses
   d. Payment of income tax
   e. Acquisition of equipment. Granite Shoals sold equipment that had book value of $15,000.
   f. Cash receipt from sale of plant assets
   g. Issuance of long-term note payable. Granite Shoals paid off $10,000 of long-term notes payable.
   h. Issuance of common stock
   i. Payment of dividends
   j. Purchase of treasury stock
2. Prepare Granite Shoals Corporation's statement of cash flows (*direct* method) for the year ended December 31, 2014. There were no noncash investing and financing activities.

Solution

1. Cash flow amounts:

   a.

   $$\begin{array}{c}\text{Collections}\\\text{from}\\\text{customers}\end{array} = \begin{array}{c}\text{Sales}\\\text{revenue}\end{array} + \begin{array}{c}\text{Decrease in}\\\text{accounts}\\\text{receivables}\end{array}$$

   $$\$191,000 = \$190,000 + \$1,000$$

   b.

   $$\begin{array}{c}\text{Payments}\\\text{for}\\\text{inventory}\end{array} = \begin{array}{c}\text{Cost of}\\\text{goods}\\\text{sold}\end{array} + \begin{array}{c}\text{Increase}\\\text{in}\\\text{inventory}\end{array} - \begin{array}{c}\text{Increase in}\\\text{accounts}\\\text{payable}\end{array}$$

   $$\$83,000 = \$85,000 + \$3,000 - \$5,000$$

   c.

   $$\begin{array}{c}\text{Payments}\\\text{for other}\\\text{operating expenses}\end{array} = \begin{array}{c}\text{Other}\\\text{operating}\\\text{expenses}\end{array} - \begin{array}{c}\text{Decrease}\\\text{in prepaid}\\\text{expenses}\end{array} + \begin{array}{c}\text{Decrease in}\\\text{accrued}\\\text{liabilities}\end{array}$$

   $$\$37,000 = \$36,000 - \$2,000 + \$3,000$$

   d.

   $$\begin{array}{c}\text{Payment of}\\\text{income tax}\end{array} = \begin{array}{c}\text{Income tax}\\\text{expense}\end{array} - \begin{array}{c}\text{Increase in}\\\text{income tax payable}\end{array}$$

   $$\$16,000 = \$18,000 - \$2,000$$

   e. Equipment, net (let X = Acquisitions)

   $$\begin{array}{c}\text{Beginning}\end{array} + \begin{array}{c}\text{Acquisitions}\end{array} - \begin{array}{c}\text{Depreciation}\\\text{expense}\end{array} - \begin{array}{c}\text{Book value}\\\text{sold}\end{array} = \begin{array}{c}\text{Ending}\end{array}$$

   $$\$79,000 + X - \$19,000 - \$15,000 = \$90,000$$
   $$X = \$45,000$$

   f. Sale of plant assets

   $$\begin{array}{c}\text{Cash}\\\text{received}\end{array} = \begin{array}{c}\text{Book value of}\\\text{assets sold}\end{array} + \begin{array}{c}\text{Gain on sale}\end{array}$$

   $$\$21,000 = \$15,000 + \$6,000$$

   g. Long-term note payable (let X = Issuance)

   $$\text{Beginning} + \text{Issuance} - \text{Payment} = \text{Ending}$$

   $$\$50,000 + X - \$10,000 = \$45,000$$
   $$X = \$5,000$$

   h. Common stock (let X = Issuance)

   $$\text{Beginning} + \text{Issuance} = \text{Ending}$$

   $$\$20,000 + X = \$31,000$$
   $$X = \$11,000$$

   i. Retained earnings (let X = Dividends)

   $$\text{Beginning} + \text{Net income} - \text{Dividends} = \text{Ending}$$

   $$\$40,000 + \$38,000 - X = \$64,000$$
   $$X = \$14,000$$

   j. Treasury stock (let X = Purchases)

   $$\text{Beginning} + \text{Purchases} = \text{Ending}$$

   $$\$2,000 + X = \$9,000$$
   $$X = \$7,000$$

2.

GRANITE SHOALS CORPORATION Statement of Cash Flows Year Ended December 31, 2014		
Cash flows from operating activities:		
Receipts:		
Collections from customers	$ 191,000	
Payments:		
To suppliers ($83,000 + $37,000)	(120,000)	
For income tax	(16,000)	
Net cash provided by operating activities		$ 55,000
Cash flows from investing activities:		
Acquisition of plant assets	$ (45,000)	
Sale of plant assets ($15,000 + $6,000)	21,000	
Net cash used for investing activities		(24,000)
Cash flows from financing activities:		
Payment of dividends	$ (14,000)	
Issuance of common stock	11,000	
Payment of note payable	(10,000)	
Purchase of treasury stock	(7,000)	
Issuance of note payable	5,000	
Net cash used for financing activities		(15,000)
Net increase in cash		$ 16,000
Cash balance, December 31, 2013		3,000
Cash balance, December 31, 2014		$ 19,000

Appendix 14A Assignments

● Short Exercises

S14A-1 ❻ **Preparing the direct method statement of cash flows [15 min]**

Jelly Bean, Inc., began 2012 with cash of $53,000. During the year Jelly Bean earned revenue of $597,000 and collected $621,000 from customers. Expenses for the year totaled $437,000, of which Jelly Bean paid $427,000 in cash to suppliers and employees. Jelly Bean also paid $145,000 to purchase equipment and a cash dividend of $54,000 to its stockholders during 2012.

Requirement

1. Prepare the company's statement of cash flows for the year ended December 31, 2012. Format operating activities by the direct method.

Experience the Power of Practice!

As denoted by the logo, all of these questions, as well as additional practice materials, can be found in *MyAccountingLab*.

Please visit myaccountinglab.com

S14A-2 ⑥ **Preparing operating activities using the direct method [5 min]**
Happy Tot's Learning Center has assembled the following data for the year ended June 30, 2012:

Payments to suppliers	$ 117,000
Purchase of equipment	42,000
Payments to employees	72,000
Payment of note payable	25,000
Payment of dividends	7,000
Cash receipt from issuance of stock	18,000
Collections from customers	190,000
Cash receipt from sale of land	60,000

Requirement

1. Prepare the *operating* activities section of the business's statement of cash flows for the year ended June 30, 2012, using the direct method.

Note: Short Exercise 14A-3 should be used only after completing Short Exercise 14A-2.

S14A-3 ⑥ **Preparing the direct method statement of cash flows [15 min]**
Use the data in Short Exercise 14A-2 and your results.

Requirement

1. Prepare the business's complete statement of cash flows for the year ended June 30, 2012, using the *direct* method for operating activities. Stop after determining the net increase (or decrease) in cash.

S14A-4 ⑥ **Preparing the direct method statement of cash flows [15 min]**
Rouse Toy Company reported the following comparative balance sheet:

	ROUSE TOY COMPANY					
	Comparative Balance Sheet					
	December 31, 2012 and 2011					
Assets	**2012**	**2011**	**Liabilities**	**2012**	**2011**
Current:			Current:		
Cash	$ 17,000	$ 11,000	Accounts payable	$ 43,000	$ 38,000
Accounts receivable	59,000	49,000	Salary payable	24,500	19,000
Inventory	78,000	84,000	Accrued liabilities	5,000	13,000
Prepaid expenses	3,100	2,100	Long-term notes payable	60,000	70,000
Long-term investments	75,000	85,000	**Stockholders' Equity**		
Plant assets, net	227,000	189,000	Common stock	42,000	39,000
			Retained earnings	284,600	241,100
Total assets	$459,100	$420,100	Total liabilities and stockholders' equity	$459,100	$420,100

Requirement

1. Compute the following for Rouse Toy Company:
   a. Collections from customers during 2012. Sales totaled $143,000.
   b. Payments for inventory during 2012. Cost of goods sold was $80,000.

• Exercises

E14A-5 ⑥ **Identifying activity categories—direct method [10–15 min]**
Consider the following transactions:

_____ a.	Collection of accounts receivable.	_____ i.	Purchase of treasury stock.
_____ b.	Issuance of note payable to borrow cash.	_____ j.	Issuance of common stock for cash.
_____ c.	Depreciation.	_____ k.	Payment of account payable.
_____ d.	Issuance of preferred stock for cash.	_____ l.	Acquisition of building by issuance of common stock.
_____ e.	Payment of cash dividend.	_____ m.	Purchase of equipment.
_____ f.	Sale of land.	_____ n.	Payment of wages to employees.
_____ g.	Acquisition of equipment by issuance of note payable.	_____ o.	Collection of cash interest.
_____ h.	Payment of note payable.	_____ p.	Sale of building

Requirement

1. Identify each of the transactions as a(n)
   - Operating activity (O)
   - Investing activity (I)
   - Financing activity (F)
   - Noncash investing and financing activity (NIF)
   - Transaction that is not reported on the statement of cash flows (N)

For each cash flow, indicate whether the item increases (+) or decreases (–) cash. The _direct_ method is used for cash flows from operating activities.

E14A-6 ⑥ **Identifying activity categories of transactions—direct method [5–10 min]**
Consider the following transactions:

a. Land	17,000		g. Salary expense	5,200	
Cash		17,000	Cash		5,200
b. Cash	9,800		h. Cash	92,000	
Equipment		9,800	Common stock		92,000
c. Bonds payable	36,000		i. Treasury stock	16,300	
Cash		36,000	Cash		16,300
d. Building	128,000		j. Cash	3,200	
Note payable		128,000	Interest revenue		3,200
e. Cash	2,200		k. Land	64,000	
Accounts receivable		2,200	Cash		64,000
f. Dividends payable	19,800		l. Accounts payable	10,200	
Cash		19,800	Cash		10,200

Requirement

1. Indicate where, if at all, each of the transactions would be reported on a statement of cash flows prepared by the _direct_ method and the accompanying schedule of noncash investing and financing activities.

E14A-7 ⑥ **Preparing operating activities cash flow—direct method [10–15 min]**

The accounting records of Fuzzy Dice Auto Parts reveal the following:

Payment of salaries and wages	$ 31,000	Net income	$ 21,000
Depreciation	13,000	Payment of income tax	11,000
Payment of interest	16,000	Collection of dividend revenue	6,000
Payment of dividends	6,000	Payment to suppliers	54,000
Collections from customers	117,000		

Requirement

1. Compute cash flows from operating activities using the *direct* method.

E14A-8 ⑥ **Identifying activity categories of transactions—direct method [5–10 min]**

Selected accounts of Printing Networks, Inc., show the following:

Accounts receivable

Beginning balance	9,100		
Service revenue	40,000	Cash collections	38,000
Ending balance	11,100		

Land

Beginning balance	87,000	
Acquisition	14,000	
Ending balance	101,000	

Long-term notes payable

		Beginning balance	274,000
Payments	73,000	Issuance for cash	84,000
		Ending balance	285,000

Requirement

1. For each account, identify the item or items that should appear on a statement of cash flows prepared by the *direct* method. Also state each item's amount and where to report the item.

E14A-9 ⑥ **Preparing the statement of cash flows—direct method [20–30 min]**

The income statement and additional data of Best Corporation follow:

BEST CORPORATION		
Income Statement		
Year Ended June 30, 2012		
Revenues:		
Sales revenue	$ 231,000	
Dividend revenue	8,000	$ 239,000
Expenses:		
Cost of goods sold	$ 102,000	
Salary expense	48,000	
Depreciation expense	28,000	
Advertising expense	13,000	
Income tax expense	11,000	
Interest expense	3,000	205,000
Net income		$ 34,000

Additional data follow:

a. Collections from customers are $15,500 more than sales.
b. Dividend revenue, interest expense, and income tax expense equal their cash amounts.
c. Payments to suppliers are the sum of cost of goods sold plus advertising expense.
d. Payments to employees are $1,000 more than salary expense.
e. Acquisition of plant assets is $102,000.
f. Cash receipts from sale of land total $24,000.
g. Cash receipts from issuance of common stock total $32,000.
h. Payment of long-term note payable is $17,000.
i. Payment of dividends is $10,500.
j. Cash balance, June 30, 2011, was $25,000; June 30, 2012 was $28,000.

Requirement

1. Prepare Best Corporation's statement of cash flows for the year ended June 30, 2012. Use the *direct* method.

E14A-10 ⑥ Computing cash flow items—direct method [10–15 min]

Consider the following facts:

a. Beginning and ending Accounts receivable are $20,000 and $24,000, respectively. Credit sales for the period total $62,000.
b. Cost of goods sold is $76,000. Beginning Inventory balance is $27,000, and ending Inventory balance is $22,000. Beginning and ending Accounts payable are $14,000 and $9,000, respectively.

Requirements

1. Compute cash collections from customers.
2. Compute cash payments for inventory.

E14A-11 ⑥ Computing cash flow items—direct method [20–30 min]

Superb Mobile Homes reported the following in its financial statements for the year ended December 31, 2012:

	2012	2011
Income Statement		
Net sales	$ 25,118	$ 21,115
Cost of sales	18,088	15,432
Depreciation	273	232
Other operating expenses	4,411	4,283
Income tax expense	536	481
Net income	$ 1,810	$ 687
Balance Sheet		
Cash and cash equivalents ...	$ 15	$ 13
Accounts receivable	799	619
Inventories	3,489	2,839
Property and equipment, net ..	4,346	3,436
Accounts payable	1,544	1,364
Accrued liabilities	941	853
Long-term liabilities	479	468
Common stock	671	443
Retained earnings	5,014	3,779

Requirement

1. Determine the following for Superb Mobile Homes during 2012:

   a. Collections from customers.
   b. Payments for inventory.
   c. Payments of operating expenses.
   d. Acquisitions of property and equipment (no sales of property during 2012).
   e. Borrowing, with Superb paying no long-term liabilities.
   f. Cash receipt from issuance of common stock.
   g. Payment of cash dividends.

● Problems (Group A)

MyAccountingLab   **P14A-12A** ⑥ **Preparing the statement of cash flows—direct method [35–45 min]**

MPG, Inc., accountants have developed the following data from the company's accounting records for the year ended April 30, 2012:

   a. Purchase of plant assets, $59,400.
   b. Cash receipt from issuance of notes payable, $46,100.
   c. Payments of notes payable, $44,000.
   d. Cash receipt from sale of plant assets, $24,500.
   e. Cash receipt of dividends, $4,800.
   f. Payments to suppliers, $374,300.
   g. Interest expense and payments, $12,000.
   h. Payments of salaries, $88,000.
   i. Income tax expense and payments, $37,000.
   j. Depreciation expense, $59,900.
   k. Collections from customers, $605,500.
   l. Payment of cash dividends, $49,400.
   m. Cash receipt from issuance of common stock, $64,900.
   n. Cash balance: April 30, 2011, $40,000; April 30, 2012, $121,700.

Requirement

1. Prepare MPG's statement of cash flows for the year ended April 30, 2012. Use the *direct* method for cash flows from operating activities.

P14A-13A ⑥ **Preparing the statement of cash flows—direct method [40 min]**

Use the Classic Reserve Rare Coins data from Problem 14-24A.

Requirements

1. Prepare Classic Reserve Rare Coins' income statement for the year ended December 31, 2012. Use the single-step format, with all revenues listed together and all expenses listed together.

2. Prepare Classic Reserve's balance sheet at December 31, 2012.

3. Prepare Classic Reserve's statement of cash flows for the year ended December 31, 2012. Format cash flows from operating activities by the *direct* method.

P14A-14A ⑥ **Preparing the statement of cash flows—direct method [30–40 min]**

Use the Rolling Hills data from Problem 14-27A.

Requirements

1. Prepare the 2012 statement of cash flows by the *direct* method.

2. How will what you learned in this problem help you evaluate an investment?

P14A-15A ⑥ Preparing the statement of cash flows—direct method [45–60 min]

To prepare the statement of cash flows, accountants for E-Mobile, Inc., have summarized 2012 activity in the Cash account as follows:

Cash

Beginning balance	87,200	Payments of operating expenses	46,800
Issuance of common stock	60,200	Payments of salaries and wages	64,500
Receipts of interest revenue	16,100	Payment of note payable	79,000
Collections from customers	308,400	Payment of income tax	7,500
		Payments on accounts payable	101,600
		Payments of dividends	1,400
		Payments of interest	21,700
		Purchase of equipment	49,500
Ending balance	99,900		

Requirement

1. Prepare E-Mobile's statement of cash flows for the year ended December 31, 2012, using the *direct* method to report operating activities.

● Problems (Group B)

P14A-16B ⑥ Preparing the statement of cash flows—direct method [35–45 min]

KSG, Inc., accountants have developed the following data from the company's accounting records for the year ended June 30, 2012:

    a. Purchase of plant assets, $57,400.
    b. Cash receipt from issuance of notes payable, $48,100.
    c. Payments of notes payable, $45,000.
    d. Cash receipt from sale of plant assets, $23,500.
    e. Cash receipt of dividends, $4,300.
    f. Payments to suppliers, $371,300.
    g. Interest expense and payments, $13,500.
    h. Payments of salaries, $92,000.
    i. Income tax expense and payments, $38,000.
    j. Depreciation expense, $56,000.
    k. Collections from customers, $607,000.
    l. Payment of cash dividends, $45,400.
    m. Cash receipt from issuance of common stock, $65,900.
    n. Cash balance: June 30, 2011, $39,300; June 30, 2012, $125,500.

Requirement

1. Prepare KSG's statement of cash flows for the year ended June 30, 2012. Use the *direct* method for cash flows from operating activities.

P14A-17B ⑥ Preparing the statement of cash flows—direct method [40 min]

Use the National Reserve Rare Coins data from Problem 14-28B.

Requirements

1. Prepare National Reserve Rare Coins' income statement for the year ended December 31, 2012. Use the single-step format, with all revenues listed together and all expenses listed together.
2. Prepare National Reserve's balance sheet at December 31, 2012.
3. Prepare National Reserve's statement of cash flows for the year ended December 31, 2012. Format cash flows from operating activities by the *direct* method.

P14A-18B ⑥ **Preparing the statement of cash flows—direct method [30–40 min]**
Use the All Wired data from Problem 14-31B.

Requirements

1. Prepare the 2012 statement of cash flows by the *direct* method.
2. How will what you learned in this problem help you evaluate an investment?

P14A-19B ⑥ **Preparing the statement of cash flows—direct method [45–60 min]**
To prepare the statement of cash flows, accountants for I-M-Mobile, Inc., have summarized 2012 activity in the Cash account as follows:

	Cash		
Beginning balance	87,900	Payments of operating expenses	46,200
Issuance of common stock	60,700	Payments of salaries and wages	64,500
Receipts of interest revenue	15,600	Payment of note payable	78,000
Collections from customers	308,700	Payment of income tax	8,000
		Payments on accounts payable	101,200
		Payments of dividends	1,200
		Payments of interest	21,400
		Purchase of equipment	56,500
Ending balance	95,900		

Requirement

1. Prepare I-M-Mobile's statement of cash flows for the year ended December 31, 2012, using the *direct* method to report operating activities.

Preparing the Indirect Statement of Cash Flows Using a Spreadsheet

The body of Chapter 14 discussed the uses of the statement of cash flows in decision making and showed how to prepare the statement using T-accounts. The T-account approach works well as a learning device. In practice, however, most companies face complex situations. In these cases, a spreadsheet can help in preparing the statement of cash flows.

The spreadsheet starts with the beginning balance sheet and concludes with the ending balance sheet. Two middle columns—one for debit amounts and the other for credit amounts—complete the spreadsheet. These columns, labeled "Transaction Analysis," hold the data for the statement of cash flows. Accountants can prepare the statement directly from the lower part of the spreadsheet. This appendix is based on the Smart Touch Learning data used in Chapter 14. We illustrate this approach only with the indirect method for operating activities. This method could be used for the direct method as well.

The *indirect* method reconciles net income to net cash provided by operating activities. Exhibit 14B-1 on the following page is the spreadsheet for preparing the statement of cash flows by the *indirect* method. Panel A shows the transaction analysis, and Panel B gives the statement of cash flows.

 7 Prepare the indirect statement of cash flows using a spreadsheet

Transaction Analysis on the Spreadsheet—Indirect Method

a. Net income of $40,000 is the first operating cash inflow. Net income is entered on the spreadsheet (Panel B) as a debit to Net income under Cash flows from operating activities and as a credit to Retained earnings on the balance sheet (Panel A).

b. Next come the adjustments to net income, starting with depreciation of $20,000—transaction (b)—which is debited to Depreciation and credited to Plant assets, net.

c. This transaction is the sale of plant assets. The $10,000 gain on the sale is entered as a credit to Gain on sale of plant assets—a subtraction from net income—under operating cash flows. This credit removes the $10,000 gain from operations because the cash proceeds from the sale were $50,000, not $10,000. The $50,000 sale amount is then entered on the spreadsheet under investing activities. Entry (c) is completed by crediting the plant assets' book value of $40,000 to the Plant assets, net account.

d. Entry (d) debits Accounts receivable for its $17,000 increase during the year. This amount is credited to Increase in accounts receivable under operating cash flows.

e. This entry credits Inventory for its $2,000 decrease during the year. This amount is debited to Decrease in inventory under operating cash flows.

f. This entry credits Accounts payable for its $40,000 increase during the year. Then, it is debited to show as Increase in accounts payable under operating cash flows.

g. This entry debits Accrued liabilities for its $5,000 decrease during the year. Then, it is credited to show as Decrease in accrued liabilities under operating cash flows.

h. This entry debits Plant assets, net for their purchase of $310,000 and credits Acquisition of plant assets under investing cash flows.

i. This entry debits Cash receipts from issuance of common stock of $120,000 under financing cash flows. The offsetting credit is to Common stock.

j. This entry is represented by a credit to Long-term notes payable and a debit under cash flows from financing activities of $90,000 (Cash receipt from issuance of notes payable).

EXHIBIT 14B-1 | **Spreadsheet for Statement of Cash Flows—Indirect Method**

		Balance 12/31/2013	Transaction Analysis		Balance 12/31/2014
1		SMART TOUCH LEARNING, INC.			
2		Spreadsheet for Statement of Cash Flows			
3		Year Ended December 31, 2014			
5	**Panel A—Balance Sheet**				
6	Cash	$ 42,000		$ 20,000 (n)	$ 22,000
7	Accounts receivable	73,000	(d) $ 17,000		90,000
8	Inventory	145,000		2,000 (e)	143,000
9	Plant assets, net	210,000	(h) 310,000	20,000 (b)	
10				40,000 (c)	460,000
11	Total assets	$470,000			$715,000
12					
13	Accounts payable	$ 50,000		40,000 (f)	$ 90,000
14	Accrued liabilities	10,000	(g) 5,000		5,000
15	Long-term notes payable	80,000	(k) 10,000	90,000 (j)	160,000
16	Common stock	250,000		120,000 (i)	370,000
17	Retained earnings	80,000	(m) 10,000	40,000 (a)	110,000
18	Treasury stock	0	(l) 20,000		(20,000)
19	Total liabilities and stockholders' equity	$470,000	$372,000	$372,000	$715,000
20					
21					
22	**Panel B—Statement of Cash Flows**				
23	Cash flows from operating activities:				
24	Net income		(a) $ 40,000		
25	Adjustments to reconcile net income to net cash provided by operating activities:				
26	Depreciation		(b) 20,000		
27	Gain on sale of plant assets			$ 10,000 (c)	
28	Increase in accounts receivable			17,000 (d)	
29	Decrease in inventory		(e) 2,000		
30	Increase in accounts payable		(f) 40,000		
31	Decrease in accrued liabilities			5,000 (g)	
32	Net cash provided by operating activities				
33	Cash flows from investing activities:				
34	Acquisition of plant assets			310,000 (h)	
35	Cash receipt from sale of plant asset		(c) 50,000		
36	Net cash used for investing activities				
37	Cash flows from financing activities:				
38	Cash receipt from issuance of common stock		(i) 120,000		
39	Cash receipt from issuance of notes payable		(j) 90,000		
40	Payment of notes payable			10,000 (k)	
41	Purchase of treasury stock			20,000 (l)	
42	Payment of dividends			10,000 (m)	
43	Net cash provided by financing activities				
44			$362,000	$382,000	
45	Net decrease in cash		(n) 20,000		
46			$382,000	$382,000	

k. This entry is the opposite of (j). It is represented by a debit (reduction) of $10,000 to Long-term notes payable and a credit under cash flows from financial activities for Payment of notes payable.

l. The purchase of treasury stock debited the Treasury stock account on the balance sheet $20,000. The corresponding cash flow entry "Purchase of treasury stock" credits $20,000 to reduce cash flow.

m. The $10,000 reduction (debit) to the Retained earnings account is the result of dividends declared and paid by the company. So, we show "Payment of dividends" as a credit in the financing section.

n. The final item in Exhibit 14B-1 on page 718 is the Net decrease in cash. It is shown as a credit to Cash and a debit to Net decrease in cash of $20,000.

Appendix 14B Assignments

● Problems (Group A)

P14B-1A ③ Preparing the statement of cash flows—indirect method [45–60 min]

The 2012 comparative balance sheet and income statement of Appleton Group, Inc., follow. Appleton had no noncash investing and financing transactions during 2012.

APPLETON GROUP, INC. Comparative Balance Sheet December 31, 2012 and 2011			
	2012	**2011**	**Increase (Decrease)**
Current assets:			
Cash and cash equivalents	$ 9,300	$ 15,300	$ (6,000)
Accounts receivable	42,000	43,200	(1,200)
Inventories	97,100	93,700	3,400
Plant assets:			
Land	41,100	16,000	25,100
Equipment, net	101,200	94,300	6,900
Total assets	$ 290,700	$ 262,500	$ 28,200
Current liabilities:			
Accounts payable	$ 25,600	$ 26,600	$ (1,000)
Accrued liabilities	24,000	22,800	1,200
Long-term liabilities:			
Notes payable	46,000	62,000	(16,000)
Stockholders' equity:			
Common stock	140,300	131,400	8,900
Retained earnings	54,800	19,700	35,100
Total liabilities and stockholders' equity	$ 290,700	$ 262,500	$ 28,200

APPLETON GROUP, INC.		
Income Statement		
Year Ended December 31, 2012		
Revenues:		
Sales revenue		$ 439,000
Interest revenue		11,800
Total revenues		$ 450,800
Expenses:		
Cost of goods sold	$ 205,500	
Salary expense	76,500	
Depreciation expense	15,500	
Other operating expense	49,500	
Interest expense	24,300	
Income tax expense	16,300	
Total expenses		387,600
Net income		$ 63,200

Requirement

1. Prepare the spreadsheet for the 2012 statement of cash flows. Format cash flows from operating activities by the *indirect* method.

P14B-2A ❸ **Preparing the statement of cash flows—indirect method [45–60 min]**
Review the data from P14-27A.

Requirement

1. Prepare the spreadsheet for Rolling Hills' 2012 statement of cash flows. Format cash flows from operating activities by the *indirect* method.

● Problems (Group B)

MyAccountingLab **P14B-3B** ❸ **Preparing the statement of cash flows—indirect method [45–60 min]**
The 2012 comparative balance sheet and income statement of Attleboro Group, Inc. follow. Attleboro had no noncash investing and financing transactions during 2012.

ATTLEBORO GROUP, INC.
Comparative Balance Sheet
December 31, 2012 and 2011

	2012	2011	Increase (Decrease)
Current assets:			
Cash and cash equivalents	$ 11,800	$ 15,200	$ (3,400)
Accounts receivable	42,200	43,900	(1,700)
Inventories	96,800	93,500	3,300
Plant assets:			
Land	39,800	14,000	25,800
Equipment, net	101,100	93,800	7,300
Total assets	$ 291,700	$ 260,400	$ 31,300
Current liabilities:			
Accounts payable	$ 25,100	$ 26,300	$ (1,200)
Accrued liabilities	24,200	22,500	1,700
Long-term liabilities:			
Notes payable	51,000	64,000	(13,000)
Stockholders' equity:			
Common stock	136,600	128,300	8,300
Retained earnings	54,800	19,300	35,500
Total liabilities and stockholders' equity	$ 291,700	$ 260,400	$ 31,300

ATTLEBORO GROUP, INC.
Income Statement
Year Ended December 31, 2012

Revenues:		
Sales revenue		$ 441,000
Interest revenue		11,300
Total revenues		$ 452,300
Expenses:		
Cost of goods sold	$ 205,300	
Salary expense	76,500	
Depreciation expense	15,100	
Other operating expense	49,600	
Interest expense	24,700	
Income tax expense	16,700	
Total expenses		387,900
Net income		$ 64,400

Requirement

1. Prepare the spreadsheet for the 2012 statement of cash flows. Format cash flows from operating activities by the *indirect* method.

P14B-4B ❸ **Preparing the statement of cash flows—indirect method [45–60 min]**
Review the data from P14-31B.

Requirement

1. Prepare the spreadsheet for All Wired's 2012 statement of cash flows. Format cash flows from operating activities by the *indirect* method.

15 Financial Statement Analysis

> How can we use the financial statement results to analyze a company?

SMART TOUCH LEARNING, INC.
Balance Sheet
May 31, 2013

Assets				Liabilities	
Current assets:				**Current liabilities:**	
Cash		$ 4,800		Accounts payable	$ 48,700
Accounts receivable		2,600		Salary payable	900
Inventory		30,500		Interest payable	100
Supplies		600		Unearned service revenue	400
Prepaid rent		2,000		Total current liabilities	50,100
Total current assets			$ 40,500	**Long-term liabilities:**	
Plant assets:				Notes payable	20,000
Furniture	$18,000			Total liabilities	70,100
Less: Accumulated depreciation—furniture	300	17,700			
Building	48,000			**Stockholders' Equity**	
Less: Accumulated depreciation—building	200	47,800		Common stock	30,000
Total plant assets			65,500	Retained earnings	5,900
				Total stockholders' equity	35,900
Total assets			$106,000	Total liabilities and stockholders' equity	$106,000

Learning Objectives

1 Perform a horizontal analysis of financial statements

2 Perform a vertical analysis of financial statements

3 Prepare and use common-size financial statements

4 Compute and evaluate the standard financial ratios

Now that you have learned some of the "how-tos" of financial statement preparation, you may be asking, "How can I use financial statements in a meaningful way to help me manage my company better? How can I compare my company's results with companies that do what I do?"

In this chapter, you'll learn tools that allow users to see beyond the pure "numbers" on the financial statements and translate them into meaningful analysis. We'll start by analyzing the statements of Smart Touch Learning and finish the chapter by analyzing Greg's Tunes.

• • •

Investors and creditors cannot evaluate a company by examining only one year's data. This is why most financial statements cover at least two periods. In fact, most financial analysis covers trends of three to five years. This chapter shows you how to use some of the analytical tools for charting a company's progress through time. These tools can be used by small business owners to measure performance, by financial analysts to analyze stock investments, by auditors to obtain an overall sense of a company's financial health, by creditors to determine credit risk, or by any other person wanting to compare financial data in relevant terms.

To accurately determine a company's performance, such as for Smart Touch, we need to compare its performance

A. from year to year.

B. with a competing company, like **Learning Tree**.

C. with the education and training industry as a whole.

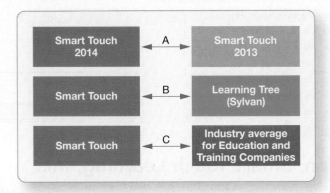

Then we will have a better idea of how to judge Smart Touch's present situation and predict what might happen in the near future.

There are three main ways to analyze financial statements:

- Horizontal analysis provides a year-to-year comparison of a company's performance in different periods.

- Another technique, vertical analysis, is a way to compare different companies.

- Comparing to the industry average provides a comparison of a company's performance in relationship to the industry in which the company operates.

We'll start with horizontal analysis.

Horizontal Analysis

Many decisions hinge on whether the numbers—sales, expenses, and net income—are increasing or decreasing. Have sales and other revenues risen from last year? By how much?

Sales may have increased by $1,723 million ($3,189 − $1,466 from Exhibit 15-1 on the next page), but considered alone, this fact is not very helpful. The *percentage change* in sales over time is more relative and, therefore, more helpful. It is better to know that sales increased by 117.5% than to know that sales increased by $1,723 million.

The study of percentage changes in comparative statements is called **horizontal analysis. Horizontal analysis compares one year to the next.** Computing a percentage change in comparative statements requires two steps:

1. Compute the dollar amount of the change from the earlier period to the later period.

2. Divide the dollar amount of change by the earlier period amount. We call the earlier period the base period.

 Perform a horizontal analysis of financial statements

EXHIBIT 15-1 | **Comparative Income Statement, Smart Touch Learning, Inc.**

SMART TOUCH LEARNING, INC.* Income Statement (Adapted) Year Ended December 31, 2014 and 2013		
(In millions)	**2014**	**2013**
Revenues (same as Net sales)	$3,189	$1,466
Expenses:		
Cost of revenues (same as Cost of goods sold)	1,458	626
Sales and marketing expense	246	120
General and administrative expense	140	57
Research and development expense	225	91
Other expense	470	225
Income before income tax	650	347
Income tax expense	251	241
Net income	$ 399	$ 106

*All values are assumed.

Illustration: Smart Touch Learning, Inc.

Horizontal analysis is illustrated for Smart Touch as follows (dollar amounts in millions):

			Increase (Decrease)	
	2014	**2013**	**Amount**	**Percentage**
Revenues (same as Net sales).........	$3,189	$1,466	$1,723	117.5%

Smart Touch sales increased by an incredible 117.5% during 2014, computed as follows:

> STEP 1: Compute the dollar amount of change in sales from 2014 to 2013:

$$\begin{array}{ccc} 2014 & 2013 & \text{Increase} \\ \$3,189 - & \$1,466 = & \$1,723 \end{array}$$

> STEP 2: Divide the dollar amount of change by the base-period amount. This computes the percentage change for the period:

$$\text{Percentage change} = \frac{\text{Dollar amount of change}}{\text{Base-period amount}}$$

$$= \frac{\$1,723}{\$1,466} = 1.175 = 117.5\%$$

Completed horizontal analyses for Smart Touch's financial statements are shown in the following exhibits:

- Exhibit 15-2 Income Statement
- Exhibit 15-3 Balance Sheet

EXHIBIT 15-2 | **Comparative Income Statement—Horizontal Analysis**

SMART TOUCH LEARNING, INC.*
Income Statement (Adapted)
Year Ended December 31, 2014 and 2013

(Dollar amounts in millions)	2014	2013	Increase (Decrease) Amount	Percentage
Revenues	$3,189	$1,466	$1,723	117.5%
Cost of revenues	1,458	626	832	132.9
Gross profit	$1,731	$ 840	$ 891	106.1
Operating expenses:				
Sales and marketing expense	$ 246	$ 120	$ 126	105.0
General and administrative expense	140	57	83	145.6
Research and development expense	225	91	134	147.3
Other expense	470	225	245	108.9
Total operating expenses	$1,081	$ 493	$ 588	119.3
Income before income tax	$ 650	$ 347	$ 303	87.3
Income tax expense	251	241	10	4.1
Net income	$ 399	$ 106	$ 293	276.4

*All values are assumed.

EXHIBIT 15-3 | **Comparative Balance Sheet—Horizontal Analysis**

SMART TOUCH LEARNING, INC.*
Balance Sheet (Adapted)
December 31, 2014 and 2013

(Dollar amounts in millions)	2014	2013	Increase (Decrease) Amount	Percentage
Assets				
Current assets:				
Cash and cash equivalents	$ 427	$149	$ 278	186.6%
Other current assets	2,266	411	1,855	451.3
Total current assets	$2,693	$560	$ 2,133	380.9
Property, plant, and equipment, net	379	188	191	101.6
Intangible assets, net	194	106	88	83.0
Other assets	47	17	30	176.5
Total assets	$3,313	$871	$ 2,442	280.4
Liabilities				
Current liabilities:				
Accounts payable	$ 33	$ 46	$ (13)	(28.3)%
Other current liabilities	307	189	118	62.4
Total current liabilities	$ 340	$235	$ 105	44.7
Long-term liabilities	44	47	(3)	(6.4)
Total liabilities	$ 384	$282	$ 102	36.2
Stockholders' Equity				
Common stock	$ 1	$ 45	$ (44)	(97.8)
Retained earnings and other equity	2,928	544	2,384	438.2
Total stockholders' equity	$2,929	$589	$ 2,340	397.3
Total liabilities and stockholders' equity	$3,313	$871	$ 2,442	280.4

*All values are assumed.

Horizontal Analysis of the Income Statement

Smart Touch's comparative income statement reveals exceptional growth during 2014. An increase of 100% occurs when an item doubles, so Smart Touch's 117.5% increase in revenues means that revenues more than doubled.

The item on Smart Touch's income statement with the slowest growth rate is income tax expense. Income taxes increased by only 4.1%. On the bottom line, net income grew by an incredible 276.4%. That is real progress!

Horizontal Analysis of the Balance Sheet

Smart Touch's comparative balance sheet also shows rapid growth in assets, with total assets increasing by 280.4%. That means total assets almost quadrupled in one year. Very few companies grow that fast.

Smart Touch's liabilities grew more slowly. Total liabilities increased by 36.2%, and Accounts payable and long-term liabilities actually decreased, as indicated by the liability figures in parentheses. This is another indicator of positive growth for Smart Touch.

Trend Analysis

Trend analysis is a form of horizontal analysis. **Trend precentages indicate the direction a business is taking.** How have sales changed over a five-year period? What trend does net income show? These questions can be answered by trend analysis over a period, such as three to five years.

Trend analysis percentages are computed by selecting a base year (the earliest year). The base year amounts are set equal to 100%. The amounts for each subsequent year are expressed as a percentage of the base amount. To compute trend analysis percentages, we divide each item for the following years by the base year amount.

$$\text{Trend \%} = \frac{\text{Any year \$}}{\text{Base year \$}} \times 100$$

Assume Smart Touch's total revenues were $1,000 million in 2010 and rose to $3,189 million in 2014. To illustrate trend analysis, review the trend of net sales during 2010–2014, with dollars in millions. The base year is 2010, so that year's percentage is set equal to 100.

(In millions)	2014	2013	2012	2011	2010
Net sales..................	$3,189	1,466	1,280	976	1,000
Trend percentages	318.9%	146.6%	128%	97.6%	100%

We want percentages for the five-year period 2010–2014. We compute these by dividing each year's amount by the 2010 net sales amount. Net sales decreased slightly in 2011 and then the rate of growth increased from 2012–2014.

You can perform a trend analysis on any one or multiple item(s) you consider important. Trend analysis is widely used to predict the future health of a company.

Vertical Analysis

As we have seen, horizontal analysis and trend analysis percentages highlight changes in an item from year to year, or over *time*. But no single technique gives a complete picture of a business, so we also need vertical analysis.

Vertical analysis of a financial statement shows the relationship of each item to its base amount, which is the 100% figure. Every other item on the statement is then reported as a percentage of that base. For the income statement, net sales is the base.

2 Perform a vertical analysis of financial statements

$$\text{Vertical analysis } \% = \frac{\text{Each income statement item}}{\text{Revenues (net sales)}} \times 100$$

Exhibit 15-4 shows the completed vertical analysis of Smart Touch's 2014 and 2013 comparative income statement.

The vertical analysis percentage for Smart Touch's cost of revenues is 45.7% of net sales ($1,458/$3,189 = 0.457 or 45.7%) in 2014 and 42.7% ($626/$1,466 = 0.427 or 42.7%) in 2013. This means that for every $1 in net sales, almost $0.46 in 2014 and almost $0.43 in 2013 is spent on cost of revenue.

On the bottom line, Smart Touch's net income is 12.5% of revenues in 2014 and 7.2% of revenues in 2013. That improvement from 2013 to 2014 is extremely good. Suppose under normal conditions a company's net income is 10% of revenues. A drop to 4% may cause the investors to be alarmed and sell their stock.

EXHIBIT 15-4 | **Comparative Income Statement—Vertical Analysis**

SMART TOUCH LEARNING, INC.*
Comparative Income Statement (Adapted)
Years Ended December 31, 2014 and 2013

(Dollar amounts in millions)	2014 Amount	2014 Percent of Total	2013 Amount	2013 Percent of Total
Revenues	$3,189	100.0%	$1,466	100.0%
Cost of revenues	1,458	45.7	626	42.7
Gross profit	$1,731	54.3	$ 840	57.3
Operating expenses:				
Sales and marketing expense	$ 246	7.7	$ 120	8.2
General and administrative expense	140	4.4	57	3.9
Research and development expense	225	7.1	91	6.2
Other expense	470	14.7	225	15.3
Total operating expenses	$1,081	33.9	$ 493	33.6
Income before income tax	$ 650	20.4	$ 347	23.7
Income tax expense	251	7.9	241	16.5^
Net income	$ 399	12.5%	$ 106	7.2%

*All values are assumed. ^The calculated percentage of 16.4 was adjusted for rounding to 16.5.

Exhibit 15-5 on the following page depicts the vertical analysis of Smart Touch's balance sheet. The base amount (100%) is total assets. The base amount is also total liabilities and equity, because they are exactly the same number, in 2014 that's $3,313. (Recall that they should always be the same number because of the accounting equation.)

EXHIBIT 15-5 | **Comparative Balance Sheet—Vertical Analysis**

SMART TOUCH LEARNING, INC.*
Balance Sheet (Adapted)
December 31, 2014 and 2013

	2014		2013	
(Dollar amount in millions)	Amount	Percent of Total	Amount	Percent of Total
Assets				
Current Assets:				
Cash and cash equivalents	$ 427	12.9%	$149	17.1%
Other current assets	2,266	68.4	411	47.2
Total current assets	$2,693	81.3	$560	64.3
Property, plant, and equipment, net	379	11.4	188	21.6
Intangible assets, net	194	5.9	106	12.1^
Other assets	47	1.4	17	2.0
Total assets	$3,313	100.0%	$871	100.0%
Liabilities				
Current Liabilities:				
Accounts payable	$ 33	1.0%	$ 46	5.3%
Other current liabilities	307	9.3	189	21.7
Total current liabilities	$ 340	10.3	$235	27.0
Long-term liabilities	44	1.3	47	5.4
Total liabilities	$ 384	11.6	$282	32.4
Stockholders' Equity				
Common stock	$ 1	0.0	$ 45	5.2
Retained earnings and other equity	2,928	88.4	544	62.4
Total stockholders' equity	$2,929	88.4	$589	67.6
Total liabilities and stockholders' equity	$3,313	100.0%	$871	100.0%

*All values are assumed. ^percents rounded to balance.

The vertical analysis of Smart Touch's balance sheet reveals several interesting things:

- Current assets make up 81.3% of total assets in 2014 and 64.3% of total assets in 2013. For most companies this percentage is closer to 30%. The 81.3% of current assets represents a great deal of liquidity and a significant increase in liquidity from 2013 to 2014.

- Property, plant, and equipment make up only 11.4% of total assets in 2014 but 21.6% of total assets in 2013. This percentage is low because of the nature of Smart Touch's business. Smart Touch's Web-based operations do not require many buildings or equipment.

- Total liabilities are only 11.6% of total assets in 2014, but were 32.4% of total assets in 2013. This improvement is positive for Smart Touch. Stockholders' equity makes up 88.4% of total assets in 2014 and 67.6% of total assets in 2013. Most of Smart Touch's equity is retained earnings and other equity—signs of a strong company because most of the equity is internally generated rather than externally generated (through stock share sales).

Key Takeaway

Vertical analysis shows the relationship of each item on the statement to a base amount. The base amount is net sales on the income statement and total assets on the balance sheet. All other items are reported as a percentage of the 100% net sales line on the income statement or the 100% total assets line on the balance sheet.

How Do We Compare One Company with Another?

 Prepare and use common-size financial statements

Horizontal analysis and vertical analysis provide much useful data about a company. As we have seen, Smart Touch's percentages depict a very successful company. But the data apply only to one business.

To compare Smart Touch to another company we can use a common-size state-ment. A **common-size statement** reports only percentages—the same percentages that appear in a vertical analysis. By only reporting percentages, it removes dollar value bias when comparing one company to another company. **Dollar value bias** is the bias one sees from comparing numbers in absolute (dollars) rather than relative (percentage) terms. For us, $1 million seems like a large number. For some large companies, it is immaterial. Smart Touch's common-size income statement is an example of removing dollar value bias. This statement comes directly from the percentages in Exhibit 15-4.

We could prepare common size statements for Smart Touch from year to year; however, we will start by preparing common size income statements for Smart Touch and **Learning Tree**, both of which compete in the service-learning industry. Which company earns a higher percentage of revenues as profits for its shareholders? Exhibit 15-6 gives both companies' common-size income statements for 2014 so that we may compare them on a relative, not absolute, basis.

EXHIBIT 15-6	**Common-Size Income Statement** **Smart Touch vs. Learning Tree**

SMART TOUCH vs. LEARNING TREE* Common-Size Income Statement Year Ended December 31, 2014		
	Smart Touch	Learning Tree
Revenues	100.0%	100.0%
Cost of revenues	45.7	36.3
Gross profit	54.3	63.7
Sales and marketing expense	7.7	21.8
General and administrative expense	4.4	7.3
Research and development expense	7.1	10.3
Other expense (income)	14.7	(11.5)
Income before income tax	20.4	35.8
Income tax expense	7.9	12.3
Net income	12.5%	23.5%

*All values are assumed.

Exhibit 15-6 shows that **Learning Tree** was more profitable than Smart Touch in 2014. **Learning Tree**'s gross profit percentage is 63.7%, compared to Smart Touch's 54.3%. This means that **Learning Tree** is earning more profit from every dollar of revenue than Smart Touch is earning. And, most importantly, **Learning Tree**'s per-centage of net income to revenues is 23.5%. That means almost one-fourth of **Learning Tree**'s revenues result in profits for the company's stockholders. Smart Touch's percentage of net income to revenues, on the other hand, is 12.5%. Both are excellent percentages; however, the common-size statement highlights **Learning Tree**'s advantages over Smart Touch.

Benchmarking

Benchmarking is the practice of comparing a company with other leading companies. It often uses the common size percentages in a graphical manner to highlight differ-ences. There are two main types of benchmarks in financial statement analysis: bench-marking against a key competitor and benchmarking against the industry average.

Benchmarking Against a Key Competitor

Exhibit 15-6 uses a key competitor, **Learning Tree**, to compare Smart Touch's profitability. The two companies compete in the same industry, so **Learning Tree** serves as an ideal benchmark for Smart Touch. The graphs in Exhibit 15-7

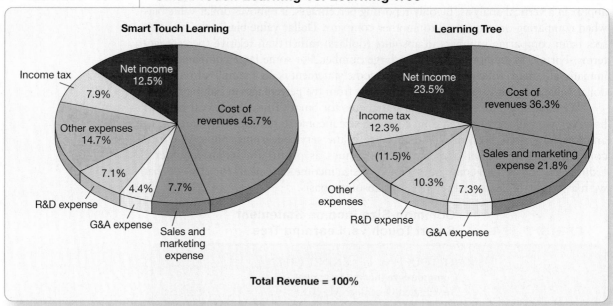

EXHIBIT 15-7

**Graphical Analysis of Common-Size Income Statement
Smart Touch Learning vs. Learning Tree**

highlight the profitability difference between the companies. Focus on the segment of the graphs showing net income. **Learning Tree** is clearly more profitable than Smart Touch.

Benchmarking Against the Industry Average

The industry average can also serve as a very useful benchmark for evaluating a company. An industry comparison would show how Smart Touch is performing alongside the average for the e-learning industry. *Annual Statement Studies*, published by the Risk Management Association, provides common-size statements for most industries. To compare Smart Touch to the industry average, we would simply insert the industry-average common-size income statement in place of **Learning Tree** in Exhibit 15-6.

Stop & Think...

As you are taking classes toward your degree, how do you know how quickly you can complete your studies? If you knew the average credit hours taken each semester was 12 credit hours, the 12 hours would be your benchmark. Comparing the number of classes you take to the average of 12 hours a semester is the same concept as benchmarking. Maybe you are taking 15 hours a semester. Then you'd be completing your degree faster than the average student. Maybe you take only 3 credit hours in the Spring so you can work a part-time job. Then, you'd be completing classes at a slower pace than average.

Now let's put your learning to practice. Work the summary problem on the following page, which reviews the concepts from the first half of this chapter.

Key Takeaway

Vertical analysis can be used to prepare common-size statements to compare companies against each other. We can benchmark (measure) a company against a key competitor or measure a company against the industry average.

Summary Problem 15-1

Requirements

Perform a horizontal analysis and a vertical analysis of the comparative income statement of Kimball Corporation, which makes iPod covers. State whether 2014 was a good year or a bad year, and give your reasons.

KIMBALL CORPORATION
Comparative Income Statement
Years Ended December 31, 2014 and 2013

	2014	2013
Net sales	$300,000	$250,000
Expenses:		
Cost of goods sold	$214,200	$170,000
Engineering, selling, and administrative expenses	54,000	48,000
Interest expense	6,000	5,000
Income tax expense	9,000	3,000
Other expense (income)	2,700	(1,000)
Total expenses	285,900	225,000
Net income	$ 14,100	$ 25,000

Solution

KIMBALL CORPORATION
Horizontal Analysis of Comparative Income Statement
Years Ended December 31, 2014 and 2013

	2014	2013	Increase (Decrease) Amount	Increase (Decrease) Percent
Net sales	$300,000	$250,000	$ 50,000	20.0%
Expenses:				
Cost of goods sold	$214,200	$170,000	$ 44,200	26.0
Engineering, selling, and administrative expenses	54,000	48,000	6,000	12.5
Interest expense	6,000	5,000	1,000	20.0
Income tax expense	9,000	3,000	6,000	200.0
Other expense (income)	2,700	(1,000)	3,700	—*
Total expenses	285,900	225,000	60,900	27.1
Net income	$ 14,100	$ 25,000	$ (10,900)	(43.6%)

*Percentage changes are typically not computed for shifts from a negative to a positive amount, and vice versa.

The horizontal analysis shows that net sales increased 20.0%. Total expenses increased by 27.1%, and net income decreased 43.6%. So, even though Kimball's net sales increased, the company's expenses increased by a larger percentage, netting an overall 43.6% reduction in net income between the years. This analysis identifies areas where management should review more data. For example, Cost of goods sold increased 26.0%. Managers would want to know why this increase occurred to determine if the company can implement cost saving strategies (such as purchasing from other, lower cost vendors).

	2014		2013	
	Amount	Percent	Amount	Percent

KIMBALL CORPORATION
Vertical Analysis of Comparative Income Statement
Years Ended December 31, 2014 and 2013

	Amount	Percent	Amount	Percent
Net sales	$300,000	100.0%	$250,000	100.0%
Expenses:				
Cost of goods sold	$214,200	71.4	$170,000	68.0
Engineering, selling, and administrative expenses	54,000	18.0	48,000	19.2
Interest expense	6,000	2.0	5,000	2.0
Income tax expense	9,000	3.0	3,000	1.2
Other expense (income)	2,700	0.9	(1,000)	(0.4)
Total expenses	285,900	95.3	225,000	90.0
Net income	$ 14,100	4.7%	$ 25,000	10.0%

The vertical analysis shows changes in the percentages of net sales. A few notable items are

- cost of goods sold—increased from 68.0% to 71.4%;
- engineering, selling, and administrative expenses—decreased from 19.2% to 18.0%.

These two items are Kimball's largest dollar expenses, so their percentage changes are important. This indicates that cost controls need to be improved, especially for COGS.

The 2014 net income declined to 4.7% of sales, compared with 10.0% the preceding year. Kimball's increase in cost of goods sold is the biggest factor in the overall decrease in net income as a percentage of sales. The horizontal analysis showed that although Net sales increased 20% from 2013 to 2014, the amount of each of those sales dollars resulting in net income decreased.

Using Ratios to Make Decisions

 Compute and evaluate the standard financial ratios

Online financial databases, such as **Lexis/Nexis** and the **Dow Jones News Retrieval Service**, provide data on thousands of companies. Suppose you want to compare some companies' recent earnings histories. You might want to compare companies' returns on stockholders' equity. The computer could then search the databases and give you the names of the 20 companies with the highest return on equity. You can use any ratio to search for information that is relevant to a particular decision.

Remember, however, that no single ratio tells the whole picture of any company's performance. Different ratios explain different aspects of a company. The ratios we discuss in this chapter may be classified as follows:

1. Evaluating the ability to pay current liabilities

2. Evaluating the ability to sell inventory and collect receivables

3. Evaluating the ability to pay long-term debt

4. Evaluating profitability

5. Evaluating stock as an investment

Evaluating the Ability to Pay Current Liabilities

Working capital is defined as follows:

> **Working capital = Current assets – Current liabilities**

Working capital measures the ability to meet short-term obligations with current assets. Two decision tools based on working-capital data are the *current ratio* and the *acid-test ratio*.

Current Ratio

The most widely used ratio is the *current ratio*, which is current assets divided by current liabilities. **The current ratio measures a company's ability to pay current liabilities with its current assets.**

Exhibit 15-8 on the following page shows the comparative income statement and balance sheet of Greg's Tunes, which we will be using in the remainder of this chapter.

The current ratios of Greg's Tunes, at December 31, 2014 and 2013, follow, along with the average for the entertainment industry:

		Greg's Tunes' Current Ratio		Industry
	Formula	**2014**	**2013**	**Average**
Current ratio =	$\dfrac{\text{Current assets}}{\text{Current liabilities}}$	$\dfrac{\$262,000}{\$142,000} = 1.85$	$\dfrac{\$236,000}{\$126,000} = 1.87$	0.60

A high current ratio indicates that the business has sufficient current assets to maintain normal business operations. Compare Greg's Tunes' current ratio of 1.85 for 2014 with the industry average of 0.60.

What is an acceptable current ratio? The answer depends on the industry. The norm for companies in most industries is around 1.50, as reported by the Risk Management Association. Greg's Tunes' current ratio of 1.85 is strong. Keep in mind that we would not want to see a current ratio that is too high, say 25.0. This would indicate that the company is too liquid and, therefore, is not using its assets effectively. For example, the company may need to reduce inventory levels so as not to tie up available resources.

EXHIBIT 15-8 | **Comparative Financial Statements**

GREG'S TUNES, INC.
Comparative Income Statement
Years Ended December 31, 2014 and 2013

	2014	2013
Net sales	$858,000	$803,000
Cost of goods sold	513,000	509,000
Gross profit	$345,000	$294,000
Operating expenses:		
Selling expenses	$126,000	$114,000
General expenses	118,000	123,000
Total operating expenses	$244,000	$237,000
Income from operations	$101,000	$ 57,000
Interest revenue	4,000	—
Interest (expense)	(24,000)	(14,000)
Income before income taxes	$ 81,000	$ 43,000
Income tax expense	33,000	17,000
Net income	$ 48,000	$ 26,000

GREG'S TUNES, INC.
Comparative Balance Sheet
December 31, 2014 and 2013

	2014	2013
Assets		
Current assets:		
Cash	$ 29,000	$ 32,000
Accounts receivable, net	114,000	85,000
Inventories	113,000	111,000
Prepaid expenses	6,000	8,000
Total current assets	$262,000	$236,000
Long-term investments	18,000	9,000
Property, plant, and equipment, net	507,000	399,000
Total assets	$787,000	$644,000
Liabilities		
Current liabilities:		
Accounts payable	$ 73,000	$ 68,000
Accrued liabilities	27,000	31,000
Notes payable	42,000	27,000
Total current liabilities	$142,000	$126,000
Long-term notes payable	289,000	198,000
Total liabilities	$431,000	$324,000
Stockholders' Equity		
Common stock, no par	$186,000	$186,000
Retained earnings	170,000	134,000
Total stockholders' equity	$356,000	$320,000
Total liabilities and stockholders' equity	$787,000	$644,000

Acid-Test Ratio

The *acid-test* (or *quick*) *ratio* tells us whether the entity could pay all its current liabilities if they came due immediately. That is, could the company pass the *acid test*?

To compute the acid-test ratio, we add cash, short-term investments (those that may be sold in the lesser of 12 months or the business operating cycle), and net current receivables (accounts and notes receivable, net of allowances) and divide this sum by current liabilities. Inventory and prepaid expenses are *not* included in the acid test because they are the least-liquid current assets. Greg's Tunes' acid-test ratios for 2014 and 2013 follow:

| | | Greg's Tunes' Acid-Test Ratio | | Industry |
Formula		2014	2013	Average
Acid-test ratio $=$	$\dfrac{\text{Cash + Short-term investments + Net current receivables}}{\text{Current liabilities}}$	$\dfrac{\$29{,}000 + \$0 + \$114{,}000}{\$142{,}000} = 1.01$	$\dfrac{\$32{,}000 + \$0 + \$85{,}000}{\$126{,}000} = 0.93$	0.46

The company's acid-test ratio improved during 2014 and is significantly better than the industry average. The norm for the acid-test ratio ranges from 0.20 for shoe retailers to 1.00 for manufacturers of equipment, as reported by the Risk Management Association. An acid-test ratio of 0.90 to 1.00 is acceptable in most industries.

Evaluating the Ability to Sell Inventory and Collect Receivables

In this section, we discuss five ratios that measure the company's ability to sell inventory and collect receivables.

Inventory Turnover

The inventory turnover ratio measures the number of times a company sells its average level of inventory during a year. A high rate of turnover indicates ease in selling inventory; a low rate indicates difficulty. A value of 4 means that the company sold its average level of inventory four times—once every three months—during the year. If the company were a seasonal company, this would be a good ratio because it would mean it turned its inventory over each season, on average.

To compute inventory turnover, we divide cost of goods sold by the average inventory for the period. We use the cost of goods sold—not sales—because both cost of goods sold and inventory are stated *at cost*. Sales at *retail* are not comparable with inventory at *cost*.

Greg's Tunes' inventory turnover for 2014 is as follows:

Formula	Greg's Tunes' Inventory Turnover	Industry Average
Inventory turnover $= \dfrac{\text{Cost of goods sold}}{\text{Average inventory}}$	$\dfrac{\$513{,}000}{\$112{,}000} = 4.6$	27.7

Cost of goods sold comes from the income statement (Exhibit 15-8). Average inventory is figured by adding the beginning inventory of $111,000 to the ending inventory of $113,000 and dividing by 2. (See the balance sheet, Exhibit 15-8.)

Inventory turnover varies widely with the nature of the business. For example, most manufacturers of farm machinery have an inventory turnover close to three times a year. In contrast, companies that remove natural gas from the ground hold their inventory for a very short period of time and have an average turnover of 30. Greg's Tunes' turnover of 4.6 times a year means on average the company has enough inventory to handle sales for over 79 days (365/4.6 times). This is very low for its industry, which has an average turnover of 27.7 times per year. This ratio has identified an area that Greg's Tunes needs to improve.

Days in Inventory

Another key measure is the number of **days in inventory ratio**. This measures the average number of days inventory is held by the company. Greg's Tunes' days in inventory for 2014 is as follows:

Formula	Greg's Tunes' Days in Inventory	Industry Average
Days in inventory $= \dfrac{365 \text{ days}}{\text{Inventory turnover ratio}}$	$\dfrac{365 \text{ days}}{4.6} = 79$ days	13 days

Days in inventory varies widely, depending on the business. Greg's Tunes' days in inventory is 79 days—too high for its industry, which has a days in inventory ratio of only 13 days. This ratio has identified an area that Greg's Tunes needs to improve. Greg's Tunes should focus on reducing average inventory held. By decreasing average inventory, the company can increase inventory turnover and lower the average days in inventory. Greg's will also be able to reduce its inventory storage and insurance costs, as well as reduce the risk of holding obsolete inventory.

Gross Profit Percentage

Gross profit (gross margin) is net sales minus the cost of goods sold. Merchandisers strive to increase the *gross profit percentage* (also called the *gross margin percentage*). This measures the profitability of each net sales dollar.

Greg's Tunes' gross profit percentage for 2014 is as follows:

Formula	Greg's Tunes' Gross Profit Percentage	Industry Average
Gross profit percentage $= \dfrac{\text{Gross profit}}{\text{Net sales}}$	$\dfrac{\$345,000}{\$858,000} = 0.402$ or 40.2%	43%

Gross profit percentage varies widely, depending on the business. Greg's Tunes' gross profit percentage is 40.2%, which is slightly lower than the industry, which has a gross profit percentage of 43%. This ratio has identified an area that Greg's Tunes needs to improve. To increase gross profit percentage, Greg's Tunes needs to decrease the cost of the merchandise and/or increase revenue (selling price). Additionally, addressing Greg's inventory turnover issues will probably help Greg's to increase its gross profit percentage.

Accounts Receivable Turnover

The **accounts receivable turnover ratio** measures the ability to collect cash from credit customers. The higher the ratio, the faster the cash collections. But a receivable turnover that is too high may indicate that credit is too tight, causing the loss of sales to good customers.

To compute accounts receivable turnover, we divide net credit sales (assuming all Greg's sales from Exhibit 15-8 are on account) by average net accounts receivable.

Greg's Tunes' accounts receivable turnover ratio for 2014 is computed as follows:

Formula	Greg's Tunes' Accounts Receivable Turnover	Industry Average
Accounts receivable turnover $=$ $\dfrac{\text{Net credit sales}}{\text{Average net accounts receivable}}$	$\dfrac{\$858,000}{\$99,500} = 8.6$	29.1

Net credit sales comes from the income statement (Exhibit 15-8). Average net accounts receivable is figured by adding the beginning Accounts receivable of $85,000 to the ending Accounts receivable of $114,000 and dividing by 2. (See the balance sheet, Exhibit 15-8.)

Greg's receivable turnover of 8.6 times per year is much slower than the industry average of 29.1. Why the difference? Greg's is a fairly new business that sells to established people who pay their accounts over time. Further, this turnover coincides with the lower than average inventory turnover. So, Greg's may achieve a higher receivable turnover by increasing its inventory turnover ratio.

Days' Sales in Receivables

The *days' sales in receivables* ratio also measures the ability to collect receivables. **Days' sales in receivables tell us how many days' sales remain in Accounts receivable.**

To compute this ratio for Greg's Tunes for 2014, we divide 365 days by the accounts receivable turnover ratio we previously calculated:

Formula	Greg's Tunes' Days' Sales in Accounts Receivable	Industry Average
Days' sales in average accounts receivable $=$ $\dfrac{365 \text{ days}}{\text{Accounts receivable turnover ratio}}$	$\dfrac{365}{8.6} = 42$ days	25 days

Greg's Tunes' ratio tells us that 42 average days' sales remain in Accounts receivable and need to be collected. The company's days' sales in receivables ratio is much higher (worse) than the industry average of 25 days. Greg's might give its customers a longer time to pay, such as 45 days versus 30 days. Alternatively, Greg's credit department may need to review the criteria it uses to evaluate individual customer's credit. Without the customers' good paying habits, the company's cash flow would suffer.

Evaluating the Ability to Pay Long-Term Debt

The ratios discussed so far yield insight into current assets and current liabilities. They help us measure ability to sell inventory, collect receivables, and pay current liabilities. Most businesses also have long-term debt. Three key indicators of a business's ability to pay long-term liabilities are the *debt ratio*, the *debt to equity ratio*, and the *times-interest-earned ratio*.

Debt Ratio

A loan officer at Metro Bank is evaluating loan applications from two companies. Both companies have asked to borrow $500,000 and have agreed to repay the loan over a five-year period. The first firm already owes $600,000 to another bank. The second company owes only $100,000. If all else is equal, the bank is more likely to lend money to Company 2 because that company owes less than Company 1.

The relationship between total liabilities and total assets—called the *debt ratio*—shows the proportion of assets financed with debt. **If the debt ratio is 1, then all the assets are financed with debt.** A debt ratio of 50% means that half the assets are financed with debt and the other half are financed by the owners of the business. The higher the debt ratio, the higher the company's financial risk.

The debt ratios for Greg's Tunes at the end of 2014 and 2013 follow:

| | | Greg's Tunes' Debt Ratio | | Industry |
	Formula	2014	2013	Average
Debt ratio =	$\dfrac{\text{Total liabilities}}{\text{Total assets}}$	$\dfrac{\$431{,}000}{\$787{,}000} = 0.548\ (54.8\%)$	$\dfrac{\$324{,}000}{\$644{,}000} = 0.503\ (50.3\%)$	0.69 (69%)

Both total liabilities and total asset amounts are from the balance sheet, presented in Exhibit 15-8. Greg's debt ratio in 2014 of 54.8% is not very high. The Risk Management Association reports that the average debt ratio for most companies ranges from 57% to 67%, with relatively little variation from company to company. Greg's debt ratio indicates a fairly low-risk position compared with the industry average debt ratio of 69%.

Debt to Equity Ratio

The relationship between total liabilities and total equity—called the **debt to equity ratio**—shows the proportion of total liabilities relative to the proportion of total equity that is financing the company's assets. Thus, this ratio measures financial leverage. If the debt to equity ratio is greater than 1, then the company is financing more assets with debt than with equity. If the ratio is less than 1, then the company is financing more assets with equity than with debt. The higher the debt to equity ratio, the higher the company's financial risk.

The debt to equity ratios for Greg's Tunes at the end of 2014 and 2013 follow:

| | | Greg's Tunes' Debt to Equity Ratio | | Industry |
	Formula	2014	2013	Average
Debt to equity =	$\dfrac{\text{Total liabilities}}{\text{Total equity}}$	$\dfrac{\$431{,}000}{\$356{,}000} = 1.21$	$\dfrac{\$324{,}000}{\$320{,}000} = 1.01$	2.23

Greg's debt to equity ratio in 2014 of 1.21 is not very high. Greg's debt to equity ratio indicates a fairly low-risk position compared with the industry average debt to equity ratio of 2.23.

Times-Interest-Earned Ratio

The debt ratio and debt to equity ratio say nothing about the ability to pay interest expense. Analysts use the **times-interest-earned ratio** to relate Earnings before interest and taxes (EBIT) to interest expense. This ratio is also called the **interest-coverage ratio**. It measures the number of times EBIT can cover (pay) interest expense. A high interest-coverage ratio indicates ease in paying interest expense; a low ratio suggests difficulty.

To compute this ratio, we divide EBIT (Net income + Income tax expense + Interest expense) by interest expense. Calculation of Greg's times-interest-earned ratio follows:

| | | Greg's Tunes' Times-Interest-Earned Ratio | | Industry |
	Formula	2014	2013	Average
Times-interest-earned ratio =	$\dfrac{\text{EBIT}}{\text{Interest expense}}$	$\dfrac{\$48{,}000 + \$33{,}000 + \$24{,}000}{\$24{,}000} = 4.38$	$\dfrac{\$26{,}000 + \$17{,}000 + \$14{,}000}{\$14{,}000} = 4.07$	7.80

The company's times-interest-earned ratios 4.38 for 2014 and 4.07 for 2013 are significantly lower than the average for the industry of 7.80 times but is slightly better than the average U.S. business. The norm for U.S. business, as reported by the Risk Management Association, falls in the range of 2.0 to 3.0. When you consider Greg's debt ratio and its times-interest-earned ratio, Greg's Tunes appears to have little difficulty *servicing its debt*, that is, paying liabilities.

Evaluating Profitability

The fundamental goal of business is to earn a profit. Ratios that measure profitability often are reported in the business press. Let's examine five profitability measures.

Rate of Return on Net Sales

In business, the term *return* is used broadly as a measure of profitability. Consider a ratio called the **rate of return on net sales**, or simply **return on sales**. (The word *net* is usually omitted for convenience, even though net sales is used to compute the ratio.) **The rate of return on net sales ratio shows the percentage of each net sales dollar earned as net income.** Greg's Tunes' rate of return on sales follows:

	Formula	Greg's Tunes' Rate of Return on Net Sales		Industry Average
		2014	**2013**	
Rate of return on net sales	$= \dfrac{\text{Net income}}{\text{Net sales}}$	$\dfrac{\$48,000}{\$858,000} = 0.056\ (5.6\%)$	$\dfrac{\$26,000}{\$803,000} = 0.032\ (3.2\%)$	0.017 (1.7%)

Both net income and net sales amounts are from the income statement presented in Exhibit 15-8. Companies strive for a high rate of return on net sales. The higher the rate of return, the more sales dollars end up as profit. The increase in Greg's rate of return on net sales from 2013 to 2014 is significant and identifies the company as more successful than the average CD sales and music service provider, whose rate of return on net sales is 1.7%.

Rate of Return on Total Assets

The *rate of return on total assets*, or simply *return on assets*, measures a company's success in using assets to earn a profit. Two groups finance a company's assets:

- Creditors have loaned money to the company, and they earn interest.
- Shareholders have invested in stock, and their return is net income.

The sum of interest expense and net income divided by average total assets is the return to the two groups that have financed the company's assets. Computation of the rate of return on total assets ratio for Greg's Tunes follows:

	Formula	Greg's Tunes' 2014 Rate of Return on Total Assets	Industry Average
Rate of return on total assets	$= \dfrac{\text{Net income} + \text{Interest expense}}{\text{Average total assets}}$	$\dfrac{\$48,000 + \$24,000}{\$715,500} = 0.101\ (10.1\%)$	0.060 (6.0%)

Net income and interest expense come from the income statement (Exhibit 15-8). Average total assets is figured by adding the beginning Total assets of $644,000 to the ending Total assets of $787,000 and dividing by 2. (See the balance sheet, Exhibit 15-8.) Greg's Tunes' rate of return on total assets ratio of 10.1% is much better than the industry average of 6.0%.

Connect To: Ethics

Ratios are carefully watched by lenders, investors, and analysts. Recall that we classify assets and liabilities as current if they will be used/settled within one year or the operating cycle, whichever is longer. The classification between current and long-term is clear, and, as you have seen, it affects many ratios. A company on the border of exceeding debt ratio levels stated in its loan agreements must carefully watch these classifications, as well as the timing of decisions it makes, in order to legally protect its status with the lender.

Asset Turnover Ratio

The **asset turnover ratio** measures the amount of net sales generated for each average dollar of total assets invested. This ratio measures how well a company is using its assets to generate sales revenues. To compute this ratio, we divide net sales by average total assets. Greg's Tunes' 2014 asset turnover ratio is as follows:

Formula	Greg's Tunes' 2014 Asset Turnover Ratio	Industry Average
Asset turnover ratio $= \dfrac{\text{Net sales}}{\text{Average total assets}}$	$\dfrac{\$858,000}{\$715,500} = 1.20$ times	3.52 times

Greg's asset turnover ratio of 1.20 is much lower than the industry average of 3.52 times. Recall that Greg's gross profit percentage was lower than the industry's also. Normally, companies with high gross profit percentages will have low asset turnover. Companies with low gross profit percentages will have high asset turnover ratios. This is another area where Greg's management must consider options to increase sales and decrease its average total assets to improve this ratio.

Rate of Return on Common Stockholders' Equity

A popular measure of profitability is *rate of return on common stockholders' equity*, often shortened to *return on equity*. This ratio shows the relationship between net income and common stockholders' equity. **The rate of return on common stockholders' equity shows how much income is earned for each $1 invested by the common shareholders.**

To compute this ratio, we first subtract preferred dividends from net income to get net income available to the common stockholders. (Greg's does not have any preferred stocks issued, so preferred dividends are zero.) Then we divide net income available to common stockholders by average common stockholders' equity during the year. Common equity is total stockholders' equity minus preferred equity. Average common stockholders' equity is the average of the beginning and ending common stockholders' equity balances [($356,000 + $320,000)/2 or $338,000].

The 2014 rate of return on common stockholders' equity for Greg's Tunes follows:

Formula	Greg's Tunes' 2014 Rate of Return on Common Stockholders' Equity	Industry Average
Rate of return on common stockholders' equity $= \dfrac{\text{Net income} - \text{Preferred dividends}}{\text{Average common stockholders' equity}}$	$\dfrac{\$48,000 - \$0}{\$338,000} = 0.142\ (14.2\%)$	$0.105\ (10.5\%)$

Greg's rate of return on common stockholders' equity of 14.2% is higher than its rate of return on total assets of 10.1%. This difference results from borrowing at one rate—say, 8%—and investing the money to earn a higher rate, such as the firm's 14.2% return on equity. This practice is called **trading on the equity,** or using *leverage*. It is directly related to the debt ratio. The higher the debt ratio, the higher the leverage. Companies that finance operations with debt are said to *leverage* their positions.

During good times, leverage increases profitability. But, leverage can have a negative impact on profitability as well. Therefore, leverage is a double-edged sword, increasing profits during good times but compounding losses during bad times. Compare Greg's Tunes' rate of return on common stockholders' equity with the industry average of 10.5%. Once again, Greg's Tunes is performing much better than the average company in its industry. A rate of return on common stockholders' equity of 15%–20% year after year is considered good in most industries. At 14.2%, Greg's is doing well.

Earnings per Share of Common Stock

Earnings per share of common stock, or simply *earnings per share (EPS)*, is perhaps the most widely quoted of all financial statistics. EPS is the only ratio that must appear on the face of the income statement. EPS is the amount of net income earned for each share of the company's outstanding *common* stock. Recall that

> Outstanding stock = Issued stock − Treasury stock

Earnings per share is computed by dividing net income available to common stockholders by the number of common shares outstanding during the year. Preferred dividends are subtracted from net income because the preferred stockholders have the first claim to dividends. Greg's Tunes has no preferred stock outstanding and, therefore, paid no preferred dividends.

The firm's EPS for 2014 and 2013 follow. (Note that Greg's had 10,000 shares of common stock outstanding throughout both years.)

		Greg's Tunes' Earnings per Share		Industry
	Formula	2014	2013	Average
Earnings per share of common stock	$= \dfrac{\text{Net income} - \text{Preferred dividends}}{\text{Number of shares of common stock outstanding}}$	$\dfrac{\$48,000 - \$0}{10,000} = \$4.80$	$\dfrac{\$26,000 - \$0}{10,000} = \$2.60$	$9.76

Greg's Tunes' EPS increased significantly in 2014 (by almost 85%). Its stockholders should not expect this big a boost in EPS every year. Most companies strive to increase EPS by 10%–15% annually, and leading companies do so. But even the most successful companies have an occasional bad year. EPS for the industry at $9.76 is a little over twice Greg's Tunes' 2014 EPS. Therefore, Greg's Tunes needs to work on continuing to increase EPS so that it is more competitive with other companies in its industry.

Evaluating Stock Investments

Investors purchase stock to earn a return on their investment. This return consists of two parts: (1) gains (or losses) from selling the stock at a price above (or below) purchase price and (2) dividends. The ratios we examine in this section help analysts evaluate stock investments.

Price/Earnings Ratio

The **price/earnings ratio** is the ratio of the market price of a share of common stock to the company's earnings per share. **The price/earnings ratio shows the market price of $1 of earnings.** This ratio, abbreviated P/E, appears in the *Wall Street Journal* stock listings.

Calculations for the P/E ratios of Greg's Tunes follow. The market price of its common stock was $60 at the end of 2014 and $35 at the end of 2013. These prices for real companies can be obtained from a financial publication, a stockbroker, or the company's Web site.

Formula	Greg's Tunes' Price/Earnings Ratio		Industry Average
	2014	2013	
P/E ratio = $\dfrac{\text{Market price per share of common stock}}{\text{Earnings per share}}$	$\dfrac{\$60.00}{\$4.80} = 12.50$	$\dfrac{\$35.00}{\$2.60} = 13.46$	17.79

The market price for Greg's common stock was stated in the previous paragraph. The earnings per share values were calculated immediately before the P/E ratio. Greg's P/E ratio for 2014 of 12.50 means that the company's stock is selling at 12.5 times one year's earnings. Net income is more controllable, and net income increased during 2014. Greg's would like to see this ratio increase in future years in order to be more in line with the industry average P/E of 17.79.

Dividend Yield

Dividend yield is the ratio of annual dividends per share to the stock's market price per share. This ratio measures the percentage of a stock's market value that is returned annually as dividends to shareholders. *Preferred* stockholders, who invest primarily to receive dividends, pay special attention to dividend yield.

Greg's paid annual cash dividends of $1.20 per share of common stock in 2014 and $1.00 in 2013. As noted previously, market prices of the company's common stock were $60 in 2014 and $35 in 2013. The firm's dividend yields on common stock follow:

Formula	Dividend Yield on Greg's Tunes' Common Stock		Industry Average
	2014	2013	
Dividend yield on common stock* = $\dfrac{\text{Annual dividends per share of common stock}}{\text{Market price per share of common stock}}$	$\dfrac{\$1.20}{\$60.00} = 0.020 \ (2\%)$	$\dfrac{\$1.00}{\$35.00} = 0.029 \ (2.9\%)$	0.036 (3.6%)

*Dividend yields may also be calculated for preferred stock.

Both the annual dividends and the market price for this calculation were given in the previous paragraph. An investor who buys Greg's Tunes' common stock for $60 can expect to receive 2% of the investment annually in the form of cash dividends. The industry, however, is paying out 3.6% annually. An investor might be willing to accept lower dividends (cash now) if the stock's market price is growing (cash later when the stock is sold).

Dividend Payout

Dividend payout is the ratio of annual dividends declared per common share relative to the earnings per share of the company. This ratio measures the percentage of earnings paid annually to common shareholders as cash dividends. Recall that Greg's paid annual cash dividends of $1.20 per share of common stock in 2014 and $1.00 in 2013. Earnings per share were calculated on the previous page as $4.80 per share for 2014 and $2.60 for 2013. So, Greg's dividend payout yields are as follows:

| | | Greg's Tunes' Dividend Payout on Common Stock | | Industry |
	Formula	2014	2013	Average
Dividend Payout =	$\dfrac{\text{Annual dividends per share}}{\text{Earnings per share}}$	$\dfrac{\$1.20}{\$4.80} = 0.25$ or 25%	$\dfrac{\$1.00}{\$2.60} = 0.38$ or 38%	0.63 or 63%

Greg's Tunes' dividend payout ratio of 25% in 2014 and 38% in 2013 is less than the industry average of 63%. Greg's, being a fairly new company, might be retaining more of its earnings for growth and expansion. An investor who buys Greg's Tunes' common stock may predict annual cash dividends to be about 25% of earnings, based on the 2014 dividend payout ratio. This investor would want to see higher market prices and higher asset turnover for Greg's Tunes' in the future for Greg's to stay competitive.

Book Value per Share of Common Stock

Book value per share of common stock is common equity divided by the number of common shares outstanding. Common equity equals total stockholders' equity less preferred equity. Greg's has no preferred stock outstanding. Its book value per share of common stock ratios follow. (Note that 10,000 shares of common stock were outstanding.)

| | | Greg's Tunes' Book Value per Share of Common Stock | |
	Formula	2014	2013
Book value per share of common stock =	$\dfrac{\text{Total stockholders' equity} - \text{Preferred equity}}{\text{Number of shares of common stock outstanding}}$	$\dfrac{\$356,000 - \$0}{10,000} = \$35.60$	$\dfrac{\$320,000 - \$0}{10,000} = \$32.00$

The industry averages are not presented for book value per share of common stock as many experts argue that book value is not useful for investment analysis. It bears no relationship to market value and provides little information beyond stockholders' equity reported on the balance sheet. But some investors base their investment decisions on book value. For example, some investors rank stocks on the basis of the ratio of market price to book value. To these investors, the lower the ratio, the more attractive the stock.

Red Flags in Financial Statement Analyses

Analysts look for *red flags* in financial statements that may signal financial trouble. Recent accounting scandals highlight the importance of these red flags. The following conditions may reveal that the company is too risky.

- **Movement of Sales, Inventory, and Receivables.** Sales, inventory, and receivables generally move together. Increased sales lead to higher receivables and may require more inventory (or higher inventory turnover) to meet demand. Unexpected or inconsistent movements among sales, inventory, and receivables make the financial statements look suspect.
- **Earnings Problems.** Has net income decreased significantly for several years in a row? Did the company report net income in previous years but now is reporting net loss? Most companies cannot survive consecutive losses year after year.
- **Decreased Cash Flow.** Cash flow validates net income. Is cash flow from operations consistently lower than net income? If so, the company is in trouble. Are the sales of plant assets a major source of cash? If so, the company may face a cash shortage.
- **Too Much Debt.** How does the company's debt ratio compare to that of major competitors? If the debt ratio is too high, the company may be unable to pay its debts.
- **Inability to Collect Receivables.** Are days' sales in receivables growing faster than for competitors? If so, a cash shortage may be looming.
- **Buildup of Inventories.** Is inventory turnover too slow? If so, the company may be unable to sell goods, or it may be overstating inventory.

Do any of these red flags apply to either Smart Touch or Greg's Tunes from the analyses we did in the chapter? No, the financial statements of both companies depict strong and growing companies. Will both Smart Touch and Greg's Tunes continue to grow? Time will tell.

The Decision Guidelines on the following page summarize the most widely used ratios.

Decision Guidelines 15-1

USING RATIOS IN FINANCIAL STATEMENT ANALYSIS

Mike and Roberta Robinson want to begin investing for retirement. Their 401(k) retirement plan allows them to choose from six different investments. How will they determine which investments to choose? They use the standard ratios discussed in this chapter.

Ratio	Computation	Information Provided
Evaluating the ability to pay current liabilities:		
1. Current ratio	$\dfrac{\text{Current assets}}{\text{Current liabilities}}$	Measures ability to pay current liabilities with current assets
2. Acid-test (quick) ratio	$\dfrac{\text{Cash} + \text{Short-term investments} + \text{Net current receivables}}{\text{Current liabilities}}$	Shows ability to pay all current liabilities if they came due immediately
Evaluating the ability to sell inventory and collect receivables:		
3. Inventory turnover	$\dfrac{\text{Cost of goods sold}}{\text{Average inventory}}$	Indicates salability of inventory—the number of times a company sells its average level of inventory during a year
4. Days in inventory	$\dfrac{365 \text{ days}}{\text{Inventory turnover ratio}}$	Measures the average number of days inventory is held by the company
5. Gross profit percentage	$\dfrac{\text{Gross profit}}{\text{Net sales}}$	Measures the profitability of each sales dollar above cost of goods sold
6. Accounts receivable turnover	$\dfrac{\text{Net credit sales}}{\text{Average net accounts receivable}}$	Measures ability to collect cash from customers
7. Days' sales in receivables	$\dfrac{365}{\text{Accounts receivable turnover ratio}}$	Shows how many days' sales remain in Accounts receivable—how many days it takes to collect the average level of receivables
Evaluating the ability to pay long-term debt:		
8. Debt ratio	$\dfrac{\text{Total liabilities}}{\text{Total assets}}$	Indicates percentage of assets financed with debt
9. Debt to equity ratio	$\dfrac{\text{Total liabilities}}{\text{Total equity}}$	Indicates ratio of debt financing relative to equity financing

Ratio	Computation	Information Provided
10. Times-interest-earned ratio	$$\frac{\text{EBIT}}{\text{Interest expense}}$$	Measures the number of times EBIT can cover (pay) interest expense

Evaluating profitability:

Ratio	Computation	Information Provided
11. Rate of return on net sales	$$\frac{\text{Net income}}{\text{Net sales}}$$	Shows the percentage of each net sales dollar earned as net income
12. Rate of return on total assets	$$\frac{\text{Net income + Interest expense}}{\text{Average total assets}}$$	Measures how profitably a company uses its assets
13. Asset turnover ratio	$$\frac{\text{Net sales}}{\text{Average total assets}}$$	Measures the amount of net sales generated for each average dollar of total assets invested
14. Rate of return on common stock-holders' equity	$$\frac{\text{Net income} - \text{Preferred dividends}}{\text{Average common stockholders' equity}}$$	Gauges how much income is earned for each dollar invested by the common shareholders
15. Earnings per share of common stock	$$\frac{\text{Net income} - \text{Preferred dividends}}{\text{Number of shares of common stock outstanding}}$$	Gives the amount of net income earned for each share of the company's outstanding common stock

Evaluating stock investments:

Ratio	Computation	Information Provided
16. Price/earnings ratio	$$\frac{\text{Market price per share of common stock}}{\text{Earnings per share}}$$	Indicates the market price of $1 of earnings
17. Dividend yield	$$\frac{\text{Annual dividends per share of common (or preferred) stock}}{\text{Market price per share of common (or preferred) stock}}$$	Measures the percentage of a stock's market value that is returned annually as dividends to stockholders
18. Dividend payout	$$\frac{\text{Annual dividends per share}}{\text{Earnings per share}}$$	Measures the percentage of earnings paid to the common shareholders as cash dividends.
19. Book value per share of common stock	$$\frac{\text{Total stockholders' equity} - \text{Preferred equity}}{\text{Number of shares of common stock outstanding}}$$	Indicates the recorded net equity amount from the balance sheet for each share of common stock outstanding

Summary Problem 15-2

JAVA, INC. Four-Year Selected Financial Data (adapted) Years Ended January 31, 2013–2010				
Operating Results*	**2013**	**2012**	**2011**	**2010**
Net sales	$13,848	$13,673	$11,635	$ 9,054
Cost of goods sold	9,704	8,599	6,775	5,318
Interest expense	109	75	45	46
Income from operations	338	1,455	1,817	1,333
Income tax expense	100	263	338	247
Net income (net loss)	(8)	877	1,127	824
Cash dividends	76	75	76	77
Financial Position				
Merchandise inventory	1,677	1,904	1,462	1,056
Total assets	7,591	7,012	5,189	3,963
Current ratio	1.48:1	0.95:1	1.25:1	1.20:1
Stockholders' equity	3,010	2,928	2,630	1,574
Average number of shares of common stock outstanding (in thousands)	860	879	895	576

*Dollar amounts are in thousands.

Requirement

Using the financial data presented above, compute the following ratios and evaluate Java's results for 2011–2013:

1. Rate of return on net sales
2. Earnings per share
3. Inventory turnover
4. Times-interest-earned ratio
5. Rate of return on common stockholders' equity
6. Gross profit percentage

Solution

	2013	2012	2011
1. Rate of return on net sales	$\dfrac{\$(8)}{\$13,848} = (0.06\%)$	$\dfrac{\$877}{\$13,673} = 6.4\%$	$\dfrac{\$1,127}{\$11,635} = 9.7\%$
2. Earnings per share	$\dfrac{\$(8)}{860} = \$(0.01)$	$\dfrac{\$877}{879} = \$1.00$	$\dfrac{\$1,127}{895} = \$1.26$
3. Inventory turnover	$\dfrac{\$9,704}{(\$1,904 + \$1,677)/2} = 5.4 \text{ times}$	$\dfrac{\$8,599}{(\$1,462 + \$1,904)/2} = 5.1 \text{ times}$	$\dfrac{\$6,775}{(\$1,056 + \$1,462)/2} = 5.4 \text{ times}$
4. Times-interest-earned ratio	$\dfrac{[\$(8) + \$100 + \$109]}{\$109} = 1.8 \text{ times}$	$\dfrac{(\$75 + \$263 + \$75)}{\$75} = 5.5 \text{ times}$	$\dfrac{(\$76 + \$338 + \$45)}{\$45} = 10.2 \text{ times}$
5. Rate of return on common stockholders' equity	$\dfrac{\$(8)}{(\$2,929 + \$3,010)/2} = (0.3\%)$	$\dfrac{\$877}{(\$2,630 + \$2,928)/2} = 31.6\%$	$\dfrac{\$1,127}{(\$1,574 + \$2,630)/2} = 53.6\%$
6. Gross profit percentage	$\dfrac{(\$13,848 - \$9,704)}{\$13,848} = 29.9\%$	$\dfrac{(\$13,673 - \$8,599)}{\$13,673} = 37.1\%$	$\dfrac{(\$11,635 - \$6,775)}{\$11,635} = 41.8\%$

Evaluation: During this period, Java's operating results deteriorated on all these measures except inventory turnover. The times-interest-earned ratio and rate of return on common stockholders' equity percentages are down sharply. From these data, it is clear that Java could sell its coffee, but not at the markups the company enjoyed in the past. The final result, in 2013, was a net loss for the year.

Review *Financial Statement Analysis*

● Accounting Vocabulary

Accounts Receivable Turnover Ratio (p. 736)
Measures a company's ability to collect cash from credit customers. To compute accounts receivable turnover, divide net credit sales by average net accounts receivable.

Asset Turnover Ratio (p. 740)
Ratio that measures the amount of net sales generated for each average dollar of assets invested.

Benchmarking (p. 729)
The practice of comparing a company with other companies that are leaders.

Common-Size Statement (p. 728)
A financial statement that reports only percentages (no dollar amounts).

Days in Inventory Ratio (p. 736)
Ratio that measures the average number of days inventory is held by the company.

Debt to Equity Ratio (p. 738)
Ratio that measures the proportion of total liabilities relative to the proportion of total equity that is financing the company's assets.

Dividend Payout (p. 743)
The ratio of dividends declared per common share relative to the earnings per share of the company.

Dividend Yield (p. 742)
Ratio of annual dividends per share of stock to the stock's market price per share. Measures the percentage of a stock's market value that is returned annually as dividends to stockholders.

Dollar Value Bias (p. 729)
The bias one sees from comparing numbers in absolute (dollars) rather than relative (percentage) terms.

Horizontal Analysis (p. 723)
Study of percentage changes in comparative financial statements.

Interest-Coverage Ratio (p. 738)
Ratio of EBIT to interest expense. Measures the number of times that EBIT can cover (pay) interest expense. Also called the **times-interest-earned ratio**.

Price/Earnings Ratio (p. 741)
Ratio of the market price of a share of common stock to the company's earnings per share. Measures the value that the stock market places on $1 of a company's earnings.

Rate of Return on Net Sales (p. 739)
Ratio of net income to net sales. A measure of profitability. Also called **return on sales**.

Return on Sales (p. 739)
Ratio of net income to net sales. A measure of profitability. Also called **rate of return on net sales**.

Times-Interest-Earned Ratio (p. 738)
Ratio of EBIT to interest expense. Measures the number of times that EBIT can cover (pay) interest expense. Also called the **interest-coverage ratio**.

Trading on the Equity (p. 740)
Earning more income on borrowed money than the related interest expense, thereby increasing the earnings for the owners of the business. Also called *leverage*.

Trend Analysis (p. 726)
A form of horizontal analysis in which percentages are computed by selecting a base year as 100% and expressing amounts for following years as a percentage of the base amount.

Vertical Analysis (p. 727)
Analysis of a financial statement that reveals the relationship of each statement item to its base amount, which is the 100% figure.

Working Capital (p. 733)
Current assets minus current liabilities. Measures a business's ability to meet its short-term obligations with its current assets.

● Destination: Student Success

Student Success Tips

The following are hints on some common trouble areas for students in this chapter:

● Remember the word "horizon" is in horizontal analysis, so it compares percentage changes from year to year (row to row)—work across the comparative statement.

● Recall that vertical analysis translates all financial statement values to percentages, with net sales being 100% on the income statement and total assets being 100% on the balance sheet. All other items are expressed as a percentage of either net sales or total assets.

● Keep in mind that common-size statements are similar to vertical analysis statements except the dollars are removed. Common-size statements allow us to compare companies that operate in the same industry.

● There are many ratios in this chapter. Remember that one ratio can't tell the whole story any more than one financial statement can. Each ratio paints a picture about the company's asset management, liquidity, solvency, or profitability.

Getting Help

If there's a learning objective from the chapter you aren't confident about, try using one or more of the following resources:

● Review Summary Problem 15-1 in the chapter to reinforce your understanding of horizontal and vertical analysis.

● Review Summary Problem 15-2 in the chapter to reinforce your understanding of ratio analysis.

● Practice additional exercises or problems at the end of Chapter 15 that cover the specific learning objective that is challenging you.

● Watch the white board videos for Chapter 15 located at myaccountinglab.com under the Chapter Resources button.

● Go to myaccountinglab.com and select the Study Plan button. Choose Chapter 15 and work the questions covering that specific learning objective until you've mastered it.

● Work the Chapter 15 pre/post tests in myaccountinglab.com.

● Visit the learning resource center on your campus for tutoring.

• Quick Check

Liberty Corporation reported the following figures:

Account	2012	2011
Cash and cash equivalents	$ 2,450	$ 2,094
Receivables	1,813	1,611
Inventory	1,324	1,060
Prepaid expenses	1,709	2,120
Total current assets	$ 7,296	$ 6,885
Other assets	18,500	15,737
Total assets	$ 25,796	$ 22,622
Total current liabilities	$ 7,230	$ 8,467
Long-term liabilities	4,798	3,792
Common stock	6,568	4,363
Retained earnings	7,200	6,000
Total liabilities and equity	$ 25,796	$ 22,622

Sales	$ 20,941
Cost of sales	7,055
Operating expenses	7,065
Operating income	$ 6,821
Interest expense	210
Income tax expense	2,563
Net income	$ 4,048

1. Horizontal analysis of Liberty's balance sheet for 2012 would report
   a. Cash as 9.50% of total assets.
   b. 17% increase in Cash.
   c. Current ratio of 1.01.
   d. Inventory turnover of 6 times.

2. Vertical analysis of Liberty's balance sheet for 2012 would report
   a. Cash as 9.50% of total assets.
   b. Inventory turnover of 6 times.
   c. Current ratio of 1.01.
   d. 17% increase in Cash.

3. A common-size income statement for Liberty would report (amounts rounded)
   a. Net income of 19%.
   b. Sales of 100%.
   c. Cost of sales at 34%.
   d. All of the above

4. Which statement best describes Liberty's acid-test ratio?
   a. Greater than 1
   b. Equal to 1
   c. Less than 1
   d. None of the above

5. Liberty's inventory turnover during 2012 was (amounts rounded)

   a. 6 times.

   b. 7 times.

   c. 8 times.

   d. Not determinable from the data given.

6. During 2012, Liberty's days' sales in receivables ratio was (amounts rounded)

   a. 34 days.

   b. 30 days.

   c. 32 days.

   d. 28 days.

7. Which measure expresses Liberty's times-interest-earned ratio? (amounts rounded)

   a. 54.7%

   b. 19 times

   c. 34 times

   d. 32 times

8. Liberty's rate of return on common stockholders' equity can be described as

   a. weak.

   b. normal.

   c. strong.

   d. average.

9. The company has 2,500 shares of common stock outstanding. What is Liberty's earnings per share?

   a. $1.62

   b. $1.75

   c. $2.73

   d. 2.63 times

10. Liberty's stock has traded recently around $48 per share. Use your answer to question 9 to measure the company's price/earnings ratio. (Round to the nearest whole number.)

   a. 1.01

   b. 30

   c. 48

   d. 78

Answers are given after Apply Your Knowledge (p. 771).

Assess Your Progress

• Short Exercises

S15-1 **❶ Horizontal analysis [5–10 min]**

McCormick, Corp., reported the following on its comparative income statement:

MyAccountingLab

(In millions)	2012	2011	2010
Revenue	$9,575	$9,300	$8,975
Cost of sales	6,000	5,975	5,900

Requirement

1. Prepare a horizontal analysis of revenues and gross profit—both in dollar amounts and in percentages—for 2012 and 2011.

S15-2 **①** **Trend analysis [5–10 min]**

Mariner, Corp., reported the following revenues and net income amounts:

(In millions)	2013	2012	2011	2010
Revenue	$9,910	$9,700	$9,210	$9,110
Net income.........................	7,475	7,400	5,495	4,690

Requirements

1. Calculate Mariner's trend analysis for revenues and net income. Use 2010 as the base year, and round to the nearest percent.
2. Which measure increased faster during 2011–2013?

S15-3 **②** **Vertical analysis [10–15 min]**

Tri-State Optical Company reported the following amounts on its balance sheet at December 31, 2012 and 2011:

	2012	2011
Cash and receivables	$ 54,530	$ 46,860
Inventory	42,435	32,670
Property, plant, and equipment, net	108,035	85,470
Total assets	$ 205,000	$ 165,000

Requirement

1. Prepare a vertical analysis of Tri-State assets for 2012 and 2011.

S15-4 **③** **Common-size income statement [10 min]**

Data for Martinez, Inc., and Rosado, Corp., follow:

	Martinez	Rosado
Net sales	$ 10,600	$ 18,600
Cost of goods sold	6,455	13,522
Other expenses	3,541	4,185
Net income	$ 604	$ 893

Requirements

1. Prepare common-size income statements.
2. Which company earns more net income?
3. Which company's net income is a higher percentage of its net sales?

S15-5 **④** **Evaluating current ratio [5–10 min]**

Win's Companies, a home improvement store chain, reported the following summarized figures:

WIN'S COMPANIES		
Income Statement		
Years Ended May 31, 2012 and 2011		
	2012	2011
Net sales	$ 50,200,000	$ 43,800,000
Cost of goods sold	28,400,000	29,300,000
Interest expense	500,000	140,000
All other expenses	5,800,000	8,400,000
Net income	$ 15,500,000	$ 5,960,000

Assets	2012	2011	Liabilities	2012	2011
		WIN'S COMPANIES			
		Balance Sheet			
		May 31, 2012 and 2011			
Cash	$ 2,000,000	$ 900,000	Total current liabilities	$ 33,000,000	$ 13,100,000
Short-term investments	28,000,000	9,000,000	Long-term liabilities	12,300,000	10,600,000
Accounts receivable	7,400,000	5,300,000	Total liabilities	$ 45,300,000	$ 23,700,000
Inventory	6,900,000	8,200,000	**Stockholders' Equity**		
Other current assets	10,000,000	1,800,000	Common stock	$ 11,000,000	$ 11,000,000
Total current assets	$ 54,300,000	$ 25,200,000	Retained earnings	32,000,000	16,500,000
All other assets	34,000,000	26,000,000	Total equity	$ 43,000,000	$ 27,500,000
Total assets	$ 88,300,000	$ 51,200,000	Total liabilities and equity	$ 88,300,000	$ 51,200,000

Requirements

1. Compute Win's Companies' current ratio at May 31, 2012 and 2011.
2. Did Win's Companies' current ratio improve, deteriorate, or hold steady during 2012?

S15-6 ❹ **Computing inventory, gross profit, and receivables ratios [10–15 min]**
Use the Win's Companies data in Short Exercise 15-5 to complete the following requirements.

Requirements

1. Compute the rate of inventory turnover, days in inventory, and gross profit percentage for 2012.
2. Compute days' sales in average receivables during 2012. Round dollar amounts to three decimal places.

S15-7 ❹ **Measuring ability to pay liabilities [5 min]**
Use the financial statements of Win's Companies in Short Exercise 15-5.

Requirements

1. Compute the debt ratio and the debt to equity ratio at May 31, 2012.
2. Is Win's ability to pay its liabilities strong or weak? Explain your reasoning.

S15-8 ❹ **Measuring profitability [10 min]**
Use the financial statements of Win's Companies in Short Exercise 15-5 to complete the following profitability measures for 2012.

Requirements

1. Compute the rate of return on net sales.
2. Compute the rate of return on total assets.
3. Compute the asset turnover ratio.
4. Compute the rate of return on common stockholders' equity.
5. Are these rates of return strong or weak? Explain your reasoning.

S15-9 ④ **Computing EPS and P/E ratio [5–10 min]**

Use the financial statements of Win's Companies in Short Exercise 15-5. Win's has 500,000 common shares outstanding during 2012.

Requirements

1. Compute earnings per share (EPS) for Win's. Round to the nearest cent.
2. Compute Win's Companies' price/earnings ratio. The market price per share of Win's stock is $68.50.

S15-10 ④ **Using ratios to reconstruct an income statement [10 min]**

A skeleton of Landmark Mills' income statement appears as follows (amounts in thousands):

Income Statement	
Net sales	$ 7,200
Cost of goods sold	(a)
Selling and admin expenses	1,830
Interest expense	(b)
Other expenses	150
Income before taxes	$ 1,325
Income tax expense	(c)
Net income	(d)

Requirement

1. Use the following ratio data to complete Landmark Mills' income statement:
   a. Inventory turnover was 3.50 (beginning inventory was $850; ending inventory was $810).
   b. Rate of return on net sales is 0.11.

S15-11 ④ **Using ratios to reconstruct a balance sheet [15–20 min]**

A skeleton of Vintage Mills' balance sheet appears as follows (amounts in thousands):

Balance Sheet				
Cash	$ 75	Total current liabilities	$ 1,900	
Receivables	(a)	Long-term note payable	(e)	
Inventories	725	Other long-term		
Prepaid expenses	(b)	liabilities	980	
Total current assets . .	$ (c)	Stockholder's equity	2,325	
Plant assets, net	(d)			
Other assets	2,000	Total liabilities and		
Total assets	$ 6,800	stockholders' equity	$ (f)	

Requirement

1. Use the following ratio data to complete Vintage Mills' balance sheet.
   a. Current ratio is 0.80.
   b. Acid-test ratio is 0.40.

• Exercises

E15-12 ❶ **Computing working capital changes [5–15 min]**

Data for Beverage Enterprises follows:

	2012	2011	2010
Total current assets	$510,000	$ 350,000	$240,000
Total current liabilities	245,000	175,000	120,000

Requirement

1. Compute the dollar amount of change and the percentage of change in Beverage Enterprises' working capital each year during 2011 and 2012. What do the calculated changes indicate?

E15-13 ❶ **Horizontal analysis—income statement [10–15 min]**

Data for Mariner Designs, Inc., follow:

MARINER DESIGNS, INC. Comparative Income Statement Years Ended December 31, 2012 and 2011		
	2012	**2011**
Net sales revenue	$ 431,000	$ 372,350
Expenses:		
Cost of goods sold	$ 200,000	$ 187,550
Selling and general expenses	99,000	91,050
Other expense	8,350	6,850
Total expenses	$ 307,350	$ 285,450
Net income	$ 123,650	$ 86,900

Requirements

1. Prepare a horizontal analysis of the comparative income statement of Mariner Designs, Inc. Round percentage changes to one decimal place.
2. Why did 2012 net income increase by a higher percentage than net sales revenue?

E15-14 ❶ **Computing trend analysis [5–10 min]**

Magic Oaks Realty's net revenue and net income for the following five-year period, using 2010 as the base year, follow:

	2014	2013	2012	2011	2010
Net revenue	$1,310,000	$1,187,000	$1,110,000	$1,011,000	$1,045,000
Net income	122,000	113,000	84,000	72,000	83,000

Requirements

1. Compute trend analysis for net revenue and net income. Round to the nearest full percent.
2. Which grew faster during the period, net revenue or net income?

E15-15 ❷ **Vertical analysis of a balance sheet [10–15 min]**
Beta Graphics, Inc., has the following data:

BETA GRAPHICS, INC. Comparative Balance Sheet December 31, 2012 and 2011		
	2012	**2011**
Assets		
Total current assets	$ 42,750	$ 59,000
Property, plant, and equipment, net	208,335	215,000
Other assets	33,915	35,500
Total assets	$ 285,000	$ 309,500
Liabilities		
Total current liabilities	$ 49,020	$ 50,100
Long-term debt	109,155	102,300
Total liabilities	$ 158,175	$ 152,400
Stockholders' Equity		
Total stockholders' equity	126,825	157,100
Total liabilities and stockholders' equity	$ 285,000	$ 309,500

Requirement

1. Perform a vertical analysis of Beta's balance sheet for each year.

E15-16 ❸ **Preparing common-size income statements [10–15 min]**
Consider the data presented in Exercise 15-13.

Requirements

1. Prepare a comparative common-size income statement for Mariner Designs, Inc., using the 2012 and 2011 data. Round percentages to one-tenth percent (three decimal places).

2. To an investor, how does 2012 compare with 2011? Explain your reasoning.

E15-17 ❹ **Computing six key ratios [10–15 min]**
The financial statements of Victor's Natural Foods include the following items:

	Current Year	Preceding Year
Balance sheet:		
Cash	$ 15,000	$ 20,000
Short-term investments	11,000	27,000
Net receivables	54,000	73,000
Inventory	77,000	69,000
Prepaid expenses	15,000	9,000
Total current assets	$ 172,000	$ 198,000
Total current liabilities	$ 133,000	$ 93,000
Income statement:		
Net credit sales	$ 462,000	
Cost of goods sold	315,000	

Requirement

1. Compute the following ratios for the current year:

   a. Current ratio
   b. Acid-test ratio
   c. Inventory turnover
   d. Days in inventory
   e. Days' sales in receivables
   f. Gross profit percentage

E15-18 ❹ **Analyzing the ability to pay liabilities [15–20 min]**
Large Land Photo Shop has asked you to determine whether the company's ability to pay current liabilities and total liabilities improved or deteriorated during 2012. To answer this question, you gather the following data:

	2012	2011
Cash	$ 58,000	$ 57,000
Short-term investments	31,000	—
Net receivables	110,000	132,000
Inventory	247,000	297,000
Total assets	585,000	535,000
Total current liabilities	255,000	222,000
Long-term note payable	46,000	48,000
Income from operations	180,000	153,000
Interest expense	52,000	39,000

Requirement

1. Compute the following ratios for 2012 and 2011:

   a. Current ratio
   b. Acid-test ratio
   c. Debt ratio
   d. Debt to equity ratio

E15-19 ❹ **Analyzing profitability [10–15 min]**
The CJ, Inc., comparative income statement follows. The 2010 data are given as needed.

CJ, INC.			
Comparative Income Statement			
Years Ended December 31, 2012 and 2011			
(Dollars in thousands)	2012	2011	2010
Net sales	$176,000	$160,000	
Cost of goods sold	93,400	86,500	
Selling and general expenses	46,000	41,000	
Interest expense	9,000	10,300	
Income tax expense	10,200	9,600	
Net income	$ 17,400	$ 12,600	
Additional data:			
Total assets	$203,000	$190,000	$175,000
Common stockholders' equity	$ 96,600	$ 90,100	$ 79,400
Preferred dividends	$ 3,500	$ 3,500	$ 0
Common shares outstanding during the year	20,500	20,500	18,000

Requirements

1. Calculate the rate of return on net sales.
2. Calculate the rate of return on total assets.
3. Calculate the asset turnover ratio.
4. Calculate the rate of return on common stockholders' equity.
5. Calculate the EPS.
6. Calculate the 2012 dividend payout on common stock.
7. Did the company's operating performance improve or deteriorate during 2012?

E15-20 ❹ **Evaluating a stock as an investment [10–15 min]**
Data for Shamrock State Bank follows:

	2012	2011
Net income	$ 61,000	$ 52,000
Dividends—common	26,000	26,000
Dividends—preferred	12,600	12,600
Total stockholders' equity at year-end		
(includes 80,000 shares of common stock)	760,000	610,000
Preferred stock, 6%	210,000	210,000
Market price per share of common stock	$ 19.50	$ 14

Requirement

1. Evaluate the common stock of Shamrock State Bank as an investment. Specifically, use the four stock ratios to determine whether the common stock has increased or decreased in attractiveness during the past year.

E15-21 ❹ **Using ratios to reconstruct a balance sheet [20–30 min]**
The following data are adapted from the financial statements of Betty's Shops, Inc.:

Total current assets	$ 1,200,000
Accumulated depreciation	$ 2,400,000
Total liabilities	$ 1,400,000
Preferred stock	$ 0
Debt ratio	64%
Current ratio	1.50

Requirement

1. Complete Betty's condensed balance sheet.

Current assets		☐
Property, plant, and equipment	☐	
Less: Accumulated depreciation	☐	☐
Total assets		☐
Current liabilities		☐
Long-term liabilities		☐
Stockholders' equity		☐
Total liabilities and stockholders' equity		☐

● Problems (Group A)

P15-22A ❶ Trend analysis and return on common equity [20–30 min]

MyAccountingLab

Net sales revenue, net income, and common stockholders' equity for Azbel Mission Corporation, a manufacturer of contact lenses, follow for a four-year period.

	2013	2012	2011	2010
Net sales revenue	$ 762,000	$ 706,000	$ 637,000	$ 665,000
Net income	58,000	44,000	37,000	43,000
Ending common stockholders' equity ...	376,000	358,000	330,000	304,000

Requirements

1. Compute trend analyses for each item for 2011–2013. Use 2010 as the base year, and round to the nearest whole percent.
2. Compute the rate of return on common stockholders' equity for 2011–2013, rounding to three decimal places.

P15-23A ❷ Vertical analysis [20–30 min]

The McConnell Department Stores, Inc., chief executive officer (CEO) has asked you to compare the company's profit performance and financial position with the average for the industry. The CEO has given you the company's income statement and balance sheet, as well as the industry average data for retailers.

MCCONNELL DEPARTMENT STORES, INC.		
Income Statement Compared with Industry Average		
Year Ended December 31, 2012		
	McConnell	Industry Average
Net sales	$ 778,000	100.0%
Cost of goods sold	522,816	65.8
Gross profit	$ 255,184	34.2
Operating expenses	161,046	19.7
Operating income	$ 94,138	14.5
Other expenses	4,668	0.4
Net income	$ 89,470	14.1%

MCCONNELL DEPARTMENT STORES, INC. Balance Sheet Compared with Industry Average December 31, 2012	McConnell	Industry Average
Current assets	$ 325,440	70.9%
Fixed assets, net	120,960	23.6
Intangible assets, net	8,640	0.8
Other assets	24,960	4.7
Total assets	$ 480,000	100.0%
Current liabilities	$ 222,720	48.1%
Long-term liabilities	107,520	16.6
Stockholders' equity	149,760	35.3
Total liabilities and stockholders' equity	$ 480,000	100.0%

Requirement

1. Prepare a vertical analysis for McConnell for both its income statement and balance sheet.

Note: Problem 15-24A should be used only after completing Problem 15-23A.

P15-24A ③ ④ **Common-size statements, analysis of profitability and financial position, comparison with the industry, and using ratios to evaluate a company [20–30 min]**

Consider the data for McConnell Department Stores presented in P15-23A.

Requirements

1. Prepare a common-size income statement and balance sheet for McConnell. The first column of each statement should present McConnell's common-size statement, and the second column, the industry averages.
2. For the profitability analysis, compute McConnell's (a) gross profit percentage and (b) rate of return on net sales. Compare these figures with the industry averages. Is McConnell's profit performance better or worse than the industry average?
3. For the analysis of financial position, compute McConnell's (a) current ratio and (b) debt to equity ratio. Compare these ratios with the industry averages. Is McConnell's financial position better or worse than the industry averages?

P15-25A ④ **Effects of business transactions on selected ratios [30–40 min]**

Financial statement data of *American Traveler Magazine* include the following items:

Cash	$ 23,000
Accounts receivable, net	79,000
Inventories	184,000
Total assets	634,000
Accounts payable	104,000
Accrued liabilities	40,000
Short-term notes payable	47,000
Long-term liabilities	221,000
Net income	74,000
Common shares outstanding	60,000

Requirements

1. Compute *American Traveler*'s current ratio, debt ratio, and earnings per share. Round all ratios to two decimal places, and use the following format for your answer:

Current Ratio	Debt Ratio	Earnings per Share

2. Compute the three ratios after evaluating the effect of each transaction that follows. Consider each transaction *separately*.

    a. Purchased inventory of $49,000 on account.

    b. Borrowed $122,000 on a long-term note payable.

    c. Issued 6,000 shares of common stock, receiving cash of $103,000.

    d. Received cash on account, $3,000.

P15-26A ❹ **Using ratios to evaluate a stock investment [40–50 min]**
Comparative financial statement data of Danfield, Inc., follow:

DANFIELD, INC.		
Comparative Income Statement		
Years Ended December 31, 2012 and 2011		
	2012	**2011**
Net sales	$ 467,000	$ 428,000
Cost of goods sold	237,000	218,000
Gross profit	$ 230,000	$ 210,000
Operating expenses	136,000	134,000
Income from operations	$ 94,000	$ 76,000
Interest expense	9,000	10,000
Income before income tax	$ 85,000	$ 66,000
Income tax expense	24,000	27,000
Net income	$ 61,000	$ 39,000

	DANFIELD, INC. Comparative Balance Sheet December 31, 2012 and 2011		
	2012	**2011**	**2010***
Current assets:			
Cash	$ 97,000	$ 95,000	
Current receivables, net	112,000	118,000	$ 102,000
Inventories	145,000	163,000	203,000
Prepaid expenses	12,000	5,000	
Total current assets	$ 366,000	$ 381,000	
Property, plant, and equipment, net	211,000	179,000	
Total assets	$ 577,000	$ 560,000	598,000
Total current liabilities	$ 225,000	$ 246,000	
Long-term liabilities	114,000	97,000	
Total liabilities	$ 339,000	$ 343,000	
Preferred stock, 3%	108,000	108,000	
Common stockholders' equity, no par	130,000	109,000	85,000
Total liabilities and stockholders' equity	$ 577,000	$ 560,000	

* Selected 2010 amounts

1. Market price of Danfield's common stock: $86.58 at December 31, 2012, and $46.54 at December 31, 2011.

2. Common shares outstanding: 12,000 during 2012 and 10,000 during 2011 and 2010.

3. All sales on credit.

Requirements

1. Compute the following ratios for 2012 and 2011:

    a. Current ratio
    b. Times-interest-earned ratio
    c. Inventory turnover
    d. Gross profit percentage
    e. Debt to equity ratio
    f. Rate of return on common stockholders' equity
    g. Earnings per share of common stock
    h. Price/earnings ratio

2. Decide (a) whether Danfield's ability to pay debts and to sell inventory improved or deteriorated during 2012 and (b) whether the investment attractiveness of its common stock appears to have increased or decreased.

P15-27A ❹ **Using ratios to decide between two stock investments [45–60 min]**

Assume that you are purchasing an investment and have decided to invest in a company in the digital phone business. You have narrowed the choice to Digitalized, Corp., and Zone Network, Inc., and have assembled the following data:

Selected income statement data for the current year:

	Digitalized	Zone Network
Net sales (all on credit) . . . . $	423,035 $	493,115
Cost of goods sold	206,000	258,000
Interest expense	——	19,000
Net income	54,000	66,000

Selected balance sheet and market price data at the *end* of the current year:

	Digitalized	Zone Network
Current assets:		
Cash . . . . $	23,000 $	21,000
Short-term investments	38,000	19,000
Current receivables, net	38,000	43,000
Inventories	64,000	96,000
Prepaid expenses	21,000	13,000
Total current assets . . . . $	184,000 $	192,000
Total assets . . . . $	266,000 $	326,000
Total current liabilities	102,000	96,000
Total liabilities	102,000	131,000
Common stock, $1 par (12,000 shares)	12,000	
$2 par (16,000 shares)		32,000
Total stockholders' equity . . . . $	164,000 $	195,000
Market price per share of common stock . . $	76.50 $	94.99
Dividends paid per common share . . . . . . $	0.50 $	0.40

Selected balance sheet data at the *beginning* of the current year:

	Digitalized	Zone Network
Balance sheet:		
Current receivables, net . . . . $	44,000 $	53,000
Inventories	80,000	86,000
Total assets	262,000	276,000
Common stock, $1 par (12,000 shares)	12,000	
$2 par (16,000 shares)		32,000

Your strategy is to invest in companies that have low price/earnings ratios but appear to be in good shape financially. Assume that you have analyzed all other factors and that your decision depends on the results of ratio analysis.

Requirement

1. Compute the following ratios for both companies for the current year, and decide which company's stock better fits your investment strategy.

   a. Acid-test ratio
   b. Inventory turnover
   c. Days' sales in receivables
   d. Debt ratio
   e. Earnings per share of common stock
   f. Price/earnings ratio
   g. Dividend payout

● Problems (Group B)

MyAccountingLab

P15-28B ① Trend analyses and return on common equity [20–30 min]

Net sales revenue, net income, and common stockholders' equity for Shawnee Mission Corporation, a manufacturer of contact lenses, follow for a four-year period.

	2013	2012	2011	2010
Net sales revenue	$ 759,000	$ 701,000	$ 639,000	$ 659,000
Net income	56,000	43,000	38,000	48,000
Ending common stockholders' equity ...	364,000	356,000	328,000	300,000

Requirements

1. Compute trend analyses for each item for 2011–2013. Use 2010 as the base year, and round to the nearest whole percent.
2. Compute the rate of return on common stockholders' equity for 2011–2013, rounding to three decimal places.

P15-29B ② Vertical analysis [20–30 min]

The Specialty Department Stores, Inc., chief executive officer (CEO) has asked you to compare the company's profit performance and financial position with the average for the industry. The CEO has given you the company's income statement and balance sheet, as well as the industry average data for retailers.

SPECIALTY DEPARTMENT STORES, INC.		
Income Statement Compared with Industry Average		
Year Ended December 31, 2012		
	Specialty	Industry Average
Net sales	$ 782,000	100.0%
Cost of goods sold	528,632	65.8
Gross profit	$ 253,368	34.2
Operating expenses	163,438	19.7
Operating income	$ 89,930	14.5
Other expenses	4,692	0.4
Net income	$ 85,238	14.1%

SPECIALTY DEPARTMENT STORES, INC. Balance Sheet Compared with Industry Average December 31, 2012		
	Specialty	Industry Average
Current assets	$ 303,750	70.9%
Fixed assets, net	117,000	23.6
Intangible assets, net	5,850	0.8
Other assets	23,400	4.7
Total assets	$ 450,000	100.0%
Current liabilities	$ 208,800	48.1%
Long-term liabilities	102,600	16.6
Stockholders' equity	138,600	35.3
Total liabilities and stockholders' equity	$ 450,000	100.0%

Requirement

1. Prepare a vertical analysis for Specialty for both its income statement and balance sheet.

Note: Problem 15-30B should be used only after completing Problem 15-29B.

P15-30B ③ ④ **Common-size statements, analysis of profitability and financial position, comparison with the industry, and using ratios to evaluate a company [20–30 min]**

Consider the data for Specialty Department Stores presented in P15-29B.

Requirements

1. Prepare a common-size income statement and balance sheet for Specialty. The first column of each statement should present Specialty's common-size statement, and the second column, the industry averages.

2. For the profitability analysis, compute Specialty's (a) gross profit percentage and (b) rate of return on net sales. Compare these figures with the industry averages. Is Specialty's profit performance better or worse than the industry average?

3. For the analysis of financial position, compute Specialty's (a) current ratio and (b) debt to equity. Compare these ratios with the industry averages. Is Specialty's financial position better or worse than the industry averages?

P15-31B ④ **Effects of business transactions on selected ratios [30–40 min]**

Financial statement data of *Road Trip Magazine* include the following items:

Cash	$ 24,000
Accounts receivable, net	82,000
Inventories	188,000
Total assets	638,000
Accounts payable	99,000
Accrued liabilities	39,000
Short-term notes payable	51,000
Long-term liabilities	223,000
Net income	72,000
Common shares outstanding . . .	20,000

Requirements

1. Compute *Road Trip*'s current ratio, debt ratio, and earnings per share. Round all ratios to two decimal places, and use the following format for your answer:

Current Ratio	Debt Ratio	Earnings per Share

2. Compute the three ratios after evaluating the effect of each transaction that follows. Consider each transaction *separately*.

   a. Purchased inventory of $45,000 on account.
   b. Borrowed $127,000 on a long-term note payable.
   c. Issued 2,000 shares of common stock, receiving cash of $105,000.
   d. Received cash on account, $7,000.

P15-32B ④ Using ratios to evaluate a stock investment [40–50 min]

Comparative financial statement data of Tanfield, Inc., follow:

TANFIELD, INC. Comparative Income Statement Years Ended December 31, 2012 and 2011		
	2012	2011
Net sales	$ 460,000	$ 422,000
Cost of goods sold	239,000	212,000
Gross profit	$ 221,000	$ 210,000
Operating expenses	138,000	136,000
Income from operations	$ 83,000	$ 74,000
Interest expense	13,000	16,000
Income before income tax	$ 70,000	$ 58,000
Income tax expense	19,000	21,000
Net income	$ 51,000	$ 37,000

			2012	2011	2010*
Current assets:					
	Cash		$ 91,000	$ 88,000	
	Current receivables, net		113,000	121,000	$ 106,000
	Inventories		144,000	158,000	204,000
	Prepaid expenses		16,000	3,000	
	Total current assets		$ 364,000	$ 370,000	
Property, plant, and equipment, net			217,000	176,000	
Total assets			$ 581,000	$ 546,000	602,000
Total current liabilities			$ 227,000	$ 240,000	
Long-term liabilities			117,000	96,000	
Total liabilities			$ 344,000	$ 336,000	
Preferred stock, 3%			92,000	92,000	
Common stockholders' equity, no par			145,000	118,000	89,000
Total liabilities and stockholders' equity			$ 581,000	$ 546,000	

TANFIELD, INC.
Comparative Balance Sheet
December 31, 2012 and 2011

* Selected 2010 amounts

1. Market price of Tanfield's common stock: $59.36 at December 31, 2012, and $46.65 at December 31, 2011.

2. Common shares outstanding: 13,000 during 2012 and 11,000 during 2011 and 2010.

3. All sales on credit.

Requirements

1. Compute the following ratios for 2012 and 2011:

   a. Current ratio

   b. Times-interest-earned ratio

   c. Inventory turnover

   d. Gross profit percentage

   e. Debt to equity ratio

   f. Rate of return on common stockholders' equity

   g. Earnings per share of common stock

   h. Price/earnings ratio

2. Decide (a) whether Tanfield's ability to pay debts and to sell inventory improved or deteriorated during 2012 and (b) whether the investment attractiveness of its common stock appears to have increased or decreased.

P15-33B ❹ **Using ratios to decide between two stock investments [45–60 min]**

Assume that you are purchasing an investment and have decided to invest in a company in the digital phone business. You have narrowed the choice to Best Digital, Corp., and Every Zone, Inc., and have assembled the following data.

Selected income statement data for the current year:

		Best Digital	Every Zone
Net sales (all on credit)	$	420,115 $	498,955
Cost of goods sold		210,000	256,000
Interest expense		—	16,000
Net income		48,000	74,000

Selected balance sheet and market price data at the *end* of the current year:

		Best Digital		Every Zone
Current assets:				
Cash	$	25,000	$	23,000
Short-term investments		42,000		21,000
Current receivables, net.		42,000		52,000
Inventories		69,000		105,000
Prepaid expenses		19,000		14,000
Total current assets	$	197,000	$	215,000
Total assets	$	268,000	$	331,000
Total current liabilities		102,000		100,000
Total liabilities		102,000		128,000
Common stock, $1 par (15,000 shares)		15,000		
$1 par (16,000 shares)				16,000
Total stockholders' equity	$	166,000	$	203,000
Market price per share of common stock	$	48.00	$	115.75
Dividends paid per common share	$	2.00	$	1.80

Selected balance sheet data at the *beginning* of the current year:

		Best Digital	Every Zone
Balance sheet:			
Current receivables, net	$	47,000 $	56,000
Inventories		83,000	92,000
Total assets		261,000	274,000
Common stock, $1 par (15,000 shares)		15,000	
$1 par (16,000 shares)			16,000

Your strategy is to invest in companies that have low price/earnings ratios but appear to be in good shape financially. Assume that you have analyzed all other factors and that your decision depends on the results of ratio analysis.

Requirement

1. Compute the following ratios for both companies for the current year, and decide which company's stock better fits your investment strategy.

   a. Acid-test ratio
   b. Inventory turnover
   c. Days' sales in receivables
   d. Debt ratio
   e. Earnings per share of common stock
   f. Price/earnings ratio
   g. Dividend payout

● Continuing Exercise

E15-34 ❷ **Vertical analysis of a balance sheet [10–15 min]**

MyAccountingLab

This exercise continues the Lawlor Lawn Service, Inc., situation from Exercise 14-32 of Chapter 14.

Requirement

1. Prepare a vertical analysis from the income statement you prepared in Chapter 4.

● Continuing Problem

P15-35 ❹ **Using ratios to evaluate a stock investment [20–25 min]**

MyAccountingLab

This problem continues the Draper Consulting, Inc., situation from Problem 14-33 of Chapter 14.

Requirement

1. Using the results from Chapter 4, and knowing that the current market price of Draper's stock is $200 per share, calculate the following ratios for the company:

    a. Current ratio
    b. Debt ratio
    c. Debt to equity ratio
    d. Earnings per share
    e. P/E ratio
    f. Rate of return on total assets
    g. Rate of return on common stockholders' equity

Apply Your Knowledge

● Decision Cases

Decision Case 15-1 ABC and XYZ companies both had a bad year in 2010; the companies' suffered net losses. Due to the losses, some of the measures of return deteriorated for both companies. Assume top management of ABC and XYZ are pondering ways to improve their ratios for the following year. In particular, management is considering the following transactions:

1. Borrow $100 million on long-term debt.
2. Purchase treasury stock for $500 million cash.
3. Expense one-fourth of the goodwill carried on the books.
4. Create a new design division at a cash cost of $300 million.
5. Purchase patents from Johnson, Co., paying $20 million cash.

Requirement

1. Top management wants to know the effects of these transactions (increase, decrease, or no effect) on the following ratios:
    a. Current ratio
    b. Debt ratio
    c. Rate of return on common stockholders' equity

Decision Case 15-2 Lance Berkman is the controller of Saturn, a dance club whose year-end is December 31. Berkman prepares checks for suppliers in December makes the proper journal entries, and posts them to the appropriate accounts in that month. However, he holds on to the checks and mails them to the suppliers in January.

Requirements

1. What financial ratio(s) is(are) most affected by the action?
2. What is Berkman's purpose in undertaking this activity?

● Ethical Issue 15-1

Ross's Ripstick Company's long-term debt agreements make certain demands on the business. For example, Ross may not purchase treasury stock in excess of the balance of retained earnings. Also, long-term debt may not exceed stockholders' equity, and the current ratio may not fall below 1.50. If Ross fails to meet any of these requirements, the company's lenders have the authority to take over management of the company.

Changes in consumer demand have made it hard for Ross to attract customers. Current liabilities have mounted faster than current assets, causing the current ratio to fall to 1.47. Before releasing financial statements, Ross's management is scrambling to improve the current ratio. The controller points out that an investment can be classified as either long-term or short-term, depending on management's intention. By deciding to convert an investment to cash within one year, Ross can classify the investment as short-term—a current asset. On the controller's recommendation, Ross's board of directors votes to reclassify long-term investments as short-term.

Requirements

1. What effect will reclassifying the investments have on the current ratio? Is Ross's true financial position stronger as a result of reclassifying the investments?
2. Shortly after the financial statements are released, sales improve; so, too, does the current ratio. As a result, Ross's management decides not to sell the investments it had reclassified as short-term. Accordingly, the company reclassifies the investments as long-term. Has management behaved unethically? Give the reasoning underlying your answer.

● Fraud Case 15-1

Allen Software was a relatively new tech company led by aggressive founder Benjamin Allen. His strategy relied not so much on producing new products as using new equity capital to buy up other software companies. To keep attracting investors, Allen had to show year-to-year revenue growth. When his normal revenue streams stalled, he resorted to the tried and true "channel stuffing" technique. First, he improperly recorded shipments to his distributors as sales revenue, shipments that far exceeded the market demand for his products. Then he offered the distributors large payments to hold the excess inventory instead of returning it for a refund. Those payments were disguised as sales promotion expenses. He was able to show a considerable growth in revenues for two years running until one savvy investor group started asking questions. That led to a complaint filed with the SEC (Securities and Exchange Commission). The company is now in bankruptcy and several criminal cases are pending.

Requirements

1. What factor may have tipped off the investor group that something was wrong?
2. In what way would those investors have been harmed?
3. If Allen had attracted enough equity capital, do you think he would have been able to conceal the scheme?

● Financial Statement Case 15-1

Amazon.com's financial statements in Appendix A at the end of this book reveal some interesting relationships. Answer these questions about **Amazon:**

Requirements

1. Compute trend analyses for net sales and net income. Use 2007 as the base year. What is the most notable aspect of this data?

2. Compute inventory turnover for 2009 and 2008. The inventory balance at December 31, 2009, was $2,171 million. Do the trend of net income from 2008 to 2009 and the change in the rate of inventory turnover tell the same story or a different story? Explain your answer.

● Team Projects

Team Project 15-1 Select an industry you are interested in, and pick any company in that industry to use as the benchmark. Then select two other companies in the same industry. For each category of ratios in the Decision Guidelines in the chapter, compute all the ratios for the three companies. Write a two-page report that compares the two companies with the benchmark company.

Team Project 15-2 Select a company and obtain its financial statements. Convert the income statement and the balance sheet to common size, and compare the company you selected to the industry average. The Risk Management Association's *Annual Statement Studies*, Dun & Bradstreet's *Industry Norms & Key Business Ratios*, and Prentice Hall's *Almanac of Business and Industrial Financial Ratios*, by Leo Troy, publish common-size statements for most industries.

● Communication Activity 15-1

In 75 words or fewer, explain the difference between horizontal and vertical analysis. Be sure to include in your answer how each might be used.

Quick Check Answers

1. *b* 2. *a* 3. *d* 4. *c* 5. *a* 6. *b* 7. *d* 8. *c* 9. *a* 10. *b*

For online homework, exercises, and problems that provide you immediate feedback, please visit myaccountinglab.com.

Comprehensive Problem for Chapter 15

Analyzing a Company for Its Investment Potential

In its annual report, WRS Athletic Supply, Inc., includes the following five-year financial summary.

WRS ATHLETIC SUPPLY, INC.
Five-Year Financial Summary (Partial; adapted)

(Dollar amounts in thousands except per share data)	2015	2014	2013	2012	2011	2010
Net sales	$244,524	$217,799	$191,329	$165,013	$137,634	
Net sales increase	12%	14%	16%	20%	17%	
Domestic comparative store sales increase	5%	6%	5%	8%	9%	
Other income—net	2,001	1,873	1,787	1,615	1,391	
Cost of sales	191,838	171,562	150,255	129,664	108,725	
Operating, selling, and general and administrative expenses	41,236	36,356	31,679	27,408	22,516	
Interest:						
Interest expense	1,063	1,357	1,383	1,045	803	
Interest income	(138)	(171)	(188)	(204)	(189)	
Income tax expense	4,487	3,897	3,692	3,338	2,740	
Net income	8,039	6,671	6,295	5,377	4,430	
Per share of common stock:						
Net income	1.81	1.49	1.41	1.21	0.99	
Dividends	0.30	0.28	0.24	0.20	0.16	
Financial Position						
Current assets, excluding inventory	$ 30,483	$ 27,878	$ 26,555	$ 24,356	$ 21,132	
Inventories at LIFO cost	24,891	22,614	21,442	19,793	17,076	$16,497
Property, plant, and equipment, net	51,904	45,750	40,934	35,969	25,973	
Total assets	94,685	83,527	78,130	70,349	49,996	
Current liabilities	32,617	27,282	28,949	25,803	16,762	
Long-term debt	22,731	21,143	17,838	18,712	12,122	
Shareholders' equity	39,337	35,102	31,343	25,834	21,112	
Financial Ratios						
Acid-test ratio	0.9	1.0	0.9	0.9	1.3	
Rate of return on total assets	10.2%	9.9%	10.3%	10.7%	9.6%	
Rate of return on shareholders' equity	21.6%	20.1%	22.0%	22.9%	22.4%	

Requirement

1. Analyze the company's financial summary for the fiscal years 2011–2015 to decide whether to invest in the common stock of WRS. Include the following sections in your analysis, and fully explain your final decision.
   a. Trend analysis for net sales and net income (use 2011 as the base year).
   b. Profitability analysis.
   c. Evaluate the ability to sell inventory (WRS uses the LIFO method).
   d. Evaluate the ability to pay debts.
   e. Evaluate the dividends.

16 Introduction to Managerial Accounting

Learning Objectives

1 Distinguish managerial accounting from financial accounting

2 Identify trends in the business environment and the role of management accountability

3 Apply ethical standards to decision making

4 Classify costs and prepare an income statement for a service company

5 Classify costs and prepare an income statement for a merchandising company

6 Classify costs and prepare an income statement and statement of cost of goods manufactured for a manufacturing company

After growing up in the south, you are excited about attending a prestigious college in the north. In addition to working toward your accounting degree, you are looking forward to participating in some winter sports. You soon have the opportunity to try ice skating. Since you have enjoyed inline skating for years, you think the transition from wheels to blades will be easy. Unfortunately, the transition is not smooth. By the end of the evening, you have sore ankles and several bruises from some embarrassing falls. While the basic concept of skating is the same, you soon discovered you have to learn some new techniques.

•   •   •

Just as you had to shift your focus from wheels to blades, from pavement to ice, we will also shift our focus in this chapter from financial accounting to managerial accounting. *Financial accounting* focuses on preparing financial statements. *Managerial* (or *management*) *accounting* focuses on the accounting tools managers use to run a business. So while the basic accounting concepts learned in financial accounting still apply, we will need to learn how to use these new tools. Anyone with an interest in owning or managing a business will find managerial accounting tools helpful in providing the information needed to make decisions. We'll explain these concepts using Smart Touch Learning and Greg's Tunes.

Management Accountability: Financial vs. Managerial Accounting

① Distinguish managerial accounting from financial accounting

Before we launch into how managers use accounting, let's think about some of the groups to whom managers must answer. We call these groups the **stakeholders** of the company because each group has an interest of some sort in the business. **Management accountability** is the manager's *responsibility* to the various stakeholders of the company. Many different stakeholders have an interest in an organization, including customers, creditors, suppliers, and owners. Exhibit 16-1 shows the links between management and the various stakeholders of a company. The exhibit is organized by the three main categories of cash-flow activities: operating, investing, and financing. It also includes actions that affect society. For each activity, we list the stakeholders and what they provide to the organization. The far-right column shows how managers are accountable to the stakeholders.

EXHIBIT 16-1 | **Management Accountability to Stakeholders**

Stakeholders	Provide	and Management is accountable for
Operating activities		
Suppliers	Products and services	Making timely payments to suppliers
Employees	Time and expertise	Providing a safe and productive work environment
Customers	Cash	Providing products and services that are safe and defect free; backing up the products and services they provide
Investing activities		
Asset vendors	Long-term assets	Making timely payments to asset vendors
Financing activities		
Owners	Cash or other assets	Providing a return on the owners' investment
Creditors	Cash	Repaying principal and interest
Actions that affect society		
Governments	Permission to operate	Obeying laws and paying taxes
Communities	Human and physical resources	Operating in an ethical manner to support the community; ensuring the company's environmental impact does not harm the community

To earn the stakeholders' trust, managers provide information about their decisions and the results of those decisions. Thus, management accountability requires two forms of accounting:

- Financial accounting for *external* reporting
- Managerial (or management) accounting for *internal* planning and control

Financial accounting provides financial statements that report results of operations, financial position, and cash flows both to managers and to external stakeholders: owners, creditors, suppliers, customers, the government, and society. Financial accounting satisfies management's accountability (responsibility) to

- owners and creditors for their investment decisions.
- regulatory agencies, such as the Securities Exchange Commission, the Federal Trade Commission, and the Internal Revenue Service.
- customers and society to ensure that the company acts responsibly.

The financial statements that you studied in Chapters 1–15 focused on financial accounting and reporting on the company as a whole.

Managerial accounting, on the other hand, provides information to help managers plan and control operations as they lead the business. This includes managing the company's plant, equipment, and human resources. Managerial accounting often requires forward-looking information because of the futuristic nature of business decisions. Additionally, managerial accounting reports may contain proprietary (company specific, non-public) information, whereas financial reports do not.

Stop & Think...

You speak differently when you are speaking to your friends than when you are speaking to your boss or parents. This is the essence of managerial and financial accounting—the accounting data is formatted differently and contains more detailed information so that it "speaks" to the correct audience of users (stakeholders).

Managers are responsible to many stakeholders, so they must plan and control operations carefully.

- **Planning** means choosing goals and deciding how to achieve them. For example, a common goal is to increase operating income (profits). To achieve this goal, managers may raise selling prices or advertise more in the hope of increasing sales. The **budget** is a mathematical expression of the plan that managers use to coordinate the business's activities. **The budget shows the expected financial impact of decisions and helps identify the resources needed to achieve goals.**

- **Controlling** means implementing the plans and evaluating operations by comparing actual results to the budget. For example, managers can compare actual costs to budgeted costs to evaluate their performance. If actual costs fall below budgeted costs, that is usually good news. But if actual costs exceed the budget, managers may need to make changes. Cost data help managers make decisions.

Exhibit 16-2 on the following page highlights the differences between managerial accounting and financial accounting. Both managerial accounting and financial accounting use the accrual basis of accounting. Many managerial accounting reports also focus on cash and the timing of cash receipts and disbursements. But managerial accounting is not required to meet external reporting requirements, such as generally accepted accounting principles. Therefore, managers have more leeway in preparing management accounting reports, as you can see in points 1–4 of the exhibit.

Managers tailor their managerial accounting system to help them make wise decisions. Managers weigh the *benefits* of the system (better information leads to more informed decisions, which hopefully create higher profits) against the *costs* to develop and run the system. Weighing the costs against the benefits is called **cost/benefit analysis**. To remain in service, a managerial accounting system's benefits must exceed its costs.

Point 5 of Exhibit 16-2 indicates that managerial accounting provides more detailed and timely information than does financial accounting. On a day-to-day basis, managers identify ways to cut costs, set prices, and evaluate employee performance. Company intranets and handheld computers provide this information with the click of a mouse. While detailed information is important to managers, summary information is more valuable to external users of financial data.

Point 6 of Exhibit 16-2 reminds us that managerial accounting reports affect people's behavior. Accountability is created through measuring results. Therefore, employees try to perform well on the parts of their jobs that the accounting system measures. For example, if a manufacturing company evaluates a plant manager based only on costs, the manager may focus on cutting costs by using cheaper materials or hiring less experienced workers. These actions will cut costs, but they can hurt profits if product quality drops and sales fall as a result. Therefore, managers must consider how their decisions will motivate company employees and if that motivation will achieve the overall results the company desires.

Key Takeaway

Managerial accounting focuses on the information needs of internal users. Generally, managerial accounting reports provide more details so that managers have the information they need to plan and control costs. The benefits of the managerial accounting system must outweigh its cost.

	Financial Accounting	Managerial Accounting
EXHIBIT 16-2	**Financial Accounting Versus Managerial Accounting**	
1. Primary users	External—investors, creditors, and government authorities	Internal—the company's managers
2. Purpose of information	Help investors and creditors make investment and credit decisions	Help managers plan and control operations
3. Focus and time dimension of the information	Relevance and reliability of the information and focus on the past—example: 2013 actual performance reported in 2014	Relevance of the information and focus on the future—example: 2014 budget prepared in 2013
4. Rules and restrictions	Required to follow GAAP. Public companies are required to be audited by an independent CPA	Not required to follow GAAP
5. Scope of information	Summary reports primarily on the company as a whole, usually on a quarterly or annual basis	Detailed reports on parts of the company (products, departments, territories), often on a daily or weekly basis
6. Behavioral	Concern about adequacy of disclosures; behavioral implications are secondary	Concern about how reports will affect employee behavior

Today's Business Environment

2 Identify trends in the business environment and the role of management accountability

Connect To: Accounting Information Systems: ERP

Enterprise resource planning (ERP) software has made huge advances in the past decade that streamline formerly time-consuming processes and provide a level of reporting not known in accounting information systems of the past. ERP systems such as those designed by Oracle and SAP allow managers to see transactions affecting costs as they are happening. This allows managers to make decisions in a timely manner. The heart of ERP systems includes virtual connectivity to vendors and customers alike.

In order to be successful, managers of both large corporations and small, privately owned businesses must consider recent business trends, such as the following:

- **Shift Toward a Service Economy.** **Service companies** provide health care, communication, banking, and other important benefits to society. **Google** and **DirecTV** do not sell products; they sell their services. In the last century, many developed economies shifted their focus from manufacturing to service, and now service companies employ more than half of the workforce. The U.S. Census Bureau expects services, such as technology and health care, to grow especially fast.

- **Global Competition.** To be competitive, many companies are moving operations to other countries to be closer to new markets. Other companies are partnering with foreign companies to meet local needs. For example, **Toyota**, a Japanese company, has five major assembly plants located in the U.S. in Huntsville, AL; Georgetown, KY; Princeton, IN: San Antonio, TX; and Buffalo, WV.

- **Time-Based Competition.** The Internet, electronic commerce (e-commerce), and express delivery speed the pace of business. Customers who instant message around the world will not want to wait two weeks to receive DVDs they purchased online. Time is the new competitive turf for world-class business. To compete, companies have developed the following time-saving responses:

    1. **Advanced Information Systems.** Many companies use **enterprise resource planning (ERP)** systems to integrate all their worldwide functions, departments, and data. **ERP systems help to streamline operations and enable companies to respond quickly to changes in the marketplace.**

2. **E-Commerce.** The Internet allows companies to sell to thousands of customers around the world by providing every product the company offers 24/7.

3. **Just-in-Time Management.** Inventory held too long becomes obsolete. Storing goods takes space and must be insured—that costs money. The just-in-time philosophy helps managers cut costs by speeding the transformation of raw materials into finished products. **Just-in-time (JIT)** means producing *just in time* to satisfy needs. Ideally, suppliers deliver materials for today's production in exactly the right quantities *just in time* to begin production, and finished units are completed *just in time* for delivery to customers.

- **Total Quality Management.** Companies must deliver high-quality goods and services in order to be successful. **Total quality management (TQM)** is a philosophy designed to integrate all organizational areas in order to provide customers with superior products and services while meeting organizational goals throughout the value chain. The **value chain** includes all the activities that add value to a company's products and services. Companies achieve this goal by continuously improving quality and reducing or eliminating defects and waste. **In TQM, each business function sets higher and higher goals to continuously improve quality.** Mark Tiffee, CEO of **A Cut Above Exteriors**, says that one example of how TQM changed his business is in the sales department. "The initial analysis showed that 78% of sales orders had errors. We saw this was a problem with our process, not our people. By working on the process, we were able to cut sales order errors down. Within eight months we had eliminated virtually all errors without any disciplinary tactics."[1]

> **Key Takeaway**
>
> Developed economies have shifted from a manufacturing focus to a service focus. Global competition, e-commerce, and the Internet have expedited both the need and the speed with which information must be available to decision makers. JIT production and TQM mean producing just in time to satisfy customer demand, while constantly improving the quality of goods and services offered to customers.

Ethical Standards

The Bernie Madoff and **Bank of America/Merrill Lynch** scandals underscore what happens when ethics are violated. The ethical path is clear and requires ethical behavior without regard to personal consequences. Consider the following examples:

3 Apply ethical standards to decision making

- Sarah Baker is examining the ending inventory records for the December 31 year end financial statements at Top-Flight's warehouses in Arizona. She discovers an inventory purchase of $1,000 that was counted as part of the ending inventory, but the inventory was shipped F.O.B. destination and arrived January 3. When asked about the invoice, Mike Flinders, purchasing manager, admits that he included the inventory in his ending count, though the goods were not yet in the warehouse. After all, the company would have the inventory in just a few days.

- As the accountant of Casey Computer, Co., you are aware of Casey's weak financial condition. Casey is close to signing a lucrative contract that should ensure its future. The controller states that the company *must* report a profit this year. He suggests: "Two customers have placed orders that are scheduled to be shipped January 3, when production of those orders is completed. Let's record the goods as finished and bill the customer on December 31 so we can show the profit from those orders in the current year."

---

[1]http://www.price-associates.com/solutions/performance/total-quality-management/a-cut-above-exteriors-case-study.aspx, 06/08/2010

Although the ethical path is clear in the two preceding examples, some situations pose ethical challenges for a manager. The Institute of Management Accountants (IMA) has developed standards to help managerial accountants meet ethical challenges. The IMA standards remind us that society expects professional accountants to exhibit the highest level of ethical behavior. An excerpt from the IMA's Statement of Ethical Professional Practice appears in Exhibit 16-3. These standards require management accountants to

- maintain their professional competence,
- preserve the confidentiality of the information they handle, and
- act with integrity and credibility.

EXHIBIT 16-3 | **IMA Statement of Ethical Professional Practice (excerpt)**

Management accountants have a commitment to ethical professional practice which includes principles of Honesty, Fairness, Objectivity, and Responsibility. The standards of ethical practice include the following:

I. COMPETENCE
1. Maintain an appropriate level of professional expertise by continually developing knowledge and skills.
2. Perform professional duties in accordance with relevant laws, regulations, and technical standards.
3. Provide decision support information and recommendations that are accurate, clear, concise, and timely.
4. Recognize and communicate professional limitations or other constraints that would preclude responsible judgment or successful performance of an activity.

II. CONFIDENTIALITY
1. Keep information confidential except when disclosure is authorized or legally required.
2. Inform all relevant parties regarding appropriate use of confidential information. Monitor subordinates' activities to ensure compliance.
3. Refrain from using confidential information for unethical or illegal advantage.

III. INTEGRITY
1. Mitigate actual conflicts of interest, regularly communicate with business associates to avoid apparent conflicts of interest. Advise all parties of any potential conflicts.
2. Refrain from engaging in any conduct that would prejudice carrying out duties ethically.
3. Abstain from engaging in or supporting any activity that might discredit the profession.

IV. CREDIBILITY
1. Communicate information fairly and objectively.
2. Disclose all relevant information that could reasonably be expected to influence an intended user's understanding of the reports, analyses, or recommendations.
3. Disclose delays or deficiencies in information, timeliness, processing, or internal controls in conformance with organization policy and/or applicable law.

Adapted with permission from IMA, www.imanet.org

To resolve ethical dilemmas, the IMA also suggests discussing ethical situations with your immediate supervisor, or with an objective adviser.

Let's return to the two ethical dilemmas. By including inventory that wasn't owned by the company in the ending inventory count, Mike Flinders violated the IMA's integrity standards (overstating the company's assets). Because Sarah Baker discovered the inflated inventory report, she would not be fulfilling her ethical responsibilities (integrity and credibility) if she allowed the inventory to be overstated and did not report Flinder's actions.

The second dilemma, in which the controller asked Sarah Baker to record goods still owned by the company as a sale, also poses problems. Clearly these acts are a violation of GAAP, so you should discuss the available alternatives and their consequences with others. Following the controller's suggestion to manipulate the company's income would violate the standards of competence, integrity, and credibility. If you refuse to make the entries in December and you simply resign without attempting to find an alternative solution, you might only hurt yourself and your family. Ideally, you could convince the controller that the income manipulation is not ethical and violates the revenue recognition principle. Therefore, no entries for these transactions would be made in December.

Key Takeaway

Issues where professional judgments must be made arise often. Determining the ethical action is usually easy. Acting ethically is where integrity and credibility prevail. The excerpt from the IMA's Statement of Ethical Professional Practice guides managerial accountants in ethical matters.

Service Companies

Service companies, such as **eBay** (online auction), **Verizon** (cell phone service), and your local car wash (cleaning services), sell services. **Basically, service companies sell their time, skills, and knowledge.** As with other types of businesses, service companies seek to provide services with the following three characteristics:

 4 Classify costs and prepare an income statement for a service company

- High quality
- Reasonable prices
- Timely delivery

We focused on financial statements for service companies in Chapters 1–4 using Smart Touch Learning, Inc.

Service companies have the simplest accounting since they carry no inventories of products for sale. All of their costs are **period costs**, those costs that are incurred and expensed in the same accounting *period*.

Let's look first at Smart Touch as it originally started out in early 2013 as a service company. Recall that this business sold e-learning. Smart Touch's income statement for the month ended May 31, 2013, reproduced from Chapter 3 with ratio analysis added, follows:

EXHIBIT 16-4 | **Income Statement—Service Company**

SMART TOUCH LEARNING, INC. Income Statement Month Ended May 31, 2013			
Revenue:			
Service revenue		$7,600	100%
Expenses:			
Salary expense	$1,800		24%
Rent expense	1,000		13%
Utilities expense	400		5%
Depreciation expense—furniture	300		4%
Depreciation expense—building	200		3%
Interest expense	100		1%
Supplies expense	100		1%
Total expenses		3,900	51%
Net income		$3,700	49%

Smart Touch had no inventory in May, so the company's income statement has no Cost of goods sold. The largest expense is for the salaries of personnel who work for the company. Salary expense was 24% of Smart Touch's revenue in May and the company earned a 49% net income.

Service companies need to know which services are most profitable, and that means evaluating both revenues and costs. Knowing the cost per service helps managers set the price of each and then calculate operating income. Service companies often consider *all* operating expenses (period costs) as part of their cost of service. In larger, more advanced service companies, the period costs may be split between service costs (part of the cost per unit of service) and non-service costs (expenses unrelated to the service). In May 2013, Smart Touch provided 1,950 e-learning services. What is the cost per service? Use the following formula to calculate the unit cost:

> Unit cost per service = Total service costs ÷ Total number of services provided
>
> = $3,900 ÷ 1,950
>
> = $2 per e-learning service

Key Takeaway

Service companies sell their time, skills, or knowledge. All of their operating expenses are normally considered period costs and are considered part of the cost of providing each service unit. In larger, more advanced service companies, the operating expenses (period costs) may be split between service costs (part of the cost per unit of service) and non-service costs (expenses unrelated to the service).

Merchandising Companies

5 Classify costs and prepare an income statement for a merchandising company

Merchandising companies, such as **Amazon.com**, **Target**, and **Best Buy**, resell products they buy from suppliers. Merchandisers keep an inventory of products, and managers are accountable for the purchasing, storage, and sale of the products. You learned about merchandising companies in Chapters 5 and 6 of this textbook.

In contrast with service companies, merchandisers' income statements report Cost of goods sold as the major expense. The cost of goods sold section of the income statement is not shown in most external financial reports, but is simply listed as one item, Cost of goods sold. This section is often detailed on internal management reports to show the flow of product costs through the inventory. These product costs are **inventoriable product costs** because the products are held in inventory, an asset, until sold. For *external reporting*, GAAP require companies to treat inventoriable product costs as an asset until the product is sold or consumed, at which time the costs are expensed.

Merchandising companies' inventoriable product costs include *only* the cost to purchase the goods plus freight in—the cost to get the goods *in* the warehouse. The activity in the Inventory account provides the information for the cost of goods sold section of the income statement as shown in the following formula:

> Beginning Inventory + Net Purchases + Freight In − Ending Inventory = Cost of Goods Sold

To highlight the roles of beginning inventory, purchases, and ending inventory, we use the periodic inventory system. However, the concepts in this chapter apply equally to companies that use perpetual inventory systems.

In managerial accounting, we distinguish inventoriable product costs from period costs. As noted previously, *period costs* are those operating costs that are expensed in the period in which they are incurred. Therefore, period costs are the expenses that are not part of inventoriable product cost.

Recall Greg's Tunes' December 31, 2014, results as presented in Chapter 5 as our merchandising example. Remember that Greg's Tunes first started as a service company selling musical services. Then, the company began selling music CDs and DVDs produced by other companies. At that point the company became a merchandiser. Exhibit 16-5 shows the income statement of Greg's Tunes for the year ended December 31, 2014, using the periodic inventory method and including ratio analysis.

EXHIBIT 16-5 | **Income Statement—Merchandising Company**

GREG'S TUNES Income Statement Year Ended December 31, 2014			
Sales revenue		$169,300	102.0%
Less: Sales returns and allowances	$ 2,000		1.2%
Sales discounts	1,400		0.8%
		3,400	2.0%
Net sales revenue		$165,900	100.0%
Cost of goods sold:			
Beginning inventory	$ 0		
Purchases and freight in	131,000		
Cost of goods available for sale	$131,000		
Ending inventory	40,200		
Cost of goods sold		90,800	54.7%
Gross profit		$ 75,100	45.3%
Operating expenses			
Selling expenses:			
Wage expense	$ 10,200		6.1%
General expenses:			
Rent expense	8,400		5.1%
Insurance expense	1,000		0.6%
Depreciation expense	600		0.4%
Supplies expense	500		0.3%
Total operating expenses		20,700	12.5%
Operating income		$ 54,400	32.8%
Other income and (expense):			
Interest expense		(1,300)	(0.8%)
Net income		$ 53,100	32.0%

Greg's was not selling DVDs and CDs in 2013, so the beginning inventory at December 31, 2013, was $0. During 2014, Greg's purchased DVDs and CDs at a total cost of $131,000. At the end of 2014, Greg's ending inventory was $40,200. (You can confirm this by reviewing the balance sheet in Exhibit 5-8.) Of the $131,000 available for sale, the cost of DVDs and CDs sold in 2014 was $90,800. Notice that cost of goods sold is 54.7% of net sales revenue (cost of goods sold divided by net sales revenue of $165,900). Managers watch the gross profit percentage (45.3% for Greg's) to make sure it does not change too much. A large decrease in the gross profit percentage may indicate that the company has a problem with inventory theft or shrinkage (waste). It may also indicate a problem with retail pricing of the products. The company's profit margin (net income divided by net sales revenue) is 32% for the year ended December 31, 2014.

Merchandising companies need to know which products are most profitable. Knowing the unit cost per product helps managers set appropriate selling prices. During the year, Greg's sold 10,000 CDs and DVDs. What is the average cost of each item sold? Use the following formula to calculate the average unit cost per item:

Unit cost per item = Total cost of goods sold ÷ Total number of items sold

= $90,800 ÷ 10,000

= $9.08 per item

Now practice what you have learned by solving Summary Problem 16-1.

Key Takeaway

Merchandising companies resell products they buy from suppliers. Merchandisers keep an inventory of products, and managers are accountable for the purchase, storage, and sale of the products. Inventory is an asset until it is sold. Cost of goods sold is the total cost of merchandise inventory sold during the period, and includes the freight to get the goods into the warehouse. COGS divided by total units sold equals the cost per unit for the merchandiser.

Summary Problem 16-1

Jackson, Inc., a retail distributor of futons, provided the following information for 2013:

Merchandise inventory, January 1	$ 20,000
Merchandise inventory, December 31	30,000
Selling expense	50,000
Delivery expense (freight out)	18,000
Net purchases of futons	265,000
Rent expense	15,000
Utilities expense	3,000
Freight in	15,000
Administrative expense	64,000
Sales revenue	500,000
Units sold during the year	2,500 futons

Requirements

1. Calculate the cost of goods sold. What is the cost per futon sold?
2. Calculate the total period costs.
3. Prepare Jackson's income statement for the year ended December 31, 2013. Do not categorize operating expenses between selling and general. What is the gross profit percentage? What is the profit margin percentage?

Solution

1.

Cost of goods sold = Beginning inventory + Net purchases + Freight in − Ending inventory

$270,000   = $20,000   + $265,000   + $15,000 − $30,000

The cost per futon sold = Cost of goods sold ÷ Number of futons sold

$108 per futon   = $270,000   ÷   2,500 futons

2. Total period costs include all expenses not included in inventory:

Selling expense	$ 50,000
Delivery expense (freight out)	18,000
Rent expense	15,000
Utilities expense	3,000
Administrative expense	64,000
Total period costs	$150,000

3. The income statement follows:

JACKSON, INC. Income Statement Year Ended December 31, 2013			
Sales revenue		$500,000	100%
Cost of goods sold:			
Merchandise inventory, January 1	$ 20,000		
Net purchases and freight in ($265,000 + $15,000)	280,000		
Cost of goods available for sale	$300,000		
Merchandise inventory, December 31	30,000		
Cost of goods sold		270,000	54%
Gross profit		$230,000	46%
Operating expenses:			
Administrative expense	$ 64,000		
Selling expense	50,000		
Delivery expense	18,000		
Rent expense	15,000		
Utilities expense	3,000	150,000	30%
Operating income		$ 80,000	16%

Gross profit % = $230,000 / $500,000 × 100 = 46%
Profit margin % = $80,000 / $500,000 × 100 = 16%

Manufacturing Companies

6   Classify costs and prepare an income statement and statement of cost of goods manufactured for a manufacturing company

Manufacturing companies use labor, equipment, supplies, and facilities to convert raw materials into finished products. Managers in manufacturing companies must use these resources to create a product that customers want at a price customers are willing to pay. Managers are responsible for generating profits and maintaining positive cash flows.

In contrast with service and merchandising companies, manufacturing companies have a broad range of production activities that require tracking costs on three kinds of inventory:

1. **Materials inventory** includes raw materials used to make a product. For example, a baker's raw materials include flour, sugar, and eggs. Materials to manufacture a DVD include casings, colored insert label, blank DVD, and software program licensed to each DVD.

2. **Work in process inventory** includes goods that are in the manufacturing process but are not yet complete. Some production activities have transformed the raw materials, but the product is not yet finished or ready for sale. A baker's work in process inventory includes dough ready for cooking. A DVD manufacturer's work in process could include the DVD and software program, but not the casing and labeling.

3. **Finished goods inventory** includes completed goods that have not yet been sold. Finished goods are the products that the manufacturer sells, such as a finished cake or boxed DVD, to a merchandiser (or directly to customers).

Types of Costs

A **direct cost** is a cost that can be directly traced to a cost object, such as a product. Direct materials and direct labor are examples of direct costs. A **cost object** is anything for which managers need a separate breakdown of its component costs. Smart Touch's DVDs are an example of a cost object. Managers may want to know the cost of a product, a department, a sales territory, or an activity. Costs that cannot be traced directly to a cost object, such as manufacturing overhead, are **indirect costs.** **Indirect costs are required to make the finished product but are not as easy or cost effective to track to ONE specific finished product.** In manufacturing companies, product costs include both direct and indirect costs.

Inventoriable Product Costs

The completed product in finished goods inventory represents the *inventoriable product cost.* The inventoriable product cost includes three components of manufacturing costs:

- **Direct materials** become a physical part of the finished product. **The cost of direct materials (purchase cost plus freight in) can be traced directly to the finished product.**
- **Direct labor** is the labor of employees who convert materials into the company's products. **The cost of direct labor can be traced *directly* to the finished products.**
- **Manufacturing overhead** refers to indirect manufacturing costs. So, it includes all manufacturing costs other than direct materials and direct labor. These costs are created by all of the supporting production activities, including storing materials, setting up machines, and cleaning the work areas. These activities incur costs of indirect materials, indirect labor, repair and maintenance, utilities, rent, insurance, property taxes, manufacturing plant managers' salaries, and depreciation on manufacturing plant buildings and equipment. Manufacturing overhead is also called **factory overhead** or **indirect manufacturing cost.**

Direct labor and manufacturing overhead combined are called **conversion cost** because the direct labor and manufacturing overhead CONVERT raw materials into a finished product.

Exhibit 16-6 on the following page summarizes a manufacturer's inventoriable product costs.

A Closer Look at Manufacturing Overhead

- Manufacturing overhead includes only those indirect costs that are related to the manufacturing operation. Insurance and depreciation on the *manufacturing plant's* building and equipment are indirect manufacturing costs, so they are part of manufacturing overhead. In contrast, depreciation on *delivery trucks* is not part of manufacturing overhead. Instead, depreciation on delivery trucks is a cost of moving the product to the customer. Its cost is delivery expense (a period cost), not an inventoriable product cost. Similarly, the cost of auto insurance for the sales force vehicles is a marketing expense (a period cost), not manufacturing overhead.
- *Manufacturing overhead includes indirect materials and indirect labor.* The spices used in cakes become physical parts of the finished product. But these costs are minor compared with the flour and sugar for the cakes. Similarly, the label is necessary but minor in relation to the DVD, case, and software. Since these low-priced materials' costs cannot conveniently be traced to a particular cake or DVD or these costs are so minor that we don't want to trace them to a specific cake or DVD,

EXHIBIT 16-6 | **Manufacturer's Inventoriable Product Costs**

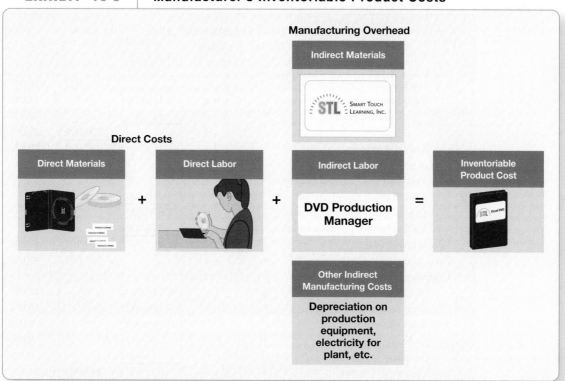

these costs are called indirect materials and become part of manufacturing overhead. Thus, **indirect materials** are materials used in making a product but whose costs either cannot conveniently be directly traced to specific finished products or whose costs are not large enough to justify tracing to the specific product.

Like indirect materials, **indirect labor** is difficult to trace to specific products so it is part of manufacturing overhead. Indirect labor is labor incurred that is necessary to make a product but whose costs either cannot conveniently be directly traced to specific finished products or whose costs are not large enough to justify tracing to the specific product. Examples include the pay of forklift operators, janitors, and plant managers. Keep in mind that with indirect costs there is often professional judgment involved as to whether a specific cost is part of the product manufacturing overhead cost (inventoriable product cost) or if the particular cost is not related to the manufacturing of the product (period cost).

Now let's assume that Smart Touch has decided in 2014 to manufacture its own brand of learning DVDs. The company's first year of operations as a manufacturer of learning DVDs is presented on the next page in the income statement in Exhibit 16-7 for the year ended December 31, 2014.

Smart Touch's cost of goods sold represents 60% of the net sales revenue. This is the inventoriable product cost of the DVDs that Smart Touch sold in 2014. Smart Touch's balance sheet at December 31, 2014, reports the inventoriable product costs of the finished DVDs that are still on hand at the end of that year. The cost of the ending inventory, $50,000, will become the beginning inventory of next year and will then be included as part of the Cost of goods sold on next year's income statement as the DVDs are sold. The operating expenses that represent 24.1% of net sales revenue are period costs.

Exhibit 16-8 summarizes the differences between inventoriable product costs and period costs for service, merchandising, and manufacturing companies. This is a reference tool that will help you determine how to categorize costs.

EXHIBIT 16-7 | **Income Statement—Manufacturing Company**

SMART TOUCH LEARNING, INC.
Income Statement
Year Ended December 31, 2014

Sales revenue		$1,200,000	120.0%
Less: Sales returns and allowances	$ 120,000		12.0%
Sales discounts	80,000		8.0%
		200,000	20.0%
Net sales revenue		$1,000,000	100.0%
Cost of goods sold:			
Beginning finished goods inventory	$ 0		
Cost of goods manufactured*	650,000		
Cost of goods available for sale	$ 650,000		
Ending finished goods inventory	50,000		
Cost of goods sold		600,000	60.0%
Gross profit		$ 400,000	40.0%
Operating expenses			
Wage expense	$ 120,000		12.0%
Rent expense	100,000		10.0%
Insurance expense	10,000		1.0%
Depreciation expense	6,000		0.6%
Supplies expense	5,000		0.5%
Total operating expenses		241,000	24.1%
Operating income		$ 159,000	15.9%
Other income and (expense):			
Interest expense		(7,600)	(0.8%)
Net income		$ 151,400	15.1%

* Calculation explained later in Exhibit 16-10

EXHIBIT 16-8 | **Inventoriable Product Costs and Period Costs for Service, Merchandising, and Manufacturing Companies**

Type of Company	Inventoriable Product Costs— Initially an asset (Inventory), and expensed (Cost of goods sold) when the inventory is sold	Period Costs— Expensed in the period incurred; never considered an asset
Service company	None	Salaries, depreciation, utilities, insurance, property taxes, advertising expenses
Merchandising company	Purchases plus freight in	Salaries, depreciation, utilities, insurance, property taxes on storage building, advertising, delivery expenses
Manufacturing company	Direct materials, direct labor, and manufacturing overhead (including indirect materials; indirect labor; depreciation on the manufacturing plant and equipment; plant insurance, utilities, and property taxes)	Delivery expense; depreciation expense, utilities, insurance, and property taxes on executive headquarters (separate from the manufacturing plant); advertising; CEO's salary

Let's compare Smart Touch's manufacturing income statement in Exhibit 16-7 with Greg's Tunes' merchandising income statement in Exhibit 16-5. The only difference is that the merchandiser (Greg's) uses *purchases* in computing cost of goods sold, while the manufacturer (Smart Touch) uses the *cost of goods manufactured*. Notice that the term **cost of goods manufactured** is in the past tense. It is the manufacturing cost of the goods that Smart Touch *completed during 2014*. The following is the difference between a manufacturer and a merchandiser:

- The manufacturer *made* the product that it later sold.
- The merchandiser *purchased* a product that was already complete and ready to be sold.

Calculating the Cost of Goods Manufactured The cost of goods manufactured summarizes the activities and the costs that take place in a manufacturing plant over the period. Let's begin by reviewing these activities. Exhibit 16-9 reminds us that the manufacturer starts by buying materials. Then the manufacturer uses direct labor and manufacturing plant and equipment (overhead) to transform (convert) these materials into work in process inventory. When inventory is completed, it becomes finished goods inventory. These are all inventoriable product costs because they are required for the inventory production process.

EXHIBIT 16-9 | **Manufacturing Company: Inventoriable Product Costs and Period Costs**

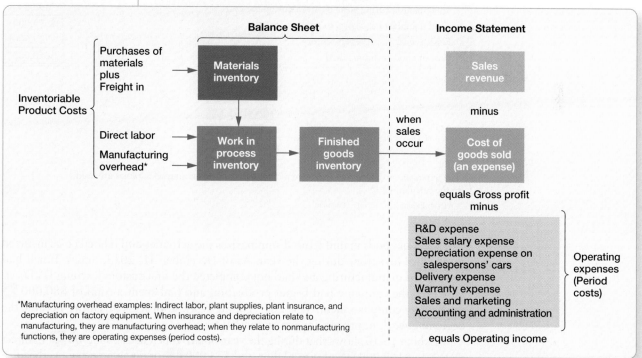

*Manufacturing overhead examples: Indirect labor, plant supplies, plant insurance, and depreciation on factory equipment. When insurance and depreciation relate to manufacturing, they are manufacturing overhead; when they relate to nonmanufacturing functions, they are operating expenses (period costs).

Finished goods are the only category of inventory that is ready to sell. The cost of the finished goods that the manufacturer sells becomes its cost of goods sold on the income statement. Costs the manufacturer incurs in nonmanufacturing activities, such as sales salaries, are operating expenses—period costs—and are expensed in the period incurred. Exhibit 16-9 shows that these operating costs are deducted from gross profit to compute operating income.

You now have a clear understanding of the flow of activities and costs in the plant, and you are ready to calculate the cost of goods manufactured. Exhibit 16-10 shows how Smart Touch computed its cost of goods manufactured for 2014 of $650,000. This is the cost of making 15,000 custom DVDs that Smart Touch *finished* during 2014.

EXHIBIT 16-10 | **Schedule of Cost of Goods Manufactured**

SMART TOUCH LEARNING, INC.
Schedule of Cost of Goods Manufactured
Year Ended December 31, 2014

A	Beginning work in process inventory			$ 80,000
	Direct materials used:			
B	Beginning direct materials inventory	$ 70,000		
C	Purchases of direct materials (including freight in)	350,000		
D	Available for use	$420,000		
E	Ending direct materials inventory	(65,000)		
F	Direct materials used		$355,000	
G	Direct labor		169,000	
	Manufacturing overhead:			
H	Indirect materials	$ 17,000		
I	Indirect labor	28,000		
J	Depreciation—plant and equipment	10,000		
K	Plant utilities, insurance, and property taxes	18,000		
L	Total manufacturing overhead		73,000	
M	Total manufacturing costs incurred during the year			597,000
N	Total manufacturing costs to account for			$677,000
O	Ending work in process inventory			(27,000)
P	Cost of goods manufactured			$650,000*

B + C = D
D − E = F
H + I + J + K = L
F + G + L = M
A + M = N
N − O = P

The letters are provided as a means to aid students in determining which lines are used in the calculations.

* refer to Exhibit 16-7 income statement

Cost of goods manufactured summarizes the activities and related costs incurred to produce inventory during the year. As of December 31, 2013, Smart Touch had just started manufacturing and had not completed the first custom learning DVD yet. However, the company had begun production and had spent a total of $80,000 **A** to partially complete them. This 2013 ending work in process inventory became the beginning work in process inventory for 2014.

Exhibit 16-10 shows that during the year, Smart Touch used $355,000 **F** of direct materials, $169,000 **G** of direct labor, and $73,000 **L** of manufacturing overhead.

Total manufacturing costs incurred during the year are the sum of the following three amounts:

Total Manufacturing Costs	
Direct materials used...	$355,000 **F**
Direct labor...	169,000 **G**
Manufacturing overhead...	73,000 **L**
Total manufacturing costs incurred during the year	$597,000 **M**

Adding total manufacturing cost for the year, $597,000 **M**, to the beginning Work in Process (WIP) Inventory of $80,000 **A** gives the total manufacturing cost to account for, $677,000 **N**. At December 31, 2014, unfinished DVDs costing only $27,000 **O** remained in WIP Inventory. The company finished 130,000 DVDs and sent them to Finished Goods (FG) Inventory. Cost of goods manufactured for the year was $650,000 **P**. The following is the computation of the cost of goods manufactured:

Beginning + WIP **A**	Direct materials used **F**	+ Direct labor **G**	+ Manufacturing overhead **L**	− Ending WIP **O**	= Cost of goods manufactured **P**
$80,000 +	355,000 +	169,000 +	73,000	− 27,000 =	$650,000

If you refer back to Smart Touch's December, 2014, income statement in Exhibit 16-7, you will find the $650,000 **P** listed as the cost of goods manufactured.

Flow of Costs Through the Inventory Accounts   Exhibit 16-11 diagrams the flow of costs through Smart Touch's inventory accounts. The format—what is on hand at the beginning of the period plus what is added during the period less what is on hand at the end of the period equals what has been used/sold—is the same for all three stages:

- Direct materials
- Work in process
- Finished goods

EXHIBIT 16-11 | **Flow of Costs Through a Manufacturer's Inventory Accounts**

Direct Materials Inventory		Work in Process Inventory		Finished Goods Inventory	
Beginning inventory	$ 70,000	Beginning inventory	$ 80,000	Beginning inventory	$ 0
+ Purchases and freight in	350,000	+ Direct materials used	$355,000	+ Cost of goods	
		+ Direct labor	169,000	manufactured	650,000
		+ Manufacturing overhead	73,000		
		Total manufacturing costs incurred during the year	$597,000		
= Direct materials available for use	$420,000	= Total manufacturing costs to account for	$677,000	= Cost of goods available for sale	$650,000
− Ending inventory	(65,000)	− Ending inventory	(27,000)	− Ending inventory	(50,000)
= Direct materials used	$355,000	= Cost of goods manufactured	$650,000	= Cost of goods sold	$600,000

Source: The authors are indebted to Judith Cassidy for this presentation.

The final amount at each stage is the beginning of the next stage. Take time to see how the schedule of cost of goods manufactured in Exhibit 16-11 uses the flows of the direct materials and work in process stages for Smart Touch's year ended December 31, 2014. Then review the income statement for Greg's Tunes in Exhibit 16-5 on page 781. Because Greg's is a merchandising company, it uses only a single Inventory account.

Calculating Unit Product Cost

Knowing the unit product cost helps managers decide on the prices to charge for each product to ensure that each product is profitable. They can then measure operating income and determine the cost of finished goods inventory. Smart Touch produced 130,000 DVDs during 2014. What did it cost to make each DVD?

Cost of goods manufactured ÷ Total units produced = Unit product cost		
$650,000 ÷	130,000 =	$5 per DVD

During 2014, Smart Touch sold 120,000 DVDs, and the company knows each DVD cost $5 to produce. With this information, Smart Touch can compute its cost of goods sold as follows:

$$
\begin{array}{ccc}
\text{Number of} & \text{Unit product} & \text{Cost of} \\
\text{units sold} & \times \quad \text{cost} & = \quad \text{goods sold} \\
120{,}000 & \times \; \$5 \text{ per DVD} & = \; \$600{,}000
\end{array}
$$

Keep in mind that the manufacturer still has period costs unrelated to the product cost that it must pay, like selling costs and administrative costs. These expenses are reported on the company's income statement because they are a necessary expense in running the business (period cost) but are not part of the product cost (inventory).

Stop & Think...

It seems lately that every time we go to the gas pump to fill up our cars, the price per gallon has changed. This change causes us to rethink our expected fuel expense each month. Similarly, the unit cost to make a product will change over time because the costs of the inputs to the production process change over time. With readily available data from computerized ERP systems, the cost of goods manufactured statement is prepared more than once (daily, monthly, yearly, or some other time interval depending on the business)—to update management's cost data about the products the company is producing and selling. By having current cost information, management can adjust the sales price to the customer, if necessary, to maintain product profitability. So back to your gas pump—this is why the price per gallon changes. Your local gas store updates the price per gallon that you pay based on updates to the cost your gas store pays per gallon.

Key Takeaway

The manufacturer creates a product from raw materials by adding direct labor and manufacturing overhead. Because at any point in time products are at various stages of completion, manufacturers have three inventory accounts: Raw materials, Work in process, and Finished goods. The schedule of cost of goods manufactured captures these production costs to determine the cost of goods manufactured for a period. Product cost per unit is calculated by dividing cost of goods manufactured by the total number of units produced.

Decision Guidelines 16-1

BUILDING BLOCKS OF MANAGERIAL ACCOUNTING

Let's review some of the building blocks of managerial accounting.

Decision	Guidelines
• What information should managerial accountants provide? What is the primary focus of managerial accounting?	Managerial accounting provides information that helps managers make better decisions; it has a • focus on *relevance* to business decisions, and • *future* orientation.
• How do you decide on a company's managerial accounting system, which is not regulated by GAAP?	Use cost/benefit analysis: Design the managerial accounting system so that benefits (from helping managers make wise decisions) outweigh the costs of the system.

• How do you distinguish among service, merchandising, and manufacturing companies? How do their balance sheets differ?	*Service companies:*
	• Provide customers with intangible services
	• Have no inventories on the balance sheet
	Merchandising companies:
	• Resell tangible products purchased ready-made from suppliers
	• Have only one category of inventory
	Manufacturing companies:
	• Use labor, plant, and equipment to transform raw materials into new finished products
	• Have three categories of inventory:
	  • Materials inventory
	  • Work in process inventory
	  • Finished goods inventory

• How do you compute the cost of goods sold?	• *Service companies:* No cost of goods sold, because they do not sell tangible goods • *Merchandising companies:* Beginning *merchandise* inventory + Purchases and freight in – Ending *merchandise* inventory = Cost of goods sold • *Manufacturing companies:* Beginning *finished goods* inventory + Cost of goods manufactured – Ending *finished goods* inventory = Cost of goods sold

Decision	Guidelines
• How do you compute the cost of goods manufactured for a manufacturer?	Beginning *work in process* inventory + Current period manufacturing costs (direct materials used + direct labor + manufacturing overhead) – Ending *work in process* inventory = Cost of goods manufactured
• How do you compute the cost per unit?	Cost of goods manufactured ÷ Total units produced = Unit product cost
• Which costs are initially treated as assets for external reporting? When are these costs expensed?	*Inventoriable product costs* are initially treated as assets (Inventory); these costs are expensed (as Cost of goods sold) when the products are sold.
• What costs are inventoriable under GAAP?	• *Service companies:* No inventoriable product costs • *Merchandising companies:* Purchases and freight in • *Manufacturing companies:* Direct materials used, direct labor, and manufacturing overhead
• Which costs are never inventoriable product costs?	Period costs. These are always expensed as incurred.

Summary Problem 16-2

Requirements

1. For a manufacturing company, identify the following as either an inventoriable product cost or a period cost:
   a. Depreciation on plant equipment
   b. Depreciation on salespersons' automobiles
   c. Insurance on plant building
   d. Marketing manager's salary
   e. Raw materials
   f. Manufacturing overhead
   g. Electricity bill for home office
   h. Production employee wages
2. Show how to compute cost of goods manufactured. Use the following amounts: direct materials used $24,000, direct labor $9,000, manufacturing overhead $17,000, beginning work in process inventory $5,000, and ending work in process inventory $4,000.
3. Using the results from Requirement 2, calculate the per unit cost for goods manufactured assuming 1,000 units were manufactured.
4. Beginning inventory had 100 units that had a unit cost of $50 each. Ending inventory has 200 units left. Calculate COGS assuming FIFO inventory costing is used.

Solution

Requirement 1

Inventoriable product cost: a, c, e, f, h
Period cost: b, d, g

Requirement 2

Cost of goods manufactured:

Beginning work in process inventory		$ 5,000
Direct materials used	$24,000	
Direct labor	9,000	
Manufacturing overhead	17,000	
Total manufacturing costs incurred during the period		50,000
Total manufacturing costs to account for		$55,000
Ending work in process inventory		(4,000)
Cost of goods manufactured		$51,000

Requirement 3

Cost of goods manufactured	÷	Total units produced	=	Unit product cost
$51,000	÷	1,000 units	=	$51 per unit

Requirement 4

Beginning finished goods inventory (100 @ $50 per unit)	$ 5,000
Cost of goods manufactured	51,000
Cost of goods available for sale	$ 56,000
Ending finished goods inventory (200 @ $51 per unit)	(10,200)
Cost of goods sold [(100 @ $50 per unit) + (800 @ $51 per unit)]	$ 45,800

Review Introduction to Managerial Accounting

● Accounting Vocabulary

Budget (p. 775)
A mathematical expression of the plan that managers use to coordinate the business's activities.

Controlling (p. 775)
Implementing plans and evaluating the results of business operations by comparing the actual results to the budget.

Conversion Costs (p. 784)
Direct labor plus manufacturing overhead.

Cost/Benefit Analysis (p. 775)
Weighing costs against benefits to help make decisions.

Cost Object (p. 784)
Anything for which managers want a separate measurement of cost.

Cost of Goods Manufactured (p. 787)
The manufacturing or plant-related costs of the goods that finished the production process in a given period.

Direct Cost (p. 784)
A cost that can be traced to a cost object.

Direct Labor (p. 784)
The compensation of employees who physically convert materials into finished products.

Direct Materials (p. 784)
Materials that become a physical part of a finished product and whose costs are traceable to the finished product.

Enterprise Resource Planning (ERP) (p. 776)
Software systems that can integrate all of a company's worldwide functions, departments, and data into a single system.

Factory Overhead (p. 784)
All manufacturing costs other than direct materials and direct labor. Also called **manufacturing overhead** or **indirect manufacturing costs**.

Finished Goods Inventory (p. 784)
Completed goods that have not yet been sold.

Indirect Costs (p. 784)
Costs that cannot be traced to a cost object.

Indirect Labor (p. 785)
Labor costs that are necessary to make a product but whose costs either cannot conveniently be directly traced to specific finished products or whose costs are not large enough to justify tracing to the specific product.

Indirect Manufacturing Cost (p. 784)
All manufacturing costs other than direct materials and direct labor. Also called **factory overhead** or **manufacturing overhead**.

Indirect Materials (p. 785)
Materials used in making a product but whose costs either cannot conveniently be directly traced to specific finished products or whose costs are not large enough to justify tracing to the specific product.

Inventoriable Product Costs (p. 780)
All costs of a product that GAAP require companies to treat as an asset for external financial reporting. These costs are not expensed until the product is sold.

Just-in-Time (JIT) (p. 777)
A system in which a company produces just in time to satisfy needs. Suppliers deliver materials just in time to begin production and finished units are completed just in time for delivery to the customer.

Management Accountability (p. 774)
The manager's responsibility to manage the resources of an organization.

Manufacturing Company (p. 783)
A company that uses labor, equipment, supplies, and facilities to convert raw materials into new finished products.

Manufacturing Overhead (p. 784)
All manufacturing costs other than direct materials and direct labor. Also called **factory overhead** or **indirect manufacturing costs**.

Materials Inventory (p. 783)
Raw materials for use in manufacturing.

Merchandising Company (p. 780)
A company that resells products previously bought from suppliers.

Period Costs (p. 779)
Operating costs that are expensed in the period in which they are incurred.

Planning (p. 775)
Choosing goals and deciding how to achieve them.

Service Companies (p. 776)
Companies that sell intangible services rather than tangible products.

Stakeholders (p. 774)
Groups that have a stake in a business.

Total Quality Management (TQM) (p. 777)
A philosophy designed to integrate all organizational areas in order to provide customers with superior products and services, while meeting organizational goals throughout the value chain.

Value Chain (p. 777)
Includes all activities that add value to a company's products and services.

Work in Process Inventory (p. 783)
Goods that have been started into the manufacturing process but are not yet complete.

● Destination: Student Success

Student Success Tips

The following are hints on some common trouble areas for students in this chapter:

● Remember the difference between service, merchandising, and manufacturing firms. Service firms sell services. Merchandisers sell products that other companies produce. Manufacturing firms take raw materials and convert them into a finished product that is sold.

Getting Help

If there's a learning objective from the chapter you aren't confident about, try using one or more of the following resources:

● Review Exhibit 16-10, the schedule of cost of goods manufactured.

● Review the Decision Guidelines in the chapter.

● Review Summary Problem 16-1 in the chapter to reinforce your understanding of merchandising companies.

● Destination: Student Success *(Continued)*

Student Success Tips

- Recall that cost per unit is cost of goods manufactured divided by the number of units produced.

- Remember the difference between direct costs and indirect costs. For example, direct labor includes the compensation of employees who physically worked on making the products. Indirect labor includes employees that are necessary but not directly involved in physically making the products.

- Keep in mind that manufacturers have three types of Inventory assets: Raw materials, Work in process, and Finished goods.

- Remember that the schedule of cost of goods manufactured is the tool a manufacturer uses to calculate the cost of goods it produced for a period. Since the cost of direct materials, direct labor, and manufacturing overhead vary, this schedule must be produced often so a company has the most current cost of production information. This schedule contains the company's inventoriable product costs.

- Keep in mind that manufacturers still have other operating expenses, like selling and administrative expenses, that are NOT part of the cost of making the product. These operating expenses are reported on the income statement.

Getting Help

- Review Summary Problem 16-2 in the chapter to reinforce your understanding of manufacturing companies.

- Practice additional exercises or problems at the end of Chapter 16 that cover the specific learning objective that is challenging you.

- Watch the white board videos for Chapter 16 located at myaccountinglab.com under the Chapter Resources button.

- Go to myaccountinglab.com and select the Study Plan button. Choose Chapter 16 and work the questions covering that specific learning objective until you've mastered it.

- Work the Chapter 16 pre/post tests in myaccountinglab.com.

- Visit the learning resource center on your campus for tutoring.

● Quick Check

1. Which is *not* a characteristic of managerial accounting information?
   a. Emphasizes the external financial statements
   b. Provides detailed information about individual parts of the company
   c. Emphasizes relevance
   d. Focuses on the future

2. World-class businesses use which of these systems to integrate all of a company's worldwide functions, departments, and data into a single system?
   a. Cost standards   c. Just-in-time management
   b. Enterprise resource planning   d. Items a, b, and c are correct

3. Today's business environment is characterized by
   a. global competition.   c. a shift toward a service economy.
   b. time-based competition.   d. Items a, b, and c are correct

4. Which of the following accounts does a manufacturing company, but not a service company, have?
   a. Advertising expense   c. Cost of goods sold
   b. Salary payable   d. Retained earnings

5. In computing cost of goods sold, which of the following is the manufacturer's equivalent to the merchandiser's purchases?
   a. Total manufacturing costs to account for
   b. Direct materials used
   c. Total manufacturing costs incurred during the period
   d. Cost of goods manufactured

6. Which of the following is a direct cost of manufacturing a sportboat?

    a. Salary of engineer who rearranges plant layout

    b. Depreciation on plant and equipment

    c. Cost of boat engine

    d. Cost of customer hotline

7. Which of the following is *not* part of manufacturing overhead for producing a computer?

    a. Manufacturing plant property taxes   c. Depreciation on delivery trucks

    b. Manufacturing plant utilities   d. Insurance on plant and equipment

Questions 8 and 9 use the data that follow. Suppose a bakery reports this information:

Beginning materials inventory	$ 8,000
Ending materials inventory	7,000
Beginning work in process inventory . . .	4,000
Ending work in process inventory	3,000
Beginning finished goods inventory . . .	3,000
Ending finished goods inventory	5,000
Direct labor	30,000
Purchases of direct materials	95,000
Manufacturing overhead	21,000

8. What is cost of direct materials used?

    a. $95,000   c. $103,000

    b. $96,000   d. $94,000

9. What is the cost of goods manufactured?

    a. $146,000   c. $144,000

    b. $148,000   d. $147,000

10. A management accountant who avoids conflicts of interest meets the ethical standard of

    a. confidentiality.   c. credibility.

    b. competence.   d. integrity.

Answers are given after Apply Your Knowledge (p. 812).

Assess Your Progress

● Short Exercises

MyAccountingLab   **S16-1**   ❶ **Managerial accounting vs. financial accounting [5–10 min]**
Managerial and financial accounting differ in many aspects.

Requirement

    1. For each of the following, indicate whether the statement relates to managerial accounting (MA) or financial accounting (FA):

            _____ a. Helps investors make investment decisions.

            _____ b. Provides detailed reports on parts of the company.

            _____ c. Helps in planning and controlling operations.

            _____ d. Reports must follow generally accepted accounting principles (GAAP).

            _____ e. Reports audited annually by independent certified public accountants.

S16-2 **❶ Management accountability and the stakeholders [10 min]**

Management has the responsibility to manage the resources of an organization in a responsible manner.

Requirement

1. For each of the following management responsibilities, indicate the primary stakeholder group to whom management is responsible. In the space provided, write the letter corresponding to the appropriate stakeholder group.

_____ 1. Providing high-quality, reliable products/services for a reasonable price in a

timely manner.

_____ 2. Paying taxes in a timely manner.

_____ 3. Providing a safe, productive work environment.

_____ 4. Generating a profit.

_____ 5. Repaying principal plus interest in a timely manner.

a. Owners
b. Creditors
c. Suppliers
d. Employees
e. Customers
f. Government
g. Community

S16-3 **❷ Business trends terminology [10 min]**

Consider the terms and definitions that follow:

_____ 1. A philosophy designed to integrate all organizational areas in order to provide

customers with superior products and services, while meeting organizational

objectives. Requires improving quality and eliminating defects and waste.

_____ 2. Use of the Internet for such business functions as sales and customer service.

Enables companies to reach thousands of customers around the world.

_____ 3. Software systems that integrate all of a company's worldwide functions,

departments, and data into a single system.

_____ 4. A system in which a company produces just in time to satisfy needs.

Suppliers deliver materials just in time to begin production, and finished

units are completed just in time for delivery to customers.

a. ERP
b. Just-in-time (JIT)
c. E-commerce
d. Total quality management

Requirement

1. Match the term with the correct definition.

S16-4 **❸ Ethical decisions [5 min]**

The Institute of Management Accountants' Statement of Ethical Professional Practice (Exhibit 16-3) requires managerial accountants to meet standards regarding the following:

- Competence
- Confidentiality
- Integrity
- Credibility

Requirement

1. Consider the following situations. Which guidelines are violated in each situation?

a. You tell your brother that your company will report earnings significantly above financial analysts' estimates.

b. You see that others take home office supplies for personal use. As an intern, you do the same thing, assuming that this is a "perk."

c. At a conference on e-commerce, you skip the afternoon session and go sightseeing.

d. You failed to read the detailed specifications of a new general ledger package that you asked your company to purchase. After it is installed, you are surprised that it is incompatible with some of your company's older accounting software.

e. You do not provide top management with the detailed job descriptions they requested because you fear they may use this information to cut a position from your department.

S16-5 ④ **Calculating income and unit cost for a service organization [5–10 min]**

Duncan and Oates provides hair cutting services in the local community. In February, the business incurred the following operating costs to cut the hair of 230 clients:

Hair supplies expense	$ 805
Building rent expense	1,150
Utilities	184
Depreciation on equipment	46

Duncan and Oates earned $5,200 in revenues from haircuts for the month of February.

Requirements

1. What is the net operating income for the month?
2. What is the cost of one haircut?

S16-6 ⑤ **Computing cost of goods sold [5 min]**

The Tinted View, a retail merchandiser of auto windshields, has the following information:

Web site maintenance	$ 7,100
Delivery expense	900
Freight in	2,900
Purchases	39,000
Ending inventory	4,900
Revenues	57,000
Marketing expenses	9,900
Beginning inventory	7,900

Requirement

1. Compute The Tinted View's cost of goods sold.

S16-7 ⑤ **Computing cost of goods sold [5–10 min]**

Consider the following partially completed income statements:

	Fit Apparel	Jones, Inc.
Sales	$ 101,000	(d)
Cost of goods sold		
Beginning inventory	(a)	$ 29,000
Purchases and freight in	48,000	(e)
Cost of goods available for sale	(b)	88,000
Ending inventory	1,900	1,900
Cost of goods sold	59,000	(f)
Gross margin	$ 42,000	$ 113,000
Selling and administrative expenses	(c)	84,000
Operating income	$ 13,000	(g)

Requirement

1. Compute the missing amounts.

S16-8   **4 5 6** **Match type of company with product and period costs [5 min]**
Consider the following costs:

Type of cost:	Type of company that reports this cost on its income statment		
Advertising costs	Manuf	Merch	Serv
1. Cost of goods manufactured			
2. The CEO's salary			
3. Cost of goods sold			
4. Building rent expense			
5. Customer service expense			

Requirement

1. For each of the costs, indicate if the cost would be found on the income statement of a service company (Serv), a merchandising company (Merch), and/or a manufacturing company (Manuf). Some costs can be found on the income statements of more than one type of company.

S16-9   **6** **Computing direct materials used [5 min]**
You are a new accounting intern at Cookie Messages. Your boss gives you the following information:

Purchases of direct materials	$ 6,400
Freight in	200
Property taxes	900
Ending inventory of direct materials	1,500
Beginning inventory of direct materials	4,000

Requirement

1. Compute direct materials used.

S16-10   **6** **Distinguishing between direct and indirect costs [5–10 min]**
Consider Granger Cards' manufacturing plant.

Requirement

1. Match one of the following terms with each example of a manufacturing cost given below:

1. Direct materials	_____ a.	Artists' wages.
2. Direct labor	_____ b.	Wages of warehouse workers.
3. Indirect materials	_____ c.	Paper
4. Indirect labor	_____ d.	Depreciation on equipment.
5. Other manufacturing overhead	_____ e.	Manufacturing plant manager's salary.
	_____ f.	Property taxes on manufacturing plant.
	_____ g.	Glue for envelopes.

S16-11   **6** **Computing manufacturing overhead [5–10 min]**
Glass Doctor Company manufactures sunglasses. Suppose the company's May records include the following items:

Glue for frames	$ 350	Company president's salary	$ 24,500
Depreciation expense on company		Plant foreman's salary	5,000
cars used by sales force	3,000	Plant janitor's wages	1,000
Plant depreciation expense	9,000	Oil for manufacturing equipment	200
Interest expense	1,500	Lenses	50,000

Requirements

1. List the items and amounts that are manufacturing overhead costs.
2. Calculate Glass Doctor's total manufacturing overhead cost in May.

S16-12 **6** **Compute cost of goods manufactured [5 min]**

All Pro Golf Company had the following inventory data for the year ended January 31, 2012:

Direct materials used	$ 12,000
Manufacturing overhead	20,000
Work in process inventory:	
Beginning	7,000
Ending	5,000
Direct labor	11,000
Finished goods inventory	9,000

Requirement

1. Compute All Pro's cost of goods manufactured for 2012.

S16-13 **6** **Inventoriable product costs vs. period costs [5–10 min]**

Manufacturer's costs are either inventoriable product costs or period costs.

Requirement

1. Classify each of a paper manufacturer's costs as either an inventoriable product cost or a period cost:

   a. Salaries of scientists studying ways to speed forest growth.
   b. Cost of computer software to track WIP inventory.
   c. Cost of electricity at a paper mill.
   d. Salaries of the company's top executives.
   e. Cost of chemicals to treat paper.
   f. Cost of TV ads.
   g. Depreciation on the gypsum board plant.
   h. Cost of lumber to be cut into boards.
   i. Life insurance on CEO.

● Exercises

MyAccountingLab   **E16-14** **1** **Management vs. financial accounting and managers' use of information [5 min]**

The following statements consider how managers use information.

a. Companies must follow GAAP in their ____ accounting systems.
b. Financial accounting develops reports for external parties, such as ____ and ____.
c. When managers compare the company's actual results to the plan, they are performing the ____ role of management.
d. ____ are decision makers inside a company.
e. ____ accounting provides information on a company's past performance.
f. ____ accounting systems are not restricted by GAAP but are chosen by comparing the costs versus the benefits of the system.
g. Choosing goals and the means to achieve them is the ____ function of management.

Requirement

1. Complete each blank with one of the terms listed here. You may use a term more than once, and some terms may not be used at all.

Budget	Creditors	Managers	Planning
Controlling	Financial	Managerial	Shareholders

E16-15 ❷ Understanding today's business environment [5 min]

The following statements relate to understanding today's business environment.

a. ____ is a management philosophy that focuses on maintaining lean inventories while producing products as needed by the customer.

b. ____ is a philosophy designed to integrate all organizational areas in order to provide customers with superior products and services, while meeting organizational objectives. It requires improving quality and eliminating defects and waste throughout the value chain.

c. ____ can integrate all of a company's worldwide functions, departments, and data into a single system.

d. Firms adopt ____ to conduct business on the Internet.

Requirement

1. Complete the statements with one of the terms listed here. You may use a term more than once, and some terms may not be used at all.

E-commerce	Just-in-time (JIT) manufacturing
Enterprise Resource Planning (ERP)	Total quality management (TQM)

E16-16 ❸ Ethical decisions [15 min]

Sue Peters is the controller at Vroom, a car dealership. Dale Miller recently has been hired as bookkeeper. Dale wanted to attend a class on Excel spreadsheets, so Sue temporarily took over Dale's duties, including overseeing a fund for filling a car's gas tank before a test drive. Sue found a shortage in this fund and confronted Dale when he returned to work. Dale admitted that he occasionally uses this fund to pay for his own gas. Sue estimated that the amount involved is close to $450.

Requirements

1. What should Sue Peters do?

2. Would you change your answer to the previous question if Sue Peters was the one recently hired as controller and Dale Miller was a well-liked, longtime employee who indicated that he always eventually repaid the fund?

E16-17 ❹ Calculating income and cost per unit for a service company [5–10 min]

Fido Grooming provides grooming services in the local community. In April, Kevin Oliver, the owner, incurred the following operating costs to groom 650 dogs:

Wages . . . . $	3,900
Grooming supplies expense . . .	1,625
Building rent expense	1,300
Utilities	325
Depreciation on equipment . . .	130

Fido Grooming earned $16,300 in revenues from grooming for the month of April.

Requirements

1. What is Fido's net operating income for April?

2. What is the cost to groom one dog?

E16-18 ❺ Preparing an income statement and computing the unit cost for a merchandising company [15 min]

Snyder Brush Company sells standard hair brushes. The following information summarizes Snyder's operating activities for 2012:

Selling and administrative expenses . . . . $	49,680
Purchases	78,000
Sales revenue	138,000
Merchandise inventory, January 1, 2012	7,500
Merchandise inventory, December 31, 2012	12,360

Requirements

1. Prepare an income statement for 2012. Compute the ratio of operating expense to total revenue and operating income to total revenue.
2. Snyder sold 6,000 brushes in 2012. Compute the unit cost for one brush.

E16-19 ⑥ Computing cost of goods manufactured [15–20 min]

Consider the following partially completed cost of goods manufactured statements.

	Boswell, Inc.	Laura's Bakery	Rustic Gear
Beginning work in process inventory	(a)	$ 40,500	$ 2,200
Direct materials used	$ 14,200	$ 35,200	(g)
Direct labor	10,800	20,700	1,400
Manufacturing overhead	(b)	10,500	300
Total manufacturing costs incurred during year ...	45,300	(d)	(h)
Total manufacturing costs to account for	$ 55,800	(e)	$ 7,400
Ending work in process inventory	(c)	(25,900)	(2,500)
Cost of goods manufactured	$ 51,200	(f)	(i)

Requirement

1. Complete the missing amounts.

E16-20 ⑥ Preparing a statement of cost of goods manufactured [15–20 min]

Knight, Corp., a lamp manufacturer, provided the following information for the year ended December 31, 2012:

Inventories:	Beginning	Ending
Materials	$ 56,000	$ 23,000
Work in process	103,000	63,000
Finished goods	41,000	48,000

Other information:			
Depreciation: plant building and equipment	$ 16,000	Repairs and maintenance–plant	$ 8,000
Materials purchases	159,000	Indirect labor	32,000
Insurance on plant	22,000	Direct labor	122,000
Sales salaries expense	46,000	Administrative expenses	59,000

Requirements

1. Prepare a schedule of cost of goods manufactured.
2. What is the unit product cost if Knight manufactured 2,160 lamps for the year?

E16-21 ⑥ Flow of costs through a manufacturer's inventory accounts [15–20 min]

Consider the following data for a manufacturer:

	Beginning of Year	End of Year
Direct materials inventory	$ 29,000	$ 32,000
Work in process inventory	44,000	37,000
Finished goods inventory	19,000	24,000
Purchases of direct materials ...		77,000
Direct labor		87,000
Manufacturing overhead		45,000

Requirement

1. Compute cost of goods manufactured and cost of goods sold.

• Problems (Group A)

P16-22A ❶ ❷ ❹ Calculating income and unit cost for a service company [15–20 min] MyAccountingLab

The Windshield People repair chips in car windshields in the company's home county. Rocky Chip, the owner, incurred the following operating costs for the month of February 2012:

Salaries and wages	$ 9,000
Windshield repair materials	4,900
Depreciation on truck	250
Depreciation on building and equipment	800
Supplies expense	600
Gasoline and utilities	2,130

The Windshield People earned $26,000 in revenues for the month of February by repairing 500 windshields. All costs shown are considered to be directly related to the repair service.

Requirements

1. Prepare an income statement for the month of February. Compute the ratio of total operating expense to total revenue and operating income to total revenue.

2. Compute the per unit cost of repairing one windshield.

3. The manager of The Windshield People must keep unit operating cost below $50 per windshield in order to get his bonus. Did he meet the goal?

4. What kind of system could The Windshield People use to integrate all its data?

P16-23A ❸ Apply ethical standards to decision making [20–25 min]

Natalia Wallace is the new controller for Smart Software, Inc., which develops and sells education software. Shortly before the December 31 fiscal year-end, James Cauvet, the company president, asks Wallace how things look for the year-end numbers. He is not happy to learn that earnings growth may be below 13% for the first time in the company's five-year history. Cauvet explains that financial analysts have again predicted a 13% earnings growth for the company and that he does not intend to disappoint them. He suggests that Wallace talk to the assistant controller, who can explain how the previous controller dealt with such situations. The assistant controller suggests the following strategies:

a. Persuade suppliers to postpone billing $13,000 in invoices until January 1.

b. Record as sales $115,000 in certain software awaiting sale that is held in a public warehouse.

c. Delay the year-end closing a few days into January of the next year, so that some of next year's sales are included as this year's sales.

d. Reduce the estimated Bad debt expense from 5% of Sales revenue to 3%, given the company's continued strong performance.

e. Postpone routine monthly maintenance expenditures from December to January.

Requirements

1. Which of these suggested strategies are inconsistent with IMA standards?

2. What should Wallace do if Cauvet insists that she follow all of these suggestions?

P16-24A ⑤ **Preparing an income statement for a merchandising company [45–55 min]**

In 2012 Charlie Snyder opened Charlie's Pets, a small retail shop selling pet supplies. On December 31, 2012, Charlie's accounting records showed the following:

Inventory on December 31, 2012	$	10,200
Inventory on January 1, 2012		15,100
Sales revenue		57,000
Utilities for shop		3,900
Rent for shop		4,100
Sales commissions		2,150
Purchases of merchandise		27,000

Requirement

1. Prepare an income statement for Charlie's Pets, a merchandiser, for the year ended December 31, 2012.

P16-25A ⑥ **Preparing cost of goods manufactured schedule and income statement for a manufacturing company [30–45 min]**

Charlie's Pets succeeded so well that Charlie decided to manufacture his own brand of chewing bone—Fido Treats. At the end of December 2012, his accounting records showed the following:

Inventories:	Beginning		Ending
Materials	$ 13,400		$ 9,500
Work in process	0		2,000
Finished goods	0		5,300

Other information:			
Direct material purchases	$ 33,000	Utilities for plant	$ 1,600
Plant janitorial services	800	Rent of plant	13,000
Sales salaries expense	5,000	Customer service hotline expense	1,400
Delivery expense	1,700	Direct labor	22,000
Sales revenue	109,000		

Requirements

1. Prepare a schedule of cost of goods manufactured for Fido Treats for the year ended December 31, 2012.
2. Prepare an income statement for Fido Treats for the year ended December 31, 2012.
3. How does the format of the income statement for Fido Treats differ from the income statement of a merchandiser?
4. Fido Treats manufactured 18,075 units of its product in 2012. Compute the company's unit product cost for the year.

P16-26A ⑥ **Preparing financial statements for a manufacturer [25–35 min]**

Certain item descriptions and amounts are missing from the monthly schedule of cost of goods manufactured and the income statement of Tioga Manufacturing Company.

TIOGA MANUFACTURING COMPANY			
_____			
_____ June 30, 2012			
Beginning _____			$ 22,000
Direct _____ :			
Beginning direct materials inventory	$ X		
Purchase of materials	54,000		
_____	$ 80,000		
Ending direct materials inventory	(23,000)		
Direct _____		$ X	
Direct _____		X	
Manufacturing overhead		43,000	
Total _____ costs _____			175,000
Total _____ costs _____			$ X
Ending _____			(29,000)
_____			$ X

TIOGA MANUFACTURING COMPANY			
_____			
_____ June 30, 2012			
Sales revenue			$ X
Cost of goods sold:			
Beginning _____		$ 112,000	
_____		X	
Cost of goods _____		$ X	
Ending _____		X	
Cost of goods sold			217,000
Gross profit			$ 283,000
_____ expenses:			
Marketing expenses		$ 94,000	
Administrative expenses		X	159,000
_____ income			$ X

Requirement

1. Fill in the missing words (____) and amounts (X).

P16-27A **6** **Flow of costs through a manufacturer's inventory accounts [20–25 min]**

Root Shoe Company makes loafers. During the most recent year, Root incurred total manufacturing costs of $26,400,000. Of this amount, $2,100,000 was direct materials used and $19,800,000 was direct labor. Beginning balances for the year were Direct materials inventory, $600,000; Work in process inventory, $800,000; and Finished goods inventory, $700,000. At the end of the year, inventory accounts showed these amounts:

	Materials	Direct Labor	Manufacturing Overhead
Direct materials inventory	$ 900,000	$ 0	$ 0
Work in process inventory	400,000	600,000	400,000
Finished goods inventory	800,000	150,000	40,000

Requirements

1. Compute Root Shoe Company's cost of goods manufactured for the year.
2. Compute Root's cost of goods sold for the year.
3. Compute the cost of materials purchased during the year.

● Problems (Group B)

MyAccountingLab

P16-28B **1** **2** **4** **Calculating income and unit cost for a service company [15–20 min]**

Total Glass Company repairs chips in car windshields in the company's home county. Gary White, the owner, incurred the following operating costs for the month of July 2012:

Salaries and wages	$ 11,000
Windshield repair materials	4,800
Depreciation on truck	550
Depreciation on building and equipment	1,200
Supplies expense	300
Gasoline and utilities	2,620

Total Glass Company earned $23,000 in revenues for the month of July by repairing 200 windshields. All costs shown are considered to be directly related to the repair service.

Requirements

1. Prepare an income statement for the month of July. Compute the ratio of total operating expense to total revenue and operating income to total revenue.
2. Compute the per unit cost of repairing one windshield.
3. The manager of Total Glass Company must keep unit operating cost below $70 per windshield in order to get his bonus. Did he meet the goal?
4. What kind of system could Total Glass Company use to integrate all its data?

P16-29B **3** **Apply ethical standards to decision making [20–25 min]**

Ava Borzi is the new controller for Halo Software, Inc., which develops and sells education software. Shortly before the December 31 fiscal year-end, Jeremy Busch, the company president, asks Borzi how things look for the year-end numbers. He is not happy to learn that earnings growth may be below 9% for the first time in the company's five-year history. Busch explains that financial analysts have again predicted a 9% earnings growth for the company and that he does not intend to disappoint them. He suggests that Borzi talk to the assistant controller, who can explain how the previous controller dealt with such situations. The assistant controller suggests the following strategies:

a. Persuade suppliers to postpone billing $18,000 in invoices until January 1.

b. Record as sales $120,000 in certain software awaiting sale that is held in a public warehouse.

c. Delay the year-end closing a few days into January of the next year so that some of next year's sales are included as this year's sales.

d. Reduce the estimated Bad debt expense from 3% of Sales revenue to 2%, given the company's continued strong performance.

e. Postpone routine monthly maintenance expenditures from December to January.

Requirements

1. Which of these suggested strategies are inconsistent with IMA standards?

2. What should Borzi do if Busch insists that she follow all of these suggestions?

P16-30B ⑤ Preparing an income statement for a merchandising company [45–55 min]

In 2012 Craig Gonzales opened Craig's Pets, a small retail shop selling pet supplies. On December 31, 2012, Craig's accounting records showed the following:

Inventory on December 31, 2012	$	10,100
Inventory on January 1, 2012		15,400
Sales revenue		58,000
Utilities for shop		3,300
Rent for shop		4,500
Sales commissions		2,850
Purchases of merchandise		26,000

Requirement

1. Prepare an income statement for Craig's Pets, a merchandiser, for the year ended December 31, 2012.

P16-31B ⑥ Preparing cost of goods manufactured schedule and income statement for a manufacturing company [30–45 min]

Craig's Pets succeeded so well that Craig decided to manufacture his own brand of chewing bone—Organic Bones. At the end of December 2012, his accounting records showed the following:

Inventories:	Beginning		Ending	
Materials	$ 13,200		$ 7,000	
Work in process	0		4,000	
Finished goods	0		5,800	

Other information:				
Direct material purchases	$ 31,000	Utilities for plant	$ 1,900	
Plant janitorial services	200	Rent on plant	11,000	
Sales salaries expense	5,400	Customer service hotline expense	1,200	
Delivery expense	1,400	Direct labor	23,000	
Sales revenue	110,000			

Requirements

1. Prepare a schedule of cost of goods manufactured for Organic Bones for the year ended December 31, 2012.

2. Prepare an income statement for Organic Bones for the year ended December 31, 2012.

3. How does the format of the income statement for Organic Bones differ from the income statement of a merchandiser?

4. Organic Bones manufactured 15,400 units of its product in 2012. Compute the company's unit product cost for the year.

P16-32B ⑥ **Preparing financial statements for a manufacturer [25–35 min]**
Certain item descriptions and amounts are missing from the monthly schedule of cost
of goods manufactured and the income statement of Pinta Manufacturing Company.

PINTA MANUFACTURING COMPANY			
_____ June 30, 2012			
Beginning _____			$ 25,000
Direct _____:			
Beginning direct materials inventory	$ X		
Purchase of materials	57,000		
_____	$ 85,000		
Ending direct materials inventory	(22,000)		
Direct _____		$ X	
Direct _____		X	
Manufacturing overhead		45,000	
Total _____ costs _____			182,000
Total _____ costs _____			$ X
Ending _____			(21,000)
_____			$ X

PINTA MANUFACTURING COMPANY		
_____ June 30, 2012		
Sales revenue		$ X
Cost of goods sold:		
Beginning _____	$ 113,000	
_____	X	
Cost of goods _____	$ X	
Ending _____	X	
Cost of goods sold		231,000
Gross profit		$ 209,000
_____ expenses:		
Marketing expenses	$ 93,000	
Administrative expenses	X	154,000
_____ income		$ X

Requirement

1. Fill in the missing words (___) and amounts (X).

P16-33B ⑥ **Flow of costs through a manufacturer's inventory accounts [20–25 min]**
Renka Shoe Company makes loafers. During the most recent year, Renka incurred
total manufacturing costs of $22,900,000. Of this amount, $2,800,000 was direct
materials used and $15,800,000 was direct labor. Beginning balances for the year
were Direct materials inventory, $900,000; Work in process inventory, $1,500,000;
and Finished goods inventory, $900,000. At the end of the year, inventory accounts
showed these amounts:

	Materials	Direct Labor	Manufacturing Overhead
Direct materials inventory	$ 800,000	$ 0	$ 0
Work in process inventory	700,000	500,000	300,000
Finished goods inventory	200,000	550,000	60,000

Requirements

1. Compute Renka Shoe Company's cost of goods manufactured for the year.
2. Compute Renka's cost of goods sold for the year.
3. Compute the cost of materials purchased during the year.

● Continuing Exercise

E16-34 ❻ **Classifying costs of a manufacturer [10–15 min]**

MyAccountingLab

This exercise continues the Lawlor Lawn Service, Inc., situation from Exercise 15-34 of Chapter 15. Lawlor is considering manufacturing a weed eater. Lawlor expects to incur the following manufacturing costs:

Shaft and handle of weed eater.

Motor of weed eater.

Factory labor for workers assembling weed eaters.

Nylon thread used by the weed eater (not traced to the job by Lawlor).

Glue to hold housing together.

Plant janitorial wages.

Depreciation on factory equipment.

Rent on plant.

Sales commission expense.

Administrative salaries

Plant utilities.

Shipping costs to deliver finished weed eaters to customers.

Requirement

1. Classify each cost as either direct materials, direct labor, factory overhead, or period costs.

● Continuing Problem

P16-35 ❻ **Classifying costs of a manufacturer [20–25 min]**

MyAccountingLab

This problem continues the Draper Consulting, Inc., situation from Problem 15-35 of Chapter 15. Draper is going to manufacture billing software. During its first month of manufacturing, Draper incurred the following manufacturing costs:

Inventories:	Beginning		Ending
Materials	$ 10,800		$ 10,300
Work in process	0		21,000
Finished goods	0		31,500

Other information:			
Direct material purchases	$ 19,000	Utilities for plant	$ 10,000
Plant janitorial services	700	Rent of plant	13,000
Sales salaries expense	5,000	Customer service hotline expense	18,000
Delivery expense	1,700	Direct labor	190,000
Sales revenue	750,000		

Requirement

1. Prepare a schedule of cost of goods manufactured for Draper for the month ended January 31, 2014.

Apply Your Knowledge

● Decision Cases

Decision Case 16-1 PowerSwitch, Inc., designs and manufactures switches used in telecommunications. Serious flooding throughout North Carolina affected PowerSwitch's facilities. Inventory was completely ruined, and the company's computer system, including all accounting records, was destroyed.

Before the disaster recovery specialists clean the buildings, Stephen Plum, the company controller, is anxious to salvage whatever records he can to support an insurance claim for the destroyed inventory. He is standing in what is left of the accounting department with Paul Lopez, the cost accountant.

"I didn't know mud could smell so bad," Paul says. "What should I be looking for?"

"Don't worry about beginning inventory numbers," responds Stephen, "we'll get them from last year's annual report. We need first-quarter cost data."

"I was working on the first-quarter results just before the storm hit," Paul says. "Look, my report's still in my desk drawer. All I can make out is that for the first quarter, material purchases were $476,000 and direct labor, manufacturing overhead, and total manufacturing costs to account for were $505,000; $245,000; and $1,425,000; respectively. Wait! Cost of goods available for sale was $1,340,000."

"Great," says Stephen. "I remember that sales for the period were approximately $1,700,000. Given our gross profit of 30%, that's all you should need."

Paul is not sure about that, but decides to see what he can do with this information. The beginning inventory numbers are

- Direct materials, $113,000
- Work in process, $229,000
- Finished goods, $154,000

He remembers a schedule he learned in college that may help him get started.

Requirements

1. Exhibit 16-11 resembles the schedule Paul has in mind. Use it to determine the ending inventories of direct materials, work in process, and finished goods.
2. Itemize a list of the book value of inventory lost.

Decision Case 16-2 The IMA's Statement of Ethical Professional Practice can be applied to more than just managerial accounting. They are also relevant to college students.

Requirement

1. Explain at least one situation that shows how each IMA standard in Exhibit 16-3 is relevant to your experiences as a student. For example, the ethical standard of competence would suggest not cutting classes!

● Ethical Issue 16-1

Becky Knauer recently resigned from her position as controller for Shamalay Automotive, a small, struggling foreign car dealer in Upper Saddle River, New Jersey. Becky has just started a new job as controller for Mueller Imports, a much larger dealer for the same car manufacturer. Demand for this particular make of car is exploding, and the manufacturer cannot produce enough to satisfy demand. The manufacturer's regional sales managers are each given a certain number of cars. Each sales manager then decides how to divide the cars among the independently owned dealerships in the region. Because of high demand for these cars, dealerships all want to receive as many cars as they can from the regional sales manager.

Becky's former employer, Shamalay Automotive, receives only about 25 cars a month. Consequently, Shamalay was not very profitable.

Becky is surprised to learn that her new employer, Mueller Imports, receives over 200 cars a month. Becky soon gets another surprise. Every couple of months, a local jeweler bills the dealer $5,000 for "miscellaneous services." Franz Mueller, the owner of the dealership, personally approves payment of these invoices, noting that each invoice is a "selling expense." From casual conversations with a salesperson, Becky learns that Mueller frequently gives Rolex watches to the manufacturer's regional sales manager and other sales executives. Before talking to anyone about this, Becky decides to work through her ethical dilemma.

Requirement

1. Put yourself in Becky's place.
   a. What is the ethical issue?
   b. What are your options?
   c. What are the possible consequences?
   d. What should you do?

● Fraud Case 16-1

Juan Gomez was the fastest rising star of a small CPA firm in West Palm Beach. Most of his clients traveled in stratospheric circles of wealth, and Juan knew that fitting in with this crowd was essential to his career. Although he made good money, it wasn't enough to live that kind of lifestyle. Meanwhile, Juan had become friends with one of his clients, Tony Russo. Knowing Russo's books inside and out, and being on close terms with him, Juan asked Tony for a personal loan. Juan was sure he'd be able to pay it back when he got his next bonus, but things stretched out, and additional loans were made. Two years later, Tony's company hit some losses, and the numbers were looking grim. Tony reminded Juan that it would not look good for his career if his CPA firm knew Juan had borrowed from a client, and so Juan changed a few numbers and signed off on clean financials for Tony's firm. This went on for three years, until one morning when Juan got a call. Russo had died; his sons had gone through the books, and the whole scheme came out. Juan did some prison time and lost his license, but he was repentant, and made an instructional video for accounting students to warn them of the temptations they may encounter in the real world of business.

Requirements

1. Although the protagonist of this story worked in public accounting, please refer to the Statement of Ethical Professional Practice in Exhibit 16-3 and discuss which of those issues are reflected in this case.

2. Could Juan have extricated himself from his situation? How?

● Team Project 16-1

Search the Internet for a nearby company that also has a Web page. Arrange an interview for your team with a managerial accountant, a controller, or other accounting/finance officer of the company.

Requirements

Before your team conducts the interview, answer the following questions:

1. Is this a service, merchandising, or manufacturing company? What is its primary product or service?

2. Is the primary purpose of the company's Web site to provide information about the company and its products, to sell online, or to provide financial information for investors?

3. Are parts of the company's Web site restricted so that you need password authorization to enter? What appears to be the purpose of limiting access?

4. Does the Web site provide an e-mail link for contacting the company?

At the interview, begin by clarifying your team's answers to questions 1 through 4, and ask the following additional questions:

5. If the company sells over the Web, what benefits has the company derived? Did the company perform a cost-benefit analysis before deciding to begin Web sales?

   Or

   If the company does not sell over the Web, why not? Has the company performed a cost-benefit analysis and decided not to sell over the Web?

6. What is the biggest cost of operating the Web site?

7. Does the company make any purchases over the Internet? What percentage?

8. How has e-commerce affected the company's managerial accounting system? Have the managerial accountant's responsibilities become more or less complex? More or less interesting?

9. Does the company use Web-based accounting applications, such as accounts receivable or accounts payable?

10. Does the company use an ERP system? If so, do managers view the system as a success? What have been the benefits? The costs?

   Your team should summarize your findings in a short paper. Provide any exhibits that enhance your explanation of key items. Provide proper references and a works cited page.

• Communication Activity 16-1

In 100 words or fewer, explain the difference between inventoriable product costs and period costs. In your explanation, explain the inventory accounts of a manufacturer.

Quick Check Answers

1. *a* 2. *b* 3. *d* 4. *c* 5. *d* 6. *c* 7. *c* 8. *b* 9. *b* 10. *d*

For online homework, exercises, and problems that provide you immediate feedback, please visit myaccountinglab.com.

17 Job Order and Process Costing

Shift Your Focus · Product Costing · Cost Allocation

Cost-Volume-Profit · Relevant Information · Capital Budgeting

Budgeting · Cost Control · Performance Measures

Learning Objectives

1. Distinguish between job order costing and process costing

2. Record materials and labor in a job order costing system

3. Record overhead in a job order costing system

4. Record completion and sales of finished goods and the adjustment for under- or overallocated overhead

5. Calculate unit costs for a service company

6. Allocate costs using a process costing system—weighted-average method (see Appendix 17A)

You're a music major completing some coursework by working at a local elementary school. You enjoy being with the children, but some of the school's musical equipment desperately needs to be replaced. However, due to budget constraints, there are no immediate plans to replace the equipment. You therefore decide to work with your college service organization to raise funds for the school's music program. You suggest a spaghetti dinner for the fund raiser, but you're concerned the members of your service organization will invest a lot of time and money into a project that will not be profitable. You need to determine how much it will cost the group to prepare each dinner and the price to charge for each spaghetti plate. The price needs to be low enough to draw a crowd but high enough to cover the cost and provide a profit. How do you do it?

• • •

This chapter shows how to measure cost in situations similar to the spaghetti dinner. This type of cost accounting system is called *job order costing* because production is arranged by the job. The appendix to this chapter then covers the other main type of costing system—called *process costing*.

Businesses face the same situation. They must draw a crowd and sell enough goods and services to earn a profit. So, regardless of the type of business you own or manage, you need to know how much it costs to produce your product or service.

For example, marketing managers must consider their unit product cost in order to set the selling price high enough to cover costs. Engineers study the materials, labor, and overhead that go into a product to pinpoint ways to cut costs. Production managers then decide whether it is more profitable to make the product or to *outsource* it (buy from an outside supplier). The Finance Department arranges financing for the venture. The Accounting Department collects all the cost data from the purchasing, design, and production departments for making these decisions.

You can see that it is important for managers in all areas to know how much it costs to make a product. This chapter shows you how to figure these costs for Smart Touch Learning.

How Much Does It Cost to Make a Product? Two Approaches

 Distinguish between job order costing and process costing

Cost accounting systems accumulate cost information so that managers can measure how much it costs to produce each unit of merchandise. For example, **Intel** must know how much each processor costs to produce. **FedEx** knows its cost of flying each pound of freight one mile. These unit costs help managers

- set selling prices that will lead to profits.
- compute cost of goods sold for the income statement.
- compute the cost of inventory for the balance sheet.

If a manager knows the cost to produce each product, then the manager can plan and control the cost of resources needed to create the product and deliver it to the customer. A cost accounting system assigns these costs to the company's product or service.

Job Order Costing

Some companies manufacture batches of unique products or provide specialized services. A **job order costing** system accumulates costs for each batch, or job. Accounting firms, music studios, health-care providers, building contractors, and furniture manufacturers are examples of companies that use job order costing systems. For example, **Dell** makes personal computers based on customer orders (see the "Customize" button on **Dell**'s Web site). As we move to a more service-based economy and with the advent of ERP systems, job order costing has become more prevalent.

Process Costing

Other companies, such as **Procter & Gamble** and **Coca-Cola** produce identical units through a series of production steps or processes. A **process costing** system accumulates the costs of each *process* needed to complete the product. So, for example, **Coca-Cola**'s process steps may include mixing, bottling, and packaging. A surfboard manufacturing company's process steps may include sanding, painting, waxing, and packaging. A medical equipment manufacturer of a blood glucose meter's process steps may include soldering, assembly, and testing. Process costing is used primarily by large producers of similar goods.

Both job order and process costing systems

- accumulate the costs incurred to make the product.
- assign costs to the products.

Accountants use **cost tracing** to assign directly traceable costs, such as direct materials and direct labor, to the product. They use a less precise technique—**cost allocation**—to assign manufacturing overhead and other indirect costs to the product. Let's see how a job order costing system works for a manufacturing company.

How Job Costs Flow Through the Accounts: An Overview

A job order costing system tracks costs as raw materials move from the storeroom, to the production floor, to finished products. Exhibit 17-1 diagrams the flow of costs through the accounts in a job order costing system. Let's consider how a manufacturer, Smart Touch, uses job order costing. For Smart Touch, each customer order is a separate job. Smart Touch uses a job cost record to accumulate the following costs for each job:

- direct materials.
- direct labor.
- manufacturing overhead.

2 Record materials and labor in a job order costing system

The company starts the job cost record when work begins on the job. As Smart Touch incurs costs, the company adds costs to the job cost record. For jobs started but not yet finished, the job cost records show costs that accumulate as costs are added to the Work in process (WIP) inventory. When Smart Touch finishes a job, the company totals the costs and transfers costs from Work in process inventory to Finished goods inventory.

When the job's units are sold, the costing system moves the costs from Finished goods inventory, an asset, to Cost of goods sold (COGS), an expense. Exhibit 17-1 summarizes this sequence.

EXHIBIT 17-1 | **Flow of Costs Through the Accounts in a Job Order Costing System**

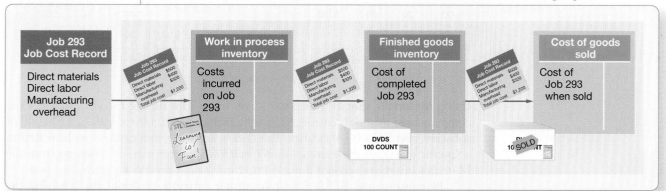

Purchasing Materials On December 31, 2013, Smart Touch had the following inventory balances:

Materials inventory	Work in process inventory	Finished goods inventory
Bal 12/31/13 70,000	Bal 12/31/13 80,000	Bal 12/31/13 0

During 2014, Smart Touch purchased direct materials of $350,000 and indirect materials of $17,000 on account. We record the purchase of materials as follows:

(1)		Materials inventory (direct) (A+)	350,000	
		Materials inventory (indirect) (A+)	17,000	
		Accounts payable (L+)		367,000

Materials inventory

Bal 12/31/13	70,000
(1) Purchased	350,000
(1) Purchased	17,000

Note that journal entry (1) shows two separate debits to Materials inventory to illustrate the source (direct and indirect materials) and to account for the materials subsidiary ledgers; however, one debit to Materials inventory for $367,000 would also be correct for the general ledger.

Materials inventory is a general ledger account. Smart Touch also uses a subsidiary ledger for materials. The subsidiary materials ledger includes a separate record for each type of material, so there is a subsidiary ledger for the blank DVDs, the paper inserts, and the casings. Exhibit 17-2 shows the subsidiary ledger of one type of casing that Smart Touch uses. The balance of the Materials inventory account in the general ledger should always equal the sum of the balances in the subsidiary materials ledger.

EXHIBIT 17-2 | **Example Subsidiary Materials Ledger Record**

SUBSIDIARY MATERIALS LEDGER RECORD

STL SMART TOUCH LEARNING, INC.

Item No. C–101   Description   5 × 6 Casings

	Received			Issued				Balance		
Date	Units	Cost	Total Cost	Mat. Req. No.	Units	Cost	Total Cost	Units	Cost	Total Cost
2014										
1–20								20	$14	$280
1–23	20	$14	$280					40	14	560
7–24				334	10	$14	$140	30	14	420

Using Materials   Smart Touch works on many jobs during the year. In 2014 the company used materials costing $355,000, including $80,000 of DVDs, $200,000 of software, and $75,000 of casings. The DVDs, software, and casings can be traced to a specific job(s), so these are all *direct materials*. Direct material costs go from the Materials inventory account directly into the Work in process inventory account.

By contrast, the $17,000 cost of printer cartridges to print the labels on the paper inserts is difficult to trace to a specific job, so the printer cartridges are *indirect materials*. The cost of indirect materials goes from the Materials inventory account into the Manufacturing overhead account. The following journal entry then records the issuance of materials into production:

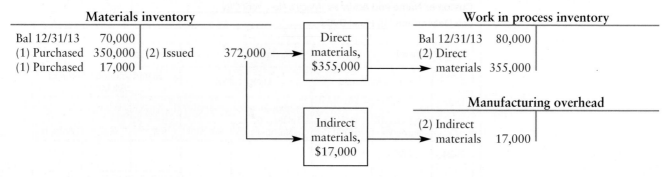

We can summarize the flow of materials costs through the T-accounts as follows:

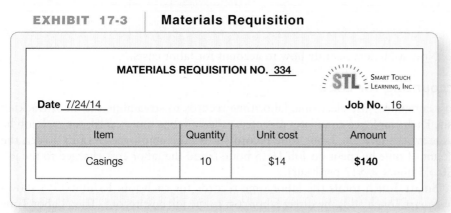

For both direct materials and indirect materials, the production team completes a document called a **materials requisition** to request the transfer of materials to the production floor. **A materials requisition sends the signal to the warehouse to bring materials into production.** These requisitions are often in electronic form rather than paper. For Job 16, Exhibit 17-3 shows Smart Touch's materials requisition for the 10 casings needed to make 10 Excel DVDs.

EXHIBIT 17-3 | **Materials Requisition**

MATERIALS REQUISITION NO. 334

STL SMART TOUCH LEARNING, INC.

Date 7/24/14

Job No. 16

Item	Quantity	Unit cost	Amount
Casings	10	$14	**$140**

Exhibit 17-4 is a **job cost record**. It assigns the cost of the direct material (casings) to Job 16. Follow the $140 cost of the casings from the materials inventory subsidiary ledger record (Exhibit 17-2), through the electronic materials requisition (Exhibit 17-3), and to the job cost record in Exhibit 17-4. Notice that all the dollar amounts in these exhibits show Smart Touch's *costs*—not the prices at which Smart Touch sells its products.

EXHIBIT 17-4 | **Direct Materials on Job Cost Record**

JOB COST RECORD

STL SMART TOUCH LEARNING, INC.

Job No. 16

Customer Name and Address Macy's New York City

Job Description 10 Excel DVDs

Date Promised		7–31	Date Started		7–24	Date Completed		
Date	Direct Materials		Direct Labor			Manufacturing Overhead Allocated		
	Requisition Numbers	Amount	Labor Time Record Numbers	Amount		Date	Rate	Amount
7–24	334	$140						
						Overall Cost Summary Direct Materials.......$ Direct Labor............. Manufacturing Overhead Allocated		
Totals						Total Job Cost.......$		

Now we'll demonstrate how to account for labor costs.

Accounting for Labor

Most companies use electronic labor/time records to streamline the labor tracking costs. Each employee completes an entry, called a labor time record, for each job he or she works on. The **labor time record** shows the employee (Ryan Oliver), the amount of time he spent on Job 16 (5 hours), and the labor cost charged to the job ($60 = 5 hours × $12 per hour).

Smart Touch totals the labor time records for each job. Exhibit 17-5 shows how Smart Touch adds the direct labor cost to the job cost record. The "Labor Time Record Numbers" show that on July 24, three employees worked on Job 16. Labor time record 251 is Ryan Oliver's ($60). Labor time records 236 and 258 indicate that two other employees also worked on Job 16. The job cost record shows that Smart Touch assigned Job 16 a total of $200 of direct labor costs for the three employees' work.

During 2014, Smart Touch incurred total labor costs of $197,000, of which $169,000 was direct labor and $28,000 was indirect labor (overhead). These amounts include the labor costs for Job 16 that we have been working with plus all the company's other jobs worked on during the year.

Smart Touch's accounting for labor cost requires the company to

- assign labor cost to individual jobs, as we saw for Ryan Oliver's work on Job 16.
- transfer labor cost incurred (Wages payable) into Work in process inventory (for direct labor) and into Manufacturing overhead (for indirect labor).

EXHIBIT 17-5 | **Direct Labor on Job Cost Record**

JOB COST RECORD

STL SMART TOUCH LEARNING, INC.

Job No. 16
Customer Name and Address Macy's New York City
Job Description 10 Excel DVDs

Date Promised		7–31	Date Started		7–24	Date Completed		
Date	Direct Materials		Direct Labor			Manufacturing Overhead Allocated		
	Requisition Numbers	Amount	Labor Time Record Numbers	Amount		Date	Rate	Amount
7–24	334	$140	236, 251, 258	$200				
Totals						Total Job Cost..........$		

Overall Cost Summary
Direct Materials..........$
Direct Labor.................
Manufacturing Over-
head Allocated............

The following journal entry records the incurrence of manufacturing wages and the amount of labor cost applied to Work in process inventory and to the Manufacturing overhead accounts.

(3)	Work in process inventory (for direct labor)	(A+)	169,000	
	Manufacturing overhead (for indirect labor)	(E+)	28,000	
	Wages payable (L+)			197,000

This entry divides total manufacturing wages between Work in process inventory ($169,000 of direct labor) and Manufacturing overhead ($28,000 of indirect labor), as shown in the following T-accounts:

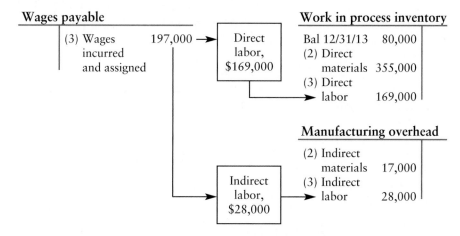

Many companies have automated these accounting procedures. The addition of labor and manufacturing overhead to materials is called **conversion costs** because the labor and overhead costs *convert* materials into a finished product.

Study the Decision Guidelines on the following page, which summarize the first half of the chapter. Then work Summary Problem 17-1 that follows.

Key Takeaway

Direct materials and direct labor associated with a specific job are tracked to a job costing record based on a job number. When direct materials costs are incurred for a job, Work in process inventory is debited and Materials inventory is credited. When direct labor costs are incurred on a job, Work in process inventory is debited and Wages payable is credited. Indirect materials and indirect labor utilized are debited to the Manufacturing overhead account to be allocated to jobs later.

Decision Guidelines 17-1

JOB ORDER COSTING: TRACING DIRECT MATERIALS AND DIRECT LABOR

Smart Touch uses a job order costing system that assigns manufacturing costs to each individual job for DVDs. These guidelines explain some of the decisions Smart Touch made in designing its system.

Decision	Guidelines
• Should we use job costing or process costing?	Use *job order costing* when the company produces unique products (DVDs) in small batches (usually a "batch" contains a specific learning program). Use *process costing* when the company produces identical products in large batches, often in a continuous flow.

• How to record:
  • Purchase and issuance (use) of materials?

Purchase of materials:

Materials inventory	XX	
Accounts payable (or Cash)		XX

Issuance of materials:

Work in process inventory (direct materials)	XX	
Manufacturing overhead (indirect materials)	XX	
Materials inventory		XX

  • Incurrence and assignment of labor to jobs?

Incurrence and assignment of labor cost to jobs:

Work in process inventory (direct labor)	XX	
Manufacturing overhead (indirect labor)	XX	
Wages payable		XX

Summary Problem 17-1

Tom Baker manufactures custom teakwood patio furniture. Suppose Baker has the following transactions:

 a. Purchased raw materials on account, $135,000.
 b. Materials costing $130,000 were requisitioned (issued) for use in production. Of this total, $30,000 were indirect materials.
 c. Labor time records show that direct labor of $22,000 and indirect labor of $5,000 were incurred (but not yet paid) and assigned.

Requirement

 1. Prepare journal entries for each transaction. Then explain each journal entry in terms of what got increased and what got decreased.

Solution

a.	Materials inventory (A+)	135,000	
	Accounts payable (L+)		135,000

When materials are purchased on account,

 • debit (increase) Materials inventory for the *cost* of the materials purchased.
 • credit (increase) Accounts payable to record the liability for the materials.

b.	Work in process inventory (A+)	100,000	
	Manufacturing overhead (E+)	30,000	
	Materials inventory (A–)		130,000

When materials are requisitioned (issued) for use in production, we record the movement of materials out of materials inventory and into production, as follows:

 • Debit (increase) Work in process inventory for the cost of the *direct* materials (in this case, $100,000—the $130,000 total materials requisitioned minus the $30,000 indirect materials).
 • Debit (increase) Manufacturing overhead for the *indirect* materials cost.
 • Credit (decrease) Materials inventory for the cost of both direct and indirect materials moved into production from the materials storage area.

c.	Work in process inventory (A+)	22,000	
	Manufacturing overhead (E+)	5,000	
	Wages payable (L+)		27,000

To record the incurrence and assignment of labor costs,

 • debit (increase) Work in process inventory for the cost of the *direct* labor.
 • debit (increase) Manufacturing overhead for the cost of the *indirect* labor.
 • credit (increase) Wages payable to record the liability for wages not paid.

Job Order Costing: Allocating Manufacturing Overhead

3 Record overhead in a job order costing system

All manufacturing overhead costs are *accumulated* as debits to a single general ledger account—Manufacturing overhead. We have already assigned the costs of indirect materials (entry 2, $17,000) and indirect labor (entry 3, $28,000) to Manufacturing overhead. In addition to indirect materials and indirect labor, Smart Touch incurred the following overhead costs:

- Depreciation on manufacturing plant and manufacturing equipment, $10,000
- Plant utilities, $7,000
- Plant insurance, $6,000 (previously paid)
- Property taxes incurred, but not yet paid, on the plant, $5,000

Entries 4 through 7 record these manufacturing overhead costs. The account titles in parentheses indicate the specific records that were debited in the overhead subsidiary ledger.

(4)	Manufacturing overhead (Depreciation—plant		
	and equipment) (E+)	10,000	
	Accumulated depreciation—plant		
	and equipment (CA+)		10,000
(5)	Manufacturing overhead (Plant utilities) (E+)	7,000	
	Cash (A–)		7,000
(6)	Manufacturing overhead (Plant insurance) (E+)	6,000	
	Prepaid insurance—plant (A–)		6,000
(7)	Manufacturing overhead (Property taxes—plant) (E+)	5,000	
	Property taxes payable (L+)		5,000

The actual manufacturing overhead costs (such as indirect materials and indirect labor, plus depreciation, utilities, insurance, and property taxes on the plant) are debited to Manufacturing overhead as they occur throughout the year. By the end of the year, the Manufacturing overhead account has accumulated all the actual overhead costs as debits:

Manufacturing overhead	
(2) Indirect materials	17,000
(3) Indirect labor	28,000
(4) Depreciation—plant and equipment	10,000
(5) Plant utilities	7,000
(6) Plant insurance	6,000
(7) Property taxes—plant	5,000
Total overhead cost	73,000

Now you have seen how Smart Touch *accumulates* (debits) actual overhead costs in the accounting records. But how does Smart Touch allocate (assign) overhead costs to individual jobs? As you can see, overhead includes a variety of costs that the company cannot trace to individual jobs. For example, it is impossible to say how much of the cost of plant utilities is related to Job 16. Yet manufacturing overhead costs are as essential as direct materials and direct labor, so Smart Touch must find some way to allocate (assign) overhead costs to specific jobs. Otherwise, each job would not bear its fair share of the total cost. Smart Touch may then set unrealistic prices for some of its DVDs and wind up losing money on some of its hard-earned sales.

1. **Compute the predetermined manufacturing overhead rate.** The **predetermined manufacturing overhead rate** is computed as follows:

$$\text{Predetermined manufacturing overhead rate} = \frac{\text{Total estimated manufacturing overhead costs}}{\text{Total estimated quantity of the manufacturing overhead allocation base}}$$

The most accurate allocation can be made only when total overhead cost is known—and that is not until the end of the period. But managers cannot wait that long for product cost information. So the predetermined manufacturing overhead rate is calculated before the period begins. Companies use this predetermined rate to allocate estimated overhead cost to individual jobs. The predetermined manufacturing overhead rate is based on two factors:

- Total *estimated* manufacturing overhead costs for the period (in Smart Touch's case, one year)
- Total *estimated* quantity of the manufacturing overhead allocation base

The key to allocating (assigning) indirect manufacturing costs to jobs is to identify a workable manufacturing overhead allocation base. The **allocation base** is a common denominator that links overhead costs to the products. **Ideally, the allocation base is the primary cost driver of manufacturing overhead—that is, the more "allocation base," the more overhead costs and vice-versa.** As the phrase implies, a **cost driver** is the primary factor that causes (drives) a cost. Traditionally, manufacturing companies have used the following as cost drivers (allocation bases):

- Direct labor hours (for labor-intensive production environments)
- Direct labor cost (for labor-intensive production environments)
- Machine hours (for machine-intensive production environments)

Smart Touch uses only one allocation base, direct labor cost, to assign manufacturing overhead to jobs. Later in the textbook, we will look at other ways to assign overhead to jobs.

2. **Allocate manufacturing overhead costs to jobs as the company makes its products.** Allocate manufacturing overhead cost to jobs as follows:

$$\text{Allocated manufacturing overhead cost} = \text{\textit{Predetermined} manufacturing overhead rate (from Step 1)} \times \text{\textit{Actual} quantity of the allocation base used by each job}$$

As we have seen, Smart Touch traces direct costs directly to each job. But how does Smart Touch allocate overhead cost to jobs? Recall that indirect manufacturing costs include plant depreciation, utilities, insurance, and property taxes, plus indirect materials and indirect labor.

1. Smart Touch uses direct labor cost as the allocation base. In 2013, Smart Touch estimated that total overhead costs for 2014 would be $68,000 and direct labor cost would total $170,000. Using this information, we can compute the predetermined manufacturing overhead rate as follows:

$$\begin{aligned} \text{Predetermined} \\ \text{manufacturing} \\ \text{overhead rate} \end{aligned} = \frac{\text{Total estimated manufacturing overhead costs}}{\text{Total estimated quantity of the manufacturing}} \\ \text{overhead allocation base}$$

$$= \frac{\text{Total estimated manufacturing overhead costs}}{\text{Total estimated direct labor cost}}$$

$$= \frac{\$68,000}{\$170,000} = 0.40 \text{ or } 40\%$$

As jobs are completed in 2014, Smart Touch will allocate overhead costs by assigning 40% of each direct labor dollar incurred for the job as manufacturing overhead cost. Smart Touch uses the same predetermined overhead rate (40% of direct labor cost) to allocate manufacturing overhead to all jobs worked on throughout the year. Now back to Job 16.

2. The total direct labor cost for Job 16 is $200 and the predetermined manufacturing overhead rate is 40% of direct labor cost. Therefore, Smart Touch allocates $80 ($200 × 0.40) of manufacturing overhead to Job 16 (the journal entry would debit Work in progress inventory $200 and credit Manufacturing overhead $200).

The completed job cost record for the Macy's order (Exhibit 17-6) shows that Job 16 cost Smart Touch a total of $420, comprised of $140 for direct materials, $200 for direct labor, and $80 of allocated manufacturing overhead. Job 16 produced 10 DVDs, so Smart Touch's cost per DVD is $42 ($420 ÷ 10).

EXHIBIT 17-6 | **Manufacturing Overhead on Job Cost Record**

JOB COST RECORD

STL SMART TOUCH LEARNING, INC.

Job No.   16

Customer Name and Address   Macy's New York City

Job Description   10 Excel DVDs

Date Promised		7–31	Date Started	7–24	Date Completed		7–29
	Direct Materials		Direct Labor		Manufacturing Overhead Allocated		
Date	Requisition Numbers	Amount	Labor Time Record Numbers	Amount	Date	Rate	Amount
7–24	334	$140	236, 251, 258	$200	7–29	40% of Direct Labor Cost	$80
					Overall Cost Summary		
					Direct Materials $140		
					Direct Labor....................200		
					Manufacturing Overhead Allocated 80		
Totals		$140		$200	Total Job Cost............$420		
					Cost per DVD.............$ 42		

Smart Touch worked on many jobs, including Job 16, during 2014. The company allocated manufacturing overhead to each of these jobs. Smart Touch's direct labor cost for 2014 was $169,000, so total overhead allocated to all jobs is 40% of the $169,000 direct labor cost, or $67,600. The journal entry to allocate manufacturing overhead cost to Work in process inventory is as follows:

(8)	Work in process inventory (A+)	67,600	
	Manufacturing overhead (E–)		67,600

After allocating manufacturing overhead to jobs for 2014, a $5,400 debit balance remains in the Manufacturing overhead account. This means that Smart Touch's actual overhead costs of $73,000 were greater than the overhead allocated to jobs in Work in process inventory of $67,600. We say that Smart Touch's Manufacturing overhead is *underallocated* because the company allocated only $67,600 to jobs but actually incurred $73,000 of manufacturing overhead. We will show how to correct this problem later in the chapter.

The flow of manufacturing overhead through the T-accounts follows:

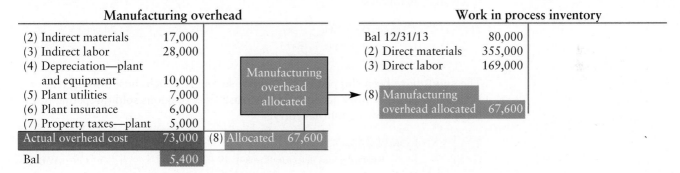

Accounting for Completion and Sale of Finished Goods and Adjusting Manufacturing Overhead

Now you know how to accumulate and assign the cost of direct materials, direct labor, and overhead to jobs. To complete the process, we must do the following:

- Account for the completion and sale of finished goods
- Adjust manufacturing overhead at the end of the period

4 Record completion and sales of finished goods and the adjustment for under- or overallocated overhead

Accounting for the Completion and Sale of Finished Goods

Study Exhibit 17-1 to review the flow of costs as a job goes from work in process to finished goods to cost of goods sold. Smart Touch reported the following inventory balances one year ago, back on December 31, 2013:

Materials inventory......................	$70,000
Work in process inventory	80,000
Finished goods inventory..............	0

The following transactions occurred in 2014:

Cost of goods manufactured	$ 644,600
Sales on account...........................	1,200,000
Cost of goods sold.........................	594,600

The $644,600 cost of goods manufactured is the cost of all jobs Smart Touch completed during 2014. (Normally, this entry would be made as each individual job is completed.) The cost of goods manufactured goes from Work in process inventory to Finished goods inventory as jobs are completed and moved into the finished goods storage area. Smart Touch records goods completed in 2014 as follows:

(9)	Finished goods inventory (A+)	644,600	
	Work in process inventory (A–)		644,600

As the DVDs are sold on account, Smart Touch records sales revenue and accounts receivable, as follows:

(10)	Accounts receivable (A+)	1,200,000	
	Sales revenue (R+)		1,200,000

The goods have been shipped to customers, so Smart Touch must also decrease the Finished goods inventory account and increase Cost of goods sold (perpetual inventory) with the following journal entry:

(10b)	Cost of goods sold (E+)	594,600	
	Finished goods inventory (A–)		594,600

The key T-accounts for Smart Touch's manufacturing costs now show:

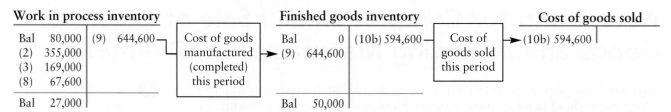

Some jobs are completed, and their costs are transferred out to Finished goods inventory, $644,600. We end the period with other jobs started but not finished ($27,000 ending balance of Work in process inventory) and jobs completed and not sold ($50,000 ending balance of Finished goods inventory).

Adjusting Manufacturing Overhead at the End of the Period

During 2014, Smart Touch

- debits Manufacturing overhead for actual overhead costs.
- credits Manufacturing overhead for amounts allocated to Work in process inventory.

The total debits to the Manufacturing overhead account rarely equal the total credits. Why? Because Smart Touch allocates overhead to jobs using a *predetermined* manufacturing overhead rate that is based on *estimates*. The predetermined manufacturing overhead rate represents the *expected* relationship between overhead costs and the allocation base. In our example, the $5,400 debit balance of Manufacturing overhead is called **underallocated overhead** because the manufacturing overhead allocated to Work in process inventory was *less* than the actual overhead cost. (If it had been **overallocated** instead, the Manufacturing overhead account would have had a credit balance.)

Accountants adjust underallocated and overallocated overhead at the end of the period when closing the Manufacturing overhead account. Closing the account means zeroing it out, so when overhead is underallocated, as in our example, a credit to Manufacturing overhead of $5,400 is needed to bring the account balance to zero. What account should we debit? Because Smart Touch *undercosted* jobs by $5,400 during the year, the adjustment should increase (debit) the Cost of goods sold:

(11)	Cost of goods sold (E+)	5,400	
	Manufacturing overhead (E–)		5,400

The Manufacturing overhead balance is now zero and the Cost of goods sold is up to date.

Manufacturing overhead				Cost of goods sold		
Actual	73,000	Allocated (8)	67,600	(10b)	594,600	
		Closed (11)	5,400	(11)	5,400	
	0				600,000	

Exhibit 17-7 summarizes the accounting for manufacturing overhead:

EXHIBIT 17-7   Summary of Accounting for Manufacturing Overhead

Before the Period

$$\text{Compute predetermined manufacturing overhead rate} = \frac{\text{Total estimated manufacturing overhead costs}}{\text{Total estimated quantity of the manufacturing overhead allocation base}}$$

During the Period

$$\text{Allocated manufacturing overhead cost} = \text{Actual quantity of the allocation base used by each job} \times \text{Predetermined manufacturing overhead rate}$$

At the End of the Period

Close the Manufacturing overhead account:

Jobs are undercosted

If actual > allocated → *Underallocated* manufacturing overhead

Need to *increase* Cost of goods sold, as follows:

	Cost of goods sold (E+)	XXX	
	Manufacturing overhead (E–)		XXX

Jobs are overcosted

If allocated > actual → *Overallocated* manufacturing overhead

Need to *reduce* Cost of goods sold, as follows:

	Manufacturing overhead (E+)	XXX	
	Cost of goods sold (E–)		XXX

Job Order Costing in a Service Company

  Calculate unit costs for a service company

As we have seen, service firms have no inventory. These firms incur only noninventoriable costs. But their managers still need to know the costs of different jobs in order to set prices for their services as follows (amounts assumed):

Cost of Job 19..	$6,000
Add standard markup of 50% ($6,000 × 0.50)......	3,000
Sale price of Job 19	$9,000

A merchandising company can set the selling price of its products this same way.

We now illustrate how service firms assign costs to jobs. The law firm of Walsh Associates considers each client a separate job. Walsh's most significant cost is direct labor—attorney time spent on clients' cases. How do service firms trace direct labor to individual jobs?

Suppose Walsh's accounting system is not automated. Walsh's employees can fill out a weekly electronic labor time record. Software totals the amount of time spent on each job. For example, attorney Lois Fox's electronic time record shows that she devoted 14 hours to client 367 and 26 hours to other clients during the week of June 10, 2014.

Fox's salary and benefits total $100,000 per year. Assuming a 40-hour workweek and 50 workweeks in each year, Fox has 2,000 available work hours per year (50 weeks × 40 hours per week). Fox's hourly pay rate is as follows:

$$\text{Hourly rate to the employer} = \frac{\$100,000 \text{ per year}}{2,000 \text{ hours per year}} = \$50 \text{ per hour}$$

Fox worked 14 hours for client 367, so the direct labor cost traced to client 367 is 14 hours × $50 per hour = $700.

Walsh's employees enter the client number into the time tracking software when they start on the client's job. The software records the time elapsed until the employee signs off on that job.

Founding partner Jacob Walsh wants to know the total cost of serving each client, not just the direct labor cost. Walsh Associates also allocates indirect costs to individual jobs (clients). The law firm develops a predetermined indirect cost allocation rate, following the same approach that Smart Touch used. In December 2013, Walsh estimates that the following indirect costs will be incurred in 2014:

Office rent..	$200,000
Office support staff...	70,000
Maintaining and updating law library for case research.......	25,000
Advertisements in the yellow pages	3,000
Sponsorship of the symphony...	2,000
Total indirect costs..	$300,000

Walsh uses direct labor hours as the allocation base, because direct labor hours are the main driver of indirect costs. He estimates that Walsh attorneys will work 10,000 direct labor hours in 2014.

STEP 1: Compute the predetermined indirect cost allocation rate.

$$\text{Predetermined indirect cost allocation rate} = \frac{\$300,000 \text{ expected indirect costs}}{10,000 \text{ expected direct labor hours}}$$

$$= \$30 \text{ per direct labor hour}$$

STEP 2: **Allocate indirect costs to jobs by multiplying the predetermined indirect cost allocation rate (Step 1) by the actual quantity of the allocation base used by each job.** Client 367, for example, required 14 direct labor hours of Fox's time, so the indirect costs are allocated as follows:

$$14 \text{ direct labor hours} \times \$30/\text{hour} = \$420$$

To summarize, the total costs assigned to client 367 are as follows:

Direct labor: 14 hours × $50/hour	$ 700
Indirect costs: 14 hours × $30/hour........	420
Total costs...	$1,120

You have now learned how to use a job order cost system for a service company and assign costs to jobs.

Stop & Think...

When you have car trouble, you probably go to your mechanic and ask him or her to give you an estimate of what it will cost to fix it. That estimated cost is based on the time the mechanic thinks it will take to fix your car. The mechanic's repair shop has overhead, such as tools, equipment, and building. When you receive the final bill for fixing your car, that bill will be based on both the time it actually took the mechanic to fix your car and an hourly rate that includes the mechanic repair shop's overhead. This is an example of service job costing. Your car problem is the job for the mechanic.

Review the Decision Guidelines on the following page to solidify your understanding.

Key Takeaway

Service firms must also allocate overhead to jobs to determine each job's real cost. Just like with manufacturing firms, a predetermined indirect cost allocation rate must be determined. The rate is then used to allocate overhead costs to service jobs.

Decision Guidelines 17-2

JOB ORDER COSTING

Companies using a job order costing system treat each job separately. The following are some of the decisions that a company makes when designing its job order costing system.

Decision	Guidelines

• Are utilities, insurance, property taxes, and depreciation
    • manufacturing overhead or
    • operating expenses?
	These costs are part of manufacturing overhead *only* if they are incurred in the manufacturing plant.
	
	 If unrelated to manufacturing, they are operating expenses. For example, if related to the research lab, they are R&D expenses. If related to executive headquarters, they are administrative expenses. If related to distribution centers, they are selling expenses. These are all operating expenses, not manufacturing overhead.

• How do we record *actual* manufacturing overhead costs?

Manufacturing overhead		XX	
Accumulated depreciation—plant and equipment			XX
Prepaid insurance—plant and equipment			XX
Utilities payable (or Cash) and so on			XX

• How do we compute a predetermined manufacturing overhead rate?

$$\frac{\text{Total estimated manufacturing overhead costs}}{\text{Total estimated quantity of the manufacturing overhead allocation base}}$$

• How do we record allocation of manufacturing overhead?

Work in process inventory		XX	
Manufacturing overhead			XX

• What is the *amount* of the allocated manufacturing overhead?

$$\text{Actual quantity of the manufacturing overhead allocation base used by each job} \times \text{Predetermined manufacturing overhead rate}$$

• How do we close Manufacturing overhead at the end of the period?

Close directly to Cost of goods sold, as follows:
For *underallocated* overhead:

Cost of goods sold		XX	
Manufacturing overhead			XX

For *overallocated* overhead:

Manufacturing overhead		XX	
Cost of goods sold			XX

Decision	Guidelines
• When providing services, how do we trace employees' direct labor to individual jobs?	Either use automated software that directly captures the amount of time employees spend on a client's job, or have employees fill out a time record.

Summary Problem 17-2

Skippy Scooters manufactures motor scooters. The company has automated production, so it allocates manufacturing overhead based on machine hours. Skippy expects to incur $240,000 of manufacturing overhead costs and to use 4,000 machine hours during 2011. At the end of 2010, Skippy reported the following inventories:

Materials inventory......................	$20,000
Work in process inventory	17,000
Finished goods inventory..............	11,000

During January 2011, Skippy actually used 300 machine hours and recorded the following transactions:

    a. Purchased materials on account, $31,000
    b. Used direct materials, $39,000
    c. Manufacturing wages incurred totaled $40,000, of which 90% was direct labor and 10% was indirect labor
    d. Used indirect materials, $3,000
    e. Incurred other manufacturing overhead, $13,000 on account
    f. Allocated manufacturing overhead for January 2011
    g. Cost of completed motor scooters, $100,000
    h. Sold scooters on account, $175,000; cost of scooters sold, $95,000

Requirements

1. Compute Skippy's predetermined manufacturing overhead rate for 2011.
2. Journalize the transactions in the general journal.
3. Enter the beginning balances and then post the transactions to the following accounts: Materials inventory, Work in process inventory, Finished goods inventory, Wages payable, Manufacturing overhead, and Cost of goods sold.
4. Close the ending balance of Manufacturing overhead. Post your entry to the T-accounts.
5. What are the ending balances in the three inventory accounts and in Cost of goods sold?

Solution

Requirement 1

$$\text{Predetermined manufacturing overhead rate} = \frac{\text{Total estimated manufacturing overhead costs}}{\text{Total estimated quantity of the manufacturing overhead allocation base}}$$

$$= \frac{\$240,000}{4,000 \text{ machine hours}}$$

$$= \$60/\text{machine hour}$$

Requirement 2

a.	Materials inventory (A+)	31,000	
	Accounts payable (L+)		31,000

b.	Work in process inventory (A+)	39,000	
	Materials inventory (A–)		39,000

c.	Work in process inventory ($40,000 × 0.90) (A+)	36,000	
	Manufacturing overhead ($40,000 × 0.10) (E+)	4,000	
	Wages payable (L+)		40,000

d.	Manufacturing overhead (E+)	3,000	
	Materials inventory (A–)		3,000

e.	Manufacturing overhead (E+)	13,000	
	Accounts payable (L+)		13,000

f.	Work in process inventory (300 × $60) (A+)	18,000	
	Manufacturing overhead (E–)		18,000

g.	Finished goods inventory (A+)	100,000	
	Work in process inventory (A–)		100,000

h.	Accounts receivable (A+)	175,000	
	Sales revenue (R+)		175,000
	Cost of goods sold (E+)	95,000	
	Finished goods inventory (A–)		95,000

Requirement 3

Post the transactions:

Materials inventory

Bal	20,000	(b)	39,000
(a)	31,000	(d)	3,000
Bal	9,000		

Work in process inventory

Bal	17,000	(g)	100,000
(b)	39,000		
(c)	36,000		
(f)	18,000		
Bal	10,000		

Finished goods inventory

Bal	11,000	(h)	95,000
(g)	100,000		
Bal	16,000		

Wages payable

		(c)	40,000

Manufacturing overhead

(c)	4,000	(f)	18,000
(d)	3,000		
(e)	13,000		
Bal	2,000		

Cost of goods sold

(h)	95,000		

Requirement 4

Close Manufacturing overhead:

i.	Cost of goods sold (E+)		2,000	
	Manufacturing overhead (E–)			2,000

Manufacturing overhead					Cost of goods sold		
(c)	4,000	(f)	18,000	(h)	95,000		
(d)	3,000	(i)	2,000	(i)	2,000		
(e)	13,000						
				Bal	97,000		

Requirement 5

Ending balances:

Materials inventory (from Requirement 3)......................	$ 9,000
Work in process inventory (from Requirement 3)	10,000
Finished goods inventory (from Requirement 3)..............	16,000
Cost of goods sold (from Requirement 4)......................	97,000

Review *Job Order and Process Costing*

● Accounting Vocabulary

Allocation Base (p. 823)
A common denominator that links indirect costs to cost objects. Ideally, the allocation base is the primary cost driver of the indirect costs.

Conversion Costs (p. 819)
Direct labor plus manufacturing overhead.

Cost Allocation (p. 815)
Assigning indirect costs (such as manufacturing overhead) to cost objects (such as jobs or production processes).

Cost Driver (p. 823)
The primary factor that causes a cost to increase or decrease based on the cost driver factor's usage. (Example: more machine hours = more total machine costs.)

Cost Tracing (p. 815)
Assigning direct costs (such as direct materials and direct labor) to cost objects (such as jobs or production processes) that used those costs.

Equivalent Units (p. 859)
Allows us to measure the amount of work done on a partially finished group of units during a period and to express it in terms of fully complete units of output.

Job Cost Record (p. 817)
Document that accumulates the direct materials, direct labor, and manufacturing overhead costs assigned to an individual job.

Job Order Costing (p. 814)
A system that accumulates costs for each job. Law firms, music studios, health-care providers, mail-order catalog companies, building contractors, and custom furniture manufacturers are examples of companies that use job order costing systems.

Labor Time Record (p. 818)
Identifies the employee, the amount of time spent on a particular job, and the labor cost charged to the job; a record used to assign direct labor cost to specific jobs.

Materials Requisition (p. 817)
Request for the transfer of materials to the production floor, prepared by the production team.

Overallocated (Manufacturing) Overhead (p. 827)
Occurs when the manufacturing overhead allocated to Work in process inventory is more than the amount of manufacturing overhead costs actually incurred.

Predetermined Manufacturing Overhead Rate (p. 823)
Estimated manufacturing overhead cost per unit of the allocation base, computed at the beginning of the period.

Process Costing (p. 814)
System for assigning costs to large numbers of identical units that usually proceed in a continuous fashion through a series of uniform production steps or processes.

Production Cost Report (p. 870)
Summarizes operations for one department for a month. Combines the costs to account for and the cost per equivalent unit and shows how those costs were assigned to the goods completed and transferred out.

Transferred-In Costs (p. 868)
Costs that were incurred in a previous process and brought into a later process as part of the product's cost.

Underallocated (Manufacturing) Overhead (p. 827)
Occurs when the manufacturing overhead allocated to Work in process inventory is less than the amount of manufacturing overhead costs actually incurred.

Weighted-Average Process Costing Method (p. 866)
Determines the average cost of all of a specific department's equivalent units of work.

● Destination: Student Success

Student Success Tips

The following are hints on some common trouble areas for students in this chapter:

● Remember the difference between job order costing and process costing: Job order costing accumulates costs for each batch or job. Process costing accumulates costs of each process needed to complete the product.

● Recall that direct materials, direct labor, and manufacturing overhead costs are the costs that make up a product, whether we cost that product using job order, process, or some other costing method.

● Recall that as costs are added while making the product, we debit Work in process. When products are finished, we move the costs from Work in process (credit) to Finished goods (debit).

● Keep in mind that the formula for calculating a predetermined manufacturing overhead rate is an estimate. Actual costs will rarely exactly equal the costs allocated based on the rate.

Getting Help

If there's a learning objective from the chapter you aren't confident about, try using one or more of the following resources:

● Review Exhibit 17-6, accounting for manufacturing overhead.

● Review Summary Problem 17-2 in the chapter to reinforce your understanding of job order costing system journal entries.

● Practice additional exercises or problems at the end of Chapter 17 that cover the specific learning objective that is challenging you.

● Watch the white board videos for Chapter 17 located at myaccountinglab.com under the Chapter Resources button.

● Go to myaccountinglab.com and select the Study Plan button. Choose Chapter 17 and work the questions covering that specific learning objective until you've mastered it.

● Work the Chapter 17 pre/post tests in myaccountinglab.com.

● Visit the learning resource center on your campus for tutoring.

● Quick Check

1. Would an advertising agency use job or process costing? What about a cell phone manufacturer?

    a. Advertising agency—process costing; Cell phone manufacturer—process costing

    b. Advertising agency—job order costing; Cell phone manufacturer—job order costing

    c. Advertising agency—process costing; Cell phone manufacturer—job order costing

    d. Advertising agency—job order costing; Cell phone manufacturer—process costing

2. When a manufacturing company *uses* direct materials, it *assigns* the cost by debiting

    a. Direct materials.   c. Manufacturing overhead.

    b. Work in process inventory.   d. Materials inventory.

3. When a manufacturing company *uses* indirect materials, it *assigns* the cost by debiting

    a. Work in process inventory.   c. Materials inventory.

    b. Indirect materials.   d. Manufacturing overhead.

4. When a manufacturing company *uses* direct labor, it *assigns* the cost by debiting

    a. Work in process inventory.   c. Direct labor.

    b. Manufacturing overhead.   d. Wages payable.

Questions 5, 6, 7, and 8 are based on the following information about Gell Corporation's manufacturing of computers. Assume that Gell

- allocates manufacturing overhead based on machine hours.
- estimated 12,000,000 machine hours and $93,000,000 of manufacturing overhead costs.
- Actually used 16,000,000 machine hours and incurred the following actual costs:

Indirect labor	$ 11,000,000
Depreciation on plant	48,000,000
Machinery repair	11,000,000
Direct labor	75,000,000
Plant supplies	6,000,000
Plant utilities	7,000,000
Advertising	35,000,000
Sales commissions	27,000,000

5. What is Gell's predetermined manufacturing overhead rate?

    a. $7.75/machine hour   c. $6.92/machine hour

    b. $5.81/machine hour   d. $5.19/machine hour

6. What is Gell's actual manufacturing overhead cost?

    a. $158,000,000   c. $145,000,000

    b. $83,000,000   d. $220,000,000

7. How much manufacturing overhead would Gell allocate?

    a. $83,000,000   c. $124,000,000

    b. $93,000,000   d. $220,000,000

8. What entry would Gell make to close the manufacturing overhead account?

a.
| Manufacturing overhead | 10,000,000 | |
| Cost of goods sold | | 10,000,000 |

b.
| Manufacturing overhead | 41,000,000 | |
| Cost of goods sold | | 41,000,000 |

c.
| Cost of goods sold | 41,000,000 | |
| Manufacturing overhead | | 41,000,000 |

d.
| Cost of goods sold | 10,000,000 | |
| Manufacturing overhead | | 10,000,000 |

9. A manufacturing company's management can use product cost information to

a. set prices of its products.

b. decide which products to emphasize.

c. identify ways to cut production costs.

d. a, b, and c are correct

10. For which of the following reasons would David Laugherty, owner of the Laughtery Associates law firm, want to know the total costs of a job (serving a particular client)?

a. For inventory valuation

b. To determine the fees to charge clients

c. For external reporting

d. a, b, and c are correct

Answers are given after Apply Your Knowledge (p. 855).

Assess Your Progress

● Short Exercises

MyAccountingLab **S17-1** **❶ Distinguishing between job costing and process costing [5 min]**
Job costing and process costing track costs differently.

Requirement

1. Would the following companies use job order costing or process costing?
   a. A manufacturer of refrigerators
   b. A manufacturer of specialty wakeboards
   c. A manufacturer of luxury yachts
   d. A professional services firm
   e. A landscape contractor
   f. A custom home builder
   g. A cell phone manufacturer
   h. A manufacturer of frozen pizzas
   i. A manufacturer of multivitamins
   j. A manufacturer of tennis shoes

S17-2 **❷ Flow of costs in job order costing [10 min]**
For a manufacturer that uses job order costing, there is a correct order that the costs flow through the accounts.

Requirement

1. Order the following from 1–4. Item 1 has been completed for you.

   __1__ a. Materials inventory

   _____ b. Finished goods inventory

   _____ c. Cost of goods sold

   _____ d. Work in process inventory

S17-3 ❷ Accounting for materials [5–10 min]

Rite Packs manufactures backpacks. Its plant records include the following materials-related transactions:

Purchases of canvas (on account)	$ 71,000
Purchases of sewing machine lubricating oil (on account) . . .	1,100
Materials requisitions:	
Canvas	64,000
Sewing machine lubricating oil	250

Requirements

1. Journalize the entries to record these transactions.
2. Post these transactions to the Materials inventory account.
3. If the company had $34,000 of Materials inventory at the beginning of the period, what is the ending balance of Materials inventory?

S17-4 ❷ Accounting for materials [10 min]

Consider the following T-accounts:

Materials inventory					Work in process inventory			
Bal	50				Bal	15		
Purchases	205	Used	☐		Direct materials	☐	Cost of goods	550
Bal	35				Direct labor	285	manufactured	
					Manufacturing overhead	135		
					Bal	45		

Requirement

1. Use the T-accounts to determine direct materials used and indirect materials used.

S17-5 ❷ Accounting for labor [5 min]

Creative Crystal, Ltd., reports the following labor-related transactions at its plant in Portland, Oregon.

Plant janitor's wages	$	570
Plant furnace operator's wages		880
Glass blower's wages		78,000

Requirement

1. Journalize the entry for the incurrence and assignment of these wages.

S17-6 ❷ Accounting for materials and labor [5 min]

Seattle Enterprises produces LCD touch screen products. The company reports the following information at December 31, 2012:

Materials inventory		Work in process inventory		Finished goods inventory	
47,000	31,400	28,000	123,000	123,000	109,000
		62,000			
		53,900			

Wages payable		Manufacturing overhead	
	74,000	3,400	53,900
		12,000	
		36,500	

Seattle began operations on January 30, 2012.

Requirements

1. What is the cost of direct materials used? The cost of indirect materials used?
2. What is the cost of direct labor? The cost of indirect labor?

S17-7 ❸ **Accounting for overhead [5 min]**

Teak Outdoor Furniture manufactures wood patio furniture. The company reports the following costs for June 2012:

Wood	$ 250,000
Nails, glue, and stain	26,000
Depreciation on saws	5,500
Indirect manufacturing labor	38,000
Depreciation on delivery truck	2,300
Assembly-line workers' wages	57,000

Requirement

1. What is the balance in the Manufacturing overhead account before overhead is applied to jobs?

S17-8 ❸ **Allocating overhead [5 min]**

Job 303 includes direct materials costs of $500 and direct labor costs of $430.

Requirement

1. If the manufacturing overhead allocation rate is 80% of direct labor cost, what is the total cost assigned to Job 303?

Note: Short Exercise 17-6 must be completed before attempting Short Exercise 17-9.

S17-9 ❹ **Comparing actual to allocated overhead [10 min]**

Refer to the data in S17-6.

Requirements

1. What is the actual manufacturing overhead of Seattle Enterprises?
2. What is the allocated manufacturing overhead?
3. Is manufacturing overhead underallocated or overallocated? By how much?

S17-10 ❹ **Under/overallocated overhead [10 min]**

The T-account showing the manufacturing overhead activity for Jackson, Corp., for 2012 is as follows:

Manufacturing overhead	
197,000	207,000

Requirements

1. What is the actual manufacturing overhead?
2. What is the allocated manufacturing overhead?
3. What is the predetermined manufacturing overhead rate as a percentage of direct labor cost, if actual direct labor costs were $165,600?
4. Is manufacturing overhead underallocated or overallocated? By how much?
5. Is Cost of goods sold too high or too low?

Note: Short Exercise 17-10 must be completed before attempting Short Exercise 17-11.

S17-11 ❹ **Closing out under/overallocated overhead [5 min]**

Refer to the data in S17-10.

Requirement

1. Journalize the entry to close out the company's Manufacturing overhead account.

S17-12 ❺ **Job order costing in a service company [5 min]**

Roth Accounting pays Jaclyn Sawyer $104,400 per year. Sawyer works 1,800 hours per year.

Requirements

1. What is the hourly cost to Roth Accounting of employing Sawyer?

2. What direct labor cost would be traced to client 507 if Sawyer works 12 hours to prepare client 507's financial statements?

Note: Short Exercise 17-12 must be completed before attempting Short Exercise 17-13.

S17-13 ❺ **Job order costing in a service company [5 min]**

Refer to the data in S17-12. Assume that Roth's accountants are expected to work a total of 8,000 direct labor hours in 2012. Roth's estimated total indirect costs are $240,000.

Requirements

1. What is Roth's indirect cost allocation rate?

2. What indirect costs will be allocated to client 507 if Sawyer works 12 hours to prepare the financial statements?

3. Calculate the total cost to prepare client 507's financial statements.

● Exercises

E17-14 ❶ **Distinguishing between job order costing and process costing [5–10 min]** *MyAccountingLab*

Consider the following incomplete statements.

  a. _____ is used by companies that produce small quantities of many different products.

  b. **Georgia-Pacific** pulverizes wood into pulp to manufacture cardboard. The company uses a _____ system.

  c. To record costs of manufacturing thousands of identical files, the file manufacturer will use a _____ system.

  d. Companies that produce large numbers of identical products use _____ systems for product costing.

  e. The computer repair service that visits your home and repairs your computer uses a _____ system.

  f. **Apple** assembles electronic parts and software to manufacture millions of iPods. **Apple** uses a _____ system.

  g. Textbook publishers produce titles of a particular book in batches. Textbook publishers use a _____ system.

  h. A company that bottles milk into one-gallon containers uses a _____ system.

  i. A company that makes large quantities of one type of tankless hot water heater uses a _____ system.

  j. A particular governmental agency takes bids for specific items it utilizes. Each item requires a separate bid. The agency uses a _____ system.

Requirement

1. Complete each of the statements with the term job order costing or the term process costing.

E17-15 ❷❸❹ **Accounting for job costs [15 min]**

Sloan Trailers' job cost records yielded the following information:

Job No.	Started	Finished	Sold	Total Cost of Job at September 30
1	August 21	September 16	September 17	$ 3,100
2	August 29	September 21	September 26	13,000
3	September 3	October 11	October 13	6,900
4	September 7	September 29	October 1	4,400

Requirement

1. Use the dates in the table to identify the status of each job. Compute Sloan's cost of (a) Work in process inventory at September 30, (b) Finished goods inventory at September 30, and (c) Cost of goods sold for September.

E17-16 ❷ ❸ ❹ **Job order costing journal entries [20–25 min]**
Consider the following transactions for Judy's Sofas:

a. Incurred and paid Web site expenses, $2,900.
b. Incurred manufacturing wages of $15,000, 60% of which was direct labor and 40% of which was indirect labor.
c. Purchased materials on account, $24,000.
d. Used in production: direct materials, $9,500; indirect materials, $4,500.
e. Recorded manufacturing overhead: depreciation on plant, $10,000; plant insurance, $1,300; plant property tax, $4,200 (credit Property tax payable).
f. Allocated manufacturing overhead to jobs, 250% of direct labor costs.
g. Completed production, $38,000.
h. Sold inventory on account, $20,000; cost of goods sold, $10,000.
i. Journalized the closing of the manufacturing overhead account.

Requirement

1. Journalize the transactions in Judy's general journal.

E17-17 ❷ ❸ ❹ **Identifying job order costing journal entries [15 min]**
Consider the following:

Materials inventory		Work in process inventory		Finished goods inventory		Accounts payable	
(a)	(b)	(b)	(f)	(f)	(g)		(a)
		(c)					
		(e)					

Wages payable		Manufacturing overhead		Cost of goods sold		Prepaid insurance	
	(c)	(b)	(e)	(g)			(d)
		(c)	(h)	(h)			
		(d)					

Requirement

1. Describe the letter transactions in the above accounts.

E17-18 ❸ ❹ **Allocating manufacturing overhead [15–20 min]**
Selected cost data for Antique Print, Co., are as follows:

Estimated manufacturing overhead cost for the year	$ 115,000
Estimated direct labor cost for the year	71,875
Actual manufacturing overhead cost for the year	119,000
Actual direct labor cost for the year	73,000

Requirements

1. Compute the predetermined manufacturing overhead rate per direct labor dollar.
2. Prepare the journal entry to allocate overhead cost for the year.
3. Use a T-account to determine the amount of underallocated or overallocated manufacturing overhead.
4. Prepare the journal entry to close the balance of the Manufacturing overhead account.

E17-19 ❸ ❹ **Allocating manufacturing overhead [15–20 min]**

Brooks Foundry uses a predetermined manufacturing overhead rate to allocate over-head to individual jobs, based on the machine hours required. At the beginning of 2012, the company expected to incur the following:

Manufacturing overhead costs	$ 840,000
Direct labor costs	1,550,000
Machine hours	70,000 hours

At the end of 2012, the company had actually incurred:

Direct labor cost	$ 1,160,000
Depreciation on manufacturing property, plant, and equipment	600,000
Property taxes on plant	40,000
Sales salaries	26,500
Delivery drivers' wages	23,500
Plant janitor's wages	17,000
Machine hours	67,000 hours

Requirements

1. Compute Brooks' predetermined manufacturing overhead rate.

2. Prepare the journal entry to allocate manufacturing overhead.

3. Post the manufacturing overhead transactions to the Manufacturing overhead T-account. Is manufacturing overhead underallocated or overallocated? By how much?

4. Close the Manufacturing overhead account to Cost of goods sold. Does your entry increase or decrease cost of goods sold?

E17-20 ❸ ❹ **Allocating manufacturing overhead [10–15 min]**

Refer to the data in E17-19. Brooks' accountant found an error in her 2012 cost records. Depreciation on manufacturing property, plant, and equipment was actually $550,000, not the $600,000 she originally reported. Unadjusted balances at the end of 2012 include:

Finished goods inventory	$ 131,000
Cost of goods sold	580,000

Requirements

1. Use a T-account to determine whether manufacturing overhead is underallocated or overallocated, and by how much.

2. Prepare the journal entry to close out the underallocated or overallocated manufacturing overhead.

3. What is the adjusted ending balance of Cost of goods sold?

E17-21 ❹ **Allocating manufacturing overhead [15–20 min]**

The manufacturing records for Krazy Kayaks at the end of the 2012 fiscal year show the following information about manufacturing overhead:

Overhead allocated to production	$ 405,900
Actual manufacturing overhead costs	$ 428,000
Overhead allocation rate for the year	$ 41 per machine hour

Requirements

1. How many machine hours did Krazy Kayaks use in 2012?

2. Was manufacturing overhead over- or underallocated for the year and by how much?

3. Prepare the journal entry to close out the over- or underallocated overhead.

E17-22 ④ **Using the Work in process inventory account [15–20 min]**

June production generated the following activity in Auto Chassis Company's Work in process inventory account:

Work in process inventory

Jun 1 Bal	20,000
Direct materials used	31,000
Direct labor assigned to jobs	33,000
Manufacturing overhead allocated to jobs	13,000

Additionally, Auto has completed Jobs 142 and 143, with total costs of $38,000 and $36,000, respectively.

Requirements

1. Prepare the journal entry for production completed in June.

2. Post the journal entry made in Requirement 1. Compute the ending balance in the Work in process account on June 30.

3. Prepare the journal entry to record the sale (on credit) of Job 143 for $46,000. Also, prepare the journal entry to record Cost of goods sold for Job 143.

4. What is the gross profit on Job 143? What other costs must gross profit cover?

E17-23 ⑤ **Job order costing in a service company [15–20 min]**

Martin Realtors, a real estate consulting firm, specializes in advising companies on potential new plant sites. The company uses a job order costing system with a predetermined indirect cost allocation rate, computed as a percentage of direct labor costs. At the beginning of 2012, managing partner Andrew Martin prepared the following budget for the year:

Direct labor hours (professionals)	19,600 hours
Direct labor costs (professionals)	$ 2,450,000
Office rent	370,000
Support staff salaries	1,282,500
Utilities	430,000

Peters Manufacturing, Inc., is inviting several consultants to bid for work. Andrew Martin estimates that this job will require about 240 direct labor hours.

Requirements

1. Compute Martin Realtors' (a) hourly direct labor cost rate and (b) indirect cost allocation rate.

2. Compute the predicted cost of the Peters Manufacturing job.

3. If Martin wants to earn a profit that equals 45% of the job's cost, how much should he bid for the Peters Manufacturing job?

● Problems (Group A)

P17-24A ① ② ③ ④ **Analyzing cost data [25–35 min]**

MyAccountingLab

Bluebird Manufacturing makes carrying cases for portable electronic devices. Its costing records yield the following information:

Job No.	Date Started	Date Finished	Sold	Total Cost of Job at October 31	Total Manufacturing Costs Added in November
1	10/3	10/12	10/13	$ 1,900	
2	10/3	10/30	11/1	1,800	
3	10/17	11/24	11/27	400	$ 1,500
4	10/29	11/29	12/3	800	1,200
5	11/8	11/12	11/14		550
6	11/23	12/6	12/9		700

Requirements

1. Which type of costing system is Bluebird using? What piece of data did you base your answer on?

2. Use the dates in the table to identify the status of each job. Compute Bluebird's account balances at October 31 for Work in process inventory, Finished goods inventory, and Cost of goods sold. Compute, by job, account balances at November 30 for Work in process inventory, Finished goods inventory, and Cost of goods sold.

3. Prepare journal entries to record the transfer of completed units from Work in process to Finished goods for October and November.

4. Record the sale of Job 3 for $2,100.

5. What is the gross profit for Job 3? What other costs must this gross profit cover?

P17-25A ② ③ ④ **Accounting for construction transactions [30–45 min]**

Quaint Construction, Inc., is a home builder in Arizona. Quaint uses a job order costing system in which each house is a job. Because it constructs houses, the company uses an account titled Construction overhead. The company applies overhead based on estimated direct labor costs. For the year, it estimated construction overhead of $1,100,000 and total direct labor cost of $2,750,000. The following events occurred during August:

a. Purchased materials on account, $400,000.

b. Requisitioned direct materials and used direct labor in construction. Record the materials requisitioned.

	Direct materials	Direct labor
House 402	$ 54,000	$ 42,000
House 403	68,000	35,000
House 404	63,000	57,000
House 405	85,000	53,000

c. The company incurred total wages of $200,000. Use the data from item b to assign the wages.

d. Depreciation of construction equipment, $6,200.

e. Other overhead costs incurred on houses 402 through 405:

Indirect labor	$	13,000
Equipment rentals paid in cash		37,000
Worker liability insurance expired . .		3,000

f. Allocated overhead to jobs.

g. Houses completed: 402, 404.

h. House sold: 404 for $250,000.

Requirements

1. Calculate Quaint's construction overhead application rate for the year.

2. Prepare journal entries to record the events in the general journal.

3. Open T-accounts for Work in process inventory and Finished goods inventory. Post the appropriate entries to these accounts, identifying each entry by letter. Determine the ending account balances, assuming that the beginning balances were zero.

4. Add the costs of the unfinished houses, and show that this total amount equals the ending balance in the Work in process inventory account.

5. Add the cost of the completed house that has not yet been sold, and show that this equals the ending balance in Finished goods inventory.

6. Compute gross profit on the house that was sold. What costs must gross profit cover for Quaint Construction?

P17-26A ❷ ❸ ❹ **Preparing and using a job cost record [30–35 min]**
Lu Technology, Co., manufactures CDs and DVDs for computer software and entertainment companies. Lu uses job order costing and has a perpetual inventory system.

On April 2, Lu began production of 5,900 DVDs, Job 423, for Stick People Pictures for $1.30 sales price per DVD. Lu promised to deliver the DVDs to Stick People by April 5. Lu incurred the following costs:

Date	Labor Time Record No.	Description	Amount
4/2	655	10 hours @ $14	$ 140
4/3	656	20 hours @ $13	260

Date	Materials Requisition No.	Description	Amount
4/2	63	31 lbs. polycarbonate plastic @ $11	$ 341
4/2	64	25 lbs. acrylic plastic @ $27	675
4/3	74	3 lbs. refined aluminum @ $42	126

Stick People provides the movie file for Lu to burn onto the DVDs at a cost of $0.50 per DVD. Lu Technology allocates manufacturing overhead to jobs based on the relation between estimated overhead of $540,000 and estimated direct labor costs of $432,000. Job 423 was completed and shipped on April 3.

Requirements

1. Prepare a job cost record similar to Exhibit 17-6 for Job 423. Calculate the predetermined overhead rate; then allocate manufacturing overhead to the job.

2. Journalize in summary form the requisition of direct materials (including the movie files) and the assignment of direct labor and manufacturing overhead to Job 423.

3. Journalize completion of the job and the sale of the 5,900 DVDs.

P17-27A ② ③ ④ **Comprehensive accounting for manufacturing transactions [90–120 min]**

Howie Stars produces stars for elementary teachers to reward their students. Howie Stars' trial balance on June 1 follows:

HOWIE STARS Trial Balance June 1, 2012		
	Balance	
Account Title	Debit	Credit
Cash	$ 14,000	
Accounts receivable	155,000	
Inventories:		
Materials	5,700	
Work in process	39,400	
Finished goods	20,400	
Plant assets	200,000	
Accumulated depreciation		$ 72,000
Accounts payable		127,000
Wages payable		1,700
Common stock		142,000
Retained earnings		91,800
Sales revenue	—	—
Cost of goods sold	—	
Manufacturing overhead	—	
Marketing and general expenses	—	
Total	$434,500	$434,500

June 1 balances in the subsidiary ledgers were as follows:

- Materials subledger: Paper, $4,700; indirect materials, $1,000
- Work in process subledger: Job 120, $39,400; $0 for Job 121
- Finished goods subledger: Large Stars, $9,400; Small Stars, $11,000

June transactions are summarized as follows:

a. Collections on account, $152,000.
b. Marketing and general expenses incurred and paid, $28,000.
c. Payments on account, $36,000.
d. Materials purchases on credit: Paper, $22,900; indirect materials, $3,800.
e. Materials used in production (requisitioned):
   - Job 120: paper, $850
   - Job 121: paper, $7,650
   - Indirect materials, $1,000
f. Wages incurred and assigned during June, $35,000. Labor time records for the month: Job 120, $3,500; Job 121, $16,600; indirect labor, $14,900.
g. Wages paid in June include the balance in the Wages payable account at May 31 and $32,200 of wages incurred during June.
h. Depreciation on plant and equipment, $2,600.
i. Manufacturing overhead was allocated at the predetermined rate of 50% of direct labor cost.
j. Jobs completed during the month: Job 120, 300,000 Large Stars at total cost of $45,500.
k. Credit sales on account: all of Job 120 for $111,000.
l. Closed the Manufacturing overhead account to Cost of goods sold.

Requirements

1. Journalize the transactions for the company. Howie uses a perpetual inventory system.

2. Open T-accounts for the general ledger, the Materials ledger, the Work in process ledger, and the Finished goods ledger. Insert each account balance as given, and use the reference Bal. Post the journal entries to the T-accounts using the transaction letters as a reference.

3. Prepare a trial balance at June 30, 2012.

4. Use the Work in process inventory T-account to prepare a schedule of cost of goods manufactured for the month of June. (You may want to review Exhibit 16-10.)

5. Prepare an income statement for the month of June. To calculate cost of goods sold, you may want to review Exhibit 16-7. (*Hint*: In transaction l, you closed any under/overallocated manufacturing overhead to Cost of goods sold. In the income statement, show this correction as an adjustment to Cost of goods sold. If manufacturing overhead is underallocated, the adjustment will increase Cost of goods sold. If overhead is overallocated, the adjustment will decrease Cost of goods sold.)

P17-28A ③ ④ **Accounting manufacturing overhead [25–35 min]**

White Woods manufactures jewelry boxes. The primary materials (wood, brass, and glass) and direct labor are traced directly to the products. Manufacturing overhead costs are allocated based on machine hours. Data for 2012 follow:

	Estimated (Budget)	Actual
Machine hours	25,000 hours	32,100 hours
Maintenance labor (repairs to equipment)	$12,000	$28,500
Plant supervisor's salary	47,000	48,000
Screws, nails, and glue	24,000	45,000
Plant utilities	41,000	96,850
Freight out	37,000	46,500
Depreciation on plant and		
equipment	87,000	83,000
Advertising expense	43,000	54,000

Requirements

1. Compute the predetermined manufacturing overhead rate.

2. Post actual and allocated manufacturing overhead to the Manufacturing overhead T-account.

3. Close the under- or overallocated overhead to Cost of goods sold.

4. The predetermined manufacturing overhead rate usually turns out to be inaccurate. Why don't accountants just use the actual manufacturing overhead rate?

P17-29A ⑤ **Job order costing in a service company [20–25 min]**

Crow Design, Inc., is a Web site design and consulting firm. The firm uses a job order costing system in which each client is a different job. Crow Design traces direct labor, licensing costs, and travel costs directly to each job. It allocates indirect costs to jobs based on a predetermined indirect cost allocation rate, computed as a percentage of direct labor costs.

At the beginning of 2012, managing partner Sally Simone prepared the following budget estimates:

Direct labor hours (professional)	6,250 hours
Direct labor costs (professional)	$1,800,000
Support staff salaries	765,000
Computer leases	46,000
Office supplies	27,000
Office rent	62,000

In November 2012, Crow Design served several clients. Records for two clients appear here:

	Delicious Treats	Mesilla Chocolates
Direct labor hours	700 hours	100 hours
Software licensing costs	$ 4,000	$ 400
Travel costs	8,000	—

Requirements

1. Compute Crow Design's direct labor rate and its predetermined indirect cost allocation rate for 2012.
2. Compute the total cost of each job.
3. If Simone wants to earn profits equal to 50% of service revenue, how much (what fee) should she charge each of these two clients?
4. Why does Crow Design assign costs to jobs?

● Problems (Group B)

P17-30B ❶ ❷ ❸ ❹ **Analyzing cost data [25–35 min]**

Stratton Manufacturing makes carrying cases for portable electronic devices. Its costing records yield the following information:

Job No.	Date Started	Date Finished	Date Sold	Total Cost of Job at October 31	Total Manufacturing Costs Added in November
1	10/3	10/12	10/13	$ 1,000	
2	10/3	10/30	11/1	1,100	
3	10/17	11/24	11/27	700	$ 1,400
4	10/29	11/29	12/3	300	1,500
5	11/8	11/12	11/14		650
6	11/23	12/6	12/9		500

Requirements

1. Which type of costing system is Stratton using? What piece of data did you base your answer on?
2. Use the dates in the table to identify the status of each job. Compute Stratton's account balances at October 31 for Work in process inventory, Finished goods inventory, and Cost of goods sold. Compute, by job, account balances at November 30 for Work in process inventory, Finished goods inventory, and Cost of goods sold.
3. Prepare journal entries to record the transfer of completed units from work in process to finished goods for October and November.
4. Record the sale of Job 3 for $2,200.
5. What is the gross profit for Job 3? What other costs must this gross profit cover?

P17-31B ❷ ❸ ❹ **Accounting for construction transactions [30–45 min]**

Cottage Construction, Inc., is a home builder in Arizona. Cottage uses a job order costing system in which each house is a job. Because it constructs houses, the company uses an account titled Construction overhead. The company applies overhead based on estimated direct labor costs. For the year, it estimated construction overhead of $1,050,000 and total direct labor cost of $3,500,000. The following events occurred during August:

a. Purchased materials on account, $460,000.

b. Requisitioned direct materials and used direct labor in construction. Record the materials requisitioned.

	Direct materials	Direct labor
House 402	$ 50,000	$ 45,000
House 403	69,000	30,000
House 404	66,000	56,000
House 405	88,000	55,000

c. The company incurred total wages of $210,000. Use the data from item b to assign the wages.

d. Depreciation of construction equipment, $6,000.

e. Other overhead costs incurred on houses 402 through 405:

Indirect labor	$ 24,000
Equipment rentals paid in cash	36,000
Worker liability insurance expired . .	8,000

f. Allocated overhead to jobs.

g. Houses completed: 402, 404.

h. House sold: 404 for $200,000.

Requirements

1. Calculate Cottage's construction overhead application rate for the year.

2. Record the events in the general journal.

3. Open T-accounts for Work in process inventory and Finished goods inventory. Post the appropriate entries to these accounts, identifying each entry by letter. Determine the ending account balances, assuming that the beginning balances were zero.

4. Add the costs of the unfinished houses, and show that this total amount equals the ending balance in the Work in process inventory account.

5. Add the cost of the completed house that has not yet been sold, and show that this equals the ending balance in Finished goods inventory.

6. Compute gross profit on the house that was sold. What costs must gross profit cover for Cottage Construction?

P17-32B ❷ ❸ ❹ **Preparing and using a job cost record [30–35 min]**

True Technology, Co., manufactures CDs and DVDs for computer software and entertainment companies. True uses job order costing and has a perpetual inventory system.

On November 2, True began production of 5,500 DVDs, Job 423, for Leopard Pictures for $1.60 sales price per DVD. True promised to deliver the DVDs to Leopard by November 5. True incurred the following costs:

Date	Labor Time Record No.	Description	Amount
11/2	655	10 hours @ $18	$ 180
11/3	656	20 hours @ $14	280

Date	Materials Requisition No.	Description	Amount
11/2	63	31 lbs. polycarbonate plastic @ $12	$ 372
11/2	64	25 lbs. acrylic plastic @ $29	725
11/3	74	3 lbs. refined aluminum @ $48	144

Leopard Pictures provides the movie file for True to burn onto the DVDs at a cost of $0.45 per DVD. True Technology allocates manufacturing overhead to jobs based on the relation between estimated overhead of $550,000 and estimated direct labor costs of $500,000. Job 423 was completed and shipped on November 3.

Requirements

1. Prepare a job cost record similar to Exhibit 17-6 for Job 423. Calculate the predetermined overhead rate, then allocate manufacturing overhead to the job.

2. Journalize in summary form the requisition of direct materials (including the movie files) and the assignment of direct labor and manufacturing overhead to Job 423.

3. Journalize completion of the job and the sale of the 5,500 DVDs.

P17-33B ②③④ **Comprehensive accounting for manufacturing transactions [90–120 min]**
School Stars produces stars for elementary teachers to reward their students. School Stars' trial balance on June 1 follows:

	SCHOOL STARS Trial Balance June 1, 2012		
		Balance	
Account Title		Debit	Credit
Cash		$ 17,000	
Accounts receivable		170,000	
Inventories:			
Materials		6,200	
Work in process		43,000	
Finished goods		21,300	
Plant assets		250,000	
Accumulated depreciation			$ 71,000
Accounts payable			133,000
Wages payable			3,300
Common stock			144,000
Retained earnings			156,200
Sales revenue		—	—
Cost of goods sold		—	
Manufacturing overhead		—	
Marketing and general expenses		—	
Total		$507,500	$507,500

June 1 balances in the subsidiary ledgers were as follows:

- Materials subledger: $4,300 paper and $1,900 indirect materials
- Work in process subledger: Job 120 $43,000; $0 for Job 121
- Finished goods subledger: $9,300 Large Stars and $12,000 Small Stars

June transactions are summarized as follows:

a. Collections on account, $155,000.
b. Marketing and general expenses incurred and paid, $22,000.
c. Payments on account, $37,000.
d. Materials purchases on credit: Paper, $26,600; indirect materials, $4,200.
e. Materials used in production (requisitioned):
   • Job 120: Paper, $900
   • Job 121: Paper, $7,850
   • Indirect materials, $1,600
f. Wages incurred and assigned during June, $43,000. Labor time records for the month: Job 120, $4,800; Job 121, $18,500; indirect labor, $19,700.
g. Wages paid in June include the balance in the Wages payable account at May 31 and $39,900 of wages incurred during June.
h. Depreciation on plant and equipment, $2,700.
i. Manufacturing overhead was allocated at the predetermined rate of 90% of direct labor cost.
j. Jobs completed during the month: Job 120, 600,000 Large Stars at total cost of $53,020.
k. Credit sales on account: all of Job 120 for $133,000.
l. Closed the Manufacturing overhead account to Cost of goods sold.

Requirements

1. Journalize the transactions for the company. School uses a perpetual inventory system.

2. Open T-accounts for the general ledger, the Materials ledger, the Work in process ledger, and the Finished goods ledger. Insert each account balance as given, and use the reference Bal. Post the journal entries to the T-accounts using the transaction letters as a reference.

3. Prepare a trial balance at June 30, 2012.

4. Use the Work in process inventory T-account to prepare a schedule of cost of goods manufactured for the month of June. (You may want to review Exhibit 16-10.)

5. Prepare an income statement for the month of June. To calculate cost of goods sold, you may want to review Exhibit 16-7. (*Hint*: In transaction l, you closed any under/overallocated manufacturing overhead to Cost of goods sold. In the income statement, show this correction as an adjustment to Cost of goods sold. If manufacturing overhead is underallocated, the adjustment will increase Cost of goods sold. If overhead is overallocated, the adjustment will decrease Cost of goods sold.)

P17-34B ❸ ❹ **Accounting for manufacturing overhead [25–35 min]**
Superior Woods manufactures jewelry boxes. The primary materials (wood, brass, and glass) and direct labor are traced directly to the products. Manufacturing overhead costs are allocated based on machine hours. Data for 2012 follow:

	Estimated (Budget)	Actual
Machine hours	28,000 hours	32,400 hours
Maintenance labor (repairs to equipment)	$16,000	$26,500
Plant supervisor's salary	46,000	47,000
Screws, nails, and glue	23,000	46,000
Plant utilities	42,000	93,850
Freight out	35,000	47,500
Depreciation on plant and equipment	83,000	82,000
Advertising expense	46,000	59,000

Requirements

1. Compute the predetermined manufacturing overhead rate.

2. Post actual and allocated manufacturing overhead to the Manufacturing overhead T-account.

3. Close the under- or overallocated overhead to Cost of goods sold.

4. The predetermined manufacturing overhead rate usually turns out to be inaccurate. Why don't accountants just use the actual manufacturing overhead rate?

P17-35B ⑤ **Job order costing in a service company [20–25 min]**

Skylark Design, Inc., is a Web site design and consulting firm. The firm uses a job order costing system in which each client is a different job. Skylark Design traces direct labor, licensing costs, and travel costs directly to each job. It allocates indirect costs to jobs based on a predetermined indirect cost allocation rate, computed as a percentage of direct labor costs.

At the beginning of 2013, managing partner Judi Jacquin prepared the following budget estimates:

Direct labor hours (professional)	8,000 hours
Direct labor costs (professional)	$2,000,000
Support staff salaries	664,000
Computer leases	47,000
Office supplies	23,000
Office rent	66,000

In November 2013, Skylark Design served several clients. Records for two clients appear here:

	Food Coop	Martin Chocolates
Direct labor hours	900 hours	100 hours
Software licensing costs	$ 3,500	$ 100
Travel costs	11,000	—

Requirements

1. Compute Skylark Design's direct labor rate and its predetermined indirect cost allocation rate for 2012.

2. Compute the total cost of each job.

3. If Jacquin wants to earn profits equal to 50% of sales revenue, how much (what fee) should she charge each of these two clients?

4. Why does Skylark Design assign costs to jobs?

● Continuing Exercise

E17-36 ③④ **Accounting for manufacturing overhead [25–35 min]**

This exercise continues the Lawlor Lawn Service, Inc., situation from Exercise 16-34 of Chapter 16. Lawlor completed a special landscaping job for Sheldon's Ideal Designs. Lawlor collected the following data about the job:

Sheldon job details:	
Direct materials	$ 700
Direct labor	$1,200

Requirements

1. Lawlor allocates overhead costs based on 60% of direct labor cost. What is the total cost of the Sheldon job?

2. If the price Sheldon paid for the job is $3,460, what is the profit or loss on the job?

• Continuing Problem

MyAccountingLab **P17-37** ❸❹ **Accounting for manufacturing overhead [25–35 min]**

This problem continues the Draper Consulting, Inc., situation from Problem 16-35 of Chapter 16. Draper Consulting uses a job order costing system in which each client is a different job. Draper traces direct labor, daily per diem, and travel costs directly to each job. It allocates indirect costs to jobs based on a predetermined indirect cost allocation rate, computed as a percentage of direct labor costs.

At the beginning of 2013, the controller prepared the following budget:

Direct labor hours (professional)	5,500	hours
Direct labor costs (professional)	$990,000	
Support staff salaries	105,000	
Computer leases	48,000	
Office supplies	15,000	
Office rent	30,000	

In November 2013, Draper served several clients. Records for two clients appear here:

	Tommy's Trains	Marcia's Cookies
Direct labor hours	730 hours	300 hours
Meal—per diem	$ 2,600	$ 600
Travel costs	11,000	0

Requirements

1. Compute Draper's predetermined indirect cost allocation rate for 2013.
2. Compute the total cost of each job.
3. If Draper wants to earn profits equal to 25% of sales revenue, how much (what fee) should it charge each of these two clients?
4. Why does Draper assign costs to jobs?

Apply Your Knowledge

• Decision Cases

Decision Case 17-1 Hiebert Chocolate, Ltd., is located in Memphis. The company prepares gift boxes of chocolates for private parties and corporate promotions. Each order contains a selection of chocolates determined by the customer, and the box is designed to the customer's specifications. Accordingly, Hiebert uses a job order costing system and allocates manufacturing overhead based on direct labor cost.

One of Hiebert's largest customers is the Goforth and Leos law firm. This organization sends chocolates to its clients each Christmas and also provides them to employees at the firm's gatherings. The law firm's managing partner, Bob Goforth, placed the client gift order in September for 500 boxes of cream-filled dark chocolates. But Goforth and Leos did not place its December staff-party order until the last week of November. This order was for an additional 100 boxes of chocolates identical to the ones to be distributed to clients.

Hiebert budgeted the cost per box for the original 500-box order as follows:

Chocolate, filling, wrappers, box	$14.00
Employee time to fill and wrap the box (10 min.)	2.00
Manufacturing overhead	1.00
Total manufacturing cost	$17.00

Ben Hiebert, president of Hiebert Chocolate, Ltd., priced the order at $20 per box.

In the past few months, Hiebert has experienced price increases for both dark chocolate and direct labor. All other costs have remained the same. Hiebert budgeted the cost per box for the second order as follows:

Chocolate, filling, wrappers, box	$15.00
Employee time to fill and wrap the box (10 min.)	2.20
Manufacturing overhead	1.10
Total manufacturing cost	$18.30

Requirements

1. Do you agree with the cost analysis for the second order? Explain your answer.

2. Should the two orders be accounted for as one job or two in Hiebert's system?

3. What sale price per box should Ben Hiebert set for the second order? What are the advantages and disadvantages of this price?

Decision Case 17-2 Nature's Own Garden manufactures organic fruit preserves sold primarily through health food stores and on the Web. The company closes for two weeks each December to enable employees to spend time with their families over the holiday season. Nature's Own Garden's manufacturing overhead is mostly straight-line depreciation on its plant, and air-conditioning costs for keeping the berries cool during the summer months. The company uses direct labor hours as the manufacturing overhead allocation base. President Cynthia Ortega has just approved new accounting software and is telling controller Jack Strong about her decision.

"I think this new software will be great," Ortega says. "It will save you time in preparing all those reports."

"Yes, and having so much more information just a click away will help us make better decisions and help control costs," replies Strong. "We need to consider how we can use the new system to improve our business practices."

"And I know just where to start," says Ortega. "You complain each year about having to predict the weather months in advance for estimating air-conditioning costs to include in the calculation of the predetermined manufacturing overhead rate, when professional meteorologists can't even get tomorrow's forecast right! I think we should calculate the predetermined overhead rate on a monthly basis."

Controller Strong is not so sure this is a good idea.

Requirements

1. What are the advantages and disadvantages of Ortega's proposal?

2. Should Nature's Own Garden compute its predetermined manufacturing overhead rate on an annual basis or monthly basis? Explain.

● Ethical Issue 17-1

Farley, Inc., is a manufacturer that produces customized computer components for several well-known computer-assembly companies. Farley's latest contract with CompWest.com calls for Farley to deliver sound cards that simulate surround sound from two speakers. Farley spent several hundred thousand dollars to design the sound card to meet CompWest.com's specifications.

Farley's president, Bryon Wilson, has stipulated a pricing policy that requires the bid price for a new job to be based on Farley's estimated costs to design, manufacture, distribute, and provide customer service for the job, plus a profit margin. Upon reviewing the contract figures, Farley's controller, Paul York, was startled to find that the cost estimates developed by Farley's cost accountant, Tony Hayes, for the CompWest.com bid were based on only the manufacturing costs. York is upset with Hayes. He is not sure what to do next.

Requirements

1. How did using manufacturing cost only, instead of using all costs associated with the CompWest.com job, affect the amount of Farley's bid for the job?

2. Identify the parties involved in Paul York's dilemma. What are his alternatives? How would each party be affected by each alternative? What should York do next?

● Fraud Case 17-1

Jerry never imagined he'd be sitting there in Washington being grilled mercilessly by a panel of congressmen. But a young government auditor picked up on his scheme last year. His company produced hi-tech navigation devices that were sold to both military and civilian clients. The military contracts were "cost-plus," meaning that payments were calculated based on actual production costs plus a profit markup. The civilian contracts were bid out in a very competitive market, and every dollar counted. Jerry knew that because all the jobs were done in the same factory, he could manipulate the allocation of overhead costs in a way that would shift costs away from the civilian contracts and into the military "cost-plus" work. That way, the company would collect more from the government and be able to shave its bids down on civilian work. He never thought anyone would discover the alterations he had made in the factory workers' time sheets, but one of his accountants had noticed and tipped off the government auditor. Now as the congressman from Michigan rakes him over the coals, Jerry is trying to figure out his chances of dodging jail time.

Requirements

1. Based on what you have read above, what was Jerry's company using as a cost driver to allocate overhead to the various jobs?

2. Name two ways that reducing costs on the civilian contracts would benefit the company.

● Team Project 17-1

Major airlines like **American**, **Delta**, and **Continental** are struggling to meet the challenges of budget carriers such as **Southwest** and **JetBlue**. Suppose the **Delta** CFO has just returned from a meeting on strategies for responding to competition from budget carriers. The vice president of operations suggested doing nothing: "We just need to wait until these new airlines run out of money. They cannot be making money with their low fares." In contrast, the vice president of marketing, not wanting to lose market share, suggests cutting **Delta's** fares to match the competition. "If **JetBlue** charges only $75 for that flight from New York, so must we!" Others, including the CFO, emphasized the potential for cutting costs. Another possibility is starting a new budget airline within **Delta**. The CEO cut the meeting short, and directed the CFO to "get some hard data."

As a start, the CFO decides to collect cost and revenue data for a typical **Delta** flight, and then compare it to the data for a competitor. Assume she prepares the following schedule:

	Delta	JetBlue
Route: New York to Tampa..................	Flight 1247	Flight 53
Distance	1,000 miles	1,000 miles
Seats per plane	142	162
One-way ticket price	$80–$621*	$75
Food and beverage	Meal	Snack

*The highest price is first class airfare.

Excluding food and beverage, the CFO estimates that the cost per available seat mile is 8.4 cents for **Delta**, compared to 5.3 cents for **JetBlue**. (That is, the cost of flying a seat for one mile—whether or not the seat is occupied—is 8.4 cents for **Delta**, and 5.3 cents for **JetBlue**.) Assume the average cost of food and beverage is $5 per passenger for snacks and $10 for a meal.

Split your team into two groups. Group 1 should prepare its response to Requirement 1 and group 2 should prepare its response to Requirement 2 before the entire team meets to consider Requirements 3 and 4.

Requirements

1. Use the data to determine the following for **Delta**:
   a. The total cost of Flight 1247, assuming a full plane (100% load factor)
   b. The revenue generated by Flight 1247, assuming a 100% load factor and average revenue per one-way ticket of $102
   c. The profit per Flight 1247, given the responses to a. and b.

2. Use the data to determine the following for **JetBlue**:
   a. The total cost of Flight 53, assuming a full plane (100% load factor)
   b. The revenue generated by Flight 53, assuming a 100% load factor
   c. The profit per Flight 53, given the responses to a. and b.

3. Based on the responses to Requirements 1 and 2, carefully evaluate each of the four alternative strategies discussed in **Delta**'s executive meeting.

4. The analysis in this project is based on several simplifying assumptions. As a team, brainstorm factors that your quantitative evaluation does not include, but that may affect a comparison of **Delta**'s operations to budget carriers.

• Communication Activity 17-1

In 100 words or fewer, explain why we use a predetermined overhead rate instead of waiting to use the "real" rate. In your answer, explain how the rate works with the Manufacturing overhead account.

Quick Check Answers

1. *d* 2. *b* 3. *d* 4. *a* 5. *a* 6. *b* 7. *c* 8. *b* 9. *d* 10. *b*

**For online homework, exercises, and problems that provide you
immediate feedback, please visit myaccountinglab.com.**

Process Costing—Weighted-Average Method

6 Allocate costs using a process costing system—weighted-average method

We saw in the chapter that companies like **Dell Computer**, **Boeing**, and Smart Touch use job order costing to determine the cost of their custom goods and services. In contrast, **BP Oil**, **Crayola**, and **Sony** use a series of steps (called *processes*) to make large quantities of similar products. These systems are called *process costing* systems. There are two methods for handling process costing: weighted-average and FIFO. We focus on the weighted-average method in this appendix.

To introduce process costing, we will look at the crayon manufacturing process. Let's divide **Crayola**'s manufacturing into three processes: mixing, molding, and packaging. **Crayola** accumulates the costs of each process. The company then assigns these costs to the crayons passing through that process.

Suppose **Crayola**'s production costs incurred to make 10,000 crayons and the costs per crayon are as follows:

	Total Costs	Cost per Crayon
Mixing	$200	$0.02
Molding	100	0.01
Packaging	300	0.03
Total cost	$600	$0.06

The total cost to produce 10,000 crayons is the sum of the costs incurred for the three processes. The cost per crayon is the total cost divided by the number of crayons, or

$$\$600/10{,}000 = \$0.06 \text{ per crayon}$$

Crayola uses the cost per unit of each process to

- control costs. The company can find ways to cut the costs where actual process costs are more than planned process costs.
- set selling prices. The company wants the selling price to cover the costs of making the crayons and it also wants to earn a profit.
- calculate the ending work in process inventory and finished goods inventory of crayons for the balance sheet and the cost of goods sold for the income statement.

At any moment, some crayons are in the mixing process, some are in the molding process, and others are in the packaging process. Computing the crayons' cost becomes more complicated when some of the units are still in process. In this appendix, you will learn how to use process costing to calculate the cost of homogeneous products, using crayons as an example.

Exhibit 17A-1 on the following page compares cost flows in

- a job order costing system for **Dell Computer**, and
- a process costing system for **Crayola**.

EXHIBIT 17A-1 **Comparison of Job Order Costing and Process Costing**

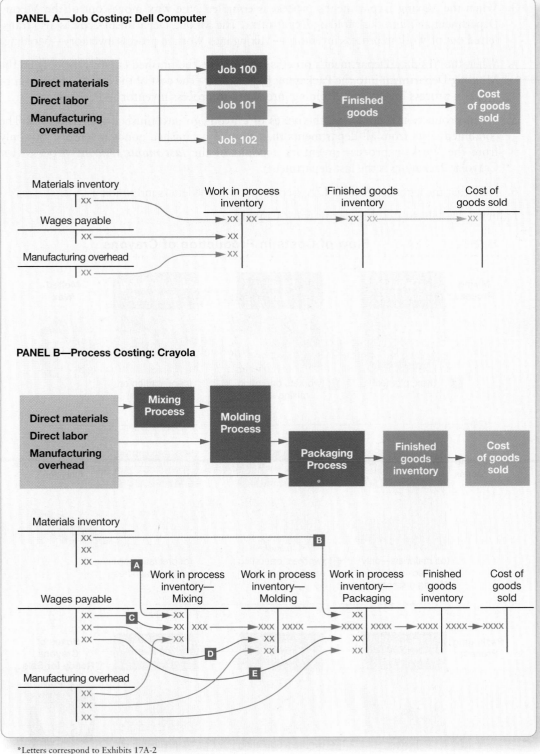

PANEL A—Job Costing: Dell Computer

PANEL B—Process Costing: Crayola

*Letters correspond to Exhibits 17A-2

Panel A shows that **Dell**'s job order costing system has a single Work in process inventory control account. The Work in process inventory account in **Dell**'s general ledger is supported by an individual subsidiary cost record for each job (for example, each custom-built computer). Panel B summarizes the flow of costs for **Crayola**. Notice the following:

1. Each process (mixing, molding, and packaging) is a separate department and each department has its own Work in process inventory account.

2. Direct materials, direct labor, and manufacturing overhead are assigned to Work in process inventory for each process that uses them.

3. When the Mixing Department's process is complete, the wax moves out of the Mixing Department and into the Molding Department. The Mixing Department's cost is also transferred out of Work in process inventory—Mixing into Work in process inventory—Molding.

4. When the Molding Department's process is complete, the finished crayons move from the Molding Department into the Packaging Department. The cost of the crayons flows out of Work in process inventory—Molding into Work in process inventory—Packaging.

5. When production is complete, the boxes of crayons go into finished goods storage. The combined costs from all departments then flow into Finished goods inventory, but only from the Work in process inventory account of the *last manufacturing process* (for **Crayola**, Packaging is the last department).

6. Note that the letters in Exhibit 17A-1 correspond to the letters in Exhibit 17A-2.

Exhibit 17A-2 illustrates this cost flow for **Crayola**.

EXHIBIT 17A-2 | **Flow of Costs in Production of Crayons**

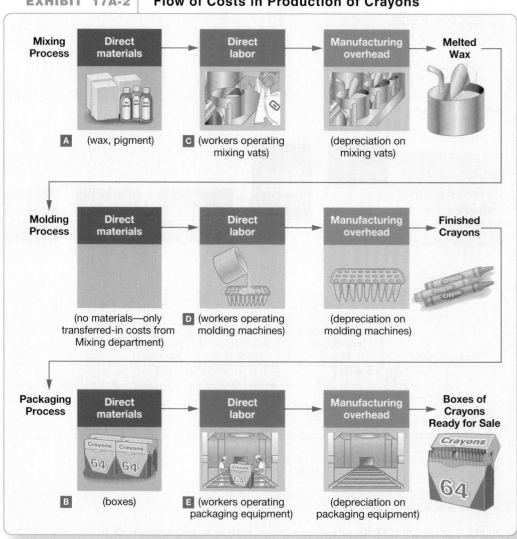

*Note letters correspond to Exhibit 17A-1

Building Blocks of Process Costing

We use two building blocks for process costing:

- Conversion costs
- Equivalent units of production

Chapter 16 introduced three kinds of manufacturing costs: direct materials, direct labor, and manufacturing overhead. Many companies are highly automated, so direct labor is a small part of total manufacturing costs. Such companies often use only two categories:

- Direct materials
- Conversion costs (direct labor plus manufacturing overhead)

Combining direct labor and manufacturing overhead in a single category simplifies the accounting. We call this category *conversion costs* because it is the cost (direct labor plus manufacturing overhead) to *convert* raw materials into finished products.

Completing most products takes time, so **Crayola** may have work in process inventories for crayons that are only partially completed. The concept of **equivalent units** allows us to measure the amount of work done on a partially finished group of units during a period and to express it in terms of fully complete units of output. Assume **Crayola**'s production plant has 10,000 crayons in ending Work in process inventory—Packaging. Each of the 10,000 crayons is 80% complete. If conversion costs are incurred evenly throughout the process, then getting 10,000 crayons 80% of the way through production is the same amount of work as getting 8,000 crayons 100% of the way through the process (10,000 × 80%).

$$
\begin{array}{ccc}
\text{Number of} & \text{Percentage of} & \text{Number of} \\
\text{partially complete units} \times & \text{process completed} = & \text{equivalent units} \\
10,000 & \times \quad 80\% \quad = & 8,000
\end{array}
$$

So, ending Work in process inventory has 8,000 equivalent units for conversion costs.

Stop & Think...

You've ordered three pepperoni pizzas, each cut into eight slices for a party. The pizzas cost $5 each. At the end of the party, the first pizza has two slices left and the second pizza has six slices left. The third pizza box is empty. How many equivalent WHOLE pizzas are still left? Well, you have eight slices in two boxes, so you really have one whole pizza left over that cost $5. That's the concept of equivalent units. So how much was the cost of pizza consumed? Two equivalent pizzas were consumed at $5 each, or $10.*

We use this formula when costs are incurred evenly throughout production. This is usually true for conversion costs. However, direct materials are often added at a specific point in the process. For example, **Crayola**'s wax is added at the beginning of production in the Mixing Department, and packaging materials are added at the end in the Packaging Department. How many equivalent units of wax, conversion costs, and packaging materials are in the ending work in process inventory of 10,000 crayons?

---

*The authors wish to thank Craig Reeder at FAMU for this suggestion.

Look at the timeline in Exhibit 17A-3. The 10,000 crayons in ending work in process inventory have

- 100% of their wax because wax was added at the very beginning. So, they have 10,000 equivalent units of wax. (10,000 × 100% have the wax material.)
- none of their boxes because that is the very last thing that happens in the Packaging Department. So, they have 0 equivalent units of packaging materials. (The crayons have not been packaged yet.)
- 8,000 equivalent units of conversion costs that we completed earlier.

EXHIBIT 17A-3 | **Crayola Production Plant Timeline**

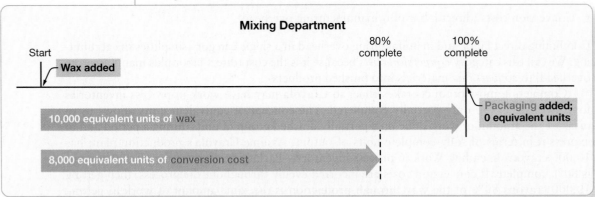

This example illustrates an important point:

> We must compute separate equivalent units for the following:
> - Direct materials
> - Conversion costs

Process Costing in the First Department with No Beginning Work in Process Inventory

To illustrate process costing, we will use Puzzle Me, a company that recycles calendars into jigsaw puzzles. Exhibit 17A-4 illustrates the two major production processes:

- The Assembly Department applies the glue to cardboard and then presses a calendar page onto the cardboard.
- The Cutting Department cuts the calendar board into puzzle pieces and packages the puzzles in a box. The box is then moved to finished goods storage.

EXHIBIT 17A-4 | **Flow of Costs in Producing Puzzles**

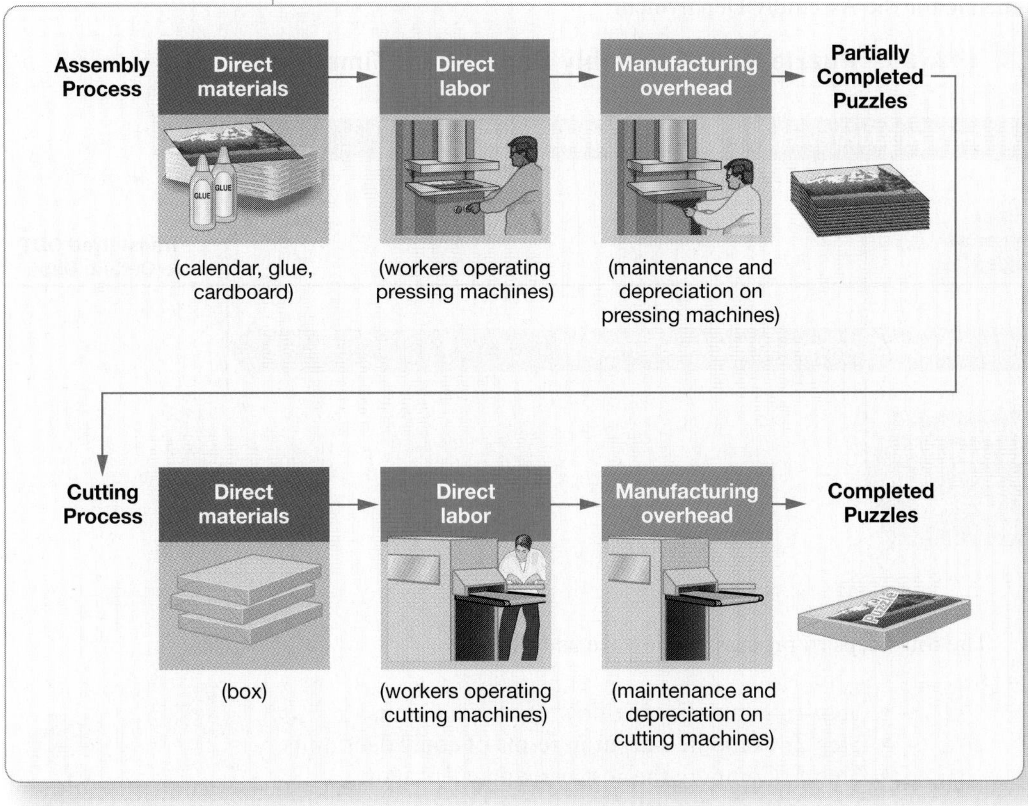

The production process uses materials, machines, and labor in both departments, and there are two Work in process inventory accounts: one for the Assembly Department and one for the Cutting Department.

During July, Puzzle Me incurred the costs shown in Exhibit 17A-5.

EXHIBIT 17A-5 | **Puzzle Me Production Costs for July**

	Assembly Dept	Cutting Dept
Units:		
Beginning WIP—units	0	5,000
Started in production	50,000	must calculate
Transferred out in July	40,000	38,000
Beginning WIP—% complete	N/A	60%
Ending WIP—% complete	25%	30%
Costs:		
Beginning WIP—Transferred in costs	$ 0	$22,000
Beginning WIP—Materials costs	$ 0	$ 0
Beginning WIP—Conversion costs	$ 0	$ 1,200
Direct materials	$140,000	$19,000
Conversion costs:		
Direct labor	$ 20,000	$ 3,840
Manufacturing overhead	$ 48,000	$11,000
Total conversion costs	$ 68,000	$14,840

The accounting period ends before all of the puzzle boards are made. Exhibit 17A-6 shows a timeline for the Assembly Department.

EXHIBIT 17A-6 | **Puzzle Me's Assembly Department Timeline**

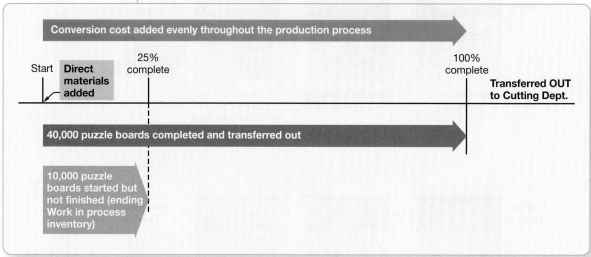

The four steps to process costing are as follows:

- Step 1: Summarize the flow of physical units.
- Step 2: Compute output in terms of equivalent units.
- Step 3: Compute the cost per equivalent unit.
- Step 4: Assign costs to units completed and to units still in ending Work in process inventory.

- "Units to account for" include the number of puzzle boards still in process at the beginning of July plus the number of puzzle boards started during July.
- "Units accounted for" shows what happened to the puzzle boards in process during July. We want to take the July costs incurred in each department and allocate them to the puzzle boards completed and to the puzzle boards still in process at the end of July.

Of the 50,000 puzzle boards started by the Assembly Department in July, 40,000 were completed and transferred out to the Cutting Department. The remaining 10,000 are only partially completed. These partially complete units are the Assembly Department's ending Work in process inventory on July 31.

The Assembly Department timeline in Exhibit 17A-6 shows that all direct materials are added at the beginning of the process. In contrast, conversion costs are incurred evenly throughout the process. This is because labor and overhead production activities occur daily. Thus, we must compute equivalent units separately for the following:

- Direct materials
- Conversion costs

The Assembly Department worked on 50,000 puzzle boards during July, as shown in Exhibit 17A-7. As Exhibit 17A-8 shows, 40,000 puzzle boards are now complete for both materials and conversion costs. Another 10,000 puzzle boards are only 25% complete. How many equivalent units did Assembly produce during July?

Equivalent Units for Materials

Equivalent units for materials total 50,000 (**A** and **D**) because all the direct materials have been added to all 50,000 units worked on during July.

Equivalent Units for Conversion Costs

Equivalent units for conversion costs total 42,500 (**G**). Conversion costs are complete for the 40,000 (**E**) puzzle boards completed and transferred out. But only 25% of the conversion work has been done on the 10,000 puzzle boards in ending Work in process inventory. Therefore, ending Work in process inventory represents only 2,500 (**F**) equivalent units for conversion costs.

Exhibits 17A-7 and 17A-8 summarize steps 1 and 2.

The cost per equivalent unit requires information about total costs and equivalent units. The computations are as follows:

$$\text{Cost per equivalent unit for direct materials} = \frac{\text{Total direct materials cost}}{\text{Equivalent units of materials}}$$

$$\text{Cost per equivalent unit for conversion costs} = \frac{\text{Total conversion cost}}{\text{Equivalent units for conversion}}$$

Exhibit 17A-5, presented earlier, summarizes the total costs to account for in the Assembly Department. The Assembly Department has 50,000 physical units and $208,000 of costs to account for. Our next task is to split these costs between the following:

- 40,000 puzzle boards transferred out to the Cutting Department
- 10,000 partially complete puzzle boards that remain in the Assembly Department's ending Work in process inventory

In step 2, we computed equivalent units for direct materials (50,000 (**D**)) and conversion costs (42,500 (**G**)). Because the equivalent units differ, we must compute a separate cost per unit for direct materials and for conversion costs. Exhibit 17A-5 shows that the direct materials costs are $140,000 (**H** + **I** = **J**). Conversion costs are $68,000 (**L** + **M** = **N**), which is the sum of direct labor of $20,000 and manufacturing overhead of $48,000.

The cost per equivalent unit of material is $2.80 (**J** ÷ **D** = **K**), and the cost per equivalent unit of conversion cost is $1.60 (**N** ÷ **G** = **O**), as shown in Exhibit 17A-9.

We must determine how much of the $208,000 total costs to be accounted for by the Assembly Department should be assigned to

- the 40,000 completed puzzle boards that have been transferred out to the Cutting Department.
- the 10,000 partially completed puzzle boards remaining in the Assembly Department's ending Work in process inventory.

Exhibit 17A-10 shows how to assign costs.

The total cost of completed puzzle boards for the Assembly Department is $176,000 (**P**), as shown in Exhibit 17A-10. The $176,000 is the sum of ($112,000 (**B** × **K**)) and conversion costs ($64,000 (**E** × **O**)). The cost of the 10,000 partially completed puzzle boards in ending Work in process inventory is $32,000 (**Q**), which is the sum of direct material costs ($28,000 (**C** × **K**)) and conversion costs ($4,000 (**F** × **O**)) allocated in Exhibit 17A-10.

Exhibit 17A-10 has accomplished our goal of splitting the $208,000 total cost between the following:

The 40,000 puzzles completed and transferred out to the Cutting Department	$176,000 **P**
The 10,000 puzzles remaining in the Assembly Department's ending Work in process inventory on July 31 ($28,000 + $4,000).....	32,000 **Q**
Total costs of the Assembly Department	$208,000

EXHIBIT 17A-7 | **Step 1: Summarize Physical Flow of Goods**

PUZZLE ME
Cost of Production—ASSEMBLY DEPT.
Month Ended July 31, 2014

Flow of Production	Whole Units	
Step 1: PHYSICAL FLOW		
Units to account for:		
Beginning work in process, June 30	0	
Started in production during July	50,000	
Total physical units to account for	50,000	**A**

Journal entries to record July costs placed into production in the Assembly Department follow (data from Exhibit 17A-5):

(1) Work in process inventory—Assembly (A+)	208,000	
Materials inventory (A–)		140,000
Wages payable (L+)		20,000
Manufacturing overhead (E–)		48,000
To assign materials, labor, and overhead cost to Assembly.		

The entry to transfer the cost of the 40,000 completed puzzles out of the Assembly Department and into the Cutting Department follows (Item **P** from Exhibit 17A-10):

P Work in process inventory—Cutting (A+)	176,000	
Work in process inventory—Assembly (A–)		176,000
To transfer costs from Assembly to Cutting.		

After these entries are posted, the Work in process inventory—Assembly account appears as follows:

Work in process inventory—Assembly

Balance, June 30	—	Transferred to Cutting	176,000 **P**
Direct materials	140,000		
Direct labor	20,000		
Manufacturing overhead	48,000		
Q Balance, July 31	32,000		

Note that the ending balance is the same $32,000 as item **Q** on Exhibit 17A-10's cost of production report.

Process Costing in a Second Department

Most products require a series of processing steps. In this section, we consider a second department—Puzzle Me's Cutting Department for July—to complete the picture of process costing.

EXHIBIT 17A-11 | **Puzzle Me's Cutting Department Timeline**

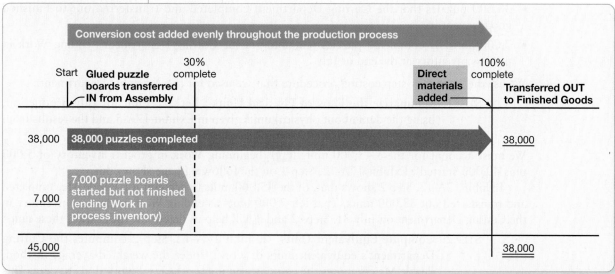

The Cutting Department receives the puzzle boards and cuts the board into puzzle pieces before inserting the pieces into the box at the end of the process. Exhibit 17A-11 shows the following:

- Glued puzzle boards are transferred in from the Assembly Department at the beginning of the Cutting Department's process.
- The Cutting Department's conversion costs are added evenly throughout the process.
- The Cutting Department's direct materials (boxes) are added at the end of the process.

Keep in mind that *direct materials* in the Cutting Department refers to the boxes added *in that department* and not to the materials (cardboard and glue) added in the Assembly Department. The materials from the Assembly Department that are *transferred into* the Cutting Department are called *transferred in costs*. Likewise, *conversion costs* in the Cutting Department refers to the direct labor and manufacturing overhead costs incurred only in the Cutting Department.

Exhibit 17A-5, presented earlier in this appendix, lists July information for both of Puzzle Me's departments. We will be referring to this data as we complete our Cutting Department allocation for July. Remember that Work in process inventory at the close of business on June 30 is both of the following:

- Ending inventory for June
- Beginning inventory for July

Exhibit 17A-5 shows that Puzzle Me's Cutting Department started the July period with 5,000 puzzle boards partially completed through work done in the Cutting Department in June. During July, the Cutting Department started work on 40,000 additional puzzle boards that were received from the Assembly Department (which we calculated earlier in Exhibits 17A-7 through 17A-10).

The weighted-average method combines the Cutting Department's

- work done last month—beginning Work in process inventory—to start the Cutting process on the 5,000 puzzle boards that were in beginning Work in process inventory.
- work done in July to complete the 5,000 puzzle boards in beginning Work in process inventory and to work on the 40,000 additional puzzle boards that were transferred in from the Assembly Department during July.

Thus, the **weighted-average process costing method** determines the average cost of all the Cutting Department's equivalent units of work on these 45,000 (**A**) puzzle boards (5,000 beginning Work in process inventory + 40,000 (**B** and **E**) transferred in from the previous department).

Just as we did for the Assembly Department, our goal is to split the total cost in the Cutting Department between the following:

- 38,000 puzzles that the Cutting Department completed and transferred out to Finished goods inventory
- 7,000 partially completed puzzles remaining in the Cutting Department's ending Work in process inventory at the end of July

We use the same four-step costing procedure that we used for the Assembly Department.

STEP 1: **Summarize the Flow of Physical Units** Let's account for July production, using the data about physical units given in Exhibit 17A-5 and the results from Exhibit 17A-10 for the Assembly Department.

We must account for these 45,000 units (**A**) (beginning Work in process inventory of 5,000 plus 40,000 started). Exhibit 17A-12, Step 1 on the following page shows this.

Exhibit 17A-12, Step 2 shows that, of the 45,000 units to account for, Puzzle Me completed and transferred out 38,000 units. That left 7,000 units as ending Work in process inventory in the Cutting Department on July 31. Steps 2 and 3 will help us determine the costs of these units.

STEP 2: **Compute Equivalent Units** Exhibit 17A-12, Step 2 computes the Cutting Department's equivalent units of work. Under the weighted-average method, Puzzle Me computes the equivalent units for the total work done to date. This includes all the work done in the current period (July), plus the work done last period (June) on the beginning Work in process inventory.

EXHIBIT 17A-12 | Cost of Production—Second Department

PUZZLE ME
Cost of Production—CUTTING DEPT.
Month Ended July 31, 2014

Flow of Production

1 Step 1: PHYSICAL FLOW	Whole Units	
Units to account for:		
Beginning work in process, June 30 (from Exhibit 17A-5)	5,000	
Started in production during July (from Exhibit 17A-10)	40,000	B E
Total physical units to account for	45,000	A

Step 2: EQUIVALENT UNITS

2	Whole Units		Transferred In		Direct Materials		Conversion Costs	
Units accounted for:								
Completed and transferred out during July (from Exhibit 17A-5)	38,000	B	38,000	B	38,000	E	38,000	H
Ending work in process, July 31	7,000	C	$7,000 \times 100\% = 7,000$	C	$7,000 \times 0\% = 0$	F	$7,000 \times 30\% = 2,100$	I
Total physical units to be assigned costs	45,000	A	45,000	D	38,000	G	40,100	J

Step 3: COST PER EQUIVALENT UNIT

3			Transferred In		Direct Materials		Conversion Costs	
Units Costs:								
Beginning work in process, June 30 (from Exhibit 17A-5)		K	$ 22,000	K	$ 0	N	$ 1,200	S
Costs added during July (from Exhibit 17A-5)		P	$176,000	P	$19,000	O	$14,840	T
Total costs to account for		K+P=L	$198,000	K+P=L	$19,000	N+O=P	$16,040	S+T=U
Total equivalent units		D	÷ 45,000	D	÷ 38,000	G	÷ 40,100	J
Cost per equivalent unit		L÷D=M	$ 4.40	L÷D=M	$ 0.50	P÷G=R	$ 0.40	U÷J=W

Step 4: ASSIGN COSTS

4							Total Costs	
Completed and transferred out during July	$38,000 \times \$4.40 = \$167,200$	B×M	$38,000 \times \$0.50 = \$19,000$	E×R	$38,000 \times \$0.40 = \$15,200$	H×W	$ 23,200	
							$209,840	
							$233,040	
Ending work in process, July 31	$7,000 \times \$4.40 = \$ 30,800$	C×M	$0 \times \$0.50 = \$ 0$	F×R	$2,100 \times \$0.40 = \$ 840$	I×W	$ 5.30	
							$201,400	X
							$ 31,640	Y
Total costs accounted for							$233,040	

We can see in Exhibit 17A-12, Step 2 that the total equivalent units with respect to

- transferred-in costs include all 45,000 (D) units because they are complete with respect to work done in the Assembly Department. The equivalent units for transferred-in costs will always be 100% of the units to account for, because these units must be 100% complete on previous work before coming to the Cutting Department.
- direct materials include only the 38,000 (E) finished puzzles because Cutting Department materials (boxes) are added at the end.
- conversion costs include the 38,000 (H) finished puzzles plus the 2,100 (I) puzzles (7,000 puzzle boards × 30%) that are still in process at the end of the month. Conversion work occurs evenly throughout the cutting process.

Exhibit 17A-12, Step 3 accumulates the Cutting Department's total costs to account for. In addition to direct material and conversion costs, the Cutting Department must account for transferred-in costs. **Transferred-in costs** are those costs that were incurred in a previous process (the Assembly Department, in this case) and brought into a later process (the Cutting Department) as part of the product's cost.

Exhibit 17A-12, Step 3 shows that the Cutting Department's total cost to account for ($233,040) is the sum of the following:

- The cost incurred in June to start the Cutting process on the 5,000 puzzles in Cutting's beginning Work in process inventory ($22,000 + $0 + $1,200) (K + N + S)
- The costs added to Work in process inventory—Cutting during July ($209,840 = $176,000 (P) transferred in from the Assembly Department + $19,000 (O) direct materials added in the Cutting Department + $14,840 (T) conversion costs added in the Cutting Department)

Exhibit 17A-12, Step 3 also shows the cost per equivalent unit. For each cost category, we divide total cost by the number of equivalent units. Perform this computation for all cost categories: transferred-in costs, direct materials, and conversion costs. In this illustration, the total cost per equivalent unit is $5.30 ($4.40 (M)+ $0.50 (R) + $0.40 (W)).

Exhibit 17A-12, Step 4 shows how Puzzle Me assigns the total Cutting Department costs of $233,040 to

- units completed and transferred out to Finished goods inventory ($201,400 (X)).
- units remaining in the Cutting Department's ending Work in process inventory ($31,640 (Y)).

We use the same approach as we used for the Assembly Department in Exhibit 17A-10. Multiply the number of equivalent units from Step 2 by the cost per equivalent unit from Step 3.

Exhibit 17A-13 shows how Exhibit 17A-12 divided the Cutting Department's costs.

The Cutting Department's journal entries previously recorded the $176,000 in transferred-in costs of puzzle boards from the Assembly Department into the Cutting Department on page 865.

The following entry records the Cutting Department's other costs during July (data from Exhibit 17A-5):

(2)	Work in process inventory—Cutting (A+)	33,840	
	Materials inventory (A–)		19,000
	Wages payable (L+)		3,840
	Manufacturing overhead (E–)		11,000
	To assign materials and conversion costs to the Cutting Dept.		

The entry to transfer the cost of completed puzzles out of the Cutting Department and into Finished goods inventory is based on the dollar amount in Exhibit 17A-12:

X	Finished goods inventory (A+)	201,400	
	Work in process inventory—Cutting (A–)		201,400
	To transfer costs from the Cutting Dept. to Finished goods.		

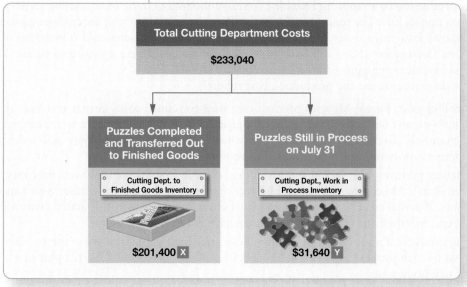

EXHIBIT 17A-13 | **Assigning Cutting Department Costs to Units Completed and Transferred Out, and to Ending Work in Process Inventory**

After posting, the key accounts appear as follows:

Work in process inventory—Assembly

(Exhibit 17A-10)			
Balance, June 30	—	Transferred to Cutting	176,000 **P**
I Direct materials	140,000		
M Direct labor	20,000		
M Manufacturing overhead	48,000		
Q Balance, July 31	32,000		

Work in process inventory—Cutting

Balance, June 30	23,200	Transferred to Finished	
P Transferred in from Assembly	176,000	goods inventory	201,400 **X**
O Direct materials	19,000		
T Direct labor	3,840		
T Manufacturing overhead	11,000		
Y Balance, July 31	31,640		

Finished goods inventory

Balance, June 30	0	
X Transferred in from Cutting	201,400	

As we saw earlier in this chapter, accountants prepare cost reports to help production managers evaluate the efficiency of their manufacturing operations. Both job order and process costing are similar in that they

- *accumulate* costs as the product moves through production.
- *assign* costs to the units (such as gallons of gasoline or number of crayons) passing through that process.

The difference between job order costing and process costing lies in the way costs are accumulated. Job order costing uses a *job cost sheet* and process costing uses a *production cost report*. (See Exhibits 17A-10 and 17A-12 that we completed for the Assembly and Cutting Departments.)

The **production cost report** in Exhibit 17A-12 summarizes Puzzle Me's Cutting Department operations during July. The report combines the costs to account for and the cost per equivalent unit. It shows how those costs were assigned to the puzzles completed and transferred out of the Cutting Department ($201,400) and how much of the costs were assigned to ending Work in process inventory remaining in the department ($31,640).

How do managers use the production cost report?

- Controlling cost: Puzzle Me uses product cost data to reduce costs. A manager may decide that the company needs to change either suppliers or a certain component to reduce the cost of its materials. To reduce labor costs, it may need either different employee skill levels paid at different hourly rates or new production equipment.

- Evaluating performance: Managers are often rewarded based on how well they meet the budget. Puzzle Me compares the actual direct materials and conversion costs with expected amounts. If actual costs are too high, managers look for ways to cut. If actual costs are less than expected, the Cutting Department's managers may receive a bonus.

- Pricing products: Puzzle Me must set its selling price high enough to cover the manufacturing cost of each puzzle ($5.30 = $4.40 + $0.50 + $0.40 in Exhibit 17A-12) plus marketing and distribution costs.

- Identifying the most profitable products: Selling price and cost data help managers figure out which products are most profitable. They can then promote these products.

- Preparing the financial statements: Finally, the production cost report aids financial reporting. It provides inventory data for the balance sheet and cost of goods sold for the income statement.

Appendix 17A Assignments

● Short Exercises

S17A-1 ❻ **Calculating conversion costs and unit cost [5–10 min]**
Spring Fresh produces premium bottled water. Spring Fresh purchases artesian water, stores the water in large tanks, and then runs the water through two processes: filtration and bottling.

During February, the filtration process incurred the following costs in processing 150,000 liters:

Wages of workers operating the filtration equipment	$ 25,950
Manufacturing overhead allocated to filtration	20,050
Water	80,000

Spring Fresh had no beginning Work in process inventory in the Filtration Department in February.

Requirements

1. Compute the February conversion costs in the Filtration Department.
2. The Filtration Department completely processed 150,000 liters in February. What was the filtration cost per liter?

Note: Short Exercise 17A-1 must be completed before attempting Short Exercise 17A-2.

S17A-2 ❻ **Drawing a timeline, and computing equivalent units [10 min]**
Refer to S17A-1. At Spring Fresh, water is added at the beginning of the filtration process. Conversion costs are added evenly throughout the process. Now assume that in February, 130,000 liters were completed and transferred out of the Filtration

Department into the Bottling Department. The 20,000 liters remaining in Filtration's ending Work in process inventory were 80% of the way through the filtration process. Recall that Spring Fresh has no beginning inventories.

Requirements

1. Draw a timeline for the filtration process.
2. Compute the equivalent units of direct materials and conversion costs for the Filtration Department.

S17A-3 ⑥ **Computing equivalent units [5 min]**

The Mixing Department of Foods for You had 65,000 units to account for in October. Of the 65,000 units, 35,000 units were completed and transferred to the next department, and 30,000 units were 40% complete. All of the materials are added at the beginning of the process. Conversion costs are added equally throughout the mixing process.

Requirement

1. Compute the total equivalent units of direct materials and conversion costs for October.

Note: Short Exercise 17A-3 must be completed before attempting Short Exercise 17A-4.

S17A-4 ⑥ **Computing the cost per equivalent unit [5 min]**

Refer to the data in S17A-3 and your results for equivalent units. The Mixing Department of Foods for You has direct materials costs of $20,800 and conversion costs of $23,500 for October.

Requirement

1. Compute the cost per equivalent unit for direct materials and for conversion costs.

Note: Short Exercises 17A-3 and 17A-4 must be completed before attempting Short Exercise 17A-5.

S17A-5 ⑥ **Computing cost of units transferred out and units in ending work in process [5 min]**

Refer to S17A-3 and S17A-4. Use Food for You's costs per equivalent unit for direct materials and conversion costs that you calculated in S17A-4.

Requirement

1. Calculate the cost of the 35,000 units completed and transferred out and the 30,000 units, 40% complete, in the ending Work in process inventory.

● Exercises

E17A-6 **6** **Drawing a timeline, computing equivalent units, and assigning cost to completed units and ending work in process; no beginning work in process inventory or cost transferred in [20 min]**

Crafty Paint prepares and packages paint products. Crafty Paint has two departments: (1) Blending and (2) Packaging. Direct materials are added at the beginning of the blending process (dyes) and at the end of the packaging process (cans). Conversion costs are added evenly throughout each process. Data from the month of May for the Blending Department are as follows:

Gallons:	
Beginning work in process inventory	0
Started production	9,000 gallons
Completed and transferred out to Packaging in May	4,000 gallons
Ending work in process inventory (30% of the way through	
blending process)	5,000 gallons
Costs:	
Beginning work in process inventory	$ 0
Costs added during May:	
Direct materials	6,750
Direct labor	1,300
Manufacturing overhead	2,000
Total costs added during May	$10,050

Requirements

1. Fill in the timeline for the Blending Department.

2. Use the timeline to help you compute the Blending Department's equivalent units for direct materials and for conversion costs.

3. Compute the total costs of the units (gallons)
   a. completed and transferred out to the Packaging Department.
   b. in the Blending Department ending Work in process inventory.

Note: Exercise 17A-6 must be completed before attempting Exercise 17A-7.

E17A-7 **6** **Preparing journal entries and posting to work in process T-accounts [15 min]**
Refer to your answers from E17A-6.

Requirements

1. Prepare the journal entries to record the assignment of direct materials and direct labor, and the allocation of manufacturing overhead to the Blending Department. Also, prepare the journal entry to record the costs of the gallons completed and transferred out to the Packaging Department.

2. Post the journal entries to the Work in process inventory—Blending T-account. What is the ending balance?

3. What is the average cost per gallon transferred out of Blending into Packaging? Why would the company managers want to know this cost?

E17A-8 **6** **Drawing a timeline, computing equivalent units, and assigning cost to completed units and ending work in process; no beginning work in process inventory or cost transferred in [20 min]**
Samson Winery in Pleasant Valley, New York, has two departments: Fermenting and Packaging. Direct materials are added at the beginning of the fermenting process (grapes) and at the end of the packaging process (bottles). Conversion costs are

added evenly throughout each process. Data from the month of March for the Fermenting Department are as follows:

Gallons:	
Beginning work in process inventory	0
Started production	9,100 gallons
Completed and transferred out to Packaging in March	7,900 gallons
Ending work in process inventory (80% of the way through fermenting process)	1,200 gallons
Costs:	
Beginning work in process inventory	$ 0
Costs added during March:	
Direct materials	9,828
Direct labor	3,500
Manufacturing overhead	3,588
Total costs added during March	$16,916

Requirements

1. Draw a timeline for the Fermenting Department.
2. Use the timeline to help you compute the equivalent units for direct materials and for conversion costs.
3. Compute the total costs of the units (gallons)
   a. completed and transferred out to the Packaging Department.
   b. in the Fermenting Department ending Work in process inventory.

Note: Exercise 17A-8 must be completed before attempting Exercise 17A-9.

E17A-9 ⑥ **Preparing journal entries and posting to work in process T-accounts [15 min]**
Refer to the data and your answers from E17A-8.

Requirements

1. Prepare the journal entries to record the assignment of Direct materials and Direct labor and the allocation of Manufacturing overhead to the Fermenting Department. Also prepare the journal entry to record the cost of the gallons completed and transferred out to the Packaging Department.
2. Post the journal entries to the Work in process inventory—Fermenting T-account. What is the ending balance?
3. What is the average cost per gallon transferred out of Fermenting into Packaging? Why would Samson Winery's managers want to know this cost?

E17A-10 ⑥ **Computing equivalent units, computing cost per equivalent unit; assigning costs; journalizing; second department, weighted-average method [25–30 min]**
Cool Spring Company produces premium bottled water. In the second department, the Bottling Department, conversion costs are incurred evenly throughout the bottling process, but packaging materials are not added until the end of the process. Costs in beginning Work in process inventory include transferred in costs of $1,700,

direct labor of $700, and manufacturing overhead of $330. February data for the Bottling Department follow:

COOL SPRING COMPANY					
Work in process inventory—Bottling					
Month Ended February 28, 2013					
	Physical Units	Dollars		Physical Units	Dollars
Beginning inventory, January 31 (40% complete)	12,000	$ 2,730	Transferred out	152,000	$?
Production started:					
Transferred in	163,000	134,800			
Direct materials		30,400			
Conversion costs:					
Direct labor		33,100			
Manufacturing overhead		16,300			
Total to account for	175,000	$217,330			
Ending inventory, February 28 (70% complete)	23,000	$?			

Requirements

1. Compute the Bottling Department equivalent units for the month of February. Use the weighted-average method.
2. Compute the cost per equivalent unit for February.
3. Assign the costs to units completed and transferred out and to ending Work in process inventory.
4. Prepare the journal entry to record the cost of units completed and transferred out.
5. Post all transactions to the Work in process inventory—Bottling Department T-account. What is the ending balance?

● Problems (Group A)

MyAccountingLab

P17A-11A ⑥ **Computing equivalent units and assigning costs to completed units and ending work in process; no beginning work in process inventory or cost transferred in [30–45 min]**

Amy Electronics makes CD players in three processes: assembly, programming, and packaging. Direct materials are added at the beginning of the assembly process. Conversion costs are incurred evenly throughout the process. The Assembly Department had no Work in process inventory on October 31. In mid-November, Amy Electronics started production on 125,000 CD players. Of this number, 95,800 CD players were assembled during November and transferred out to the Programming Department. The November 30 Work in process inventory in the Assembly Department was 25% of the way through the assembly process. Direct materials costing $437,500 were placed in production in Assembly during November, and Direct labor of $200,800 and Manufacturing overhead of $134,275 were assigned to that department.

Requirements

1. Compute the number of equivalent units and the cost per equivalent unit in the Assembly Department for November.
2. Assign total costs in the Assembly Department to (a) units completed and transferred to Programming during November and (b) units still in process at November 30.
3. Prepare a T-account for Work in process inventory—Assembly to show its activity during November, including the November 30 balance.

P17A-12A ⑥ **Computing equivalent units and assigning costs to completed units and ending work in process; no beginning work in process inventory or cost transferred in [30–45 min]**

Reed Paper, Co., produces the paper used by wallpaper manufacturers. Reed's four-stage process includes mixing, cooking, rolling, and cutting. During March, the Mixing Department started and completed mixing for 4,520 rolls of paper. The department started but did not finish the mixing for an additional 500 rolls, which were 20% complete with respect to both direct materials and conversion work at the end of March. Direct materials and conversion costs are incurred evenly throughout the mixing process. The Mixing Department incurred the following costs during March:

Work in process inventory—Mixing

Bal, Mar 1	0
Direct materials	5,775
Direct labor	620
Manufacturing overhead	6,310

Requirements

1. Compute the number of equivalent units and the cost per equivalent unit in the Mixing Department for March.

2. Show that the sum of (a) cost of goods transferred out of the Mixing Department and (b) ending Work in process inventory—Mixing equals the total cost accumulated in the department during March.

3. Journalize all transactions affecting the company's mixing process during March, including those already posted.

P17A-13A ⑥ **Computing equivalent units and assigning costs to completed units and ending work in process inventory; two materials, added at different points; no beginning work in process inventory or cost transferred in [30–45 min]**

Smith's Exteriors produces exterior siding for homes. The Preparation Department begins with wood, which is chopped into small bits. At the end of the process, an adhesive is added. Then the wood/adhesive mixture goes on to the Compression Department, where the wood is compressed into sheets. Conversion costs are added evenly throughout the preparation process. January data for the Preparation Department are as follows:

Sheets			Costs	
Beginning work in process inventory	0	sheets	Beginning work in process inventory	$ 0
Started production	3,700	sheets	Costs adding during January:	
Completed and transferred out to			Wood	3,108
Compression in January	2,000	sheets	Adhesives	1,240
			Direct labor	558
Ending work in process inventory (30%	_____		Manufacturing overhead	1,450
of the way through preparation process)	1,700	sheets	Total costs	$ 6,356

Requirements

1. Draw a timeline for the Preparation Department.

2. Use the timeline to help you compute the equivalent. (*Hint*: Each direct material added at a different point in the production process requires its own equivalent-unit computation.)

3. Compute the total costs of the units (sheets)
   a. completed and transferred out to the Compression Department.
   b. in the Preparation Department's ending Work in process inventory.

4. Prepare the journal entry to record the cost of the sheets completed and transferred out to the Compression Department.

5. Post the journal entries to the Work in process inventory—Preparation T-account. What is the ending balance?

P17A-14A ⑥ **Computing equivalent units for a second department with beginning work in process inventory; preparing a production cost report and recording transactions on the basis of the report's information; weighted-average method [45–60 min]**

Christine Carpet manufactures broadloom carpet in seven processes: spinning, dyeing, plying, spooling, tufting, latexing, and shearing. In the Dyeing Department, direct materials (dye) are added at the beginning of the process. Conversion costs are incurred evenly throughout the process. Christine uses weighted-average process costing. Information for November 2012 follows:

Units:		
Beginning work in process inventory	90	rolls
Transferred in from Spinning Department during November	540	rolls
Completed during November	510	rolls
Ending work in process (80% complete as to		
conversion work)	120	rolls
Costs:		
Beginning work in process (transferred-in cost, $4,900;		
materials cost, $1,390; conversion costs, $4,900)	$ 11,190	
Transferred in from Spinning Department during November	22,190	
Materials cost added during November	11,210	
Conversion costs added during November (manufacturing		
wages, $8,225; manufacturing overhead, $43,839)	52,064	

Requirements

1. Prepare a timeline for Christine's Dyeing Department.

2. Use the timeline to help you compute the equivalent units, cost per equivalent unit, and total costs to account for in Christine's Dyeing Department for November.

3. Prepare the November production cost report for Christine's Dyeing Department.

4. Journalize all transactions affecting Christine's Dyeing Department during November, including the entries that have already been posted.

P17A-15A ⑥ **Computing equivalent units for a second department with beginning work in process inventory; assigning costs to completed units and ending work in process; weighted-average method [50–60 min]**

WaterBound uses three processes to manufacture lifts for personal watercraft: forming a lift's parts from galvanized steel, assembling the lift, and testing the completed lifts. The lifts are transferred to finished goods before shipment to marinas across the country.

WaterBound's Testing Department requires no direct materials. Conversion costs are incurred evenly throughout the testing process. Other information follows:

Units:		
Beginning work in process	2,000	units
Transferred in from the Assembling Dept. during the period	7,000	units
Completed during the period	4,000	units
Ending work in process (40% complete as to		
conversion work)	5,000	units
Costs:		
Beginning work in process (transferred-in cost, $93,000;		
conversion costs, $18,000)	$ 111,000	
Transferred in from the Assembling Dept. during the period	672,000	
Conversion costs added during the period	54,000	

The cost transferred into Finished goods inventory is the cost of the lifts transferred out of the Testing Department. WaterBound uses weighted-average process costing.

Requirements

1. Draw a timeline for the Testing Department.
2. Use the timeline to compute the number of equivalent units of work performed by the Testing Department during the period.
3. Compute WaterBound's transferred-in and conversion costs per equivalent unit. Use the unit costs to assign total costs to (a) units completed and transferred out of Testing and (b) units in Testing's ending Work in process inventory.
4. Compute the cost per unit for lifts completed and transferred out to Finished goods inventory. Why would management be interested in this cost?

● Problems (Group B)

P17A-16B ⑥ **Computing equivalent units and assigning costs to completed units and ending work in process; no beginning work in process inventory or cost transferred in [30–45 min]**

Beth Electronics makes CD players in three processes: assembly, programming, and packaging. Direct materials are added at the beginning of the assembly process. Conversion costs are incurred evenly throughout the process. The Assembly Department had no work in process inventory on March 31. In mid-April, Beth Electronics started production on 115,000 CD players. Of this number, 99,000 CD players were assembled during April and transferred out to the Programming Department. The April 30 work in process inventory in the Assembly Department was 45% of the way through the assembly process. Direct materials costing $345,000 were placed in production in Assembly during April, and direct labor of $150,000 and manufacturing overhead of $62,400 were assigned to that department.

Requirements

1. Compute the number of equivalent units and the cost per equivalent unit in the Assembly Department for April.
2. Assign total costs in the Assembly Department to (a) units completed and transferred to Programming during April and (b) units still in process at April 30.
3. Prepare a T-account for Work in process inventory—Assembly to show its activity during April, including the April 30 balance.

P17A-17B ⑥ **Computing equivalent units and assigning costs to completed units and ending work in process; no beginning work in process inventory or cost transferred in [30–45 min]**

Smith Paper, Co., produces the paper used by wallpaper manufacturers. Smith's four-stage process includes mixing, cooking, rolling, and cutting. During September, the Mixing Department started and completed mixing for 4,405 rolls of paper. The department started but did not finish the mixing for an additional 600 rolls, which were 20% complete with respect to both direct materials and conversion work at the end of September. Direct materials and conversion costs are incurred evenly throughout the mixing process. The Mixing Department incurred the following costs during September:

Work in process inventory–Mixing

Bal, Sep 1	0
Direct materials	5,430
Direct labor	550
Manufacturing overhead	5,785

Requirements

1. Compute the number of equivalent units and the cost per equivalent unit in the Mixing Department for September.

2. Show that the sum of (a) cost of goods transferred out of the Mixing Department and (b) ending Work in process inventory—Mixing equals the total cost accumulated in the department during September.

3. Journalize all transactions affecting the company's mixing process during September, including those already posted.

P17A-18B ⑥ **Computing equivalent units and assigning costs to completed units and ending work in process inventory; two materials, added at different points; no beginning work in process inventory or cost transferred in [30–45 min]**

Bert's Exteriors produces exterior siding for homes. The Preparation Department begins with wood, which is chopped into small bits. At the end of the process, an adhesive is added. Then the wood/adhesive mixture goes on to the Compression Department, where the wood is compressed into sheets. Conversion costs are added evenly throughout the preparation process. January data for the Preparation Department are as follows:

Sheets			Costs		
Beginning work in process inventory	0	sheets	Beginning work in process inventory	$	0
Started production	3,900	sheets	Costs adding during January:		
Completed and transferred out to			Wood		3,120
Compression in January	2,700	sheets	Adhesives		1,836
			Direct labor		990
Ending work in process inventory (25%			Manufacturing overhead		2,100
of the way through the preparation process)	1,200	sheets	Total costs	$	8,046

Requirements

1. Draw a timeline for the Preparation Department.

2. Use the timeline to help you compute the equivalent units. (*Hint*: Each direct material added at a different point in the production process requires its own equivalent-unit computation.)

3. Compute the total costs of the units (sheets)
   a. completed and transferred out to the Compression Department.
   b. in the Preparation Department's ending Work in process inventory.

4. Prepare the journal entry to record the cost of the sheets completed and transferred out to the Compression Department.

5. Post the journal entries to the Work in process inventory—Preparation T-account. What is the ending balance?

P17A-19B ⑥ **Computing equivalent units for a second department with beginning work in process inventory; preparing a production cost report and recording transactions on the basis of the report's information; weighted-average method [45–60 min]**

Carol Carpet manufactures broadloom carpet in seven processes: spinning, dyeing, plying, spooling, tufting, latexing, and shearing. In the Dyeing Department, direct materials (dye) are added at the beginning of the process. Conversion costs are incurred evenly throughout the process. Carol uses weighted-average process costing. Information for July 2012 follows:

Units:	
Beginning work in process inventory	65 rolls
Transferred in from Spinning Department during July	570 rolls
Completed during July	520 rolls
Ending work in process (80% complete as to	
conversion work)	115 rolls
Costs:	
Beginning work in process (transferred-in cost, $3,900;	
materials cost, $1,625; conversion costs, $5,555)	$ 11,080
Transferred in from Spinning Department during July	19,595
Materials cost added during July	9,805
Conversion costs added during July (manufacturing	
wages, $9,450; manufacturing overhead, $43,135)	52,585

Requirements

1. Prepare a timeline for Carol's Dyeing Department.
2. Use the timeline to help you compute the equivalent units, cost per equivalent unit, and total costs to account for in Carol's Dyeing Department for July.
3. Prepare the July production cost report for Carol's Dyeing Department.
4. Journalize all transactions affecting Carol's Dyeing Department during July, including the entries that have already been posted.

P17A-20B ⑥ **Computing equivalent units for a second department with beginning work in process inventory; assigning costs to completed units and ending work in process; weighted average method [50–60 min]**

OceanBound uses three processes to manufacture lifts for personal watercrafts: forming a lift's parts from galvanized steel, assembling the lift, and testing the completed lifts. The lifts are transferred to finished goods before shipment to marinas across the country.

OceanBound's Testing Department requires no direct materials. Conversion costs are incurred evenly throughout the testing process. Other information follows:

Units:	
Beginning work in process	2,200 units
Transferred in from the Assembling Dept. during the period	7,100 units
Completed during the period	4,200 units
Ending work in process (40% complete as to	
conversion work)	5,100 units
Costs:	
Beginning work in process (transferred in cost, $93,800;	
conversion costs, $18,200)	$ 112,000
Transferred in from the Assembling Dept. during the period	706,000
Conversion costs added during the period	44,200

The cost transferred into Finished goods inventory is the cost of the lifts transferred out of the Testing Department. OceanBound uses weighted-average process costing.

Requirements

1. Draw a timeline for the Testing Department.
2. Use the timeline to compute the number of equivalent units of work performed by the Testing Department during the period.
3. Compute OceanBound's transferred-in and conversion costs per equivalent unit. Use the unit costs to assign total costs to (a) units completed and transferred out of Testing and (b) units in Testing's ending Work in process inventory.
4. Compute the cost per unit for lifts completed and transferred out to Finished goods inventory. Why would management be interested in this cost?

18

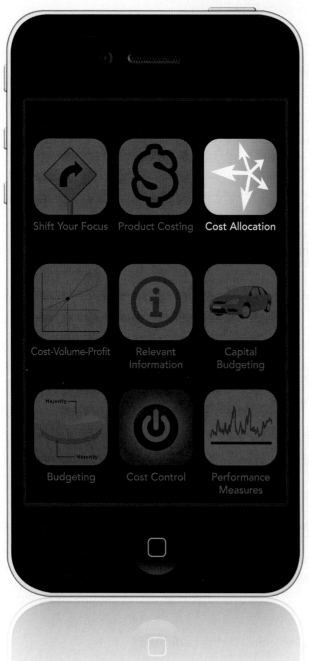

Activity-Based Costing and Other Cost Management Tools

Learning Objectives

1. Develop activity-based costs (ABC)

2. Use activity-based management (ABM) to achieve target costs

3. Describe a just-in-time (JIT) production system, and record its transactions

4. Use the four types of quality costs to make decisions

David Larimer, Matt Sewell, and Brian Jobe are college friends who share an apartment. They split the monthly costs equally as shown below:

Rent and utilities	$570
Cable TV	50
High-speed Internet access	40
Groceries	240
Total monthly costs	**$900**

Each roommate's share is $300 ($900/3).

Things go smoothly the first few months. But then David calls a meeting. "Since I started having dinner at Amy's, I shouldn't have to pay a full share for the groceries." Matt then pipes in, "I'm so busy on the Internet that I never have time to watch TV. I don't want to pay for the cable TV any more. And Brian, since your friend Jennifer eats here most evenings, you should pay a double share of the grocery bill." Brian retorts, "Matt, then you should pay for the Internet access, since you're the only one around here who uses it!"

What happened? The friends originally shared the costs equally. But they are not participating equally in eating, watching TV, and using the Internet. Splitting these costs equally is not the best arrangement.

The roommates could better match their costs with the people who participate in each activity. This means splitting cable TV between David and Brian, letting Matt pay for

Internet access, and allocating the grocery bill 1/3 to Matt and 2/3 to Brian. Exhibit 18-1 compares the results of this refined system with the original system.

		David	Matt	Brian
EXHIBIT 18-1	**More-Refined Versus Original Cost Allocation System**			
More-refined cost allocation system:				
Rent and utilities		$190	$190	$190
Cable TV		25	—	25
High-speed Internet access		—	40	—
Groceries		—	80	160
Total costs allocated		$215	$310	$375
Original cost allocation system		$300	$300	$300
Difference		$ (85)	$ 10	$ 75

No wonder David called the meeting! The original system cost him $300 a month, but under the refined system, David pays only $215.

●   ●   ●

Large companies such as **Microsoft** or **Sony**, as well as smaller companies like Smart Touch Learning, face situations like this every day. What is the best way to allocate our costs to the things we do? Fair allocations have high stakes: friendships for David, Matt, and Brian and profits and losses for companies. Businesses that offer multiple products and/or services use a similar approach to link the various types of production and non-manufacturing costs to their various products or services.

Refining Cost Systems

Now we turn to a more accurate method to attach costs to products, called activity-based costing. We'll discuss how to develop an ABC system and compare it to traditional methods you learned about in the previous chapter.

 1 Develop activity-based costs (ABC)

Sharpening the Focus: Assigning Costs Based on the Activities That Caused the Costs

Let's illustrate cost refinement by looking at Smart Touch. In today's competitive market, Smart Touch needs to know what it costs to make a DVD. The cost information helps Smart Touch set a selling price to cover costs and provide a profit. To remain competitive with other learning DVD manufacturers, Smart Touch must hold its costs down.

We have seen that direct costs (materials and labor) are easy to assign to products. But indirect costs (utilities, supervisor salaries, and plant depreciation) are another story. It is the indirect costs—and they are significant—that must be allocated somehow. One way to manage costs is to refine the way indirect costs are allocated. Exhibit 18-2 provides an example. The first column of Exhibit 18-2 starts with Smart Touch's production function—making the DVDs. Production is where most companies begin refining their cost systems.

Before business got so competitive, managers could limit their focus to a broad business function such as production, and use a single plant-wide rate to allocate manufacturing overhead cost to their inventory, as we demonstrated in Chapter 17. But today's environment calls for more refined cost accounting. Managers need better data to set prices and identify the most profitable products. They drill down to focus on the costs incurred by each activity within the production function, as shown on the right side of Exhibit 18-2. This has led to a better way to allocate indirect cost to production, called activity-based costing.

EXHIBIT 18-2 | **Focus on the Activities That Cause the Costs—Smart Touch**

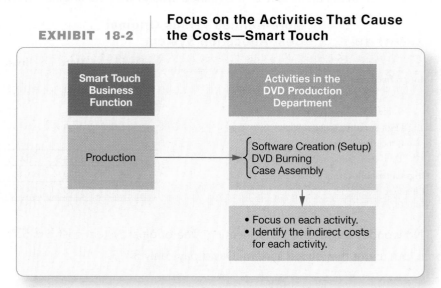

Activity-based costing (ABC) focuses on *activities*. For example, a tire factory that produces five models of tires has a complex warehousing operation, a casting operation, a quality inspection operation, and a packaging operation, each of which is an "activity." A landscaping service company has a yard maintenance operation, a landscape design operation, a tree service operation, and a commercial turf planting operation, each of which is considered a separate activity.* Smart Touch's activities in the DVD production department are software creation, DVD burning, and case assembly. The costs of those activities become the building blocks for measuring (allocating) the costs of products and services. **Activity-based costing divides the total production process into activities and then assigns costs to products based on how much the production USES those activities to make the product.** Companies like **Dell**, **Coca-Cola**, and **American Express** use ABC.

Each activity has its own (usually unique) cost driver. For example, one of Smart Touch's activities is case assembly, and Smart Touch allocates indirect case assembly activity costs to DVDs based on the number of inserts a worker must put in the DVD case. DVDs that require more inserts cost more to manufacture. Exhibit 18-3 shows some representative activities and cost drivers for manufacturing companies.

EXHIBIT 18-3 | **Examples of Activities and Cost Drivers**

---

*The authors wish to thank Craig Reeder of FAMU for his suggestions.

Stop & Think...

You go to a restaurant with three of your friends and the waiter brings one bill for $100. How do you split it up? The meal you ordered only cost $20 of the total bill. Do you pay ¼ of the bill, $25, or do you pay based on the cost of what you ordered, $20? Paying based on what you ordered is the key to activity-based costing. Production costs get allocated based on the amount of each activity of production that the products use.

Developing an Activity-Based Costing System

The main difference between ABC and traditional systems is that ABC uses a separate allocation rate for each activity. Traditional systems, as demonstrated in Chapter 17, usually use one rate. ABC requires four steps, as outlined in Exhibit 18-4, using Smart Touch's data for the case assembly activity.

EXHIBIT 18-4 | **Activity-Based Costing in Four Easy Steps**

ABC Step	Application
1. Identify each activity and estimate its total indirect cost.	Activity Case Assembly Estimated total indirect cost per year $10,000
2. Identify the cost driver for each activity and estimate the total quantity of each driver's allocation base.	Cost driver for case assembly Number of inserts Estimated total number of inserts each year 100,000
3. Compute the cost allocation rate for each activity. $$\text{Cost allocation rate} = \frac{\text{Estimated total indirect cost of the activity}}{\text{Estimated total quantity of the allocation base (activity)}}$$	$$\text{Cost allocation rate} = \frac{\$10,000}{100,000 \text{ inserts}} = \$0.10 \text{ per insert}$$
4. Allocate indirect costs to the cost object—in this case, all the inserts put in DVD cases during January. $$\text{Allocated activity cost} = \frac{\text{Cost allocation rate for the activity}}{} \times \text{Actual quantity of the allocation base used by the cost object}$$	$$\begin{aligned}\text{Cost of DVD Assembly for January} &= \$0.10 \times \begin{array}{c}8{,}000 \text{ inserts}\\ \text{during January}\end{array}\\ &= \underline{\$800}\end{aligned}$$

The first step in developing an activity-based costing system is to identify the activities. Analyzing all the activities required for a product or service forces managers to think about how each activity might be improved—or whether it is necessary at all.

Traditional Versus Activity-Based Costing Systems: Smart Touch Learning

To illustrate an ABC system, we use Smart Touch. Smart Touch produces hundreds of different learning DVDs, including mass quantities of large audience DVDs and small quantities of "specialty" learning DVDs for specific companies.

We begin with a traditional cost system using a plant-wide manufacturing overhead allocation rate to show its weakness. You will see shortly that the ABC system that follows is clearly superior.

A Traditional Cost System

Smart Touch's cost system allocates all manufacturing overhead the traditional way—based on a single allocation rate: 40% of direct labor cost. Smart Touch's controller, James Kolen, gathered data for two of the company's products:

- **Microsoft** Excel Training DVD (Multiple customers use this DVD)
- Specialty DVD created for a company's custom software application (A single customer uses this DVD)

Based on Smart Touch's traditional cost system, Kolen computed each product's gross profit as shown in Exhibit 18-5.

EXHIBIT 18-5	Smart Touch's Manufacturing Cost and Gross Profit Using Traditional Overhead Allocation	

	Excel DVD	Specialty DVD
Sale price per DVD	$12.00	$70.00
Less: Manufacturing cost per DVD:		
Direct materials	2.40	2.40
Direct labor	4.00	34.00
Manufacturing overhead (40% of Direct labor cost)	1.60	13.60
Total manufacturing cost per DVD	8.00	50.00
Gross profit per DVD	$ 4.00	$20.00

The gross profit for the specialty DVD is $20 per DVD—five times as high as the $4 gross profit for the Excel DVD. Smart Touch CEO Sheena Bright is surprised that the specialty DVD appears so much more profitable. She asks Kolen to check this out. Kolen confirms that the gross profit per DVD is five times as high for the specialty DVD. Bright wonders whether Smart Touch should produce more specialty DVDs.

Key Point: Because direct labor cost is the single allocation base for all products, Smart Touch allocates far more total dollars of overhead cost to the Excel DVDs than to the specialty DVDs. However, total dollars of overhead are spread over more DVDs, which is why the per unit cost per DVD is less for Excel DVDs than for specialty DVDs. This costing is accurate only if direct labor really is the overhead cost driver, and only if the Excel DVD really does cause more overhead than the specialty DVD.

Noriko Kitagawa, Smart Touch's marketing manager, reviews the gross profit data and calls a meeting with production foreman Ryan Oliver and controller Kolen. At the meeting, Kitagawa suggests that the company should try expanding sales of the specialty product and reduce sales of the Excel DVD. Kolen says he is not sure that's the right answer because there may be some distortion in the way overhead is allocated. Intuitively, he feels like the specialty DVD does not really require that much more in overhead resources than the Excel product, but because it uses higher labor cost, the Excel DVD is getting more total manufacturing overhead costs allocated to the product.

Kolen fears that the problem could be Smart Touch's cost accounting system. Kolen suggests that Smart Touch break down overhead costs by activities and then look at the gross profit data again before making such an important strategic marketing decision. Exhibit 18-6 compares the traditional single-allocation-base system (Panel A) to the new ABC system that Kolen's team developed (Panel B).

Activity-Based Cost System

Panel B of Exhibit 18-6 shows that Smart Touch's ABC team identifies three activities: setup, DVD burning, and case assembly. (*Setup* is when the company prepares the manufacturing line—sets it up—to produce a different product.) Each activity has its own cost driver. But exactly how does ABC work? The ABC team develops the new system by following the four steps described in Exhibit 18-4.

EXHIBIT 18-6 | **Overview of Smart Touch's Traditional and ABC Systems**

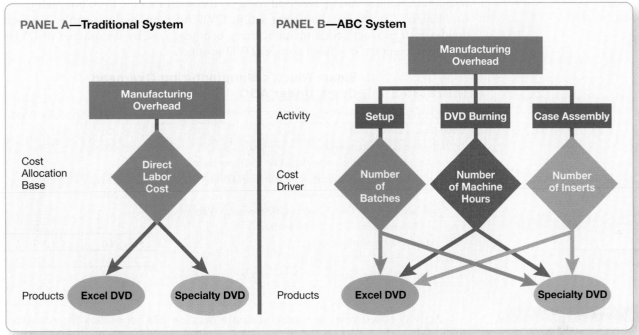

Let's see how an ABC system works, with a focus on the setup activity. Exhibit 18-7 develops Smart Touch's ABC system. Follow the details of each step. Make sure you understand exactly how each ABC step applies to Smart Touch's setup process.

EXHIBIT 18-7 | **Smart Touch's ABC System**

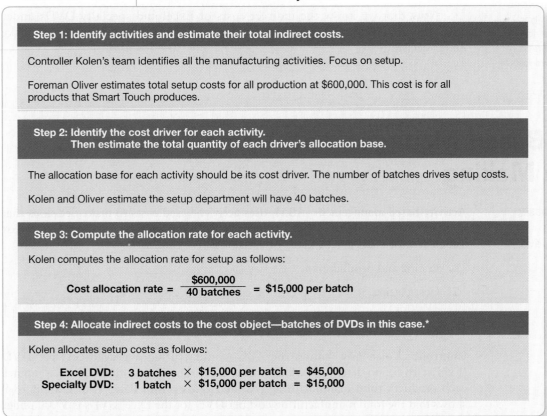

*Other Smart Touch products represent the remaining 36 batches.

Controller Kolen then uses the ABC costs allocated from Exhibit 18-7 to recompute manufacturing overhead costs, as shown in Exhibit 18-8. For each product, Kolen adds the total costs of setup, DVD burning, and assembly. He then divides each product's total manufacturing overhead cost by the number of DVDs produced to get the overhead cost per DVD product.

EXHIBIT 18-8 | **Smart Touch's Manufacturing Overhead Costs Under ABC**

Manufacturing Overhead Costs	Excel DVD	Specialty DVD
Setup (from Exhibit 18-7)	$ 45,000	$15,000
DVD Burning (amounts assumed)	5,000	1,500
Case Assembly (from Exhibit 18-4, based on $0.10 per insert).		
Each Excel DVD has 1 insert. (100,000 Excel DVDs × 1 insert per DVD × $0.10 per insert)	10,000	
Each specialty DVD has 7 inserts. (500 specialty DVDs × 7 inserts per DVD × $0.10 per insert)		350
Total manufacturing overhead cost	$ 60,000	$16,850
Divide by number of DVDs produced	100,000	500
Manufacturing overhead cost per DVD under ABC	$ 0.60	$ 33.70

Activity-based costs are more accurate because ABC considers the resources (activities) each product actually uses. Focus on the bottom line of Exhibit 18-8. Manufacturing overhead costs of

- Excel DVDs are $0.60 per DVD, which is less than the $1.60 manufacturing overhead cost allocated under the old system (shown in color in Exhibit 18-5).

- specialty DVDs are $33.70 per DVD, which far exceeds the $13.60 manufacturing overhead cost under the old system (shown in color in Exhibit 18-5).

Now that we know the indirect costs of Excel and specialty DVDs under ABC, let's see how Smart Touch's managers *use* the ABC cost information to make better decisions.

Activity-Based Management: Using ABC for Decision Making

 Use activity-based management (ABM) to achieve target costs

Activity-based management (ABM) uses activity-based costs to make decisions that increase profits while meeting customer needs. In this section, we show how Smart Touch can use ABC in two kinds of decisions:

1. Pricing and product mix

2. Cost cutting

Pricing and Product Mix Decisions

Controller Kolen now knows the ABC manufacturing overhead cost per DVD (Exhibit 18-8). To determine which products are the most profitable, he recomputes each product's total manufacturing cost and gross profit. Panel A of Exhibit 18-9 shows that the total manufacturing cost per DVD for the Excel DVDs is $7.00 under the ABC system. Contrast this with the $8.00 cost per DVD under Smart Touch's traditional cost system, as shown in Panel B. More important, the ABC data in Panel A show that the specialty DVDs cost $70.10 per DVD, rather than the $50 per DVD indicated by the old system (Panel B). Smart Touch has been losing $0.10 on each specialty DVD—and this is *before* selling, administrative, and distribution expenses! It seems that specialty DVDs are not currently profitable for Smart Touch.

EXHIBIT 18-9 | **Smart Touch's Cost Comparison— ABC vs. Traditional Allocation**

PANEL A—Manufacturing Cost per DVD and Gross Profit Under ABC

	Excel DVD	Specialty DVD
Sale price per DVD	$12.00	$70.00
Less: Manufacturing cost per DVD:		
Direct materials	2.40	2.40
Direct labor	4.00	34.00
Manufacturing overhead (from Exhibit 18-8)	0.60	33.70
Total manufacturing cost per DVD	7.00	70.10
Gross profit **per DVD**	$ 5.00	$ (0.10)

PANEL B—Manufacturing Cost per DVD and Gross Profit Under Traditional Allocation of Costs

	Excel DVD	Specialty DVD
Sale price per DVD	$12.00	$70.00
Less: Manufacturing cost per DVD:		
Direct materials	2.40	2.40
Direct labor	4.00	34.00
Manufacturing overhead (40% of Direct labor cost)	1.60	13.60
Total manufacturing cost per DVD	8.00	50.00
Gross profit **per DVD**	$ 4.00	$20.00

This illustration shows that ABC is the more accurate way to allocate the cost of manufacturing a product. With better cost and profitability information, Smart Touch can make better decisions that increase company profits.

Armed with a better measure of the cost of each product, Smart Touch may want to evaluate the production process to identify potential ways to reduce manufacturing overhead costs. If Smart Touch cannot cut costs enough to earn a profit on the specialty DVDs, then the company may decide to increase the sale price of the specialty DVDs. If customers will not pay more, Smart Touch may decide to drop the specialty DVDs. *This is the exact opposite of the strategy suggested by cost data from the traditional system. That system favored specialty DVDs.* This is a product mix decision. Product mix considers overall production capacity and serves to focus on producing the mix of products that is most profitable, considering limited production capabilities.

Cutting Costs

Most companies adopt ABC to get better product costs for pricing and product-mix decisions. However, they often benefit more by cutting costs. ABC and value engineering can work together. **Value engineering** means reevaluating activities to reduce costs. It requires the following cross-functional teams:

- Marketers to identify customer needs
- Engineers to design more efficient products
- Accountants to estimate costs

Why are managers turning to value engineering? Because it gets results! Companies like **Apple** and **Carrier Corporation** are following Japanese automakers **Toyota** and **Nissan** and setting sale prices based on **target prices**—what customers

Connect To: Business

How do businesses create an atmosphere for implementing cost-cutting strategies? One technique is to simply ask employees for suggestions that either cut costs or create new revenues. Rewarding employees for recommendations that are implemented by offering bonuses based on a percentage of the amount of savings generated is an incentive and motivator. Who better to see ideas to help save the company money than those who work there every day?

are willing to pay for the product or service. Exhibit 18-10 compares target pricing to cost-based pricing. Study each column separately.

EXHIBIT 18-10 | **Target Pricing Versus Cost-Based Pricing**

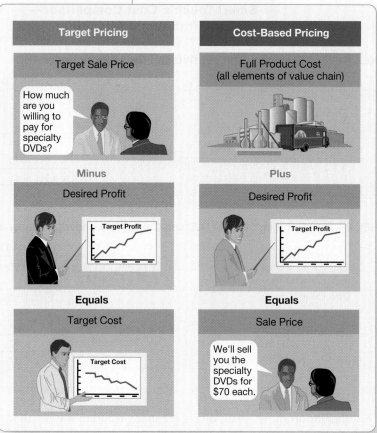

Instead of starting with product cost and then adding a profit to determine the sale price (right column of the exhibit), target pricing (left column) does just the opposite. Target pricing starts with the price that customers are willing to pay and then subtracts the company's desired profit to determine the **target cost**. Then the company works backward to develop the product at the target cost. The company's goal is to achieve the target cost.

Let's return to our Smart Touch illustration. The ABC analysis in Exhibit 18-9, Panel A, prompts CEO Sheena Bright to push Excel DVDs because it appears that the specialty DVD is losing money. The marketing department says the selling price of the Excel DVDs is likely to fall to $10.00 per DVD. Bright wants to earn a profit equal to 20% of the sale price.

Full-product costs consider *all* production costs (direct materials, direct labor, and allocated manufacturing overhead) plus all nonmanufacturing costs (operating expenses, such as administrative and selling expenses) when determining target costs and target profits. What is Smart Touch's target full-product cost per Excel DVD? The following is the computation:

Target sale price per Excel DVD	$10.00
− Desired profit ($10.00 × 20%)	(2.00)
= Target cost per Excel DVD	$ 8.00

Does Smart Touch's current full-product cost meet this target? Let's see:

Current total manufacturing cost per Excel DVD	$7.00
+ Nonmanufacturing costs (operating expenses—amount assumed)	1.10
= Current full-product cost per Excel DVD	$8.10

Smart Touch's current cost does not meet the target cost.

Because Smart Touch's current full-product cost, $8.10, exceeds the target cost of $8.00, Bright assembles a value engineering team to identify ways to cut costs. The team analyzes each production activity. For each activity, the team considers how to

- cut costs, given Smart Touch's current production process.
- redesign the production process to further cut costs.

Of the team's several proposals, Bright decides to *redesign setup to reduce the setup cost per batch*. Smart Touch will do this by grouping raw materials that are used together to reduce the time required to assemble the materials for each setup. Estimated total cost saving is $160,000, and the number of batches remains unchanged at 40.

Will this change allow Smart Touch to reach the target cost? Exhibit 18-11 shows how controller Kolen recomputes the cost of Setup based on the value engineering study.

EXHIBIT 18-11 | **Recomputing Activity Costs After a Value Engineering Study—Excel DVDs**

		Manufacturing Overhead		
	Setup	DVD Burning	Assembly	Total Manufacturing Overhead Cost
Estimated total indirect costs of activity:				
Setup ($600,000 − $160,000)	$440,000			
Estimated total quantity of each allocation base	40 batches			
Compute the cost allocation rate for each activity:				
(Divide estimated indirect cost by estimated	$440,000	Amounts	Amounts	
quantity of the allocation base)	÷ 40 batches	from	from	
Cost allocation rate for each activity	= $11,000 per batch	Exhibit	Exhibit	
Actual quantity of each allocation base used		18-8	18-8	
by Excel DVDs:				
Setup (from Exhibit 18-7; Excel DVDs				
require three batches)	× 3 batches			
Total Allocated Manufacturing Costs	= $ 33,000	+ $5,000	+ $10,000	= $48,000

Exhibit 18-11 shows that value engineering cuts total manufacturing overhead cost of the Excel DVDs to $48,000 from $60,000 (in Exhibit 18-8). Now Kolen totals the revised cost estimates for Excel DVDs in Exhibit 18-12.

EXHIBIT 18-12 | **ABC Manufacturing Overhead Costs After Value Engineering Study—Excel DVDs**

PANEL A—Manufacturing Cost Under ABC After Value Engineering Study

	Excel DVD
Manufacturing overhead costs	
Setup (from Exhibit 18-11)	$ 33,000
DVD Burning (from Exhibit 18-11)	5,000
Case Assembly (from Exhibit 18-11)	10,000
Total manufacturing overhead cost	$ 48,000
Divide by number of DVDs produced	100,000
Manufacturing overhead cost per DVD under ABC after value engineering study	$ 0.48

PANEL B—Total Manufacturing Cost and Full Product Cost Under ABC After Value Engineering Study

	Excel DVD
Manufacturing cost per DVD:	
Direct materials	$2.40
Direct labor	4.00
Manufacturing overhead (from Panel A)	0.48
Total manufacturing cost per DVD after value engineering study	$6.88
Non manufacturing costs per DVD (assumed)	1.10
Full product cost after value engineering study per DVD	$7.98

Cost of $6.88 is quite an improvement from the prior manufacturing cost of $7.00 per DVD (Exhibit 18-9, Panel A). Now Smart Touch's full cost of $7.98 is less than its target full product cost of $8.00. Value engineering worked.

Next, we'll review Decision Guidelines 18-1, which cover ABC systems and ABC management.

Key Takeaway

Activity-based management (ABM) uses activity-based costs to make decisions that increase profits while meeting customer needs. Most companies adopt ABC to get better product costs for pricing and product-mix decisions. However, they often benefit more by cutting costs. Target pricing takes the sales price and subtracts desired profit to determine the target cost of manufacturing. ABC and value engineering work together to reevaluate activities with the goal of reducing manufacturing overhead costs to meet the target cost. By reducing costs, companies can maintain desired profit levels.

Decision Guidelines 18-1

ACTIVITY-BASED COSTING

You are the manager of operations for a hi-tech electronics manufacturing company. The company's production has doubled in the last year. The company decides to adopt an ABC system. What decisions will your company face as it begins refining its cost system?

Decision	Guidelines
• How does a company develop an ABC system?	1. Identify each activity and estimate its total indirect costs. 2. Identify the cost driver for each activity. Then estimate the total quantity of each driver's allocation base. 3. Compute the cost allocation rate for each activity. 4. Allocate indirect costs to the cost object.
• How do we compute a cost allocation rate for an activity?	$$\frac{\text{Estimated total indirect cost of the activity}}{\text{Estimated total quantity of the allocation base (activity)}}$$
• How do we allocate an activity's cost to the cost object?	$$\frac{\text{Cost allocation}}{\text{rate for the activity}} \times \frac{\text{Actual quantity of the allocation}}{\text{base used by the cost object}}$$
• For what kinds of decisions do managers use ABC?	Managers use ABC data to decide on the following: • Pricing and product mix • Cost cutting
• How are target costs set?	Target sale price (based on market research) − Desired profit = Target cost
• How can a company achieve target costs?	Use value engineering to cut costs by improving product design and production processes.
• What are the main benefits of ABC?	• More accurate product cost information helps managers determine which products are most profitable to produce. • More detailed information on the costs of activities and their cost drivers helps managers control costs.

Summary Problem 18-1

Indianapolis Auto Parts (IAP) has a Seat Manufacturing Department that uses activity-based costing. IAP's system has the following activities:

Activity	Allocation Base	Cost Allocation Rate
Purchasing	Number of purchase orders	$50.00 per purchase order
Assembling	Number of parts	$0.50 per part
Packaging	Number of finished seats	$1.00 per finished seat

Each auto seat has 20 parts. Direct materials cost per seat is $1. Direct labor cost per seat is $10. Suppose **Ford** has asked IAP for a bid on 50,000 built-in baby seats that would be installed as an option on some **Ford** SUVs. IAP will use a total of 200 purchase orders if **Ford** accepts IAP's bid.

Requirements

1. Compute the total cost IAP will incur to (a) purchase the needed materials and then (b) assemble and (c) package 50,000 baby seats. Also, compute the average cost per seat.
2. For bidding, IAP adds a 30% markup to total cost. What total price will IAP bid for the entire **Ford** order?
3. Suppose that instead of an ABC system, IAP has a traditional product costing system that allocates indirect costs other than direct materials and direct labor at the rate of $65 per direct labor hour. The baby-seat order will require 10,000 direct labor hours. What price will IAP bid using this system's total cost?
4. Use your answers to Requirements 2 and 3 to explain how ABC can help IAP make a better decision about the bid price to offer **Ford**.

Solution

Requirement 1

Direct materials, 50,000 seats × $1.00	$	50,000
Direct labor, 50,000 seats × $10.00		500,000
Activity costs:		
Purchasing, 200 purchase orders × $50.00		10,000
Assembling, 50,000 seats × 20 parts per seat × $0.50		500,000
Packaging, 50,000 seats × $1.00		50,000
Total cost of order		$1,110,000
Divide by number of seats	÷	50,000
Average cost per seat	$	22.20

Requirement 2

Bid price (ABC system): ($1,110,000 × 130%) .... <u>$1,443,000</u>

Requirement 3

Direct materials, 50,000 seats × $1.00	$	50,000
Direct labor, 50,000 seats × $10.00		500,000
Indirect costs, 10,000 direct labor hours × $65.00		650,000
Total cost of order...		$1,200,000
Bid price (traditional system): ($1,200,000 × 130%)...		$1,560,000

Requirement 4

IAP's bid would be $117,000 higher using the traditional system than using ABC ($1,560,000 – $1,443,000). Assuming the ABC system more accurately captures the costs caused by the order, the traditional system over-costs the order. This leads to a higher bid price and reduces IAP's chance of winning the order. The ABC system can increase IAP's chance of winning the order by bidding a lower price.

Just-in-Time (JIT) Systems

Competition is fierce, especially in manufacturing and technology-related services. Chinese and Indian companies are producing high-quality goods at very low costs. As we saw in the discussion of activity-based costing, there is a never-ending quest to cut costs.

The cost of buying, storing, and moving inventory can be significant for companies like **Home Depot, Toyota,** and **Dell.** To lower inventory costs, many companies use a just-in-time (JIT) system.

Companies with JIT systems buy materials and complete finished goods *just in time* for delivery to customers. In traditional manufacturing, materials would be ordered in large quantities to obtain volume discounts and to have surplus materials on hand in case some of the materials turn out to be defective. Under the JIT system, the manufacturer contracts with suppliers to deliver small quantities of goods, as needed. Deliveries are small and frequent, and the suppliers must guarantee a close to zero defect rate. That way the manufacturers hold only small amounts of raw materials in the warehouse, use only materials as needed, and because of the zero defect rate and quick delivery, can be assured they won't run out of materials and have to shut down production. Because of JIT, relationships with suppliers of raw materials must be very reliable to ensure that the company has raw materials just when needed to manufacture products. Because products are made as ordered, finished goods inventories are kept to a minimal amount. This reduces the company's cost to store and insure inventory. It also allows the company to minimize the resources it has invested in raw materials and in inventory. Lastly, because the inventories are low, the risk of the inventory becoming "obsolete" or unsaleable is very small.

Production in JIT systems is completed in self-contained work cells, as shown in Exhibit 18-13. **A work cell is an area where everything needed to complete a manufacturing process is readily available.** Each work cell includes the machinery and labor resources to manufacture a product. Employees work in a team in the work cell and are empowered to complete the work without supervision. Workers complete a small batch of units and are responsible for inspecting for quality throughout the process. As the completed product moves out of the work cell, the suppliers deliver more materials to the work cell just in time to keep production moving along.

By contrast, traditional production systems separate manufacturing into various processing departments that focus on a single activity. Work in process must be moved from one department to another. More movements waste time, and wasted time is wasted money.

3 Describe a just-in-time (JIT) production system, and record its transactions

EXHIBIT 18-13 | **Production Flow Comparison: Just-in-Time Versus Traditional Production**

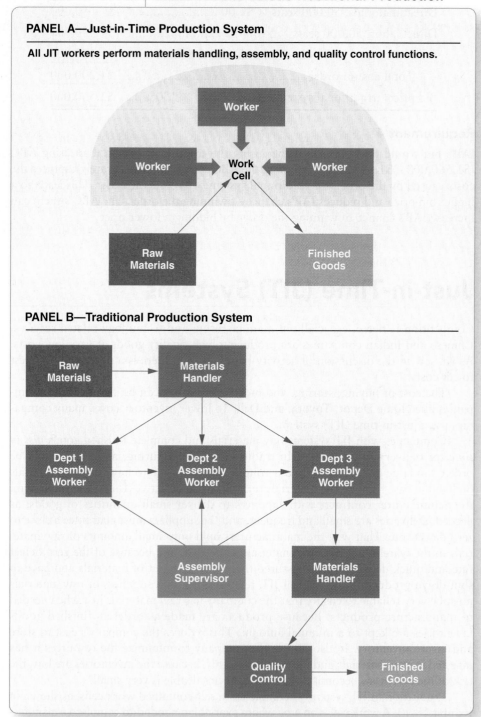

PANEL A—Just-in-Time Production System

All JIT workers perform materials handling, assembly, and quality control functions.

PANEL B—Traditional Production System

Under JIT, a customer's order—customer demand—triggers manufacturing. The sales order "pulls" materials, labor, and overhead into production. This "demand–pull" system extends back to the suppliers of materials. As noted previously, suppliers make frequent deliveries of defect-free materials *just in time* for production. Purchasing only what customers demand reduces inventory. Less inventory frees floor space (and resources) for more productive use. Thus, JIT systems help to reduce waste. Exhibit 18-13 shows a traditional production system in Panel B. The traditional system requires more inventory, more workers, and costs more to operate than a JIT system.

Companies like **Toyota, Carrier,** and **Dell** credit JIT for saving them millions of dollars. But JIT systems are not without problems. With little or no inventory buffers, JIT users lose sales when they cannot get materials on time, or when poor-quality materials arrive just in time. There is no way to make up for lost time. As a result, as noted earlier, strong relationships with quality raw materials vendors are very important to JIT. Additionally, many JIT companies still maintain small inventories of critical materials.

Just-in-Time Costing

JIT costing leads many companies to simplify their accounting. **Just-in-time costing,** sometimes called **backflush costing,** seems to work backwards. JIT costing starts with output that has been completed and then assigns manufacturing costs to units sold and to inventories. There are three major differences between JIT costing and traditional standard costing, as shown in Exhibit 18-14:

1. JIT costing does not track the cost of products from Materials inventory (or Raw materials inventory) to Work in process inventory to Finished goods inventory. Instead, JIT costing waits until the units are completed to record the cost of production.

2. JIT costing combines Materials inventory and Work in process inventory accounts into a single account called **Raw and in-process inventory.**

3. Under the JIT philosophy, workers perform many tasks. Most companies using JIT combine labor and manufacturing overhead costs into a single account called Conversion costs. *Conversion costs* is a temporary account that works just like the Manufacturing overhead account. Actual conversion costs accumulate as debits in the Conversion costs account and allocated conversion costs are credited to the account as units are completed. Accountants close any under- or overallocated conversion costs to Cost of goods sold at the end of the period, just like they do for under- or overallocated manufacturing overhead.

EXHIBIT 18-14 | **Comparison of Traditional and Just-in-Time Costing**

	Traditional	Just-in-Time
Recording production activity	Build the costs of products as they move from materials into work in process and on to finished goods inventory	Record the costs of products when units are completed
Inventory accounts	Materials inventory Work in process inventory Finished goods inventory	Raw and in-process inventory Finished goods inventory
Manufacturing costs	Direct materials Direct labor Manufacturing overhead	Direct materials Conversion costs

JIT Costing Illustrated: Smart Touch

To illustrate JIT costing, we'll continue with our Smart Touch example. Smart Touch has only one direct material cost: blank DVDs. This cost is recorded in the Raw and in-process inventory account. All other manufacturing costs—including labor, various indirect materials, and overhead—are indirect costs of converting the "raw" DVDs into finished goods (DVD learning systems). All these indirect costs are collected in the Conversion costs account.

As noted previously, JIT does not use a separate Work in process inventory account. Instead, it uses only two inventory accounts:

- Raw and in-process inventory, which combines direct materials with work in process
- Finished goods inventory

Assume that on January 31, Smart Touch had $100,000 of beginning Raw and in-process inventory, and $200,000 of beginning Finished goods inventory. During February, Smart Touch uses JIT costing to record the following transactions:

1. Smart Touch purchased $240,000 of direct materials (blank DVDs) on account.

1.	Raw and in-process inventory (A+)	240,000	
	Accounts payable (L+)		240,000
	Purchased direct materials on account.		

2. Smart Touch spent $590,000 on labor and overhead.

2.	Conversion costs (E+)	590,000	
	Wages payable, Accumulated depreciation, etc.		590,000
	Incurred conversion costs.		

3. Smart Touch completed 115,000 Excel DVDs that it moved to Finished goods. Recall that the standard cost of each Excel DVD in Exhibit 18-9 is $7 ($2.40 direct materials + $4.60 conversion costs). The debit (increase) to Finished goods inventory is at standard cost of $805,000 (115,000 completed Excel DVDs × $7). There is no separate Work in process inventory account in JIT costing, so Smart Touch credits the following:

3.	Finished goods inventory (115,000 × $7) (A+)	805,000	
	Raw and in-process inventory (115,000 × $2.40) (A–)		276,000
	Conversion costs (115,000 × $4.60) (E–)		529,000
	Completed production.		

- Raw and in-process inventory is credited for the blank DVDs, $276,000 (115,000 completed Excel DVDs × $2.40 standard raw material cost per DVD).
- Conversion costs is credited for the labor and other indirect costs allocated to the finished DVDs, $529,000 (115,000 completed Excel DVDs × $4.60 standard conversion cost per DVD).

This is the key to JIT costing. The system does not track costs as the DVDs move through manufacturing. Instead, *completion* of the DVDs triggers the accounting system to go back and move costs from Raw and in-process inventory (credit) and to allocate conversion costs (credit) to attach those costs to the finished products (debit).

4. Smart Touch sold 110,000 Excel DVDs (110,000 DVDs × cost of $7 per DVD = $770,000). The cost of goods sold entry is as follows:

4.	Cost of goods sold (E+)	770,000	
	Finished goods inventory (A–)		770,000
	Cost of sales.		

Exhibit 18-15 shows Smart Touch's relevant accounts. Combining the Materials inventory account with the Work in process inventory account to form the single Raw and in-process inventory account eliminates detail.

EXHIBIT 18-15 | **Smart Touch's JIT Costing Accounts**

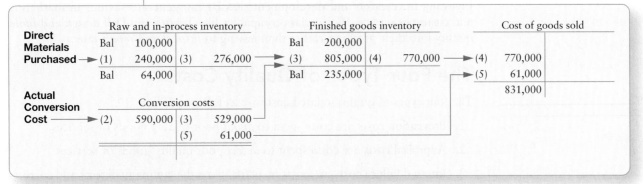

5. You can see from Exhibit 18-15 that conversion costs are underallocated by $61,000 (actual cost of $590,000 – applied cost of $529,000). Under- and overallocated conversion costs are treated just like under- and overallocated manufacturing overhead and closed to Cost of goods sold, as follows:

5.	Cost of goods sold (E+)	61,000	
	Conversion costs (E–)		61,000
	Closed conversion costs.		

In the final analysis, cost of goods sold for February is $831,000, as shown in the T-account in Exhibit 18-15.

Stop Think...

If you were to go to the grocery store today, you could either buy just the ingredients you need to make dinner tonight or you could purchase enough groceries to last you two weeks. If you purchase for two weeks, can you be sure you'll use all the groceries you buy or will some of it "go bad" before you eat it? Choosing to purchase just enough to get you through a short period (today) is like just-in-time costing. Companies purchase just enough raw materials for the production needs of the next day or two, rather than purchasing large amounts of raw materials that have to be stored.

Continuous Improvement and the Management of Quality

Because just-in-time production systems have very little inventory on hand, companies are far more vulnerable to production shutdowns if they receive poor-quality or defective direct materials. For this reason, it is critical that a company's direct materials be nearly defect free.

To meet this challenge, each business function monitors its activities to improve quality and eliminate defects and waste. Continuous improvement is the goal of total quality management (TQM), and it is monitored many ways. For example, companies compare the cost of any changes they want to make against the benefits of the changes as one measure that aids decision making. Say a company is considering reorganizing a work cell to improve efficiency. The reorganization costs $40,000, but the change is expected to result in a $100,000 reduction in costs. Would the company want to implement the change considering its cost and benefits? Absolutely! Why? The change is expected to net the company an additional $60,000 in profit.

4 Use the four types of quality costs to make decisions

Well-designed products reduce inspections, rework, and warranty claims. Investing in research and development (R&D) can generate savings in marketing and customer service. World-class companies like **Toyota** and **Dell** *design* and *build* quality into their products rather than having to *inspect* and *repair* later.

The Four Types of Quality Costs

The four types of quality-related costs are as follows:

1. **Prevention costs** are costs spent to *avoid* poor-quality goods or services.

2. **Appraisal costs** are costs spent to *detect* poor-quality goods or services.

3. **Internal failure costs** are costs incurred when the company detects and corrects poor-quality goods or services before delivery to customers.

4. **External failure costs** are costs spent after the company *delivers poor-quality goods or services* to customers and then has to make things right with the customer.

Exhibit 18-16 gives examples of the four types of quality costs. Most prevention costs occur in the R&D stage of the value chain. In contrast, most appraisal and internal failure costs occur while the product is being made; thus, they ultimately become part of the cost of the finished product. External failure causes an increase in customer service costs, or it could cause lost sales due to an unhappy customer. External failure costs ultimately affect warranty expense claims or worse, potential lawsuit liability exposure. Prevention is much cheaper than external failure.

EXHIBIT 18-16 | **Four Types of Quality Costs**

Prevention Costs	Appraisal Costs
Employee training	Inspection at various stages of production
Improved quality of materials	Inspection of final products or services
Preventive maintenance on equipment	Product testing
Internal Failure Costs	**External Failure Costs**
Any production problem that causes manufacturing to stop	Lost sales due to unhappy customers
Reworking of substandard products	Warranty costs
Rejected product units	Service costs at customer sites
	Sales returns due to product defects

Stop & Think...

Do you go to the dentist every six months to have your teeth cleaned? The cost of the cleaning is a prevention cost. By investing in the care of your teeth, not only do your teeth look nice, but you hope to *prevent* decay in your teeth. Preventing that decay helps you to avoid a bigger dentist bill for repairing your teeth in the future. The same is true for producing products. Monies spent ensuring consistent quality standards and screening for defective products before they ship to customers is cheaper than monies spent on returned products and warranty claims, or revenues lost from losing a customer.

Deciding Whether to Adopt a New Quality Program

Let's revisit Smart Touch. CEO Sheena Bright is considering spending the following on a new quality program:

Inspect raw materials	$100,000
Reengineer to improve product quality	750,000
Inspect finished goods	150,000
Preventive maintenance of equipment	100,000

Smart Touch expects this quality program to reduce costs by the following amounts:

Avoid lost profits due to unhappy customers	$800,000
Fewer sales returns	50,000
Decrease the cost of rework	250,000
Lower warranty costs...	100,000

Bright asks controller Kolen to

1. classify each cost into one of the four categories (prevention, appraisal, internal failure, external failure). Total the estimated cost for each category.

2. recommend whether Smart Touch should undertake the quality program. Kolen uses Exhibit 18-17 to compare the costs to

   - undertake the quality program, or
   - not undertake the quality program.

> **Key Takeaway**
>
> The four types of quality-related costs are prevention, appraisal, internal failure, and external failure costs. Quality improvement programs that reduce internal and external failure costs by more than the increased cost to prevent or appraise the product are smart total quality management decisions.

	Analysis of Smart Touch's
EXHIBIT 18-17	**Proposed Quality Program**

Undertake the Quality Program		Do Not Undertake the Quality Program	
Prevention		**Internal Failure**	
Reengineer to improve product quality	$ 750,000	Cost of rework	$ 250,000
Preventive maintenance of equipment	100,000	Total internal failure costs	$ 250,000
Total prevention costs	$ 850,000		
		External Failure	
		Lost profits due to unhappy customers	$ 800,000
Appraisal		Sales returns	50,000
Inspect raw materials	$ 100,000	Warranty costs	100,000
Inspect finished goods	150,000	Total external failure costs	$ 950,000
Total appraisal costs	$ 250,000	**Total costs of not undertaking the**	
Total costs of the quality program	$1,100,000	**quality program**	$1,200,000

Decision: Undertake the Quality Program and Save $100,000.

These estimates suggest that Smart Touch would save $100,000 ($1,200,000 − $1,100,000) by undertaking the quality program.

Quality costs can be hard to measure. For example, it is very hard to measure external failure costs. Lost profits due to unhappy customers do not appear in the accounting records! Therefore, TQM uses many nonfinancial measures, such as the number of customer complaints and the volume of incoming customer-service phone calls, as a means to measure success or failure.

Next, we'll review the Decision Guidelines for JIT and quality costs.

Decision Guidelines 18-2

JUST-IN-TIME AND QUALITY COSTS

Now, consider you are the production foreman for a soft drink manufacturer. Could implementing JIT and total quality management help you make better decisions?

Decision	Guidelines	
• How do we change from traditional production to JIT?	*Traditional* Similar machines grouped together Larger batches Higher inventories Each worker does a few tasks Many suppliers	*JIT* Work cells Smaller batches Lower inventories Each worker does a wide range of tasks Fewer but well-coordinated suppliers
• How does costing work under JIT?	Under JIT costing, 1. the Materials and Work in process inventory accounts are combined into a single Raw and in-process inventory account. 2. labor and overhead are combined into a Conversion costs account. 3. summary journal entries are recorded *after* units are completed.	
• What are the four types of quality costs?	Prevention Appraisal Internal failure External failure	
• How can we manage the four types of quality costs?	Invest up front in prevention and appraisal to reduce internal and external failure costs.	

Summary Problem 18-2

Flores Company manufactures cell phones and uses JIT costing. The standard unit cost is $30 is comprised of $20 direct materials and $10 conversion costs. Direct materials purchased on account during June totaled $2,500,000. Actual conversion costs totaled $1,100,000. Flores completed 100,000 cell phones in June and sold 98,000.

Requirements

1. Journalize these transactions.
2. Were conversion costs under- or overallocated? *Hint*: You may want to prepare a T-account for the Conversion costs account. Explain your answer and then make the entry to close the Conversion costs account.
3. What is the ending balance of the Raw and in-process inventory account? How much Cost of goods sold did Flores have in June?

Solution

Requirement 1

Raw and in-process inventory (A+)	2,500,000	
Accounts payable (L+)		2,500,000
Conversion costs (E+)	1,100,000	
Wages payable, Accumulated depreciation, etc.		1,100,000
Finished goods inventory (A+)	3,000,000	
Raw and in-process inventory (100,000 × $20) (A−)		2,000,000
Conversion costs (100,000 × $10) (E−)		1,000,000
Cost of goods sold (98,000 × $30) (E+)	2,940,000	
Finished goods inventory (A−)		2,940,000

Requirement 2

Conversion costs

1,100,000	1,000,000
Bal 100,000	

Conversion costs were underallocated. Actual costs ($1,100,000) exceeded the cost allocated to inventory ($1,000,000).

Cost of goods sold (E+)	100,000	
Conversion costs (E−)		100,000

Requirement 3

Raw and in-process inventory

2,500,000	2,000,000
Bal 500,000	

COGS = $3,040,000 ($2,940,000 + $100,000)

Review *Activity-Based Costing and Other Cost Management Tools*

● Accounting Vocabulary

Activity-Based Costing (ABC) (p. 882)
Focuses on activities as the fundamental cost objects. The costs of those activities become the building blocks for allocating the costs of products and services.

Activity-Based Management (ABM) (p. 886)
Using activity-based cost information to make decisions that increase profits while satisfying customers needs.

Appraisal Costs (p. 898)
Costs incurred to detect poor-quality goods or services.

Backflush Costing (p. 895)
A costing system that starts with output completed and then assigns manufacturing costs to units sold and to inventories. Also called **just-in-time costing**.

External Failure Costs (p. 898)
Costs incurred when the company does not detect poor-quality goods or services until after delivery to customers.

Internal Failure Costs (p. 898)
Costs incurred when the company detects and corrects poor-quality goods or services before delivery to customers.

Just-in-Time (JIT) Costing (p. 895)
A costing system that starts with output completed and then assigns manufacturing costs to units sold and to inventories. Also called **backflush costing**.

Prevention Costs (p. 898)
Costs incurred to avoid poor-quality goods or services.

Raw and In-Process Inventory (p. 895)
Combined account for raw materials and work in process inventories under JIT systems.

Target Cost (p. 888)
The maximum cost to develop, produce, and deliver the product or service and earn the desired profit. Equals target price minus desired profit.

Target Price (p. 887)
What customers are willing to pay for the product or service.

Value Engineering (p. 887)
Reevaluating activities to reduce costs while satisfying customer needs.

● Destination: Student Success

Student Success Tips

The following are hints on some common trouble areas for students in this chapter:

● Remember ABC costing measures manufacturing overhead by activities. By allocating costs to products based on how much they USE the activities, more accurate product costing results.

● Keep in mind that an allocation base (such as number of parts) can be used by more than one activity for ABC costing.

● Keep in mind that the goal of ABC is not only accurate costing but providing better information for Total Quality Management decision-making.

● Recall that JIT processing focuses on better vendor relationships so there is no need to maintain large raw materials inventories. Streamlined JIT production allows for streamlined accounting.

● Review the costs of quality. Keep in mind how dollars spent in preventing/appraising the process often reduce dollars spent repairing internal/external failures later.

Getting Help

If there's a learning objective from the chapter you aren't confident about, try using one or more of the following resources:

● Review Exhibit 18-4, the four steps of ABC.

● Review Decision Guidelines 18-1 in the chapter to review ABC systems.

● Review Exhibit 18-16, the four types of quality costs.

● Review Summary Problem 18-2 in the chapter to reinforce your understanding of JIT and quality costs.

● Practice additional exercises or problems at the end of Chapter 18 that cover the specific learning objective that is challenging you.

● Watch the white board videos for Chapter 18 located at myaccountinglab.com under the Chapter Resources button.

● Go to myaccountinglab.com and select the Study Plan button. Choose Chapter 18 and work the questions covering that specific learning objective until you've mastered it.

● Work the Chapter 18 pre/post tests in myaccountinglab.com.

● Consult the Check Figures for End of Chapter starters, exercises, and problems, located at myaccountinglab.com.

● Visit the learning resource center on your campus for tutoring.

● Quick Check

1. Which statement is *false*?

    a. Information technology makes it feasible for most companies to adopt ABC.

    b. An ABC system is more refined than one that uses a company-wide overhead rate.

    c. ABC focuses on indirect costs.

    d. ABC is used ONLY for manufacturing companies.

Use the following information for questions 2–4. Two of Compute It's production activities are *kitting* (assembling the raw materials needed for each computer in one kit) and *boxing* the completed products for shipment to customers. Assume that Compute It spends $12,000,000 a month on kitting and $22,000,000 a month on boxing. Compute It allocates the following:

- Kitting costs based on the number of parts used in the computer
- Boxing costs based on the cubic feet of space the computer requires

Suppose Compute It estimates it will use 400,000,000 parts a month and ship products with a total volume of 20,000,000 cubic feet.

Assume that each desktop computer requires 125 parts and has a volume of 10 cubic feet.

2. What is the activity cost allocation rate?

	Kitting	Boxing
a.	$0.03/part	$0.05/cubic foot
b.	$0.60/part	$0.06/cubic foot
c.	$0.03/part	$1.10/cubic foot
d.	$33.33/part	$0.91/cubic foot

3. What are the kitting and boxing costs assigned to one desktop computer?

	Kitting	Boxing
a.	$ 3.75	$ 11.00
b.	$ 0.30	$137.50
c.	$11.00	$ 3.75
d.	$ 4.05	$148.50

4. Compute It contracts with its suppliers to pre-kit certain component parts before delivering them to Compute It. Assume this saves $2,000,000 of the kitting cost and reduces the total number of parts by 200,000,000 (because Compute It considers each pre-kit as one part). If a desktop now uses 90 parts, what is the new kitting cost assigned to one desktop?

    a. $4.50   c. $2.70

    b. $1.00   d. $3.75

5. Compute It can use ABC information for what decisions?

    a. Cost cutting   c. Product mix

    b. Pricing   d. Items a, b, and c are all correct

6. Which of the following would be true for a computer manufacturing company?

    a. ABC helps the company make more informed decisions about products.

    b. Manufacturing computers use only a few activities, so a companywide overhead allocation rate would work well.

    c. Most of the company's costs are for direct materials and direct labor. Indirect costs are a small proportion of total costs.

    d. All the above are true.

7. Companies enjoy many benefits from using JIT. Which is not a benefit of adopting JIT?

   a. Ability to respond quickly to changes in customer demand

   b. Lower inventory carrying costs

   c. Ability to continue production despite disruptions in deliveries of raw materials

   d. More space available for production

8. Which account is *not* used in JIT costing?

   a. Finished goods inventory   c. Work in process inventory

   b. Raw and in-process inventory   d. Conversion costs

9. The cost of lost future sales after a customer finds a defect in a product is which type of quality cost?

   a. Prevention cost   c. Internal failure cost

   b. Appraisal cost   d. External failure cost

10. Spending on testing a product before shipment to customers is which type of quality cost?

   a. External failure cost   c. Appraisal cost

   b. Prevention cost   d. None of the above

Answers are given after Apply Your Knowledge (p. 923).

Assess Your Progress

● Short Exercises

MyAccountingLab

S18-1   **❶ Activity-based costing [5–10 min]**
Activity-based costing requires four steps.

Requirement

1. Rank the following steps in the order in which they would be completed. Number the first step as "1" until you have ranked all four steps.
   a. Compute the cost allocation rate for each activity.
   b. Identify the cost driver for each activity and estimate the total quantity of each driver's allocation base.
   c. Allocate indirect costs to the cost object.
   d. Identify each activity and estimate its total indirect cost.

S18-2   **❶ Calculating costs using traditional and ABC [10 min]**
Brian and Gary are college friends planning a skiing trip to Killington before the New Year. They estimated the following costs for the trip:

	Estimated		Activity Allocation	
	Costs	Cost Driver	Brian	Gary
Food	$ 550	Pounds of food eaten	24	26
Skiing	240	# of lift tickets	3	0
Lodging	320	# of nights	4	4
	$ 1,110			

Requirements

1. Brian suggests that the costs be shared equally. Calculate the amount each person would pay.

2. Gary does not like the idea because he plans to stay in the room rather than ski. Gary suggests that each type of cost be allocated to each person based on the above listed cost driver. Using the activity allocation for each person, calculate the amount that each person would pay based on his own consumption of the activity.

S18-3 **1** **Computing indirect manufacturing costs per unit [15 min]**

Day, Corp., is considering the use of activity-based costing. The following information is provided for the production of two product lines:

Activity	Cost	Cost Driver
Setup	$ 106,000	Number of setups
Machine maintenance	55,000	Machine hours
Total indirect manufacturing costs	$ 161,000	

	Product A	Product B	Total
Direct labor hours	6,500	5,500	12,000
Number of setups	20	180	200
Number of machine hours	1,600	2,400	4,000

Day plans to produce 400 units of Product A and 375 units of Product B.

Requirement

1. Compute the ABC indirect manufacturing cost per unit for each product.

S18-4 **1** **Computing indirect manufacturing costs per unit [15 min]**

The following information is provided for the Orbit Antenna, Corp., which manufactures two products: Lo-Gain antennas, and Hi-Gain antennas for use in remote areas.

Activity	Cost	Cost Driver
Setup	$ 57,000	Number of setups
Machine maintenance	27,000	Machine hours
Total indirect manufacturing costs	$ 84,000	

	Lo-Gain	Hi-Gain	Total
Direct labor hours	1,400	3,600	5,000
Number of setups	30	30	60
Number of machine hours	1,800	1,200	3,000

Orbit plans to produce 75 Lo-Gain antennas and 150 Hi-Gain antennas.

Requirements

1. Compute the ABC indirect manufacturing cost per unit for each product.
2. Compute the indirect manufacturing cost per unit using direct labor hours from the single-allocation-base system.

S18-5 **1** **Using ABC to compute product costs per unit [15 min]**

Accel, Corp., makes two products: C and D. The following data have been summarized:

	Product C	Product D
Direct materials cost per unit	$ 700	$ 2,000
Direct labor cost per unit	300	100
Indirect manufacturing cost per unit	?	?

Indirect manufacturing cost information includes the following:

Activity	Allocation Rate	Product C	Product D
Setup	$1,500/per setup	38 setups	75 setups
Machine maintenance	$ 12/per hour	1,400 hours	4,000 hours

The company plans to manufacture 150 units of each product.

Requirement

1. Calculate the product cost per unit for Products C and D using activity-based costing.

S18-6   **① Using ABC to compute product costs per unit [15 min]**

Jaunkas, Corp., manufactures mid-fi and hi-fi stereo receivers. The following data have been summarized:

	Mid-Fi	Hi-Fi
Direct materials cost per unit	$ 400	$ 1,300
Direct labor cost per unit	400	300
Indirect manufacturing cost per unit	?	?

Indirect manufacturing cost information includes the following:

Activity	Allocation Rate	Mid–Fi	Hi–Fi
Setup	$1,700/per setup	39 setups	39 setups
Inspections	$ 400/per hour	45 hours	15 hours
Machine maintenance	$ 10/per machine hour	1,900 machine hours	1,200 machine hours

The company plans to manufacture 200 units of the mid-fi receivers and 250 units of the hi-fi receivers.

Requirement

1. Calculate the product cost per unit for both products using activity-based costing.

S18-7   **① Allocating indirect costs and computing income [10 min]**

Pacific, Inc., is a technology consulting firm focused on Web site development and integration of Internet business applications. The president of the company expects to incur $775,000 of indirect costs this year, and she expects her firm to work 5,000 direct labor hours. Pacific's systems consultants provide direct labor at a rate of $310 per hour. Clients are billed at 160% of direct labor cost. Last month Pacific's consultants spent 150 hours on Crockett's engagement.

Requirements

1. Compute Pacific's indirect cost allocation rate per direct labor hour.
2. Compute the total cost assigned to the Crockett engagement.
3. Compute the operating income from the Crockett engagement.

Note: Short Exercise 18-7 must be completed before attempting Short Exercise 18-8.

S18-8   **① Computing ABC allocation rates [5 min]**

Refer to Short Exercise 18-7. The president of Pacific suspects that her allocation of indirect costs could be giving misleading results, so she decides to develop an ABC system. She identifies three activities: documentation preparation, information technology support, and training. She figures that documentation costs are driven by the number of pages, information technology support costs are driven by the number of software applications used, and training costs are driven by the number of direct labor hours worked. Estimates of the costs and quantities of the allocation bases follow:

Activity	Estimated Cost	Allocation Base	Estimated Quantity of Allocation Base
Documentation preparation	$ 102,000	Pages	3,000 pages
Information technology support	156,000	Applications used	780 applications
Training	517,000	Direct labor hours	4,700 hours
Total indirect costs	$ 775,000		

Requirement

1. Compute the cost allocation rate for each activity.

Note: Short Exercises 18-7 and 18-8 must be completed before attempting Short Exercise 18-9.

S18-9   **① Using ABC to allocate costs and compute profit [10–15 min]**
Refer to Short Exercises 18-7 and 18-8. Suppose Pacific's direct labor rate was $310 per hour, the documentation cost was $34 per page, the information technology support cost was $200 per application, and training costs were $110 per direct labor hour. The Crockett engagement used the following resources last month:

Cost Driver	Crockett
Direct labor hours	150
Pages	320
Applications used	75

Requirements

1. Compute the cost assigned to the Crockett engagement, using the ABC system.
2. Compute the operating income from the Crockett engagement, using the ABC system.

Note: Short Exercise 18-9 must be completed before attempting Short Exercise 18-10.

S18-10   **② Using ABC to achieve target profit [10–15 min]**
Refer to Short Exercise 18-9. Pacific desires a 25% target profit after covering all costs.

Requirement

1. Considering the total costs assigned to the Crockett engagement in S18-9, what would Pacific have to charge the customer to achieve that profit?

Note: Short Exercise 18-5 must be completed before attempting Short Exercise 18-11.

S18-11   **② Using ABC to achieve target profit [10–15 min]**
Refer to Short Exercise 18-5. Accel, Corp., desires a 25% target profit after covering all costs.

Requirement

1. Considering the total costs assigned to the Products C and D in S18-5, what would Accel have to charge the customer to achieve that profit?

S18-12   **③ Just-in-time characteristics [5–10 min]**
Consider the following characteristics of either a JIT production system or a traditional production system.

    a. Products are produced in large batches.
    b. Large stocks of finished goods protect against lost sales if customer demand is higher than expected.
    c. Suppliers make frequent deliveries of small quantities of raw materials.
    d. Employees do a variety of jobs, including maintenance and setups as well as operating machines.
    e. Machines are grouped into self-contained production cells or production lines.
    f. Machines are grouped according to function. For example, all cutting machines are located in one area.
    g. The final operation in the production sequence "pulls" parts from the preceding operation.
    h. Each employee is responsible for inspecting his or her own work.
    i. Management works with suppliers to ensure defect-free raw materials.

Requirement

1. Indicate whether each is characteristic of a JIT production system or a traditional production system.

S18-13 ❸ **Recording JIT costing journal entries [10 min]**
Quality Products uses a JIT system to manufacture trading pins for the **Hard Rock Café**. The standard cost per pin is $2 for raw materials and $3 for conversion costs. Last month Quality recorded the following data:

Number of pins completed	4,000 pins	Raw material purchases	$	9,500
Number of pins sold	3,300 pins	Conversion costs	$	14,000

Requirement

1. Use JIT costing to prepare journal entries for the month, including the entry to close the Conversion costs account.

S18-14 ❹ **Matching cost-of-quality examples to categories [5–10 min]**
Sammy, Inc., manufactures motor scooters. Consider each of the following examples of quality costs.

_____ 1. Preventive maintenance on machinery.

_____ 2. Direct materials, direct labor, and manufacturing overhead costs incurred to rework a defective scooter that is detected in-house through inspection.

_____ 3. Lost profits from lost sales if company's reputation was hurt because customers previously purchased a poor-quality scooter.

_____ 4. Costs of inspecting raw materials, such as chassis and wheels.

_____ 5. Working with suppliers to achieve on-time delivery of defect-free raw materials.

_____ 6. Cost of warranty repairs on a scooter that malfunctions at customer's location.

_____ 7. Costs of testing durability of vinyl.

_____ 8. Cost to re-inspect reworked scooters.

Requirement

1. Indicate which of the following quality cost categories each example represents.
   - P   Prevention costs
   - A   Appraisal costs
   - IF   Internal failure costs
   - EF   External failure costs

● Exercises

MyAccountingLab **E18-15** ❶ **Product costing in an activity-based costing system [15–20 min]**
Fortunado, Inc., uses activity-based costing to account for its chrome bumper manufacturing process. Company managers have identified four manufacturing activities: materials handling, machine setup, insertion of parts, and finishing. The budgeted activity costs for 2012 and their allocation bases are as follows:

Activity	Total Budgeted Cost	Allocation Base
Materials handling	$ 9,000	Number of parts
Machine setup	3,900	Number of setups
Insertion of parts	42,000	Number of parts
Finishing	82,000	Finishing direct labor hours
Total	$ 136,900	

Fortunado expects to produce 500 chrome bumpers during the year. The bumpers are expected to use 4,000 parts, require 10 setups, and consume 1,000 hours of finishing time.

Requirements

1. Compute the cost allocation rate for each activity.
2. Compute the indirect manufacturing cost of each bumper.

E18-16 ❶ Product costing in an activity-based costing system [15–20 min]

Turbo Champs, Corp., uses activity-based costing to account for its motorcycle manufacturing process. Company managers have identified three supporting manufacturing activities: inspection, machine setup, and machine maintenance. The budgeted activity costs for 2012 and their allocation bases are as follows:

Activity	Total Budgeted Cost	Allocation Base
Inspection	$ 6,000	Number of inspections
Machine setup	32,000	Number of setups
Machine maintenance	5,000	Maintenance hours
Total	$ 43,000	

Turbo Champs expects to produce 20 custom-built motorcycles for the year. The motorcycles are expected to require 100 inspections, 20 setups, and 100 maintenance hours.

Requirements

1. Compute the cost allocation rate for each activity.
2. Compute the indirect manufacturing cost of each motorcycle.

E18-17 ❶ Product costing in an activity-based costing system [20–30 min]

Elton Company manufactures wheel rims. The controller budgeted the following ABC allocation rates for 2012:

Activity	Allocation Base	Cost Allocation Rate	
Materials handling	Number of parts	$ 4.00	per part
Machine setup	Number of setups	500.00	per setup
Insertion of parts	Number of parts	23.00	per part
Finishing	Finishing hours	50.00	per hour

The number of parts is now a feasible allocation base because Elton recently purchased bar coding technology. Elton produces two wheel rim models: standard and deluxe. Budgeted data for 2012 are as follows:

	Standard	Deluxe
Parts per rim	6.0	9.0
Setups per 500 rims	17.0	17.0
Finishing hours per rim	5.0	6.5
Total direct labor hours per rim	6.0	7.0

The company expects to produce 500 units of each model during the year.

Requirements

1. Compute the total budgeted indirect manufacturing cost for 2012.

2. Compute the ABC indirect manufacturing cost per unit of each model. Carry each cost to the nearest cent.

3. Prior to 2012, Elton used a direct labor hour single-allocation-base system. Compute the (single) allocation rate based on direct labor hours for 2012. Use this rate to determine the indirect manufacturing cost per wheel rim for each model, to the nearest cent.

E18-18 ❶ ❷ **Using activity-based costing to make decisions [10 min]**
Dino Dog Collars uses activity-based costing. Dino's system has the following features:

Activity	Allocation Base	Cost Allocation Rate
Purchasing	Number of purchase orders	$65.00 per purchase order
Assembling	Number of parts	$ 0.36 per part
Packaging	Number of finished collars	$ 0.25 per collar

Each collar has 4 parts; direct materials cost per collar is $9. Direct labor cost is $4 per collar. Suppose Animal Hut has asked for a bid on 25,000 dog collars. Dino will issue a total of 150 purchase orders if Animal Hut accepts Dino's bid.

Requirements

1. Compute the total cost Dino will incur to purchase the needed materials and then assemble and package 25,000 dog collars. Also compute the cost per collar.

2. For bidding, Dino adds a 40% markup to total cost. What total price will the company bid for the entire Animal Hut order?

3. Suppose that instead of an ABC system, Dino has a traditional product costing system that allocates indirect costs other than direct materials and direct labor at the rate of $9.60 per direct labor hour. The dog collar order will require 12,000 direct labor hours. What total price will Dino bid using this system's total cost?

4. Use your answers to Requirements 2 and 3 to explain how ABC can help Dino make a better decision about the bid price it will offer Animal Hut.

Note: Exercise 18-17 must be completed before attempting Exercise 18-19.

E18-19 ❷ **Using activity-based costing to make decisions [15–20 min]**
Refer to Exercise 18-17. For 2013, Elton's managers have decided to use the same indirect manufacturing costs per wheel rim that they computed in 2012. In addition to the unit indirect manufacturing costs, the following data are budgeted for the company's standard and deluxe models for 2013:

	Standard	Deluxe
Sales price	800.00	940.00
Direct materials	31.00	50.00
Direct labor	45.00	56.00

Because of limited machine-hour capacity, Elton can produce *either* 2,000 standard rims *or* 2,000 deluxe rims.

Requirements

1. If Elton's managers rely on the ABC unit cost data computed in E18-17, which model will they produce? Carry each cost to the nearest cent. (Ignore operating expenses for this calculation.)

2. If the managers rely on the single-allocation-base cost data, which model will they produce?

3. Which course of action will yield more income for Elton?

Note: Exercises 18-17 and 18-19 must be completed before attempting Exercise 18-20.

E18-20 ❷ **Activity-based management and target cost [10 min]**

Refer to Exercises 18-17 and 18-19. Controller Michael Bender is surprised by the increase in cost of the deluxe model under ABC. Market research shows that for the deluxe rim to provide a reasonable profit, Elton will have to meet a target manufacturing cost of $656 per rim. A value engineering study by Elton's employees suggests that modifications to the finishing process could cut finishing cost from $50 to $40 per hour and reduce the finishing direct labor hours per deluxe rim from 6.5 hours to 6 hours. Direct materials would remain unchanged at $50 per rim, as would direct labor at $56 per rim. The materials handling, machine setup, and insertion of parts activity costs also would remain the same.

Requirement

1. Would implementing the value engineering recommendation enable Elton to achieve its target cost for the deluxe rim?

E18-21 ❸ **Recording manufacturing costs in a JIT costing system [15–20 min]**

Lancer, Inc., produces universal remote controls. Lancer uses a JIT costing system. One of the company's products has a standard direct materials cost of $9 per unit and a standard conversion cost of $35 per unit. During January 2012, Lancer produced 600 units and sold 595. It purchased $6,300 of direct materials and incurred actual conversion costs totaling $17,500.

Requirements

1. Prepare summary journal entries for January.
2. The January 1, 2012, balance of the Raw and in-process inventory account was $50. Use a T-account to find the January 31 balance.
3. Use a T-account to determine whether conversion costs are over- or underallocated for the month. By how much? Prepare the journal entry to close the Conversion costs account.

E18-22 ❸ **Recording manufacturing costs in a JIT costing system [10–15 min]**

Dubuc produces electronic calculators. Suppose Dubuc's standard cost per calculator is $27 for materials and $63 for conversion costs. The following data apply to August production:

Materials purchased	$ 6,700	
Conversion costs incurred	14,000	
Number of calculators produced		200 calculators
Number of calculators sold		195 calculators

Requirements

1. Prepare summary journal entries for August using JIT costing, including the entry to close the Conversion costs account.
2. The beginning balance of Finished goods inventory was $1,700. Use a T-account to find the ending balance of Finished goods inventory.

E18-23 ❹ **Classifying quality costs [5–10 min]**

Delance & Co. makes electronic components. Chris Delance, the president, recently instructed vice president Jim Bruegger to develop a total quality control program. "If we don't at least match the quality improvements our competitors are making," he told Bruegger, "we'll soon be out of business." Bruegger began by listing various "costs of quality" that Delance incurs. The first six items that came to mind were:

a. Costs incurred by Delance customer representatives traveling to customer sites to repair defective products, $15,000.
b. Lost profits from lost sales due to reputation for less-than-perfect products, $60,000.
c. Costs of inspecting components in one of Delance's production processes, $25,000.
d. Salaries of engineers who are redesigning components to withstand electrical overloads, $80,000.
e. Costs of reworking defective components after discovery by company inspectors, $40,000.
f. Costs of electronic components returned by customers, $55,000.

Requirement

1. Classify each item as a prevention cost, an appraisal cost, an internal failure cost, or an external failure cost. Then, determine the total cost of quality by category.

E18-24 ❹ **Classifying quality costs and using these costs to make decisions [15–20 min]**

Clarke, Inc., manufactures door panels. Suppose Clarke is considering spending the following amounts on a new total quality management (TQM) program:

Strength-testing one item from each batch of panels	$ 62,000
Training employees in TQM	25,000
Training suppliers in TQM	38,000
Identifying suppliers who commit to on-time delivery of	
perfect-quality materials	56,000

Clarke expects the new program would save costs through the following:

Avoid lost profits from lost sales due to disappointed customers	$ 94,000
Avoid rework and spoilage	60,000
Avoid inspection of raw materials	55,000
Avoid warranty costs	20,000

Requirements

1. Classify each cost as a prevention cost, an appraisal cost, an internal failure cost, or an external failure cost.
2. Should Clarke implement the new quality program? Give your reason.

E18-25 ❹ **Classifying quality costs and using these costs to make decisions [10–15 min]**

Kane manufactures high-quality speakers. Suppose Kane is considering spending the following amounts on a new quality program:

Additional 20 minutes of testing for each speaker	$ 620,000
Negotiating with and training suppliers to obtain higher-quality	
materials and on-time delivery	410,000
Redesigning the speakers to make them easier to manufacture	1,350,000

Kane expects this quality program to save costs, as follows:

Reduce warranty repair costs	$ 225,000
Avoid inspection of raw materials	540,000
Avoid rework because of fewer defective units	800,000

It also expects this program to avoid lost profits from the following:

Lost sales due to disappointed customers	$ 940,000
Lost production time due to rework	278,000

Requirements

1. Classify each of these costs into one of the four categories of quality costs (prevention, appraisal, internal failure, external failure).
2. Should Kane implement the quality program? Give your reasons.

● Problems (Group A)

P18-26A ① **Product costing in an ABC system [15–20 min]**

MyAccountingLab ⯈

The August Manufacturing Company in Rochester, Minnesota, assembles and tests electronic components used in handheld video phones. Consider the following data regarding component T24:

Direct materials cost	$ 82.00
Direct labor cost	$ 23.00
Activity costs allocated	?
Manufacturing product cost	$?

The activities required to build the component follow:

Activity	Allocation Base	Cost Allocated to Each Unit					
Start station	Number of raw component chasis	6	× $	1.60	= $	9.60
Dip insertion	Number of dip insertions	?	× $	0.20	=	5.20
Manual insertion	Number of manual insertions	10	× $	0.40	=	?
Wave solder	Number of components soldered	6	× $	1.70	=	10.20
Backload	Number of backload insertions	8	× $	?	=	6.40
Test	Testing hours	0.43	× $	60.00	=	?
Defect analysis	Defect analysis hours	0.13	× $	?	= $	5.20
Total indirect activity costs					$	?

Requirements

1. Complete the missing items for the two tables.
2. Why might managers favor this ABC system instead of August's older system, which allocated all conversion costs on the basis of direct labor?

P18-27A ① ② **Product costing in an ABC system [20–30 min]**

Prescott, Inc., manufactures bookcases and uses an activity-based costing system. Prescott's activity areas and related data follow:

Activity	Budgeted Cost of Activity	Allocation Base	Cost Allocation Rate
Materials handling	$ 230,000	Number of parts	$ 0.50
Assembly	3,200,000	Direct labor hours	16.00
Finishing	180,000	Number of finished units	4.50

Prescott produced two styles of bookcases in October: the standard bookcase and an unfinished bookcase, which has fewer parts and requires no finishing. The totals for quantities, direct materials costs, and other data follow:

Product	Total Units Produced	Total Direct Materials Costs	Total Direct Labor Costs	Total Number of Parts	Total Assembling Direct Labor Hours
Standard bookcase	3,000	$ 36,000	$ 45,000	9,000	4,500
Unfinished bookcase	3,500	35,000	35,000	7,000	3,500

Requirements

1. Compute the manufacturing product cost per unit of each type of bookcase.

2. Suppose that pre-manufacturing activities, such as product design, were assigned to the standard bookcases at $7 each, and to the unfinished bookcases at $2 each. Similar analyses were conducted of post-manufacturing activities such as distribution, marketing, and customer service. The post-manufacturing costs were $22 per standard bookcase and $14 per unfinished bookcase. Compute the full product costs per unit.

3. Which product costs are reported in the external financial statements? Which costs are used for management decision making? Explain the difference.

4. What price should Prescott's managers set for unfinished bookcases to earn $15 per bookcase?

P18-28A ❶ ❷ **Comparing costs from ABC and single-rate systems [30–40 min]**

Corbertt Pharmaceuticals manufactures an over-the-counter allergy medication. The company sells both large commercial containers of 1,000 capsules to health-care facilities and travel packs of 20 capsules to shops in airports, train stations, and hotels. The following information has been developed to determine if an activity-based costing system would be beneficial:

Activity	Estimated Indirect Activity Costs	Allocation Base	Estimated Quantity of Allocation Base
Materials handling	$ 95,000	Kilos	19,000 kilos
Packaging	219,000	Machine hours ..	5,475 hours
Quality assurance	124,500	Samples	2,075 samples
Total indirect costs	$ 438,500		

Other production information includes the following:

	Commerical Containers	Travel Packs
Units produced	3,500 containers	57,000 packs
Weight in kilos	14,000	5,700
Machine hours	2,625	570
Number of samples	700	855

Requirements

1. Compute the cost allocation rate for each activity.

2. Use the activity-based cost allocation rates to compute the activity costs per unit of the commercial containers and the travel packs. (*Hint*: First compute the total activity costs allocated to each product line, and then compute the cost per unit.)

3. Corbertt's original single-allocation-base costing system allocated indirect costs to products at $157 per machine hour. Compute the total indirect costs allocated to the commercial containers and to the travel packs under the original system. Then compute the indirect cost per unit for each product.

4. Compare the indirect activity-based costs per unit to the indirect costs per unit from the single-allocation-base system. How have the unit costs changed? Explain why the costs changed.

P18-29A ❸ **Recording manufacturing costs for a JIT costing system [15–25 min]**

High Point produces fleece jackets. The company uses JIT costing for its JIT production system.

High Point has two inventory accounts: Raw and in-process inventory and Finished goods inventory. On February 1, 2012, the account balances were Raw and in-process inventory, $7,000; Finished goods inventory, $2,200.

The standard cost of a jacket is $37, comprised of $13 direct materials plus $24 conversion costs. Data for February's activities follow:

| Number of jackets completed | 20,000 | Direct materials purchased | $ 257,500 |
| Number of jackets sold | 19,600 | Conversion costs incurred | $ 580,000 |

Requirements

1. What are the major features of a JIT production system such as that of High Point?
2. Prepare summary journal entries for February. Under- or overallocated conversion costs are closed to Cost of goods sold monthly.
3. Use a T-account to determine the February 29, 2012, balance of Raw and in-process inventory.

P18-30A ④ Analyzing costs of quality [20–30 min]

Christi, Inc., is using a costs-of-quality approach to evaluate design engineering efforts for a new skateboard. Christi's senior managers expect the engineering work to reduce appraisal, internal failure, and external failure activities. The predicted reductions in activities over the 2-year life of the skateboards follow. Also shown are the cost allocation rates for each activity.

Activity	Predicted Reduction in Activity Units	Activity Cost Allocation Rate Per Unit
Inspection of incoming materials	420	$ 37
Inspection of finished goods	420	26
Number of defective units discovered in-house	1,400	56
Number of defective units discovered by customers	325	75
Lost sales to dissatisfied customers	150	103

Requirements

1. Calculate the predicted quality cost savings from the design engineering work.
2. Christi spent $103,000 on design engineering for the new skateboard. What is the net benefit of this "preventive" quality activity?
3. What major difficulty would Christi's managers have in implementing this costs-of-quality approach? What alternative approach could they use to measure quality improvement?

● Problems (Group B)

P18-31B ① Product costing in an ABC system [15–20 min]

The Abram Manufacturing Company in Rochester, Minnesota, assembles and tests electronic components used in handheld video phones. Consider the following data regarding component T24:

Direct materials cost	$ 81.00
Direct labor cost	$ 21.00
Activity costs allocated	?
Manufacturing product cost	$?

The activities required to build the component follow:

Activity	Allocation Base	Cost Allocated to Each Unit		
Start station	Number of raw component chasis	1 × $ 1.20 =	$	1.20
Dip insertion	Number of dip insertions	? × $ 0.35 =		11.20
Manual insertion	Number of manual insertions	11 × $ 0.20 =		?
Wave solder	Number of components soldered	1 × $ 1.60 =		1.60
Backload	Number of backload insertions	4 × ? =		2.80
Test	Testing hours	0.38 × $ 50.00 =		?
Defect analysis	Defect analysis hours	0.14 × ? =		5.60
Total indirect activity costs			$	?

Requirements

1. Complete the missing items for the two tables.
2. Why might managers favor this ABC system instead of Abram's older system, which allocated all conversion costs on the basis of direct labor?

P18-32B ❶ ❷ **Product costing in an ABC system [20–30 min]**
McKnight, Inc., manufactures bookcases and uses an activity-based costing system. McKnight's activity areas and related data follow:

Activity	Budgeted Cost of Activity	Allocation Base	Cost Allocation Rate
Materials handling	$ 240,000	Number of parts	$ 1.00
Assembly	3,300,000	Direct labor hours	17.00
Finishing	150,000	Number of finished units	2.50

McKnight produced two styles of bookcases in April: the standard bookcase and an unfinished bookcase, which has fewer parts and requires no finishing. The totals for quantities, direct materials costs, and other data follow:

Product	Total Units Produced	Total Direct Materials Costs	Total Direct Labor Costs	Total Number of Parts	Total Assembling Direct Labor Hours
Standard bookcase	2,000	$ 24,000	$ 30,000	8,000	3,000
Unfinished bookcase	2,600	26,000	26,000	7,800	2,600

Requirements

1. Compute the manufacturing product cost per unit of each type of bookcase.
2. Suppose that pre-manufacturing activities, such as product design, were assigned to the standard bookcases at $4 each, and to the unfinished bookcases at $3 each. Similar analyses were conducted of post-manufacturing activities such as distribution, marketing, and customer service. The post-manufacturing costs were $20 per standard bookcase and $15 per unfinished bookcase. Compute the full product costs per unit.
3. Which product costs are reported in the external financial statements? Which costs are used for management decision making? Explain the difference.
4. What price should McKnight's managers set for unfinished bookcases to earn $16 per bookcase?

P18-33B ❶ ❷ **Comparing costs from ABC and single-rate systems [30–40 min]**
Sawyer Pharmaceuticals manufactures an over-the-counter allergy medication. The company sells both large commercial containers of 1,000 capsules to health-care facilities and travel packs of 20 capsules to shops in airports, train stations, and

hotels. The following information has been developed to determine if an activity-based costing system would be beneficial:

Activity	Estimated Indirect Activity Costs	Allocation Base	Estimated Quantity of Allocation Base
Materials handling ..... $	115,000	Kilos	23,000 kilos
Packaging	204,000	Machine hours ..	4,160 hours
Quality assurance	114,000	Samples	1,900 samples
Total indirect costs ..... $	433,000		

Other production information includes the following:

	Commerical Containers		Travel Packs	
Units produced	3,400	containers	55,000	packs
Weight in kilos	17,000		16,500	
Machine hours	2,720		550	
Number of samples	340		825	

Requirements

1. Compute the cost allocation rate for each activity.

2. Use the activity-based cost allocation rates to compute the activity costs per unit of the commercial containers and the travel packs. (*Hint*: First compute the total activity costs allocated to each product line, and then compute the cost per unit.)

3. Sawyer's original single-allocation-base costing system allocated indirect costs to products at $150 per machine hour. Compute the total indirect costs allocated to the commercial containers and to the travel packs under the original system. Then compute the indirect cost per unit for each product.

4. Compare the indirect activity-based costs per unit to the indirect costs per unit from the single-allocation-base system. How have the unit costs changed? Explain why the costs changed as they did.

P18-34B ❸ **Recording manufacturing costs for a JIT costing system [15–25 min]**
Deep Freeze produces fleece jackets. The company uses JIT costing for its JIT production system.

Deep Freeze has two inventory accounts: Raw and in-process inventory and Finished goods inventory. On February 1, 2012, the account balances were Raw and in-process inventory, $10,000; Finished goods inventory, $1,600.

The standard cost of a jacket is $39, comprised of $16 direct materials plus $23 conversion costs. Data for February's activities follow:

Number of jackets completed	19,000	Direct materials purchased	$ 301,500
Number of jackets sold	18,600	Conversion costs incurred	$ 538,000

Requirements

1. What are the major features of a JIT production system such as that of Deep Freeze?

2. Prepare summary journal entries for February. Under- or overallocated conversion costs are closed to Cost of goods sold monthly.

3. Use a T-account to determine the February 29, 2012, balance of Raw and in-process inventory.

P18-35B ❹ **Analyzing costs of quality [20–30 min]**
Roxi, Inc., is using a costs-of-quality approach to evaluate design engineering efforts for a new skateboard. Roxi's senior managers expect the engineering work to reduce appraisal, internal failure, and external failure activities. The predicted reductions in

activities over the 2-year life of the skateboards follow. Also shown are the cost allocation rates for each activity.

Activity	Predicted Reduction in Activity Units	Activity Cost Allocation Rate Per Unit
Inspection of incoming materials	385	$ 39
Inspection of finished goods	385	22
Number of defective units discovered in-house	1,200	55
Number of defective units discovered by customers	300	73
Lost sales to dissatisfied customers	100	97

Requirements

1. Calculate the predicted quality cost savings from the design engineering work.
2. Roxi spent $109,000 on design engineering for the new skateboard. What is the net benefit of this "preventive" quality activity?
3. What major difficulty would Roxi's managers have in implementing this costs-of-quality approach? What alternative approach could they use to measure quality improvement?

● Continuing Exercise

MyAccountingLab **E18-36** **❶ Product costing in an ABC system [15–20 min]**

This exercise continues the Lawlor Lawn Service, Inc., situation from Exercise 17-34 of Chapter 17. Recall that Lawlor completed a special landscaping job for Sheldon's Ideal Designs. If Lawlor had used activity-based costing, Lawlor's data about the job, including ABC information, would be as follows:

Sheldon Job details:
Direct materials $700
Direct labor $1,200

ABC Costing Rates:
$275 per setup
$15 per plant

Requirements

1. Lawlor uses one setup for the Sheldon job and installs 35 plants. What is the total cost of the Sheldon job?
2. If Sheldon paid $3,900 for the job, what is the profit or loss under ABC?

● Continuing Problem

MyAccountingLab **P18-37** **❶❷ Comparing costs from ABC and single-rate systems [30–40 min]**

This problem continues the Draper Consulting, Inc., situation from Problem 17-35 of Chapter 17. Recall that Draper allocated indirect costs to jobs based on a predetermined indirect cost allocation rate, computed as a percentage of direct labor costs. Because Draper provides a service, there are no direct materials costs. Draper is now considering using an ABC system. Information about ABC costs follows:

Activity	Budgeted Cost of Activity	Allocation Base	Cost Allocation Rate
Design	$ 350,000	Number of designs	$ 7,000
Programming	550,000	Direct labor hours	110
Testing	288,000	Number of tests	3,500

Records for two clients appear here:

Job	Total Direct Labor Costs	Total Number of Designs	Total Programming Direct Labor Hours	Number of Tests
Tommy's Trains	$ 13,600	3	730	6
Marcia's Cookies	600	5	300	8

Requirements

1. Compute the total cost of each job.

2. Is the job cost greater or less than that computed in Problem 17-35 for each job? Why?

3. If Draper wants to earn gross profit equal to 25% of cost, how much (what fee) should it charge each of these two clients?

Apply Your Knowledge

● Decision Cases

Decision Case 18-1 Harris Systems specializes in servers for workgroup, e-commerce, and ERP applications. The company's original job costing system has two direct cost categories: direct materials and direct labor. Overhead is allocated to jobs at the single rate of $22 per direct labor hour.

A task force headed by Harris's CFO recently designed an ABC system with four activities. The ABC system retains the current system's two direct cost categories. Overhead costs are reflected in the four activities. Pertinent data follow:

Activity	Allocation Base	Cost Allocation Rate
Materials handling	Number of parts	$ 0.85
Machine setup	Number of setups	500.00
Assembling	Assembling hours	80.00
Shipping	Number of shipments	1,500.00

Harris Systems has been awarded two new contracts, which will be produced as Job A and Job B. Budget data relating to the contracts follow:

	Job A	Job B
Number of parts...............................	15,000	2,000
Number of setups............................	6	4
Number of assembling hours............	1,500	200
Number of shipments.......................	1	1
Total direct labor hours	8,000	600
Number of units produced	100	10
Direct materials cost.........................	$220,000	$30,000
Direct labor cost...............................	$160,000	$12,000

Requirements

1. Compute the product cost per unit for each job, using the original costing system (with two direct cost categories and a single overhead allocation rate).

2. Suppose Harris Systems adopts the ABC system. Compute the product cost per unit for each job using ABC.

3. Which costing system more accurately assigns to jobs the costs of the resources consumed to produce them? Explain.

Decision Case 18-2 To remain competitive, Harris Systems' management believes the company must produce Job B-type servers (from Decision Case 18-1) at a target cost of $5,400. Harris Systems has just joined a B2B e-market site that management believes will enable the firm to cut direct materials costs by 10%. Harris's management also believes that a value engineering team can reduce assembly time.

Requirement

1. Compute the assembling cost savings per Job B-type server required to meet the $5,400 target cost. (*Hint*: Begin by calculating the direct materials, direct labor, and allocated activity costs per server.)

● Ethical Issue 18-1

Cassidy Manning is assistant controller at LeMar Packaging, Inc., a manufacturer of cardboard boxes and other packaging materials. Manning has just returned from a packaging industry conference on activity-based costing. She realizes that ABC may help LeMar meet its goal of reducing costs by 5% over each of the next three years.

LeMar Packaging's Order Department is a likely candidate for ABC. While orders are entered into a computer that updates the accounting records, clerks manually check customers' credit history and hand-deliver orders to shipping. This process occurs whether the sales order is for a dozen specialty boxes worth $80, or 10,000 basic boxes worth $8,000.

Manning believes that identifying the cost of processing a sales order would justify (1) further computerization of the order process and (2) changing the way the company processes small orders. However, the significant cost savings would arise from elimination of two positions in the Order Department. The company's sales order clerks have been with the company many years. Manning is uncomfortable with the prospect of proposing a change that will likely result in terminating these employees.

Requirement

1. Use the IMA's ethical standards (see Chapter 16) to consider Manning's responsibility when cost savings come at the expense of employees' jobs.

● Fraud Case 18-1

Anu Ghai was a new production analyst at RHI, Inc., a large furniture factory in North Carolina. One of her first jobs was to update the activity rates for factory production costs. This was normally done once a year, by analyzing the previous year's actual data, factoring in projected changes, and calculating a new rate for the coming year. What Anu found was strange. The activity rate for "maintenance" had more than doubled in one year, and she was puzzled how that could have happened. When she spoke with Larry McAfee, the factory manager, she was told to spread the increases out over the other activity costs to "smooth out" the trends. She was a bit intimidated by Larry, an imposing and aggressive man, but she knew something wasn't quite right. Then one night she was at a restaurant and overheard a few employees who worked at RHI talking. They were joking about the work they had done fixing up Larry's home at the lake last year. Suddenly everything made sense. Larry had been using factory labor, tools, and supplies to have his lake house renovated on the weekends. Anu had a distinct feeling that if she went up against Larry on this issue, she would come out the loser. She decided to look for work elsewhere.

Requirements

1. Besides spotting irregularities, like the case above, what are some other ways that ABC cost data are useful for manufacturing companies?
2. What are some of the other options that Anu might have considered?

● Team Project 18-1

Bronson Shrimp Farms, in Brewton, Alabama, has a Processing Department that processes raw shrimp into two products:

* Headless shrimp
* Peeled and deveined shrimp

Bronson recently submitted bids for two orders: (1) headless shrimp for a cruise line and (2) peeled and deveined shrimp for a restaurant chain. Bronson won the first bid but lost the second. The production and sales managers are upset. They believe that Bronson's state-of-the-art equipment should have given the company an edge in the peeled and deveined market. Consequently, production managers are starting to keep their own sets of product cost records.

Bronson is reexamining both its production process and its costing system. The existing costing system has been in place since 1991. It allocates all indirect costs based on direct labor hours. Bronson is considering adopting activity-based costing. Controller Heather Barefield and a team of production managers performed a preliminary study. The team identified six activities, with the following (department-wide) estimated indirect costs and cost drivers for 2014:

Activity	Estimated Total Cost of Activity	Allocation Base
Redesign of production process (costs of changing process and equipment)	$ 5,000	Number of design changes
Production scheduling (production scheduler's salary)	6,000	Number of batches
Chilling (depreciation on refrigerators)	1,500	Weight (in pounds)
Processing (utilities and depreciation on equipment)	19,200	Number of cuts
Packaging (indirect labor and depreciation on equipment)	1,425	Cubic feet of surface exposed
Order filling (order-takers' and shipping clerks' wages)	7,000	Number of orders
Total indirect costs for the entire department	$40,125	

The raw shrimp are chilled and then cut. For headless shrimp, employees remove the heads, then rinse the shrimp. For peeled and deveined shrimp, the headless shrimp are further processed—the shells are removed and the backs are slit for deveining. Both headless shrimp and peeled and deveined shrimp are packaged in foam trays and covered with shrink wrap. Order-filling personnel assemble orders of headless shrimp as well as peeled and deveined shrimp.

Barefield estimates that Bronson will produce 10,000 packages of headless shrimp and 50,000 packages of peeled and deveined shrimp in 2014. The two products incur the following costs and activities per package:

	Costs and Activities per Package	
	Headless Shrimp	Peeled and Deveined Shrimp
Shrimp	$3.50	$4.50
Foam trays	$0.05	$0.05
Shrink wrap	$0.05	$0.02
Number of cuts	1 cut	3 cuts
Cubic feet of exposed surface ...	1 cubic foot	0.75 cubic foot
Weight (in pounds)..................	2.5 pounds	1 pound
Direct labor hours...................	0.01 hour	0.05 hour

Bronson pays direct laborers $20 per hour. Barefield estimates that each product line also will require the following *total* resources:

	Headless Shrimp		Peeled and Deveined Shrimp	
Design changes	1 change	for all	4 changes	for all
Batches	40 batches	10,000	20 batches	50,000
Sales orders	90 orders	packages	110 orders	packages

Requirements

Form groups of four students. All group members should work together to develop the group's answers to the three requirements.

1. Using the original costing system with the single indirect cost allocation base (direct labor hours), compute the total budgeted cost per package for the headless shrimp and then for the peeled and deveined shrimp. (*Hint*: First, compute the indirect cost allocation rate—that is, the predetermined overhead rate. Then, compute the total budgeted cost per package for each product.)

2. Use activity-based costing to recompute the total budgeted cost per package for the headless shrimp and then for the peeled and deveined shrimp. (*Hint*: First, calculate the budgeted cost allocation rate for each activity. Then, calculate the total indirect costs of (a) the entire headless shrimp product line and (b) the entire peeled and deveined shrimp product line. Next, compute the indirect cost per package of each product. Finally, calculate the total cost per package of each product.)

3. Write a memo to Bronson CEO Gary Pololu explaining the results of the ABC study. Compare the costs reported by the ABC system with the costs reported by the original system. Point out whether the ABC system shifted costs toward headless shrimp or toward peeled and deveined shrimp, and explain why. Finally, explain whether Pololu should feel more comfortable making decisions using cost data from the original system or from the new ABC system.

● Communication Activity 18-1

In 75 words or fewer, explain the difference between allocating manufacturing overhead using traditional cost allocation and activity-based costing allocations.

Quick Check Answers

1. *d* 2. *c* 3. *a* 4. *a* 5. *d* 6. *a* 7. *c* 8. *c* 9. *d* 10. *c*

For online homework, exercises, and problems that provide you immediate feedback, please visit myaccountinglab.com.

19

Cost-Volume-Profit Analysis

Learning Objectives

1. Identify how changes in volume affect costs

2. Use CVP analysis to compute breakeven points

3. Use CVP analysis for profit planning, and graph the CVP relations

4. Use CVP methods to perform sensitivity analyses

5. Calculate the breakeven point for multiple products or services

6. Distinguish between variable costing and absorption costing (see Appendix 19A, located at myaccountinglab.com)

You and your friends head out to a favorite restaurant for dinner. The restaurant serves a meat dish with three side dishes for a reasonable price. The combination of good food at a good price has made this "meat and three" restaurant popular. However, when you arrive at the restaurant this time, it is not as crowded as usual. You also notice the restaurant has increased the price for a meal.

After you are seated and order, you and your friends discuss the changes. No one seems surprised by the price increase. You've all noticed that food prices have increased at the grocery store and speculate that the restaurant's supplier has also increased prices. If food costs increase, the business would have to increase the sales price per meal in order for the meals to remain profitable. Is this what is keeping some customers away? What will be the effect on profits if the restaurant charges more per meal but serves fewer meals? At what point will the business begin to operate at a loss rather than a profit? How long will the restaurant remain open if it loses a large number of customers?

These are the type of questions asked by managers in every business—what is the relationship among costs, volume, and profit? In this chapter, you'll learn about **cost-volume-profit (CVP) analysis**, a tool managers use to answer these questions. We continue this analysis using Greg's Tunes in this chapter.

Cost Behavior

Some costs, like COGS, increase as the volume of activity increases. Other costs, like straight-line depreciation expense, are not affected by volume changes. Managers need to know how a business's costs are affected by changes in its volume of activity. Let's look at the three different types of costs:

① Identify how changes in volume affect costs

- Variable costs
- Fixed costs
- Mixed costs

Variable Costs

Variable costs are those costs that increase or decrease in total in direct proportion to increases or decreases in the volume of activity. **Total variable costs** change in direct proportion to changes in the volume of activity. Volume is the measure or degree of an activity of a business action that affects costs—the more volume, the more cost is incurred. Those activities include selling, producing, driving, and calling. The volume of activities can be measured in many different ways, such as number of units sold, number of units produced, number of miles driven by a delivery vehicle, and the number of phone calls placed.

As you may recall, Greg's Tunes offers DJ services for parties, weddings, and other events. For each event, Greg's spends $15 for equipment rental. Greg's can perform at 15 to 30 events per month. To calculate total variable costs, Natalie Blanding, the office manager, would show the following:

Number of Events per Month	Equipment Rental Cost per Event	Total Equipment Rental Cost per Month
15	$15	$225
20	$15	$300
30	$15	$450

As you can see, the total variable cost of equipment rental increases proportionately as the number of events increases. But the equipment rental cost per event does not change. Exhibit 19-1 graphs total variable cost for equipment rental as the number of events increases from 0 to 30, but the cost for each equipment rental stays at $15 per event.

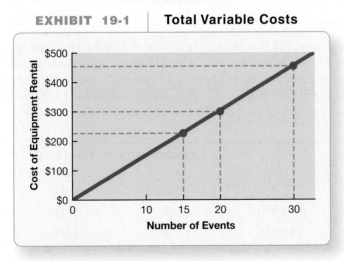

EXHIBIT 19-1 | Total Variable Costs

If there are no events, Greg's incurs no equipment rental cost, so the total variable cost line begins at the bottom left corner. This point is called the *origin*, and it represents zero volume and zero cost. The *slope* of the variable cost line is the change in equipment rental cost (on the vertical axis) divided by the change in the number of events (on the horizontal axis). The slope of the graph equals the variable cost per unit. In Exhibit 19-1, the slope of the variable cost line is 15 because Greg's spends $15 on equipment rental for each event.

If Greg's Tunes performs at 15 events during the month, it will spend a total of $225 (15 events × $15 each) for equipment rental. Follow this total variable cost line to the right to see that doubling the number of events to 30 likewise doubles the total variable cost to $450 (30 × $15 = $450). Exhibit 19-1 shows how the *total variable cost* of equipment rental varies directly with the number of events. But again, note that *the per-event cost remains constant* at $15.

Remember this important fact about *variable costs*:

> **Total variable costs fluctuate with changes in volume, but the variable cost per unit remains constant.**

Fixed Costs

In contrast, **total fixed costs** are costs that do not change over wide ranges of volume. **Fixed costs** tend to remain the same in amount, regardless of variations in level of activity. Greg's fixed costs include depreciation on the cars, as well as the part-time manager's salary. Greg's has these fixed costs regardless of the number of events—15, 20, or 30.

Suppose Greg's incurs $12,000 of fixed costs each month, and the number of monthly events is between 15 and 30. Exhibit 19-2 graphs total fixed costs as a flat line that intersects the cost axis at $12,000, because Greg's will incur the same $12,000 of fixed costs regardless of the number of events.

EXHIBIT 19-2 | **Total Fixed Costs**

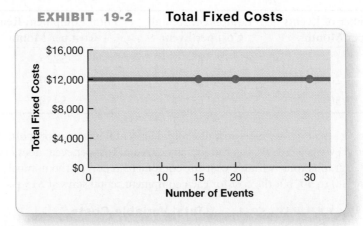

Total fixed cost does not change, as shown in Exhibit 19-2. But the *fixed cost per event* depends on the number of events. If Greg's Tunes performs at 15 events, the fixed cost per event is $800 ($12,000 ÷ 15 events). If the number of events doubles to 30, the fixed cost per event is cut in half to $400 ($12,000 ÷ 30 events). Therefore, the fixed cost per event is *inversely* proportional to the number of events, as follows:

Total Fixed Costs	Number of Events	Fixed Cost per Event
$12,000	15	$800
$12,000	20	$600
$12,000	30	$400

Remember the following important fact about *fixed costs*:

> Total fixed costs remain constant, but the fixed cost per unit is inversely proportional to volume.

Mixed Costs

Costs that have both variable and fixed components are called **mixed costs**. For example, Greg's Tunes' cell phone company charges $10 a month to provide the service and $0.15 for each minute of use. If the cell phone is used for 100 minutes, the company will bill Greg's $25 [$10 + (100 minutes × $0.15)].

Exhibit 19-3 shows how Greg's can separate its cell-phone bill into fixed and variable components. The $10 monthly charge is a fixed cost because it is the same no matter how many minutes the company uses the cell phone. The $0.15-per-minute charge is a variable cost that increases in direct proportion to the number of minutes of use. If Greg's uses the phone for 100 minutes, its total variable cost is $15 (100 minutes × $0.15). If it doubles the use to 200 minutes, total variable cost also doubles to $30 (200 minutes × $0.15), and the total bill rises to $40 ($10 + $30).

EXHIBIT 19-3 | **Mixed Costs**

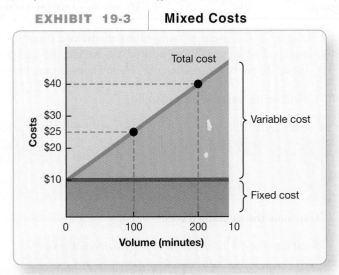

Stop & Think...

Think about your costs related to taking this class. Which ones are fixed? Which ones are variable? The cost of your tuition and books are fixed costs, because you pay one price for the class and your books, no matter how many days you come to class. If you drive to class, the cost of gas put in your car is variable, because you only incur gas costs when you come to class. Are there any mixed costs associated with your class? Maybe your cell phone provider charges you a flat fee each month for a certain amount of minutes. If you go over that limit because you call your classmates a lot, then that would be a mixed cost associated with your class.

High-Low Method to Separate Fixed Costs from Variable Costs

An easy method to separate mixed costs into variable and fixed components is the **high-low method**. This method requires you to identify the highest and lowest levels of activity over a period of time. Using this information, complete the following three steps:

> **STEP 1:** Calculate the variable cost per unit.

Variable cost per unit = Change in total cost ÷ Change in volume of activity

STEP 2: Calculate the total fixed cost.

Total fixed cost = Total mixed cost – Total variable cost

STEP 3: Create and use an equation to show the behavior of a mixed cost.

Total mixed cost = (Variable cost per unit × number of units) + Total fixed costs

Let's revisit the Greg's Tunes illustration. A summary of Greg's Tunes' music equipment maintenance costs for the past year shows the following costs for each quarter:

	Event-Playing Hours	Total Maintenance Cost	
1st Quarter	360	$1,720	
2nd Quarter	415	1,830	
3rd Quarter	480	1,960	←——— Highest Volume
4th Quarter	240	1,480	←——— Lowest Volume

The highest volume is 480 event-playing hours in the 3rd quarter of the year, and the lowest volume is 240 event-playing hours. We can use the high-low method to identify Greg's Tunes' fixed and variable costs of music equipment maintenance.

STEP 1: Calculate the variable cost per unit.

Variable cost per unit = Change in total cost ÷ Change in volume of activity
= ($1,960 – $1,480) ÷ (480 hours – 240 hours)
= $480 ÷ 240 hours
= $2 per event-playing hour

STEP 2: Calculate the total fixed cost.

Total fixed cost = Total mixed cost – Total variable cost
= $1,960 – ($2 × 480)
= $1,960 – $960
= $1,000

This example uses the highest cost and volume to calculate the total fixed cost, but you can use any volume and calculate the same $1,000 total fixed cost.

STEP 3: Create and use an equation to show the behavior of a mixed cost.

Total mixed cost = (Variable cost per unit × number of units) + Total fixed cost
Total equipment maintenance cost = ($2 per event-playing hour × no. of hours) + $1,000

Using this equation, the estimated music equipment maintenance cost for 400 event-playing hours would be as follows:

($2 × 400 event-playing hours) + $1,000 = $1,800

This method provides a rough estimate of fixed and variable costs for cost-volume-profit analysis. The high and low volumes become the relevant range, which we discuss in the next section. Managers find the high-low method to be quick and easy, but regression analysis provides the most accurate estimates and is discussed in cost accounting textbooks.

Relevant Range

The **relevant range** is the range of volume where total fixed costs remain constant and the variable cost *per unit* remains constant. **The relevant range is the range of events (or other activity) where total fixed costs and variable cost per unit stays the same.** To estimate costs, managers need to know the relevant range. Why? Because,

- total "fixed" costs can differ from one relevant range to another.
- the variable cost *per unit* can differ in various relevant ranges.

Exhibit 19-4 shows fixed cost for Greg's Tunes over three different relevant ranges. If the company expects to offer 15,000 event-playing hours next year, the relevant range is between 10,000 and 20,000 event-playing hours, and managers budget fixed cost of $144,000.

EXHIBIT 19-4 | **Relevant Range**

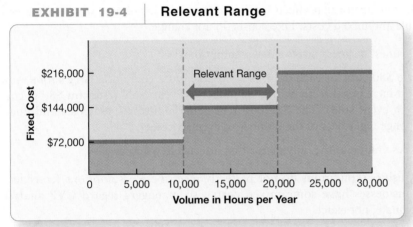

To offer 22,000 event-playing hours, Greg's will have to expand the company. This will increase total fixed costs for added rent and equipment costs. Exhibit 19-4 shows that total fixed cost increases to $216,000 as the relevant range shifts to this higher band of volume. Conversely, if Greg's expects to offer only 8,000 event-playing hours, the company will budget only $72,000 of fixed cost. Managers will have to lay off employees or take other actions to cut fixed costs.

Variable cost per unit can also change outside the relevant range. For example, Greg's Tunes may get a quantity discount for equipment maintenance if it can provide more than 20,000 event-playing hours.

Now, let's apply CVP analysis to answer some interesting management questions.

Key Takeaway

Variable costs are those costs that increase or decrease in total as the volume of activity increases or decreases. Fixed costs are costs that do not change over wide ranges of volume. Costs that have both variable and fixed components are called mixed costs. The high-low method is an easy way to separate mixed costs into variable and fixed components by requiring you to identify the highest and lowest levels of activity over a period of time. The relevant range is the range of activity where total fixed cost stays the same and variable cost per unit stays the same.

Basic CVP Analysis: What Must We Sell to Break Even?

Greg's Tunes is considering expanding its events coverage to include weddings. Greg's first analyzes its existing costs, partially covered in the previous section. (For simplicity, we ignore the mixed costs.) Variable costs are $15 for equipment rental per event plus $65 in contracted labor per event. All the other monthly business expenses are fixed costs, $12,000. Average sales price per event is $200.

 Use CVP analysis to compute breakeven points

Selling price per event.................	$ 200
Variable cost per event..............	$ 80
Fixed costs	$12,000

Greg's Tunes faces several important questions:

- How many DJ services (hereinafter, events) must the company sell to break even?
- What will profits be if sales double?
- How will changes in selling price, variable costs, or fixed costs affect profits?

Before getting started, let's review the assumptions required for CVP analysis to be accurate.

Assumptions

CVP analysis assumes that

1. managers can classify each cost as either variable or fixed.

2. the only factor that affects total costs is change in volume, which increases variable and mixed costs. Fixed costs do not change.

Greg's Tunes' business meets these assumptions:

1. The $80 cost for each event is a variable cost. Therefore, Greg's *total variable cost* increases directly with the number of events sold (an extra $80 in cost for each event sold). The $12,000 represents monthly fixed costs and does not change regardless of the number of events worked.

2. Sales volume is the only factor that affects Greg's costs.

Most business conditions do not perfectly meet these assumptions (consider that most businesses have some mixed costs), so managers regard CVP analysis as approximate, not exact.

How Much Must Greg Sell to Break Even? Three Approaches

Virtually all businesses want to know their breakeven point. The **breakeven point** is the sales level at which operating income is zero: Total revenues equal total costs (expenses). Sales below the breakeven point result in a loss. Sales above break even provide a profit. Greg's Tunes needs to know how many DJ events must be held to break even.

There are several ways to figure the breakeven point, including the

- income statement approach and the
- contribution margin approach.

We start with the income statement approach because it is the easiest method to remember. You are already familiar with the income statement.

The Income Statement Approach

Let's start by expressing income in equation form and then breaking it down into its components:

$$\text{Sales revenue} - \underbrace{\text{Total costs}} = \text{Operating income}$$
$$\text{Sales revenue} - \text{Variable costs} - \text{Fixed costs} = \text{Operating income}$$

Sales revenue equals the unit sale price ($200 per event in this case) multiplied by the number of units (events) sold. Variable costs equal variable cost per unit ($80 in this case) times the number of units (events) sold. Greg's fixed costs total $12,000. At the breakeven point, operating income is zero. We use this information to solve the income statement equation for the number of DJ events Greg's must sell to break even.

Sales revenue	−	Variable costs	− Fixed costs = Operating income
$\left(\begin{array}{c}\text{Sale price} \\ \text{per unit}\end{array} \times \text{Units sold}\right)$	−	$\left(\begin{array}{c}\text{Variable cost} \\ \text{per unit}\end{array} \times \text{Units sold}\right)$	− Fixed costs = Operating income

$$(\$200 \times \text{Units sold}) - (\$80 \times \text{Units sold}) - \$12,000 = \$0$$
$$(\$200 - \$80) \times \text{Units sold} - \$12,000 = \$0$$
$$\$120 \times \text{Units sold} = \$12,000$$
$$\text{Units sold} = \$12,000 \div \$120$$
$$\text{Breakeven sales in units} = 100 \text{ events}$$

Greg's Tunes must sell 100 events to break even. The breakeven sales level in dollars is $20,000 (100 events × $200).

Be sure to check your calculations. "Prove" the breakeven point by substituting the breakeven number of units into the income statement. Then check to ensure that this level of sales results in zero profit.

Proof	Sales revenue − Variable costs − Fixed costs = Operating income
	$(\$200 \times 100) - (\$80 \times 100) - \$12,000 = \$0$
	$\$20,000 - \$8,000 - \$12,000 = \$0$

The Contribution Margin Approach: A Shortcut

This shortcut method of computing the breakeven point uses Greg's contribution margin. The **contribution margin** is sales revenue minus variable costs (expenses). It is called the *contribution margin* because the excess of sales revenue over variable costs contributes to covering fixed costs and then to providing operating income.

The **contribution margin income statement** shows costs by cost behavior—variable costs or fixed costs—and highlights the contribution margin. The format shows the following:

Sales revenue
− Variable costs
= Contribution margin
− Fixed costs
= Operating income

Now let's rearrange the income statement formula and use the contribution margin to develop a shortcut method for finding the number of DJ events Greg's must hold to break even.

Sales revenue	−	Variable costs	− Fixed costs = Operating income
$\left(\begin{array}{c}\text{Sale price} \\ \text{per unit}\end{array} \times \text{Units sold}\right)$	−	$\left(\begin{array}{c}\text{Variable cost} \\ \text{per unit}\end{array} \times \text{Units sold}\right)$	− Fixed costs = Operating income
$\left(\begin{array}{c}\text{Sale price} \\ \text{per unit}\end{array} - \begin{array}{c}\text{Variable cost} \\ \text{per unit}\end{array}\right) \times \text{Units sold}$			= Fixed costs + Operating income
Contribution margin per unit × Units sold			= Fixed costs + Operating income

Dividing both sides of the equation by the contribution margin per unit yields the alternate equation:

$$\text{Units sold} = \frac{\text{Fixed costs} + \text{Operating income}}{\text{Contribution margin per unit}}$$

Greg's Tunes can use this contribution margin approach to find its breakeven point. Fixed costs total $12,000. Operating income is zero at break even. The contribution margin per event is $120 ($200 sale price − $80 variable cost). Greg's breakeven computation is as follows:

$$\text{Breakeven sales in units} = \frac{\$12,000}{\$120}$$
$$= 100 \text{ events}$$

Why does this shortcut method work? Each event Greg's Tunes sells provides $120 of contribution margin. To break even in one month, Greg's must generate enough contribution margin to cover $12,000 of monthly fixed costs. At the rate of $120 per event, Greg's must sell 100 events ($12,000/$120) to cover monthly fixed costs. You can see that the contribution margin approach just rearranges the income statement equation, so the breakeven point is the same under both methods.

To "prove" the breakeven point, you can also use the contribution margin income statement format:

GREG'S TUNES, INC.	
Income Statement	
For one month	
Sales revenue ($200 × 100 events)	$20,000
Variable costs ($80 × 100 events)	8,000
Contribution margin ($120 × 100 events)	$12,000
Fixed costs	12,000
Operating income	$ 0

Using the Contribution Margin Ratio to Compute the Breakeven Point in Sales Dollars

Companies can use the contribution margin ratio to compute their breakeven point in terms of *sales dollars*. The **contribution margin ratio** is the ratio of contribution margin to sales revenue. For Greg's Tunes, we have the following:

$$\text{Contribution margin ratio} = \frac{\text{Contribution margin}}{\text{Sales revenue}} = \frac{\$120}{\$200} = 0.60 \text{ or } 60\%$$

The 60% contribution margin ratio means that each dollar of sales revenue contributes $0.60 toward fixed costs and profit.

The contribution margin *ratio* approach differs from the shortcut contribution margin approach we have just seen in only one way: Here we use the contribution margin *ratio* rather than the dollar amount of the contribution margin.

$$\text{Breakeven sales in dollars} = \frac{\text{Fixed costs}}{\text{Contribution margin ratio}}$$

Using this ratio formula, Greg's breakeven point in sales dollars is as follows:

$$\text{Breakeven sales in dollars} = \frac{\$12,000}{0.60}$$
$$= \$20,000$$

This is the same $20,000 breakeven sales revenue we calculated in the contribution margin approach.

Why does the contribution margin ratio formula work? Each dollar of Greg's sales contributes $0.60 to fixed costs and profit. To break even, Greg's must generate enough contribution margin at the rate of 60% of sales to cover the $12,000 fixed costs ($12,000 ÷ 0.60 = $20,000).

Key Takeaway

The breakeven point is the sales level at which operating income is zero: Total revenues equal total costs. The breakeven point can be found by using the income statement approach, using zero for operating income. The breakeven point can also be found by dividing total fixed cost by the contribution margin per unit (sales price per unit − variable cost per unit).

Now, we have seen how companies use *contribution margin* to estimate breakeven points in CVP analysis. But managers use the contribution margin for other purposes too, such as motivating the sales force. Salespeople who know the contribution margin of each product can generate more profit by emphasizing high-margin products over low-margin products. This is why many companies base sales commissions on the contribution margins produced by sales rather than on sales revenue alone.

Using CVP to Plan Profits

For established products and services, managers are more interested in the sales level needed to earn a target profit than in the breakeven point. **Target profit** is the operating income that results when sales revenue minus variable costs and minus fixed cost equals management's profit goal. Managers of new business ventures are also interested in the profits they can expect to earn. For example, now that Greg's Tunes knows it must sell 100 events to break even, Natalie Blanding, the controller for Greg's, wants to know how many more events must be sold to earn a monthly operating profit of $6,000.

③ Use CVP analysis for profit planning, and graph the CVP relations

How Much Must Greg's Sell to Earn a Profit?

What is the only difference from our prior analysis? Here, Greg's wants to know how many events must be sold to earn a $6,000 profit. We can use the income statement approach or the shortcut contribution margin approach to find the answer. Let's start with the income statement approach.

	Sales revenue	−	Variable costs	− Fixed costs	= Operating income
	($200 × Units sold)	−	($80 × Units sold) −	$12,000	= $ 6,000
	[($200 − 80) × Units sold]			− $12,000	= $ 6,000
	$120 × Units sold				= $18,000
				Units sold	= $18,000 ÷ $120
				Units sold	= 150 events
Proof	($200 × 150)	−	($80 × 150)	− $12,000	= Operating income
	$30,000	−	$12,000	− $12,000	= $6,000

This analysis shows that Greg's must sell 150 events each month to earn an operating profit of $6,000. This is 150 − 100 = 50 more events than the breakeven sales level (100 events).

The proof shows that Greg's needs sales revenues of $30,000 to earn a profit of $6,000. Alternatively, we can compute the dollar sales necessary to earn a $6,000 profit directly, using the contribution margin ratio form of the CVP formula:

$$\text{Target sales in dollars} = \frac{\text{Fixed costs} + \text{Operating income}}{\text{Contribution margin ratio}}$$

$$= \frac{\$12,000 + \$6,000}{0.60}$$

$$= \frac{\$18,000}{0.60}$$

$$= \$30,000$$

This shows that Greg's needs $30,000 in sales revenue to earn a $6,000 profit.

Graphing Cost-Volume-Profit Relations

Controller Natalie Blanding can graph the CVP relations for Greg's Tunes. A graph provides a picture that shows how changes in the levels of sales will affect profits. As in the variable-, fixed-, and mixed-cost graphs of Exhibits 19-1, 19-2, and 19-3, Blanding shows the volume of units (events) on the horizontal axis and dollars on the vertical axis. Then she follows four steps to graph the CVP relations for Greg's Tunes, as illustrated in Exhibit 19-5.

EXHIBIT 19-5 | **Cost-Volume-Profit Graph**

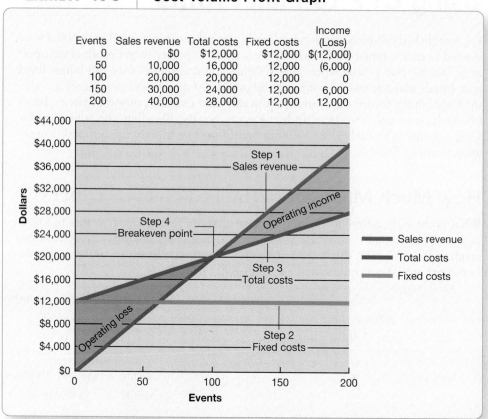

Events	Sales revenue	Total costs	Fixed costs	Income (Loss)
0	$0	$12,000	$12,000	$(12,000)
50	10,000	16,000	12,000	(6,000)
100	20,000	20,000	12,000	0
150	30,000	24,000	12,000	6,000
200	40,000	28,000	12,000	12,000

STEP 1: Choose a sales volume, such as 200 events. Plot the point for total sales revenue at that volume: 200 events × $200 per event = sales of $40,000. Draw the *sales revenue line* from the origin (0) through the $40,000 point. Why start at the origin? If Greg's sells no events, there is no revenue.

STEP 2: Draw the *fixed cost line*, a horizontal line that intersects the dollars axis at $12,000. The fixed cost line is flat because fixed costs are the same, $12,000, no matter how many events are sold.

STEP 3: Draw the *total cost line*. Total costs are the sum of variable costs plus fixed costs. Thus, total costs are *mixed*. So the total cost line follows the form of the mixed cost line in Exhibit 19-3. Begin by computing variable costs at the chosen sales volume: 200 events × $80 per event = variable costs of $16,000. Add variable costs to fixed costs: $16,000 + $12,000 = $28,000. Plot the total cost point of $28,000 for 200 events. Then draw a line through this point from the $12,000 fixed cost intercept on the dollars vertical axis. This is the *total cost line*. The total cost line starts at the fixed cost line because even if Greg's Tunes sells no events, the company still incurs the $12,000 of fixed costs.

STEP 4: Identify the *breakeven point* and the areas of operating income and loss. The breakeven point is where the sales revenue line intersects the total cost line. This is where revenue exactly equals total costs—at 100 events, or $20,000 in sales.

Mark the *operating loss* area on the graph. To the left of the breakeven point, total costs exceed sales revenue—leading to an operating loss, indicated by the orange zone.

Mark the *operating income* area on the graph. To the right of the breakeven point, the business earns a profit because sales revenue exceeds total cost, as shown by the green zone.

Why bother with a graph? Why not just use the income statement approach or the shortcut contribution margin approach? Graphs like Exhibit 19-5 help managers quickly estimate the profit or loss earned at different levels of sales. The income statement and contribution margin approaches indicate income or loss for only a single sales amount.

Summary Problem 19-1

Happy Feet buys hiking socks for $6 a pair and sells them for $10. Management budgets monthly fixed costs of $10,000 for sales volumes between 0 and 12,000 pairs.

Requirements

1. Use both the income statement approach and the shortcut contribution margin approach to compute the company's monthly breakeven sales in units.
2. Use the contribution margin ratio approach to compute the breakeven point in sales dollars.
3. Compute the monthly sales level (in units) required to earn a target operating income of $6,000. Use either the income statement approach or the shortcut contribution margin approach.
4. Prepare a graph of Happy Feet's CVP relationships, similar to Exhibit 19-5. Draw the sales revenue line, the fixed cost line, and the total cost line. Label the axes, the breakeven point, the operating income area, and the operating loss area.

Solution

Requirement 1
Income statement approach:

Sales revenue	−	Variable costs		− Fixed costs = Operating income
$\left(\dfrac{\text{Sale price}}{\text{per unit}} \times \text{Units sold}\right)$	−	$\left(\dfrac{\text{Variable cost}}{\text{per unit}} \times \text{Units sold}\right)$		− Fixed costs = Operating income
($10 × Units sold) −		($6 × Units sold)	− $10,000	= $0
($10 −		$6) × Units sold		= $10,000
		$4 × Units sold		= $10,000
		Units sold		= $10,000 ÷ $4
	Breakeven sales in units			= 2,500 units

Shortcut contribution margin approach:

$$\text{Units sold} = \frac{\text{Fixed costs} + \text{Operating income}}{\text{Contribution margin per unit}}$$

$$\text{Breakeven sales in units} = \frac{\$10,000 + \$0}{\$10 - \$6}$$

$$= \frac{\$10,000}{\$4}$$

$$= 2,500 \text{ units}$$

Requirement 2

$$\text{Breakeven sales in dollars} = \frac{\text{Fixed costs} + \text{Operating income}}{\text{Contribution margin ratio}}$$

$$= \frac{\$10,000 + \$0}{0.40^*}$$

$$= \$25,000$$

$$^*\text{Contribution margin ratio} = \frac{\text{Contribution margin per unit}}{\text{Sale price per unit}} = \frac{\$4}{\$10} = 0.40$$

Requirement 3

Income statement equation approach:

Sales revenue	–	Variable costs	– Fixed costs = Operating income
$\left(\begin{array}{c}\text{Sale price}\\\text{per unit}\end{array} \times \text{Units sold}\right)$ –		$\left(\begin{array}{c}\text{Variable cost}\\\text{per unit}\end{array} \times \text{Units sold}\right)$	– Fixed costs = Operating income
($10 × Units sold) –		($6 × Units sold)	– $10,000 = $6,000
($10 –		$6) × Units sold	= $10,000 + $6,000
		$4 × Units sold	= $16,000
		Units sold	= $16,000 ÷ $4
		Units sold	= 4,000 units

Shortcut contribution margin approach:

$$\text{Units sold} = \frac{\text{Fixed costs} + \text{Operating income}}{\text{Contribution margin per unit}}$$

$$= \frac{\$10,000 + \$6,000}{\$10 - \$6}$$

$$= \frac{\$16,000}{\$4}$$

$$= 4,000 \text{ units}$$

Requirement 4

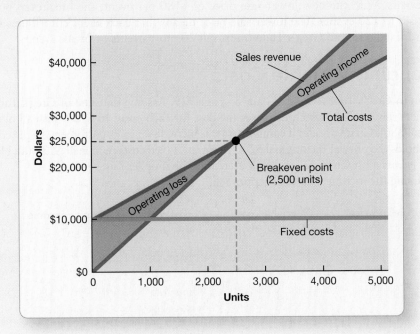

Using CVP for Sensitivity Analysis

Managers often want to predict how changes in sale price, costs, or volume affect their profits. Managers can use CVP relationships to conduct sensitivity analysis. **Sensitivity analysis** is a "what if" technique that asks what results are likely if selling price or costs change, or if an underlying assumption changes. So sensitivity analysis allows managers to see how various business strategies will affect how much profit the company will make and thus empowers managers with better information for decision making. Let's see how Greg's Tunes can use CVP analysis to estimate the effects of some changes in its business environment.

4 Use CVP methods to perform sensitivity analyses

Changing the Selling Price

Competition in the DJ event services business is so fierce that Greg's Tunes believes it must cut the selling price to $180 per event to maintain market share. Suppose Greg's Tunes' variable costs remain $80 per event and fixed costs stay at $12,000. How will the lower sale price affect the breakeven point?

Using the income statement approach, the results are as follows:

Sales revenue	–	Variable costs	–	Fixed costs	= Operating income
($180 × Units sold)	–	($80 × Units sold) –		$12,000	= $0
[($180 – $80) × Units sold]			–	$12,000	= $0
$100 × Units sold					= $12,000
				Units sold	= $12,000 ÷ $100
				Units sold	= 120 events

Proof	($180 × 120)	–	($80 × 120)	–	$12,000	= Operating income
	$21,600	–	$9,600	–	$12,000	= $0

With the original $200 sale price, Greg's Tunes' breakeven point was 100 events. With the new lower sale price of $180 per event, the breakeven point increases to 120 events. The lower sale price means that each event contributes less toward fixed costs, so Greg's Tunes must sell 20 more events to break even.

Changing Variable Costs

Return to Greg's Tunes' original data on page 929. Assume that one of Greg's Tunes' suppliers raises prices, which increases the cost for each event to $120 (instead of the original $80). Greg's decides it cannot pass this increase on to its customers, so the company holds the price at the original $200 per event. Fixed costs remain at $12,000. How many events must Greg's sell to break even after the supplier raises prices?

Using the income statement approach,

Sales revenue	−	Variable costs	−	Fixed costs	= Operating income
($200 × Units sold)	−	($120 × Units sold)	−	$12,000	= $0
[($200 − 120) × Units sold]			−	$12,000	= $0
$80 × Units sold					= $12,000
				Units sold	= $12,000 ÷ $80
				Units sold	= 150 events

Proof	($200 × 150)	−	($120 × 150)	−	$12,000	= Operating income
	$30,000	−	$18,000	−	$12,000	= $0

Higher variable costs per event reduce Greg's Tunes' per-unit contribution margin from $120 per event to $80 per event. As a result, Greg's must sell more events to break even—150 rather than the original 100. This analysis shows why managers are particularly concerned with controlling costs during an economic downturn. Increases in cost raise the breakeven point, and a higher breakeven point can lead to problems if demand falls due to a recession.

Of course, a decrease in variable costs would have the opposite effect. Lower variable costs increase the contribution margin on each event and, therefore, lower the breakeven point.

Changing Fixed Costs

Return to Greg's original data on page 929. Controller Natalie Blanding is considering spending an additional $3,000 on Web site banner ads. This would increase fixed costs from $12,000 to $15,000. If the events are sold at the original price of $200 each and variable costs remain at $80 per event, what is the new breakeven point?

Using the income statement approach,

Sales revenue	−	Variable costs	−	Fixed costs	= Operating income
($200 × Units sold)	−	($80 × Units sold)	−	$15,000	= $0
[($200 − $80) × Units sold]			−	$15,000	= $0
$120 × Units sold					= $15,000
				Units sold	= $15,000 ÷ $120
				Units sold	= 125 events

Proof	($200 × 125)	−	($80 × 125)	−	$15,000	= Operating income
	$25,000	−	$10,000	−	$15,000	= $0

Higher fixed costs increase the total contribution margin required to break even. In this case, increasing the fixed costs from $12,000 to $15,000 increases the breakeven point to 125 events (from the original 100 events).

Managers usually prefer a lower breakeven point to a higher one. But do not overemphasize this one aspect of CVP analysis. Even though investing in the Web banner ads increases Greg's Tunes' breakeven point, the company should pay the extra $3,000 if that would increase both sales and profits.

Exhibit 19-6 shows how all of these changes affect the contribution margin per unit and the breakeven point.

EXHIBIT 19-6 | **How Changes in Selling Price, Variable Costs, and Fixed Costs Affect the Contribution Margin per Unit and the Breakeven Point**

Cause	Effect	Result
Change	Contribution Margin per Unit	Breakeven Point
Selling Price per Unit Increases	Increases	Decreases
Selling Price per Unit Decreases	Decreases	Increases
Variable Cost per Unit Increases	Decreases	Increases
Variable Cost per Unit Decreases	Increases	Decreases
Total Fixed Cost Increases	Is not affected	Increases
Total Fixed Cost Decreases	Is not affected	Decreases

Margin of Safety

The **margin of safety** is the excess of expected sales over breakeven sales. **The margin of safety is therefore the "cushion" or drop in sales that the company can absorb without incuring an operating loss.**

Managers use the margin of safety to evaluate the risk of both their current operations and their plans for the future. Let's apply the margin of safety to Greg's Tunes.

Greg's Tunes' original breakeven point was 100 events. Suppose the company expects to sell 170 events. The margin of safety is as follows:

Expected sales – Breakeven sales = Margin of safety in units
170 events   –   100 events   =   70 events

Margin of safety in units × Sales price = Margin of safety in dollars
70 events   × $200   = $14,000

Sales can drop by 70 events, or $14,000, before Greg's incurs a loss. This margin of safety (70 events) is 41.2% of total expected sales (170 events). That is a comfortable margin of safety.

Margin of safety focuses on the sales part of the equation—that is, how many sales dollars the company is generating above breakeven sales dollars. Conversely, target profit focuses on how much operating income is left over from sales revenue after covering all variable and fixed costs.

Stop & Think...

If you have done really well on all your assignments in a particular course for the semester and currently have an A, you have created a sort of "margin of safety" for your grade. That is, by performing above the minimum (C, or break even), you have a cushion to help you maintain a good grade even if you happen to perform poorly on a future assignment.

Key Takeaway

Sensitivity analysis is a "what if" technique that asks what results are likely if selling price or costs change or if an underlying assumption changes. The income statement approach to break even is just adjusted for the new proposed values. The margin of safety is the "cushion" or drop in sales that the company can absorb before incurring a loss.

Effect of Sales Mix on CVP Analysis

5 Calculate the breakeven point for multiple products or services

Most companies sell more than one product. Selling price and variable costs differ for each product, so each product makes a different contribution to profits. The same CVP formulas we used earlier apply to a company with multiple products.

To calculate break even for each product, we must compute the *weighted-average contribution margin* of all the company's products. The sales mix provides the weights that make up total product sales. The weights equal 100% of total product sales. **Sales mix** (or *product mix*) is the combination of products that make up total sales. For example, Cool Cat Furniture sold 6,000 cat beds and 4,000 scratching posts during the past year. The sales mix of 6,000 beds and 4,000 posts creates a ratio of 6,000/10,000 or 60% cat beds and 4,000/10,000 or 40% scratching posts. You could also convert this to the least common ratio, as 6/10 is the same as 3/5 cat beds and 4/10 is the same as 2/5 scratching posts. So, we say the sales mix or product mix is 3:2, or for every three cat beds, Cool Cat expects to sell two scratching posts.

Cool Cat's total fixed costs are $40,000. The cat bed's unit selling price is $44 and variable cost per bed are $24. The scratching post's unit selling price is $100 and variable cost per post is $30. To compute breakeven sales in units for both products Cool Cat completes the following three steps.

STEP 1: Calculate the weighted-average contribution margin per unit, as follows:

	Cat Beds	Scratching Posts	Total
Sale price per unit	$ 44	$100	
Variable cost per unit	24	30	
Contribution margin per unit	$ 20	$ 70	
Sales mix in units	× 3	× 2	5
Contribution margin	$ 60	$140	$200
Weighted-average contribution margin per unit ($200/5)			$ 40

STEP 2: Calculate the breakeven point in units for the "package" of products:

$$\text{Breakeven sales in total units} = \frac{\text{Fixed costs} + \text{Operating income}}{\text{Weighted-average contribution margin per unit}}$$

$$= \frac{\$40,000 + \$0}{\$40}$$

$$= 1,000 \text{ items}$$

STEP 3: Calculate the breakeven point in units for each product. Multiply the "package" breakeven point in units by each product's proportion of the sales mix.

Breakeven sales of cat beds (1,000 × 3/5) .... 600 cat beds
Breakeven sales of scratching posts (1,000 × 2/5) .... 400 scratching posts

In this example, the calculations yield round numbers. When the calculations do not yield round numbers, round your answer up to the next whole number.

The overall breakeven point in sales dollars is $66,400:

600 cat beds at $44 selling price each............................	$26,400
400 scratching posts at $100 selling price each	40,000
Total sales revenue	$66,400

We can prove this breakeven point by preparing a contribution margin income statement:

		Cat Beds	Scratching Posts	Total
Sales revenue:				
	Cat beds (600 × $44)	$26,400		
	Scratching posts (400 × $100)		$40,000	$ 66,400
Variable costs:				
	Cat beds (600 × $24)	14,400		
	Scratching posts (400 × $30)		12,000	26,400
Contribution margin		$12,000	$28,000	$ 40,000
Fixed costs				(40,000)
Operating income				$ 0

If the sales mix changes, then Cool Cat can repeat this analysis using new sales mix information to find the breakeven points for each product.

In addition to finding the breakeven point, Cool Cat can also estimate the sales needed to generate a certain level of operating profit. Suppose Cool Cat would like to earn operating income of $20,000. How many units of each product must Cool Cat now sell?

$$\text{Breakeven sales in total units} = \frac{\text{Fixed costs} + \text{Operating income}}{\text{Weighted-average contribution margin per unit}}$$

$$= \frac{\$40,000 + \$20,000}{\$40}$$

$$= 1,500 \text{ items}$$

Breakeven sales of cat beds (1,500 × 3/5) .... 900 cat beds
Breakeven sales of scratching posts (1,500 × 2/5) .... 600 scratching posts

We can prove this planned profit level by preparing a contribution margin income statement:

		Cat Beds	Scratching Posts	Total
Sales revenue:				
	Cat beds (900 × $44)	$39,600		
	Scratching posts (600 × $100)		$60,000	$99,600
Variable costs:				
	Cat beds (900 × $24)	21,600		
	Scratching posts (600 × $30)		18,000	39,600
Contribution margin		$18,000	$42,000	$60,000
Fixed costs				40,000
Operating income				$20,000

You have learned how to use CVP analysis as a managerial tool. Now you can review the CVP Analysis Decision Guidelines on the next page to make sure you understand these basic concepts.

Key Takeaway

Most companies sell more than one product. Selling price and variable costs differ for each product, so each product makes a different contribution to profits. To calculate break even for each product, we compute the weighted-average contribution margin of all the company's products. The combination of products that make up total sales, called the sales mix (or product mix), provides the weights that make up total product sales.

Decision Guidelines 19-1

COST-VOLUME-PROFIT ANALYSIS

As a manager, you will find CVP very useful. Here are some questions you will ask, and guidelines for answering them.

Decision	Guidelines

- How do changes in volume of activity affect

• total costs?
Total *variable* costs → Change in proportion to changes in volume (number of products or services sold)

Total *fixed* costs → No change

• cost per unit?
Variable cost per unit → No change

• fixed cost per unit?
Decreases when volume rises (fixed costs are spread over *more* units)

Increases when volume drops (fixed costs are spread over *fewer* units)

- How do I calculate the sales needed to break even or earn a target operating income

• in units?

Income Statement Approach:

$$\text{Sales revenue} - \text{Variable costs} - \text{Fixed costs} = \text{Operating income}$$

$$\left(\begin{array}{c}\text{Sale price}\\\text{per unit}\end{array} \times \text{Units sold}\right) - \left(\begin{array}{c}\text{Variable cost}\\\text{per unit}\end{array} \times \text{Units sold}\right) - \text{Fixed costs} = \text{Operating income}$$

Shortcut Contribution Margin Approach:

$$\left(\begin{array}{c}\text{Sale price}\\\text{per unit}\end{array} - \begin{array}{c}\text{Variable cost}\\\text{per unit}\end{array}\right) \times \text{Units sold} = \text{Fixed costs} + \text{Operating income}$$

$$\text{Contribution margin per unit} \times \text{Units sold} = \text{Fixed costs} + \text{Operating income}$$

$$\text{Units sold} = \frac{\text{Fixed Costs} + \text{Operating income}}{\text{Contribution margin per unit}}$$

• in dollars?

Shortcut Contribution Margin Ratio Approach:

$$\frac{\text{Fixed costs} + \text{Operating income}}{\text{Contribution margin ratio}}$$

Decision	Guidelines		
• How will changes in sale price, variable costs, or fixed costs affect the breakeven point?	**Cause**	**Effect**	**Result**
	Change	**Contribution Margin per Unit**	**Breakeven Point**
	Selling price per unit increases	Increases	Decreases
	Selling price per unit decreases	Decreases	Increases
	Variable cost per unit increases	Decreases	Increases
	Variable cost per unit decreases	Increases	Decreases
	Total fixed cost increases	Is not affected	Increases
	Total fixed cost decreases	Is not affected	Decreases

• How do I use CVP analysis to measure risk?

Margin of safety in units = Expected sales – Breakeven sales

• How do I calculate my breakeven point when I sell more than one product or service?

Step 1: Compute the weighted-average contribution margin per unit.
Step 2: Calculate the breakeven point in units for the "package" of products.
Step 3: Calculate the breakeven point in units for each product. Multiply the "package" breakeven point in units by each product's proportion of the sales mix.

Summary Problem 19-2

Happy Feet buys hiking socks for $6 a pair and sells them for $10. Management budgets monthly fixed costs of $12,000 for sales volumes between 0 and 12,000 pairs.

Requirements

Consider each of the following questions separately by using the foregoing information each time.

1. Calculate the breakeven point in units.
2. Happy Feet reduces its selling price from $10 a pair to $8 a pair. Calculate the new breakeven point in units.
3. Happy Feet finds a new supplier for the socks. Variable costs will decrease by $1 a pair. Calculate the new breakeven point in units.
4. Happy Feet plans to advertise in hiking magazines. The advertising campaign will increase total fixed costs by $2,000 per month. Calculate the new breakeven point in units.
5. In addition to selling hiking socks, Happy Feet would like to start selling sports socks. Happy Feet expects to sell one pair of hiking socks for every three pairs of sports socks. Happy Feet will buy the sports socks for $4 a pair and sell them for $8 a pair. Total fixed costs will stay at $12,000 per month. Calculate the breakeven point in units for both hiking socks and sports socks.

Solution

Requirement 1

$$\text{Units sold} = \frac{\text{Fixed costs}}{\text{Contribution margin per unit}}$$

$$\text{Breakeven sales in units} = \frac{\$12,000}{\$10 - \$6}$$

$$= \frac{\$12,000}{\$4}$$

$$= 3,000 \text{ units}$$

Requirement 2

$$\text{Units sold} = \frac{\text{Fixed costs}}{\text{Contribution margin per unit}}$$

$$\text{Breakeven sales in units} = \frac{\$12,000}{\$8 - \$6}$$

$$= \frac{\$12,000}{\$2}$$

$$= 6,000 \text{ units}$$

Requirement 3

$$\text{Units sold} = \frac{\text{Fixed costs}}{\text{Contribution margin per unit}}$$

$$\text{Breakeven sales in units} = \frac{\$12,000}{\$10 - \$5}$$

$$= \frac{\$12,000}{\$5}$$

$$= 2,400 \text{ units}$$

Requirement 4

$$\text{Units sold} = \frac{\text{Fixed costs}}{\text{Contribution margin per unit}}$$

$$\text{Breakeven sales in units} = \frac{\$14,000}{\$10 - \$6}$$

$$= \frac{\$14,000}{\$4}$$

$$= 3,500 \text{ units}$$

Requirement 5

STEP 1: Calculate the weighted-average contribution margin:

		Hiking	Sports	
Sale price per unit		$10.00	$ 8.00	
Variable cost per unit		6.00	4.00	
Contribution margin per unit		$ 4.00	$ 4.00	
Sales mix in units		× 1	× 3	4
Contribution margin		$ 4.00	$12.00	$16.00
Weighted-average CM ($16/4)				$ 4.00

STEP 2: Calculate breakeven point for "package" of products:

$$\text{Breakeven sales in units} = \frac{\text{Fixed costs}}{\text{Contribution margin per unit}}$$

$$= \frac{\$12,000}{\$4}$$

$$= 3,000 \text{ units}$$

STEP 3: Calculate breakeven point for each product:

Number of hiking socks (3,000 × (1/4))	750
Number of sport socks (3,000 × (3/4))	2,250

Review *Cost-Volume-Profit Analysis*

● Accounting Vocabulary

Breakeven Point (p. 930)
The sales level at which operating income is zero: Total revenues equal total expenses (costs).

Contribution Margin (p. 931)
Sales revenue minus variable expenses (costs).

Contribution Margin Income Statement (p. 931)
Income statement that groups costs by cost behavior—variable costs or fixed costs—and highlights the contribution margin.

Contribution Margin Ratio (p. 932)
Ratio of contribution margin to sales revenue.

Cost-Volume-Profit (CVP) Analysis (p. 924)
Expresses the relationships among costs, volume, and profit or loss.

Fixed Costs (p. 926)
Costs that tend to remain the same in amount, regardless of variations in level of activity.

High-Low Method (p. 927)
A method used to separate mixed costs into variable and fixed components, using the highest and lowest activity levels.

Margin of Safety (p. 939)
Excess of expected sales over breakeven sales. A drop in sales that a company can absorb without incurring an operating loss.

Mixed Costs (p. 927)
Costs that have both variable and fixed components.

Relevant Range (p. 929)
The range of volume where total fixed costs remain constant and the variable cost per unit remains constant.

Sales Mix (p. 940)
Combination of products that make up total sales.

Sensitivity Analysis (p. 937)
A "what if" technique that asks what results are likely if selling price or costs change, or if an underlying assumption changes.

Target Profit (p. 933)
The operating income that results when sales revenue minus variable and minus fixed costs equals management's profit goal.

Total Fixed Costs (p. 926)
Costs that do not change over wide ranges in volume.

Total Variable Costs (p. 925)
Costs that change in total in direct proportion to changes in volume.

Variable Costs (p. 925)
Costs that increase or decrease in total in direct proportion to increases or decreases in the volume of activity.

● Destination: Student Success

Student Success Tips

The following are hints on some common trouble areas for students in this chapter:

● Remember the difference between variable, fixed, and mixed costs.

● Keep in mind that breakeven means the company has neither net income NOR net loss.

● Recall that the income statement approach to breakeven is really just the income statement you learned in Chapter 1.

● Consider that the breakeven formula can be used to make different assumptions about sales price, variable costs, fixed costs, and target profits.

● Keep in mind when calculating breakeven values whether the calculation is asking for number of units or for a dollar amount.

● Recall that the high-low method is a way to separate mixed costs into fixed and variable portions.

● Remember the margin of safety is the amount of sales dollars above breakeven, so it's the safety net of extra profit the company has before profits go to zero or worse, a net loss.

● Remember that most companies make more than one product, so sales mix must be considered in finding a weighted-average contribution margin to determine breakeven for multiple products.

Getting Help

If there's a learning objective from the chapter you aren't confident about, try using one or more of the following resources:

● Review the Decision Guidelines 19-1 in the chapter.

● Review Summary Problem 19-1 in the chapter to reinforce your understanding of breakeven and sensitivity analysis.

● Review Exhibit 19-6 for information about how CVP changes affect contribution margin per unit and breakeven point.

● Review Summary Problem 19-2 in the chapter to reinforce your understanding of breakeven point for multiple products.

● Practice additional exercises or problems at the end of Chapter 19 that cover the specific learning objective that is challenging you.

● Watch the white board videos for Chapter 19, located at myaccountinglab.com under the Chapter Resources button.

● Go to myaccountinglab.com and select the Study Plan button. Choose Chapter 19 and work the questions covering that specific learning objective until you've mastered it.

● Work the Chapter 19 pre/post tests in myaccountinglab.com.

● Consult the Check Figures for End of Chapter short exercises, exercises, and problems, located at myaccountinglab.com.

● Visit the learning resource center on your campus for tutoring.

● Quick Check

1. For Frank's Funky Sounds, units of production depreciation on the trucks is a

   a. variable cost.

   b. fixed cost.

   c. mixed cost.

   d. high-low cost.

2. Assume Intervale Railway is considering hiring a reservations agency to handle passenger reservations. The agency would charge a flat fee of $13,000 per month, plus $3 per passenger reservation. What is the total reservation cost if 200,000 passengers take the trip next month?

   a. $613,000

   b. $3.07

   c. $600,000

   d. $13,000

3. If Intervale Railway's fixed costs total $90,000 per month, the variable cost per passenger is $45, and tickets sell for $75, what is the breakeven point in units?

   a. 1,200 passengers

   b. 2,000 passengers

   c. 225,000 passengers

   d. 3,000 passengers

4. Suppose Intervale Railway's total revenues are $4,000,000, its variable costs are $2,000,000, and its fixed costs are $800,000. Compute the breakeven point in dollars.

   a. $4,000,000

   b. $800,000

   c. $1,600,000

   d. $2,000,000

5. If Intervale Railway's fixed costs total $90,000 per month, the variable cost per passenger is $45, and tickets sell for $75, how much revenue must the Railway generate to earn $120,000 in operating income per month?

   a. $350,000

   b. $210,000

   c. $7,000

   d. $525,000

6. On a CVP graph, the total cost line intersects the vertical (dollars) axis at

   a. the origin.

   b. the level of the fixed costs.

   c. the breakeven point.

   d. the level of the variable costs.

7. If a company increases its selling price per unit for Product A, then the new breakeven point will

   a. increase.

   b. decrease.

   c. remain the same.

8. If a company increases its fixed costs for Product B, then the contribution margin per unit will

   a. increase.

   b. decrease.

   c. remain the same.

9. The Best Appliances had the following revenue over the past five years:

2007	$ 600,000
2008	700,000
2009	900,000
2010	800,000
2011	1,000,000

   To predict revenues for 2012, The Best uses the average for the past five years. The company's breakeven revenue is $800,000 per year. What is The Best's predicted margin of safety for 2012?

   a. $800,000

   b. $0

   c. $200,000

   d. $100,000

10. Rocky Mountain Waterpark sells half of its tickets for the regular price of $75. The other half go to senior citizens and children for the discounted price of $35. Variable cost per passenger is $15 for both groups, and fixed costs total $60,000 per month. What is Rocky Mountain's breakeven point in total guests? Regular guests? Discount guests?

a. 2,000/1,000/1,000
c. 750/375/375
b. 800/400/400
d. 1,500/750/750

Answers are given after Apply Your Knowledge (p. 961).

Assess Your Progress

● Short Exercises

MyAccountingLab

S19-1 ❶ Variable, fixed, and mixed costs [5–10 min]
Philadelphia Acoustics builds innovative speakers for music and home theater systems. Consider the following costs:

1. Units of production depreciation on routers used to cut wood enclosures.
2. Wood for speaker enclosures.
3. Patents on crossover relays.
4. Total compensation to salesperson, who receives a salary plus a commission based on meeting sales goals.
5. Crossover relays.

6. Straight-line depreciation on manufacturing plant.
7. Grill cloth.
8. Cell phone costs of salesperson (plan includes 1,200 minutes; overseas calls are charged at an average of $0.15 per minute).
9. Glue.
10. Quality inspector's salary.

Requirement
1. Identify the costs as variable (V), fixed (F), or mixed (M).

S19-2 ❶ Variable, fixed, and mixed costs [5–10 min]
Holly's DayCare has been in operation for several years. Consider the following costs:

1. Building rent.
2. Toys.
3. Salary of office manager, who also receives a bonus based on number of students enrolled.
4. Afternoon snacks.
5. Lawn service contract at $200 a month; any extra work needed is billed at an hourly rate based on the time needed to complete the job.

6. Holly's salary.
7. Wages of afterschool employees.
8. Drawing paper for student art work.
9. Straight-line depreciation of tables, chairs, and playground equipment.
10. Fee paid to security company for monthly service (contract includes up to four responses in a month; responses over four in a month incur an additional fee per response).

Requirement
1. Identify the costs as variable (V), fixed (F), or mixed (M).

S19-3 ❶ Mixed costs—high-low method [5–10 min]
Martin owns a machine shop. In reviewing his utility bill for the last 12 months, he found that his highest bill of $2,800 occurred in August when his machines worked 1,400 machine hours. His lowest utility bill of $2,600 occurred in December when his machines worked 900 machine hours.

Requirements

1. Calculate (a) the variable rate per machine hour and (b) Martin's total fixed utility cost.
2. Show the equation for determining the total utility cost for Martin's.
3. If Martin's anticipates using 1,200 machine hours in January, predict his total utility bill using the equation from Requirement 2.
4. Draw a graph illustrating your total cost under this plan. Label the axes, and show your costs at 900, 1,200, and 1,400 machine hours.

S19-4   ❷ **Computing breakeven point in sales units [5–10 min]**
Story Park competes with Splash World by providing a variety of rides. Story sells tickets at $50 per person as a one-day entrance fee. Variable costs are $10 per person, and fixed costs are $240,000 per month.

Requirement

1. Compute the number of tickets Story must sell to break even. Perform a numerical proof to show that your answer is correct.

Note: Short Exercise 19-4 must be completed before attempting Short Exercise 19-5.

S19-5   ❷ **Computing breakeven point in sales dollars [5 min]**
Refer to Short Exercise 19-4.

Requirements

1. Compute Story Park's contribution margin ratio. Carry your computation to two decimal places.
2. Use the contribution margin ratio CVP formula to determine the sales revenue Story Park needs to break even.

S19-6   ❷ ❸ **Computing contribution margin, breakeven point, and units to achieve operating income [10–15 min]**
Consider the following facts:

	A	B	C
Number of units	1,300	3,600	7,500
Sale price per unit	$ 100	$ 40	$ 125
Variable costs per unit	40	10	100
Total fixed costs	72,000	60,000	40,000
Target operating income	180,000	75,000	100,000
Calculate:			
Contribution margin per unit	_____	_____	_____
Contribution margin ratio	_____	_____	_____
Breakeven points in units	_____	_____	_____
Breakeven point in sales dollars	_____	_____	_____
Units to achieve target operating income	_____	_____	_____

Requirement

1. Compute the missing information.

Note: Short Exercise 19-4 must be completed before attempting Short Exercise 19-7.

S19-7 ④ **Sensitivity analysis of changing sale price and variable costs on breakeven point [10 min]**
Refer to Short Exercise 19-4.

Requirements

1. Suppose Story Park cuts its ticket price from $50 to $40 to increase the number of tickets sold. Compute the new breakeven point in tickets and in sales dollars.
2. Ignore the information in Requirement 1. Instead, assume that Story Park increases the variable cost from $10 to $20 per ticket. Compute the new breakeven point in tickets and in sales dollars.

Note: Short Exercise 19-4 must be completed before attempting Short Exercise 19-8.

S19-8 ④ **Sensitivity analysis of changing fixed cost on breakeven point [5–10 min]**
Refer to Short Exercise 19-4. Suppose Story Park reduces fixed costs from $240,000 per month to $170,000 per month.

Requirement

1. Compute the new breakeven point in tickets and in sales dollars.

Note: Short Exercise 19-4 must be completed before attempting Short Exercise 19-9.

S19-9 ④ **Computing margin of safety [5–10 min]**
Refer to Short Exercise 19-4.

Requirement

1. If Story Park expects to sell 6,200 tickets, compute the margin of safety in tickets and in sales dollars.

S19-10 ⑤ **Calculating weighted-average contribution margin [5–10 min]**
Wet Weekend Swim Park sells individual and family tickets, which include a meal, three beverages, and unlimited use of the swimming pools. Wet Weekend has the following ticket prices and variable costs for 2012:

	Individual	Family
Sale price per ticket	$ 30	$ 90
Variable cost per ticket . . .	15	60

Wet Weekend expects to sell two individual tickets for every four family tickets. Wet Weekend's total fixed costs are $75,000.

Requirements

1. Compute the weighted-average contribution margin per ticket.
2. Calculate the total number of tickets Wet Weekend must sell to break even.
3. Calculate the number of individual tickets and the number of family tickets the company must sell to break even.

Note: Short Exercise 19-10 must be completed before attempting Short Exercise 19-11.

S19-11 ⑤ **Calculating breakeven point for two products [5–10 min]**
Refer to Short Exercise 19-10. For 2013, Wet Weekend expects a sales mix of two individual tickets for every three family tickets.

Requirements

1. Compute the new weighted-average contribution margin per ticket.
2. Calculate the total number of tickets Wet Weekend must sell to break even.
3. Calculate the number of individual tickets and the number of family tickets the company must sell to break even.

● Exercises

E19-12 ❶ CVP definitions [15 min]

Consider the following terms and definitions.

_____ 1. Costs that do not change in total despite wide changes in volume.

_____ 2. The sales level at which operating income is zero: Total revenues equal total costs.

_____ 3. Drop in sales a company can absorb without incurring an operating loss.

_____ 4. Combination of products that make up total sales.

_____ 5. Sales revenue minus variable costs.

_____ 6. Describes how costs change as volume changes.

_____ 7. Costs that change in total in direct proportion to changes in volume.

_____ 8. The band of volume where total fixed costs remain constant and the variable cost *per unit* remains constant.

a. Breakeven
b. Contribution margin
c. Cost behavior
d. Margin of safety
e. Relevant range
f. Sales mix
g. Fixed costs
h. Variable costs

Requirement

1. Match the terms with the correct definitions.

E19-13 ❶ Mixed costs—the high-low method [10–15 min]

The manager of Able Car Inspection reviewed his monthly operating costs for the past year. His costs ranged from $4,000 for 1,000 inspections to $3,600 for 600 inspections.

Requirements

1. Calculate the variable cost per inspection.
2. Calculate the total fixed costs.
3. Write the equation and calculate the operating costs for 800 inspections.
4. Draw a graph illustrating your total cost under this plan. Label the axes, and show your costs at 600, 800, and 1,000 inspections.

E19-14 ❷ Preparing contribution margin income statements and calculating breakeven sales [15 min]

For its top managers, Worldwide Travel formats its income statement as follows:

WORLDWIDE TRAVEL		
Contribution Margin Income Statement		
Three Months Ended March 31, 2012		
Sales revenue	$	317,500
Variable costs		95,250
Contribution margin	$	222,250
Fixed costs		175,000
Operating income	$	47,250

Worldwide's relevant range is between sales of $245,000 and $364,000.

Requirements

1. Calculate the contribution margin ratio.
2. Prepare two contribution margin income statements: one at the $245,000 level and one at the $364,000 level. (*Hint*: The proportion of each sales dollar that goes toward variable costs is constant within the relevant range.)
3. Compute breakeven sales in dollars.

E19-15 ❷ **Computing breakeven sales by the contribution margin approach [15 min]**

Trendy Toes, Co., produces sports socks. The company has fixed costs of $95,000 and variable costs of $0.95 per package. Each package sells for $1.90.

Requirements

1. Compute the contribution margin per package and the contribution margin ratio. (Round your answers to two decimal places.)

2. Find the breakeven point in units and in dollars, using the contribution margin approach.

E19-16 ❸ **Computing a change in breakeven sales [10–15 min]**

Owner Yinan Song is considering franchising her Noodles restaurant concept. She believes people will pay $7.50 for a large bowl of noodles. Variable costs are $3.00 per bowl. Song estimates monthly fixed costs for a franchise at $9,000.

Requirements

1. Use the contribution margin ratio approach to find a franchise's breakeven sales in dollars.

2. Song believes most locations could generate $40,000 in monthly sales. Is franchising a good idea for Song if franchisees want a minimum monthly operating income of $13,500?

E19-17 ❸ **Computing breakeven sales and operating income or loss under different conditions [10–15 min]**

Gary's Steel Parts produces parts for the automobile industry. The company has monthly fixed costs of $660,000 and a contribution margin of 75% of revenues.

Requirements

1. Compute Gary's monthly breakeven sales in dollars. Use the contribution margin ratio approach.

2. Use contribution margin income statements to compute Gary's monthly operating income or operating loss if revenues are $530,000 and if they are $1,040,000.

3. Do the results in Requirement 2 make sense given the breakeven sales you computed in Requirement 1? Explain.

E19-18 ❸ **Analyzing a cost-volume profit graph [15–20 min]**

John Kyler is considering starting a Web-based educational business, e-Prep MBA. He plans to offer a short-course review of accounting for students entering MBA programs. The materials would be available on a password-protected Web site; students would complete the course through self-study. Kyler would have to grade the course assignments, but most of the work is in developing the course materials, setting up the site, and marketing. Unfortunately, Kyler's hard drive crashed before he finished his financial analysis. However, he did recover the following partial CVP chart:

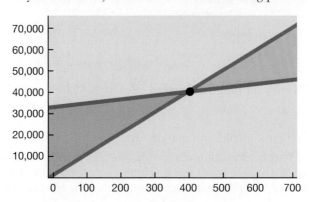

Requirements

1. Label each axis, the sales revenue line, the total costs line, the fixed costs, the operating income area, and the breakeven point.
2. If Kyler attracts 300 students to take the course, will the venture be profitable?
3. What are the breakeven sales in students and dollars?

E19-19 ④ **Impact on breakeven point if sale price, variable costs, and fixed costs change [15 min]**
Dependable Drivers Driving School charges $250 per student to prepare and administer written and driving tests. Variable costs of $100 per student include trainers' wages, study materials, and gasoline. Annual fixed costs of $75,000 include the training facility and fleet of cars.

Requirements

1. For each of the following independent situations, calculate the contribution margin per unit and the breakeven point in units by first referring to the original data provided:
   a. Breakeven point with no change in information.
   b. Decrease sales price to $220 per student.
   c. Decrease variable costs to $50 per student.
   d. Decrease fixed costs to $60,000.
2. Compare the impact of changes in the sales price, variable costs, and fixed costs on the contribution margin per unit and the breakeven point in units.

E19-20 ④ **Computing margin of safety [15 min]**
Rodney's Repair Shop has a monthly target operating income of $15,000. Variable costs are 75% of sales, and monthly fixed costs are $10,000.

Requirements

1. Compute the monthly margin of safety in dollars if the shop achieves its income goal.
2. Express Rodney's margin of safety as a percentage of target sales.

E19-21 ⑤ **Calculating breakeven point for two products [15–20 min]**
Speedy's Scooters plans to sell a standard scooter for $55 and a chrome scooter for $70. Speedy's purchases the standard scooter for $30 and the chrome scooter for $40. Speedy expects to sell one standard scooter for every three chrome scooters. His monthly fixed costs are $23,000.

Requirements

1. How many of each type of scooter must Speedy's Scooters sell each month to break even?
2. To earn $25,300?

• Problem (Group A)

P19-22A ❶ ❷ ❸ **Calculating cost-volume profit elements [45–60 min]**

The budgets of four companies yield the following information:

	Company			
	Blue	Red	Green	Yellow
Sales revenue	$ 960,000	$ (4)	$ 770,000	$ (10)
Variable costs	(1)	132,000	462,000	162,000
Fixed costs	(2)	145,000	220,000	(11)
Operating income (loss)	$ 32,000	$ (5)	$ (7)	$ 93,000
Units sold	160,000	11,000	(8)	(12)
Contribution margin per unit	$ 2.70	$ (6)	$ 77.00	$ 16.00
Contribution margin ratio	(3)	0.70	(9)	0.40

Requirements

1. Fill in the blanks for each missing value. (Round the contribution margin per unit to the nearest cent.)
2. Which company has the lowest breakeven point in sales dollars?
3. What causes the low breakeven point?

P19-23A ❷ ❸ **Break even sales; sales to earn a target operating income; contribution margin income statement [30–45 min]**

England Productions performs London shows. The average show sells 1,300 tickets at $60 per ticket. There are 150 shows a year. No additional shows can be held as the theater is also used by other production companies. The average show has a cast of 65, each earning a net average of $340 per show. The cast is paid after each show. The other variable cost is a program-printing cost of $8 per guest. Annual fixed costs total $728,000.

Requirements

1. Compute revenue and variable costs for each show.
2. Use the income statement equation approach to compute the number of shows England Productions must perform each year to break even.
3. Use the contribution margin approach to compute the number of shows needed each year to earn a profit of $5,687,500. Is this profit goal realistic? Give your reasoning.
4. Prepare England Productions' contribution margin income statement for 150 shows performed in 2012. Report only two categories of costs: variable and fixed.

P19-24A ❷ ❸ ❹ **Analyzing CVP relationships [30–45 min]**

Kincaid Company sells flags with team logos. Kincaid has fixed costs of $583,200 per year plus variable costs of $4.80 per flag. Each flag sells for $12.00.

Requirements

1. Use the income statement equation approach to compute the number of flags Kincaid must sell each year to break even.
2. Use the contribution margin ratio CVP formula to compute the dollar sales Kincaid needs to earn $33,000 in operating income for 2012. (Round the contribution margin to two decimal places.)
3. Prepare Kincaid's contribution margin income statement for the year ended December 31, 2012, for sales of 72,000 flags. Cost of goods sold is 70% of variable costs. Operating costs make up the rest of variable costs and all of fixed costs. (Round your final answers to the nearest whole number.)

4. The company is considering an expansion that will increase fixed costs by 21% and variable costs by $0.60 per flag. Compute the new breakeven point in units and in dollars. Should Kincaid undertake the expansion? Give your reasoning. Round your final answers to the nearest whole number.

P19-25A ② ③ ④ **Computing breakeven sales and sales needed to earn a target operating income; graphing CVP relationships; sensitivity analysis [30–45 min]**
National Investor Group is opening an office in Portland. Fixed monthly costs are office rent ($8,500), depreciation on office furniture ($2,000), utilities ($2,100), special telephone lines ($1,100), a connection with an online brokerage service ($2,800), and the salary of a financial planner ($4,500). Variable costs include payments to the financial planner (8% of revenue), advertising (13% of revenue), supplies and postage (3% of revenue), and usage fees for the telephone lines and computerized brokerage service (6% of revenue).

Requirements
1. Use the contribution margin ratio CVP formula to compute National's breakeven revenue in dollars. If the average trade leads to $1,000 in revenue for National, how many trades must be made to break even?
2. Use the income statement equation approach to compute the dollar revenues needed to earn a target monthly operating income of $12,600.
3. Graph National's CVP relationships. Assume that an average trade leads to $1,000 in revenue for National. Show the breakeven point, the sales revenue line, the fixed cost line, the total cost line, the operating loss area, the operating income area, and the sales in units (trades) and dollars when monthly operating income of $12,600 is earned.
4. Suppose that the average revenue National earns increases to $1,200 per trade. Compute the new breakeven point in trades. How does this affect the breakeven point?

P19-26A ④ ⑤ **Calculating breakeven point for two products; margin of safety [20 min]**
The contribution margin income statement of Delectable Donuts for August 2012 follows:

DELECTABLE DONUTS		
Contribution Margin Income Statement		
For the Month of August 2012		
Sales revenue		$ 150,000
Variable costs:		
Cost of goods sold	$ 41,000	
Marketing costs	15,000	
General and administrative costs	4,000	60,000
Contribution margin		$ 90,000
Fixed costs:		
Marketing costs	37,800	
General and administrative costs	12,600	50,400
Operating income		$ 39,600

Delectable sells four dozen plain donuts for every dozen custard-filled donuts. A dozen plain donuts sells for $4, with total variable cost of $1.60 per dozen. A dozen custard-filled donuts sells for $5, with total variable cost of $2 per dozen.

Requirements
1. Calculate the weighted-average contribution margin.
2. Determine Delectable's monthly breakeven point in dozens of plain donuts and custard-filled donuts. Prove your answer by preparing a summary contribution

margin income statement at the breakeven level of sales. Show only two categories of costs: variable and fixed.

3. Compute Delectable's margin of safety in dollars for August 2012.

4. If Delectable can increase monthly sales revenue from August's level by 20%, what will operating income be? (The sales mix remains unchanged.)

● Problem (Group B)

MyAccountingLab

P19-27B ① ② ③ Calculating cost-volume profit elements [45–60 min]

The budgets of four companies yield the following information:

	Company			
	Up	Down	Left	Right
Sales revenue	$ 900,000	$ (4)	$ 710,000	$ (10)
Variable costs	(1)	208,000	319,500	240,000
Fixed costs	(2)	135,000	235,000	(11)
Operating income (loss)	$ 10,000	$ (5)	$ (7)	$ 49,000
Units sold	100,000	16,000	(8)	(12)
Contribution margin per unit	$ 3.60	$ (6)	$ 78.10	$ 10.00
Contribution margin ratio	(3)	0.60	(9)	0.20

Requirements

1. Fill in the blanks for each missing value. (Round the contribution margin to the nearest cent.)

2. Which company has the lowest breakeven point in sales dollars?

3. What causes the low breakeven point?

P19-28B ② ③ Breakeven sales; sales to earn a target operating income; contribution margin income statement [30–45 min]

British Productions performs London shows. The average show sells 900 tickets at $65 per ticket. There are 155 shows a year. No additional shows can be held as the theater is also used by other production companies. The average show has a cast of 55, each earning a net average of $330 per show. The cast is paid after each show. The other variable cost is program-printing cost of $9 per guest. Annual fixed costs total $580,500.

Requirements

1. Compute revenue and variable costs for each show.

2. Use the income statement equation approach to compute the number of shows British Productions must perform each year to break even.

3. Use the contribution margin approach to compute the number of shows needed each year to earn a profit of $4,128,000. Is this profit goal realistic? Give your reasoning.

4. Prepare British Productions' contribution margin income statement for 155 shows performed in 2012. Report only two categories of costs: variable and fixed.

P19-29B ② ③ ④ Analyzing CVP relationships [30–45 min]

Kincaid Company sells flags with team logos. Kincaid has fixed costs of $664,000 per year plus variable costs of $4.50 per flag. Each flag sells for $12.50.

Requirements

1. Use the income statement equation approach to compute the number of flags Kincaid must sell each year to break even.

2. Use the contribution margin ratio CVP formula to compute the dollar sales. Kincaid needs to earn $33,600 in operating income for 2012. (Round the contribution margin to two decimal places.)

3. Prepare Kincaid's contribution margin income statement for the year ended December 31, 2012, for sales of 75,000 flags. Cost of goods sold is 60% of variable costs. Operating costs make up the rest of variable costs and all of fixed costs. (Round your final answers to the nearest whole number.)

4. The company is considering an expansion that will increase fixed costs by 24% and variable costs by $0.25 per flag. Compute the new breakeven point in units and in dollars. Should Kincaid undertake the expansion? Give your reasoning. (Round your final answers to the nearest whole number.)

P19-30B ❷ ❸ ❹ **Computing breakeven sales and sales needed to earn a target operating income; graphing CVP relationships; sensitivity analysis [30–45 min]**

Diversified Investor Group is opening an office in Boise. Fixed monthly costs are office rent ($8,100), depreciation on office furniture ($1,600), utilities ($2,500), special telephone lines ($1,200), a connection with an online brokerage service ($2,700), and the salary of a financial planner ($4,900). Variable costs include payments to the financial planner (8% of revenue), advertising (14% of revenue), supplies and postage (1% of revenue), and usage fees for the telephone lines and computerized brokerage service (7% of revenue).

Requirements

1. Use the contribution margin ratio CVP formula to compute Diversified's breakeven revenue in dollars. If the average trade leads to $750 in revenue for Diversified, how many trades must be made to break even?

2. Use the income statement equation approach to compute the dollar revenues needed to earn a target monthly operating income of $10,500.

3. Graph Diversified's CVP relationships. Assume that an average trade leads to $750 in revenue for Diversified. Show the breakeven point, the sales revenue line, the fixed cost line, the total cost line, the operating loss area, the operating income area, and the sales in units (trades) and dollars when monthly operating income of $10,500 is earned.

4. Suppose that the average revenue Diversified earns increases to $1,000 per trade. Compute the new breakeven point in trades. How does this affect the breakeven point?

P19-31B ❹ ❺ **Calculating breakeven point for two products; margin of safety [20 min]**

The contribution margin income statement of Dandy Donuts for May 2012 follows:

DANDY DONUTS		
Contribution Margin Income Statement		
For the Month of May 2012		
Sales revenue		$ 190,000
Variable costs:		
Cost of goods sold	$ 56,000	
Marketing costs	20,000	
General and administrative costs	19,000	95,000
Contribution margin		$ 95,000
Fixed costs:		
Marketing costs	50,700	
General and administrative costs	27,300	78,000
Operating income		$ 17,000

Dandy sells three dozen plain donuts for every dozen custard-filled donuts. A dozen plain donuts sells for $6, with a variable cost of $3 per dozen. A dozen custard-filled donuts sells for $8, with a variable cost of $4 per dozen.

Requirements

1. Calculate the weighted-average contribution margin.
2. Determine Dandy's monthly breakeven point in dozens of plain donuts and custard-filled donuts. Prove your answer by preparing a summary contribution margin income statement at the breakeven level of sales. Show only two categories of costs: variable and fixed.
3. Compute Dandy's margin of safety in dollars for May 2012.
4. If Dandy can increase the monthly sales revenue from May's level by 25%, what will operating income be? (The sales mix remains unchanged.)

• Continuing Exercise

MyAccountingLab **E19-32** ❸ **Computing contribution margin, breakeven point, and units to achieve operating income [10–15 min]**

This exercise continues the Lawlor Lawn Service, Inc., situation from Exercise 18-36 of Chapter 18. Lawlor Lawn Service currently charges $100 for a standard lawn service and incurs $60 in variable cost. Assume fixed costs are $1,400 per month.

Requirements

1. What is the number of lawns that must be serviced to reach break even?
2. If Lawlor desires to make a profit of $1,800, how many lawns must be serviced?

• Continuing Problem

MyAccountingLab **P19-33** ❷❸❹ **Computing breakeven sales and sales needed to earn a target operating income; sensitivity analysis [30–45 min]**

This problem continues the Draper Consulting, Inc., situation from Problem 18-37 of Chapter 18. Draper Consulting provides consulting service at an average price of $175 per hour and incurs variable cost of $100 per hour. Assume average fixed costs are $5,250 a month.

Requirements

1. What is the number of hours that must be billed to reach break even?
2. If Draper desires to make a profit of $3,000, how many consulting hours must be completed?
3. Draper thinks it can reduce fixed cost to $3,990 per month, but variable cost will increase to $105 per hour. What is the new break even in hours?

Apply Your Knowledge

• Decision Case 19-1

Steve and Linda Hom live in Bartlesville, Oklahoma. Two years ago, they visited Thailand. Linda, a professional chef, was impressed with the cooking methods and the spices used in the Thai food. Bartlesville does not have a Thai restaurant, and the Homs are contemplating opening one. Linda would supervise the cooking, and Steve would leave his current job to be the maitre d'. The restaurant would serve dinner Tuesday–Saturday.

Steve has noticed a restaurant for lease. The restaurant has seven tables, each of which can seat four. Tables can be moved together for a large party. Linda is planning two seatings per evening, and the restaurant will be open 50 weeks per year.

The Homs have drawn up the following estimates:

Average revenue, including beverages and dessert	$	45 per meal
Average cost of food	$	15 per meal
Chef's and dishwasher's salaries.......................................	$	5,100 per month
Rent (premises, equipment)..	$	4,000 per month
Cleaning (linen and premises)..	$	800 per month
Replacement of dishes, cutlery, glasses............................	$	300 per month
Utilities, advertising, telephone.......................................	$	2,300 per month

Requirements

1. Compute the *annual* breakeven number of meals and sales revenue for the restaurant.

2. Also compute the number of meals and the amount of sales revenue needed to earn operating income of $75,600 for the year.

3. How many meals must the Homs serve each night to earn their target income of $75,600?

4. What factors should the Homs consider before they make their decision as to whether to open the restaurant or not?

● Ethical Issue 19-1

You have just begun your summer internship at Omni Instruments. The company supplies sterilized surgical instruments for physicians. To expand sales, Omni is considering paying a commission to its sales force. The controller, Matthew Barnhill, asks you to compute: (1) the new breakeven sales figure, and (2) the operating profit if sales increase 15% under the new sales commission plan. He thinks you can handle this task because you learned CVP analysis in your accounting class.

You spend the next day collecting information from the accounting records, performing the analysis, and writing a memo to explain the results. The company president is pleased with your memo. You report that the new sales commission plan will lead to a significant increase in operating income and only a small increase in breakeven sales.

The following week, you realize that you made an error in the CVP analysis. You overlooked the sales personnel's $2,800 monthly salaries and you did not include this fixed marketing cost in your computations. You are not sure what to do. If you tell Matthew Barnhill of your mistake, he will have to tell the president. In this case, you are afraid Omni might not offer you permanent employment after your internship.

Requirements

1. How would your error affect breakeven sales and operating income under the proposed sales commission plan? Could this cause the president to reject the sales commission proposal?

2. Consider your ethical responsibilities. Is there a difference between: (a) initially making an error, and (b) subsequently failing to inform the controller?

3. Suppose you tell Matthew Barnhill of the error in your analysis. Why might the consequences not be as bad as you fear? Should Barnhill take any responsibility for your error? What could Barnhill have done differently?

4. After considering all the factors, should you inform Barnhill or simply keep quiet?

● Fraud Case 19-1

Amanda Jackson loved reading obituaries. She was retired, but she had worked many bookkeeping jobs in her day and had made herself an expert in creating false invoices and opening bank accounts for fake companies. The scam was easy. When someone dies, the whole family is in grief, and one of the family members must clean up the deceased person's paperwork, close out accounts, pay the last bills, etc. If the now deceased person had ordered a pricey box set of classical music CDs, or had his ventilation system cleaned out, or even gotten therapeutic massages, who would bother questioning the bill? Sometimes the families of the deceased person paid Amanda's fake bills, and sometimes they didn't, but nobody ever looked any further. Yes, Amanda Jackson loved reading obituaries.

Requirements

1. Although this fraud pertains to individuals, how do businesses make sure they do not pay fake invoices?

2. If a person dies, is anyone liable for paying the remaining bills of the deceased?

● Team Project 19-1 (Based on Online Appendix 19A)

FASTPACK Manufacturing produces filament packaging tape. In 2014, FASTPACK produced and sold 15,000,000 rolls of tape. The company has recently expanded its capacity, so it now can produce up to 30,000,000 rolls per year. FASTPACK's accounting records show the following results from 2014:

Sale price per roll	$ 3.00
Variable manufacturing costs per roll................................	$ 2.00
Variable marketing and administrative costs per roll............	$ 0.50
Total fixed manufacturing overhead costs...........................	$8,400,000
Total fixed marketing and administrative costs....................	$1,100,000
Sales..	15,000,000 rolls
Production	15,000,000 rolls

There were no beginning or ending inventories in 2014.

In January 2015, FASTPACK hired a new president, Kevin McDaniel. McDaniel has a one-year contract that specifies he will be paid 10% of FASTPACK's 2015 absorption costing operating income, instead of a salary. In 2015, McDaniel must make two major decisions:

- Should FASTPACK undertake a major advertising campaign? This campaign would raise sales to 24,000,000 rolls. This is the maximum level of sales FASTPACK can expect to make in the near future. The ad campaign would add an additional $2,300,000 in fixed marketing and administrative costs. Without the campaign, sales will be 15,000,000 rolls.

- How many rolls of tape will FASTPACK produce?

At the end of the year, FASTPACK's Board of Directors will evaluate McDaniel's performance and decide whether to offer him a contract for the following year.

Requirements

Within your group, form two subgroups. The first subgroup assumes the role of Kevin McDaniel, FASTPACK's new president. The second subgroup assumes the role of FASTPACK's Board of Directors. McDaniel will meet with the Board of Directors shortly after the end of 2014 to decide whether he will remain at FASTPACK. Most of your effort should be devoted to advance preparation for this meeting. Each subgroup should meet separately to prepare for the meeting between the Board and McDaniel.

Kevin McDaniel should

1. compute FASTPACK's 2014 operating income.

2. decide whether to adopt the advertising campaign. Prepare a memo to the Board of Directors explaining this decision. Give this memo to the Board of Directors as soon as possible (before the joint meeting).

3. assume FASTPACK adopts the advertising campaign. Decide how many rolls of tape to produce in 2015.

4. (given the response to Requirement 3) prepare an absorption costing income statement for the year ended December 31, 2015, ending with operating income before bonus. Then compute the bonus separately. The variable cost per unit and the total fixed costs (with the exception of the advertising campaign) remain the same as in 2014. Give this income statement and bonus computation to the Board of Directors as soon as possible (before the meeting with the Board).

5. decide whether he wishes to remain at FASTPACK for another year. He currently has an offer from another company. The contract with the other company is identical to the one he currently has with FASTPACK—he will be paid 10% of absorption costing operating income instead of a salary.

The Board of Directors should

1. compute FASTPACK's 2014 operating income.

2. determine whether FASTPACK should adopt the advertising campaign.

3. determine how many rolls of tape FASTPACK should produce in 2015.

4. evaluate McDaniel's performance, based on his decisions and the information he provided the Board. (*Hint*: You may want to prepare a variable costing income statement.)

5. evaluate the contract's bonus provision. Is the Board satisfied with this provision? If so, explain why. If not, recommend how it should be changed.

After McDaniel has given the Board his memo and income statement, and after the Board has had a chance to evaluate McDaniel's performance, McDaniel and the Board should meet. The purpose of the meeting is to decide whether it is in their mutual interest for McDaniel to remain with FASTPACK, and if so, the terms of the contract FASTPACK will offer McDaniel.

● Communication Activity 19-1

In 25 words or fewer, explain what it means for a company to break even.

<hr>

Quick Check Answers

1. *a* 2. *a* 3. *d* 4. *c* 5. *d* 6. *b* 7. *b* 8. *c* 9. *b* 10. *d*

For online homework, exercises, and problems that provide you immediate feedback, please visit myaccountinglab.com.

20

Short-Term Business Decisions

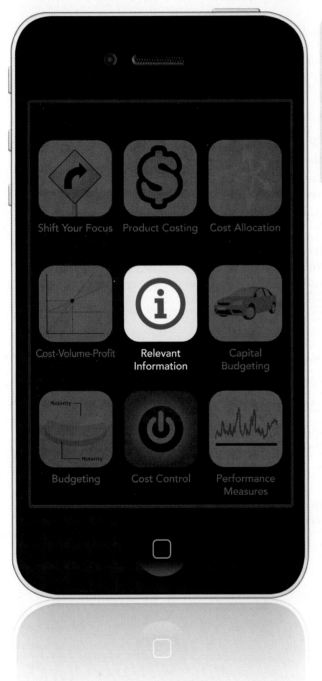

Learning Objectives

1. Describe and identify information relevant to business decisions

2. Make special order and pricing decisions

3. Make dropping a product and product-mix decisions

4. Make outsourcing and sell as is or process further decisions

Most major companies receive special order requests at reduced pricing as they grow. Smart Touch Learning, Inc., is considering a special order for its Excel DVDs. But why would Smart Touch consider selling its Excel DVDs at a reduced price? What costs and other information must Smart Touch consider in making the decision to accept or reject the order?

• • •

In Chapter 19, we saw how managers use cost behavior to determine the company's breakeven point and to estimate the sales volume needed to achieve target profits. In this chapter, we will see how managers use their knowledge of cost behavior to make six special business decisions, such as whether or not to accept a special order. The decisions we will discuss in this chapter pertain to short periods of time so managers do not need to worry about the time value of money. In other words, they do not need to compute the present value of the revenues and expenses relating to the decision. In Chapter 21 we will discuss longer-term decisions (such as plant expansions) in which the time value of money becomes important. Before we look at the six business decisions in detail, let's consider a manager's decision-making process and the information managers need to evaluate their options.

How Managers Make Decisions

Exhibit 20-1 illustrates how managers make decisions among alternative courses of action. Managerial accountants help with the third step: gathering and analyzing *relevant information* to compare alternatives.

1 Describe and identify information relevant to business decisions

EXHIBIT 20-1 | **How Managers Make Decisions**

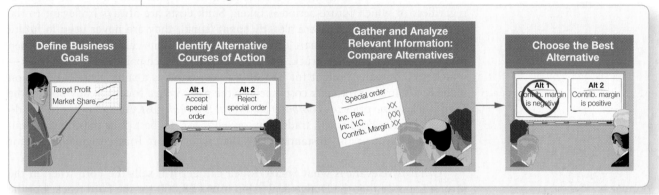

Relevant Information

When managers make decisions, they focus on costs and revenues that are relevant to the decisions. Exhibit 20-2 shows that **relevant information** is

1. expected *future* data that
2. *differs* among alternatives.

   Relevant costs are those costs that are relevant to a particular decision. To illustrate, if Smart Touch were considering purchasing a Dodge or a **Toyota** delivery truck, the cost of the truck, the sales tax, and the insurance premium costs would all be relevant because these costs

- are incurred in the *future* (after Smart Touch decides which truck to buy), and
- *differ between alternatives* (each truck has a different invoice price, sales tax, and insurance premium).

   These costs are *relevant* because they can affect the decision of which truck to purchase.

EXHIBIT 20-2 | **Relevant Information**

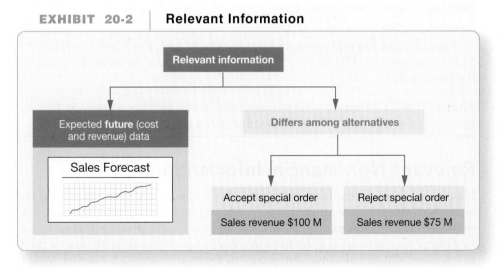

Irrelevant costs are costs that *do not* affect the decision. For example, because the Dodge and **Toyota** both have similar fuel efficiency and maintenance ratings, we do not expect the truck operating costs to differ between those two alternatives. Because these costs do not differ, they do not affect Smart Touch's decision. In other words, they are *irrelevant* to the decision. Similarly, the cost of an annual license tag is also irrelevant because the tag costs the same whether Smart Touch buys the Dodge or the **Toyota**.

Sunk costs are costs that were incurred in the *past* and cannot be changed regardless of which future action is taken. Sunk costs are always irrelevant to the decision. **Since sunk costs are already spent (sunk), they are never used in future decision making.** Perhaps Smart Touch wants to trade in its current **Ford** truck when the company buys the new truck. The amount Smart Touch paid for the **Ford** truck— which the company bought for $15,000 a year ago—is a sunk cost. No decision made *now* can alter the sunk costs spent in the past. Smart Touch already bought the **Ford** truck so *the price the company paid for it is a sunk cost.* All Smart Touch can do *now* is keep the **Ford** truck, trade it in, or sell it for the best price the company can get, even if that price is substantially less than what Smart Touch originally paid for the truck.

What *is* relevant is what Smart Touch can get if it sells the **Ford** truck in the future. Suppose that the Dodge dealership offers $8,000 for the **Ford** truck, but the **Toyota** dealership offers $10,000. Because the amounts differ and the transaction will take place in the future, the trade-in cost *is* relevant to Smart Touch's decision. Why? Because the trade-in values are different.

The same principle applies to all situations—*only relevant data affect decisions.* Let's consider another application of this principle.

Suppose Smart Touch is deciding whether to use DVDs made from new materials or DVDs made from recycled materials for its Excel Learning DVDs. Assume Smart Touch predicts the following costs under the two alternatives:

	New Materials	Recycled Materials	Cost Difference
Manufacturing cost per DVD:			
Direct materials	$2.40	$2.60	$0.20
Direct labor	$4.00	$4.00	$0.00

The cost of direct materials is relevant because this cost differs between alternatives (the recycled DVDs cost $0.20 more per DVD than the new material DVDs). The labor cost is irrelevant because that cost is the same for both.

Stop & Think...

You are considering replacing your old computer with the latest model. Is the $1,200 you spent in 2005 on the computer relevant to your decision about buying the new model?

Answer: The $1,200 cost of your old computer is irrelevant. It is a *sunk* cost that you incurred in the past so it is the same whether or not you buy the new computer.

Relevant Nonfinancial Information

Nonfinancial, or qualitative factors, also play a role in managers' decisions. For example, closing manufacturing plants and laying off employees can seriously hurt employee morale. **Outsourcing**, the decision to buy or subcontract a product or service rather than produce it in-house, can reduce control over delivery time or product quality. Offering discounted prices to select customers can upset regular customers and tempt them to take their business elsewhere. Managers must always consider the potential quantitative *and* qualitative effects of their decisions.

Managers who ignore qualitative factors can make serious mistakes. For example, the City of Nottingham, England, spent $1.6 million on 215 solar-powered parking meters after seeing how well the parking meters worked in countries along the Mediterranean Sea. However, they did not consider that British skies are typically overcast. The result was that the meters did not always work because of the lack of sunlight. The city *lost* money because people parked for free! Relevant qualitative information has the same characteristics as relevant financial information. The qualitative effect occurs in the *future* and it *differs* between alternatives. In the parking meter example, the amount of *future* sunshine required *differed* between alternatives. The mechanical meters did not require any sunshine, but the solar-powered meters needed a lot of sunshine.

Keys to Making Short-Term Special Decisions

Our approach to making short-term special decisions is called the **relevant information approach,** or the **incremental analysis approach.** Instead of looking at the company's *entire* income statement under each decision alternative, we will just look at how operating income would *differ* under each alternative. Using this approach, we will leave out irrelevant information—the costs and revenues that will not differ between alternatives. We will consider six kinds of short-term special decisions in this chapter:

1. Special sales orders

2. Pricing

3. Dropping products, departments, and territories

4. Product mix

5. Outsourcing (make or buy)

6. Selling as is or processing further

As you study these decisions, keep in mind the two keys in analyzing short-term special business decisions shown in Exhibit 20-3:

1. **Focus on relevant revenues, costs, and profits.** Irrelevant information only clouds the picture and creates information overload.

2. **Use a contribution margin approach that separates variable costs from fixed costs.** Because fixed costs and variable costs behave differently, they must be analyzed separately. Traditional (absorption costing) income statements, which blend fixed and variable costs together, can mislead managers. Contribution margin income statements, which isolate costs by behavior (variable or fixed), help managers gather the cost-behavior information they need. Keep in mind that unit manufacturing costs are mixed costs, too, so they can also mislead managers. If you use unit manufacturing costs in your analysis, be sure to first separate the unit cost into its fixed and variable portions.

We will use these two keys in each decision.

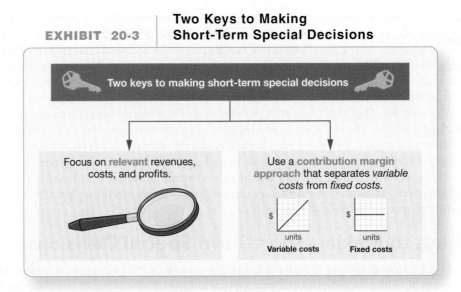

EXHIBIT 20-3

**Two Keys to Making
Short-Term Special Decisions**

Special Sales Order and Regular Pricing Decisions

2 Make special
order and pricing
decisions

We will start our discussion by looking at special sales order decisions and regular pricing decisions. In the past, managers did not consider pricing to be a short-term decision. However, product life cycles are getting shorter in most industries. Companies often sell products for only a few months before replacing them with an updated model, even if the updating is small. The clothing and technology industries have always had short life cycles. Even auto and housing styles change frequently. Pricing has become a shorter-term decision than it was in the past.

First, we'll examine a special sales order in detail. Then we'll discuss regular pricing decisions.

When to Accept a Special Sales Order

A special order occurs when a customer requests a one-time order at a *reduced* sale price. Before agreeing to the special deal, management must consider the questions shown in Exhibit 20-4.

EXHIBIT 20-4	Special Order Considerations

- Does the company have excess capacity available to fill this order?

- Will the reduced sales price be high enough to cover the *incremental* costs of filling the order (the variable costs and any additional fixed costs)?

- Will the special order affect regular sales in the long run?

First, managers must consider available manufacturing capacity. If the company is already using all its existing manufacturing capacity and selling all units made at its *regular* sales price, it would not be profitable to fill a special order at a *reduced* sales price. Therefore, available excess capacity is a necessity for accepting a special order. This is true for service firms as well as manufacturers.

Second, managers need to consider whether the special reduced sales price is high enough to cover the incremental costs of filling the special order. The special price *must* be greater than the variable costs of filling the order or the company will lose money on the deal. In other words, the special order must provide a *positive* contribution margin.

Next, the company must consider fixed costs. If the company has excess capacity, fixed costs probably will not be affected by producing more units (or delivering more service). However, in some cases, management may have to incur some other fixed cost to fill the special order, such as additional insurance premiums. If so, they will need to consider whether the special sales price is high enough to generate a positive contribution margin *and* cover the additional fixed costs.

Finally, managers need to consider whether the special order will affect regular sales in the long run. Will regular customers find out about the special order and demand a lower price? Will the special order customer come back *again and again*, asking for the same reduced price? Will the special order price start a price war with competitors? Managers should determine the answers to these questions and consider how customers will respond. Managers may decide that any profit from the special sales order is not worth these risks.

Let's consider a special sales order example. We learned in Chapter 18 that Smart Touch normally sells its Excel DVDs for $12.00 each. Assume that a company has offered Smart Touch $67,500 for 10,000 DVDs, or $6.75 per DVD. This sale

- will use manufacturing capacity that would otherwise be idle (excess capacity).
- will not change fixed costs.
- will not require any variable *nonmanufacturing* expenses (because no extra marketing costs are incurred with this special order).
- will not affect regular sales.

We have addressed every consideration except one: Is the special sales price high enough to cover the variable *manufacturing* costs associated with the order? First, we'll review the *wrong* way and then we'll review the *right* way to figure out the answer to this question.

Suppose Smart Touch made and sold 100,000 DVDs before considering the special order. Using the traditional (absorption costing) income statement on the left-hand side of Exhibit 20-5, the ABC manufacturing cost per unit is $7.00 (from Chapter 18, Exhibit 18-9). A manager who does not examine these numbers carefully may believe that Smart Touch should *not* accept the special order at a sale price of $6.75 because each DVD costs $7.00 to manufacture. But appearances can be deceiving! Recall that the unit manufacturing cost of the DVD, $7.00, is a *mixed* cost, containing both fixed and variable cost components. To correctly answer our question, we need to find only the *variable* portion of the manufacturing unit cost.

The right-hand side of Exhibit 20-5 shows the contribution margin income statement that separates variable expenses from fixed expenses. The contribution margin income statement allows us to see that the *variable* manufacturing cost per DVD is only $6.50 ($650,000 ÷ 100,000). The special sales price of $6.75 per DVD is *higher* than the variable manufacturing cost of $6.50. Therefore, the special order will provide a positive contribution margin of $0.25 per DVD ($6.75 – $6.50). Since the special order is for 10,000 DVDs, Smart Touch's total contribution margin should increase by $2,500 (10,000 DVDs × $0.25 per DVD) if it accepts this order.

EXHIBIT 20-5 **Traditional (Absorption Costing) Format and Contribution Margin Format Income Statements**

SMART TOUCH LEARNING, INC.		
Income Statement (at a production and sales level of 100,000 Excel DVDs)		
Year Ended December 31, 2013		

Traditional (Absorption Costing) Format			Contribution Margin Format			
Sales revenue		$1,200,000	Sales revenue			$1,200,000
Cost of goods sold		700,000	Variable expenses:			
Gross profit		$ 500,000	Manufacturing		$640,000	
Marketing and administrative expenses		110,000	Marketing and administrative		10,000	650,000
			Contribution margin			$ 550,000
			Fixed expenses:			
			Manufacturing		$ 60,000	
			Marketing and administrative		100,000	160,000
Operating income		$ 390,000	Operating income			$ 390,000

Using an incremental analysis approach, Smart Touch compares the additional revenues from the special order with the incremental expenses to see if the special order will contribute to profits. Exhibit 20-6 shows that the special sales order will increase revenue by $67,500 (10,000 × $6.75) but will also increase variable manufacturing cost by $65,000 (10,000 × $6.50). As a result, Smart Touch's contribution margin will increase by $2,500, as previously shown. The other costs seen in Exhibit 20-5 are not relevant to the decision. Variable marketing and administrative expenses will be the same whether or not Smart Touch accepts the special order, because Smart Touch made no special efforts to get this sale. Fixed manufacturing expenses will not change because Smart Touch has enough idle capacity to produce 10,000 extra Excel DVDs without needing additional facilities. Fixed marketing and administrative expenses will not be affected by this special order either. Because there are no additional fixed costs, the total increase in contribution margin flows directly to operating income. As a result, the special sales order will increase operating income by $2,500.

EXHIBIT 20-6 **Incremental Analysis of Special Sales Order of 10,000 Excel DVDs**

Expected increase in revenues (10,000 DVDs × $6.75)	$ 67,500
Expected increase in variable manufacturing costs (10,000 DVDs × $6.50)	(65,000)
Expected increase in operating income	$ 2,500

Notice that the analysis follows the two keys to making short-term special business decisions discussed earlier: (1) Focus on relevant data (revenues and costs that *will change* if Smart Touch accepts the special order) and (2) use of a contribution margin approach that separates variable costs from fixed costs.

To summarize, for special sales orders, the decision rule is as follows:

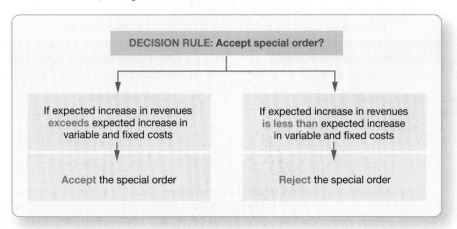

How to Set Regular Prices
=========================

In the special order decision, Smart Touch decided to sell a limited quantity of DVDs for $6.75 each, even though the normal price was $12.00 per unit. But how did Smart Touch decide to set its regular price at $12.00 per DVD? Exhibit 20-7 shows that managers start with three basic questions when setting regular prices for their products or services.

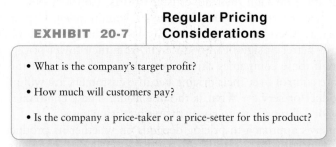

EXHIBIT 20-7 | **Regular Pricing Considerations**

- What is the company's target profit?

- How much will customers pay?

- Is the company a price-taker or a price-setter for this product?

    The answers to these questions are complex and ever-changing. Stockholders expect the company to achieve certain profits. Economic conditions, historical company earnings, industry risk, competition, and new business developments all affect the level of profit that stockholders expect. Stockholders usually tie their profit expectations to the amount of assets invested in the company. For example, stockholders may expect a 10% annual return on their investment. A company's stock price tends to decline if it does not meet target profits, so managers must keep costs low while generating enough revenue to meet target profits.

    This leads to the second question: How much will customers pay? Managers cannot set prices above what customers are willing to pay or sales will decline. The amount customers will pay depends on the competition, the product's uniqueness, the effectiveness of marketing campaigns, general economic conditions, and so forth.

    To address the third pricing question, imagine a horizontal line with price-takers at one end and price-setters at the other end. A company's products and services fall somewhere along this line, shown in Exhibit 20-8. Companies are price-takers when they have little or no control over the prices of their products or services. This occurs when their products and services are *not* unique or when competition is intense. Examples include food commodities (milk and corn), natural resources (oil and lumber), and generic consumer products and services (paper towels, dry cleaning, and banking).

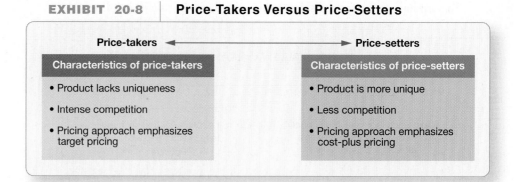

EXHIBIT 20-8 | **Price-Takers Versus Price-Setters**

Companies are price-setters when they have more control over pricing—in other words, they can "set" the price to some extent. Companies are price-setters when their products are unique, which results in less competition. Unique products, such as original art and jewelry, specially manufactured machinery, patented perfume scents, and the latest technological gadget (like an iPad), can command higher prices.

Obviously, managers would rather be price-setters than price-takers. To gain more control over pricing, companies try to differentiate their products. They want to make their products unique in terms of features, service, or quality, or at least make the buyer *think* their product is unique or somehow better. Companies achieve this differentiation through their advertising efforts. Consider **Nike**'s tennis shoes, **Starbucks'** coffee, **Kleenex**'s tissues, **Tylenol**'s acetaminophen, **Capital One**'s credit cards, **Shell**'s gas, **Abercrombie and Fitch**'s jeans—the list goes on and on. Are these products really better or significantly different from their lower-priced competitors? It is possible. If these companies can make customers *believe* that this is true, they will gain more control over their pricing because customers are willing to pay *more* for their product or service. What is the downside? These companies must charge higher prices or sell more just to cover their advertising costs.

A company's approach to pricing depends on whether its product or service is on the price-taking or price-setting side of the spectrum. Price-takers emphasize a target-pricing approach. Price-setters emphasize a cost-plus pricing approach. Keep in mind that many products fall somewhere along the horizontal line in Exhibit 20-8. Therefore, managers tend to use both approaches to some extent. We will now discuss each approach in turn.

Stop & Think...

It is lunchtime....you want a hamburger. Where do you go—**Wendy's**, **McDonald's**, or your college's cafeteria? Why? A hamburger is the same wherever you go, right? The answer to that question is the key to changing a product (a hamburger) from a commodity to a unique product (a **Wendy's** hamburger). The advertising, conditioning of your family, etc. have possibly made you think that the three companies' hamburgers are different. The perceived uniqueness of the hamburger helps the company (say **Wendy's**) be a price-setter instead of a price-taker.

Target Pricing

When a company is a price-taker, it emphasizes a target pricing approach to managing costs and profits. Target pricing starts with the market price of the product (the price customers are willing to pay) and then subtracts the company's desired profit to determine the maximum allowed **target full product cost**—the *full* cost to develop, produce, and deliver the product or service.

Revenue at market price		Revenue (at market price)
Less: Desired profit	O	– COGS (Target full product cost)
Target full product cost	R	Target net income (Desired profit)

In this relationship, the market price is "taken." Recall from Chapter 16 that a product's *full* cost contains all elements from the value chain—both inventoriable costs and period costs. It also includes fixed and variable costs. If the product's current cost is higher than the target full cost, the company must find ways to reduce the product's cost or it will not meet its profit goals. Managers often use ABC costing along with value engineering (as discussed in Chapter 18) to find ways to cut costs.

Assume that Excel Learning DVDs are a commodity, and that the current market price is $11.00 per DVD (not the $12.00 sales price assumed in the earlier Smart Touch example). Because the DVDs are a commodity, Smart Touch will emphasize a target-pricing approach. Assume Smart Touch's stockholders expect a 10% annual return on the company's assets. If the company has $3,000,000 average assets, the desired profit is $300,000 ($3,000,000 × 10%). Exhibit 20-9 calculates the target full cost at the current sales volume of 100,000 DVDs. Once we know the target full cost, we can analyze the fixed and variable cost components separately.

EXHIBIT 20-9 | **Calculating Target Full Cost**

	Calculations	
Revenue at market price	100,000 DVDs × $11.00 sales price	$1,100,000
Less: Desired profit	10% × $3,000,000 average assets	300,000
Target full cost		$ 800,000

Can Smart Touch make and sell 100,000 Excel Learning DVDs at a full cost of $800,000? We know from Smart Touch's contribution margin income statement (Exhibit 20-5) that the company's variable costs are $6.50 per unit ($650,000 ÷ 100,000 units). This variable cost per unit includes both manufacturing costs ($6.40 per unit) and marketing and administrative costs ($0.10 per unit). We also know the company incurs $160,000 in fixed costs in its current relevant range. Again, some fixed costs stem from manufacturing and some from marketing and administrative activities. *In setting regular sales prices, companies must cover **all** of their costs—whether the costs are inventoriable or period, fixed or variable.*

Making and selling 100,000 DVDs currently costs the company $810,000 [(100,000 units × $6.50 variable cost per unit) + $160,000 of fixed costs], which is more than the target full cost ($800,000). So, what are Smart Touch's options?

1. Accept the lower operating income of $290,000, which is a 9.67% return, not the 10% target return required by stockholders.

2. Reduce fixed costs by $10,000 or more.

3. Reduce variable costs by $10,000 or more.

4. Use other strategies. For example, Smart Touch could attempt to increase sales volume. Recall that the company has excess manufacturing capacity, so making and selling more units would only affect variable costs; however, it would mean that current fixed costs are spread over more units. The company could also consider changing or adding to its product mix. Finally, it could attempt to differentiate its Excel Learning DVDs from the competition to gain more control over sales prices (be a price-setter).

Let's look at some of these options. Smart Touch may first try to cut fixed costs. As shown in Exhibit 20-10, the company would have to reduce fixed costs to $150,000 to meet its target profit level.

EXHIBIT 20-10 | **Calculating Target Fixed Cost**

	Calculations	
Target full cost	(From Exhibit 20-9)	$ 800,000
Less: Current variable costs	100,000 DVDs × $6.50	650,000
Target fixed cost		$ 150,000

If the company cannot reduce its fixed costs by $10,000 ($160,000 current fixed costs – $150,000 target fixed costs), it would have to lower its variable cost to $6.40 per unit, as shown in Exhibit 20-11.

EXHIBIT 20-11 | **Calculating Target DVD Variable Cost**

	Calculations	
Target full cost	(From Exhibit 20-9)	$ 800,000
Less: Current fixed costs	(From Exhibit 20-5)	160,000
Target total variable costs		$ 640,000
Divided by the number of DVDs		÷ 100,000
Target variable cost per unit		$ 6.40

If Smart Touch cannot reduce variable cost per unit to $6.40, then the company could try to meet its target profit through a combination of lowering both fixed costs and variable costs.

Another strategy would be to increase sales. Smart Touch's managers can use CVP analysis, as you learned in Chapter 19, to figure out how many Excel Learning DVDs the company would have to sell to achieve its target profit. How could the company increase demand for the Excel Learning DVDs? Perhaps it could reach new markets or advertise. How much would advertising cost—and how many extra Excel Learning DVDs would the company have to sell to cover the cost of advertising? These are only some of the questions managers must ask. As you can see, managers do not have an easy task when the current cost exceeds the target full cost. Sometimes companies just cannot compete given the current market price. If that is the case, they may have no other choice than to quit making that product.

Cost-Plus Pricing

When a company is a price-setter, it emphasizes a cost-plus approach to pricing. This pricing approach is essentially the *opposite* of the target-pricing approach. Cost-plus pricing starts with the company's full costs (as a given) and *adds* its desired profit to determine a cost-plus price.

> Full product cost
> Plus: Desired profit
> Cost-plus price

When the product is unique, the company has more control over pricing. The company still needs to make sure that the cost-plus price is not higher than what customers are willing to pay. Now, back to our original Smart Touch example. This time, assume the Excel Learning DVDs benefit from brand recognition so the company has some control over the price it charges for its DVDs. Exhibit 20-12 takes a cost-plus pricing approach, assuming the current level of sales.

EXHIBIT 20-12 | Calculating Cost-Plus Price

	Calculations	
Current variable costs	100,000 DVDs × $6.50	$ 650,000
Plus: Current fixed costs	(From Exhibit 20-5)	160,000
Full product cost		$ 810,000
Plus: Desired profit	10% × $3,000,000 average assets	300,000
Target revenue		$1,110,000
Divided by the number of DVDs		÷ 100,000
Cost-plus price per DVD		$ 11.10

If the current market price for generic Excel Learning DVDs is $11.00, as we assumed earlier, can Smart Touch sell its brand-name DVDs for $11.10, or more, each? The answer depends on how well the company has been able to differentiate its product or brand name. The company may use focus groups or marketing surveys to find out how customers would respond to its cost-plus price. The company may find out that its cost-plus price is too high, or it may find that it could set the price even higher without losing sales.

Notice how pricing decisions used our two keys to decision making: (1) focus on relevant information and (2) use a contribution margin approach that separates variable costs from fixed costs. In pricing decisions, all cost information is relevant because the company must cover *all* costs along the value chain before it can generate a profit. However, we still need to consider variable costs and fixed costs separately because they behave differently at different volumes.

Our pricing decision rule is as follows:

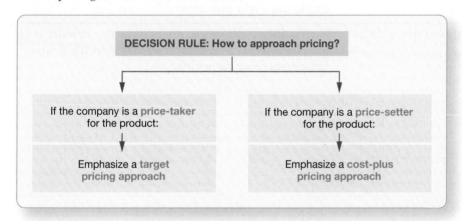

Now take some time to review the Decision Guidelines on the next page.

Key Takeaway

Managers must consider three things when considering a special order: 1) Does the company have excess manufacturing capacity? 2) Does the special sales price cover the incremental costs of filling the special order? and 3) Will fixed costs change because of the special order? If the expected increase in revenues exceeds the expected increase in costs, the company should accept the special order. When setting prices, the company must consider its target profit goal, how much customers will pay for the product, and whether the company is a price-taker or a price-setter. Price setters use a cost-plus pricing approach to pricing, whereas price-takers use a target pricing approach.

Decision Guidelines 20-1

RELEVANT INFORMATION FOR BUSINESS DECISIONS

Nike makes special order and regular pricing decisions. Even though it sells mass-produced tennis shoes and sport clothing, **Nike** has differentiated its products with advertising and with athlete endorsements. **Nike's** managers consider both quantitative and qualitative factors as they make pricing decisions. Here are key guidelines **Nike's** managers follow in making their decisions.

Decision	Guidelines
• What information is relevant to a short-term special business decision?	Relevant data 1. are expected *future* data. 2. *differ* between alternatives.
• What are two key guidelines in making short-term special business decisions?	1. Focus on *relevant* data. 2. Use a *contribution margin* approach that separates variable costs from fixed costs.
• Should **Nike** accept a lower sale price than the regular price for a large order from a customer in Labadee, Haiti?	If the revenue from the order exceeds the extra variable and fixed costs incurred to fill the order, then accepting the order will increase operating income.
• What should **Nike** consider in setting its regular product prices?	**Nike** considers 1. the profit stockholders expect it to make. 2. the price customers will pay. 3. whether it is a price-setter or a price-taker.
• What approach should **Nike** take to pricing?	**Nike** has differentiated its products by advertising. Thus, **Nike** tends to be a price-setter. **Nike's** managers can emphasize a cost-plus approach to pricing.
• What approach should discount shoe stores, such as **Payless Shoes**, take to pricing?	**Payless Shoes** sells generic shoes (no-name brands) at low prices. **Payless** is a price-taker so managers use a target-pricing approach to pricing.

Summary Problem 20-1

MC Alexander Industries makes tennis balls. Its only plant can produce up to 2,500,000 cans of balls per year. Current production is 2,000,000 cans. Annual manufacturing, selling, and administrative fixed costs total $700,000. The variable cost of making and selling each can of balls is $1.00. Stockholders expect a 12% annual return on the company's $3,000,000 of assets.

Requirements

1. What is MC Alexander's current full cost of making and selling 2,000,000 cans of tennis balls? What is the current full *unit* cost of each can of tennis balls?
2. Assume MC Alexander is a price-taker, and the current market price is $1.45 per can of balls (this is the price at which manufacturers sell to retailers). What is the *target* full cost of producing and selling 2,000,000 cans of balls? Given MC Alexander's current costs, will the company reach stockholders' profit goals?
3. If MC Alexander cannot change its fixed costs, what is the target variable cost per can of balls?
4. Suppose MC Alexander could spend an extra $100,000 on advertising to differentiate its product so that it could be a price-setter. Assuming the original volume and costs, plus the $100,000 of new advertising costs, what cost-plus price will MC Alexander want to charge for a can of balls?
5. **Nike** has just asked MC Alexander to supply the company with 400,000 cans of balls at a special order price of $1.20 per can. **Nike** wants MC Alexander to package the balls under the **Nike** label (MC Alexander will imprint the **Nike** logo on each ball and can). MC Alexander will have to spend $10,000 to change the packaging machinery. Assuming the original volume and costs, should MC Alexander accept this special order? (Unlike the chapter problem, assume MC Alexander will incur variable selling costs as well as variable manufacturing costs related to this order.)

Solution

Requirement 1

The full unit cost is as follows:

Fixed costs	$ 700,000
Plus: Total variable costs (2,000,000 cans × $1.00 per unit) ...	+ 2,000,000
Total full product costs	$2,700,000
Divided by the number of cans...	÷ 2,000,000
Full product cost per can..	$ 1.35

Requirement 2

The target full cost is as follows:

	Calculations	Total			
Revenue at market price	2,000,000 units × $1.45 price =	$2,900,000	**O**	Revenue	$2,900,000
Less: Desired profit	12% × $3,000,000 of assets	360,000	**R**	COGS	2,540,000
Target *full* product cost		$2,540,000		Target net income	$ 360,000

MC Alexander's current total full product costs ($2,700,000 from Requirement 1) are $160,000 higher than the target full product cost ($2,540,000). If MC Alexander cannot reduce product costs, it will not be able to meet stockholders' profit expectations.

Requirement 3

Assuming MC Alexander cannot reduce its fixed costs, the target variable cost per can is as follows:

	Total
Target *full* product cost (from Requirement 2)	$2,540,000
Less: Fixed costs	700,000
Target total variable cost	$1,840,000
Divided by the number of units	÷2,000,000
Target variable cost per unit	$ 0.92

Since MC Alexander cannot reduce its fixed costs, it needs to reduce variable costs by $0.08 per can ($1.00 − $0.92) to meet its profit goals. This would require an 8% cost reduction, which may not be possible.

Requirement 4

If MC Alexander can differentiate its tennis balls, it will gain more control over pricing. The company's new cost-plus price would be as follows:

Current total costs (from Requirement 1)	$2,700,000
Plus: Additional cost of advertising	+ 100,000
Plus: Desired profit (from Requirement 2)	+ 360,000
Target revenue	$3,160,000
Divided by the number of units	÷ 2,000,000
Cost-plus price per unit	$ 1.58

MC Alexander must study the market to determine whether retailers would pay $1.58 per can of balls.

Requirement 5

Nike's special order price ($1.20) is less than the current full cost of each can of balls ($1.35 from Requirement 1). However, this should not influence management's decision. MC Alexander could fill Nike's special order using existing excess capacity. MC Alexander takes an incremental analysis approach to its decision, comparing the extra revenue with the incremental costs of accepting the order. Variable costs will increase if MC Alexander accepts the order, so the variable costs are relevant. Only the *additional* fixed costs of changing the packaging machine ($10,000) are relevant since all other fixed costs will remain unchanged.

Revenue from special order (400,000 × $1.20 per unit)	$ 480,000
Less: Variable cost of special order (400,000 × $1.00)	400,000
Contribution margin from special order	$ 80,000
Less: Additional fixed costs of special order	10,000
Operating income provided by special order	$ 70,000

MC Alexander should accept the special order because it will increase operating income by $70,000. However, MC Alexander also needs to consider whether its regular customers will find out about the special price and demand lower prices too.

When to Drop Products, Departments, or Territories

Managers must often decide whether to drop products, departments, or territories that are not as profitable as desired. How do managers make these decisions? Exhibit 20-13 lists some of the questions managers must consider when deciding whether to drop a product, department, or territory.

 3 Make dropping a product and product-mix decisions

EXHIBIT 20-13	Considerations for Dropping Products, Departments, or Territories

- Does the product, department, or territory provide a positive contribution margin?

- Will fixed costs continue to exist, even if the company drops the product?

- Are there any direct fixed costs that can be avoided if the company drops the product, department, or territory?

- Will dropping the product, department, or territory affect sales of the company's other products?

- What could the company do with the freed manufacturing capacity?

Once again, we follow the two key guidelines for special business decisions: (1) focus on relevant data and (2) use a contribution margin approach. The relevant financial data are still the changes in revenues and expenses. But now we are considering a *decrease* in volume rather than an *increase*, as we did in the special sales order decision. In the following example, we will consider how managers decide to drop a product. Managers would use the same process in deciding whether to drop a department or territory.

Earlier, we focused on only one of Smart Touch's products—Excel Learning DVDs. Now we'll focus on both of its products—the Excel Learning DVDs and the specialty DVDs we covered in Chapter 18. Exhibit 20-14 shows the company's contribution margin income statement by product, assuming fixed costs are shared by both products. Because the specialty DVD line has an operating *loss* of $420, management is considering dropping the product.

EXHIBIT 20-14	Contribution Margin Income Statements by Product

SMART TOUCH LEARNING, INC. Income Statement For the Month Ended January 31, 2014		Products	
		Excel DVDs	**Specialty DVDs**
		(100,000 DVDs)	**(350 DVDs)**
	Total	**(From Exhibit 20-5)**	
Sales revenue	$1,224,500	$1,200,000	$24,500
Variable expenses:			
Manufacturing	652,740	640,000	12,740
Marketing and administrative	10,035	10,000	35
Total variable expenses	662,775	650,000	12,775
Contribution margin	$ 561,725	$ 550,000	$11,725
Fixed expenses:			
Manufacturing	71,795	60,000	11,795
Marketing and administrative	100,350	100,000	350
Total fixed expenses	172,145	160,000	12,145
Operating income (loss)	$ 389,580	$ 390,000	$ (420)

The first question management should ask is "Does the product provide a positive contribution margin?" If the product has a negative contribution margin, then the product is not even covering its variable costs. Therefore, the company should drop the product. However, if the product has a positive contribution margin, then it is *helping* to cover some of the company's fixed costs. In Smart Touch's case, the specialty DVDs provide a positive contribution margin of $11,725. Smart Touch's managers now need to consider fixed costs.

Suppose Smart Touch allocates fixed costs using the ABC costs per unit calculated in Chapter 18, Exhibit 18-9 ($7.00 per unit). Smart Touch could allocate fixed costs in many different ways, and each way would allocate a different amount of fixed costs to each product. Therefore, allocated fixed costs are *irrelevant* because they are arbitrary in amount. What is relevant are the following:

1. Will the fixed costs continue to exist *even if* the product is dropped?

2. Are there any *direct* fixed costs of the specialty DVDs that can be avoided if the product is dropped?

Dropping Products Under Various Assumptions

Now we'll consider various assumptions when dropping products.

Fixed Costs Will Continue to Exist and Will Not Change

Fixed costs that will continue to exist even after a product is dropped are often called unavoidable fixed costs. Unavoidable fixed costs are *irrelevant* to the decision because they *will not change* if the company drops the product. Let's assume that all of Smart Touch's fixed costs of $172,145 will continue to exist even if the company drops the specialty DVDs. Assume that Smart Touch makes the specialty DVDs in the same plant using the same machinery as the Excel Learning DVDs. Thus, only the contribution margin the specialty DVDs provide is relevant. If Smart Touch drops the specialty DVDs, it will lose the $11,725 contribution margin.

The incremental analysis shown in Exhibit 20-15 verifies the loss. If Smart Touch drops the specialty DVDs, revenue will decrease by $24,500, but variable expenses will decrease by only $12,775, resulting in a net $11,725 decrease in operating income. Because fixed costs are unaffected, they are not included in the analysis. This analysis suggests that management should *not* drop specialty DVDs. It is actually more beneficial for Smart Touch to lose $420 than to drop the specialty DVDs and lose $11,725 in operating income.

EXHIBIT 20-15	**Incremental Analysis for Dropping a Product When Fixed Costs Will *Not* Change**

Expected decrease in revenues (350 specialty DVDs × $70.00)	$(24,500)
Expected decrease in variable costs (From Exhibit 20-14, $12,740 + $35)	12,775
Expected *decrease* in operating income	$(11,725)

Direct Fixed Costs Will Change

Since Smart Touch allocates its fixed costs using ABC costing, some of the fixed costs *belong* only to the specialty DVD product. These would be direct fixed costs of the specialty DVDs only.[1] Assume that $12,000 of the fixed costs will be avoidable

---

[1]To aid in decision-making, companies should separate direct fixed costs from indirect fixed costs on their contribution margin income statements. Companies should *trace direct fixed costs* to the appropriate product and only *allocate indirect fixed costs* among products.

if Smart Touch drops the specialty DVD product. Then, $12,000 are avoidable fixed costs and *are relevant* to the decision because they would change (go away) if the product is dropped.

Exhibit 20-16 shows that, in this situation, operating income will *increase* by $275 if Smart Touch drops the specialty DVDs. Why? Because revenues will decline by $24,500 but expenses will decline even more—by $24,775. The result is a net increase to operating income of $275. This analysis suggests that management should drop specialty DVDs.

EXHIBIT 20-16	**Incremental Analysis for Dropping a Product When Fixed Costs *Will* Change**	

Expected decrease in revenues (350 specialty DVDs × $70.00)		$(24,500)
Expected decrease in variable costs (From Exhibit 20-14, $12,740 + $35)	12,775	
Expected decrease in fixed costs	12,000	
Expected decrease in total expenses		24,775
Expected increase in operating income		$ 275

Other Considerations

Management must also consider whether dropping the product, department, or territory would hurt other product sales. In the examples given so far, we assumed that dropping the specialty DVDs would not affect Smart Touch's other product sales. However, think about a grocery store. Even if the produce department is not profitable, would managers drop it? Probably not, because if they did, they would lose customers who want one-stop shopping. In such situations, managers must also include the loss of contribution margin from *other* departments affected by the change when deciding whether to drop a department.

Management should also consider what it could do with freed manufacturing capacity. In the Smart Touch example, we assumed that the company produces both Excel Learning DVDs and specialty DVDs using the same manufacturing equipment. If Smart Touch drops the specialty DVDs, could it make and sell another product using the freed machine hours? Is product demand strong enough that Smart Touch could make and sell more of the Excel Learning DVDs? Managers should consider whether using the machinery to produce a different product or expanding existing product lines would be more profitable than using the machinery to produce specialty DVDs.

Special decisions should take into account all costs affected by the choice of action. Managers must ask the following questions: What total costs—variable and fixed—will change? Are there additional environmental costs (for example, waste water disposal) that should be considered? As Exhibits 20-15 and 20-16 show, the key to deciding whether to drop products, departments, or territories is to compare the lost revenue against the costs that can be saved and to consider what would be done with the freed capacity. The decision rule is as follows:

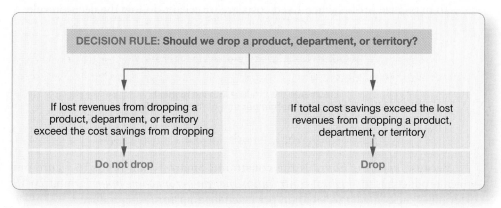

Product Mix: Which Product to Emphasize?

Companies do not have unlimited resources. **Constraints** that restrict production or sale of a product vary from company to company. For a manufacturer like Smart Touch, the production constraint may be labor hours, machine hours, or available materials. For a merchandiser like **Walmart**, the primary constraint is cubic feet of display space. Other companies are constrained by sales demand. Competition may be stiff, and so the company may be able to sell only a limited number of units. In such cases, the company produces only as much as it can sell. However, if a company can sell all the units it can produce, which products should it emphasize? For which items should production be increased? Companies facing constraints consider the questions shown in Exhibit 20-17.

EXHIBIT 20-17	Product Mix Considerations

- What constraint(s) stop(s) the company from making (or displaying) all the units the company can sell?

- Which products offer the highest contribution margin per unit of the constraint?

- Would emphasizing one product over another affect fixed costs?

Let's return to our Smart Touch example. Assume the company can sell all the Excel DVDs and all the specialty DVDs it produces, but it only has 2,000 machine hours of manufacturing capacity. The company uses the same machines to make both types of DVDs. In this case, machine hours is the constraint. Note that this is a short-term decision because in the long run, Smart Touch could expand its production facilities to meet sales demand if it made financial sense to do so. The data in Exhibit 20-18 suggest that specialty DVDs are more profitable than Excel DVDs.

EXHIBIT 20-18	Smart Touch's Contribution Margin per Unit

	Excel DVD	Specialty DVD
Sale price per DVD	$12.00	$70.00
Variable cost per DVD	6.50	36.50
Contribution margin	5.50	33.50
Contribution margin ratio		
Excel DVDs $5.50/$12.00	46%	
Specialty DVDs $33.50/$70.00		48%

However, an important piece of information is missing—the time it takes to make each product. Assume that Smart Touch can produce either 80 Excel DVDs *or* 10 specialty DVDs per machine hour. *The company will incur the same fixed costs either way so fixed costs are irrelevant.* Which product should it emphasize?

To maximize profits when fixed costs are irrelevant, follow the decision rule:

> **DECISION RULE: Which product to emphasize?**
>
> ↓
>
> Emphasize the product with the highest contribution margin per unit of the constraint.

Because *machine hours* is the constraint, Smart Touch needs to figure out which product has the *highest contribution margin per machine hour*. Exhibit 20-19 determines the contribution margin per machine hour for each product.

EXHIBIT 20-19	Smart Touch's Contribution Margin per Machine Hour	Excel DVD	Specialty DVD
	(1) DVDs that can be produced each machine hour	80	10
	(2) Contribution margin per DVD from Exhibit 20-18	$ 5.50	$ 33.50
	Contribution margin per machine hour (1) × (2)	$ 440	$ 335
	Available capacity—number of machine hours	2,000	2,000
	Total contribution margin at full capacity	$880,000	$670,000

Excel DVDs have a higher contribution margin per machine hour, $440, than specialty DVDs, $335. Smart Touch will earn more profit by producing Excel DVDs. Why? Because even though Excel DVDs have a lower contribution margin *per unit*, Smart Touch can make eight times as many Excel DVDs as specialty DVDs in the 2,000 available machine hours. Exhibit 20-19 also proves that Smart Touch earns more total profit by making Excel DVDs. Multiplying the contribution margin per machine hour by the available number of machine hours shows that Smart Touch can earn $880,000 of contribution margin by producing only Excel DVDs, but only $670,000 by producing only specialty DVDs.

To maximize profit, Smart Touch should make 160,000 Excel DVDs (2,000 machine hours × 80 Excel DVDs per hour) and zero specialty DVDs. Why should Smart Touch make zero specialty DVDs? Because for every machine hour spent making specialty DVDs, Smart Touch would *give up* $105 of contribution margin ($440 per hour for Excel DVDs versus $335 per hour for specialty DVDs).

We made two assumptions here: (1) Smart Touch's sales of other products will not be hurt by this decision and (2) Smart Touch can sell as many Excel DVDs as it can produce. Let's challenge these assumptions. First, how could making only Excel DVDs hurt sales of other products? By producing the specialty DVDs, Smart Touch also sells many of its standard offerings like the Excel DVDs that coordinate with the specialty DVDs. Other DVD sales might fall if Smart Touch no longer offers specialty DVDs.

Let's challenge our second assumption. Suppose that a new competitor has decreased the demand for Smart Touch's Excel DVDs. Now the company can only sell 120,000 Excel DVDs. Smart Touch should only make as many Excel DVDs as it can sell and use the remaining machine hours to produce specialty DVDs. How will this constraint in sales demand change profitability?

Recall from Exhibit 20-19 that Smart Touch will make $880,000 of contribution margin by using all 2,000 machine hours to produce Excel DVDs. However, if Smart Touch only makes 120,000 Excel DVDs, it will only use 1,500 machine hours (120,000 Excel DVDs ÷ 80 Excel DVDs per machine hour). That leaves 500 machine hours available for making specialty DVDs. Smart Touch's new contribution margin will be as shown in Exhibit 20-20.

EXHIBIT 20-20	Smart Touch's Contribution Margin per Machine Hour—Limited Market for Product	Excel DVD	Specialty DVD	Total
	(1) DVDs that can be produced each machine hour	80	10	
	(2) Contribution margin per DVD from Exhibit 20-18	$ 5.50	$ 33.50	
	Contribution margin per machine hour (1) × (2)	$ 440	$ 335	
	Machine hours devoted to product	1,500	500	
	Total contribution margin at full capacity	$660,000	$167,500	$827,500

Because of the change in product mix, Smart Touch's total contribution margin will fall from $880,000 to $827,500, a $52,500 decrease. Smart Touch had to give up $105 of contribution margin per machine hour ($440 − $335) on the 500 hours it spent producing specialty DVDs rather than Excel DVDs. However, Smart Touch had no choice—the company would have incurred an *actual loss* from producing Excel DVDs that it could not sell. If Smart Touch had produced 160,000 Excel DVDs but only sold 120,000, the company would have spent $220,000 to make the unsold DVDs (40,000 Excel DVDs × $5.50 variable cost per Excel DVD), yet received no sales revenue from them.

What about fixed costs? In most cases, changing the product mix emphasis in the short run will not affect fixed costs, so fixed costs are irrelevant. However, it is possible that fixed costs could differ by emphasizing a different product mix. What if Smart Touch had a month-to-month lease on a production camera used only for making specialty DVDs? If Smart Touch only made Excel DVDs, it could *avoid* the production camera cost. However, if Smart Touch makes any specialty DVDs, it needs the camera. In this case, the fixed costs become relevant because they differ between alternative product mixes (specialty DVDs only *versus* Excel DVDs only, or both products).

Notice that the analysis again follows the two guidelines for special business decisions: (1) focus on relevant data (only those revenues and costs that differ) and (2) use a contribution margin approach, which separates variable from fixed costs.

Outsourcing and Sell as Is or Process Further Decisions

 Make outsourcing and sell as is or process further decisions

Now let's consider other management decisions, such as whether the company should outsource or sell a product as it is or process it further. We'll start with outsourcing decisions.

When to Outsource

Delta outsources much of its reservation work and airplane maintenance. **IBM** outsources most of its desktop production of personal computers. Make-or-buy decisions are often called outsourcing decisions because managers must decide whether to buy a component product or service, or produce it in-house. The heart of these decisions is *how best to use available resources*.

How do managers make outsourcing decisions? Greg's Tunes, a manufacturer of music CDs, is deciding whether to make the paper liners for the CD cases in-house or whether to outsource them to Becky's Box Designs, a company that specializes in producing paper liners. Greg's Tunes' cost to produce 250,000 liners is as follows:

	Total Cost (250,000 liners)
Direct materials..	$ 40,000
Direct labor...	20,000
Variable manufacturing overhead	15,000
Fixed manufacturing overhead..............................	50,000
Total manufacturing cost	$125,000
Number of liners..	÷ 250,000
Cost per liner	$ 0.50

Becky's Box Designs offers to sell Greg's Tunes the liners for $0.37 each. Should Greg's Tunes make the liners or buy them from Becky's Box Designs? Greg's Tunes' $0.50 cost per unit to make the liner is $0.13 higher than the cost of buying it from Becky's Box Designs. Initially, it seems that Greg's Tunes should outsource the liners. But the correct answer is not so simple. Why? Because manufacturing unit costs contain both fixed and variable components. In deciding whether to outsource, managers must assess fixed and variable costs separately. Exhibit 20-21 shows some of the questions managers must consider when deciding whether to outsource.

EXHIBIT 20-21 | **Outsourcing Considerations**

- How do the company's variable costs compare to the outsourcing cost?

- Are any fixed costs avoidable if the company outsources?

- What could the company do with the freed manufacturing capacity?

How do these considerations apply to Greg's Tunes? By purchasing the liners, Greg's Tunes can avoid all variable manufacturing costs—$40,000 of direct materials, $20,000 of direct labor, and $15,000 of variable manufacturing overhead. In total, the company will save $75,000 in variable manufacturing costs, or $0.30 per liner ($75,000 ÷ 250,000 liners). However, Greg's Tunes will have to pay the variable outsourcing price of $0.37 per unit, or $92,500 for the 250,000 liners. Based only on variable costs, the lower cost alternative is to manufacture the liners in-house. However, managers must still consider fixed costs.

Assume first that Greg's Tunes cannot avoid any of the fixed costs by outsourcing. In this case, the company's fixed costs are irrelevant to the decision because Greg's Tunes would continue to incur $50,000 of fixed costs either way (the fixed costs do not differ between alternatives). Greg's Tunes should continue to make its own liners because the variable cost of outsourcing the liners, $92,500, exceeds the variable cost of making the liners, $75,000.

However, what if Greg's Tunes can avoid some fixed costs by outsourcing the liners? Assume that management can reduce fixed overhead cost by $10,000 by outsourcing the liners. Greg's Tunes will still incur $40,000 of fixed overhead ($50,000 – $10,000) if it outsources the liners. In this case, fixed costs become relevant to the decision because they differ between alternatives. Exhibit 20-22 shows the differences in costs between the make and buy alternatives under this scenario.

EXHIBIT 20-22 | **Incremental Analysis for Outsourcing Decision**

Liner Costs	Make Liners	Buy Liners	Difference
Variable costs:			
Direct materials	$ 40,000	—	$40,000
Direct labor	20,000	—	20,000
Variable overhead	15,000	—	15,000
Purchase cost from Becky's			
(250,000 × $0.37)	—	$ 92,500	(92,500)
Fixed overhead	50,000	40,000	10,000
Total cost of liners	$125,000	$132,500	$ (7,500)

Exhibit 20-22 shows that even with the $10,000 reduction in fixed costs, it would still cost Greg's Tunes less to make the liners than to buy them from Becky's Box Designs. The net savings from making 250,000 liners is $7,500. Exhibit 20-22 also shows that outsourcing decisions follow our two key guidelines for special business decisions: (1) Focus on relevant data (differences in costs in this case) and (2) use a contribution margin approach that separates variable costs from fixed costs.

Note how the unit cost—which does *not* separate costs according to behavior—can be deceiving. If Greg's Tunes' managers made their decision by comparing the total manufacturing cost per liner ($0.50) to the outsourcing unit cost per liner ($0.37), they would have incorrectly decided to outsource. Recall that the manufacturing unit cost ($0.50) contains both fixed and variable components, whereas the outsourcing cost ($0.37) is strictly variable. To make the correct decision, Greg's Tunes had to separate the two cost components and analyze them separately.

Our decision rule for outsourcing is as follows:

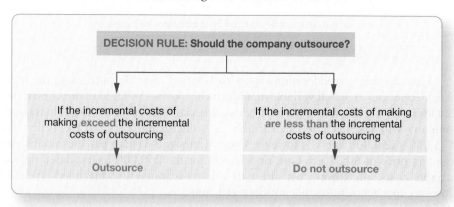

We have not considered what Greg's Tunes could do with the freed manufacturing capacity it would have if it outsourced the liners. The analysis in Exhibit 20-22 assumes there is no other use for the production facilities if Greg's Tunes buys the liners from Becky's Box Designs. But suppose Greg's Tunes has an opportunity to use its freed-up facilities to make more CDs, which have an expected profit of $18,000. Now, Greg's Tunes must consider its **opportunity cost**—the benefit given up by not choosing an alternative course of action. In this case, Greg's Tunes' opportunity cost of making the liners is the $18,000 profit it gives up if it does not free its production facilities to make the additional CDs.

How do Greg's Tunes' managers decide among three alternatives?

1. Use the facilities to make the liners.

2. Buy the liners and leave facilities idle (continue to assume $10,000 of avoidable fixed costs from outsourcing liners).

3. Buy the liners and use facilities to make more CDs (continue to assume $10,000 of avoidable fixed costs from outsourcing liners).

The alternative with the lowest *net* cost is the best use of Greg's Tunes' facilities. Exhibit 20-23 compares the three alternatives.

EXHIBIT 20-23 | **Best Use of Facilities, Given Opportunity Costs**

		Buy Liners	
	Make Liners	Facilities Idle	Make Additional CDs
Expected cost of 250,000 liners (From Exhibit 20-22)	$125,000	$132,500	$132,500
Expected *profit* from additional CDs	—	—	(18,000)
Expected net cost of obtaining 250,000 liners	$125,000	$132,500	$114,500

Greg's Tunes should buy the liners from Becky's Box Designs and use the freed manufacturing capacity to make more CDs. If Greg's Tunes makes the liners, or if it buys the liners from Becky's Box Designs but leaves its production facilities idle, it will give up the opportunity to earn $18,000.

Greg's Tunes' managers should consider qualitative factors as well as revenue and cost differences in making their final decision. For example, Greg's Tunes' managers may believe they can better control quality by making the liners themselves. This is an argument for Greg's to continue making the liners.

Stop & Think...

Assume you purchase a new desk for your room. The desk requires assembly. You can choose to either put the desk together yourself or pay someone (outsource) to put the desk together for you. If you choose to pay someone to put the desk together for you, what can you do with the time you save? Maybe you can put in a few extra hours at your job and earn more than what you'll pay to have your desk put together. This is similar to the outsourcing decision—by focusing on doing what jobs you do best (your job versus putting together a desk), your overall financial position is better.

Outsourcing decisions are increasingly important in today's globally wired economy. In the past, make-or-buy decisions often ended up as "make" because coordination, information exchange, and paperwork problems made buying from suppliers too inconvenient. Now, companies can use the Internet to tap into information systems of suppliers and customers located around the world. Paperwork vanishes, and information required to satisfy the strictest JIT delivery schedule is available in real time. As a result, companies are focusing on their core competencies and are outsourcing more functions.

Sell As Is or Process Further?

At what point in processing should a company sell its product? Many companies, especially in the food processing and natural resource industries, face this business decision. Companies in these industries process a raw material (milk, corn, livestock, crude oil, lumber, to name a few) to a point before it is saleable. For example, **Kraft** pasteurizes raw milk before it is saleable. **Kraft** must then decide whether it should sell the pasteurized milk "as is" or process it further into other dairy products (reduced-fat milk, butter, sour cream, cheese, and other dairy products). Managers consider the questions shown in Exhibit 20-24 when deciding whether to sell as is or process further.

EXHIBIT 20-24 | **Sell As Is or Process Further Considerations**

- How much revenue will the company receive if we sell the product as is?

- How much revenue will the company receive if the company sells the product after processing it further?

- How much will it cost to process the product further?

Consider one of **Chevron**'s sell as is or process further decisions. Suppose **Chevron** spent $125,000 to process crude oil into 50,000 gallons of regular gasoline, as shown in Exhibit 20-25. After processing crude oil into regular gasoline, should **Chevron** sell the regular gas as is or should it spend more to process the gasoline into premium grade? In making the decision, **Chevron**'s managers consider the following relevant information:

EXHIBIT 20-25 | **Sell As Is or Process Further Decision**

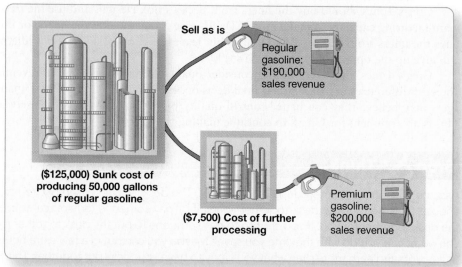

- **Chevron** could sell premium gasoline for $4.00 per gallon, for a total of $200,000 (50,000 × $4.00).

- **Chevron** could sell regular gasoline for $3.80 per gallon, for a total of $190,000 (50,000 × $3.80).

- **Chevron** would have to spend $0.15 per gallon, or $7,500 (50,000 gallons × $0.15), to further process regular gasoline into premium-grade gas.

Notice that **Chevron**'s managers do *not* consider the $125,000 spent on processing crude oil into regular gasoline. Why? It is a *sunk* cost. Recall from our previous discussion that a sunk cost is a past cost that cannot be changed regardless of which future action the company takes. **Chevron** has incurred $125,000—regardless of whether it sells the regular gasoline as is or processes it further into premium gasoline. Therefore, the cost is *not* relevant to the decision.

By analyzing only the relevant costs in Exhibit 20-26, managers see that they can increase profit by $2,500 if they convert the regular gasoline into premium gasoline. The $10,000 extra revenue ($200,000 − $190,000) outweighs the incremental $7,500 cost of the extra processing.

EXHIBIT 20-26 | **Incremental Analysis for Sell As Is or Process Further Decision**

	Sell As Is	Process Further	Difference
Expected revenue from selling 50,000 gallons of regular gasoline at $3.80 per gallon	$190,000		
Expected revenue from selling 50,000 gallons of premium gasoline at $4.00 per gallon		$200,000	$10,000
Additional costs of $0.15 per gallon to convert 50,000 gallons of regular gasoline into premium gasoline		(7,500)	(7,500)
Total net revenue	$190,000	$192,500	$ 2,500

Thus, the decision rule is as follows:

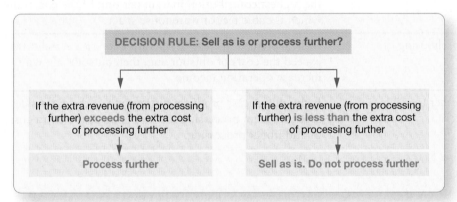

Recall that our keys to decision making include (1) focusing on relevant information and (2) using a contribution margin approach that separates variable costs from fixed costs. The analysis in Exhibit 20-26 includes only those *future* costs and revenues that *differ* between alternatives. We assumed **Chevron** already has the equipment and labor necessary to convert regular gasoline into premium grade gasoline. Because fixed costs would not differ between alternatives, they were irrelevant. However, if **Chevron** has to acquire equipment or hire employees to convert the gasoline into premium grade gasoline, the extra fixed costs would be relevant. Once again, we see that fixed costs are only relevant if they *differ* between alternatives.

Next, take some time to review the Decision Guidelines for short-term business decisions on the next page.

Key Takeaway

When a company is considering outsourcing, if the incremental costs of making the product exceed the incremental costs of outsourcing, then the company should outsource the product. When a company is considering selling a product as is or processing it further, if the extra revenue from processing the product further exceeds the extra costs to process the product further, then the company should process the product further.

Decision Guidelines 20-2

SHORT-TERM SPECIAL BUSINESS DECISIONS

Amazon.com has confronted most of the special business decisions we have covered in this chapter. Here are the key guidelines Amazon.com's managers follow in making their decisions.

Decision	Guidelines
• Should **Amazon** drop its electronics product line?	If the cost savings exceed the lost revenues from dropping the electronics product line, then dropping the product will increase operating income.
• Given limited warehouse space, which products should **Amazon** focus on selling?	**Amazon.com** should focus on selling the products with the highest contribution margin per unit of the constraint, which is cubic feet of warehouse space.
• Should **Amazon** outsource its warehousing operations?	If the incremental costs of operating its own warehouses exceed the costs of outsourcing, then outsourcing will increase operating income.
• How should **Amazon** decide whether to sell a product as is or process it further?	It should process products further only if the extra sales revenue (from processing further) exceeds the extra costs of additional processing.

Summary Problem 20-2

Shelly's Shades produces standard and deluxe sunglasses:

	Standard	Deluxe
Sale price per pair...	$20	$30
Variable expenses per pair.............................	16	21

The company has 15,000 machine hours available. In one machine hour, Shelly's can produce 70 pairs of the standard model or 30 pairs of the deluxe model.

Requirements

1. Which model should Shelly's emphasize?
2. Shelly's incurs the following costs for 20,000 of its hiking shades:

Direct materials..	$ 20,000
Direct labor...	80,000
Variable manufacturing overhead	40,000
Fixed manufacturing overhead...	80,000
Total manufacturing cost	$220,000
Cost per pair ($220,000 ÷ 20,000).................................	$ 11

Another manufacturer has offered to sell similar shades to Shelly's for $10, a total purchase cost of $200,000. If Shelly's outsources *and* leaves its plant idle, it can save $50,000 of fixed overhead cost. Or, it can use the freed manufacturing facilities to make other products that will contribute $70,000 to profits. In this case, the company will not be able to avoid any fixed costs. Identify and analyze the alternatives. What is the best course of action?

Solution

Requirement 1

	Standard	Deluxe
Sale price per pair...	$ 20	$ 30
Variable expense per pair.............................	16	21
Contribution margin per pair.........................	$ 4	$ 9
Units produced each machine hour	× 70	× 30
Contribution margin per machine hour.........	$ 280	$ 270
Capacity—number of machine hours	× 15,000	× 15,000
Total contribution margin at full capacity	$4,200,000	$4,050,000

Decision: Emphasize the standard model because it has the higher contribution margin per unit of the constraint—machine hours.

Requirement 2

	Make Shades	Buy Shades	
		Facilities Idle	Make Other Products
Relevant costs:			
Direct materials	$ 20,000	—	—
Direct labor	80,000	—	—
Variable overhead...........................	40,000	—	—
Fixed overhead	80,000	$ 30,000	$ 80,000
Purchase cost (20,000 × $10)........	—	200,000	200,000
Total cost of obtaining shades	220,000	230,000	280,000
Profit from other products.............	—	—	(70,000)
Net cost of obtaining shades	$220,000	$230,000	$210,000

Decision: Shelly's should buy the shades from the outside supplier and use the freed manufacturing facilities to make other products.

Review *Short-Term Business Decisions*

● Accounting Vocabulary

Constraint (p. 980)
A factor that restricts production or sale of a product.

Incremental Analysis Approach (p. 965)
A method that looks at how operating income would *differ* under each decision alternative. Leaves out irrelevant information—the costs and revenues that will not differ between alternatives. Also called the **relevant information approach.**

Irrelevant Costs (p. 964)
Costs that *do not* affect a decision.

Opportunity Cost (p. 984)
The benefit given up by not choosing an alternative course of action.

Outsourcing (p. 964)
The decision to buy or subcontract a component product or service rather than produce it in-house.

Relevant Costs (p. 963)
Costs that *do* affect a decision.

Relevant Information (p. 963)
Expected *future* data that *differs* among alternatives.

Relevant Information Approach (p. 965)
A method that looks at how operating income would *differ* under each decision alternative. Leaves out irrelevant information—the costs and revenues that will not differ between alternatives. Also called the **incremental analysis approach.**

Sunk Cost (p. 964)
A past cost that cannot be changed regardless of which future action is taken.

Target Full Product Cost (p. 970)
The total cost in developing, producing, and delivering a product or service.

● Destination: Student Success

Student Success Tips

The following are hints on some common trouble areas for students in this chapter:

● Remember the difference between relevant costs, irrelevant costs, and sunk costs.

● Keep in mind the two keys to short-term special decisions: Focus on relevant revenues, costs, and profits; and use a contribution margin approach that separates variable and fixed costs.

● Recall the special sales order considerations in Exhibit 20-4 and the incremental analysis approach used to analyze these special orders.

● Consider the difference between price-setters and price-takers. Companies are price-setters when they have more control over pricing because their product is unique—that is, they can "set" the price. Companies are price-takers when the competition is intense and the product is not unique.

● Recall the considerations for dropping product lines, departments, or territories in Exhibit 20-13.

● Remember the considerations for outsourcing a function or component: How will variable and/or fixed costs change? What can the company do with the freed manufacturing capacity? If the incremental costs of making the product exceed the incremental costs of outsourcing, then the company should outsource the product.

● Keep in mind that when a company is considering selling a product as is or processing it further, if the extra revenue from processing the product further exceeds the extra costs to process the product further, then the company should process the product further.

Getting Help

If there's a learning objective from the chapter you aren't confident about, try using one or more of the following resources:

● Review the Decision Guidelines 20-1 in the chapter.

● Review Summary Problem 20-1 in the chapter to reinforce your understanding of make or buy decisions.

● Review Summary Problem 20-2 in the chapter to reinforce your understanding of production constraints.

● Practice additional exercises or problems at the end of Chapter 20 that cover the specific learning objective that is challenging you.

● Watch the white board videos for Chapter 20 located at myaccountinglab.com under the Chapter Resources button.

● Go to myaccountinglab.com and select the Study Plan button. Choose Chapter 20 and work the questions covering that specific learning objective until you've mastered it.

● Work the Chapter 20 pre/post tests in myaccountinglab.com.

● Consult the Check Figures for End of Chapter starters, exercises, and problems, located at myaccountinglab.com.

● Visit the learning resource center on your campus for tutoring.

● Quick Check

1. In making short-term special decisions, you should
   a. use a traditional absorption costing approach.
   b. focus on total costs.
   c. separate variable from fixed costs.
   d. only focus on quantitative factors.

2. Which of the following is relevant to Kitchenware.com's decision to accept a special order at a lower sale price from a large customer in China?
   a. The cost of shipping the order to the customer
   b. The cost of Kitchenware.com's warehouses in the United States
   c. Founder Eric Crowley's salary
   d. Kitchenware.com's investment in its Web site

3. Which of the following costs are irrelevant to business decisions?
   a. Avoidable costs   c. Sunk costs
   b. Costs that differ between alternatives   d. Variable costs

4. When making decisions, managers should consider
   a. revenues that differ between alternatives.
   b. costs that do not differ between alternatives.
   c. only variable costs.
   d. sunk costs in their decisions.

5. When pricing a product or service, managers must consider which of the following?
   a. Only period costs   c. Only variable costs
   b. Only manufacturing costs   d. All costs

6. When companies are price-setters, their products and services
   a. are priced by managers using a target-pricing emphasis.
   b. tend to have a lot of competitors.
   c. tend to be commodities.
   d. tend to be unique.

7. In deciding whether to drop its electronics product line, Kitchenware.com would consider
   a. how dropping the electronics product line would affect sales of its other products like CDs.
   b. the costs it could save by dropping the product line.
   c. the revenues it would lose from dropping the product line.
   d. All of the above

8. In deciding which product lines to emphasize, Kitchenware.com should focus on the product line that has the highest
   a. contribution margin per unit of product.
   b. contribution margin per unit of the constraining factor.
   c. profit per unit of product.
   d. contribution margin ratio.

9. When making outsourcing decisions
   a. expected use of the freed capacity is irrelevant.
   b. the variable cost of producing the product in-house is relevant.
   c. the total manufacturing unit cost of making the product in-house is relevant.
   d. avoidable fixed costs are irrelevant.

10. When deciding whether to sell as is or process a product further, managers should ignore which of the following?

  a. The costs of processing the product thus far

  b. The cost of processing further

  c. The revenue if the product is sold as is

  d. The revenue if the product is processed further

Answers are given after Apply Your Knowledge (p. 1009).

Assess Your Progress

● Short Exercises

S20-1 **❶ Describing and identifying information relevant to business decisions [5 min]**

MyAccountingLab

You are trying to decide whether to trade in your inkjet printer for a more recent model. Your usage pattern will remain unchanged, but the old and new printers use different ink cartridges.

Requirement

1. Indicate if the following items are relevant or irrelevant to your decision:

   a. The price of the new printer
   b. The price you paid for the old printer
   c. The trade-in value of the old printer
   d. Paper costs
   e. The difference between ink cartridges' costs

S20-2 **❷ Making special order and pricing decisions [10 min]**

Mount Snow operates a Rocky Mountain ski resort. The company is planning its lift ticket pricing for the coming ski season. Investors would like to earn a 16% return on the company's $109,375,000 of assets. The company primarily incurs fixed costs to groom the runs and operate the lifts. Mount Snow projects fixed costs to be $35,000,000 for the ski season. The resort serves about 700,000 skiers and snowboarders each season. Variable costs are about $12 per guest. Currently, the resort has such a favorable reputation among skiers and snowboarders that it has some control over the lift ticket prices.

Requirements

1. Would Mount Snow emphasize target pricing or cost-plus pricing. Why?

2. If other resorts in the area charge $83 per day, what price should Mount Snow charge?

Note: Short Exercise 20-2 must be completed before attempting Short Exercise 20-3.

S20-3 **❷ Making special order and pricing decisions [10 min]**

Consider Mount Snow from Short Exercise 20-2. Assume that Mount Snow's reputation has diminished and other resorts in the vicinity are only charging $80 per lift ticket. Mount Snow has become a price-taker and will not be able to charge more than its competitors. At the market price, Mount Snow managers believe they will still serve 700,000 skiers and snowboarders each season.

Requirements

1. If Mount Snow cannot reduce its costs, what profit will it earn? State your answer in dollars and as a percent of assets. Will investors be happy with the profit level?

2. Assume Mount Snow has found ways to cut its fixed costs to $32,900,000. What is its new target variable cost per skier/snowboarder?

S20-4 **③ Making dropping a product and product-mix decisions [5–10 min]**

Deela Fashions operates three departments: Men's, Women's, and Accessories. Departmental operating income data for the third quarter of 2012 are as follows:

DEELA FASHIONS				
Income Statement				
For the quarter ended September 30, 2012				
	Department			
	Men's	Women's	Accessories	Total
Sales revenue	$ 108,000	$ 55,000	$ 100,000	$ 263,000
Variable expenses	58,000	30,000	92,000	180,000
Fixed expenses	26,000	21,000	26,000	73,000
Total expenses	84,000	51,000	118,000	253,000
Operating income (loss)	$ 24,000	$ 4,000	$ (18,000)	$ 10,000

Assume that the fixed expenses assigned to each department include only direct fixed costs of the department:

- Salary of the department's manager
- Cost of advertising directly related to that department

If Deela Fashions drops a department, it will not incur these fixed expenses.

Requirement

1. Under these circumstances, should Deela Fashions drop any of the departments? Give your reasoning.

S20-5 **③ Making dropping a product and product-mix decisions [15 min]**

StoreAll produces plastic storage bins for household storage needs. The company makes two sizes of bins: large (50 gallon) and regular (35 gallon). Demand for the product is so high that StoreAll can sell as many of each size as it can produce. The company uses the same machinery to produce both sizes. The machinery can only be run for 3,300 hours per period. StoreAll can produce 9 large bins every hour, whereas it can produce 15 regular bins in the same amount of time. Fixed costs amount to $110,000 per period. Sales prices and variable costs are as follows:

	Regular	Large
Sales price per unit...................................	$9.00	$10.80
Variable cost per unit..............................	$3.10	$ 4.20

Requirements

1. Which product should StoreAll emphasize? Why?
2. To maximize profits, how many of each size bin should StoreAll produce?
3. Given this product mix, what will the company's operating income be?

S20-6 **④ Making outsourcing and sell as is or process further decisions [10 min]**

Suppose a Roasted Olive restaurant is considering whether to (1) bake bread for its restaurant in-house or (2) buy the bread from a local bakery. The chef estimates that variable costs of making each loaf include $0.52 of ingredients, $0.24 of variable overhead (electricity to run the oven), and $0.70 of direct labor for kneading and forming the loaves. Allocating fixed overhead (depreciation on the kitchen equipment and building) based on direct labor assigns $0.96 of fixed overhead per loaf. None of the fixed costs are avoidable. The local bakery would charge $1.75 per loaf.

Requirements

1. What is the unit cost of making the bread in-house (use absorption costing)?
2. Should Roasted Olive bake the bread in-house or buy from the local bakery? Why?
3. In addition to the financial analysis, what else should Roasted Olive consider when making this decision?

S20-7 **④ Making outsourcing decisions [10–15 min]**

Priscilla Nailey manages a fleet of 375 delivery trucks for Jones Corporation. Nailey must decide if the company should outsource the fleet management function. If she outsources to Fleet Management Services (FMS), FMS will be responsible for maintenance and scheduling activities. This alternative would require Nailey to lay off her five employees. However, her own job would be secure; she would be Jones's liaison with FMS. If she continues to manage the fleet she will need fleet-management software that costs $8,250 a year to lease. FMS offers to manage this fleet for an annual fee of $285,000. Nailey performed the following analysis:

JONES CORPORATION			
Outsourcing Decision Analysis			
	Retain In-House	Outsource to FMS	Difference
Annual leasing fee for software	$ 8,250	$ —	$ 8,250
Annual maintenance of trucks	147,000	—	147,000
Total annual salaries of five other fleet management employees	175,000	—	175,000
Fleet Management Services' annual fee	—	285,000	(285,000)
Total cost / cost savings	$ 330,250	$ 285,000	$ 45,250

Requirements

1. Which alternative will maximize Jones's short-term operating income?
2. What qualitative factors should Jones consider before making a final decision?

S20-8 **④ Sell as is or process further decisions [10 min]**

Cocoaheaven processes cocoa beans into cocoa powder at a processing cost of $9,500 per batch. Cocoaheaven can sell the cocoa powder as is or it can process the cocoa powder further into either chocolate syrup or boxed assorted chocolates. Once processed, each batch of cocoa beans would result in the following sales revenue:

Cocoa powder..	$ 16,500
Chocolate syrup	$102,000
Boxed assorted chocolates.......................	$196,000

The cost of transforming the cocoa powder into chocolate syrup would be $70,000. Likewise, the company would incur a cost of $176,000 to transform the cocoa powder into boxed assorted chocolates. The company president has decided to make boxed assorted chocolates due to its high sales value and to the fact that the cocoa bean processing cost of $9,500 eats up most of the cocoa powder profits.

Requirement

1. Has the president made the right or wrong decision? Explain your answer. Be sure to include the correct financial analysis in your response.

Exercises

MyAccountingLab

E20-9   **1** **Describing and identifying information relevant to business decisions [5–10 min]**

Dan Jacobs, production manager for GreenLife, invested in computer-controlled production machinery last year. He purchased the machinery from Superior Design at a cost of $3,000,000. A representative from Superior Design has recently contacted Dan because the company has designed an even more efficient piece of machinery. The new design would double the production output of the year-old machinery but would cost GreenLife another $4,500,000. Jacobs is afraid to bring this new equipment to the company president's attention because he convinced the president to invest $3,000,000 in the machinery last year.

Requirement

1. Explain what is relevant and irrelevant to Jacobs' dilemma. What should he do?

E20-10   **2** **Making special order and pricing decisions [10–15 min]**

Suppose the Baseball Hall of Fame in Cooperstown, New York, has approached Hobby-Cardz with a special order. The Hall of Fame wishes to purchase 57,000 baseball card packs for a special promotional campaign and offers $0.41 per pack, a total of $23,370. Hobby-Cardz's total production cost is $0.61 per pack, as follows:

Variable costs:	
Direct materials	$ 0.13
Direct labor	0.06
Variable overhead	0.12
Fixed overhead	0.30
Total cost	$ 0.61

Hobby-Cardz has enough excess capacity to handle the special order.

Requirements

1. Prepare an incremental analysis to determine whether Hobby-Cardz should accept the special sales order.
2. Now assume that the Hall of Fame wants special hologram baseball cards. Hobby-Cardz will spend $5,900 to develop this hologram, which will be useless after the special order is completed. Should Hobby-Cardz accept the special order under these circumstances?

E20-11   **2** **Making special order and pricing decisions [20–25 min]**

San Jose Sunglasses sell for about $157 per pair. Suppose that the company incurs the following average costs per pair:

Direct materials	$ 39
Direct labor	15
Variable manufacturing overhead	8
Variable marketing expenses	2
Fixed manufacturing overhead	20*
Total cost	$ 84

* $2,200,000 total fixed manufacturing overhead ÷ 110,000 pairs of sunglasses

San Jose has enough idle capacity to accept a one-time-only special order from Washington Shades for 25,000 pairs of sunglasses at $80 per pair. San Jose will not incur any variable marketing expenses for the order.

Requirements

1. How would accepting the order affect San Jose's operating income? In addition to the special order's effect on profits, what other (longer-term qualitative) factors should San Jose's managers consider in deciding whether to accept the order?

2. San Jose's marketing manager, Peter Bing, argues against accepting the special order because the offer price of $80 is less than San Jose's $84 cost to make the sunglasses. Bing asks you, as one of San Jose's staff accountants, to explain whether his analysis is correct.

E20-12 ❷ **Making special order and pricing decisions [10–15 min]**

Stenback Builders builds 1,500 square-foot starter tract homes in the fast-growing suburbs of Atlanta. Land and labor are cheap, and competition among developers is fierce. The homes are a standard model, with any upgrades added by the buyer after the sale. Stenback Builders' costs per developed sub-lot are as follows:

Land	$ 59,000
Construction	$ 124,000
Landscaping	$ 6,000
Variable marketing costs	$ 5,000

Stenback Builders would like to earn a profit of 14% of the variable cost of each home sale. Similar homes offered by competing builders sell for $208,000 each.

Requirements

1. Which approach to pricing should Stenback Builders emphasize? Why?

2. Will Stenback Builders be able to achieve its target profit levels?

3. Bathrooms and kitchens are typically the most important selling features of a home. Stenback Builders could differentiate the homes by upgrading the bathrooms and kitchens. The upgrades would cost $22,000 per home but would enable Stenback Builders to increase the selling prices by $38,500 per home. (Kitchen and bathroom upgrades typically add about 175% of their cost to the value of any home.) If Stenback Builders makes the upgrades, what will the new cost-plus price per home be? Should the company differentiate its product in this manner?

E20-13 ❸ **Making dropping a product and product-mix decisions [10 min]**

Top managers of Movie Street are alarmed by their operating losses. They are considering dropping the VCR-tape product line. Company accountants have prepared the following analysis to help make this decision:

			DVD	VCR
		Total	Discs	Tapes
Sales revenue	$	432,000	$ 305,000	$ 127,000
Variable expenses		246,000	150,000	96,000
Contribution margin	$	186,000	$ 155,000	$ 31,000
Fixed expenses:				
Manufacturing		128,000	71,000	57,000
Marketing and administrative		67,000	52,000	15,000
Total fixed expenses		195,000	123,000	72,000
Operating income (loss)	$	(9,000)	$ 32,000	$ (41,000)

MOVIE STREET
Income Statement
For the Year Ended December 31, 2012

Total fixed costs will not change if the company stops selling VCR tapes.

Requirement

1. Prepare an incremental analysis to show whether Movie Street should drop the VCR-tape product line. Will dropping VCR tapes add $41,000 to operating income? Explain.

Note: Exercise 20-13 must be completed before attempting Exercise 20-14.

E20-14 ❸ **Making dropping a product and product-mix decisions [10 min]**
Refer to Exercise 20-13. Assume that Movie Street can avoid $41,000 of fixed expenses by dropping the VCR-tape product line (these costs are direct fixed costs of the VCR product line).

Requirement

1. Prepare an incremental analysis to show whether Movie Street should stop selling VCR tapes.

E20-15 ❸ **Product mix under production constraints [15 min]**
Lifemaster produces two types of exercise treadmills: regular and deluxe. The exercise craze is such that Lifemaster could use all its available machine hours to produce either model. The two models are processed through the same production departments. Data for both models is as follows:

	Per Unit	
	Deluxe	Regular
Sale price	$ 1,020	$ 560
Costs:		
Direct materials	300	90
Direct labor	88	188
Variable manufacturing overhead	264	88
Fixed manufacturing overhead*	138	46
Variable operating expenses	111	65
Total cost	901	477
Operating income	$ 119	$ 83

*Allocated on the basis of machine hours.

Requirements

1. What is the constraint?
2. Which model should Lifemaster produce? (*Hint:* Use the allocation of fixed manufacturing overhead to determine the proportion of machine hours used by each product.)
3. If Lifemaster should produce both models, compute the mix that will maximize operating income.

E20-16 ❸ **Making dropping a product and product-mix decisions [10–15 min]**
Klintan sells both designer and moderately priced fashion accessories. Top management is deciding which product line to emphasize. Accountants have provided the following data:

	Per Item	
	Designer	Moderately Priced
Average sale price	$ 210	$ 81
Average variable expenses	90	26
Average contribution margin	$ 120	$ 55
Average fixed expenses (allocated)	15	5
Average operating income	$ 105	$ 50

The Klintan store in Grand Junction, Colorado, has 9,000 square feet of floor space. If Klintan emphasizes moderately priced goods, it can display 630 items in the store.

If Klintan emphasizes designer wear, it can only display 270 designer items. These numbers are also the average monthly sales in units.

Requirement

1. Prepare an analysis to show which product the company should emphasize.

E20-17   **③ Making dropping a product and product-mix decisions [15–20 min]**
Each morning, Ned Stenback stocks the drink case at Ned's Beach Hut in Myrtle Beach, South Carolina. The drink case has 115 linear feet of refrigerated drink space. Each linear foot can hold either six 12-ounce cans or three 20-ounce bottles.

Ned's Beach Hut sells three types of cold drinks:
1. Yummy Time in 12-oz. cans, for $1.45 per can
2. Yummy Time in 20-oz. bottles, for $1.75 per bottle
3. Pretty Pop in 20-oz. bottles, for $2.30 per bottle

Ned's Beach Hut pays its suppliers:
1. $0.15 per 12-oz. can of Yummy Time
2. $0.35 per 20-oz. bottle of Yummy Time
3. $0.65 per 20-oz. bottle of Pretty Pop

Ned's Beach Hut's monthly fixed expenses include:

Hut rental	$	360
Refrigerator rental		80
Ned's salary		1,500
Total fixed expenses	$	1,940

Ned's Beach Hut can sell all the drinks stocked in the display case each morning.

Requirements

1. What is Ned's Beach Hut's constraining factor? What should Ned stock to maximize profits?

2. Suppose Ned's Beach Hut refuses to devote more than 75 linear feet to any individual product. Under this condition, how many linear feet of each drink should Ned's stock? How many units of each product will be available for sale each day?

E20-18   **④ Making outsourcing decisions [10–15 min]**
Fiber Systems manufactures an optical switch that it uses in its final product. The switch has the following manufacturing costs per unit:

Direct materials	$ 9.00
Direct labor	1.50
Variable overhead	5.00
Fixed overhead	9.00
Manufacturing product cost	$ 24.50

Another company has offered to sell Fiber Systems the switch for $18.50 per unit. If Fiber Systems buys the switch from the outside supplier, the manufacturing facilities that will be idled cannot be used for any other purpose, yet none of the fixed costs are avoidable.

Requirement

1. Prepare an outsourcing analysis to determine if Fiber Systems should make or buy the switch.

Note: Exercise 20-18 must be completed before attempting Exercise 20-19.

E20-19   **④ Making outsourcing decisions [10–15 min]**
Refer to Exercise 20-18. Fiber Systems needs 84,000 optical switches. By outsourcing them, Fiber Systems can use its idle facilities to manufacture another product that will contribute $253,000 to operating income.

Requirements

1. Identify the *incremental* costs that Fiber Systems will incur to acquire 84,000 switches under three alternative plans.

2. Which plan makes the best use of Fiber System's facilities? Support your answer.

E20-20 **④ Making sell as is or process further decisions [10 min]**

Naturalmaid processes organic milk into plain yogurt. Naturalmaid sells plain yogurt to hospitals, nursing homes, and restaurants in bulk, one-gallon containers. Each batch, processed at a cost of $800, yields 600 gallons of plain yogurt. Naturalmaid sells the one-gallon tubs for $7 each and spends $0.16 for each plastic tub. Naturalmaid has recently begun to reconsider its strategy. Naturalmaid wonders if it would be more profitable to sell individual-size portions of fruited organic yogurt at local food stores. Naturalmaid could further process each batch of plain yogurt into 12,800 individual portions (3/4 cup each) of fruited yogurt. A recent market analysis indicates that demand for the product exists. Naturalmaid would sell each individual portion for $0.54. Packaging would cost $0.07 per portion, and fruit would cost $0.11 per portion. Fixed costs would not change.

Requirement

1. Should Naturalmaid continue to sell only the gallon-size plain yogurt (sell as is), or convert the plain yogurt into individual-size portions of fruited yogurt (process further)? Why?

● Problems (Group A)

P20-21A ① ② Identifying which information is relevant, and making special order and pricing decisions [15–20 min]

Buoy manufactures flotation vests in Charleston, South Carolina. Buoy's contribution margin income statement for the month ended December 31, 2012, contains the following data:

BUOY	
Income Statement	
For the Month Ended December 31, 2012	
Sales in units	32,000
Sales revenue	$ 544,000
Variable expenses:	
Manufacturing	96,000
Marketing and administrative	110,000
Total variable expenses	$ 206,000
Contribution margin	$ 338,000
Fixed expenses:	
Manufacturing	127,000
Marketing and administrative	95,000
Total fixed expenses	$ 222,000
Operating income	$ 116,000

Suppose Overboard wishes to buy 3,900 vests from Buoy. Acceptance of the order will not increase Buoy's variable marketing and administrative expenses. The Buoy plant has enough unused capacity to manufacture the additional vests. Overboard has offered $8.00 per vest, which is below the normal sale price of $17.

Requirements

1. Identify each cost in the income statement as either relevant or irrelevant to Buoy's decision.

2. Prepare an incremental analysis to determine whether Buoy should accept this special sales order.

3. Identify long-term factors Buoy should consider in deciding whether to accept the special sales order.

P20-22A ❷ **Making special order and pricing decisions [15–20 min]**

Green Thumb operates a commercial plant nursery where it propagates plants for garden centers throughout the region. Green Thumb has $4,800,000 in assets. Its yearly fixed costs are $600,000, and the variable costs for the potting soil, container, label, seedling, and labor for each gallon-size plant total $1.35. Green Thumb's volume is currently 470,000 units. Competitors offer the same plants, at the same quality, to garden centers for $3.60 each. Garden centers then mark them up to sell to the public for $9 to $12, depending on the type of plant.

Requirements

1. Green Thumb's owners want to earn a 10% return on the company's assets. What is Green Thumb's target full cost?

2. Given Green Thumb's current costs, will its owners be able to achieve their target profit?

3. Assume Green Thumb has identified ways to cut its variable costs to $1.20 per unit. What is its new target fixed cost? Will this decrease in variable costs allow the company to achieve its target profit?

4. Green Thumb started an aggressive advertising campaign strategy to differentiate its plants from those grown by other nurseries. Monrovia Plants made this strategy work so Green Thumb has decided to try it, too. Green Thumb does not expect volume to be affected, but it hopes to gain more control over pricing. If Green Thumb has to spend $115,000 this year to advertise, and its variable costs continue to be $1.20 per unit, what will its cost-plus price be? Do you think Green Thumb will be able to sell its plants to garden centers at the cost-plus price? Why or why not?

P20-23A ❸ **Making dropping a product and product-mix decisions [20–25 min]**

Members of the board of directors of Safe Zone have received the following operating income data for the year ended May 31, 2012:

		SAFE ZONE		
		Income Statement		
		For the Year Ended May 31, 2012		
		Product Line		
		Industrial Systems	Household Systems	Total
Sales revenue		$ 370,000	$ 390,000	$ 760,000
Cost of goods sold:				
Variable		36,000	42,000	78,000
Fixed		260,000	65,000	325,000
Total cost of goods sold		$ 296,000	$ 107,000	$ 403,000
Gross profit		$ 74,000	$ 283,000	$ 357,000
Marketing and administrative expenses:				
Variable		66,000	75,000	141,000
Fixed		44,000	24,000	68,000
Total marketing and administrative exp.		$ 110,000	$ 99,000	$ 209,000
Operating income (loss)		$ (36,000)	$ 184,000	$ 148,000

Members of the board are surprised that the industrial systems product line is losing money. They commission a study to determine whether the company should drop the line. Company accountants estimate that dropping industrial systems will decrease fixed cost of goods sold by $84,000 and decrease fixed marketing and administrative expenses by $14,000.

Requirements

1. Prepare an incremental analysis to show whether Safe Zone should drop the industrial systems product line.

2. Prepare contribution margin income statements to show Safe Zone's total operating income under the two alternatives: (a) with the industrial systems line and (b) without the line. Compare the *difference* between the two alternatives' income numbers to your answer to Requirement 1.

3. What have you learned from the comparison in Requirement 2?

P20-24A ❸ **Making dropping a product and product-mix decisions [10–15 min]**

Brik, located in Port St. Lucie, Florida, produces two lines of electric toothbrushes: deluxe and standard. Because Brik can sell all the toothbrushes it can produce, the owners are expanding the plant. They are deciding which product line to emphasize. To make this decision, they assemble the following data:

	Per Unit	
	Deluxe Toothbrush	Standard Toothbrush
Sale price	$ 88	$ 52
Variable expenses	24	16
Contribution margin	$ 64	$ 36
Contribution margin ratio	72.7%	69.2%

After expansion, the factory will have a production capacity of 4,900 machine hours per month. The plant can manufacture either 60 standard electric toothbrushes or 28 deluxe electric toothbrushes per machine hour.

Requirements

1. Identify the constraining factor for Brik.

2. Prepare an analysis to show which product line to emphasize.

P20-25A ❹ **Making outsourcing decisions [20–30 min]**

Outdoor Life manufactures snowboards. Its cost of making 2,000 bindings is as follows:

Direct materials	$ 17,550
Direct labor	3,400
Variable overhead	2,040
Fixed overhead	6,300
Total manufacturing costs for 2,000 bindings	$ 29,290

Suppose Lancaster will sell bindings to Outdoor Life for $14 each. Outdoor Life would pay $3 per unit to transport the bindings to its manufacturing plant, where it would add its own logo at a cost of $0.70 per binding.

Requirements

1. Outdoor Life's accountants predict that purchasing the bindings from Lancaster will enable the company to avoid $2,100 of fixed overhead. Prepare an analysis to show whether Outdoor Life should make or buy the bindings.

2. The facilities freed by purchasing bindings from Lancaster can be used to manufacture another product that will contribute $2,700 to profit. Total fixed costs will be the same as if Outdoor Life had produced the bindings. Show which alternative makes the best use of Outdoor Life's facilities: (a) make bindings, (b) buy bindings and leave facilities idle, or (c) buy bindings and make another product.

P20-26A ④ **Making sell as is or process further decisions [20–25 min]**
Smith Petroleum has spent $204,000 to refine 62,000 gallons of petroleum distillate, which can be sold for $6.40 a gallon. Alternatively, Smith can process the distillate further and produce 56,000 gallons of cleaner fluid. The additional processing will cost $1.75 per gallon of distillate. The cleaner fluid can be sold for $9.00 a gallon. To sell the cleaner fluid, Smith must pay a sales commission of $0.13 a gallon and a transportation charge of $0.18 a gallon.

Requirements

1. Diagram Smith's decision alternatives, using Exhibit 20-26 as a guide.
2. Identify the sunk cost. Is the sunk cost relevant to Smith's decision?
3. Should Smith sell the petroleum distillate or process it into cleaner fluid? Show the expected net revenue difference between the two alternatives.

● Problems (Group B)

P20-27B ① ② **Identifying which information is relevant, and making special order and pricing decisions [15–20 min]**   *MyAccountingLab*
Safe Sailing manufactures flotation vests in Tampa, Florida. Safe Sailing's contribution margin income statement for the month ended December 31, 2012, contains the following data:

SAFE SAILING	
Income Statement	
For the Month Ended December 31, 2012	
Sales in units	41,000
Sales revenue	$ 820,000
Variable expenses:	
Manufacturing	205,000
Marketing and administrative	105,000
Total variable expenses	$ 310,000
Contribution margin	$ 510,000
Fixed expenses:	
Manufacturing	126,000
Marketing and administrative	91,000
Total fixed expenses	$ 217,000
Operating income	$ 293,000

Suppose Overtown wishes to buy 3,800 vests from Safe Sailing. Acceptance of the order will not increase Safe Sailing's variable marketing and administrative expenses. The Safe Sailing plant has enough unused capacity to manufacture the additional vests. Overtown has offered $12.00 per vest, which is below the normal sale price of $20.00.

Requirements

1. Identify each cost in the income statement as either relevant or irrelevant to Safe Sailing's decision.

2. Prepare an incremental analysis to determine whether Safe Sailing should accept this special sales order.

3. Identify long-term factors Safe Sailing should consider in deciding whether to accept the special sales order.

P20-28B ② **Making special order and pricing decisions [15–20 min]**

Nature Place operates a commercial plant nursery, where it propagates plants for garden centers throughout the region. Nature Place has $5,100,000 in assets. Its yearly fixed costs are $650,000 and the variable costs for the potting soil, container, label, seedling, and labor for each gallon-size plant total $1.40. Nature Place's volume is currently 480,000 units. Competitors offer the same plants, at the same quality, to garden centers for $3.75 each. Garden centers then mark them up to sell to the public for $7 to $10, depending on the type of plant.

Requirements

1. Nature Place's owners want to earn a 11% return on the company's assets. What is Nature Place's target full cost?

2. Given Nature Place's current costs, will its owners be able to achieve their target profit?

3. Assume Nature Place has identified ways to cut its variable costs to $1.25 per unit. What is its new target fixed cost? Will this decrease in variable costs allow the company to achieve its target profit?

4. Nature Place started an aggressive advertising campaign strategy to differentiate its plants from those grown by other nurseries. Monrovia Plants made this strategy work so Nature Place has decided to try it, too. Nature Place does not expect volume to be affected, but it hopes to gain more control over pricing. If Nature Place has to spend $125,000 this year to advertise, and its variable costs continue to be $1.25 per unit, what will its cost-plus price be? Do you think Nature Place will be able to sell its plants to garden centers at the cost-plus price? Why or why not?

P20-29B ③ **Making dropping a product and product-mix decisions [20–25 min]**

Members of the board of directors of Control One have received the following operating income data for the year ended March 31, 2012:

	Product Line		
CONTROL ONE			
Income Statement			
For the Year Ended March 31, 2012			
	Industrial Systems	Household Systems	Total
Sales revenue	$ 330,000	$ 370,000	$ 700,000
Cost of goods sold:			
Variable	33,000	47,000	80,000
Fixed	240,000	69,000	309,000
Total cost of goods sold	$ 273,000	$ 116,000	$ 389,000
Gross profit	$ 57,000	$ 254,000	$ 311,000
Marketing and administrative expenses:			
Variable	64,000	73,000	137,000
Fixed	39,000	27,000	66,000
Total marketing and administrative exp.	$ 103,000	$ 100,000	$ 203,000
Operating income (loss)	$ (46,000)	$ 154,000	$ 108,000

Members of the board are surprised that the industrial systems product line is losing money. They commission a study to determine whether the company should drop the line. Company accountants estimate that dropping industrial systems will decrease fixed cost of goods sold by $82,000 and decrease fixed marketing and administrative expenses by $15,000.

Requirements

1. Prepare an incremental analysis to show whether Control One should drop the industrial systems product line.

2. Prepare contribution margin income statements to show Control One's total operating income under the two alternatives: (a) with the industrial systems line and (b) without the line. Compare the *difference* between the two alternatives' income numbers to your answer to Requirement 1.

3. What have you learned from this comparison in Requirement 2?

P20-30B ❸ **Making dropping a product and product-mix decisions [10–15 min]**
Breit, located in San Antonio, Texas, produces two lines of electric toothbrushes: deluxe and standard. Because Breit can sell all the toothbrushes it can produce, the owners are expanding the plant. They are deciding which product line to emphasize. To make this decision, they assemble the following data:

	Per Unit	
	Deluxe Toothbrush	Standard Toothbrush
Sale price	$ 90	$ 50
Variable expenses	23	18
Contribution margin	$ 67	$ 32
Contribution margin ratio	74.4%	64.0%

After expansion, the factory will have a production capacity of 4,300 machine hours per month. The plant can manufacture either 65 standard electric toothbrushes or 27 deluxe electric toothbrushes per machine hour.

Requirements

1. Identify the constraining factor for Breit.

2. Prepare an analysis to show which product line the company should emphasize.

P20-31B ❹ **Making outsourcing decisions [20–30 min]**
Cool Boards manufactures snowboards. Its cost of making 2,100 bindings is as follows:

Direct materials	$ 17,580
Direct labor	2,600
Variable overhead	2,100
Fixed overhead	6,500
Total manufacturing costs for 2,100 bindings	$ 28,780

Suppose Lewis will sell bindings to Cool Boards for $15 each. Cool Boards would pay $1 per unit to transport the bindings to its manufacturing plant, where it would add its own logo at a cost of $0.40 per binding.

Requirements

1. Cool Boards' accountants predict that purchasing the bindings from Lewis will enable the company to avoid $2,600 of fixed overhead. Prepare an analysis to show whether Cool Boards should make or buy the bindings.

2. The facilities freed by purchasing bindings from Lewis can be used to manufacture another product that will contribute $3,500 to profit. Total fixed costs will be the same as if Cool Boards had produced the bindings. Show which alternative makes the best use of Cool Boards' facilities: (a) make bindings, (b) buy bindings and leave facilities idle, or (c) buy bindings and make another product.

P20-32B ❹ Make sell as is or process further decisions [20–25 min]

Cole Petroleum has spent $206,000 to refine 63,000 gallons of petroleum distillate, which can be sold for $6.30 a gallon. Alternatively, Cole can process the distillate further and produce 53,000 gallons of cleaner fluid. The additional processing will cost $1.80 per gallon of distillate. The cleaner fluid can be sold for $9.20 a gallon. To sell the cleaner fluid, Cole must pay a sales commission of $0.12 a gallon and a transportation charge of $0.15 a gallon.

Requirements

1. Diagram Cole's decision alternatives, using Exhibit 20-26 as a guide.
2. Identify the sunk cost. Is the sunk cost relevant to Cole's decision?
3. Should Cole sell the petroleum distillate or process it into cleaner fluid? Show the expected net revenue difference between the two alternatives.

● Continuing Exercise

E20-33 ❷ Making special order and pricing decisions [15–20 min]

This exercise continues the Lawlor Lawn Service, Inc., situation from Exercise 19-32 of Chapter 19. Lawlor Lawn Service currently charges $100 for a standard lawn service and incurs $60 in variable cost. Assume fixed costs are $1,400 per month. Lawlor has been offered a special contract for $80 each for 20 lawns in one subdivision. This special contract will not affect Lawlor's other business.

Requirements

1. Should Lawlor take the special contract?
2. What will Lawlor's incremental profit be on the special contract?

● Continuing Problem

P20-34 ❹ Make sell as is or process further decisions [20–25 min]

This problem continues the Draper Consulting, Inc., situation from Problem 19-33 of Chapter 19. Draper Consulting provides consulting service at an average price of $175 per hour and incurs variable costs of $100 per hour. Assume average fixed costs are $5,250 a month.

Draper has developed new software that will revolutionize billing for companies. Draper has already invested $200,000 in the software. It can market the software as is at $30,000 a client and expects to sell to eight clients. Draper can develop the software further, adding integration to **Microsoft** products at an additional development cost of $120,000. The additional development will allow Draper to sell the software for $38,000 each, but to 20 clients.

Requirement

1. Should Draper sell the software as is or develop it further?

Apply Your Knowledge

● Decision Case 20-1

BKFin.com provides banks access to sophisticated financial information and analysis systems over the Web. The company combines these tools with benchmarking data access, including e-mail and wireless communications, so that banks can instantly evaluate individual loan applications and entire loan portfolios.

BKFin.com's CEO Jon Wise is happy with the company's growth. To better focus on client service, Wise is considering outsourcing some functions. CFO Jenny Lee suggests that the company's e-mail may be the place to start. She recently attended a conference and learned that companies like **Continental Airlines**, **DellNet**, **GTE**, and **NBC** were outsourcing their e-mail function. Wise asks Lee to identify costs related to BKFin.com's in-house Microsoft Exchange mail application, which has 2,300 mailboxes. This information follows:

Variable costs:	
E-mail license...	$7 per mailbox per month
Virus protection license	$1 per mailbox per month
Other variable costs..	$8 per mailbox per month
Fixed costs:	
Computer hardware costs...	$94,300 per month
$8,050 monthly salary for two information technology	
staff members who work only on e-mail	$16,100 per month

Requirements

1. Compute the *total cost* per mailbox per month of BKFin.com's current e-mail function.
2. Suppose Mail.com, a leading provider of Internet messaging outsourcing services, offers to host BKFin.com's e-mail function for $9 per mailbox per month. If BKFin.com outsources its e-mail to Mail.com, BKFin.com will still need the virus protection software, its computer hardware, and one information technology staff member, who would be responsible for maintaining virus protection, quarantining suspicious e-mail, and managing content (e.g., screening e-mail for objectionable content). Should CEO Wise accept Mail.com's offer?
3. Suppose for an additional $5 per mailbox per month, Mail.com will also provide virus protection, quarantine, and content-management services. Outsourcing these additional functions would mean that BKFin.com would not need either an e-mail information technology staff member or the separate virus protection license. Should CEO Wise outsource these extra services to Mail.com?

● Ethical Issue 20-1

Mary Tan is the controller for Duck Associates, a property management company in Portland, Oregon. Each year Tan and payroll clerk Toby Stock meet with the external auditors about payroll accounting. This year, the auditors suggest that Tan consider outsourcing Duck Associates' payroll accounting to a company specializing in payroll processing services. This would allow Tan and her staff to focus on their primary responsibility: accounting for the properties under management. At present, payroll requires 1.5 employee positions—payroll clerk Toby Stock and a bookkeeper who spends half her time entering payroll data in the system.

Tan considers this suggestion, and she lists the following items relating to outsourcing payroll accounting:

a. The current payroll software that was purchased for $4,000 three years ago would not be needed if payroll processing were outsourced.
b. Duck Associates' bookkeeper would spend half her time preparing the weekly payroll input form that is given to the payroll processing service. She is paid $450 a week.

c. Duck Associates would no longer need payroll clerk Toby Stock, whose annual salary is $42,000.

d. The payroll processing service would charge $2,000 a month.

Requirements

1. Would outsourcing the payroll function increase or decrease Duck Associates' operating income?

2. Tan believes that outsourcing payroll would simplify her job, but she does not like the prospect of having to lay off Stock, who has become a close personal friend. She does not believe there is another position available for Stock at his current salary. Can you think of other factors that might support keeping Stock, rather than outsourcing payroll processing? How should each of the factors affect Tan's decision if she wants to do what is best for Duck Associates and act ethically?

● Fraud Case 20-1

Frank Perdue had built up a successful development company. When he became City Commissioner, everyone said it was good to have a businessman on the Commission. Businessmen know how to control costs and make sound economic decisions, they said, and Frank could help the city tighten its belt. One of his first projects was an analysis of the Human Resources Department. He claimed that if the whole function was outsourced, it would save the taxpayers money. A year later, after painful layoffs and a bumpy transition, the new contractor, NewSoft, was in place. Two years later, NewSoft's billing rates had steadily increased, and there were complaints about service. After five years, the supposed savings had vanished, and Frank had moved on to state government, his campaigns fueled by "generous" campaign contributions from companies like NewSoft.

Requirements

1. Although this case differs from "fraud" in the usual sense, describe the conflict of interest in this case. Who benefitted and who did not?

2. When making business decisions of this sort, some factors are quantitative and some are not. Discuss some of the non-quantitative factors related to this case. (Challenge)

● Team Project 20-1

John Menard is the founder and sole owner of **Menards**. Analysts have estimated that his chain of home improvement stores scattered around nine midwestern states generate about $3 billion in annual sales. But how can **Menards** compete with giant **Home Depot**?

Suppose Menard is trying to decide whether to produce **Menards'** own line of Formica countertops, cabinets, and picnic tables.

Assume **Menards** would incur the following unit costs in producing its own product lines:

	Countertops	Cabinets	Picnic Tables
Direct materials per unit......................................	$15	$10	$25
Direct labor per unit...	10	5	15
Variable manufacturing overhead per unit	5	2	6

Rather than making these products, assume that **Menards** could buy them from outside suppliers. Suppliers would charge **Menards** $40 per countertop, $25 per cabinet, and $65 per picnic table.

Whether Menard makes or buys these products, assume that he expects the following annual sales:

- Countertops—487,200 at $130 each
- Picnic tables—100,000 at $225 each
- Cabinets—150,000 at $75 each

Assume that **Menards** has a production facility with excess capacity that could be used to produce these products with no additional fixed costs. If "making" is sufficiently more profitable than outsourcing, Menard will start production of his new line of products. John Menard has asked your consulting group for a recommendation.

Requirements

1. Are the following items relevant or irrelevant in Menard's decision to build a new plant that will manufacture his own products?
   a. The unit sale prices of the countertops, cabinets, and picnic tables (the sale prices that **Menards** charges its customers)
   b. The prices outside suppliers would charge **Menards** for the three products, if **Menards** decides to outsource the products rather than make them
   c. The direct materials, direct labor, and variable overhead **Menards** would incur to manufacture the three product lines
   d. John Menard's salary

2. Determine whether **Menards** should make or outsource the countertops, cabinets, and picnic tables. In other words, what is the annual difference in cash flows if **Menards** decides to make rather than outsource each of these three products?

3. Write a memo giving your recommendation to John Menard. The memo should clearly state your recommendation, along with a brief summary of the reasons for your recommendation.

● Communication Activity 20-1

In 50 words or fewer, explain the difference between relevant costs, irrelevant costs, and sunk costs.

Quick Check Answers

1. *c* 2. *a* 3. *c* 4. *a* 5. *d* 6. *d* 7. *d* 8. *b* 9. *b* 10. *a*

For online homework, exercises, and problems that provide you immediate feedback, please visit myaccountinglab.com.

21

Capital Investment Decisions and the Time Value of Money

Shift Your Focus · Product Costing · Cost Allocation

Cost-Volume-Profit · Relevant Information · **Capital Budgeting**

Budgeting · Cost Control · Performance Measures

Learning Objectives

1. Describe the importance of capital investments and the capital budgeting process

2. Use the payback period and rate of return methods to make capital investment decisions

3. Use the time value of money to compute the present and future values of single lump sums and annuities

4. Use discounted cash flow models to make capital investment decisions

Your car wouldn't start again this morning. Now you know you're going to be late to work for the second time this week, and your manager is not going to be happy. As you wait for the bus, you realize you have to make a decision about the car before you lose your job. You have already taken it to a repair shop and received a large estimate on the cost of repairs. Now you need to decide if you will repair the car or trade it in for a new one. This is a major decision with long-term effects, so you want to carefully consider your options. Should you invest more money in your current car? If you do, how long will the repairs last before the car needs more work? What does it cost you to operate the current car? If you buy a new, more energy-efficient car, you will make a large initial investment—more than repairing the current car—but any needed repairs in the next few years will be covered by the warranty. Also, day-to-day operating costs will be lower with the new, more efficient model. Will these cost savings be enough to make the large initial investment a wise choice? Should you repair your current car or buy a new one?

Most people have limited resources and want to make the best decision about how to use those resources. In this chapter, we'll see how companies like Smart Touch Learning and Greg's Tunes, which also have limited resources, use capital investment analysis techniques to decide which long-term capital investments to make.

Capital Budgeting

The process of making capital investment decisions is often referred to as **capital budgeting. Capital budgeting is planning to invest in long-term assets in a way that returns the most profitability to the company.** Companies make capital investments when they acquire *capital assets*—assets used for a long period of time. Capital investments include buying new equipment, building new plants, automating production, and developing major commercial Web sites. In addition to affecting operations for many years, capital investments usually require large sums of money.

Capital investment decisions affect all businesses as they try to become more efficient by automating production and implementing new technologies. Grocers and retailers, such as **Walmart**, have invested in expensive self-scan check-out machines, while airlines, such as **Delta** and **Continental**, have invested in self check-in kiosks. These new technologies cost money. How do managers decide whether these expansions in plant and equipment will be good investments? They use capital budgeting analysis. Some companies, such as **Georgia-Pacific**, employ staff solely dedicated to capital budgeting analysis. They spend thousands of hours a year determining which capital investments to pursue.

> **1** Describe the importance of capital investments and the capital budgeting process

Four Methods of Capital Budgeting Analysis

In this chapter, we discuss four popular methods of analyzing potential capital investments:

1. Payback period

2. Rate of return (ROR)

3. Net present value (NPV)

4. Internal rate of return (IRR)

The first two methods, payback period and rate of return, are fairly quick and easy and work well for capital investments that have a relatively short life span, such as computer equipment and software that may have a useful life of only three to five years. Payback period and rate of return are also used to screen potential investments from those that are less desirable. The payback period provides management with valuable information on how fast the cash invested will be recouped. The rate of return shows the effect of the investment on the company's accrual-based income.

However, these two methods are inadequate if the capital investments have a longer life span. Why? Because these methods do not consider the time value of money. The last two methods, net present value and internal rate of return, factor in the time value of money so they are more appropriate for longer-term capital investments, such as Smart Touch's expansion to manufacturing DVDs. Management often uses a combination of methods to make final capital investment decisions.

Capital budgeting is not an exact science. Although the calculations these methods require may appear precise, remember that they are based on predictions about an uncertain future—estimates. These estimates must consider many unknown factors, such as changing consumer preferences, competition, the state of the economy, and government regulations. The further into the future the decision extends, the more likely that actual results will differ from predictions. Long-term decisions are riskier than short-term decisions.

Focus on Cash Flows

Generally accepted accounting principles (GAAP) are based on accrual accounting, but capital budgeting focuses on cash flows. The desirability of a capital asset depends on its ability to generate net cash inflows—that is, inflows in excess of outflows—over the asset's useful life. Recall that operating income based on accrual accounting contains noncash expenses, such as depreciation expense and bad-debt expense. The capital investment's *net cash inflows,* therefore, will differ from its operating income. Of the four capital budgeting methods covered in this chapter, only the rate of return method uses accrual-based accounting income. The other three methods use the investment's projected *net cash inflows.*

What do the projected *net cash inflows* include? Cash *inflows* include future cash revenue generated from the investment, any future savings in ongoing cash operating costs resulting from the investment, and any future residual value of the asset. How are these cash inflows projected? Employees from production, marketing, materials management, accounting, and other departments provide inputs to aid managers in estimating the projected cash flows. Good estimates are a critical part of making the best decisions.

To determine the investment's *net* cash inflows, the inflows are *netted* against the investment's *future cash outflows,* such as the investment's ongoing cash operating costs and cash paid for refurbishment, repairs, and maintenance costs. The initial investment itself is also a significant cash outflow. However, in our calculations, *we will always consider the amount of the investment separately from all other cash flows related to the investment.* The projected net cash inflows are "given" in our examples and in the assignment material. In reality, much of capital investment analysis revolves around projecting these figures as accurately as possible using input from employees throughout the organization (production, marketing, and so forth, depending on the type of capital investment).

Capital Budgeting Process

The first step in the capital budgeting process is to identify potential investments—for example, new technology and equipment that may make the company more efficient, competitive, and/or profitable. Employees, consultants, and outside sales vendors often offer capital investment proposals to management. After identifying potential capital investments, managers project the investments' net cash inflows and then analyze the investments using one or more of the four capital budgeting methods previously described. Sometimes the analysis involves a two-stage process. In the first stage, managers screen the investments using one or both of the methods that do *not* incorporate the time value of money—payback period or rate of return. These simple methods quickly weed out undesirable investments. Potential investments that "pass stage one" go on to a second stage of analysis. In the second stage, managers further analyze the potential investments using the net present value and/or internal rate of return methods. Because these methods consider the time value of money, they provide more accurate information about the potential investment's profitability.

Some companies can pursue all of the potential investments that meet or exceed their decision criteria. However, because of limited resources, other companies must engage in **capital rationing,** and choose among alternative capital investments. Based on the availability of funds, managers determine if and when to make specific capital investments. **So, capital rationing occurs when the company has limited assets available to invest in long-term assets.** For example, management may decide to wait three years to buy a certain piece of equipment because it considers other investments more important. In the intervening three years, the company will reassess whether it should still invest in the equipment. Perhaps technology has changed, and even better equipment is available. Perhaps consumer tastes have changed so the company no longer needs the equipment. Because of changing factors, long-term capital budgets are rarely set in stone.

Most companies perform **post-audits** of their capital investments. After investing in the assets, they compare the actual net cash inflows generated from the investment to the projected net cash inflows. **Post-audits help companies determine whether the investments are going as planned and deserve continued support, or whether they should abandon the project and sell the assets.** Managers also use feedback from post-audits to better estimate net cash flow projections for future projects. If managers expect routine post-audits, they will more likely submit realistic net cash flow estimates with their capital investment proposals.

Using Payback Period and Rate of Return to Make Capital Investment Decisions

Next, we'll review two capital investment decision tools that companies use to initially screen capital investment choices—payback period and rate of return. When we review formulas, we'll also show you the Excel formulas with an "X" symbol. Note that these Excel formulas are provided as an alternate tool only.

2 Use the payback period and rate of return methods to make capital investment decisions

Payback Period

Payback is the length of time it takes to recover, in net cash inflows, the cost of the capital outlay. The payback model measures how quickly managers expect to recover their investment dollars. All else being equal, the shorter the payback period, the more attractive the asset. Computing the payback period depends on whether net cash inflows are equal each year, or whether they differ over time. We consider each in turn.

Payback with Equal Annual Net Cash Inflows

Smart Touch is considering investing $240,000 in hardware and software to upgrade its Web site to provide a business-to-business (B2B) portal. Employees throughout the company will use the B2B portal to access company-approved suppliers. Smart Touch expects the portal to save $60,000 a year for each of the six years of its useful life. The savings will arise from reducing the number of purchasing personnel the company employs and from lower prices on the goods and services purchased. Net cash inflows arise from an increase in revenues, a decrease in expenses, or both. In Smart Touch's case, the net cash inflows result from lower expenses.

When net cash inflows are equal each year, managers compute the payback period as shown in Exhibit 21-1.

EXHIBIT 21-1 | **Calculating Payback Period— Equal Cash Flows**

$$\text{Payback period} = \frac{\text{Amount invested}}{\text{Expected annual net cash inflow}}$$

Smart Touch computes the investment's payback period as follows:

=SUM(240,000/60,000)

$$\text{Payback period for B2B portal} = \frac{\$240,000}{\$60,000} = 4 \text{ years}$$

Exhibit 21-2 verifies that Smart Touch expects to recoup the $240,000 investment in the B2B portal by the end of year 4, when the accumulated net cash inflows total $240,000.

Smart Touch is also considering investing $240,000 to upgrade its Web site. The company expects the upgraded Web site to generate $80,000 in net cash inflows each year of its three-year life. The payback period is computed as follows:

=SUM(240,000/80,000)

$$\text{Payback period for Web site development} = \frac{\$240,000}{\$80,000} = 3 \text{ years}$$

Exhibit 21-2 verifies that Smart Touch will recoup the $240,000 investment for the Web site upgrade by the end of year 3, when the accumulated net cash inflows total $240,000.

EXHIBIT 21-2 | **Payback—Equal Annual Net Cash Inflows**

	Net Cash Outflows	Net Cash Inflows			
		B2B Portal		Web Site Upgrade	
Year	Amount Invested	Annual	Accumulated	Annual	Accumulated
0	240,000	—	—	—	—
1	—	$60,000	$ 60,000	$80,000	$ 80,000
2	—	60,000	120,000	80,000	160,000
3	—	60,000	180,000	80,000	240,000
4	—	60,000	240,000		
5	—	60,000	300,000		
6	—	60,000	360,000		

Payback with Unequal Net Cash Inflows

The payback equation in Exhibit 21-1 only works when net cash inflows are the same each period. When periodic cash flows are unequal, you must total net cash inflows until the amount invested is recovered. Assume that Smart Touch is considering an alternate investment, the Z80 portal. The Z80 portal differs from the B2B portal and the Web site in two respects: (1) It has *unequal* net cash inflows during its life and (2) it has a $30,000 residual value at the end of its life. The Z80 portal will generate net cash inflows of $100,000 in year 1, $80,000 in year 2, $50,000 each year in years 3 and 4, $40,000 each in years 5 and 6, and $30,000 in residual value when it is sold at the end of its life. Exhibit 21-3 shows the payback schedule for these unequal annual net cash inflows.

EXHIBIT 21-3	**Payback: Unequal Annual Net Cash Inflows**

Net Cash Outflows Z80 Portal		Net Cash Inflows Z80 Portal		
Year	Amount Invested	Annual		Accumulated
0	$240,000	—		—
1	—	100,000	*Useful Life*	$100,000
2	—	80,000		180,000
3	—	50,000		230,000
4	—	50,000		280,000
5	—	40,000		320,000
6	—	40,000		360,000
6–Residual Value		30,000		390,000

By the end of year 3, the company has recovered $230,000 of the $240,000 initially invested, so it is only $10,000 short of payback. Because the expected net cash inflow in year 4 is $50,000, by the end of year 4 the company will have recovered *more* than the initial investment. Therefore, the payback period is somewhere between three and four years. Assuming that the cash flow occurs evenly throughout the fourth year, the payback period is calculated as follows:

$$\text{Payback} = 3 \text{ years} + \frac{\$10,000 \text{ (amount needed to complete recovery in year 4)}}{\$50,000 \text{ (net cash inflow in year 4)}}$$

$$= 3.2 \text{ years}$$

Criticism of the Payback Period Method

A major criticism of the payback period method is that it focuses only on time, not on profitability. The payback period considers only those cash flows that occur *during* the payback period. This method ignores any cash flows that occur *after* that period. For example, Exhibit 21-2 shows that the B2B portal will continue to generate net cash inflows for two years after its payback period. These additional net cash inflows amount to $120,000 ($60,000 × 2 years), yet the payback period method ignores this extra cash. A similar situation occurs with the Z80 portal. As shown in Exhibit 21-3, the Z80 portal will provide an additional $150,000 of net cash inflows, including residual value, after its payback period of 3.2 years ($390,000 total accumulated cash inflows – $240,000 amount invested). However, the Web site's useful life, as shown in Exhibit 21-2, is the *same* as its payback period (three years). No cash flows are ignored, yet the Web site will merely cover its cost and provide no profit. Because this is the case, the company has no financial reason to invest in the Web site.

Exhibit 21-4 compares the payback period of the three investments. As the exhibit illustrates, the payback period method does not consider the asset's profitability. The method only tells management how quickly it will recover the cash. Even though the Web site has the shortest payback period, both the B2B portal and the Z80 portal are better investments because they provide profit. The key point is that the investment with the shortest payback period is best *only if all other factors are the same.* Therefore, managers usually use the payback period method as a screening device to "weed out" investments that will take too long to recoup. They rarely use payback period as the sole method for deciding whether to invest in the asset.

When using the payback period method, managers are guided by following decision rule:

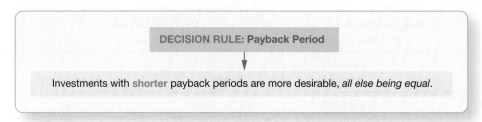

DECISION RULE: Payback Period

Investments with **shorter** payback periods are more desirable, *all else being equal*.

| EXHIBIT 21-4 | **Comparing Payback Periods Between Investments** |

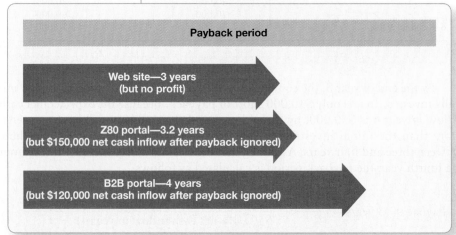

Payback period

Web site—3 years
(but no profit)

Z80 portal—3.2 years
(but $150,000 net cash inflow after payback ignored)

B2B portal—4 years
(but $120,000 net cash inflow after payback ignored)

Stop & Think...

Let's say you loan $50 to a friend today (a Friday). The friend says he will pay you $25 next Friday when he gets paid and another $25 the following Friday. What is your payback period? The friend will pay you back in 2 weeks.

Rate of Return (ROR)

Companies are in business to earn profits. One measure of profitability is the **rate of return (ROR)** on an asset. The formula for calculating ROR is shown in Exhibit 21-5.

| EXHIBIT 21-5 | **Calculating Rate of Return** |

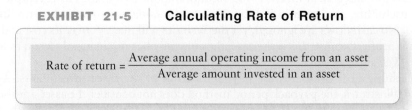

$$\text{Rate of return} = \frac{\text{Average annual operating income from an asset}}{\text{Average amount invested in an asset}}$$

The ROR focuses on the *operating income, not the net cash inflow,* an asset generates. **The ROR measures the *average* accounting rate of return over the asset's entire life.** Let's first consider investments with no residual value.

Recall the B2B portal, which costs $240,000, has equal annual net cash inflows of $60,000, a six-year useful life, and no (zero) residual value.

Let's look at the average annual operating income in the numerator first. The average annual operating income of an asset is simply the asset's total operating income over the course of its operating life divided by its lifespan (number of years).

Operating income is based on *accrual accounting*. Therefore, any noncash expenses, such as depreciation expense, must be subtracted from the asset's net cash inflows to arrive at its operating income. Exhibit 21-6 displays the formula for calculating average annual operating income.

EXHIBIT 21-6	**Calculating Average Annual Operating Income from Asset**

Total net cash inflows during operating life of the asset	A
Less: Total depreciation during operating life of the asset (Cost – Residual Value)	B
Total operating income during operating life	(A – B)
Divide by: Asset's operating life in years	C
Average annual operating income from asset	[(A – B)/C]

The B2B portal's average annual operating income is as follows:

Total net cash inflows during operating life of the asset ($60,000 × 6 years)	$ 360,000
Less: Total depreciation during operating life of asset (cost – any salvage value)	240,000
Total operating income during operating life of asset	$ 120,000
Divide by: Asset's operating life (in years)	÷ 6 years
Average annual operating income from asset	$ 20,000

Now let's look at the denominator of the ROR equation. The *average* amount invested in an asset is its *net book value* at the beginning of the asset's useful life plus the net book value at the end of the asset's useful life divided by 2. Another way to say that is the asset's cost plus the asset's residual value divided by 2. The net book value of the asset decreases each year because of the annual depreciation shown in Exhibit 21-6.

Because the B2B portal does not have a residual value, the *average* amount invested is $120,000 [($240,000 cost + $0 residual value) ÷ 2].

We calculate the B2B's ROR as follows:

$$\text{Rate of return} = \frac{\$20,000}{(\$240,000 + \$0)/2} = \frac{\$20,000}{\$120,000} = 0.167 = 16.70\%$$

=SUM(20000/((240000+0)/2))

Now consider the Z80 portal (data from Exhibit 21-3). Recall that the Z80 portal differed from the B2B portal only in that it had unequal net cash inflows during its life and a $30,000 residual value at the end of its life. Its average annual operating income is calculated as follows:

Total net cash inflows *during* operating life of asset (does not include the residual value at end of life) (Year 1 + Year 2, etc.)	$ 360,000
Less: Total depreciation during operating life of asset (cost – any salvage value) ($240,000 cost – $30,000 residual value)	210,000
Total operating income during operating life of asset	$ 150,000
Divide by: Asset's operating life (in years)	÷ 6 years
Average annual operating income from asset	$ 25,000

Notice that the Z80 portal's average annual operating income of $25,000 is higher than the B2B portal's operating income of $20,000. Since the Z80 asset has a residual value at the end of its life, less depreciation is expensed each year, leading to a higher average annual operating income.

Now let's calculate the denominator of the ROR equation, the average amount invested in the asset. For the Z80, the average asset investment is as follows:

=SUM(25000/((240000+30000)/2))

Average amount invested = (Amount invested in asset + Residual value)/2

$135,000 = ($240,000 + $30,000) /2

We calculate the Z80's ROR as follows:

$$\text{Rate of return} = \frac{\$25,000}{(\$240,000 + \$30,000)/2} = \frac{\$25,000}{\$135,000} = 0.185 = 18.5\%$$

Companies that use the ROR model set a minimum required rate of return. If Smart Touch requires a ROR of at least 20%, then its managers would not approve an investment in the B2B portal or the Z80 portal because the ROR for both investments is less than 20%.

The decision rule is as follows:

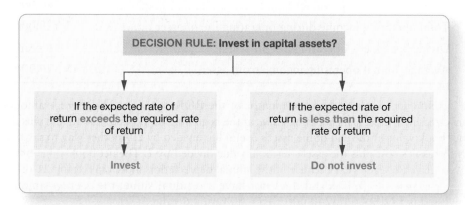

DECISION RULE: Invest in capital assets?

If the expected rate of return **exceeds** the required rate of return → **Invest**

If the expected rate of return **is less than** the required rate of return → **Do not invest**

Next, let's take some time to review the Decision Guidelines for capital budgeting on the following page.

Decision Guidelines 21-1

CAPITAL BUDGETING

Amazon.com started as a virtual retailer. It held no inventory. Instead, it bought books and CDs only as needed to fill customer orders. As the company grew, its managers decided to invest in their own warehouse facilities. Why? Owning warehouse facilities allows **Amazon** to save money by buying in bulk. Also, shipping all items in the customer's order in one package, from one location, saves shipping costs. Here are some of the guidelines **Amazon**'s managers used as they made the major capital budgeting decision to invest in building warehouses.

Decision	Guidelines
• Why is this decision important?	Capital budgeting decisions typically require large investments and affect operations for years to come.
• What method shows us how soon we will recoup our cash investment?	The payback period method shows managers how quickly they will recoup their investment. This method highlights investments that are too risky due to long payback periods. However, it does not reveal any information about the investment's profitability.
• Does any method consider the impact of the investment on accrual accounting income?	The rate of return (ROR) is the only capital budgeting method that shows how the investment will affect accrual accounting income, which is important to financial statement users. All other methods of capital investment analysis focus on the investment's net cash inflows.
• How do we compute the payback period if cash flows are *equal*?	$$\text{Payback period} = \frac{\text{Amount invested}}{\text{Expected annual net cash inflow}}$$
• How do we compute the payback period if cash flows are *unequal*?	Accumulate net cash inflows until the amount invested is recovered.
• How do we compute the ROR?	$$\text{Rate of return} = \frac{\text{Average annual operating income from an asset}}{\text{Average amount invested in an asset}}$$

Summary Problem 21-1

Dyno-max is considering buying a new water treatment system for its Austin, Texas, plant. The company screens its potential capital investments using the payback period and rate of return methods. If a potential investment has a payback period of less than four years and a minimum 12% rate of return, it will be considered further. The data for the water treatment system follow:

Cost of water treatment system..	$48,000
Estimated residual value..	$ 0
Estimated annual net cash inflow (each year for 5 years) from anticipated environmental cleanup savings	$13,000
Estimated useful life	5 years

Requirements

1. Compute the water treatment system's payback period.
2. Compute the water treatment system's ROR.
3. Should Dyno-max turn down this investment proposal or consider it further?

Solution

Requirement 1

$$\text{Payback period} = \frac{\text{Amount invested}}{\text{Expected annual net cash inflow}} = \frac{\$48,000}{\$13,000} = 3.7 \text{ years (rounded)}$$

Requirement 2

$$\text{Rate of return} = \frac{\text{Average annual operating income from an asset}}{\text{Average amount invested in an asset}}$$

$$= \frac{\$3,400^*}{(\$48,000 + \$0)/2}$$

$$= \frac{\$3,400}{\$24,000}$$

$$= 0.142 \text{ (rounded)}$$

$$= 14.2\%$$

*Total net cash inflows during life ($13,000 × 5 years)	$ 65,000
Less: total depreciation during life	48,000
Total operating income during life	$ 17,000
Divided by: life of the asset	÷ 5 years
Average annual operating income	$ 3,400

Requirement 3

The water treatment system proposal passes both initial screening tests. The payback period is slightly less than four years, and the rate of return is higher than 12%. Dyno-max should further analyze the proposal using a method that incorporates the time value of money.

A Review of the Time Value of Money

A dollar received today is worth more than a dollar to be received in the future. Why? Because you can invest today's dollar and earn extra income so you'll have more money next year. The fact that invested money earns income over time is called the *time value of money*, and this explains why we would prefer to receive cash sooner rather than later. The time value of money means that the timing of capital investments' net cash inflows is important. Two methods of capital investment analysis incorporate the time value of money: the net present value (NPV) and internal rate of return (IRR). This section reviews time value of money to make sure you have a firm foundation for discussing these two methods.

3 Use the time value of money to compute the present and future values of single lump sums and annuities

Factors Affecting the Time Value of Money

The time value of money depends on several key factors:

1. The principal amount (*p*)
2. The number of periods (*n*)
3. The interest rate (*i*)

The principal (*p*) refers to the amount of the investment or borrowing. Because this chapter deals with capital investments, we will primarily discuss the principal in terms of investments. However, the same concepts apply to borrowings (which we covered in Chapter 8). We state the principal as either a single lump sum or an annuity. For example, if you win the lottery, you have the choice of receiving all the winnings now (a single lump sum) or receiving a series of equal payments for a period of time in the future (an annuity). An **annuity** is a stream of *equal installments* made at *equal time intervals under the same interest rate*.[1] **For example, $100 a month for 12 months at 5% is an annuity.**

The number of periods (*n*) is the length of time from the beginning of the investment until termination. All else being equal, the shorter the investment period, the lower the total amount of interest earned. If you withdraw your savings after four years rather than five years, you will earn less interest. In this chapter, the number of periods is stated in years.[2]

The interest rate (*i*) is the annual percentage earned on the investment. **Simple interest** means that interest is calculated *only* on the principal amount. **Compound interest** means that interest is calculated on the principal *and* on all previously earned interest. *Compound interest assumes that all interest earned will remain invested and earn additional interest at the same interest rate.* Exhibit 21-7 compares simple interest (6%) on a five-year, $10,000 CD with interest compounded yearly (rounded to the nearest dollar). As you can see, the amount of compound interest earned yearly grows as the base on which it is calculated (principal plus cumulative interest to date) grows. Over the life of this investment, the total amount of compound interest is more than the total amount of simple interest. Most investments yield compound interest so we assume compound interest, rather than simple interest, for the rest of this chapter.

Fortunately, time value calculations involving compound interest do not have to be as tedious as those shown in Exhibit 21-7. Formulas and tables (or proper use of business calculators programmed with these formulas, or spreadsheet software such as Microsoft Excel) simplify the calculations. In the next sections, we will discuss how to use these tools to perform time value calculations.

---

[1] An *ordinary annuity* is an annuity in which the installments occur at the *end* of each period. An *annuity due* is an annuity in which the installments occur at the beginning of each period. Throughout this chapter, we use ordinary annuities because they are better suited to capital budgeting cash flow assumptions.

[2] The number of periods can also be stated in days, months, or quarters. If so, the interest rate needs to be adjusted to reflect the number of time periods in the year.

EXHIBIT 21-7	**Simple Versus Compound Interest for a Principal Amount of $10,000, at 6%, over 5 Years**

Year	Simple Interest Calculation	Simple Interest	Compound Interest Calculation	Compound Interest
1	$10,000 × 6% =	$ 600	$10,000 × 6% =	$ 600
2	$10,000 × 6% =	600	($10,000 + 600) × 6% =	636
3	$10,000 × 6% =	600	($10,000 + 600 + 636) × 6% =	674
4	$10,000 × 6% =	600	($10,000 + 600 + 636 + 674) × 6% =	715
5	$10,000 × 6% =	600	($10,000 + 600 + 636 + 674 + 715) × 6% =	758
	Total interest	$3,000	Total interest	$3,383

Future Values and Present Values: Points Along the Time Line

Consider the time line in Exhibit 21-8. The future value or present value of an investment simply refers to the value of an investment at different points in time.

EXHIBIT 21-8	**Present Value and Future Value Along the Time Continuum**

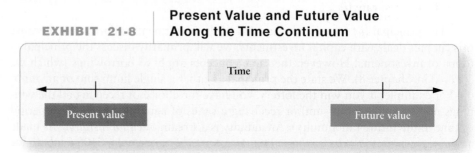

We can calculate the future value or the present value of any investment by knowing (or assuming) information about the three factors we listed earlier: (1) the principal amount, (2) the period of time, and (3) the interest rate. For example, in Exhibit 21-7, we calculated the interest that would be earned on (1) a $10,000 principal, (2) invested for five years, (3) at 6% interest. The future value of the investment is simply its worth at the end of the five-year time frame—the original principal *plus* the interest earned. In our example, the future value of the investment is as follows:

$$\text{Future value} = \text{Principal} + \text{Interest earned}$$
$$= \$10,000 + \quad \$3,383$$
$$= \$13,383$$

If we invest $10,000 *today*, its *present value* is simply $10,000. So another way of stating the future value is as follows:

$$\text{Future value} = \text{Present value} + \text{Interest earned}$$

We can rearrange the equation as follows:

$$\text{Present value} = \text{Future value} - \text{Interest earned}$$
$$\$10,000 \quad = \quad \$13,383 \quad - \quad \$3,383$$

The only difference between present value and future value is the amount of interest that is earned in the intervening time span.

Future Value and Present Value Factors

Calculating each period's compound interest, as we did in Exhibit 21-7, and then adding it to the present value to determine the future value (or subtracting it from the future value to determine the present value) is tedious. Fortunately, mathematical formulas have been developed that specify future values and present values for unlimited combinations of interest rates (i) and time periods (n). Separate formulas exist for single lump-sum investments and annuities.

These formulas are programmed into most business calculators so that the user only needs to correctly enter the principal amount, interest rate, and number of time periods to find present or future values. These formulas are also programmed into spreadsheet functions in Microsoft Excel. In this chapter, we will use tables and show the Excel formulas to demonstrate these calculations. Note that since the table values are rounded, your Excel results will differ slightly. These tables contain the results of the formulas for various interest rate and time period combinations.

The formulas and resulting tables are shown in Appendix B at the end of this book:

1. Present Value of $1 (Appendix B, Table B-1)—*used to calculate the value today of one future amount (a lump sum)*

2. Present Value of Annuity of $1 (Appendix B, Table B-2)—*used to calculate the value today of a series of equal future amounts (annuities)*

3. Future Value of $1 (Appendix B, Table B-3)—*used to calculate a value at a future date of one present amount (lump sum)*

4. Future Value of Annuity of $1 (Appendix B, Table B-4)—*used to calculate a value at a future date of a series of equal amounts (annuities)*

Take a moment to look at these tables because we are going to use them throughout the rest of the chapter. Note that the columns are interest rates (i) and the rows are periods (n).

The data in each table, known as future value factors (FV factors) and present value factors (PV factors), are for an investment (or loan) of $1. To find the future value of an amount other than $1, you simply multiply the FV factor by the present amount. To find the present value of an amount other than $1, you multiply the PV factor by the future amount.

The annuity tables are derived from the lump-sum tables. For example, the Annuity PV factors (in the Present Value of Annuity of $1 table) are the *sums* of the PV factors found in the Present Value of $1 tables for a given number of time periods. The annuity tables allow us to perform "one-step" calculations rather than separately computing the present value of each annual cash installment and then summing the individual present values.

Calculating Future Values of Single Sums and Annuities Using FV Factors

Let's go back to our $10,000 lump-sum investment. If we want to know the future value of the investment five years from now at an interest rate of 6%, we determine the FV factor from the table labeled Future Value of $1 (Appendix B, Table B-3). We use this table for lump-sum amounts. We look down the 6% column, and across the 5 periods row, and find the future value factor is 1.338. We finish our calculations as follows:

> Future value = Principal amount × (FV factor for i = 6%, n = 5)
> = $10,000 × (1.338)
> = $13,380

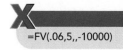

=FV(.06,5,,-10000)

Excel note: Excel results will differ slightly than results calculated using the tables because all table values are rounded to three decimal places.

This figure materially agrees with our earlier calculation of the investment's future value of $13,383 in Exhibit 21-7. (The difference of $3 is due to two facts: (1) The tables round the FV and PV factors to three decimal places and (2) we rounded our earlier yearly interest calculations in Exhibit 21-7 to the nearest dollar.)

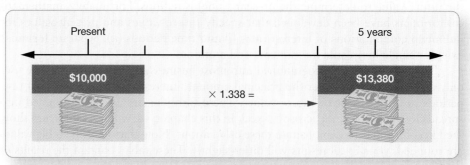

Let's also consider our alternative investment strategy, investing $2,000 at the end of each year for five years. The procedure for calculating the future value of an *annuity* is quite similar to calculating the future value of a lump-sum amount. This time, we use the Future Value of Annuity of $1 table (Appendix B, Table B-4). Assuming 6% interest, we once again look down the 6% column. Because we will be making five annual installments, we look across the row marked 5 periods. The Annuity FV factor is 5.637. We finish the calculation as follows:

=FV(.06,5,-2000)

> Future value = Amount of each cash installment × (Annuity FV factor for i = 6%, n = 5)
> = $2,000 × (5.637)
> = $11,274

This is considerably less than the future value of $13,380 of the lump sum of $10,000, even though we have invested $10,000 out-of-pocket either way. The difference is that we didn't invest $10,000 for the *entire* five years—we invested $2,000 each year. So, we earned less interest.

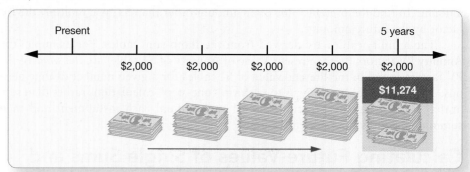

Calculating Present Values of Single Sums and Annuities Using PV Factors

The process for calculating present values—often called discounting cash flows—is similar to the process for calculating future values. The difference is the point in time at which you are assessing the investment's worth. Rather than determining its value at a future date, you are determining its value at an earlier point in time (today). For our example, assume you have just won the lottery after purchasing one $5 lottery ticket. The state offers you the following three payout options for your after-tax prize money:

Option #1: $1,000,000 now

Option #2: $150,000 at the end of each year for the next 10 years

Option #3: $2,000,000 10 years from now

Which alternative should you take? You might be tempted to wait 10 years to "double" your winnings. You may be tempted to take the money now and spend it. However, assume you plan to prudently invest all money received—no matter when you receive it—so that you have financial flexibility in the future (for example, for buying a house, retiring early, or taking exotic vacations). How can you choose among the three payment alternatives, when the total amount of each option varies ($1,000,000 versus $1,500,000 versus $2,000,000) and the timing of the cash flows varies (now versus some each year versus later)? Comparing these three options is like comparing apples to oranges—we just cannot do it—unless we find some common basis for comparison. Our common basis for comparison will be the prize-money's worth at a certain point in time—namely, today. In other words, if we convert each payment option to its *present value*, we can compare apples to apples.

We already know the principal amount and timing of each payment option, so the only assumption we will have to make is the interest rate. The interest rate will vary, depending on the amount of risk you are willing to take with your investment. Riskier investments (such as stock investments) command higher interest rates; safer investments (such as FDIC-insured bank deposits) yield lower interest rates. Let's say that after investigating possible investment alternatives, you choose an investment contract with an 8% annual return. We already know that the present value of Option #1 is $1,000,000 because we would receive that $1,000,000 today. Let's convert the other two payment options to their present values so that we can compare them. We will need to use the Present Value of Annuity of $1 table (Appendix B, Table B-2) to convert payment Option #2 (since it is an annuity) and the Present Value of $1 table (Appendix B, Table B-1) to convert payment Option #3 (since it is a single-lump-sum). To obtain the PV factors, we will look down the 8% column and across the 10 period row. Then, we finish the calculations as follows:

Option #2

Present value = Amount of each cash installment × (Annuity PV factor for *i* = 8%, *n* = 10)
Present value = $150,000 × (6.710)
Present value = $1,006,500

=PV(.08,10,-150000)

Option #3

Present value = Principal amount × (PV factor for *i* = 8%, *n* = 10)
Present value = $2,000,000 × (0.463)
Present value = $926,000

=PV(.08,10,,-2000000)

Exhibit 21-9 shows that we have converted each payout option to a common basis—its worth *today*—so we can make a valid comparison among the options. Based on this comparison, we should choose Option #2 because its worth, in today's dollars, is the highest of the three options.

EXHIBIT 21-9 | **Present Value of Lottery Payout Options**

Payment Options	Present Value of Lottery Payout (*i* = 8%, *n* = 10)
Option #1	$1,000,000
Option #2	$1,006,500
Option #3	$ 926,000

Now that you have reviewed time value of money concepts, we will discuss the two capital budgeting methods that incorporate the time value of money: net present value (NPV) and internal rate of return (IRR).

Using Discounted Cash Flow Models to Make Capital Investment Decisions

4 Use discounted cash flow models to make capital investment decisions

Neither the payback period nor the ROR recognizes the time value of money. That is, these models fail to consider the *timing* of the net cash inflows an asset generates. *Discounted cash flow models*—the NPV and the IRR—overcome this weakness. These models incorporate compound interest by assuming that companies will reinvest future cash flows when they are received. Over 85% of large industrial firms in the United States use discounted cash-flow methods to make capital investment decisions. Companies that provide services also use these models.

The NPV and IRR methods rely on present value calculations to *compare* the amount of the investment (the investment's initial cost) with its expected net cash inflows. Recall that an investment's *net cash inflows* includes all *future* cash flows related to the investment, such as future increased sales or cost savings netted against the investment's cash operating costs. Because the cash outflow for the investment occurs *now*, but the net cash inflows from the investment occur in the *future*, companies can only make valid "apple-to-apple" comparisons if they convert the cash flows to the *same point in time*—namely the present value. Companies use the present value to make the comparison (rather than the future value) because the investment's initial cost is already stated at its present value.[3]

If the present value of the investment's net cash inflows exceeds the initial cost of the investment, that's a good investment. In terms of our earlier lottery example, the lottery ticket turned out to be a "good investment" because the present value of its net cash inflows (the present value of the lottery payout under *any* of the three payout options) exceeded the cost of the investment (the lottery ticket cost $5 to purchase). Let's begin our discussion by taking a closer look at the NPV method.

Net Present Value (NPV)

Greg's Tunes is considering producing CD players and digital video recorders (DVRs). The products require different specialized machines that each cost $1,000,000. Each machine has a five-year life and zero residual value. The two products have different patterns of predicted net cash inflows, as shown in Exhibit 21-10.

EXHIBIT 21-10 | **Expected Cash Inflows for Two Projects**

	Annual Net Cash Inflows	
Year	CD Players	DVRs
1	$ 305,450	$ 500,000
2	$ 305,450	350,000
3	$ 305,450	300,000
4	$ 305,450	250,000
5	$ 305,450	40,000
Total	$1,527,250	$1,440,000

The CD-player project generates more net cash inflows, but the DVR project brings in cash sooner. To decide how attractive each investment is, we find its **net present value (NPV)**. The NPV is the *net difference* between the present value of the investment's net cash inflows and the investment's cost (cash outflows). We *discount* the net cash inflows—just as we did in the lottery example—using Greg's minimum desired rate of

---

[3] If the investment is to be purchased through lease payments, rather than a current cash outlay, we would still use the current cash price of the investment as its initial cost. If no current cash price is available, we would discount the future lease payments back to their present value to estimate the investment's current cash price.

return. This rate is called the **discount rate** because it is the interest rate used for the present value calculations. **The discount rate is the interest rate that discounts or reduces future amounts to their lesser value in the present (today).** It is also called the **required rate of return** or **hurdle rate** because the investment must meet or exceed this rate to be acceptable. **To help you understand what a hurdle rate is, visualize a runner jumping over a hurdle at a track—the hurdle is the minimum height the runner must jump.** The discount rate depends on the riskiness of investments. The higher the risk, the higher the discount (interest) rate. Greg's discount rate for these investments is 14%.

We then compare the present value of the net cash inflows to the investment's initial cost to decide which projects meet or exceed management's minimum desired rate of return. In other words, management is deciding whether the $1,000,000 option is worth more (because the company would give it up now to invest in the project) or whether the project's future net cash inflows are worth more. Management can only make a valid comparison between the two sums of money by comparing them at the *same* point in time—namely, at their present value.

NPV with Equal Periodic Net Cash Inflows (Annuity)

Greg's expects the CD-player project to generate $305,450 of net cash inflows each year for five years. Because these cash flows are equal in amount, and occur every year, they are an annuity. Therefore, we use the Present Value of Annuity of $1 table (Appendix B, Table B-2) to find the appropriate Annuity PV factor for $i = 14\%, n = 5$.

The present value of the net cash inflows from Greg's CD-player project is as follows:

> Present value = Amount of each cash net cash inflow × (Annuity PV factor for
> $i = 14\%, n = 5$)
> = $305,450 × (3.433)
> = $1,048,610

X
=NPV(.14,305450,305450,
305450,305450,305450)
or
=PV(.14,5,-305450)
Then subtract the $1,000,000
initial investment

Next, we simply subtract the investment's initial cost of $1,000,000 (cash outflows) from the present value of the net cash inflows of $1,048,610. The difference of $48,610 is the *net* present value (NPV), as shown in Exhibit 21-11.

EXHIBIT 21-11	**NPV of Equal Net Cash Inflows—CD-Player Project**			
Time		Annuity PV Factor ($i = 14\%, n = 5$)	Net Cash Inflow	Present Value
1–5 yrs	Present value of annuity of equal annual net cash inflows for 5 years at 14%	3.433*	× $305,450 =	$ 1,048,610
0	Investment			(1,000,000)
	Net present value of the CD-player project			$ 48,610

*Annuity PV Factor is found in Appendix B, Table B-2.

A *positive* NPV means that the project earns *more* than the required rate of return. A negative NPV means that the project earns less than the required rate of return. This leads to the following decision rule:

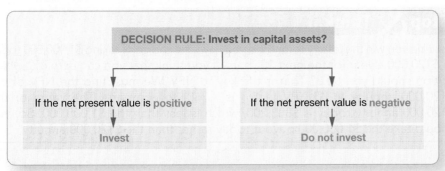

DECISION RULE: Invest in capital assets?

If the net present value is positive → Invest

If the net present value is negative → Do not invest

In Greg's Tunes' case, the CD-player project is an attractive investment. The $48,610 positive NPV means that the CD-player project earns *more than* Greg's Tunes' 14% target rate of return.

Another way managers can use present value analysis is to start the capital budgeting process by computing the total present value of the net cash inflows from the project to determine the *maximum* the company can invest in the project and still earn the target rate of return. For Greg's, the present value of the net cash inflows is $1,048,610. This means that Greg's Tunes can invest a maximum of $1,048,610 and still earn the 14% target rate of return (i.e., if Greg's invests $1,048,610, NPV will be 0 and return will be exactly 14%). Because Greg's Tunes' managers believe they can undertake the project for $1,000,000, the project is an attractive investment.

NPV with Unequal Periodic Net Cash Inflows

In contrast to the CD-player project, the net cash inflows of the DVR project are unequal—$500,000 in year 1, $350,000 in year 2, and so on. Because these amounts vary by year, Greg's Tunes' managers *cannot* use the annuity table to compute the present value of the DVR project. They must compute the present value of each individual year's net cash inflows *separately (as separate lump sums received in different years)*, using the Present Value of $1 table (Appendix B, Table B-1). Exhibit 21-12 shows that the $500,000 net cash inflow received in year 1 is discounted using a PV factor of $i = 14\%, n = 1$, while the $350,000 net cash inflow received in year 2 is discounted using a PV factor of $i = 14\%, n = 2$, and so forth. After separately discounting each of the five year's net cash inflows, we add each result to find that the *total* present value of the DVR project's net cash inflows is $1,078,910. Finally, we subtract the investment's cost of $1,000,000 (cash outflows) to arrive at the DVR project's NPV: $78,910.

=NPV(.14,500000,350000, 300000,250000,40000)

Then subtract the $1,000,000 initial investment

EXHIBIT 21-12 | **NPV with Unequal Net Cash Inflows—DVR Project**

Year		PV Factor ($i = 14\%$)		Net Cash Inflow		Present Value
	Present value of each year's net cash inflows discounted at 14%					
1	Year 1 ($n = 1$)	0.877†	×	$500,000	=	$ 438,500
2	Year 2 ($n = 2$)	0.769	×	350,000	=	269,150
3	Year 3 ($n = 3$)	0.675	×	300,000	=	202,500
4	Year 4 ($n = 4$)	0.592	×	250,000	=	148,000
5	Year 5 ($n = 5$)	0.519	×	40,000	=	20,760
	Total present value of net cash inflows					$ 1,078,910
0	Investment					(1,000,000)
	Net present value of the DVR project					$ 78,910

†PV Factors are found in Appendix B, Table B-1.

Because the NPV is positive, Greg's Tunes expects the DVR project to earn more than the 14% target rate of return, making this an attractive investment.

Stop & Think...

Assume you win the lottery today and you have the choice of taking $1,000,000 today or $120,000 a year for the next 10 years. If you think that you can earn 6%, which option should you take? That is the key to NPV. We must find the NPV of the $120,000 annuity at 6% (PV factor is 7.360) to compare. The value of the $120,000 annuity today is $883,200, which is less than the $1,000,000. So, you should take the $1,000,000 payout today rather than the $120,000 annuity.

Capital Rationing and the Profitability Index

Exhibits 21-11 and 21-12 show that both the CD player and DVR projects have positive NPVs. Therefore, both are attractive investments. Because resources are limited, companies are not always able to invest in all capital assets that meet their investment criteria. As mentioned earlier, this is called *capital rationing*. For example, Greg's may not have the funds to invest in both the DVR and CD-player projects at this time. In this case, Greg's should choose the DVR project because it yields a higher NPV. The DVR project should earn an additional $78,910 beyond the 14% required rate of return, while the CD-player project returns an additional $48,610.

This example illustrates an important point. The CD-player project promises more *total* net cash inflows. But the *timing* of the DVR cash flows—loaded near the beginning of the project—gives the DVR investment a higher NPV. The DVR project is more attractive because of the time value of money. Its dollars, which are received sooner, are worth more now than the more-distant dollars of the CD-player project.

If Greg's had to choose between the CD and DVR project, the company would choose the DVR project because it yields a higher NPV ($78,910). However, comparing the NPV of the two projects is *only* valid because both projects require the same initial cost—$1,000,000. In contrast, Exhibit 21-13 summarizes three capital investment options faced by Smart Touch. Each capital project requires a different initial investment. All three projects are attractive because each yields a positive NPV. Assuming Smart Touch can only invest in one project at this time, which one should it choose? Project B yields the highest NPV, but it also requires a larger initial investment than the alternatives.

EXHIBIT 21-13 | **Smart Touch Capital Investment Options**

Cash Flows	Project A	Project B	Project C
Present value of net cash inflows	$ 150,000	$ 238,000	$ 182,000
Investment	(125,000)	(200,000)	(150,000)
Net present value (NPV)	$ 25,000	$ 38,000	$ 32,000

To choose among the projects, Smart Touch computes the **profitability index** (also known as the **present value index**). The profitability index is computed as follows:

> Profitability index = Present value of net cash inflows ÷ Investment

The profitability index computes the number of dollars returned for every dollar invested, *with all calculations performed in present value dollars*. It allows us to compare alternative investments in present value terms (like the NPV method), but it also considers differences in the investments' initial cost. Let's compute the profitability index for all three alternatives.

Present value of net cash inflows	÷ Investment	= Profitability index
Project A: $150,000	÷ $125,000 =	1.20
Project B: $238,000	÷ $200,000 =	1.19
Project C: $182,000	÷ $150,000 =	1.21

The profitability index shows that Project C is the best of the three alternatives because it returns $1.21 (in present value dollars) for every $1.00 invested. Projects A and B return slightly less.

Let's also compute the profitability index for Greg's Tunes' CD-player and DVR projects:

CD-player: $1,048,610 ÷ $1,000,000 = 1.049
DVR: $1,078,910 ÷ $1,000,000 = 1.079

The profitability index confirms our prior conclusion that the DVR project is more profitable than the CD-player project. The DVR project returns $1.079 (in present value dollars) for every $1.00 invested (beyond the 14% return already used to discount the cash flows). We did not need the profitability index to determine that the DVR project was preferable because both projects required the same investment ($1,000,000). Because Greg's chose the DVR project over the CD-player project, the CD-player project is the opportunity cost. *Opportunity cost is the benefit foregone by not choosing an alternative course of action.*

NPV of a Project with Residual Value

Many assets yield cash inflows at the end of their useful lives because they have residual value. Companies discount an investment's residual value to its present value when determining the *total* present value of the project's net cash inflows. The residual value is discounted as a single lump sum—not an annuity—because it will be received only once, when the asset is sold. In short, it is just another type of cash inflow of the project.

Suppose Greg's expects that the CD project equipment will be worth $100,000 at the end of its five-year life. To determine the CD-player project's NPV, we discount the residual value of $100,000 using the Present Value of $1 table ($i = 14\%$, $n = 5$). (See Appendix B, Table B-1.) We then *add* its present value of $51,900 to the present value of the CD project's other net cash inflows we calculated in Exhibit 21-11 ($1,048,610). This gives the new net present value calculation as shown in Exhibit 21-14:

EXHIBIT 21-14 | NPV of a Project with Residual Value

=NPV(.14,305450,305450,
305450,305450,405450)

Then subtract the $1,000,000
initial investment

Year		PV Factor ($i = 14\%$, $n = 5$)	Net Cash Inflow	Present Value
1–5	Present value of annuity	3.433 ×	$305,450 =	$ 1,048,610
5	Present value of residual value (single lump sum)	0.519 ×	$100,000 =	51,900
	Total present value of net cash inflows			$ 1,100,510
0	Investment			(1,000,000)
	Net present value (NPV)			$ 100,510

Because of the expected residual value, the CD-player project is now more attractive than the DVR project. If Greg's could pursue only the CD or DVR project because of capital rationing, Greg's would now choose the CD project, because its NPV of $100,510 is higher than the DVR project's NPV of $78,910, and both projects require the same investment of $1,000,000.

Sensitivity Analysis

Capital budgeting decisions affect cash flows far into the future. Greg's managers might want to know whether their decision would be affected by any of their major assumptions, for example,

- changing the discount rate from 14% to 12% or to 16%.
- changing the net cash flows by 10%.

After reviewing the basic information for NPV analysis, managers perform sensitivity analyses to recalculate and review the results.

Internal Rate of Return (IRR)

Another discounted cash flow model for capital budgeting is the internal rate of return. The **internal rate of return (IRR)** is the rate of return (based on discounted cash flows) a company can expect to earn by investing in a capital asset. *It is the interest rate that makes the NPV of the investment equal to zero.*

Let's look at this concept in another light by substituting in the definition of NPV:

> Present value of the investment's net cash inflows – Investment's cost (Present value of cash outflows) = 0

In other words, the IRR is the *interest rate* that makes the cost of the investment equal to the present value of the investment's net cash inflows. The higher the IRR, the more desirable the project.

IRR with Equal Periodic Net Cash Inflows (Annuity)

Let's first consider Greg's CD-player project, which would cost $1,000,000 and result in five equal yearly cash inflows of $305,450. We compute the IRR of an investment with equal periodic cash flows (annuity) by taking the following steps:

1. The IRR is the interest rate that makes the cost of the investment *equal to* the present value of the investment's net cash inflows, so we set up the following equation:

> Investment's cost = Present value of investment's net cash inflows
> Investment's cost = Amount of each equal net cash inflow × Annuity PV factor (i = ?, n = given)

2. Next, we plug in the information we do know—the investment cost, $1,000,000, the equal annual net cash inflows, $305,450, but assume there is no residual value, and the number of periods (five years):

> $1,000,000 = $305,450 × Annuity PV factor (i = ?, n = 5)

3. We then rearrange the equation and solve for the Annuity PV factor (i = ?, n = 5):

> $1,000,000 ÷ $305,450 = Annuity PV factor (i = ?, n = 5)
> 3.274 = Annuity PV factor (i = ?, n = 5)

4. Finally, we find the interest rate that corresponds to this Annuity PV factor. Turn to the Present Value of Annuity of $1 table (Appendix B, Table B-2). Scan the row corresponding to the project's expected life—five years, in our example. Choose the column(s) with the number closest to the Annuity PV factor you calculated in step 3. The 3.274 annuity factor is in the 16% column. Therefore, the IRR of the CD-player project is 16%. Greg's expects the project to earn an internal rate of return of 16% over its life. Exhibit 21-15 confirms this result: Using a 16% discount rate, the project's NPV is zero. In other words, 16% is the discount rate that makes the investment cost equal to the present value of the investment's net cash inflows.

> **X**
> Enter the values in cells A1 through A6 as follows:
> -1000000
> 305450
> 305450
> 305450
> 305450
> 305450
> Then, =IRR(A1:A6)

EXHIBIT 21-15 | **IRR—CD-Player Project**

Years		Annuity PV Factor (i = 16%, n = 5)	Net Cash Inflow		Total Present Value
1–5	Present value of annuity of equal annual net cash inflows for 5 years at 16%	3.274 ×	$305,450	=	$1,000,000†
0	Investment				(1,000,000)
	Net present value of the CD-player project				$ 0‡

†Slight rounding of $43.
‡The zero difference proves that the IRR is 16%.

To decide whether the project is acceptable, compare the IRR with the minimum desired rate of return. The decision rule is as follows:

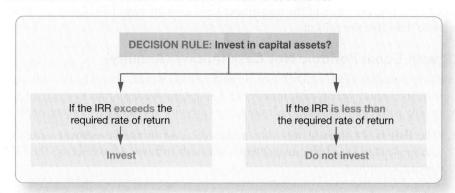

Recall that Greg's Tunes' required rate of return or hurdle rate is 14%. Because the CD project's IRR (16%) is higher than the hurdle rate (14%), Greg's would invest in the project.

In the CD-player project, the exact Annuity PV factor (3.274) appears in the Present Value of an Annuity of $1 table (Appendix B, Table B-2). Many times, the exact factor will not appear in the table. For example, let's find the IRR of Smart Touch's B2B Web portal from Exhibit 21-2. Recall the B2B portal had a six-year life with annual net cash inflows of $60,000. The investment costs $240,000. We find its Annuity PV factor using the same steps:

Enter the values in cells A1 through A7 as follows:
-240000
60000
60000
60000
60000
60000
60000
Then, =IRR(A1:A7)

Investment's cost	= Present value of investment's net cash inflows
Investment's cost	= Amount of each equal net cash inflow ×
	Annuity PV factor (i = ?, n = given)
$240,000	= $60,000 × Annuity PV factor (i = ?, n = 6)
$240,000 ÷ $60,000	= Annuity PV factor (i = ?, n = 6)
4.00	= Annuity PV factor (i = ?, n = 6)

Now look in the Present Value of Annuity of $1 table in the row marked 6 periods (Appendix B, Table B-2). You will not see 4.00 under any column. The closest two factors are 3.889 (at 14%) and 4.111 (at 12%). Thus, the B2B portal's IRR must be somewhere between 12% and 14%. If we need a more precise figure, we could interpolate, or use a business calculator or Microsoft Excel to find the portal's exact IRR of 12.978% (see Excel formula in margin). If Smart Touch had a 14% required rate of return, it would *not* invest in the B2B portal because the portal's IRR is less than 14%.

IRR with Unequal Periodic Cash Flows

Because the DVR project has unequal cash inflows, Greg's cannot use the Present Value of Annuity of $1 table to find the asset's IRR. Rather, Greg's must use a trial-and-error procedure to determine the discount rate making the project's NPV equal to zero. For example, because the company's minimum required rate of return is 14%, Greg's might start by calculating whether the DVR project earns at least 14%. Recall from Exhibit 21-12 that the DVR's NPV using a 14% discount rate is $78,910. Since the NPV is *positive*, the IRR must be *higher* than 14%. Greg's continues the trial-and-error process using *higher* discount rates until the company finds the rate that brings the net present value of the DVR project to *zero*. Exhibit 21-16 shows that at 16%, the DVR has an NPV of $40,390. Therefore, the IRR must be higher than 16%. At 18%, the NPV is $3,980, which is very close to zero. Thus, the IRR must be slightly higher than 18%. If we use a business calculator or Excel, rather than the trial-and-error procedure, we would find the IRR is 18.23%.

EXHIBIT 21-16 | **Finding the DVR's IRR Through Trial-and-Error**

Years		Net Cash Inflow	PV Factor (for i = 16%)		Present Value at 16%	Net Cash Inflow	PV Factor (for i = 18%)		Present Value at 18%
1	Inflows	$500,000	× 0.862*	=	$ 431,000	$500,000	× 0.847*	=	$ 423,500
2	Inflows	350,000	× 0.743	=	260,050	350,000	× 0.718	=	251,300
3	Inflows	300,000	× 0.641	=	192,300	300,000	× 0.609	=	182,700
4	Inflows	250,000	× 0.552	=	138,000	250,000	× 0.516	=	129,000
5	Inflows	40,000	× 0.476	=	19,040	40,000	× 0.437	=	17,480
	Total present value of net cash inflows				$ 1,040,390				$ 1,003,980
0	Investment				(1,000,000)				(1,000,000)
	Net present value (NPV)				$ 40,390				$ 3,980

*PV Factors are found in Appendix B, Table B-1.

The DVR's internal rate of return is higher than Greg's 14% required rate of return so the DVR project is attractive.

Comparing Capital Budgeting Methods

We have discussed four capital budgeting methods commonly used by companies to make capital investment decisions. Two of these methods do not incorporate the time value of money: payback period and ROR. Exhibit 21-17 summarizes the similarities and differences between these two methods.

EXHIBIT 21-17 | **Capital Budgeting Methods That *Ignore* the Time Value of Money**

Payback period	Rate of return
• Simple to compute	• The only method that uses accrual accounting figures
• Focuses on the time it takes to recover the company's cash investment	• Shows how the investment will affect operating income, which is important to financial statement users
• Ignores any cash flows occurring after the payback period, including any residual value	• Measures the profitability of the asset over its entire life
• Highlights risks of investments with longer cash recovery periods	• Ignores the time value of money
• Ignores the time value of money	

The discounted cash-flow methods are superior because they consider both the time value of money and profitability. These methods compare an investment's initial cost (cash outflow) with its future net cash inflows—all converted to the *same point in time*—the present value. Profitability is built into the discounted cash-flow methods because they consider *all* cash inflows and outflows over the project's life. Exhibit 21-18 considers the similarities and differences between the two discounted cash-flow methods.

X

Enter the values in cells A1 through A6 as follows:

-1000000
500000
350000
300000
250000
40000
Then, =IRR(A1:A6)

Key Takeaway

The NPV is the net difference between the present value of the investment's net cash inflows and the investment's cost (cash outflows), discounted at the company's required rate of return (hurdle) rate. The investment must meet or exceed the hurdle rate to be acceptable. The IRR is the interest rate that makes the cost of the investment equal to the present value of the investment's net cash inflows. Capital investment (budgeting) methods that consider the time value of money (like NPV and IRR) are best for decision making.

EXHIBIT 21-18 | **Capital Budgeting Methods That _Incorporate_ the Time Value of Money**

Net present value	Internal rate of return
• Incorporates the time value of money and the asset's net cash flows over its entire life	• Incorporates the time value of money and the asset's net cash flows over its entire life
• Indicates whether the asset will earn the company's minimum required rate of return	• Computes the project's unique rate of return
• Shows the excess or deficiency of the asset's present value of net cash inflows over its initial investment cost	• No additional steps needed for capital rationing decisions
• The profitability index should be computed for capital rationing decisions when the assets require different initial investments	

Managers often use more than one method to gain different perspectives on risks and returns. For example, Smart Touch could decide to pursue capital projects with positive NPVs, provided that those projects have a payback of four years or fewer.

Next, let's review the Decision Guidelines on the following page, which cover the two capital budgeting methods that consider the time value of money.

Decision Guidelines 21-2

CAPITAL BUDGETING

Here are more of the guidelines **Amazon.com**'s managers used as they made the major capital budgeting decision to invest in building warehouses.

Decision	Guideline
• Which capital budgeting methods are best?	Discounted cash-flow methods (NPV and IRR) are best because they incorporate both profitability and the time value of money.
• Why do the NPV and IRR models use the present value?	Because an investment's cash inflows and cash outflows occur at different points in time, they must be converted to a common point in time to make a valid comparison (that is, to determine whether inflows exceed cash outflows). These methods use the *present* value as the common point in time.
• How do we know whether investing in warehouse facilities will be worthwhile?	An investment in warehouse facilities may be worthwhile if the NPV is positive or the IRR exceeds the required rate of return.
• How do we compute the net present value with	
• equal annual cash flows?	Compute the present value of the investment's net cash inflows using the Present Value of an Annuity of $1 table and then subtract the investment's cost.
• unequal annual cash flows?	Compute the present value of each year's net cash inflows using the Present Value of $1 (lump sum) table, sum the present values of the inflows, and then subtract the investment's cost.
• How do we compute the internal rate of return (IRR) with	
• equal annual cash flows?	Find the interest rate that yields the following PV factor: $$\text{Annuity PV factor} = \frac{\text{Investment cost}}{\text{Expected annual net cash inflow}}$$
• unequal annual cash flows?	Trial and error, spreadsheet software, or business calculator

Summary Problem 21-2

Recall from Summary Problem 21-1 that Dyno-max is considering buying a new water treatment system. The investment proposal passed the initial screening tests (payback period and rate of return) so the company now wants to analyze the proposal using the discounted cash flow methods. Recall that the water treatment system costs $48,000, has a five-year life, and no residual value. The estimated net cash inflows from environmental cleanup savings are $13,000 per year over its life. The company's required rate of return is 16%.

Requirements

1. Compute the water treatment system's NPV.
2. Find the water treatment system's IRR (exact percentage is not required).
3. Should Dyno-max buy the water treatment system? Why?

Solution

Requirement 1

Present value of annuity of equal annual net cash inflows at 16% ($13,000 × 3.274*).....................................	$ 42,562
Investment...	(48,000)
Net present value	$ (5,438)

*Annuity PV factor ($i = 16\%, n = 5$)

Requirement 2

Investment's cost = Amount of each equal net cash inflow × Annuity PV factor

$$(i = ?, n = 5)$$

$$\$48,000 = \$13,000 \times \text{Annuity PV factor } (i = ?, n = 5)$$

$$\$48,000 \div \$13,000 = \text{Annuity PV factor } (i = ?, n = 5)$$

$$3.692 = \text{Annuity PV factor } (i = ?, n = 5)$$

Enter the values in cells A1 through A6 as follows:
-48000
13000
13000
13000
13000
13000
Then, =IRR(A1:A6)

Because the cash flows occur for five years, we look for the PV factor 3.692 in the row marked $n = 5$ on the Present Value of Annuity of $1 table (Appendix B, Table B-2). The PV factor is 3.605 at 12% and 3.791 at 10%. Therefore, the water treatment system has an IRR that falls between 10% and 12%. (*Optional:* Using a business calculator or Excel, we find an 11.03864% internal rate of return.)

Requirement 3

Decision: Do not buy the water treatment system. It has a negative NPV and its IRR falls below the company's required rate of return. Both methods consider profitability and the time value of money. Since the savings came mainly from the estimated environmental cleanup savings, the company may want to study this issue further to ensure all environmental savings, both short term and long term, were considered in the initial evaluation.

Review *Capital Investment Decisions and the Time Value of Money*

● Accounting Vocabulary

Annuity (p. 1021)
A stream of equal installments made at equal time intervals under the same interest rate.

Capital Budgeting (p. 1011)
The process of making capital investment decisions. Companies make capital investments when they acquire *capital assets*—assets used for a long period of time.

Capital Rationing (p. 1012)
Choosing among alternative capital investments due to limited funds.

Compound Interest (p. 1021)
Interest computed on the principal *and* all previously earned interest.

Discount Rate (p. 1027)
Management's minimum desired rate of return on an investment. Also called the **required rate of return** and **hurdle rate**.

Hurdle Rate (p. 1027)
The rate an investment must meet or exceed in order to be acceptable. Also called the **discount rate** and **required rate of return**.

Internal Rate of Return (IRR) (p. 1031)
The rate of return (based on discounted cash flows) that a company can expect to earn by investing in a capital asset. The interest rate that makes the NPV of the investment equal to zero.

Net Present Value (NPV) (p. 1026)
The net *difference* between the present value of the investment's net cash inflows and the investment's cost (cash outflows).

Payback (p. 1013)
The length of time it takes to recover, in net cash inflows, the cost of a capital outlay.

Post-Audits (p. 1013)
Comparing a capital investment's actual net cash inflows to its projected net cash inflows.

Present Value Index (p. 1029)
An index that computes the number of dollars returned for every dollar invested, *with all calculations performed in present value dollars*. Computed as present value of net cash inflows divided by investment. Also called the **profitability index**.

Profitability Index (p. 1029)
An index that computes the number of dollars returned for every dollar invested, *with all calculations performed in present value dollars*. Computed as present value of net cash inflows divided by investment. Also called the **present value index**.

Rate of Return (ROR) (p. 1016)
A measure of profitability computed by dividing the average annual operating income from an asset by the average amount invested in the asset.

Required Rate of Return (p. 1027)
The rate an investment must meet or exceed in order to be acceptable. Also called the **discount rate** and **hurdle rate**.

Simple Interest (p. 1021)
Interest computed *only* on the principal amount.

● Destination: Student Success

Student Success Tips

The following are hints on some common trouble areas for students in this chapter:

● Remember that the payback period and rate of return don't consider the time value of money. NPV and IRR do consider the time value of money.

● Keep in mind the definition of an annuity: equal amounts, equal time periods, and a constant interest rate.

● Consider that NPV discounts the future cash inflows that come from investing in an asset to the present value today because the decision will be made today (in the present).

● Keep in mind that the discount rate where NPV equals zero is the IRR.

● Recall the discounted cash flow values can be calculated using the tables in Appendix B, a business calculator, or Excel. The results between the table values and the other methods will vary slightly due to rounding in the Appendix B tables.

● Remember that when deciding between two investments where both are positive, capital rationing may come into play. Capital rationing means the company has limited resources available for capital investments; thus, it will choose the investment that has the highest NPV.

Getting Help

If there's a learning objective from the chapter you aren't confident about, try using one or more of the following resources:

● Consider drawing a time line to help you visualize when cash inflows and outflows are occurring.

● Review Decision Guidelines 21-1 and 21-2 in the chapter.

● Review Summary Problems 21-1and 21-2 in the chapter to reinforce your understanding of payback period, ROR, NPV and IRR.

● Practice additional exercises or problems at the end of Chapter 21 that cover the specific learning objective that is challenging you.

● Watch the white board videos for Chapter 21, located at myaccountinglab.com under the Chapter Resources button.

● Go to myaccountinglab.com and select the Study Plan button. Choose Chapter 21 and work the questions covering that specific learning objective until you've mastered it.

● Work the Chapter 21 pre/post tests in myaccountinglab.com.

● Consult the Check Figures for End of Chapter starters, exercises, and problems, located at myaccountinglab.com.

● Visit the learning resource center on your campus for tutoring.

● Quick Check

1. What is the first step of capital budgeting?

   a. Gathering the money for the investment

   b. Identifying potential projects

   c. Getting the accountant involved

   d. All of the above

2. Ian, Corp., is considering two expansion projects. The first project streamlines the company's warehousing facilities. The second project automates inventory utilizing bar code scanners. Both projects generate positive NPV, yet Ian, Corp., only chooses the bar coding project. Why?

   a. The payback period is greater than the warehouse project's life.

   b. The internal rate of return of the warehousing project is less than the company's required rate of return for capital projects.

   c. The company is practicing capital rationing.

   d. All of the above are true.

3. Which of the following methods does not consider the investment's profitability?

   a. ROR   c. NPV

   b. Payback   d. IRR

4. Suppose Francine Dunkelberg's Sweets is considering investing in warehouse-management software that costs $550,000, has $75,000 residual value, and should lead to cost savings of $130,000 per year for its five-year life. In calculating the ROR, which of the following figures should be used as the equation's denominator (average amount invested in the asset)?

   a. $275,000   c. $625,000

   b. $237,500   d. $312,500

5. Your rich aunt has promised to give you $2,000 a year at the end of each of the next four years to help you pay for college. Using a discount rate of 12%, the present value of the gift can be stated as

   a. PV = $2,000 (PV factor, $i = 4\%$, $n = 12$).

   b. PV = $2,000 (Annuity PV factor, $i = 12\%$, $n = 4$).

   c. PV = $2,000 (Annuity FV factor, $i = 12\%$, $n = 4$).

   d. PV = $2,000 \times 12\% \times 4$.

6. Which of the following affects the present value of an investment?

   a. The type of investment (annuity versus single lump sum)

   b. The number of time periods (length of the investment)

   c. The interest rate

   d. All of the above

7. Which of the following is true regarding capital rationing decisions?

   a. Companies should always choose the investment with the highest NPV.

   b. Companies should always choose the investment with the highest ROR.

   c. Companies should always choose the investment with the shortest payback period.

   d. None of the above

8. In computing the IRR on an expansion at Mountain Creek Resort, Vernon Valley would consider all of the following *except?*

   a. Present value factors

   b. Depreciation on the assets built in the expansion

   c. Predicted cash inflows over the life of the expansion

   d. The cost of the expansion

9. The IRR is

   a. the interest rate at which the NPV of the investment is zero.

   b. the firm's hurdle rate.

   c. the same as the ROR.

   d. None of the above

10. Which of the following is the most reliable method for making capital budgeting decisions?

   a. ROR method   c. NPV method

   b. Post-audit method   d. Payback method

Answers are given after Apply Your Knowledge (p. 1049).

Assess Your Progress

● Short Exercises

S21-1   **1** **The importance of capital investments and the capital budgeting process**   *MyAccountingLab*
[10 min]
Review the following activities of the capital budgeting process:

   a. Budget capital investments.

   b. Project investments' cash flows.

   c. Perform post-audits.

   d. Make investments.

   e. Use feedback to reassess investments already made.

   f. Identify potential capital investments.

   g. Screen/analyze investments using one or more of the methods discussed.

Requirement

   1. Place the activities in sequential order as they occur in the capital budgeting process.

S21-2 ❷ **Using the payback period and rate of return methods to make capital investment decisions [10 min]**

Consider how Smith Valley Snow Park Lodge could use capital budgeting to decide whether the $13,500,000 Snow Park Lodge expansion would be a good investment.

Assume Smith Valley's managers developed the following estimates concerning the expansion:

Number of additional skiers per day	117
Average number of days per year that weather	
conditions allow skiing at Smith Valley	142
Useful life of expansion (in years)	10
Average cash spent by each skier per day	$ 236
Average variable cost of serving each skier per day . . .	$ 76
Cost of expansion	$13,500,000
Discount rate	10%

Assume that Smith Valley uses the straight-line depreciation method and expects the lodge expansion to have a residual value of $1,000,000 at the end of its 10-year life.

Requirements

1. Compute the average annual net cash inflow from the expansion.
2. Compute the average annual operating income from the expansion.

Note: Short Exercise 21-2 must be completed before attempting Short Exercise 21-3.

S21-3 ❷ **Using the payback method to make capital investment decisions [5 min]**

Refer to the Smith Valley Snow Park Lodge expansion project in S21-2.

Requirement

1. Compute the payback period for the expansion project.

Note: Short Exercise 21-2 must be completed before attempting Short Exercise 21-4.

S21-4 ❷ **Using the rate of return method to make capital investment decisions [5–10 min]**

Refer to the Smith Valley Snow Park Lodge expansion project in S21-2.

Requirement

1. Calculate the ROR.

Note: Short Exercise 21-2 must be completed before attempting Short Exercise 21-5.

S21-5 ❷ **Using the payback and rate of return methods to make capital investment decisions [5–10 min]**

Refer to the Smith Valley Snow Park Lodge expansion project in S21-2. *Assume the expansion has zero residual value.*

Requirements

1. Will the payback period change? Explain your answer and recalculate if necessary.
2. Will the project's ROR change? Explain your answer and recalculate if necessary.
3. Assume Smith Valley screens its potential capital investments using the following decision criteria:

Maximum payback period	5.3 years
Minimum rate of return	16.55%

Will Smith Valley consider this project further, or reject it?

S21-6 **2** **Using the payback and rate of return methods to make capital investment decisions [5–10 min]**
Suppose Smith Valley is deciding whether to purchase new accounting software. The payback period for the $28,575 software package is three years, and the software's expected life is eight years. Smith Valley's required rate of return is 14.0%.

Requirement

1. Assuming equal yearly cash flows, what are the expected annual cash savings from the new software?

S21-7 **3** **Using the time value of money to compute the present and future values of single lump sums and annuities [10–15 min]**
Your grandfather would like to share some of his fortune with you. He offers to give you money under one of the following scenarios (you get to choose):

1. $8,750 a year at the end of each of the next seven years.
2. $50,050 (lump sum) now.
3. $100,250 (lump sum) seven years from now.

Requirement

1. Calculate the present value of each scenario using a 6% discount rate. Which scenario yields the highest present value? Would your preference change if you used a 12% discount rate?

S21-8 **3** **Using the time value of money to compute the present and future values of single lump sums and annuities [5–10 min]**
Assume you make the following investments:

a. You invest $8,000 for five years at 14% interest.
b. In a different account earning 14% interest, you invest $1,750 at the end of each year for five years.

Requirement

1. Calculate the value of each investment at the end of five years.

S21-9 **3** **Using the time value of money to compute the present and future values of single lump sums and annuities [10–15 min]**
Refer to the lottery payout options summarized in Exhibit 21-9.

Requirement

1. Rather than comparing the payout options at their present values (as done in the chapter), compare the payout options at their future value, 10 years from now.
   a. Using an 8% interest rate, what is the future value of each payout option?
   b. Rank your preference among payout options.
   c. Does computing the future value rather than the present value of the options change your preference between payout options? Explain your reasoning.

S21-10 **3** **Using the time value of money to compute the present and future values of single lump sums and annuities [10–15 min]**
Use the Present Value of $1 table (Appendix B, Table B-1) to determine the present value of $1 received one year from now. Assume an 8% interest rate. Use the same table to find the present value of $1 received two years from now. Continue this process for a total of five years.

Requirements

1. What is the *total* present value of the cash flows received over the five-year period?
2. Could you characterize this stream of cash flows as an annuity? Why or why not?
3. Use the Present Value of Annuity of $1 table (Appendix B, Table B-2) to determine the present value of the same stream of cash flows. Compare your results to your answer to Requirement 1.
4. Explain your findings.

Note: Short Exercise 21-2 must be completed before attempting Short Exercise 21-11.

S21-11 ❹ **Using discounted cash flow models to make capital investment decisions [10–15 min]**
Refer to the Smith Valley Snow Park Lodge expansion project in S21-2.

Requirement

1. What is the project's NPV? Is the investment attractive? Why?

Note: Short Exercise 21-2 must be completed before attempting Short Exercise 21-12.

S21-12 ❹ **Using discounted cash flow models to make capital investment decisions [10–15 min]**
Refer to S21-2. *Assume the expansion has no residual value.*

Requirement

1. What is the project's NPV? Is the investment attractive? Why?

Note: Short Exercise 21-12 must be completed before attempting Short Exercise 21-13.

S21-13 ❹ **Using discounted cash flow models to make capital investment decisions [10–15 min]**
Refer to S21-12. *Continue to assume that the expansion has no residual value.*

Requirement

1. What is the project's IRR? Is the investment attractive? Why?

● Exercises

MyAccountingLab **E21-14** ❶ **The importance of capital investments and the capital budgeting process [15–20 min]**
You have just started a business and want your new employees to be well informed about capital budgeting.

Requirement

1. Match each definition with its capital budgeting method.

METHODS
1. Rate of return.
2. Internal rate of return.
3. Net present value.
4. Payback period.

DEFINITIONS
A. Is only concerned with the time it takes to get cash outflows returned.
B. Considers operating income but not the time value of money in its analyses.
C. Compares the present value of cash out to the cash in to determine investment worthiness.
D. The true rate of return an investment earns.

E21-15 ❷ **Using the payback and rate of return methods to make capital investment decisions [5–10 min]**
Preston, Co., is considering acquiring a manufacturing plant. The purchase price is $1,100,000. The owners believe the plant will generate net cash inflows of $297,000 annually. It will have to be replaced in six years.

Requirement

1. Use the payback method to determine whether Preston should purchase this plant.

E21-16 ❷ **Using the payback and rate of return methods to make capital investment decisions [5–10 min]**

Robinson Hardware is adding a new product line that will require an investment of $1,454,000. Managers estimate that this investment will have a 10-year life and generate net cash inflows of $300,000 the first year, $270,000 the second year, and $260,000 each year thereafter for eight years.

Requirement

    1. Compute the payback period.

Note: Exercise 21-16 must be completed before attempting Exercise 21-17.

E21-17 ❷ **Using the payback and rate of return methods to make capital investment decisions [10–15 min]**

Refer to the Robinson Hardware information in E21-16. Assume the project has no residual value.

Requirement

    1. Compute the ROR for the investment.

E21-18 ❸ **Using the time value of money to compute the present and future values of single lump sums and annuities [15–20 min]**

Assume you want to retire early at age 52. You plan to save using one of the following two strategies: (1) save $3,000 a year in an IRA beginning when you are 22 and ending when you are 52 (30 years), or (2) wait until you are 37 to start saving and then save $6,000 per year for the next 15 years. Assume you will earn the historic stock market average of 14% per year.

Requirements

    1. How much "out-of-pocket" cash will you invest under the two options?

    2. How much savings will you have accumulated at age 52 under the two options?

    3. Explain the results.

    4. If you were to let the savings continue to grow for 10 more years (with no further out-of-pocket investments), what would the investments be worth when you are age 62?

E21-19 ❸ **Using the time value of money to compute the present and future values of single lump sums and annuities [15–20 min]**

Your best friend just received a gift of $7,000 from his favorite aunt. He wants to save the money to use as "starter" money after college. He can invest it (1) risk-free at 6%, (2) taking on moderate risk at 8%, or (3) taking on high risk at 14%.

Requirement

    1. Help your friend project the investment's worth at the end of four years under each investment strategy and explain the results to him.

E21-20 ❸ **Using the time value of money to compute the present and future values of single lump sums and annuities [5–10 min]**

Janice wants to take the next five years off work to travel around the world. She estimates her annual cash needs at $28,000 (if she needs more, she will work odd jobs). Janice believes she can invest her savings at 8% until she depletes her funds.

Requirements

    1. How much money does Janice need now to fund her travels?

    2. After speaking with a number of banks, Janice learns she will only be able to invest her funds at 4%. How much does she need now to fund her travels?

E21-21 ❸ **Using the time value of money to compute the present and future values of single lump sums and annuities [10–15 min]**

Congratulations! You have won a state lotto. The state lottery offers you the following (after-tax) payout options:

Option #1: $15,000,000 after five years.

Option #2: $2,150,000 per year for the next five years.

Option #3: $13,000,000 after three years.

Requirement

1. Assuming you can earn 8% on your funds, which option would you prefer?

E21-22 ❹ **Using discounted cash flow models to make capital investment decisions [15–20 min]**

Use the NPV method to determine whether Kyler Products should invest in the following projects:

- *Project A*: Costs $260,000 and offers seven annual net cash inflows of $57,000. Kyler Products requires an annual return of 16% on projects like A.
- *Project B*: Costs $375,000 and offers 10 annual net cash inflows of $75,000. Kyler Products demands an annual return of 14% on investments of this nature.

Requirements

1. What is the NPV of each project?
2. What is the maximum acceptable price to pay for each project?
3. What is the profitability index of each project?

E21-23 ❹ **Using discounted cash flow models to make capital investment decisions [15–20 min]**

Sprocket Industries is deciding whether to automate one phase of its production process. The manufacturing equipment has a six-year life and will cost $905,000. Projected net cash inflows are as follows:

Year 1	$260,000
Year 2	$254,000
Year 3	$225,000
Year 4	$215,000
Year 5	$205,000
Year 6	$173,000

Requirements

1. Compute this project's NPV using Sprocket's 16% hurdle rate. Should Sprocket invest in the equipment?
2. Sprocket could refurbish the equipment at the end of six years for $103,000. The refurbished equipment could be used one more year, providing $75,000 of net cash inflows in year 7. Additionally, the refurbished equipment would have a $54,000 residual value at the end of year 7. Should Sprocket invest in the equipment and refurbishing it after six years? (*Hint:* In addition to your answer to Requirement 1, discount the additional cash outflow and inflows back to the present value.)

Note: Exercise 21-22 must be completed before attempting Exercise 21-24.

E21-24 ❹ **Using discounted cash flow models to make capital investment decisions [15 min]**

Refer to the data regarding Kyler Products in E21-22.

Requirement

1. Compute the IRR of each project and use this information to identify the better investment.

E21-25 ④ **Using discounted cash flow models to make capital investment decisions [10–15 min]**
Brighton Manufacturing is considering three capital investment proposals. At this time, Brighton only has funds available to pursue one of the three investments.

	Equipment A	Equipment B	Equipment C
Present value of net cash inflows	$ 1,735,915	$ 1,969,888	$ 2,207,765
Investment	(1,563,887)	(1,669,397)	(1,886,979)
NPV	$ 172,028	$ 300,491	$ 320,786

Requirement

1. Which investment should Brighton pursue at this time? Why?

● Problems (Group A)

P21-26A ① **Describing the importance of capital investments and the capital budgeting process [10–15 min]**   *MyAccountingLab*
Consider the following statements about capital budgeting.

a. _____ is (are) more appropriate for long-term investments.

b. _____ highlights risky investments.

c. _____ shows the effect of the investment on the company's accrual-based income.

d. _____ is the interest rate that makes the NPV of an investment equal to zero.

e. In capital rationing decisions, management must identify the discount rate when the _____ method is used.

f. _____ provides management with information on how fast the cash invested will be recouped.

g. _____ is the rate of return, using discounted cash flows, a company can expect to earn by investing in the asset.

h. _____ does not consider the asset's profitability.

i. _____ uses accrual accounting rather than net cash inflows in its computation.

Requirement

1. Fill in each statement with the appropriate capital budgeting method: Payback period, ROR, NPV, or IRR.

P21-27A ② ④ **Using payback, rate of return, discounted cash flow models, and profitability index to make capital investment decisions [20–30 min]**
Water Planet is considering purchasing a water park in Atlanta, Georgia, for $1,870,000. The new facility will generate annual net cash inflows of $460,000 for eight years. Engineers estimate that the facility will remain useful for eight years and have no residual value. The company uses straight-line depreciation, and its stockholders demand an annual return of 10% on investments of this nature.

Requirements

1. Compute the payback period, the ROR, the NPV, the IRR, and the profitability index of this investment.

2. Recommend whether the company should invest in this project.

P21-28A ② ④ **Using payback, rate of return, discounted cash flow models, and profitability index to make capital investment decisions; Calculating IRR [30–45 min]**

Leches operates a chain of sandwich shops. The company is considering two possible expansion plans. Plan A would open eight smaller shops at a cost of $8,400,000. Expected annual net cash inflows are $1,500,000, with zero residual value at the end of 10 years. Under Plan B, Leches would open three larger shops at a cost of $8,250,000. This plan is expected to generate net cash inflows of $1,080,000 per year for 10 years, the estimated useful life of the properties. Estimated residual value for Plan B is $1,000,000. Leches uses straight-line depreciation and requires an annual return of 10%.

Requirements

1. Compute the payback period, the ROR, the NPV, and the profitability index of these two plans. What are the strengths and weaknesses of these capital budgeting models?

2. Which expansion plan should Leches choose? Why?

3. Estimate Plan A's IRR. How does the IRR compare with the company's required rate of return?

P21-29A ③ **Using the time value of money to compute the present and future values of single lump sums and annuities [15–20 min]**

You are planning for a very early retirement. You would like to retire at age 40 and have enough money saved to be able to draw $235,000 per year for the next 40 years (based on family history, you think you will live to age 80). You plan to save by making 15 equal annual installments (from age 25 to age 40) into a fairly risky investment fund that you expect will earn 12% per year. You will leave the money in this fund until it is completely depleted when you are 80 years old.

Requirements

1. How much money must you accumulate by retirement to make your plan work? (*Hint:* Find the present value of the $235,000 withdrawals.)

2. How does this amount compare to the total amount you will draw out of the investment during retirement? How can these numbers be so different?

3. How much must you pay into the investment each year for the first 15 years? (*Hint:* Your answer from Requirement 1 becomes the future value of this annuity.)

4. How does the total "out-of-pocket" savings compare to the investment's value at the end of the 15-year savings period and the withdrawals you will make during retirement?

● Problems (Group B)

MyAccountingLab ⏺ **P21-30B** ① **Describing the importance of capital investments and the capital budgeting process [10–15 min]**

Consider the following statements about capital budgeting.

a. _____ is (are) often used by management to screen potential investments from those less desired.

b. _____ does not consider the asset's profitability.

c. _____ is calculated by dividing the average amount invested by the asset's average annual operating income.

d. _____ is the rate of return, using discounted cash flows, a company can expect to earn by investing in the asset.

e. In capital rationing decisions, the profitability index must be computed to compare investments requiring different initial investments when the _____ method is used.

f. _____ ignores any residual value.

g. _____ is the interest rate that makes the NPV of an investment equal to zero.

h. _____ highlights risky investments.

i. _____ shows the effect of the investment on the company's accrual-based income.

Requirement

1. Fill in each statement with the appropriate capital budgeting method: Payback period, ROR, NPV, or IRR.

P21-31B ❷ ❹ **Using payback, rate of return, discounted cash flow models, and profitability index to make capital investment decisions [20–30 min]**

Splash World is considering purchasing a water park in Omaha, Nebraska, for $1,820,000. The new facility will generate annual net cash inflows of $472,000 for eight years. Engineers estimate that the facility will remain useful for eight years and have no residual value. The company uses straight-line depreciation, and its stockholders demand an annual return of 10% on investments of this nature.

Requirements

1. Compute the payback period, the ROR, the NPV, the IRR, and the profitability index of this investment.
2. Recommend whether the company should invest in this project.

P21-32B ❷ ❹ **Using payback, rate of return, discounted cash flow models, and profitability index to make capital investment decisions; Calculating IRR [30–45 min]**

Lulus operates a chain of sandwich shops. The company is considering two possible expansion plans. Plan A would open eight smaller shops at a cost of $8,450,000. Expected annual net cash inflows are $1,750,000, with zero residual value at the end of eight years. Under Plan B, Lulus would open three larger shops at a cost of $8,000,000. This plan is expected to generate net cash inflows of $1,020,000 per year for eight years, which is the estimated useful life of the properties. Estimated residual value for Plan B is $1,200,000. Lulus uses straight-line depreciation and requires an annual return of 6%

Requirements

1. Compute the payback period, the ROR, the NPV, and the profitability index of these two plans. What are the strengths and weaknesses of these capital budgeting models?
2. Which expansion plan should Lulus choose? Why?
3. Estimate Plan A's IRR. How does the IRR compare with the company's required rate of return?

P21-33B ❸ **Using the time value of money to compute the present and future values of single lump sums and annuities [15–20 min]**

You are planning for an early retirement. You would like to retire at age 40 and have enough money saved to be able to draw $240,000 per year for the next 35 years (based on family history, you think you will live to age 75). You plan to save by making 10 equal annual installments (from age 30 to age 40) into a fairly risky investment fund that you expect will earn 16% per year. You will leave the money in this fund until it is completely depleted when you are 75 years old.

Requirements

1. How much money must you accumulate by retirement to make your plan work? (*Hint:* Find the present value of the $240,000 withdrawals.)

2. How does this amount compare to the total amount you will draw out of the investment during retirement? How can these numbers be so different?

3. How much must you pay into the investment each year for the first 10 years? (*Hint:* Your answer from Requirement 1 becomes the future value of this annuity.)

4. How does the total "out-of-pocket" savings compare to the investment's value at the end of the 10-year savings period and the withdrawals you will make during retirement?

● Continuing Exercise

MyAccountingLab **E21-34** **② ④** **Using payback, accounting rate of return, discounted cash flow, and IRR to make capital investment decisions [30–45 min]**

This exercise continues the Lawlor Lawn Service, Inc., situation from Exercise 20-33 of Chapter 20. Lawlor Lawn Service is considering purchasing a mower that will generate cash inflows of $9,000 per year. The mower has a zero residual value and an estimated useful life of three years. The mower costs $20,000. Lawlor's required rate of return is 12%.

Requirements

1. Calculate payback period, rate of return, net present value, and IRR for the mower investment.

2. Should Lawlor invest in the new mower?

● Continuing Problem

MyAccountingLab **P21-35** **② ④** **Using payback, accounting rate of return, discounted cash flow, and IRR to make capital investment decisions [30–45 min]**

This problem continues the Draper Consulting, Inc., situation from Problem 20-34 of Chapter 20. Draper Consulting is considering purchasing two different types of servers. Server A will generate cash inflows of $25,000 per year and has a zero residual value. Server A's estimated useful life is three years and it costs $40,000.

Server B will generate cash inflows of $25,000 in year 1, $11,000 in year 2, and $4,000 in year 3. Server B has a $4,000 residual value and an estimated life of three years. Server B also costs $40,000. Draper's required rate of return is 14%.

Requirements

1. Calculate payback period, rate of return, net present value, and IRR for both server investments.

2. Assuming capital rationing applies, which server should Draper invest in?

Apply Your Knowledge

● Decision Case 21-1

Dominic Hunter, a second-year business student at the University of Utah, will graduate in two years with an accounting major and a Spanish minor. Hunter is trying to decide where to work this summer. He has two choices: work full-time for a bottling plant or work part-time in the accounting department of a meat-packing plant. He probably will work at the same place next summer as well. He is able to work 12 weeks during the summer.

The bottling plant will pay Hunter $380 per week this year and 7% more next summer. At the meat-packing plant, he could work 20 hours per week at $8.75 per hour. Hunter believes that the experience he gains this summer will qualify him for a full-time accounting position with the meat-packing plant next summer. That position will pay $550 per week.

Hunter sees two additional benefits of working part-time this summer. By working only part-time, he could take two accounting courses this summer (tuition is $225 per hour for each of the four-hour courses) and reduce his studying workload during the Fall and Spring semesters. Second, he would have the time to work as a grader in the university's accounting department during the 15-week fall term and make additional income. Grading pays $50 per week.

Requirements

1. Suppose that Hunter ignores the time value of money in decisions that cover this short time period. Suppose also that his sole goal is to make as much money as possible between now and the end of next summer. What should he do? What nonquantitative factors might Hunter consider? What would *you* do if you were faced with these alternatives?

2. Now suppose that Hunter considers the time value of money for all cash flows that he expects to receive one year or more in the future. Which alternative does this consideration favor? Why?

● Fraud Case 21-1

John Johnson's landscape company was on its last legs, so when John got a call from Capital Funding, Ltd., offering a non-secured loan, he thought it might be his last chance to keep the business afloat. The loan officer explained that the government was promoting loans to keep small businesses from folding during the recession, and that his company qualified. John knew his credit rating was terrible, but he didn't want to lay off his staff of six and look for work himself, so he put aside his doubts and showed up at the office to fill out the paperwork. The gentleman was professional and reassuring. Two days later, John got a call assuring him that the funds would be transferred as soon as they received a "processing fee" of $900. This was a bit of shock for John, but he delivered the check. He could hardly sleep that night, and he called back first thing the next morning. There was no answer. He drove by the loan office. It was vacant. They had vanished without a trace.

Requirements

1. Did John have reason to be suspicious? What were the warning signs?
2. What should small businesses do when they are in financial trouble?

● Communication Activity 21-1

In 70 words or fewer, explain the difference between NPV and IRR.

Quick Check Answers

1. *b* 2. *c* 3. *b* 4. *d* 5. *b* 6. *d* 7. *d* 8. *b* 9. *a* 10. *c*

For online homework, exercises, and problems that provide you immediate feedback, please visit myaccountinglab.com.

22

The Master Budget and Responsibility Accounting

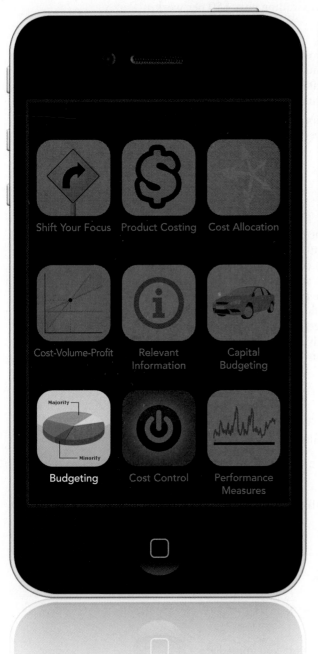

Shift Your Focus · Product Costing · Cost Allocation

Cost-Volume-Profit · Relevant Information · Capital Budgeting

Budgeting · Cost Control · Performance Measures

Learning Objectives

1. Learn why managers use budgets

2. Understand the components of the master budget

3. Prepare an operating budget

4. Prepare a financial budget

5. Use sensitivity analysis in budgeting

6. Prepare performance reports for responsibility centers and account for traceable and common shared fixed costs

Y ou're set to graduate in a few weeks and already have a great job offer. Your excitement, however, is paired with some anxiety. You'll be financially independent for the first time, not relying on your parents for financial support. You want to make sure you'll be able to live within your means. You've heard of friends who graduated and quickly created a financial mess by carelessly using credit cards, so you've decided to make a budget for your first year out of college. Your salary will be your only source of income. Your expenses will include rent, food, utilities, car operation and maintenance, insurance, and entertainment. You also need a more professional wardrobe and will have some expenses related to setting up your new apartment. Also, you have a student loan that will need to be repaid beginning six months after graduation, so you need to include your student loan payment in your budget. Some of these expenses will be the same each month, like your rent. Some will vary from month to month, like interest expense on your student loan.

Creating a budget will help you make critical decisions, such as how much rent you can afford. You'll also use the budget to plan and control your other expenses. Careful budgeting helps both individuals and businesses set goals that help plan for the future.

As you will see throughout this chapter, knowing how *costs* behave continues to be important when organizations are forming budgets. Total fixed costs will not change as volume changes within the relevant range. However, total variable costs must be adjusted when sales volume is expected to fluctuate. In this chapter, we'll continue to use Smart Touch Learning and Greg's Tunes to demonstrate budgeting.

Why Managers Use Budgets

Let's continue our study of budgets by moving from your personal budget to see how a small service business develops a simple budget. When Smart Touch Learning, Inc., first began, it was a small online service company that provided e-learning services to customers. Assume Smart Touch wants to earn $550,000 a month and expects to sell 20,000 e-learning services per month at a price of $30 each. Over the past six months, it paid an average of $18,000 a month to its Internet service provider, and spent an additional $20,000 per month on salaries. Smart Touch expects these monthly costs to remain about the same, so these are the monthly fixed costs. Smart Touch spent 5% of its revenues for banner ads on other Web sites. Smart Touch also incurs $2.25 in server space expense for each e-learning service provided. Because advertising and server space expenses fluctuate with revenue, advertising and server space expenses are variable.

Exhibit 22-1 shows how to compute a budgeted income statement using the variable costing approach. The **budgeted income statement** projects operating income for the period. **A budgeted income statement shows *estimated* (budgeted) values, whereas an income statement shows *actual* results.**

> **1** Learn why managers use budgets

EXHIBIT 22-1 | **Service Company Budget**

SMART TOUCH LEARNING, INC. Budgeted Income Statement For the Month Ended May 31, 2014	
Service revenue (20,000 × $30 each)	$600,000
Variable expenses:	
Server space expense (20,000 × $2.25 each)	$ 45,000
Advertising expense (5% × $600,000 revenue)	30,000
Total variable expenses	75,000
Contribution margin	$525,000
Fixed expenses:	
Salary expense	$ 20,000
Internet access expense	18,000
Total fixed expenses	38,000
Budgeted operating income	$487,000

As you can see from the exhibit, Smart Touch's contribution margin is strong, at $525,000. For each e-learning service sold, 87.5% ($525,000/$600,000) of revenue is contributing to the covering of fixed costs and to making a profit. Smart Touch's budgeted operating income of $487,000 will not meet its $550,000 per month operating income goal. It will have to increase revenue (perhaps through word-of-mouth advertising) or cut expenses (perhaps by reducing server space expense of $2.25 per service or by reducing the other variable and/or fixed costs).

Using Budgets to Plan and Control

Large international for-profit companies, such as **Amazon.com,** and nonprofit organizations, such as **Habitat for Humanity,** use budgets for the same reasons as you do in your personal life or in your small business—to plan and control actions and the related revenues and expenses. Managers also use budgets to plan for technology upgrades, other capital asset replacements, improvements, or expansions. Strategic as well as operational plans are budgeted for as well. Exhibit 22-2 shows how managers use budgets in fulfilling their major responsibilities. First, they develop strategies—overall business goals like **Amazon**'s goal to expand its international operations, or **Gateway**'s goal to be a value leader in the personal computer market while diversifying into other markets. Companies then plan and budget for specific actions to achieve those goals. The next step is to act. For example, **Amazon** planned for and then added a grocery feature to its Web sites.

EXHIBIT 22-2 | **Managers Use Budgets to Plan and Control Business Activities**

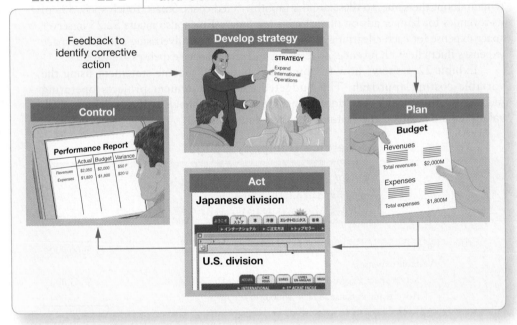

After acting, managers compare actual results with the budget. This feedback allows them to determine what, if any, corrective action to take. If, for example, **Amazon** spent more than expected to add the grocery feature to its Web sites, managers must cut other costs or increase revenues. These decisions affect the company's future strategies and plans.

Amazon has a number of budgets, as its managers develop budgets for their own divisions. Software then combines the division budgets to create an organization-wide budget for the whole company. Managers also prepare both long-term and short-term budgets. Some of the budgets are long-term forecasts that project demand for various business segments for the next 20 years. Keep in mind that all budgets incorporate management's strategic and operational plans.

However, most companies budget their cash flows monthly, weekly, and even daily to ensure that they have enough cash. They also budget revenues and expenses—and operating income—for months, quarters, and years. This chapter focuses on short-term budgets of one year or less. Chapter 21 explained how companies budget for major capital expenditures on property, plant, and equipment.

Benefits of Budgeting

Exhibit 22-3 summarizes three key benefits of budgeting. Budgeting forces managers to plan, promotes coordination and communication, and provides a benchmark for evaluating actual performance. The budget really represents the plan the company has in place to achieve its goals.

EXHIBIT 22-3 | **Benefits of Budgeting**

Budgets force managers to plan.

Budgets promote coordination and communication.

Budgets provide a benchmark that motivates employees and helps managers evaluate performance against planned goals.

Planning

Exhibit 22-1 shows the expected income from Smart Touch's online e-learning business is $487,000. This is short of the target operating income of $550,000. The sooner Smart Touch learns of the expected shortfall, the more time it has to modify its plan and to devise strategies to increase revenues or cut expenses so the company can achieve its planned goals. The better Smart Touch's plan, and the more time it has to act on the plan, the more likely it will be to find a way to meet the target.

Coordination and Communication

The master budget coordinates a company's activities. Creating a master budget facilitates coordination and communication by requiring managers at different levels and in different functions across the entire value chain to work together to make a single, unified, comprehensive plan for the business. For example, **Amazon** stimulates sales by offering free shipping on orders over a specified dollar amount. If sales increase, the shipping department may have to hire additional employees to handle the increase in shipments. The budget encourages communication among managers to ensure that the extra profits from increased sales outweigh the revenue lost from not charging for shipping.

Benchmarking

Budgets provide a benchmark that motivates employees and helps managers evaluate performance. In most companies, part of the manager's performance evaluation depends on how actual results compare to the budget. So, for example, the budgeted expenses for international expansion encourage **Amazon**'s employees to increase the efficiency of international warehousing operations and to find less-expensive technology to support the Web sites.

Let's return to Smart Touch's e-learning business. Suppose that comparing actual results to the budget in Exhibit 22-1 leads to the performance report in Exhibit 22-4.

EXHIBIT 22-4

Service Company Income Statement Performance Report

	SMART TOUCH LEARNING, INC. Income Statement Performance Report For the Month Ended May 31, 2014		
	Actual	**Budget**	**Variance (Actual–Budget)**
Number of e-learning services:	19,000	20,000	(1,000)
Service revenue	$589,000	$600,000	$(11,000)
Variable expenses:			
Server space expense	$ 38,000	$ 45,000	$ (7,000)
Advertising expense	29,450	30,000	(550)
Total variable expenses	67,450	75,000	(7,550)
Contribution margin	$521,550	$525,000	$ (3,450)
Fixed expenses:			
Salary expense	$ 20,000	$ 20,000	$ —
Internet access expense	18,000	18,000	—
Total fixed expenses	38,000	38,000	—
Budgeted operating income	$483,550	$487,000	$ (3,450)

This report identifies areas where the actual results differed from the budget. The differences are itemized below:

1. Actual service revenue was $11,000 less than budgeted service revenue. This was caused by two factors. First, Smart Touch sold 1,000 fewer services than it planned to sell (19,000 actual – 20,000 budgeted). Second, Smart Touch was able to sell at a higher average price per service $31 ($589,000/19,000 services) than the $30 per service it planned.

2. Variable expenses were less than budgeted for both server space expense and advertising expense. Actual server space expense was less than budgeted server space expense because Smart Touch sold 1,000 fewer services and because Smart Touch reduced the server space expense per service from $2.25 budgeted to $2.00 ($38,000/19,000 services) actual per service. Advertising expense remained constant at 5% of revenues, but due to the $11,000 reduction in revenues, advertising expense was $550 less ($11,000 × 5%).

3. Actual fixed expenses were exactly the same as budgeted fixed expenses. Although not common, considering Smart Touch's fixed expenses, one wouldn't expect these to change unless Smart Touch changed the pay rate or number of employees or unless Smart Touch negotiated a new contract with its Internet service provider.

After management reviews the variances, Smart Touch will want to consider how it can implement new strategies to meet its goals. Can Smart Touch increase the number of services sold at the new higher price? Should the company increase its advertising budget in hopes of increasing the number of services sold? Can Smart Touch reduce any of its fixed expenses?

Smart Touch needs to know the answers to these kinds of questions to decide how to meet its goals.

Key Takeaway

A budgeted income statement shows estimated amounts, whereas the income statement shows actual results. Managers use budgets to develop strategies (overall business goals) and to create plans and follow actions that enable them to achieve those goals. They also review results against the goals (control), often using a performance report that compares budgeted amounts to actual amounts.

Understanding the Components of the Master Budget

Now that you know *why* managers go to the trouble of developing budgets, let's consider the steps managers take to prepare a budget.

2 Understand the components of the master budget

Components of the Master Budget

The **master budget** is the set of budgeted financial statements and supporting schedules for the entire organization. Exhibit 22-5 shows the order in which managers prepare the components of the master budget for a merchandiser such as **Amazon** or Greg's Tunes.

EXHIBIT 22-5	Master Budget for a Merchandising Company

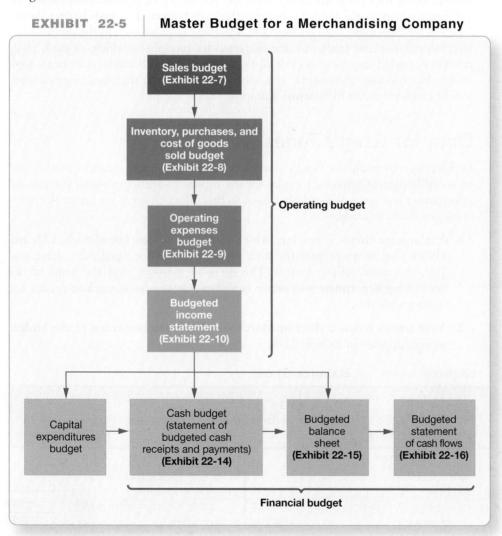

The exhibit shows that the master budget includes three types of budgets:

1. The operating budget
2. The capital expenditures budget
3. The financial budget

The **operating budget** is the set of budgets that project sales revenue, cost of goods sold, and operating expenses, leading to the budgeted income statement that projects operating income for the period. The first component of the operating budget is the sales budget, the cornerstone of the master budget. Why? Because sales affect most other components of the master budget. After projecting sales revenue, cost of goods sold, and operating expenses, management prepares the end result of the operating budget: the budgeted income statement that projects operating income for the period.

The second type of budget is the **capital expenditures budget**. This budget presents the company's plan for purchasing property, plant, equipment, and other long-term assets.

The third type of budget is the **financial budget**. Prior components of the master budget, including the budgeted income statement and the capital expenditures budget, along with plans for raising cash and paying debts, provide information for the first element of the financial budget: the cash budget. The **cash budget** details how the business expects to go from the beginning cash balance to the desired ending cash balance and feeds into the budgeted balance sheet, which, in turn, feeds into the budgeted statement of cash flows. These budgeted financial statements look exactly like ordinary statements. The only difference is that they list budgeted (projected) amounts rather than actual amounts.

Data for Greg's Tunes

In this chapter, we will use Greg's Tunes to see how managers prepare operating and financial budgets. Chapter 21 explained the capital budgeting process. Here is the information you have. We will refer back to this information as we create the operating and financial budgets.

1. **You manage Greg's Tunes, Inc., which carries a complete line of music CDs and DVDs.** You are to prepare the store's master budget for April, May, June, and July, the main selling season. The division manager and the head of the accounting department will arrive from headquarters next week to review the budget with you.

2. **Your store's balance sheet at March 31, 2014, the beginning of the budget period, appears in Exhibit 22-6.**

EXHIBIT 22-6 | **Balance Sheet**

GREG'S TUNES, INC. Balance Sheet March 31, 2014				
Assets			**Liabilities**	
Current assets:			Current liabilities:	
Cash	$ 16,400		Accounts payable	$ 16,800
Accounts receivable	16,000		Salary and commissions payable	4,250
Inventory	48,000		Total liabilities	$ 21,050
Prepaid insurance	1,800			
Total current assets	$ 82,200		**Stockholders' Equity**	
Plant assets:			Common stock, no par	20,000
Equipment and fixtures	32,000		Retained earnings	60,350
Less: Accumulated depreciation	12,800		Total stockholders' equity	$ 80,350
Total plant assets	$ 19,200		Total liabilities and stockholders'	
Total assets	$101,400		equity	$101,400

3. **Sales in March were $40,000. The sales manager predicts the following monthly sales:**

April..	$50,000
May	80,000
June...	60,000
July	50,000
August..	40,000

Sales are 60% cash and 40% on credit (on account). Greg's Tunes collects all credit sales the month after the sale. The $16,000 of accounts receivable at March 31, 2014, is March's credit sales ONLY (40% of $40,000). There are no other accounts receivable. Uncollectible accounts are immaterial and thus aren't included in the master budget.

4. **Greg's Tunes has a rule of thumb for maintaining enough inventory so that it does not run out of stock and potentially lose sales. It wants to have inventory at the end of each month of $20,000, plus it wants to keep an additional amount equal to 80% of what it expects to sell in the coming month.** So the rule is that ending inventory should be equal to $20,000 plus 80% of next month's cost of goods sold. Cost of goods sold averages 70% of sales. This is a variable cost.

5. **The accounts payable balance is only inventory purchases not yet paid.** Greg's pays for inventory purchases as follows: 50% during the month of purchase and 50% the month after purchase. Accounts payable consists of inventory purchases only. March purchases were $33,600, so accounts payable on Greg's March 31, 2014, balance sheet shows $16,800 ($33,600 × 0.50).

6. **Monthly payroll is salary of $2,500 plus sales commissions equal to 15% of sales.** This is a mixed cost, with both a fixed and a variable component. The company pays half this amount during the month and half early in the following month. Therefore, at the end of each month, Greg's reports salary and commissions payable equal to half the month's payroll. The $4,250 balance in Salaries and commissions payable in Exhibit 22-6 is half the March payroll of $8,500:

March payroll = Salary of $2,500 + Sales commissions of $6,000 (0.15 × $40,000)
 = $8,500

7. **Other monthly expenses are as follows:**

Rent expense (fixed cost).........................	$2,000, paid as incurred
Depreciation expense, including truck (fixed cost)	500
Insurance expense (fixed cost)................	200 expiration of prepaid amount
Miscellaneous expenses (variable cost)....	5% of sales, paid as incurred

8. **Greg's plans to purchase a used delivery truck in April for $3,000 cash.**

9. **Greg's requires a minimum cash balance of $10,000 before financing at the end of each month.** The store can borrow money in $1,000 increments at an annual interest rate of 12%. Management borrows no more than the amount needed to maintain the $10,000 minimum cash balance before financing. Total interest expense will vary (variable cost) as the amount of borrowing varies from month to month. Notes payable require $1,000 payments of principal, plus

monthly interest on the unpaid principal balance. Borrowing and all principal and interest payments occur at the end of the month.

10. **Income taxes are ignored in order to simplify the process.**

As you prepare the master budget, remember that you are developing the store's operating and financial plan for the next four months. The steps in this process may seem mechanical, but are easily calculated with the use of Excel. (Workpapers in Excel are provided in myaccountinglab.com for every end of chapter problem.) Additionally, the template for the two Summary Problems is provided in myaccountinglab.com as a tool for you to use. In creating the master budget, you must think carefully about pricing, product lines, job assignments, needs for additional equipment, and negotiations with banks. Successful managers use this opportunity to make decisions that affect the future course of business.

Preparing the Operating Budget

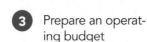

Prepare an operating budget

The first three components of the operating budget as shown in Exhibit 22-5 are as follows:

1. Sales budget (Exhibit 22-7)
2. Inventory, purchases, and cost of goods sold budget (Exhibit 22-8)
3. Operating expenses budget (Exhibit 22-9)

The results of these three budgets feed into the fourth element of the operating budget: the budgeted income statement (Exhibit 22-10). We consider each, in turn.

The Sales Budget

The forecast of sales revenue is the cornerstone of the master budget because the level of sales affects expenses and almost all other elements of the master budget. Budgeted total sales for each product equals the sales price multiplied by the expected number of units sold. The overall sales budget in Exhibit 22-7 is the sum of the budgets for the individual products. Trace the April through July total sales of $240,000 to the budgeted income statement in Exhibit 22-10.

EXHIBIT 22-7 | **Sales Budget**

GREG'S TUNES, INC. Sales Budget April–July 2014					
	April	May	June	July	April–July Total
Cash sales, 60%	$30,000	$48,000	$36,000	$30,000	
Credit collections, one month after sale, 40%	20,000	32,000	24,000	20,000	
Total sales, 100%	$50,000	$80,000	$60,000	$50,000	$240,000

The Inventory, Purchases, and Cost of Goods Sold Budget

This budget determines cost of goods sold for the budgeted income statement, ending inventory for the budgeted balance sheet, and purchases for the cash budget. The familiar cost of goods sold computation specifies the relations among these items:

Beginning inventory + Purchases − Ending inventory = Cost of goods sold

Beginning inventory is known from last month's balance sheet, budgeted cost of goods sold averages 70% of sales, and budgeted ending inventory is a computed amount. Recall that Greg's minimum inventory rule is as follows: Ending inventory should be equal to $20,000 plus 80% of next month's cost of goods sold. You must solve for the budgeted purchases figure. To do this, rearrange the previous equation to isolate purchases on the left side:

> Purchases = Cost of goods sold + Ending inventory − Beginning inventory

This equation makes sense. How much inventory does Greg's Tunes need to purchase? Greg's should have the minimum amount of inventory to be sure the company balances providing goods to customers with turning over (selling) the inventory efficiently. Keeping inventory at the minimum level that meets these needs helps reduce inventory storage costs, insurance costs, and warehousing costs, and reduces the potential for inventory to become obsolete (not sellable). Exhibit 22-8 shows Greg's inventory, purchases, and cost of goods sold budget.

EXHIBIT 22-8 | **Inventory, Purchases, and Cost of Goods Sold Budget**

GREG'S TUNES, INC.
Inventory, Purchases, and Cost of Goods Sold Budget
April–July 2014

	April	May	June	July	April–July Total	Source
Cost of goods sold (70% × sales)	$ 35,000	$ 56,000	$ 42,000	$ 35,000	$168,000	Exhibit 22-7
Desired ending inventory [$20,000 + (80% × COGS for next month)]	64,800†	53,600	48,000	42,400^		
Total inventory required	$ 99,800	$109,600	$ 90,000	$ 77,400		
Beginning inventory	(48,000)*	(64,800)	(53,600)	(48,000)		
Purchases	$ 51,800	$ 44,800	$ 36,400	$ 29,400		

†$20,000 + (0.80 × $56,000) = $64,800
*Balance at March 31 (Exhibit 22-6)
^$20,000 + [0.80 × (0.70 × $40,000)]

Trace the total budgeted cost of goods sold from Exhibit 22-8 of $168,000 to the budgeted income statement in Exhibit 22-10. We will use the budgeted inventory and purchases amounts later.

The Operating Expenses Budget

Recall that Greg's operating expenses include variable and fixed expenses. One of Greg's expenses is fixed salaries of $2,500. One of Greg's variable expenses is sales commissions equal to 15% of sales (from item 6 on page 1057). Half the total salary and commission expense is paid in the month incurred and the remaining half is paid in the following month. Greg's variable operating expenses also include miscellaneous expenses of 5% of sales for the month. Greg's also has other fixed expenses of $2,000 rent, $500 depreciation, and $200 of insurance expense (from item 7 on page 1057). Exhibit 22-9 shows the operating expenses budget. Study each expense to make sure you know how it is computed. For example, sales commissions and miscellaneous expenses fluctuate with sales (variable). Salary, rent, depreciation, and insurance are the same each month (fixed).

Trace the April through July totals from the operating expenses budget in Exhibit 22-9 (commissions of $36,000, miscellaneous expenses of $12,000, and so on) to the budgeted income statement in Exhibit 22-10.

EXHIBIT 22-9 | **Operating Expenses Budget**

GREG'S TUNES, INC.
Operating Expenses Budget
April–July 2014

	April	May	June	July	April–July Total	Source
Variable operating expenses:						
Commission expense, 15% of sales	$ 7,500	$12,000	$ 9,000	$ 7,500	$36,000	Exhibit 22-7
Miscellaneous expenses, 5% of sales	2,500	4,000	3,000	2,500	12,000	Exhibit 22-7
Total variable operating expenses:	$10,000	$16,000	$12,000	$10,000	$48,000	
Fixed operating expenses:						
Salary expense, fixed amount	2,500	2,500	2,500	2,500	10,000	
Rent expense, fixed amount	2,000	2,000	2,000	2,000	8,000	
Depreciation expense, fixed amount	500	500	500	500	2,000	
Insurance expense, fixed amount	200	200	200	200	800	
Total fixed operating expenses	$ 5,200	$ 5,200	$ 5,200	$ 5,200	$20,800	
Total operating expenses	$15,200	$21,200	$17,200	$15,200	$68,800	

The Budgeted Income Statement

Use the sales budget (Exhibit 22-7); the inventory, purchases, and cost of goods sold budget (Exhibit 22-8); and the operating expenses budget (Exhibit 22-9) to prepare the budgeted income statement in Exhibit 22-10. (We explain the computation of interest expense as part of the cash budget in the next section.) Notice that the income statement highlights the contribution margin, which you learned about in Chapter 19. Recall that the contribution margin is Revenue minus Variable costs. The contribution margin should be large enough to cover fixed expenses and to make a profit for Greg's.

EXHIBIT 22-10 | **Budgeted Income Statement**

GREG'S TUNES, INC.
Budgeted Income Statement
Four Months Ending July 31, 2014

		Amount	Source
Sales revenue		$240,000	Exhibit 22-7
Cost of goods sold		168,000	Exhibit 22-8
Gross profit		$ 72,000	
Variable operating expenses:			
Commissions expense	$36,000		Exhibit 22-9
Miscellaneous expenses	12,000		Exhibit 22-9
Total variable operating expenses		48,000	
Contribution margin		$ 24,000	
Fixed operating expenses:			
Salary expense	$10,000		Exhibit 22-9
Rent expense	8,000		Exhibit 22-9
Depreciation expense	2,000		Exhibit 22-9
Insurance expense	800		Exhibit 22-9
Total fixed operating expenses		20,800	
Operating income		$ 3,200	
Interest expense		(210)	*Exhibit 22-14
Net income (loss)		$ 2,990	

* $80 + $70 + $60

Key Takeaway

The first three components of the operating budget include the sales budget; the inventory, purchases, and cost of goods sold budget; and the operating expenses budget. The sales budget depicts the breakdown of sales based on the terms of collection. The inventory, purchases, and cost of goods sold budget aids in planning for adequate inventory to meet sales (COGS) and for inventory purchases. The operating expenses budget captures the planned variable and fixed operating expenses necessary for normal operations. The three budgets help to form the budgeted income statement. Together these form the operational budget that depicts the company's operational strategy for a period of time.

Take this opportunity to solidify your understanding of operating budgets by carefully working out Summary Problem 22-1.

Summary Problem 22-1

Review the Greg's Tunes example. You now think July sales might be $40,000 instead of the projected $50,000 in Exhibit 22-7. You also assume a change in sales collections as follows:

60% in the month of the sale

20% in the month after the sale

19% two months after the sale

1% never collected

You want to see how this change in sales affects the budget.

Requirement

1. Revise the sales budget (Exhibit 22-7); the inventory, purchases, and cost of goods sold budget (Exhibit 22-8); and the operating expenses budget (Exhibit 22-9). Prepare a revised budgeted income statement for the four months ended July 31, 2014.

Solution

Requirement

1. Revised figures appear in color for emphasis.

EXHIBIT 22-7R | **Revised—Sales Budget**

GREG'S TUNES, INC.
Revised—Sales Budget
April–July 2014

	April	May	June	July	April–July Total
Cash sales, 60%	$30,000	$48,000	$36,000	$24,000	
Credit collections, one month after sale, 20%	10,000	16,000	12,000	8,000	
Credit collections, two months after sale, 19%	9,500	15,200	11,400	7,600	
Bad debts, 1%	500	800	600	400	
Total sales, 100%	$50,000	$80,000	$60,000	$40,000	$230,000

EXHIBIT 22-8R | **Revised—Inventory, Purchases, and Cost of Goods Sold Budget**

GREG'S TUNES, INC.
Revised—Inventory, Purchases, and Cost of Goods Sold Budget
April–July 2014

	April	May	June	July	April–July Total	Source
Cost of goods sold, (70% × sales)	$ 35,000	$ 56,000	$ 42,000	$ 28,000	$161,000	Exhibit 22-7R
Desired ending inventory [$20,000 + (80% × COGS for next month)]	64,800	53,600	42,400	42,400		
Total inventory required	$ 99,800	$109,600	$ 84,400	$ 70,400		
Beginning inventory	(48,000) *	(64,800)	(53,600)	(42,400)		
Purchases	$ 51,800	$ 44,800	$ 30,800	$ 28,000		

*March 31 inventory balance (Exhibit 22-6)

EXHIBIT 22-9R | **Revised—Operating Expenses Budget**

GREG'S TUNES, INC.
Revised—Operating Expenses Budget
April–July 2014

	April	May	June	July	April–July Total	Source
Variable operating expenses:						
Commission expense, 15% of sales	$ 7,500	$12,000	$ 9,000	$ 6,000	$34,500	Exhibit 22-7R
Miscellaneous expenses, 5% of sales	2,500	4,000	3,000	2,000	11,500	Exhibit 22-7R
Bad debt expense, 1% of sales	500	800	600	400	2,300	Exhibit 22-7R
Total variable operating expenses:	$10,500	$16,800	$12,600	$ 8,400	$48,300	
Fixed operating expenses:						
Salary expense, fixed amount	2,500	2,500	2,500	2,500	10,000	
Rent expense, fixed amount	2,000	2,000	2,000	2,000	8,000	
Depreciation expense, fixed amount	500	500	500	500	2,000	
Insurance expense, fixed amount	200	200	200	200	800	
Total fixed operating expenses	$ 5,200	$ 5,200	$ 5,200	$ 5,200	$20,800	
Total operating expenses	$15,700	$22,000	$17,800	$13,600	$69,100	

EXHIBIT 22-10R | **Revised—Budgeted Income Statement**

GREG'S TUNES, INC.
Revised—Budgeted Income Statement
Four Months Ending July 31, 2014

			Source
Sales revenue		$230,000	Exhibit 22-7R
Cost of goods sold		161,000	Exhibit 22-8R
Gross profit		$ 69,000	
Variable operating expenses:			
Commission expense	$34,500		Exhibit 22-9R
Miscellaneous expenses	11,500		Exhibit 22-9R
Bad debt expense	2,300		
Total variable operating expenses		48,300	
Contribution margin		$ 20,700	
Fixed operating expenses:			
Salary expense	$10,000		Exhibit 22-9R
Rent expense	8,000		Exhibit 22-9R
Depreciation expense	2,000		Exhibit 22-9R
Insurance expense	800		Exhibit 22-9R
Total fixed operating expenses		20,800	
Operating income (loss)		$ (100)	
Interest expense		(450)	*Exhibit 22-14R
Net income (loss)		$ (550)	

* $160 + $150 + $140

Preparing the Financial Budget

Armed with a clear understanding of Greg's Tunes' operating budget, you are now ready to prepare the financial budget. Exhibit 22-5 shows that the financial budget includes the cash budget, the budgeted balance sheet, and the budgeted statement of cash flows. We start with the cash budget.

④ Prepare a financial budget

Preparing the Cash Budget

The *cash budget*, or statement of budgeted cash receipts and payments, details how the business expects to go from the beginning cash balance to the desired ending balance. The cash budget has four major parts:

- Budgeted cash collections from customers (Exhibit 22-11)
- Budgeted cash payments for purchases (Exhibit 22-12)
- Budgeted cash payments for operating expenses (Exhibit 22-13)
- Budgeted cash payments for capital expenditures (for example, the $3,000 capital expenditure to acquire the delivery truck). Recall that we don't cover the preparation of the capital expenditures budget in this chapter.

Cash collections and payments depend on revenues and expenses, which appear in the operating budget. This is why you cannot prepare the cash budget until you have finished the operating budget.

Budgeted Cash Collections from Customers

Recall from item 3 on page 1057 that Greg's sales are 60% cash and 40% on credit. The 40% credit sales are collected the month after the sale is made. Exhibit 22-11 shows that April's budgeted cash collections consist of two parts: (1) April's cash sales from the sales budget in Exhibit 22-7 ($30,000) plus (2) collections of March's credit sales ($16,000 from the March 31 balance sheet, Exhibit 22-6). Trace April's $46,000 ($30,000 + $16,000) total cash collections to the cash budget in Exhibit 22-14 on page 1066.

EXHIBIT 22-11 | Budgeted Cash Collections

	April	May	June	July	April–July Total	Source
GREG'S TUNES, INC. Budgeted Cash Collections from Customers April–July 2014						
Cash sales, 60%	$30,000	$48,000	$36,000	$30,000		Exhibit 22-7
Credit collections, one month after sale, 40%	16,000*	20,000	32,000	24,000		Exhibit 22-7
Total collections	$46,000	$68,000	$68,000	$54,000	$236,000	

*March 31 accounts receivable (Exhibit 22-6)

Budgeted Cash Payments for Purchases

Recall from item 5 on page 1057 that Greg's pays for inventory purchases 50% during the month of purchase and 50% the month after purchase. Exhibit 22-12 uses the inventory, purchases, and cost of goods sold budget from Exhibit 22-8 to compute budgeted cash payments for purchases of inventory. April's cash payments for purchases consist of two parts: (1) payment of 50% of March's purchases ($16,800 accounts payable balance from the March 31 balance sheet, Exhibit 22-6) plus (2) payment for 50% of April's purchases (50% × $51,800 = $25,900). Trace April's $42,700 ($16,800 + $25,900) cash payment for purchases to the cash budget in Exhibit 22-14.

EXHIBIT 22-12 | **Budgeted Cash Payments for Purchases**

| | | | | | April–July | |
	April	May	June	July	Total	Source
			GREG'S TUNES, INC.			
		Budgeted Cash Payments for Purchases				
			April–July 2014			
50% of last month's purchases	$16,800*	$25,900	$22,400	$18,200		Exhibit 22-8
50% of this month's purchases	25,900	22,400	18,200	14,700		Exhibit 22-8
Total payments for purchases	$42,700	$48,300	$40,600	$32,900	$164,500	

*March 31 accounts payable (Exhibit 22-6)

Budgeted Cash Payments for Operating Expenses

Exhibit 22-13 uses the operating expenses budget (Exhibit 22-9) and Greg's payment information to compute cash payments for operating expenses. Greg's pays half the salary in the month incurred and half in the following month. Recall that Greg's operating expenses also include $2,000 rent, $500 depreciation, $200 of insurance expense, and miscellaneous expenses of 5% of sales for the month (from item 7 on page 1057). Greg's pays all those expenses in the month incurred except for insurance and depreciation. Recall that the insurance was prepaid insurance, so the cash payment for insurance was made before this budget period; therefore, no cash payment is made for insurance during April–July. Depreciation is a noncash expense, so it's not included in the budgeted cash payments for operating expenses. April's cash payments for operating expenses consist of four items:

Payment of 50% of March's salary and commissions (from March 31 balance sheet, Exhibit 22-6)	$ 4,250
Payment of 50% of April's salary and commissions (50% × $10,000, Exhibit 22-9)......................	5,000
Payment of rent expense (Exhibit 22-9).................................	2,000
Payment of miscellaneous expenses (Exhibit 22-9)	2,500
Total April cash payments for operating expenses...................	$13,750

Follow April's $13,750 cash payments for operating expenses from Exhibit 22-13 to the cash budget in Exhibit 22-14.

EXHIBIT 22-13 | **Budgeted Cash Payments for Operating Expenses**

GREG'S TUNES, INC
Budgeted Cash Payments for Operating Expenses
April–July 2014

	April	May	June	July	April–July Total	Source
Variable operating expenses						
50% of last month's commission expenses	$ 3,000	$ 3,750	$ 6,000	$ 4,500		Exhibit 22-9
50% of this month's commission expenses	3,750	6,000	4,500	3,750		Exhibit 22-9
Miscellaneous expenses, 5% of sales	2,500	4,000	3,000	2,500		Exhibit 22-9
Total payments for variable operating expenses	9,250	13,750	13,500	10,750		
Fixed operating expenses:						
50% of last month's salary expenses	$ 1,250	$ 1,250	$ 1,250	$ 1,250		Exhibit 22-9
50% of this month's salary expenses	1,250	1,250	1,250	1,250		Exhibit 22-9
Rent expense	2,000	2,000	2,000	2,000		Exhibit 22-9
Total payments for fixed operating expenses	4,500	4,500	4,500	4,500		
Total payments for operating expenses	$13,750	$18,250	$18,000	$15,250	$65,250	

Stop & Think...

Why are depreciation expense and insurance expense from the operating expenses budget (Exhibit 22-9) *excluded* from the budgeted cash payments for operating expenses in Exhibit 22-13?

Answer: These expenses do not require cash outlays in the current period. Depreciation is the periodic write-off of the cost of the equipment and fixtures that Greg's Tunes acquired previously. Insurance expense is the expiration of insurance paid for in a previous period; thus, no cash payment was made to the insurance company this period.

The Cash Budget

To prepare the cash budget in Exhibit 22-14, start with the beginning cash balance (Exhibit 22-6) and add the budgeted cash collections from Exhibit 22-11 to determine the cash available. Then, subtract cash payments for purchases (Exhibit 22-12), operating expenses (Exhibit 22-13), and any capital expenditures. This yields the ending cash balance before financing.

Item 9 on page 1057 states that Greg's Tunes requires a minimum cash balance before financing of $10,000. April's $2,950 budgeted cash balance before financing falls $7,050 short of the minimum required ($10,000 – $2,950). To be able to access short-term financing, Greg's must have secured an existing line of credit with the company's bank. Securing this credit in advance is crucial to having the credit available to draw upon when cash shortages arise. Because Greg's borrows in $1,000 increments, the company will have to borrow $8,000 to cover April's expected shortfall. The budgeted ending cash balance equals the "ending cash balance before financing," adjusted for the total effects of the financing (an $8,000 inflow in April). Exhibit 22-14 shows that Greg's expects to end April with $10,950 of cash ($2,950 + $8,000). Recall additionally that when Greg's borrows, the amount borrowed is to be paid back in $1,000 installments plus interest at 12% annually. Note that in May, Greg's begins to pay the $8,000 borrowed in April. Greg's must also pay interest at 12%. For May, the interest paid is calculated as $8,000 owed × 12% × ½ of the year, or $80 interest. For June, Greg's interest owed will change because the principal of the note has been paid down $1,000 in May. June interest is calculated as ($8,000 – $1,000) owed × 12% × ½ of the year, or $70 interest. For July, interest is ($8,000 – $1,000 – $1,000) owed × 12% × ½ of the year, or $60 interest. Exhibit 22-14 also shows the cash balance at the end of May, June, and July.

EXHIBIT 22-14 | **Cash Budget**

GREG'S TUNES, INC.
Cash Budget
Four Months Ending July 31, 2014

	April	May	June	July	Source
Beginning cash balance	$ 16,400*	$ 10,950	$ 11,320	$ 19,650	
Cash collections	46,000	68,000	68,000	54,000	Exhibit 22-11
Cash available	$ 62,400	$ 78,950	$ 79,320	$ 73,650	
Cash payments:					
Purchases of inventory	42,700	48,300	40,600	32,900	Exhibit 22-12
Operating expenses	13,750	18,250	18,000	15,250	Exhibit 22-13
Purchase of delivery truck	3,000				
Total cash payments	59,450	66,550	58,600	48,150	
(1) Ending cash balance before financing	$ 2,950	$ 12,400	$ 20,720	$ 25,500	
Minimum cash balance desired	(10,000)	(10,000)	(10,000)	(10,000)	
Cash excess (deficiency)	$ (7,050)	$ 2,400	$ 10,720	$ 15,500	
Financing of cash deficiency:					
Borrowing (at end of month)a	8,000	—	—	—	
Principal payments (at end of month, at $1,000)		(1,000)	(1,000)	(1,000)	
Interest expense (at 12% annually)b		(80)	(70)	(60)	
(2) Total effects of financing	8,000	(1,080)	(1,070)	(1,060)	
Ending cash balance (1) + (2)	$ 10,950	$ 11,320	$ 19,650	$ 24,440	

*March 31 cash balance (Exhibit 22-6)
a Borrowing occurs in multiples of $1,000 and only for the amount needed to maintain a minimum cash balance before financing of $10,000
b Interest expense: May: $8,000 × (0.12 × 1/12) = $80; June: ($8,000 − $1,000) × (0.12 × 1/12) = $70; July: ($8,000 − $1,000 − $1,000) × (0.12 × 1/12) = $60

The cash balance at the end of July of $24,440 is the cash balance in the July 31 budgeted balance sheet in Exhibit 22-15.

EXHIBIT 22-15 | **Budgeted Balance Sheet**

GREG'S TUNES, INC.
Budgeted Balance Sheet
July 31, 2014

Assets		Source
Current assets:		
Cash	$ 24,440	Exhibit 22-14
Accounts receivable	20,000	Exhibit 22-7
Inventory	42,400	Exhibit 22-8
Prepaid insurance	1,000	Beg. Bal. $1,800 – (Exhibit 22-9) ($200 per month expiration × 4 months)
Total current assets	$ 87,840	
Plant assets:		
Equipment and fixtures	$ 35,000	Beg. Bal. $32,000 + (Item 8, p 1057) $3,000 truck acquisition
Less: Accumulated depreciation	14,800	Beg. Bal. $12,800 + (Exhibit 22-9) ($500 per month depreciation × 4 months)
Total plant assets	20,200	
Total assets	$108,040	
Liabilities		
Current liabilities:		
Accounts payable	$ 14,700	July purchases from Exhibit 22-8 of $29,400 × 50% paid in month after purchase
Salary and commissions payable	5,000	(July salary of $2,500 plus July commissions of $7,500 from Exhibit 22-9) × 50% paid in month after incurred
Short-term notes payable	5,000	$8,000 borrowed in April (revised cash budget) – ($1,000 principal repayments × 3 months) (Exhibit 22-14)
Total liabilities	$ 24,700	
Stockholders' Equity		
Common stock, no par	$ 20,000	Exhibit 22-6
Retained earnings	63,340	Beg. Bal. $60,350 + net income from Exhibit 22-10 income statement $2,990
Total stockholders' equity	83,340	
Total liabilities and stockholders' equity	$108,040	

The Budgeted Balance Sheet

To prepare the budgeted balance sheet, project each asset, liability, and stockholders' equity account based on the plans outlined in the previous exhibits.

Study the budgeted balance sheet in Exhibit 22-15 to make certain you understand the computation of each figure. For example, on the budgeted balance sheet as of July 31, 2014, budgeted cash equals the ending cash balance from the cash budget in Exhibit 22-14. Accounts receivable as of July 31 equal July's credit sales of $20,000, shown in the sales budget (Exhibit 22-7). July 31 inventory of $42,400 is July's desired ending inventory in the inventory, purchases, and cost of goods sold budget in Exhibit 22-8. Detailed computations for each of the other accounts appear in Exhibit 22-15.

The Budgeted Statement of Cash Flows

The final step is preparing the budgeted statement of cash flows. Use the information from the schedules of cash collections and payments, the cash budget, and the beginning balance of cash to project cash flows from operating, investing, and financing activities. Take time to study Exhibit 22-16 on the next page and make sure you understand the origin of each figure.

EXHIBIT 22-16 | **Budgeted Statement of Cash Flows**

GREG'S TUNES, INC.
Budgeted Statement of Cash Flows
Four Months Ending July 31, 2014

			Source
Cash flows from operating activities:			
Receipts:			
Collections from customers	$ 236,000		Exhibit 22-11
Total cash receipts		$ 236,000	
Payments:			
To suppliers for purchases of inventory	(164,500)		Exhibit 22-12
For operating expenses	(65,250)		Exhibit 22-13
For interest	(210)		Exhibit 22-14
Total cash payments		(229,960)	
Net cash provided by operating activities		$ 6,040	
Cash flows from investing activities:			
Acquisition of delivery truck	(3,000)		
Net cash used by investing activities		(3,000)	
Cash flows from financing activities:			
Proceeds from issuance of notes payable	8,000		Exhibit 22-14
Payment of notes payable	(3,000)		Exhibit 22-14
Net cash provided by financing activities		5,000	
Net increase in cash		$ 8,040	
Cash balance, April 1, 2014		16,400	Exhibit 22-6
Cash balance, July 31, 2014		$ 24,440	Exhibit 22-14

Getting Employees to Accept the Budget

What is the most important part of Greg's Tunes' budgeting system? Despite all the numbers we have crunched, it is not the mechanics. It is getting managers and employees to accept the budget so Greg's can reap the planning, coordination, and control benefits illustrated in Exhibit 22-3.

Few people enjoy having their work monitored and evaluated. So if managers use the budget as a benchmark to evaluate employees' performance, managers must first motivate employees to accept the budget's goals. Here is how they can do it:

- Managers must support the budget themselves, or no one else will.
- Managers must show employees how budgets can help them achieve better results.
- Managers must have employees participate in developing the budget.

But these principles alone are not enough. As the manager of Greg's, your performance is evaluated by comparing actual results to the budget. When you develop the company's budget, you may be tempted to build in *slack*. For example, you might want to budget fewer sales and higher purchases than you expect. This increases the chance that actual performance will be better than the budget and that you will receive a good evaluation. But adding slack into the budget makes it less accurate—and less useful for planning and control. When the division manager and the head of the accounting department arrive from headquarters next week, they will scour your budget to find any slack you may have inserted.

Now, we'll continue our budget example started in Summary Problem 22-1 in Summary Problem 22-2.

Key Takeaway

The cash budget details how the business expects to go from the beginning cash balance to the desired ending balance each period. The cash budget has four major parts: cash collections from customers, cash payments for purchases, cash payments for operating expenses, and cash payments for capital expenditures. The results of these budgets are combined to form the cash budget. After preparing the cash budget, the rest of the financial statement budgets are prepared, including the budgeted balance sheet and budgeted statement of cash flows. These budgets depict the financial plan that implements the strategic goals of the company.

Summary Problem 22-2

Continue the revised Greg's Tunes illustration from Summary Problem 22-1. Recall that you think July sales will be $40,000 instead of $50,000, as projected in Exhibit 22-7. You also assume a change in sales collections as follows:

60% in the month of the sale

20% in the month after the sale

19% two months after the sale

1% never collected

How will this affect the financial budget?

Requirements

1. Revise the schedule of budgeted cash collections (Exhibit 22-11), the schedule of budgeted cash payments for purchases (Exhibit 22-12), and the schedule of budgeted cash payments for operating expenses (Exhibit 22-13).

2. Prepare a revised cash budget (Exhibit 22-14), a revised budgeted balance sheet at July 31, 2014 (Exhibit 22-15), and a revised budgeted statement of cash flows for the four months ended July 31, 2014 (Exhibit 22-16). *Note: Round values to the nearest dollar.*

Solution

Requirement 1

1. Revised figures appear in color for emphasis.

EXHIBIT 22-11R | **Revised—Budgeted Cash Collections from Customers**

	April	May	June	July	April–July Total	Source
GREG'S TUNES, INC. Revised—Budgeted Cash Collections from Customers April–July 2014						
Cash sales, 60%	$30,000	$48,000	$36,000	$24,000		Exhibit 22-7R
Credit collections, one month after sale, 20%	8,000	10,000	16,000	12,000		Exhibit 22-7R
Credit collections, two months after sale, 19%	^	7,600	9,500	15,200		Exhibit 22-7R
Total collections	$38,000	$65,600	$61,500	$51,200	$216,300	

*Notice that $400 (1% × $40,000 sales) of the March 31 Accounts receivable balance (Exhibit 22-6) of $16,000 is never collected (bad debt) and thus should appear as an expense on the March 31 income statement and will reduce the March 31 balance in Retained earnings.
^There were no accounts receivable for February.

EXHIBIT 22-12R | **Revised—Budgeted Cash Payments for Purchases**

	April	May	June	July	April–July Total	Source
GREG'S TUNES, INC. Revised—Budgeted Cash Payments for Purchases April–July 2014						
50% of last month's purchases	$16,800*	$25,900	$22,400	$15,400		Exhibit 22-8R
50% of this month's purchases	25,900	22,400	15,400	14,000		Exhibit 22-8R
Total payments for purchases	$42,700	$48,300	$37,800	$29,400	$158,200	

*March 31 accounts payable (Exhibit 22-6)

EXHIBIT 22-13R | **Revised—Budgeted Cash Payments for Operating Expenses**

GREG'S TUNES, INC
Revised—Budgeted Cash Payments for Operating Expenses
April–July 2014

	April	May	June	July	April–July Total	Source
Variable operating expenses:						
50% of last month's commission expense	$ 3,000	$ 3,750	$ 6,000	$ 4,500		Exhibit 22-9R
50% of this month's commission expense	3,750	6,000	4,500	3,000		Exhibit 22-9R
Miscellaneous expenses, 5% of sales	2,500	4,000	3,000	2,000		Exhibit 22-9R
Total payments for variable operating expenses	9,250	13,750	13,500	9,500		
Fixed operating expenses:						
50% of last month's salary expense	$ 1,250	$ 1,250	$ 1,250	$ 1,250		Exhibit 22-9R
50% of this month's salary expense	1,250	1,250	1,250	1,250		Exhibit 22-9R
Rent expense	2,000	2,000	2,000	2,000		Exhibit 22-9R
Total payments for fixed operating expenses	4,500	4,500	4,500	4,500		
Total payments for operating expenses	$13,750	$18,250	$18,000	$14,000	$64,000	

Requirement 2

EXHIBIT 22-14R | **Revised—Cash Budget**

GREG'S TUNES, INC.
Revised—Cash Budget
Four Months Ending July 31, 2014

	April	May	June	July	Source
Beginning cash balance	$ 16,400*	$ 10,950	$ 8,840	$ 13,390	
Cash collections	38,000	65,600	61,500	51,200	Exhibit 22-11R
Cash available	$ 54,400	$ 76,550	$ 70,340	$ 64,590	
Cash payments:					
Purchases of inventory	42,700	48,300	37,800	29,400	Exhibit 22-12R
Operating expenses	13,750	18,250	18,000	14,000	Exhibit 22-13R
Purchase of delivery truck	3,000				
Total cash payments	59,450	66,550	55,800	43,400	
(1) Ending cash balance before financing	$ (5,050)	$ 10,000	$ 14,540	$ 21,190	
Minimum cash balance desired	(10,000)	(10,000)	(10,000)	(10,000)	
Cash excess (deficiency)	$(15,050)	$ —	$ 4,540	$ 11,190	
Financing of cash deficiency					
Borrowing (at end of month)[a]	16,000	—	—	—	
Principal payments (at end of month, at $1,000)		(1,000)	(1,000)	(1,000)	
Interest expense (at 12% annually)[b]		(160)	(150)	(140)	
(2) Total effects of financing	16,000	(1,160)	(1,150)	(1,140)	
Ending cash balance (1) + (2)	$ 10,950	$ 8,840	$ 13,390	$ 20,050	

*March 31 cash balance (Exhibit 22-6)
[a] Borrowing occurs in multiples of $1,000 and only for the amount needed to maintain a minimum cash balance before financing of $10,000
[b] Interest expense: May: $16,000 × (0.12 × 1/12) = $160; June: ($16,000 − $1,000) × (0.12 × 1/12) = $150; July: ($16,000 − $1,000 − $1,000) × (0.12 × 1/12) = $140

EXHIBIT 22-15R | **Revised—Budgeted Balance Sheet**

GREG'S TUNES, INC.
Revised—Budgeted Balance Sheet
July 31, 2014

Assets		Source
Current assets:		
Cash	$ 20,050	Revised cash budget (Exhibit 22-14R)
Accounts receivable	27,000	Revised sales budget (Exhibit 22-7R)—collections not made yet
		(June, $11,400 + July, $8,000 + July, $7,600)
Inventory	42,400	Revised inventory, purchases, and COGS budget (Exhibit 22-8R)
Prepaid insurance	1,000	Beg. Bal. $1,800 – (200 per month expiration × 4 months)
Total current assets	$ 90,450	
Plant assets:		
Equipment and fixtures	$ 35,000	April Beg. Bal. $32,000 (Exhibit 22-6) + $3,000 truck acquisition
Less: Accumulated depreciation	14,800	April Beg. Bal. $12,800 (Exhibit 22-6) + ($500 per month
		depreciation × 4 months)
Total plant assets	20,200	
Total assets	$110,650	
Liabilities		
Current liabilities:		
Accounts payable	$ 14,000	July purchases of $28,000 × 50% paid in month after purchase
Salary and commissions payable	4,250	July salary and comissions of $8,500 × 50% paid in month
		after incurred
Short-term notes payable	13,000	$16,000 borrowed in April (revised cash budget Exhibit 22-14R) –
		($1,000 principal repayments × 3 months)
Total liabilities	$ 31,250	
Stockholders' Equity		
Common stock	$ 20,000	Exhibit 22-6
Retained earnings	59,400	Beg. Bal. $60,350 – March accounts receivable never collected
		$400 – loss from revised income statement $550
Total stockholders' equity	79,400	
Total liabilities and stockholders' equity	$110,650	

EXHIBIT 22-16R | **Revised—Budgeted Statement of Cash Flows**

GREG'S TUNES, INC.
Revised—Budgeted Statement of Cash Flows
Four Months Ending July 31, 2014

			Source
Cash flows from operating activities:			
Receipts:			
Collections from customers	$216,300		Revised budgeted cash collections (Exhibit 22-11R)
Total cash receipts		$ 216,300	
Payments:			
To suppliers for purchases of inventory	(158,200)		Revised budgeted cash payments for purchases (Exhibit 22-12R)
For operating expenses	(64,000)		Revised budgeted cash payments for operating expenses (Exhibit 22-13R)
For interest	(450)		Revised cash budget (Exhibit 22-14R)
Total cash payments		(222,650)	
Net cash provided by operating activities		$ (6,350)	
Cash flows from investing activities:			
Acquisition of delivery truck	(3,000)		
Net cash used by investing activities		(3,000)	
Cash flows from financing activities:			
Proceeds from issuance of notes payable	16,000		Revised cash budget (Exhibit 22-14R)
Payment of notes payable	(3,000)		Revised cash budget (Exhibit 22-14R)
Net cash provided by financing activities		13,000	
Net increase in cash		$ 3,650	
Cash balance, April 1, 2014		16,400	Exhibit 22-6
Cash balance, July 31, 2014		$ 20,050	Exhibit 22-14R

Using Information Technology for Sensitivity Analysis and Rolling Up Unit Budgets

5 Use sensitivity analysis in budgeting

Exhibits 22-7 through 22-16 show that managers must prepare many calculations to develop the master budget for just one of the retail stores in the Greg's Tunes merchandising chain. Technology makes it more cost-effective for managers to

- conduct sensitivity analysis on their own unit's budget, and
- combine individual unit budgets to create the companywide master budget.

Sensitivity Analysis

The master budget models the company's *planned* activities. Top management pays special attention to ensure that the results of the budgeted income statement (Exhibit 22-10), the cash budget (Exhibit 22-14), and the budgeted balance sheet (Exhibit 22-15) support key strategies.

But actual results often differ from plans, so management wants to know how budgeted income and cash flows would change if key assumptions turned out to be incorrect. In Chapter 19, we defined *sensitivity analysis* as a *what-if* technique that asks *what* a result will be *if* a predicted amount is not achieved or *if* an underlying assumption changes. *What if* the stock market crashes? How will this affect **Amazon.com**'s sales? Will it have to postpone a planned expansion in Asia and Europe? *What* will Greg's Tunes' cash balance be on July 31 *if* the period's sales are 45% cash, not 60% cash? Will Greg's have to borrow more cash?

Most companies use computer spreadsheet programs like Excel to prepare master budget schedules and statements. Today, what-if budget questions are easily changed within Excel with a few keystrokes. (Note: All the budgets presented in the chapter material and in both Summary Problems are available online at myaccountinglab.com for your use.)

Technology makes it cost-effective to perform more comprehensive sensitivity analyses. Armed with a better understanding of how changes in sales and costs are likely to affect the company's bottom line, today's managers can react quickly if key assumptions underlying the master budget (such as sales price or quantity) turn out to be wrong. Summary Problems 22-1 and 22-2 are examples of sensitivity analysis for Greg's Tunes.

Rolling Up Individual Unit Budgets into the Companywide Budget

Greg's Tunes operates three retail stores. As Exhibit 22-17 shows, Greg's Tunes' headquarters must roll up the budget data from each of the stores to prepare the companywide master budgeted income statement. This roll-up can be difficult for companies whose units use different spreadsheets to prepare the budgets.

EXHIBIT 22-17 | **Rolling Up Individual Unit Budgets into the Companywide Budget**

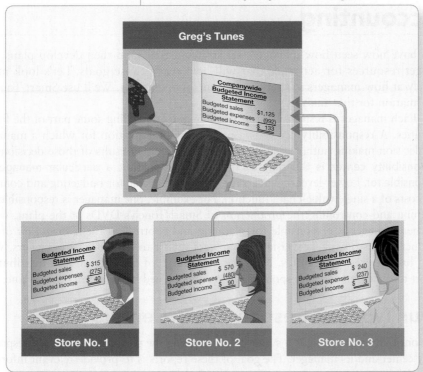

Companies like **Sunoco** turn to budget-management software to solve this problem. Often designed as a component of the company's Enterprise Resource Planning (ERP) system (or data warehouse), this software helps managers develop and analyze budgets.

Software allows managers to conduct sensitivity analyses on their own unit's data. When the manager is satisfied with his or her budget, he or she can enter it in the companywide budget easily. His or her unit's budget automatically rolls up with budgets from all other units around the world.

Whether at headquarters or on the road, top executives can log into the budget system through the Internet and conduct their own sensitivity analyses on individual units' budgets or on the companywide budget. The result: Managers spend less time compiling and summarizing data and more time analyzing and making decisions that ensure the budget leads the company to achieve its key strategic goals.

Key Takeaway

Sensitivity budgeting was once a time-consuming task. Now, with technology, modifying the budget assumptions is easy. Individual managers can easily modify the budgets of their specific units, and that data is automatically updated in the companywide budget plans. Being able to modify this data easily allows managers to be more responsive to business changes and plan better; thus, better, more timely decisions that benefit the company may be made.

Stop & Think...

Consider two budget situations: (1) Greg's Tunes' marketing analysts produce a forecast for four-month sales of $4,500,000 for the company's three stores. (2) Much uncertainty exists about the period's sales. The most likely amount is $4,500,000, but marketing considers any amount between $3,900,000 and $5,100,000 to be possible. How will the budgeting process differ in these two circumstances?

Answer: Greg's will prepare a master budget for the expected sales level of $4,500,000 in either case. Because of the uncertainty in the second situation, executives will want a set of budgets covering the entire range of volume rather than a single level. Greg's Tunes' managers may prepare budgets based on sales of, for example, $3,900,000, $4,200,000, $4,500,000, $4,800,000, and $5,100,000. These budgets will help managers plan for sales levels throughout the forecasted range.

Responsibility Accounting

 Prepare performance reports for responsibility centers and account for traceable and common shared fixed costs.

You have now seen how managers set strategic goals and then develop plans and budget resources for activities that will help reach those goals. Let's look more closely at how managers *use* reports to control operations. We'll use Smart Touch's information for this analysis.

Each manager is responsible for planning and controlling some part of the firm's activities. A **responsibility center** is a part of the organization for which a manager has decision-making authority and accountability for the results of those decisions. **A responsibility center is the part of the organization that a particular manager is responsible for.** Lower-level managers are often responsible for budgeting and controlling costs of a single value-chain function. For example, one manager is responsible for planning and controlling the *production* of Smart Touch's DVDs at the plant, while another manager is responsible for planning and controlling the *distribution* of the product to customers. Lower-level managers report to higher-level managers, who have broader responsibilities. Managers in charge of production and distribution report to senior managers responsible for profits earned by an entire product line.

Four Types of Responsibility Centers

Responsibility accounting is a system for evaluating the performance of each responsibility center and its manager. The goal of these reports is to provide relevant information to those managers empowered to make decisions.

This decentralization highlights the need for reports on individual *segments*, which are parts of the company for which managers need reports. Segments are typically defined as one of the types of responsibility centers illustrated in Exhibit 22-18. The four types of responsibility centers are as follows:

1. **In a cost center, managers are accountable for costs (expenses) only.** Manufacturing operations, such as the CD production lines, are cost centers. The line foreman

EXHIBIT 22-18 | **Four Types of Responsibility Centers**

1. In a **cost center**, such as a production line for CDs, managers are responsible for costs.

2. In a **revenue center**, such as the Midwest sales region, managers are responsible for generating sales revenue.

3. In a **profit center**, such as a line of products, managers are responsible for both revenues and costs.

4. In an **investment center**, such as the CD, DVD, and e-learning divisions, managers are responsible for investments, revenues, and costs.

controls costs by monitoring materials costs, repairs and maintenance expenses, employee costs (wages, salaries, and benefits), and employee efficiency. The foreman is *not* responsible for generating revenues because he or she is not involved in selling the product. The plant manager evaluates the foreman on his or her ability to control *costs* by comparing actual costs to budgeted costs (covered in the next chapter).

2. **In a revenue center, managers are primarily accountable for revenues.** Examples include the Midwest and Southeast sales regions of businesses that carry Smart Touch's products, such as CDs and DVDs.

3. **In a profit center, managers are accountable for both revenues and costs (expenses) and, therefore, profits.** The (higher-level) manager responsible for the entire CD product line would be accountable for increasing sales revenue *and* controlling costs to achieve the profit goals. Profit center reports include both revenues and expenses to show the profit center's income.

4. **In an investment center, managers are accountable for investments, revenues, and costs (expenses).** Examples include the **Chevrolet** division (subsidiary) of **General Motors** and the DVD division of Smart Touch. Managers of investment centers are responsible for (1) generating sales, (2) controlling expenses, (3) managing the amount of capital required to earn the income (revenues minus expenses), and (4) planning future investments for growth and expansion of the company.

Top management often evaluates investment center managers based on return on investment (ROI), residual income (RI), or economic value added (EVA). Chapter 24 explains how these measures are calculated and used. All else being equal, the manager will receive a more favorable evaluation if the division's actual ROI, RI, or EVA exceeds the amount budgeted.

Responsibility Accounting Performance Reports

Exhibit 22-19 shows how an organization like Smart Touch may assign responsibility.

At the top level, the CEO oversees each of the three divisions. Division managers generally have broad responsibility, including deciding how to use assets to maximize ROI. Most companies classify divisions as *investment centers*.

EXHIBIT 22-19 | **Partial Organization Chart**

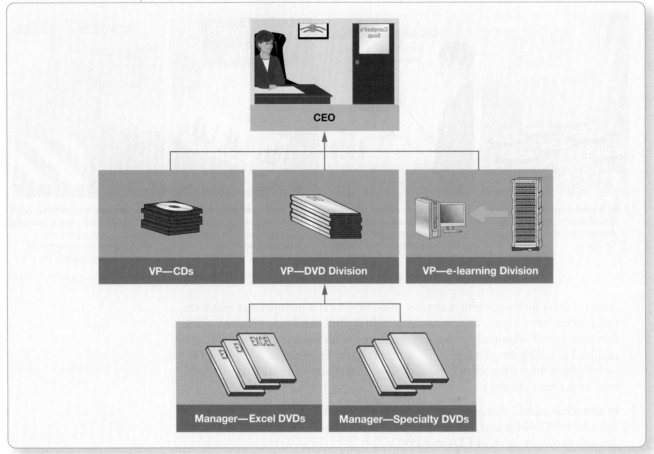

Each division manager supervises all the product lines in that division. Exhibit 22-19 shows that the VP of the DVD division oversees the Excel and Specialty DVD lines. Product lines are generally considered *profit centers*. Thus, the manager of the Excel DVD product line is responsible for evaluating lower-level managers of both

- *cost centers* (such as plants that make Excel DVD products) and
- *revenue centers* (such as managers responsible for selling Excel DVD products).

Learn about Service Departments

In most companies, there are departments that provide services to multiple departments or divisions for the company. These shared resources are often called *service departments* because they provide *services* to other departments at the same company. Another common characteristic of service departments is that they usually do not generate revenues. This is similar to the shared production overhead we allocated in the activity-based costing chapter, only now we are talking about nonproduction related service departments. Some examples of service departments follow:

- Payroll and Human Resources
- Accounting
- Copying/Graphic Services

- Physical Plant (repairs and maintains administrative and production facilities)
- Advertising (companywide, not specific products)
- Mail and Shipping Services
- Shared Facilities (such as meeting rooms used by various departments)
- Legal Services
- Travel Booking Services

This list is not all-inclusive, but merely some common centralized functions. For example, at your college or university, there are many similar shared services that support academic departments such as the library, admissions, counseling center and information technology. The key is that a service department is a centralized, nonrevenue generating department that provides services to many departments within a company.

It is clear these service costs provide value to other parts of the company. But should we charge these costs to those divisions, products, or segments? The key to that question is to determine if the cost is *traceable* to a particular product, division, or business segment. If the costs are purely variable, tracing those costs to a specific product, division, or segment is easily identifiable. If the costs are fixed, it becomes a bit more challenging. **Traceable fixed costs** are fixed costs that can be directly associated with an individual product, division, or business segment. **A traceable fixed cost would disappear if the company discontinued making the product or discontinued operating the division or the segment.** For example, Smart Touch's DVD manager's salary is traceable to the DVD product line. **Untraceable fixed costs (or common fixed costs)** are those fixed costs that cannot be directly associated with an individual product, division, or business segment. For example, the salary of Sheena Bright, president of Smart Touch, is not traceable to a specific product line, division, or business segment. Therefore, her salary would be an untraceable fixed cost.

Assigning Traceable Service Department Costs

So, how do companies charge various departments for their use of service departments? Let's start with an example. Suppose Smart Touch incurs $40,000 per month to operate the Centralized Ordering Department. $30,000 is considered traceable fixed costs of the three divisions: CDs, DVDs, and e-Learning. $10,000 of the total $40,000 of Centralized Ordering Department costs are considered untraceable (common). How should the company assign the $30,000 traceable fixed cost among the three divisions? Splitting the cost equally—charging each division $10,000—may not be fair, especially if the three units do not use the services equally. Smart Touch's data for assigning the payroll costs follows in Exhibit 22-20, showing not only the three divisions but also a further separation of information, for the DVD division.

Ideally, the company should assign the $30,000 traceable fixed costs based on each division's use of centralized ordering services. The company should use the primary activity that drives (increases or decreases) the cost of central ordering services as the assignment base. As you may recall from Chapter 18, companies identify cost drivers when they implement activity-based costing (ABC). Therefore, a company that has already implemented ABC should know what cost drivers would be suitable for assigning traceable service department charges. For example, order processing cost may be driven by the number of orders placed. Exhibit 22-21 provides several examples of centralized services and common assignment bases.

EXHIBIT 22-20 | **Smart Touch Learning's Data for Traceable Cost Assignment**

Divisions Sharing Order Processing Services	Number of Orders (assignment base)	Sales Revenue	Variable Expenses (includes variable COGS)
CD	100,000	$3,600,000	$3,040,000
DVD	140,000	1,200,000	850,000
e-Learning	160,000	3,840,000	3,350,000
Total	400,000	$8,640,000	$7,240,000

Departments in the DVD Division Sharing Order Processing Services	Number of Orders (assignment base)	Sales Revenue	Variable Expenses (includes variable COGS)
Excel DVDs	84,000	$ 960,000	$680,000
Specialty DVDs	56,000	240,000	170,000
Total	140,000	$1,200,000	$850,000

EXHIBIT 22-21 | **Common Service Departments**

Centralized Service Departments	Examples of Departments' Cost	Typical Base Used to Assign Traceable Portion
Payroll and Human Resources	Payroll and human resources' salaries, depreciation on equipment and facilities, payroll software	Number of employees
Accounting	Accounting personnel salaries, depreciation on equipment and facilities used by accounting staff, accounting software costs	Number of reports prepared
Copying/Graphic Services	Copier depreciation, toner and paper, salaries of Copying/Graphic Services	Number of copies made for department
Physical Plant	Salaries of physical plant employees, depreciation on physical plant equipment, cost of repair and maintenance parts, plant supplies (glue, bolts, small tools)	Number of repairs made
Order Processing	Cost of telephone lines and employee salaries	Number of orders
Mail and Shipping Services	Cost of shipping/mailing, salaries of shipping personnel, depreciation on equipment and facilities used by mail personnel	Pieces of mail processed
Shared Facilities	Depreciation on furniture and fixtures, utilities cost	Allocation based on hours of use
Legal	Salaries of legal department personnel, depreciation on legal department equipment, software costs	Number of hours spent on legal matters
Travel	Salaries of travel department personnel, depreciation on travel department equipment, software costs	Number of business trips booked

Based on the data in Exhibit 22-20, Smart Touch would probably chose the "number of orders" as the cost driver for assigning the $30,000 in traceable fixed ordering costs as this would closely match how much each division uses the Order Processing Department. First, Smart Touch would calculate a cost per order of $0.075 ($30,000/400,000 orders). Smart Touch's data is in Exhibit 22-20. Exhibit 22-22 shows the assignment of the $30,000 traceable costs based on the total number of orders placed for each division.

EXHIBIT 22-22 | **Smart Touch's Assignment of Traceable Order Processing Services (Three Divisions) Using Number of Orders**

Divisions Sharing Order Processing Services	Number of Orders (assignment base)	Cost per Order	Service Department Charge (Orders × $0.075 per order)
CD	100,000	$0.075	$ 7,500
DVD	140,000	$0.075	10,500
e-Learning	160,000	$0.075	12,000
Total	400,000	$0.075	$30,000

The assignment of the Order Processing Department's traceable costs for Smart Touch can be further broken down by product line. We determined in Exhibit 22-22 that the DVD division was allocated $10,500 of the total $30,000 traceable Order Processing Department costs when we used number of orders as an activity base. From earlier chapters we know that Smart Touch's DVD division mainly produces two types of DVDs—Excel DVDs and Specialty DVDs. Of the $10,500 in traceable order processing costs of the DVD division, only $7,000 of those costs are traceable to the two products and $3,500 of those costs are untraceable (common). We need to assign the $7,000 in traceable order processing costs for the DVD division to the two product lines within the DVD division to determine the profit from each product line. First, Smart Touch would calculate a cost per order of $0.05 ($7,000/140,000 orders). Then, Smart Touch would assign the $7,000 traceable order processing costs between Excel and Specialty DVDs as before and as shown in Exhibit 22-23.

EXHIBIT 22-23 | **Smart Touch's Assignment of Traceable Order Processing Services (DVD Division) Using Number of Orders**

Divisions Sharing Order Processing Services	Number of Orders (assignment base)	Cost per Order	Service Department Charge (orders × $0.05)
Excel DVD	84,000	$0.05	$4,200
Specialty DVD	56,000	$0.05	2,800
Total	140,000	$0.05	$7,000

Step 3 would calculate income by division and by product line after assigning all traceable costs. To simplify the example, we assume the only traceable fixed costs are from the Order Processing Department. Exhibit 22-24 illustrates responsibility accounting reports for each of the levels of management shown in Exhibit 22-19. **Responsibility accounting reports show the results of the segment or division for which a particular manager is responsible.** This is illustrated in Exhibit 22-24 for the divisions and the whole company, and in Exhibit 22-25 for the DVD division and its products only.

Notice the headings in blue for the segment-specific income: Divisional segment margin and Product segment margin. Assume you were Smart Touch's DVD division manager. How would this information help you make better decisions? By highlighting costs in a contribution margin format and reporting results by division, it helps managers to have the best information to make decisions. As shown in previous chapters' analyses, the Excel DVD division continues to stand out as the most profitable product for the DVD division.

EXHIBIT 22-24 | **Smart Touch Income Statement—Segments Defined as Divisions**

SMART TOUCH LEARNING, INC.
Income Statement
For the Year Ended December 31, 2014

	Total Company	CD	DVD	e-Learning
Sales revenue	$8,640,000	$3,600,000	$1,200,000	$3,840,000
Less: Variable expenses	7,240,000	3,040,000	850,000	3,350,000
Contribution margin	1,400,000	560,000	350,000	490,000
Less: Traceable fixed expenses (Exhibit 22-22)	30,000	7,500	10,500	12,000
Divisional segment margin	1,370,000	$ 552,500	$ 339,500	$ 478,000
Less: Common fixed expenses not traceable to specific divisions	10,000			
Net operating income (loss)	$1,360,000			

EXHIBIT 22-25 | **Smart Touch Income Statement—Segments Defined as Product Lines Within the DVD Division**

SMART TOUCH LEARNING, INC.
Divisional Income Statement
For the Year Ended December 31, 2014

	DVD Division	Excel DVD	Specialty DVD
Sales revenue	$1,200,000	$960,000	$240,000
Less: Variable expenses	850,000	680,000	170,000
Contribution margin	350,000	280,000	70,000
Less: Traceable fixed expenses (Exhibit 22-23)	7,000	4,200	2,800
Product segment margin	343,000	$275,800	$ 67,200
Less: Common fixed expenses not traceable to specific products	3,500		
Divisional segment margin	$ 339,500		

Further, managers could compare these values to the budgeted values to determine where the actual results differed from the budget plan, which we'll review in the next chapter.

Stop & Think...

Say you and your roommate share groceries at your apartment. The last grocery trip was $200. How do you split up the costs? There are many ways you could divide the grocery bill. You could split the total grocery cost between the two of you evenly, $100 each. You could split the bill based on the number of meals each of you eats a week. If you eat at the apartment 5 times a week, but your roommate eats at the apartment 15 times a week, then your roommate would rightfully pay a bigger part of the grocery bill ($200 × 15/20 meals, or $150). Your roommate may balk at this, arguing that your meals are larger than hers. Then how do you split the bill? This is the same logic we use in assigning shared cost. Maybe there's an item on the grocery bill, such as spices, that isn't really traceable to either roommate but is more of a common cost. No system is perfect, but you aim for the assignment that best measures the traceable costs to the correct business segment.

The Decision Guidelines on the next page review budgets and responsibility accounting. Study these guidelines before working on Summary Problem 22-3.

Key Takeaway

Responsibility centers are parts of the company for which managers have decision-making authority and accountability over. Responsibility accounting is performance reporting for those responsibility centers. There are four types of responsibility centers: cost centers, revenue centers, profit centers, and investment centers. Traceable fixed costs are those costs that would disappear if a company quit making a particular product or discontinued a division or segment. Common fixed costs (untraceable) are those costs that aren't traceable to a specific product, division, or segment.

Decision Guidelines 22-1

THE MASTER BUDGET AND RESPONSIBILITY ACCOUNTING

Amazon.com's initial strategy was to "get big fast." But without a budget, spending got out of control. So founder and CEO Jeff Bezos added a second strategic goal—to become the world's most cost-efficient, high-quality e-tailer. Today, **Amazon**'s managers use budgets to help reach both the growth and cost-efficiency goals. Let's consider some of the decisions **Amazon** made as it set up its budgeting process.

Decision	Guidelines
• What benefits should **Amazon** expect to obtain from developing a budget?	• Requires managers to *plan* how to increase sales and how to cut costs • Promotes *coordination and communication*, such as communicating the importance of the cost-efficiency goal • Provides a *benchmark* that motivates employees and helps managers evaluate how well employees contributed to the sales growth and cost-efficiency goals
• In what order should **Amazon**'s managers prepare the components of the master budget?	Begin with the *operating budget*. • Start with the *sales budget*, which feeds into all other budgets. • The sales budget determines the *inventory, purchases, and cost of goods sold budget*. • The sales, cost of goods sold, and *operating expenses budgets* determine the *budgeted income statement*. Next, prepare the *capital expenditures budget*. Finally, prepare the *financial budget*. • Start with the *cash budget*. • The cash budget provides the ending cash balance for the *budgeted balance sheet* and the details for the *budgeted statement of cash flows*.
• What extra steps should **Amazon** take given the uncertainty of Internet-based sales forecasts?	Prepare a *sensitivity analysis* and project budgeted results at different sales levels.
• How does **Amazon** compute budgeted purchases?	$$\text{Purchases} = \frac{\text{Cost of}}{\text{goods sold}} + \frac{\text{Ending}}{\text{inventory}} - \frac{\text{Beginning}}{\text{inventory}}$$
• What kind of a responsibility center does each manager supervise?	• *Cost center*: The manager is responsible for costs. • *Revenue center*: The manager is responsible for revenues. • *Profit center*: The manager is responsible for both revenues and costs, and, therefore, profits. • *Investment center*: The manager is responsible for revenues, costs, and the amount of the investment required to earn the income.
• What is the difference between traceable fixed costs and common fixed costs?	*Traceable fixed costs* are fixed costs that can be directly associated with an individual product, division, or business segment. A traceable fixed costs would disappear if the company discontinued making the product or discontinued operating the division or segment. *Common fixed costs* (or *untraceable fixed costs*) are those fixed costs that cannot be directly associated with an individual product, division, or segment.

Summary Problem 22-3

Wilke's Tool-a-Rama manufactures small tools and tool sets. The company utilizes a shared warehouse facility that stores the inventory. The Small Tools division uses 150,000 square feet of the warehouse and the Tool Set division uses 100,000 square feet of the warehouse. The total cost of the warehouse facility was $30,000, of which $25,000 are traceable fixed costs. Further, the Small Tools division has two main products: wrenches and screwdrivers. The wrenches use 60,000 square feet of the warehouse and the screwdrivers use 75,000 square feet. The remaining 15,000 square feet is used by the Small Tools division manager, so it isn't traceable to either Small Tools division product. Additionally, income and expense data for each division for the month of August 2013 follows.

Additional data:	Small Tools		Tool Set
	Wrenches	Screwdrivers	
Sales revenue	$65,000	$35,000	$140,000
Variable cost of goods sold	31,200	16,800	56,000
Fixed cost of goods sold	12,000	8,000	25,000
Variable selling expenses	8,000	10,000	13,000

Requirements

1. Calculate the cost per square foot for the warehouse facility and show the cost used by each division. Calculate the cost used by each product of the Small Tools division.
2. Prepare an income statement by division and by product for the month ended August 31, 2013.

Solution

Requirements

1. $25,000/250,000 square feet of space = $0.10 per square foot.

Divisions Sharing Warehouse Facilities	Number of Square Feet (assignment base)	Cost per Square Foot	Traceable Warehouse Costs (number of square feet × $0.10 per square foot)
Small Tools	150,000	$0.10	$15,000
Tools Sets	100,000	$0.10	10,000
Total	250,000	$0.10	$25,000

Products Sharing Warehouse Facilities	Number of Square Feet (assignment base)	Cost per Square Foot	Traceable Warehouse Costs (number of square feet × $0.10 per square foot)
Wrenches	60,000	$0.10	$ 6,000
Screwdrivers	75,000	$0.10	7,500
Total	135,000	$0.10	$13,500

2.

WILKE'S TOOL-A-RAMA			
Income Statement			
For the Month Ended August 31, 2013			
	Total Company	**Small Tools**	**Tool Set**
Sales revenue	$240,000	$100,000	$140,000
Less: Variable COGS	104,000	48,000	56,000
Variable selling expenses	31,000	18,000	13,000
Contribution margin	$105,000	$ 34,000	$ 71,000
Less: Fixed COGS	45,000	20,000	25,000
Traceable fixed expenses (from Requirement 1)	25,000	15,000	10,000
Divisional segment margin	$ 35,000	$ (1,000)	$ 36,000
Less: Common fixed expenses not traceable			
to specific divisions	5,000		
Net operating income (loss)	$ 30,000		

WILKE'S TOOL-A-RAMA			
Divisional Income Statement			
For the Month Ended August 31, 2013			
	Small Tools Division	**Wrenches**	**Screwdrivers**
Sales revenue	$100,000	$65,000	$35,000
Less: Variable COGS	48,000	31,200	16,800
Variable selling expenses	18,000	8,000	10,000
Contribution margin	$ 34,000	$25,800	$ 8,200
Less: Fixed COGS	20,000	12,000	8,000
Traceable fixed expenses (from Requirement 1)	13,500	6,000	7,500
Product segment margin	$ 500	$ 7,800	$ (7,300)
Less: Common fixed expenses not traceable to			
specific products	1,500		
Divisional segment margin	$ (1,000)		

Review *The Master Budget and Responsibility Accounting*

● Accounting Vocabulary

Budgeted Income Statement (p. 1051)
Statement that projects operating income for a period.

Capital Expenditures Budget (p. 1056)
A company's plan for purchases of property, plant, equipment, and other long-term assets.

Cash Budget (p. 1056)
Details how the business expects to go from the beginning cash balance to the desired ending cash balance.

Common Fixed Costs (p 1077)
Fixed costs that cannot be directly associated with an individual product, division, or business segment. Also called **untraceable fixed costs.**

Financial Budget (p. 1056)
The cash budget (cash inflows and outflows), the budgeted income statement, the budgeted balance sheet, and the budgeted statement of cash flows.

Master Budget (p. 1055)
The set of budgeted financial statements and supporting schedules for the entire organization. Includes the operating budget, the capital expenditures budget, and the financial budget.

Operating Budget (p. 1056)
Set of budgets that project sales revenue, cost of goods sold, and operating expenses, leading to the budgeted income statement that projects operating income for the period.

Responsibility Accounting (p. 1074)
A system for evaluating the performance of each responsibility center and its manager.

Responsibility Center (p. 1074)
A part of the organization for which a manager has decision-making authority and accountability for the results of those decisions.

Traceable Fixed Costs (p. 1077)
Fixed costs that can be directly associated with an individual product, division, or business segment. A traceable fixed cost would disappear if the company discontinued making the product or discontinued operating the division or the segment.

Untraceable Fixed Costs (p. 1077)
Fixed costs that cannot be directly associated with an individual product, division, or business segment. Also called **common fixed costs.**

● Destination: Student Success

Student Success Tips

The following are hints on some common trouble areas for students in this chapter:

● Remember that the master budget represents the company's plan of action.

● Keep in mind the three types of budgets within the master budget: operating, capital expenditures, and financial.

● Recall that the operating budget includes the sales budget; the inventory, purchases, and COGS budget; the operating expenses budget; and the income statement. These budgets show the accrual basis planned operations.

● Keep in mind that the capital expenditures budget shows the company's plan for purchasing long-term assets.

● Recall the financial budget includes many budgets. The cash collections from customers, cash payments for purchases, and cash payments for operating expenses budgets help create the cash budget. The budgeted balance sheet and budgeted statement of cash flows round out the financial budgets.

● Keep in mind the four different types of responsibility centers: cost centers, revenue centers, profit centers, and investment centers.

● Remember that traceable fixed costs are those costs that would eventually disappear if the company ceased to sell the individual segment (such as a product). Common fixed costs (untraceable) are those costs that cannot be traced to a specific product, division, or segment.

Getting Help

If there's a learning objective from the chapter you aren't confident about, try using one or more of the following resources:

● Review the Excel templates at myaccountinglab.com for the in-chapter problem and for Summary Problems 22-1 and 22-2.

● Review Decision Guidelines 22-1 in the chapter.

● Review Summary Problem 22-1 in the chapter to reinforce your understanding of the operating budget.

● Review Summary Problem 22-2 in the chapter to reinforce your understanding of the financial budget.

● Review Summary Problem 22-3 in the chapter to reinforce your understanding of segment performance reporting and traceable fixed costs.

● Practice additional exercises or problems at the end of Chapter 22 that cover the specific learning objective that is challenging you.

● Watch the white board videos for Chapter 22 located at myaccountinglab.com under the Chapter Resources button.

● Go to myaccountinglab.com and select the Study Plan button. Choose Chapter 22 and work the questions covering that specific learning objective until you've mastered it.

● Work the Chapter 22 pre/post tests in myaccountinglab.com.

● Consult the Check Figures for End of Chapter starters, exercises, and problems, located at myaccountinglab.com.

● Visit the learning resource center on your campus for tutoring.

● Quick Check

1. **Amazon.com** expected to receive which of the following benefits when it started its budgeting process?

    a. The budget provides **Amazon.com**'s managers with a benchmark against which to compare actual results for performance evaluation.

    b. The planning required to develop the budget helps managers foresee and avoid potential problems before they occur.

    c. The budget helps motivate employees to achieve **Amazon.com**'s sales growth and cost-reduction goals.

    d. All of the above

2. Which of the following is the cornerstone (or most critical element) of the master budget?

    a. The operating expenses budget

    b. The budgeted balance sheet

    c. The sales budget

    d. The inventory, purchases, and cost of goods sold budget

3. The budgeted statement of cash flows is part of which element of **Amazon.com**'s master budget?

    a. The financial budget

    b. The operating budget

    c. The capital expenditures budget

    d. None of the above

Use the following information to answer questions 4 through 6. Suppose Mallcentral sells 1,000,000 hardcover books a day at an average price of $30. Assume that Mallcentral's purchase price for the books is 75% of the selling price it charges retail customers. Mallcentral has no beginning inventory, but it wants to have a three-day supply of ending inventory. Assume that operating expenses are $1,000,000 per day.

4. Compute Mallcentral's budgeted sales for the next (seven-day) week.

    a. $157,500,000

    b. $217,000,000

    c. $435,000,000

    d. $210,000,000

5. Determine Mallcentral's budgeted purchases for the next (seven-day) week.

    a. $300,000,000

    b. $225,000,000

    c. $157,500,000

    d. $75,000,000

6. What is Mallcentral's budgeted contribution margin for a (seven-day) week?

    a. $157,500,000

    b. $52,500,000

    c. $45,500,000

    d. $164,500,000

7. Which of the following expenses would *not* appear in Mallcentral's cash budget?

    a. Depreciation expense

    b. Marketing expense

    c. Interest expense

    d. Wages expense

8. Information technology has made it easier for **Amazon.com**'s managers to perform all of the following tasks *except*

    a. preparing responsibility center performance reports that identify variances between actual and budgeted revenues and costs.

    b. rolling up individual units' budgets into the companywide budget.

    c. sensitivity analyses.

    d. removing slack from the budget.

9. Which of the following managers is responsible for revenues and expenses but not ROI?

    a. Investment center manager

    b. Cost center manager

    c. Profit center manager

    d. Revenue center manager

10. Suppose Reeder, Corp., has three divisions, all using the warehouse: Pipes, Seals, and Flanges. The total warehousing cost is $40,000. Total warehouse space is 100,000 square feet, of which Pipes uses 30,000 square feet, Seals uses 25,000 square feet, and Flanges uses 20,000 square feet. The remaining warehouse space is used by the warehouse manager. Which of the following is true?

a. Traceable fixed costs are $30,000.   c. Traceable fixed costs are $40,000.

b. Common fixed costs are $40,000.   d. Common fixed costs are $30,000.

Answers are given after Apply Your Knowledge (p. 1104).

Assess Your Progress

● Short Exercises

S22-1 **❶ Why managers use budgets [5 min]**
Consider the budget for any business.

Requirement

1. List the three key benefits companies get from preparing the budget.

S22-2 **❷ Understanding the components of the master budget [5–10 min]**
The following are some of the components included in the master budget.

> a. Budgeted balance sheet
> b. Sales budget
> c. Capital expenditures budget
> d. Budgeted income statement
> e. Cash budget
> f. Inventory, purchases, and cost of goods sold budget
> g. Budgeted statement of cash flows

Requirement

1. List in order of preparation the items of the master budget.

S22-3 **❸ Preparing an operating budget [5 min]**
Grippers sells its rock-climbing shoes worldwide. Grippers expects to sell 8,500 pairs of shoes for $180 each in January, and 3,500 pairs of shoes for $190 each in February. All sales are cash only.

Requirement

1. Prepare the sales budget for January and February.

Note: Short Exercise 22-3 must be completed before attempting Short Exercise 22-4.

S22-4 **❸ Preparing an operating budget [10 min]**
Review your results from S22-3. Grippers expects cost of goods sold to average 60% of sales revenue, and the company expects to sell 4,100 pairs of shoes in March for $260 each. Grippers' target ending inventory is $10,000 plus 50% of the next month's cost of goods sold.

Requirement

1. Use this information and the sales budget prepared in S22-3 to prepare Grippers' inventory, purchases, and cost of goods sold budget for January and February.

Note: Short Exercise 22-3 must be completed before attempting Short Exercise 22-5.

S22-5 ❹ **Preparing a financial budget [15–20 min]**
Refer to the Grippers sales budget that you prepared in S22-3. Now assume that Grippers' sales are collected as follows:
November sales totaled $400,000 and December sales were $425,000.

50% in the month of the sale
30% in the month after the sale
18% two months after the sale
2% never collected

Requirement

1. Prepare a schedule for the budgeted cash collections for January and February. Round answers to the nearest dollar.

Note: Short Exercises 22-3 and 22-4 must be completed before attempting Short Exercise 22-6.

S22-6 ❹ **Preparing a financial budget [15–20 min]**
Refer to the Grippers inventory, purchases, and cost of goods sold budget your prepared in S22-4. Assume Grippers pays for inventory purchases 50% in the month of purchase and 50% in the month after purchase.

Requirement

1. Prepare a schedule for the budgeted cash payments for purchases for January and February.

Note: Short Exercises 22-5 and 22-6 must be completed before attempting Short Exercise 22-7.

S22-7 ❹ **Preparing a financial budget [5–10 min]**
Grippers has $12,500 in cash on hand on January 1. Refer to S22-5 and S22-6 for cash collections and cash payment information. Assume Grippers has cash payment for operating expenses including salaries of $50,000 plus 1% of sales, all paid in the month of sale. The company requires a minimum cash balance of $10,000.

Requirement

1. Prepare a cash budget for January and February. Will Grippers need to borrow cash by the end of February?

Note: Short Exercise 22-5 must be completed before attempting Short Exercise 22-8.

S22-8 ❺ **Using sensitivity analysis in budgeting [10–15 min]**
Refer to the Grippers cash collections from customers budget that you prepared in S22-5. Now assume that Grippers' sales are collected as follows:

Requirement

60% in the month of the sale
30% in the month after the sale
8% two months after the sale
2% never collected

1. Prepare a revised schedule for the budgeted cash collections for January and February.

S22-9 ⑤ **Using sensitivity analysis in budgeting [10–15 min]**
Maplehaven Sporting Goods Store has the following sales budget:

MAPLEHAVEN SPORTING GOODS STORE					
Sales Budget					
April–July					
	April	May	June	July	April–July Total
Cash sales, 80%	$ 40,800	$ 64,000	$ 51,200	$ 40,800	
Credit sales, 20%	10,200	16,000	12,800	10,200	
Total sales, 100%	$ 51,000	$ 80,000	$ 64,000	$ 51,000	$ 246,000

Suppose June sales are expected to be $80,000 rather than $64,000.

Requirement

1. Revise Maplehaven's sales budget.

S22-10 ⑥ **Preparing performance reports for responsibility centers [5 min]**
Consider the following list of responsibility centers and phrases.

A cost center	A revenue center
An investment center	Lower
A profit center	Higher
A responsibility center	

Requirement

1. Fill in the blanks with the phrase that best completes the sentence.

   a. The maintenance department at the San Diego Zoo is _____.
   b. The concession stand at the San Diego Zoo is _____.
   c. The menswear department at **Bloomingdale's**, which is responsible for buying and selling merchandise, is _____.
   d. A production line at a Palm Pilot plant is _____.
   e. _____ is any segment of the business whose manager is accountable for specific activities.
   f. Gatorade, a division of **Quaker Oats**, is _____.
   g. The sales manager in charge of **Nike's** northwest sales territory oversees _____.
   h. Managers of cost and revenue centers are at _____ levels of the organization than are managers of profit and investment centers.

S22-11 ⑥ **Preparing performance reports for responsibility centers [5–10 min]**
Wham-O is a distributor of board games and water toys manufactured by other companies. The company utilizes a shared Testing Facility where toys are safety tested. The Board Games division uses 3,000 testing hours a month. The Water Toys division uses 6,000 testing hours a month. The additional 1,000 hours are used testing R&D projects for the company. The total fixed costs of the Testing Facility were $100,000. Additionally, income and expense data for each division for the month of April 2012 follows:

	Board Games	Water Toys
Sales revenue	$450,000	$300,000
Variable cost of goods sold ...	216,000	120,000
Fixed cost of goods sold	120,000	140,000
Variable selling expenses	60,000	40,000

Requirements

1. Calculate the rate per hour for Testing Facilities. Calculate the traceable fixed costs for each division.

2. Prepare an income statement for the company using the contribution margin approach. Calculate divisional segment margin for both divisions.

● Exercises

E22-12 ① Why managers use budgets [15 min]

Doug Ramirez owns a chain of travel goods stores. Last year, his sales staff sold 20,000 suitcases at an average sale price of $190. Variable expenses were 75% of sales revenue, and the total fixed expense was $250,000. This year, the chain sold more expensive product lines. Sales were 15,000 suitcases at an average price of $290. The variable expense percentage and the total fixed expenses were the same both years. Ramirez evaluates the chain manager by comparing this year's income with last year's income.

Requirement

1. Prepare a performance report for this year, similar to Exhibit 22-4. How would you improve Ramirez's performance evaluation system to better analyze this year's results?

E22-13 ② Understanding the components of the master budget [15–20 min]

Sarah Edwards, division manager for Pillows Plus, is speaking to the controller, Diana Rothman, about the budgeting process. Sarah states, "I'm not an accountant, so can you explain the three main parts of the master budget to me and tell me their purpose?"

Requirement

1. Answer Sarah's question.

E22-14 ③ Preparing an operating budget [15–20 min]

Tremont, Inc., sells tire rims. Its sales budget for the nine months ended September 30 follows:

	Quarter Ended			Nine-Month
	March 31	June 30	September 30	Total
Cash sales, 20%	$ 24,000 $	34,000 $	29,000 $	87,000
Credits sales, 80% . . .	96,000	136,000	116,000	348,000
Total sales, 100%	$ 120,000 $	170,000 $	145,000 $	435,000

In the past, cost of goods sold has been 40% of total sales. The director of marketing and the financial vice president agree that each quarter's ending inventory should not be below $20,000 plus 10% of cost of goods sold for the following quarter. The marketing director expects sales of $220,000 during the fourth quarter. The January 1 inventory was $32,000.

Requirement

1. Prepare an inventory, purchases, and cost of goods sold budget for each of the first three quarters of the year. Compute cost of goods sold for the entire nine-month period.

Note: Exercise 22-14 must be completed before attempting Exercise 22-15.

E22-15 ③ Preparing an operating budget [15–20 min]

Consider the facts presented in E22-14. Tremont's operating expenses include the following:

> Rent, $2,000 a month
> Salary, $3,000 a month
> Commissions, 3% of sales
> Depreciation, $1,000 a month
> Miscellaneous expenses, 1% of sales

Requirement

1. Prepare an operating expenses budget for each of the three quarters of 2012 and totals for the nine-month period.

E22-16 ④ Preparing a financial budget [20–30 min]

Agua Pure is a distributor of bottled water.

Requirement

1. For each of the Items a. through c., compute the amount of cash receipts or payments Agua Pure will budget for September. The solution to one item may depend on the answer to an earlier item.

   a. Management expects to sell equipment that cost $20,000 at a gain of $5,000. Accumulated depreciation on this equipment is $5,000.

   b. Management expects to sell 7,300 cases of water in August and 9,800 in September. Each case sells for $14. Cash sales average 10% of total sales, and credit sales make up the rest. Three-fourths of credit sales are collected in the month of sale, with the balance collected the following month.

   c. The company pays rent and property taxes of $4,300 each month. Commissions and other selling expenses average 20% of sales. Agua Pure pays one-half of commissions and other selling expenses in the month incurred, with the balance paid in the following month.

E22-17 ④ ⑤ Preparing a financial budget, and using sensitivity analysis in budgeting [15–20 min]

Ling Auto Parts, a family-owned auto parts store, began January with $10,200 cash. Management forecasts that collections from credit customers will be $11,700 in January and $15,000 in February. The store is scheduled to receive $7,000 cash on a business note receivable in January. Projected cash payments include inventory purchases ($14,500 in January and $13,900 in February) and operating expenses ($2,900 each month).

Ling Auto Parts' bank requires a $10,000 minimum balance in the store's checking account. At the end of any month when the account balance dips below $10,000, the bank automatically extends credit to the store in multiples of $1,000. Ling Auto Parts borrows as little as possible and pays back loans in quarterly installments of $2,500, plus 5% interest on the entire unpaid principal. The first payment occurs three months after the loan. (*Note: We recommend you use the Excel work papers provided at myaccountinglab.com.*)

Requirements

1. Prepare Ling Auto Parts' cash budget for January and February.

2. How much cash will Ling Auto Parts borrow in February if collections from customers that month total $14,000 instead of $15,000?

E22-18 ④ Preparing a financial budget [20 min]

You recently began a job as an accounting intern at Reilly Golf Park. Your first task was to help prepare the cash budget for April and May. Unfortunately, the computer with the budget file crashed, and you did not have a backup or even a paper copy.

You ran a program to salvage bits of data from the budget file. After entering the following data in the budget, you may have just enough information to reconstruct the budget.

REILLY GOLF PARK Cash Budget April and May		
	April	May
Beginning cash balance	$ 18,000	$?
Cash collections	?	82,000
Cash from sale of plant assets	0	2,100
Cash available	113,000	?
Cash payments:		
Purchase of inventory	$?	$ 44,000
Operating expenses	46,000	?
Total cash payments	97,000	?
Ending cash balance before financing	?	22,100
Less: Minimum cash balance required	20,000	20,000
Cash excess (deficiency)	$?	$?
Financing of cash deficiency:		
Borrowing (at end of month)	?	?
Principal repayments (at end of month)	?	?
Interest expense	?	?
Total effects of financing	?	?
Ending cash balance	$?	$?

Reilly Golf Park eliminates any cash deficiency by borrowing the exact amount needed from First Street Bank, where the current interest rate is 6%. Reilly Golf Park first pays interest on its outstanding debt at the end of each month. The company then repays all borrowed amounts at the end of the month with any excess cash above the minimum required but after paying monthly interest expenses.

Requirement

1. Complete the cash budget.

E22-19 ❹ **Preparing a financial budget [25–30 min]**

Consider the following June actual ending balances and July 31, 2012, budgeted amounts for Oleans.com:

a. June 30 inventory balance, $17,750
b. July payments for inventory, $4,300
c. July payments of accounts payable and accrued liabilities, $8,200
d. June 30 accounts payable balance, $10,600
e. June 30 furniture and fixtures balance, $34,500; accumulated depreciation balance, $29,830
f. June 30 equity, $28,360
g. July depreciation expense, $900
h. Cost of goods sold, 50% of sales
i. Other July expenses, including income tax, total $6,000, paid in cash
j. June 30 cash balance, $11,400
k. July budgeted credit sales, $12,700
l. June 30 accounts receivable balance, $5,140
m. July cash receipts, $14,200

Requirement

1. Prepare a budgeted balance sheet.

E22-20 ⑥ **Preparing performance reports for responsibility centers [5 min]**

Consider the following:

 a. The bakery department of a **Publix** supermarket reports income for the current year.

 b. **Pace Foods** is a subsidiary of **Campbell Soup Company.**

 c. The personnel department of **State Farm Insurance Companies** prepares its budget and subsequent performance report on the basis of its expected expenses for the year.

 d. The shopping section of **Burpee.com** reports both revenues and expenses.

 e. **Burpee.com**'s investor relations Web site provides operating and financial information to investors and other interested parties.

 f. The manager of a **BP** service station is evaluated based on the station's revenues and expenses.

 g. A charter airline records revenues and expenses for each airplane each month.

 h. The manager of the Southwest sales territory is evaluated based on a comparison of current period sales against budgeted sales.

Requirement

 1. Identify each responsibility center as a cost center, a revenue center, a profit center, or an investment center.

E22-21 ⑥ **Preparing performance reports for responsibility centers [15–20 min]**

Love My Phone is based in Kingswood, Texas. The merchandising company has two divisions: Cell Phones and MP3 Players. The Cell Phone division has two main product lines: Basic and Advanced. The Basic product line includes phones whose primary function is storing contacts and making/receiving calls. The Advanced product line includes multi-application phones that, in addition to the Basic phones usage, contain a variety of applications. Applications include texting, surfing the Internet, interfacing to Outlook, creating documents, taking pictures, and so on. The company uses a shared order processing department. There are $25,000 in fixed order processing costs each month, of which $20,000 are traceable to the two divisions by the number of orders placed. 3,000 orders a month are processed by the MP3 Player division and 7,000 orders a month are processed by the Cell Phone division. 1,000 of the orders processed for the Cell Phone division cannot be traced to either product line. Facts related to the divisions and products for the month ended September 30, 2012, follow:

	Cell Phones Division		
	Basic	Advanced	MP3 Players Division
Number of orders processed per month . . .	2,000	4,000	3,000
Sales revenue	$75,000	$300,000	$150,000
COGS (variable)	52,500	180,000	60,000
Fixed selling expenses	12,000	9,000	25,000
Variable selling expenses	9,000	16,000	14,000

Requirements

 1. Calculate the rate per order for Order Processing. Calculate the traceable fixed costs for each division and for each product in the Cell Phone division.

 2. Prepare an income statement for the company using the contribution margin approach. Calculate net income for the company, divisional segment margin for both divisions, and product segment margin for both products.

● Problems (Group A)

P22-22A ❸ Preparing an operating budget [30 min]

MyAccountingLab

Thumbtack's March 31, 2012, budgeted balance sheet follows:

THUMBTACK OFFICE SUPPLY Budgeted Balance Sheet March 31, 2012					
Assets			**Liabilities**		
Current assets:			Current liabilities:		
Cash		$18,000	Accounts payable		$12,500
Accounts receivable		12,000	Salary and commissions payable		1,400
Inventory		16,000	Total liabilities		$13,900
Prepaid insurance		2,200			
Total current assets		$48,200	**Stockholders' Equity**		
Plant assets:			Common stock		16,000
Equipment and fixtures	45,000		Retained earnings		33,300
Less: Accumulated depreciation	30,000		Total stockholders' equity		$49,300
Total plant assets		$15,000			
Total assets		$63,200	Total liabilities and stockholders' equity		$63,200

The budget committee of Thumbtack Office Supply has assembled the following data.

a. Sales in April were $40,000. You forecast that monthly sales will increase 2% over April's sales in May. June's sales will increase 4% over April's sales. July's sales will increase 20% over April's sales. Collections are 80% in the month of sale and 20% in the month following sale.

b. Thumbtack maintains inventory of $11,000 plus 25% of the COGS budgeted for the following month. COGS = 50% of sales revenue. Purchases are paid 30% in the month of purchase and 70% in the month following the purchase.

c. Monthly salaries amount to $7,000. Sales commissions equal 5% of sales for that month. Salaries and commissions are paid 30% in the month incurred and 70% in the following month.

d. Other monthly expenses are as follows:

Rent expense	$2,400, paid as incurred
Depreciation expense	$200
Insurance expense	$100, expiration of prepaid amount
Income tax	20% of operating income, paid as incurred

Requirements

1. Prepare Thumbtack's sales budget for April and May, 2012. Round *all* amounts to the nearest $1.

2. Prepare Thumbtack's inventory, purchases, and cost of goods sold budget for April and May.

3. Prepare Thumbtack's operating expenses budget for April and May.

4. Prepare Thumbtack's budgeted income statement for April and May.

Note: We recommend you solve this and the related problems (P22-23A and P22-24A) using Excel templates that you create.

Note: Problem 22-22A must be completed before attempting Problem 22-23A.

P22-23A ❹ **Preparing a financial budget [30 min]**
Refer to P22-22A.

Requirements

1. Prepare the schedule of budgeted cash collections from customers for April and May.
2. Prepare the schedule of budgeted cash payments for purchases for April and May.
3. Prepare the schedule of budgeted cash payments for operating expenses for April and May.
4. Prepare the cash budget for April and May. Assume no financing took place.

Note: Problems 22-22A and 22-23A must be completed before attempting Problem 22-24A.

P22-24A ❹ **Preparing a financial budget [30 min]**
Refer to P22-22A and P22-23A.

Requirements

1. Prepare a budgeted balance sheet as of May 31, 2012.
2. Prepare the budgeted statement of cash flows for the two months ended May 31, 2012. (Note: You should omit sections of the cash flow statements where the company has no activity.)

P22-25A ❸ ❹ **Preparing an operating and a financial budget [50–60 min]**
Class Printing Supply of Baltimore has applied for a loan. **Bank of America** has requested a budgeted balance sheet at April 30, 2012, and a budgeted statement of cash flows for April. The March 31, 2012, budgeted balance sheet follows:

CLASS PRINTING SUPPLY				
Budgeted Balance Sheet				
March 31, 2012				
Assets			**Liabilities**	
Current assets:			Current liabilities:	
Cash	$ 50,500		Accounts payable	$ 8,600
Accounts receivable	12,800			
Inventory	11,900		Total liabilities	$ 8,600
Total current assets	$ 75,200		**Stockholders' Equity**	
Plant assets:			Common stock	42,000
Equipment and fixtures	81,100		Retained earnings	93,200
Less: Accumulated depreciation	12,500		Total stockholders' equity	$135,200
Total plant assets	$ 68,600			
Total assets	$143,800		Total liabilities and stockholders' equity	$143,800

As Class Printing's controller, you have assembled the following additional information:

a. April dividends of $2,500 were declared and paid.
b. April capital expenditures of $16,400 budgeted for cash purchase of equipment.
c. April depreciation expense, $700.
d. Cost of goods sold, 40% of sales.
e. April operating expenses, including salaries, total $38,000, 20% of which will be paid in cash and the remainder will be paid next month.
f. Additional April operating expenses also include miscellaneous expenses of 5% of sales, all paid in April.
g. April budgeted sales, $89,000, 60% is collected in April and 40% in May.
h. April cash payments of March 31 liabilities incurred for March purchases of inventory, $8,600.
i. April purchases of inventory, $10,900 for cash and $37,500 on credit. Half the credit purchases will be paid in April and half in May.

Requirements

1. Prepare the sales budget for April.
2. Prepare the operating expenses budget for April.
3. Prepare the budgeted income statement for April.
4. Prepare the budgeted cash collections from customers for April.
5. Prepare the budgeted cash payments for operating expenses for April.
6. Prepare the cash budget for April.
7. Prepare the budgeted balance sheet for Class Printing at April 30, 2012.
8. Prepare the budgeted statement of cash flows for April.

Note: Problems 22-22A through 22-24A must be completed before attempting Problem 22-26A.

P22-26A ③ ⑤ Preparing an operating budget using sensitivity analysis [30–40 min]

Refer to your results from P22-22A, P22-23A, and P22-24A. Assume the following changes to the original facts:

a. Collections of receivables are 60% in the month of sale, 38% in the month following the sale, and 2% are never collected. Assume the March receivables balance is net of the allowance for uncollectibles.
b. Minimum required inventory levels are $8,000 plus 30% of next month's COGS.
c. Purchases of inventory will be paid 20% in the month of purchase, 80% in the month following purchase.
d. Salaries and commissions are paid 60% in the month incurred and 40% in the following month.

Requirements

1. Prepare Thumbtack's revised sales budget for April and May. Round all calculations to the nearest dollar.
2. Prepare Thumbtack's revised inventory, purchases, and cost of goods sold budget for April and May.
3. Prepare Thumbtack's revised operating expenses budget for April and May.
4. Prepare Thumbtack's revised budgeted income statement for April and May.

Note: Problem 22-26A must be completed before attempting Problem 22-27A.

P22-27A ④ ⑤ Preparing a financial budget using sensitivity analysis [30–40 min]

Refer to the original data in P22-22A and the revisions presented in P22-26A.

Requirements

1. Prepare the schedule of budgeted cash collections from customers for April and May.
2. Prepare the schedule of budgeted cash payments for purchases for April and May.
3. Prepare the schedule of budgeted cash payments for operating expenses for April and May.
4. Prepare the cash budget for April and May. Assume no financing took place.

Note: Problems 22-26A and 22-27A must be completed before attempting Problem 22-28A.

P22-28A ④ ⑤ Preparing a financial budget using sensitivity analysis [30 min]

Refer to P22-26A and P22-27A.

Requirements

1. Prepare a budgeted balance sheet as of May 31, 2012.
2. Prepare the budgeted statement of cash flows for the two months ended May 31, 2012. (Note: You should omit sections of the cash flow statements where the company has no activity.)

P22-29A ⑥ **Preparing performance reports for responsibility centers [25–40 min]**

Jalapenos! is based in Pleasant Hill, California. The merchandising company has three divisions: Clothing, Food, and Spices. The Clothing division has two main product lines: T-shirts and Sweatshirts. The company uses a shared warehousing facility. There are $50,000 in fixed warehousing costs each month, of which $40,000 are traceable to the three divisions based on the amount of square feet used. There is 100,000 square feet of warehouse space in the facility. The clothing division uses 60,000 square feet of the space, but 5,000 of that space isn't traceable to t-shirts or sweatshirts. Facts related to the divisions and products for the month ended October 31, 2012, follow:

	Clothing		Food	Spices
	T-shirts	Sweatshirts		
Square feet used	40,000	15,000	30,000	10,000
Sales revenue	$300,000	$100,000	$150,000	$80,000
COGS (variable)	$210,000	$ 60,000	$ 60,000	$32,000
Fixed selling expenses	$ 7,000	$ 5,000	$ 3,000	$ 1,000
Variable selling expenses	$ 9,000	$ 8,500	$ 11,000	$ 2,500

Requirements

1. Calculate the rate per square foot for Warehousing. Calculate the traceable fixed costs for each division and for each product in the Clothing division.
2. Prepare an income statement for the company using the contribution margin approach. Calculate net income for the company, divisional segment margin for both divisions, and product segment margin for both products.

● Problems (Group B)

P22-30B ③ **Preparing an operating budget [30 min]**

Clipboard Office Supply's March 31, 2012, budgeted balance sheet follows:

CLIPBOARD OFFICE SUPPLY			
Budgeted Balance Sheet			
March 31, 2012			
Assets		**Liabilities**	
Current assets:		Current liabilities:	
Cash	$28,000	Accounts payable	$10,500
Accounts receivable	11,500	Salary and commissions payable	1,200
Inventory	15,000	Total liabilities	$11,700
Prepaid insurance	1,000		
Total current assets	$55,500	**Stockholders' Equity**	
Plant assets:		Common stock	25,000
Equipment and fixtures	55,000	Retained earnings	53,800
Less: Accumulated depreciation	20,000	Total stockholders' equity	$78,800
Total plant assets	$35,000		
Total assets	$90,500	Total liabilities and stockholders' equity	$90,500

The budget committee of Clipboard Office Supply has assembled the following data.

a. Sales in April were $48,000. You forecast that monthly sales will increase 5% over April's sales in May. June's sales will increase 10% over April's sales. July's sales will increase 15% over April's sales. Collections are 80% in the month of sale and 20% in the month following sale.

b. Clipboard maintains inventory of $9,000 plus 25% of the COGS budgeted for the following month. COGS = 50% of sales revenue. Purchases are paid 40% in the month of purchase and 60% in the month following the purchase.

c. Monthly salaries amount to $6,000. Sales commissions equal 5% of sales for that month. Salaries and commissions are paid 60% in the month incurred and 40% in the following month.

d. Other monthly expenses are as follows:

Rent expense	$2,800, paid as incurred
Depreciation expense	$300
Insurance expense	$100, expiration of prepaid amount
Income tax	25% of operating income, paid as incurred

Requirements

1. Prepare Clipboard's sales budget for April and May, 2012.
2. Prepare Clipboard's inventory, purchases, and cost of goods sold budget for April and May.
3. Prepare Clipboard's operating expenses budget for April and May.
4. Prepare Clipboard's budgeted income statement for April and May.

Note: We recommend you solve this and the related problems (P22-31B and P22-32B) using Excel templates that you create.

Note: Problem 22-30B must be completed before attempting Problem 22-31B.

P22-31B ④ Preparing a financial budget [30 min]
Refer to P22-30B.

Requirements

1. Prepare the schedule of budgeted cash collections from customers for April and May.
2. Prepare the schedule of budgeted cash payments for purchases for April and May.
3. Prepare the schedule of budgeted cash payments for operating expenses for April and May.
4. Prepare the cash budget for April and May. Assume no financing took place.

Note: Problems 22-30B and 22-31B must be completed before attempting Problem 22-32B.

P22-32B ④ Preparing a financial budget [30 min]
Refer to P22-30B and P22-31B.

Requirements

1. Prepare a budgeted balance sheet as of May 31, 2012.
2. Prepare the budgeted statement of cash flows for the two months ended May 31, 2012. (Note: You should omit sections of the cash flow statements where the company has no activity.)

P22-33B ③ ④ **Preparing an operating and a financial budget [50–60 min]**

Alliance Printing of Baltimore has applied for a loan. **Bank of America** has requested a budgeted balance sheet at April 30, 2012, and a budgeted statement of cash flows for April. The March 31, 2012, budgeted balance sheet follows:

<table>
<tr><td colspan="4" align="center">**ALLIANCE PRINTING**
Budgeted Balance Sheet
March 31, 2012</td></tr>
<tr><td colspan="2" align="center">Assets</td><td colspan="2" align="center">Liabilities</td></tr>
<tr><td>Current assets:</td><td></td><td>Current liabilities:</td><td></td></tr>
<tr><td>Cash</td><td>$ 51,100</td><td>Accounts payable</td><td>$ 7,800</td></tr>
<tr><td>Accounts receivable</td><td>14,900</td><td>Total liabilities</td><td>$ 7,800</td></tr>
<tr><td>Inventory</td><td>12,100</td><td></td><td></td></tr>
<tr><td>Total current assets</td><td>$ 78,100</td><td align="center">Stockholders' Equity</td><td></td></tr>
<tr><td>Plant assets:</td><td></td><td>Common stock</td><td>36,000</td></tr>
<tr><td>Equipment and fixtures</td><td>80,800</td><td>Retained earnings</td><td>102,800</td></tr>
<tr><td>Less: Accumulated depreciation</td><td>12,300</td><td>Total stockholders' equity</td><td>$138,800</td></tr>
<tr><td>Total plant assets</td><td>$ 68,500</td><td></td><td></td></tr>
<tr><td>Total assets</td><td>$146,600</td><td>Total liabilities and stockholders' equity</td><td>$146,600</td></tr>
</table>

As Alliance Printing's controller, you have assembled the following information:

a. April dividends of $8,000 were declared and paid.

b. April capital expenditures of $16,700, budgeted for cash purchase of equipment.

c. April depreciation expense, $400.

d. Cost of goods sold, 30% of sales.

e. April operating expenses, including salaries, total $35,000, 40% of which will be paid in cash and the remainder will be paid next month.

f. Additional April operating expenses also include miscellaneous expenses of 5% of sales, all paid in April.

g. April budgeted sales, $85,000, 60% is collected in April and 40% in May.

h. April cash payments of March 31 liabilities incurred for March purchases of inventory, $7,800.

i. April purchases of inventory, $11,200 for cash and $37,300 on credit. Half the credit purchases will be paid in April and half in May.

Requirements

1. Prepare the sales budget for April.

2. Prepare the operating expenses budget for April.

3. Prepare the budgeted income statement for April.

4. Prepare the budgeted cash collections from customers for April.

5. Prepare the budgeted cash payments for operating expenses for April.

6. Prepare the cash budget for April.

7. Prepare the budgeted balance sheet for Alliance Printing at April 30, 2012.

8. Prepare the budgeted statement of cash flows for April.

Note: Problems 22-30B through 22-32B must be completed before attempting Problem 22-34B.

P22-34B ❸ ❺ **Preparing an operating budget and using sensitivity analysis [30–40 min]**
Refer to your results from P22-30B, P22-31B, and P22-32B. Assume the following changes to the original facts:

a. Collections of receivables are 60% in the month of sale, 35% in the month following the sale, and 5% are never collected. Assume the March receivables balance is net of the allowance for uncollectibles.
b. Minimum required inventory levels are $5,000 plus 40% of next month's COGS.
c. Purchases of inventory will be paid 30% in the month of purchase, 70% in the month following purchase.
d. Salaries and commissions are paid 40% in the month incurred and 60% in the following month.

Requirements
1. Prepare Clipboard's revised sales budget for April and May. Round all calculations to the nearest dollar.
2. Prepare Clipboard's revised inventory, purchases, and cost of goods sold budget for April and May.
3. Prepare Clipboard's revised operating expenses budget for April and May.
4. Prepare Clipboard's revised budgeted income statement for April and May.

Note: Problem 22-34B must be completed before attempting Problem 22-35B.

P22-35B ❹ ❺ **Preparing a financial budget using sensitivity analysis [30-40 min]**
Refer to the original data in P22-30B and the revisions presented in P22-34B.

Requirements
1. Prepare the schedule of budgeted cash collections from customers for April and May.
2. Prepare the schedule of budgeted cash payments for purchases for April and May.
3. Prepare the schedule of budgeted cash payments for operating expenses for April and May.
4. Prepare the cash budget for April and May. Assume no financing took place.

Note: Problems 22-34B and 22-35B must be completed before attempting Problem 22-36B.

P22-36B ❹ ❺ **Preparing a financial budget using sensitivity analysis [30 min]**
Refer to P22-34B and P22-35B.

Requirements
1. Prepare a budgeted balance sheet as of May 31, 2012.
2. Prepare the budgeted statement of cash flows for the two months ended May 31, 2012. (Note: You should omit sections of the cash flow statements where the company has no activity.)

P22-37B ❻ **Preparing performance reports for responsibility centers [25-40 min]**
Ensalada is based in Pleasant Hill, California. The merchandising company has three divisions: Clothing, Food, and Spices. The Clothing division has two main product lines: T-shirts and Sweatshirts. The company uses a shared warehousing facility. There are $65,000 in fixed warehousing costs each month, of which $30,000 are traceable to the three divisions based on the amount of square feet used. There is 100,000 square feet of warehouse space in the facility. The clothing division uses 50,000 square feet of the space, but 5,000 of that space isn't traceable to T-shirts or sweatshirts. Facts related to the divisions and products for the month ended October 31, 2012, follow:

	Clothing		Food	Spices
	T-shirts	Sweatshirts		
Square feet used	30,000	15,000	10,000	40,000
Sales revenue	$440,000	$150,000	$ 80,000	$180,000
COGS (variable).................	$308,000	$ 90,000	$ 32,000	$ 72,000
Fixed selling expenses	$ 5,000	$ 10,000	$ 6,000	$ 700
Variable selling expenses	$ 14,000	$ 9,000	$ 8,500	$ 2,100

Requirements

1. Calculate the rate per square foot for Warehousing. Calculate the traceable fixed costs for each division and for each product in the Clothing division.
2. Prepare an income statement for the company using the contribution margin approach. Calculate net income for the company, divisional segment margin for both divisions, and product segment margin for both products.

● Continuing Exercise

MyAccountingLab **E22-38** ❸ **Preparing an operating budget [30 min]**

This exercise continues the Lawlor Lawn Service, Inc., situation from Exercise 21-34 of Chapter 21. Lawlor Lawn Service is projecting sales for July of $100,000. August's sales will be 8% higher than July's. September's sales are expected to be 10% higher than August's. October's sales are expected to be 5% higher than September's. COGS is expected to be 30% of sales. Lawlor desires to keep minimum inventory of $1,000 plus 10% of next month's COGS. Beginning inventory on June 30 is $11,000. Purchases are paid for in the month of purchase. Operating expenses are estimated to be $10,000 a month for rent, and $750 per month in depreciation.

Requirements

1. Prepare a sales budget for the quarter ended September 30, 2013.
2. Prepare an inventory, purchases, and cost of goods sold budget for the quarter ended September 30, 2013.
3. Prepare an operating expenses budget for the quarter ended September 30, 2013.
4. Prepare a budgeted income statement for the quarter ended September 30, 2013.

● Continuing Problem

MyAccountingLab **P22-39** ❹ **Preparing a financial budget [30 min]**

This problem continues the Draper Consulting, Inc., situation from P21-35 of Chapter 21. Assume Draper Consulting began January with $29,000 cash. Management forecasts that collections from credit customers will be $49,000 in January and $51,500 in February. Projected cash payments include equipment purchases ($17,000 in January and $40,000 in February) and operating expenses ($6,000 each month).

Draper's bank requires a $20,000 minimum balance in the store's checking account. At the end of any month when the account balance dips below $20,000, the bank automatically extends credit to the store in multiples of $5,000. Draper borrows as little as possible and pays back loans each month in $1,000 increments, plus 5% interest on the entire unpaid principal. The first payment occurs one month after the loan.

Requirements

1. Prepare Draper Consulting's cash budget for January and February 2013.
2. How much cash will Draper borrow in February if collections from customers that month total $21,500 instead of $51,500?

Apply Your Knowledge

● Decision Cases

Decision Case 22-1 Donna Tse has recently accepted the position of assistant manager at Cycle World, a bicycle store in St. Louis. She has just finished her accounting courses. Cycle

World's manager and owner, Jeff Towry, asks Tse to prepare a budgeted income statement for 2015 based on the information he has collected. Tse's budget follows:

CYCLE WORLD
Budgeted Income Statement
For the Year Ending July 31, 2015

Sales revenue		$244,000
Cost of goods sold		177,000
Gross profit		$ 67,000
Operating expenses:		
Salary and commission expense	$ 46,000	
Rent expense	8,000	
Depreciation expense	2,000	
Insurance expense	800	
Miscellaneous expenses	12,000	68,800
Operating loss		$ (1,800)
Interest expense		(225)
Net loss		$ (2,025)

Requirement

1. Tse does not want to give Towry this budget without making constructive suggestions for steps Towry could take to improve expected performance. Write a memo to Towry outlining your suggestions.

Decision Case 22-2 Each autumn, as a hobby, Anne Magnuson weaves cotton place mats to sell through a local craft shop. The mats sell for $20 per set of four. The shop charges a 10% commission and remits the net proceeds to Magnuson at the end of December. Magnuson has woven and sold 25 sets each for the last two years. She has enough cotton in inventory to make another 25 sets. She paid $7 per set for the cotton. Magnuson uses a four-harness loom that she purchased for cash exactly two years ago. It is depreciated at the rate of $10 per month. The accounts payable relate to the cotton inventory and are payable by September 30.

Magnuson is considering buying an eight-harness loom so that she can weave more intricate patterns in linen. The new loom costs $1,000; it would be depreciated at $20 per month. Her bank has agreed to lend her $1,000 at 18% interest, with $200 payment of principal, plus accrued interest payable each December 31. Magnuson believes she can weave 15 linen place mat sets in time for the Christmas rush if she does not weave any cotton mats. She predicts that each linen set will sell for $50. Linen costs $18 per set. Magnuson's supplier will sell her linen on credit, payable December 31.

Magnuson plans to keep her old loom whether or not she buys the new loom. The balance sheet for her weaving business at August 31, 2014, is as follows:

ANNE MAGNUSON, WEAVER
Balance Sheet
August 31, 2014

Current assets:			Current liabilities:	
Cash	$ 25		Accounts payable	$ 74
Inventory of cotton	175			
		200		
Fixed assets:				
Loom	500		Stockholders' equity	386
Less: Accumulated depreciation	240			
		260		
Total assets		$ 460	Total liabilities and owner's equity	$460

Requirements

1. Prepare a cash budget for the four months ending December 31, 2014, for two alternatives: weaving the place mats in cotton using the existing loom, and weaving the place mats in linen using the new loom. For each alternative, prepare a budgeted income statement for the four months ending December 31, 2014, and a budgeted balance sheet at December 31, 2014.

2. On the basis of financial considerations only, what should Magnuson do? Give your reason.

3. What nonfinancial factors might Magnuson consider in her decision?

• Ethical Issue 22-1

Residence Suites operates a regional hotel chain. Each hotel is operated by a manager and an assistant manager/controller. Many of the staff who run the front desk, clean the rooms, and prepare the breakfast buffet work part-time or have a second job so turnover is high.

Assistant manager/controller Terry Dunn asked the new bookkeeper to help prepare the hotel's master budget. The master budget is prepared once a year and is submitted to company headquarters for approval. Once approved, the master budget is used to evaluate the hotel's performance. These performance evaluations affect hotel managers' bonuses and they also affect company decisions on which hotels deserve extra funds for capital improvements.

When the budget was almost complete, Dunn asked the bookkeeper to increase amounts budgeted for labor and supplies by 15%. When asked why, Dunn responded that hotel manager Clay Murry told her to do this when she began working at the hotel. Murry explained that this budgetary cushion gave him flexibility in running the hotel. For example, because company headquarters tightly controls capital improvement funds, Murry can use the extra money budgeted for labor and supplies to replace broken televisions or pay "bonuses" to keep valued employees. Dunn initially accepted this explanation because she had observed similar behavior at the hotel where she worked previously.

Requirements

Put yourself in Dunn's position. In deciding how to deal with the situation, answer the following questions:

1. What is the ethical issue?

2. What are my options?

3. What are the possible consequences?

4. What should I do?

• Fraud Case 22-1

Patrick had worked in the garment business for years and had set up a small clothing outlet as a front for a scheme. At first, he placed small orders with a few carefully chosen manufacturers and made sure to pay promptly. After a few months, he used those companies as credit references, and placed progressively larger orders with bigger outfits. Then, with a good track record of payments, he started buying from FiestaWear, a trendy, upmarket apparel factory in Los Angeles. After two years, he sprung the trap. He placed a $280,000 order for garments from FiestaWear and asked them to "expedite" the delivery. The moment the merchandise arrived, his rented trucks rushed the goods to Mexico, he closed up his outlet, and vanished into the woodwork. When FiestaWear realized that something was fishy, it called the FBI. The company had been duped by a ploy known as the "overbuy." The merchandise was easy for Patrick to sell on the black market.

Requirements

1. What can a company do to protect against this kind of business risk?

2. Where does the expense for uncollectible accounts get reported in the financial statements?

● Team Project 22-1

Xellnet provides e-commerce software for the pharmaceuticals industry. Xellnet is organized into several divisions. A companywide planning committee sets general strategy and goals for the company and its divisions, but each division develops its own budget.

Lonnie Draper is the new division manager of wireless communications software. His division has two departments: Development and Sales. Chad Sanchez manages the 20 or so programmers and systems specialists typically employed in the development department to create and update the division's software applications. Liz Smith manages the sales department.

Xellnet considers the divisions to be investment centers. To earn his bonus next year, Draper must achieve a 30% return on the $3 million invested in his division. Within the wireless division, development is a cost center, while sales is a revenue center.

Budgeting is in progress. Sanchez met with his staff and is now struggling with two sets of numbers. Alternative A is his best estimate of next year's costs. However, unexpected problems can arise when writing software, and finding competent programmers is an ongoing challenge. He knows that Draper was a programmer before he earned an MBA so he should be sensitive to this uncertainty. Consequently, he is thinking of increasing his budgeted costs (Alternative B). His department's bonuses largely depend on whether the department meets its budgeted costs.

XELLNET Wireless Division Development Budget 2013		
	Alternative A	**Alternative B**
Salaries expense (including overtime and part time)	$2,400,000	$2,640,000
Software expense	120,000	132,000
Travel expense	65,000	71,500
Depreciation expense	255,000	255,000
Miscellaneous expense	100,000	110,000
Total expense	$2,940,000	$3,208,500

Liz Smith is also struggling with her sales budget. Companies have made their initial investments in communications software so it is harder to win new customers. If things go well, she believes her sales team can maintain the level of growth achieved over the last few years. This is Alternative A in the sales budget. However, if Smith is too optimistic, sales may fall short of the budget. If this happens, her team will not receive bonuses. Therefore, Smith is considering reducing the sales numbers and submitting Alternative B.

XELLNET Wireless Division Sales Budget 2013		
	Alternative A	**Alternative B**
Sales revenue	$5,000,000	$4,500,000
Salaries expense	360,000	360,000
Travel expense	240,000	210,500

Split your team into three groups. Each group should meet separately before the entire team meets.

Requirements

1. The first group plays the role of development manager Chad Sanchez. Before meeting with the entire team, determine which set of budget numbers you are going to present to Lonnie Draper. Write a memo supporting your decision. Give this memo to the third group before the team meeting.

2. The second group plays the role of sales manager Liz Smith. Before meeting with the entire team, determine which set of budget numbers you are going to present to Lonnie Draper. Write a memo supporting your decision. Give this memo to the third group before the team meeting.

3. The third group plays the role of division manager Lonnie Draper. Before meeting with the entire team, use the memos that Sanchez and Smith provided you to prepare a division budget based on the sales and development budgets. Your divisional overhead costs (additional costs beyond those incurred by the development and sales departments) are approximately $390,000. Determine whether the wireless division can meet its targeted 30% return on assets given the budgeted alternatives submitted by your department managers.

During the meeting of the entire team, the group playing Draper presents the division budget and considers its implications. Each group should take turns discussing its concerns with the proposed budget. The team as a whole should consider whether the division budget must be revised. The team should prepare a report that includes the division budget and a summary of the issues covered in the team meeting.

● Communication Activity 22-1

In 75 words or fewer, explain the difference between traceable fixed costs and common fixed costs.

Quick Check Answers

1. *d* 2. *c* 3. *a* 4. *d* 5. *b* 6. *b* 7. *a* 8. *d* 9. *c* 10. *a*

For online homework, exercises, and problems that provide you immediate feedback, please visit myaccountinglab.com.

23

Flexible Budgets and Standard Costs

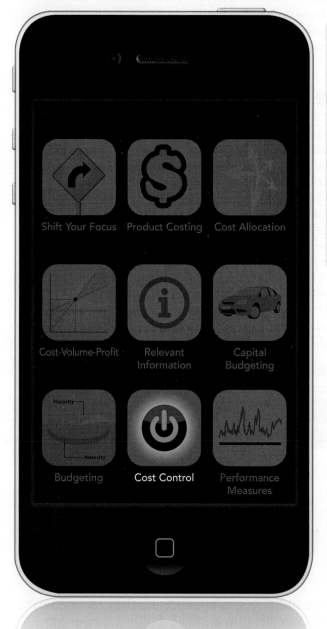

Learning Objectives

1. Prepare a flexible budget for the income statement

2. Prepare an income statement performance report

3. Identify the benefits of standard costs and learn how to set standards

4. Compute standard cost variances for direct materials and direct labor

5. Analyze manufacturing overhead in a standard cost system

6. Record transactions at standard cost and prepare a standard cost income statement

Remember your personal budget from the previous chapter? You prepared a budget for your first year out of college to help you plan and control your spending. Now that you've been working for a few months, you need to reevaluate your situation. Have you been able to keep spending within the budget limits, or did you underestimate some expenses?

After comparing the budgeted amount for utilities with the actual amount you spent, you find you have been spending more than expected. What changes do you need to make? You have to either increase your earnings or decrease your spending. Could you use less electricity by lowering the thermostat in the winter? Should you consider getting a part-time job to supplement your salary? Should you make up the difference by taking lunch to work rather than eating out every day? Or would a combination of changes be best?

Just as we sometimes have to make hard decisions about our personal budgets, businesses have to make similar decisions. An economic downturn or increased competition may cause a decrease in sales. If that happens, spending must also decrease in order for the company to remain profitable.

This chapter builds on your knowledge of budgeting. A *budget variance* is just the difference between an actual amount and a budgeted figure. This chapter shows how managers use variances to operate a business. It is important to know *why* actual amounts differ from the budget. That will enable you to identify problems and decide what action to take.

In this chapter, you will learn how to figure out *why* actual results differ from your budget. This is the first step in correcting problems. You will also learn to use another management tool—standard costing.

How Managers Use Flexible Budgets

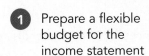 Prepare a flexible budget for the income statement

Let's consider Smart Touch Learning, Inc. At the beginning of the year, Smart Touch's managers prepared a master budget. The master budget is a **static budget**, which means that it is prepared for only *one* level of sales volume. The static budget does not change after it is developed.

Exhibit 23-1 shows that Smart Touch's actual operating income for the month of June is $16,000. This is $4,000 higher than expected from the static budget. This is a $4,000 favorable variance for June operating income. A **variance** is the difference between an actual amount and the budgeted amount. The variances in the third column of Exhibit 23-1 are as follows:

- Favorable (F) if an actual amount increases operating income (Actual revenue > Budgeted revenue; Actual cost (expense) < Budgeted cost (expense))
- Unfavorable (U) if an actual amount decreases operating income (Actual revenue < Budgeted revenue; Actual cost (expense) > Budgeted cost (expense))

EXHIBIT 23-1 | **Actual Results Versus Static Budget**

		Actual Results	Static Budget	Variance
	Units (DVDs)	10,000	8,000	2,000 F
	Sales revenue	$121,000	$96,000	$25,000 F
	Variable expenses	86,000	64,000	22,000 U
	Contribution margin	$ 35,000	$32,000	$3,000 F
	Fixed expenses	19,000	20,000	1,000 F
	Operating income	$ 16,000	$12,000	$4,000 F

SMART TOUCH LEARNING, INC.
Comparison of Actual Results with Static Budget
Month Ended June 30, 2014

Smart Touch's variance for operating income is favorable primarily because Smart Touch sold 10,000 learning DVDs rather than the 8,000 DVDs it budgeted to sell during June. But there is more to this story. Smart Touch needs a *flexible budget* to show budgeted income at different sales levels. Let's see how to prepare and use a flexible budget.

What Is a Flexible Budget?

The report in Exhibit 23-1 is hard to analyze because the static budget is based on 8,000 DVDs, but the actual results are for 10,000 DVDs. This report raises more questions than it answers—for example,

- why did the $22,000 unfavorable variable expense variance occur?
- did workers waste materials?

- did the cost of materials suddenly increase?
- how much of the additional expense arose because Smart Touch sold 10,000 rather than 8,000 DVDs?
- how was the company able to reduce fixed expenses by $1,000?

We need a flexible budget to help answer these questions.

A **flexible budget** summarizes costs (expenses) and revenues for several different volume levels within a relevant range. **Flexible budgets separate variable costs from fixed costs; the variable costs put the "flex" in the flexible budget.** To create a flexible budget, you need to know the following:

- Budgeted selling price per unit
- Variable cost per unit (which includes variable cost of goods sold and all variable operating expenses)
- Total fixed costs (such as fixed cost of goods sold and fixed operating expenses)
- Different volume levels within the relevant range

Exhibit 23-2 is a flexible budget for Smart Touch's revenues and costs that shows what will happen if sales reach 5,000, 8,000, or 10,000 DVDs during June. The budgeted sale price per DVD is $12. Budgeted variable costs are $8 per DVD, and budgeted fixed costs total $20,000.

EXHIBIT 23-2 | **Flexible Budget**

SMART TOUCH LEARNING, INC.
Flexible Budget
Month Ended June 30, 2014

	Per Unit	By Units (DVDs)		
Units (DVDs)		5,000	8,000	10,000
Sales revenue	$12	$60,000	$96,000	$120,000
Variable expenses	$ 8	40,000	64,000	80,000
Contribution margin		$20,000	$32,000	$ 40,000
Fixed expenses*		20,000	20,000	20,000
Operating income		$ 0	$12,000	$ 20,000

* Fixed expenses are usually given as a total rather than as a cost per unit

Notice in Exhibit 23-2 that sales revenue, variable costs, and contribution margin increase as more DVDs are sold. But fixed costs remain constant regardless of the number of DVDs sold within the relevant range of 5,000–10,000 DVDs. *Variable cost per unit and total fixed cost only stay constant within a specific relevant range of output.* Why? Because fixed costs and the variable cost per DVD may change outside this range. In our example, Smart Touch's relevant range is 5,000–10,000 DVDs. If the company sells 12,000 DVDs, it will have to rent additional equipment, which will increase total fixed costs above the current $20,000. Smart Touch may also have to pay workers for overtime pay, so the variable cost per DVD may be more than $8.

Stop & Think...

Assume you are a waiter or waitress. Each night, you cannot be sure how much you will receive in tips from your customers. The more tips you receive, the more income you have to spend on gas, CDs, or possibly to save for a vacation. Informally, you probably figure in your head how much you will receive each night in tips and of that amount, how much you want to save or spend. The flexible budget is just a formalization of that same process for a business.

Using the Flexible Budget: Why Do Actual Results Differ from the Static Budget?

2 Prepare an income statement performance report

It is not enough to know that a variance occurred. That is like knowing you have a fever. The doctor needs to know *why* your temperature is above normal.

Managers must know *why* a variance occurred in order to pinpoint problems and take corrective action. As you can see in Exhibit 23-1, the static budget underestimated both sales and variable costs. The variance in Exhibit 23-1 is called a *static budget variance* because actual activity differed from what was expected in the static budget. To develop more useful information, managers divide the static budget variance into two broad categories:

- **Flexible budget variance**—arises because the company had different revenues and/or costs than expected for the *actual* units sold. The flexible budget variance occurs because sales price per unit, variable cost per unit, and/or fixed cost was different than planned on the budget.

- **Sales volume variance**—arises because the actual number of units sold differed from the number of units on which the static budget was based. Sales volume variance is the volume difference between actual sales and budgeted sales.

Exhibit 23-3 diagrams these variances.

EXHIBIT 23-3	**The Static Budget Variance: The Sales Volume Variance and the Flexible Budget Variance**

Actual Results	Flexible Budget based on **actual** number of units sold	Static (Master) Budget based on **expected** number of units sold
	Flexible Budget Variance	Sales Volume Variance
	Static Budget Variance	

Following are the formulas for computing the two variances:

$$\text{Flexible Budget Variance} = \begin{pmatrix} \text{Actual Results} \\ \text{for the number of units} \\ \text{actually sold} \\ \text{10,000 DVDs} \end{pmatrix} - \begin{pmatrix} \text{Flexible Budget} \\ \text{for the number of units} \\ \text{actually sold} \\ \text{10,000 DVDs} \end{pmatrix}$$

$$\text{Sales Volume Variance} = \begin{pmatrix} \text{Flexible Budget} \\ \text{for the number of units} \\ \text{actually sold} \\ \text{10,000 DVDs} \end{pmatrix} - \begin{pmatrix} \text{Static (Master) Budget} \\ \text{for the number of units} \\ \text{expected to be sold} \\ \text{8,000 DVDs} \end{pmatrix}$$

We have seen that Smart Touch budgeted (planned to sell) 8,000 DVDs during June. Actual sales were 10,000 DVDs. We will need to compute the flexible budget variance and the sales volume variance for Smart Touch. Exhibit 23-4 is Smart Touch's income statement performance report for June. Recall the variances in the second and fourth column of Exhibit 23-4 are

- favorable (F) if an actual amount increases operating income.

- unfavorable (U) if an actual amount decreases operating income.

EXHIBIT 23-4	Income Statement Performance Report

SMART TOUCH LEARNING, INC.
Income Statement Performance Report
Month Ended June 30, 2014

	1	2 (1) – (3)	3	4 (3) – (5)	5
	Actual Results at Actual Prices*	**Flexible Budget Variance**	**Flexible Budget for Actual Number of Units Sold~**	**Sales Volume Variance**	**Static (Master) Budget***
Units (DVDs)	10,000	0	10,000	2,000 F	8,000
Sales revenue	$121,000	$1,000 F	$120,000	$24,000 F	$96,000
Variable expenses	86,000	6,000 U	80,000	16,000 U	64,000
Contribution margin	$ 35,000	$5,000 U	$ 40,000	$ 8,000 F	$32,000
Fixed expenses	19,000	1,000 F	20,000	0	20,000
Operating income	$ 16,000	$4,000 U	$ 20,000	$ 8,000 F	$12,000

Flexible budget variance,
$4,000 U

Sales volume variance,
$8,000 F

Static budget variance, $4,000 F

*Values from Exhibit 23-1
~Values from Exhibit 23-2

Column 1 of the performance report shows the actual results—based on the 10,000 DVDs actually sold. Operating income was $16,000 for June.

Column 3 is Smart Touch's flexible budget (shown in Exhibit 23-2) for the 10,000 DVDs actually sold. Operating income should have been $20,000.

Column 5 (originally shown in Exhibit 23-1) gives the static budget for the 8,000 DVDs expected to be sold for June. Smart Touch budgeted earnings of $12,000.

The budget variances appear in columns 2 and 4 of the exhibit. Let's begin with actual results in column 1. This data comes from Exhibit 23-1.

Column 1 of Exhibit 23-4 gives the actual results for June—10,000 DVDs and operating income of $16,000. Operating income is $4,000 less than Smart Touch would have expected for 10,000 DVDs (column 3, flexible budget for actual number of units sold). Managers want to know why operating income did not measure up to the flexible budget.

- It was not because the selling price of DVDs took a dive. Sales revenue was $1,000 more than expected for 10,000 DVDs.
- Variable costs were $6,000 too high for 10,000 DVDs.
- Fixed costs were $1,000 too low for 10,000 DVDs.

So, managers would focus on why the variable costs were higher than expected to determine whether the increase is controllable (can be reduced) or uncontrollable (due to some abnormal or isolated event). Overall, expenses rose by $5,000 ($6,000 increase in variable expenses minus $1,000 decrease in fixed expenses) above the flexible budget, while sales revenue only increased by $1,000, resulting in the overall $4,000 unfavorable flexible budget variance.

Now let's look at column 4, the sales volume variance, which is the difference between column 3 and column 5.

The flexible budget for 10,000 units from Exhibit 23-2 is in column 3. The static budget for 8,000 units from Exhibit 23-1 is in column 5. The differences between the static budget and the flexible budget—column 4—arise only because Smart Touch sold 10,000 DVDs rather than the number of DVDs it planned to sell, 8,000.

Connect To: AIS—ERP

Preparing flexible budgets is easy with the use of spreadsheets and/or enterprise resource planning (ERP) software. The key is getting the right information about the inputs (standard costs) and what is projected for sales, the economy, the availability of materials and labor, etc. Further, managers need timely feedback via the income statement performance report to continuously evaluate the decisions made and how those decisions affected performance. The biggest question managers ask is "Was the difference (variance) controllable?" If so, management can make decisions that will enhance future profitability based on this information. If the variance was uncontrollable, management can determine whether the variance is an isolated event or something that will affect future standards. If so, that must be reflected in the flexible budget and standard costs so management will have the most relevant and up-to-date information on which to make decisions.

Column 4 shows the sales volume variances. Sales revenue is $24,000 more than Smart Touch planned (2,000 more DVDs sold at $12 budgeted sales price). Variable expenses were $16,000 higher (unfavorable) than planned for the same reason (2,000 more DVDs sold at $8 variable cost per DVD = $16,000). Fixed expenses were the same for both budgets as the units were within the relevant range. Overall, operating income is favorable by $8,000 because Smart Touch sold more DVDs than it planned to sell (10,000 sold rather than the 8,000 budgeted). Notice this is also the planned contribution margin difference of $8,000 (2,000 more DVDs sold at $4 contributed per DVD). The static budget is developed *before* the period. The performance report in Exhibit 23-4 is prepared after the *end* of the period. Why? Because *the actual units sold are not known until the end of the period.*

Next, take some time to review the Decision Guidelines on the following page.

Decision Guidelines 23-1

FLEXIBLE BUDGETS

You and your roommate have started a business that prints T-shirts (for example, for school and student organizations). How can you use flexible budgets to plan and control your costs?

Decision	Guidelines
• How do you estimate sales revenue, costs, and profits within your relevant range?	Prepare a set of flexible budgets for different sales levels, as in Exhibit 23-2.
• How do you use budgets to help control costs?	Prepare an income statement performance report, as in Exhibit 23-4. Review the results to determine which variances are controllable and which are uncontrollable. Managers will focus on the controllable variances.
• On which output level is the budget based?	Static (master) budget—*expected* number of T-shirts, estimated before the period
• On which output level do managers compare actual results to?	Flexible budget—*actual* number of T-shirts, not known until the end of the period
• Why does your actual income differ from budgeted income?	Prepare an income statement performance report comparing actual results, flexible budget for the actual number of T-shirts sold, and static (master) budget, as in Exhibit 23-4. This report will highlight differences for you to investigate further.
• How much of the difference occurs because revenues and costs are not what they should have been for the actual number of T-shirts sold?	Compute the flexible budget variance (FBV) by comparing actual results with the flexible budget. • Favorable FBV—Actual sales revenue > Flexible budget sales revenue • Favorable FBV—Actual cost (expense) < Flexible budget cost (expense) • Unfavorable FBV—Actual sales revenue < Flexible budget sales revenue • Unfavorable FBV—Actual cost (expense) > Flexible budget cost (expense)
• How much of the difference arises because the actual number of T-shirts sold does not equal budgeted sales?	Compute the sales volume variance (SVV) by comparing the flexible budget with the static budget. • Favorable SVV—Actual number of T-shirts sold > Expected number of T-shirts sold • Unfavorable SVV—Actual number of T-shirts sold < Expected number of T-shirts sold
• What actions can you take to avoid an unfavorable sales volume variance?	• Design more attractive T-shirts to increase demand. • Provide marketing incentives to increase the number of T-shirts sold.
• What actions can you take to avoid an unfavorable flexible budget variance?	• Avoid an unfavorable flexible budget variance for *sales revenue* by maintaining (not discounting) your selling price. • Avoid an unfavorable flexible budget variance for *costs* by controlling variable costs, such as the cost of the T-shirts, dye, and labor, and by controlling fixed costs.

Summary Problem 23-1

Exhibit 23-4 shows that Smart Touch sold 10,000 DVDs during June. Now assume that Smart Touch sold 7,000 DVDs (instead of 10,000) and that the actual sale price averaged $12.50 per DVD. Actual variable costs were $57,400, and actual fixed costs were $19,000.

Requirements

1. Prepare a revised income statement performance report using Exhibit 23-4 as a guide. (*Hint:* You will need to calculate the flexible budget amounts for 7,000 DVDs.)
2. As the company owner, which employees would you praise or criticize after you analyze this performance report?

Solution

Requirement 1

SMART TOUCH LEARNING, INC.
Income Statement Performance Report
Month Ended June 30, 2014

	1	2 (1) – (3)	3	4 (3) – (5)	5
	Actual Results at Actual Prices	Flexible Budget Variance	Flexible Budget for Actual Number of Units Sold	Sales Volume Variance	Static (Master) Budget~
Units (DVDs)	7,000	0	7,000	1,000 U	8,000
Sales revenue	$87,500	$3,500 F	$84,000	$12,000 U	$96,000
Variable expenses	57,400	1,400 U	56,000	8,000 F	64,000
Contribution margin	$30,100	$2,100 F	$28,000	$ 4,000 U	$32,000
Fixed expenses	19,000	1,000 F	20,000	0	20,000
Operating income	$11,100	$3,100 F	$ 8,000	$ 4,000 U	$12,000

Flexible budget variance, $3,100 F   Sales volume variance, $4,000 U

Static budget variance, $900 U

~Values from Exhibit 23-1

Requirement 2

As the company owner, you should determine the *causes* of the variances before praising or criticizing employees. It is especially important to determine whether the variance is due to factors the manager can control. For example

- the $1,000 favorable flexible budget variance for fixed costs could be due to a reduction in insurance premiums. The savings might have come from delaying a scheduled overhaul of equipment that decreased fixed expenses in the short term, but could increase the company's costs in the long run.
- the $4,000 unfavorable sales volume variance could be due to an ineffective sales staff or it could be due to a long period of snow that made it difficult for employees to get to work and brought work to a standstill.

Smart managers use variances to raise questions and direct attention, not to fix blame.

Standard Costing

Most companies use **standard costs** (expenses) to develop their flexible budgets. **Think of a standard cost as a budget for a single unit.** For example, Smart Touch's standard variable cost is $8 per DVD (Exhibit 23-2). This $8 variable cost includes the standard cost of inputs like the direct materials, direct labor, and variable overhead needed for one DVD.

3 Identify the benefits of standard costs and learn how to set standards

In a standard cost system, each input has both a price standard and a quantity standard. Smart Touch has a standard for the following:

- Price it pays per square foot of vinyl (this determines the price standard)
- Amount of vinyl for making the DVDs (this determines the quantity standard)

Let's see how managers set these price and quantity standards.

Price Standards

The price standard for direct materials starts with the base purchase cost of each unit of inventory. Accountants help managers set a price standard for materials after considering early-pay discounts, freight in, and receiving costs.

World-class businesses demand efficient, lean production, while providing the highest quality product and excellent customer service. Lean production cost savings can be achieved several ways. A company can work with existing suppliers to cut its costs. A company could also use the Internet to solicit price quotes from suppliers around the world.

For direct labor, accountants work with human resource managers to determine standard labor rates. They must consider basic pay rates, payroll taxes, and fringe benefits. Job descriptions reveal the level of experience needed for each task. A big part of this is ensuring that employees receive training for the job and are paid fairly for the job.

Accountants work with production managers to estimate manufacturing overhead costs. Production managers identify an appropriate allocation base such as direct labor hours or direct labor cost, as you learned in Chapter 17, or allocate overhead using activity-based costing, as you learned in Chapter 18. Accountants then compute the standard overhead rates. Exhibit 23-5 summarizes the setting of standard costs.

EXHIBIT 23-5 | **Summary of Standard Setting Issues**

	Price Standard	Quantity Standard
Direct Materials	Responsibility: Purchasing manager Factors: Purchase price, discounts, delivery requirements, credit policy	Responsibility: Production manager and engineers Factors: Product specifications, spoilage, production scheduling
Direct Labor	Responsibility: Human resource managers Factors: Wage rate based on experience requirements, payroll taxes, fringe benefits	Responsibility: Production manager and engineers Factors: Time requirements for the production level and employee experience needed
Manufacturing Overhead	Responsibility: Production managers Factors: Nature and amount of resources needed for support activities (e.g., moving materials, maintaining equipment, and inspecting output)	

Application

Let's see how Smart Touch might determine its production cost standards for materials, labor, and overhead.

The manager in charge of purchasing for Smart Touch indicates that the purchase price, net of discounts, is $1.90 per square foot of vinyl. Delivery, receiving, and inspection add an average of $0.10 per square foot. Smart Touch's hourly wage for workers is $8 and payroll taxes and fringe benefits total $2.50 per direct labor hour. Variable overhead will total $6,400 based on 8,000 DVDs (static budget), fixed overhead is $9,600, and overhead is allocated based on 3,200 estimated direct-labor hours. Now let's compute Smart Touch's cost standards for direct materials, direct labor, and overhead based on the static budget of 8,000 DVDs:

Direct materials price standard for vinyl:

Purchase price, net of discounts...	$1.90 per square foot
Delivery, receiving, and inspection	0.10 per square foot
Total standard cost per square foot of vinyl.........................	$2.00 per square foot

Direct labor price (or rate) standard:

Hourly wage	$ 8.00 per direct labor hour
Payroll taxes and fringe benefits.............................	2.50 per direct labor hour
Total standard cost per direct labor hour................	$10.50 per direct labor hour

Variable overhead price (or rate) standard:

$$= \frac{\text{Estimated variable overhead cost}}{\text{Estimated quantity of allocation base}}$$

$$= \frac{\$6,400}{3,200 \text{ direct labor hours}}$$

$$= \$2.00 \text{ per direct labor hour}$$

Fixed overhead price (or rate) standard:

$$= \frac{\text{Estimated fixed overhead cost}}{\text{Estimated quantity of allocation base}}$$

$$= \frac{\$9,600}{3,200 \text{ direct labor hours}}$$

$$= \$3.00 \text{ per direct labor hour}$$

Quantity Standards

Production managers and engineers set direct material and direct labor *quantity standards*. To set its labor standards, **Westinghouse Air Brake**'s Chicago plant analyzed every moment in the production of the brakes.

To eliminate unnecessary work, **Westinghouse** rearranged machines in tight U-shaped work cells so that work could flow better. Workers no longer had to move parts all over the plant floor, as illustrated in the following diagram.

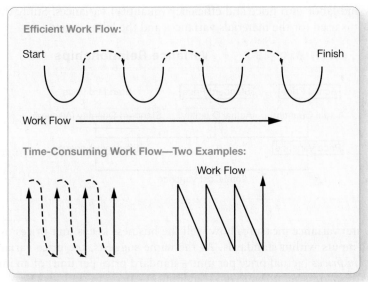

*Note: Solid lines indicate production processes whereas dotted lines indicate moving parts and/or WIP to a different location in the plant.

Westinghouse conducted time-and-motion studies to streamline various tasks. For example, the plant installed a conveyer at waist height to minimize bending and lifting. The result? Workers slashed one element of standard time by 90%.

Companies from the **Ritz-Carlton** to **Federal Express** develop quantity standards based on "best practices." This is often called *benchmarking*. The *best practice* may be an internal benchmark from other plants or divisions within the company or it may be an external benchmark from other companies. Internal benchmarks are easy to obtain, but managers can also purchase external benchmark data. For example, **Riverside Hospital** in Columbus, Ohio, can compare its cost of performing an appendectomy with the "best practice" cost developed by a consulting firm that compares many different hospitals' costs for the same procedure.

Why Do Companies Use Standard Costs?

U.S. surveys show that more than 80% of responding companies use standard costing. Over half of responding companies in the United Kingdom, Ireland, Sweden, and Japan use standard costing. Why? Standard costing helps managers

- prepare the master budget,
- set target levels of performance (static budget),
- identify performance standards (standard quantities and standard costs),
- set sales prices of products and services, and
- decrease accounting costs.

Standard cost systems might appear to be expensive. Indeed, the company must invest up front to develop the standards. But standards can save accounting costs. It is cheaper to value inventories at standard rather than actual costs. With standard costs, accountants avoid the LIFO, FIFO, or average-cost computations.

Variance Analysis

Once we establish standard costs, we can use the standards to assign costs to production. At least once a year, we will compare our actual production costs to the standard costs to locate variances. Exhibit 23-6 shows how to separate total variances for materials and labor into price and efficiency (quantity) variances. Study this exhibit carefully. It is used for the materials variances and the labor variances.

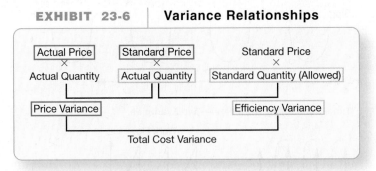

EXHIBIT 23-6 | **Variance Relationships**

A **price (rate) variance** measures how well the business keeps unit prices of material and labor inputs within standards. As the name suggests, the price variance is the *difference in prices* (actual price per unit – standard price per unit) of an input, multiplied by the *actual quantity* used of the input:

> Price Variance = (Actual Price × Actual Quantity) – (Standard Price × Actual Quantity)
> Or, Price Variance = (Actual Price – Standard Price) × Actual Quantity
>
> = (AP – SP) × AQ

An **efficiency (or quantity) variance** measures how well the business uses its materials or human resources. The efficiency variance measures the difference in quantities (actual quantity of input used – standard quantity of input allowed for the actual number of units produced), multiplied by the standard price per unit of the input:

> Efficiency Variance = (Standard Price × Actual Quantity) – (Standard Price × Standard Quantity)
> Or, Efficiency Variance = (Actual Quantity – Standard Quantity) × Standard Price
>
> = (AQ – SQ) × SP

Exhibit 23-7 illustrates these variances and emphasizes two points:

EXHIBIT 23-7 | **The Relationships Among Price, Efficiency, Flexible Budget, Sales Volume, and Static Budget Variances**

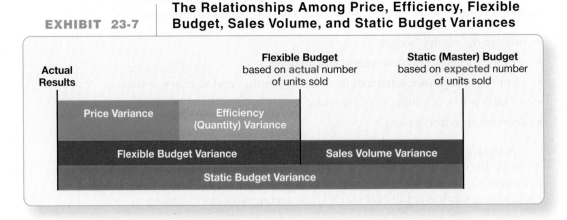

- First, the price and efficiency variances add up to the flexible budget variance.
- Second, static budgets like column 5 of Exhibit 23-4 play no role in the price and efficiency variances.

The static budget is used only to compute the sales volume variance (the variance caused because the company sold a different quantity than it thought it would sell when it created the budget)—never to compute the flexible budget variance or the price and efficiency cost variances for materials and labor.

Stop & Think...

When you go to the gas station, do you fill up your car? How many miles per gallon does your car normally get? What is the usual price per gallon that you pay for gas? Assume you normally pay $4.00 per gallon and buy 10 gallons of gas. That is your standard cost for gas for your car. But what if the next time you need to fill up, you have to pay $4.25 per gallon, but you only have to buy 9.8 gallons of gas? The price variance is unfavorable because it is $0.25 more per gallon, but your car is using the gas more efficiently because you used .2 gallons less than normal.

> **Key Takeaway**
>
> Most companies use standard costs to develop their flexible budgets. Standard cost is a budget for a single unit of materials, labor, and overhead. Price variances measure the difference in actual and standard prices. Efficiency variances measure the difference in actual and standard quantities used.

How Smart Touch Uses Standard Costing: Analyzing the Flexible Budget Variance

Now we'll return to our Smart Touch example. Exhibit 23-4 showed that the main cause for concern at Smart Touch is the $4,000 unfavorable flexible budget variance for operating income. The first step in identifying the causes of the cost variance is to identify the variable and fixed costs, as shown in Panel A of Exhibit 23-8.

Carefully study Exhibit 23-8 on the next page. Panel A shows the $5,000 flexible budget variance from Exhibit 23-4 for 10,000 DVDs. Panel B shows how to compute the flexible budget amounts for 10,000 DVDs. Panel C shows how to compute actual materials and labor costs for 10,000 DVDs. Trace the following:

4 Compute standard cost variances for direct materials and direct labor

- Flexible budget amounts from Panel B to column (2) of Panel A
- Actual costs from Panel C to column (1) of Panel A

Column 3 of Panel A gives the flexible budget variances for direct materials and direct labor. For now, focus on materials and labor. We will cover overhead later.

Direct Materials Variances

There are two types of direct materials variances. We'll cover both next.

Direct Materials Price Variance

Let's investigate the $2,800 unfavorable variance for direct materials in Exhibit 23-8, Panel A. Recall that the direct materials standard price was $2.00 per square foot, and 10,000 square feet are needed for 10,000 DVDs (1 square foot per DVD × 10,000 DVDs). The actual price of materials was $1.90 per square foot, and 12,000 square feet were actually used to make 10,000 DVDs. Using the formula, the materials price variance is $1,200 favorable. The calculation follows:

Materials Price Variance = (AP − SP) × AQ

= ($1.90 per square foot − $2.00 per square foot) × 12,000 square feet

= −$0.10 per square foot × 12,000 square feet

= −$1,200, or $1,200 F

EXHIBIT 23-8 | **Data for Standard Costing Example**

PANEL A—Comparison of Actual Results with Flexible Budget for 10,000 DVDs

SMART TOUCH LEARNING, INC.
Comparison of Actual Results with Flexible Budget
Month Ended June 30, 2014

	Actual Results at Actual Prices	Flexible Budget for 10,000 DVDs	Flexible Budget Variance
Variable costs:			
Direct materials	$ 22,800	$ 20,000	$2,800 U
Direct labor	41,800	42,000	200 F
Variable overhead	9,000	8,000	1,000 U
Marketing and administrative costs	12,400	10,000	2,400 U
Total variable costs	86,000	80,000	6,000 U
Fixed costs:			
Fixed overhead	12,300	9,600‡	2,700 U
Marketing and administrative expense	6,700	10,400	3,700 F
Total fixed costs	19,000	20,000	1,000 F
Total costs	$105,000	$100,000	$5,000 U

‡Fixed overhead was budgeted at $9,600 per month (Application Answer on page 1114).

PANEL B—Computation of Flexible Budget for Direct Materials, Direct Labor, and Variable Overhead for 10,000 DVDs—Based on Standard Costs

	(1) Standard Quantity of Inputs Allowed for 10,000 DVDs	(2) Standard Price per Unit of Input	(3) (1) × (2) Flexible Budget for 10,000 DVDs
Direct materials	1 square foot per DVD × 10,000 DVDs = 10,000 square feet	$ 2.00	$20,000
Direct labor	.40 hours per DVD × 10,000 DVDs = 4,000 hours	$10.50	42,000
Variable overhead	.40 hours per DVD × 10,000 DVDs = 4,000 hours	$ 2.00	8,000

PANEL C—Computation of Actual Costs for Direct Materials and Direct Labor for 10,000 DVDs

	(1) Actual Quantity of Inputs Used for 10,000 DVDs	(2) Actual Price per Unit of Input	(3) (1) × (2) Actual Cost for 10,000 DVDs
Direct materials	12,000 square feet actually used	$1.90 actual cost/square foot	$22,800
Direct labor	3,800 hours actually used	$11.00 actual cost/hour	41,800

The $1,200 direct materials price variance (from page 1117) is *favorable* because the purchasing manager spent $0.10 *less* per square foot of vinyl than budgeted ($1.90 actual price – $2.00 standard price).

Direct Materials Efficiency Variance

Now let's see what portion of the unfavorable materials variance was due to the quantity used.

The standard quantity of inputs is the *quantity that should have been used* for the actual units produced. For Smart Touch, the *standard quantity of inputs (vinyl) that workers should have used for the actual number of DVDs produced* (10,000 DVDs) is 1 square foot of vinyl per DVD, or a total of 10,000 square feet. The direct materials efficiency variance is as follows:

$$
\begin{aligned}
\text{Direct Materials Efficiency Variance} &= (AQ - SQ) \times SP \\
&= (12{,}000 \text{ square feet} - 10{,}000 \text{ square feet}) \times \$2.00 \text{ per square foot} \\
&= +\,2{,}000 \text{ square feet} \times \$2.00 \text{ per square foot} \\
&= +\$4{,}000, \text{ or } \$4{,}000 \text{ U}
\end{aligned}
$$

The $4,000 direct materials efficiency variance is *unfavorable* because workers used 2,000 *more* square feet of vinyl than they planned (budgeted) to use for 10,000 DVDs.

Summary of Direct Materials Variances

Exhibit 23-9 summarizes how Smart Touch splits the $2,800 unfavorable direct materials flexible budget variance into price and efficiency effects.

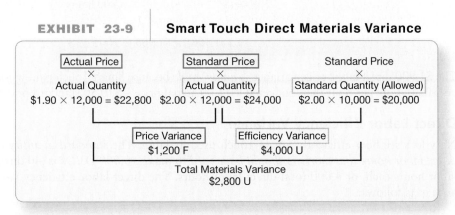

EXHIBIT 23-9 | **Smart Touch Direct Materials Variance**

In summary, Smart Touch spent $2,800 more than it should have for vinyl because

- a good price for the vinyl increased profits by $1,200, but
- inefficient use of the vinyl reduced profits by $4,000.

Let's consider why each variance may have occurred and who may be responsible.

1. The purchasing manager is in the best position to explain the favorable price variance. Smart Touch's purchasing manager may have negotiated a good price for vinyl.

2. The manager in charge of making DVDs can explain why workers used so much vinyl to make the 10,000 DVDs. Was the vinyl of lower quality? Did workers waste materials? Did the production equipment malfunction? Smart Touch's top management needs this information to decide what corrective action to take.

These variances raise questions that can help pinpoint problems. But be careful! A favorable variance does not always mean that a manager did a good job, nor does an unfavorable variance mean that a manager did a bad job. Perhaps Smart Touch's purchasing manager got a lower price by purchasing inferior-quality materials. This could lead to wasted materials. If so, the purchasing manager's decision hurt the company. This illustrates why good managers

- use variances as a guide for investigation rather than merely to assign blame.
- investigate favorable as well as unfavorable variances.

Direct Labor Variances

Smart Touch uses a similar approach to analyze the direct labor flexible budget variance.

Let's review Exhibit 22-8 to determine why Smart Touch spent $200 less on labor than it should have spent for 10,000 DVDs. To determine this, Smart Touch computes the labor price and efficiency variances in exactly the same way as it did for direct materials. Recall from Exhibit 22-8 the standard price for direct labor is $10.50 per hour, and 4,000 hours were budgeted for 10,000 DVDs (.40 hours per DVD $\times$ 10,000 DVDs). But actual direct labor cost was $11.00 per hour, and it took 3,800 hours to make 10,000 DVDs.

Direct Labor Price (Rate) Variance

Using the formula, the direct labor price variance was $1,900 unfavorable. The calculation follows:

$$
\begin{aligned}
\text{Direct Labor Price Variance} &= (\text{AP} - \text{SP}) \times \text{AH} \\
&= (\$11.00 - \$10.50) \times 3{,}800 \text{ hours} \\
&= \$0.50 \times 3{,}800 \text{ hours} \\
&= +\$1{,}900, \text{ or } \$1{,}900 \text{ U}
\end{aligned}
$$

The $1,900 direct labor price variance is *unfavorable* because Smart Touch paid workers $0.50 *more* per hour than budgeted ($11.00 actual price – $10.50 standard price).

Direct Labor Efficiency Variance

Now let's see how efficiently Smart Touch used its labor. The *standard quantity of direct labor hours that workers should have used to make 10,000 DVDs* is .40 direct labor hours each, or 4,000 total direct labor hours. The direct labor efficiency variance is as follows:

$$
\begin{aligned}
\text{Direct Labor Efficiency Variance} &= (\text{AH} - \text{SH}) \times \text{SP} \\
&= (3{,}800 \text{ hours} - 4{,}000 \text{ hours}) \times \$10.50 \text{ per hour} \\
&= -200 \text{ hours} \times \$10.50 \\
&= -\$2{,}100, \text{ or } \$2{,}100 \text{ F}
\end{aligned}
$$

The $2,100 direct labor efficiency variance is *favorable* because laborers actually worked 200 *fewer* hours than the budget called for.

Summary of Direct Labor Variances

Exhibit 23-10 summarizes how Smart Touch computes the direct labor price and efficiency variances.

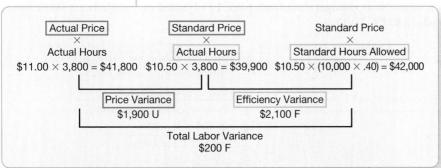

EXHIBIT 23-10 | Smart Touch—Direct Labor Variance

The $200 favorable direct labor variance suggests that total labor costs were close to expectations. But to manage Smart Touch's labor costs, we need to gain more insight:

- Smart Touch paid its employees an average of $11.00 per hour in June instead of the standard rate of $10.50—for an unfavorable price variance.
- Workers made 10,000 DVDs in 3,800 hours instead of the budgeted 4,000 hours—for a favorable efficiency variance.

This situation reveals a trade-off. Smart Touch hired more experienced (and thus more expensive) workers and had an unfavorable price variance. But the workers turned out more work than expected, and the strategy was successful. The overall effect on profits was favorable. This possibility reminds us that managers should take care in using variances to evaluate performance. Go slow, analyze the data, and then take action.

> **Key Takeaway**
>
> Standard cost variances for direct materials and direct labor are each split between the price variance and efficiency variance. The price variance measures the difference between actual and standard price for direct materials and labor used. The efficiency variance measures the difference between actual and standard usage for direct materials and labor based on standard prices. In analyzing each variance, management must consider the overall effect of each decision and how it affected overall results for the production period.

Manufacturing Overhead Variances

In this section of the chapter, we use the terms *manufacturing overhead* and *overhead* interchangeably. The total overhead variance is the difference between

Actual overhead cost	and	Standard overhead allocated to production

Exhibit 23-8 shows that Smart Touch actually incurred $21,300 of overhead: $9,000 variable and $12,300 fixed. The next step is to see how Smart Touch allocates overhead in a standard cost system.

5 Analyze manufacturing overhead in a standard cost system

Allocating Overhead in a Standard Cost System

In a standard costing system, the manufacturing overhead allocated to production is as follows:

$$\text{Overhead allocated to production} = \text{Standard (predetermined) overhead rate} \times \text{Standard quantity of the allocation base allowed for } \textit{actual} \text{ output}$$

Let's begin by computing Smart Touch's standard variable and fixed overhead rates as follows (static budget data from page 1114 based on 3,200 direct labor hours to produce 8,000 DVDs):

$$\text{Standard overhead rate} = \frac{\text{Budgeted manufacturing overhead cost}}{\text{Budgeted direct labor hours}}$$

$$= \frac{\text{Variable overhead} + \text{Fixed overhead}}{\text{Budgeted direct labor hours}}$$

$$= \frac{\$6,400 + \$9,600}{3,200 \text{ direct labor hours}}$$

$$= \frac{\$6,400}{3,200} + \frac{\$9,600}{3,200}$$

$$= \$2.00 \text{ variable} + \$3.00 \text{ fixed}$$

$$= \$5.00 \text{ per direct labor hour}$$

So Smart Touch uses a $2.00 per direct labor hour rate to apply variable overhead to jobs and $3.00 per direct labor hour rate to apply fixed overhead to jobs. Now, let's analyze the variances for variable and fixed overhead.

Variable Overhead Variances

Smart Touch uses a similar approach to analyze the variable overhead flexible budget variance as it did to analyze the direct materials and direct labor variances.

Let's review Exhibit 23-8 to determine why Smart Touch spent $1,000 more on variable overhead than it should have spent for 10,000 DVDs. To determine this, Smart Touch computes the variable overhead spending (price) and efficiency variances. Recall from Exhibit 23-8 the standard price for variable overhead is $2.00 per hour, and 4,000 hours were budgeted for 10,000 DVDs (.40 hours per DVD × 10,000 DVDs). But actual variable overhead cost was $9,000 (AP × AH), and it took 3,800 hours to make 10,000 DVDs.

Variable Overhead Spending (Price) Variance

Using the formula, the variable overhead spending (price) variance was $1,400 unfavorable. The calculation is the same formula we used before—we just have to rearrange the equation as follows:

$$\text{Variable Overhead Spending (Price) Variance} = (\text{AP} - \text{SP}) \times \text{AH}$$
$$(\text{AP} \times \text{AH}) - (\text{SP} \times \text{AH})$$
$$= (\$9,000) - (\$2.00 \times 3,800 \text{ hours})$$
$$= \$9,000 - \$7,600$$
$$= +\$1,400, \text{ or } \$1,400 \text{ U}$$

The $1,400 variable overhead spending (price) variance is *unfavorable* because Smart Touch actually spent $1,400 more than budgeted for variable overhead.

Variable Overhead Efficiency Variance

Now let's see how efficiently Smart Touch used its variable overhead. Since variable overhead is applied based on direct labor hours used, this variance will also be favorable, as the direct labor efficiency variance was favorable. The *standard quantity of direct labor hours that workers should have used to make 10,000 DVDs is .40 direct labor hours each, or 4,000 total direct labor hours.*

The variable overhead efficiency variance is as follows:

Variable Overhead Efficiency Variance = (AH − SH) × SP

= (3,800 hours − 4,000 hours) × \$2.00 per hour

= − 200 hours × \$2.00

= −\$400, or \$400 F

The \$400 variable overhead efficiency variance is *favorable* because laborers actually worked 200 *fewer* hours than the budget called for and variable overhead is applied based on direct labor hours.

Summary of Variable Overhead Variances

Exhibit 23-11 summarizes how Smart Touch computes the variable overhead spending (price) and efficiency variances.

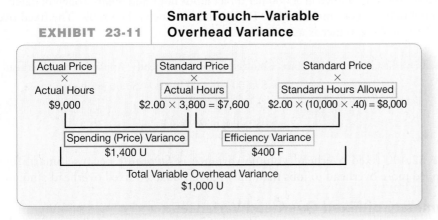

EXHIBIT 23-11 | **Smart Touch—Variable Overhead Variance**

The \$1,000 unfavorable variable overhead variance indicates that variable overhead costs have increased more than expected. To manage Smart Touch's variable overhead costs, we need to get more insight:

- Smart Touch incurred \$1,400 higher than anticipated actual variable overhead costs—for an unfavorable spending (price) variance.
- Workers made 10,000 DVDs in 3,800 hours instead of the budgeted 4,000 hours—for a favorable efficiency variance.

Management will want to investigate the variable overhead spending variance further to determine if the extra costs were controllable or uncontrollable.

Fixed Overhead Variances

Smart Touch uses a similar approach to analyze the fixed overhead variances.

Let's review Exhibit 22-8 to determine why Smart Touch spent \$300 more on fixed overhead than it budgeted. To determine this, Smart Touch computes the *fixed overhead spending* and *volume variances* in exactly the same way as it did for direct materials. Recall that the budgeted fixed overhead was \$9,600. But actual fixed overhead cost was \$12,300 (AP × AH) to make 10,000 DVDs.

Fixed Overhead Spending Variance

The **fixed overhead spending variance** measures the difference between actual fixed overhead and budgeted fixed overhead to determine the controllable portion of total fixed overhead variance. Using the formula, the fixed overhead spending variance was $2,700 unfavorable. The calculation is the same formula we used before—we just have to rearrange the equation as follows:

> Fixed Overhead Spending Variance = Actual fixed overhead − Budgeted fixed overhead
> = $12,300 − $9,600
> = +$2,700, or $2,700 U

The $2,700 fixed overhead spending variance is *unfavorable* because Smart Touch actually spent $2,700 more than budgeted for fixed overhead.

Fixed Overhead Volume Variance

Now let's see how efficiently Smart Touch used its fixed overhead. The **fixed overhead volume variance** measures the difference between the budgeted fixed overhead and the amount of overhead that should have been applied to jobs based on the output. Since fixed overhead is applied at $3.00 per direct labor hour and Smart Touch budgeted to spend 4,000 hours to make 10,000 DVDs, this variance is favorable. The fixed overhead efficiency variance is as follows:

> Fixed Overhead Volume Variance = Budgeted Fixed Overhead − Applied Fixed Overhead
> = $9,600 − (4,000 hours × $3.00 per hour)
> = $9,600 − $12,000
> = −$2,400, or $2,400 F

The $2,400 fixed overhead volume variance is *favorable* because Smart Touch applied more overhead to jobs than the $9,600 budgeted fixed overhead amount.

Summary of Fixed Overhead Variances

Exhibit 23-12 summarizes how Smart Touch computes the fixed overhead spending and volume variances.

EXHIBIT 23-12 | Smart Touch—Fixed Overhead Variance

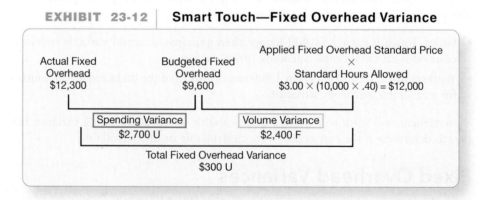

The $300 unfavorable fixed overhead variance indicates that fixed overhead costs have increased more than expected. To manage Smart Touch's fixed overhead costs, we need to get more insight:

- Smart Touch incurred $2,700 higher than anticipated actual fixed overhead costs applied in actual allocations based on production—for an unfavorable spending variance.
- Workers made 10,000 DVDs, which would normally take 4,000 hours but actually only took 3,800 hours; thus, more overhead was applied to the job than was budgeted, which resulted in a $2,400 favorable volume variance. The volume variance can be misleading though because Smart Touch produced more than the static budget of 8,000 DVDs, but this was because workers were efficient.

Management will want to investigate the fixed overhead spending variance further to determine whether the extra costs were controllable or uncontrollable.

Summary of Overhead Variances

Most companies compile cost information for the individual items of overhead, such as indirect materials, indirect labor, and utilities. Managers drill down by comparing actual to budgeted costs for each item. For example, Smart Touch's analysis might reveal that variable overhead costs were higher than expected because utility rates increased or because workers used more power than expected. Perhaps spending on fixed overhead increased because Smart Touch purchased new equipment and its depreciation increased.

Standard Cost Accounting Systems

Next we'll cover standard cost journal entries and standard cost income statements.

Journal Entries

We use Smart Touch's June transactions to demonstrate standard costing journal entries in a job costing context. Management needs to know about variances to address each problem. Therefore, Smart Touch records variances from standards as soon as possible. This means that Smart Touch records direct materials price variances when materials are purchased. It also means that Work in process inventory is debited (DVDs are recorded) at standard input quantities and standard prices. The entries for the month of June follow:

6 Record transactions at standard cost and prepare a standard cost income statement

1.		Materials inventory (12,000 square feet AQ × $2.00 SP) (A+)	24,000	
		Direct materials price variance (CE+)		1,200
		Accounts payable (12,000 AQ × $1.90 AP) (L+)		22,800
		To record purchase of direct materials.		

Entry 1 records the debit to Materials inventory, which is recorded at the *actual quantity* of vinyl purchases (12,000 square feet) at the *standard price* ($2 per square foot). In contrast, the credit to Accounts payable is for the *actual quantity* of vinyl purchased (12,000 square feet) at the *actual price* ($1.90 per square foot). Maintaining Materials inventory at the $2.00 *standard price* allows Smart Touch to record the direct materials price variance at the time of purchase. Recall that Smart Touch's direct materials price variance was $1,200 favorable. A favorable variance has a credit balance and is a contra expense. An unfavorable variance means more expense has been incurred than planned and would have a debit balance.

2.		Work in process inventory (10,000 square feet SQ × $2.00 SP) (A+)	20,000	
		Direct materials efficiency variance (E+)	4,000	
		Materials inventory (12,000 AQ × $2.00 SP) (A−)		24,000
		To record use of direct materials.		

In entry 2, Smart Touch debits Work in process inventory for the *standard cost* of the 10,000 square feet of direct materials that should have been used to make 10,000 DVDs. This maintains Work in process inventory at standard cost. Materials inventory is credited for the *actual quantity* of materials put into production (12,000 square feet) costed at the *standard price*.

Smart Touch's direct materials efficiency variance was $4,000 unfavorable. An unfavorable variance has a debit balance, which increases expense and decreases profits.

3.			
	Manufacturing wages (3,800 AQ hours × $10.50 SP) (E+)	39,900	
	Direct labor price variance (E+)	1,900	
	Wages payable (3,800 AQ × $11.00 AP) (L+)		41,800
	To record direct labor costs incurred.		

In entry 3, manufacturing wages is debited for the $10.50 *standard price* of 3,800 direct labor hours actually used. (The Manufacturing wages account contains both direct and indirect labor. Note entry 4 applies the amount of wages from the Manufacturing wages account to the Work in process inventory and Manufacturing overhead accounts for direct and indirect labor used.) Wages payable is credited for the *actual cost* (the *actual* hours worked at the *actual* wage rate) because this is the amount Smart Touch must pay the workers. The direct labor price variance is $1,900 unfavorable, a debit amount.

4.			
	Work in process inventory (4,000 hours SQ × $10.50 SP) (A+)	42,000	
	Direct labor efficiency variance (CE+)		2,100
	Manufacturing wages (3,800 AQ × $10.50 SP) (E−)		39,900
	To allocate direct labor cost to production.		

In entry 4, Smart Touch debits Work in process inventory for the standard cost per direct labor hour ($10.50) that should have been used for 10,000 DVDs (4,000 hours), like direct materials entry 2. Manufacturing wages is credited to close its prior debit balance for entry 3. The Direct labor efficiency variance is credited for the $2,100 favorable variance. This maintains Work in process inventory at standard cost.

5.			
	Manufacturing overhead (actual cost) (E+)	21,300	
	Various accounts		21,300
	To record actual overhead costs incurred.		

Entry 5 records Smart Touch's actual overhead cost for June. $9,000 actual variable overhead plus $12,300 actual fixed overhead equals $21,300 actual Manufacturing overhead. Various accounts may include Accounts payable, Accumulated depreciation, or other related overhead accounts.

6.			
	Work in process inventory (4,000 SQ hours × $5.00 SP) (A+)	20,000	
	Manufacturing overhead (E−)		20,000
	To allocate overhead to production.		

Entry 6 shows the overhead allocated to Work in process inventory computed as the standard overhead rate ($5.00 per hour) × standard quantity of the allocation base allowed for actual output (4,000 hours for 10,000 DVDs).

7.			
	Finished goods inventory (A+)	82,000	
	Work in process inventory (A−)		82,000
	To record completion of 10,000 DVDs ($20,000 of materials +		
	$42,000 of labor + $20,000 of manufacturing overhead),		
	all at standard cost.		

Entry 7 transfers the standard cost of the 10,000 DVDs completed during June from Work in process inventory to Finished goods.

8.	Cost of goods sold (E+)	82,000	
	Finished goods inventory (A–)		82,000
	To record the cost of sales of 10,000 DVDs at standard cost.		

Entry 8 transfers the cost of sales of the 10,000 DVDs completed at standard cost of $8.20 per DVD.

9.	Variable overhead spending (price) variance (E+)	1,400	
	Fixed overhead spending variance (E+)	2,700	
	Fixed overhead volume variance (CE+)		2,400
	Variable overhead efficiency variance (CE+)		400
	Manufacturing overhead (E–)		1,300
	To record overhead variances and close the Manufacturing		
	overhead account.		

Entry 9 closes the Manufacturing overhead account and records the overhead variances.

Exhibit 23-13 shows the relevant Smart Touch accounts after posting these entries.

EXHIBIT 23-13 | **Smart Touch's Flow of Costs in a Standard Costing System**

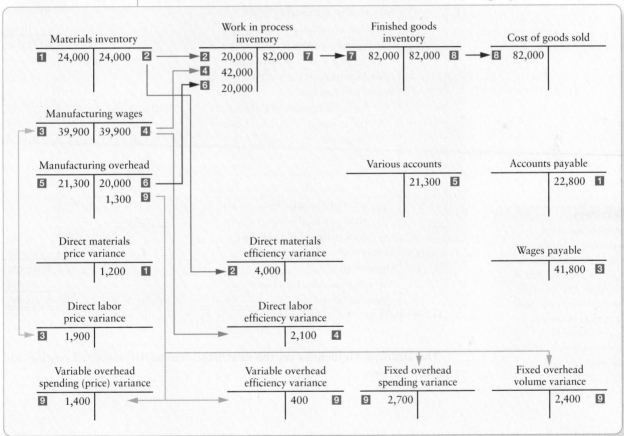

Standard Cost Income Statement for Management

Smart Touch's top management needs to know about the company's cost variances. Exhibit 23-14 shows a standard cost income statement that highlights the variances for management.

The statement starts with sales revenue at standard and adds the favorable sales revenue variance of $1,000 (Exhibit 23-4) to yield actual sales revenue. Next, the statement shows the cost of goods sold at standard cost. Then the statement separately lists each manufacturing cost variance, followed by cost of goods sold at actual cost. At the end of the period, all the variance accounts are closed to zero out their balances. Operating income is thus closed to Income summary.

The income statement shows that the net effect of all the manufacturing cost variances is $3,900 unfavorable. Therefore, June's operating income is $3,900 lower than it would have been if all the actual manufacturing costs had been equal to their standard costs.

EXHIBIT 23-14 | **Standard Cost Income Statement**

SMART TOUCH LEARNING, INC. Standard Cost Income Statement Month Ended June 30, 2014			
Sales revenue at standard (10,000 × $12)			$120,000
Sales revenue variance			1,000
Sales revenue at actual			$121,000
Cost of goods sold at standard cost		$82,000	
Manufacturing cost variances (parentheses denote a credit balance):			
Direct materials price variance	$(1,200)		
Direct materials efficiency variance	4,000		
Direct labor price variance	1,900		
Direct labor efficiency variance	(2,100)		
Variable overhead spending (price) variance	1,400		
Variable overhead efficiency variance	(400)		
Fixed overhead spending variance	2,700		
Fixed overhead volume variance	(2,400)		
Total manufacturing variance		3,900	
Cost of goods sold at actual cost			85,900
Gross profit			$ 35,100
Marketing and administrative expense*			19,100
Operating income			$ 16,000

*$12,400 + $6,700 from Exhibit 23-8, Panel A.

The Decision Guidelines on the next page summarize standard costing and variance analysis.

Decision Guidelines 23-2

STANDARD COSTS AND VARIANCE ANALYSIS

Now you have seen how managers use standard costs and variances to identify potential problems. Variances help managers see *why* actual costs differ from the budget. This is the first step in determining how to correct problems. Let's review how Smart Touch made some key decisions in setting up and using its standard cost system.

Decision	Guidelines
• How do companies set standards?	• Historical performance data • Engineering analysis/time-and-motion studies • Continuous improvement standards • Benchmarking
• How do companies compute a price variance for materials, labor, or variable overhead?	$$\text{Price variance} = \left(\begin{array}{c} \text{Actual price} \\ \text{per input unit} \end{array} - \begin{array}{c} \text{Standard price} \\ \text{per input unit} \end{array} \right) \times \begin{array}{c} \text{Actual quantity} \\ \text{of input} \end{array}$$
• How do companies compute an efficiency variance for materials, labor, or variable overhead?	$$\text{Efficiency variance} = \left(\begin{array}{c} \text{Actual} \\ \text{quantity} \\ \text{of input} \end{array} - \begin{array}{c} \text{Standard} \\ \text{quantity of input} \\ \text{for actual output} \end{array} \right) \times \begin{array}{c} \text{Standard price} \\ \text{per input unit} \end{array}$$

• Who is best able to explain a(n)
  • sales volume variance?
  • sales revenue variance?
  • direct material price variance?
  • direct material efficiency variance?
  • direct labor price variance?
  • direct labor efficiency variance?
  • overhead variance?
	
	The Marketing Department
	The Marketing Department
	The Purchasing Department
	The Production Department
	The Human Resources Department
	The Production Department
	The Production Department

• How do companies compute fixed overhead variances?	$$\begin{array}{c} \text{Fixed overhead} \\ \text{spending} \\ \text{variance} \end{array} = \begin{array}{c} \text{Actual} \\ \text{fixed} \\ \text{overhead} \end{array} - \begin{array}{c} \text{Budgeted} \\ \text{fixed} \\ \text{overhead} \end{array}$$ $$\begin{array}{c} \text{Fixed overhead} \\ \text{volume} \\ \text{variance} \end{array} = \begin{array}{c} \text{Budgeted} \\ \text{fixed} \\ \text{overhead} \end{array} - \begin{array}{c} \text{Standard overhead} \\ \text{applied based} \\ \text{on actual output} \end{array}$$
• How do companies record standard costs in the accounts?	• Materials inventory: Actual quantity at standard price • Work in process inventory (and Finished goods inventory and Cost of goods sold): Standard quantity of inputs allowed for actual outputs, at standard price of inputs
• How do companies analyze cost variances?	• Debit balance → more expense (E+) • Credit balance → less expense (CE+)

Summary Problem 23-2

Exhibit 23-8 indicates that Smart Touch sold 10,000 DVDs in June. Suppose Smart Touch had sold 7,000 DVDs instead of 10,000 and that *actual costs* were as follows:

Direct materials (vinyl)...............	7,400 square feet @ $2.00 per square foot
Direct labor.................................	2,740 hours @ $10.00 per hour
Variable overhead	$5,400
Fixed overhead...........................	$11,900

Requirements

1. Given these new data, prepare an exhibit similar to Exhibit 23-8. Ignore marketing and administrative expense.
2. Compute price and efficiency variances for direct materials, direct labor, and variable overhead. Compute the spending and volume variances for fixed overhead.

Solution

Requirement 1

PANEL A—Comparison of Actual Results with Flexible Budget for 7,000 DVDs

<table>
<tr><td colspan="4" align="center">SMART TOUCH LEARNING, INC.
Revised Data for Standard Costing Example
Month Ended June 30, 2014</td></tr>
<tr><td></td><td>Actual Results at Actual Prices</td><td>Flexible Budget for 7,000 DVDs</td><td>Flexible Budget Variance</td></tr>
<tr><td>Variable costs:</td><td></td><td></td><td></td></tr>
<tr><td>Direct materials</td><td>$14,800</td><td>$14,000</td><td>$ 800 U</td></tr>
<tr><td>Direct labor</td><td>27,400</td><td>29,400</td><td>2,000 F</td></tr>
<tr><td>Variable overhead</td><td>5,400</td><td>5,600</td><td>200 F</td></tr>
<tr><td>Total variable costs</td><td>47,600</td><td>49,000</td><td>1,400 F</td></tr>
<tr><td>Fixed costs:</td><td></td><td></td><td></td></tr>
<tr><td>Fixed overhead</td><td>11,900</td><td>9,600‡</td><td>2,300 U</td></tr>
<tr><td>Total costs</td><td>$59,500</td><td>$58,600</td><td>$ 900 U</td></tr>
</table>

‡Fixed overhead was budgeted at $9,600 per month.

PANEL B—Computation of Flexible Budget for Direct Materials, Direct Labor, and Variable Overhead for 7,000 DVDs—Based on Standard Costs

	(1) Standard Quantity of Inputs Allowed for 7,000 DVDs	(2) Standard Price per Unit of Input	(3) (1) × (2) Flexible Budget for 7,000 DVDs
Direct materials	1 square foot per DVD × 7,000 DVDs = 7,000 square feet	$ 2.00	$14,000
Direct labor	.40 hours per DVD × 7,000 DVDs = 2,800 hours	$10.50	29,400
Variable overhead	.40 hours per DVD × 7,000 DVDs = 2,800 hours	$ 2.00	5,600

PANEL C—Computation of Actual Costs for Direct Materials and Direct Labor for 7,000 DVDs

	(1) Actual Quantity of Inputs Used for 7,000 DVDs	(2) Actual Price per Unit of Input	(3) (1) × (2) Actual Cost for 7,000 DVDs
Direct materials	7,400 square feet actually used	$2.00 actual cost/square foot	$14,800
Direct labor	2,740 hours actually used	$10.00 actual cost/hour	27,400

Requirement 2

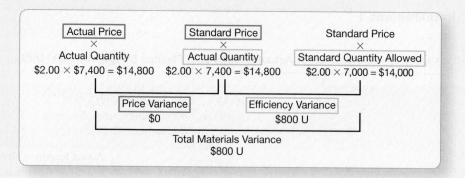

Actual Price
×
Actual Quantity
$2.00 × $7,400 = $14,800

Standard Price
×
Actual Quantity
$2.00 × 7,400 = $14,800

Standard Price
×
Standard Quantity Allowed
$2.00 × 7,000 = $14,000

Price Variance
$0

Efficiency Variance
$800 U

Total Materials Variance
$800 U

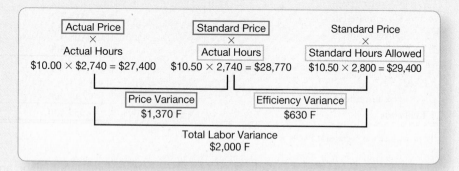

Actual Price
×
Actual Hours
$10.00 × $2,740 = $27,400

Standard Price
×
Actual Hours
$10.50 × 2,740 = $28,770

Standard Price
×
Standard Hours Allowed
$10.50 × 2,800 = $29,400

Price Variance
$1,370 F

Efficiency Variance
$630 F

Total Labor Variance
$2,000 F

Actual Price
×
Actual Hours
$5,400

Standard Price
×
Actual Hours
$2.00 × 2,740 = $5,480

Standard Price
×
Standard Hours Allowed
$2.00 × 2,800 = $5,600

Spending (Price) Variance
$80 F

Efficiency Variance
$120 F

Total Variable Overhead Variance
$200 F

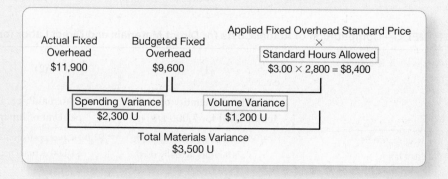

Actual Fixed
Overhead
$11,900

Budgeted Fixed
Overhead
$9,600

Applied Fixed Overhead Standard Price
×
Standard Hours Allowed
$3.00 × 2,800 = $8,400

Spending Variance
$2,300 U

Volume Variance
$1,200 U

Total Materials Variance
$3,500 U

Review *Flexible Budgets and Standard Costs*

● Accounting Vocabulary

Efficiency (Quantity) Variance (p. 1116)
Measures whether the quantity of materials or labor used to make the actual number of units produced is within the standard allowed for that number of units produced. Computed as the difference in quantities (actual quantity of input used minus standard quantity of input allowed for the actual number of units produced) multiplied by the standard price per unit of the input.

Fixed Overhead Spending Variance (p. 1123)
Measures the difference between actual fixed overhead and budgeted fixed overhead to determine the controllable portion of total fixed overhead variance.

Fixed Overhead Volume Variance (p. 1124)
Measures the difference between the budgeted fixed overhead and the amount of overhead that should have been applied to jobs based on the output.

Flexible Budget (p. 1107)
A summarized budget that managers can easily compute for several different volume levels; separates variable costs from fixed costs.

Flexible Budget Variance (p. 1108)
The difference arising because the company had more or less revenue, or more or less cost, than expected for the *actual* level of units sold.

Price (Rate) Variance (p. 1116)
Measures how well the business keeps unit prices of material and labor inputs within standards. Computed as the difference in prices (actual price per unit minus standard price per unit) of an input multiplied by the actual quantity of the input.

Sales Volume Variance (p. 1108)
The difference arising only because the actual number of units sold differed from the number of units on which the static budget was based. Equals the difference between a static budget amount and a flexible budget amount.

Standard Cost (p. 1113)
A budget for a single unit.

Static Budget (p. 1106)
The budget prepared for only one level of sales volume. Also called the *master budget*.

Variance (p. 1106)
The difference between an actual amount and the budgeted amount. Labeled as favorable if it increases operating income and unfavorable if it decreases operating income.

● Destination: Student Success

Student Success Tips

The following are hints on some common trouble areas for students in this chapter:

● Keep in mind that a static budget shows revenues and expenses at the expected output level for the period.

● Recall that a flexible budget shows revenues and expenses for multiple output levels.

● Remember that the income statement performance report compares actual results to flexible budget amounts to determine the flexible budget variance. The flexible budget is then compared to the static budget to determine the sales volume variance.

● Recall a price variance measures the difference in actual and standard price based on the actual amount used.

● Remember an efficiency variance measures the difference in the actual amount used and the standard amount based on the standard price.

● Keep in mind that overhead variances are measured separately for the variable and fixed portion of overhead.

● Remember that the journal entries in a standard cost system record WIP based on standard costs.

● Remember the differences in a standard costing income statement and the one you learned about in earlier chapters: 1) It shows all the variances individually on the statement. 2) Operating income is the same whether the company uses standard costing or not.

Getting Help

If there's a learning objective from the chapter you aren't confident about, try using one or more of the following resources:

● Review Decision Guidelines 23-1 and 23-2 in the chapter.

● Review Summary Problem 23-1 in the chapter to reinforce your understanding of flexible budgets and the income statement performance report.

● Review Summary Problem 23-2 in the chapter to reinforce your understanding of variances.

● Practice additional exercises or problems at the end of Chapter 23 that cover the specific learning objective that is challenging you.

● Watch the white board videos for Chapter 23, located at myaccountinglab.com under the Chapter Resources button.

● Go to myaccountinglab.com and select the Study Plan button. Choose Chapter 23 and work the questions covering that specific learning objective until you've mastered it.

● Work the Chapter 23 pre/post tests in myaccountinglab.com.

● Consult the Check Figures for End of Chapter starters, exercises, and problems, located at myaccountinglab.com.

● Visit the learning resource center on your campus for tutoring.

● Quick Check

Questions 1–4 rely on the following data. MajorNet Systems is a start-up company that makes connectors for high-speed Internet connections. The company has budgeted variable costs of $145 for each connector and fixed costs of $7,500 per month.

MajorNet's static budget predicted production and sales of 100 connectors in August, but the company actually produced and sold only 84 connectors at a total cost of $21,000.

1. MajorNet's total flexible budget cost for 84 connectors per month is
   - a. $14,500.
   - b. $12,180.
   - c. $19,680.
   - d. $21,000.

2. MajorNet's sales volume variance for total costs is
   - a. $1,320 U.
   - b. $1,320 F.
   - c. $2,320 U.
   - d. $2,320 F.

3. MajorNet's flexible budget variance for total costs is
   - a. $1,320 U.
   - b. $1,320 F.
   - c. $2,320 U.
   - d. $2,320 F.

4. MajorNet Systems' managers could set direct labor standards based on
   - a. time-and-motion studies.
   - b. continuous improvement.
   - c. benchmarking.
   - d. past actual performance.
   - e. Items a, b, c, and d are all correct.

Questions 5–7 rely on the following data. MajorNet Systems has budgeted three hours of direct labor per connector, at a standard cost of $17 per hour. During August, technicians actually worked 189 hours completing 84 connectors. All 84 connectors actually produced were sold. MajorNet paid the technicians $17.80 per hour.

5. What is MajorNet's direct labor price variance for August?
   - a. $67.20 U
   - b. $151.20 U
   - c. $201.60 U
   - d. $919.80 U

6. What is MajorNet's direct labor efficiency variance for August?
   - a. $919.80 F
   - b. $1,071.00 F
   - c. $1,121.40 F
   - d. $3,364.20 F

7. The journal entry to record MajorNet's *use* of direct labor in August is which of the following?

a.
Manufacturing wages		
Direct labor efficiency variance		
Work in process inventory		

b.
Work in process inventory		
Direct labor efficiency variance		
Manufacturing wages		

c.
Work in process inventory		
Direct labor efficiency variance		
Manufacturing wages		

d.
Manufacturing wages		
Direct labor efficiency variance		
Work in process inventory		

Questions 8–10 rely on the following data. FrontGrade Systems allocates manufacturing overhead based on machine hours. Each connector should require 11 machine hours. According to the static budget, FrontGrade expected to incur the following:

>1,100 machine hours per month (100 connectors × 11 machine hours per connector)
>$5,500 in variable manufacturing overhead costs
>$8,250 in fixed manufacturing overhead costs

During August, FrontGrade actually used 1,000 machine hours to make 110 connectors and spent $5,600 in variable manufacturing costs and $8,300 in fixed manufacturing overhead costs.

8. FrontGrade's predetermined standard *variable* manufacturing overhead rate is
   a. $5.00 per machine hour.
   b. $5.50 per machine hour.
   c. $7.50 per machine hour.
   d. $12.50 per machine hour.

9. Calculate the variable overhead spending variance for FrontGrade.
   a. $450 F
   b. $600 U
   c. $1,050 F
   d. $1,650 F

10. Calculate the variable overhead efficiency variance for FrontGrade.
    a. $450 F
    b. $600 U
    c. $1,050 F
    d. $1,650 F

Answers are given after Apply Your Knowledge (p. 1150).

Assess Your Progress

● Short Exercises

S23-1   ❶ Matching terms [10 min]

Consider the following terms:

a. Flexible Budget
b. Flexible Budget Variance
c. Sales Volume Variance
d. Static Budget
e. Variance

Consider the following definitions:

_____ 1. A summarized budget for several levels of volume that separates variable costs from fixed costs.

_____ 2. The budget prepared for only one level of sales volume.

_____ 3. The difference between an actual amount and the budget.

_____ 4. The difference arising because the company actually earned more or less revenue, or incurred more or less cost, than expected for the actual level of output.

_____ 5. The difference arising only because the number of units actually sold differs from the static budget units.

Requirement

1. Match each term to the correct definition.

S23-2 ● **Matching terms [10 min]**
Consider the following terms:

a. Benchmarking
b. Efficiency Variance
c. Fixed Overhead Spending Variance
d. Price Variance
e. Fixed Overhead Volume Variance
f. Standard Cost

Consider the following definitions:

_____ **1.** Measures whether the quantity of materials or labor used to make the actual number of outputs is within the standard allowed for that number of outputs.

_____ **2.** Using standards based on "best practice."

_____ **3.** Measures how well the business keeps unit prices of material and labor inputs within standards.

_____ **4.** A budget for a single unit.

_____ **5.** Compares actual overhead spent to budgeted overhead costs.

_____ **6.** Arises when budgeted overhead differs from applied overhead.

Requirement

1. Match each term to the correct definition.

S23-3 ● **Flexible budget preparation [10 min]**
Moje, Inc., manufactures travel locks. The budgeted selling price is $19 per lock, the variable cost is $8 per lock, and budgeted fixed costs are $15,000.

Requirement

1. Prepare a flexible budget for output levels of 4,000 locks and 7,000 locks for the month ended April 30, 2012.

S23-4 ● **Flexible budget variance [10–15 min]**
Consider the following partially completed income statement performance report for Gaje, Inc.

GAJE, INC. Income Statement Performance Report (partial) Month Ended April 30, 2012					
	Actual Results at Actual Prices		Flexible Budget Variance	Flexible Budget for Actual Number of Units Sold	
Output units		6,000			6,000
Sales revenue	$	90,000		$	78,000
Variable expenses		52,200			49,500
Contribution margin	$	37,800		$	28,500
Fixed expenses		16,200			15,300
Operating income	$	21,600		$	13,200

Requirement

1. Complete the flexible budget variance analysis by filling in the blanks in the partial income statement performance report for 6,000 travel locks.

S23-5 ❸ **Identifying the benefits of standard costs [5 min]**
Setting standards for a product may involve many employees of the company.

Requirement

1. Identify some of the employees who may be involved in setting the standard costs and describe what their role might be in setting those standards.

S23-6 ❹ **Calculate materials variances [10–15 min]**
Johnson, Inc., is a manufacturer of lead crystal glasses. The standard materials quantity is 0.8 pound per glass at a price of $0.30 per pound. The actual results for the production of 6,900 glasses was 1.1 pounds per glass, at a price of $0.40 per pound.

Requirement

1. Calculate the materials price variance and the materials efficiency variance.

S23-7 ❹ **Calculate labor variances [10–15 min]**
Johnson, Inc., manufactures lead crystal glasses. The standard direct labor time is 0.3 hour per glass, at a price of $13 per hour. The actual results for the production of 6,900 glasses were 0.2 hour per glass, at a price of $10 per hour.

Requirement

1. Calculate the labor price variance and the labor efficiency variance.

Note: Short Exercises 23-6 and 23-7 should be completed before attempting Short Exercise 23-8.

S23-8 ❹ **Interpreting material and labor variances [5–10 min]**
Refer to your results from S23-6 and S23-7.

Requirements

1. For each variance, who in Johnson's organization is most likely responsible?
2. Interpret the direct materials and direct labor variances for Johnson's management.

Note: Short Exercises 23-6 and 23-7 should be completed before attempting Short Exercise 23-9.

S23-9 ❺ **Standard overhead rates [5 min]**
Refer to the data from Johnson, Inc., in S23-6 and S23-7. The following information relates to the company's overhead costs:

Static budget variable overhead	$ 9,000
Static budget fixed overhead	$ 4,500
Static budget direct labor hours	1,800 hours
Static budget number of glasses	6,000

Johnson allocates manufacturing overhead to production based on standard direct labor hours. Last month, Johnson reported the following actual results: actual variable overhead, $10,200; actual fixed overhead, $2,830.

Requirement

1. Compute the standard variable overhead rate and the standard fixed overhead rate.

Note: Short Exercises 23-6, 23-7, and 23-9 should be completed before attempting Short Exercise 23-10.

S23-10 ❺ **Computing overhead variances [10–20 min]**
Refer to the Johnson data in S23-6, S23-7, and S23-9.

Requirements

1. Compute the variable and fixed overhead variances. Use Exhibits 23-11 and 23-12 as guides.
2. Explain why the variances are favorable or unfavorable.

Note: Short Exercises 23-6, 23-7, and 23-10 should be completed before attempting Short Exercise 23-11.

S23-11 ⑥ **Journalizing variances [15–25 min]**
Refer to your results from S23-6, S23-7, and S23-10.

Requirement

1. Prepare the nine journal entries to record direct materials, labor, variable and fixed overhead, and the variances. Record the transfer to finished goods and COGS, assuming all production is sold. Last, record the entry to close the Manufacturing overhead account.

S23-12 ⑥ **Materials journal entries [5–10 min]**
The following materials variance analysis was performed for Brookman.

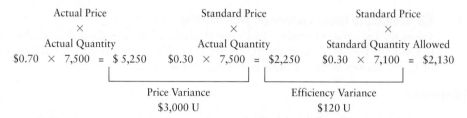

Actual Price	Standard Price	Standard Price
×	×	×
Actual Quantity	Actual Quantity	Standard Quantity Allowed
$0.70 × 7,500 = $ 5,250	$0.30 × 7,500 = $2,250	$0.30 × 7,100 = $2,130

Price Variance	Efficiency Variance
$3,000 U	$120 U

Requirements

1. Record Brookman's direct materials journal entries.
2. Explain what management will do with this variance information.

S23-13 ⑥ **Labor journal entries [5–10 min]**
The following labor variance analysis was performed for Longman.

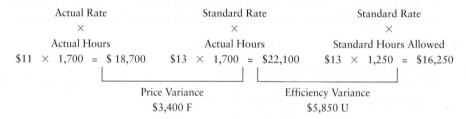

Actual Rate	Standard Rate	Standard Rate
×	×	×
Actual Hours	Actual Hours	Standard Hours Allowed
$11 × 1,700 = $ 18,700	$13 × 1,700 = $22,100	$13 × 1,250 = $16,250

Price Variance	Efficiency Variance
$3,400 F	$5,850 U

Requirements

1. Record Longman's direct labor journal entries.
2. Explain what management will do with this variance information.

S23-14 ⑥ **Standard cost income statement [10–15 min]**
Consider the following information:

Cost of goods sold	$367,000	Direct labor efficiency variance	$18,000 F
Sales revenue	$550,000	Variable overhead efficiency variance	$ 3,400 U
Direct materials price variance	$ 8,000 U	Fixed overhead volume variance	$12,000 F
Direct materials efficiency variance	$ 2,800 U	Marketing and administrative costs	$77,000
Direct labor price variance	$ 42,000 U	Variable overhead spending variance	$ 700 F
Fixed overhead spending variance	$ 1,900 F		

Requirement

1. Use the above information to prepare a standard cost income statement for Whitmer, using Exhibit 23-14 as a guide. Remember that unfavorable variances increase cost of goods sold.

● Exercises

E23-15 **❶** **Preparing a flexible budget [10–15 min]**

OfficePlus sells its main product, ergonomic mouse pads, for $12 each. Its variable cost is $5.20 per pad. Fixed costs are $205,000 per month for volumes up to 65,000 pads. Above 65,000 pads, monthly fixed costs are $280,000.

Requirement

1. Prepare a monthly flexible budget for the product, showing sales revenue, variable costs, fixed costs, and operating income for volume levels of 45,000, 55,000, and 75,000 pads.

E23-16 **❷** **Preparing an income statement performance report [15–20 min]**

Stenback Pro Company managers received the following incomplete performance report:

	Actual Results at Actual Prices	Flexible Budget Variance	Flexible Budget for Actual Number of Units Sold	Sales Volume Variance	Static (Master) Budget
Output units	39,000	——	39,000	3,000 F	——
Sales revenue	$ 218,000	——	$ 218,000	$ 27,000 F	——
Variable expenses	84,000	——	81,000	10,000 U	——
Contribution margin	$ 134,000	——	$ 137,000	$ 17,000 F	——
Fixed expenses	108,000	——	101,000	0	——
Operating income	$ 26,000	——	$ 36,000	$ 17,000 F	——

STENBACK PRO COMPANY
Income Statement Performance Report
Year Ended July 31, 2012

Requirement

1. Complete the performance report. Identify the employee group that may deserve praise and the group that may be subject to criticism. Give your reasoning.

E23-17 **❷** **Preparing an income statement performance report [20–25 min]**

Top managers of Kyler Industries predicted 2012 sales of 14,800 units of its product at a unit price of $8.50. Actual sales for the year were 14,600 units at $10.50 each. Variable costs were budgeted at $2.20 per unit, and actual variable costs were $2.30 per unit. Actual fixed costs of $41,000 exceeded budgeted fixed costs by $4,500.

Requirement

1. Prepare Kyler's income statement performance report. What variance contributed most to the year's favorable results? What caused this variance?

E23-18 **❸** **❹** **Defining the benefits of setting cost standards, and calculating materials and labor variances [10–15 min]**

Premium, Inc., produced 1,000 units of the company's product in 2012. The standard quantity of materials was three yards of cloth per unit at a standard price of $1.05 per yard. The accounting records showed that 2,600 yards of cloth were used and the company paid $1.10 per yard. Standard time was two direct labor hours per unit at a standard rate of $9.75 per direct labor hour. Employees worked 1,400 hours and were paid $9.25 per hour.

Requirements

1. What are the benefits of setting cost standards?
2. Calculate the materials price variance and the materials efficiency variance, as well as the labor price and efficiency variances.

E23-19 ④ **Calculating materials and labor variances [20–30 min]**

Great Fender, which uses a standard cost accounting system, manufactured 20,000 boat fenders during the year, using 144,000 feet of extruded vinyl purchased at $1.05 per square foot. Production required 420 direct labor hours that cost $13.50 per hour. The materials standard was seven feet of vinyl per fender, at a standard cost of $1.10 per square foot. The labor standard was 0.025 direct labor hour per fender, at a standard price of $12.50 per hour.

Requirement

1. Compute the price and efficiency variances for direct materials and direct labor. Does the pattern of variances suggest Great Fender's managers have been making trade-offs? Explain.

Note: Exercise 23-19 should be completed before attempting Exercise 23-20.

E23-20 ⑤ **Computing overhead variances [20–30 min]**

Review the data from Great Fender given in E23-19. Consider the following additional information:

Static budget variable overhead	$ 5,500
Static budget fixed overhead	$22,000
Static budget direct labor hours	550 hours
Static budget number of units	22,000

Great Fender allocates manufacturing overhead to production based on standard direct labor hours. Great Fender reported the following actual results for 2012: actual variable overhead, $4,950; actual fixed overhead, $23,000.

Requirements

1. Compute the variable and fixed overhead variances. Use Exhibits 23-11 and 23-12 as guides.
2. Explain why the variances are favorable or unfavorable.

Note: Exercise 23-18 should be completed before attempting Exercise 23-21.

E23-21 ⑤ **Calculating overhead variances [10–15 min]**

Review the data from Premium, Inc., given in Exercise 23-18. Consider the following additional information:

Static budget variable overhead	$1,600
Static budget fixed overhead	$3,200
Static budget direct labor hours	1,600 hours
Static budget number of units	800

Premium allocates manufacturing overhead to production based on standard direct labor hours. Premium reported the following actual results for 2012: actual variable overhead, $1,900; actual fixed overhead, $3,300.

Requirements

1. Compute the variable and fixed overhead variances. Use Exhibits 23-11 and 23-12 as guides.
2. Explain why the variances are favorable or unfavorable.

E23-22 ⑥ **Preparing a standard cost income statement [15 min]**

The May 2012 revenue and cost information for Houston Outfitters, Inc., follows:

Sales revenue	$ 540,000	
Cost of goods sold (standard)	341,000	
Direct materials price variance	1,100	F
Direct materials efficiency variance	6,100	F
Direct labor price variance	4,200	U
Direct labor efficiency variance	2,400	F
Variable overhead spending variance	3,300	U
Fixed overhead volume variance	8,100	F
Fixed overhead spending variance	1,400	U
Variable overhead efficiency variance	1,400	U

Requirement

1. Prepare a standard cost income statement for management through gross profit. Report all standard cost variances for management's use. Has management done a good or poor job of controlling costs? Explain.

Note: Exercises 23-18 and 23-21 should be completed before attempting Exercise 23-23.

E23-23 ⑥ **Preparing journal entries [20–30 min]**

Review the results from E23-18 and E23-21.

Requirement

1. Record the journal entries to record materials, labor, variable overhead, and fixed overhead. Record the journal entries to record the movement to finished goods and sale of all production for the year. Close out the manufacturing overhead account.

Note: Exercise 23-19 and 23-20 should be completed before attempting Exercise 23-24.

E23-24 ⑥ **Preparing journal entries [20–30 min]**

Review the results from E23-19 and E23-20.

Requirement

1. Record the journal entries to record materials, labor, variable overhead, and fixed overhead. Record the journal entries to record the movement to finished goods and sale of all production for the year. Close out the manufacturing overhead account.

Note: Exercises 23-19, 23-20, and 23-24 should be completed before attempting Exercise 23-25.

E23-25 ⑥ **Preparing a standard cost income statement [15–20 min]**

Review your results from E23-19, E23-20, and E23-24. Assume each fender sold for $60 and total marketing and administrative costs were $400,000.

Requirement

1. Prepare a standard cost income statement for 2012 for Great Fender.

Problems (Group A)

P23-26A ❶ ❸ ❹ ❺ **Preparing a flexible budget and computing standard cost variances [60–75 min]**

Preston Recliners manufactures leather recliners and uses flexible budgeting and a standard cost system. Preston allocates overhead based on yards of direct materials. The company's performance report includes the following selected data:

	Static Budget (1,000 recliners)	Actual Results (980 recliners)
Sales (1,000 recliners × $ 495)	$ 495,000	
(980 recliners × $ 475)		$ 465,500
Variable manufacturing costs:		
Direct materials (6,000 yds @ $8.80/yard)	52,800	
(6,150 yds @ $8.60/yard)		52,890
Direct labor (10,000 hrs @ $9.20/hour)	92,000	
(9,600 hrs @ $9.30/hour)		89,280
Variable overhead (6,000 yds @ $5.00/yard)	30,000	
(6,150 yds @ $6.40/yard)		39,360
Fixed manufacturing costs:		
Fixed overhead	60,000	62,000
Total cost of goods sold	$ 234,800	$ 243,530
Gross profit	$ 260,200	$ 221,970

Requirements

1. Prepare a flexible budget based on the actual number of recliners sold.
2. Compute the price variance and the efficiency variance for direct materials and for direct labor. For manufacturing overhead, compute the variable overhead spending, variable overhead efficiency, fixed overhead spending, and fixed overhead volume variances.
3. Have Preston's managers done a good job or a poor job controlling materials, labor, and overhead costs? Why?
4. Describe how Preston's managers can benefit from the standard costing system.

P23-27A ❷ **Preparing an income statement performance report [30 min]**

AllTalk Technologies manufactures capacitors for cellular base stations and other communications applications. The company's January 2012 flexible budget income statement shows output levels of 6,500, 8,000, and 10,000 units. The static budget was based on expected sales of 8,000 units.

		ALLTALK TECHNOLOGIES		
		Flexible Budget Income Statement		
		Month Ended January 31, 2012		
	Per Unit	By Units (Capacitors)		
		6,500	8,000	10,000
Sales revenue	$24	$ 156,000	$ 192,000	$ 240,000
Variable expenses	$10	65,000	80,000	100,000
Contribution margin		$ 91,000	$ 112,000	$ 140,000
Fixed expenses		53,000	53,000	53,000
Operating income		$ 38,000	$ 59,000	$ 87,000

The company sold 10,000 units during January, and its actual operating income was as follows:

ALLTALK TECHNOLOGIES	
Income Statement	
Month Ended January 31, 2012	
Sales revenue	$ 246,000
Variable expenses	104,500
Contribution margin	$ 141,500
Fixed expenses	54,000
Operating income	$ 87,500

Requirements

1. Prepare an income statement performance report for January.
2. What was the effect on AllTalk's operating income of selling 2,000 units more than the static budget level of sales?
3. What is AllTalk's static budget variance? Explain why the income statement performance report provides more useful information to AllTalk's managers than the simple static budget variance. What insights can AllTalk's managers draw from this performance report?

P23-28A ④ ⑤ ⑥ **Computing and journalizing standard cost variances [45 min]**
Java manufactures coffee mugs that it sells to other companies for customizing with their own logos. Java prepares flexible budgets and uses a standard cost system to control manufacturing costs. The standard unit cost of a coffee mug is based on static budget volume of 60,200 coffee mugs per month:

Direct materials (0.2 lbs @ $0.25 per lb)		$ 0.05
Direct labor (3 minutes @ $0.12 per minute)		0.36
Manufacturing overhead:		
Variable (3 minutes @ $0.05 per minute)	$ 0.15	
Fixed (3 minutes @ $0.14 per minute)	0.42	0.57
Total cost per coffee mug		$ 0.98

Actual cost and production information for July 2012 follow:

a. Actual production and sales were 62,900 coffee mugs.
b. Actual direct materials usage was 10,000 lbs., at an actual price of $0.17 per lb.
c. Actual direct labor usage was 202,000 minutes at a total cost of $30,300.
d. Actual overhead cost was $10,000 variable and $30,500 fixed.
e. Marketing and administrative costs were $115,000.

Requirements

1. Compute the price and efficiency variances for direct materials and direct labor.
2. Journalize the usage of direct materials and the assignment of direct labor, including the related variances.
3. For manufacturing overhead, compute the variable overhead spending and efficiency variances and the fixed overhead spending and volume variances.
4. Journalize the actual manufacturing overhead and the applied manufacturing overhead. Journalize the movement of all production from WIP. Journalize the closing of the manufacturing overhead account.
5. Java intentionally hired more-skilled workers during July. How did this decision affect the cost variances? Overall, was the decision wise?

Note: Problem 23-28A should be completed before attempting Problem 23-29A.

P23-29A ⑥ Prepare a standard costing income statement [20 min]

Review your results from P23-28A. Java's sales price per mug is $3.

Requirement

1. Prepare the standard costing income statement for July 2012.

P23-30A ④⑤⑥ Computing standard cost variances and reporting to management [45–60 min]

HearSmart manufactures headphone cases. During September 2012, the company produced and sold 107,000 cases and recorded the following cost data:

Standard Cost Information:

	Quantity	Price
Direct materials	2 parts	$ 0.16 per part
Direct labor	0.02 hours	$ 8.00 per hour
Variable manufacturing overhead	0.02 hours	$ 9.00 per hour
Fixed manufacturing overhead ($32,980 for static budget volume of 97,000 units and 1,940 hours, or $17 per hour)		

Actual Information:

Direct materials (210,000 parts @ $0.21 per part = $44,100)
Direct labor (1,640 hours @ $8.15 per hour = $13,366)
Variable manufacturing overhead $8,000
Fixed manufacturing overhead $30,000

Requirements

1. Compute the price and efficiency variances for direct materials and direct labor.
2. For manufacturing overhead, compute the variable overhead spending and efficiency variances and the fixed overhead spending and volume variances.
3. HearSmart's management used better quality materials during September. Discuss the trade-off between the two direct material variances.

• Problems (Group B)

P23-31B ①③④⑤ **Preparing a flexible budget and computing standard cost variances [60–75 min]** MyAccountingLab

Relaxing Recliners manufactures leather recliners and uses flexible budgeting and a standard cost system. Relaxing allocates overhead based on yards of direct materials. The company's performance report includes the following selected data:

	Static Budget (975 recliners)	Actual Results (955 recliners)
Sales (975 recliners × $505)	$ 492,375	
(955 recliners × $485)		$ 463,175
Variable manufacturing costs:		
Direct materials (5,850 yds @ $8.90/yard)	52,065	
(6,000 yds @ $8.70/yard)		52,200
Direct labor (9,750 hrs @ $9.00/hour)	87,750	
(9,350 hrs @ $9.10/hour)		85,085
Variable overhead (5,850 yds @ $5.30/yard)	31,005	
(6,000 yds @ $6.70/yard)		40,200
Fixed manufacturing costs:		
Fixed overhead	60,255	62,255
Total cost of goods sold	$ 231,075	$ 239,740
Gross profit	$ 261,300	$ 223,435

Requirements

1. Prepare a flexible budget based on the actual number of recliners sold.
2. Compute the price variance and the efficiency variance for direct materials and for direct labor. For manufacturing overhead, compute the variable overhead spending, variable overhead efficiency, fixed overhead spending, and fixed overhead volume variances.
3. Have Relaxing's managers done a good job or a poor job controlling materials, labor, and overhead costs? Why?
4. Describe how Relaxing's managers can benefit from the standard costing system.

P23-32B ② **Preparing an income statement performance report [30 min]**

Network Technologies manufactures capacitors for cellular base stations and other communication applications. The company's July 2012 flexible budget income statement shows output levels of 7,000, 8,500, and 10,500 units. The static budget was based on expected sales of 8,500 units.

NETWORK TECHNOLOGIES Flexible Budget Income Statement Month Ended July 31, 2012				
	Per Unit	By Units (Capacitors)		
		7,000	8,500	10,500
Sales revenue	$25	$ 175,000	$ 212,500	$ 262,500
Variable expenses	$13	91,000	110,500	136,500
Contribution margin		$ 84,000	$ 102,000	$ 126,000
Fixed expenses		56,000	56,000	56,000
Operating income		$ 28,000	$ 46,000	$ 70,000

The company sold 10,500 units during July, and its actual operating income was as follows:

NETWORK TECHNOLOGIES

Income Statement

Month Ended July 31, 2012

Sales revenue	$ 269,500
Variable expenses	141,500
Contribution margin	$ 128,000
Fixed expenses	57,000
Operating income	$ 71,000

Requirements

1. Prepare an income statement performance report for July 2012.
2. What was the effect on Network's operating income of selling 2,000 units more than the static budget level of sales?
3. What is Network's static budget variance? Explain why the income statement performance report provides more useful information to Network's managers than the simple static budget variance. What insights can Network's managers draw from this performance report?

P23-33B ④⑤⑥ **Computing and journalizing standard cost variances [45 min]**

McKnight manufactures coffee mugs that it sells to other companies for customizing with their own logos. McKnight prepares flexible budgets and uses a standard cost system to control manufacturing costs. The standard unit cost of a coffee mug is based on static budget volume of 59,800 coffee mugs per month:

Direct materials (0.2 lbs @ $0.25 per lb)		$ 0.05
Direct labor (3 minutes @ $0.11 per minute)		0.33
Manufacturing overhead:		
Variable (3 minutes @ $0.06 per minute)	$ 0.18	
Fixed (3 minutes @ $0.15 per minute)	0.45	0.63
Total cost per coffee mug		$ 1.01

Actual cost and production information for July 2012 follow:

a. Actual production and sales were 62,500 coffee mugs.
b. Actual direct materials usage was 10,000 lbs., at an actual price of $0.17 per lb.
c. Actual direct labor usage of 198,000 minutes at a total cost of $25,740.
d. Actual overhead cost was $8,500 variable and $32,100 fixed.
e. Marketing and administrative costs were $110,000.

Requirements

1. Compute the price and efficiency variances for direct materials and direct labor.
2. Journalize the usage of direct materials and the assignment of direct labor, including the related variances.
3. For manufacturing overhead, compute the variable overhead spending and efficiency variances and the fixed overhead spending and volume variances.
4. Journalize the actual manufacturing overhead and the applied manufacturing overhead. Journalize the movement of all production from WIP. Journalize the closing of the manufacturing overhead account.
5. McKnight intentionally hired more-skilled workers during July. How did this decision affect the cost variances? Overall, was the decision wise?

Note: Problem 23-33B should be completed before attempting Problem 23-34B.

P23-34B ❻ **Prepare a standard costing income statement [20 min]**

Review your results from P23-33B. McKnight's sales price per mug is $5.

Requirement

1. Prepare the standard costing income statement for July 2012.

P23-35B ❹❺❻ **Computing standard cost variances and reporting to management [45–60 min]**

SoundSmart manufactures headphone cases. During September 2012, the company produced 108,000 cases and recorded the following cost data:

Standard Cost Information:

	Quantity	Price
Direct materials	2 parts	$ 0.16 per part
Direct labor	0.02 hours	$ 7.00 per hour
Variable manufacturing overhead	0.02 hours	$11.00 per hour
Fixed manufacturing overhead ($29,400 for static budget volume of 98,000 units and 1,960 hours, or $15 per hour)		

Actual Information:

Direct materials (193,000 parts @ $0.21 per part = $40,530)
Direct labor (1,760 hours @ $7.15 per hour = $12,584)
Variable manufacturing overhead $12,000
Fixed manufacturing overhead, $30,000

Requirements

1. Compute the price and efficiency variances for direct materials and direct labor.
2. For manufacturing overhead, compute the variable overhead spending and efficiency variances and the fixed overhead spending and volume variances.
3. SoundSmart's management used better quality materials during September. Discuss the trade-off between the two direct material variances.

● Continuing Exercise

E23-36 ❹❻ **Calculating labor variances and journalizing labor transactions [15 min]** *MyAccountingLab*

This exercise continues the Lawlor Lawn Service, Inc., situation from Exercise 22-38 of Chapter 22. Lawlor's budgeted static production volume for the month was 440 lawns. The standard direct labor cost was $15.00 per hour and two hours standard per lawn.

Lawlor actually mowed 500 lawns in June. Actual labor costs were $20.00 per hour, and 900 hours were worked during June.

Requirements

1. Compute the direct labor price and efficiency variances.
2. Journalize the transactions to record the incurrence and usage of direct labor in June for Lawlor.
3. Analyze the labor variances for Lawlor.

Continuing Problem

P23-37 ④ ⑥ **Calculating materials and labor variances and preparing journal entries [20–25 min]**

This problem continues the Draper Consulting, Inc., situation from Problem 22-39 of Chapter 22. Assume Draper has created a standard cost card for each job. Standard direct materials include 14 software packages at a cost of $900 per package. Standard direct labor costs per job include 90 hours at $120 per hour. Draper plans on completing 12 jobs during October.

Actual direct materials costs for October included 90 software packages at a total cost of $81,450. Actual direct labor costs included 100 hours per job at an average rate of $125 per hour. Draper completed all 12 jobs in October.

Requirements

1. Calculate direct materials price and efficiency variances.
2. Calculate direct labor price and efficiency variances.
3. Prepare journal entries to record the use of both materials and labor for October for the company.

Apply Your Knowledge

Decision Cases

Decision Case 23-1 Movies Galore distributes DVDs to movie retailers, including dot.coms. Movies Galore's top management meets monthly to evaluate the company's performance. Controller Allen Walsh prepared the following performance report for the meeting:

MOVIES GALORE Income Statement Performance Report Month Ended July 31, 2010	Actual Results	Static Budget	Variance
Sales revenue	$1,640,000	$1,960,000	$320,000 U
Variable costs:			
Cost of goods sold	775,000	980,000	205,000 F
Sales commisions	77,000	107,800	30,800 F
Shipping cost	43,000	53,900	10,900 F
Total variable costs	$ 895,000	$1,141,700	$246,700 F
Contribution margin	745,000	818,300	73,300 U
Fixed costs:			
Salary cost	311,000	300,500	10,500 U
Depreciation cost	209,000	214,000	5,000 F
Rent cost	129,000	108,250	20,750 U
Advertising cost	81,000	68,500	12,500 U
Total fixed costs	$ 730,000	$ 691,250	$ 38,750 U
Operating income	$ 15,000	$ 127,050	$112,050 U

Walsh also revealed that the actual sale price of $20 per movie was equal to the budgeted sale price and that there were no changes in inventories for the month.

Management is disappointed by the operating income results. CEO Jilinda Robinson exclaims, "How can actual operating income be roughly 12% of the static budget amount when there are so many favorable variances?"

Requirements

1. Prepare a more informative performance report. Be sure to include a flexible budget for the actual number of DVDs bought and sold.

2. As a member of Movies Galore's management team, which variances would you want investigated? Why?

3. Robinson believes that many consumers are postponing purchases of new movies until after the introduction of a new format for recordable DVD players. In light of this information, how would you rate the company's performance?

Decision Case 23-2 Suppose you manage the local Scoopy's ice cream parlor. In addition to selling ice-cream cones, you make large batches of a few flavors of milk shakes to sell throughout the day. Your parlor is chosen to test the company's "Made-for-You" system. This new system enables patrons to customize their milk shakes by choosing different flavors.

Customers like the new system and your staff appears to be adapting, but you wonder whether this new made-to-order system is as efficient as the old system in which you just made a few large batches. Efficiency is a special concern because your performance is evaluated in part on the restaurant's efficient use of materials and labor. Your superiors consider efficiency variances greater than 5% to be unacceptable.

You decide to look at your sales for a typical day. You find that the parlor used 390 pounds of ice cream and 72 hours of direct labor to produce and sell 2,000 shakes. The standard quantity allowed for a shake is 0.2 pound of ice cream and 0.03 hour of direct labor. The standard prices are $1.50 per pound for ice cream and $8 an hour for labor.

Requirements

1. Compute the efficiency variances for direct labor and direct materials.

2. Provide likely explanations for the variances. Do you have reason to be concerned about your performance evaluation? Explain.

3. Write a memo to Scoopy's national office explaining your concern and suggesting a remedy.

● Ethical Issues

Rita Lane is the accountant for Outdoor Living, a manufacturer of outdoor furniture that is sold through specialty stores and Internet companies. Lane is responsible for reviewing the standard costs. While reviewing the standards for the coming year, two ethical issues arise.

Ethical Issue 23-1 Lane has been approached by Casey Henderson, a former colleague who worked with Lane when they were both employed by a public accounting firm. Henderson has recently started his own firm, Henderson Benchmarking Associates, which collects and sells data on industry benchmarks. He offers to provide Lane with benchmarks for the outdoor furniture industry free of charge if she will provide him with the last three years of Outdoor Living's standard and actual costs. Henderson explains that this is how he obtains most of his firm's benchmarking data. Lane always has a difficult time with the standard-setting process and believes that the benchmark data would be very useful.

Ethical Issue 23-2 Outdoor Living's management is starting a continuous improvement policy that requires a 10% reduction in standard costs each year for the next three years. Dan Jacobs, manufacturing foreman of the Teak furniture line, asks Lane to set loose standard costs this year before the continuous improvement policy is implemented. Jacobs argues that there is no other way to meet the tightening standards while maintaining the high quality of the Teak line.

Requirements

1. Use the IMA's ethical guidelines (https://www.imanet.org/PDFs/Statement%20of%20 Ethics_web.pdf) to identify the ethical dilemma in each situation.

2. Identify the relevant factors in each situation and suggest what Lane should recommend to the controller.

● Fraud Case 23-1

Aja could tell that this "patron" was not her store's usual type. She could see he did not care about fashion, and the customers that came to her shop in the Jacksonville mall were all tuned in to the latest styles. He came up to the register and took two pairs of jeans and an expensive sweater out of a bag to return. He didn't have a receipt. Aja looked at the garments. They weren't even close to his size. She had not seen him before, but she knew there were shoplifters who had been stealing from her company's stores throughout the state. They grabbed clothing from one location and returned it to another. He knew—and she knew—that her store had a loose return policy. Receipts were not required and cash was given. She knew it would be pointless to call security; there was no proof. She remained courteous and professional. Although his returns would not impact her own performance stats, she couldn't help feeling angry. A month later when the company changed its policy, Aja was relieved.

Requirements

1. What factors does a company consider when it decides on a policy for returns?
2. How is theft of this type handled in the accounting system?

● Team Project 23-1

Lynx, Corp., manufactures windows and doors. Lynx has been using a standard cost system that bases price and quantity standards on Lynx's historical long-run average performance. Suppose Lynx's controller has engaged your team of management consultants to advise him or her whether Lynx should use some basis other than historical performance for setting standards.

Requirements

1. List the types of variances you recommend that Lynx compute (for example, direct materials price variance for glass). For each variance, what specific standards would Lynx need to develop? In addition to cost standards, do you recommend that Lynx develop any nonfinancial standards?
2. There are many approaches to setting standards other than simply using long-run average historical prices and quantities.
   a. List three alternative approaches that Lynx could use to set standards, and explain how Lynx could implement each alternative.
   b. Evaluate each alternative method of setting standards, including the pros and cons of each method.
   c. Write a memo to Lynx's controller detailing your recommendations. First, should Lynx retain its historical data-based standard cost approach? If not, which of the alternative approaches should it adopt?

● Communication Activity 23-1

In 75 words or fewer, explain what a price variance is and describe its potential causes.

Quick Check Answers

1. *c* 2. *d* 3. *a* 4. *e* 5. *b* 6. *b* 7. *b* 8. *a* 9. *b* 10. *c*

For online homework, exercises, and problems that provide you immediate feedback, please visit myaccountinglab.com.

24 Performance Evaluation and the Balanced Scorecard

Learning Objectives

1. Explain why and how companies decentralize

2. Explain why companies use performance evaluation systems

3. Describe the balanced scorecard and identify key performance indicators for each perspective

4. Use performance reports to evaluate cost, revenue, and profit centers

5. Use ROI, RI, and EVA to evaluate investment centers

Our lives need balance. Even while we are students and our main focus is on our studies, we still need balance. Working accounting problems keeps our minds sharp, but we also need to take care of our physical well-being by eating properly, exercising, and getting enough sleep. And we need to take care of our emotional well-being by cultivating friendships and taking time to relax. An intellectual goal may be to earn an A in accounting, a physical goal may be to work out at the gym three times a week, and an emotional goal may be to take Friday nights off to spend time with friends. It is the combination of goals that keeps our lives in balance.

Many experts recommend writing down goals and posting them where we can see them every day, such as on a bulletin board. Keeping our goals in sight helps us remember and work toward achieving them.

Businesses also have goals they must communicate to their employees. Goals motivate employees to make decisions that are in the best interest of the company. Businesses often use a system—such as the *balanced scorecard*—for communicating the company's strategy to employees and for measuring how well they are achieving the goals. Communicating goals becomes more challenging as companies grow and decentralize decision making.

In this chapter, you'll learn about key performance indicators and the balanced scorecard. Later in the chapter we'll revisit Smart Touch Learning, but first we'll look at the advantages and disadvantages of decentralization.

Decentralized Operations

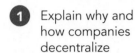

In a small company, the owner or top manager often makes all planning and operating decisions. Small companies are most often considered to be **centralized companies** because centralizing decision making is easier due to the smaller scope of their operations. However, when a company grows, it is impossible for a single person to manage the entire organization's daily operations. Therefore, most companies decentralize as they grow. These are called **decentralized companies**.

Companies decentralize by splitting their operations into different divisions or operating units. Top management delegates decision-making responsibility to the unit managers. Top management determines the type of decentralization that best suits the company's strategy. For example, decentralization may be based on geographic area, product line, customer base, business function, or some other business characteristic. **Citizen's Bank** segments its operations by state (different geographic areas). **Sherwin-Williams** segments by customer base (commercial and consumer paint divisions). **PepsiCo** segments by brands (**Pepsi, Frito-Lay, Quaker, Gatorade,** and **Tropicana**). UPS segments first by function (domestic packaging, international packaging, and nonpackaging services), then by geographic area. Smart Touch thinks it will segment by product line (DVDs and Web-based learning).

Advantages of Decentralization

What advantages does decentralization offer large companies? Let's take a look.

Frees Top Management Time

By delegating responsibility for daily operations to unit managers, top management can concentrate on long-term strategic planning and higher-level decisions that affect the entire company. It also naturally places the decision makers (top management) closer to the source of the decisions.

Supports Use of Expert Knowledge

Decentralization allows top management to hire the expertise each business unit needs to excel in its own specific operations. For example, decentralizing by state allows **Citizens Bank** to hire managers with specialized knowledge of the banking laws in each state. Such specialized knowledge can help unit managers make better decisions than could the company's top managers about product and business improvements within the business unit (state).

Improves Customer Relations

Unit managers focus on just one segment of the company. Therefore, they can maintain closer contact with important customers than can upper management. Thus, decentralization often leads to improved customer relations and quicker customer response time.

Provides Training

Decentralization also provides unit managers with training and experience necessary to become effective top managers. For example, companies often choose CEOs based on their past performance as division managers.

Improves Motivation and Retention

Empowering unit managers to make decisions increases managers' motivation and retention. This improves job performance and satisfaction.

Disadvantages of Decentralization

Despite its advantages, decentralization can also cause potential problems, including those outlined here.

Duplication of Costs

Decentralization may cause the company to duplicate certain costs or assets. For example, each business unit may hire its own payroll department and purchase its own payroll software. Companies can often avoid such duplications by providing centralized services. For example, **Doubletree Hotels** segments its business by property, yet each property shares one centralized reservations office and one centralized Web site.

Problems Achieving Goal Congruence

Goal congruence occurs when unit managers' goals align with top management's goals. Decentralized companies often struggle to achieve goal congruence. Unit managers may not fully understand the "big picture" of the company. They may make decisions that are good for their division but could harm another division or the rest of the company. For example, the purchasing department may buy cheaper components to decrease product cost. However, cheaper components may hurt the product line's quality, and the company's brand, *as a whole*, may suffer. Later in this chapter, we will see how managerial accountants can design performance evaluation systems that encourage goal congruence.

Although we've discussed some disadvantages of decentralization, it's important to note that the advantages of decentralization usually outweigh the disadvantages.

Responsibility Centers

Decentralized companies delegate responsibility for specific decisions to each subunit, creating responsibility centers. Recall from Chapter 22 that a *responsibility center* is a part or subunit of an organization whose manager is accountable for specific activities. Exhibit 24-1 reviews the four most common types of responsibility centers.

> **Key Takeaway**
>
> As companies grow, they often decentralize by geographic area, product line, customer base, business function, or some other characteristic. Decentralization frees top management's time by delegating decision making, supports the use of expert knowledge, improves customer relations, provides training for managers, and improves employee motivation and retention. Disadvantages of decentralization include possible cost duplications and difficulty achieving goal congruence among decentralized divisions.

EXHIBIT 24-1 | **The Four Most Common Types of Responsibility Centers**

Responsibility Center	Manager is responsible for...	Examples
Cost center	Controlling costs	Production line at Dell Computer; legal department and accounting departments at Nike
Revenue center	Generating sales revenue	Midwest sales region at Pace Foods; central reservation office at Delta
Profit center	Producing profit through generating sales and controlling costs	Product line at Anheuser-Busch; individual Home Depot stores
Investment center	Producing profit and managing the division's invested capital	Company divisions, such as Walt Disney World Resorts and Toon Disney

Performance Measurement

2 Explain why companies use performance evaluation systems

Once a company decentralizes operations, top management is no longer involved in running the subunits' day-to-day operations. Performance evaluation systems provide top management with a framework for maintaining control over the entire organization.

Goals of Performance Evaluation Systems

When companies decentralize, top management needs a system to communicate its goals to subunit managers. Additionally, top management needs to determine whether the decisions being made at the subunit level are effectively meeting company goals. Let's look at the primary goals of performance evaluation systems.

Promoting Goal Congruence and Coordination

As previously mentioned, decentralization increases the difficulty of achieving goal congruence. Unit managers may not always make decisions consistent with the overall goals of the organization. A company will be able to achieve its goals only if each unit moves, in a synchronized fashion, toward the overall company goals. The performance measurement system should provide incentives for coordinating the subunits' activities and direct them toward achieving the overall company goals.

Communicating Expectations

To make decisions that are consistent with the company's goals, unit managers must know the goals and the specific part their unit plays in attaining those goals. The performance measurement system should spell out the unit's most critical objectives. Without a clear picture of what management expects, unit managers have little to guide their daily operating decisions.

Motivating Unit Managers

Unit managers are usually motivated to make decisions that will help to achieve top management's expectations. For additional motivation, upper management may offer bonuses to unit managers who meet or exceed performance targets. Top management must exercise extreme care in setting performance targets, however. For example, managers measured solely by their ability to control costs may take whatever actions are necessary to achieve that goal, including sacrificing quality or customer service. But such actions would *not* be in the best interests of the firm as a whole. Therefore, upper management must consider the ramifications of the performance targets it sets for unit managers.

Providing Feedback

As noted previously, in decentralized companies, top management is not involved in the day-to-day operations of each subunit. Performance evaluation systems provide upper management with the feedback it needs to maintain control over the entire organization, even though it has delegated responsibility and decision-making authority to unit managers. If targets are not met at the unit level, upper management will take corrective actions, ranging from modifying unit goals (if the targets were unrealistic) to replacing the unit manager (if the targets were achievable, but the manager failed to reach them).

Benchmarking

Performance evaluation results are often used for benchmarking, which is the practice of comparing the company's achievements against the best practices in the industry. Comparing results against industry benchmarks is often more revealing than comparing results against budgets. To survive, a company must keep up with its competitors. Benchmarking helps the company determine whether it is performing at least as well as its competitors.

Stop & Think...

Do companies only benchmark subunit performance against competitors and industry standards?

Answer: No. Companies also benchmark performance against the subunit's past performance. Historical trend data (measuring performance over time) helps managers assess whether their decisions are improving, having no effect, or adversely affecting subunit performance. Some companies also benchmark performance against other subunits with similar characteristics.

Limitations of Financial Performance Measurement

In the past, performance measurement revolved almost entirely around *financial* performance. For example, until 1995, 95% of **UPS**'s performance measures were financial. On the one hand, this focus makes sense because the ultimate goal of a company is to generate profit. On the other hand, *current* financial performance tends to reveal the results of *past* actions rather than indicate *future* performance. For this reason, financial measures tend to be **lag indicators** (after the fact) rather than **lead indicators** (future predictors). Management needs to know the results of past decisions, but it also needs to know how current decisions may affect the future. To adequately assess the company, managers need both lead indicators and lag indicators.

Another limitation of financial performance measures is that they tend to focus on the company's short-term achievements rather than on long-term performance. Why is this the case? Because financial statements are prepared on a monthly, quarterly, or annual basis. To remain competitive, top management needs clear signals that assess and predict the company's performance over longer periods of time.

> **Key Takeaway**
>
> Performance evaluation systems provide top management with a framework for maintaining control over the entire organization once it is decentralized. Such systems should help management promote goal congruence, provide a tool for communications, motivate unit managers, provide feedback, and allow for benchmarking. These measures should not revolve around just financial performance measures, however.

The Balanced Scorecard

In the early 1990s, Robert Kaplan and David Norton introduced the **balanced scorecard**.[1] The balanced scorecard recognizes that management must consider *both* financial performance measures (which tend to measure the results of actions already taken—lag indicators) and operational performance measures (which tend to drive future performance—lead indicators) when judging the performance of a company and its subunits. These measures should be linked with the company's goals and its strategy for achieving those goals. The balanced scorecard represents a major shift in corporate performance measurement. Rather than treating financial indicators as the sole measure of performance, companies recognize that they are only one measure among a broader set. Keeping score of operating measures *and* traditional financial measures gives management a "balanced" view of the organization.

3 Describe the balanced scorecard and identify key performance indicators for each perspective

---

[1]Robert Kaplan and David Norton, "The Balanced Scorecard—Measures That Drive Performance," *Harvard Business Review on Measuring Corporate Performance*, Boston, 1991, pp. 123–145; Robert Kaplan and David Norton, *Translating Strategy into Action: The Balanced Scorecard*, Boston, Harvard Business School Press, 1996.

Kaplan and Norton use the analogy of an airplane pilot to illustrate the necessity for a balanced scorecard approach to performance evaluation. The pilot of an airplane cannot rely on only one factor, such as wind speed, to fly a plane. Rather, the pilot must consider other critical factors, such as altitude, direction, and fuel level. Likewise, management cannot rely on only financial measures to guide the company. Management needs to consider other critical factors, such as customer satisfaction, operational efficiency, and employee excellence. Similar to the way a pilot uses cockpit instruments to measure critical factors, management uses *key performance indicators*—such as customer satisfaction ratings and revenue growth—to measure critical factors that affect the success of the company. As shown in Exhibit 24-2, **key performance indicators (KPIs)** are summary performance measures that help managers assess whether the company is achieving its goals.

EXHIBIT 24-2 | **Linking Company Goals to Key Performance Indicators (KPIs)**

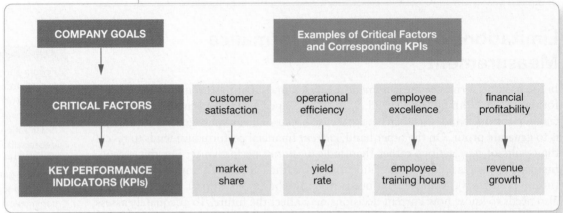

Four Perspectives of the Balanced Scorecard

The balanced scorecard views the company from four different perspectives, each of which evaluates a specific aspect of organizational performance:

1. Financial perspective
2. Customer perspective
3. Internal business perspective
4. Learning and growth perspective

Exhibit 24-3 on the following page illustrates how the company's strategy affects, and, in turn, is affected by all four perspectives. Additionally, it shows the cause-and-effect relationship linking the four perspectives.

Companies that adopt the balanced scorecard usually have specific goals they wish to achieve within each of the four perspectives. Once management clearly identifies the goals, it develops KPIs that will assess how well the goals are being achieved. That is, they measure actual results of KPIs against goal KPIs. The difference is the variance. If an individual KPI variance is positive, the company exceeded its goal. If an individual KPI variance is negative, the company did not meet the goal. This allows management to focus attention on the most critical elements and prevent information overload. Management should take care to use only a few KPIs for each perspective. Let's look at each of the perspectives and discuss the links among them.

EXHIBIT 24-3 | **The Four Perspectives of the Balanced Scorecard**

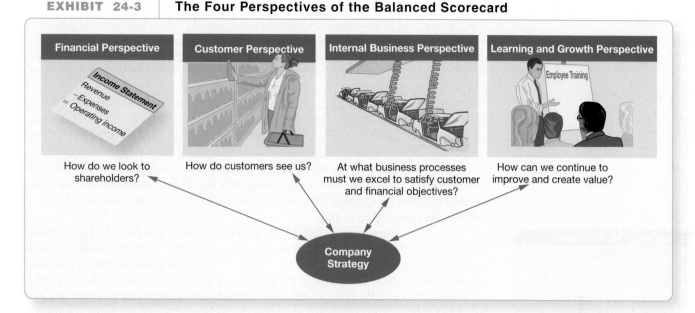

Financial Perspective

This perspective helps managers answer the question, "How do we look to share-holders?" The ultimate goal of companies is to generate income for their owners. Therefore, company strategy revolves around increasing the company's profits through increasing revenue growth and productivity. Companies grow revenue by introducing new products, gaining new customers, and increasing sales to existing customers. Companies increase productivity through reducing costs and using the company's assets more efficiently. Managers may implement seemingly sensible strategies and initiatives, but the test of their judgment is whether these decisions increase company profits. The financial perspective focuses management's attention on KPIs that assess financial objectives, such as revenue growth and cost cutting. Some commonly used financial perspective KPIs include *sales revenue growth, gross margin growth,* and *return on investment.* The latter portion of this chapter discusses in detail the most commonly used financial perspective KPIs.

Customer Perspective

This perspective helps managers evaluate the question, "How do customers see us?" Customer satisfaction is a top priority for long-term company success. If customers are not happy, they will not come back. Therefore, customer satisfaction is critical to achieving the company's financial goals outlined in the financial perspective of the balanced scorecard. Customers are typically concerned with four specific product or service attributes: (1) the product's price, (2) the product's quality, (3) the service quality at the time of sale, and (4) the product's delivery time (the shorter the better). Since each of these attributes is critical to making the customer happy, most companies have specific objectives for each of these attributes.

Businesses commonly use customer perspective KPIs, such as *customer satisfaction ratings,* to assess how they are performing on these attributes. No doubt you have filled out a customer satisfaction survey. Because customer satisfaction is crucial, customer satisfaction ratings often determine the extent to which bonuses are granted to restaurant managers. For example, if customer satisfaction ratings are greater than average, the KPI will be positive. If customer satisfaction ratings are lower than average, management will want to devise measures to improve customer satisfaction. Other typical customer perspective KPIs include *percentage of market share, increase in the number of customers, number of repeat customers,* and *rate of on-time deliveries.*

Internal Business Perspective

This perspective helps managers address the question, "At what business processes must we excel to satisfy customer and financial objectives?" The answer to this question incorporates three factors: innovation, operations, and post-sales service. All three factors critically affect customer satisfaction, which will affect the company's financial success.

Satisfying customers once does not guarantee future success, which is why the first important factor of the internal business perspective is innovation. Customers' needs and wants constantly change. Just a couple of years ago, iPads and mini-computers did not exist. Companies must continually improve existing products (such as adding more applications to cell phones) and develop new products (such as the iPad) to succeed in the future. Companies commonly assess innovation using internal business perspective KPIs, such as the *number of new products developed* or *new-product development time*.

The second important factor of the internal business perspective is operations. Lean and effective internal operations allow the company to meet customers' needs and expectations. For example, the time it takes to manufacture a product (*manufacturing cycle time*) affects the company's ability to deliver quickly to meet a customer's demand. Production efficiency (*number of units produced per hour*) and product quality (*defect rate*) also affect the price charged to the customer. To remain competitive, companies must be at least as good as the industry leader at those internal operations that are essential to their business.

The third factor of the internal business perspective is post-sales service. How well does the company service customers after the sale? Claims of excellent post-sales service help to generate more sales. Management assesses post-sales service through the following typical internal business perspective KPIs: *number of warranty claims received*, *average repair time*, and *average wait time on the phone for a customer service representative*. So, for example, if the number of warranty claims is greater than the number of expected (or acceptable) warranty claims, the KPI will be negative. Management will want to devise measures to improve the quality of its products so it can reduce the number of warranty claims. If the number of warranty claims is less than the number of expected (or acceptable) warranty claims, that will be a positive KPI.

Learning and Growth Perspective

This perspective helps managers assess the question, "How can we continue to improve and create value?" The learning and growth perspective focuses on three factors: (1) employee capabilities, (2) information system capabilities, and (3) the company's "climate for action." The learning and growth perspective lays the foundation needed to improve internal business operations, sustain customer satisfaction, and generate financial success. Without skilled employees, updated technology, and a positive corporate culture, the company will not be able to meet the objectives of the other perspectives.

Let's consider each of these factors. First, because most routine work is automated, employees are freed up to be critical and creative thinkers who, therefore, can help achieve the company's goals. The learning and growth perspective measures employees' skills, knowledge, motivation, and empowerment. Learning and growth perspective KPIs typically include *hours of employee training*, *employee satisfaction*, *employee turnover*, and *number of employee suggestions implemented*. Second, employees need timely and accurate information on customers, internal processes, and finances; therefore, other KPIs measure the maintenance and improvement of the company's information system. For example, KPIs might include the *percentage of employees having online access to information about customers*, and the *percentage of processes with real-time feedback on quality, cycle time, and cost*. Finally, management must create a corporate culture that supports and encourages communication, change, and growth. For example, a company may use the balanced scorecard to communicate strategy to every employee and to show each employee how his or her daily work contributed to company success. So, for example, managers might review the employee turnover KPI to determine whether the company is attracting and retaining skilled employees. If the data show the employee turnover rate is greater than the expected employee turnover rate, the KPI would be negative. Management will want to devise measures to identify the reasons for the increase in employee turnover and devise measures to increase employee retention. If the employee turnover rate is less than the expected employee turnover rate, that would be a positive KPI.

So far, we have looked at why companies decentralize, why they need to measure subunit performance, and how the balanced scorecard can help. In the second half of the chapter, we will focus on how companies measure the financial perspective of the balanced scorecard.

The Decision Guidelines and Summary Problem on the next pages ask you to put these concepts to use.

Key Takeaway

The balanced scorecard focuses performance measurement on progress toward the company's goals in each of the four perspectives. In designing the scorecard, managers start with the company's goals and its strategy for achieving those goals and then identify the *most* important measures of performance that will predict long-term success. Some of these measures are lead indicators, while others are lag indicators. Managers must consider the linkages between strategy and operations and how those operations will affect finances now and in the future.

Decision Guidelines 24-1

As Smart Touch expanded its business operations, it had to make the following types of decisions when it decentralized and developed its balanced scorecard for performance evaluation.

Decision	Guidelines
• On what basis should the company be decentralized?	The manner of decentralization should fit the company's strategy. Many companies decentralize based on geographic region, product line, business function, or customer type.
• Will decentralization have any negative impact on the company?	Decentralization usually provides many benefits; however, decentralization also has potential drawbacks: • Subunits may duplicate costs or assets. • Subunit managers may not make decisions that are favorable to the entire company.
• How can responsibility accounting be incorporated at decentralized companies?	Subunit managers are given responsibility for specific activities and are only held accountable for the results of those activities. Subunits generally fall into one of the following four categories according to their responsibilities: 1. Cost centers—responsible for controlling costs 2. Revenue centers—responsible for generating revenue 3. Profit centers—responsible for controlling costs and generating revenue 4. Investment centers—responsible for controlling costs, generating revenue, and efficiently managing the division's invested capital (assets)
• Is a performance evaluation system necessary?	While not mandatory, most companies will reap many benefits from implementing a well-designed performance evaluation system. Such systems promote goal congruence, communicate expectations, motivate managers, provide feedback, and enable benchmarking.
• Should the performance evaluation system include lag or lead measures?	Better performance evaluation systems include *both* lag and lead measures. Lag measures indicate the results of past actions, while lead measures try to predict future performance.
• What are the four balanced scorecard perspectives?	1. Financial perspective 2. Customer perspective 3. Internal business perspective 4. Learning and growth perspective
• Must all four perspectives be included in the company's balanced scorecard?	Every company's balanced scorecard will be unique to its business and strategy. Because each of the four perspectives is causally linked, most companies will benefit from developing performance measures for each of the four perspectives.

Summary Problem 24-1

The balanced scorecard gives performance perspective from four different viewpoints.

Requirements

1. Each of the following describes a key performance indicator. Determine which of the balanced scorecard perspectives is being addressed (financial, customer, internal business, or learning and growth):
   a. Employee turnover
   b. Earnings per share
   c. Percentage of on-time deliveries
   d. Revenue growth rate
   e. Percentage of defects discovered during manufacturing
   f. Number of warranty claims
   g. New product development time
   h. Number of repeat customers
   i. Number of employee suggestions implemented

2. Read the following company initiatives and determine which of the balanced scorecard perspectives is being addressed (financial, customer, internal business, learning and growth):
   a. Purchasing efficient production equipment
   b. Providing employee training
   c. Updating retail store lighting
   d. Paying quarterly dividends to stockholders
   e. Updating the company's information system

Solution

Requirement 1
   a. Learning and growth
   b. Financial
   c. Customer
   d. Financial
   e. Internal business
   f. Internal business
   g. Internal business
   h. Customer
   i. Learning and growth

Requirement 2
   a. Internal business
   b. Learning and growth
   c. Customer
   d. Financial
   e. Learning and growth

Measuring the Financial Performance of Cost, Revenue, and Profit Centers

4 Use performance reports to evaluate cost, revenue, and profit centers

In this half of the chapter, we will take a more detailed look at how companies measure the financial perspective of the balanced scorecard for different subunits of the company. We will focus now on the financial performance measurement of each type of responsibility center.

Responsibility accounting performance reports capture the financial performance of cost, revenue, and profit centers. Recall from Chapter 22 that responsibility accounting performance reports compare *actual* results with *budgeted* amounts and display a variance, or difference, between the two amounts. Because *cost centers* are only responsible for controlling costs, their performance reports only include information on actual traceable costs versus budgeted *costs*. Likewise, performance reports for *revenue centers* only contain actual revenue versus budgeted *revenue*. However, *profit centers* are responsible for both controlling costs and generating revenue. Therefore, their performance reports contain actual and budgeted information on both their *revenues and costs*.

Cost center performance reports typically focus on the *flexible budget variance*—the difference between actual results and the flexible budget (as described in Chapter 23). Exhibit 24-4 shows an example of a cost center performance report for a regional payroll processing department of Smart Touch. Because the payroll processing department only incurs expenses and does not generate revenue, it is classified as a cost center.

EXHIBIT 24-4 | **Example of a Cost Center Performance Report**

SMART TOUCH LEARNING, INC.
Payroll Processing Department Performance Report
July 2014

	Actual	Flexible Budget	Flexible Budget Variance (U or F)	% Variance* (U or F)
Salary and wages	$18,500	$18,000	$ 500 U	2.8% U
Payroll benefits	6,100	5,000	1,100 U	22.0% U
Equipment depreciation	3,000	3,000	0	0%
Supplies	1,850	2,000	150 F	7.5% F
Other expenses	1,900	2,000	100 F	5.0% F
Total expenses	$31,350	$30,000	$1,350 U	4.5% U

*% Variance = Flexible budget variance/flexible budget

Managers use *management by exception* to determine which variances in the performance report are worth investigating. **Management by exception** directs management's attention to important differences between actual and budgeted amounts. For example, management may only investigate variances that exceed a certain dollar amount (i.e., over $1,000) or a certain percentage of the budgeted figure (i.e., over 10%). Smaller variances signal that operations are close to target and do not require management's immediate attention. Consider the cost center performance report illustrated in Exhibit 24-4. Management might only investigate payroll benefits because the variance exceeds both $1,000 and 10%. Companies that use standard costs can compute price and efficiency variances, as described in Chapter 23, to better understand why significant flexible budget variances occurred.

Revenue center performance reports often highlight both the flexible budget variance and the sales volume variance. The performance report for the specialty

DVD department of Smart Touch might look similar to Exhibit 24-5, with detailed sales volume and revenue shown for each brand and type of DVD sold. (For simplicity, the exhibit shows volume and revenue for only one item.) The cash register bar-coding system provides management with the sales volume and sales revenue generated by individual products.

EXHIBIT 24-5	Example of a Revenue Center Performance Report

SMART TOUCH LEARNING, INC.
Specialty DVD Department Performance Report
July 2014

Sales revenue	Actual Sales	Flexible Budget Variance	Flexible Budget	Sales Volume Variance	Static (Master) Budget
Number of Specialty DVDs	2,480	–0–	2,480	155 F	2,325
Specialty DVDs	$40,920	$3,720 U	$44,640	$2,790 F	$41,850

Recall from Chapter 23 that the sales volume variance is due strictly to volume differences—selling more or fewer units (DVDs) than originally planned. The flexible budget variance, however, is due strictly to differences in the sales price—selling units for a higher or lower price than originally planned. Both the sales volume variance and the flexible budget variance help revenue center managers understand why they have exceeded or fallen short of budgeted revenue.

Managers of profit centers are responsible for both generating revenue and controlling costs so their performance reports include both revenues and expenses. Exhibit 24-6 shows an example of a profit center performance report for the DVD department.

EXHIBIT 24-6	Example of a Profit Center Performance Report

SMART TOUCH LEARNING, INC.
DVD—Performance Report
July 2014

	Actual	Flexible Budget	Flexible Budget Variance	% Variance (U or F)
Sales revenue	$5,243,600	$5,000,000	$243,600 F	4.9% F
Variable expenses	4,183,500	4,000,000	183,500 U	4.6% U
Contribution margin	1,060,100	1,000,000	60,100 F	6.0% F
Traceable fixed expenses	84,300	75,000	9,300 U	12.4% U
Divisional segment margin	$ 975,800	$ 925,000	$ 50,800 F	5.5% F

Notice how this profit center performance report contains a line called "Traceable fixed expenses." Recall that one drawback of decentralization is that subunits may duplicate costs or assets. Many companies avoid this problem by providing centralized service departments where several subunits, such as profit centers, share assets or costs. For example, the payroll processing cost center shown in Exhibit 24-4 serves all of Smart Touch. In addition to centralized payroll departments, companies often provide centralized human resource departments, legal departments, and information systems.

When subunits share centralized services, should those services be "free" to the subunits? If they are free, the subunit's performance report will *not* include any charge for using those services. However, if they are not free, the performance report will show a charge for the traceable portion of those expenses, as you see in Exhibit 24-6. Most companies charge subunits for their use of centralized services because the subunit would incur a cost to buy those services on its own. For example, if Smart Touch did not operate a centralized payroll department, the DVD department would have to hire its own payroll department personnel and purchase computers, payroll software, and supplies necessary to process the department's payroll. As an alternative, it could outsource payroll to a company, such as **Paychex** or **ADP**. In either event, the department would incur a cost for processing payroll. It only seems fair that the department is charged for using the centralized payroll processing department. Notice we have excluded common fixed expenses not traceable to the DVD division.

Regardless of the type of responsibility center, performance reports should focus on information, not blame. Analyzing budget variances helps managers understand the underlying *reasons* for the unit's performance. Once management understands these reasons, it may be able to take corrective actions. But some variances are uncontrollable. For example, the 2010 **BP** oil spill in the Gulf of Mexico has caused damage to many businesses along the coast, as well as environmental damage to the wetlands and wildlife. Consequently, the price of seafood from the Gulf of Mexico increased because of the decreased supply. These price increases resulted in unfavorable cost variances for many restaurants and seafood retailers. Managers should not be held accountable for conditions they cannot control. Responsibility accounting can help management identify the causes of variances, thereby allowing them to determine what was controllable and what was not.

We have just looked at the detailed financial information presented in responsibility accounting performance reports. In addition to these *detailed* reports, upper management often uses *summary* measures—financial KPIs—to assess the financial performance of cost, revenue, and profit centers. Examples include the *cost per unit of output* (for cost centers), *revenue growth* (for revenue centers), and *gross margin growth* (for profit centers). KPIs such as these are used to address the financial perspective of the balanced scorecard for cost, revenue, and profit centers. In the next section, we will look at the most commonly used KPIs for investment centers.

Stop & Think...

We have just seen that companies like Smart Touch use responsibility accounting performance reports to evaluate the financial performance of cost (payroll processing), revenue (specialty DVDs), and profit centers (DVD division). Are these types of responsibility reports sufficient for evaluating the financial performance of investment centers? Why or why not?

Answer: Investment centers are responsible not only for generating revenue and controlling costs, but also for efficiently managing the subunits' invested capital. The performance reports we have just seen address how well the subunits control costs and generate revenue, but they do not address how well the subunits manage their assets. Therefore, these performance reports will be helpful but not sufficient for evaluating investment center performance.

Measuring the Financial Performance of Investment Centers

 Use ROI, RI, and EVA to evaluate investment centers

Investment centers are typically large divisions of a company, such as the media division of **Amazon.com** or of Smart Touch. The duties of an investment center manager are similar to those of a CEO. The CEO is responsible for maximizing income, in relation to the company's invested capital, by using company assets efficiently.

Likewise, investment center managers are responsible not only for generating profit, but also for making the best use of the investment center's assets.

How does an investment center manager influence the use of the division's assets? An investment center manager has the authority to open new stores or close old stores. The manager may also decide how much inventory to hold, what types of investments to make, how aggressively to collect accounts receivable, and whether to invest in new equipment. In other words, the manager has decision-making responsibility over all of the division's assets.

Companies cannot evaluate investment centers the way they evaluate profit centers, based only on operating income. Why? Because operating income does not indicate how *efficiently* the division is using its assets. The financial evaluation of investment centers must measure two factors: (1) how much operating income the division is generating and (2) how efficiently the division is using its assets.

Consider Smart Touch. In addition to its DVD Division, it also has an online e-learning Division. Operating income, average total assets, and sales for the two divisions for July follow:

Smart Touch	e-learning	DVD
Operating income	$ 450,000	$ 975,800
Average total assets	2,500,000	6,500,000
Sales	7,500,000	5,243,600

Based on operating income alone, the DVD Division (with operating income of $975,800) appears to be more profitable than the e-learning Division (with operating income of $450,000). However, this comparison is misleading because it does not consider the assets invested in each division. The DVD Division has more assets than does the e-learning Division.

To adequately evaluate an investment center's financial performance, companies need summary performance measures—or KPIs—that include *both* the division's operating income *and* its assets (see Exhibit 24-7). In the next sections, we discuss three commonly used performance measures: return on investment (ROI), residual income (RI), and economic value added (EVA). All three measures incorporate both the division's assets and its operating income. For simplicity, we will leave the word *divisional* out of the equations. However, keep in mind that all of the equations use divisional data when evaluating a division's performance. Also, we will round each ratio to the nearest percentage.

EXHIBIT 24-7 | **KPIs for Investment Centers**

KPIs for Investment Centers

These three KPIs take into consideration
1. the division's operating income and
2. the division's average total assets.

Return on Investment (ROI)

Economic Value Added (EVA)

Residual Income (RI)

Return on Investment (ROI)

Return on investment (ROI) is one of the most commonly used KPIs for evaluating an investment center's financial performance. Companies typically define ROI as follows:

$$ROI = \frac{\text{Operating income}}{\text{Average total assets}}$$

ROI measures the amount of operating income an investment center earns relative to the amount of its average total assets. **The ROI formula focuses on the amount of operating income earned before other revenue/expense items (such as interest expense) by utilizing the average total assets employed for the year (denominator).** Each division's ROI is calculated as follows:

$$\text{e-learning Division's ROI} = \frac{\$450,000}{\$2,500,000} = 0.18, \text{ or } 18\%$$

$$\text{DVD Division's ROI} = \frac{\$975,800}{\$6,500,000} = 0.15, \text{ or } 15\%$$

Although the DVD Division has a higher operating income than the e-learning Division, the DVD Division is actually *less* profitable than the e-learning Division when we consider that the DVD Division requires more average total assets to generate its operating income.

If you had $1,000 to invest, would you rather invest it in the DVD Division or the e-learning Division? The DVD Division earns operating income of $0.15 on every $1.00 of average total assets, but the e-learning Division earns $0.18 on every $1.00 of average total assets. When top management decides how to invest excess funds, it often considers each division's ROI. A division with a higher ROI is more likely to receive extra funds because it has a history of providing a higher return.

In addition to comparing ROI across divisions, management also compares a division's ROI across time to determine whether the division is becoming more or less profitable in relation to its average total assets. Additionally, management often benchmarks divisional ROI with other companies in the same industry to determine how each division is performing compared to its competitors.

To determine what is driving a division's ROI, management often restates the ROI equation in its expanded form. Notice that Sales is incorporated in the denominator of the first term, and in the numerator of the second term. When the two terms are multiplied together, Sales cancels out, leaving the original ROI formula.

$$ROI = \frac{\text{Operating income}}{\text{Sales}} \times \frac{\text{Sales}}{\text{Average total assets}} = \frac{\text{Operating income}}{\text{Average total assets}}$$

Why do managers rewrite the ROI formula this way? Because it helps them better understand how they can improve their ROI. The first term in the expanded equation is called the **profit margin:**

$$\text{Profit margin} = \frac{\text{Operating income}}{\text{Sales}}$$

The profit margin shows how much operating income the division earns on every $1.00 of sales, so this term focuses on profitability. Each division's profit margin is calculated as follows:

$$\text{e-learning Division's profit margin} = \frac{\$450,000}{\$7,500,000} = 0.06, \text{ or } 6\%$$

$$\text{DVD Division's profit margin} = \frac{\$975,800}{\$5,243,600} = 0.186, \text{ or } 19\%$$

The e-learning Division has a profit margin of 6%, meaning that it earns operating income of $0.06 on every $1.00 of sales. The DVD Division, however, is much more profitable with a profit margin of 19%, earning $0.19 on every $1.00 of sales.

Asset turnover is the second term of the expanded ROI equation:

$$\text{Asset turnover} = \frac{\text{Sales}}{\text{Average total assets}}$$

Asset turnover shows how efficiently a division uses its average total assets to generate sales. Rather than focusing on profitability, asset turnover focuses on efficiency. Each division's asset turnover is calculated as follows:

$$\text{e-learning Division's asset turnover} = \frac{\$7,500,000}{\$2,500,000} = 3$$

$$\text{DVD Division's asset turnover} = \frac{\$5,243,600}{\$6,500,000} = 0.81$$

The e-learning Division has an asset turnover of 3. This means that the e-learning Division generates $3.00 of sales with every $1.00 of average total assets. The DVD Division's asset turnover is only 0.81. The DVD Division generates only $0.81 of sales with every $1.00 of average total assets. The e-learning Division uses its average total assets much more efficiently in generating sales than the DVD Division.

Putting the two terms back together in the expanded ROI equation gets the following:

	Profit margin	×	Asset turnover	= ROI
e-learning Division:	6%	×	3	= 0.18 or 18%
DVD Division:	19%	×	0.81	= 0.15 or 15%

As you can see, the expanded ROI equation gives management more insight into the division's ROI. Management can now see that the DVD Division is more profitable on its sales (profit margin of 19%) than the e-learning Division (profit margin of 6%), but the e-learning Division is doing a better job of generating sales with its average total assets (asset turnover of 3) than the DVD Division (asset turnover of 0.81). Consequently, the e-learning Division has a higher ROI of 18%.

If managers are not satisfied with their division's asset turnover rate, how can they improve it? They might try to eliminate nonproductive assets, for example, by being more aggressive in collecting accounts receivables or by decreasing inventory levels. They might decide to change retail-store layout to increase sales.

What if management is not satisfied with the current profit margin? To increase the profit margin, management must increase the operating income earned on every dollar of sales. Management may cut product costs or selling and administrative costs, but it needs to be careful when trimming costs. Cutting costs in the short term can hurt long-term ROI. For example, sacrificing quality or cutting back on research and development could decrease costs in the short run but may hurt long-term sales. The balanced scorecard helps management carefully consider the consequences of cost-cutting measures before acting on them.

ROI has one major drawback. Evaluating division managers based solely on ROI gives them an incentive to adopt *only* projects that will maintain or increase their current ROI. Say that top management has set a company-wide target ROI of 16%. Both divisions are considering investing in in-store video display equipment that shows customers how to use featured products. This equipment will increase sales because customers are more likely to buy the products when they see these infomercials. The equipment would cost each division $100,000 and is expected to provide each division with $17,000 of annual operating income. The *equipment's* ROI is as follows:

$$\text{Equipment ROI} = \frac{\$17,000}{\$100,000} = 17\%$$

Upper management would want the divisions to invest in this equipment since the equipment will provide a 17% ROI, which is higher than the 16% target rate. But what will the managers of the divisions do? Because the DVD Division currently has an ROI of 15%, the new equipment (with its 17% ROI) will *increase* the division's *overall* ROI. Therefore, the DVD Division manager will buy the equipment. However, the e-learning Division currently has an ROI of 18%. If the e-learning Division invests in the equipment, its *overall* ROI will *decrease*. Therefore, the manager of the e-learning Division will probably turn down the investment. In this case, goal congruence is *not* achieved— only one division will invest in equipment. Yet top management wants both divisions to invest in the equipment because the equipment return exceeds the 16% target ROI. Next, we discuss a performance measure that overcomes this problem with ROI.

Residual Income (RI)

Residual income (RI) is another commonly used KPI for evaluating an investment center's financial performance. Similar to ROI, RI considers both the division's operating income and its average total assets. RI measures the division's profitability and the efficiency with which the division uses its average total assets. RI also incorporates another piece of information: top management's target rate of return (ROI) (such as the 16% target return in the previous example). The target rate of return is the minimum acceptable rate of return that top management expects a division to earn with its average total assets. You will learn how to calculate target rate of return in your finance class. For now, we provide the target rate of return for you.

RI compares the division's actual operating income with the minimum operating income expected by top management *given the size of the division's average total assets*. **RI is the "extra" operating income above the minimum operating income.** A positive RI means that the division's operating income exceeds top management's target rate of return. A negative RI means the division is not meeting the target rate of return. Let's look at the RI equation and then calculate the RI for both divisions using the 16% target rate of return from the previous example.

$$\text{RI} = \text{Operating income} - \text{Minimum acceptable operating income}$$

In this equation, the minimum acceptable operating income is defined as top management's target rate of return multiplied by the division's average total assets. Therefore,

$$\text{RI} = \text{Operating income} - (\text{Target rate of return} \times \text{Average total assets})$$

$$\begin{aligned} \text{e-learning Division RI} &= \$450,000 - (16\% \times \$2,500,000) \\ &= \$450,000 - \$400,000 \\ &= \$50,000 \end{aligned}$$

The positive RI indicates that the e-learning Division exceeded top management's 16% target rate of return expectations. The RI calculation also confirms what we learned about the e-learning Division's ROI. Recall that the e-learning Division's ROI was 18%, which is higher than the target rate of return of 16%.

Now let's calculate the RI for the DVD Division:

$$\begin{aligned} \text{DVD Division RI} &= \$975,800 - (16\% \times \$6,500,000) \\ &= \$975,800 - \$1,040,000 \\ &= \$(64,200) \end{aligned}$$

The DVD Division's RI is negative. This means that the DVD Division did not use its average total assets as effectively as top management expected. Recall that the DVD Division's ROI of 15% fell short of the target rate of return of 16%.

Why would a company prefer to use RI over ROI for performance evaluation? The answer is that RI is more likely to lead to goal congruence than ROI. Consider the video display equipment that both divisions could buy. In both divisions, the equipment is expected to generate a 17% return. If the divisions are evaluated based on ROI, we learned that the DVD Division will buy the equipment because it will increase the division's ROI. The e-learning Division, on the other hand, will probably not buy the equipment because it will lower the division's ROI.

However, if management evaluates divisions based on RI rather than ROI, what will the divisions do? The answer depends on whether the project yields a positive or negative RI. Recall that the equipment would cost each division $100,000, but will provide $17,000 of operating income each year. The RI provided by *just* the equipment would be as follows:

$$\begin{aligned} \text{Equipment RI} &= \$17,000 - (\$100,000 \times 16\%) \\ &= \$17,000 - \$16,000 \\ &= \$1,000 \end{aligned}$$

If purchased, this equipment will *improve* each division's current RI by $1,000 each year. As a result, both divisions will be motivated to invest in the equipment. Goal congruence is achieved because both divisions will take the action that top management desires. That is, both divisions will invest in the equipment.

Another benefit of RI is that management may set different target returns for different divisions. For example, management might require a higher target rate of return from a division operating in a riskier business environment. If the DVD industry were riskier than the e-learning industry, top management might decide to set a higher target rate of return—perhaps 17%—for the DVD Division.

Economic Value Added (EVA)

Economic value added (EVA) is a special type of RI calculation. Unlike the RI calculation we have just discussed, EVA looks at a division's RI through the eyes of the company's primary stakeholders: its investors (stockholders) and long-term creditors (such as bondholders). Since these stakeholders provide the company's capital, management often wishes to evaluate how efficiently a division is using its assets from these two stakeholders' viewpoints. EVA calculates RI for these stakeholders by specifically considering the following:

1. The after-tax operating income available to these stakeholders

2. The assets used to generate after-tax operating income for these stakeholders

3. The minimum rate of return required by these stakeholders (referred to as the **weighted average cost of capital**, or WACC)

Let's compare the EVA equation with the RI equation and then examine the differences in more detail:

RI = Operating income   − (Average total assets   × Target rate of return)

EVA = After-tax operating income − [(Average total assets − Current liabilities) × WACC%]

Both equations calculate whether any operating income was created by the division above and beyond expectations. They do this by comparing actual operating income with the minimum acceptable operating income. But note the differences in the EVA calculation:

1. The EVA calculation uses *after-tax operating income*, which is the operating income left over after subtracting income taxes. Why? Because the portion of operating income paid to the government is not available to investors (stockholders) and long-term creditors.

2. *Average total assets are reduced by current liabilities.* Why? Because funds owed to short-term creditors, such as suppliers (accounts payable) and employees (salary payable), will be paid in the immediate future and will not be available for generating operating income in the long run. The division is not expected to earn a return for investors (stockholders) and long-term creditors on those funds that will soon be paid out to short-term creditors.

3. The *WACC replaces management's target rate of return.* Since EVA focuses on investors (stockholders) and long-term creditors, it is *their* expected rate of return that should be used, not management's expected rate of return. The WACC, which represents the minimum rate of return expected by *investors (stockholders) and long-term creditors*, is the company's cost of raising capital from both groups of stakeholders. The riskier the business, the higher the WACC. The less risky the business, the lower the WACC. Management's target rate of return must at LEAST be equal to the cost of the capital (WACC) that the business is incurring to break even.

In summary, EVA incorporates all the elements of RI from the perspective of investors (stockholders) and long-term creditors. The goal for the company is positive EVA; therefore, after-tax operating income should be greater than the cost of the capital being employed [(Average total assets – current liabilities) × WACC%]. Now that we have walked through the equation's components, let's calculate EVA for the e-learning and DVD Divisions discussed earlier. We will need the following additional information:

Effective income tax rate	30%
WACC	13%
e-learning Division's current liabilities	$150,000
DVD Division's current liabilities	$250,000

The 30% effective income tax rate means that the government takes 30% of the company's operating income, leaving only 70% to the company's stakeholders. Therefore, we calculate *after-tax operating income* by multiplying the division's operating income by 70% (100% – effective income tax rate of 30%).

EVA = After-tax operating income – [(Average total assets – Current liabilities) × WACC%]

e-learning Division EVA = ($450,000 × 70%) – [($2,500,000 – $150,000) × 13%]
= $315,000 – ($2,350,000 × 13%)
= $315,000 – $305,500
= $9,500

DVD Division EVA = ($975,800 × 70%) – [($6,500,000 – 250,000) × 13%]
= $683,060 – ($6,250,000 × 13%)
= $683,060 – $812,500
= $(129,440)

These EVA calculations show that the e-learning Division has generated after-tax operating income in excess of expectations for its investors (stockholders) and long-term creditors, whereas the DVD Division has not.

Many firms, such as **Coca-Cola, Amazon.com**, and **J.C. Penney**, measure the financial performance of their investment centers using EVA. EVA promotes goal congruence, just as RI does. Additionally, EVA looks at the after-tax operating income generated by the division in excess of expectations, solely from the perspective of investors (stockholders) and long-term creditors. Therefore, EVA specifically addresses the financial perspective of the balanced scorecard that asks, "How do we look to stakeholders?"

Exhibit 24-8 summarizes the three KPIs commonly used to evaluate an investment center's financial performance, and some of their advantages.

EXHIBIT 24-8 | **Three Investment Center KPIs: A Summary**

Equation	ROI = $\dfrac{\text{Operating income}}{\text{Sales}} \times \dfrac{\text{Sales}}{\text{Average total assets}} = \dfrac{\text{Operating income}}{\text{Average total assets}}$
Advantages	• The expanded equation provides management with additional information on profitability and efficiency • Management can compare ROI across divisions and with other companies • ROI is useful for resource allocation
Equation	RI = Operating income − (Average total assets × Target rate of return)
Advantages	• Promotes goal congruence better than ROI • Incorporates management's minimum required rate of return • Management can use different target rates of return for divisions with different levels of risk
Equation	EVA = After-tax operating income − [(Average total assets − Current liabilities) × WACC%]
Advantages	• Considers after-tax operating income generated for investors (stockholders) and long-term creditors in excess of their expectations • Positive EVA clearly illustrates a positive return above the cost of capital (WACC) • Promotes goal congruence

Limitations of Financial Performance Measures

We have just finished looking at three KPIs (ROI, RI, and EVA) commonly used to evaluate the financial performance of investment centers. As discussed in the following sections, all of these measures have drawbacks that management should keep in mind when evaluating the financial performance of investment centers.

Measurement Issues

The ROI, RI, and EVA calculations appear to be very straightforward; however, management must make some decisions before these calculations can be made. For example, all three equations use the term *average total assets*. Recall that total assets is a balance sheet figure, which means that it is a snapshot at any given point in time. Because the total assets figure will be *different* at the beginning of the period and at the end of the period, most companies choose to use a simple average of the two figures in their ROI, RI, and EVA calculations.

Management must also decide if it really wants to include *all* assets in the average total asset figure. Many firms, such as **Walmart**, are continually buying land on which to build future retail outlets. Until those stores are built and opened, the land (including any construction in progress) is a nonproductive asset, which is not adding to the company's operating income. Including nonproductive assets in the average total asset figure will naturally drive down the ROI, RI, and EVA figures. Therefore, some firms will not include nonproductive assets in these calculations.

Another asset measurement issue is whether to use the gross book value of assets (the historical cost of the assets), or the net book value of assets (historical cost less accumulated depreciation). Many firms will use the net book value of assets because the figure is consistent with and easily pulled from the balance sheet. Because depreciation expense factors into the firm's operating income, the net book value concept is also consistent with the measurement of operating income. However, using the net book value of assets has a definite drawback. Over time, the net book value of assets decreases because accumulated depreciation continues to grow until the assets are fully depreciated. Therefore, ROI, RI, and EVA get *larger* over time *simply because of depreciation* rather than from actual improvements in operations. In addition, the rate of this depreciation effect will depend on the depreciation method used.

In general, calculating ROI based on the net book value of assets gives managers incentive to continue using old, outdated equipment because its low net book value results in a higher ROI. However, top management may want the division to invest in new technology to create operational efficiency (internal business perspective of the balanced scorecard) or to enhance its information systems (learning and growth perspective). The long-term effects of using outdated equipment may be devastating, as competitors use new technology to produce and sell at lower cost. Therefore, to create *goal congruence*, some firms prefer calculating ROI based on the gross book value of assets. The same general rule holds true for RI and EVA calculations—All else being equal, using net book value will increase RI and EVA over time.

Short-Term Focus

One serious drawback of financial performance measures is their short-term focus. Companies usually prepare performance reports and calculate ROI, RI, and EVA figures over a one-year time frame or less. If upper management uses a short time frame, division managers have an incentive to take actions that will lead to an immediate increase in these measures, even if such actions may not be in the company's long-term interest (such as cutting back on R&D or advertising). On the other hand, some potentially positive actions considered by subunit managers may take longer than one year to generate income at the targeted level. Many product life cycles start slow, even incurring losses in the early stages, before generating profit. If managers are measured on short-term financial performance only, they may not introduce new products because they are not willing to wait several years for the positive effect to show up in their financial performance measures.

As a potential remedy, management can measure financial performance using a longer time horizon, such as three to five years. Extending the time frame gives subunit managers the incentive to think long term rather than short term and make decisions that will positively impact the company over the next several years.

The limitations of financial performance measures confirm the importance of the balanced scorecard. The deficiencies of financial measures can be overcome by taking a broader view of performance—including KPIs from all four balanced scorecard perspectives rather than concentrating on only the financial measures.

Next, take some time to review the Decision Guidelines and Summary Problem on the next pages.

Key Takeaway

To evaluate an investment center's financial performance, companies need summary performance measures—or KPIs—that include both the division's operating income and its assets. Commonly used KPIs for evaluating an investment center's financial performance are return on investment (ROI), residual income (RI), and economic value added (EVA). Each of these financial KPIs must be considered in conjunction with KPIs that come from all four of the balanced scorecard perspectives.

Decision Guidelines 24-2

When managers at Smart Touch developed the financial perspective of their balanced scorecard, they had to make decisions such as the examples that follow.

Decision	Guidelines
• How should the financial section of the balanced scorecard be measured for cost, revenue, and profit centers?	Responsibility accounting performance reports measure the financial performance of cost, revenue, and profit centers. These reports typically highlight the variances between budgeted and actual performance.
• How should the financial section of the balanced scorecard be measured for investment centers?	Investment centers require measures that take into account the division's operating income *and* the division's assets. Typical measures include the following: • Return on investment (ROI) • Residual income (RI) • Economic value added (EVA)
• How is ROI computed and interpreted?	$$\text{ROI} = \text{Operating income} \div \text{Average total assets}$$ ROI measures the amount of operating income earned by a division relative to the size of its average total assets—the higher, the better.
• Can managers learn more by writing the ROI formula in its expanded form?	In its expanded form, ROI is written as follows: $$\text{ROI} = \text{Profit margin} \times \text{Asset turnover}$$ where, $$\text{Profit margin} = \text{Operating income} \div \text{Sales}$$ $$\text{Asset turnover} = \text{Sales} \div \text{Average total assets}$$ Profit margin focuses on profitability (the amount of operating income earned on every dollar of sales), while asset turnover focuses on efficiency (the amount of sales generated with every dollar of average total assets).
• How is RI computed and interpreted?	$$\text{RI} = \text{Operating income} - \left(\text{Target rate of return} \times \text{Average total assets} \right)$$ If RI is positive, the division is earning operating income at a rate that exceeds management's minimum expectations.
• How does EVA differ from RI?	EVA is a special type of RI calculation that focuses on the after-tax operating income (in excess of expectations) created by the division for two specific stakeholders: investors (stockholders) and long-term creditors.
• When calculating ROI, RI, or EVA, are there any measurement issues of concern?	If the net book value of assets is used to measure average total assets, ROI, RI, and EVA will "artificially" rise over time due to the depreciation of the assets. Using gross book value to measure average total assets eliminates this measurement issue. Many firms use the average balance of total assets, rather than the beginning or ending balance of assets, when they calculate ROI, RI, and EVA.

Summary Problem 24-2

Assume Smart Touch expects each division to earn a 16% target rate of return. Smart Touch's weighted average cost of capital (WACC) is 13% and its effective income tax rate is 30%. Assume the company's original CD Division (an investment center) had the following results last year:

Operating income	$ 1,450,000,000
Average total assets	16,100,000,000
Current liabilities	3,600,000,000
Sales	26,500,000,000

Requirements

1. Compute the CD Division's profit margin, asset turnover, and ROI. Round your results to three decimal places. Interpret the results in relation to the e-learning and DVD Divisions discussed in the chapter.
2. Compute and interpret the CD Division's RI.
3. Compute the CD Division's EVA. What does this tell you?
4. What can you conclude based on all three financial performance KPIs?

Solution

Requirement 1

ROI =	Profit margin	×	Asset turnover
=	(Operating income ÷ Sales)	×	(Sales ÷ Average total assets)
= ($1,450,000,000 ÷ $26,500,000,000) × ($26,500,000,000 ÷ $16,100,000,000)			
=	0.055	×	1.646
=	0.091		

The original CD Division is far from meeting top management's expectations. Its ROI is only 9.1%. The profit margin of 5.5% is slightly lower than the e-learning Division and significantly lower than both divisions (6% for e-learning and 19% for the DVD Division). The asset turnover (1.646) is much lower than the e-learning Division (3 asset turnover) but much higher than the DVD Division asset turnover of 0.81. This means that the original CD Division is not generating sales from its average total assets as efficiently as the e-learning Division but is more efficient than the DVD Division. Division management needs to consider ways to increase the efficiency with which it uses divisional average total assets.

Requirement 2

RI = Operating income − (Target rate of return × Average total assets)
= $ 1,450,000,000 − (16% × $16,100,000,000)
= $ 1,450,000,000 − $2,576,000,000
= $(1,126,000,000)

The negative RI confirms the ROI results: The division is not meeting management's target rate of return.

Requirement 3

$$EVA = \text{After-tax operating income} - [(\text{Average total assets} - \text{Current liabilities}) \times \text{WACC\%}]$$

$$= (\$1,450,000,000 \times 70\%) - [(\$16,100,000,000 - \$3,600,000,000) \times 13\%]$$

$$= \$1,015,000,000 - (\$12,500,000,000) \times 13\%)$$

$$= \$1,015,000,000 - \$1,625,000,000$$

$$= \$(610,000,000)$$

The negative EVA means that the division is not generating after-tax operating income for investors (stockholders) and long-term creditors at the rate desired by these stakeholders.

Requirement 4

All three investment center financial performance KPIs (ROI, RI, and EVA) point to the same conclusion: The original CD Division is not meeting financial expectations. Either top management and stakeholders' expectations are unrealistic or the division is not *currently* performing up to par. Recall, however, that financial performance measures tend to be lag indicators—measuring the results of decisions made in the past. The division's managers may currently be implementing new initiatives to improve the division's future profitability. Lead indicators should be used to project whether such initiatives are pointing the company in the right direction.

Review *Performance Evaluation and the Balanced Scorecard*

● Accounting Vocabulary

Asset Turnover (p. 1167)
The amount of sales revenue generated for every dollar of average total assets; a component of the ROI calculation, computed as sales divided by average total assets.

Balanced Scorecard (p. 1155)
Recognition that management must consider both financial performance measures and operational performance measures when judging the performance of a company and its subunits.

Centralized Companies (p. 1152)
Companies in which all major planning and operating decisions are made by top management.

Decentralized Companies (p. 1152)
Companies that are segmented into different divisions or operating units; unit managers make planning and operating decisions for their unit.

Economic Value Added (EVA) (p. 1169)
A residual income measure calculating the amount of after-tax operating income generated by the company or its divisions in excess of stockholders' and long-term creditors' expectations.

Goal Congruence (p. 1153)
Aligning the goals of unit managers with the goals of top management.

Key Performance Indicator(s) (KPIs) (p. 1156)
Summary performance measures that help managers assess whether the company is achieving its goals.

Lag Indicators (p. 1155)
Performance measures that indicate past performance.

Lead Indicators (p. 1155)
Performance measures that forecast future performance.

Management by Exception (p. 1162)
Directs management's attention to important differences between actual and budgeted amounts.

Profit Margin (p. 1166)
The amount of operating income earned on every dollar of sales; a component of the ROI calculation, computed as operating income divided by sales.

Residual Income (RI) (p. 1168)
A measure of profitability and efficiency, computed as the excess of actual operating income over a specified minimum acceptable operating income.

Return on Investment (ROI) (p. 1166)
A measure of profitability and efficiency, computed as operating income divided by average total assets.

Weighted Average Cost of Capital (WACC) (p. 1169)
The company's cost of capital; the minimum rate of return expected by stockholders and long-term creditors.

● Destination: Student Success

Student Success Tips

The following are hints on some common trouble areas for students in this chapter:

● Recall that companies decentralize as they grow.

● Keep in mind the advantages and disadvantages of decentralization.

● Remember that performance measurement systems are in place to help management communicate and evaluate goals to the various subunits in the company.

● Keep in mind the four perspectives of the balanced scorecard: financial, customer, internal business, and learning and growth perspective.

● Recall that the performance reports highlight variances between the budget plan and actual results. These variances signal to managers where to focus their time.

● Keep in mind that ROI, RI, and EVA are all financial performance measurement KPIs. Review Exhibit 24-8 for the formulas and advantages of each.

Getting Help

If there's a learning objective from the chapter you aren't confident about, try using one or more of the following resources:

● Review Decision Guidelines 24-1 and 24-2 in the chapter.

● Review Summary Problem 24-1 in the chapter to reinforce your understanding of the four perspectives of the balanced scorecard.

● Review Summary Problem 24-2 in the chapter to reinforce your understanding of ROI, RI, and EVA.

● Practice additional exercises or problems at the end of Chapter 24 that cover the specific learning objective that is challenging you.

● Watch the white board videos for Chapter 24, located at myaccountinglab.com under the Chapter Resources button.

● Go to myaccountinglab.com and select the Study Plan button. Choose Chapter 24 and work the questions covering that specific learning objective until you've mastered it.

● Work the Chapter 24 pre/post tests in myaccountinglab.com.

● Visit the learning resource center on your campus for tutoring.

● Quick Check

1. Which is *not* one of the potential advantages of decentralization?

    a. Improves motivation and retention   c. Improves customer relations

    b. Supports use of expert knowledge   d. Increases goal congruence

2. The **Quaker Foods** division of **PepsiCo** is most likely treated as a(n)

    a. revenue center.   c. investment center.

    b. cost center.   d. profit center.

3. Decentralization is often based on all the following except

    a. revenue size.   c. business function.

    b. geographic region.   d. product line.

4. Which of the following is NOT a goal of performance evaluation systems?

    a. Promoting goal congruence and coordination

    b. Communicating expectations

    c. Providing feedback

    d. Reprimanding unit managers

5. Which of the following balanced scorecard perspectives essentially asks, "Can we continue to improve and create value?"

    a. Customer   c. Financial

    b. Learning and growth   d. Internal business

The following data applies to questions 6 through 9. Assume the Residential Division of Kipper Faucets had the following results last year:

Sales..................... $	4,160,000	Management's target rate of return	18%
Operating income...........	1,040,000	WACC.................................	15%
Average total assets	5,200,000		
Current liabilities	200,000		

6. What is the division's profit margin?

    a. 400%   c. 25%

    b. 20%   d. 80%

7. What is the division's asset turnover?

    a. 0.20   c. 1.25

    b. 0.80   d. 0.25

8. What is the division's ROI?

    a. 20%   c. 500%

    b. 25%   d. 80%

9. What is the division's RI?

    a. $(140,000)   c. $140,000

    b. $104,000   d. $(104,000)

10. The performance evaluation of a cost center is typically based on its

    a. sales volume variance.   c. static budget variance.

    b. ROI.   d. flexible budget variance.

Answers are given after Apply Your Knowledge (p. 1190).

Experience the Power of Practice!

As denoted by the logo, all of these questions, as well as additional practice materials, can be found in *MyAccountingLab*.

Please visit myaccountinglab.com

Assess Your Progress

● Short Exercises

S24-1 ❶ **Explaining why and how companies decentralize [5 min]**
Decentralization divides company operations into various reporting units. Most decentralized subunits can be described as one of four different types of responsibility centers.

Requirements

1. Explain why companies decentralize. Describe some typical methods of decentralization.

2. List the four most common types of responsibility centers and describe their responsibilities.

S24-2 ❶ **Explaining why and how companies decentralize [5 min]**
Each of the following managers has been given certain decision-making authority:

    a. Manager of Holiday Inn's Central Reservation Office
    b. Managers of various corporate-owned Holiday Inn locations
    c. Manager of the Holiday Inn Corporate Division
    d. Manager of the Housekeeping Department at a Holiday Inn
    e. Manager of the Holiday Inn Express Corporate Division
    f. Manager of the complimentary breakfast buffet at a Holiday Inn Express

Requirement

1. Classify each of the managers according to the type of responsibility center they manage.

S24-3 ❷ **Explaining why companies use performance evaluation systems [5 min]**
Well-designed performance evaluation systems accomplish many goals. Consider the following actions:

a. Comparing targets to actual results
b. Providing subunit managers with performance targets
c. Comparing actual results with industry standards
d. Providing bonuses to subunit managers who achieve performance targets
e. Aligning subunit performance targets with company strategy
f. Comparing actual results to the results of competitors
g. Taking corrective actions
h. Using the adage, "you get what you measure," when designing the performance evaluation system

Requirement

1. State which goal is being achieved by the action.

S24-4 ❸ **Describing the balanced scorecard and identifying key performance indicators for each perspective [5–10 min]**

Consider the following key performance indicators:

a. Number of employee suggestions implemented
b. Revenue growth
c. Number of on-time deliveries
d. Percentage of sales force with access to real-time inventory levels
e. Customer satisfaction ratings
f. Number of defects found during manufacturing
g. Number of warranty claims
h. ROI
i. Variable cost per unit
j. Percentage of market share
k. Number of hours of employee training
l. Number of new products developed
m. Yield rate (number of units produced per hour)
n. Average repair time
o. Employee satisfaction
p. Number of repeat customers

Requirement

1. Classify each of the preceding key performance indicators according to the balanced scorecard perspective it addresses. Choose from financial perspective, customer perspective, internal business perspective, or learning and growth perspective.

S24-5 ❹ **Using performance reports to evaluate cost, revenue, and profit centers [5 min]**

Management by exception is a term often used in performance evaluation.

Requirement

1. Describe management by exception and how it is used in the evaluation of cost, revenue, and profit centers.

S24-6 ❺ **Using ROI, RI, and EVA to evaluate investment centers [5–10 min]**

Consider the following data:

	Domestic	International
Operating income	$ 7,000,000	$ 8,000,000
Average total assets	23,000,000	31,000,000

Requirement

1. Which of the corporate divisions is more profitable? Explain.

S24-7 ⑤ **Using ROI, RI, and EVA to evaluate investment centers [5–10 min]**

Extreme Sports Company makes snowboards, downhill skis, cross-country skis, skateboards, surfboards, and in-line skates. The company has found it beneficial to split operations into two divisions based on the climate required for the sport: Snow sports and Non-snow sports. The following divisional information is available for the past year:

	Sales	Operating Income	Average Total Assets	Current Liabilities	ROI
Snow sports	$ 5,500,000	$ 935,000	$ 4,500,000	$ 420,000	20.8%
Non-snow sports	8,400,000	1,428,000	6,700,000	695,000	21.3%

Extreme's management has specified a 16% target rate of return. The company's weighted average cost of capital (WACC) is 10% and its effective tax rate is 38%.

Requirement

1. Calculate each division's profit margin. Interpret your results.

Note: Short Exercise 24-7 should be completed before attempting Short Exercise 24-8.

S24-8 ⑤ **Using ROI, RI, and EVA to evaluate investment centers [10 min]**

Refer to the information in S24-7.

Requirements

1. Compute each division's asset turnover (round to two decimal places). Interpret your results.
2. Use your answers to Requirement 1, along with the profit margin, to recalculate ROI using the expanded formula. Do your answers agree with the basic ROI in S24-7?

Note: Short Exercise 24-7 should be completed before attempting Short Exercise 24-9.

S24-9 ⑤ **Using ROI, RI, and EVA to evaluate investment centers [5–10 min]**

Refer to the information in S24-7.

Requirement

1. Compute each division's RI. Interpret your results. Are your results consistent with each division's ROI?

Note: Short Exercise 24-7 should be completed before attempting Short Exercise 24-10.

S24-10 ⑤ **Using ROI, RI, and EVA to evaluate investment centers [10–15 min]**

Refer to the information in S24-7.

Requirement

1. Compute each division's EVA. Interpret your results.

● Exercises

MyAccountingLab **E24-11** ① **Identifying responsibility centers after decentralization [10 min]**

Grandpa Joe's Cookie Company sells homemade cookies made with organic ingredients. His sales are strictly Web based. The business is taking off more than Grandpa Joe ever expected, with orders coming from across the country from both consumers and corporate event planners. Grandpa decides to decentralize and hires a full-time baker who will manage production and product cost and a Web designer/sales manager who will focus on increasing sales through the Web site. Grandpa Joe can no longer handle the business on his own, so he hires a business manager to work with the other employees to ensure the company is best utilizing its assets to produce profit. Grandpa will then have time to focus on new product development.

Requirement

1. Now that Grandpa Joe's Cookie Company has decentralized, identify the type of responsibility center that each manager is managing.

E24-12 ❷ **Explaining why companies use performance evaluation systems [5–10 min]**
Financial performance is measured in many ways.

Requirements

1. Explain the difference between lag and lead indicators.

2. The following is a list of financial measures. Indicate whether each is a lag or a lead indicator:

   a. Income statement shows net income of $100,000.
   b. Listing of next week's orders of $50,000.
   c. Trend showing that average hits on the redesigned Web site are increasing at 5% per week.
   d. Price sheet from vendor reflecting that cost per pound of sugar for next month is $2.
   e. Contract signed last month with large retail store that guarantees a minimum shelf space for Grandpa's Overloaded Chocolate Cookies for the next year.

E24-13 ❷ **Explaining why companies use performance evaluation systems [10 min]**
Well-designed performance evaluation systems accomplish many goals.

Requirement

1. Describe the potential benefits performance evaluation systems offer.

E24-14 ❸ **Describing the balanced scorecard and identifying key performance indicators for each perspective [10–15 min]**
Consider the following key performance indicators:

   a. Number of customer complaints
   b. Number of information system upgrades completed
   c. EVA
   d. New product development time
   e. Employee turnover rate
   f. Percentage of products with online help manuals
   g. Customer retention
   h. Percentage of compensation based on performance
   i. Percentage of orders filled each week
   j. Gross margin growth
   k. Number of new patents
   l. Employee satisfaction ratings
   m. Manufacturing cycle time (average length of production process)
   n. Earnings growth
   o. Average machine setup time
   p. Number of new customers
   q. Employee promotion rate
   r. Cash flow from operations
   s. Customer satisfaction ratings
   t. Machine downtime
   u. Finished products per day per employee
   v. Percentage of employees with access to upgraded system
   w. Wait time per order prior to start of production

Requirement

1. Classify each indicator according to the balanced scorecard perspective it addresses. Choose from the financial perspective, customer perspective, internal business perspective, or the learning and growth perspective.

E24-15 ❹ **Using performance reports to evaluate cost, revenue, and profit centers [10–15 min]**

One subunit of Mountain Sports Company had the following financial results last month:

Mountain—Subunit X	Actual	Flexible Budget	Flexible Budget Variance (U or F)	% Variance (U or F)
Direct materials	$ 28,500	$ 26,400		
Direct labor	13,400	14,100		
Indirect labor	26,200	22,700		
Utilities	12,100	11,100		
Depreciation	26,000	26,000		
Repairs and maintenance	4,000	4,900		
Total	$ 110,200	$ 105,200	$	

Requirements

1. Complete the performance evaluation report for this subunit. Enter the variance percent as a percentage rounded to two decimal places.
2. Based on the data presented, what type of responsibility center is this subunit?
3. Which items should be investigated if part of management's decision criteria is to investigate all variances exceeding $2,500 or 10%?
4. Should only unfavorable variances be investigated? Explain.

E24-16 ❹ **Using performance reports to evaluate cost, revenue, and profit centers [15–20 min]**

The accountant for a subunit of Mountain Sports Company went on vacation before completing the subunit's monthly performance report. This is as far as she got:

Mountain—Subunit X Revenue by Product	Actual Results at Actual Prices	Flexible Budget Variance	Flexible Budget for Actual Number of Units Sold	Sales Volume Variance	Static (Master) Budget
Downhill—RI	$ 326,000			$ 19,000 F	$ 301,000
Downhill—RII	154,000		$ 164,000		148,000
Cross—EXI	280,000	$ 1,000 U	281,000		297,000
Cross—EXII	254,000		249,000	16,500 U	265,500
Snow—LXI	424,000	2,000 F			402,000
Total	$ 1,438,000	$	$	$	$ 1,413,500

Requirements

1. Complete the performance evaluation report for this subunit.
2. Based on the data presented, what type of responsibility center is this subunit?
3. Which items should be investigated if part of management's decision criteria is to investigate all variances exceeding $10,000?

E24-17 ⑤ **Using ROI, RI, and EVA to evaluate investment centers [10–15 min]**
Zooms, a national manufacturer of lawn-mowing and snow-blowing equipment, segments its business according to customer type: professional and residential. The following divisional information was available for the past year:

	Sales	Operating Income	Average Total Assets	Current Liabilities
Residential	$ 520,000	$ 64,320	$ 192,000	$ 62,000
Professional	1,020,000	158,760	392,000	143,000

Management has a 26% target rate of return for each division. Zooms' weighted average cost of capital is 13% and its effective tax rate is 27%.

Requirements

1. Calculate each division's ROI. Round all of your answers to four decimal places.
2. Calculate each division's profit margin. Interpret your results.
3. Calculate each division's asset turnover. Interpret your results.
4. Use the expanded ROI formula to confirm your results from Requirement 1. What can you conclude?

Note: Exercise 24-17 should be completed before attempting Exercise 24-18.

E24-18 ⑤ **Using ROI, RI, and EVA to evaluate investment centers [10–15 min]**
Refer to the data in E24-17.

Requirements

1. Calculate each division's RI. Interpret your results.
2. Calculate each division's EVA. Interpret your results.

● Problems (Group A)

P24-19A ① ② ③ ④ **Explaining why and how companies decentralize and why they use performance evaluation systems [30–45 min]** *MyAccountingLab*
One subunit of Boxing Sports Company had the following financial results last month:

Subunit X	Flexible Budget for Actual Number of Units Sold	Actual Results at Actual Prices	Flexible Budget Variance (U or F)	% Variance (U or F)
Sales	$ 453,000	$ 479,000		
Variable expenses	250,000	260,000		
Contribution margin	$ 203,000	$ 219,000		
Fixed expenses	52,000	56,000		
Operating income before traceable service department charges	$ 151,000	$ 163,000		
Traceable fixed expenses	33,000	38,000		
Divisional segment margin	$ 118,000	$ 125,000	$	

Requirements

1. Complete the performance evaluation report for this subunit (round to two decimal places).
2. Based on the data presented and your knowledge of the company, what type of responsibility center is this subunit?

3. Which items should be investigated if part of management's decision criteria is to investigate all variances equal to or exceeding $5,000 *and* exceeding 10% (both criteria must be met)?

4. Should only unfavorable variances be investigated? Explain.

5. Is it possible that the variances are due to a higher-than-expected sales volume? Explain.

6. Will management place equal weight on each of the $5,000 variances? Explain.

7. Which balanced scorecard perspective is being addressed through this performance report? In your opinion, is this performance report a lead or a lag indicator? Explain.

8. List one key performance indicator for the three other balanced scorecard perspectives. Make sure to indicate which perspective is being addressed by the indicators you list. Are they lead or lag indicators? Explain.

P24-20A ⑤ **Using ROI, RI, and EVA to evaluate investment centers [30–45 min]**
Consider the following condensed financial statements of Money Freedom, Inc. The company's target rate of return is 10% and its WACC is 7%:

MONEY FREEDOM, INC.		
Comparative Balance Sheet		
As of December 31, 2012 and 2011		
Assets	2012	2011
Cash	$ 77,000	$ 66,000
Account receivable	62,500	28,400
Supplies	500	600
Property, plant, and equipment, net	300,000	200,000
Patents, net	160,000	105,000
Total assets	$ 600,000	$ 400,000
Liabilities and Stockholders' Equity		
Accounts payable	$ 32,000	$ 34,000
Short-term notes payable	146,000	48,000
Long-term notes payable	200,000	130,000
Common stock, no par	200,000	167,500
Retained earnings	22,000	20,500
Total liabilities and stockholders' equity	$ 600,000	$ 400,000

MONEY FREEDOM, INC.	
Income Statement	
For the Year Ended December 31, 2012	
Sales revenue	$5,000,000
COGS	2,900,000
Gross profit	$2,100,000
Operating expenses	1,900,000
Operating income	$ 200,000
Other: Interest expense	(20,000)
Income before income tax expense	$ 180,000
Income tax expense	(63,000)
Net income	$ 117,000

Requirements

1. Calculate the company's profit margin. Interpret your results.

2. Calculate the company's asset turnover. Interpret your results.

3. Use the expanded ROI formula to confirm your results from Requirement 1. Interpret your results.

4. Calculate the company's RI. Interpret your results.

5. Calculate the company's EVA. Interpret your results.

P24-21A ⑤ Using ROI, RI, and EVA to evaluate investment centers [30–45 min]

San Diego Paints is a national paint manufacturer and retailer. The company is segmented into five divisions: Paint stores (branded retail locations), Consumer (paint sold through stores like **Sears** and **Lowe's**), Automotive (sales to auto manufacturers), International, and Administration. The following is selected divisional information for its two largest divisions: Paint stores and Consumer.

	Sales	Operating Income	Average Total Assets	Current Liabilities
Paint stores	$ 3,960,000	$ 476,000	$ 1,400,000	$ 340,000
Consumer	1,275,000	188,000	1,580,000	600,000

Management has specified a 19% target rate of return. The company's weighted average cost of capital is 15%. The company's effective tax rate is 36%.

Requirements

1. Calculate each division's profit margin. Interpret your results.

2. Calculate each division's asset turnover. Interpret your results.

3. Use the expanded ROI formula to confirm your results from Requirement 1. Interpret your results.

4. Calculate each division's RI. Interpret your results and offer a recommendation for any division with negative RI.

5. Calculate each division's EVA. Interpret your results.

6. Describe some of the factors that management considers when setting its minimum target rate of return.

● Problems (Group B)

P24-22B ① ② ③ ④ Explaining why and how companies decentralize and why they use performance evaluation systems [30–45 min]   *MyAccountingLab*

One subunit of Freeway Sports Company had the following financial results last month:

Subunit X	Flexible Budget for Actual Number of Units Sold	Actual Results at Actual Prices	Flexible Budget Variance (U or F)	% Variance (U or F)
Sales	$ 450,000	$ 478,000		
Variable expenses	253,000	263,000		
Contribution margin	$ 197,000	$ 215,000		
Fixed expenses	50,000	55,000		
Operating income before traceable service department charges	$ 147,000	$ 160,000		
Traceable fixed expenses	30,000	40,000		
Divisional segment margin	$ 117,000	$ 120,000	$	

Requirements

1. Complete the performance evaluation report for this subunit (round to two decimal places).

2. Based on the data presented and your knowledge of the company, what type of responsibility center is this subunit?

3. Which items should be investigated if part of management's decision criteria is to investigate all variances equal to or exceeding $10,000 *and* exceeding 10% (both criteria must be met)?

4. Should only unfavorable variances be investigated? Explain.

5. Is it possible that the variances are due to a higher-than-expected sales volume? Explain.

6. Will management place equal weight on each of the $10,000 variances? Explain.

7. Which balanced scorecard perspective is being addressed through this performance report? In your opinion, is this performance report a lead or a lag indicator? Explain.

8. List one key performance indicator for the three other balanced scorecard perspectives. Make sure to indicate which perspective is being addressed by the indicators you list. Are they lead or lag indicators? Explain.

P24-23B ⑤ **Using ROI, RI, and EVA to evaluate investment centers [30–45 min]**
Consider the following condensed financial statements of Secure Life, Inc. The company's target rate of return is 12% and its WACC is 9%:

SECURE LIFE, INC. Comparative Balance Sheet As of December 31, 2013 and 2012		
Assets	**2013**	**2012**
Cash	$ 82,000	$ 50,000
Accounts receivable	54,000	20,500
Supplies	1,000	500
Property, plant, and equipment, net	275,000	180,000
Patents, net	138,000	99,000
Total assets	$550,000	$350,000
Liabilities and Stockholders' Equity		
Accounts payable	$ 40,000	$ 32,000
Short-term notes payable	135,000	45,000
Long-term notes payable	170,000	125,000
Common stock, no par	150,000	130,000
Retained earnings	55,000	18,000
Total liabilities and stockholders' equity	$550,000	$350,000

SECURE LIFE, INC. Income Statement For the Year Ended December 31, 2013	
Sales revenue	$6,750,000
COGS	3,200,000
Gross profit	$3,550,000
Operating expenses	1,525,000
Operating income	$2,025,000
Other: Interest expense	(17,000)
Income before income tax expense	$2,008,000
Income tax expense	(702,800)
Net income	$1,305,200

Requirements

1. Calculate the company's profit margin. Interpret your results.

2. Calculate the company's asset turnover. Interpret your results.

3. Use the expanded ROI formula to confirm your results from Requirement 1. Interpret your results.

4. Calculate the company's RI. Interpret your results.

5. Calculate the company's EVA. Interpret your results.

P24-24B 5 **Using ROI, RI, and EVA to evaluate investment centers [30–45 min]**

Bear Paints is a national paint manufacturer and retailer. The company is segmented into five divisions: Paint stores (branded retail locations), Consumer (paint sold through stores like **Sears** and **Lowe's**), Automotive (sales to auto manufacturers), International, and Administration. The following is selected divisional information for its two largest divisions: Paint stores and Consumer:

	Sales	Operating Income	Average Total Assets	Current Liabilities
Paint stores	$ 3,940,000	$ 477,000	$ 1,410,000	$ 343,000
Consumer	1,310,000	185,000	1,575,000	605,000

Management has specified a 21% target rate of return. The company's weighted average cost of capital is 14%. The company's effective tax rate is 34%.

Requirements

1. Calculate each division's profit margin. Interpret your results.

2. Calculate each division's asset turnover. Interpret your results.

3. Use the expanded ROI formula to confirm your results from Requirement 1. Interpret your results.

4. Calculate each division's RI. Interpret your results and offer a recommendation for any division with negative RI.

5. Calculate each division's EVA. Interpret your results.

6. Describe some of the factors that management considers when setting its minimum target rate of return.

• Continuing Exercise

E24-25 ⑤ **Calculating profit margin for an investment center [10–15 min]**

This exercise continues the Lawlor Lawn Service, Inc., situation from Exercise 23-38 of Chapter 23. Lawlor Lawn Service experienced sales of $500,000 and operating income of $65,000 for 2013. Total assets were $250,000 and total liabilities were $25,000 at the end of 2013. Lawlor's target rate of return is 16% and WACC is 12%. Its 2013 tax rate was 32%.

Requirement

1. Calculate Lawlor's profit margin for 2013.

• Continuing Problem

P24-26 ⑤ **Using ROI, RI, and EVA to evaluate investment centers [10–15 min]**

This problem continues the Draper Consulting, Inc., situation from Problem 23-39 of Chapter 23. Draper Consulting reported 2013 sales of $3,750,000 and operating income of $210,000. Average total assets during 2013 were $600,000 and total liabilities at the end of 2013 were $180,000. Draper's target rate of return is 14% and WACC is 7%. Its 2013 tax rate was 36%.

Requirement

1. Calculate Draper's profit margin, asset turnover, and EVA for 2013.

Apply Your Knowledge

• Decision Case 24-1

Colgate-Palmolive operates two product segments. Using the company Web site, locate segment information for the company's latest published annual report. (*Hint*: Go to the company Web site and look under "for investors." From there, find the information on the "10-K." Within the 10-K, find the Financial Statements and Supplemental Data and look for one of the notes to the financial statements that provides Segment Information.)

Requirements

1. What are the two product segments? Gather data about each segment's net sales, operating income, and identifiable assets.
2. Calculate ROI for each segment.
3. Which segment has the highest ROI? Explain why.
4. If you were on the top management team and could allocate extra funds to only one division, which division would you choose? Why?

● Ethical Issue 24-1

Dixie Irwin is the department manager for Religious Books, a manufacturer of religious books that are sold through Internet companies. Irwin's bonus is based on reducing production costs.

Requirement

1. Irwin has identified a supplier, Cheap Paper, that can provide paper products at a 10% cost reduction. The paper quality is not the same as that of the current paper used in production. If Irwin uses the supplier, he will certainly achieve his personal bonus goals; however, other company goals may be in jeopardy. Identify the key performance issues at risk and recommend a plan of action for Irwin.

● Fraud Case 24-1

Everybody knew Ed McAlister was a brilliant businessman. He had taken a small garbage collection company in Kentucky and built it up to be one of the largest and most profitable waste management companies in the Midwest. But when he was convicted of a massive financial fraud, what surprised everyone was how crude and simple the scheme was. To keep the earnings up and the stock prices soaring, he and his cronies came up with an almost foolishly simple scheme: First, they doubled the useful lives of the dumpsters. That allowed them to cut depreciation expense in half. The following year, they simply increased the estimated salvage value of the dumpsters, allowing them to further reduce depreciation expense. With thousands of dumpsters spread over 14 states, these simple adjustments gave the company an enormous boost to the bottom line. When it all came tumbling down, McAlister had to sell everything he owned to pay for his legal costs and was left with nothing.

Requirements

1. If an asset has either too long a useful life or too high an estimated salvage value, what happens, from an accounting perspective, when that asset is worn out and has to be disposed of?
2. Do the rules of GAAP (generally accepted accounting principles) mandate specific lives for different types of assets? What is the role of the outside auditor in evaluating the reasonableness of depreciation lives and salvage values?

● Team Project 24-1

Each group should identify one public company's product that it wishes to evaluate. The team should gather all the information it can about the product.

Requirement

1. Develop a list of key performance indicators for the product.

● Communication Activity 24-1

In 150 words or fewer, list each of the four perspectives of the balanced scorecard. Give an example of one KPI from each of the perspectives and explain what measure the KPI provides for a retailing business.

Quick Check Answers

1. *d* 2. *c* 3. *a* 4. *d* 5. *b* 6. *c* 7. *b* 8. *a* 9. *b* 10. *d*

For online homework, exercises, and problems that provide you immediate feedback, please visit myaccountinglab.com.

P Partnerships

BRIGHT & GONZALEZ SOFTWARE — Balance Sheet — June 1, 2013			
Assets		**Liabilities**	
Cash	$ 15,000	Accounts payable	$ 80,000
Inventory	40,000	**Owners' Equity**	
Computer equipment	55,000	**Bright, capital**	**25,000**
Computer software	18,000	**Gonzalez, capital**	**23,000**
Total assets	$128,000	Total liabilities and owners' equity	$128,000

Partnerships have two or more owners.

Learning Objectives

1. Identify the characteristics and types of partnerships

2. Account for partner investments

3. Allocate profits and losses to the partners

4. Account for the admission of a new partner

5. Account for a partner's withdrawal from the firm

6. Account for the liquidation of a partnership

7. Prepare partnership financial statements

Sheena Bright is considering starting a new software business with her friend, Martin Gonzalez. They have already talked about the product development, marketing, and sales goals. Now they just have to finalize how they will operate. They decide a **partnership** will work best for their needs and decide to draft a plan for the Bright & Gonzalez partnership.

Forming a partnership is easy. It requires no permission from the government and no outside legal procedures. A partnership combines the assets and abilities of the partners. New opportunities may open up as Sheena Bright and Martin Gonzalez pool their talents and resources. By forming a partnership, they can offer a fuller range of goods and services than each one of them alone can provide.

Partnerships come in all sizes. Many have just two owners, but some are quite large. Exhibit P-1 lists the largest U.S. accounting firms that are organized as partnerships.

EXHIBIT P-1 | **The Four Largest U.S. Accounting Firms**

Deloitte & Touche
Ernst & Young
PricewaterhouseCoopers
KPMG

Source: Adapted from *Accounting Today,* Top 100 Firms 2010 (http://digital.webcpa.com/top100firms/2010#pg18)

You have learned how to account for sole proprietorships and corporations. However, partnership accounting is different. In this chapter, we'll address these differences using Bright and Gonzalez's new partnership.

● ● ●

Characteristics and Types of Partnerships

1 Identify the characteristics and types of partnerships

Let's look at some characteristics and types of partnerships.

Partnership Characteristics

A partnership is voluntary. You can't be forced to join one, and you can't be forced to accept another person as a partner. Partnerships differ from proprietorships and corporations in the following ways.

The Written Agreement

A partnership is somewhat like a marriage. To be successful, the partners must cooperate. But, the partners don't vow to remain together for life. To increase the partners' understanding of how the business is run, they should draw up a **partnership agreement,** also called the **articles of partnership.** This agreement is a contract between the partners and is governed by contract law. **The partnership agreement outlines the rules of the partnership.** The articles of partnership should specify the following:

1. Name, location, and nature of the business

2. Name, capital investment, and duties of each partner

3. Procedures for admitting a new partner

4. Method of sharing profits and losses among the partners

5. Drawing of assets by the partners

6. Procedures for settling up with a partner who withdraws from the firm

7. Procedures for liquidating the partnership—selling the assets, paying the liabilities, and giving any remaining cash to the partners

Limited Life

A partnership has a limited life. Any change in the existing partners, whether someone withdraws, dies, or a new partner is added, causes the old partnership to dissolve. **Dissolution** is the ending of a partnership. The addition of a new partner dissolves the old partnership but creates a new partnership.

Mutual Agency

Mutual agency means that every partner is a mutual agent of the firm. Any partner can bind the business to a contract within the scope of its regular business operations. If Sheena Bright, a partner in the firm of Bright & Gonzalez, contracts to pay a debt, then the firm of Bright & Gonzalez—not just Bright—owes the liability. If Bright signs a contract to buy her own car, however, the partnership is not liable because it is a personal matter for Bright.

Unlimited Liability

Each partner has **unlimited personal liability** for the debts of the business. When a partnership can't pay its debts, the partners must pay with their personal assets.

Suppose Bright & Gonzalez can't pay a $20,000 business debt. Then Bright & Gonzalez each become personally liable for the $20,000 because each partner has *unlimited liability* for the business's debts. If either partner can't pay his or her part of the debt, the other partner must pay the total. For example, if Bright can pay only $5,000 of the liability, Gonzalez must pay $15,000. If Bright can't pay anything, Gonzalez must pay the full $20,000.

Co-Ownership of Property

Any asset—cash, inventory, computers, and so on—that a partner invests in the partnership becomes the property of the partnership. The partner who invested the asset is no longer its sole owner.

No Partnership Income Tax

A partnership pays no business income tax. Instead, the net income of the business flows through and becomes the individual taxable income of the partners. Suppose the Bright & Gonzalez firm earned net income of $200,000, shared equally by the partners. The firm pays no income tax *as a business entity.* But Bright and Gonzalez each pay personal income tax on $100,000 of partnership income.

Partners' Capital Accounts

Accounting for a partnership is much like accounting for a proprietorship. Since a partnership has more than one partner (owner), each partner needs a separate capital account. For example, the equity account for Sheena Bright is Bright, capital. Similarly, each partner has a withdrawal account such as Bright, drawing.

Exhibit P-2 lists the advantages and disadvantages of partnerships (compared with proprietorships and corporations). As you can see, most features of a proprietorship also apply to a partnership:

- Limited life
- Unlimited liability
- No business income tax

| EXHIBIT P-2 | Advantages and Disadvantages of Partnerships |

Partnership Advantages	Partnership Disadvantages
Versus Proprietorships: 1. Partnership can raise more capital. 2. Partnership brings together the abilities of more than one person. 3. Partners working well together can add more value than by working alone. $1 + 1 > 2$ in a good partnership. *Versus Corporations:* 1. Partnership is less expensive to organize than a corporation, which requires a charter from the state. 2. There's no double taxation. Partnership income is taxed only to the partners as individuals.	1. Partnership agreement may be difficult to formulate. Each time a new partner is admitted or a partner withdraws, the business needs a new partnership agreement. 2. Relations among partners may be fragile. 3. Mutual agency and unlimited liability create personal obligations for each partner.

Types of Partnerships

There are two basic types of partnerships: general and limited.

General Partnership

A **general partnership** is the basic form. Each partner is a co-owner of the business with all the privileges and risks of ownership. The profits and losses of the partnership pass through to the partners, who then pay personal income tax on their income. All the other features we just covered also apply to a general partnership.

Limited Partnership

A **limited partnership** has at least two classes of partners. There must be at least one *general partner,* who takes primary responsibility. The general partner also takes most of the risk if the partnership goes bankrupt. Usually, the general partner is the last owner to receive a share of profits and losses. But the general partner often gets all the excess profit after the limited partners get their share of the income.

The *limited partners* have limited liability for partnership debts. Their liability is limited to their investment in the business. Limited partners usually have first claim to profits and losses, but only up to a certain limit. In exchange for their limited liability, their potential for profits is also limited.

Most accounting firms—including those in Exhibit P-1—are organized as **limited liability partnerships,** or **LLPs.** That means each partner's personal liability for business debts is limited to a certain amount. The LLP must carry a large insurance policy to protect the public in case the partnership is found guilty of malpractice. Medical, legal, and other professional firms are also organized as LLPs.

There are other forms of business that have some characteristics that are similar to a partnership.

Other Forms of Business

Limited Liability Company (LLC)

A **limited liability company (LLC)** is its own form of business organization—neither a partnership nor a corporation. It combines the advantages of both. The LLC form is perhaps the most flexible way to organize a business because the owners, called *members,* have numerous choices.

The features of a limited liability company that parallel a *corporation* are as follows:

- The LLC must file articles of organization with the state.
- The business name must include "LLC" or a similar designation to alert the public about the limited liability of the members.
- The members are *not* personally liable for the business's debts. This is one of the chief advantages of an LLC compared to a proprietorship or a partnership.

The features of an LLC similar to a *partnership* are as follows:

- The LLC can elect *not* to pay business income tax. The income of the LLC can be taxed to the members as though they were partners. This is the other big advantage of an LLC as compared to a corporation. Corporations pay a corporate income tax. Then the stockholders pay personal income tax on any dividends they receive from the corporation. This is why we say that corporations face *double taxation.*
- The members (owners of the LLC) can participate actively in management of the business.
- The accounting for an LLC follows the pattern for a partnership.

S Corporation

An **S corporation** is a corporation with fewer than 100 stockholders that elects to be taxed as a partnership. This form of business organization comes from Subchapter S of the U.S. Internal Revenue Code. An S corporation offers its owners the benefits of a corporation—no personal liability for business debts—and of a partnership—no double taxation. An ordinary (Subchapter C) corporation is subject to double taxation.

An S corporation pays no corporate income tax. Instead, the corporation's income flows through to the stockholders (on a K-1 form), who pay personal income tax on their share of the S corporation's income.

Exhibit P-3 summarizes this section by showing the features of the different types of business organization.

EXHIBIT P-3 | **Features of the Different Types of Business Organization**

Organization	Legal Entity	Personal Liability of the Owners	Pays Business Income Tax
Proprietorship	No	Unlimited	No
Partnership	No		No
General partners		Unlimited	
Limited partners		Limited	
Limited Liability			
Company (LLC)	Yes	Limited	No*
S Corporation	Yes	Limited	No
C Corporation	Yes	Limited	Yes

*In some states, a limited liability company can elect to pay corporate income tax.

The Start-Up of a Partnership

 Account for partner investments

Let's examine the start-up of a partnership. The partners may invest both assets and liabilities. These contributions are journalized the same as for a proprietorship—debit the assets and credit the liabilities. The excess—assets minus liabilities—measures each partner's capital contribution.

Suppose Sheena Bright and Martin Gonzalez form a partnership to sell computer software on June 1, 2013. The partners agree on the following values:

Bright's Investment
- Cash, $10,000; inventory, $40,000; and accounts payable, $80,000 (The current market values for these items equal Bright's values.)
- Computer equipment—cost, $80,000; accumulated depreciation, $20,000; *current market value, $55,000*

Gonzalez's Investment
- Cash, $5,000
- Computer software: cost, $20,000; *market value, $18,000*

The partnership records the partners' investments at *current market value*. Why? Because the partnership is buying the assets and assuming the liabilities at their current market values. The partnership journal entries are as follows:

2013				
June 1	Cash (A+)		10,000	
	Inventory (A+)		40,000	
	Computer equipment (A+)		55,000	
		Accounts payable (L+)		80,000
		Bright, capital (Q+)		25,000
	To record Bright's investment.			
June 1	Cash (A+)		5,000	
	Computer software (A+)		18,000	
		Gonzalez, capital (Q+)		23,000
	To record Gonzalez's investment.			

The initial partnership balance sheet appears in Exhibit P-4. The assets and liabilities are the same for a proprietorship and a partnership.

EXHIBIT P-4 | **Partnership Balance Sheet**

BRIGHT & GONZALEZ SOFTWARE
Balance Sheet
June 1, 2013

Assets		Liabilities	
Cash	$ 15,000	Accounts payable	$ 80,000
Inventory	40,000	**Owners' Equity**	
Computer equipment	55,000	Bright, capital	25,000
Computer software	18,000	Gonzalez, capital	23,000
Total assets	$128,000	Total liabilities and owners' equity	$128,000

Key Takeaway

When a partnership is started, each partner contributes assets and liabilities at their current market values. The partnership balance sheet is similar to other balance sheets you've learned about—the main difference is that there are separate capital accounts for each partner.

Sharing Profits and Losses, and Partner Drawings

Allocating profits and losses among partners can be challenging. The partners can agree to any profit-and-loss-sharing method they desire. Typical arrangements include the following:

3 Allocate profits and losses to the partners

1. Sharing of profits and losses based on a stated fraction for each partner, such as 50/50 for two partners or 4:3:3 for three partners (which means you first add the parts, 4 + 3 + 3 parts for 10 total parts, so 4/10 to Partner A, 3/10 to B, and 3/10 to C)

2. Sharing based on each partner's investment

3. Sharing based on each partner's service

4. Sharing based on a combination of stated fractions, investments, and service

If the partners have no agreement as to how to divide profits and losses, then they share equally. If the agreement specifies a method for sharing profits but not losses, then losses are shared the same way as profits. For example, a partner who gets 75% of the profits will absorb 75% of any losses.

Let's see how some of these profit-and-loss-sharing methods work.

Sharing Based on a Stated Fraction

The agreement may state each partner's fraction of the profits and losses. Suppose Bright and Gonzalez allocate 2/3 of the profits and losses to Bright and 1/3 to Gonzalez. This sharing rule can also be expressed as 2:1. If their net income for the year is $60,000, the Income summary account has a credit balance of $60,000 prior to the third closing entry.

The entry to close net income to the partners' capital accounts is as follows:

Clo 3	Dec 31	Income summary	60,000	
		Bright, capital ($60,000 × 2/3) (Q+)		40,000
		Gonzalez, capital ($60,000 × 1/3) (Q+)		20,000
		To close net income to the partners.		

After posting, the accounts appear as follows:

Income summary		
Clo 3	60,000	60,000
	Bal	0

Bright, capital		
	Jun 1	25,000
	Clo 3	40,000
	Bal	65,000

Gonzalez, capital		
	Jun 1	23,000
	Clo 3	20,000
	Bal	43,000

If instead the partnership had a net loss of $15,000, the Income summary account would have a debit balance of $15,000, as follows:

Income summary	
Bal	15,000

In that case, Bright takes a hit for 2/3 of the loss, and records the closing entry as follows:

Clo 3	Dec 31	Bright, capital ($15,000 × 2/3) (Q–)	10,000	
		Gonzalez, capital ($15,000 × 1/3) (Q–)	5,000	
		Income summary		15,000
		To close net loss to the partners.		

After posting the loss, the account balances are as follows:

Income summary		
15,000	Clo 3	15,000
Bal 0		

Bright, capital		
	Jun 1	$25,000
Clo 3	10,000	
	Bal	$15,000

Gonzalez, capital		
	Jun 1	$23,000
Clo 3	5,000	
	Bal	$18,000

Sharing Based on Capital Balances and on Service

One partner may invest more capital. Another may work more hours in the business. Even among partners who log equal time, one partner may have contributed more capital to the firm. Therefore, the profits and losses may be divided based on a combination of partner capital balances *and* service.

Let's reconsider Bright & Gonzalez's original agreement. Bright invested $25,000 in capital, whereas Gonzalez invested only $23,000. But Gonzalez devotes more time to the business. Accordingly, the two partners have agreed to share profits as follows:

1. The first allocations are based on 10% of partner capital balances.

2. The next $40,000 is allocated based on service, with Bright getting $16,000 and Gonzalez $24,000.

3. Any remaining profit is allocated equally.

Since the agreement specifies three steps, all three steps must be performed whenever the partnership allocates profits or losses. The partnership's net income for the first year is still $60,000, but the partners share this profit as follows:

		Bright	Gonzalez	Total
	Total net income			$60,000
1	Sharing 10% of capital balances:			
	Bright ($25,000 × 10%)	$ 2,500		
	Gonzalez ($23,000 × 10%)		$ 2,300	
	Total			(4,800)
	Net income remaining for allocation			$55,200
2	Sharing of next $40,000, based on service:	16,000	24,000	(40,000)
	Net income remaining for allocation			15,200
3	Remainder shared equally: ($15,200 × 1/2)	7,600	7,600	(15,200)
	Net income remaining for allocation			$ 0
	Net income allocated to the partners	$26,100	$33,900	$60,000

For this allocation, the closing entry would now be as follows:

Clo 3	Dec 31	Income summary		60,000	
		Bright, capital (Q+)			26,100
		Gonzalez, capital (Q+)			33,900
		To close net income to the partners.			

What happens if this same income sharing agreement were in place, but Bright & Gonzalez incurred total net loss of $15,000? Since the partnership sharing agreement has three steps, the allocation of the net loss also goes through all three steps as follows:

		Bright	Gonzalez	Total
	Total net loss			$(15,000)
1	Sharing 10% of capital balances:			
	Bright: $25,000 × 10%	$ 2,500		
	Gonzalez: $23,000 × 10%		$ 2,300	
	Total			(4,800)
	Net loss remaining for allocation			$(19,800)
2	Sharing of next $40,000, based on service:	16,000	24,000	(40,000)
	Net loss remaining for allocation			$(59,800)
3	Remainder shared equally: [($59,800) × 1/2]	(29,900)	(29,900)	59,800
	Net loss remaining for allocation			$ 0
	Net loss allocated to the partners	$(11,400)	$(3,600)	$(15,000)

The closing entry to allocate the $15,000 loss under this three-level sharing agreement is as follows:

Clo 3	Dec 31	Bright, capital (Q–)	11,400	
		Gonzalez, capital (Q–)	3,600	
		Income summary		15,000
		To close net loss to the partners.		

Stop & Think...

Dave, Mike, and Joe decide to buy a pizza. The pizza is pre-cut into eight slices. How will they divide up the pizza? Maybe they decide that Dave will get four slices and Mike and Joe will each get two slices. If Dave is not as hungry and only has two slices, Mike and Joe will each get three slices. The dividing of the pizza is like a partnership profit-and-loss-sharing agreement. In the first example, the sharing would be 4:2:2; in the second example, it would be 2:3:3.

Partner Drawings of Cash and Other Assets

Partners don't earn a salary; rather, they withdraw cash or other assets from the partnership based on what is allowed by the written partnership agreement. Drawings (withdrawals) from a partnership are recorded in a contra equity account. Assume that Sheena Bright and Martin Gonzalez each made withdrawals of $3,000. The partnership records the December 31 withdrawals with the following entry:

	Dec 31	Bright, drawing (D+)	3,000	
		Gonzalez, drawing (D+)	3,000	
		Cash (A–)		6,000
		Partner withdrawals of cash.		

The general ledger shows these partner drawing accounts:

Bright, drawing		Gonzalez, drawing	
Dec 31	3,000	Dec 31	3,000

The drawing accounts are closed at the end of the period, exactly as for a proprietorship: Credit each partner's drawing account and debit his or her capital account:

Clo 4	Dec 31	Bright, capital (Q–)	3,000	
		Gonzalez, capital (Q–)	3,000	
		Bright, drawing (D–)		3,000
		Gonzalez, drawing (D–)		3,000
		To close the partners' drawing accounts.		

Key Takeaway

The partnership agreement should specify how the partners will share profits and losses. If the agreement is silent, the partners share profits and losses equally. If the agreement has multiple steps, all steps must be applied each time the partnership allocates profits or losses. Each partner has a separate drawing account. That account is closed to the partner's capital account during the closing process.

Now, what would Bright and Gonzalez's capital accounts look like assuming the $60,000 net income with the three-level sharing agreement and the drawings as shown previously?

Bright, capital				Gonzalez, capital			
		Jun 1	$25,000			Jun 1	$23,000
		Clo 3	26,100			Clo 3	33,900
Clo 4	3,000			Clo 4	3,000		
		Bal	$48,100			Bal	$53,900

Admission of a Partner

Admitting a new partner dissolves the old partnership and begins a new one. **Any time the partner mix changes, the old partnership ceases to exist and a new partnership begins.** Often, the new partnership continues the original partnership's type of business. Let's look at the ways a new owner can be added to a partnership.

4 Account for the admission of a new partner

Admission by Purchasing an Existing Partner's Interest

A person can become a partner by purchasing an existing partner's interest. First, however, the new person must gain the approval of the other partners.

The Bright & Gonzalez partnership has these balances at December 31, 2013:

EXHIBIT P-5 | **Partnership Balance Sheet**

BRIGHT & GONZALEZ
Balance Sheet
December 31, 2013

Assets		Liabilities and Owners' Equity	
Cash	$ 40,000	Accounts payable	$ 70,000
Inventory	76,000	Bright, capital	48,100
Computer equipment, net	44,000	Gonzalez, capital	53,900
Computer software, net	12,000		
Total assets	$172,000	Total liabilities and owners' equity	$172,000

Suppose Bright wants out and Barry Holt, an outside party, buys Bright's interest on January 1, 2014.

Gonzalez accepts Holt as a partner, and Bright agrees to accept $50,000. The partnership records the transfer of capital interest with the following entry:

Jan 1	Bright, capital	(Q–)		48,100	
	Holt, capital	(Q+)			48,100
	To transfer Bright's equity to Holt.				

Bright, capital				Holt, capital			Gonzalez, capital		
Jan 1	48,100	Bal	48,100		Bal	48,100		Jan 1	53,900
			0						

The debit closes Bright's capital account, and the credit sets up Holt's capital, as shown in the T-accounts. The entry amount is Bright's capital balance of $48,100 and not the $50,000 that Holt paid Bright. Why $48,100?

In this example, the partnership receives no cash because the transaction was between Holt and Bright, not between Holt and the partnership. The full $50,000 went to Bright. Suppose Holt pays Bright less than her capital balance—say, $40,000. The entry on the partnership books is not affected. Bright's equity is transferred to Holt at book value of $48,100.

The old partnership of Bright & Gonzalez has dissolved. Gonzalez and Holt draw up a new agreement with a new profit-and-loss-sharing method and continue in business. If Gonzalez does not accept Holt as a partner, then Holt gets no voice in management. But under the Uniform Partnership Act, Holt shares in the profits and losses of the firm and in its assets at liquidation.

Admission by Investing in the Partnership

A person can enter a partnership by investing directly in the business. (This is different from buying out an existing partner, as in the preceding example.) Here the new partner invests assets—for example, cash or equipment—in the business. Refer back to Exhibit P-5, the balance sheet of Bright & Gonzalez on December 31, 2013 (before the Holt transaction).

Let's consider several possible alternate ways to add a new partner.

Admission by Investing in the Partnership at Book Value—No Bonus to Any Partner

Cheryl Kaska wants into the Bright & Gonzalez partnership on January 1, 2014.

Kaska can invest land with a market value of $51,000. Bright and Gonzalez agree to dissolve their partnership and start up a new one, giving Kaska a 1/3 interest in the new partnership for her $51,000 investment, as follows:

Partnership capital before Kaska is admitted ($48,100 + $53,900)........	$102,000
Kaska's investment in the partnership..	51,000
Partnership capital after Kaska is admitted..	$153,000
Kaska's capital in the new partnership ($153,000 × 1/3)	$ 51,000

Notice that Kaska is buying into the partnership at book value because her 1/3 investment of $51,000 equals 1/3 of the new partnership's total capital of $153,000. The partnership's entry to record Kaska's investment is as follows:

2014			
Jan 1	Land (A+)	51,000	
	Kaska, capital (Q+)		51,000
	To admit Kaska as a partner.		

Kaska's 1/3 interest does not necessarily entitle her to 1/3 of the profits. Remember: The sharing of profits and losses is a separate element from the creation of the partnership agreement.

Admission by Investing in the Partnership—Bonus to the Old Partners

A successful partnership may require a higher payment from a new partner. The old partners may demand a bonus, which will increase their capital accounts.

Refer back to Exhibit P-5, the balance sheet of Bright & Gonzalez on December 31, 2013. Assume instead that Bright and Gonzalez admit Nancy Fry to a 1/4 interest in the new partnership for Fry's cash investment of $98,000. Fry's capital balance on the new partnership books is only $48,000, computed as follows:

Partnership capital before Fry is admitted ($48,100 + $53,900)	$102,000
Fry's investment in the partnership	98,000
Partnership capital after Fry is admitted	$200,000
Fry's capital in the partnership ($200,000 × 1/4)	$ 50,000
Bonus to the old partners ($98,000 − $50,000)	$ 48,000

In effect, Fry had to buy into the partnership at a price ($98,000) above the book value of her 1/4 interest ($50,000). Fry's higher-than-book-value investment creates a *bonus* for Bright and Gonzalez. Assuming Bright and Gonzalez's original partnership agreement had them sharing profits and losses equally, the partnership entry to record the receipt of Fry's investment is as follows:

2014			
Jan 1	Cash (A+)	98,000	
	Fry, capital (Q+)		50,000
	Bright, capital ($48,000 × 1/2) (Q+)		24,000
	Gonzalez, capital ($48,000 × 1/2) (Q+)		24,000
	To admit Fry as a partner.		

Fry's capital account was credited for her 1/4 interest in the new partnership, $50,000. The *bonus* was allocated to Bright and Gonzalez based on their original profit-and-loss-sharing ratio (equally).

Admission by Investing in the Partnership—Bonus to the New Partner

A new partner may be so valuable that the old partners offer a partnership share that includes a bonus to the new person.

Let's go back to our Fry partner admission. On January 2, 2014, Fry gives Bright and Gonzalez $98,000 but instead, gets a 60% interest in the new partnership. The computation of Fry's 60% equity in the new partnership is as follows:

Partnership capital before Fry is admitted ($48,100 + $53,900)	$102,000
Fry's investment in the partnership	98,000
Partnership capital after Fry is admitted	$200,000
Fry's capital in the partnership ($200,000 × 60%)	$120,000
Bonus to the new partner ($120,000 − $98,000)	$ 22,000

In this case, Fry entered the partnership at a price less than the book value of her equity of $120,000. The bonus of $22,000 went to Fry from the other partners so their capital accounts are debited (reduced) for the bonus. The old partners share this decrease in capital as though it were a loss, on the basis of their profit-and-loss-sharing ratio (equally). The entry to record Fry's investment is as follows:

2014			
Jan 2	Cash (A+)	98,000	
	Bright, capital ($22,000 × 1/2) (Q–)	11,000	
	Gonzalez, capital ($22,000 × 1/2) (Q–)	11,000	
	Fry, capital (Q+)		120,000
	To admit Fry as a partner.		

Now let's see how to account for the withdrawal of a partner from the firm.

Withdrawal of a Partner

 5 Account for a partner's withdrawal from the firm

A partner may leave the business for many reasons, including retirement, death, or a dispute. The withdrawal of a partner dissolves the old partnership. The agreement should specify how to settle up with a withdrawing partner. **Any time the partner mix changes, the old partnership ceases to exist and a new partnership begins.**

In the simplest case, a partner may sell his or her interest to another party in a personal transaction. This is the same as admitting a new person who purchases an existing partner's interest, as we saw earlier. The journal entry simply debits the withdrawing partner's capital account and credits the new partner's capital. The dollar amount is the old partner's capital balance, as illustrated for Bright and Holt on page P-11.

Often, however, the withdrawal is more complex, as we shall see next.

Revaluation of Assets

The withdrawing partner may receive assets other than cash. Then the question is what value to assign to the assets—book value or current market value? The settlement procedure often specifies an independent appraisal to determine current market value. If market values are different than book values, the partnership must revalue its assets. The partners share any market-value changes in their profit-and-loss-sharing ratio.

Let's revisit the latest partnership balance sheet for Bright, Gonzalez, and Fry, assuming Fry was admitted with a bonus from the old partners (the $120,000 Fry, capital) on January 2, 2014.

Before any asset appraisal, the partnership balance sheet reports the following:

EXHIBIT P-6 | **Partnership Balance Sheet—After Admitting Fry with a Bonus from the Existing Partners**

BRIGHT, GONZALEZ, & FRY
Balance Sheet
January 2, 2014

Assets		Liabilities and Owners' Equity	
Cash ($40,000 + $98,000)	$138,000	Accounts payable	$ 70,000
Inventory	76,000	Bright, capital ($48,100 – $11,000)	37,100
Computer equipment, net	44,000	Gonzalez, capital ($53,900 – $11,000)	42,900
Computer software, net	12,000	Fry, capital	120,000
Total assets	$270,000	Total liabilities and owners' equity	$270,000

On January 31, 2014, an independent appraiser revalues the inventory at $70,000 (down from $76,000) and the computer equipment at $45,200 (up from $44,000). The partners share the differences between market value and book value on the basis of their profit-and-loss-sharing ratio.

The partnership agreement allocates 1/6 to Bright, 2/6 to Gonzalez, and 3/6 (or 1/2) to Fry. (This ratio may be written 1:2:3.) For each share that Bright has, Gonzalez gets two and Fry gets three. The entries to record the revaluation of the inventory and computer equipment are as follows:

2014			
Jan 31	Bright, capital ($6,000 × 1/6) (Q–)	1,000	
	Gonzalez, capital ($6,000 × 2/6) (Q–)	2,000	
	Fry, capital ($6,000 × 3/6) (Q–)	3,000	
	Inventory ($76,000 – $70,000) (A–)		6,000
	To revalue the inventory.		
31	Computer equipment ($45,200 – $44,000) (A+)	1,200	
	Bright, capital ($1,200 × 1/6) (Q+)		200
	Gonzalez, capital ($1,200 × 2/6) (Q+)		400
	Fry, capital ($1,200 × 3/6) (Q+)		600
	To revalue the computer equipment.		

After the revaluations, the partnership balance sheet reports the following:

EXHIBIT P-7 | **Partnership Balance Sheet—After Revaluation**

BRIGHT, GONZALEZ, & FRY
Balance Sheet
January 31, 2014

Assets		Liabilities and Owners' Equity	
Cash	$138,000	Accounts payable	$ 70,000
Inventory ($76,000 – $6,000)	70,000	Bright, capital ($37,100 – $1,000 + $200)	36,300
Computer equipment, net ($44,000 + $1,200)	45,200	Gonzalez, capital ($42,900 – $2,000 + $400)	41,300
Computer software, net	12,000	Fry, capital ($120,000 – $3,000 + $600)	117,600
Total assets	$265,200	Total liabilities and owners' equity	$265,200

The books now carry the assets at market value, which becomes the new book value, and the capital accounts are up-to-date. As the balance sheet shows, Bright has a claim to $36,300 in partnership assets. Now we can account for Bright's withdrawal from the business.

Withdrawal at Book Value

If Bright withdraws by receiving cash for her book value, the entry will be as follows:

	2014			
	Jan 31	Bright, capital (Q–)	36,300	
		Cash (A–)		36,300
		To record withdrawal of Bright from the partnership.		

Withdrawal at Less Than Book Value

The withdrawing partner may be so eager to depart that she will take less than her full equity interest (capital balance). Assume that Bright withdraws from the business and agrees to receive cash of $10,000 and the new partnership's $20,000 note payable. This $30,000 settlement is $6,300 less than Bright's $36,300 capital balance. The remaining partners share this $6,300 difference—a bonus to them—according to their existing profit-and-loss-sharing ratio. This means the former 1:2:3 ratio is now 2:3 (Gonzalez's and Fry's parts only).

The entry to record Bright's withdrawal at less than her book value is as follows:

	2014			
	Jan 31	Bright, capital (Q–)	36,300	
		Cash (A–)		10,000
		Note payable (L+)		20,000
		Gonzalez, capital ($6,300 × 2/5) (Q+)		2,520
		Fry, capital ($6,300 × 3/5) (Q+)		3,780
		To record withdrawal of Bright from the partnership.		

Bright's capital account is closed, and Gonzalez and Fry may or may not continue in the new partnership of Gonzalez & Fry. If they continue, they will need to draft a new partnership agreement and determine a new profit-and-loss-sharing ratio.

Withdrawal at More Than Book Value

A withdrawing partner may receive assets worth more than the book value of his or her equity. This situation creates the following:

- A bonus to the withdrawing partner
- A decrease in the remaining partners' capital accounts, shared in their profit-and-loss-sharing ratio

Let's assume instead that Bright is given cash of $20,000 and a note payable of $20,000, the total of which is $3,700 ($40,000 – $36,300) more than Bright's capital account of $36,300. The entry for Bright to withdraw under these new assumptions is as follows:

Key Takeaway

The treatment of a partner withdrawal is similar to the treatment of admitting a new partner. First, the partners can agree to a revaluation. Then, the withdrawing partner can be withdrawn at an amount either exactly equal to his or her capital balance or another amount, higher or lower than his or her capital balance. If the withdrawing partner is given an amount different than his or her capital balance, a bonus to either the remaining partners or to the withdrawing partner occurs.

2014				
Jan 31	Bright, capital (Q–)	36,300		
	Gonzalez, capital ($3,700 × 2/5) (Q–)	1,480		
	Fry, capital ($3,700 × 3/5) (Q–)	2,220		
	Cash (A–)		20,000	
	Note payable (L+)		20,000	
	To record withdrawal of Bright from the partnership.			

Liquidation of a Partnership

As we've seen, the admission or withdrawal of a partner dissolves the partnership. However, it may continue operating with no apparent change to outsiders. In contrast, **liquidation** shuts down the firm by selling its assets and paying its liabilities.

6 Account for the liquidation of a partnership

The final step in liquidation is to *distribute any remaining cash to the partners based on their capital balances.* Before a business is liquidated, its books should be adjusted and closed (the four closing steps). Liquidation includes three additional steps:

STEP L1: Sell the assets. Allocate the gain or loss to the partners' capital accounts based on the profit-and-loss-sharing ratio.

STEP L2: Pay all partnership liabilities.

STEP L3: Pay the remaining cash, if any, to the partners based on their capital balances, **NOT** their profit-and-loss-sharing agreement.

The key to liquidation is that all accounts of the company are closed (zeroed out). The liquidation of a business can stretch over weeks or months—a year or longer for a big company. To avoid excessive detail in our illustrations, we include only two asset categories—Cash and Noncash assets—and a single liability—Accounts payable. Our examples assume that the business sells the assets in a single transaction and then pays the liabilities at once.

Akers, Bloch, and Crane have shared profits and losses in the ratio of 3:1:1. (This ratio is equal to 3/5, 1/5, 1/5, or 60%, 20%, 20%, respectively.) The partners decide to liquidate the partnership. After the books are adjusted and closed, the following accounts remain:

EXHIBIT P-8 | **Partnership Balance Sheet—Before Liquidation**

AKERS, BLOCH, AND CRANE
Balance Sheet
October 31, 2014

Assets		Liabilities and Owners' Equity	
Cash	$ 10,000	Accounts payable	$ 30,000
Noncash assets	90,000	Akers, capital	40,000
		Bloch, capital	20,000
		Crane, capital	10,000
Total assets	$100,000	Total liabilities and owners' equity	$100,000

Sale of Assets at a Gain

Assume that Akers, Bloch, and Crane sell the noncash assets for $150,000 (book value, $90,000). The partnership realizes a gain of $60,000, allocated to the partners based on their profit-and-loss ratio. The entry to record this sale and allocate the gain is as follows:

	2014			
L1	Oct 31	Cash (A+)	150,000	
		Noncash assets (A–)		90,000
		Akers, capital ($60,000 × 60%) (Q+)		36,000
		Bloch, capital ($60,000 × 20%) (Q+)		12,000
		Crane, capital ($60,000 × 20%) (Q+)		12,000
		To sell assets.		

Now the partner capital accounts have the following balances:

Akers, capital			Bloch, capital			Crane, capital	
Oct 31	40,000		Oct 31	20,000		Oct 31	10,000
L1	36,000		L1	12,000		L1	12,000
Bal	76,000		Bal	32,000		Bal	22,000

The partnership then pays off its liabilities:

	2014			
L2	Oct 31	Accounts payable (L–)	30,000	
		Cash (A–)		30,000
		To pay liabilities.		

If there is insufficient cash in the partnership to pay its liabilities, the shortfall is a loss to the partnership. Because it's a loss, the partners must contribute cash according to their profit-and-loss-sharing ratio. Remember that partners are personally liable for the debts of the partnership. The final liquidation transaction pays all remaining cash, if any, to the partners *according to their capital balances.*

The amount of cash left in the partnership is $130,000, as follows:

Cash			
Oct 31	10,000	L2	30,000
L1	150,000		
End Bal	130,000		

The partners divide the remaining cash according to their capital balances shown on the previous page:

	2014			
L3	Oct 31	Akers, capital (Q–)	76,000	
		Bloch, capital (Q–)	32,000	
		Crane, capital (Q–)	22,000	
		Cash (A–)		130,000
		To distribute remaining cash based on partners' capital balances.		

Remember:

- Upon liquidation, gains and losses on the sale of assets are divided according to the *profit-and-loss-sharing ratio*.
- The final cash payment to the partners is based on *capital balances*.

After the payment of cash to the partners, the business has no assets, liabilities, or equity. All final balances are zero.

Sale of Assets at a Loss

Liquidation of a business often includes the sale of assets at a loss. When a loss occurs, the partner capital accounts are debited based on the profit-and-loss ratio. Otherwise, the accounting follows the pattern illustrated for the sale at a gain.

Stop & Think...

You and your roommate have just graduated with finance degrees. You decide to have a garage sale and sell everything you both had in your apartment. Before the sale, you put price tags on each item. Red price tags are on your stuff. Yellow price tags are on your friend's stuff. Green price tags are for items you shared. After each sale, you put the red price tags in one column, the yellow in another column, and the green in the last column. At the end of the sale, how would you divide the cash? Take the green tag total and split it 1/2 red and 1/2 yellow. Then, total the red tag total and the yellow tag total. The red tag total + 1/2 the green tag total represents your "capital" account. The yellow tag total + 1/2 the green tag total represents your friend's "capital" account. So, like in a liquidation, you just pay the cash based on the balance in each of your individual capital accounts.

Key Takeaway

To liquidate a partnership, first the partnership must perform the normal end-of-period closing of revenues, expenses, income summary, and drawing accounts. Then, the partnership sells its assets. Any gain or loss on the sale of the assets is allocated to the partners based on their profit-and-loss-sharing ratio from the partnership agreement. Next, the partnership pays off any liabilities it has. Last, if cash remains, the partners' capital balances are paid. When a partnership is completely liquidated, all account balances are zero.

Partnership Financial Statements

 7 Prepare partnership financial statements

Partnership financial statements are similar to the the statements of a proprietorship, but with the following differences:

- A partnership income statement shows the division of net income to the partners. For example, the partnership of Bright & Gonzalez can report its income statement with the three-tiered sharing discussed earlier in the chapter on pages P-8 and P-9 and as shown in Exhibit P-9 below.

- A partnership balance sheet reports a separate capital account for each partner, as shown previously in Exhibit P-5 on page P-11.

EXHIBIT P-9 | **Income Statement of a Partnership**

BRIGHT & GONZALEZ
Income Statement
Year Ended December 31, 2013

Revenues		$470,000
Expenses		410,000
Net income		$ 60,000
Allocation of net income:		
	To Bright	$ 26,100
	To Gonzalez	33,900
Total net income allocated to the partners		$ 60,000

Now turn to the Decision Guidelines on the following page for a summary of the accounting for partnerships.

Key Takeaway

The key difference in a partnership income statement and other types of company income statements is that the allocation of net income/loss is shown on the face of the statement. The key difference in the partnership balance sheet from other balance sheets is the individual capital accounts for each partner are listed in the equity section.

Decision Guidelines P-1

ACCOUNTING FOR PARTNERSHIPS

Suppose you have a friend who's a biology major. He has achieved amazing success cross-breeding fruit trees. He knows trees but has no sense for business, so the two of you form a partnership to take advantage of your respective skills. How do you organize? What decisions must you make? Consider these decision guidelines.

Decision	Guidelines
• How do you organize the business?	Consider forming a partnership, a limited liability partnership, or an S corporation.
• On what matters should the partners agree?	The written partnership agreement should cover all matters of the partnership, including profit sharing, admitting/withdrawing partners, and liquidation.
• At what value does the partnership record assets and liabilities?	Current market value on the date of acquisition.

• How are partnership profits and losses shared among the partners?	• Equally if there is no written profit-and-loss-sharing agreement.
	• As provided in the partnership agreement. Can be based on any combination of the partners'
	  a. Stated fractions
	  b. Capital contributions or a percentage of capital balances
	  c. Service to the partnership

• How are new partners admitted to the partnership?	• *Purchase a partner's interest directly from the partner.* The old partnership is dissolved. The remaining partners may admit the new partner to the partnership. Close the withdrawing partner's capital account balance, and open a capital account for the new partner with the capital balance of the withdrawing partner. • *Invest in the partnership.* Buying in at book value creates no bonus to any partner. Buying in at a price above book value creates a bonus to the old partners. Buying in at a price below book value creates a bonus for the new partner.
• What happens when a partner withdraws from the firm?	The old partnership dissolves. The remaining partners may or may not form a new partnership.

• How does the partnership account for the withdrawal of a partner?	• First, adjust and close the books up to the date of the partner's withdrawal from the business.
	• Second, appraise the assets and liabilities at current market value and record adjusting entries to reflect the market values.
	• Third, account for the partner's withdrawal.
	  a. At book value (no change in remaining partners' capital balances)
	  b. At less than book value (increase the remaining partners' capital balances)
	  c. At more than book value (decrease the remaining partners' capital balances)

• What happens if the partnership goes out of business?	Adjust and close the books up to the date of liquidation. Then, liquidate the partnership, as follows:
	  L1: Sell the partnership's assets. Allocate gain or loss to the partners based on their profit-and-loss-sharing ratio.
	  L2: Pay the partnership liabilities.
	  L3: Pay any remaining cash to the partners based on their capital balances.

Summary Problem P-1

The partnership of Red & White admits Blue as a partner on January 1, 2014. The partnership has these balances on December 31, 2013:

<table>
<tr><td colspan="4" align="center">RED & WHITE
Balance Sheet
December 31, 2013</td></tr>
<tr><td colspan="2" align="center">Assets</td><td colspan="2" align="center">Liabilities and Owners' Equity</td></tr>
<tr><td>Cash</td><td>$ 9,000</td><td>Accounts payable</td><td>$ 50,000</td></tr>
<tr><td>Other assets</td><td>110,000</td><td>Red, capital</td><td>45,000</td></tr>
<tr><td></td><td></td><td>White, capital</td><td>24,000</td></tr>
<tr><td>Total assets</td><td>$119,000</td><td>Total liabilities and owners' equity</td><td>$119,000</td></tr>
</table>

Red's share of profits and losses is 60%, and White gets 40%.

Requirements
(Items 1, 2, and 3 are independent)

1. Suppose Blue pays White $30,000 to buy out White. Red approves Blue as a partner.
   a. Record the transfer of equity on the partnership books on January 1, 2014.
   b. Prepare the partnership balance sheet immediately after Blue is admitted as a partner.
2. Suppose Blue becomes a partner by investing $31,000 cash on January 1, 2014, to acquire a one-fourth interest in the business.
   a. Compute Blue's capital balance, and determine whether there's any bonus. If so, who gets the bonus?
   b. Journalize Blue's investment in the business.
   c. Prepare the partnership balance sheet immediately after Blue is admitted as a partner. Include the heading.
3. Assume the Red & White partnership liquidates by selling its other assets for $100,000. Prepare the entries to liquidate the partnership on January 1, 2014.

Solution

Requirement 1

a.

<table>
<tr><td>Jan 1</td><td>White, capital   (Q–)</td><td>24,000</td><td></td></tr>
<tr><td></td><td>   Blue, capital   (Q+)</td><td></td><td>24,000</td></tr>
<tr><td></td><td>To transfer White's equity to Blue.</td><td></td><td></td></tr>
</table>

b. The balance sheet for the partnership of Red and Blue is almost identical to the balance sheet given for Red and White in the problem, except that Blue replaces White in the title and in the listing of capital accounts, and the date of the balance sheet is January 1, 2014: